PENGUIN REFERENCE

The Penguin Dictionary of Philosophy

Thomas Mautner is Visiting Fellow in the School of Humanities at the Australian National University. Amongst his teaching and research interests are seventeenth- and eighteenth-century philosophy, moral and political thought, and natural law and natural rights. He has published papers in academic journals, and his other publications include *Francis Hutcheson: Two Texts on Human Nature* (1993).

The Penguin Dictionary of
Philosophy

Thomas Mautner

PENGUIN BOOKS

PENGUIN BOOKS

Published by the Penguin Group
Penguin Books Ltd, 27 Wrights Lane, London W8 5TZ, England
Penguin Putnam Inc., 375 Hudson Street, New York, New York 10014, USA
Penguin Books Australia Ltd, Ringwood, Victoria, Australia
Penguin Books Canada Ltd, 10 Alcorn Avenue, Toronto, Ontario, Canada M4V 3B2
Penguin Books India (P) Ltd, 11, Community Centre, Panchsheel Park, New Delhi – 110 017, India
Penguin Books (NZ) Ltd, Private Bag 102902, NSMC, Auckland, New Zealand
Penguin Books (South Africa) (Pty) Ltd, 5 Watkins Street, Denver Ext 4, Johannesburg 2094, South Africa

Penguin Books Ltd, Registered Offices: Harmondsworth, Middlesex, England

First published by Blackwell Publishers 1996
Published with revisions in Penguin Books 1997, 1999, 2000

7

Typeset by Rowland Phototypesetting Ltd, Bury St Edmunds, Suffolk
Printed in England by Clays Ltd, St Ives plc

CONTENTS

PREFACE

Philosophy is fascinating, but studying it is not without its problems: terms of obscure provenance or meaning turn up; unknown names are mentioned; even pronunciation can be a puzzle in some cases. This dictionary is designed to provide genuine help. Its guiding principle is simple: to include information that will make it easier for newcomers to come to terms with philosophical texts.

Accordingly, the dictionary contains entries on a large number of important thinkers in which their views are presented. A special feature are the philosophical self-portraits by a number of eminent contemporary philosophers.

There is also a large number of entries which explain the vocabulary used in philosophy, and many that also serve the related purpose of demystification, by giving information on the origin of words and word-elements. Many philosophical terms sound strange because of their foreign origin – usually Greek, which in the beginning was the language of philosophy, or Latin, which came later. Since the seventeenth century, the use of these languages in philosophy gradually decreased, but much of the existing philosophical terminology was imported or transposed into the vernacular. Moreover, when a need was felt for a new word or phrase, it was usually met by drawing on Greek or Latin. To mention only two examples out of many hundreds, 'idealism' was created in the eighteenth century, 'agnosticism' in the nineteenth, and in the twentieth century the practice of creating new terms from Greek or Latin roots is continuing, indeed flourishing. This is why, in philosophy, the origin of a term is frequently an important clue to its present meaning. Also, once the origin of seemingly mysterious words is known, they will lose some of their exotic glamour, but in return they will make more sense.

Philosophers and concepts belonging to non-western traditions of thought lie outside the scope of this dictionary. Given the great variety and richness of the Indian, Chinese, and other non-western traditions, the attempt to cover them within this volume would be a vain presumption. For that task, special expertise and a separate dictionary are needed.

The boundaries of philosophy are not sharply defined, and the dictionary also supplies information which is arguably on the periphery of philosophy, especially for terms that have several meanings, some philosophical, some not. One example among many is 'functionalism'. Some terms that belong to fields adjacent to philosophy, such as grammar or rhetoric, are also included. It would be unhelpful to exclude them, because it is not always easy for a reader to tell whether an unknown word that occurs in a philosophical text is a technical term in philosophy or in a neighbouring area.

Explanations are also offered of a number of expressions, for example *ceteris paribus*, *de jure*, *ipso facto*, *non sequitur*, which, although not part of the vocabulary of any particular discipline, occur fairly frequently in philosophical discourse.

It is hoped that the information on pronunciation of words and names will be welcome. For some foreign words or names, like 'Descartes', there is an established English pronunciation, and in such cases both the English and the foreign pronunciations are indicated. But for most foreign words or names only the foreign pronunciation is indicated. This is for information. In ordinary English speech the words or names would of course be pronounced in an anglicized manner, in line with standard phonetic patterns. The pronunciation indicated for Greek and Latin expressions is one likely to be heard from English speakers generally, but may not be as authentic as that preferred by classicists.

The dictionary also includes a select number of words that were used in the past in a sense that is no longer current. They often lead to misunderstanding of classical philosophical texts – for example, those of Hobbes, Locke, Hume, Bentham or Mill. It is typical of false friends – as these treacherous words are sometimes described – that they do not announce their deceptiveness. For this reason, words of this kind, which set traps for the unwary and which have entries in this dictionary, are listed below.

amuse, -ment
awful
careless
character
civilian
compact
complacency
diffidence
discover
event
experiment
fond
humane
impose upon
indifference
insult
just
logical truth
nice
obnoxious
own
pathology, -ical
pretend
vicissitude

radical	science	system
receive	sophistication	use
repugnancy	specious	want(ing)
revolution	speculation	without

A note on conventions

In standard academic usage, the surname alone is often sufficient to indicate who is meant: for instance, 'Russell's theory of descriptions', 'Moore's theory of sense-data', and philosophers are often referred to by surname alone: 'Kant', 'Leibniz', 'Popper', 'Ryle'.

When a more complete form of the name is used, there are two common variants. Some philosophers are called by their first name and surname. Thus, the author of *An Inquiry into Meaning and Truth* is known as Bertrand Russell (not 'B. Russell'). Other philosophers are referred to by two initials and surname. Thus, the author of *Principia Ethica* is known as G. E. Moore (not 'George Edward Moore').

These are mere conventions without any deeper significance. Still, awareness of them can be useful. In this dictionary they are indicated by means of parentheses. For instance, *Skinner, B(urrhus) F(rederick)* indicates that one usually says 'B. F. Skinner'.

A note on the Penguin edition

The present edition of this *Dictionary of Philosophy* is on the whole the same as the hardback edition published by Blackwell in 1996. Some corrections have, however, been carried out and there are also some other changes. The booklist at the end of the volume has been reviewed. A small number of entries have been reformulated (e.g. *Church's Thesis*, *Church's Theorem*, *philosophy*, *realization*, *Thomasius*) or brought up to date, and a few new entries (e.g. *personal identity*, *Turing*) have been added. The 1999 reprint contained a few additional improvements. Three entries were added (*quad*, *truism*, *world*) and in the 2000 reprint the list of books in print has again been updated.

ACKNOWLEDGEMENTS

When working on this dictionary, it was my good fortune to have the support of John Passmore (Australian National University). During the time that the work was in progress, the prospect of receiving the comments of such an eminent philosopher and historian of philosophy served as a great source of encouragement. He showed great generosity in carrying out a thorough examination of a full-length draft, a fact that adds to my debt of gratitude for all the good advice I received.

The list of those to whom my thanks are owed is long. Brenda Almond (University of Hull) reviewed earlier full-length drafts with great care, and it is thanks to her that the number of infelicities of style and substance was substantially reduced. In order further to ensure a high degree of reliability, I also consulted subject specialists about selected groups of entries. A very large number of entries on logic and on classical Greek philosophy were examined by David Bostock (Merton College, Oxford), and Robert Barnes (Australian National University) did likewise with a very large number of entries relating to theological and to Greek and hellenistic subjects. Smaller, but still substantial, numbers of entries were critically examined by Reinhart Brandt (University of Marburg), William Grey (University of Queensland), Frank Jackson (Australian National University), Barry Hindess (Australian National University), Dominic Hyde (University of Queensland), Kimon Lycos (University of Melbourne), Lindis Masterman (La Trobe University) and my colleagues Peter Röper and Paul Thom.

The advice kindly proffered by all these friends had two functions. In part (indeed, for the most part) it confirmed that the entries were sound. But it also helped to remove many infelicities or mistakes, and to introduce many improvements.

This applies equally to advice received from other helpers who looked at smaller numbers of entries or even a single one, and who likewise kindly helped with their comments; their names follow. The list also includes a few persons who helped by supplying preliminary drafts which, although not used as such, were of great value and in some cases virtually indispensable for getting the entry into shape. It has been gratifying to meet with so much helpfulness combined with expertise all round the world, and I wish to express my most sincere thanks also to Karl-Otto Apel (Frankfurt), John Bishop (University of Auckland), David Boucher (University College of Swansea), David Braddon-Mitchell (University of Auckland), Geoffrey Brennan (ANU), Richard Campbell (ANU), Roderick Chisholm (Brown University), David Cooper (University of Durham), David Cullen (University of Auckland), Murray Domney (Ministry of Defence, Canberra), Jean Gassin (La Trobe University), Moira Gatens (University of Sydney), James Grieve (ANU), Colin Groves (ANU), Eduard Khamara (Monash University, Melbourne), John Kilcullen (Macquarie University, Sydney), Peter Lamarque (University of Hull), Loren Lomasky (Bowling Green University), Jennifer MacMahon (ANU), Anthony O'Hear (University of Bradford), Graham Oppy (ANU), Paul Patton (University of Sydney), Philip Pettit (ANU), Bill Readings (Toronto), Nicolaas Rupke (Göttingen), Thomas Sheehan (Loyola University, Chicago), Robin Small (Monash University, Melbourne), J. J. C. Smart (ANU), M. A. Stewart (University of Lancaster), Suzanne Uniacke (University of Wollongong), and my colleagues Bruin Christensen, Hugh Clapin, Penelope Deutscher, Chris Falzon, Brian Garrett, Natalie Stoljar and Udo Thiel. James Tiles (University of Hawaii) helped to improve the 1999 reprint (the 'cave' entry).

A special check-up was necessary in respect of phonetics and etymology: James Grieve (ANU) helped with French words, and Colin Mayrhofer (ANU) helped with Latin and Greek words and gave useful hints on what may be described as their correct mispronunciation in English.

The need for the entries to be written – as far as possible – in a manner accessible to the general reader was not overlooked. In order to meet it, reactions to selected entries were sought at an early stage from a few undergraduate students and other members of the reading public – an instructive exercise – and at a later stage, Yvonne Parrey (ANU) rendered great service in surveying the whole text from this point of view.

It is, in fact, difficult to give full expression to my sentiments of appreciation and gratitude to all those mentioned, whose expert comment and advice have benefited this project. It is important to note, however, that many parts of the text have been further revised since they saw it. So if any errors or infelicities remain it would be unsafe to assign blame to my generous advisers.

Equally deserving of acknowledgement and thanks are, of course, the contributors who supplied a large number of entries for this dictionary.

Among those who have written a considerable number of entries within a subject area are: Daniel Graham (Brigham Young University) – ancient Greek philosophy; George Hughes (Victoria University, Wellington) – logic; John Marenbon (Trinity College, Cambridge) – medieval philosophy; Alan Musgrave (University of Otago, Dunedin) – philosophy of science; Richard Popkin (Washington University, St Louis and University of California Los Angeles) – early modern philosophy; Robert Solomon (University of Texas, Austin) – existentialism and phenomenology; Harold Tarrant (University of Newcastle, N.S.W.) – Hellenistic philosophy; Alan White (University of Hull) – modern British philosophy.

Many of these entries cover great philosophers, including Plato and Aristotle. Other illustrious past philosophers have been covered as follows: Hans Burkhardt (University of Erlangen) has written about Leibniz; John Cottingham (University of Reading) about Descartes; Edwin Curley (University of Michigan) about Spinoza; John Haldane (University of St Andrews) about Augustine; Michael Inwood (Trinity College, Oxford) about Hegel; Manfred Kuehn (Purdue University) about Kant; David Pears (Christ Church, Oxford) about Wittgenstein; Terence Penelhum (University of Calgary) about Hume; Alan Ryan (New College, Oxford) about Mill; Tom Sorell (University of Essex) about Hobbes; Udo Thiel (ANU) about Locke.

The external contributions mentioned so far are not the only ones. Many other experts from all over the world have also contributed. They are mentioned in the following complete list of the authors of contributed entries in this dictionary:

Brenda Almond (University of Hull), David Armstrong (University of Sydney), Judith Armstrong (University of Melbourne), Robert Barnes (ANU), David Bennett (Australian Academy of the Humanities), Sir Isaiah Berlin (All Souls, Oxford), John Bishop (University of Auckland), David Braddon-Mitchell (University of Auckland), Barry Brundell (Pontifical Gregorian University, Rome), Hans Burkhardt (University of Erlangen), Keith Campbell (University of Sydney), Richard Campbell (ANU), Colin Cheyne (University of Otago, Dunedin), Roderick Chisholm (Brown University), Bruin Christensen (ANU), Tim Clark (University of Durham), Jack Copeland (University of Canterbury, Christchurch), John Cottingham (University of Reading), Edwin Curley (University of Michigan), Gregory Currie (Flinders University), Chris Falzon (ANU), Brian Garrett (ANU), Quentin Gibson (ANU), Daniel Graham (Brigham Young University),

Knud Haakonssen (Boston University), John Haldane (University of St Andrews), R. M. Hare (University of Florida), Bernard Harrison (University of Utah), Kathleen Higgins (University of Texas at Austin), Barry Hindess (ANU), Carl Huffman (DePauw University), George Hughes (Victoria University, Wellington), Dominic Hyde (University of Queensland), Michael Inwood (Trinity College, Oxford), Frank Jackson (ANU), John Kilcullen (Macquarie University, Sydney), Manfred Kuehn (Purdue University), Chandran Kukathas (University College of the University of New South Wales (Canberra)), Peter Lamarque (University of Hull), John Lechte (Macquarie University, Sydney), Alasdair MacIntyre (Duke University), John Marenbon (Trinity College, Cambridge), Karis Muller (ANU), Alan Musgrave (University of Otago, Dunedin), Yvonne Parrey (ANU), John Passmore (ANU), Paul Patton (University of Sydney), David Pears (Christ Church, Oxford), Terence Penelhum (University of Calgary), Richard Popkin (Washington University, St Louis, and University of California Los Angeles), Dag Prawitz (University of Stockholm), Ruth Anna Putnam (Wellesley College), Willard V. O. Quine (Harvard University), Charles Reagan (Kansas State University), Peter Röper (ANU), Richard Rorty (University of Virginia), Jennifer Rutherford (ANU), Alan Ryan (New College, Oxford), John Searle (University of California, Berkeley), Jeremy Shearmur (ANU), Peter Singer (Monash University, Melbourne), J. J. C. Smart (ANU), Robert Solomon (University of Texas at Austin), Tom Sorell (University of Essex), Timothy Sprigge (University of Edinburgh), M. A. Stewart (University of Lancaster), Natalie Stoljar (ANU), Göran Sundholm (University of Leiden), Richard Sylvan (ANU), Godfrey Tanner (University of Newcastle, N.S.W.), Harold Tarrant (University of Newcastle, N.S.W.), Udo Thiel (ANU), Paul Thom (ANU), Pavel Tichý (University of Otago, Dunedin), Tim van Gelder (University of Indiana, Bloomington), Alan White (University of Hull), Graham White (Clare Hall, Cambridge), Kevin Wilkinson (ANU), Robert Wokler (University of Manchester).

It is, however, with great sadness that I have to record that six of those who helpfully responded to my request for assistance during the long gestation of this dictionary died before it was completed: George Hughes, Kimon Lycos, Bill Readings, Richard Sylvan, Pavel Tichý, and Alan White. My debt of gratitude to them remains.

TM

LIST OF CONTRIBUTORS' INITIALS

AM	Alan Musgrave	HB	Hans Burkhardt
AMC	Alasdair MacIntyre	HT	Harold Tarrant
AR	Alan Ryan	IB	Isaiah Berlin
AW	Alan White	JA	Judith Armstrong
BA	Brenda Almond	JB	John Bishop
BB	Barry Brundell	JCD	Jack Copeland
BC	Bruin Christensen	JCM	John Cottingham
BG	Brian Garrett	JH	John Haldane
BHA	Bernard Harrison	JK	John Kilcullen
BHI	Barry Hindess	JL	John Lechte
BR	Bill Readings	JM	John Marenbon
CC	Colin Cheyne	JP	John Passmore
CF	Chris Falzon	JR	Jennifer Rutherford
CH	Carl Huffman	JSE	John Searle
CK	Chandran Kukathas	JSH	Jeremy Shearmur
CR	Charles Reagan	JSM	J. J. C. Smart
DA	David Armstrong	JT	James Tiles
DB	David Bennett	KC	Keith Campbell
DBM	David Braddon-Mitchell	KHA	Knud Haakonssen
DG	Daniel Graham	KHI	Kathleen Higgins
DH	Dominic Hyde	KM	Karis Muller
DPE	David Pears	KW	Kevin Wilkinson
DPR	Dag Prawitz	MI	Michael Inwood
EC	Edwin Curley	MK	Manfred Kuehn
FJ	Frank Jackson	MS	M. A. Stewart
GC	Gregory Currie	NS	Natalie Stoljar
GH	George Hughes	PL	Peter Lamarque
GS	Göran Sundholm	PP	Paul Patton
GT	Godfrey Tanner	PR	Peter Röper
GW	Graham White	PS	Peter Singer

PTH	Paul Thom	RSY	Richard Sylvan
PTI	Pavel Tichý	RW	Robert Wokler
QG	Quentin Gibson	TC	Tim Clark
RB	Robert Barnes	TP	Terence Penelhum
RCA	Richard Campbell	TSO	Tom Sorell
RCH	Roderick M. Chisholm	TSP	Timothy Sprigge
RH	Richard M. Hare	TVG	Tim van Gelder
RPO	Richard Popkin	UT	Udo Thiel
RPU	Ruth Anna Putnam	WQ	Willard V. O. Quine
RR	Richard Rorty	YP	Yvonne Parrey
RSO	Robert Solomon		

LIST OF ABBREVIATIONS

Af.	Afrikaans	*conj.*	conjunction
Dan.	Danish	*n.*	noun
Du.	Dutch	*n. sing.*	noun with plural form but singular in number (e.g. physics)
Eng.	English	*pl.*	plural
Fr.	French	*prep.*	preposition
Gm.	German	*pron.*	pronoun
Gr.	Greek	*sing.*	singular
Heb.	Hebrew	*syn.*	synonym
It.	Italian	*vb.*	verb
Lat.	Latin	*c.*	circa
Po.	Polish	cf.	compare
Port.	Portuguese	d.	died
Rus.	Russian	edn	edition
Sans.	Sanskrit	*fl.*	floruit
Sp.	Spanish	rev.	revised
Sw.	Swedish	transl.	translated
adj.	adjective	viz.	videlicet
adv.	adverb		
ant.	antonym		

LOGICAL SYMBOLS

For an explanation of the logical symbols used in this dictionary, see the entries as indicated in the following table:

$\sim$	tilde	$\forall x$	quantifier
&	conjunction	$\exists x$	quantifier
$\wedge$	conjunction	$\Box$	modal logic
$\vee$	disjunction	$\Diamond$	modal logic
$\supset$	conditional	$\Box\!\!\rightarrow$	counterfactual conditional
$\equiv$	biconditional		

PRONUNCIATION KEY

The symbols used in the pronunciation transcriptions (enclosed within two slashes thus: / /) in this dictionary are taken from the International Phonetic Alphabet. The following orthographic symbols have their usual value: *b*, *d*, *f*, *h*, *k*, *l*, *m*, *n*, *p*, *r*, *s*, *t*, *v*, *w*, *z* and the list below gives the pronunciation for the other symbols used.

symbol	**as in**
a	French *ami* (ami); German *Mann* (man)
aː	French *art* (aːʀ); German *Vater* (ˈfaːtər)
æ	*act* (ækt); *hat* (hæt)
ɑː	*father* (fɑːðe); *heart* (hɑːt)
ɑ	French *bas* (bɑ)
aɪ	*eye* (aɪ); *height* (haɪt)
aɪɔ	*fire* (faɪə)
aʊ	*how* (haʊ)
aʊə	*flour* (flaʊə)
ɛ	*get* (gɛt)
e	French *été* (ete); German *sehr* (zer)
ɜː	*learn* (lɜːn); *term* (tɜːm)
eɪ	*day* (deɪ)
ɛə	*fair* (fɛə); *where* (wɛə)
ɪ	*hit* (hɪt)
ɪə	*here* (hɪə)
i	French *il* (il); German *Idee* (iˈde)
iː	*she* (ʃiː)
ɒ	*hot* (hɒt)
əʊ	*bone* (bəʊn)
ɔ	French *bonne* (bɔn)
ɔː	*false* (fɔːls)
ɔɪ	*joy* (dʒɔɪ)
o	French *rose* (ʀoz); German *so* (zo)
œ	French *peur* (pœʀ); German *zwölf* (tsvœlf)

symbol	**as in**
ø	French *deux* (dø); German *schön* (ʃøn)
ʊ	*book* (bʊk)
u	French *pour* (puʀ)
uː	*true* (truː)
y	French *tu* (ty); German *über* (ybər)
ʌ	*mother* (ˈmʌðə); *sun* (sʌn)
ə	unstressed vowel, as in *the reader* (ðə ˈriːdə)
g	*give* (gɪv)
ʃ	*ship* (ʃɪp)
ʒ	*measure* (ˈmɛʒə)
tʃ	*chicken* (tʃɪkn) – (this is a digraph representing one sound, and not t+ʃ)
dʒ	*join* (dʒɔɪn) – (this is a digraph representing one sound, and not d+ʒ)
ɲ	French *vigne* (viɲ)
ŋ	*long* (lɒŋ)
θ	*thin* (θɪn)
ð	*this* (ðɪs)
x	Scottish *loch* (lɒx); German *ach* (ax)
ç	German *ich* (iç)
j	*young* (jʌŋ)
ɣ	Spanish *luego* (lʊˈɛɣɔ)

Vowel Length The symbol ː is used to indicate length as applied to vowels.

Nasalization ˜ above a vowel indicates a nasal sound, as in French *an*, *vin*, *bon*, *un*.

Stress Primary stress is marked by the symbol ˈ before the syllable to which the stress is applied.

THE GREEK ALPHABET

upper-case	*lower-case*	*name*		*transliteration*
Α	α	alpha	ˈælfə	a
Β	β	beta	ˈbiːtə	b
Γ	γ	gamma	ˈgæmə	g
Δ	δ	delta	ˈdɛltə	d
Ε	ε	epsilon	ˈɛpsɪlɒn	e
Ζ	ζ	zeta	ˈziːtə	z
Η	η	eta	ˈiːtə	ē
Θ	ϑ, θ	theta	ˈθiːtə	th
Ι	ι	iota	aɪˈəʊtə	i
Κ	κ	kappa	ˈkæpə	k or c
Λ	λ	lambda	ˈlæmdə	l
Μ	μ	mu	mjuː	m
Ν	ν	nu	njuː	n
Ξ	ξ	xi	ksaɪ	x
Ο	ο	omicron	ˈɒmikrɒn	o
Π	π	pi	paɪ	p
Ρ	ϱ	rho	rəʊ	r or rh
Σ	σ, ς	sigma	ˈsɪgmə	s
Τ	τ	tau	taʊ, tɔː	t
Υ	υ	upsilon	ˈʌpsɪlɒn	y (or u)
Φ	φ, ϕ	phi	faɪ	ph
Χ	χ	chi	kaɪ	ch
Ψ	ψ	psi	psaɪ	ps
Ω	ω	omega	ˈəʊmɪgə	ō

abduction *n.* **1** (in Aristotle) a syllogistic inference from a major premiss which is certain, and a merely probable minor premiss, to a merely probable conclusion (*Prior Analytics* 2,25 69^{a}20ff.).
2 (in C. S. Peirce) reasoning of this form: (a) facts of type B have been observed; (b) a true statement of the form *If A then B* can explain B. Therefore, probably A.

Peirce called this pattern abduction, believing that he used the term in the Aristotelian sense. He held that abduction is the standard form of setting up scientific hypotheses, and can count as the third kind of inference, together with induction and deduction. Since then, it has been stressed that what makes A probable is that it is the *best* explanation we can think of. Scientifically useful abduction is, then, INFERENCE TO THE BEST EXPLANATION. The general form of such an inference is: (1) D is a collection of data; (2) H (a hypothesis) would, if true, explain D; (3) no other hypothesis can explain D as well as H does. (4) Therefore, H is probably true. Of course, abductive reasoning is common also in everyday life, whenever we try to find answers to questions why something is the case. *Syn.* retroduction.

Abelard /ˈæbəlaːd/, Pierre (1079–1142) Taught by the outstanding masters of his day – Roscelin, William of Champeaux and Anselm of Laon (with each of whom he quarrelled), Abelard had established himself by *c.* 1115 as the leading Parisian logic master. He married Heloïse, a pupil, but later became a monk. In the 1130s he had, however, resumed teaching logic and theology in the Parisian schools.

Abelard's main logical works were commentaries on Porphyry's *Isagoge* and Aristotle's *Categories* and *De interpretatione*, and an independent treatise, the *Dialectica*. A striking feature of these works is Abelard's wish to limit things to individual substances (such as this man or that dog) and individual forms (such as this whiteness or that rationality). There are, he held, no universal things, merely words (*voces* or, the term he later preferred, *sermones*) which refer not just to one individual but to all individuals of the same sort: so 'man' refers to all men and no one man in particular, just as, if I say that I want a hat, I do not mean that I want this hat or that hat. Members of a given species do indeed share in the *status* of being the sort of thing they are. Men, for instance, all have the status of being a man – that is, being a rational, mortal substance. A status, however, is not a thing, but rather a way in which things are. Similarly, the *dictum* of a statement – what a statement says is the case – is not a thing.

Abelard also devoted great energy to the logic of inference. He transformed the system of topical inferences, inherited from antiquity through Boethius, from a rhetorical guide to success in disputation to an analysis of the conditions for entailment. He insisted that for p to entail q, the impossibility of (p and not-q) is not enough; in addition, p must *require* that q be the case.

Abelard's logic had important applications to theology, which are explored both in the logical commentaries themselves and in his *Theologia Summi Boni*, revised and extended to form his *Theologia Christiana* and further revised to become the *Theologia Scholarium*. Abelard tried to explore various theological problems by analysing the correct logical form of the sentences in which they were stated. He believed that whilst the mysteries of the Trinity are ultimately beyond human comprehension, it is possible to indicate, in the language of Porphyry, how God can be three persons without compromise to his unity.

Abelard's thoughts about ethics are mostly found in his unfinished *Scito teipsum* (Know thyself), sometimes called his *Ethics*, and his *Dialogue between a Christian, a Philosopher and a Jew* (or *Collationes*). According to Abelard, wrongness lies in the intention at the root of an action, rather than in the action itself: I am no less guilty of a crime I fully intended to carry out because I happened to be thwarted. Intention, however, must be distinguished from wish (*voluntas*). I may wish, for instance, to sleep with another man's wife, but resist my desire to do so – in which case I will by no means have sinned. Or, by contrast, I may sleep with his wife whilst wishing that she were not already married – and be an adulterer, despite my wish. A person sins by *consenting* to a course of action which he believes to be contrary to God's will. This formulation might seem to lead to a complete subjectivism in morality, especially since Abelard was ready to say that every course of action which is actually realized belongs to God's providential order and so accords with his will. But Abelard considered that there are certain precepts of natural law – mostly prohibitions, such as 'Do not murder' or 'Do not commit adultery' – which are known to all men. Moreover, intention is not the measure of how good (as opposed to how bad) an action is. For the goodness of actions, Abelard turned to a theory of virtues, which he took from Cicero, but greatly modified, so that justice becomes the central virtue, strengthened by courage and temperance and made possible by wisdom. JM

ab esse ad posse valet consequentia Lat. the inference from the actual to the possible is valid. As an axiom in modal logic, this principle is sometimes called the axiom of possibility. *See also* MODALITIES.

absolute (Lat. *ab* from + *solutum* free, released) **1** *adj.* unrelated. Among its synonyms are: independent, non-relative, unconditioned, unmodified, unrestricted, without qualification, etc. *Ant.* relative.
2 *n.* Traditional metaphysics has a concept of the Absolute, an ultimate, all-embracing reality, that which necessarily exists and depends on nothing else, sometimes conceived as a personal or quasi-personal being. This 'God of the philosophers' (contrasted by Pascal with the God experienced in an intense personal encounter) can be found in many metaphysical theories, including those of the neo-Platonists, Nicholas of Cusa, Spinoza, Leibniz, Fichte, Schelling and Hegel.

The concept was important in Spencer's philosophy, and it plays a central part in the metaphysics of absolute idealists like Bradley, for whom the Absolute is the whole of existence; a timeless, harmonious totality.

The use of the word as a noun can be traced to Nicholas of Cusa's *De docta ignorantia* 1440 (On learned ignorance) but seems not to have re-emerged until Mendelssohn's and Jacobi's debate about Spinoza in the 1770s. It then came into general philosophical use with Schelling and Hegel in the early nineteenth century.

absolutism *n.* **1** a system of government in which a ruler's power is not subject to constitutional limitations. **2** the view that certain moral rules admit of no exceptions. **3** the metaphysics of the Absolute, especially Bradley's. **4** anti-relativism.

abstract (Lat. *abstrahere* to draw away) *adj.* A quality, idea or concept is said to be abstract when it is thought of in isolation from the object to which it belongs. For example, triangles of different shapes are all triangular.

Berkeley rejected abstract ideas in sections 10–12 of the introduction to his *Principles of Human Knowledge*. In his view, the abstract idea of triangularity would be the idea of a shape shared by all triangles – and yet, triangles have very different shapes.

Among abstract entities are not only concepts that may be supposed to originate from a process of abstraction, but also numbers, classes, propositions, etc. Some features which may be used to distinguish them from concrete entities are causal inefficacy, no location in space-time, and necessary existence.

In Hegelian-style philosophy, not only qualities, ideas and concepts, but also individual objects are said to be abstract, in so far as they are thought of in isolation from the whole to which they belong. For instance, an individual human being, considered in isolation from his social relations, is said to be abstract. In this view everything is abstract to some degree, except the all-encompassing whole. In this philosophy, the only truth is the whole truth: all abstraction involves some falsification.

abstraction *n.* **1** the process of considering only some aspects of a whole. **2** the result of this process. **3** (in set theory) defining a set as the set of all objects that have a certain property. **4** (in logic) an operation by which a predicate is formed from an open sentence. For instance, from the open sentence Fx, which can be read 'x is F', one can form the expression $\hat{x}$ (Fx) which designates the property F. Similarly, $\hat{x}$(Fx & Gx) designates the property of being both F and G, $\hat{x}\hat{y}$(Fxy) designates the two-place property, i.e. the relation F, etc.

abstraction, axiom of *See* COMPREHENSION, AXIOM OF.

absurd *adj.* (The Latin *absurdus* meant literally *out of tune, ill-sounding*, but the word was also used like its present-day English counterpart.) irrational; self-contradictory, patently false.

Generally, the absurd is that which violates rules of logic or is otherwise flagrantly wrong-headed. Some existentialists say that human existence is absurd because it lacks an ultimate purpose and thus is 'meaningless'. **absurdity** *n.*

absurdum, reductio ad See *REDUCTIO*.

academic philosophy **1** The academic philosophy, i.e. the philosophy of the Academy, was initially Platonist. Later, however, when in the third century BC the school was headed by Arcesilaus, Philo and others, academic philosophy came to be sceptical. The term has since also been used for a kind of scepticism, less radical than PYRRHONISM, by Cicero in the first century BC, by Hume in the eighteenth century, and many others. **2** In the present-day sense, academic philosophy is the philosophy studied in universities.

The use of the adjective 'academic' to suggest irrelevance or impracticality can be traced back to the 1880s.

academy *n.* **1** the name of an area in ancient Athens, and of the school which Plato founded there about 385 BC. In the fifth century AD it was a centre for neo-Platonic opposition to Christian doctrine, and the Emperor Justinian's decree in 529 against the public teaching of philosophy by pagans led to its closure. **2** beginning in Italy during the Renaissance, a society organized for the cultivation of letters, arts, science, medicine, technology, etc. An early notable example was the Platonic Academy at Florence (*see* FICINO). **3** Educational institutions in England and Ireland in the seventeenth and eighteenth centuries were often called academies. Some of these 'dissenting academies' provided advanced courses of study for non-Anglicans who did not have access to the universities.

acatalepsy (Gr. *akatalēpsia* unintelligibility; non-understanding) *n.* 'The radical sceptic's denial of the mind's capacity to comprehend truth' (Francis Bacon, *The New Organon* I, 126).

acausal (*a-* (Gr. privative prefix) + Lat. *causa*) *adj.* non-causal. A hybrid neologism.

accessibility relation a technical term employed in giving semantics for modal logics. It is a structural relation between worlds, used in defining truth-conditions for modal statements. Thus, *possibly p* is true at a world w, if and only if p is true in some world accessible from w, and *necessarily p* is true at a world w, if and only if p is true in all worlds accessible from w.

This is a refinement, dating from the mid-twentieth century, of the traditional idea that *possibly p* is true if and only if p is true in some possible world, and *necessarily p* is true if and only if p is true in every possible world.

The accessibility relation can be specified in different ways. For instance, if it is reflexive and transitive, the theorems of a modal system known as S4 will come out true. By varying the properties (transitivity, symmetry, and the like) of the accessibility relation, different classes of modal logics are obtained, and thus different concepts of necessity and possibility. DH

accident *n.* **1** a property that a thing can have but need not have. In contrast, an essential property is one that a thing must have, in order to be what it is. **2** something which cannot exist on its own, but only as inhering in a substance.

accidentally *adv.* contingently; in the manner of an accident.

Achilles and the tortoise *See* ZENO OF ELEA.

acosmism (Gr. *a-* (privative prefix) + *cosmos* (world-)order) *n.* denial of the reality of the world. Salomon Maimon (*c.* 1752–1800) used the term, and, somewhat later, Hegel did too, to characterize Spinoza's identification of God and Nature. Hegel took Spinoza to deny the real existence of individual things and to assert all that exists is God (*Encyclopedia*, section 151, addendum), but this interpretation is questionable.

acrasia *n.*, **acratic** *adj. See* AKRASIA.

acroamatic (Gr. *akroamatikos* to be heard, oral) *adj.* pertaining to lecturing. This was contrasted with other teaching methods, such as the EROTEMATIC.

Aristotle's lectures within the school were acroamatic, and contrasted with his EXOTERIC teaching.

actant *n.* a technical term in the semiotics of A. J. Greimas. An actant is a basic role-type in a story. Greimas initially distinguished six: subject, object, sender, receiver, helper, opponent, but the term has also been applied to other character-types which have a distinct function in the structure of a literary work (e.g. the fool; the innocent victim). In a plot, different actors can represent the same actant – e.g. many villains may assail the hero – and one person can represent more than one actant.

act-consequentialism *See* ACT-UTILITARIANISM.

actor *n.* **1** a person who performs a part in a play. **2** a person who acts, an agent.

act psychology a kind of theory which gives a central place to the distinction between the character and the content of a mental act. This line of inquiry goes back to Brentano, who taught that what distinguishes the mental from the physical is the intentional nature of mental acts: i.e. that the content of a mental act may be something that is non-existent. Examples are belief in the existence of unicorns, or a groundless fear. A number of writers influenced by Brentano, among them Meinong, Stumpf, Höfler, Husserl, Kreibig and Witasek, developed theories in which this act/content distinction plays a significant part. *See also* MEINONG.

Acts and Omissions doctrine the view that acts and omissions are morally different, even if the consequences are the same; especially, the view that performing an act with certain foreseen bad consequences is morally worse than a failure to act which has the same foreseen bad consequences. For instance, other things being equal, that killing is worse than merely letting die. Another label for the view that it is worse to do harm than to allow harm to be done, is the *Doctrine of Doing and Allowing*.

actualism *n.* 1 the view that what is actual exists, but that what is merely possible does not exist. It is held by Alvin Plantinga, Robert Stalnaker et al. This view stands in opposition to a view sometimes called possibilism but more often (modal) realism, held by David Lewis, that non-actual possible worlds exist.
2 the theory that it is the actual and not the expected consequences of an action that are relevant when determining its rightness is called actualism by Michael Slote in his *From Morality to Virtue* 1992, with *expectabilism* (previously: *probabilism*) as the contrasting term.
3 the theory that in a choice between options, the right thing to do is to choose the best option, given what the agent *will* subsequently do. This is contrasted with *possibilism*, according to which the right thing to do is to choose the best option, given what the agent *can* subsequently do. The contrast can be illustrated as in Table 1.

According to possibilism, A *can* do what is best, so the right action for A is to promise. (If A does not promise, A cannot do what is best.) According to actualism, A *will* not do what is best, so the right action for A is not to promise.

The debate around this contrast began with an article by Frank Jackson and Robert Pargetter in *Philosophical Review* 95 (1986).
4 a kind of idealist philosophy, represented by Gentile, de Ruggiero, etc.

Table 1 Alternative courses of action

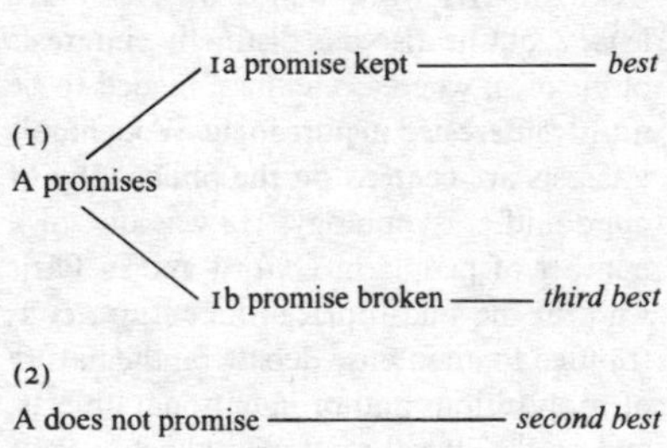

act-utilitarianism *n.* According to act-utilitarianism, it is the value of the consequences of *the particular act* that counts when determining whether the act is right. Bentham's theory is act-utilitarian, and so is that of J. J. C. Smart.

One objection to act-utilitarianism is that it seems to be too permissive, capable of justifying any crime, and even making it morally obligatory, if only the value of the consequences of the particular act is great enough. Another objection is that act-utilitarianism seems better in theory than in practice, since we hardly ever have the time and the knowledge to predict the consequences of an act, assess their value, and make comparisons with possible alternative acts.

Modern act-utilitarians think that these objections can be met. Others have developed alternatives to act-utilitarianism, e.g. RULE-UTILITARIANISM, and other forms of indirect utilitarianism (UTILITARIANISM, INDIRECT).

For the terminological variation between 'utilitarianism' and 'consequentialism', see CONSEQUENTIALISM.

ad Lat. to, towards; at. *See also ARGUMENTUM AD.*

Adam of Wodeham (*c.* 1298–1358) a disciple and close associate of William of Ockham. His work builds on Ockham's legacy, but he also has distinctive interests of his own; whereas Ockham tended to be mostly interested in pure logic, Wodeham's interests are centred on the philosophy of mind and epistemology. He was one of a number of people in Oxford and in Paris who, in the mid-fourteenth century, contributed to an intense debate on the nature of propositions and of intentional objects, and on the structure of mental acts. GW

ad baculum /æd'bækjʊləm/ *See ARGUMENTUM AD BACULUM.*

addition *n.* inference from a sentence to a disjunction in which the sentence is one of the disjuncts:

$$\frac{p}{p \vee q} \quad \frac{q}{p \vee q}$$

In natural deduction systems the rule permitting this inference is usually called the rule of ∨-introduction.

ad fin(em) Lat. *ad finem* at the end (of a paragraph, a page, a chapter, etc.).

ad hoc Lat. for this, to this; for this special purpose. A theory undermined by contrary evidence can always be saved by the introduction of an additional hypothesis. The complaint that such a hypothesis has been introduced *ad hoc* implies that the hypothesis has no independent merit, but has been introduced *merely* for that purpose.

ad hominem /æd'hɒmɪnɛm/ *See ARGUMENTUM AD HOMINEM.*

adiaphoron (*sing.*), **adiaphora** /aːdɪ'æfərə/ (*pl.*) (Gr. indifferent) *n.* **1** matters indifferent from a moral point of view. In Stoic philosophy, most things commonly taken to be important are regarded as adiaphora by the wise man. **2** matters indifferent from a religious point of view. In heated debates among the early Protestant reformers in the sixteenth century, Melanchton argued that certain decisions concerning the liturgy were of this kind, a view passionately rejected by others, e.g. Matthias Flacius Illyricus.

ad infinitum /æd ɪnfɪ'naɪtəm/ (Lat. *ad* towards; *in-* un-; *finis* end, boundary, limit) without limit; forever.

adjunction *See* CONJUNCTION.

ad lib(itum) Lat. at one's pleasure; as one likes.

ad misericordiam *See ARGUMENTUM AD MISERICORDIAM.*

Adorno, Theodor (Wiesengrund-) (1903–69) a leading member of the Frankfurt School, in exile 1934–49, mainly in the United States. As a musicologist and critic of contemporary culture, Adorno saw a prospect for human autonomy at the cultural level in Schönberg's atonal music, and a serious threat to it in mass musical culture, especially jazz, which he emphatically condemned. He was a collaborator in the collective work entitled *The Authoritarian Personality* 1950, an empirical investigation of the personality traits peculiar to those who are attracted by fascism or Nazism. The important *Dialektik der Aufklärung* 1947 (*Dialectic of Enlightenment*), written together with Horkheimer, argues that once reason triumphed over myth and gained control over nature, the individual's subjection to nature was replaced by the social domination of the individual, and Enlightenment philosophy was therefore bound to harbour totalitarian tendencies. The analysis of society and the approach to sociology represented by himself and others of the Frankfurt School was criticized by Popper, Hans Albert et al. in a famous debate in the 1960s, published as *Der Positivismusstreit in der deutschen Soziologie* 1969 (*The Positivist Dispute in German Sociology*). Critics and adherents alike have found his writings obscure: this includes his *Negative Dialektik* 1966 (Negative dialectics), where the concept of non-identity is employed in a critique of ever-threatening reification, commodification and dehumanization. *See also* AUTHORITARIAN PERSONALITY.

adventitious (Lat. *ad* to + *venire* to come) *adj.* Adventitious ideas (*idées adventices*) are those that come to us from without, through our senses. Descartes distinguishes them in the third of the *Meditations* from innate ideas and from ideas that we ourselves create.

Adventitious rights and obligations are those that a person acquires, by entering into an agreement, or by some other act. Pufendorf distinguishes them from innate rights and obligations in his *Law of Nature and Nations* 1672.

Some present-day writers use the word differently, simply as a synonym for 'accidental' or 'inessential'.

ad verecundiam *See* *ARGUMENTUM AD VERECUNDIAM.*

Aegidius Romanus /iːˈdʒɪdɪəs rəʊˈmaːnəs/ *See* GILES OF ROME.

Aenesidemus /aɪnɪsɪˈdiːməs/ (1st century BC) sceptical philosopher. He saw scepticism as a way of life in which serene peace of mind, *ataraxia*, is achieved by suspension of judgement, *epochē*. Abandoning the academic scepticism of Arcesilaus and Carneades, whom he accused of lapsing into the holding of definite opinions, he claimed Pyrrho as the founder of genuine scepticism.

Some arguments of his about causal inferences anticipate Hume's: we can neither perceive nor understand the link between physical causes and effects. And, even if we could, we would remain unable to distinguish between actual and supposed causes.

He formulated ten tropes, or modes, of withholding assent (which, it has been argued, reveal an influence from Plato's *Theaetetus*). Reflection on them would show that opposing arguments had equal weight, and such a balance would make it easier to suspend judgement. Objects appear differently: (1) to different animals; (2) to different human beings; (3) to different sense-organs; (4) in different conditions; (5) in different positions; (6) with different accompanying sensations; (7) in different quantities; (8) in different relations; (9) according to frequency of occurrence; (10) according to different traditions.

None of his writings survive, and some interpreters have considered the possibility that he presented difficulties for the theory of knowledge without, however, insisting on a sceptical answer. The major sources of information are writings by Photius and Sextus Empiricus.

Note: The title 'Aenesidemus' was used for an important early critique of Kant's philosophy. This was an anonymous treatise defending Humean scepticism; its author was Gottlob Ernst Schulze (1761–1833).

aeon /'iːən; 'iːɒn/ *n.* in Gnosticism, a hypostatized divine attribute, conceived of as a very powerful being. *See also* EON.

aestheticism /ɪs'θɛtɪsɪzm/ *n.* **1** giving priority to aesthetic values. **2** theory, often summed up in the French *l'art pour l'art*, that art has intrinsic value and should be valued for its own sake only, and not for other purposes or functions that it may have. This theory had many advocates in the nineteenth century. (An extreme formulation was: 'Whatever is useful is ugly'.)

aesthetics /ɪs'θɛtɪks; ɛs-/ (Gr. *aisthēsis* sense-perception, sensation) *n. sing.* **1** the study of what is immediately pleasing to our visual or auditory perception or to our imagination: the study of the nature of beauty; also, the theory of taste and criticism in the creative and performing arts.

The word was first used in this sense by Alexander Baumgarten (1714–62) in a dissertation of 1735, and in his *Aesthetica* 1750. Plato, Aristotle, Hutcheson, Hume, Kant, Hegel and Schopenhauer are but a few of the philosophers who in the past made important contributions to this study. **2** In Kant's *Critique of Pure Reason*, the Transcendental Aesthetic is the investigation of the way our external and internal senses convey knowledge of objects. The main result is that space and time must be presupposed as forms of all sensory intuition.

aetiology /iːtɪ'ɒlədʒɪ/ (Gr. *aitia* cause, explanatory factor; that which is responsible for an outcome) *n.* **1** inquiry into, or theory of, the causes of a particular phenomenon or of phenomena of a certain kind.
2 the cause(s) of a particular phenomenon or of phenomena of a certain kind.

affection *n.* **1** a contingent, alterable, state or quality of a being. **2** feeling; emotion. **3** positive feeling towards someone, as in friendship.

affective fallacy (in literary theory) evaluating a literary work through its impact on the reader's subjective, emotional response rather than by considering the qualities of the work itself. W. K. Wimsatt and Monroe Beardsley, *The Verbal Icon* 1954, argued that this was an error and gave it this name.

affirmative action action designed to give special support to members of disadvantaged sections of society, e.g. by facilitating access to education or employment.

The expression is of recent origin, and so is the debate concerning the merits of affirmative action. In favour, it can be argued that affirmative action is necessary in order to compensate for past injustice or in order to create genuine equality of opportunity. Against, it can be argued that affirmative action is itself unfair and discriminatory, by not giving preference on the basis of individual merit.

affirmative proposition (in syllogistic logic) a proposition of the form *All S is P* or of the form *Some S is P*.

affirming the antecedent a form of inference, also known as MODUS PONENS.

affirming the consequent a kind of fallacious reasoning. For example: 'If Jill loves Jack, she cooks his meals. Jill cooks Jack's meals. Therefore, Jill loves Jack.' This is a fallacy. The conclusion can be false even if the premisses are true. The general form of the fallacy is:

If p then q   q
―――――――――
p

This pattern may deceive the unwary because of its similarity to MODUS PONENS.

a fortiori /aː fɔːtɪ'ɔːrɪ; eɪ fɔːtɪ'ɔːraɪ/ Lat. *a fortiori argumento* for a stronger reason; all the more; with all the more reason; with even greater certainty.

agape /'ægəpɪ/ (Gr. *agapē* love) *n.* the word commonly used for Christian love. In contrast to *eros*, a kind of love which even in its higher manifestations retains an element of self-seeking desire, *agape* is the wholly unselfish, outgoing form of love, and is Christian love properly so called, according to the Swedish theologian Anders Nygren (*Agape and Eros* 1932–9), who argued that Augustine conflated the two and that his influence had subsequently led much Christian theology astray.

agathon /'ægəθɒn/ Gr. the good *n.* This is the word used by Aristotle when he states at the beginning of the *Nicomachean Ethics* that the good is that at which all things aim.

agent *n.* a person who acts. In philosophical usage it is not implied that the action is on someone else's behalf.

agent-neutral Agent-neutral reasons relate to what an agent ought to value independently of any particular relation to himself. *Agent-relative* reasons, in contrast, refer to the particular characteristics or circumstances of the agent. Thomas Nagel, for instance, writes (*Equality and Partiality* 1991, p. 40) 'Each of us has an agent-neutral reason to care about everyone, and in addition an agent-relative reason to care more particularly about himself.' These two kinds of reasons are both universal, in that they are taken to apply to any agent. The distinction, first introduced by Nagel (*The Possibility of Altruism* 1970) in terms of objective and subjective reasons, is often observed in recent moral theory.

agent-relative *See* AGENT-NEUTRAL.

Age of Reason The ENLIGHTENMENT.

agglomeration, principle of If a person has a duty, for instance a moral duty, to do A and a duty to do B, it seems reasonable to infer that that person has a duty to do both A and B. In DEONTIC LOGIC, this rule of inference, in its general form, has been called the principle of agglomeration. It states that O(A) & O(B) entails O(A & B), where O signifies some concept of moral necessity ('shall', 'ought', 'is obligatory', 'is commanded' etc.).

There are objections to this deontic principle of agglomeration. It has been argued, for instance, that it does not hold for moral duties since there can be genuine moral dilemmas in which a person has a duty to do A but also a duty to do B, although it is impossible to do both, and therefore no duty to do both. A similar objection can be made in respect of the concept of legal duty.

The principle was so named by Bernard Williams in his 'Ethical Consistency', *Proceedings of the Aristotelian Society, Supplementary Volume 39* (1965), 103–24.

Instead of *agglomeration*, the word *combination* is sometimes used in these contexts.

The converse principle has been called the *principle of division*. It states that O(A & B) entails O(A) & O(B).

This principle has also been disputed. Examples can easily be found where it seems that unless both duties are performed, there is no duty to do only one: for instance, soaking a garment and washing it.

agnosticism (Gr. *a-* (privative prefix) + *gnōsis* knowledge) *n.* a theory according to which things within a specified realm are unknowable. Especially: (1) the view that we cannot know whether or not God exists; (2) the view, to be found in positivist theories like those of du Bois-Reymond and Spencer, that ultimate reality is unknowable. Kant's philosophy is sometimes interpreted in this way. The term was created by Thomas Huxley in 1869 (*Collected Essays*, vol. 5, p. 239).

agonistic (Gr. *agōn* contest) *adj.* polemical; combative (in the context of physical, psychological, ideological, etc. conflict).

Agrippa /ə'grɪpə/ (*fl.* AD 230?) Roman sceptical philosopher. Little is known about him, except that he summarized the arguments for scepticism in five 'tropes': (1) the diversity of opinion about the same object; (2) the infinite regress in every proof, since every premiss has to be proved in turn; (3) the variety of ways in which an object appears to observers, varying with differences between them and differences in the object's environment; (4) the arbitrariness in all efforts to cut off an infinite regress dogmatically; (5) the question-begging nature of every proof. The last point, elaborated by Sextus Empiricus, and reasserted by John Stuart Mill about 1600 years later, is that, for instance, in a syllogism: *Every man is mortal, Socrates is a man, Therefore Socrates is mortal*, the conclusion must be known before we can know that the first premiss is true.

Agrippa of Nettesheim /ə'grɪpə əv 'nɛtəs-haɪm/, Heinrich Cornelius (1486–1535) born in Cologne; a colourful Renaissance intellectual and controversialist. He took a keen interest in cabbalism, alchemy, astrology, numerology, etc., but later in life he turned both against these disciplines and also against the more respectable, established forms of learning in his *Invective Declamation on the Uncertainty and Vanity of the Sciences* 1526, in favour of scepticism and simple fideist (FIDEISM) piety.

aidōs /'aɪdɒs/ Gr. sense of shame, shyness, modesty, respect *n.* having and showing proper respect towards persons who deserve it. It is the subject of a speech by Protagoras in Plato's dialogue of that name. In Aristotle, it is described as a mean between bashfulness and impudence.

Aidōs is not in Aristotle's list of virtues, because he classifies it as a sentiment, not as a disposition.

aitia /'aɪtɪə/ Gr. cause, explanatory factor; culpability, responsibility.

Ajdukiewicz /aɪduːkɪ'evɪtʃ/, Kasimierz (1890–1963) a leading representative of the logical-analytical tradition in Polish philosophy, with strong empiricist leanings. His philosophical interests ranged widely, and his influence as an intellectual was considerable. His view of logic and the theory of knowledge has been described as radical conventionalism. He maintained that in our natural languages there is no strict distinction between analytic and synthetic statements, nor between rules of logical inference and scientific hypotheses. In the face of certain new discoveries, for instance in quantum physics, it can on this view be a matter of convenience and convention whether we revise the rules or the hypotheses. His categorial grammar (1935) was an important source for Richard Montague's work.

akrasia /ə'krɑːzɪə/ (Gr. *a-* (privative prefix) + *kratos* power, rule, control) *n.* weakness of will; lack of self-control. To fail to act although one judges that one has sufficient reason to act, is to be akratic. Weakness of will is expressed in Ovid's *video meliora proboque, deteriora sequor*: I see the better course and approve, and yet I follow the worse. It is well known to those who wish to give up a bad habit but yield to temptation.

According to certain moral theories, approving of a course of action, or judging a proposed action to be the right one, consists in having an intention to perform the action, or at least to try. For theories of this kind, weakness of will becomes an important problem.

The first extended discussion is in Aristotle's *Nicomachean Ethics*, Book 7. (In some translations *akrasia* is translated by *incontinence* and an akratic person is said to be *incontinent*.) **akratic** *adj.*

Alain /alɛ̃/ (= Emile Chartier) (1868–1951) In his books and daily newspaper columns ('*Propos*'), Alain, who was a *lycée* professor of philosophy, dealt eclectically and edifyingly with the major thinkers and the grand themes of philosophy. He was particularly concerned to defend the idea of human freedom and moral responsibility. His political stance was radical in the French sense, i.e. republican, secular, liberal. More an essayist than a systematic philosopher, Alain has had a remarkably strong influence in twentieth-century French intellectual life, not least because of the entrenched position of his writings in the French philosophy curriculum.

Albert /albɛrt/, Hans (1921–) German philosopher and social theorist, professor at Mannheim until 1989. His best-known work, *Traktat über kritische Vernunft* 1968, revised edn 1991 (*Treatise on Critical Reason*) advocates a critical rationalism, influenced by Popper's. Relativism is rejected and dogmatism criticized for its reliance on 'immunization strategies' calculated to deflect legitimate criticism. Albert formulated 'the Münchhausen trilemma', arguing against foundationalism that it would have to accept for the justification of knowledge-claims either an infinite regress, or a logical circle, or an arbitrary cut-off. All three are uninviting. In Albert's view, all knowledge-claims are in principle fallible and open to revision. In the German POSITIVISM DISPUTE that reached its peak in the early 1960s, Albert and Popper were the main opponents of Adorno and Habermas. AM/ed.

Albertus Magnus /æl'bɜːtəs 'mægnəs/ (*c.* 1200–1280) Also known as Albert the Great, he became a Dominican, taught at Cologne and Paris, and was a teacher of Thomas Aquinas. A great polymath, his interests included the natural sciences, and the Greek and Islamic learning in these and other disciplines. He began what Aquinas continued: the reception of Aristotle into mainstream Western philosophy. He wrote a *Summa Theologiae*, and commentaries on works by Aristotle.

alchemy *n.* a kind of theory about material substances, based on close analogies between material qualities and relations on the one hand, mental or spiritual ones on the other. Among its practical applications was the preparation of medicines, but best known is the attempt to make gold out of base metals. That process required a catalyst, known as the philosopher's stone. Alchemy flourished in the late Middle Ages and the Renaissance.

Alembert *See* D'ALEMBERT.

aleph *n.* **1** the first letter in the Hebrew alphabet: ℵ. **2** (in transfinite mathematics) any infinite cardinal number. $\aleph_0$ (aleph nought) designates the smallest infinite cardinality, i.e. that of the natural numbers.

alethic modalities (Gr. *alētheia* truth) name commonly given to the modal concepts *possible*, *necessary*, *impossible* and *contingent*, to distinguish them from, e.g. *epistemic* modalities such as *known*, *believed*, and from *deontic* modalities such as *obligatory*, *permissible*, *optional*. GH

Alexander of Aphrodisias /ælɪg'zændə əv æfrəʊ'diːsɪəs/ (*fl. c.* 200 BC) Aristotelian philosopher. Of his commentaries on Aristotle's works, many survive. The commentary on the first five books of the *Metaphysics* is by him – the commentary on the rest is by another author, some eight centuries later. His *On Fate* was written against Stoicism, and he is thought to have influenced Plotinus. HT/ed.

Alexander, Samuel (1859–1938) an Australian who, after studies in Oxford, followed by a fellowship there, obtained a chair in philosophy at Manchester. He became from the turn of the century an important figure in the realist movement, insisting that knowledge is of a world that exists independently of the knowing subject. Alexander differed, however, from others in this movement in his construction of a naturalistic metaphysical system on a realist basis. It was a historical hypothesis of the emergent evolutionary kind, resulting from reflection on the features of our experience, and designed to account for all of them. He presented this theory in his Gifford Lectures from 1916 to 1918, which were published in 1920 under the title *Space, Time, and Deity*. Space-time is conceived of as the basic stuff of the universe, the categories – the ones of which Kant had given an account in the *Critique of Pure Reason* – are its pervasive features, and from it evolve the qualities of matter, the secondary qualities, and the qualities of life and mind. All of these are *emergent* qualities. At any stage, but in particular from the stage where mind has emerged, Deity is that which is the next higher quality to emerge – Deity is that which is beyond and as yet unrealized. There are no 'degrees of reality' as envisaged by the idealists, and minds, in particular, simply exist alongside everything else. Values, conceived of as arising from a certain relation between minds and the world, were the subject of a further volume, *Beauty and Other Forms of Value*, published in 1933. QG

Alexandrian School a Platonic school which is said to have flourished in Alexandria for three centuries until the Arab conquest in 642. The extent to which the thinkers in that city belonged to a single school is now in doubt. Important neo-Platonists from Alexandria were Hierocles, Hypatia, Hermias, John Philoponus (*c.* 490–570) and Olympiodorus. The Alexandrian neo-Platonists were more accommodating to Christian thought than the Academy in Athens, which also favoured neo-Platonism, but where paganism was more entrenched. They believed that there were natural moral and religious notions common to man, so that religious differences were really nothing more than different symbols or allegories for the same underlying truth.

algebraic number a real number which is a solution to an equation of the form

$$a_0x^n + a_1x^{n-1} + a_2x^{n-2} \ldots + a_{n-1}x + a_n = 0$$

where all the a's are rational numbers. Real numbers that are not algebraic are called transcendental.

al-Ghazali, Abu Hamid Muhammad (1058–1111) Persian Islamic philosopher, known as Algazel in medieval Europe. Using philosophical techniques in theology, he nevertheless argued against the rationalist elements in the theories of Avicenna and other leading thinkers in his *Incoherence of the Philosophers* (to which Averroes later replied with a *Incoherence of the Incoherence*). Al-Ghazali emphasized the contingency of everything and God's complete freedom of decision, and inclined towards a neo-Platonic mysticism. His philosophy became well-known, and influential on Jewish and Christian thought.

algorithm *n.* procedure for carrying out ('mechanically') a mathematical or formal calculation: an effective process that transforms one expression into another in a finite number of steps.

The word is derived from the name of the Arab mathematician al-Khuwarizmi (*fl.* 830).

alienans (Lat. alienating, estranging, casting off) *n.*, *adj.* If an adjective A qualifies a term N so that something can be A+N without being an N, the adjective is said to be (an) alienans. Examples: *X is an expectant mother* does not imply that X *is* a mother; *Y is a reformed thief* does not imply that Y *is* a thief; *Z is a potential victim* does not imply that Z *is* a victim; etc.

This can be contrasted with the cases in which an A+N has to be an N: *X is a doting mother* implies that X is a mother; *Y is a cunning thief* implies that Y is a thief; *Z is a helpless victim* implies that Z is a victim.

Sometimes the term is given a narrower sense, so that A is an alienans if and only if being A+N implies not being N.

alienation *n.* **1** the renunciation or transfer to another party of something that is one's own. An inalienable right is, accordingly, a right that cannot be renounced or transferred; whether it can be forfeited is unclear.

2 (in older medical terminology) not being in one's senses; in older usage, a psychiatrist is known as an alienist.

3 (a) a process of estrangement or isolation from a natural or social context; (b) the condition arising as a result of such a process; (c) the subjective experience of being in such a condition.

The connotation is negative: the word signifies something undesirable or unwelcome.

This concept became a focus of interest once Marx's early economic and philosophical manuscripts of 1844 were published for the first time in 1932 (and in English translation not until 1959), and especially from the late 1940s to the late 1970s, when the word also became a modish expression of political, personal or general discontent.

Hegel had used this concept in his account of the history of the absolute mind or consciousness, which posits difference within itself and then does its best to overcome this self-alienation to regain unity. He also used it in his analysis of human activity, whose products, be they material objects, social institutions, or cultural achievements, become separate from their origin. This alienation can be overcome by achieving full knowledge of the object.

Influenced by Hegel, Feuerbach also believed that alienation is overcome by the gaining of insight. In his analysis of religion, he argued that through a fateful error, human beings fail to recognize that human nature is in itself good. Instead, they project the good qualities that belong to human nature to an imaginary being, God, who is supposed to be the bearer of all perfections. Through this alienation, man comes to regard himself as being worthless, and ascribes everything worthwhile to another being. By gaining insight into the nature of man and the nature of religion, the alienation and the sense of worthlessness that goes with it can be overcome. Freed from this obstacle, individuals can actualize the full potential of their human nature.

This approach was generalized by Marx. It is not only in religion, but also in other cultural manifestations, as well as in actually existing political institutions and economic activity, especially because of the worker's lack of control over the conditions of work, that human beings lose some of their human nature or essence, i.e. are alienated, and thus become incapable of self-development and self-fulfilment. Some political movements of Marxist inspiration have seen it as their aim to restructure human society, including the production of goods, so that alienation is overcome and individuals can actualize their full human potential.

Five senses of *alienation* were distinguished by M. Seeman, writing in the *American Sociological Review* 1959, at a time when the concept was emerging as the central one in social and political theory: powerlessness, meaninglessness, social isolation, normlessness, self-estrangement. Used in this way, the term describes a variety of conditions, irrespective of how they have arisen. This goes beyond the earlier usage, which applied the term only to conditions that are the result of a *process* of alienation.

aliorelative *See* REFLEXIVE.

allegory (Gr. *allos* other + *agoreuein* to address an assembly) *n.* a story which in addition to its apparent meaning also carries another moral, political or spiritual message. Examples are Bunyan's *Pilgrim's Progress* and Orwell's *Animal Farm.*

allocratic (Gr. *allos* other + *kratein* to rule) *adj.* In the theory of interpretation, E. D. Hirsch has contrasted allocratic and autocratic norms of interpretation. Allocratic norms allow for the revision of an interpretation in the light of new evidence and new theories. Autocratic interpretation makes the reader the ultimate authority for the validity of an interpretation, and is not susceptible to revision (unless the reader changes his mind).

allographic (Gr. *allos* other + *graphein* to write) *adj.* Every accurate copy (of the text, the score, etc.) of an *allographic* work of art genuinely represents the work. Literary works, musical compositions, are allographic. In contrast, every copy of an *autographic* work of art is an imitation or a forgery. Paintings, and prints from an original plate, are autographic. The distinction, introduced by Nelson Goodman in *Languages of Art* 1968, applies to works of art for which there is a criterion of identity. An autographic work is identified through the history of its production, an allographic work is not. In the beginning, he suggests, there was only autography: the existence and use of a suitable notation are necessary conditions for allography.

Almagest an encyclopedic work on mathematics and astronomy, in 13 books, compiled *c.* 140 by Ptolemy (Claudius Ptolemaeus of Alexandria). Its name is that of the Arabic translation of 827. It contains, *inter alia*, the Ptolemaic astronomy which prevailed until the Copernican revolution.

als ob /als ɔp (Gm.)/ Gm. as if. The expression is sometimes used with allusion to Vaihinger's fictionalism.

alter /ˈæltə; ˈɔːltə/ Lat. other, the other.

alter ego /ˈæltə iːgəʊ; ˈɔltə iːgəʊ/ Lat. another self; a second self.

To regard another person truly as a friend is to regard him as an *alter ego*, according to Aristotle (*Nicomachean Ethics* 1166ᵃ32; 1169ᵇ7).

alterity *n.* otherness. Sartre also uses 'alterity' to denote separation, in contrast to reciprocity.

alternation *n.* **1** inclusive disjunction: p or q is true if and only if at least one of p and q is true. **2** exclusive disjunction: p or q is true if and only if exactly one of p and q is true.

Usage varies. A few writers use the term in the first sense, others in the second. *See also* DISJUNCTION.

Althusser /altysɛːʀ (Fr.)/, Louis (1918–90) a professional philosopher and an active member of the French Communist Party. His most influential works were *Pour Marx* 1965 (For Marx), *Lire le Capital* 1968 (*Reading Capital*) and the essays collected in *Lenin and Philosophy and other essays*

1971. These essays are a sustained attempt to establish Marxism as a science of history and to argue, against the claims of Marxist humanism, that there is a radical discontinuity between the ideas of the young Marx and the scientific analysis set out in *Capital*. Althusser's anti-humanism was a major influence on the French left-wing intelligentsia in the 1960s. Althusser retracted some of his most important theses in *Elements d'autocritique* 1974 ('Elements of self-criticism' in: *Essays in Self-Criticism*) and later writings, but these works had little impact. His public life ended in 1980, after he strangled his wife and was committed to a psychiatric clinic.

Adapting an argument of Gaston Bachelard, Althusser maintains that each new science emerges as the product of an epistemological break, involving revolutionary reconstruction of an ideologically generated set of problems that precedes it, and he insists that such a break can be detected in the difference between the humanistic writings of the early Marx and the scientific texts of his maturity. Althusser describes scientific knowledge as the outcome of a practice governed, not by the intentions of scientists themselves, but rather by the system of concepts, or problematic, which determines the questions to be investigated, the kinds of evidence to be sought, and the difficulties that are recognized as important – much as an assembly line determines the tasks to be performed by those who work on it.

He defines ideology in terms of the 'lived' or 'imaginary' relation between individuals and the social conditions of their existence – thereby suggesting that ideology is an inescapable feature of the human condition. Theoretical ideologies (e.g. Aristotelian physics and the non-Marxist social sciences) are elaborated versions of those imaginary relations: they appear to be governed by their own distinctive range of problems, but they also reflect the forms of human subjectivity and the class relations in which those forms are constituted. While, in Althusser's view, the sciences have an autonomous dynamic of their own, theoretical ideologies are subject to the play of contending social forces. This distinction between science and theoretical ideology has proved difficult to sustain – especially since Althusser also maintains (in *Lénine et la philosophie*) that the principal task of philosophy is to defend the sciences against the encroachment of ideology.

Marxists have generally insisted that while the economic foundation of society plays a fundamental role, law, politics and ideology nevertheless have some degree of autonomy. What most distinguishes Althusser's account of Marxism as a science is his insistence that both Marxist humanism and Marxist orthodoxy have mistakenly analysed societies in historicist terms, that is, in terms of the 'expressive' causality of a 'Hegelian' theoretical ideology – which allows law, politics and ideology to be read as expressions of an essence located either in the economic foundation itself or in the class relations to which it gives rise. In fact, Althusser claims, the argument of Marx's *Capital* makes use of a structural causality, a relationship between a structure and its parts such that the structure secures the conditions of existence of its parts while the parts provide the conditions of existence of the structure. This suggests that, once existing, the structure will be self-perpetuating, a conclusion that is difficult to reconcile with Althusser's own insistence in other contexts on the historical importance of class struggle. This concept of structural causality is an integral part of Althusser's anti-humanism: it suggests that human individuals should not be seen as independent creative subjects but rather as bearers of functions that arise from their location within a structure. BHI

altruism (Lat. *alter* (the) other) *n.* benevolent concern for the interests and welfare of other persons. The term was created by Auguste Comte in his *Cours de philosophie positive* 1830–42, and gained currency in English from the 1850s through the writings of G. H. Lewes (1817–78) and Herbert Spencer (*Principles of Psychology*, part 8). Initially, 'altruism', 'egoism', and their cognates sounded scientific, but are now part of common language. The contrast had previously been marked by other pairs of terms: benevolence/self-love; public affection/private affection; kindness/selfishness, etc.

Nobody doubts that motivation can be egoistic, but the possibility of genuine altruism has been keenly debated for centuries. Sceptical moralists have shown how ulterior motives of self-interest hide behind much apparent altruism. Others have made the stronger claim that altruism is nothing over and above egoism. They hold that benevolent concern for others is nothing but a subtler way to satisfy one's own desires or interests. This view, now known as PSYCHOLOGICAL EGOISM, was in the eighteenth century attacked by Hutcheson, Butler and Hume. Their objections have become widely accepted.

It has been argued that some motivation is neither altruistic nor egoistic, but may be merely disinterested. *See* NON-TUISM.

Note: 'Egoism' can denote either a quality of character and conduct, or a psychological or ethical theory; 'altruism' is not used to denote a theory.

ambiguity *n.* the presence of two (or more) meanings. There are two main kinds of ambiguity. An example of *semantic* (or *lexical*) ambiguity is provided by the word 'bank', which can mean a financial institution or the sloping border of a river. *Syntactic* (or *structural*) ambiguity arises from the structure of a clause: '. . . restoration after 15 years of a Labour government' can be taken to imply either that Labour has been in power for 15 years, or that it has not.

Ambiguities can be dispelled by means of explanation. To prevent them from arising, care in the choice of words helps, but sometimes what is needed is attention to punctuation (or intonation). A comma can make a great difference: if one says 'Call me, Ishmael' the person addressed is presumably so named, but if one says 'Call me Ishmael', there is no ground for such a presumption. A hyphen makes all the difference between the noun-phrase 'virtue-rules' and the sentence 'virtue rules'. The hyphen can also help to save – or wreck – a marriage: note the difference between 'extra-marital sex' and 'extra marital sex'.

ambiguity, intolerance of inability or unwillingness to accept that no definite conclusion can be reached on the basis of insufficient evidence. For instance, at first sight we do not normally have enough information to tell what the person whom we have just met is really like. The only rational thing to do is to suspend judgement. But those who cannot tolerate ambiguity are unable to do so. They rush to judgement, perhaps by relying on some theory of character types supplied by biology (a theory of racial types, say), psychology, astrology, numerology, etc. To the person unable to keep an open mind the scientific credentials of the theory are inessential: what is sought is satisfaction of the need for certainty.

The concept was first used by Else Frenkel-Brunswik in the 1940s in the description of the AUTHORITARIAN PERSONALITY.

Different from this is of course the 'intolerance' shown when ambiguities that underlie fallacious reasoning are revealed and rejected.

amoral (Gr. *a-* (privative prefix) + moral) *adj.* 1 having no moral awareness or moral concerns. 2 having no moral dimension; non-moral.

This hybrid neologism was created by Jean Guyau.

amor fati /ˈæmɔː ˈfɑtɪ/ Lat. *amor* love; *fatum* fate; the willing acceptance, indeed love, of one's fate. Nietzsche sees it as constitutive of human greatness, in his *Ecce homo* (written in late 1888). His concept is a more extreme variant of the Stoic notion of willing submission to one's destiny.

amour de soi /amuʀ də swa (Fr.)/ Fr. love of self. Rousseau's concept of *amour de soi* includes (1) the natural, innocent, benign instinct of self-preservation, (2) the concern for one's own interests that can express itself without detriment to others; and (3) proper self-esteem. He distinguishes it from *amour-propre*. His concept of the latter is usually taken to be the tendency to assert oneself competitively at the expense of others; it can display itself as selfishness, arrogance, vanity, etc. It has been argued, however, that this misrepresents his real view: *amour-propre* expresses itself in these negative ways only because of the corrupting influence of society, and in itself *amour-propre* need not be more than the proper assertion of oneself as an equal of other persons.

amour-propre /amuʀ proprə (Fr.)/ Fr. self-love. *See* AMOUR DE SOI.

amphiboly (Gr. *amphibolia* throwing in two directions) *n.* equivocation, ambiguity. Aristotle distinguished (*Sophistical Refutations* 4, 106^{a}22) amphiboly, i.e. syntactic ambiguity, from what he called homonymy, i.e. semantic ambiguity.

In an appendix to the Transcendental Analytic in the *Critique of Pure Reason*, Kant discusses the 'amphiboly of concepts of reflection'. These are the concepts identity/difference; compatibility/opposition; internal/external; matter/form. When these concepts are applied, we have to be clear about whether we relate them to the domain of the intellect or to the domain of phenomena. Lack of clarity on this point leads to confusion, and is, in Kant's view, a shortcoming in Leibniz's metaphysics.

ampliation *n.* In medieval logic, *ampliation* is the widening of the extension of a term. An *ampliative judgement* is a synthetic judgement in Kant's sense: the predicate is not contained in the concept of the subject. In contrast, a clarificatory judgement spells out something that is contained in the concept of the subject. *Ampliative reasoning*, in the terminology of C. S. Peirce, is so called because it yields a conclusion that contains more information than the premisses, as in induction from a finite number of observed instances to a general causal relationship. *Ant.* restriction.

amplification (Lat. *amplificare* to increase, to augment) *n.* the expansion of a statement for rhetorical effect.

amuse *vb.* (in older usage) to bewilder, to lead astray.

anachronism (Gr. *anachronismos* (cf. *ana-* back; up; against + *chronos* time) an incorrect time reference) *n.* 1 an error of chronology. 2 something occurring out of its historical setting; for example, a goose-quill in a modern office can be called an anachronism.

anachrony *n.* (in literature) discrepancy between the order of events and the order in which they are told: a flashback (analepsis) or a 'flashforward' (prolepsis).

anacoluthon /ænəkəˈluːθɒn/ *n.* (in grammar and rhetoric) a break in the syntax of a sentence which begins in one construction and ends in another.

anagoge, anagogy /'ænəgɒdʒɪ/ (Gr. *anagōge* leading up; raising) *n.* **1** spiritual or allegorical interpretation of an uplifting kind, especially of Scripture. **2** (in Aristotle's syllogistics) direct reduction to a syllogism in the first figure, in contrast to *apagoge*, indirect reduction.

analepsis /ænə'lɛpsɪs/ (*sing.*); **analepses** /anə'lɛpsiːz/ (*pl.*) (Gr. *ana*-back + *lēpsis* a taking) *n.* (in literature) an account of what had happened earlier, a flashback.

analogia entis /ænə'lɔdʒɪə 'ɛntɪs/ Lat. analogy of being.

analogies of experience This is Kant's designation (*Critique of Pure Reason* B 218-B 265; *Prolegomena* 57) of three *a priori* principles that are presupposed for all empirical knowledge: (1) that there is something permanent underlying every change; (2) that nothing that happens can be preceded by 'empty time', i.e. that every event has a cause (B 237); (3) that all things perceived as coexisting in space, interact.

Kant called these principles analogies, because the 'inference' from the perception of certain qualities to a substance in which they inhere, or from an event to an antecedent cause, etc., resembles inferences by analogy.

analogy *n.* similarity, likeness.

One of the uses of this concept is in attempts to explain how religious statements can make sense. The problem is that if our words are used in their ordinary sense, God is reduced to human proportions, but if they are not, what sense can they make? One important discussion is in Aquinas, *Summa Theologiae* 1a, q.13, 5 and 6: a few predicates, all of them negative, apply univocally to God, e.g. 'eternal', 'simple'. But for the most part, predicates are applied to God neither univocally, nor equivocally, but by analogy. The *analogy of being* is based on the idea that God, being the cause of whatever is good in a kind of thing, can be described by the predicate that expresses the perfection in that kind of thing. Distinct from this is the *analogy of proportion*: God is to man as a shepherd to his sheep.

analysandum (*sing.*); **analysanda** (*pl.*) *n.* that which is to be analysed.

analysans *n.* that which gives the analysis of an analysandum.

analysis (*sing.*); **analyses** (*pl.*) (Gr. *analysis* taking apart, decomposition) *n.* **1** the process of separating the constituents of a whole and discerning the manner in which they are interrelated. **2** the result of this process.

(In philosophy) *conceptual analysis*, or *philosophical analysis*, is, in general, the process (or its result) of explaining a concept, a belief, a theory, etc. by drawing attention to its constituents, its presuppositions, its implications, etc. This can in turn serve as a basis for a critical assessment.

Sometimes philosophical analysis is more narrowly conceived as *reductive* analysis: showing how concepts, beliefs, theories, etc. can be reduced to elements belonging to some basic category. An example would be the analysis of statements about a physical object into sets of reports about sense-data.

Philosophical analyses can take different forms. It is sometimes taken for granted that all of them have the same basic form, such as: (1) BC is the same as A; or (2) BC is a necessary and sufficient condition for A.

An example is this analysis of the concept of *widowhood*: *being a widow* is the same as *being female, and not being married, having been married, having one's last marriage ended by the husband's death*.

Another example is this analysis of the concept of *validity*: Necessarily, an argument is *valid* if and only if *it is impossible that all the premisses be true and the conclusion false*.

But it is a mistake to think that all philosophical analyses follow such patterns. For instance, the analysis of ought-statements as essentially having a motivating force cannot be accommodated to this model.

(In psychology) psychoanalysis.

(In mathematics) differential and integral calculus was in the past also called infinitesimal analysis. In current mathematical usage, analysis is that branch which deals with limits of functions, sequences and series.

analysis, non-standard a mathematical theory devised by Abraham Robinson (1918–74). It rehabilitates the concept of infinitesimal numbers (smaller than any given positive real number, and yet not equal to zero) and its use in the theory of derivatives and integrals. He devised non-standard models of a first-order theory of elementary arithmetic, and showed that these models can be extended so as to be models of a first-order theory of real numbers, in which the old notion of an infinitesimal can be defined. It is not liable to the cogent objections that Berkeley, in *The Analyst* 1734, directed against Newton's and Leibniz's use of infinitesimals.

analysis, paradox of There is a problem with philosophical analyses of forms such as *BC is the same as A*. The problem is that if such a statement is correct, then 'A' and 'BC' are synonyms: they have the same meaning. That may be of interest to a learner of the language, but trivial and uninformative from the point of view of philosophical inquiry. But if the two expressions do not have the same meaning, then the analysis is not correct. It seems, therefore, that a philosophical analysis cannot be both interesting (i.e. non-trivial) and correct.

The paradox was first presented by C(ooper) H(arold) Langford in 1942 in his contribution to P. A. Schilpp (ed.), *The Philosophy of G. E. Moore*. Since then, it has been extensively discussed.

Analytic(s) *n.* Aristotle's *Prior Analytics* and *Posterior Analytics* are two works on logic, constituting the third part of his *Organon*. The former contains his theory of the syllogism, the latter his theory of scientific knowledge and demonstration, definitions, and the origin of knowledge.

In Kant's *Critique of Pure Reason*, the Transcendental Analytic is that part of the Transcendental Logic section which investigates the *a priori* principles which determine the scope and validity of the operations of the mind, whilst the Transcendental Dialectic is that part which deals with the sophistries and illusions to which the human mind is prone. Kant adopted these terms from the logic of his time, where the part called analytic formulates (negative) tests of truth, and the part called dialectic explains how error and sophistry come about.

analytic *adj.* The important distinction between *analytic* and *synthetic* was foreshadowed in Locke and Leibniz, but the current terminology was introduced by Kant. His definitions are: An analytic statement is one in which the predicate is contained in the concept of the subject. A synthetic statement is one in which the predicate is not contained in the concept of the subject. Examples: *All red roses are red* is analytic, since the predicate *red* is contained in the concept *red roses*. *All bachelors are unmarried* is analytic, once it is assumed that the predicate *unmarried* is contained in the concept *bachelor*.

In a synthetic statement, the predicate adds something new. For example, *All roses are red* is synthetic, since the predicate *red* is not contained in the concept *rose*. Again, *All bachelors are happy* is synthetic, since the predicate *happy* is not contained in the concept *bachelor*.

Note that Kant's formulation is '. . . contained in *the concept of* the subject', and not simply '. . . contained in the subject'. The reason is that in his terminology, the predicate is contained in the subject in *every* true statement, but is contained in the concept of the subject only in *some* true statements, i.e. the analytic ones.

Kant's definitions apply only to subject-predicate statements. The more recent definitions apply also to statements of other kinds, e.g.: 'An analytic statement is one which is true in virtue of its meaning.' All statements that are analytic in Kant's sense are so in the modern sense, and all that are synthetic in Kant's sense are so in the modern sense.

An analytic statement cannot be denied without self-contradiction; a synthetic statement can. So if a statement is analytic, it is logically necessary, and if it is synthetic, it is logically contingent.

The distinction has been challenged in contemporary philosophy. One early well-known attack is that of W. V. O. Quine in his famous article 'Two dogmas of empiricism' in *Philosophical Review 60* (1951), reprinted in *From a Logical Point of View* 1953.

analytical geometry coordinate geometry, devised by Descartes in his *La Géometrie* 1637.

analytical jurisprudence a kind of legal theory which gives special emphasis to the precise analysis and articulation of basic legal concepts and principles, sometimes on the assumption that these are present in every legal system properly so called. John Austin (1790–1859) has been regarded as its main representative.

analytic philosophy a philosophical trend in the twentieth century which sees analysis as the proper method to resolve definitively the problems that are within the ken of philosophy. Behind this trend is at least one of two following assumptions: that the problems of philosophy arise from conceptual confusion capable of being dispelled by analysis, and that analysis consists in carefully discerning and exhibiting the simple constituents of more complex notions. The search for conceptual clarity led to a painstaking attention to detail, in contrast to the broad imaginative sweeps of grander theory. The objects of analysis were said to be concepts or propositions, but by the 1930s a linguistic turn became clearly noticeable. Language came to be regarded as the fundamental object of analysis, and analytic philosophy was often called linguistic.

Early in the twentieth century, Bertrand Russell and G. E. Moore in Cambridge were prominent representatives of this tendency, but similar movements emerged independently in other places, such as Uppsala, Warsaw and Vienna. At the time, the influence of analytic philosophy was limited, but it became reinforced in anglophone countries by exiled continental philosophers in the 1930s and 1940s. After the war it had gained hegemony there and also in the Nordic countries. Elsewhere, its influence grew, albeit later and more slowly.

Critics accuse the analytical movement of aridity and irrelevance; sympathizers see merit in its respect for rationality and its suspicion of rhetorical posturing and false profundity. It has been described as an antidote to 'the semantic pollution of the intellectual environment' (Stegmüller). The use of the label 'analytic philosophy' seems to have taken on after the publication of Arthur Pap's *Elements of Analytic Philosophy* 1949.

anamnesis /ænæmˈniːsɪs/ (Gr. *anamnēsis* recollection, remembrance) *n.* In Plato's dialogue *Meno* (80e–86c), an untutored slave-boy is able to display geometrical knowledge by merely answering questions put to him by Socrates. The explanation proposed is that the boy already has this knowledge although he was unaware of it, and that Socrates's questioning only helped to bring it to awareness. Indeed, recollection is invoked to explain our ability to reason logically. In the dialogue *Phaedo* (72e–77a) it is argued that we have ideas of various kinds of perfection which cannot be based on experience, since nothing in the world we experience is perfect; so recollection is invoked to explain our grasp of certain concepts that are not adequately exemplified in experience. In both passages Plato suggests that the soul is remembering what it had once seen or learnt in a previous existence, not in this world.

anankē /əˈnæŋkɪ/ Gr. necessity.

anaphora /əˈnæfərə/ (Gr. a bringing back, a carrying back) *n.* **1** (in grammar and logic) referring back; the use of a word as a substitute for a preceding expression. In the sentence *John bought a car and so did I*, the words *so* and *did* are used anaphorically. The use of third-person pronouns is usually anaphoric. **2** (in rhetoric) repetition of the same expression in successive clauses. An example is the use of 'blessed' in the Sermon on the Mount.

anarchism (Gr. *an-* (privative prefix) + *archē* rule, ruling power) *n.* a theory or a political movement which interprets the ideals of human freedom and equality very strictly, so as to exclude all relations of domination; particularly important is the refusal to accept the legitimacy of state power. All political structures in which there are rulers and subjects, all relations of authority and subordination, are rejected as being unjust and ultimately based on brute force. Political and economic institutions, organized or protected ultimately by the power of the state, are to be abolished. Instead, social organization should be based on small autonomous communities in which individuals freely cooperate towards common goals and engage in cooperative forms of production. Only under such conditions can human beings flourish and reach their full potential.

Modern anarchism can be traced to William Godwin's *An Enquiry Concerning the Principles of Political Justice* 1793, 3rd rev. edn 1798. Proudhon, the first to use the term, linked the anarchist ideal with the abolition of private property. Another leading early anarchist was Bakunin. From the outset, anarchist anti-authoritarianism led to theoretical and political conflict with socialism and communism. The hostility to the existing structures of domination also made some anarchist groups take recourse to 'propaganda through the deed' (i.e. acts of terrorism). As a political movement, anarchism was probably at its strongest in the period 1871–1914.

There are also libertarian varieties of anarchism, less radical, which advocate a minimal state which provides maximal scope for private initiative and free competition.

anarchy *n.* **1** a condition of political and social disorder (especially if due to absence of governmental control). **2** the political condition advocated by anarchism.

anatomic (Gr. *an-* (privative prefix) + *atomos* indivisible) *adj.* An anatomic property is one which is necessarily shared: it cannot be uniquely possessed. *Being a sibling* is anatomic, since it is impossible that one and exactly one person is a sibling. In contrast, an 'atomic' property is one that can belong to one thing only.

This new usage occurs in J. Fodor and

E. LePore, *Holism: A Shopper's Guide* 1992.

Anaxagoras /ænək'sægərəs/ (*c.* 500–428 BC) Anaxagoras of Clazomenae first made Mind a principle of philosophical explanation. After spending thirty years in Athens as an associate of Pericles and other important political leaders, he retired to Lampsacus to escape a prosecution for impiety. His philosophy was an attempt to provide an adequate basis for natural philosophy in the face of Parmenides's objections. Accepting from Parmenides the principle (1) that nothing is generated or destroyed, he defends the reality of change by maintaining (2) that there is a universal mixture of everything in everything, (3) that matter is infinitely divisible, and (4) that whatever predominates in a given mixture determines the character of that mixture.

Since there is no generation and destruction, every substance we meet in experience must always exist; when one substance appears to change into another, for instance when water appears to change into air through evaporation, what we are really witnessing is the emergence or 'separating off' of a second substance previously contained in the first: air was already in the water. Since water predominated in the mixture, we did not perceive the air, but it was there nonetheless. And since any substance can eventually produce any other, we must suppose that traces of every substance are in every other substance. On this account there must be an element corresponding to every kind of substance we perceive: water, air, blood, bone, etc. While Anaxagoras's physical theory is less economical than that of his contemporary Empedocles, who gets by with only four elements, Anaxagoras can claim that his theory satisfies Parmenides's requirements better because it does not require the generation of new substances from the elements, as does Empedocles's theory.

Like most of his contemporaries, Anaxagoras attempted to describe the origin and nature of the universe. He posited an initial chaos in which no distinct substance was discernible, but which had 'seeds' of all things in it. Besides the mixture of substances there was Mind (*nous*), which, though extended in space, does not mix with anything else, but has a principle of self-rule and a power to control physical substances. Mind began a circular motion which separated substances into different regions, forming a disc-shaped Earth surrounded by heavens moving in a vortex motion. The speed of the vortex picked up rocks and caused them to glow by its friction, producing the heavenly bodies. Anaxagoras's naturalistic account of the heavenly bodies seems to have occasioned the charge of impiety against him.

Anaxagoras maintained that Mind ordered all things, whether past, present, or future. Plato and Aristotle praised Anaxagoras for making Mind the cause of order in the universe, but they criticized him for failing to exploit his insight, for he appealed to mechanical causes rather than to reasons and purposes to tell how the universe came to be. Nevertheless, he did for the first time make a categorial distinction between mind and matter, and he did assign an essential causal role to mind. DG

Anaximander /ænæksɪm'ændə/ (*c.* 612–545 BC) The second major philosopher of ancient Greece, he was a native of Miletus and a successor of Thales. Like Thales, he thought that there was a single material source of all things, but for him it was not any determinate element but the APEIRON or boundless. The world arose when something productive of hot and cold was separated off, from which appeared Earth, surrounded by mist and a wall of fire. The fire broke into concentric rings surrounded by mist; through holes in the mist we see the light of the stars (in the ring or band closest to Earth), the moon (middle ring) and the sun (outermost ring). A disc-shaped Earth is balanced in the midst because of the symmetry of the world. The seasons arise from the predominance of hot or cold, wet or dry, powers; these powers come to be and perish into their opposites in an order determined by the assessment of Time, a quasi-personified agent. Anaximander drew a map of the Earth and explained meteorological phenomena by appealing to natural powers and processes. He also explained the appearance of life by a simple evolutionary process. Through his bold conjectures Anaximander seems to have set the tone and defined the content of early Greek philosophy. DG

Anaximenes /ænæk'sɪmənɪːz/ (*fl. c.* 545 BC) The third major philosopher of ancient Greece, he was, like Thales and Anaximander, a native of Miletus. He held that the original matter of the universe was air. When air is rarefied it becomes fire; when it is condensed or 'felted' it becomes successively wind, clouds, water, earth, and stones. A flat Earth rides on a cushion of air, while the heavens revolve around it like a felt cap. The cosmos is surrounded by a boundless expanse of air, which is divine, and may control the world, as air is the principle of life which controls humans. Anaximenes uses his physical theory to explain meteorological and geological phenomena. His notion of rarefaction and condensation as principles of physical transformation points the way towards a scientific approach to nature. DG

ancestral relation In the ordinary, biological, sense of 'ancestor', my ancestors (i.e. those who stand in the relation *ancestor of* to me) consist of my parents, the parents of my parents, the parents of the parents of my parents, and so on indefinitely. As the term is commonly used by logicians, the *ancestral relation* with respect to any given two-place relation R (commonly written R*) is that relation which stands to R as *ancestor of* stands to *parent of*. That is, x is R*-related to y if x is either R-related to y, or R-related to something that is R-related to y, or . . . For convenience, x is counted as being R*-related to itself, provided that it is R-related to anything or anything is R-related to it. For instance, in the field of the natural numbers, *equal to or greater than* is the ancestral relation of *successor of*. The notion of an ancestral relation is important in proofs by mathematical induction. GH

Anderson, John (1893–1962) Scottish-Australian philosopher. Born in Lanarkshire, educated in the University of Glasgow, at first in mathematics and natural philosophy (i.e. physics), then in philosophy, he was appointed professor of philosophy in Sydney in 1927, after lecturing in Welsh and Scottish universities.

Glasgow under Edward Caird had been a centre for a broadly-based, tolerant Hegelianism, but by the time Anderson arrived in Australia he was a realist, positivist, Marxist and empiricist. This last was in a special sense, for he rejected both the classical distinction between analytic and synthetic propositions and the view that our immediate experience is of elementary sense-data. Such 'empiricism', he argued, should rather be described as 'rationalism' in so far as it was a quest for certainty, even if it sought that certainty in our experience of sense-data rather than in first principles. In fact, we experience nothing less than complex states of affairs, situations, which in virtue of their infinite complexity we can always be mistaken about. By calling himself an 'empiricist' he was asserting that we have no other source of information about these states of affairs than what we can gather from observation and experiment, even if never in such a way as to exclude all risk of error.

His ontology was in general terms Heraclitean. Things persist in so far as there is a degree of balance between the forces that make them up: this is as true of the mind, where the conflict is between passions, and of society, where it is between social movements, as it is in the world at large. There are no conflict-free entities whether in the form of God, selves, or societies. He broke with Marxism to see in conflict something both perpetual and desirable.

Both in his ethics and his aesthetics he defended objectivism. Some forms of human activity have the property of being good, some works of art of being beautiful. In logic he defended a considerably elaborated version of the traditional logic; in mathematics, an empiricist version. His better-known pupils include John Mackie, David Armstrong and John Passmore, but he has also won the attention of political and legal thinkers and anthropologists. Where Plato saw philosophers as potential kings, Anderson saw them as perpetual critics.

An inveterate controversialist and a conscientious teacher of large classes, Anderson published no substantial books. His influence was mainly exerted through his lectures; but some of his views can be gathered in outline through the succinct essays published as *Studies in Empirical Philosophy* 1962, *Education and Inquiry* 1980 and *Art and Reality* 1982. JP

andreia Gr. manliness, bravery, valour, courage *n.* One of the four CARDINAL VIRTUES.

androcentrism (Gr. *anēr* man) *n.* male-centred bias; emphasis on masculine interests or points of view. Cf. GYNOCENTRISM.

androgyny (Gr. *anēr* man; *gynē* woman) *n.* hermaphroditism; uncertain sexual identity, combining male and female characteristics.

In feminist theory, the word is often used to signify a gender-free condition, i.e. absence of socially-induced differences between the sexes. In this usage, the guardians in Plato's republic are said to have an androgynous character in the sense that males and females have the same education, lifestyle and virtues. Jungian psychology is another area where the concept is of importance.

a necesse ad esse valet consequentia Lat. the inference from the necessary to the actual is valid. As an axiom in modal logic, this principle is sometimes called the axiom of necessity. *See also* MODALITIES.

***Angst*, angst** /aŋst (Gm.), æŋst (Eng.)/ (Gm., Dan. anxiety, anguish, dread) *n.* Like other moods, anxiety has no intentional object, in contrast to e.g. fear, which is fear *of* something. It was introduced as a philosophical topic by Kierkegaard in *Begrebet Angest* 1844 (The concept of dread). It is the state of mind of a person who comes to realize that he can use his freedom, when the path that may be chosen is not understood and yet exercises an attraction. In Heidegger, it is the state of mind that arises when contemplating sheer nothingness, as exemplified by death, when the standard way of looking at the world loses its obviousness. It is possible that this should be interpreted as implying that *Angst* is the state of mind that arises when one becomes aware of the fact that the framework we take for granted when we see ourselves as existing in the world is not given once and for all: anxiety arises from the thought that the framework we use to make sense of ourselves and of the world in which we see ourselves placed is not the only possible one.

animism (Lat. *anima* breath, vital principle; soul; spirit) *n.* the belief that material objects and the physical environment are imbued with some kind of soul or spirit. The term was introduced by the anthropologist E. B. Tylor (1832–1917) to designate what he took to be the earliest stage of the evolution of religion, common among primitive peoples. For philosophical theories that all matter contains an element of mind, the term *panpsychism* is more appropriate.

anomalous monism a kind of materialist theory of the mind, proposed and named in Donald Davidson's article 'Mental Events' in the early 1970s. According to the theory, every occurrence of a mental event is identical with some occurrence of a physiological, primarily neurological, event. This view is monistic because it rejects mind–body dualism, and takes every mental event also to be a physical one. Davidson calls his theory anomalous because it denies that there can be any strict laws connecting the physical to the mental. That is, a token mental event (i.e. a particular occurrence of a mental event of a certain kind) can be identified with a particular physical state, but there are no true general propositions that all mental occurrences of a certain kind are identical with physical states of a certain kind. This is contrary to the programme of the earlier identity theory of the mind, which assumes 'type–type' identity; anomalous monism assumes 'token–token' identity without any bridging laws linking tokens of the two kinds. *See also* MONISM.

anomie /'ænɔmɪ/ (Fr. *anomie*, from the Greek privative *a-* and *nomos* law, order) *n.* **1** a condition in which traditional social bonds and personal ties have been dissolved, and with them the individual's sense of attachment to society. An increase in crime and suicide rates is a symptom of this condition. The use of the word in this sense became established through the writings of Emile Durkheim published in the 1890s, especially his *Le Suicide* 1897 (Suicide). **2** The term had, however, been coined earlier and given a more favourable sense (now obsolete) by Jean Guyau in his *Esquisse d'une morale sans obligation ni sanction* 1885 (A sketch of morality independent of obligation or sanction) to designate the essential feature of the morality of the future: the individual would no longer be oppressed by a legalistic morality which lays down duties with penalties for non-compliance. Instead, the higher morality of the future would be guided by ideal values freely adopted by the individual. *See also* ANTINOMIANISM.

Anschauung /'anʃaʊʊŋ/ Gm. a looking at *n.* **1** view, opinion, outlook. *Weltanschauung* = world-view; *Lebensanschauung* = life-view: i.e. a view of the meaning of life and the destiny of man. **2** intuition; immediate awareness, immediate perception.

The word is used by Kant and many others as the equivalent of the Latin *intuitio*. In the *Critique of Pure Reason*, space and time are the form of sensory *Anschauung* (i.e. of our sense-experiences). Translators of Kant and Hegel regularly use *intuition* as the English equivalent.

Anscombe /'ænskəm/, Elizabeth (1919–) belonged to the inner circle around the later Wittgenstein, and held a chair at Cambridge until 1986. Her own work, much of it against the current, covers ethics, philosophy of mind, philosophy of religion, and is noted for its analytical incisiveness and a strongly anti-utilitarian, absolutist tendency on certain questions of ethics. She is the author of *Intention* 1957, *Three Philosophers* 1963 (jointly with her husband P. T. Geach), and a considerable number of articles, many of them in her *Collected Papers* (3 vols) 1981.

Anselm of Canterbury (1033–1109) Born at Aosta in Italy, Anselm became a monk and then abbot of Bec, in Normandy, and in 1093 Archbishop of Canterbury. From 1070 onwards he produced a series of treatises on important problems in theology and what would now be called the philosophy of religion. They included a daringly innovative explanation of why God became man (*Cur Deus Homo*), and discussions of truth, justice, sin, free will and the Trinity. Although Anselm was deeply influenced both by the Church Fathers (especially Augustine) and by Scripture, he never makes a parade of authorities. His treatises, sometimes in dialogue form, seem to be reflections considering a subject from first principles. There is a deceptive simplicity to their manner which often disguises a sophisticated and rigorous logic. One short monograph, *De grammatico*, shows more explicitly Anselm's interest in the logical problems raised by Aristotle's *Categories* and the theory of signification.

Anselm is known to philosophers above all as the deviser of the famous 'ontological' argument for the existence of God, proposed near the beginning of his *Proslogion*. God, he says, is that than which nothing greater can be thought. Suppose someone denies that God exists – that is to say, that he exists in reality: still, he can understand the concept of that than which nothing greater can be thought. That than which nothing greater can be thought exists, therefore, in his mind. But, Anselm argues, it is greater to exist both in reality and in the mind, than in the mind alone. If that than which nothing greater can be thought were to exist in the mind only, something could be thought which was like it in every way except that it existed in reality as well as in thought. It would therefore be greater than it. But this cannot be the case, if it is that than which nothing greater can be thought. Therefore that than which nothing greater can be thought must exist both in the mind and in reality, otherwise it would not be that than which nothing greater can be thought.

The ontological argument was discussed throughout the Middle Ages and later. Aquinas rejected it, remarking that the existence of God is not, as the argument suggests, self-evident. Duns Scotus accepted a greatly modified and sophisticated version of it. Descartes made his own peculiar adaptation of the argument one of the bases of his thought, whereas Kant dismissed it. Five pounds are greater than three pounds; but it is wrong, he urged, to say that five real pounds are greater than five imaginary pounds. The ontological argument relies on this type of reasoning, in which existence is treated as a perfection. Some twentieth-century philosophers, however, have reformulated the argument in ways which are not open to this objection, and Anselm's argument continues to be of interest to modal logicians and philosophers of religion. JM

an sich/für sich See IN ITSELF.

antecedent *n.* the clause in a conditional statement which states the condition. In a conditional of the form *if p then q*, *p* is the antecedent. The other statement, *q*, is called the consequent.

In Gentzen's sequent calculus, the part to the left in a sequent is called the antecedent, and the part on the right the *succedent*. The rule of MODUS PONENS is sometimes called the rule of affirming the antecedent. There is a fallacy known as DENYING THE ANTECEDENT.

antecedentialism *n.* moral theories according to which antecedent circumstances can be relevant in determining whether an action is right. Such moral theories can be contrasted with consequentialism, according to which only the value of the consequences of an action determines whether it is right.

The difference can be illustrated as follows. On an antecedentialist standpoint, the brave rescuer of a trapped accident victim *deserves* a reward, and this is why it is right to offer a reward. On a consequentialist standpoint, backward-looking considerations are, as such, irrelevant: it is right to offer a reward if and only if doing so will, on the whole, have beneficial consequences.

The word is a neologism, introduced in the late 1980s as a contrasting term to 'consequentialism', but is very seldom used. There is also a variant form 'antecedentalism'.

anthropic principle An anthropic principle states that the existence of intelligent human life places certain constraints on physical or metaphysical theories. A principle of this kind was proposed by the physicist Robert H. Dicke in 1961. A number of different principles have since been so called: (1) the weak anthropic principle: since human beings now exist, the basic constants of physics and other features of the physical universe, including its age, must be such as to permit this to have come to pass; (2) the strong anthropic principle: the basic constants of physics and other features of the universe must be such as to permit life to develop within it at some stage; (3) the participatory anthropic principle: no universe (including our own) can exist unless there are conscious intelligent observers. This variant is a version of philosophical idealism but is claimed to have scientific backing; (4) the final anthropic principle: intelligent observation must come into being, and once this has happened it cannot die out.

Also, together with the premisses (independently argued for) that there are conscious observers only on Earth, and that the existing universe cannot self-annihilate, it can be inferred that, once begun, life on Earth cannot be destroyed.

The term 'anthropic principle' for this kind of cosmological principle seems first to have been proposed by the astrophysicist B. Carter in 1974.

These and cognate versions of the anthropic principle are obviously debatable, and have indeed been keenly debated by philosophers and physicists. Prominent advocates are J. D. Barrow and F. J. Tipler. Martin Gardner is a well-known critic.

anthropocentrism (Gr. *anthrōpos* man, human being + *kentron* centre) *n.* an outlook that places mankind at the centre of the universe; a tendency to ascribe a particular significance to human beings and to human concerns in the general scheme of things.

This tendency is present in many traditional religious or philosophical worldviews, and in early science. It comes to expression, for instance, in the view that everything in nature exists for the sake of man. In the modern era, opposition to this tendency has been on the increase. An early important critic was Spinoza.

anthropology (Gr. *anthrōpos* man, human being) *n.* literally: the science of man. Various kinds of theory and discipline have been so called: (1) (in philosophical anthropology) theory of human nature; (2) (in physical anthropology) the scientific study of physical differences between members of different human groups; (3) (in social anthropology) the scientific study of social customs and institutions of human groups and societies; usually defined more narrowly to denote the study of primitive societies only; (4) (in cultural anthropology) the scientific study of cultures, especially of societies that have not been significantly influenced by Western civilization. One important strand (F. Boas, R. Benedict, M. Mead, R. Linton, A. Kardiner) has given special emphasis to the interplay between cultural norms and the emergence of certain personality types.

anthropomorphism (Gr. *anthrōpos* man, human being + *morphē* shape, form) *n.* the ascription of human characteristics to non-human beings. Views which represent God (or gods) as closely resembling a human being are anthropomorphic. Of the known attacks on religious anthropomorphism the first was made by Xenophanes.

More generally, the use of concepts that properly apply only to human beings when describing, interpreting and explaining non-human behaviour (of animals, plants, ecosystems or inanimate objects) is said to be anthropomorphic. It was G. H. Lewes (1817–78), the consort of the novelist George Eliot, who introduced this usage in the late 1850s.

anthropomorphite *n.* adherent of a fourth-century heresy which interpreted certain biblical descriptions of God very literally, and thus conceived God in the image of man.

anthropophobia (Gr. *anthrōpos* man, human being + *phobos* fear, dread, horror) (in Kant:) dislike of human company, although compatible with benevolence towards mankind. This is how the word is defined by Kant in his *Metaphysics of Morals*, in §26 of the Theory of Virtue.

anthroposcopism (Gr. *anthrōpos* man, human being + *skopia* a looking at, a watching) *n.* the view that human beings alone fall within the purview of moral theory, and that the moral relevance of non-human entities (animals, the environment) is indirect and secondary.

The use of the word in this sense in the early 1990s is of uncertain viability. In a different sense, *anthroposcopy* was used in the nineteenth century as a synonym of *physiognomy* (the art of judging a person's character from physical, especially facial, features).

anthroposophy *n.* a comprehensive system of ideas of a theosophical kind, developed by Rudolf Steiner (1861–1925). Its aim is to guide the individual, by way of a process of self-development, towards regaining contact with a spiritual world.

anticipations of perception Under this heading, Kant (*Critique of Pure Reason* B207–B218) formulates an *a priori* principle of experience: In every perception, the real that is an object of sensation has a certain intensive magnitude, i.e. a certain degree.

antihumanism *n.* in general, a view which rejects humanism (in any of the many senses of that term). In particular, *anti-humanism* has since the 1960s been used for the view held by prominent French intellectuals (structuralists, Althusserians), that human freedom is largely illusory. Human action is determined by structures (social, economic, linguistic) over which no individual can be in control. The later Heidegger saw humanism, represented by Descartes, Sartre• and others, as 'self-centred' and rejected it in favour of an attitude of 'openness, attentiveness, to Being'.

antilogism /æn'tɪlədʒɪzm/ *n.* **1** a group of three propositions {p_1, p_2, not-q} such that the joint truth of any two of them implies the falsity of the third. The term was introduced in this sense by Christine Ladd-Franklin. It allows for a very succinct formulation of a criterion for the validity of a syllogistic form. Let p_1, p_2 and q be categorical propositions. The syllogistic argument

$$\frac{p_1 \quad p_2}{q}$$

is valid if and only if {p_1, p_2, not-q} is an antilogism. **2** more generally, the antilogism of a syllogistic argument from premisses p_1, . . . p_n to the conclusion q has been defined as the group of the n + 1 propositions {p_1, . . . p_n, not-q}.

antinomianism (Gr. *anti-* against + *nomos* law) *n.* the view that laws cannot determine what conduct is right: what is right becomes evident for individuals when they consult their conscience.

This view has often been combined with the doctrine that those who have received divine grace are in a state of sinless perfection. Hence they are exempt from the law, and can do no wrong. This is an interpretation of the Pauline doctrine that the Law has been superseded by the Gospel. Although espoused by some Christian individuals and sects, it is widely rejected by all major churches. Antinomian sectarians have often blurred the distinction between liberty and licentiousness.

antinomy /æn'tɪnəmɪ/ *n.* **1** in modern logic, a logically impossible conclusion, established by an apparently correct proof. Frank Ramsey (1903–30) distinguished semantic antinomies, which require for their formulation notions like naming, meaning, truth, from logical, or set-theoretical, antinomies. *The Liar*, *Grelling's paradox* and *Richard's paradox* are usually counted as semantic antinomies, whilst *Russell's*, *Cantor's* and *Burali-Forti's* antinomies are of the logical kind. The word 'paradox' is also often used for these antinomies.
2 In the section called Transcendental Dialectic in Kant's *Critique of Pure Reason* (B432–B595), he presents four antinomies: four pairs of thesis and antithesis, both of which are supplied with proofs. (He also refers to them collectively in the singular, as 'the antinomy of pure reason'.) The first thesis is that the world has a beginning in time and is limited in space. The second thesis is that there are ultimately simple substances. The third thesis is that not everything in the world is determined by natural causes, that is to say, there is freedom. The fourth thesis is that there exists an absolutely necessary being, that is to say, that not everything exists contingently. Each of the four theses expresses a demand of reason to find an ultimate basis for everything conditioned (for instance a First Cause), and the antithesis in each case expresses a demand of reason to regard every condition as being in turn conditioned (for instance, to regard every cause as in turn an effect of something else). Kant resolves the antinomies by asserting that in each antinomy, one of the two conflicting statements can be thought to apply to phenomena (things as they appear to us), the other to noumena (things as they are in themselves). In a similar manner, he presents an antinomy of practical reason in the *Critique of Practical Reason*, and two further ones in the *Critique of Judgment*.

Antiochus /æn'taiəkəs/ **of Ascalon** (*c.* 125–*c.* 68 BC) Under the headship of Antiochus, the Academy made a turn from scepticism towards Platonism. His philosophical views were anti-sceptical, and he argued that the differences between the doctrines of Plato, Aristotle and the Stoics were inessential. His theory of knowledge comes to expression through 'Lucullus' in Cicero's *Academica*, and his moral views in Book 5 of *De finibus*. HT/ed.

antiphasis /æn'tɪfəsɪs/ (Gr. *anti-* contra- + *phasis* speech, diction) *n.* **1** contradiction; the affirmation (*kataphasis*) and denial (*apophasis*) of the same proposition. **2** contradictory; the denial of a given proposition.

anti-realism *n.* in general, a view which rejects realism (in any of the many senses of that term). In particular, *anti-realism* has since the 1960s been used for the view that a statement cannot be said to be true or false if the evidence for or against it is unavailable in principle. In other words, anti-realism in this sense is the rejection of the principle of bivalence for a certain class of statements. *See also* VERIFICATIONISM.

Antisthenes /æn'tɪsθəniːz/ (*c.* 445–*c.* 360 BC) a friend of Socrates, regarded as the founder of the CYNICAL School. Only some fragments of his many writings are extant. He held the view, later adopted by the Stoics, that wisdom once gained cannot be lost, and that the truly wise (who are obviously few in number) cannot ever act foolishly. He used Hercules as a symbol of the ideal life: *acting* well, especially by overcoming adversity, is virtue and produces happiness.

anti-symmetric(al) *adj. See* SYMMETRIC(AL).

antithesis /æn'tɪθəsɪs/ (*sing.*); **antitheses** /æn'tɪθəsiːz/ (*pl.*) (Gr. *anti-* against + *thesis* position; proposition) *n.* **1** an opposite statement: a contrary or a contradictory. **2** (in rhetoric) a striking contrast; a phrase containing a balanced juxtaposition of two contrasting ideas.

Each of the four antinomies (ANTINOMY) discussed by Kant consists of two propositions: a thesis and an antithesis. In Hegel's philosophy, the terms 'thesis' and 'antithesis' are applied not only to propositions but also to historical or social forces that stand in conflict to each other. Such conflicts, called 'contradictions' in Hegel's philosophy, reach a resolution in a synthesis in which the conflicting elements have been absorbed.

antonym *n.* a word opposite in meaning to another. For instance, *internal* and *external* are antonyms; so are *synonym* and *antonym*.

apagoge *n.* Gr. reduction.

apathy (Gr. *apatheia*, from *a-* (privative prefix) + *pathos* affection, emotion) *n.* a state of serene detachment or indifference in which one remains unaffected by the vicissitudes of life; regarded by the Stoics as the condition most to be desired, since, in their view, emotions were irrational and therefore contrary to nature. They insisted that it must not be confused with mere callousness and insensitivity.

apeiron Gr. from *a-* (privative prefix) + *peras* boundary, limit *n.* the indeterminate, boundless, the unlimited, the infinite. It is the ultimate source of reality out of which definite particular beings emerge and back to which they eventually return, according to Anaximander, as reported in Aristotle's *Physics* 1,3.

Apel /'aːpəl/, Karl-Otto (1922–) German philosopher, professor at the universities of Kiel, Saarbrücken, and from 1972 to 1990 at Frankfurt. The main direction of Apel's philosophical effort has been towards a modernized version of Kant's transcendental philosophy. Kant intended to determine the universal and necessary conditions for empirical knowledge. But, in Apel's view, the advance of science since Kant's day has shown that it is not possible to take particular categories (e.g. causality) and forms of intuition (e.g. three-dimensional Euclidean space) to be universal and necessary. Instead, what can be established are the universal and necessary conditions under which agreement can be reached when people make opposing validity-claims. Apel calls this transformation of Kant's approach 'transcendental pragmatics': 'transcendental' because it is the study of universal and necessary presuppositions; 'pragmatics' because the objects of investigation are *acts* – speech-acts such as asserting, denying, proving, refuting, etc.

When people enter into argument in order to reach agreement about the truth of the matter under discussion, they make the following four important claims: (1) that what is said makes sense; (2) that it is true; (3) that it is sincere (i.e. the speaker believes it to be true); (4) that it is communicated in a normatively correct way. This last condition, as explained by Apel, carries with it an implicit acknowledgement of the equality and autonomy of all interlocutors. Indeed, he sees it as implying that when we engage in discourse with others, we implicitly acknowledge the notion of a *community* of participants in discourse – even if this is a regulative ideal rather than actual practice.

Apel, following Peirce, regards the truth-claim mentioned in the second condition as a claim that under ideal conditions and involving all possible rational beings, agreement would be reached. In short: truth is universal consensus in the long run. This is a limiting concept, like a Kantian regulative idea – we can move towards the goal, but never entirely reach it.

These four presuppositions are necessary in the sense that a rejection of them is self-refuting, in the same way that 'I do not exist' is refuted (but not contradicted) by my saying so. Apel uses the expression 'pragmatic contradiction' (PRAGMATIC PARADOX) to distinguish self-refutation from logical contradiction.

This theory of necessary presuppositions enables Apel to oppose relativist tendencies in twentieth-century philosophy, and to set limits to the kind of fallibilism represented by Quine, Popper, Albert, etc. To assert, as they do, that all theories and hypotheses are in principle refutable, presupposes that there is some fixed point: their standpoint requires at least that the concept of refutation itself is fixed. Apel's anti-relativism is also applied to ethics. Here, the presupposition of ideal consensus between rational agents (he cites Kohlberg's conception of a presupposed 'universal reciprocity of role-taking') leads to a DISCOURSE ETHICS with distinctively deontological ingredients of a Kantian kind.

Among translated writings are: *Towards a Transformation of Philosophy* 1980, *Understanding and Explanation* 1988, *Towards a Transcendental Semiotics* 1994.

BC

aphairesis /ə'faɪərəsɪs/ *n.* Gr. **1** (in Aristotle) abstraction. **2** (in neo-Platonism) negation, as a method of forming a conception of the highest being.

aphorism *n.* a concise statement expressing a striking insight. Among eminent writers who present philosophical ideas in aphoristic form are Francis Bacon, Pascal, La Rochefoucauld, Diderot, Lichtenberg, Nietzsche and Wittgenstein.

apocalypse /ə'pɒkəlɪps/ *n.* **1** prophetic revelation. **2** a sequence of final disasters. The second sense has arisen because the last book of the New Testament, called The Apocalypse, or Revelation (short for The Revelation of St John the Divine), foretells destruction, followed by doom, on the day of the Last Judgement.

apocatastasis /æpɒkə'tæstəsɪs/ (Gr. *apokatastasis* a setting up again) *n.* restoration. The term is often used with reference to Origen's doctrine of an *apokatastasis pantōn*, a restoration of all things at the end of time, except inherently or incurably evil individuals, who will lapse into non-existence. It follows from this that the torments of the damned are not eternal. The major Christian churches have rejected this (first at the Council of Constantinople in 553) as a heresy and have strongly asserted the eternity of hell.

apocryphal /ə'pɒkrɪfəl/ *adj.* of doubtful authenticity, authority or authorship. *See also* CANON.

apodeictic /æpə'daɪktɪk/ (Gr. *apodeiktikos* demonstrative) *adj.* An apodeictic proposition states what *must be* the case, in contrast to an assertoric one, which states what *is* the case, and to a problematic one, which states what *can be* the case. These are the terms used by Kant for the partition between the necessary, the actual, and the possible. *See also* APODEIXIS.

Note: The word is sometimes written *apodictic*.

apodeixis /æpəʊ'daɪksɪs/ Gr. a pointing out, a pointing towards; demonstration, proof *n.*

apodosis /ə'pɒdəsɪs/ *n.* the consequent in a conditional statement. The correlated term for the antecedent is *protasis.*

Apollonian *adj.* A contrast between the two fundamental tendencies in human life, the Apollonian and the Dionysiac (or Dionysian), was drawn by Nietzsche in *The Birth of Tragedy from the Spirit of Music* 1872. He used Apollo to symbolize classical harmony, balance and self-control; Dionysus was the type for exuberant life-force, capable of excess. The Apollonian spirit of serenity is expressed in classical sculpture and painting; music and lyrical poetry convey the life-affirming Dionysian spirit.

apologetics (Gr. *apologia* defence (against an accusation)) *n. sing.* defence against adverse criticism. The word is often used for defence of religious beliefs and for the branch of theology concerned with this defence.

apophansis (Gr. assertion, statement) *n.* Aristotle's term for (categorical) proposition. His term for an affirmative one is *kataphasis*, for a negative, *apophasis.* In *On Interpretation*, Aristotle distinguishes apophantic speech, which by means of affirmation or denial presents something as true or false, from other forms of speech: (a) prayer (in religion); (b) pragmatic speech (the subject-matter of rhetoric); (c) poetry and fiction (the subject-matter of poetics).

apophantics *n. sing.* in Husserl's terminology, the general theory of propositional meaning and truth.

apophasis /ə'pɒfəsɪs/ (Gr. denial) *n.* Aristotle's term for a negative (categorical) proposition. (In rhetoric) the feigned denial of one's intention, e.g., 'far be it from me to draw attention to my opponent's sordid past . . .'

apophatic theology negative theology. A theology which emphasizes the limitations of the human intellect and the impossibility for us of saying anything of God except what he is not. The term is used especially, but not exclusively, for a theological tradition which has its roots in the Hellenistic world, with mystical and neo-Platonic ingredients. *Ant.* kataphatic theology.

apophthegm /'æpəθɛm/ *n.* a terse and pithy saw.

aporia /ə'pɔːriə/ (Gr. *a-* (privative prefix) + *poros* path, passage) *n.* a seemingly insoluble difficulty; a puzzle or paradox; a condition of being at a loss what to think.

Aristotle suggests that inquiry should take its starting point in a survey of aporias. He did so himself, e.g. in listing fifteen of them in *Metaphysics*, Book B 1–6.

(In rhetoric) feigned or genuine doubt about what to do or say.

The word has come into fashion in recent literary theory to refer to the self-contradictory or self-undermining character of a text. **aporetic**, **aporematic** *adj.*

a posteriori /ɑː pɒstɛri'ɔːrɪ; eɪ pɒstɛri'ɔːraɪ/ Lat. from what comes after *adv.*, *adj.* *A posteriori* knowledge and *a posteriori* truth-claims are those which are based on, dependent on, or derived from, experience. *See* A PRIORI.

apostrophe /əˈpɒstrəfɪ/ (Gr. *apostrophe* a turning aside, away) *n.* a temporary digression, in which the speaker directly addresses an absent or present, abstract or concrete, personal or non-personal being, for instance a poet's invocation of a muse.

This figure of speech is rare in philosophical writings. Kant, imitating Rousseau, has a famous one, addressed to duty. It begins: 'Duty! Thou sublime and mighty name that dost embrace nothing charming or insinuating but requirest submission and yet seekest not to move the will by threatening aught that would arouse natural aversion or terror, but only holdest forth a law' (*Critique of Practical Reason*, AA p. 87; with apologies for the quaintly archaic translation).

apotheosis /əpɒθɪˈəʊsis/ (Gr. *apo-* away, off + *theos* god) *n.* deification; bestowing divine status on a being.

appearance *n.* In Kantian and idealist philosophy, the term is used in a technical sense. *See* PHENOMENON.

apperception *n.* awareness of one's own mental representations; also, consciousness of one's own self. The term was introduced by Leibniz in *Principles of Nature and Grace* 4.

applied ethics the philosophical examination, from a moral standpoint, of particular problems in private and public life that are matters of moral judgement. Subjects dealt with include personal relationships, medical science and practice, questions of race relations, political terrorism, and environmental issues.

The acceptance of applied ethics as a branch of philosophical inquiry implies a rejection of the view that philosophy can only analyse and clarify moral problems but is unable to take on the task of seeking answers to them. BA/ed.

applied philosophy the philosophical examination of a range of issues, including those that come under the heading of applied ethics, but also including inquiry of a more metaphysical kind into man's place in nature, the nature of personhood, agency, and autonomy, the social implications of scientific and technological change, etc.

The term is also used with particular reference to the project of exploring, often in cooperation with specialists in other fields, philosophical and ethical issues in contentious practical areas, including environment, biomedicine, and personal, social and political relationships.

a priori; a posteriori /ɑː prɪˈɔːrɪ, eɪ praɪˈɔːraɪ; ɑː pɒstɛrɪˈɔːrɪ, eɪ pɒstɛrɪˈɔːraɪ/ Lat. from what is earlier; from what comes after *adv.*, *adj.* **1** The pair of terms marks a distinction between reasoning *from ground to consequence* and reasoning *from consequence to ground* which goes back to Aristotle, and was adopted by medieval Arabic and Christian philosophers, including Thomas Aquinas. Albert of Saxony (*c.* 1316–90) is often mentioned as the originator of this pair of terms. This usage can also be found in Samuel Clarke (1675–1729): the ontological argument for God's existence is *a priori*, whilst the argument (in Descartes's *Third Meditation*) from my idea of God to his existence is *a posteriori*.
2 The pair of terms was later applied not to two kinds of reasoning, but two kinds of *knowledge*, of *propositions* and of *concepts*. Knowledge *a posteriori* is *based on experience*, knowledge *a priori* is *independent of experience*. The two kinds of knowledge were assigned to different faculties of the mind (sensibility v. intellect). The new usage can be found in Leibniz, *Discours de métaphysique* section 8, and Kant, *Critique of Pure Reason*, 2nd edn, Introduction, section 1.

Traditionally, the truths of metaphysics, mathematics, geometry and logic have been considered to be knowable, and indeed some of them known, *a priori*. Certain moral truths, for instance that promise-keeping is a duty, have also been so regarded. The following four examples give an idea of what truths are known *a priori*, according to many classical theories.

To give an example from *metaphysics*, we know *a priori* that every event has a cause. Observation and experience will not make us change our mind on this matter. If we do not find a cause of some event we do not infer that there is none – we assume that there is one, not yet discovered.

The same is true of our knowledge that 2 + 2 = 4. There is no observation or experience that could make us change our mind. Generally, our knowledge of *mathematical* truths is *a priori*.

To give an example from *logic*, we know *a priori* that any argument of this form (modus ponens) is valid:

$$\frac{A \quad \text{If A then B}}{B}$$

That is to say, our knowledge that it is valid does not *depend on* observation and experience.

Again, in *ethics*, our knowledge that promises ought to be kept does not depend on observation or experience.

Against all this, it could be argued that in these examples, these truths could not possibly be known to us independently of prior experience: we have to learn a language, we have to be instructed in arithmetic, and so on. In reply, it may be said that the truth-claims exemplified above do not *depend on* such experience, and that the general idea of the *a priori* can be formulated more precisely: 'It can be known *a priori* that p, if anyone whose experience is enough for him to know what "p" means, requires no *further* experience in order to know that p.' So 2 + 2 = 4 is known *a priori*, because someone who has learnt to understand what the expression '2 + 2 = 4' means needs no further experience to know that 2 + 2 = 4.

There is a great variety of philosophical opinion regarding claims that knowledge of a certain kind is *a priori*. Many anti-metaphysical philosophers consider all metaphysical knowledge-claims to be spurious. Moral non-cognitivists claim that there is no such thing as moral knowledge. Other philosophers accept that there is metaphysical knowledge, moral knowledge, etc., but argue that it is not *a priori*, but *a posteriori*.

Note: A priori/a posteriori form a pair of opposites; so do *necessary/contingent* and *analytic/synthetic*. There is no synonymy between any two of these pairs. But are any two of them coextensive? For instance, are all synthetic statements *a posteriori*, and vice versa? Are all necessary statements analytic? On these questions, there are marked differences of philosophical opinion.

aptitude *n.* A creditor has a right to be paid; an innocent victim of misfortune deserves, but does not have a right, to be helped. Grotius (1583–1645) used the Latin nouns *ius* (right) and *aptitudo* (desert, worthiness, aptness), rendered 'aptitude' by some translators, to mark this distinction.

Aquinas /ə'kwaɪnəs/, Thomas (*c.* 1225–74) Aquinas was born into an aristocratic family at Roccasecca in the south of Italy. As a teenager, he studied Aristotle at the university of Naples and then, against his family's wishes, he became a Dominican friar. After studying with Albert the Great at Cologne, Aquinas went to the university of Paris. The rest of his career was divided between Paris and Italy.

Aquinas's best-known work is his

Summa theologiae (1266–73), an attempt, unsuccessful at the time, to replace Peter Lombard's *Sentences* as the standard textbook for students of theology. Among his other writings are his own commentary on the *Sentences*, dating from the beginning of his teaching career; another, earlier *summa* (*Summa contra gentiles*; the full title is, in translation: On the truth of the catholic faith against the errors of unbelievers); disputations on truth, the soul, power and evil; commentaries on the Bible; and commentaries on Aristotle, designed, like those of Averroes, to expound in detail the Greek philosopher's arguments.

Aquinas's thought is often presented in terms of its Aristotelianism. A contrast is drawn between the theologians of the mid-thirteenth century such as Alexander of Hales, Robert Grosseteste and St Bonaventure, who – though familiar with a wide range of Aristotle's works – preferred to follow Augustine and, to an extent, Avicenna; and Aquinas's contemporaries in the Faculty of Arts, such as Siger of Brabant and Boethius of Dacia, who tried (with the guidance of Averroes) to follow Aristotle with complete fidelity. Aquinas is supposed to have taken the middle course between these extremes and achieved a 'synthesis' between Aristotelianism and Christianity; but this description is misleading in two important ways. Aquinas was entirely a Christian theologian, for whom the revealed doctrine of the faith could not be a mere element to be combined with others at choice. At the same time, he knew Aristotle more deeply and widely than any of the arts masters, and he was able to adopt what he took to be Aristotelian positions in many important areas of epistemology, ethics and metaphysics – in part at least because his reading of Aristotle, for all its precision and perceptiveness, was one which modern scholars would regard as anachronistic. For Aquinas, Aristotle was a firm theist (although one who held that the universe is eternal) and an upholder of the immortality of the individual soul.

As a theologian fully aware of the claims of philosophy, Aquinas saw the need to ask why, if every type of being is considered by one or other of the branches of philosophy, there is any need for a further subject, theology. Aquinas's answer reflects the twofold purpose he attributed to divine revelation. On the one hand, God reveals certain things (for instance his existence, unity, omnipotence and eternity) which man can also discover by using his (God-given) reason. Such revelation is required because, without it, only a few people would grasp these truths, and then perhaps only mixed with error. On the other hand, divine revelation makes known truths (such as God's trinity) which unaided human reason could never discover. The theologian such as Aquinas is consequently engaged in a mixed enterprise. At times his inquiry is the same as that of a purely rational philosopher; and, in these cases, he is often seeking to provide a rational demonstration of what he and other Christians already know by revelation. At other times, Aquinas builds his reasoning on premisses provided by revelation, which take the place of the self-evident truths on which Aristotle insisted that each branch of knowledge must be based.

This mixed enterprise bears out Aquinas's two main principles about the relation between faith and reason. The first is that reason, rightly used, will never discover anything contrary to faith, since both reason and faith grasp the truth. Where reasoning issues in a conclusion incompatible with Christianity, there must be some error in it. The second principle is that there are questions where rational argument cannot prove the position which revelation holds, nor even disprove the position contrary to that required by the faith, although it is always possible (in accord with the first principle) to show that any arguments against the Christian position are themselves inconclusive. For instance, Christians know that the world is not eternal. Some of Aquinas's contemporaries, such as St Bonaventure, believed that (using arguments which go back to St John Philoponus) they could *demonstrate* that this is the case. Aquinas considered that none of these arguments was conclusive, although neither was any of the arguments designed to demonstrate that the world is eternal. That the world had a beginning is something which Christians must accept on faith alone.

Aquinas's celebrated 'FIVE WAYS' – five arguments to show the existence of God – are a clear example of his working like a purely rational philosopher, without using revealed premisses. Aquinas rejects the possibility of demonstrating God's existence solely by considering the type of being he is (as Anselm had tried to do in his ontological argument) and instead tries to show that there must be a God by considering the created universe.

In his ontology, too, Aquinas might seem to be reasoning in a manner which would have been open to a non-Christian philosopher. He differentiates between the being (*essentia*, 'essence') of a thing – what a thing is as an existent: a man, a horse, a stone – and the fact of its being, its existence. Aquinas insists on the real distinction between essence and existence: this man or this stone might not have existed; there is nothing about the sort of thing it is which means that it must in fact be. For God, however, it is otherwise. In his case, and in his case alone, essence and existence are identified: what God is, is to be. In terms of Aristotle's distinction between act and potency, God is pure act. All this seems to be a piece of rational, metaphysical analysis. Yet some scholars have claimed that at its centre is a revealed, rather than a self-evident, truth: the God of Genesis naming himself as 'I am', so introducing an ontological notion of God as pure being, absent from Aristotle's idea of the Prime Mover or of intellect contemplating itself.

Aquinas's epistemology and philosophy of mind is far more clearly reliant on revealed premisses, although it is worked out with fine logic and makes ample use of Aristotle. Indeed, at first sight this part of Aquinas's thought is strikingly Aristotelian. Like Aristotle, Aquinas presents intellectual cognition as a process in which the intellect is informed by the form of the thing perceived. The form is that which makes a thing perceived the sort of thing it is. Moreover, Aquinas held (by contrast with contemporaries and predecessors such as Alexander of Hales and St Bonaventure) that the 'active intellect' – the capacity to discern these essential forms within sense-impressions – was something which belongs to each man individually. Man does not depend on divine illumination for each act of understanding. Yet Aquinas's view of the complex procedure of forming a proposition, making an argument and arriving at the truth depends on seeing human thought as the lowest form of intellectual cognition – an imperfect version of the way in which angels infallibly and effortlessly arrive at the truth.

Aquinas's ethical thought, too, uses Aristotelian terminology and ideas, but ends up being very different from Aristotle's. Aquinas keeps an important place for the Aristotelian virtues, such as fortitude and temperance. But practical knowledge is not for him, as it was for Aristotle, knowledge only of means. Just as the intellect is made so as to grasp the fundamental self-evident principles of the branches of theoretical knowledge, so practical reason infallibly grasps the fundamental principles of action, the natural law. Conscience can err in its reasonings based on these premisses, but not over the premisses themselves. Again unlike Aristotle, when he studies human behaviour, Aquinas does not see himself presented with the simple phenomenon: man. The men around him are, for Aquinas, men who because of original sin have lost some, although not all, of their capacity for acting well in accord with their reason. Some of these men have had their powers of acting well restored by God's free, unmerited gift of grace. Aristotle, as a pagan who lived long before the coming of Christ, knew none of this and so, for all his wisdom, based himself on a simplistic view of human nature.

Aquinas is often honoured by historians of political thought as the first medieval thinker to value the state positively, by stressing (in accord with Aristotle) man's nature as a social animal, whose capacities are developed to the full only within a political community. It is true that Aquinas was one of the first medieval writers to exploit Aristotle's *Politics*; yet there was already a tradition, stretching back at least as far as Abelard, which regarded states – especially those of antiquity – in an idealizing fashion. In any case, political theory was marginal to Aquinas's concerns. JM

Method of citation of the *Summa Theologiae*: name of part, number of question, number of article, number of response. Of the three main parts the second is subdivided: 1a (prima = the first part); 1a2ae (prima secundae = the first division of the second part); 2a2ae (secunda secundae = the second division of the second part); 3a (tertia = the third part). JM

Arcesilaus (*c.* 315–240 BC) sceptical philosopher, head of the Academy in Athens. No writings of his are extant. He rejected the dogmatic Platonic metaphysics which had been cultivated in the Academy, and the dogmatic claims to knowledge made by the Stoics. He is credited with having been the first to employ the concept of *epochē*, suspension of judgement. He did, however, admit that even in the absence of genuine knowledge, one can think and act on grounds which, although not certain, are 'reasonable'.

archē /'ɑːkɪ/ Gr. beginning, origin; ruling principle *n.* In philosophy the term was used early, in the theories of the Ionian philosophers (Thales, Anaximander, Anaximenes) to refer to the primordial reality; but, like *principle*, it has a number of related senses.

archetype /'ɑːkɪtaɪp/ (Gr. *archetypos* model, original) *n.* an original pattern or model: **1** (in epistemology) The concept occurs in Descartes, Malebranche, Cudworth, Locke, Berkeley, and others. In the *Meditations* (III, 33), Descartes insists that a series of ideas that generate one another must have a beginning in an archetype. Locke uses the word 'pattern' as a synonym, and takes an archetype to be that to which our ideas must conform in order to be adequate (*Essay Concerning Human Understanding* 2,20,1); but he also holds that most complex ideas are archetypes of the mind's own making (4,4,5). In Malebranche and Berkeley, archetypes are ideas in God's mind, independently of and prior to their being perceived by a human mind. Correlated term: *ectype*. An ectype relates to an archetype as a copy to its original. Cudworth (*True Intellectual System* ... 1678 (37,3,1,1), Locke and Berkeley were among those who used the word. **2** (in comparative religion) In his *The Golden Bough* 1890–1915, a large-scale historical and cross-cultural study of religion, ritual and myth, Sir James Frazer (1854–1941) applied the term to patterns shared by a great variety of religious and cultural traditions. **3** (in Jungian psychology) C. G. Jung (1885–1961) proposed, first in 1912, that the patterns and symbols in individuals' dreams and imagery, and in religions and myths all over the world, display striking similarities, and described these common features as archetypes (a term that he had found in Augustine). They are universal predispositions to form certain images, present in the collective unconscious as residues of inherited ancestral memory.

Arendt /ˈærənt (Eng.); ˈaːrɛnt (Gm.)/, Hannah (1906–75) German-Jewish political philosopher. Among her teachers were Husserl and Heidegger, but the major influence was from Jaspers. In exile after 1933, she escaped from France to the United States in 1941. *The Origins of Totalitarianism* 1951 relates the decline of the traditional state, the rise of imperialism, and the anti-semitism of the nineteenth century to the emergence of Nazi and Bolshevik dictatorships, unpredictable in their policy because of their raw lust for power. Notable also are *The Human Condition* 1958, *On Revolution* 1963 and *On Violence* 1970. Much of her work is an analysis and diagnosis of the ills of modern society: among them, the breakdown of the barrier between the public and the private realm and the intrusion of commercialism and economic concerns in all aspects of life. Combined with her concern for the downtrodden, the pariahs (proletariat, immigrants, refugees) and victims of political injustice, there is in her political stance a different strand, centred on an idealized conception of politics symbolized by New England town hall meetings in days past and by ancient Greek political assemblies, where able public-spirited individuals distinguish themselves politically through their persuasive rhetoric.

Areopagitica /ærɪɒpəˈdʒɪtɪkə/ a pamphlet published in 1644 by John Milton, in which he argued for the freedom of the press and against pre-publication censorship. The title alludes to pleadings of the kind heard before the tribunal whose sessions were held at the Areopagus in ancient Athens.

aretaic *adj.* pertaining to virtue-concepts.

aretē /ˈærətɪ/ *n.* The Greek *aretē* signifies excellence, good quality, good disposition. In English translations 'virtue' is often used as an equivalent. This is acceptable if understood in the older, general sense, which allows us, e.g., to talk of the virtues of a medicine. The so-called moral virtues are only *one* variety of *aretē*.

arguable *adj.* That an opinion or theory is *arguable* implies that there are plausible reasons *in its favour*. That an opinion or theory is *debatable* implies that there are plausible reasons *against* it.

argument *n.* **1** a set of propositions of which one, the conclusion, is supposed to follow from the other ones, the premisses. An argument is valid or invalid; correct or incorrect; sound or unsound; it cannot be said to be true or false. Of course, each of the constituent propositions, including the premisses and the conclusion, can be said to be true or false. **2** (in mathematics and logic) a member of the domain of a function. In standard notation, the letter x marks the argument-place of the function represented by f(x), and x,y are letters that mark the argument-places of the function f(x,y). **3** quarrel. **4** debate. **5** précis of a work of literature, i.e. a brief statement of its main content. *See also* COSMOLOGICAL ARGUMENT; DESIGN, ARGUMENTS FROM; ONTOLOGICAL ARGUMENT.

argumentum ad ... Many forms of persuasion, often described as fallacies, i.e. mistakes in reasoning, have Latin names of the form *argumentum ad* ... Many of these names are recently invented.

argumentum ad baculum (Lat. *baculum* stick) an appeal to the stick, i.e. a veiled or open threat, issued in order to gain assent to a proposition. This is sometimes described as a fallacy, but it could be said that 'making an offer that cannot be refused' is not a fallacy: it cannot be an invalid piece of reasoning, since it is not a piece of reasoning by which the truth of the conclusion is supposed to be established. An appeal to the stick is rather a method of gaining assent to a proposition by a method other than reasoned argument. For the same reason other forms of persuasion are not fallacies either.

argumentum ad hominem (Lat. *homo* man) An argument is said to be *ad hominem* if it is designed to reject the opponent's opinion by attacking him for being inconsistent, untrustworthy or insincere. This can be done in different ways: (1) one method is by showing that the opinion in question is incompatible with other opinions professed by the opponent. In Locke's formulation (*Essay Concerning Human Understanding* 4,17,21): 'to press a man with consequences drawn from his own principles or concessions'. An example of this usage occurs in John Mackie, 'Simple Truth', in his *Truth, Probability and Paradox* 1973, p. 26. He discusses the view that simple truth is unavailable to us, and that all we have access to is the usefulness of a proposition. This view can be rebutted, he writes, by the *ad hominem* argument that somebody who asserts that a certain theory *is* useful implicitly claims simple truth for that assertion; (2) another method is by pointing to defects in the opponent's character: 'given *your* record of dishonesty, we will not accept your opinion'; (3) yet another method is by showing that the opinion defended is self-serving, i.e. that the opponent adopts it from ulterior motives of self-interest.

Arguments *ad hominem* are traditionally regarded as fallacious, because an opinion *can* be correct even if the person holding it is a fool (muddled in his thinking) or a knave (insincere, unreliable, dishonest, etc.), and even if the opinion is in accord with the person's private interests. But although such an opinion *can* be correct, it will, under certain conditions, *probably* be false: it is unwise to place too much trust in the opinions of a foolish, dishonest, or biased person. There is nothing fallacious in this. In the assessment of testimony, we are normally right in relying less on a person with a record of dishonesty. So an argument of this kind can be a sound probable inference.

argumentum ad misericordiam (Lat. *misericordia* pity) an appeal to pity in order to gain assent.

argumentum ad populum (Lat. *populus* people) an appeal to popular opinion in order to gain assent.

argumentum ad verecundiam (Lat. *verecundia* respect) urging respect for authority, seniority, etc. in order to gain assent.

Arianism a theological doctrine about the nature of the Godhead, named after *Arius* (*c.* 250–*c.* 336), a presbyter in Alexandria, according to which Christ is not of the same substance as God the Father, who is the Supreme Being. This view was held to be incompatible with the doctrine of God's incarnation in Christ, and was condemned by the Council of Nicaea, the first ecumenical council, in 325. The so-called Nicene Creed, a reformulated version of trinitarian resolutions adopted by that council, has long been accepted as orthodox. From the seventeenth century onwards a number of important writers, including philosophers such as Locke and Samuel Clarke, held Arian or Socinian (SOCINIANISM) beliefs.

Aristippus /ærɪ'stɪpəs/ (*c.* 435–*c.* 355 BC) Greek philosopher, a follower of Socrates, from Cyrene in North Africa, whence the Cyrenaic philosophy derives its name. He is said to have taught that the enjoyment of the present moment is the highest good.

aristocracy (Gr. *aristokratia* rule of the best) *n.* **1** a class of persons enjoying high status and hereditary privileges. **2** a state ruled by a privileged upper class, usually with hereditary membership. **3** a system of government by those considered best or most capable for the task. **4** the governing body in such a system.

In the *Politics*, Aristotle discusses at length the relative merits of aristocracy, monarchy and democracy, and the relative demerits of their degenerate forms, oligarchy, tyranny, and what was later called ochlocracy (mob rule).

Aristotelian logic This expression is often used to refer to the syllogistic logic as it is traditionally taught. It should be kept in mind that some parts of it do not emanate from Aristotle, nor did he confine his logical labours to categorical syllogisms only.

Aristotle /'ærɪstɒtl/ (384–322 BC) Born in Stagira in northern Greece, Aristotle produced the most thoroughgoing and powerful philosophical system of antiquity. Through his father, physician to King Amyntas II, Aristotle had connections to the royal house of Macedonia. He enrolled in Plato's Academy in 367. Aristotle spent twenty years in the Academy as a student, colleague, lecturer and writer. About the time of Plato's death, *c.* 347, Aristotle joined a group of philosophers at the court of Hermias in Assos on the northern Aegean coast of Asia Minor, where he married the ruler's niece. After about two years he departed for the adjacent island of Lesbos, apparently doing biological research with his colleague Theophrastus. In 343/2 he joined the court of Philip of Macedonia to teach the crown prince Alexander. In 336 Alexander became king on the death of his father, and about a year later Aristotle returned to Athens to set up a school of philosophy, the Lyceum or the Peripatos. Leading thinkers gathered at his school to study philosophy and science. Aristotle retired from Athens soon after Alexander's death in 323 to escape persecution from an anti-Macedonian faction, and died in Chalcis.

Writings: although deeply influenced by Plato's work, Aristotle seems never to have been an orthodox Platonist. Evidently he developed many of his characteristic doctrines while he was still in the Academy, and he contended for leadership of Plato's followers at Plato's death, but lost out to Speusippus. Aristotle published dialogues and other popular writings from an early period, but the publication of his lectures years after his death eventually caused the dialogues to be neglected; they are known to us now only from fragments and reports. The extensive treatises that have come down to us represent many, but not all, of his lectures. The range of his interests is indicated by a list of some of his more important writings: *Categories* (kinds of predication, or basic classification of existing things); *Prior Analytics* (the first treatise ever written on formal logic); *Posterior Analytics* (philosophy of science and theory of knowledge); *Physics* (principles of science); *De Anima* (psychology); *Metaphysics* (metaphysics); *Nicomachean Ethics* (moral theory); *Politics* (political theory); *Poetics* (theory of literature). In addition he wrote extensively on biology and on such diverse topics as dialectic, rhetoric, chemistry, geology, meteorology and cosmology.

Basic principles: Aristotle's most basic philosophical commitment was to common sense: opposed both to Plato's ideal Forms and to the atomists' material atoms, he sought a theory that would at once allow a place for moral values and for scientific truths – a theory, moreover, which would not posit invisible and unknowable entities such as Forms and atoms. His solution was the theory of substance (*ousia*). In the *Categories* he explains that substances are the ultimate subjects for all properties. Socrates is a man and Socrates is pale; manhood and paleness are thus characteristics belonging to Socrates. The ultimate realities ('primary substances') are concrete things, and of concrete things Aristotle's preferred examples are biological individuals such as Socrates. Concrete things are the ultimate realities because, if they did not exist, nothing else would exist either. In other words, if there were no such things as Socrates and Callias, characteristics such as manhood and paleness would have nothing to belong to, and hence they would not exist. (One could well ask how Socrates would exist without characteristics such as manhood and paleness, but the problem does not seem to arise for Aristotle.)

Aristotle also recognizes 'secondary' substances such as Man, which is the class or defining property of Socrates, and features such as Paleness (elsewhere called 'accidents'), which Socrates can lose without ceasing to be Socrates – for instance when he gets a suntan. Furthermore, Aristotle distinguishes elsewhere between 'universals', such as manhood and paleness, which can belong to many things (e.g. to Socrates and Callias), and 'individuals' such as Socrates, which are unique. The ultimate realities, the primary substances, are individual substances.

Armed with this theory of being, Aristotle could argue that Plato's Forms are basically universals which Plato mistakenly treats as individuals. There really are universals, but they depend for their existence on particular objects such as Socrates, rather than, as Plato contends, particular objects depending on Forms. The ultimate realities are just the things that we are acquainted with in our experience, people and dogs and horses.

Logic and science: every primary substance falls under a secondary substance, e.g. Socrates is a Man. Among secondary substances Aristotle distinguishes between the lower-level class or property, called a species – e.g. Man, Horse – and the higher-level one, called a genus – e.g. Animal. Every species has an 'essence' or definable nature, which consists of the 'differentia' or specification of a genus, e.g. Man is a Rational Animal. Using these relationships between universals, Aristotle is able to derive a *logic* of relations between universals (*Prior Analytics*). For instance, if all men are animals, and all animals are living things, then all men are living things, i.e. in general, if all A are B and all B are C, then all A are C. Thus we can produce logical rules for inferring new sentences from given sentences having a given logical form: we can deduce conclusions from premisses. Aristotle's system of logic provided the standard model of logic until the nineteenth century.

Using his notion of logic, Aristotle developed for the first time the conception of science as a body of knowledge having a logical structure (*Posterior Analytics*). A science, e.g. geometry, will start from first principles, which are true and necessary, and will deduce from those principles all the truths of the science. But how will we know the first principles? They cannot be deduced from other principles, for then those others will be the principles, and we must in turn ask how we know them. Nor can they be deduced from our conclusions, for then our proof will be circular. We must somehow know them by some other way than by deduction. We begin from experience, and by induction arrive at ever more general truths, using a faculty Aristotle calls 'insight' (*nous*).

Given that Aristotle characterizes science as a logical structure, we might expect his scientific treatises to be rigorously deductive. They are, however, much more dialectical than demonstrative. For Aristotle the basic concept of natural philosophy or 'physics' is that of motion or change. Natural bodies differ from artificial bodies because they have a source of motion or change in themselves (*Physics*, Book 2). For instance, plants grow, animals move around, and the four elements recognized by the Greeks – earth, water, air and fire – move by themselves to their natural places: earth to the centre of the universe, water around it (the seas), air around the water, and fire around air. Thus the natural scientist must understand change, and change presupposes three principles: the privation, the subject, and the form. For instance, when Socrates learns music, we have a subject (Socrates) who was not-musical (privation) receiving a form (musical) (*Physics*, Book 1). But there is one important change that is difficult to analyse: it is a fact that Socrates himself comes to be, is born. How can we understand that event?; for Socrates is an apparently indivisible substance. If we follow the model, we must suppose that some subject comes to be a man from not-being a man; but what is the subject? By analogy to e.g. a statue coming to be formed out of bronze, we may understand the subject to be 'matter' (*hyle*). Thus we arrive at a form-matter analysis of substance: sensible substances are not really simple but are composed of some form in some matter.

Aristotle recognizes four 'causes', which he regards as different answers to why-questions, i.e. different kinds of explanation. Why is there a statue here? Because it was made by Pheidias (efficient or moving cause) with the shape of Athena (formal cause) out of bronze (material cause) to adorn the temple (final cause). In nature as in art, the most important cause is the final cause. For in natural objects, e.g. animals, the parts exist for the sake of the whole. Indeed, the whole universe is ordered as a whole of parts which function harmoniously together, a large but finite sphere with a spherical Earth at the centre. In his extensive writings on biology and cosmology, Aristotle attempts to bring out the role of form and function in nature. The end-directed nature of the universe is emphasized even more by the presence of a 'first unmoved mover', which Aristotle identifies with God, and which causes the outermost sphere of the heavens to rotate. The unmoved mover, conceived as an unembodied mind, serves as the goal and ideal of all heavenly motions.

Aristotle's writings show the tireless efforts of an acute mind both to extend the range of human knowledge and to organize all knowledge according to a few central insights. Aristotle was one of the great scientists of antiquity because of his ability to carry out detailed observations in the service of a systematic inquiry. His most lasting contributions to empirical science are in biology, where his writings include the results of dissections and extensive field observations, including some reports of phenomena not reconfirmed until the nineteenth century. While Aristotle was a diligent observer, he recognized no experimental method. His most powerful tool for disposing of incorrect theories was reasoned analysis rather than experimental evidence.

Metaphysics: whereas Aristotle's physical science is largely obsolete, his metaphysics retains its intrinsic interest. In one sense metaphysics is Wisdom, dealing with the ultimate principles and causes, e.g. the four causes in their application to nature (*Metaphysics*, Book 1). But in another sense it is First Philosophy, the study of 'being as being', i.e. of Being itself rather than in some restricted role such as being in motion (studied by physics (ibid., Book 4). In different contexts Aristotle recognizes the role of first philosophy as that of defending first principles (ibid., Book 4), of identifying the highest kind of substance, i.e. God (ibid., Book 6, Book 12), or of revealing what the ultimate reality is (ibid., Books 7–8). The last question is crucial, because by dividing substance into form and matter, Aristotle reopened the question of what was the ultimate entity: is it now the composite of form and matter (e.g. Socrates), or the matter (his body), or the form (his soul)? Aristotle tends towards the last answer, but not without encountering serious difficulties, which lead him to raise the question of how form and matter are related. In Book 9 he discusses his theory of potentiality and actuality, the states which apply, respectively, to matter and form. Aristotle explains that potentiality exists for the sake of actuality, but he does not clearly show how this fact solves the problem of Books 7–8. Aristotle's final view on what the ultimate reality is remains unclear, and is the subject of considerable scholarly controversy.

Ethical and political theory: in ethical theory Aristotle uses human nature to determine the good life. Everyone says the good life is happiness, but people do not agree on what happiness consists of. The answer, according to Aristotle, must depend on understanding what human beings essentially are – their distinctive function. Happiness, the good life, consists in functioning well. Since the distinctive human capacity is reason, the distinctively human life is life lived in accordance with reason, and consequently the good life for human beings is the life of reason lived 'with excellence' (or 'with virtue' – *kat'aretēn*) (*Nicomachean Ethics*, Book 1). Aristotle seems to waver between declaring the good life to be a life dominated by a single activity, namely contemplation of the results of (theoretical) reasoning, or a life inclusive of many different activities. The latter account seems much more defensible, but in Book 10 of the *Nicomachean Ethics* Aristotle seems to advocate the former. Aristotle distinguishes between moral excellence and intellectual excellence, the one being attained by habituation, the other by learning (*Nicomachean Ethics*, Book 2). Moral excellence is the acquired rational capacity to choose the mean between extremes; e.g. courage is the tendency to act with the right amount of boldness so as to avoid cowardly fear on the one hand and foolhardy overconfidence on the other hand. For Aristotle, political theory is continuous with ethics, for man is a political or social animal by nature. Hence it is natural for humans to live in societies and to behave morally towards one another (*Politics*, Book 1). Rejecting Plato's concept of an ideal state, Aristotle distinguishes good from bad forms of government according to whether or not government is constitutional or arbitrary, and recommends a mixed constitution favouring the middle class (ibid., Book 4).

Influence: Aristotle seems to have influenced the first generation of Hellenistic philosophers, including Epicurus and Zeno the Stoic. But his writings suffered a long period of neglect, only to be revived in the first century BC. From that time on, scholars studied and commented on Aristotle continuously in the ancient world, often making major contributions to science as observations on or corrections to Aristotle. In general his world-view of a finite, end-directed universe seems to have dominated ancient thinking. At the time of the fall of the Roman Empire his works, with the exception of a few treatises translated by Boethius, were lost to the West because they had not been translated into Latin, and Western scholars could no longer read Greek. In the East, however, Aristotle's treatises were still studied in the Greek Byzantine empire, and translated into Syriac (fourth to eighth centuries AD) and then Arabic (ninth century), so as to provide the intellectual basis of a flourishing Arabic culture.

In Europe, what little was known of Aristotle inspired the debate on universals (eleventh and twelfth centuries). In the twelfth century Aristotle's works caused a sensation when they began to be translated into Latin from Arabic and Greek manuscripts. In the thirteenth century the growth of universities allowed and encouraged intensive study of this vast and rigorous body of knowledge; revised translations were made, and Greek and Arabic commentaries were translated. Early fears about pagan elements in Aristotle's works were allayed when Thomas Aquinas made Aristotelian theory the basis for Catholic theology. Aristotle quickly became the dominant influence on medieval 'scholastic' philosophy.

In the fifteenth and sixteenth centuries Renaissance scholars tended to side with either Plato or Aristotle in philosophy. But with the coming of the Scientific Revolution, Aristotelian theory came under attack by progressive thinkers such as Galileo Galilei and Francis Bacon. Scholastic philosophy continued to dominate university studies for some time, but Aristotle was increasingly thought of as theoretical and anti-empirical by association with scholastic professors. Aristotle again began to be appreciated by anti-idealistic philosophers in the nineteenth century, and in the twentieth century his works have been intensively studied by both continental and Anglo-American philosophers.

Aristotle's influence has been so pervasive that many of his conceptions have become indispensable for philosophical analysis, and even for everyday use; for example his notions of categories, particulars and universals, substance, essence, property, accident, matter and form, potentiality and actuality. Aristotle sharpened the understanding of every subject he investigated, e.g. distinguishing between voluntary, involuntary and deliberate action in ethics; identifying plot and character as elements of literary analysis; discussing genus, species and differentia in classification; providing identity conditions for events; and setting out the basic notions of logic, e.g. proposition, premiss, conclusion, deduction, induction, necessity, possibility, axiom, demonstration. While the basic notion of systematic philosophy originates from Plato, Aristotle enriched that notion with an impulse to conceptual precision, compartmentalization, and attention to detail which encouraged scientific specialization on the one hand and philosophical rigour on the other. From Aristotle the world learned what a scientific world-view would look like. DG

Method of citation: two methods of reference are used, singly or jointly: (1) name of the work, number of book, number of chapter. For example: *Nicomachean Ethics*, Book 2, chapter 5; (2) name of the work, page number and, optionally, line number in the Bekker edition, Berlin 1831–70. For example, 1037^a7 means page 1037, column a, line 7. The books of the *Metaphysics* are often cited not by number, but by Greek letters, as follows: Α (I); α (II); Β (III); Γ (IV); Δ (V); Ε (VI); Ζ (VII); Η (VIII); Θ (IX); Ι (X); Κ (XI); Λ (XII); Μ (XIII); Ν (XIV).

Arminianism a theological outlook, named after the Reformed Dutch theologian Jacob Arminius (1560–1609). It was semi-Pelagian, and rejected the doctrine of predestination. At the important synod of Dort

(Dordrecht) 1618–19, the Arminian remonstrances were condemned in favour of a more rigorous Calvinism; a prominent member of the defeated party was GROTIUS. In effect, though not in name, it has prevailed in Methodist, Baptist, and many established Protestant churches.

Armstrong /ˈɑːmstrɔŋ/, David (Malet) (1926–) professor of philosophy at the University of Sydney 1964–91.

A philosophical self-portrait: Becoming a student of John Anderson at the University of Sydney in the late 1940s was crucial to my intellectual formation. While my own thinking eventually diverged from Anderson's in a number of respects, I always accepted Anderson's (then unfashionable) insistence on the need for a philosopher to work out a systematic position. I further accepted Anderson's naturalism: that reality was constituted by the single spatiotemporal system, with humanity having no privileged place in that system. I also came to accept Anderson's pluralistic theory of society and his critique of totalitarianism, in particular communism, a movement of which Anderson had earlier thought himself an ally.

Initially, my work was on the theory of perception. *Perception and the Physical World* 1961 argues that perception is no more than the acquiring of sub-verbal beliefs or information about the perceiver's current environment and bodily state. Passing to the more general topic of the mind–body problem, I argued in *A Materialist Theory of the Mind* 1968 that the mental should be *defined* in purely causal terms, but then *identified* with purely physical processes in, and states of, the brain. In further work (1973), inspired here by the views of F. P. Ramsey, beliefs were identified with maps in the mind by which we steer, and knowledge with the empirical reliability of the map.

In 1978 I published a two-volume work on the theory of *universals* (*Universals and Scientific Realism*). Accepting, as Anderson had, the objective, mind-independent, existence of qualities and relations, I argued that it was up to total science, and not the philosophers, to tell us just what properties and relations the world contains. Like Anderson, I held that where we speak of the *same* properties and relations, this is to be taken strictly as betokening that different particulars can have the very same quality or be related by the very same relation. In philosophers' parlance this meant that I upheld the existence of universals, a relatively unusual position for an empiricist.

This was followed up in 1983 by a work on the nature of laws of nature (*What is a Law of Nature?*). With some others I argued, against the prevailing orthodoxy which holds that laws are mere regularities in the behaviour of things, that laws are connections of universals, which *explain* the regularities. Most recently (*Universals*, 1989) I have tried to develop a *combinatorial* theory of possibility, possibilities being taken to be (fictional) recombinations of actually existing elements. An important role is taken in this theory by the contention, deriving from Anderson, that the world should be seen as a world of what can be called *states of affairs* – something having a property, or two or more things having a relation – instead of a world of *things*. This view is quite close to that of Anderson. DA

Arnauld /aʀno (Fr.)/, Antoine (1612–94) French theologian, philosopher and controversialist; the leading figure among the Port-Royal Jansenists. Co-author with Pierre Nicole of the *Port-Royal Logic* 1662. His philosophical writings show great penetration and lucidity. In his objections to Descartes's *Meditations* (the fourth set) he was the first to raise the problem of the

Cartesian Circle. Much later, he engaged in an extended debate, to which belongs his *Traité des vraies et des fausses idées* 1683 (Treatise on true and false ideas), with Malebranche. In a number of other writings, and in a correspondence with Leibniz that began in 1686, he subjected the *Discourse on Metaphysics* to incisive criticism: Leibniz held that the individual concept of an individual, e.g. a human being, contains every truth about that individual, but Arnauld objected that this would rule out human freedom.

Arnold, Matthew (1822–88) English poet, literary critic, social and political thinker. A liberal-minded critic of dogmatic religion, he argued in *Literature and Dogma* 1873 for a new, more enlightened faith. He also criticized the culture of contemporary society, composed, as he saw it, from the top down of 'barbarians', 'philistines', and the 'populace'. Improvement would require positive government action, especially in the area of education.

Aron /aʀɔ̃ (Fr.)/, Raymond (1905–83) French political thinker, professor of sociology at the Sorbonne 1955–68, and at the Collège de France 1970–79. Like most intellectuals who rose to prominence in France after 1945, he kept his distance from Gaullist politics, although he had associated himself with the Free French forces in London, editing the monthly *La France libre* from 1940 to 1944, but he differed from many of them, e.g. Merleau-Ponty, by also rejecting Marxist theory and communist practice. This led to a break with Sartre, until then a close friend, about 1946. A full-scale attack on the tendency, not uncommon among Western intellectuals, to condemn their own political system and condone the systematic inhumanity of Soviet communism, came in *L'Opium des intellectuels* 1955 (The opium of the intellectuals). (He always rejected with equal firmness the ideas and aims of the political right.) In this and other writings, Aron also criticized the Marxist belief in historical laws. Nor did he accept the view that abstract models can be a useful tool for explaining and predicting political events. In his view, historical explanation is based on understanding the actions of historical agents.

In post-war French intellectual public life, Aron was virtually alone in being familiar with and taking a positive interest in the philosophical ideas current in the English-speaking world.

In his moral outlook, Aron rejected the view that history, class interests, or the demand for social conformity could provide ultimate moral criteria. Rejecting ideological justifications of evil, he urged, in a Kantian spirit, that human agents can and should let principle prevail over ideology and 'pragmatism'. There remains, however, a tension, brought to the fore in Kant's political writings, between the moral ideals by which action should be judged, and the actual forces that have in fact shaped history. Much of what we now value in modern civilization is the result of force and fraud. Given this, how we are to view history? Such questions naturally led to a study of Thucydides; Aron also wrote a major study on Clausewitz: *Penser la Guerre* 1976 (transl. as *Clausewitz: Philosopher of War*).

In Aron's view, the basis for critical reflection on society must be the values and ideals widely accepted in contemporary society: liberty, equality, social justice, technological progress, etc. But he insisted that such ideals are bound to come into conflict. For instance, how can the demands of wealth-creating modern technology be reconciled with human equality? No general theory or ideology can offer an answer.

arrow paradox *See* ZENO OF ELEA.

Arrow's theorem an important impossibility theorem concerning collective choice. Individual members of the public have their individual preferences, and when these are aggregated one obtains what the public on the whole prefers. This assumption seems plausible enough. Without it, the ideal of a government respecting the preferences of the governed seems impossible. But there are unexpected difficulties: they were first revealed in Condorcet's VOTING PARADOX, which can be generalized as follows.

Given a number of options, we assume that the preferences are *transitive*. That is, if option A is preferred to B, and B to C, then A is preferred to C. We also assume that the preferences are *complete*. That is, for any two options, either one is preferred to the other, or they are ranked equal. We further assume that there are three or more parties involved. On these assumptions, Arrow's impossibility theorem (proved 1951; improved 1963, named after its discoverer, the American economist Kenneth J. Arrow (1921–)) shows that there is no method of aggregation that ensures that the following four conditions apply: (1) each possible configuration of individual preferences will determine a collective preference; (2) if at least one individual prefers A to B and no one prefers B to A, then the collective preference will rank A above B; (3) the collective ranking of two alternatives A and B will be determined by individuals' preferences concerning A and B, and will be independent of their preferences regarding C, D, E, etc. If, for instance, A . . . E are candidates in an election, and one drops out after the votes have been cast, the relative preferences for the other candidates will remain unchanged; (4) the way that the collective preference is determined is non-dictatorial, i.e. the preferences of one individual will not necessarily determine the collective preference.

ascent *See* SEMANTIC ASCENT.

ascriptivism *n.* a theory about the meaning of sentences which state that an action was voluntary, intentional, etc. According to ascriptivism, such statements do not *describe* the act as having been caused in a certain way. They *ascribe* it to the agent: the point of such statements is to hold the agent responsible for it, and such ascriptions of responsibility express a certain moral attitude but are neither true nor false.

The term was introduced by P. T. Geach (1916–) in a short article with this title in *Philosophical Review 69* (1960).

aseity /eɪˈsiːɪtɪ/ (Lat. *aseitas*, from *a* from, by + *se* oneself, itself) *n.* the property of having within itself the ground for its existence, depending on nothing else for its existence. The word occurs in late scholastic philosophy. Schopenhauer ascribed aseity to the Will, Eduard von Hartmann to the Unconscious. The word is now rarely used.

Some writers draw a subtle distinction between *ens a se* (a being by itself), which depends on *nothing* for its existence, and *causa sui* (a self-caused being), which depends on *itself* for its existence. Anselm and Duns Scotus described God as *ens a se*.

assertion sign the 'turnstile', ⊢, was introduced by Frege to symbolize that the thought expressed in a sentence is asserted as true.

In standard formal-logical notation, ⊢A indicates that A is a theorem of the system in question, and B ⊢A indicates that A is deducible from B.

assertoric *adj.* An *assertoric* proposition is one which simply claims that something is or is not the case, as distinct from an *apodeictic* one which claims that something is bound to be the case, and from a *problem-*

atic one which claims that something may be the case. The word *assertoric* in this sense has come into common philosophical use from its employment in Kant's *Critique of Pure Reason* 1781. GH

associative law (in logic and mathematics) a law of the following form, where the asterisk represents a binary operation: (a*b)*c is equivalent to a*(b*c).

In propositional logic, conjunction and disjunction are associative; implication is not. In mathematics, addition and multiplication are associative; subtraction and division are not.

astrology *n.* the ancient art of divination based on the supposed influence of the celestial bodies on human affairs and human character.

Many ancient thinkers accepted various forms of divination, including astrology; others were undecided. A few opposed it staunchly, among them Xenophanes, Epicurus and his school, Carneades, and Panaitios. In Christian thought, astrology has often been rejected. Augustine argued (*City of God*, Book 5) that if a person's fate is written in the stars, there can be no place for human freedom and no possibility freely to accept or reject grace.

The present-day view of astrology is that the apparent successes of astrological soothsaying have no probative force. There are three kinds of distorting factors: one is selectivity: hits are recorded, misses are not; another is vagueness: the description of a personality, or the prediction of an event, is so indefinite that it can fit almost any outcome; a third is imposture and fraud.

asylum ignorantiae /ə'saɪləm ɪgnɔ'rænsiːaɪ/ Lat. sanctuary of ignorance. An obscure concept or method, not open to critical scrutiny, to which one resorts in order to disguise one's ignorance or lack of critical reflection.

asymmetric(al) *adj. See* SYMMETRIC(AL).

asyndeton /æ'sɪndɪtən/ (*sing.*); **asyndeta** /æ'sɪndɪtə/ (*pl.*) *n.* the omission of connecting words between clauses: e.g. 'I came, I saw, I conquered', where 'and' is omitted.

ataraxia /ætə'ræksɪə/ *n.* Gr. unperturbedness serenity, peace of mind. The Epicureans taught that *ataraxia* is the essential ingredient in happiness, the most desirable state of human existence, and so did Pyrrho and other ancient sceptics. It was sometimes contrasted with the Stoic *apatheia* (APATHY), but at times the two were eclectically identified.

atheism /'eɪθɪɪzm/ (Gr. *a-* (privative prefix) + *theos* god) *n.* the view that there is no divine being, no God. Sometimes a distinction is made between theoretical and practical atheism. A theoretical atheist *believes* that there is no divine being, no God. *Practical atheism* has been used in two entirely different senses. In one sense that occurs in Cudworth, it is the (Epicurean) view that the gods exist but do not do anything that has a bearing on human affairs. In the other, more usual sense, a practical atheist is one whose actions are not influenced by any belief in God and whose actions are accordingly presumed to be under no moral constraint. An early opponent of this presumption was Bayle.

Atheism can be distinguished from *pantheism* and from *agnosticism*. Pantheism is the view that God and the world are in some sense identical. Opinions have varied on the question of whether this is a form of atheism. Agnosticism (in religion) is the view that it is impossible for us to know whether God exists.

atheology *n.* a theory designed to disprove God's existence. The word was first used in the seventeenth century.

atom *See* ATOMISM.

atomic facts *See* LOGICAL ATOMISM.

atomism (Gr. *atomos* indivisible) *n.* atomism is the name given to a materialist theory according to which nothing exists except atoms and the void. Atoms are indivisible particles of matter. The void is that in which they move. Differences between atoms of a quantitative kind (size, shape and the like) and the various speeds and directions of the atoms' movement in the void are used to explain the fact that in the world there are all kinds of different things and events. The theory originated with Leucippus and Democritus. It was subsequently adopted, with some modifications, by Epicurus and Lucretius and was revived in the modern era by Gassendi.

Different from this metaphysical view that *everything* is composed of atoms, is the scientific view that *everything material* is so composed. This scientific hypothesis has for a long time proved very fruitful, although the items identified as atoms were eventually discovered to be neither qualitatively indistinguishable, nor indivisible. Consequently, they do not strictly deserve the name 'atom', which has, however, continued in use for reasons of convenience. **atomic** *adj. See also* EPICUREANISM; LOGICAL ATOMISM.

attitude/belief *n.* two persons may agree on all the relevant facts, and yet have a genuine disagreement when evaluating them. This is a problem for the emotivist theory of ethics, according to which in such a situation there are no facts – and hence nothing – to disagree about. The solution proposed by Charles Stevenson introduces a distinction: the disagreement when evaluating the facts is not a disagreement in *belief*, but a disagreement in *attitude*. He developed this distinction in *Ethics and Language* 1944.

attitude-utilitarianism *See* UTILITARIANISM, INDIRECT.

attribute *n.* **1** a property. **2** an essential property.

Descartes distinguishes qualities, which are contingent, like the softness of a piece of wax, from attributes, which are non-contingent, like the spatial extension of a piece of wax. The same terminological distinction was observed earlier, e.g. by Aquinas: God's properties are non-contingent and they are accordingly called (divine) attributes: simplicity, perfection, immutability, etc. (*Summa contra gentiles* 1,1,14; *Summa Theologiae* 1a, qq. 3–14). According to Spinoza, the substance, alias Nature, alias God, has an infinite number of attributes. Only two are known to us: consciousness and extension.

attributive/predicative *adj.* Adjectival expressions can be variously placed. In an attributive position, they immediately qualify a noun (e.g. 'this is a black label'). In a *predicative* position, they constitute the predicate of a sentence (e.g. 'this label is black'). Certain kinds of adjectival expressions fit in only one type of construction. 'This is a future champion' makes sense; 'this champion is future' does not.

attributive/referential *adj.* Definite descriptions, i.e. phrases of the form 'the so-and-so', can be used in two different ways. They are used attributively in an assertion that states something about whoever or whatever is so-and-so. They are used *referentially* in an assertion to indicate the particular individual about which they are made. For example 'The man who murdered Smith must be insane' is used attributively if it means that whoever the murderer may be, he must be insane; but is used referentially if the speaker uses the definite description 'the man who murdered Smith' to direct the hearer's attention to a particular person (whom the speaker takes to have committed the crime). The distinction was formulated in these terms by Keith Donnellan in 'Reference and definite descriptions', *Philosophical Review* 75 (1966).

attrition *See* REPENTANCE.

aufheben /ˈaʊheːbən (Gm.)/Gm. to supersede, to cancel, to sublate *vb.* (In Hegel's philosophy) in a synthesis, the thesis and antithesis are *aufgehoben*, i.e. superseded (in some translations, 'sublated'); at the same time they are also preserved, *aufbewahrt*.

Aufklärung /ˈaʊfklɛːrʊŋ (Gm.)/ Gm. Enlightenment.

Augustine /ɔːˈgʌstɪn/ (354–430) St Augustine was born in Tagaste in North Africa in 354. His father, Patricius, was a pagan (though he subsequently converted) and his mother, St Monica, a pious Christian. The meeting of the worlds of classical antiquity (dominated by the ideal of abstract thought) and of Christianity (built upon Judaic belief in sacred history and the New Testament doctrine of the incarnation of God in Jesus Christ) was the general background of Augustine's intellectual and spiritual development. In the course of his classical literary education he moved from Christianity towards paganism and then to the Manichaean heresy which claimed that the world is the product of two Gods – one good and the other evil. From there he was drawn towards philosophical scepticism and subsequently read certain neo-Platonist writings (probably the *Enneads* of Plotinus) which turned him away from Manichaeism back towards Christianity. One important element in this conversion was the neo-Platonic claim that evil is not a something, a substance or property, but is rather the absence of what should be, a *privation*. This idea obviated the need to look for a creative source of evil and also offered a way of reconciling the state of the world with the existence of an all-good creator ('All things that exist, therefore, seeing that the Creator of them all is supremely good, are themselves good . . . but their good may be diminished' – *Enchiridion*, 12).

Augustine thought of philosophy as a search after wisdom and saw this as continuous with the religious impulse. But he held that while reason can establish the existence of God it cannot, unlike the scriptural revelation, disclose the historical truths of creation, fall, incarnation and redemption, knowledge of which is necessary for salvation; nor can reason, unlike spiritual prayer, bring the seeker into beatific union with God – for these there have to be grace and faith. However, reason may prepare the soul and help it to understand and better appreciate what grows there.

Once Augustine became committed to Christianity he began to write a series of works in which philosophical argumentation is put to the service of attacking opposing doctrines and defending the Catholic faith. For example, he tries to refute scepticism by showing that doubt presupposes the existence of the doubter and his knowledge of his immediate thoughts ('*Si fallor sum*' – 'even if I err I am', *City of God* XI, 26). Similarly, he defends the Christian doctrine that God created the world out of nothing (*ex nihilo*) against the charge that this is incoherent because, for example, one can always ask what happened prior to some event, by arguing that the objection erroneously regards time itself as being like the events that occur within it ('time is nothing but a stretching out in length' (*Confessions* XI, 26, 33)).

Although Augustine's philosophical

reflections are motivated by theological concerns he is such a powerful thinker that what he produces is often of lasting philosophical interest. At the same time, however, he is a deeply historical figure both in the sense that he is committed to a historical revelation, and in the sense that his position in the history of philosophy makes him a transitional thinker, shaped by, and reacting in terms of, earlier thought (in particular neo-Platonism) and laying the foundation for the development of a more systematic Christian philosophy of the sort synthesized by the medieval scholastics, especially Aquinas. It is sometimes said that Aquinas replaces Augustine's Platonic dualism (of body and soul, sense and intellect, empirical worlds and transcendental reality) with a more naturalistic metaphysics inspired by Aristotle. But as one reads *Summa Theologiae* it quickly becomes clear that Aquinas is indebted to Augustine and that he seeks to avoid contradicting him while nevertheless constructing a more extensive synthesis of scripture and philosophy. Even if Aquinas's efforts are more successful, they could not have been embarked upon had it not been for Augustine – the first great Christian philosopher.

JH

Austin /ˈɒstɪn/, John (1790–1859) English moral and legal philosopher, for some time professor of jurisprudence at University College, London. In the first part of his *Lectures on Jurisprudence*, which was published separately under the title *The Province of Jurisprudence Determined* 1832, Austin developed with great clarity a utilitarian moral theory and an analysis of the concept of a law and of a legal system. Following Bentham, Austin maintained that all law properly so called is a command by a superior. Superiority consists in the ability to enforce obedience. The action commanded is a duty.

Following Locke, Austin distinguished three kinds of duties. The *religious* duties are those which conform with the principle of utility or the greatest happiness principle. They are commanded by God, since God desires our greatest happiness. Austin calls them duties because they are commanded by a superior, and he calls them religious because the superior in question is God. (Today, it would be natural to think of these as moral duties, since they are the ones that conform to the principle of utility.) The *moral* duties, in Austin's (and Bentham's) terminology, are those laid down by the moral code prevailing in a society. They are called duties because they are the commands of society. The *legal* duties are the ones commanded ultimately by the sovereign power in a political society. It is therefore possible for a legal duty to be incompatible with a moral duty, and with a 'religious' duty. The existence of a law is one thing, Austin wrote, its merit or demerit another.

Austin believed that a number of basic and general legal concepts, such as rights, obligations, contract, law and sovereignty, are common to every legal system properly so called, and attempted to give a precise analysis of them. This approach to the theory of law, which focuses on analysis and in principle leaves the historical, social or moral dimensions of the law out of account, is often called analytical jurisprudence.

Austin, John Langshaw (1911–60) professor of philosophy at Oxford from 1952 and the leading spirit of so-called 'ordinary language' or linguistic philosophy. Its characteristic method of investigating the nature of ideas such as perception, knowledge, intention, act or freedom, which are of interest to philosophers, was a rigorous, detailed, patient, comprehensive and co-operative examination of the ways in which these terms are normally used in ordinary language. This approach, which is a variation on a method as old as Aristotle but dominant only in the twentieth century, is most clearly seen in his 'A Plea for Excuses' in his *Philosophical Papers*. His hope was thereby to make philosophy more like the empirical sciences. His influence was exercised mainly by his teaching during his life and by the posthumous publication of his lectures on perception, *Sense and Sensibilia*, and on speech acts, *How to do Things with Words*.

In the former lectures he attacked the traditional theory, familiar in the eighteenth century as the 'way of ideas' and in the twentieth as the theory of sense-data – specifically in a version published by A. J. Ayer – that all we really, actually or directly perceive (that is, see, hear, smell, etc.) are the appearances of objects and not the objects themselves: a theory that had always borrowed much of its plausibility from the so-called 'argument from illusion' which seemed to show that what we really see, both when we see a dagger and when we have the illusion of seeing one, is only the appearance of a dagger. We are misled in supposing that there will be some entity called 'a look' because we can properly say 'that looks red'.

In the latter lectures Austin distinguished between three different kinds of speech acts we might be performing, that is, three kinds of things we might be doing when we make an utterance: namely, what we say (a locution), e.g. 'There is a bull in that field', what we do *in* saying that (an illocution), e.g. warn someone not to enter the field, and what we do *by* saying that (a perlocution), e.g. convince him that he should not enter. AW

autarchy /'ɔːtaːkɪ/ (Gr. *auto-* self + ARCHĒ rule) *n.* **1** autocracy. **2** self-government (rarely). *See also* AUTARKY.

autarky (or **autarchy**) (Gr. *auto-* self + *arkein* to suffice) *n.* **1** self-sufficiency. An important condition for the good life, according to the teachings of Cynics and Stoics. **2** economic self-sufficiency of a country (rarely).

authenticity *n.* the quality of being genuine, being true to oneself. The notion of authenticity has been one of the central and certainly most influential concerns of the philosophy of existentialism, although its roots go back through much of Western philosophy. Socrates could easily be viewed as a philosopher concerned with the authenticity of the self – the genuineness of his thoughts and actions. He sought to rise beyond mere opinion to attain knowledge, self-knowledge in particular: self-knowledge, he argued, is needed to be true to oneself and only then can a person have virtue. Augustine was concerned with the spiritual nature of the 'true' self as opposed to the inauthentic demands of desire and the body. Jean-Jacques Rousseau also contrasted the true, authentic, natural self which he, in strong opposition to the dominant tradition, emphatically declared to be essentially good, with the 'corruption' imposed by society. Kierkegaard, the first existentialist, insisted that the authentic self was the personally *chosen* self, as opposed to one's public or 'herd' identity. This opposition of the genuine individual versus the public or 'the herd' was taken up by Nietzsche fifty years later, and both Kierkegaard and Nietzsche influenced Martin Heidegger, whose conception of authenticity (Gm. *Eigentlichkeit*) came to dominate contemporary existentialist thought. To be authentic or genuine was to recognize resolutely one's own individuality and distinguish one's own essential being-in-the-world from one's public identity as *das Man*, Heidegger's name for the anonymous social self. Jean-Paul Sartre utilized what

Theodor Adorno later called 'the jargon of authenticity' in his conception of 'bad faith' (*mauvaise foi*), which was clearly based on Heidegger's notion of inauthenticity. The positive notion of authenticity ('good faith') remained a problem for Sartre, however, and one of the continuing criticisms of existentialism is the unclarity or impossibility of the ideal of authenticity. RS

authoritarianism *n.* **1** a system of decision-making without due consultation with the parties concerned. **2** attitude favouring decision-making without due consultation with the parties concerned. For instance, the preference for a political system in which an élite rules without regard to the opinions of the ruled.

authoritarian personality a personality type characterized by domination/submission, conformism, racism, prejudice, intellectual rigidity, and intolerance of ambiguity. The concept was introduced in a major work with this title, published in 1950, by T. Adorno, E. Frenkel-Brunswik, D. Levinson and R. Sanford, in the context of an inquiry into the social and psychological origins of fascism and Nazism. They found that this personality type was particularly common in that kind of political movement.

authority *n.* **1** a right, a power (in the deontic sense), to decide on matters within a given area. **2** a person or an institution vested with an authority in sense (1). **3** the quality of a source of information, in virtue of which it can be safely relied on to determine matters in doubt or dispute. **4** a source of information (a person, a book, a tradition) possessing authority in sense (3).

autocracy (Gr. *auto-* self + *kratia* power, might, strength) *n.* **1** absolute rule, i.e. monarchic rule without constitutional limitations. **2** a state under absolute rule. **3** (metaphorically, e.g. in Kant, but now rare) self-mastery, the ability to control one's inclinations. **4** in literary theory, the adjective (autocratic) is used as a contrasting term to ALLOCRATIC.

autodidact *n.* a self-taught person.

autographic *See* ALLOGRAPHIC.

autological *adj.* self-describing. *See* GRELLING'S PARADOX.

autonomy/heteronomy (Gr. *autos/heteros* self/other + *nomos* law) *n.* **1** (in politics) self-government; self-rule; political independence.

2 (in ethics) a person's capacity for self-determination; the ability to see oneself as the author of a moral law by which one is bound.

This is a central concept in Kant's ethics: autonomy is displayed when a person freely decides, out of respect for a moral demand, to act morally, independently of any external incentives.

Kant was inspired by Rousseau's political theory (*Social Contract* 1762) which sees the people as both sovereign and subject. In this theory, the people are bound by laws, but only those they have themselves made. Kant applied a similar conception to the individual person at the end of chapter 2 of *Foundations of the Metaphysics of Morals* 1785. He used it to describe how we can be strictly bound by a demand of morality, and yet have the freedom and dignity essential to personhood. Our compliance with a demand of morality has genuine moral worth only if it is done out of respect for a law which is seen as springing from our self-legislation (*Critique of Practical Reason* 1,1, section 8).

The opposite is HETERONOMY. The authority of the law is placed outside oneself. When doing one's duty heteronomously, one is determined by hope for or fear of something external. The four kinds of heteronomous principles are, according to Kant, those in which one's moral action is determined by a desire for (1) well-being for oneself; (2) social approval; (3) increased perfection of oneself; or (4) divine approval.

3 (in philosophical analysis) some philosophers use *autonomy* as a synonym for *logical* or *conceptual independence*. Thus, 'autonomy of ethics' has been used for the view that ethical concepts and statements constitute a category of their own, and cannot be deduced from or reduced to non-ethical concepts and statements. One writer even uses 'autonomy of colour' for the independence or irreducibility of colour-concepts and some writers have used the expression 'autonomy of institutions' (of groups, of practices) for the view that statements about institutions are not reducible to statements about the individuals that constitute them. (In this usage, 'autonomy of universities' does not mean that they are or ought to be self-governing and independent of church and state; it means that a university is not identical with a collection of buildings and other parts.)

autonymy (Gr. self-naming) *n.* the use of an expression, preferably together with a suitable device such as quotation marks, to name itself. Thus 'dog' refers autonymously to the *word* dog but 'the three-letter word composed, in order, of the fourth, the fifteenth and the seventh letters of the alphabet' refers to the same word, not autonymously but heteronymously. The term was introduced by Carnap in *The Logical Syntax of Language*. **autonymous** *adj.*

autotelic (Gr. *auto-* self + *telos* purpose) *adj.* having its purpose within itself.

Avenarius /avɛ'naːrɪʊs (Gm.)/, Richard (1843–96) German philosopher, professor in Zürich from 1877. Avenarius claimed in *Kritik der reinen Erfahrung* 1888–1900 (Critique of pure experience), like his contemporary, Ernst Mach, that knowledge can only be based on pure experience, that metaphysics is to be eliminated, and that what appears as a distinction between mind and body is simply a matter of different relations between elements of a single, neutral kind. Nor is there any difference in principle between inner and external experience. His psychologism was criticized in Husserl's *Logical Investigations* 1900, and his positivism castigated in Lenin's *Materialism and Empirio-Criticism* 1908. GC

Averroes /ə'vɛrəʊiːz/ (1126–98) the name commonly used in the West for Ibn Rushd. He lived in Spain at the time when it was under Islamic rule. He both continued and reacted against Avicenna's Aristotelianism by attempting to purify it of Platonizing additions, and also by resisting his predecessor's effort to harmonize it with Islamic teaching. Unlike preceding Islamic philosophers, Averroes sharply distinguished the realms of faith and reason, but it would be incorrect to ascribe to him the doctrine of double truth of which the so-called Latin Averroists, e.g. Boethius of Dacia and Siger of Brabant, were later accused. Besides his treatise *Tahāfut Al-Tahāfut* (*The Incoherence of the Incoherence*), designed to refute a work by Al-Ghazālī (1058–1111) which criticized Aristotelianism from the point of view of Islamic orthodoxy, Averroes's most important writings were his long commentaries on Aristotle, where he attempted to expound Aristotle's arguments as carefully as possible.

These commentaries were very influential in the Christian West from the early thirteenth century onwards. They provided an almost indispensable guide to Aristotle's puzzling texts. They – or possibly a misinterpretation of them – were also the source for the particular doctrine which became known as Averroism. According to this view, people are individuated by their bodies and their senses, but there is just one intellect which is shared by everyone. Since this theory conflicts with Christian ideas of individual immortality, reward and punishment, it was cited by Western thinkers mainly in order to reject it, although some arts masters in the 1260s and 1270s, such as Siger of Brabant, seem to have claimed that it was correct, at least as an interpretation of Aristotle. JM

Avicenna /ævɪˈsɛnə/ (980–1037) the name commonly used in the West for Ibn Sīnā. He lived in Persia and wrote in both Persian and Arabic. He inherited a tradition of Aristotelianism which went back in the Islamic world to the ninth century, when Syrian versions of Aristotle had been translated into Arabic. Alongside the *kalām*, a scholastic theology concerned to defend and elaborate the truths of faith as laid down in the Koran, there emerged a school of philosophy, based especially on Aristotle. Avicenna's most important work, the *Kitāb Al-Shifā* (*Book of Healing*), is a paraphrase and commentary on much of Aristotle's writing. Although Avicenna believes that he is presenting Aristotle's system as the Greek philosopher intended it, in fact he transforms his ideas in a neo-Platonic and theistic direction. God is described as a necessary being, whereas every other being in the universe is merely possible: it might not have existed. From God there emanates a series of Intelligences, the lowest of which is the Agent Intellect through which human beings can engage in intellectual cognition.

Much of the *Shifā* was translated into Latin in the twelfth century and exercised a strong influence on Christian thinkers early in the thirteenth century. Avicenna's Platonizing Aristotelianism proved attractive to thinkers familiar with Augustine; but even after the mid-thirteenth century, when a closer understanding of Aristotle's own texts became more common, Avicenna remained an important source for Christian theologians, and he was still read enthusiastically in the Renaissance.

avowal *n.* a statement about one's own present state of mind (or, more precisely, a first-person present-tense self-ascription of an occurrent psychological state).

It was proposed by Ryle (*The Concept of Mind* 1949) that avowals do not describe, truly or falsely, an inaccessible private inner state. Uttering 'I feel gloomy' is like moping: neither true nor false. Both express, but do not describe, a state of mind. Avowals are similar to cries, smiles and frowns except that they are linguistic and play a defined part in interpersonal communication.

Wittgenstein (*Philosophical Investigations* 1953) has commonly been taken to offer the same view. It has been argued, however, that the point Wittgenstein wished to make was a different one: he did not wish to deny that utterances like 'I am in pain' can be true or false. What he did wish to reject was the view that my avowals ascribe to an inner, independently-existing self a certain property or state (e.g. being depressed, having a toothache) which I alone am able to discover.

axiarchism /ˈæksɪaːkɪzm/, **axiarchy** /ˈæksɪaːkɪ/ Gr. *axia* worthiness, value + *-archē* ruling principle *n.* axiarchy is the determination of reality by the good, by that which is ethically valuable or required; axiarchism is the theory that reality is so determined, largely or entirely. The term axiarchy was coined by John Leslie (1940–), who himself favours a theory of this kind:

> Until this century most philosophers had axiarchistic beliefs. One is that there exists an all-powerful, benevolent creator. Another is that all things are ani-

> mated by a desire for good. The one I find most intriguing views the universe as the product of a directly active ethical requirement, a requirement which as a matter of fact proves sufficient to create things. . . (John Leslie, *Value and Existence* 1979, p. 6).

He re-states the same view, which he takes to have close affinities to neo-Platonism, in his *Universes* 1989, but the new term is not used there.

axiology /æksɪ'ɔlədʒɪ/ (Gr. *axia* value, worthiness) *n.* theory of value. It seems that the term was first used by Lotze, and then by Brentano, Husserl, Scheler, Nicolai Hartmann and others, chiefly for a general formal theory of value. Scheler contrasted it with praxeology, a general theory of action, but it has for the most part been contrasted with deontology, a theory of morally right action.

axiom /'æksɪəm/ (*sing.*) **axiomata** or **axioms** (*pl.*) (Gr. *axiōma* something worthy of approval, of esteem, of acceptance) *n.* an axiom is a formula (i.e. a proposition, or a well-formed expression which on interpretation yields a proposition) that belongs to an axiomatic system, without being derived from any other formula in that system.

Traditionally, propositions taken as axioms were so selected because they were thought to be self-evidently and indubitably true: neither capable of proof nor requiring any; this was how Euclid's axioms were regarded. These assumptions are abandoned in the modern concept of axioms.

Among the basic propositions of an axiomatic system, a distinction is sometimes made between axioms and POSTULATES.

axiom(atic) system a collection of formulae specified as consisting of all and only those which can be derived from a given set of formulae (the *axioms* of the system) by a finite number of applications of certain rules (the transformation rules of the system). The formulae so derivable are known as the *theorems* of the system. It is required (1) that the axioms be stated in such a way that it can be effectively determined for any formula whether it is an axiom or not; and (2) that the transformation rules be stated in such a way that it can be effectively determined of any purported application of them whether it is a genuine application of them or not.

The axioms in axiomatic systems of logic are also theorems, since they can be (trivially) derived from themselves.

Soundness and completeness are two important properties that axiomatic systems can have. Suppose we have (1) a given class of formulae, (2) some criterion of validity which divides these formulae into valid and invalid ones, and (3) an axiomatic system whose theorems belong to the given class. Then if all the theorems of that system are valid by that criterion, the system is said to be *sound* (with respect to that criterion); and if all formulae valid by that criterion are theorems of that system, the system is said to be *complete* (with respect to that criterion). If the system is both sound and complete (with respect to the criterion), it is said to provide an *axiomatization* of the formulae valid by that criterion. GH

axiom of choice Informally expressed, this is a proposition in set theory which states that if we have any collection of sets, each of which is non-empty and no two of which have any member in common, then there is a set which contains precisely one member taken from each of the sets in question. This proposition is easily proved if the original collection of sets is finite. But if the original collection is infinite, this axiom gives the simplest and best-known example of an axiom that asserts the existence of sets that we cannot specify. Those who approach set theory from a nominalist or conceptualist point of view tend to reject it. GH

axiom of infinity (in set theory) an axiom to the effect that there is a set with infinitely many individuals as members.

axioms of intuition In Kant's *Critique of Pure Reason* (B202–B207), these are principles for all perceptual experience: every empirical phenomenon, which is spatiotemporal, has extensive magnitude, i.e. it can be understood as an aggregate of parts. It is by virtue of these axioms that mathematics and geometry is applicable to the world of experience.

Ayer /ɛə/, (Sir) A(lfred) J(ules) (1910–89) Professor of philosophy at London 1946–59 and at Oxford 1959–78, he achieved early fame by his attractively written popularization, *Language, Truth and Logic* 1936, of an analytical approach to philosophy which combined a British tradition originating from Hume in the eighteenth century and influential in Moore and Russell in the early twentieth century, with a continental method formulated by the Vienna Circle, with whose views he had become familiar during a postgraduate stay in Vienna. This version was known as logical positivism. It divided everything capable of being true or false into two categories: one was that of the necessarily true propositions typical of logic and mathematics; the other that of the contingently true propositions of science and everyday discourse. The former were held to be true in virtue of the meaning of the words which express them, and the latter by agreement with the experience of our senses. Underlying this division was the verifiability criterion of meaning, which rejected as meaningless all statements that were in principle unverifiable by either of these methods. Hence, what is said in morals, aesthetics, theology and especially metaphysics, was declared to be factually meaningless. A place was found for morals in the suggestion that to say that something is good or right or ought to be done is not to say anything true or false about it and, therefore, anything meaningful, but is to express an emotion of approval towards it. *Foundations of Empirical Knowledge* 1940 offers a linguistic approach to the traditional doctrine of sense-data as the basis of what we really perceive. In his later work, Ayer gradually moved away from the doctrines of his first book, and his *The Problem of Knowledge* 1956 does not endorse the verification theory of meaning. Ayer modified, but did not abandon, his basic empiricist outlook, which is also presented in a mature version in *The Central Questions of Philosophy* 1973. AW

B

Baader /ˈbaːdər (Gm.)/, Franz von (1765–1841) German thinker. A mineralogist by profession, Baader turned exclusively to philosophy and theology later in life, and taught at Munich from the 1820s until his death. He represented a romantic-mystical outlook, wishing to remain within the bounds of the Roman Catholic faith and opposing the modern faith in reason and human progress promoted in the Enlightenment era. This outlook was similar to Schelling's, and there was a reciprocal influence between them. His *Fermenta cognitionis* 1822–5 (Leavening of knowledge) consists of 161 'Reflections' on the harmony between the light of grace and the light of reason. The aim is to reassert a religious and mystical tradition with roots in Gnosticism and neo-Platonism: the revival of interest in Jacob Boehme owes much to Baader. God is better understood as a process of self-creation than as a being, and nature should be understood as a system not of mechanical but of vital forces, which make themselves known especially in occult and paranormal phenomena. Important is also *Sätze aus der erotischen Philosophie* 1828 (Propositions from the erotic philosophy).

The contact with William Godwin during a four-year stay in London in the 1790s had made Baader aware of the acute misery of the lower classes. He did not accept Godwin's radical anarchism, but came to the view that the proper social and political order, under the dual threats of despotism and liberal democracy, is one that is divinely ordained and should be guided by religious authority. He was, however, critical of the exercise of political and ecclesiastical power of the Holy See, which eventually condemned his writings.

Baboeuf /babœf (Fr.)/, Gracchus (François-Noël) (1760–97) French journalist and political activist. His political thought was strongly egalitarian. The motto of the French Revolution had been 'liberty, equality, fraternity'. This ought, in his view, to include economic equality (hence his byname Gracchus), which would require radical changes in the existing distribution of wealth. Considering that the ideals of the Revolution had been betrayed by conservative forces, he was in 1796 one of the leaders of an unsuccessful revolutionary conspiracy.

Bachelard /baʃlaːʀ (Fr.)/, Gaston (1884–1962) French thinker. Initially a scientist, Bachelard later turned to philosophy and taught at Dijon from 1930, and at the Sorbonne 1940–54. Rejecting the neo-Kantian and positivist theories of scientific knowledge, and anticipating Nelson Goodman, Thomas Kuhn and Paul Feyerabend on a number of points, Bachelard argues in *Le Nouvel esprit scientifique* 1934 (The new scientific spirit) that a scientific theory is not simply determined by basic data: it is always a creative construction. The concept of an epistemological break (*rupture*) is central: science breaks with everyday knowledge, and there are radical discontinuities in the history of science, when the inconsistencies of a theory make it collapse with the advance of a rival. Scientific theory is the work of the imagination, controlled by rational thought. In many works, Bachelard also discusses the place of imagination in poetry, drawing on psychoanalytic, especially Jungian, theory. Like science, poetry deals creatively with basic experiences, but in a non-rational way that can be fruitfully compared and contrasted with that of science.

Bacon /ˈbeɪkən/, Francis (Baron Verulam, Viscount St Albans) (1561–1626) English lawyer, statesman and philosopher, traditionally regarded as the first important figure in the history of British empiricism and in the development of the modern scientific world-view. He planned to write a major work, *Instauratio magna*, but only parts of it were completed. One, *De dignitate et augmentis scientiarum* 1623 (On the dignity and growth of the sciences) was a revised version of *The Advancement of Learning* 1605 (the first major philosophical work written in English – the second was Hobbes's *Leviathan*). The title of another part, the *Novum Organum* 1620 (The new Organon), gave a clear hint that the predominant Aristotelianism ought to be superseded. Science should aim at collecting empirical data and use them for inductive generalizations, instead of seeking explanations in terms of final causes (i.e. purposes). In a simile, he likens the proper scientific method to that of bees, who collect systematically and erect a structure, in contrast to ants (i.e. EMPIRICS), who amass a disordered heap, and spiders (i.e. speculative metaphysicians), who spin beautiful webs that have no contact with reality. The aim of inquiry is practical: knowledge of nature gives us power over it. Bacon draws attention to the remarkable changes wrought by the invention of printing, gunpowder, and the magnet. In order to achieve success, the sources of error have to be understood. One source is hasty generalization. There are also common habits that tend to lead us astray: Bacon gives a famous account of the four kinds of 'IDOLS'.

Bacon /ˈbeɪkən/, Roger (*c.* 1215–*c.* 1292) English Franciscan thinker. He studied and taught at Oxford, and at Paris in the 1230s was among the first to lecture on the newly rediscovered books by Aristotle. Later, however, he condemned the study of Aristotle as a complete waste of time. Bacon developed a grand project of unified science that would include all forms of knowledge. Parts of the project have a distinctly occult character (astrology, alchemy, numerology). Bacon claimed, for instance, to have worked out the date for the coming of the Antichrist, predicted in the visionary writings of Joachim a Fiore. But there are also important anticipations of the method and outlook of modern science, in the insistence on controlled experiment and the use of mathematics.

Baden /ˈbaːdən (Gm.)/ **School** a group of neo-Kantian philosophers. Its leading representatives were Wilhelm Windelband, Heinrich Rickert, who succeeded him in the Heidelberg chair of philosophy, and Emil Lask (d. 1915). It was also known as the South-West-German School.

bad faith (Fr. *mauvaise foi*) as expounded by Sartre consists in viewing oneself as being determined by one's relatively fixed character and by external circumstances beyond one's control. This pretence of unfreedom allows a person to disclaim responsibility in good conscience.

Bakunin /bəˈkuːnɪn/, Mikhail Alexandrovich (1814–76) Russian political thinker and revolutionary activist, and the leader of the political movement known as ANARCHISM. Its aim was a far-reaching decentralization of economic and political power. In its opposition to state power, acts of violence were not ruled out as a means. His opposition to Marxism led to a split in the emerging working-class movement.

Balguy /ˈbɔːlgɪ/, John (1686–1748) English clergyman. In *A Letter to a Deist* 1726 and *The Foundation of Moral Goodness* 1728 he opposed the moral-sense theories of Shaftesbury and Hutcheson. His own view, similar to Samuel Clarke's, was that our moral knowledge must be based on rational insight into objectively existing moral relations.

barber paradox a homely variant of Russell's paradox: there is a village in which there is a barber who shaves all and only those who do not shave themselves. If this barber shaves himself, then he does not shave himself. If he does not shave himself, then he does shave himself.

Barbeyrac /baʀbeʀak (Fr.)/, Jean (1674–1744) A refugee from religious persecution in his native France, Barbeyrac held chairs in Lausanne and, from 1717, in Groningen. His main claim to fame rests on his translations into French of the major Latin works on natural law by Grotius, Pufendorf and Cumberland, each supplied with copious annotations and discussions of his own. He defended Pufendorf against Leibniz's adverse opinion, and wrote against what he saw as dubious moral teachings of the Church Fathers in his *Traité de la morale des pères de l'Eglise* 1728 (Treatise on the moral teachings of the church fathers).

Barcan formula Barcan proposed as a thesis (an equivalent version of) the formula

$$\forall x \Box Fx \supset \Box \forall x Fx$$

which is standardly read: 'if everything necessarily has the property F, then necessarily everything has the property F'. It can be interpreted to mean that if everything is F in the actual world and is F also in every possible non-actual world, then in each possible world everything is F.

This is plausible on the assumption that even if a thing may *have a property* in a possible world but lack that property in the actual world, it is not the case that a thing may *exist* in a possible world but fail to exist in the actual world. Those who find this implausible, arguing that possible worlds may contain things which do not exist in the actual world, prefer systems of modal logic which do not have this formula as a thesis.

Barcan Marcus /ˈbaːkən ˈmaːkəs/, Ruth (1921–) American logician and philosopher, since the mid-1960s professor at Illinois, Northwestern and Yale. She was the first (in *Journal of Symbolic Logic* 1946) to develop a system of quantified modal logic, i.e. a system with formulae containing both modal operators and quantifiers. Examples of such mixed formulae are $\forall x \Diamond Fx$ (for every x, possibly Fx) and $\Diamond \forall x Fx$ (possibly for every x, Fx). These two formulae are not equivalent: it is one thing to say for every runner, that that runner will possibly win, and another to say that it is possible that all the runners will win.

W. V. O. Quine found Barcan's theories at variance with the extensionalism favoured by him, and with his view that some identity-statements are contingent. This gave rise to an important debate. It can be tracked through L. Linsky (ed.), *Reference and Modality* 1971. A number of her papers are collected in her *Modalities* 1993.

Barth /baːt (Eng.), bart (Gm.)/, Karl (1886–1968) Swiss theologian, perhaps the most influential Protestant theologian of the twentieth century, and the founder of so-called dialectical theology. Barth taught at Göttingen, Münster, and Bonn, whence he was dismissed in 1934 for political reasons. He held a chair at Basel 1935–61. He opposed the liberal tendency in Protestant theology that had begun with eighteenth-century NEOLOGY and been reinforced by Schleiermacher and Harnack, because of its attempt to accommodate faith to human reason. For the same reason he rejected all forms of medieval or modern NATURAL RELIGION, and the attempts to underpin theology by metaphysics. Nor should faith compromise with the world in cultural and political matters. He regarded the nineteenth-century belief in progress as an illusion; he rejected the view that God was on anyone's side in the Great War; and he stated early, publicly and emphatically that authentic Christianity could not acquiesce in Nazi politics. Among his works are *The Epistle to the Romans* 1st edn 1919, 2nd edn 1922, in which commentary is interspersed with philosophical observations which reveal a strong influence of Kierkegaard, and the *Church Dogmatics*.

Barthes /baʀt (Fr.)/, Roland (1915–80) French writer, literary theorist, and critic of French culture and society. He opposed the conventions of the bourgeois establishment, and attacked the prevailing attitude to language and literature which had its historical roots in the classical period and had for long been fostered within the centralized French education system, arguing that the standards accepted as natural, neutral and normal were nothing of the kind.

Mythologies 1957 is a collection of essays taking a critical look at the unacknowledged codes adopted by the mass media. Barthes's alternative approach to the understanding of linguistic and other symbolic forms of communication was based on STRUCTURALISM. He explored the sociology of signs, and applied semiological analysis to non-verbal cultural phenomena, discussing, for instance, how a garment or a building can 'make a statement', in his *Système de la mode* 1967 (System of fashion).

basic action an action not performed by means of another action. Actions can be divided into two kinds. One kind of action consists in doing something *by means of* doing something else. For instance, a person with one arm paralysed can raise it by lifting it with the other normal arm. In contrast, raising one's normal arm is a basic action, because it is *not* done *by means of* some other action.

The term was introduced by Arthur Danto in *Journal of Philosophy 60* (1963) and *American Philosophical Quarterly 2* (1965).

Bataille /bataɪj/, Georges (1897–1962) author of novels and poetry as well as philosophical and other essays, a crucial figure in the genealogy of modern philosophy in the domains of deconstruction and French anti-humanism. Bataille's thinking, which he supported by a career as a librarian, emerges from the aesthetic avant-garde of the 1920s and 1930s, when he was associated with the surrealist movement and was briefly a member of the Communist Party (1933–4). Bataille is known in the English-speaking world as the founding editor of *Critique* and for his intensely 'erotic' novels, and a collection of poems. His thinking, which first emerged in early essays such as 'La Notion de dépense' 1933 (The concept of expenditure) and 'The psychological structure of fascism' 1934, has been characterized as a philosophy of virulent nihilism. Bataille continues Nietzsche's project of a transvaluation of all values, thinking through the implications of the death of God to produce a radically anti-intellectualist atheist theology without salvation or hope. Its heart is a 'Summa Atheologica' whose three volumes are *The Inner Experience* 1943, *Guilty* 1944 and *On Nietzsche* 1945. For Bataille, much modern thought and many social and economic structures are modes of denial of the fundamental nature of being as a Dionysian process without stable identity or meaningful direction, an expenditure and squandering of force that is no more than its own end – compare the second law of thermodynamics. The principle of reason and the laws of logic are seen as mere fictions necessary for leaving some scope for human control and a temporary illusion of cognitive mastery. Both, however, are doomed as merely isolated effects of moments of stasis in that overall process of dissolution with which Bataille advocates a quasi-mystical fusion, achieved through forms of extreme experience that cultivate a breakdown of the illusory sense of individuality.

Later works extend these ideas into various domains outside philosophy. Literature, for instance, is understood as a realm in which is affirmed a force of violence and transgression that Bataille sees as integral to subjectivity and whose outlet in precapitalist societies was sacrifice or the rituals of war, but which is now denigrated as 'evil' (*Literature and Evil* 1957). *Theory of Religion* 1948 traces the origins of modern capitalism as a doomed denial of the general principle of universal expenditure and useless consumption, in the interests of utility, industry and production, while *Eroticism* 1957 studies human sexuality as a realm of prodigality and loss in which the continuance of the species is necessarily the destruction of the progenitor. Bataille's *Oeuvres complètes* have appeared in 12 volumes from Gallimard (1970–88). TC

Bauer /'baʊə (Eng.); 'bauər (Gm.)/, Bruno (1809–82) German radical theologian and social critic who taught at Berlin and Bonn. His work on the New Testament texts led him to the view that their historical basis was doubtful. His theory of religion as alienated human consciousness is similar to Feuerbach's. His critical analysis of traditional Christian doctrines led eventually to his dismissal in 1842. In the same year he published *Die gute Sache der Freiheit* (The good cause of freedom) in which he argued, in a Hegelian manner, that church and state were incompatible, since the former was in its essence oppressive whilst the true state is one in which freedom is realized. In subsequent writings he attacked weaknesses in the philosophical and political ideas of left and right alike. He was the target of a lengthy polemic by Marx and Engels in *The German Ideology*.

Baumgarten /'baʊmgartən (Gm.)/, Alexander Gottlieb (1714–62) German philosopher, follower of Wolff's philosophy. He taught at Berlin and Frankfurt an der Oder. Kant used his textbooks on ethics and metaphysics for his lectures, but he is most notable for his *Aesthetica* (1750–58), intended to fill a gap in Wolff's system, which contains a theory of perceptual knowledge and an attempt to formulate a comprehensive theory of what since the publication of that work has come to be called aesthetics.

Bayes'(s) /beɪz/ **theorem** a theorem of probability theory named after the Reverend Thomas Bayes (1702–61). In its simplest form it says that the probability of A given B is equal to the probability of A multiplied by the probability of B given A (the 'likelihood' of B), divided by the probability of B. It interests some philosophers (the 'Bayesians') because it seems to them to explain how evidence confirms hypotheses. Let A be the hypothesis and B the evidence. The degree to which the hypothesis is confirmed by the evidence (that is, the probability of A given B) is given by the 'prior probability' of the hypothesis (that is, the probability of A) multiplied by the 'likelihood' of the evidence, divided by the 'prior probability' of the evidence (that is, the probability of B). Bayesians claim that many intuitions about what is good evidence for a hypothesis are captured here.

Evidence which is highly probable anyway (highly probable in the absence of the hypothesis in which we are interested) will not confirm much. To be confirmed by some piece of evidence, a hypothesis must make the evidence probable. The chief objection to Bayesian theories of confirmation concerns the difficulty of attributing precise non-zero values to the 'prior probabilities' of the evidence and, especially, of the hypothesis. AM

Bayle /bɛl (Fr.)/, Pierre (1647–1706) a French Protestant, trained at the Jesuit college in Toulouse, where for a brief period he was a convert to Catholicism, and at the Calvinist university in Geneva. He taught in France until (in 1681) he had to flee, like many other Huguenots. At first he taught philosophy at Rotterdam, while writing criticisms of intolerant and dogmatic views of Catholics and Protestants alike. He became editor of one of the first learned journals, *Nouvelles de la république des lettres* (News from the republic of letters), and then went on to produce his most important work, *The Historical and Critical Dictionary* 1697, 2nd edn 1702, published in three huge folio volumes with a myriad of footnotes and digressions. Further editions, which included manuscript additions and amendments of Bayle's, were published posthumously. It was a biographical dictionary of persons from the Bible, Greek mythology, the ancient and medieval world, and the political, philosophical, scientific and theological figures of modern times. The main entries are short, but have a vast number of notes, many of them of the length of a short article. In these notes, Bayle tried to correct the errors of earlier historians and chroniclers, to set the historical record straight; but above all, he critically discussed philosophical theories and religious beliefs, from antiquity up to Leibniz, Malebranche and other contemporaries. His examination showed up the internal difficulties in the received views, and his arguments were studied and used by Berkeley, Hume, Voltaire and indeed all eighteenth-century intellectuals. Bayle professed scepticism about all kinds of philosophies and theologies. This led him to argue that religion must be accepted on the basis of faith alone (FIDEISM), and to advocate complete toleration of all views, heretical, non-Christian and even atheist ones. Already in his first book, ostensibly written to demonstrate that the comet visible in December 1680 was not a portent of future calamities, he argued at length that false religion is not preferable to atheism, that atheists can be morally upright members of society, and that they ought to be tolerated. An important part of the argument is played by his view that human conduct is determined by passion rather than reason: passion will make a person commit a crime even if his reason tells him that he will burn in hell. People then and thereafter have had difficulty determining whether Bayle was sincere in his view that religion should be accepted on the basis of faith alone. His opponents believed that he was really trying to undermine all religious beliefs by showing that they were irrational and intellectually indefensible. His sceptical arguments and his ridicule of biblical figures made his text what Voltaire called 'the arsenal of the Enlightenment'. He continued to urge toleration, to defend his sceptical arguments, and to challenge philosophers and theologians of every school up to the very end of his life. Bayle died a few moments after finishing an attack on some of the most important French Protestant thinkers. He influenced almost all eighteenth-century intellectuals positively or negatively; but his influence gradually waned as the *Dictionary* became obsolete and was replaced by modern encyclopedias. RPO

Beauvoir, Simone de /bovwaːʀ, simon də (Fr.)/ (1908–86) French author. She was influenced by the existentialism of Jean-Paul Sartre, her lifelong companion, but influenced him in turn to a greater awareness of the social dimension of human existence. This is an important feature in her *Le Deuxième Sexe* 1949 (published in translation, not entirely complete, under the title *The Second Sex*) which gave a powerful analysis of the role, secondary in almost every respect, assigned to women by social customs and institutions. This book, and her essays, short stories, novels and autobiographical writings, have come to be regarded as a starting-point for modern feminist thought.

begging the question a defect in reasoning which consists in assuming that which one wants to argue for; taking that for granted which is the very point in question. For example, a person wants to argue that *God exists*. He argues from the two premisses (1) *The Bible says that God exists* and (2) *What the Bible says is true*. He supports the second premiss by the two assumptions *God is perfectly veracious* and *the Bible is His word*. Each of these presupposes that *God exists*. This way of arguing begs the question.

Note: Begging the question is *not* the same as raising or giving rise to a question.

behaviourism *n.* **1** a method of psychological inquiry formulated by the American psychologist J. B. Watson in 1913 and explained at length in his *Behaviorism* 1925: psychology ought to be a strictly empirical science, and should therefore study nothing except 'what an organism does and says' in order to establish correlations between stimuli and reactions. To apply this method is, as it were, to 'feign anaesthesia'. **2** a theory according to which statements about mental phenomena can be analysed without residue into statements about behaviour and behavioural dispositions. A theory of this kind is proposed in Gilbert Ryle, *The Concept of Mind* 1949, and Carl Hempel, 'The Logical Analysis of Psychology' in H. Feigl & W. Sellars (eds), *Readings in Philosophical Analysis* 1949.

bellum omnium contra omnes /'bɛləm 'ɒmnɪəm 'kɒntrə 'ɒmneɪz/ Lat. war of all against all.

beneficence /bɪ'nɛfɪsəns/ *n.* well doing; the activity of benefiting others.

benevolence /bɪ'nɛvələns/ *n.* goodwill; the disposition to benefit others.

Bentham /'bɛnθəm/, Jeremy (1748–1832) English utilitarian philosopher and social reformer. He first attracted attention as critic of the leading legal theorist in eighteenth-century England, Sir William Blackstone. Bentham's campaign for social and political reforms in all areas, most notably the criminal law, had its theoretical basis in his UTILITARIANISM, expounded in *An Introduction to the Principles of Morals and Legislation*, a work written in 1780 but not published until 1789. In it he formulated the principle of utility, which approves of an action in so far as the action has an overall tendency to promote the greatest amount of happiness. Happiness is identified with pleasure and the absence of pain. To work out the overall tendency of an action, Bentham sketched a felicific ('happiness-making') calculus, which takes into account the intensity, duration, likelihood, extent, etc. of pleasures and pains.

In Bentham's theory, an action conforming to the principle of utility is right or at least not wrong; it ought to be done, or at least it is not the case that it ought not to be done. But Bentham does not use the word 'duty' here. For Bentham, duties and rights are legal notions, linked with the notions of command and sanction. What we call moral duties and rights would require a moral legislator (a divine being, presumably), but theological notions are outside the scope of his theory. To talk of natural rights and duties suggests, as it were, a law without a legislator, and is nonsensical in the same way as talk of a son without a parent. Apart from theoretical considerations, Bentham also condemned the belief in natural rights on the grounds that it inspired violence and bloodshed, as seen in the excesses of the French Revolution.

Bentham at first believed that enlightened and public-spirited statesmen would overcome conservative stupidity and institute progressive reforms to promote public happiness. When disillusionment set in, he developed greater sympathy for democratic reform and an extension of the franchise. He believed that with the gradual improvement in the level of education in society, people would be more likely to decide and vote on the basis of rational calculation of what would be for their own long-term benefit, and individual rational decision-making would therefore, in aggregate, increasingly tend to promote the greater general happiness.

Bentham had first-hand knowledge of the legal profession and criticized it vehemently. He also wrote a highly entertaining *Handbook of Political Fallacies* 1824, which deals with the logic and rhetoric of political debate.

Bentham figured importantly among a small number of men who became known as PHILOSOPHICAL RADICALS, but his utilitarianism was not much discussed among philosophers until the latter half of the nineteenth century. His prolific writings were published in part by devoted disciples, but some were published for the first time in the 1940s and after, and the publication of his complete works is still in progress. Among these writings is an analysis of the logic of DEONTIC concepts, and *On Laws in General* contains a carefully elaborated theory of jurisprudence.

Berdyaev /bɪr'djajɪf (Rus.)/, Nicolai Alexandrovich (1874–1948) Russian philosopher, in exile in Paris after 1922. Initially he was attracted to the universalism implicit in Marxism, and he always maintained a critical distance from church institutions, although his later thought took a Christian-existentialist turn. In works like *The Destiny of Man* and *The Meaning of History* he interpreted the Christian doctrine of the Fall of man metaphysically, as a symbol of the division between the spirit and the world of objects, and in the same vein the Christian doctrine of final redemption and restoration of all things is interpreted as pointing towards an entirely different kind of existence, beyond society and history.

Bergson /bɛʀgsɔ̃ (Fr.)/, Henri (1859–1941) professor at Collège de France 1897–1921, winner of the 1927 Nobel Prize for Literature. Bergson was at first influenced by Herbert Spencer's philosophy, but soon rejected it because of its mechanistic assumptions. His analysis of time in *Essai sur les données immédiates de la conscience* 1889 (An essay on the immediate data of consciousness, transl. as *Time and Free Will*) distinguishes the scientific concept of time (ultimately a fiction, albeit a useful one), as something divisible into equal intervals and measurable by clocks, from the intuitive experience of (real) time as continuous duration where every moment is unique. Introspection also reveals a continuing free self that is present throughout the flow of time. In *L'Evolution créatrice* 1907 (Creative evolution) he argued that evolution must be explained in terms of a basic life-force (*élan vital*): a merely mechanistic-causal explanation will not do. On the whole, he emphasized the limited scope of discursive thought, and hence of science with its determinism and mechanism; the phenomena of life, consciousness and human freedom can only be known in immediate intuition. In *Les Deux sources de la morale et de la religion* 1932 (The two sources of morality and religion), history is presented as a struggle between two types of society: the open society is free, expansive, creative – it has a place for reformers and innovators; the closed society is hidebound, dominated by established customs, conservative and unfree. Bergson's thought, with its emphasis on intuition and human freedom, exercised a major influence in France, but also internationally, which only began to wane towards the mid-century.

Berkeley /'bɑːklɪ/, George (1685–1753) Irish philosopher, Bishop of Cloyne from 1734. He was concerned to refute materialism for a number of reasons, not least because it provided a basis for unbelief, and accordingly regarded the question of what it is to say that something 'exists' as a basic problem of philosophy. His answer was that for a material thing, such as a chair or a tree, to exist is to be perceived by the senses – often quoted in his Latin phrase *esse est percipi* – and for a non-material thing, such as the mind or spirit of man or God, to exist is to perceive, by either the senses, the feelings, imagination, or thought – in Latin *esse est percipere*. We have *ideas* of that which is perceived, and *notions* of the mind or spirit that does the perceiving. His views on the existence of material things were published in the first and only surviving part of his main work, *The Principles of Human Knowledge* 1710; his views on the existence of minds or spirits were discussed in a proposed second part, the manuscript of which was irretrievably lost during a journey in Italy and never rewritten.

The acceptance of the principle that to be is to be perceived, sometimes called IDEALISM, had as one consequence a denial of the commonly held view that such objects as chairs and trees are composed not only of perceivable qualities like colours, smells and sounds, which may depend on being perceived, but also of some unperceivable matter like atoms and molecules, which is the cause of the perceivable qualities. It had as another consequence that these chairs and trees cease to exist when not being perceived by any mind or spirit. This gave rise to two problems for Berkeley. First, if the existence of the chairs and trees we perceive around us depends on their being perceived, what causes these perceptions of ours on which this existence depends? Locke and the scientists had answered that the unperceivable qualities, what they called the matter, of the objects cause us to perceive them. Secondly, if these chairs and trees continue to exist when we ourselves do not perceive them, as Berkeley agreed we all do properly believe, how can this be? His answer to both these questions was to introduce an infinite mind or spirit, which he identified with God, as one who, on the one hand, causes us to have the perceptions we do have when we perceive chairs and trees, and who, on the other hand, perpetually and continuously perceives those chairs and trees when we are not perceiving them. Berkeley thought that this answer both avoided the difficulties about the nature of the scientists' matter, which Locke himself had called 'something we know not what', and also gave in terms of spirit a better account of the cause of an object's colour, smell and sound, since we are all familiar with our own mental power to cause things but cannot, he thought, understand how an inert matter could cause anything. It provided, in addition, a refutation both of scepticism about the nature and the very existence of objects in the world, and also of atheism. He explicitly preferred it to an alternative, which he had seriously considered in his *Commonplace Book* and which has been adopted by modern phenomenalists like Russell and Ayer, in terms of possible future perceptions of them.

Berkeley argued already in his earliest work, *A New Theory of Vision* 1709, that objects do not exist at a distance from us. He held that the perceptions of sight 'do not suggest or mark out to us things actually existing at a distance, but only admonish us what ideas of touch will be imprinted on our minds at such and such distance of time'. In a somewhat similar way he substituted for the scientists' postulation of unobservable entities such as atoms and molecules, our ability to make predictions from any present set of observations to some future sets – what he regarded as learning the language of God. Such a view is nowadays held, without its theological implications, under the name of INSTRUMENTALISM.

Though Berkeley confidently identified a material object as a collection of its perceived or perceivable qualities – a theory sometimes called phenomenalism – he wavered on the question, which may have been treated in the second and lost part of his *Principles*, of whether a mind or spirit was likewise to be identified wholly with its perception or as an entity which has such perceptions. It was left to Hume to take the bolder step.

Berkeley always insisted that he was doing no more than recalling us to common sense from the scepticism which he thought inevitable in Locke's views, yet his arguments led him inexorably to a highly debatable system of immaterialism and idealist metaphysics.

Berkeley also expounded his idealism in the more popular *Three Dialogues between Hylas and Philonous* 1713, in which Hylas maintains that matter (Gr. *hylē*) exists, but is refuted by Philonous (Gr. friend of reason), who defends Berkeley's immaterialism. Berkeley's phenomenalism anticipated that of Mach and later twentieth-century empiricists, and so did his important critique of Newtonian dynamics, including the rejection of the idea of absolute space, in *De Motu* 1721 (On motion). *The Analyst* 1734 contains a well-argued critique of the concept of infinitesimals. In *Alciphron* 1732, a set of seven dialogues, Christian and especially Anglican beliefs are defended against various kinds of free-thinkers: notable is the attack on Shaftesbury. *The Querist* and other occasional writings contain a large number of proposals for economic and political reform, designed to improve the condition of pauperized Ireland. AW/ed.

Berlin /bɜː'lɪn/, Sir Isaiah (1909–97)

A philosophical self-portrait: Certain topics have always preoccupied me: the possibility of final solutions to problems of thought and life; freedom of the will; the incompatibility of ultimate values; the search for political solutions by the French Enlightenment, Marxists and the forerunners of the Russian Revolution; the concept of political freedom. All these topics and my treatment of them are linked.

In mid-life, influenced especially by the Russian radical Alexander Herzen, I abandoned philosophy for the history of ideas: I believe in the dominant influence of ideas, which seems to me at least as powerful as that of impersonal forces. But in the early 1930s, in Oxford, I was mainly concerned with logical positivism. I tried to point out certain faults in the doctrine, arguing that verification is an insufficient criterion of meaning or truth for many types of statement. Yet I have never departed from an empirical viewpoint, derived mainly from Kant and Hume, nor sought light in metaphysics.

My published lectures attacking historical determinism and on the distinction between negative and positive liberty, the contrast between the empirical and the 'true' or 'real' selves, and their ethical and political distortions, have led to very widespread comment and controversy, which still continue.

The problem of free will appears to me still unsolved. I argue that if determinism is true, ordinary moral concepts cannot begin to be retained (but not that we can prove determinism to be false).

I emphasize that certain ultimate values are in principle, not merely in practice, incompatible: for example, that complete liberty is incompatible with complete equality, justice with mercy, knowledge with happiness, and so on. I deny that the pursuit by individuals or societies of some of these values rather than others leads to relativism. Rather, my view is pluralist: values are not subjective, but understandable even by those who do not adopt or who oppose them. Human communication depends on the fact that most people in most places at most times have accepted overlapping constellations of values, which are in this sense objective. Save for some Greek sophists I have not found true relativism much in evidence, even in Hume and Montesquieu, until the nineteenth century, when it is largely due to Marxism, which maintains that the productive process or the class struggle determines values, and that no common human interests exist until the final order is ushered in by the final revolution.

The first thinker, in my view, who truly distinguishes between values that are equally ultimate, but incompatible, is Machiavelli, who thought that successful statesmanship conflicted with Christian values. The German thinker J. G. Herder understood the differences between cultures, and their values, but recognized that men in one culture were capable of an empathetic understanding of other cultures, both in the past and in other parts of the world. These and other writers led me to a general investigation of political values, and of the possibility of a liberal society, where a variety of values are followed.

I have been particularly deeply impressed by the Italian philosopher G. B. Vico, the first thinker to understand what a culture is, who led me to consider the difference between the sciences and the humanities, and the fallacious application of concepts derived from the former to the latter, as by many modern sociologists.

The idea of final solutions seems to me a fallacy not merely in practice but in principle, since if ultimate values are incompatible, a perfect world in which all ultimate values – goodness, truth, justice, liberty, self-realization, equality, mercy, beauty – are combined cannot be conceived, let alone exist. This fallacy has made possible the most destructive social and political movements of this century, including right-wing authoritarianism, but particularly Lenin's application of Marxism.

It was romanticism, despite some of its unhappy results, that mounted the first serious challenge to the underlying doctrine that to all real questions there is only one answer. The romantics held that our values are not objective truths, not discovered but invented – by individuals or groups or larger individualities such as the Church, the class, the nation, or even such 'forces' as History, Progress, the World Spirit.

I have attempted to explain that we are today the products of both the Enlightenment and romanticism, which creates certain irreconcilable conflicts. I have tried to analyse the relation of modern nationalism to the idea of final solutions. My more recent essays (collected in *The Crooked Timber of Humanity* 1990) examine the implications of this idea, and its incompatibility with the psychological and practical possibilities open to mankind. IB

Among other writings of Isaiah Berlin are *Karl Marx* (1939; 4th edn 1978); *Four Essays on Liberty* (1969); *Vico and Herder* (1976); *Russian Thinkers* (1978); *Concepts and Categories: Philosophical Essays* (1978); *Against the Current: Essays in the History of Ideas* (1979); and *The Magus of the North: J. G. Hamann and the Origins of Modern Irrationalism* (1993).

Berry's paradox The English librarian C. J. Berry proposed this simplified version of Richard's paradox: when we name integers in ordinary English, some of them can be named in only *one* syllable, for example 2, 5, 12. Similarly, other integers cannot be named in less than *two* syllables, for example 7, 13, 40. Note that 25 can also be named in only two syllables, namely the syllables 'five squared'.

We can similarly define sets of integers which cannot be named in less than *three* syllables, and again *four*, *five*, etc. Continuing, we come to the set of integers that cannot be named in less than 28 syllables. Among the integers in this set, one will be the least. Call that integer N.

Since N belongs to this set, N *cannot* be named with less than 28 syllables. And yet, N *can* be named with less than 28 syllables, since it *is* so named in the phrase: 'the least integer which cannot be named in ordinary English with less than 28 syllables'!

This constitutes a paradox: an apparently sound proof of a contradictory conclusion.

biconditional *n.*, *adj.* a conjunction of two conditional sentences: *if p then q* and *if q then p*. This can also be expressed *p if and only if q*, and is sometimes abbreviated *p iff q*. When such a sentence is interpreted truth-functionally, the truth-table (with ≡ symbolizing iff) is as in Table 2.

Two sentences A and B are said to be logically equivalent if and only if the biconditional *A iff B* is logically true.

Table 2 Truth-table for the biconditional

p	q	$p \equiv q$
T	T	T
T	F	F
F	T	F
F	F	T

binary (Lat. *bini* by twos, pairwise) **notation** the representation of integers in terms of powers of 2. For instance, the number 13 ($=1 \times 10^1 + 3 \times 10^0$) in our ordinary decimal notation is written 1101 ($=1 \times 2^3 + 1 \times 2^2 + 0 \times 2^1 + 1 \times 2^0$) in binary notation. It was first devised and explored by Leibniz.

binary number number written in binary notation.

binary operation a logical or mathematical operation that applies to *two* items, e.g. conjunction (between two propositions) or division (of one number by another).

binary opposition an expression frequently used by structuralists and post-structuralists for a pair of concepts that are in some way contrasted, e.g. raw / cooked; presence / absence; necessary / possible; speech / writing; male / female. According to Derrida, one term in a binary opposition is subconsciously or implicitly assigned dominance over the other, and it is a philosophical task to reveal and eliminate the imbalance. The oppositions discussed by him and his followers are always construed as being hierarchical.

Note: Opposites come in pairs, so the word 'binary' in 'binary opposition' and 'binary opposites' is redundant in many contexts. It is certainly superfluous in pleonastic solecisms like 'binary dichotomization'.

binary relation a relation between *two* terms; a two-place predicate.

biocentrism *n.* the view that the existence of organic life, including human life, has a central place in the general scheme of things, as an ultimate value, an ultimate purpose, or both.

bisexuality *n.* **1** hermaphroditism. **2** the presence of both male and female psychological traits in one individual. **3** desiring or having sexual partners of both sexes.

bivalence /baɪˈveɪləns/ *n.* having two values.

bivalence, principle of the principle that there are exactly two truth-values, true and false, and that, within a certain area of discourse, every statement has exactly one of them.

Under the influence of the work of Michael Dummett, the point of difference between realism and anti-realism is often formulated in terms of bivalence. Realism (with respect to a certain class of statements) is defined as the view that the principle of bivalence applies to every statement (of that class) even if it should be impossible *for us* to have any grounds for assent or dissent to it. Anti-realism is the opposite view that the principle does not apply unless there is some way in which we can have some ground for assent or dissent: truth is defined as warranted assertibility.

One class of statements to which the principle does not apply, in the view of some philosophers, is the class of statements such as 'All of John's children are asleep'. It is argued that this statement is true if John has children who are all asleep, and false if John has children not all of whom are asleep, but neither true nor false if John has no children. *See also* EXCLUDED MIDDLE and FUTURE CONTINGENTS.

Blackstone /ˈblækstəʊn/, Sir William (1723–80) author of the *Commentaries on the Laws of England* (1765–9), the first major work in English jurisprudence since Sir Edward Coke's *Institutes* (1628–44). Blackstone was the target of Bentham's first published book, *A Fragment on Government* 1776, in which he was criticized for his eclectic use of modern natural law ideas and for his acceptance, often uncritically conservative, of the principles and practices of English law.

Blanshard /ˈblænʃɑːd/, Brand (1892–1987) American philosopher, who taught at Yale University. His philosophical standpoint was idealist, closely related to British neo-Hegelianism, which he expounded in an unusually clear way. In *The Nature of Thought* 1939 he criticized contemporary empiricism.

Blavatsky /bləˈvætskɪ/, Helena Petrovna, *née* Hahn (1831–91) Russian writer. She gave the name *theosophy* to her eclectic blend of occultism and spiritualism generously laced with mystical and Gnostic ingredients, and was a co-founder of the Theosophical Society in 1875. In 1885, the Society for Psychical Research in London established that the evidence proffered by her to support her claims to paranormal psychical powers was spurious. Her writings, e.g. *Isis Unveiled* 1879 and *The Secret Doctrine* 1888, are likely to be of marginal interest to students of philosophy.

Bloch /blɔx (Gm.)/, Ernst (1885–1977) German philosopher, twice in exile because of his unorthodox Marxism (from Germany in 1933; from East to West Germany in 1961). Among his prolific writings are *Das Prinzip Hoffnung* 1954–9 (The principle of hope), *Naturrecht und menschliche Würde* 1961 (Natural law and human dignity) and *Atheismus im Christentum* 1968 (Atheism in Christianity). Bloch regarded the welcoming of 'the end of history' as a bourgeois aberration, because of its acceptance, in principle, of the present condition of mankind. For Bloch, the actual state of the world should be understood as harbouring potentialities. His principle of hope, the basis for a wide-ranging synthesis of a metaphysical outlook and Marxist themes, especially those in the young Marx, is a 'philosophy of the future'. It implies the possibility of a better world, a world without exploitation and oppression. Bloch's metaphysical and humanist Marxism was condemned by orthodox Marxists, but highly esteemed by the New Left.

Blondel /blɔ̃dɛl (Fr.)/, Maurice (1861–1941) French Christian existentialist, professor of philosophy at Aix-en-Provence 1897–1927. His main work is *L'Action* 1893; rev. edn 1937.

Bodin /bɔdɛ̃ (Fr.)/, Jean (1530–96) French political thinker. In his *Six Livres de la république* 1576 (Six books on the commonwealth) he introduced the concept of sovereignty, i.e. authority not constrained by any law (except God's), and argued that the ruler of a political society should be sovereign. In this he anticipated Hobbes, and did so from a similar background of violent civil and religious conflict, where sovereign authority alone could safeguard civil peace. He did, however, allow for constitutional constraints on the ruler, which puts some strain on the consistency of his theory. Bodin accepted many of the superstitions of his time, like numerology and astrology, and wrote a tract against witchcraft (*De la Démonomanie des sorciers* 1580). On the other hand, his *Heptaplomeres* ... (Dialogue of seven wise men) is an eloquent plea for religious toleration.

Boehme /'bømə/, Jacob (1575–1624) A cobbler by trade, working in his home town of Görlitz in Saxony, Boehme had a series of mystical-religious experiences which inspired an original metaphysics which he presented in non-technical language. It combined a boldly speculative use of traditional concepts with elements of contemporary alchemy and natural philosophy. His aim was to develop a theory that would do justice to his states of mystical exaltation and at the same time overcome the perennial difficulties in Christian thought, such as the apparent incompatibilities between divine perfection and the existence of evil, and between divine providence and human freedom. The marked difference from orthodox theology led to conflict with the Lutheran church authorities. Boehme has been regarded as one of the great speculative mystics and was an important source of inspiration for Hamann, Schelling, von Baader and other romantic idealists. In England all his writings were available in translation as early as the mid-seventeenth century, and exercised an influence on religious thought there.

Boethius /bəʊ'iːθɪəs/, Anicius Manlius Severinus (*c.* 480–524/6) an aristocratic Roman who served Theodoric, the Ostrogothic ruler of Italy, and devoted his leisure to philosophy until he was imprisoned and executed on trumped-up charges of disloyalty. His Latin translations of most of Aristotle's logical works were standard in the Middle Ages, and his commentaries (two each on Porphyry's *Isagoge* and Aristotle's *De interpretatione*, and one on the *Categories*) and logical textbooks (especially his work on the theory of topics, *De topicis differentiis*) were among the most important sources for logicians before the thirteenth century. They transmitted the Aristotelian tradition of formal logic which had become accepted within the neo-Platonic schools. Boethius also wrote five *Opuscula sacra* (Short theological treatises). Three of them (I, II and V) use techniques of logical analysis to clarify orthodox Christian doctrine about the Trinity and christology and defend it against heretical distortion. One (III) is a brief neo-Platonic treatise, designed to explain how all things, although good by virtue of existing, are none the less distinct from God, the supreme good and source of all goodness.

Boethius's most famous work, *De consolatione philosophiae* (The consolation of philosophy) was written when he was in prison, awaiting execution. Boethius represents himself as overcome by grief and despairing at the order of a world in which evil seems to triumph and good go unrewarded. A personification of Philosophy appears in his cell and, without making any explicit appeal to Christian revelation, sets about convincing him by reasoning that the universe is in fact justly ordered by God. Gifts of fortune, such as power, riches, honour, fame and pleasure turn out, Philosophy argues, to be illusory when pursued individually. They are desirable because each reflects something of the supreme good. But the wise man should seek this supreme good itself, which is the same as God. Evil is not a reality but a privation of being. The closer a man adheres to God, the less he is at the mercy of fate (which is simply the day-to-day working out of divine providence), and the more free he becomes. In the final book, the discussion becomes more logically analytic, and Boethius returns to a problem he had discussed in his commentary on Aristotle's *De interpretatione*. He puts into his own mouth the following argument: if God foreknows all that will happen, then everything which happens, happens of necessity, and so humans do not have freedom of will and cannot rightly be rewarded or punished for their behaviour. Philosophy replies by distinguishing between strict necessity, which applies in cases of natural invariance, such as the rising of the sun every morning, and conditional necessity, which depends on the relationship between statements. If I know that a man is sitting, then it is conditionally necessary that he is sitting. God, she continues, does not *fore*know events, since he lives in an eternal presentness. Rather, he knows all things, past, present and future, in a single, instantaneous glimpse. Just as a man's freedom to sit or stand is not affected by my knowledge that he is sitting, so the conditional necessity of all actual states of affairs, because God knows them, does not affect freedom of action. JM

Boethius of Dacia (*fl.* 1275) a teacher at Paris, accused together with Siger of Brabant of advancing Averroistic doctrines. He had great faith in human reason and its potential, and his thought seems to have had a distinctly secular character. Conflicts between rational insight and faith could be resolved by assigning a higher, and separate, status to faith. This seems to come close to FIDEISM, and was condemned as a doctrine of a 'double truth'. The name indicates his Swedish-Danish (not Romanian) origin; he belonged as a Dominican to his home province.

Bois-Reymond *See* DU BOIS-REYMOND.

Bolingbroke /'bɒlɪŋbrʊk/, Henry St John, Viscount (1678–1751) Tory politician and minister of state and, after his return from exile in 1723, a leading opponent of the Walpole administration. The style of his writings on politics and on history was much admired. His free-thinking advocacy of deism and natural morality aroused controversy; in these writings the philosophical penetration does not match the felicity of expression.

Bolzano /bɔltsa'no (Gm.)/, Bernard (1781–1848) Bohemian philosopher and mathematician of a generally anti-Kantian outlook who anticipated, somewhat incompletely, later developments in logic and mathematical analysis. In particular he had some grasp of the notion, important in formal logic, that a valid inference is one where any interpretation of the terms of the premisses that makes the premisses true makes the conclusion true also. In mathematics, he rejected the view that concepts like continuity are ultimately to be understood by appeal to direct intuition of space and time, and showed how they can be theoretically defined. He also anticipated the later anti-psychologism of Frege and Husserl in his theory of propositions as non-mental abstract entities.

Many of Bolzano's writings remained in manuscript or were prohibited by the censors. In his philosophy of religion and in his social and political writings he represented an enlightened progressive Catholicism, and was therefore removed from his chair at Prague in 1819. GC

bona fide; bona fides /'bəʊnə 'faɪdɪ; -iːz/ Lat. in good faith; good faith.

Bonaventure /'bɒnəvɛntʃə/, St (Giovanni di Fidanza) (1221–74) scholastic philosopher and theologian who taught at Paris, a member and eventually minister-general of the Franciscan order, author of a biography of St Francis. Mainly influenced by Augustine, he accepted that philosophy (using reason alone) is capable of reaching truth in many fields of inquiry, but for the full truth, especially in metaphysics, theology (based on faith) is indispensable. Plato and Aristotle, he argued, had each seen only part of metaphysical truth: Augustine had achieved the synthesis, in seeing that God as a creator uses the Platonic Forms as exemplar causes. He linked this philosophical exemplarism with a theology based on the beginning of the fourth gospel. The *Itinerarium mentis in Deum* 1259 (The mind's journey to God) and other writings contain classical arguments for God's existence, including a re-assertion of Anselm's ontological argument. Like Aquinas, Maimonides and others, he rejected the Aristotelian view that the world has no beginning in time. But he differed from them by maintaining that this view could be refuted by rational argument, whilst they considered the Aristotelian view philosophically possible and rejected it only for theological reasons.

Boole /buːl/, George (1815–64) Irish mathematician and logician, professor of mathematics at Queen's College, Cork, and a pioneer of mathematical logic. His chief work was *The Laws of Thought* 1854. Boole applied algebraic techniques to traditional Aristotelian logic, with some surprising results. It turned out that arguments which had been thought valid since Aristotle were actually invalid. Boole is now chiefly remembered for BOOLEAN ALGEBRA, which is named after him. AM

Boolean algebra A Boolean algebra is a set in which the elements are related to one another by three operations: the *complement*, the *join* (or Boolean sum) and the *meet* (or Boolean product), and characteristic axioms. Any group of things with appropriate operations which satisfy these axioms constitutes a Boolean algebra. Thus there is a Boolean algebra of classes of sets (the Boolean sum of two sets is their union and the product is their intersection) and a Boolean algebra of propositions (the Boolean product of two propositions is their conjunction and the complement of a proposition is its negation). PR

Bosanquet /'bəʊzənkɛt, 'bəʊznkɪt/, Bernard (1848–1923) English philosopher. He taught at University College, Oxford 1870–81, and at St Andrews 1903–8 and, in addition to writing a large number of books and essays, was active in educational and charitable organizations. The main influences on his thought came from Hegel and Lotze. In his metaphysics he argued that there is only one individual, the Absolute, reality as a whole. What we regard as individuals are so only in an attenuated sense; they are comparatively constant manifestations of some qualities. Underpinning the metaphysics was a set of logical doctrines which, like those of Bradley, were the main target of the analytical onslaught of Moore and Russell early in the twentieth century. In his social philosophy he opposed the excesses of individualism, stressing community values. His *History of Aesthetics* was for a long time the definitive work on that subject in Britain.

Bossuet /bɔsyɛ (Fr.)/, Jacques Bénigne (1627–1704) French clergyman of remarkable eloquence, for a long time a favourite at the court of Louis XIV. He defended the divine right of kings and the supremacy of the church, and insisted on the necessity of obedient submission to authority in his *Politique inspirée de l'écriture sainte* (Politics drawn from Scripture). In this and other writings, admirable for their brilliant classical style, he points to the obvious dangers of civil liberty and equality; as for freedom of conscience, the Protestants constitute a warning example. His ideas now carry conviction only with a waning band of French Catholic-conservative monarchists, but are otherwise of interest mainly to students of intellectual history.

bound variable (in predicate logic) a variable that falls within the scope of a quantifier. For example, in (∀x)(∃y)Fxy, both x and y are bound. In (∃y)Fxy, x is not bound, i.e. x is free. *See also* FREE VARIABLE.

Bourbaki /buʀbaki (Fr.); bʊ'bækɪ; 'bɔːbəkɪ (Eng.)/, Nicolas. A pseudonym for a group of French mathematicians. Since 1939 the group has published a history of mathematics, many articles, and close to 40 volumes of *Eléments de mathématiques*. Mathematics is understood not as a science of mathematical objects (numbers, vectors, spaces) but as the general science of abstract structures. The membership of the group is changing and secret. It is known, however, to have included H. Cartan, Cl. Chevallerey, J. Dieudonné, Ch. Ehresmann, A. Weil *et al.*

bourgeois /buʀʒwɑ (Fr.)/ (Fr. person with full citizenship rights in a city) in Marxist theory, a member of the bourgeoisie, i.e. the class of owners of property, especially industrial and commercial. Its class interest is in conflict with the interest of the class of wage-labourers, the working class.

Boyle /bɔɪl/, Robert (1627–91) English natural philosopher, now best remembered for his experimental work on air and gases. In works like *The Origin of Forms and Qualities* 1666 and *The Excellency and Grounds of the Mechanical Hypothesis* 1674, he explored the nature and status of the corpuscular theory of matter. He argued its superiority over traditional Aristotelian and alchemical theories, on both theoretical and experimental grounds, and showed how it could form the basis for an account of the nature of species. He sought to show that the chemical, medicinal, etc. properties of substances, as well as the 'sensible' qualities of colour, taste, sound, etc., can be reduced to the 'mechanical affections' of matter; that is, the 'primary moods' (extension, impenetrability, motion, shape, size) of its 'particles', the combination of particles into 'corpuscles', and the relations of corpuscles in the texture of more complex structures. This is different from Locke's account of secondary qualities, in dispensing altogether with the concept of 'powers'. Boyle's studies confirmed in him a deeply theistic view of the world and of scientific laws, defended in works on *The Excellency of Theology* 1674, *The Notion of*

Nature 1686 and *Final Causes* 1688. He was an indefatigable but unoriginal exponent of the Design argument. In *The Christian Virtuoso* 1690 he discussed the nature of 'natural and civil history', showing how it can extend even to the acceptance of antecedently improbable events, and turned this to the defence of the biblical miracles which vindicated the Christian revelation. He left some youthful unpublished manuscripts on ethics which are predominantly Stoic in inspiration. MS

bracketing *n.* (in phenomenology) *See* EPOCHĒ.

Bradley /ˈbrædlɪ/, F(rancis) H(erbert) (1846–1924) fellow of Merton College, Oxford from 1870. Bradley's philosophy, a bold metaphysics presented in *Appearance and Reality* 1893 with pugnacious verve, takes feeling (undifferentiated intuition in which there is no distinction between the experience and what is experienced) to be the only kind of mental act that can avoid the contradictions inherent in the basic categories (thing, quality, relation, etc.) that are used in all rational, discursive thought. We have to use these categories, although they are inadequate; but reality must be a consistent totality, and it follows that our intellect cannot grasp it. Reality must also be a *single* whole, for all plurality forces us to use categories that are self-contradictory. For the same reason, reality must be something in which there is no duality between knowing and the known. The total whole – or, what is the same, the experience of it all with nothing omitted – is what Bradley calls the Absolute.

Like his other writings, *Principles of Logic* 1883 shows an influence from Hegel. It contains a number of objections to traditional logic which have later gained general acceptance: that not all judgements have a subject-predicate form; that there are valid arguments that cannot be reduced to categorical syllogisms; that a universal statement (e.g. All S is P) does not have existential import (i.e. does not imply that there are S's). Fundamental to his logical views is a kind of holism: if inferences from what is particular are valid at all, it can only be on the basis of presuppositions of a universal kind. Linked with this is the rejection of psychologism: logical relations are universal, and hold between meanings; mental occurrences, in contrast, are particulars that come and go.

Ethical Studies 1876 objects to the individualism and utilitarianism of writers like John Stuart Mill and Herbert Spencer, and makes a strong case for the moral relevance of the community. Socially defined roles are a part of what a person is. They determine the duties to oneself and to others. If understood as something contrary to this, moral equality is neither possible nor desirable.

Moore's article 'The Refutation of Idealism' 1903, and other writings of his and of Bertrand Russell in the early years of the twentieth century, had Bradley's and Bosanquet's idealism as their principal target.

Bradwardine /ˈbrædwədiːn/, Thomas (*c.* 1290–1349) fellow of Merton College, Oxford. His theory of bodily motion in space was an early attempt to improve on Aristotle's *Physics*. In his polemic against Ockham and against Pelagianism on the question of the relation between grace and human free will, Bradwardine used metaphysical rather than scriptural arguments against human free will, stressing the necessity of divine grace. His theory has difficulties in explaining why God is not the author of sin.

Braithwaite /ˈbreɪθweɪt/, R(ichard) B(evan) (1900–1990) English philosopher who taught at Cambridge from 1928. Scientific method was one of his major interests, and

Scientific Explanation 1953 is an attempt to develop a rigorously empiricist philosophy of science, in treating questions such as 'What is a law of nature?', 'What is a scientific theory?', etc., and it contains a theory for assessing the acceptability of probability-statements that would be consistent with an empiricist philosophy. Of seminal influence was his *Theory of Games as a Tool for the Moral Philosopher* 1955. In his *An Empiricist's View of the Nature of Religious Belief* 1957 he proposed a non-cognitivist interpretation of religious statements.

Brentano /brɛn'taːno (Gm.)/, Franz (Clemens) (1837–1917) philosopher and psychologist, taught at the universities of Würzburg and Vienna. His lectures were extraordinarily influential upon subsequent continental philosophy. Among those who came to hear him were Sigmund Freud, Edmund Husserl, Anton Marty, Thomas Masaryk (the first president of Czechoslovakia), Alexius Meinong, and Konrad Twardowski (the founder of contemporary Polish philosophy). Brentano was also a close associate of Christian von Ehrenfels, the founder of Gestalt psychology.

Brentano made significant contributions to almost every branch of philosophy. His general approach is best understood by reference to what he called 'descriptive, or phenomenological, psychology' (what has also come to be called 'analytic phenomenology').

In the *Psychology from an Empirical Standpoint* 1874, Brentano emphasizes that modern philosophy has neglected intentionality; examples are thinking, believing, wondering, hoping, desiring, liking and disliking. (Russell was later to call these phenomena 'propositional attitudes'.) Brentano's views are notable for his defence of the thesis of the '*primacy of the intentional*'. Where some have held that the meaning of our thoughts is to be understood by reference to an inner language, Brentano held that the meaning of any language can be understood only by reference to the thoughts – the intentional phenomena – that that language may be used to express.

Even if intentional phenomena are always accompanied by sensible or sensational phenomena, they are not themselves sensational or sensible. The presence of such attitudes may be at least as certain and indubitable for us as is the presence of our sensations. In knowing that I have such an attitude, I can know directly and immediately that there is a certain individual thing – namely, the one who has that attitude. And *I*, of course, am the one who does my thinking.

If, say, I hope for rain, then I can know that I hope for rain; and, as a rational being, I can conceive what it is to hope for rain and in so doing I can see that the only type of entity that can have the property of hoping for rain is an individual thing or substance.

Following Leibniz, Brentano distinguishes two types of certainty: the certainty we can have with respect to the existence of our conscious states, and that *a priori* certainty which may be directed upon necessary truths. I may be certain *a priori* that there cannot be believing, desiring, hoping and fearing unless there is a *substance* that believes, desires, hopes and fears. In such a case, it will be certain for me (Brentano says that I will 'perceive') that there is a substance that believes, desires, hopes and fears. Having an especially rigid theory of knowledge, Brentano also contends that, if one is certain that a given substance exists, one is identical with that substance; our beliefs about substances *other* than ourselves are at best only *probable*.

Brentano's principal ethical writing was *Our Knowledge of the Origin of Right and Wrong* 1889. His ethics is based upon the analogy he believes to hold between intellectual and emotive attitudes. In each case, the attitude is either positive or negative. We may *affirm* or *deny* the object of the idea, and we may *love* or *hate* that object. And the emotive attitudes, like the intellectual attitudes, may be *correct* or *incorrect*. To say that a thing is intrinsically good, according to him, is to say that it is *correct to love* that thing as an end, and to say that a thing is intrinsically bad is to say that it is *correct to hate* that thing as an end. Brentano believed that we can be immediately aware of the correctness of certain of our emotive attitudes, just as we can be immediately aware of the correctness (i.e. the truth) of certain of our intellectual attitudes. In each case, the correctness consists in a relation of appropriateness or fittingness between the attitude and its object. RCH

Bridgewater Treatises a series of eight works published 1833–6, generously funded through a bequest by the eighth Earl of Bridgewater (1756–1829), for the purpose of demonstrating the power, wisdom and goodness of God as manifested in the Creation, in the light of the most recent scientific discoveries. Four of the authors were theologians, four were scientists. Among them was Thomas Chalmers (the Scottish churchman and philanthropist), P. M. Roget (best known for his thesaurus) and William Whewell. All the treatises sold well and were frequently reprinted. Charles Babbage, the calculating-machine designer, produced an unsubsidized 'Ninth Bridgewater Treatise', in which he challenged Hume's argument against miracles.

Bridgman /ˈbridʒmən/, P(ercy) W(illiams) (1882–1961) American physicist, professor at Harvard University, winner of the Nobel Prize for Physics in 1946. In *The Logic of Modern Physics* 1927 he presented an operationalist (OPERATIONALISM) theory of scientific concepts: 'in general, we mean by a concept nothing more than a set of operations'. If a specific question has meaning, it must be possible to find operations that give the answer.

Broad /brɔːd/, C(harlie) D(unbar) (1887–1971) English philosopher, fellow of Trinity College, Cambridge, a prominent representative of analytical philosophy. In his view, there is no place for the misty or poetic in philosophy, nor should philosophy yield to the deliverances of common sense. His writings, elegant and lucid, contain careful clarifications of concepts and problems in many areas of philosophy (perhaps with the exception of his *Five Types of Ethical Theory* 1930, in which the treatment of a few classical moral philosophers is debatable). One of his most important works, *The Mind and Its Place in Nature* 1925, distinguishes a vast number of possible theories of the relation between matter and mind. Broad tentatively indicates a preference for a theory that allows for the possibility of independently existing mental phenomena. This is in line with the cautious but favourable attitude to parapsychology evident in his *Lectures on Psychical Research*, 1963.

broad/narrow A *narrow* description of a state or entity does not depend on anything external to it; a *broad* description does depend on something external. For instance, the statement 'the watch shows 11 o'clock' is a broad description since the position of the hands depends on certain conventions. No narrow description – of the parts of the watch and their interrelations – can include that statement.

Brouwer /ˈbraʊwər (Du.)/, Luitzen Egbertus Jan (1881–1966) Dutch mathematician and philosopher. Impressed by the logical paradoxes discovered at the beginning of this century, he advocated, influenced by Kantian ideas, a 'constructivist' theory of mathematics according to which numbers and other mathematical entities are brought into existence by human thought rather than existing independently, as the Platonists have it. This led him to suppose that certain statements in mathematics are neither true nor false, thus contradicting the orthodox logicians' 'law of excluded middle'. The logical principles that codify this new approach constitute INTUITIONISTIC LOGIC. Wittgenstein's return to philosophy after an interlude following the *Tractatus* is said to have been partly the result of his attending a lecture given by Brouwer. GC

Bruno, Giordano (1548–1600) Italian philosopher from Naples, a Dominican. He was an unorthodox thinker, a travelling intellectual adventurer. His lectures and writings shocked his audiences in Oxford, Paris and elsewhere because of their bold theories of astral magic and other strands of HERMETICISM. The revelation that much of what he offered was plagiarized from other Renaissance philosophers (Ficino, Agrippa) administered a further shock. Bruno held that neither the Earth nor the sun was the centre of the universe, argued that the universe is infinite, and identified it pantheistically with God. Condemned by the Inquisition to be executed for heresy, he was burned alive. Two centuries later, his fate made radicals and liberals – especially in Italy – see him as a martyr in the cause of enlightenment and a symbol in the struggle against reactionary Catholic-conservative oppression; in Germany, his pantheism and mysticism inspired romantic philosophy.

Brunschvicg /brœʃviːg (Fr.)/, Léon (1869–1944) French philosopher, professor at the Sorbonne 1909–40. He adhered to a neo-Kantian idealism, combining it with a belief in progress, both intellectual-scientific and moral, which will ultimately break down the barriers that separate people.

brute fact/institutional fact Brute facts, like volcanic eruptions or the number of electrons in a hydrogen atom, do not depend for their existence on human conventions or institutions; institutional facts, like those involving money, property, government, marriage, promising, games, etc., do so depend. Anscombe used 'brute' in this sense in her 'On brute facts', *Analysis 18* (1958), and Searle introduced 'institutional' as a contrasting term, in 'What is a Speech Act' in Max Black (ed.), *Philosophy in America* 1965, and has elaborated on this distinction in later publications.

The distinction has some affinity with that made by Pufendorf between physical and moral entities.

Some anti-realists maintain that the distinction has no application: all facts are institutional. There is considerable controversy around this denial of brute facts.

Buber /'buːbə/, Martin (1878–1965) Jewish philosopher and religious thinker, born in Vienna; professor of Jewish religion and ethics at Frankfurt am Main 1924–33, and at the Hebrew University in Jerusalem from 1938. He was a strong advocate of conciliation between Jews and Arabs in Palestine. In his philosophy, Buber stresses the importance of the relation between self and other (I–Thou) and its radical difference from the relation between self and object (I–It). In *Ich und Du* 1922 (I and Thou) Buber elaborates on how central dimensions of human existence (authenticity, sense of community, etc.) are lost for a person whose relations are all of the self–object kind. Genuine religion must regard God as essentially a Thou; the mistake of much traditional natural and revealed theology is to conceive of the relation between self and God in analogy with that between self and object.

Büchner /ˈbyːçnər (Gm.)/, Ludwig (1824–99) German physician and philosopher. His *Kraft und Stoff* 1855 (Force and matter) was a best-selling statement of scientific naturalism and monism: force and matter being different manifestations of the same thing. He advocated a utilitarian ethics, and rejected supernaturalist religious and moral doctrines as being both false and harmful.

Bultmann /ˈbʊltman (Gm.)/, Rudolf (1884–1976) German Protestant theologian, professor at the University of Marburg 1921–51. In his view, stated in *Kerygma und Mythos* 1948 (Kerygma and myth) and other works, the historical reliability of the gospel texts is open to doubt. This does not, however, undermine the Christian faith. What is essential is not whether the message is fact or myth: what matters is the content of the message. To get the message across to a secularized world, a demythologized interpretation of the gospel becomes necessary. An existentialist interpretation is, for Bultmann, what makes sense of the gospel in our time. See e.g. *History and Eschatology* (based on his Gifford Lectures 1957).

Buridan /ˈbjʊərɪdən (Eng.); byʀidɑ̃ (Fr.)/, John (*c.* 1295–*c.* 1358) born in the diocese of Arras; attended the University of Paris, and was a Master of Arts (i.e. a professor) around 1320. He had a distinguished career at that university, being rector twice; he is last mentioned in records in 1358, and may have died of the plague in that year.

His interests lay in logic and in what were then known as the 'natural sciences'; in the former, he developed a sophisticated theory of propositions and, on the basis of this, did outstanding work on logical paradoxes. His work in science is important for a new conception of scientific methodology, open to observation and without explanation by final causes, and also for several innovative new concepts: the idea of 'impetus', as a non-Aristotelian explanation of projectile motion, and also for the idea that the Earth might rotate, rather than the heavens. According to his theory of volition, we will what our reason tells us is best. If it should come to pass that two choices are equally good and no other choice is better, the agent would 'freeze'. The classical illustration is known as 'Buridan's ass': the hungry beast is placed at equal distance between two equal bales of hay – and starves. GW

Burke /bɜːk/, Edmund (1729–97) Irish philosopher and politician. His *Philosophical Enquiry into the Origin of our Ideas of the Sublime and the Beautiful* 1757 is a classic in the history of modern aesthetics. His analysis associates the beautiful with a sense of disinterested benevolence; and the sense of the sublime arises from fear linked with the awareness that there is no real danger. In his political writings, Burke's sympathies were with the revolution of 1688 and with the American colonies in their conflict with the Crown, but he condemned the French Revolution in his *Reflections on the Revolution in France* 1790, which has become a classic of conservative political thought. The underlying principle is one of respect for inherited rights and for established customs, and opposition to the attempts (respectively by James II, George III and the French revolutionaries) to abolish them. In Burke's view, there is a general, though not infallible, presumption in favour of tradition in social and political matters. If an established social fabric is torn apart, the future prospects for the society are unpromising.

Butler, Joseph (1692–1752) Butler was born in Wantage in England and was a younger contemporary of Samuel Clarke, with whom he corresponded. His career was within the Anglican church, his final office being that of Bishop of Durham.

Butler's ethical ideas are conveyed with great clarity and economy of exposition in his *Fifteen Sermons* 1726. Indeed, he specifically advocates directness and simplicity in ethical reasoning, claiming that morality must appeal to what we call plain common sense.

The preface to the *Fifteen Sermons* sums up the elements of his position. These include a theory of human nature and the nature of obligation. There is, in addition, a refutation of psychological hedonism or egoism.

Butler claims that his approach to the question of human nature, which he called man's 'economy' or 'constitution', is one of empirical investigation. However, he actually proceeds by analogy, making use of the Aristotelian notion that the nature of a thing is related to its function or purpose. Just as a watch can only be understood when its parts are seen as forming a *system* in relation to each other, for the purpose of telling the time, so the parts of man's nature – the appetites, passions, affections and the principle of reflection – must be seen in relation to each other, and in particular in relation to the authority of reflection or conscience, further explained in his *Dissertation on the Nature of Virtue*. Butler argues that human nature is adapted to virtue in the way in which the nature of the watch is adapted to measure time.

Nevertheless, he believed that humans have free will and can therefore choose whether or not to follow conscience. He criticized Shaftesbury, whose 'sentimentalist' views made morality dependent on feeling rather than reason, for leaving conscience out of his account of morality and relating morality instead entirely to human happiness. Butler, in contrast, saw conscience as forming the peak of the hierarchy which constituted human nature. He saw self-love and benevolence as important but lesser principles, while at the bottom of the hierarchy came the particular passions and appetites.

Butler sees conscience as a reliable guide in particular situations to any fair-minded person who is prepared to sit down and think about a course of action in moral terms. He assumes that the deliverances of conscience, because their ultimate source is God, are likely to be similar for different individuals, but admits that education or sophistication can adversely affect judgement. Whether conscience *in fact* determines one's conduct is a different question: conscience has *authority*, but will not always have the requisite *power*.

Butler's refutation of egoism appears in Sermon 11. He is particularly concerned to refute the type of egoism that he attributed to Hobbes, which regards the idea of a disinterested, generous or public-spirited action as inconceivable. He argues that we must have a direct desire for certain objects, other than our own satisfaction, in order to be able to obtain satisfaction from attaining those objects. Self-love in the sense required for the egoist argument would, he points out, be essentially empty. If it was not possible to want anything but self-gratification, the self could never be gratified. Indulging *any* of the particular passions – greed or cruelty, as well as benevolence – is a case of disinterested action which refutes the claims of the psychological egoist.

In relation to this argument, it is important to notice that Butler distinguishes two kinds of self-love. True and long-term self-love, which he called 'cool self-love', he sees as a beneficial trait, as useful to other people's interest as to one's own. The more immediate kind of selfishness – passionate or sensual selfishness – he sees as being actually contrary to this. Most people, he argued, spend a large part of their time pursuing the satisfaction of particular passions, but a well-thought-out policy of cool self-love would actually coincide to a very considerable extent with a policy of pursuing virtue for its own sake.

The *Sermons* were among the readings most frequently prescribed for university study in nineteenth-century England, and so was Butler's *Analogy of Religion* 1736, then regarded as an excellent apologetic tract. In this work, Butler assumes that it is reasonable for a person to accept the arguments in support of natural religion (deism), and argues that, given that assumption and given the features of the natural world, it would be unreasonable to reject the arguments in support of Christian revelation. BA

C

Cabanis /kabanis (Fr.)/, Pierre-Jean-Georges (1757–1808) adoptive son of Mme Helvétius. He studied medicine and wrote on that subject, but is best known for his essays on the relation between man's physical and mental constitution, published in 1802 under the title *Rapports du physique et du moral de l'homme* (The connections between the physical and the moral in man). Physiological and psychological data provided the basis for a theory of human nature, a theory which differs from Condillac's by taking into account not only external stimuli but also internal dispositions and sensations. Like many later nineteenth-century positivists, Cabanis held that human nature, like other natural phenomena, can be analysed and explained in a materialist and mechanistic way, but that we will remain ignorant of any more ultimate explanations.

Cabbala *See* KABBALA.

Cabet /kabɛ (Fr.)/, Etienne (1788–1856) utopian communist, who achieved great fame through the bestseller *Voyage en Icarie* 1840 (Voyage to Icaria).

cacodaemon (Gr. *kakos* bad, evil) *n.* an evil spirit.

Cajetan, Thomas de Vio (1468–1534) a Dominican, of Neapolitan origin, who taught at Padua and Rome, and was eventually created a cardinal. He wrote important commentaries on Aquinas's *Summa Theologiae* and on some of Aristotle's works. He also produced a number of independent treatises. Important among them is *De nominum analogia* 1498 (On the analogy of names), with its classical account of the Thomist doctrine that our statements about God are analogical. *See also* ANALOGY.

calculus (*sing.*); **calculi** (*pl.*) *n.* **1** any set of rules which can be applied for calculation in mathematics or logic. The term is also used for a formal theory that yields such rules, e.g. *propositional* (or *sentential*) calculus and *predicate* calculus. **2** short for the branches of mathematics known as the *differential* and *integral* calculus, or as the INFINITESIMAL calculus.

Callicles /ˈkælɪkliːz/ In Plato's dialogue *Gorgias*, Callicles advocates an extreme doctrine of natural justice as the right of the strongest, and scorns the artificial, unnatural constraints of morality. The character is probably not fictitious but there is no other historical evidence.

Calvin /ˈkælvɪn/, Jean (1509–64) Protestant reformer, whose theological and political teachings had a decisive influence in Geneva and other Swiss cantons, in the Reformed churches in France, the Netherlands and Germany, and in most Presbyterian churches and sects, especially in Scotland and North America. In his main work, the *Institutes of the Christian Religion*, which underwent major revisions leading up to the final version of 1560, emphasis is placed on the doctrine that man's intellect, will and conscience, although not impaired because of the Fall, have come to be employed in a manner corrupt and sinful. The traditional proofs of God's existence appeal only to reason, and are therefore of no avail; this is why

Calvin omits them. Likewise, the purely intellectual understanding of Scripture is insufficient for salvation.

Scientific and rational insight are, then, at a level distinct from that of faith. Moses did not give the correct scientific account of the creation of the world, although he knew it, but gave instead, in Genesis, the account that is the proper basis for faith. Salvation is by faith which justifies the sinner. This faith comes about by God's grace. God has decided in advance on whom it will be bestowed. Whether God decided on this before or after the Fall is a matter of dispute between SUPRA- and INFRALAPSARIANS. Those who are not saved will suffer eternal punishment in a future state.

Calvin rejected the view that religious authority should be subordinated to civil authority, and Geneva became a symbol for a polity in which church discipline and religious doctrine were strictly imposed.

Cambridge change Cambridge philosophers such as Russell and McTaggart analysed the concept of change as follows: 'x has changed if some predicate F applies to x at some time and does not apply to x at some other time.' This is so permissive as to be implausible. According to the criterion, a tree itself changes, for instance: if it comes to be overshadowed by its growing offspring; if a tree elsewhere on Earth grows to surpass its height; if it happens to be admired by a passer-by.

Peter Geach, in *God and the Soul* 1969, called changes that satisfy the criterion 'Cambridge changes', and distinguished *mere* Cambridge changes from genuine changes.

Cambridge Platonists Many Platonizing seventeenth-century theologians and philosophers were connected with two Cambridge colleges, Emmanuel and Christ's. Among them were Benjamin Whichcote (1609–83), Henry More (1614–87), Ralph Cudworth (1617–88) and John Smith (1618–52). They strongly urged the primacy of reason in religion, ethics and science, and endeavoured to develop a rational understanding of Christian religion, in opposition to sects and doctrines which appealed directly to revelation and sought to make faith immune to rational scrutiny. They also urged that the Church be willing to accept members holding a wide range of different theological opinions, a view which came to be called latitudinarianism. Although Platonic or neo-Platonic in inspiration, some of their views differed from Plato's, but their insistence that an action is loved by God because of its goodness, and not vice versa, clearly echoes Plato's dialogue *Euthyphro*.

Cambridge School Bertrand Russell (1872–1970), G. E. Moore (1873–1958) and C. D. Broad (1887–1971) were the leading representatives of what may rather loosely be called a 'school'. Many historical accounts of twentieth-century analytical philosophy are structured around locations such as Vienna, Warsaw, Uppsala and Berlin and assign, in that context, priority to Cambridge, but many elements of the distinctively analytical approach can also be seen in Brentano and his followers, and in Frege.

Campanella /kampa'nɛlla (It.)/, Tommaso (1568–1639) Italian Dominican of Neapolitan origin. He was a prolific writer on philosophical and theological subjects, sided with the new science against the scholastic tradition, wrote a defence of Galileo (*Apologia pro Galilaeo* 1616), but is best known for his utopia *Civitas solis* 1623 (The city of the sun), in which there is social equality, no private property, work for everyone, and a citizenry imbued with patriotism and a sense of civic responsibility. Much of his life was spent in the dungeons of the Inquisition for reasons partly political, partly theological.

Camus /kamy (Fr.)/, Albert (1913–60) French author. Camus grew up in a poor working-class environment in Algiers, became a journalist, essayist and novelist, and was awarded the Nobel Prize for Literature in 1957. Among French intellectuals, he was the first to give serious attention to the Algerian problem. His condemnation of communist tyranny in *L'Homme révolté* 1951 (The Rebel) led to a cooling of his long-standing relations with the political left and to a break with Sartre; his strong critique of fascism and McCarthyism gained him few friends on the right.

At the centre of Camus's thought is the thesis that human existence is absurd. An analogy can illustrate his point. We have eyes for seeing. But for seeing actually to occur, there must be something that is actually seen. Suppose now that everything that can be seen were hidden from view. We should then have a faculty of seeing that took us nowhere, and we should be aware of living in an unending night. Camus maintains that such a situation, in which the capacity of seeing is forever unsatisfied, is absurd.

This can be applied to man's search for unity, and to the search for meaning in human existence. We are aware of our demand for meaning and, with the demise of traditional religion and its substitutes in the forms of metaphysics and historicist political ideologies, we have also become aware of the fact that this demand cannot be satisfied. We can then see the absurdity of the human condition. With this awareness goes a sense of despair. There seems to be no reason for not committing suicide.

In *Le Mythe de Sisyphe* 1943 (The Myth of Sisyphus), Camus asserts that by a refusal to knuckle under, man (symbolized by Sisyphus) can create meaning through a free act of affirmation in which he gives meaning to a situation which until then had none. In focus here are the evils inherent in the human condition generally; the experience of communist and fascist tyranny (Camus was active in the French Resistance) led him to a greater concern with the evils created through human action.

Some interpreters have argued that Camus came to see the metaphysical revolt implicit in *The Myth of Sisyphus* as one that expresses itself in suicide or (as in the communist and fascist revolutions) in homicide. Behind it is the urge to destroy the existing world, with its evils. Condemning this urge and the revolutionary violence it releases, Camus argued in his later writings that not every act of self-affirmation could be acceptable. Moral integrity and an ideal of human solidarity are essential ingredients in our revolt against meaninglessness: *La Peste* 1947 (The Plague).

Candide /kɑ̃did (Fr.)/ the name of the main character in Voltaire's short novel *Candide, ou l'optimisme* 1759. At the beginning of the story Candide is an ingenuous young man whose tutor, Dr Pangloss, assures him that ours is the best of all possible worlds (a theory proposed by Leibniz), but the things Candide experiences in his adventures are evidence to the contrary.

canon (Gr. *kanōn* measuring rod, ruler) *n.* a rule by which something can be tested. It is in this sense that Kant, following Epicurean usage, calls logic a canon for the use of our intellect.

Especially, 'canon' is used for (a) the rule by which a set of writings is declared to be sacred, authentic or authoritative; (b) the set of writings so declared. As for the Bible, there are differences between some Protestant and the Roman Catholic canons. Works that are not fully approved for inclusion are collectively known as apocrypha. The word 'canon' is also used in an extended sense in literary studies, to denote collectively the works of literature that are considered to be of lasting importance.

Canon Law the ecclesiastical law of the Roman Catholic church.

Cantor /ˈkæntə (Eng.); ˈkantɔr (Gm.)/, Georg (1845–1918) professor of mathematics at the University of Halle; creator of set theory and the theory of transfinite numbers. *See also* DIAGONAL PROCEDURE.

Cantor's paradox Cantor proved that every set has more subsets than it has members. A paradox arises when this theorem is applied to the infinite set S which has all sets as its members. By the definition of S, every set *is* a member of S. And yet, some set *is not* a member of S, since, by the theorem, S has more subsets than it has members.

cardinality *See* CARDINAL NUMBER.

cardinal number, cardinality *n.* The numbers one, two, three, . . . , are cardinal numbers. Two sets are said to have *the same cardinality* if and only if there is a strictly 'monogamous' pairing of each member of the one set with a member of the other. For example, if one set consists of five apples, and another of five children, the two sets have the same cardinality just because there is an apple for each child and a child for each apple.

This definition applies also to infinite sets. For example, the infinite set of natural numbers 1,2,3, . . . has the same cardinality as the infinite set of even numbers 2,4,6, . . . since they can be paired in a one-to-one correspondence: 1–2, 2–4, 3–6, etc. Every number in one set has one 'mate' in the other, i.e. no number in either set is left out of the pairing, since for every number n in the first set, there is a number 2n in the second, and vice versa.

cardinal virtues (Lat. *cardo* a hinge) The four classical cardinal virtues, as listed in Plato's *Republic*, are as in Table 3. In medieval philosophy, the three theological virtues faith, hope, and charity, were added to this list.

Table 3 The four cardinal virtues

English	*Latin*	*Greek*
justice	*iustitia*	*dikaiosynē*
wisdom (or prudence)	*sapientia* (or *prudentia*)	*phronēsis*
courage	*fortitudo*	*andreia*
self-control (or moderation, being sensible)	*temperantia*	*sōphrosynē*

careless *adj.* (in older texts, e.g. Hume) carefree; unconcerned.

Carlyle /kɑːˈlaɪl/, Thomas (1795–1881) exercised, as a literary, cultural and social critic, a major influence in nineteenth-century Britain, where his translations and essays made the great German writers like Kant and Goethe more widely known. In German thought of the Romantic period he found a sense of spiritual values, lacking in the coarse and materialistic mentality which, in his view, had emerged from the promotion of Enlightenment ideals such as utilitarianism, egalitarianism, political democracy, etc.: where once there had been greatness, there was now only greed. In his writings on heroism and the hero he advocated a political system in which the many are guided and ruled by the superior few. This was of course in marked conflict with the contemporary rise of liberal and democratic ideals.

carnal (Lat. *caro* flesh) *adj.* In the New Testament, the word signifies the body, in contrast to mind or soul, but there is frequently the further implication of egoism and sin.

Carnap /'kɑnæp (Eng.); 'karnap (Gm.)/, Rudolf (1891–1970) After studies in Freiburg and Jena, where he attended lectures given by Frege, Carnap taught at the universities of Vienna 1926–31, Prague 1931–6, Chicago, and from 1952 California at Los Angeles. He became a leading member of the Vienna Circle, and articulated its anti-metaphysical outlook in two famous articles, 'Pseudo-problems in philosophy' 1928 and 'Elimination of metaphysics through logical analysis of language' 1932. Metaphysical statements are rejected as meaningless, since they cannot be empirically confirmed or refuted: like French positivists and like many of Brentano's followers, Carnap warned against confusing philosophy and poetry. The question of whether to adopt realism or phenomenalism in the theory of knowledge is one example of a pseudo-problem. The choice is one between linguistic frameworks, and can only be determined by convenience and convention. This is one application of what he calls the 'principle of tolerance' in his *Logische Syntax der Sprache* 1934 (*The Logical Syntax of Language*). Another application is in the choice between logics: 'In logic there are no morals. Everyone is at liberty to build up his own logic, i.e. his own form of language, as he wishes.' Thus the question whether, e.g., numbers exist makes sense only if understood as a question of whether a given language can accommodate number-terms.

In *Der logische Aufbau der Welt* 1928 (The logical construction of the world) Carnap proposed one framework constructed on a very slender basis consisting of one relation, 'remembrance of similarity', and basic data. The basic data are occurrences of total immediate experiences, and so-called sense-data are logical constructions based on those. A sensory quality is in turn defined on that basis. It did, however, become clear to critics, and to Carnap himself, that this construction project was too daring.

Of major significance were Carnap's contributions to formal semantics (*Meaning and Necessity* 1947) and to the philosophy of science (*Logical Foundations of Probability* 1950).

Carneades /kaː'niːədiːz/ (214–129 BC) When in Rome in 155 BC he displayed his intellectual and rhetorical virtuosity in public lectures by arguing on one day the cause of justice, and on the following day, with equal eloquence, the cause of injustice. This performance was much admired by the leisured Roman youth, which caused Cato to issue a ban against public philosophizing in the city.

Carneades was head of the Academy in Athens and, being a sceptic like his predecessor Arcesilaus, he extended the latter's attack on Stoicism to any school proposing a criterion of truth. He did, however, accept that there are opinions on which we can rely to the degree that they are more or less probable: we may assume, but we should not assert. This admission of probability was the main point of difference from the so-called Pyrrhonian scepticism later outlined by Sextus Empiricus.

Much of our knowledge of his views comes from Cicero. Book 3 of *De natura deorum* (On the nature of the gods) presents his objections to Stoic theology. In his view, it was absurd: God must be conceived as both infinite and finite, simple and complex, permitting and prohibiting evil, etc. In ethics, he is famous for the 'Carneadean division' in Cicero's *De finibus* 5, 16ff, which distinguished nine plausible opinions about the goal of life. He presented good reasons for all nine – and against. HT

Carroll /'kærəl/, Lewis pseudonym for Charles Lutwidge Dodgson (1832–98), student (i.e. fellow) of Christ Church College, Oxford, author of *Alice in Wonderland* 1865, but also of logical-mathematical puzzles and works in elementary logic that show great ingenuity and often go beyond the level of mere pastimes (*A Tangled Tale* 1885; *Game of Logic* 1887; *Symbolic Logic* 1893; *Pillow Problems* 1893). His logic diagrams are preferred to the Venn diagrams in some logic texts. His *A Method of taking votes on more than two issues* 1876, unduly neglected for a long time, was an early contribution to the theory of collective decision-making, which deals with VOTING PARADOXES, etc.

Cartesian *adj.* pertaining to Descartes.

Cartesian circle a circular argument, alleged to be inherent in Descartes's philosophy: we can be certain that what we perceive clearly and distinctly is true, because God exists. But we can be certain that God exists only because we clearly and distinctly perceive it. This problem was raised by Arnauld, in the fourth set of Objections appended to Descartes's *Meditations*.

Cartesius the Latin name-form for Descartes.

case, just in **1** 'I will take an umbrella (just) in case there will be rain'; i.e. *because of the possibility that* there will be rain. **2** More recently, some philosophers and logicians have used the phrase to mean *if and only if*, as in 'a conjunction is true just in case (= if and only if) all its conjuncts are true'.

Cassirer /ka'siːrər (Gm.)/, Ernst (1874–1945) professor of philosophy at Hamburg 1919–33, then forced into exile, first in Oxford, then in Göteborg 1935–41, and thereafter at Yale and Columbia universities. Influenced by the neo-Kantianism of the Marburg School (Cohen and Natorp), he developed a philosophy in which the concept of symbolism is at the centre: *Philosophie der symbolischen Formen* 1923–9 (Philosophy of symbolic forms). Symbols are the medium of mental activity, in myth, in religion, in art, and in the human, natural and exact sciences. These symbolic forms play the part in this theory that the categories and the forms of sensory intuition play in Kant's philosophy, and Cassirer saw his own philosophy as a generalization of the Kantian analysis of pure understanding.

castration (complex) (In psychoanalytic theory) at an early age boys are, or believe they are, threatened with castration, and girls believe themselves to have been the victim of same. The psychic efforts to overcome the fear or the sense of castration are the main formative influence on personality development.

Critics do not find this a likely story. Some of its defenders explain that the doubts are due to misunderstanding: 'castration' does not really mean castration, but means birth, absence, loss, deprivation, death, etc.

In Jacques Lacan's psychoanalytic theory, castration, defined as a symbolic lack of an imaginary object, is distinguished from frustration (an imaginary lack of a real object) and from privation (a real lack of a symbolic object).

casuistry /'kæzjʊɪstrɪ/ *n.* the determination of what is permissible or obligatory in cases of conscience, or, more generally, in cases of clashing moral or religious duties. In religious contexts the theory of casuistry is known as moral theology.

The use of this word to denote devious moral reasoning designed to justify action that is morally dubious – or worse – has its origin in the seventeenth century. Jesuit confessors to persons of rank were said to employ such methods in order to justify disregard of moral and religious scruples, and Jesuit writers wrote in defence of such alleged moral laxity. The criticism came particularly from Jansenist opponents. The most renowned attack was that of Pascal in his *Lettres provinciales*.

casus *See* DOLUS.

catachresis /kætə'kriːsɪs/ (*sing.*); **catachreses** /kætə'kriːsiːs/ (*pl.*) *n.* **1** the erroneous use of a word: for example, the use of 'refute' to mean deny; or of 'mitigate' to mean militate. **2** the illogical use of a word in order to obtain a striking effect: a paradoxical metaphor. **3** the extended use of a word to fill a lexical gap, i.e. to apply to things that do not have a name of their own.

catallactics (Gr. *katallatein* to exchange; to admit into a community) *n. sing.* inquiry into, or theory of, market mechanisms.

catallaxy *n.* the order spontaneously brought about by the mutual adjustments arising from market transactions. This word was coined by F. A. Hayek, but is rarely used.

catastrophe /kə'tæstrəfɪ/ *n.* **1** (in general usage) a disaster. **2** (in literary theory) the turning point, the climax, the dénouement, in drama, especially tragedy.

catastrophe theory a mathematical theory devised in the 1960s by the French mathematician René Thom. It gives a systematic mathematical characterization of basic types of abrupt changes or jumps, i.e. discontinuities.

categorematic /kætɪgɒrɪ'mætɪk/ *adj.* Originally, categorematic expressions were those that could occur as terms, i.e. as a subject or as a predicate, in a CATEGORICAL proposition. In medieval logic, the expression applies to *all* symbols that have independent meaning: 'man', 'animal', 'whiteness', etc. Categorematic expressions were thought to *stand for* something, in contrast to *syncategorematic* expressions, e.g., 'all', 'every', 'only', 'in so far as'.

categorial *adj.* pertaining to a category.

categorical *adj.* **1** In Aristotelian logic, a *categorical proposition* is a proposition of one of these four forms:

All S is P	No S is P
Some S is P	Some S is not P

Thus defined, every categorical proposition is either universal affirmative, or universal negative, or particular affirmative, or particular negative. Often the first four vowels of the alphabet are used for abbreviation, and the four types are then written:

SaP	SeP
SiP	SoP

There is a mnemonic device, using the Latin *affirmo* (I affirm) and *nego* (I deny):

```
        n
S a P   S e P
  ff      g
S i P   S o P
  r
  m
  o
```

A *categorical syllogism* is a syllogism in which all the propositions are categorical.

Subsequently, all kinds of propositions in which a predicate is said to belong to a subject were called categorical, to distinguish them from hypothetical and disjunctive propositions.

2 Kant distinguished between *categorical* and *hypothetical* ought-statements (he actually called them 'imperatives'). The hypothetical ones state what an agent ought to do, given the condition that a certain end is desired by the agent. The categorical ones state what ought to be done, independently of any such condition. According to Kant, an action has genuine moral worth only if the ought-statement that motivates the agent is categorical.

Kant also introduces a principle of morality which, perhaps somewhat confusingly, he calls *The Categorical Imperative*. In its general formulation, it is: 'Always so act that you are able to will that the maxim of your action be also a universal law.'

Kant also provides three subsidiary formulations of the principle. The first enjoins that the agent should be able to will that the maxim be also a law of nature. The second enjoins that persons never be treated as means only, but always also as ends-in-themselves. The third enjoins that the agent should be able to regard his maxim also as part of a universal legislation. This implies that one regard oneself both as legislator and as subject of the moral law.

category (Gr. *katēgoria* accusation; attribution; predication; kind of predication) *n.*
1 The term was introduced by Aristotle. Primarily, a category is a *kind of predication*: the *manner* in which a predicate is attributed to the subject; but the term has been used mainly to designate a *kind of predicate*. Aristotle deals with this in *Topics* 9, 103b, and in *Categories* 4, 1b, where he enumerates ten: substance, quantity, quality, relation, place, time, position, possession, activity, and passivity.

The categories can also be understood as *kinds of being*. Later ancient philosophers reduced the list; the Stoics regarded only the first four as fundamental. The theory was on the agenda throughout the Middle Ages thanks to Boethius's translation of *Categories* into Latin. The medieval thinkers introduced a theory of TRANSCENDENTALS, i.e. concepts that can belong to more than one category.
2 Kant used the term for the twelve forms, present in all discursive thought, by which the intellect structures all experience. He derived these forms, or categories, from the division of judgements adopted in traditional logical theory. They are set out in Table 4.

Table 4 Kant's categories

Quantity	*Quality*	*Relation*	*Modality*
unity	reality	inherence	possibility
plurality	negation	cause/effect	existence
totality	limitation	reciprocity	necessity

Kant's argument to show that these are necessary elements in all possible knowledge is presented in the transcendental deduction (i.e. justification) of them in the *Critique of Pure Reason*.
3 Analytical philosophers have attempted to use the concept, especially for the purpose of philosophical refutation. 'The number 5 is even' is merely false, in that it allocates 5 to the *wrong class*; 'The number 5 is green' is not merely false, but is a *category-mistake*, according to Gilbert Ryle, who introduced this concept in his essay, 'Categories' 1938. In *The Concept of Mind* 1949 he used it against mind–body dualism. Although it has proved difficult to develop a coherent theory of category-mistakes, the term remains in semi-technical use for certain kinds of *a priori* inadmissibility, especially of expressions which are grammatically well-formed, but which are nevertheless quite naturally classified as 'nonsense'. (Chomsky offers the example 'colourless green ideas sleep furiously'.)

catharsis /kə'θaːsɪs/ (*sing.*); **catharses** /kə'θaːsiːz/ (*pl.*) (Gr. *katharsis* cleansing, purging) *n.* According to Aristotle's *Poetics*, chapter 6, tragedy arouses passions of pity and fear but then – this is its cathartic effect – brings relief from these passions. Elsewhere, he uses the word to describe the effect of emotional arousal produced by music in cultic ceremonies. The term is also used in Freudian psychoanalytic theory for the relief gained by bringing repressed ideas and emotions to awareness.

cathexis /kə'θɛksɪs/ (*sing.*); **cathexes** /kə'θɛksiːz/ (*pl.*) (Gr. a firm grasp) *n.* (in psychoanalytic theory) concentration of psychic energy in one direction.

causality, principle of states that every change, or every event, has a cause.

Our faith in this principle goes deep. We always assume that there is some answer to the question of what caused an event to occur, a change to take place, a thing to begin to exist, even if we do not find an answer. Is our acceptance of this principle rationally defensible? It is supposed to apply without *any* exception. That cannot be established from experience. Can the principle be justified in some other way?

causal theory of knowledge According to this theory, S knows that p if and only if: (1) p is true; (2) S believes that p; (3) S is justified in believing p. The theory adds to this something that will guarantee, against the examples first proposed by Gettier, (GETTIER PROBLEM), that the three conditions do not hold merely by happy coincidence. What is added is the condition that p causes S's belief that p.

The American philosopher Alvin Goldman gave a modern formulation of the theory in *Journal of Philosophy 64* (1967).

causal theory of perception the theory according to which an expression of the form 'S has a sensory experience of O' implies that S's sensory experience was caused by O.

causal theory of reference a theory according to which names (and similarly, other referring expressions) relate to what they name if and only if there is a causal relation linking the two. On this view, names are not, as Frege and Russell thought, abbreviated definite descriptions. Rather, the relation between a name and that which is named is established by an act of naming, a 'baptism' so to speak, which forms the starting-point of a causal chain. The theory was proposed by Saul Kripke, Keith Donnellan and Hilary Putnam in the 1970s, and has been applied to proper names and natural-kind terms (water, gold, shark). Stephen P. Schwartz (ed.), *Naming, Necessity, and Natural Kinds* 1977, contains lucid expositions and discussions of the theory.

causa sui /'kaʊzə 'suːɪ/ Lat. cause of itself; that which produces itself (Plotinus, *Enneads* 6,8,14–16); 'self-originate cause' (Berkeley, *Alciphron*, the 4th dialogue). In medieval and modern metaphysics, to be the cause of itself is an essential property of absolute being. This is Descartes's view (*Meditations*, in the appended Reply to Arnauld's objections), and *causa sui* is the first concept that Spinoza defines in *Ethics*, Book 1: 'that whose essence implies existence, or that whose nature cannot be conceived as not existing'. Spinoza identifies it with God (or Nature, or Substance). In early post-Kantian philosophy, that which is its own cause is identified with the self (Fichte, Schelling).

cause *n.* Aristotle distinguished (in *Physics* 2, 3 194^{b}16ff and *Metaphysics* A 3 983^{a}24ff and Δ 2, 1013^{a}24ff) four kinds of 'cause' (Gr. *aitia*), but they should rather be called 'explanatory factors': (1) the *material* cause (*causa materialis*) is the stuff (*hylē*) out of which something is made; (2) the *formal* cause (*causa formalis*) is that in virtue of which something is what it is; (3) the *efficient* cause (*causa efficiens*) is that which brings about a change, e.g. produces an object; (4) the *final* cause (*causa finalis*) is the purpose (*telos*), that for the sake of which an action, a change or a thing comes about.

The classical illustration is that of a

bronze statue. The formal cause is that which the statue represents, its shape; the material cause is the bronze; the efficient cause is the sculptor; the final cause is the purpose that the statue is to serve.

Aristotle held that the same thing may have all four kinds of 'causes' like the bronze statue (or a building, as in *Metaphysics* Book B, 996ᵇ5ff), but did not hold the view that all things do.

cave, image of the a simile in Plato's *Republic*, Book 7: we are chained inside a cave are forced to face a wall on which shadows are cast by graven images moved about behind our backs but in front of a fire. We mistake these shadows for reality. By breaking free of the chains (of habit and sensual desire), we can examine the sources of the shadows and how they are distortedly projected, e.g. by the popular arts. Full enlightenment, however, requires the mind to escape from the cave (the sensible world) and explore the archetypes, such as the Form of Justice, of which our actual institutions (the graven images) are highly imperfect instances. Knowledge of these Forms, moreover, is incomplete, unless the mind graps the highest of them, the form of the Good. JT/ed.

central-state materialism See IDENTITY THEORY OF MIND.

ceteris paribus /ˈkɛtərɪs ˈpærɪbʊs/ Lat. *caeteris paribus* other things being equal.

Note: Both spellings are in use.

chaos (Gr. gaping void) *n.* a state of disorder supposed, in Greek mythology, to have preceded the beginning of the cosmos, the ordered universe.

chaos theory a branch of mathematical physics dealing with systems that exhibit an exponential sensitivity to very small changes in their initial states. The weather is such a system: the usually innocuous flight of a butterfly may, if initial conditions change only slightly, trigger a tornado. Although the systems are deterministic, their equations of motion generate sequences that vary from the highly regular to those indistinguishable from the outputs of a random process. James Clark Maxwell, Jacques Hadamard, Pierre Duhem and Henri Poincaré were among the first to see the mathematical possibility and physical importance of these systems, but it was only with the advent of modern computers that their properties could be explored by conducting numerical experiments. Chaos theory has been used to model such diverse systems as lasers, chemical reactions, wildlife population growth, the spread of epidemics, neural networks, weather patterns, and even social phenomena such as commodity prices and the behaviour of stock markets. It is still unclear to what extent mathematical chaos exists in nature and, in particular, whether quantum mechanical effects are chaotic. KW

character *n.* the personality traits of an individual. In older usage, the word was often used for a person's reputation or 'image'.

charisma /kəˈrɪzmə/ (Gr. favour; grace) *n.* a divine gift or endowment. Max Weber (1864–1920) distinguishes three types of legitimacy and authority. Apart from the traditional and the legal-bureaucratic, there is the charismatic type, where legitimacy springs from the perceived personal qualities of a leader.

charity *n.* together with faith and hope, one of the three theological virtues, listed together with the four cardinal virtues since the Middle Ages. In the modern era, duties of charity are commonly contrasted with duties of justice, the latter being described as PERFECT DUTIES, the former imperfect.

charity, principle of a principle recommending favourable interpretation: if a speaker's utterances can be understood in different ways, one should prefer the one which maximizes the number of statements which come out true, or which invite assent. For Quine (*Word and Object*, Chapter 2), this principle is a precondition for the possibility of radical translation, i.e. for translation from a language previously completely unknown. For Davidson ('Radical Interpretation' in *Inquiries into Truth and Interpretation*) it is a precondition for radical interpretation. Davidson has subsequently replaced the principle with a new 'principle of humanity'. It does not require that the interpretation should make most of the utterances come out *true*, but only that they come out as being *reasonable*. In either form it is a principle of benefit of doubt. This semantic principle was given an early formulation in Neil Wilson, 'Substances without substrata', *Review of Metaphysics 12* 1959.

Charron /ʃarɔ̃ (Fr.)/, Pierre (1541–1603) French lawyer and theologian. His writings express a philosophical effort to overcome the religious conflicts of his time. His sympathy for the Stoic ethical tradition in his best-known work *De la Sagesse* 1601 (*On Wisdom*) is similar to that of his friend Montaigne (1533–92) and other neo-Stoics, like Lipsius (1547–1606) and du Vair. Charron held the view that religious and metaphysical knowledge is beyond our grasp, but moral truth is inscribed in man's heart and can be known and accepted without any religious dogma.

Chartier /ʃartje (Fr.)/, Emile *See* ALAIN.

chastity *n.* **1** Like other virtues, it consists in following a middle course between excess and deficiency, according to Thomas Aquinas, *Summa Theologiae* 2a 2ae q. 151. **2** a virtue consisting in complete sexual abstinence. Moral theologians consider it not as a strict duty on everyone, but it is recommended together with poverty and obedience in the three evangelical counsels.

chauvinism /'ʃəʊvɪnɪzm/ *n.* excessive and aggressive patriotism. Chauvin, a character in a French stage-play from the 1830s, was modelled on a soldier of that name in Napoleon's army, famed for his blind devotion to his country.

Since the 1970s, the word has often been used in transferred senses. In radical feminist circles, *male chauvinism* is used as a synonym for SEXISM. In radical environmental thought, *human chauvinism* was introduced by Richard and Val Routley in 1980 to criticize views which assign to the human race a privileged position in the universe, and others have since spoken of *species chauvinism*, etc.

chiliasm /'kɪlɪæzm/ (Gr. *chilioi* a thousand) *n.* millenarianism; the doctrine that Christ will return and rule for 1000 years.

chimaera /kaɪ'mɪərə, kɪ'mɪrə/ *n.* a beast described in Homer as having a lion's head, a goat's body, and a serpent's (or dragon's) tail. It has remained the standard example of a fictitious non-existent object since it was cast in that role in Aristotle's *Posterior Analytics*.

chimpanzees, typing This is an illustration used in support of the argument from design for God's existence: imagine a vast assembly of chimpanzees, each with a typewriter on which they merrily hammer away at random. The probability of one of them producing even one correct line from Shakespeare is extremely slight. They would have to keep at it for a very long time before success could reasonably be expected. So when we read a typescript with lines from Shakespeare, we do not believe that it was produced in that way.

The orderly structures of the physical universe are almost infinitely more improbable. It would then be utterly unreasonable to think that they came about randomly. Admittedly, they could occur by chance in the very long run. But the run of this world has been too short by far. So, as in the above example, the existence of these structures must be due to design.

The illustration comes from the French mathematician Emile Borel (*Le Hasard* 1914), but the point was anticipated long before the typewriter was invented in the late nineteenth century. In Cicero's *On the Nature of the Gods* (45 BC), the thought-experiment is to let an appropriate number of letter-shaped pieces of metal be tossed in the air. It is extremely improbable that they will fall to the ground so as to form a correct line of the *Iliad*.

Chinese Room Argument a much-debated argument, first proposed by John Searle in 1980 to demonstrate that even the cleverest computer does not have a mind:

> Imagine that someone who understands no Chinese is locked in a room with a lot of Chinese symbols and a computer program for answering questions in Chinese. The input consists in Chinese symbols in the form of questions; the output of the system consists in Chinese symbols in answer to the questions. We might suppose that the program is so good that the answers to the questions are indistinguishable from those of a native Chinese speaker. But all the same, neither the person inside nor any other part of the system literally understands Chinese (J. Searle, *The Rediscovery of the Mind* 1992).

This is so because the system is formal, syntactical, whilst minds have mental or semantic contents.

Chisholm /ˈtʃɪzm/, Roderick (1916–99) American philosopher, professor at Brown University, an incisive critic of many of the predominant forms of contemporary reductionism: phenomenalism, extensionalism and physicalism. His alternative position is influenced by Brentano and his circle (Meinong, Husserl, etc.), and his writings have stimulated interest in them in the anglophone world. His writings include *The First Person* 1981 and *Theory of Knowledge* 3rd edn 1989.

Chodorow, Nancy Julia (1944–) In opposition to Freud and Lacan, she argues that basic psychological differences between the sexes originate in the fact that, almost universally, girls are looked after by a person of their own sex, while boys are not. The typical gender differences, in short, arise from the fact that it is women who do the mothering. Her writings have reinforced the influence of psychoanalytic theory on anglophone feminism. See e.g. *Feminism and Psychoanalytic Theory* 1989.

choice, axiom of *See* AXIOM OF CHOICE.

Chomsky /ˈtʃɒmskɪ/, Noam (1928–) professor at Massachusetts Institute of Technology, where he has taught since 1955. He has written extensively in the areas of linguistics, philosophy of mind, and contemporary politics. He has had a decisive influence on twentieth-century theory of language and thought, in the first instance due to his development, in *Syntactic Structures* 1957 and later works, of a theory of generative grammar, as a tool for the syntactical analysis of natural languages, by which deep structures underlying the surface structures can be discerned. This elucidates the command that language-users have of a language. In opposition to empiricist and behaviourist theories – he is a strong opponent of the theories of B. F. Skinner – Chomsky has developed a theory, compatible with materialism, of innate mental abilities. He argues, in *Cartesian Linguistics* 1966, that the very complex cognitive performances of human beings cannot entirely be the product of abilities acquired by learning. Linguistic competence is a case in point: as evidence for this he notes the rapidity with which a child grasps the rules of a language and is able to formulate an indefinite number of new but correct sentences. The similarities between the deep structures of different languages provide further evidence. He has suggested that this innatism, related to the Cartesian tradition, implies that human beings are basically similar. He contrasts it with the anti-innatism of the empiricist, Lockean tradition which, he argues, leaves more scope for the possibility of human inequality and hence racism. *Knowledge of Language* 1986 is a more recent statement of his position.

Chomsky has also become well known as a writer on social and political questions in the anarcho-syndicalist tradition. His attacks on the US political establishment for its post-war policies in Latin America, in Vietnam and elsewhere, e.g. in *American Power and the New Mandarins* 1969, gained widespread attention and much support, but subsequently his stand on other political questions has not gained a favourable reception to the same extent.

chrematistics /kriːmə'tɪstɪks/ (Gr. *chrēmatistikē* acquisition of goods; money-making) *n. sing.* **1** the art of acquisition; **2** inquiry or theory that deals with questions of fair pricing for goods and services, whether charging of interest is morally acceptable, etc. The subject-matter is dealt with in Aristotle's *Nicomachean Ethics*, Book 5, 5–7 and his *Politics*, Book 1, 8–11, and discussed by many medieval writers, e.g. in Aquinas's *Summa Theologiae* 1a 2ae, q.2, art.1 and 2a 2ae, q.78.

Note: In Aristotle the word is also used for the art of acquisition of material wealth in general, but also more narrowly for the art of selfish monetary gain.

Chrysippus /kraɪ'sɪpəs; krɪ'sɪpəs/ (*c.* 280–208 BC) the third head of the Stoic school, after Zeno of Citium and Cleanthes. Of his prolific writings very little is extant. He had a great reputation as a logician, continuing the development of propositional logic that had begun with the Megarians, and seems to have been the first clearly to formulate truth-conditions for conditional (i.e. 'if . . . then') statements. *See also* DISJUNCTIVE SYLLOGISM. His Stoic physics and metaphysics is materialistic, but does recognize an active power called spirit, reason, or God. He adopted the doctrine of eternal return: the whole history of the whole universe comes to an end and is then re-played. This is then repeated, again and again. Like the other Stoics he extolled virtue, which consists in rational wisdom, as a necessary and sufficient condition for happiness.

Church, Alonzo (1903–95) professor at Princeton and Los Angeles; one of the leading logicians of the twentieth century; author of *Introduction to Mathematical Logic* 1956.

Church's Theorem the proposition that the set of theorems of the first-order predicate calculus is not recursive, proved by Church in 1936. This is equivalent to the proposition proved by Turing in the same year, that there is no TURING MACHINE capable of answering all questions of the form: 'Is the formula p in the first-order predicate calculus a theorem?' In conjunction with CHURCH'S THESIS, the theorem implies that the first-order predicate calculus is undecidable, i.e. that there is no effective method for settling all questions of the form just given in a finite number of steps. (Fragments of the predicate calculus are, however, decidable.) This was the first important negative answer to a DECISION PROBLEM; others soon followed. The theorem implies that there are limits to what can be done by existing computers, since they are all equivalent to Turing machines. JCD

Church's Thesis A mathematical method is termed effective if it can be set out in the form of a list of instructions that can be followed by an obedient human clerk who is perfectly reliable, who works until the procedure is completed, totally lacking in insight or ingenuity, and unaided by any machinery except paper and pencil. In 1936 Church put forward the thesis that whenever there is an effective method for calculating the values of a function on the positive integers then the function is recursive. Also in 1936 Turing put forward the slightly more general but broadly equivalent thesis that any effective mathematical method can be carried out by a Turing machine. The thesis cannot be proved formally, since there is no way of ruling out the possibility that someone will in the future produce a method that cannot be carried out by a Turing machine but which the mathematical community agrees is effective. Nevertheless, few doubt that the thesis is true. JCD

Cicero /'sɪsərəʊ/, Marcus Tullius (106–43 BC) Roman statesman, orator, philosopher and man of letters. His philosophical works, most of which have been preserved, are an important source of information on the philosophy of the Hellenistic period. Most are in dialogue form, and they have been much studied as school and university texts, e.g. in the Renaissance and in the eighteenth and nineteenth centuries. Along with Cicero's partial translation of Plato's *Timaeus*, they have contributed much to philosophical terminology in Latin and modern European languages. The *De re publica* (On the state) and *De legibus* (On the laws), whose titles are borrowed from Plato, are somewhat idealized discussion of the Roman constitution and laws. The *Academica* is a discussion of academic scepticism, particularly in epistemology, in which Cicero defends a sceptical position. The *De finibus* (On [moral] ends) compares the Epicurean, Stoic and academic ethical systems. The *Tusculanae disputationes* (Disputations at Tusculum) discusses death, pain, distress and other evils. The *De natura deorum* (On the nature of the gods), a discussion of Epicurean and Stoic theology, includes a classic presentation of Stoic arguments from design for the existence of the gods, which David Hume was to argue against in his *Dialogues Concerning Natural Religion*. It should be noted that Cicero himself also criticizes these arguments from a sceptical point of view. The *De officiis* (On duties) is an equally classic attempt to overcome the apparent conflict between virtue and expediency in ethics. Cicero also wrote influential works on rhetoric, in which he argued *inter alia* that an orator needs a solid training in philosophy. RB

circular argument a set of propositions which together constitute an argument and in which one of the premisses is identical with the conclusion. A person who uses a circular argument for the purpose of establishing the conclusion will often be guilty of BEGGING THE QUESTION.

circular definition A definition is circular if (1) it is to serve the purpose of explaining the meaning of an expression; (2) the definiens cannot itself be explained without use of the definiendum.

circulus vitiosus /'sɜːkjələs vɪsɪ'əʊsəs/ Lat. VICIOUS CIRCLE.

civilian *n.* (in older usage) an expert in civil law; a jurisprudentialist.

civil law 1 the law of ancient Rome and the Roman Empire, codified under Justinian in *Corpus Iuris Civilis* 529–34. It had a considerable influence in most of Europe, especially after its systematic study was resumed in Italy in the twelfth and thirteenth centuries, and has since been the basis for private law in most of continental Europe. **2** the law of a particular jurisdiction. **3** law that concerns rights and obligations relating to property, contract, torts, etc., often contrasted with criminal law.

civil society Until the nineteenth century, the term was used as a synonym for political society, or state. Hegel introduced a terminological distinction: civil society is a social formation intermediate between the family and the state.

clairvoyance /kleə'vɔɪəns/ (Fr. clear sight) a paranormal way of knowing things hidden or distant.

Clarke, Samuel (1675–1729) English philosopher and theologian. He was one of the first to appreciate Newton's achievement. Partly 'ghosted' by Newton, he defended his theories in correspondence with Leibniz. The first set of his Boyle Lectures, *A Demonstration of the Being and Attributes of God* 1705 included a new kind of *a priori* demonstration of God's existence, and in the second set, *A Discourse Concerning the Unchangeable Obligations of Natural Religion and the Truth and Certainty of Christian Revelation* 1706, he argued that there are objective moral qualities or relations, which can be known by rational insight, in analogy with our mathematical knowledge. What is morally right or good – fitting – is so in itself and not because of God's legislative command. On this point, Clarke was in agreement with Grotius, the Cambridge Platonists, Leibniz *et al.*, and, like them, he also believed that in order to act in accordance with our moral insight into what is fitting, most or all of us have to be motivated by the prospect of rewards and punishments in a future state.

In his theological writings, Clarke had doubts about the trinitarian doctrine and was accused of ARIANISM.

Clarke's ethical rationalism was one of the main targets of the objections from Hutcheson and Hume, and his natural theology did not meet with approval in Hume's *Dialogues Concerning Natural Religion*; Rousseau, in contrast, used it in support of the deism advocated by the 'Savoyard Vicar' in *Emile*.

class *n.* In most modern versions of set theory, classes are defined differently from sets. Expressions of the form $x \in M$ (where $\in$ stands for 'is a member of') are ill-formed if x stands for a class, but not if x stands for a set. In this way, Russell's paradox can be avoided.

classic (*adj.*; *n.*), **classical** (*adj.*) The Latin *classicus* refers to class (*classis*) of taxpayers, especially the top class, and thus to persons of wealth and rank. The various current senses, of which a few are given here, spring from an ancient metaphor: persons of rank were supposed to have class, and this admirable quality was then by extension ascribed to eminent authors and to their works. For example, **1** (a work) of great and lasting value. **2** pertaining to the culture of ancient Greece and Rome. **3** the character of an achievement that is authoritative, significant, or of great merit, although it may have been superseded. In this sense we speak of classical physics, classical natural law theory, etc. Classical literature is the great works of the past by Shakespeare, Milton, Racine, Corneille, Goethe, Schiller, and others comparable to them. Classical style in the arts is contrasted with the romantic, naturalistic, modernist, etc.

class paradox *See* RUSSELL'S PARADOX.

Cleanthes /klɪ'ænθiːz/ (331–232 BC) the successor of Zeno of Citium as head of the Stoa. The longest fragment extant from early Stoicism is from his hymn to Zeus, who is a symbol of divine providence, the soul of an organic universe where each part has a lot assigned by destiny. He held the characteristically Stoic view that virtue is the highest good, and seems to have been the first to define virtue as living according to nature, identified with universal reason.

clear and distinct ideas a pair of terms frequently used by Descartes. In his *Meditations* he lays down the principle that everything that I perceive clearly and distinctly is true. The terms are not synonymous: all distinct perceptions are clear, but some clear perceptions, e.g. of a burning pain, are not distinct (*Principles of Philosophy* I §45–46).

A clear distinction between a *clear* idea and a *distinct* idea was attempted by Leibniz (*Discourse on Metaphysics* §24): my idea of a thing is *clear* if I can recognize examples of the thing; but it is *distinct* only if I can explain by what marks the idea is distinguished from other ones.

Clement /ˈklɛmənt/ of Alexandria (*c.* 150–*c.* 219) Church Father. He accepted the view that philosophy (especially Platonism) could be in harmony with and could help the understanding of Christian doctrine. Accepting a view held by Plato and Philo, he held that our knowledge of God can only be negative.

clistic *See* NEUSTIC.

closed interval (in mathematics) an interval which includes its end-points.

closed sentence a sentence which contains no free variables.

closed society *See* OPEN SOCIETY.

closure *n.* **1** A closure clause indicates that certain specified conditions are the *only* ones that apply. For instance, when specifying what is to count as a well-formed formula, certain conditions are stated, and to them is added a closure clause that a formula that does not meet these conditions is not well-formed. **2** A set S is said to be closed under an operation ∗, if for any members x,y of the set, (x∗y) is also a member of the set.

cogito ergo sum /ˈkɒgitəʊ ˈɜːgəʊ ˈsʊm/ Lat. I think, therefore I am. *See* DESCARTES.

cognition *n.* knowledge.

cognitive *adj.* pertaining to knowledge.

cognitive meaning The term *cognitive meaning* is used in certain theories of meaning for the (true or false) information conveyed by a statement. Cognitive meaning is contrasted, for instance, with the EMOTIVE MEANING of a linguistic expression.

cognitive science **1** the collective name for branches of existing disciplines (cognitive psychology, neurophysiology, computer science, epistemology, etc.) which have cognition as their object of inquiry. **2** The term is also used in narrower senses, e.g. for inquiry which has cognitive processes as its subject-matter and which is based on the assumption that they are computations in the brain.

cognitivism *n.* **1** the view, with respect to a certain area, that there are facts that can, in principle, be known. In ethics, it is the view that there are knowable ethical facts. Some recent writers prefer the term 'realism' for this kind of view, and reserve 'cognitivism' for the view that the *statements* within an area of discourse *purport* to state facts, so that in ethics, 'cognitivism' denotes the view that moral statements purport to state moral facts. *See also* NON-COGNITIVISM. **2** (in psychology and in philosophy of mind) the view that behaviour must be explained in terms of inner, physical, information-processing states and episodes. This view is assumed in much of present-day cognitive psychology. **3** (in philosophy of mind) the view that cognition consists in the operations of mental items which are symbols for real entities. It is usually assumed that these mental symbols are identifiable with neural states. These states, and the neural processes, can be understood by analogy with computers. The contrasting term is CONNECTIONISM.

Cohen /ˈkəʊɪn (Eng.); ˈkoːən (Gm.); later koˈhɛn (see note)/, Hermann (1842–1918) German-Jewish philosopher, together with Paul Natorp the leading name in the neo-Kantian Marburg School. He interpreted Kant's theory of knowledge not as a psychological theory, but as a theory of the presuppositions of knowledge. He rejected the view that we have to presuppose the existence of a thing-in-itself. The principle that secures the validity of knowledge-claims must come from ourselves. If it had another source, we could not assume without question-begging that our claim to know it was valid. Our *a priori* knowledge of objects only grasps what we, as knowers, have put there. In his ethical theory, Cohen attempted a synthesis of Jewish, Kantian and socialist elements, and gave the idea of justice a central place.

Note: Later in life Cohen came to identify more closely with Jewish tradition; /koˈhɛn/ then became his preferred pronunciation.

Cohen, Morris Raphael (1889–1947) American philosopher, who taught in New York and Chicago. He adopted a moderate realist position both in his theory of law and in his philosophy of science. Among his writings are *Law and Social Order* 1933 and (with Ernest Nagel) *An Introduction to Logic and Scientific Method* 1934.

coherence theories According to the coherence theories *of truth*, a statement is true if it coheres with a designated class of statements.

The coherence relation is variously specified, but is usually assumed to involve more than mere compatibility. At the extreme, some idealists have even insisted that the relation between any two true statements must be one of mutual implication. Others account for coherence in terms of mutual support of a kind weaker than implication. It is not only the accounts of coherence that vary; there are also different views about the designated class of statements. How do we distinguish the class of true statements from a self-consistent fairy-tale? One feature that may be found attractive in coherence theories of truth is that they bypass the problems arising from trying to give an account of 'correspondence with facts', the central concept in the rival correspondence theory of truth.

Likc other so-called theories of truth, coherence theories can be variously interpreted: as offering only a criterion of truth, or an account of the nature of truth.

According to coherence theories *of justification of belief*, proposed in twentieth-century epistemology, a belief is justified if it fits in with a set of beliefs, appropriately specified. Again, there are different accounts of the nature of the fit.

The main alternative to coherence theories is FOUNDATIONALISM.

Coleridge, Samuel Taylor (1772–1834) English poet, critic and philosopher. In the 1790s he advocated, together with Robert Southey, a utopian, strictly egalitarian polity called pantisocracy (from Greek *pant-* all + *isokratia* equal rule). Although not a systematic thinker, he exercised a great influence, to which J. S. Mill's essay on him bears witness, by introducing into Britain the Kantian and the post-Kantian Romantic philosophy. The Romantic philosophers sought to revive a forgotten, mostly medieval, cultural and philosophical past, but Coleridge himself turned to the CAMBRIDGE PLATONISTS for an alternative to the materialism and utilitarianism of his time.

Collingwood, R(obin) G(eorge) (1889–1943) English philosopher and archaeologist of Roman Britain, variously inspired by Plato, Hegel and the Italian idealists de Ruggiero, Gentile and Croce. Professor of philosophy at Oxford 1934–41, he was an unfashionable figure in an Oxford and an English philosophical world preoccupied with the theory of perception, but his later writings, especially, have attracted the attention of philosophers of art, history and science.

Philosophy begins from experience. This does not consist in the passive reception of sensations but rather in the practice of such forms of activity as art, science and religion. Each presents the philosopher with reflective mirrors of the world and of related concepts. In such works as his *Essay on Philosophical Method* 1933, Collingwood sees the philosopher as, in a quasi-Platonic manner, classifying, defining and ordering such concepts in a manner peculiar to philosophy itself, the concepts with which it is concerned – such concepts as truth and reality – cutting across species and the definitions 'placing' concepts in relation to an ideal form.

In his later, more influential writings he brings together his archaeological and his historical interests, first in his widely read *Autobiography* 1939. A proposition is not to be thought of as a picture of the world, true when it pictures the world correctly, but rather as an attempt to answer a question; it is true when it is the 'right answer' to a particular question in a particular complex of questions and answers, that is, when it helps inquiry to proceed. These questions, and the acceptability of a particular answer, vary over time, depending on the 'presuppositions' prevailing at that time. Philosophy is an essentially historical inquiry, attempting to unravel the presuppositions holding at a particular time, to bring them to light. There are no permanent philosophical problems, but there is a permanent philosophical task.

His views about history and the arts, both of them greatly influenced by Croce, are most fully presented in his *The Principles of Art* 1938 and his posthumous *The Idea of History* 1946. In the philosophy of history his principal theme is that historical understanding depends on our capacity, by putting ourselves in their position, to rethink why the historical agents acted as they did; if they acted in a way which, given the presuppositions of the time, was quite irrational, we have no way of understanding their actions. There is less emphasis on history in his philosophy of art. He closely links art with emotions – not, however, the simple expression of emotion and not an attempt to arouse emotion, which is characteristic only of what he calls the 'magical' – but rather the finding of a 'language', which need not, as it is not in the case of music and the pictorial arts, be verbal. The work of art exists in the mind of the artist; to understand it is to have access to the artist's mind.

In accordance with his general approach, his posthumous *The Idea of Nature* 1945 argues that science is essentially historical, depending as it does on records of experience. JP

Collins, Anthony (1676–1729) English free-thinker. He wrote extensively in criticism of the dogmas of the established churches, arguing, like Herbert of Cherbury and Locke before him, that we should be free to reflect critically on the claims of religion and accept nothing that is contrary to reason. *A Discourse of Free-Thinking* 1712 is the best-known of his many works, which display clarity and wit. His *A Discourse Concerning Ridicule and Irony in Writing* 1727 is a defence of the practice in the spirit of Shaftesbury.

combination, principle of *See* AGGLOMERATION, PRINCIPLE OF.

commensurable *See* INCOMMENSURABILITY.

common notions (Gr. *koinai ennoiai*; Lat. *notiones communes*) in Stoic philosophy, innate insights common to all. They are true, self-evident, and at the basis of all inquiry. In Euclid's *Elements*, the axioms are called common notions.

commonplace book a notebook used by an author to record observations, quotations and reflections for later reference.

communicable (in scholastic terminology) capable of being shared. Universals are communicable, since it is possible for two individuals to have a property in common, e.g. *humanness*. On the other hand, individuality, i.e. being *this* individual, is not communicable. Some of God's attributes, such as benevolence, are communicable, while other ones, e.g. infinitude, are not.

communism *n.* **1** a condition in which property is in common ownership. Especially, the political condition that, according to Marxist theory, will emerge when the self-destructive tendencies of the capitalist system have led to its collapse and when the following transitional period of the dictatorship of the proletariat has come to an end. In that condition, there will be no private ownership of the means of production, no exploitation of man by man, but a society based on free cooperation between individuals who flourish in a state of general economic, cultural and personal well-being. **2** a theory, a political movement, or a political system that advocates or practises abolition of private ownership. Especially, the political system in the Soviet Union as it developed after the October Revolution 1917 until approximately 1991, in China from 1949, and in other so-called people's democracies after the war.

communitarianism *n.* a social and political theory which rejects the individualism considered to be inherent in liberal political theory, and which puts an emphasis on values and goals of a collective nature – cultural or national values, say – which are held to be inaccessible in a society concerned only to protect and promote individual freedom and self-determination.

The ethical theory of writers who advocate communitarianism is in many cases virtue-orientated, in opposition to an ethics of individual autonomy, and it is argued that the virtues needed for human flourishing can only be exercised in a society which has a distinctive communal way of life. The opposition between the two schools of thought echoes that between Kant, for whom autonomy is the essence of morality, and Hegel, with his concept of *Sittlichkeit*, the ethical life, for which the individual's belonging to a community is essential.

The term has come into general use in this sense in the 1980s, to describe the views of a number of recent critics of liberalism, including Michael Sandel, Alasdair MacIntyre, Michael Walzer and Charles Taylor. On the opposite side are John Rawls, Robert Nozick, Ronald Dworkin, Bruce Ackerman and James Buchanan. The debate is by no means confined to the United States; in Germany, for instance, Jürgen Habermas has defended a theory of liberal autonomy against communitarian virtue-ethics.

commutative justice Commutative justice, also called *corrective* or *rectificatory justice*, concerns all kinds of 'exchange': Aristotle includes in Book 5 of the *Nicomachean Ethics* exchanges freely undertaken, like payment for a service, but also compensation for damage incurred, and punishment for a crime. In all of these, justice consists in observing the right proportion, maintaining a balance, observing a certain equality. In contrast, *distributive justice* concerns the right way of allocating benefits and burdens. Principles such as 'to each according to need', 'to each according to merit' are examples of principles of distributive justice.

commutative law a proposition that the arguments of a certain function or operator can change place without affecting the result. Examples are addition, since for any two numbers x and y, $x + y = y + x$, and disjunction, since for any two propositions p and q, $p \vee q$ has the same truth-value as $q \vee p$. On the other hand, subtraction is not commutative, since $5 - 7 \neq 7 - 5$, nor is the conditional, since $p \supset q$ and $q \supset p$ are not equivalent.

compact *n.* (in older usage, e.g. Locke) contract; pact.

compatibilism *n.* a view according to which two supposedly incompatible beliefs or facts are compatible; especially, the view that natural causality does not rule out the possibility of free will.

compatible *adj.* Two beliefs, theories, etc. are compatible if and only if they can be true together. Two facts, events, states of affairs, etc. are compatible if and only if the occurrence of one does not rule out the occurrence of the other.

Compatible and *consistent* are near-synonyms. There are, however, some subtle differences: one point of difference is that *compatible* is mainly used in respect of exactly *two* items, whilst *consistent* is used in respect of any number of items. Another point of difference is that when two items are both objects, events, states of affairs (rather than thoughts, beliefs, statements, theories), they are said to be *compatible* (rather than consistent). Similarly, we say that two colours are incompatible; to say that they are inconsistent would sound odd.

complacency *n.* **1** (in older usage) the state of being pleased with something. **2** (in current usage) smug self-satisfaction.

complementarity principle formulated by the Danish physicist Niels Bohr (1885–1962) in September 1927 and first published in 1928. It states that electrons and other items at the sub-atomic level can be described both as wave-like and as particle-like. One or other of the descriptions is more appropriate, depending on the conditions, but the two cannot be combined into a single coherent theory.

Some writers have used this to argue against the principles of classical logic, such as the law of non-contradiction, but such arguments do not seem tenable. What does seem to follow is that electrons are not quite like billiard balls, and not quite like waves either.

completeness *n.* a property of certain formal systems, e.g. in logic. Intuitively, it implies that the system contains all that it should contain and that any further additions would lead to trouble. Standard propositional logic is *semantically complete* in that every tautology is a theorem. It is also *syntactically complete*, in the sense that inconsistency results if a non-thesis is added. (There are other concepts of syntactic completeness, for which this does not hold.) The ordinary first-order predicate logic is semantically complete, but not syntactically complete. Gödel's incompleteness theory for elementary arithmetic states that no axiomatization of it can be both semantically complete (i.e. imply all the truths of arithmetic and none of the falsehoods) and consistent.

complex number a number of the form a + ib, where a and b are real numbers and i is the imaginary number $\sqrt{-1}$. Alternatively, complex numbers can be defined as ordered pairs for which the following conditions apply: (1) the members of the pairs are real numbers; (2) addition: $\langle a,b\rangle + \langle c,d\rangle = \langle a + c, b + d\rangle$; (3) multiplication: $\langle a,b\rangle \times \langle c,d\rangle = \langle ac - bd, ad + bc\rangle$.

composition, fallacy of an inference which relies on the invalid principle that whatever is true of every part is also true of the whole. For instance: assume that every proper part of a stone weighs less than 1 kg; we cannot infer that the stone itself weighs less than 1 kg. Or assume that every member of a committee is capable of rational decision-making; we cannot infer that the committee as a whole is.

There *are* properties such that if they belong to every part they also belong to the whole. Nelson Goodman has called them EXPANSIVE.

comprehension *n.* INTENSION (of a concept). The term was introduced in *The Port-Royal Logic*.

comprehension, axiom of (in set theory) for every property expressible in the notation of set theory, there is a set consisting of all and only those things which possess that property. This principle, although plausible at first sight, generates set-theoretic paradoxes like Russell's paradox. This proposition is also called the *principle of comprehension*, or the *axiom of abstraction*.

Comte /kɔ̃t (Fr.)/, Auguste (1798–1857) acquired an encyclopedic knowledge in many branches of study, and this formed a basis for his privately organized lectures in Paris and for their subsequent publication in his *Cours de philosophie positive* 1830–42. Analysing the underlying tendencies of human history, he conceived a theory, first sketched in an outline published in 1822, of three major stages in the individual and the historical development of the human mind. This law of three stages also applied to social evolution. The first stage is the *theological*. It is the most primitive, and is characterized by open superstition and animist patterns of thought. These do not disappear entirely, but become refined at the second or *metaphysical* stage with the development of abstract speculation and reflection. In the third and highest, *positive* stage, of which Hume is a major precursor and Comte himself the first major philosophical representative, superstition and metaphysics give way to science.

In Comte's view, many of the special sciences were already reaching the third level, but the crowning one, sociology, had yet to come into being. Its task, first undertaken by Comte himself, was to discover the laws that govern human society. Comte divided it into two major but interdependent branches: social statics and social dynamics. His study of history provided him with the inductive basis for many of the sociological laws that he put forward.

Comte called his philosophy 'positive'. This was partly to express his optimistic faith in intellectual and moral progress (he believed that the two were inseparable). But he used the word 'positive' mainly in order to indicate that inquiry must be true to the data of experience, that it should establish laws on the basis of these data, but that it must not go beyond them in a fruitless search for causes at a supposed deeper level. In this sense, all science can do is to *describe* particular facts, establish general regularities, and make predictions; it cannot *explain* anything, if that is taken to imply a descent to something underlying experience.

Comte also held that political development is characterized by three stages. They are, in turn: brute force of arms; legalism; and finally the system appropriate for modern industrialized society; and their predominant mode of action is, respectively, predatory, individualistic, communitarian. He thought that the moral regeneration of mankind, necessary to bring the third stage into being, would have to rely in particular on the working class, because of its general good sense and dislike of war, and on women, because of their inherent benevolence and submissive disposition.

Comte was in contact with many leading radical and progressive intellectuals, including John Stuart Mill, but in many cases initially cordial relations cooled, since Comte disagreed with their liberal and individualistic principles. He had a strong preference for a highly ordered and unified society, in which traditional, superstitious religion would be replaced by his Religion of Humanity. It would overcome the conflict between religion and science which had arisen and become increasingly acute over the preceding two centuries. He wrote a positivist catechism, and designed a calendar for the new positivist church, with the ancient mathematician Diophantus, Shakespeare and Adam Smith among its saints, and months with names like Archimedes. A small number of positivist congregations were actually formed.

Comte's rejection of traditional religion and metaphysics, his faith in science and progress, his theory of history, and his pioneering work in sociology, have all had a strong and persistent influence on subsequent thought.

con-attitude *n.* an unfavourable attitude. Patrick Nowell-Smith (*Ethics* 1954) introduced the word as a contrasting term to PRO-ATTITUDE.

conatus /kəʊˈneɪtəs/ Lat. endeavour, effort *n.* a dynamic tendency. In Spinoza, *conatus* is a dynamic principle, the endeavour of a thing to persist in its own being. It comes to awareness as a drive for self-preservation.

concept *n.* Concepts can be signified by simple or compound terms. It is important to note that 'true' and 'false' do not apply to concepts or terms. It is sentences, statements, propositions, beliefs, theories and doctrines that can be said to be true or false.

conceptualism *n.* the theory that universals – properties, relations, etc. – are concepts existing in the mind. It opposes nominalism, according to which there are no universals, only names or words, and it also opposes realism, according to which universals have mind-independent existence.

conceptual realism *See* REALISM.

conclusion *n.* **1** a proposition inferred from other propositions. **2** the last part of a piece of discourse. **3** the endpoint of a piece of discourse.

concrete *See* ABSTRACT.

concrete universal *See* UNIVERSAL, CONCRETE

Condillac /kɔ̃dijak (Fr.)/, Etienne Bonnot de (1715–80) French Enlightenment philosopher, brother of Mably and cousin of d'Alembert, on terms of close friendship with Turgot, Diderot, Rousseau, etc. His first work, *Essai sur l'origine des connaissances humaines* 1746 (Essay on the origin of human knowledge), established him as the major empiricist thinker in the history of French philosophy. His theory, influenced by Locke, was revised and improved throughout his life, as can be seen from the changes in the successive editions of his first work and in other works of his, but there is a core that remains constant: all knowledge derives from sensations; the faculties and the ideas of the mind are not innate but come into being gradually; the development of knowledge is due to the development of language. In his *Traité des sensations* 1754 (Treatise on sensations), Condillac uses a marble statue as a model to give an ingenious genetic account of how we come to have knowledge of a world: We will make good progress already with the sense of smell alone, and other senses will add to the picture, but only the sense of touch will make us form a conception of a world external to ourselves.

condition *n.* **1** that which is signified by the if-clause in a conditional statement. **2** that which is signified by a propositional that-clause.

conditional *adj.*, *n.* A compound statement of the form 'if p, then q' is called a *conditional statement* or a *conditional*. The statement in the if-clause (here symbolized by the letter p) is called the *antecedent* and the statement in the then-clause (here symbolized by the letter q) is called the *consequent*.

A conditional statement is false if the antecedent is true but the consequent false.

A conditional statement is often used to assert a connection of some kind between the antecedent and consequent. But in certain contexts, it can be interpreted purely as a *truth-function*. So interpreted, it is called a *material conditional* (or, less felicitously, a *material implication*). (These terms are also used to denote the operation on two statements p, q, which results in the formation of such a compound statement.) When understood truth-functionally, 'if p then q', like the equivalent 'not both p and not-q', implies nothing whatever about any connection between p and q. In propositional logic, the conditional is variously symbolized as $p \supset q$ or $p \rightarrow q$ or Cpq. Its truth-table is shown in Table 5. *See also* COUNTERFACTUAL CONDITIONAL.

Table 5 Truth-table for the conditional

p	q	$p \supset q$
T	T	T
T	F	F
F	T	T
F	F	T

conditionalization *n.* **1** the turning of an argument into a corresponding conditional statement. For example, the argument: 'If it is night, then it is dark; It is night; Therefore, it is dark' becomes, when conditionalized: 'If (if it is night, then it is dark), then, if it is night, then it is dark.'

In formal systems, conditionalization consists in turning an inference: '$P_1, P_2, \ldots P_n$, therefore C' into a conditional formula of the form: '$P_1 \supset (P_2 \supset (\ldots (P_n \supset C) \ldots))$'. **2** a logical rule, also called rule of CONDITIONAL PROOF.

conditional proof, rule of also called the rule of $\supset$-introduction (in systems of natural deduction). It states that if q is derivable from a set of premisses that include p, then $p \supset q$ is derivable from the set of premisses remaining after the removal of p.

conditional syllogism In the past, this expression was used for valid two-premiss argument-forms with exactly one conditional premiss, i.e. MODUS PONENS and MODUS TOLLENS.

conditioned *See* RELATIVE.

condition, necessary and/or sufficient In statements of the form *If A then B*, A is a sufficient condition for B, and B is a necessary condition for A. The same is the case for statements of the form *A only if B*.

conditio sine qua non /kɒn'dɪsɪəʊ 'saɪnɪ kweɪ nɒn/ Lat. a condition without which not; a necessary condition.

Condorcet /kɔ̃dɔ̃rsɛ (Fr.)/, Marquis de (1743–94) Enlightenment philosopher, also active in public life, where he campaigned for economic freedom, religious toleration, legal reform, the abolition of slavery, and the removal of the privileges of the nobility. During the French Revolution his liberal and tolerant constitutionalism and his opposition to the death penalty aroused the wrath of the Jacobins, and he died in prison. His most famous work, not complete, is his *Esquisse d'un tableau historique des progrès de l'esprit humain* 1795 (A sketch for a historical picture of the progress of the human mind), which advances the theory that in the course of history, mankind describes a path of progress. Although a major proponent of this view, he was not the first: there are similar views in Turgot 1750, in d'Alembert's 'Preliminary Discourse' to the *Grande Encyclopédie* 1753, in Lessing's 'Education of the Human Race' 1780, etc. Condorcet analysed nine distinguishable periods up to his time. The tenth, which he hoped would follow upon the success of the French Revolution, would see the abolition of social, political and international inequalities, and politics rationally conducted by the use of mathematical techniques. His other main claim to fame rests indeed on his pioneering work in developing mathematical methods (probability calculus, statistics) for application to social and political matters, for instance demography, voting, and decision-making under uncertainty.

Condorcet's paradox *See* VOTING PARADOX.

confirmation, paradox of If an observation O_1 supports a proposition P_1, and if P_1 is logically equivalent to P_2, then O_1 also confirms P_2. Let P_2 be the proposition that *all ravens are black*. Let P_1 be the proposition that *all non-black things are non-ravens*. The two propositions are logically equivalent. (The first can be symbolized $(\forall x)(Rx \supset Bx)$ and the second $(\forall x)(\sim Bx \supset \sim Rx)$.)

I now observe a white sheet of paper. What I am observing is a non-black non-raven. My observation supports the proposition that all non-black things are non-ravens. Therefore it also supports the equivalent proposition that all ravens are black.

It follows that the proposition that all ravens are black is supported not only by observing black ravens, but also by observing white paper, blue books, transparent window-panes, a grey cloud, and so on.

The paradox arises from the fact that the raven's true colours are *not* discovered by observing non-black non-ravens.

conjugation *n.* (in grammar) **1** the main inflections of a verb. **2** a class of verbs having the same main inflections.

conjunction *n.* **1** (in logic) a compound statement of the form 'p and q'. In this compound statement, p and q are called *conjuncts*.

The term is also used to denote the operation on two statements p, q, which results in the formation of such a compound statement.

In many contexts, conjunction is *truth-functional*. If so understood, 'p and q' takes the value *true* if and only if each is true, and otherwise *false*. In formal logic, conjunction is variously symbolized as pq, p·q, p&q, $p \wedge q$ or Kpq. Its truth-table is as Table 6.

The term is also used for the rule permitting the derivation of a conclusion of the form p&q from two premisses, p and q:

$$\frac{p \quad q}{p\&q}$$

Table 6 Truth-table for conjunction

p	q	p&q
T	T	T
T	F	F
F	T	F
F	F	F

The rule of conjunction is also, though rarely, called adjunction, and in natural deduction systems it is called &-introduction.

2 (in grammar) an expression such as *and*, *but*, *or*, *although*, or *because*, that links two sentences, e.g. 'Jill stayed although Jack left', or two members of the same word-class, e.g. 'bread and butter', 'poor but honest', 'on or about'.

connatural *adj.* having the same nature.

connected *adj.* A relation R is said to be (weakly) connected iff for all x, y in the domain, x = y or Rxy or Ryx. (R is said to be strongly connected iff for all x, y in the domain, Rxy or Ryx.) For example, in the domain of positive integers, the relation 'less than' is (weakly) connected, while 'less than or equal to' is strongly connected.

connectionism *n.* a research programme in cognitive science. Connectionists are distinguished by one essential feature: they all use networks of neural units as models of cognitive processes. The neural units are broadly similar to real biological neurons as found in the brain, but are highly simplified. Corresponding to the firing rate of real neurons, connectionist neural units have a numerical activity level. The neural units are connected together to form networks (hence the name). Each neural unit changes its activity level over time as a function of the activity of other units to which it is connected and the 'strength' of those connections. Much connectionist research consists in finding ways to adapt the connection strengths in a network so that the network as a whole comes to behave in ways qualitatively or even quantitatively similar to the ways humans perform on cognitive tasks. Connectionism is most usefully contrasted with the mainstream computational approach to cognition, which models cognitive processes as the rule-governed manipulation of symbolic structures, i.e. as processes of broadly the same kind as are found in a desktop digital computer.

Aside from this essential commitment, connectionism is a very diverse programme. Nevertheless, connectionism should be carefully distinguished from at least two other research programmes. Neural network research is the general exploration of the capacities of networks of neural units, and has no particular interest in the study of cognitive functions. Neural modelling is the detailed mathematical modelling of the behaviour of real biological neurons and assemblies of neurons. TVG

connective *n.* This term is used in propositional logic for truth-functional operators (conjunction, disjunction, etc.) which combine two propositions into one. Occasionally negation, a monadic operator, is also called a connective.

connotation/denotation The connotation of a term, often called its meaning, is made up of one or more properties which belong to each of those things to which the term applies. The denotation of a term is sometimes said to be any object to which the term applies, sometimes the class of the object to which it applies. Thus, the denotation of 'white' is any white object, or the class of all white objects.

Two terms with different connotations

can have the same denotation. A traditional example is 'rational animal' and 'featherless biped'. These two expressions have different connotations but both denote human beings.

Warning: these terms are given a different, almost opposite sense in non-philosophical, especially literary, contexts. The overtones of a word, things suggested without being part of the meaning of the word, are called its *connotation*. The primary meaning, as usually specified by a dictionary, is called its *denotation*. In this usage, 'home' *denotes* the place where one lives but *connotes* privacy, intimacy and cosiness. 'Horse' and 'steed' are said to *denote* the same quadruped, but 'steed' has a different *connotation* from 'horse'.

conscience *n.* the faculty of judging morally one's own actions. This is the standard sense: my conscience does not judge *your* actions, only my own. But in the past, the word was sometimes also used to signify moral judgement generally.

Warning: the French word *conscience* is used both for conscience and consciousness. Beware of mistranslations.

consensus gentium /kɒn'sɛnsəs 'dʒɛnsɪəm/ Lat. consent of the nations; the universal or very wide agreement between peoples all over the world in respect of certain customs and beliefs. It has sometimes been regarded as strong evidence for the soundness of a custom or a belief.

consequence *n.* something that *follows from* something else: an effect, a result, or an outcome.

consequent *n.* the clause in a conditional statement which states what is or would be the case, given the condition stated. In a conditional of the form *if p then q*, q is the consequent. The other statement, p, is called the antecedent.

consequentia /kɔnsɪ'kwɛnsɪə/ (*sing.*); ***consequentiae*** /kɔnsɪ'kwɛnsɪaɪ/ (*pl.*) Lat. consequence(s) *n.* entailment proposition(s). The theory of consequences was one of the branches of the new logic, the *logica modernorum*, which medieval logicians, particularly in the fourteenth century, elaborated with great theoretical subtlety. JM

consequentialism *n.* the term was first used for (1) a theory concerning *responsibility*, but is now commonly used for (2) a theory concerning *right and wrong*.

1 the view that an agent is equally responsible for the intended consequences of an act and its unintended but foreseen consequences. Elizabeth Anscombe created the new term *consequentialism* for this view in her article 'Modern Moral Philosophy' (*Philosophy 33* (1958), and often reprinted) and criticized Sidgwick and later utilitarians for holding it. The view differs, according to her, from the versions of utilitarianism proposed before Sidgwick. These had not rejected the distinction between foreseen and intended consequences as far as responsibility is concerned. Her objection to consequentialism is that since it looks at consequences only, the character of the act itself is left out of account, and this has the unacceptable consequence that an agent is equally responsible for the foreseen but unintended consequences of an act, no matter whether the act is courageous or cowardly.

2 the view that an action is right if and only if its total outcome is the best possible. This is the basic form of consequentialism; there are, however, many varieties, a few of which will be noted below. What they all have in common is that *consequences alone should be taken into account when making judgements about right or wrong*.

This is how the term has been used since the late 1960s. Previously, 'utilitarianism' was the term commonly used for consequentialism, and that use remains; but many writers now use the term 'utilitarianism' to designate a *kind* of consequentialism. Some of them reserve the term 'utilitarianism' for the view that combines consequentialism with the hedonistic assumption that *pleasure* alone has intrinsic value. Others reserve the term for the view that combines consequentialism with the eudaimonistic assumption that *happiness* (welfare, well-being) alone has intrinsic value. These two views are not always clearly distinguished. Others again use 'utilitarianism' for the kind of consequentialism that takes *preference-satisfaction* alone to have intrinsic value.

Another way of making a terminological distinction between utilitarianism and other kinds of consequentialism is by reserving the label 'utilitarianism' for those consequentialist theories that include the *maximizing* assumption: that only the best is good enough.

A survey (no doubt incomplete) of some of the varieties of consequentialism can be obtained by starting with Bentham's *principle*[a] of utility: an *act*[b] is *right*[c] if and only if *it*[d] *tends*[e] to *maximize*[f] the *net overbalancing sum total*[g] of *pleasure over pain*[h] for *all parties concerned*[i] (superscript letters refer to paragraphs below).

(a) Bentham's principle can be understood in two distinct ways: as a guide for *decision* as to what action to take, or as a guide for the *evaluation* of an action (one's own or someone else's). If the principle is taken as a guide to decision-making, it invites the objection that there is not enough time to consider all the consequences and perform, for each set of possible consequences, all the necessary calculations of their value. If the principle is taken as a guide for evaluation, there may be less time-pressure. (Even so, evaluating all the possible consequences will take a very long time.)

(b) Some versions of consequentialism evaluate things other than acts – attitudes, for instance, or rules.

(c) Some formulations do not use 'right' but introduce other words: 'ought', 'obligation' or 'duty'.

(d) Act-consequentialism considers the consequences of the act. Other theories consider the consequences of adopting a rule under which the act falls, or adopting an attitude that will result in acting in a certain way. Again, does the rightness of my keeping a promise depend on the fact that *my* adoption of the rule of promise-keeping tends to promote the good, or on the fact that the adoption *by people generally* does?

(e) There is a diversity of consequentialist theories as the actual, or the probable, or the foreseen consequences are held to be the relevant ones. Moreover, the very notion of a consequence varies. Some authors even include the very performance of an action among its consequences and hold that one of the consequences of performing an act of loyalty is the fact that an act of loyalty has occurred.

(f) Maximizing implies comparison with all relevant alternatives. Some criterion is needed to tell which alternatives are relevant; different criteria can be devised. Moreover, some versions of consequentialism reject maximizing and settle for less. They hold the view that not only the best is good enough and favour satisficing. *See also* SATISFICE.

(g) In what way, and to what extent, can one individual's goods be compared with one another? If they can be compared, can they be added together, like financial assets and liabilities? Answers to these questions differ. Again, to what extent are interpersonal comparisons or summations possible? Can B's loss be outbalanced by A's gain? In so far as we deny this we are insisting on the distinctness or SEPARATENESS OF PERSONS.

Distributive principles can also vary. Consider a situation in which ten persons are all quite happy. Five of them enjoy 20 units of the good, and the other five enjoy 60 units of the good. Compare this with a situation in which, again, they are all quite happy, all ten enjoying 40 units of the good. Is one of these situations preferable to the other? There are a variety of answers to this, and to a vast number of similar questions of distribution.

(h) The value to be maximized was, in Bentham's *hedonistic* utilitarianism, pleasure and the absence of pain. Moore's *ideal* utilitarianism takes experiences of beauty and relations of friendship to have intrinsic value. The most common present-day variety is *preference*-utilitarianism: the good consists in the satisfaction of preferences, i.e. in people having what they want. In other formulations *welfare* is said to be the good.

(i) Consequentialist theories also differ in yet another respect. On the 'total view', an increase of the total number of people is an improvement (other things being equal), as long as the additional individuals have a positive welfare or happiness score, however marginal. On the 'average view', the important thing is to seek to increase average pleasure, happiness, welfare, or the like. A situation in which there are a larger number of people would not be better (other things being equal) if the average welfare remained the same.

conservatism *n.* a view of politics and society which finds much of value in the traditions of a society and is specially aware of the risks of reforms which may bring unforeseen adverse consequences despite the reformers' best intentions. Conservative attitudes incorporate that part of popular wisdom that is expressed in adages such as 'better the devil you know . . .' and 'if it ain't broke, don't fix it'. The conservative presumption is in favour of tradition and the established order. The contrast between conservatives and their opponents is not necessarily that between rich and poor, right and left, or capitalism and socialism. The term came into use in the early nineteenth century and then designated views like those of Burke and de Maistre which condemned the ideals of the French Revolution and in general opposed radical change. Therefore there is nothing anomalous in describing Russian Communist politicians of the mid-1990s as conservatives. The Conservative government that introduced radical social and cultural change in Britain in the 1980s did not have the full approval of genuine conservatives.

consilience (Lat. *con-* with + *salire* to jump) *n.* the concurrence of evidence that occurs when data from very dissimilar fields provide support for the same scientific hypothesis.

consistency *n. A set of sentences* is consistent if all of the sentences in that set could be or could have been true together. By a natural extension, one can also say that *one sentence* is consistent if it could be or could have been true.

There are various technical definitions of consistency of a *formal system*. They capture in different ways the idea that a well-formed formula and its negation are not both theses of a consistent system.

constant *n.* In formal logic, logical constants are operators with a specified meaning. In propositional logic the connectives, like ~ (negation), & (conjunction), etc., are logical constants.

In mathematics, an expression with a fixed numerical value, or an expression treated as if it has a fixed numerical value, is called a constant. In a related sense, schematic letters used in formal logic to represent (a particular instance of) a variable are also sometimes so called. Thus, predicate-letters (usually 'F', 'G', etc.) used for predicates are called constants, in contrast to predicate-variables (usually 'φ' 'ψ'). Name-letters (usually 'a', 'b', 'c' . . .), used for individuals, are called constants, in contrast to individual variables (usually x, y, z . . .). And 'f', or 'o', representing a particular false proposition, is called a constant, in contrast to propositional variables (usually 'p', 'q', 'r' . . .).

Constant /kɔ̃stɑ̃ (Fr.)/, Benjamin (1767–1830) Born in Lausanne, Constant spent periods of his eventful life in Belgium, Germany, England, Scotland and France. He was politically active, and occupied important positions in France, before entering into opposition against Napoleon, and again after 1814; he incurred gambling debts; of his romantic entanglements the most notable was his affair with Mme de Staël, prominent as a novelist and as an intellectual; he wrote the novel *Adolphe*, and major works on the history and philosophy of religion. His view of ethics was influenced by Stoicism and Kantianism, but he disagreed with Kant's unconditional rejection of lying, following the view of Grotius and Pufendorf that our duty to tell the truth extends only to those who have a right to be told the truth. Constant is, however, best known for his political writings, with their powerful advocacy of liberalism. He attacked despotism and oligarchic rule, which was the main political enemy at the time, for its corrupting influence on society at large and for its suppression of authentic individuality.

constative *n.*, *adj.* a term introduced by J. L. Austin to describe those utterances in the indicative mood which are typically used to make true or false statements, in contrast to PERFORMATIVE utterances. This distinction was partly superseded by his later theory of SPEECH ACTS.

constitution *n.* **1** the written or unwritten laws that regulate the manner in which the highest positions of authority in a state are filled, and the scope and limits of such authority.
2 In Carnap's *Der logische Aufbau der Welt* 1928 (*The Logical Construction of the World*) a constitutional definition is one that transforms a statement in which an object A is mentioned into a statement with the same truth-value, in which other (more basic) objects, but not A, are mentioned. The aim is to provide a minimal basis for a world-description in the sense that the *kinds* of basic entities are very few in number. A similar attempt is made in Nelson Goodman's *The Structure of Appearance* 1951.
3 In phenomenological philosophy, to constitute an object is an activity. It consists in performing a mental operation which results in having the object as such in one's consciousness. Thus, in Husserl's theory of phenomenological constitution, a mental act A is constitutive of an object F, if A is constitutive of that mental act B in which F is most immediately experienced. For Husserl, it is all in the thinking mind; in contrast, Heidegger claimed that not only consciousness but also practical activity and interaction with people and things in the world enters into this activity, especially in the formation of the concepts of self and other; and Sartre and Merleau-Ponty added to this by stressing the part the subject's body plays in the constitution of these concepts.

constitutive *adj.* Kant distinguishes the constitutive from the regulative use of the Ideas of reason. The former use leads to error, the latter to a desirable advancement of knowledge. For instance, it is a mistake to think that we could ultimately come to know a first cause, but in the conduct of theoretical inquiry it is sound practice to go on in the search for further causes: there is no point at which we can be entitled to think that it is the end-point to inquiry.

Searle distinguishes between constitutive and regulative rules. The distinction is well illustrated by comparing the relation between chess and the laws of chess with the relation between driving and the laws relating to driving. Without the laws of chess, there would be no game of chess; driving, on the other hand, would be possible (but more hazardous) even without any rules of the road.

construction, logical a kind of philosophical analysis, by which certain concepts, which seem in some way problematic, are shown to be reducible to other ones which cause less trouble. Russell, John Wisdom and A. J. Ayer, among others, have used this method. For instance, the proposal that a table is a logical construction from sense-data means that any statement about a table is equivalent to a set of statements about sense-data.

constructive dilemma *See* DILEMMA.

constructivism *n.* **1** (in epistemology) the theory that knowledge is not something we *acquire* but something that we *produce*; that the objects in an area of inquiry are not there to be discovered, but are invented or constructed. **2** (in mathematics) the view that mathematical objects are admissible in a theory only if there is an effective method by which they can, ideally, be constructed. For instance, any natural number is admissible, since a procedure of counting will (at least in the very long run) lead to it, but the 'actually-infinite' set of all natural numbers is not. Brouwer's intuitionism is constructivist.

contextual definition definition in which the expression to be defined is mentioned not in isolation but in its characteristic context. If we wish to define 'divided by', the natural method would be to define the characteristic context 'a divided by b' by 'the number x such that bx = a'. This is a contextual definition of 'divided by'.

continence *See* AKRASIA.

continental philosophy The term has been used as a contrasting term to ANALYTIC PHILOSOPHY. Terminologically this is not a proper contrast, since 'continental' is a geographical term, referring to the European continent, whereas 'analytic' signifies a certain method of philosophizing.

There are, however, contrasts in style, choice of topics, and manner of writing. On the 'continental' side are Hegel, Nietzsche, Croce, Heidegger, Jaspers, Collingwood, Adorno, Sartre, Foucault, Lyotard, Derrida, etc. Critics find their projects over-ambitious and their writings obscure. On the 'analytic' side are Frege, Meinong, Russell, Moore, Wittgenstein, Carnap, Ryle, Popper, Quine, Austin, Stegmüller, Searle, etc. Their attention to logic, language, and conceptual questions makes critics accuse them of excessive attention to relatively unimportant matters, and of being more interested in sharpening tools than in using them.

The gulf between the two styles widened between the wars. After the Second World War, attempts to bridge it were few and tentative until the 1970s. Since then, mutual interest has grown, as can be seen from the increasingly numerous translations of 'analytic' writings into French, German, Italian, etc. and of 'continental' writings into English.

contingency argument an argument *from* the contingent nature of the world *to* the existence of a necessary being. Some traditional arguments for the existence of God are of this kind.

contingent *adj.* **1** (of a proposition, a statement, etc.) neither necessary nor impossible. A contingent proposition can be true but does not have to be true. This is the primary sense in contemporary philosophical usage. A contingently false proposition can be (could have been) true, but is not. A contingently true proposition can be (could have been) false, but is not. **2** (of a fact, an event, etc.) occurring without this necessarily being the case, i.e. it might not have occurred. **3** In a different sense, contingency may designate a relation between events. One event can be said to be contingent upon another. This means that the first would not happen (would not have happened) but for the second. This is the concept of contingency that plays an important part e.g. in Oakeshott.

contingent identity *The President of France in 1994* does not *mean* the same as *François Mitterrand*, but, as a matter of fact, the President of France in 1994 *was* François Mitterrand. Hence, the identity asserted is contingent: it could have been otherwise.

One important philosophical theory which employs a concept of contingent identity is the identity theory of mind, according to which mental phenomena are contingently identical with states and processes in the nervous system. Statements about a mental image, for instance, refer (as a matter of fact) to the same thing as statements about some brain-process, but they do not have the same meaning.

The theory has been much debated. Objections on the basis of doubts about the idea of contingent identity have been raised especially by Kripke.

continuum *n.* the set of real numbers; any other set of the same order of magnitude.

continuum problem To formulate the problem, the concept of a power set has first to be explained.

For example, consider a set with three members: {a,b,c}. Call it S. S has the following subsets: {0}, {a}, {b}, {c}, {a,b}, {a,c}, {b,c} and {a,b,c}. The set which has these subsets as its members is called the *power set* of S.

In this example, S has three members, and the power set of S has $8 = 2^3$ members. In general, if a set has n members, its power set has 2^n members.

Similarly, the infinite set of the integers, 1, 2, 3, ... has the cardinal number $\aleph_0$ (aleph-nought), and the cardinal number of its power set (the set of its infinitely many subsets) is written $2^{\aleph_0}$.

It can be shown that $\aleph_0 < 2^{\aleph_0}$. The problem is whether there are any cardinal numbers in between. The problem is called the continuum problem, because $2^{\aleph_0}$ is the cardinal number of the continuum, i.e. the set of real numbers.

Generalized, the continuum problem is whether for any infinite set, its power set is the next larger. It was a major discovery by Paul Cohen, in 1963, that the standard axioms of set theory imply neither an affirmative nor a negative answer.

contractarianism the view that the rules of justice governing private conduct and political structures must derive their validity from actual agreements between the parties concerned or from agreements they would have entered into under certain hypothetical conditions. *Syn.* contractualism.

contradiction *n.* Two statements, one of which affirms what the other denies, are said to be *contradictories*, to *contradict* each other, and together to form a *contradiction*. They cannot both be true and they cannot both be false. A standard way of expressing a contradiction is by statement-negation: *p* and *It is not the case that p*. A *self-contradictory* statement is one which consists of or implies two statements which contradict each other.

Contradiction is a logical relation that holds between statements or propositions. In the Hegelian tradition, the term is used more freely, and relations of antagonism and conflict in the physical or social world are described as contradictions.

contrafactive *See* FACTIVE.

contrafactual conditional *See* COUNTERFACTUAL CONDITIONAL.

contraposition *n.* **1** in propositional logic contraposition, also called *transposition*, consists in negating the antecedent and the consequent of a conditional, and letting them change places. The resulting conditional will be equivalent to the original one. Accordingly, inferences of this form are valid:

If A then B
―――――――――
If not-B then not-A

2 in syllogistic logic the contrapositive of a given categorical proposition is obtained in three steps: OBVERSION, CONVERSION, and obversion. In the case of universal affirmative propositions, contraposition is valid:

Every man is an animal
―――――――――
Every non-animal is a non-man

contrariety *n.* Two statements which cannot both be true, although they can both be false, are *contraries*, and their logical relation is *contrariety*. For instance, if the two statements, *Hume was born in Wales* and *Hume was born in England* refer to the same eminent Scottish philosopher, they cannot be true together, but they can be false together – indeed, they are.

contrary-to-fact conditional *See* COUNTERFACTUAL CONDITIONAL.

contrition *See* REPENTANCE.

conversion *n.* **1** The conversion of a CATEGORICAL proposition consists in interchanging the subject- and predicate-terms. For instance, the converse of *Every S is P* is *Every P is S*.

The conversion of the particular affirmative is valid, and so is that of the universal negative. In other words: *Some S is P* implies its converse *Some P is S*. *No S is P* implies its converse *No P is S*. But the conversion of *Every S is P* is not valid, nor is that of *Some S is not P*.

2 (in propositional logic) the converse of a conditional is obtained by interchanging antecedent and consequent: the converse of $p \supset q$ is $q \supset p$. A conditional does not imply its converse.

Copernicus, Nicolaus (1473–1543) Polish man of learning, physician and astronomer. His revolutionary theory, published in *De revolutionibus orbium caelestium* 1543 (On the revolutions of the heavenly orbs), placed the sun close to the centre of the universe, and the Earth in a circular orbit.

Copleston, Frederick (1907–94) English philosopher. He entered the Jesuit order in 1930, and had a long association with Heythrop College. Pre-eminent among his writings is the nine-volume *History of Philosophy* 1946–75.

copula *n.* the expression which joins the predicate to the subject in a sentence. For instance, in the sentence *Socrates is wise*, the copula is *is*. When the predicate is joined directly to the subject, there is no copula, as in the sentence *Socrates thinks*.

co-referential *adj.* having reference to the same thing.

corollary (related to Lat. *corolla* an adorning garland) *n.* a consequence that can be easily inferred from a proposition of which a proof has been given.

cosmogony /kɒzˈmɒgənɪ/ (Gr. *kosmos* order, world-order, world + *-goneia* birth, genesis, origination) *n.* a mythical account, or a scientific theory, of the origin of the world.

cosmological argument argument from some pervasive feature of the world, for instance the fact that there is motion or change in the material universe, to the existence of a first cause, usually identified with God. *Contingency arguments* are often also brought in under this heading. These consist in reasoning from the contingent nature of things in the world to the existence of a necessary being, often identified with God.

cosmology *n.* As a philosophical discipline, *rational cosmology* was defined by C. Wolff in 1731 as one of the three branches of what he called special metaphysics, viz. the one that deals with the general features of the physical universe which can be known *a priori*. (The other two branches were rational psychology and rational theology.) Wolff distinguished it from *empirical cosmology*, which is *a posteriori*. Kant argued in the *Critique of Pure Reason* (B435) that rational cosmology is not a genuine science but that like the other branches of metaphysics it is an expression of the natural tendency of human reason to overstep its boundaries.

As a branch of science, cosmology includes parts of theoretical physics and astrophysics.

cosmopolitanism (Gr. *kosmos* order; world-order; world + *politēs* citizen) *n.* the view, first proposed by Sophists and Stoics, that all human beings are by nature fellow citizens of a world community and are divided into particular societies only by convention.

cosmos (Gr. *kosmos* order; world-order, world) *n.* world.

countable *adj.* A countable set is finite or DENUMERABLE.

counterfactual conditional Proposition or sentence of the form (or equivalent to one of the form): 'If it had been the case that p, then it would have been the case that q', or 'If it were the case that p, then it would be the case that q'. A conditional is called counterfactual because its use seems to presuppose that the user believes its antecedent ('p' in the above formulation) to be false. Some writers go further and insist that for a conditional to count as a counterfactual, its antecedent must actually be false, but the commonest use of the term does not seem to require this.

The truth-conditions of counterfactuals are not the same as for the material conditional, commonly symbolized $p \supset q$, where the falsity of p automatically makes the conditional true.

The question of what the truth-conditions of counterfactuals are has been much debated. Most views fall into one of three main types: (1) one type holds that 'If it were the case that p, then it would be the case that q' is true if and only if an inference having 'p' and some other propositions of certain kinds (just *what* kinds is a matter of debate) as its premisses, and 'q' as its conclusion, is valid. This is the view of Chisholm, Goodman, Rescher, etc.; (2) a second type regards a counterfactual as an abbreviated version of such an inference itself, and hence holds that counterfactuals are to be evaluated as valid or invalid, rather than as true or false; (3) a third type of view holds that 'If it were the case that p, then it would be the case that q' is true if and only if at every possible world at which it is the case that p, and which is otherwise as similar as possible to the actual world, it is also the case that q. This is the view of Lewis, Pollock, Stalnaker et al.

Counterfactuals are subjunctive conditionals, but there are subjunctive conditionals which are not counterfactuals, such as 'If it were to be the case that p, then it would be the case that q'.

Since the early 1970s, many writers have used the symbol A □→ B for 'If A were the case, then B would be the case' (or 'If A had been the case, then B would have been the case'). *Syn.* contrafactual conditional; contrary-to-fact conditional. GH

counterpart theory Since the 1950s modal concepts are often explained in terms of possible worlds, so that *necessarily p* is interpreted as *p is true in every possible world*, and *possibly p* as *p is true in some possible world*.

One might then think that 'Jack could have been taller than he actually is' is true if and only if in some possible world Jack exists and *is* taller than he is in this world. Such an account implies that the same individual Jack exists in more than one world. Quite a few logicians, including David Lewis, feel uncomfortable about this, and propose that an individual can exist only in *one* world, and that 'Jack could have been taller than he actually is' is true if and only if in some possible world there is a taller *counterpart* to Jack. A counterpart to Jack in a possible world is defined as an individual sufficiently similar to Jack, and more similar to Jack than anything else in that world.

The theory is the subject of a lively debate. One apparent difficulty is that a statement about what *I could have done* (but did not do) will be equivalent to a statement about what *someone else* (i.e. my counterpart) *has done* in some possible world. But what has that got to do with *me*?

count noun *See* MASS NOUN.

courage *n.* one of the four CARDINAL VIRTUES.

Cournot /kuʀno (Fr.)/, Antoine (1801–77) made important contributions to probability theory and economics. He was one of the most prominent French men of learning in his time. In his philosophical writings he attacked materialism, favouring a vitalism that would later be taken further by Bergson, and advocated a realist world-view. Where Laplace had regarded our ideas of chance as an expression of our ignorance of the relevant laws and initial conditions, Cournot, although remaining a determinist, argued for an objective conception: chance events arise from the confluence of independent causal sequences.

Cousin /kuzɛ̃ (Fr.)/, Victor (1792–1867) As a senior civil servant and as minister of education in the 1830s and 1840s, Cousin exercised a profound and lasting influence on the study of philosophy in France, giving it a historical, liberal, anti-materialist, anti-clerical (though certainly not anti-religious) orientation. He was the first French philosopher to write extensively about the history of philosophy. His works reveal an outlook that is best described as eclectic. It shows influences from Vico, Schelling and many others, but the philosopher that he held in special esteem was Thomas Reid, the Scottish philosopher of common sense.

Couturat /kutyʀa (Fr.)/, Louis (1868–1914) was the first to introduce modern set theory and formal logic into France. His *La Logique de Leibniz* 1901 was the first publication to make known the logical papers of Leibniz. He also published a study on Kant, and conducted a correspondence with Bertrand Russell.

Crates /ˈkreɪtiːz/ (*c.* 365–285 BC) Cynic philosopher, whose quest for independence and self-sufficiency made him renounce his large fortune and restrict himself to a frugal way of life. Together with his wife Hipparchia he led the life of an itinerant philosophical sage and counsellor.

creationism *n.* the view that the biblical account of the creation of the world is entirely correct, that it is incompatible with generally accepted scientific theories, and that these therefore ought to be rejected.

credo quia absurdum; credo quia impossibile /ˈkreɪdəʊ ˈkwiːə æbˈsɛːdəm; ɪmpɒsˈiːbɪleɪ/ Lat. I believe because it is absurd, I believe because it is impossible. Tertullian, the Church Father, used these words, perhaps for rhetorical effect, about the death and resurrection of Jesus, but they can be taken in a FIDEIST sense. JM

credo ut intelligam /ˈkreidəʊ ʊt ɪnˈtelɪgœm/ Lat. I believe in order that I might understand. St Anselm's motto for his *Proslogion.* The statement reflects an important element also in the thought of St Augustine.

criterion /kraɪˈtɪərɪən/ (*sing.*); **criteria** (*pl.*) (Gr. *kritērion, -a*) *n.* a distinguishing mark; a standard or rule for judgement or decision. The debates among the ancients (especially Stoics and sceptics) about 'the criterion' concerned the criterion by which we would be able to distinguish true opinions from false ones.

Critias /ˈkraɪtɪəs/ (*c.* 453–403 BC) Athenian politician, uncle of Plato. His is the earliest statement on record that religion is invented by politicians in order to control the people.

Critical Philosophy Kantian philosophy.

critical rationalism the description used by Karl Popper of his philosophical outlook. The contrast implied by 'rationalism' is not with empiricism, but with irrationalism. The view is that progress in our search for knowledge is possible and comes about by taking bold conjectures as hypotheses and subjecting these to severe tests. There is an asymmetry in the method: a negative test-result may serve as a refutation; a positive result cannot serve as a conclusive proof. This view of knowledge-acquisition is also anti-FOUNDATIONALIST. In matters moral and political, the central place assigned to free inquiry and criticism leads critical rationalists to favour civil liberties, individualism and anti-authoritarianism, and generally the ideals of liberal democracy.

Prominent adherents of critical rationalism are H. Albert, I. Lakatos, J. Watkins, A. Musgrave, J. Agassi, W. W. Bartley, G. Radnitzky, and E. Topitsch.

Critical Realism a philosophical theory of our knowledge of the external world, which flourished from the late nineteenth century until the 1940s. Its proponents, e.g. G. Dawes Hicks (d. 1941) in Cambridge and R. W. Sellars in the USA, rejected idealism, but instead of accepting the 'direct' or 'naive' realism of the New Realists, they developed a theory according to which our knowledge of the external world always involves a subject, a percept, and an object.

Critical Theory the theoretical approach of the Frankfurt School, especially that of Adorno and Horkheimer, so named by the latter, and contrasted programmatically by him with traditional theory, which takes the natural sciences as its paradigm. The critical theorist maintains that in the social and human realm there is not, as in the natural sciences, a given rational basis of eternal verities; on the contrary, a rational form of social existence is something not yet existing, a task to be achieved. Whilst traditional theory is disinterested, critical theory is determined by an interest in human emancipation and so committed to seeking radical social change.

criticism *n.* From the Greek *krisis* = sifting; discerning; judging. This word, its derivatives and their cognates can be taken in two different senses. In one sense, a critic of a work is a person who subjects it to careful examination. The upshot may be, but does not have to be, negative. In another sense, criticism implies censure. In philosophical contexts, the first sense is often the one intended. **criticize** *vb*; **critique** *n.*

Criticism, Higher The study and interpretation of biblical texts by the same methods as those appropriate for secular historical texts: regard to the historical context; estimation of probabilities; no recourse to supernatural explanations, etc. Early writers who applied this method were Spinoza, *Tractatus Theologico-Philosophicus* 1670 and Richard Simon (1638–1712), *Histoire critique du Vieux Testament* 1687 (A critical history of the Old Testament). The expression 'Higher Criticism' is mostly used for nineteenth-century work of this kind.

In contrast, the expression *lower criticism* is occasionally used for the textual criticism (CRITICISM, TEXTUAL) of biblical texts.

The 'higher criticism' was strongly resisted by many theologians and believers for fear that it would undermine the authority of Scripture.

criticism, textual the scholarly study of manuscripts, editions and other source material with the aim of establishing a reliable version of a text.

Few classical English-language philosophical works have been published in reliable scholarly editions, but there are exceptions: excellent examples of text-critical editions are P. Nidditch's edition of Locke's *Essay Concerning Human Understanding* (Oxford 1975), and H. Warrender's edition of Hobbes's *De Cive* (Oxford 1983).

criticize *See* CRITICISM.

Critique . . . The titles of Kant's three most important works are *Critique of Pure Reason* (*Kritik der reinen Vernunft* 1781; 2nd edn 1787), *Critique of Practical Reason* (*Kritik der praktischen Vernunft* 1788), and *Critique of Judgement* (*Kritik der Urteilskraft* 1790). In these titles, 'critique' means examination and does not imply censure. *See also* CRITICISM.

Croce /ˈkrotʃe (It.)/, Benedetto (1866–1952) a major figure in the cultural and intellectual life of modern Italy. His wider reputation lies principally in his work in aesthetics, where his influence on the English philosopher R. G. Collingwood is most notable. Although his thinking on aesthetics changed during his life, from his early *Estetica come scienza dell'espressione e linguistica generale* 1902 (*Aesthetics as Science of Expression and General Linguistics*) to *La poesia: introduzione alla critica e storia della poesia* 1936 (transl. as *Poetry and Literature: An introduction to its criticism and history*), he retained the central idealist notion of art as intuition and expression. The work of art *per se* should not be identified with any physical artefact or external manifestation but with an inner state of knowledge (intuition) that transforms and unifies impressions aided by imagination (a process he called expression). Croce's work, and Collingwood's, helped to establish ontology – the kind of being possessed by works of art – as a core issue in analytic aesthetics.

In his more general philosophy, initially influenced by positivism and Marxism but later by the work of Vico and Hegel, he distinguished four levels of mental activity, each with a characteristic value-dimension. The first two are theoretical, the last two practical: (1) at the aesthetic level, intellectual and emotional aspects are united; the values are beauty/ugliness; (2) the logical level is the locus for intellectual analysis and synthesis; the values are truth/falsity; (3) at the economic level, the guiding principle is utilitarian and self-interested; the values are benefit/harm; (4) the movement towards the universal is characteristic of the ethical level; the values are morally good/morally evil. Many mistakes, particularly in aesthetic theory, arise from a lack of distinction between these levels. In his theory of history, Croce eventually moved away from Vico and Hegel and rejected, like Windelband, the view that history should seek to establish general laws. He associated history with art: both are concerned with the particular and concrete, not the general and abstract. PL/ed.

Cudworth /ˈkʌdwɜːθ/, Ralph (1617–88) one of the Cambridge Platonists, student at Emmanuel College and fellow there from 1639, and later, from 1654, master of Christ's College (where Henry More was a fellow). His *True Intellectual System of the Universe* 1678 is directed against atheism, which, in his view, has its foundation in *materialism* or in *hylozoism*. The former teaches that everything is inert matter, the latter that everything is animate matter. He accused both of absurdity since they cannot allow for the existence of minds. Our experiences are not physical effects of physical causes; further, both false belief and the distinctively active character of the mind completely defy explanation in purely material terms. It follows that something immaterial exists, and thus a major obstacle to belief in God is removed. To explain various active phenomena which do not spring from the workings of a conscious mind, Cudworth employed the notion of PLASTIC NATURES which explain the workings and the purposiveness of many natural phenomena.

In ethics, he insisted in his *Eternal and Immutable Morality* (published posthumously in 1731, although it may have been previously known in manuscript) that 'things are what they are not by will but by nature', so that God cannot by his mere command make an action right or wrong. This was against Ockham, Calvin, and Hobbes, all of whom he held to have taken the opposite view.

cui bono? /kwiː ˈbəʊnəʊ/ Lat. for whose benefit?; who stands to gain?

culpa Lat. fault; guilt. *See also* DOLUS.

cultural relativism This term is used for at least two different views. The first is uncontroversial, the second is not: (1) different cultures have different customs, social institutions, moralities, etc.; (2) the view that those who belong to one culture cannot form a valid judgement of any custom, institution, belief, etc. which is part of a culture which differs significantly from their own. The view is that there is no non-relative ('absolute') basis from which to judge, and that proper judgements can only be made from inside, i.e. from the standpoint of the culture judged.

Cumberland /ˈkʌmbələnd/, Richard (1632–1718) English clergyman and philosopher, fellow of Magdalene College, Cambridge, and later, from 1691, Bishop of Peterborough. The stated aim of his major work, *De legibus naturae* 1672 (On the laws of nature), is to refute a number of errors of Hobbes. He rejects especially a view that Hobbes was often accused of holding, namely that there is no foundation for morality in nature, but that it is simply laid down by decree of the sovereign ruler in a state. In maintaining that morality has a natural foundation, Cumberland also rejects the view that it is arbitrarily determined by divine decree. Cumberland formulates a principle of universal benevolence; he argues both that there is a natural inclination of that kind, and that an action is morally right if and only if it tends to promote the general good of all. In this respect he anticipates subsequent utilitarian theories.

De legibus naturae is a long and rambling treatise. Locke's friend James Tyrrell produced an abridged English version in 1692. A translation of the whole work by John Maxwell was published in 1727, and another by John Towers in 1750.

Cusa /'kjuːzə/, Nicholas of *See* NICHOLAS OF CUSA.

cybernetics (Gr. *kybernētēs* helmsman, steersman) *n. sing.* the general theory of self-regulating systems and control systems. The term was introduced in this sense by Norbert Wiener in 1947.

Cynic /'sɪnɪk/ *n.* The ancient Cynics, foremost among them Antisthenes, a follower of Socrates, and Diogenes of Sinope, advocated the view that nothing natural is shameful. Some went far in their contempt for conventional manners and morals, rejecting on principle even basic decencies – a few lurid anecdotes survive. This attitude was part of the quest for personal independence. It was for the sake of this that they strove to reduce their needs, to become indifferent to external conditions, and to maintain composure in the face of adversity. The goal was self-sufficiency (autarchy). Cynicism was never a fully elaborated doctrine but rather a way of life characterized by self-sufficiency and independence, advocated and practised by the members of this philosophical sect. Some of the ideas of the Cynics were taken up by the Stoics.

The name is related to the Greek *kyōn* dog, and derives from the name of the place in Athens where the doctrine was taught (*kynosarges*). A rival ancient opinion, less reliable, is that shameless immodesty, also to be found in the canine species, gave the school its name.

Other, modern, senses are: (a) an attitude of pessimistic disillusionment, especially about people's hidden ulterior motives; (b) a tendency to deal manipulatively with others, using them merely as means to further one's own ends. When used in these modern senses, the word is spelled with a lower-case c. **cynicism** *n.*

Cyrenaic /saɪrə'neɪɪk/ *adj.* The Cyrenaic school was so named after Aristippus of Cyrene, a follower of Socrates. It flourished in the fourth century BC. Its main concern was ethical: how to live a good life. It advocated the hedonistic doctrine that the pleasure of the moment is the highest good. In the development of this doctrine, a rationally led life of pleasure was the ideal, in contrast to the Cynic advocacy of abstinence.

D

dada(ism) *n.* an avant-garde artistic movement that began in Zürich during the First World War and swiftly spread to other European cities. Its anti-war and anti-bourgeois sentiments, which were inspired at least in part in reaction against the insanity of human mass sacrifice through exploitation and war, and against the hypocrisy of its defenders, was the basis for the radical challenge to established standards of art, rationality and morality. The dadaists produced stage-performances, poetry and photo-montages that seemed to be, or indeed were, nonsensical or nihilistic. The impulse came from Tristan Tzara, a Romanian poet who settled in France. Associated with dadaism were Marcel Duchamp, Jean Arp, Max Ernst, etc. Its most active years were 1916–22. In the early 1920s it was succeeded by surrealism. **dadaist** *adj.*

daimon /daɪmɒn/ (Gr. *daimōn* a spiritual being) *n.* a spiritual being that influences the fate of an individual. In Plato's dialogues, Socrates's daimon was an inner voice that warned him against unjust or unwise decisions (*Apol.* 21b, 33c; *Crito* 44a; *Phaedo* 60e; *Phaedrus* 242b). The word also signifies lesser divinities, e.g. Eros, in *Symposium* (202d–203a).

d'Alembert /dalɑ̃bɛːʀ (Fr.)/, Jean Le Rond (1717–83) An eminent mathematician, one of the luminaries of the French Enlightenment, he was, until 1759, together with Diderot, joint editor-in-chief of the *Encyclopédie* (1751–66). His *Preliminary Discourse* to the Encyclopedia outlines an empiricism derived from Bacon and Locke. In religious matters, his correspondence shows that he moved gradually from deism and agnosticism towards a materialistic atheism.

Darwinism The essence of the theory is revealed by the title of Charles Darwin's (1809–82) classical work *On the Origin of Species by Means of Natural Selection* 1859.

This work, and *The Descent of Man* 1871, provoked an intense debate. They seemed to invalidate the arguments from DESIGN for God's existence. These arguments had been proposed by the Stoics, they had enjoyed a remarkable vogue since the late seventeenth century, they had been restated in PALEY's *Natural Theology, or Evidences of the Existence and Attributes of the Deity* 1802, in the BRIDGEWATER TREATISES etc., and they had continued to enjoy general acceptance despite the powerful philosophical objections raised in Hume's *Dialogues Concerning Natural Religion* 1779 and Kant's *Critique of Pure Reason* 1781. The Darwinian account also increased the doubts about the biblical account of the Creation which had already been undermined by geology. There was also strong resistance to Darwinism since it was taken to detract from the pride and dignity of human beings. The major churches, however, gradually abandoned their initial condemnations, and their view of evolutionist biological theories is accommodating.

Dasein /ˈdaːzaɪn/ *n.* a standard German word for *existence*. (Literally, it means 'being-here' or 'being-there'.) JASPERS uses *Dasein* to signify existence in the ordinary sense, and reserves *Existenz* for the authentic mode of human existence. HEIDEGGER uses *Dasein* as a technical term for one kind of existence: the manner in which human individuals exist. The central distinguishing characteristic of existence of this kind is that it belongs only to those entities whose being is 'an issue' for them. The existence of individual objects is of a different kind. The account of the many distinctive features of *Dasein* is at the core of Heidegger's philosophy.

Heidegger uses many turns of phrase like '*Dasein* is a being that self-intends and self-interprets', '*Dasein's* forgetfulness', etc. It seems that '*Dasein*' is used to denote *individuals* (whose existence is of that kind) rather than *existence* of a certain kind. Some critics find this puzzling: people can interpret or forget – but can we say that their existence forgets or understands?

datum /ˈdeɪtəm; ˈdaːtəm/ (*sing.*); **data** /deɪtə; daːta/ (*pl.*) (Lat. *datum* given) *n.* **1** a piece of information. **2** a fact or a proposition from which inferences can be drawn. **3** something immediately presented to the mind. A sense-datum is something directly grasped by our senses.

Davidson, Donald (1917–) a major figure in American analytic philosophy, much influenced by Quine, under whom he studied at Harvard; latterly a professor at the University of California, Berkeley. Davidson's principal work is in the philosophy of language and its applications to the philosophy of mind and the philosophy of action. He has also written on Hume and Aristotle. Many of his influential articles have been re-published in his *Essays on Actions and Events* 1980 and *Inquiries into Truth and Interpretation* 1984. Davidson sought to apply Tarski's formal truth-theory to the semantics of natural language, emphasizing the idea that for a language to be learnable its semantics must depend on a finite number of axioms. He argued that an adequate semantics for a language should, in principle, show how from a finite set of axioms stating denotation and satisfaction-conditions for the basic vocabulary (names and general terms) of the language, along with rules governing truth-functional connectives ('and', 'or', 'not') and quantifiers ('all', 'some'), together with rules for well-formedness of sentences, the truth-conditions for each of an infinite number of declarative sentences of the language could be derived. These derived theorems are not of the form *s (a sentence) means that p* but, following Tarski, *s is true if and only if p*. In effect, the meaning of a sentence is given by the conditions under which it is true. Davidson's semantics has been worked out in practice only for tiny fragments of English, though he himself offered a detailed analysis of the logical form of sentences containing action-verbs.

Davidson's formal theory of meaning is supplemented by a theory of interpretation. In interpreting the language of a native speaker, according to Davidson, we presuppose ideals of rationality and adopt a principle of charity (CHARITY, PRINCIPLE OF), in trying to make sense of the speaker's utterances. These normative principles of rationality cannot be assimilated into a purely scientific discourse. Yet they are crucial, on Davidson's view, to what it is to be human and indeed to have mental states. Assigning meanings to utterances, intentions to actions, and mental states such as beliefs and desires to agents, are all subject to a holistic explanation which assumes that humans are rational for the most part and have an overall coherence in what they think, say and do. Davidson also uses this argument as a basis for the rejection of extreme scepticism, the view that all beliefs about the world might be false.

In the philosophy of mind, Davidson holds a version of non-reductive materialism which he has called anomalous monism. Although each mental event is identical with some neurophysiological event, there are no true universal statements of the form 'mental events of kind F are identical with neurophysiological events of kind G'. Similarly, although every action is caused by beliefs and desires, there are no universal laws connecting beliefs and desires to actions. Psychology is not reducible to physics. PL

de /deɪ/ *prep.* **1** Lat. from; about, concerning. The word often occurs in book titles of learned works written in Latin. The standard form was '*n* books concerning . . .', as in the title of Grotius's major work, *De iure belli ac pacis libri tres* (Three books concerning the law of war and peace). **2** /də (Fr.)/ Fr. of, from.

debatable *See* ARGUABLE.

decisionism *n.* the view that in a given area, such as morality, politics or law, there are no ultimate objective grounds for reaching a decision.

The German *Dezisionismus* was coined by Carl Schmitt and the term is often used to allude to his theory of political amoralism. In a different sense, the term can be used as a near-synonym of (moral) NON-COGNITIVISM.

decision problem A decision procedure is a procedure for determining whether an object belongs to a particular class. The procedure must be formulated in terms of mechanically applicable rules and be capable of yielding a definite answer in a finite number of steps in each case. The question whether there is such a procedure for a given class is called the *decision problem* for that class. If there is such a procedure, the decision problem for that class is said to be *solvable*, and the class is said to be *decidable*; if there is not, the decision problem is said to be *unsolvable*, and the class is said to be *undecidable*. Of particular interest is the decision problem for the class of valid formulae in a logical system. The decision problem for the class of valid formulae of the standard two-valued propositional calculus is solvable (e.g. by the method of truth-tables); that for the class of valid formulae of first-order predicate calculus is not. GH

deconstruction *n.* a form of textual analysis, usually combined with theoretical revision. Its aim is to unmask and overcome hidden (conceptual or theoretical) privilege. Deconstructive activity seeks to show that key concepts used in texts of various kinds (philosophical, literary, legal, theological, etc.) suppress an opposite concept which in fact they presuppose. To give some examples, each of the concepts of reason, the transcendent, the male, the sacred, is linked to and presupposes an opposite that is marginalized, excluded, suppressed and hidden: respectively passion, the empirical, the female, and the profane. And yet, the privileged concept could not even make sense without presupposing its opposite. One important stage or aspect of deconstruction consists in undermining the primacy of a concept by showing that priority genuinely rests with the suppressed concept, since it is presupposed by the privileged one. By this reversal, primacy is then assigned to the formerly suppressed concept. Or, privilege is replaced by equality at a second stage of deconstruction in which the conflicting claims to privileged status are resolved by a new concept which can incorporate the two former opposites, somewhat in the manner of a Hegelian synthesis.

As a reading technique, deconstruction seeks to take a text apart in order to show how it inevitably works against itself. The words used in the text have, as it were, a hidden agenda which destabilizes the ostensible meaning of the text. Ultimately, the very notion that the text has a definite meaning becomes problematic.

This is a key concept in the writings of Jacques DERRIDA. Among leading literary theorists practising this method, many of whom have been associated with Yale and Johns Hopkins universities, are Paul de Man, Geoffrey Hartman, J. Hillis Miller, Harold Bloom and Stanley Fish.

It has been thought that Derrida's theorizing implies that there can be no determinate explanation of deconstruction. If this should be the case, what has been stated so far must of course be taken with a grain of salt. On this point, hostile critics seem to agree with sympathetic observers, one of whom has written that the very appearance of 'deconstruction' in an encyclopedia is paradoxical, since various passages in Derrida make it clear that to provide an explanation or definition of this notion proves that it has not been properly understood, even if some people have been 'driven to definitions'. It has also been observed that 'Derrida has the problem of saying what he means without meaning what he says.' JA

decorum /dɪˈkɔːrəm/ Lat. proper, fitting, becoming, seemly *n.*, *adj.* The *decorum* are those actions that deserve approval although they are not perfect or imperfect duties. *Decorum* has been contrasted with the *justum* (the duties of justice, the perfect duties) and the *honestum* (the duties of morality, the imperfect duties). The terms were defined differently by THOMASIUS.

de dicto; de re /deɪ ˈdɪktəʊ; deɪ ˈreɪ/ Lat. concerning a statement; concerning a thing. The distinction arises in connection with certain terms which can be used either (*de re*) to modify a predicate which is asserted to belong to a subject, or (*de dicto*) to make some assertion about the subject-predicate statement as a whole. Some examples may make this clearer.

(1) 'Someone is bound to win the prize' is ambiguous. It may mean that what is asserted by the statement 'Someone wins the prize' is bound to be the case; this is the *de dicto* interpretation. Or it may mean that there is some specific person who is bound to win the prize; this is the *de re* interpretation, since it attributes *being bound to win the prize* to some *thing*. It is easy to envisage circumstances in which the former would be true but the latter false.

(2) If 'Some white thing could have been black' if taken, *de dicto*, to mean that the statement 'Something that is white is also black' expresses a possibility, it is false; but if it is taken, *de re*, to mean that there is something which is in fact white but might become, or might have been, black instead, it is true.

(3) Suppose it is known that someone was here yesterday, but not known who this was. Then the *de dicto* proposition 'It is known that someone was here yesterday' is true, but the corresponding *de re* proposition 'Someone is known to have been here yesterday' is false.

There are many other terms besides 'bound to', 'possible' and 'known' in connection with which the *de re/de dicto* distinction can be drawn. Some philosophers, however, believe that all *de re* propositions can be analysed into *de dicto* ones, though others deny this.

The distinction itself goes back to Aristotle. The terms '*de re*' and '*de dicto*' are found in the Middle Ages, and may have originated then. Medieval logicians themselves, however, more frequently used the terms '*in sensu diviso*' ('in a divided sense') and '*in sensu composito*' ('in a compounded sense') instead of '*de re*' and '*de dicto*' respectively. (In medieval logic 'dictum' was a technical term for a noun-clause or noun-phrase corresponding to an indicative statement; e.g. the dictum of 'Something white is black' could be 'that something white is black' or 'for something white to be black'. In Latin an accusative-with-infinitive construction was normally used.) GH

deduction *n.* The premisses in a deduction do not have to be general, or necessary. But in that respect, older concepts of deduction differed:
1 a deduction is a valid inference from *necessary* premisses. This is a traditional concept of deduction. Descartes defined it as an operation by which we have insight into something which follows necessarily from other things that are known with certainty (Rule III in *Règles pour la direction de l'esprit* (Rules for the direction of the mind)). **2** a deduction is a valid inference from more *general* premisses to a less general, i.e. a more specific, conclusion. It is contrasted with induction, which is an inference from particular instances to a general conclusion. This is the classical Aristotelian concept. **3** (in older jurisprudence) a deduction establishes the legal, in contradistinction to the factual, grounds for action in a court of law. This is the sense used metaphorically by Kant in the *Critique of Pure Reason*. His 'transcendental deduction' of the categories is the justification of the application of the categories to objects, i.e. the account of why the categories necessarily apply to all objects of experience. **4** in the modern sense, a valid deduction or a valid deductive inference is one in which the conclusion is a necessary consequence of the premisses, so that the conclusion cannot be false if all the premisses are true. In contrast, the conclusion of a sound INDUCTION is supported by the premisses and may be very probable, given the premisses, but it can be false even if all the premisses are true.

deduction, natural *See* NATURAL DEDUCTION.

deduction theorem In systems of formal logic, a deduction theorem is the counterpart to conditionalizing a valid argument in such a way that the conclusion of the argument is turned into the consequent of a conditional statement. As an example, take: 'All believers are saved; John is a believer; Therefore, John is saved.' This is a valid argument. Therefore, the following is also a valid argument. 'All believers are saved; Therefore, if John is a believer, then John is saved.' And the following is a necessary truth: 'If all believers are saved, then, if John is a believer, John is saved.'

Similarly, for many systems of propositional logic which include an operator for the conditional, a deduction theorem can be proved. It is a metatheorem, a theorem *about* the proofs and theorems in the system. It states that if in the system a formula B can be derived from well-formed formulas $A_1, A_2, \ldots A_n$, then $A_n \supset B$ can be derived from $A_1, A_2, \ldots A_{n-1}$; and $A_{n-1} \supset (A_n \supset B)$ can be derived from $A_1, A_2, \ldots A_{n-2}$; and so on; and $A_1 \supset (A_2 \supset (\ldots \supset (A_n \supset B) \ldots))$ is a theorem. *See also* CONDITIONAL PROOF.

deductive inference *See* DEDUCTION.

deductive logic the study of, or a system of, the principles of sound deductive inferences.

Deep Ecology an environmental movement with a philosophical core founded and given its name in 1973 by the Norwegian philosopher Arne NAESS. It combines practical prescriptions with normative principles. The philosophical core of Deep Ecology is called *ecosophy*, from the Greek words for 'household' and 'wisdom'. Ecosophy is the wisdom of living in harmony with what is one's household in the broadest sense, that is, nature. Fundamentally, a holistic view of nature is implied: even the boundary between a person and everything else is of no ultimate significance – all is a seamless whole. Natural things other than human beings have value in themselves, and are sometimes worth more than human beings or the things valued by human beings.

A precursor of Deep Ecology was Aldo Leopold, author of *The Conservation Ethic* 1933 and *Sand County Almanac* 1949. DB

de facto; de jure / deɪ 'fæktəʊ; deɪ 'dʒʊəreɪ/ (Lat. *de + factum* deed, fact; *ius* law, right) These two expressions mark the contrast between what actually exists and what is lawful. A person can be married *de facto* or *de jure*; a usurping group of revolutionaries may gain international recognition *de facto* or *de jure*.

definiens, definiendum *See* DEFINITION.

definist fallacy an alternative name (proposed by W. Frankena) for an error labelled 'the NATURALISTIC FALLACY' by G. E. Moore in *Principia Ethica* 1903. Among the various ways in which Moore had described the fallacy, the one which in Frankena's view catches its essence is that it consists in trying to define an indefinable concept.

definite descriptions, theory of A definite description is a phrase of the form 'the φ', where φ is a singular common noun or noun-phrase.

The 'theory of (definite) descriptions' is the name commonly given to a certain kind of analysis, due chiefly to Bertrand Russell, of propositions in which definite descriptions occur. According to this account, what a proposition of the form 'The φ is γ' means is 'There is exactly one thing which is φ and that thing is γ', or equivalently, and in some ways more conveniently, 'At least one thing is φ, at most one thing is φ, and whatever is φ is γ'. Thus, using Russell's example, which has become famous, 'The King of France is bald' means 'There is at least one King of France, there is at most one King of France, and whatever is a King of France is bald'. This type of analysis can easily be extended to other types of proposition containing definite descriptions. In general, 'The φ is the γ' becomes 'Exactly one thing is φ, exactly one thing is γ, and whatever is φ is γ'.

Russell's earliest version of the theory was in a paper entitled 'On Denoting' in *Mind 14* (1905); its more developed form occurs in vol. 1 of Whitehead and Russell, *Principia Mathematica* 1910.

In this kind of analysis the definite description itself is not directly defined in the sense of being shown to be replaceable by some other expression. Rather it is given what is called a 'contextual definition', i.e. the proposition which contains it is treated as a whole and displayed as equivalent to one in which no definite description occurs at all, but which differs systematically from the original in other ways as well.

One important feature of the theory of descriptions is that it makes a clear distinction between (1) the contradictory of 'The φ is γ' and (2) 'The φ is not γ'. The analysis given above of 'The King of France is bald', for example, shows that its contradictory is 'Either there is no King of France at all, or there is more than one King of France, or there is a King of France who is not bald'; but by a parallel analysis 'The King of France is not bald' becomes 'There is exactly one King of France and he is not bald', which says something importantly different.

One merit which many philosophers have seen in the theory of descriptions is that it shows clearly how to locate the fallacy in the following argument: ' "The φ is γ" and "The φ is not γ" are contradictories. Hence, one of them must be true. *But each implies that something is a φ.* Therefore, there is a φ (a King of France, a round square, a golden mountain, etc. etc.).' For by the theory, the first premiss is false. 'The φ is γ' and 'The φ is not γ' are not contradictories and can be false together; and in fact they both will be false if there is no φ at all or if there is more than one φ. GH

definition *n.* 1 a statement of what a thing is: a statement which states the essential properties of the things to which a given concept applies. Such a statement is called a real definition. 2 a statement concerning linguistic meaning, which states that the meaning of the expression to be defined (the *definiendum*) is the same as the meaning of the defining expression (the *definiens*).

There is an important distinction between reportive and stipulative definitions. A *reportive definition* states that a given linguistic expression has a certain meaning. Such a statement can be correct or incorrect. A *stipulative definition* lays down that a given linguistic expression is to have a certain meaning. This is why stipulative definitions cannot be said to be correct or incorrect.

The definitions mentioned so far can all be described as direct definitions of the explicit kind: definiens can replace definiendum without further ado. Another kind of direct definition are the contextual ones. In a contextual definition, only the whole statement containing the definiens can replace the whole statement containing the definiendum.

The other type, indirect definitions, includes implicit definitions and recursive definitions. The undefined terms in a set of axioms are often said to be implicitly defined by the axioms. An example of a recursive definition is: 'y is an ancestor of x $=_{df}$ y is a parent of x, or y is a parent of an ancestor of x'.

In a derived sense, there are also *ostensive* (or *deictic*) definitions: they explain what an expression means by pointing to an object, action, event, etc. denoted by the expression.

Controversies in philosophy, for example about the nature of *entailment*, *personhood*, *violence*, often deal with substantive issues, although they are formulated as if they concerned definitions.

de gustibus non disputandum /deɪ 'gʌstɪbəs nɒn dɪspju'tændəm/ Lat. matters of taste are not open to argument.

deictic *adj.* /'daɪktɪk/ (Gr. *deiktikos* demonstrative) This word and its noun (*deixis* /'daɪksɪs/ (Gr. demonstration)) have two related senses, like *demonstrate* and its cognates. One sense is that of *pointing out* directly, the other is that of *proving* directly, with the antonym *elenctic*.

deictic definition *See* OSTENSIVE DEFINITION.

deictic expression words like 'here', 'that one', 'now'. Their reference depends on the situation in which they are uttered. In philosophy, the term more commonly used is *indexical*.

deictic proof direct proof. In the terminology of ancient logic, the contrast between deictic proof and elenctic proof is that between direct and indirect proof. In the former, the conclusion is derived directly from the premisses; in the latter, the negation of the conclusion is refuted.

deism /'diːɪzm; 'deɪɪzm/ (Lat. *deus* god) *n.* belief in God as a perfect personal being; differs from THEISM by not accepting doctrines that require belief in revelation.

Post-Reformation religious conflicts led many thinkers to attempt systems of NATURAL RELIGION which would be based on rational insight, independently of any revelation, and therefore universally acceptable. They were also driven in this direction by the difficulties arising from the attempts to reconcile reason and religion. The word *deism*, which can be traced back to French writings in the 1560s, was used for many of these systems. (So was the word *theism*: its modern sense is quite recent.)

Herbert of Cherbury is commonly regarded as the first English thinker to have provided a formulation of deism, in the 1620s. He held that there are five basic tenets or common notions of natural religion: (1) there is one supreme God; (2) God ought to be worshipped; (3) worship consists in virtue and piety; (4) wrongdoing should be repented; (5) there are divine rewards and punishments in this life and the next. These tenets are rationally knowable and constitute the basis for a true universal religion.

The main thrust of deism comes to expression in the titles of works like John Toland's (1670–1722) *Christianity not mysterious: or a treatise showing that there is nothing in the Gospel contrary to reason, nor above it: and that no Christian doctrine can be properly called a mystery* 1696, and Mathew Tindal's (*c.* 1657–1733) *Christianity as old as the creation: or, the Gospel the republication of the religion of nature* 1730. True religion is identified with Christianity – but a reinterpreted 'rational' Christianity which has no place for any special revelation. A classical formulation of a deistic view is Rousseau's 'The profession of faith of the Savoyard vicar' in Book 4 of his *Emile* 1762.

deixis *See* DEICTIC.

Deleuze /dəløːz (Fr.)/, Gilles (1925–95) One of the most influential post-war French philosophers, Deleuze, who retired from his chair in philosophy at the University of Paris in 1987, is most widely known for his work with the psychoanalyst Félix Guattari (1930–92): their critique of the prevailing Freudian-Marxist orthodoxy among the post-1968 left intelligentsia – *L'Anti-Oedipe* 1972 (Anti-Oedipus) – was a *succès de scandale*. It laid the groundwork for a collaborative attempt to develop a new style of thought and writing which was pursued in *Kafka: pour une littérature mineure* 1975 (Kafka: towards a minor literature) and in *Mille Plateaux* 1980 (*A Thousand Plateaus*). The final product of this partnership, *Qu'est-ce que la philosophie?* (What is philosophy?), outlines the vision of philosophy as a process of creating concepts which informed the earlier works.

Deleuze's earlier *Nietzsche et la philosophie* 1962 (*Nietzsche and philosophy*) is credited with having inaugurated the considerable influence of Nietzsche on post-structuralist French philosophy. He also published a series of monographs on Hume, Proust, Kant and Bergsonism. However, his major philosophical work is contained in three books published at the end of the 1960s: *Différence et répétition* 1968 (Difference and repetition), *Spinoza et le problème de l'expression* 1968 (transl. as *Expressionism in Philosophy: Spinoza*) and *Logique du sens* 1969 (The logic of sense). *Différence et répétition* draws upon the earlier studies in the history of philosophy, as well as upon aspects of contemporary science and art, in order to weave together a physics and a metaphysics of difference. This enterprise is also presented as being a critique of the philosophy of representation which has dominated European thought since Plato. For Deleuze, experience is not the representation of a transcendental object by means of intuitions and concepts, but the expression or actualization of Ideas by means of a complex process of 'differentiation'. The metaphysics is 'grounded' only in the repetition of ideal problems, which are themselves defined in terms of differences, and which therefore amount precisely to a non-ground or groundlessness. *The Logic of Sense* develops a parallel theory of meaning, with reference to Lewis Carroll, as generated by the absence of meaning, i.e. non-sense, and revealed in paradoxes.

Since then, Deleuze continued to develop his vision of philosophy as the creation of concepts in relation to a variety of non-philosophical activities, including theatre (*Superpositions*, with C. Bene 1979), painting (*Francis Bacon: logique de la sensation* 1981) and cinema (*Cinéma 1 – L'image-mouvement* 1983 and *Cinéma 2 – L'image-temps* 1985). He also published a book on Foucault, an essay on Leibniz (*Le Pli* 1988 (*The fold: Leibniz and the Baroque*)), a collection of interviews (*Pourparlers* 1990), and a collection of essays, *Critique et clinique* 1993. PP

de Maistre /də mɛstʀ (Fr.)/, Joseph (1753–1821) Savoyard political thinker. He directed sharp and eloquent attacks on the democratic and egalitarian ideas of the French Revolution and on its reforming spirit, favouring traditional authority, ultimately with a religious basis (*Considérations sur la France* 1796). His book on popular sovereignty closely examined Rousseau's political thought and rejected it. He presented a spirited defence of the dogma of papal infallibility in *Du Pape* 1819 (On the pope); he rose in support of the Spanish Inquisition, which had for a while been abolished by liberal reformers; he defended traditional family values, argued for the legal subordination of women, and extolled the glorious task assigned to the public executioner. Starting from the plausible premiss of man's weakness and corruptibility, his writings remain of interest as they develop a clearly articulated opposition to democratic political ideals and, as hinted at in the title of Isaiah Berlin's 'Joseph de Maistre and the origins of fascism' (in *The Crooked Timber of Humanity* 1990), they are not without present-day relevance.

Demiurge /ˈdɛmɪɜːdʒ/ (Gr. *dēmiourgos* worker, craftsman) In Plato's dialogue *Timaeus*, the artificer of the world. The Demiurge is not all-powerful, but does as best he can, given the constraints imposed by the Forms and by Necessity. In Gnostic speculation, he is an inferior deity, subordinate to the highest God, producer of the sensible world, and thus the originator of imperfection and evil.

democracy (Gr. *dēmokratia* rule by the people) *n.* **1** a system of government in which all citizens are entitled to participate in political decision-making, be it directly, or indirectly through elected representatives. **2** a state democratically governed.

Although in the modern world the rule of law and respect for basic human rights is chiefly to be found in democracies, there is no necessary connection between the two. Democracy has had a bad reputation since ancient times when it was direct and often led to a tyranny of the majority in which the rule of the many replaced the rule of law. During the last two centuries, it is indirect, representative democracy that has come to be more widely regarded as a desirable system of government.

Democritus /dɪˈmɒkrɪtəs/ (*c.* 460–371 BC) ancient Greek philosopher of Abdera, who developed atomism as a major philosophical theory. Apparently deriving his principles from Leucippus, about whom little is known, he wrote many works developing and applying atomism. He accepted Parmenides's argument that there is no generation or destruction, but he rejected the further argument that there is no motion. Motion is made possible by a void, which is a kind of not-being, but not nothing at all. In the infinite void an infinite number of everlasting microscopic particles, the atoms, move about. The atoms are solid and internally unchanging, possessing infinitely various shapes and perhaps having the property of weight. Their motion is everlasting and uncaused. Atoms combine to form macroscopic objects, and the changes of macroscopic objects result from rearrangements of their component atoms. Just as many different words are composed of a few letters, so many kinds of substances can be composed of a few kinds of atoms.

In Democritus's cosmology, a chance concentration of atoms in empty space begins a circular motion impelled by collisions. The motion becomes a vortex surrounded by a spherical membrane, within which a cosmos, or world, is formed. Our cosmos consists of a flat Earth surrounded by heavenly bodies. There are innumerable worlds, each with its own arrangement, but we cannot see them because our own vision is limited by the membrane about our cosmos, within which the stars of our cosmos are located. In our cosmos, life arose from the seas and spread to land, where the human race arose and developed cultures and civilizations. Eventually our cosmos will perish like all other combinations of atoms.

Although Democritus uses human analogies to explain cosmic processes, he explains all natural events as the products of mechanical forces. Like substances combine in the cosmos as like sizes of pebbles are sifted out by the sea. Even the soul is a compound of atoms, in particular of fine, spherical atoms. Physical objects emit films of atoms from their surfaces, which strike the senses and are transmitted by atomic motions to the soul, accounting for sense-perception. Immoderate experiences cause imbalance in the soul, resulting in misery. Thus we should seek *euthymia* (equanimity, cheerfulness) by cultivating contentment and avoiding envy and emulation. This was the reason for his by-name 'the laughing philosopher'. The person who has equanimity will live in a lawlike manner and have a harmonious life in the state. Hence Democritus is able to derive a detailed, if rather conventional, ethical theory from his physical principles.

Democritus recognizes a tension between his physics and his account of knowledge. Our knowledge comes from sense-experience, but sense-experience is not able to reveal the atoms to us. We know the sensible qualities such as sweet, bitter, hot, cold, coloured, only by 'convention'. The real objects and their real qualities are not perceived. Moreover, our perception changes with our physical state. But if we reject the senses, we seem to have no knowledge at all. Consequently, Democritus distinguishes between 'bastard' knowledge deriving from the senses, and legitimate knowledge deriving apparently from reasoning. Our knowledge of the atoms must be of the latter kind.

Although Democritus had no immediate successors, his theory was revived later by Epicurus, who put it to use as the basis of his philosophy of consolation. Through the Epicurean school atomist ideas were conveyed to the early modern period, when they became the basis of philosophical and scientific theories from which the present atomic theory of matter is descended. DG

demonstration *n.* demonstrative knowledge is indirect, attained by proof, in contrast to intuition, i.e. immediate knowledge. The contrast has been marked in these terms by many philosophers, including Locke (*Essay Concerning Human Understanding*, 4,2) and Hume (*Treatise of Human Nature* 1,3,1).

Another contrast, in Hume, is between demonstrative knowledge which is indubitable since its denial implies a self-contradiction, and more or less probable beliefs about matters of fact.

de Morgan's laws two logical rules, stated by Ockham in the fourteenth century, by Geulincx in the seventeenth, but now named after the nineteenth-century logician Augustus de Morgan (1806–71). As rules or as theorems, the two laws belong to standard propositional logic: (1) not-(p and q) is equivalent to not-p or not-q; (2) not-(p or q) is equivalent to not-p and not-q. In other words, the negation of a conjunction implies, and is implied by, the disjunction of the negated conjuncts. And the negation of a disjunction implies, and is implied by, the conjunction of the negated disjuncts.

demotic (Gr. *dēmos* (common) people) *adj.*, *n.* pertaining to ordinary speech, in contrast to a more literary or high-flown style. *Syn.* vernacular.

demythologize *vb.* the reinterpretation of a religious (political, historical, etc.) doctrine so that its mythical elements are not taken literally.

Demythologizing plays a very important part in the interpretation of Christian doctrine proposed by the German Protestant theologian Rudolf Bultmann (1884–1976). The aim is to show that the essentials of the faith are independent of the rationally more indigestible parts of the traditional dogma. Scripture should not be taken too literally. What really matters in the dogmas are those things which matter to the modern believer.

denial *See* NEGATION.

denotation *n.* A general term is said to *denote* each object to which it refers; a singular term or a proper name is said to *designate* that to which it refers. Some writers do not make this terminological distinction, but say also of singular terms that they denote. *See also* CONNOTATION.

dénouement /deɪˈnuːmã (Eng.); denumɑ̃ (Fr.)/ Fr. an untying. (in literature and drama) the unravelling of a plot, the resolution of themes in a story.

de novo /deɪ ˈnəʊvəʊ/ Lat. anew, afresh.

dense order (in mathematics) a dense order is one in which, between any two elements, there is another. For example, the order of rational numbers (i.e. fractions) is dense. The order of integers is not dense: there is no integer greater than 11 and smaller than 12.

denumerable *adj.* a set is said to be denumerable if and only if its members can be put in a one-to-one correspondence with the positive integers. The definition implies that all denumerable sets are infinite, since there are infinitely many positive integers. But some writers also call finite sets denumerable, making the term synonymous with *countable*.

denying the antecedent a kind of fallacious reasoning. This is an example: 'If Jill loves Jack, she cooks his meals; Jill does not love Jack; Therefore, Jill does not cook Jack's meals.'

This is a fallacy. The conclusion can be false even if the premisses are true. Jill may fall out of love, say, and yet carry on grimly with her domestic chores.

The general form of the fallacy is:

$$\frac{\text{If A then B} \quad \text{Not A}}{\text{Not B}}$$

Note, however, that by replacing 'If' above with 'Only if' the resulting argument-form would be valid.

deo gratias Lat. thanks to God.

deontic /diːˈɒntɪk/ (Gr. *to deon* fit, fitting, becoming, proper) *adj.* pertaining to the concepts of permissibility and obligatoriness. The word was introduced by G. H. von Wright in his pioneering article 'Deontic Logic', *Mind 60* (1951). It was suggested to him by C. D. Broad.

deontic concepts the concepts of permissibility and obligatoriness. These can be expressed e.g. by *may*, *must*, *shall*, etc. They are sometimes called *deontic modalities*, and their logic shows certain analogies with the logic of necessity and possibility. Deontic concepts can be compared and contrasted with *normative* concepts, of which *right* and *wrong* are among the most general, and *axiological* concepts of *good* and *bad*, *good* and *evil*, etc.

deontic hexagon a diagram, similar in nature to the square of opposition for CATEGORICAL propositions which sets out the basic logical relations between simple deontic statements. It seems first to have been devised in the mid-twentieth century. Arrows symbolize implication; forks symbolize contradiction (see Figure 1).

deontic logic the logic of deontic statements. This inquiry can be said to have commenced with von Wright's 1951 article (see DEONTIC), although there had been anticipations in writings by Ernst Mally in the 1920s, and, much earlier, in Bentham and Leibniz.

deontic modalities *See* DEONTIC CONCEPTS.

deontic sentences Deontic sentences are used to affirm or deny that a certain action or state of affairs is obligatory or is permissible. Simple deontic sentences can be schematically represented by the forms *May p*, *Shall p* and their negations.

deontological *adj.* Moral theories according to which the rightness or obligatoriness of at least some actions – the fulfilment of a promise, say – is not exclusively determined by the overall value of the consequences have been called deontological. The contrasting term is TELEOLOGICAL.

Note: The use of this pair of terms to mark the contrast non-consequentalism/consequentialism seems infelicitious. As the terms are defined, Benthams's deontology is not deontological, and, even more strangely, Aristotle's ethics is not teleological.

Note: C. D. Broad first used the terms in 1930 for two different applications of 'ought': to say that an action of a certain type ought to be done regardless of the value of the probable consequences, is to make a deontological application of 'ought'. In contrast, to say that everyone

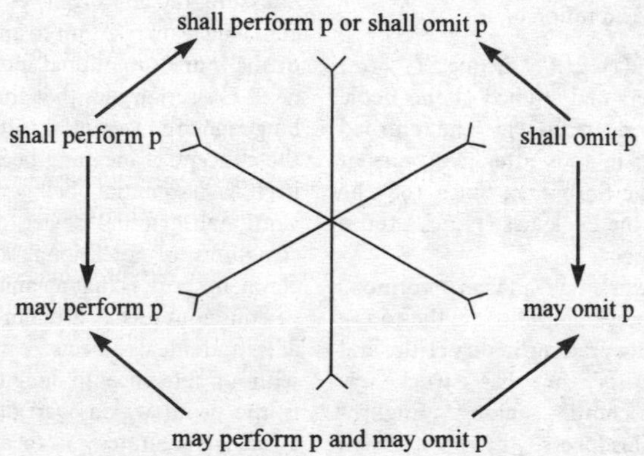

Figure 1 The logical relations between simple deontic statements

ought to act so as to promote a specified ultimate end (the agent's own happiness, or everyone's happiness, etc.), is to make a teleological application of 'ought'. In 1932, J. H. Muirhead used the terms for two 'points of view' in ethics.

deontology /diːɒn'tɒlədʒɪ/ *n.* 1 This word was devised by Jeremy Bentham (1748–1832), and used by him to mean the 'science of morality'. He also used the word as a name for his whole ethical theory, including both the basic principle of utility and a vast number of detailed applications. Bentham's *Deontology* 1834 was compiled by his editor in a way frowned upon by many of Bentham's followers, including John Stuart Mill. 2 a code of ethics for certain professions, e.g. the medical profession.

deo volente Lat. God willing.

De Rerum Natura /deɪ 'reərəm nə'tʃuːrə/ Lat. on the nature of things; a didactic philosophical work, written in hexameters by Lucretius about 50 BC.

derivation *n.* 1 (in logic generally) an inference. 2 (in Pareto) a rationalization, i.e. an ideological construction that serves the purpose of making a non-rational feeling or prejudice seem rational.

Derrida /dɛʀida (Fr.)/, Jacques (1930–) Born in Algiers and studied at the Ecole Normale Supérieure, to which he returned as a professor in 1965 after five years of teaching at the Sorbonne. Since 1985 he has taught at the Ecole des Hautes Etudes en Sciences Sociales.

Derrida's work has had an enormous vogue, perhaps waning a little in the 1990s, among English-speaking literary critics and 'critical theorists', but has struck few sympathetic chords among English-speaking philosophers, the most usual grounds given for rejecting it being that it is not merely incomprehensible but mystificatory, and that so far as it can be understood it represents an attempt to call into question the very possibility of rational inquiry.

For those who wish to undertake an independent assessment of the justice of these charges, the best place to start is probably at the beginning, with Derrida's earliest essay, *La Voix et le phénomène* 1967 (*Speech and Phenomena*). It is an attack on the theory of meaning expounded in the first of Edmund Husserl's *Logical Investigations* (1900–1901). Husserl there defends the view that meaning is primarily grasped by the mind through its apprehension of the intentional acts by which it constitutes ideal objects (numbers, physical objects considered as transcending sensation, etc.). The apprehension of meaning is therefore, on Husserl's view, something essentially timeless, transcendental and belonging to the inner life (the *pure Present*) of consciousness. Language, by contrast, is none of these things. The 'life' of linguistic signs is material, social, imbued with the histories constituted by particular languages and etymologies, and in general and essentially dependent upon features (indexicality, the structural patterns of difference noted by Saussure, the contingencies of metonymy, etc.) which are resistant to analysis in terms of the 'pure' intentional life of consciousness. Husserl argues that these features of language are inessential to the analysis of the concept of meaning because language itself is inessential, being merely a conventional, 'external' device for representing structures of intentional acts. Husserl's claim, in short, is that meaning, and the life of consciousness as a realm of intentional acts and ideal objects, can be specified without reference to language; and this is the claim which Derrida proceeds to attack. His strategy is to argue in detail not merely that the Husserlian 'inwardness' of intentionality and consciousness cannot be rigorously separated from the alleged 'externalities' of language, but that the entire project of Husserlian phenomenology is made possible only by a systematic dependence upon the supposedly 'inessential' resources of language: a dependence which the phenomenologist must therefore systematically disavow and relegate to the 'margins' of his/her theoretical life.

This last move contains in germ the central thought of DECONSTRUCTION, the critical method with which Derrida's name has come to be chiefly associated. To 'deconstruct' a theory or body of writing is to bring to light the considerations contrary to its view of things which it presupposes and yet effaces and marginalizes as a condition of its existence. Deconstruction is made necessary by the tendency (of which Husserl's theory of signs is a striking example, but which, Derrida claims, descends from Plato's *Cratylus* and is endemic in the Western philosophical tradition) to seek to privilege the terms of a favoured conceptual scheme by grounding them in some source of meaning outside language. This is what Derrida calls *logocentrism*. Logocentrism involves the privileging of speech over writing, the ideal and extra-temporal over the material and temporal, and the private intentions of speakers on particular occasions over what is public and repeatable (*iterable*) in our use of signs. Some critics, and some philosophers, have taken Derrida's critique of logocentrism to imply that no utterance can have any determinate meaning or relationship to reality, and therefore that rational discourse and the pursuit of truth are impossible. Derrida's reply, hinted at in a recent interview, would perhaps be that the concept of rationality is no more ideal or atemporal in character than any other concept, and that deconstruction releases us from the ossification of thought involved in thinking that a favoured conceptual scheme is privileged over others by virtue of being extralinguistically grounded. It may thus constitute not so much a demonstration of the vacuity of the concept of rationality as an invitation to contemplate extending the range of the concept to admit new forms of rationality.

Some works by Derrida: *La Voix et le phénomène* 1967 (*Speech and Phenomena*); *De la Grammatologie* 1967 (*Of Grammatology*); *L'Écriture et la différence* 1967 (*Writing and Difference*); *Marges de la philosophie* 1972 (*Margins of Philosophy*); *La Dissémination* 1972 (*Dissemination*); *Glas* 1974; *La Vérité en peinture* 1978 (*The Truth in Painting*); *La Carte postale* 1980 (*The Postcard*); *Psyche* 1987; *De l'Esprit* 1989 (Of spirit). BHA

de Ruggiero /de ru'dʒero (It.)/, Guido (1888–1948) Italian philosopher, adherent of actualism, a variety of idealism similar to Gentile's. Author of a major history of philosophy. His *Storia del liberalismo* 1925 (transl. as *History of European Liberalism*) was translated by R. G. Collingwood.

Descartes /'deɪkaːt (Eng.); dekaʀt (Fr.)/, René (1596–1650) Universally acknowledged as one of the chief architects of the modern age, Descartes bequeathed two principal doctrines to the philosophical world. The first was a comprehensive physico-mathematical reductionism: all observed phenomena were ultimately to be explained by reference to the interactions of particles describable solely in terms of size, shape and motion. The second was a conception of the mind as lying outside the purview of physics – a phenomenon *sui generis* whose nature could be grasped only from within, via introspective reflection.

René Descartes was born in the town between Tours and Poitiers (formerly La Haye) which now bears his name. He was educated by the Jesuits at the newly founded college of La Flèche, where he received a firm grounding in the scholastic philosophy he was later to challenge. As a young man, he was roused from his dogmatic slumbers by the Dutch mathematician Isaac Beeckman. 'You alone,' he wrote to Beeckman in 1619, 'aroused me from my state of indolence'; he went on to speak of the 'gigantic task' which he had set himself, that of producing a 'completely new science, which would provide a general solution to all possible equations involving any sort of quantity'. The vision of a complete, mathematically based physics was one which finally found expression in the mammoth *Principles of Philosophy*, published in Latin in 1644. Here Descartes outlined an explanatory schema, based on a simple definition of matter as 'extended substance' (that which has length, breadth and depth), and such that all the various forms and qualities of observed phenomena could be accounted for merely by reference to the geometrical properties of size and shape, plus certain fundamental covering laws (such as the law of the conservation of motion). 'I freely acknowledge,' Descartes wrote at the end of Part II of the *Principles*, 'that I recognize no matter in corporeal things apart from that which the geometers call quantity, and take as the object of their demonstrations, i.e. that to which every kind of division, shape and motion is applicable. Moreover, my consideration of such matter involves absolutely nothing apart from these divisions, shapes and motions: and even with regard to these, I will admit as true only what has been deduced from indubitable common notions so evidently that it is fit to be considered as a mathematical demonstration.'

Elements of this mathematically inspired vision had been explored by Descartes in his early work, the *Regulae ad directionem ingenii* (Rules for the direction of the mind), written in the late 1620s (although not published until 1701). 'I came to see,' Descartes observes there, 'that the exclusive concern of mathematics is with questions of order or measure and that it is irrelevant whether the measure in question involves numbers, shapes, stars, sounds, or any object whatever. This made me realize that there must be a general science which explains all the points that can be raised concerning order and measure irrespective of the subject-matter.' Some of Descartes's early scientific work was concerned with pure mathematics, some with applied; and in a set of three essays which he released to the public anonymously in 1637, he provided examples of his new method in the fields of geometry, optics and meteorology. Prefaced to these 'specimen essays' was an extended intellectual autobiography (written in French), the *Discourse on the Method of Rightly conducting Reason and reaching the Truth in the Sciences*.

The *Discourse* is notable for its rejection of past authority and 'preconceived opinion', and for its appeal to the unclouded reflective insights of the ordinary person of 'good sense', that 'best distributed thing in the world'. Although Descartes insisted on the importance of observation and experiment in deciding between rival hypotheses, he maintained that the fundamental axioms of the new science were to be uncovered simply by the innate powers of the human intellect: 'I noticed certain laws which God has so established in nature, and of which he has implanted such notions in our minds, that after adequate reflection we cannot doubt that they are exactly observed in everything which exists or occurs in the world.' The appeal to God as implanter, and in a certain sense guarantor, of the relevant laws introduces a central theme of Cartesian philosophy: the vision of science as a unified system which is based on secure metaphysical foundations. Part IV of the *Discourse* outlines the route to such secure foundations, proceeding from Descartes's celebrated 'method of doubt'. Customary routes to knowledge, such as the deliverances of the senses, are rejected as unreliable, and instead a basis for certainty is sought in premisses that cannot be shaken by any sceptical hypothesis, however extreme. There then follows what is probably Descartes's best-known contribution to philosophy, the famous 'Cogito' argument: 'Immediately I noticed that while I was trying thus to think everything false, it was necessary that I, who was thinking this, was something. And observing that this truth "I am thinking therefore I exist" (*je pense, donc je suis*) was so firm and sure that all the most extravagant suppositions of the sceptics were incapable of shaking it, I decided that I could accept it without scruple as the first principle of the philosophy I was seeking.'

These reflections are considerably amplified in Descartes's metaphysical masterpiece, the *Meditations on First Philosophy*, written in Latin and published in Paris in 1641. The *Meditations* had been precirculated in manuscript to some of the leading philosophers and theologians of the day (including Thomas Hobbes, Antoine Arnauld and Pierre Gassendi), and their critical comments, together with Descartes's responses, formed the six sets of *Objections and Replies* which were included with the first edition (the definitive second edition, including a seventh set of Objections by the Jesuit Pierre Bourdin, appeared the following year in Amsterdam). In the *Meditations*, Descartes traces the path of the lonely meditator from doubt and disorientation to certain and reliable knowledge. Having doubted the very existence of the world around him (using the fiction of a supremely powerful deceiver 'who employs all his cunning in order to deceive me' – First Meditation), the meditator discovers one irrefutable certainty: 'let him deceive me as much as he can, he will never bring it about that I am nothing so long as I think that I am something'. It is then argued that the self of which I am aware is 'in the strict sense only a thing that thinks' (*res cogitans*), that is, a thing that 'doubts, understands, affirms, denies, is willing, is unwilling, imagines and senses' (Second Meditation). From a reflection on the ideas found within this conscious self, the meditator identifies one idea, that of an infinite and perfect being, whose content so far exceeds my capacity that I could not have constructed it from my own resources; it follows that the infinite being, God, really exists, and 'placed the idea of himself within me to be as it were the mark of the craftsman impressed on his work' (Third Meditation). A further proof of God's existence is later offered, based on the claim that existence is contained within the very definition or essence of a perfect being. This is Descartes's version of the so-called 'ontological argument' (Fifth Meditation). Having established the existence of God, the meditator is able to reconstruct solid foundations for knowledge, based on the mind's 'clear and distinct ideas', whose reliability is guaranteed by God; this opens the possibility of 'full and certain knowledge both of God and other things whose nature is intellectual, and also concerning the whole of that nature which is the subject-matter of pure mathematics' (Fifth Meditation).

The Cartesian programme of 'foundationalist metaphysics' has called forth endless debate and criticism, both in respect of the details of the controversial proofs of God's existence, and also by reason of an alleged structural flaw in the entire procedure: if God is to be used to underwrite the reliability of the mind's perceptions, how can we rely on the premisses needed to prove his existence in the first place? (This worry, known as the 'Cartesian circle', was first raised by Descartes's contemporary critics, Marin Mersenne and Antoine Arnauld.) Perhaps the most controversial part of Descartes's metaphysics, however, is the claim (made in the Sixth Meditation) that the nature of the mind as a pure thinking substance is entirely distinct from the nature of body, or extended substance, and hence 'it is certain that I am really distinct from the body, and can exist without it'. There are two main problems with Descartes's 'dualistic' theory of mind and body. The first is that, granted that Descartes has managed to form *some* conception of himself as a conscious being, without reference to the body, it remains to be shown that the conception so formed is logically complete and adequate, so that we can really have a coherent conception of the thinking self apart from any physical substrate (compare Arnauld's critique in the Fourth Set of Objections). The second problem concerns those aspects of our mental life, notably sensation and emotion, which bear testimony to the fact that we are, as Descartes himself conceded, 'not merely present in the body, but closely conjoined and intermingled with it'. In his last book, the *Passions of the Soul* 1649, Descartes explored this further. The work grew out of a correspondence with Elizabeth of Bohemia, in which he spoke of a 'substantial union' between mind and body: purely intellectual and volitional activities belonged to the mind alone, physiological events (such as digestion) to the body alone, but emotions and sensations could not be understood without reference to the union of the two. Descartes himself insisted that this union was a 'primitive notion', but was unable to give a clear account of its nature: while the concepts of mind and body were transparent to the intellect, the nature of the union simply had to be 'experienced'.

Twentieth-century critics such as Gilbert Ryle have argued that the Cartesian conception of a ghostly mind inhabiting a mechanical body is radically confused. Others, notably Ludwig Wittgenstein, have cast doubt on the very coherence of Descartes's assumption that an account of the mental can be given from the 'private', first-personal perspective of the solitary thinker. But although the tenor of philosophy today is largely anti-Cartesian, it remains true that the framework of the 'mind–body problem' is still very largely structured by the set of problems which Descartes uncovered about the nature of consciousness and its relation to the physical world. For better or for worse, Descartes's writings have exerted an enduring influence on our ideas of human nature, the place of man in the cosmos, and the nature of the philosophical enterprise itself.

Method of citation: by reference to volume and page of the standard edition: *Oeuvres de Descartes*, ed. C. Adam and P. Tannery, rev. edn 1964–76. JCM

descriptions, theory of *See* DEFINITE DESCRIPTIONS.

descriptive ethics inquiry into, or theory of, the moral beliefs, attitudes and practices of a group or a society.

descriptivism *n.* a theory, especially in meta-ethics, which commits what J. L. Austin called 'the descriptive fallacy', i.e. the error of supposing that the meaning of an utterance is descriptive when in fact it is not.

The word 'descriptivism' was introduced in 1963 by R. M. Hare in a paper so called, as a contrasting term to his own prescriptivism. He used it to characterize the view of some of his critics (Elizabeth Anscombe, Philippa Foot) who, in his view, were committing the descriptive fallacy in their rejection of his descriptive/evaluative dualism.

design, argument(s) from Arguments from design proceed by two major steps. The first infers from observations of the world around us the conclusion that there is a certain order or design among natural phenomena, and the second infers from this to the existence of a designer, who is identified with God. *See also* TELEOLOGICAL ARGUMENT(S).

designate *n.* a singular term or a proper name is said to designate that to which it refers. *See also* DENOTATION.

designator, rigid *See* RIGID DESIGNATOR.

detachment *n.* **1** impartiality; attitude of indifference. **2** (in logic) short for *rule of detachment*: from A ⊃ B and A, B can be inferred. This rule of inference is also known as MODUS PONENS. In natural deduction system it is called the rule of ⊃-elimination.

determinable/determinate *n., adj. Shape* is a determinable of which *square*, *round*, *oblong*, etc. are determinates. Similarly, *colour* is a determinable of which *red*, *green*, *blue*, etc. are determinates. Other determinables are *size*, *weight*, etc.

This contrast is different from that between genus and species. The genus *animal* and the specific difference *rational* together define the species *rational animal* (i.e. human beings). Here, the two predicates ('rational' and 'animal') can be defined independently of each other. This is not the case with determinables and determinates.

These concepts were known to medieval logicians, but the modern discussion began with W. E. Johnson's *Logic* 1921.

determinism/indeterminism *n.* Determinism is the thesis that all events and states of affairs are determined by antecedent events and states of affairs. This claim can be made precise in several different ways, and it is advisable in reading discussions of determinism to take careful account of each author's definition. The thesis has at its core the idea that everything that happens is *fully* determined by what has gone before it: every event has antecedent causes which were sufficient to ensure its occurrence. While many philosophers do admit the notion of a 'probabilistic' cause – that is, a cause which renders it probable to a given degree (less than 1) that the effect will follow – a world in which some events had merely probabilistic causes would not be a 'deterministic' world. For determinism to be true of a world, each and every event in that world must have a deterministic cause – i.e. a cause which *ensures* its occurrence.

Views about causation, then, affect the formulation of the thesis of determinism. So, for example, those who adopt a 'regularity' account of causation may typically formulate a basic thesis of determinism as the claim that, for every event or state of affairs *e*, there are antecedent events or states of affairs *c* such that the occurrence of *e* may be deduced from the occurrence of *c* plus a true statement of the (relevant) laws of nature. (Some philosophers would revise this to allow for the possibility of causes which are simultaneous with, rather than antecedent to, their effects.)

Determinism is often expressed in terms of predictability 'in principle', and this yields a distinct formulation of the thesis which is not entailed by the basic formulation just given. The idea is that if one were, *per impossibile*, to know everything that is true about the universe at a particular instant of time, and also have complete knowledge of the laws of nature, then, if determinism is true, one would be able to derive from this knowledge a true and complete account of the state of the universe at any subsequent time. A further, distinct formulation of the thesis may be obtained by omitting the qualification that the time about which knowledge is derived must be subsequent to the time at which the total state of the universe is presumed to be known. On this formulation, in a deterministic universe, its total state at *any* other time is deducible from knowledge of its total state at any one time, given complete knowledge of the universe's ways of working.

The contemporary physical theory of quantum mechanics postulates that the most fundamental level of reality is *indeterministic* – that is, that events at this level do not have determining causes, and are understandable as falling under statistical laws only. Newtonian physics remains, however, quite adequate for our practical dealings with the medium-sized objects of everyday experience, and so we do a lot of our ordinary explaining and predicting on the basis of the deterministic assumption which Newtonian physics makes.

Philosophical discussion of determinism has often been motivated by the question whether human freedom of action is possible if the universe behaves as (or, near enough as) a deterministic system. If everything I do has some prior event as its determining cause, how can any of it be a matter of my own free choice? If my current behaviour is fixed by the way things were long before I was born, and by the eternal laws of nature, surely the idea that I am freely in control of my own actions must be some kind of illusion? Philosophers who agree that there can be no free action in a deterministic world are known as *incompatibilists*. Those who go on to assert the existence of free action, and so to infer that the actual world is indeterministic, are known as *libertarians*, whereas those who affirm determinism and so conclude that freedom of action is illusory are known as *hard determinists*. Compatibilists maintain that freedom is possible under determinism, and, if they also affirm determinism, they are known as *soft determinists*. JB

deus ex machina /'deɪʊs ɛks 'mækɪnə/ Lat. a god (descending) from (stage) machinery. The god would disentangle a plot that had become too complicated for the merely human participants.

deus sive natura /'deɪʊs 'sɪveɪ nə'tjuːrə/ Lat. God or nature. Spinoza uses either term to designate the one substance in which all attributes and their modifications inhere.

Dewey /'djuːɪ/, John (1859–1952) John Dewey was born in Burlington, Vermont, and died in New York. He was for many years the best-known philosopher in the United States and was widely regarded as a kind of philosophical conscience to the American people. As with individual conscience, they rarely did what he advised them to do, but they had an uneasy feeling that he was generally right. He was one of the first generation of Americans to be able to do graduate work in America; after attending the University of Vermont, he took a PhD at Johns Hopkins University, where he was taught by C. S. Peirce, G. Stanley Hall, and George Sylvester Morris. In 1884, he began teaching at the University of Michigan; in 1894, he moved to the University of Chicago as head of its newly created department of philosophy, psychology and pedagogy; in 1904, he moved to Columbia University, where he remained until he retired in 1930. After retirement, he was an active emeritus professor, and only retired more thoroughly in 1939. He was married twice, fathered six children, and adopted three – unusually among philosophers, even among those who write at length about education, Dewey very much liked small children.

Dewey was a shy man; this may explain why his *Collected Works* run to 37 volumes – he was most at ease behind his battered typewriter. His work falls into three phases, though they are only loosely defined. He began (1880–95) by accepting a version of Idealism from which he was weaned by reading William James's *Principles of Psychology* 1891: he thereafter espoused what he variously called *pragmatism*, *instru-*

mentalism, and his favoured label, *experimentalism*. During the 1920s, his interests moved away from logical and epistemological issues towards religion, art, contemporary politics and the like. It was in these years that he wrote *Experience and Nature* 1925, *The Quest for Certainty* 1929, *Art as Experience* 1933 and *A Common Faith* 1934, and essays on politics such as *Liberalism and Social Action* 1935.

To the public at large, Dewey is best known as a theorist of education; he somewhat resented any suggestion that he was 'an educator', rightly believing himself to be a philosopher first and foremost. Still, the public's perception was not wholly wrong. At Chicago, Dewey created the Laboratory School, where the syllabus and teaching methods were designed around his philosophy of education. *The School and Society* 1899 was Dewey's first best-selling book, even though it began ostensibly as a simple report on the Lab School's first years of operation. It was followed by *The Child and the Curriculum* 1901, *How We Think* 1910, and *Democracy and Education* 1916. Dewey's view was that children neither had a fixed nature such that teachers could stand back and let them grow – what he thought of as the exaggeration of 'child-centred' education – nor had such plastic natures that teachers could simply mould them into anything they liked. Dewey believed that human thinking was essentially a matter of problem-solving; education was a matter of giving children the widest possible problem-solving skills. Because Dewey thought that human beings needed a social setting in order to flourish, these problem-solving skills included what one might call 'moral skills'.

Dewey's philosophical work defies ready classification. Although he wrote a very successful textbook on moral philosophy – *Ethics* 1908, rev. edn 1932 – it is mostly not concerned with the sort of issues that obsess most moral philosophers, such as the problem of deriving ought from is, or distinguishing the right from the good. Much of it is descriptive. What we are concerned to do is adjust ourselves to our environment and our environment to ourselves, and Dewey spends much of his time characterizing the ways in which we do it. Morality is not a search for ultimate principles by sophisticated reflection on what we already do. The same intellectual approach is visible at what one might think of as the other end of the intellectual spectrum in *Logic: The Theory of Inquiry* 1938. The philosophy of science starts from the fact that science is already an ongoing social activity; there is no real room for philosophers to tell scientists how to conduct their own operations – for why should they take any notice of such advice? What philosophy can do is give a general description of what the internal logic of such an activity is, and thus of where it fits in among all the other ways in which we approach the world.

This allowed Dewey to argue with a confidence unusual in the twentieth century that different ways of understanding the world might be complementary to, rather than competitive with, each other; thus art (*Art as Experience* 1934) and religion (*A Common Faith* 1934) were genuinely concerned with an 'objective' reality rather than merely 'subjective' sentiments. Dewey was eager to reassure his readers that they were not adrift in a cold and alien world, and that the comforts of poetry, religion and art were not private consolations, but as reputable in their own way as science and mathematics themselves. This lent all his work a somewhat preacherly tone that is nowadays unfashionable, but the intrinsic interest of his ideas has gained Dewey many admirers in recent years. AR

diachronic /daɪə'krɒnɪk/ (Gr. *dia-* through, throughout + *chronos* time) *adj.* pertaining to change over time. The term, together with its antonym SYNCHRONIC, gained currency through Ferdinand de SAUSSURE, who used them to distinguish two kinds of linguistic theory: one concerned with the evolution of language, the other with its structure.

diagonal procedure a proof device in mathematics and logic. It was invented by G. Cantor (1845–1918), who used it to prove, *inter alia*, that the infinite set of real numbers is greater than the infinite set of natural numbers, in the sense that the real numbers cannot be brought into a one-to-one correspondence with the natural numbers; in other words, that the set of real numbers is non-denumerable.

The proof starts with the assumption that the real numbers *can* be brought into a one-to-one correspondence with the natural numbers, and derives the denial of the assumption, thereby refuting it.

Every real number can be represented as an infinite decimal fraction (and every infinite decimal fraction represents a real number). Assume that the real numbers *can* be brought into a one-to-one correspondence with the natural numbers. If so, in a list with line-numbers 1,2,3, . . . , every real number would occur sooner or later.

The beginning of the list could look like this (where every ‘x’ is one of the numbers 0, 1, 2, . . .9):

1 0. $x_{11}\ x_{12}\ x_{13}\ x_{14} \ldots x_{1n}$ . . . . . .
2 0. $x_{21}\ x_{22}\ x_{23}\ x_{24} \ldots x_{2n}$ . . . . . .
3 0. $x_{31}\ x_{32}\ x_{33}\ x_{34} \ldots x_{3n}$ . . . . . .
. . . .
. . . .
. . . .
. . . .
. . . .
k 0. $x_{k1}\ x_{k2}\ x_{k3}\ x_{k4} \ldots x_{kn}$ . . . . . .
. . . .
. . . .
. . . .

Cantor showed that no matter how long one makes this list, some real number is bound to be left out. Therefore, it is not possible that every real number will occur sooner or later in this list. This is how he showed it: Consider the diagonal number

0. $x_{11}\ x_{22}\ x_{33}\ x_{44} \ldots x_{kk} \ldots$

Each x_{nn} either equals 1, or does not equal 1. Now devise a new real number as follows:

In the *first* decimal place, write 9 if $x_{11} = 1$, and write 1 if $x_{11} \neq 1$.

In the *second* decimal place, write 9 if $x_{22} = 1$, and write 1 if $x_{22} \neq 1$.

.

.

.

In the *kth* decimal place, write 9 if $x_{kk} = 1$, and write 1 if $x_{kk} \neq 1$.

And so on.

This new real number differs, in its first decimal place, from the first number on the list above. It differs, in its second decimal place, from the second number on the list . . . It differs in its k*th* decimal place, from the k*th* number on the list . . . And so on. Therefore, it differs from every number on the list, so we have described a real number not on the list. This refutes the assumption that every real number was listed. Therefore, there is no one-to-one correspondence between the natural numbers and the real numbers.

The same technique can be used to prove Cantor's Theorem: that every set has more subsets than it has elements.

dialect *n.* a variety of a natural language; a variety of a language that deviates from language that is taken to be standard.

dialectic(s) (Gr. *dialektikē (technē)* (the art of) argumentation, reasoning, disputation) *n. sing.* **1** In ancient Greece, dialectic was a kind of disputation undertaken as a game or exercise in which questions were asked and answers for the most part had to be 'yes' or 'no'. It resembled the formal cross-examination of a witness in a trial. **2** Dialectic is the art of discourse by which we either refute or establish some proposition by means of question and answer on the part of the interlocutors (Diogenes Laertius 3, 48). This is, for Plato, a method pre-eminently suited to finding truth, no matter whether the dialogue is carried on with another person or in one's own mind. Aristotle deals with dialectic in his *Topics*, Books 7 and 8, and contrasted it with the inferior methods of disputation used by Sophists. But Aristotle also thought that dialectic, which teaches how to argue for or against a certain opinion, is inferior to logic, which teaches how to establish proofs. **3** In the terminology introduced by Kant in the *Critique of Pure Reason*, Transcendental Dialectic is the heading he gives to the discussion of the illusions to which human reason is prey. The dialectic is the process of fallacious reasoning by which reason arrives at untenable knowledge-claims concerning the self, the world as a whole, and God. (These are dealt with, respectively, in the three main subsections of the Transcendental Dialectic: Paralogism, Antinomy, Ideal of Reason.) **4** Hegel used the term *dialectic* to designate a process which brings forth an opposition, between a thesis and an antithesis, which has within it an urge to be resolved by a synthesis, a combination in which the conflicting elements are preserved and somehow reconciled. One example is the opposition between being and not-being, overcome in its synthesis, becoming. Every synthesis will in turn bring forth a new opposite, and so on. The whole chain does, however, have a beginning and an end. Hegel conceived of these oppositions both as contradictions and as conflicts. The resolutions were conceived both as thought-processes in which two contrary concepts are absorbed into a new concept, and as processes in the real world. In the real world, there is a dialectical process in the physical world, in society and in the history of mankind. Opposition between physical forces, conflict between social forces, or a struggle between historical forces, lead to outcomes which in turn call forth a new step in the dialectic.

dialectical materialism *See* MATERIALISM.

dialectical theology arose in reaction against rationalistic and liberal tendencies in Protestant theology. A guiding idea, derived from Kierkegaard, is that the difference between God and man is so great that the usual constraints on rational discourse (non-contradiction, etc.) can have only limited application: the very core of faith contains paradox, since the tension between finite human existence and infinite divine being cannot be rationally resolved. The first major statement representing this view was Karl Barth's (1886–1968) commentary, *The Epistle to The Romans* 1919. Emil Brunner (1889–1966) and Friedrich Gogarten (1887–1967) were among the leading representatives of this tendency, which also influenced Rudolf Bultmann (1884–1976).

dialetheism /daɪəˈliːθeɪzm/ (Gr. *dia-* through + *alētheia* truth) *n.* the view that contradictions may be true. *See also* PARACONSISTENT LOGIC.

dialethic logic systems of formal logic which allow for some contradictions being true, or which allow for some propositions to be both true and false. Such systems may or may not contain the law of non-contradiction. Systems of this kind are proposed in the Australian logician Graham Priest's *In Contradiction* 1987.

dianoia /daɪəˈnɔɪə/ (Gr. *dianoia* intelligence, mind, intellect) *n.* Aristotle distinguishes between dianoetic (intellectual) and ethical (moral) excellence. Important kinds of intellectual excellence are *phronēsis*, good judgement in practical matters, *technē*, practical skill, and *sophia*, theoretical wisdom, i.e. high intelligence. **dianoetic** *adj.*

diaspora /daɪˈæspərə/ (Gr. dispersion) *n.* The term is used to designate collectively nationals who do not live in their homeland.

dichotomy /daɪˈkɒtəmɪ/ (Gr. *dichotomia* cutting in two) *n.* dividing into two; especially, division of a class into two subclasses that are mutually exclusive and jointly exhaustive.

dictionary of philosophy A list of philosophical terms with explanations in Book Δ of Aristotle's *Metaphysics* may be the earliest.

Diderot /ˈdiːdərəʊ (Eng.); didʀo (Fr.)/, Denis (1713–84) a leading Enlightenment thinker, editor-in-chief of the *Encyclopédie*. He was remarkably versatile, writing novels, satires, dramas, critical essays on art and literature, essays on natural science and medicine, and letters on most subjects. His philosophical outlook underwent a change: from radical deism to an even more radical atheism. In developing his materialist philosophy he rebutted the classical objections that it cannot account for the origin of motion, of life, and of mind, arguing that nothing prevents us from assuming that among the basic characteristics of every particle of matter are the potential for motion, life and mind; there is, then, no need to assume an immaterial or supernatural agency. His political philosophy was radical: sovereignty ultimately resides with the people. He also gave a powerful criticism of the political institutions of his time. As is evident from the *Encyclopédie*, he saw the value of technology. He admired the ingenuity and skill of human achievements in the mechanical arts, and understood their enormous potential to eliminate drudgery and so improve the human condition.

diegesis /daɪəˈdʒiːsɪs/ (Gr. *diēgēsis* a narrative) *n.* **1** the relation of events by a narrator. The standard contrast, since Plato, is between diegesis (telling) and mimesis (showing, enacting).

2 In modern literary theory, the term seems to be used in various senses: (a) in one sense, the diegesis of a work is, so to speak, a background narrative, the implied setting, the fictitious or real world which constitutes the *frame* within which the content of a film, a novel or a play is situated; (b) in another sense, the diegesis is the main narrative, the sequence of events that constitutes a story, in contrast to other aspects of the work. In both senses there is an implied contrast to other kinds of text: a dialogue, a description, a commentary. The diegetic level of the narrative is that of the main story. The higher level, standing outside the sphere of the main story, is *extradiegetic*. An embedded tale within the tale is *hypodiegetic*.

The word is used both for the *process* of narrating and for the *product* of that process, i.e. the narration, the story.

différance /difeʀɑ̃ːs (Fr.)/ *n.* a French neologism coined by Derrida, pronounced in the same way as *différence* (difference). *Différance* is ambiguous, and can mean *deferment* (i.e. postponement) or *deference* (i.e. yielding to someone or something).

On one interpretation of Derrida, it is in his view a concept that defies explanation because every attempt to explain it is an attempt to go beyond the limits of language. *See also* DIFFERENCE, METAPHYSICS OF.

difference *n.* a very general notion, like its opposites, *similarity* and *identity*. Difference is *not* the same as incompatibility. Two things can be different without being incompatible.

difference, metaphysics of Some French philosophers have challenged the priority accorded to the notions of identity and similarity within the Western metaphysical tradition, arguing that in Plato, for example, the self-identity of the Forms is considered basic, while empirical reality is understood in terms of its difference from these ultimate realities. Deleuze and Derrida, drawing upon Nietzsche, Heidegger and Freud, have sought to displace this 'metaphysics of identity' (or 'presence') in favour of a metaphysics of difference.

Deleuze argues that a conception of the world in which difference is the primary term requires not only that we reconceptualize identity and similarity as secondary notions, but that the difference between identity and difference itself must be reconfigured: he proposes a complex notion of repetition.

Following Saussure, who argues that a language is defined not by the positive content of its signifying material (sounds or inscriptions) but by the structure of differences between them, Derrida coins the term *différance* to refer to the movement by which such differences come into being. This movement may be understood spatially as well as temporally. Because *différance* refers to the quasi-transcendental conditions of consciousness, conceptuality or linguistic meaning as such, Derrida insists that it is neither a word nor a concept nor any kind of being in the traditional sense. It is his avowedly paradoxical name for the primordial movement or 'play' of being which gives rise to differences. PP

difference, method of one of the methods of experimental inquiry described by John Stuart Mill (*Logic* 3,8). Suppose that an event occurs in one case but not in another, and that the two cases are exactly alike, except for one circumstance; then that one circumstance is the cause, or a necessary part of the cause.

difference, politics of Some present-day feminist writers use 'difference' as short for sexual difference, for instance in a phrase like 'the politics of difference'.

There are, however, feminist and postmodernist writers who do not adopt this usage as a mere shortcut, but against the background of their taking up the political dimension of the claim that Western thought privileges identity at the expense of difference. They argue that the failure to recognize sexual or racial differences, ultimately due to an erroneous 'metaphysics of presence', contributes to social oppression, and call for a politics that respects such differences. PP/ed.

difference principle The name given by John Rawls to the second of his two basic principles of justice in *A Theory of Justice* 1971 (section 11, p. 60; section 13; section 47). It concerns the social and economic inequalities which may remain even when the first of his two principles of justice is observed. The principle is (1) that there should be equality of opportunity for all members of society, and (2) that other inequalities should be removed, unless their retention can be reasonably expected to benefit the least well-off.

differend (Fr. *différend* disagreement, dispute) *n.* a central concept in Lyotard, defined by him as a conflict in which a rational or equitable resolution is called for, although it is impossible. He brings under this heading a heterogeneous variety of oppositions, from logical paradoxes to practical conflicts – for instance, those in which a wronged party has been silenced.

diffidence *n.* **1** (in older usage) distrust (of others). **2** (in current usage) lack of self-confidence.

dikaiosynē Gr. justice; morality. One of the four CARDINAL VIRTUES. *See* JUST; JUSTICE.

dilemma *n.* **1** the name given to various valid patterns of inference. In systems of natural deduction, the rule of dilemma (∨-elimination) states that if c is derivable from p (perhaps together with other premisses) and if c is derivable from q (perhaps together with other premisses), then c is derivable from p∨q (together with those other premisses). Schematically, the pattern is

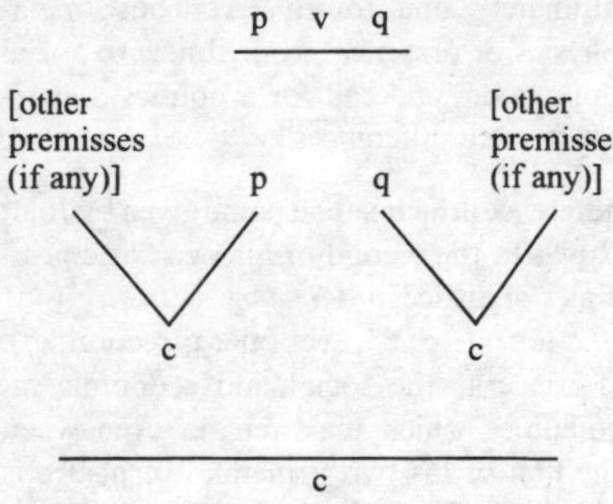

(This is a generalized version of simple constructive dilemma, shown below.)

In traditional logic the three inferences shown in Table 7 were called dilemmas. The last was called a negative dilemma, the first two positive dilemmas. In more recent logic texts, patterns of inference called dilemmas are (using a more modern layout) mainly these four:

simple constructive dilemma:

If p then q   If r then q   p or r
―――――――――――――――
q

Table 7 Forms of dilemmas

I	II	III
p or not-p	p or not-p	if q then m or n
if p then q	if p then q	if m then r
if not-p then q	if not-p then r	if n then s
q	not-r	not-r
	q	not-s
		not-q

complex constructive dilemma:

If p then q   If r then s   p or r
―――――――――――――――
q or s

simple destructive dilemma:

If p then q   If p then r   not-q or not-r
―――――――――――――――
not-p

complex destructive dilemma:

If p then q   If r then s   not-q or not-s
―――――――――――――――
not-p or not-r

2 In ordinary non-technical usage, a dilemma is a situation requiring a difficult choice between alternatives.

Dilthey /ˈdɪltaɪ (Gm.)/, Wilhelm (1833–1911) German philosopher who held chairs in various universities, finally in Berlin 1882–1905. In opposition to scientistic and positivist philosophy, Dilthey stressed the radical difference between natural sciences (*Naturwissenschaft*) and the human or cultural sciences (*Geisteswissenschaft*) such as history, psychology, philology, philosophy, etc. In the former we seek causes and ask for *explanation*, in the latter we seek *understanding* by means of interpretation. He had a decisive influence on twentieth-century hermeneutics.

Ding an sich /diŋ æn sɪk (Eng.); diŋ an zɪç (Gm.)/ Gm. thing-in-itself. *See* NOUMENON.

Diodorus Cronus /daɪə'dɔːrəs 'krəʊnəs/ (d. *c.* 284 BC (not 307)) a philosopher of the Megarian School. His so-called master argument (the reason for this name is unknown) turns on the thesis that the present and the future are no more under our control than the past. There are grounds for thinking that Diodorus was responding to what Aristotle had written on the problem of future contingents in *De Interpretatione* chapter 9, and *Metaphysics*, Book IX, 3. This problem was later stated by Epictetus (2, 19) in the form of an inconsistent triad in which any two imply the denial of the third: (1) all truths about the past are necessary; (2) no impossible proposition follows from premisses that are possibly true; (3) some proposition is possibly true although it neither is true nor will become true. We are told that Cleanthes denied the first, Chrysippus the second and Diodorus the third.

Diogenes /daɪ'ɒdʒɪniːz/ of Apollonia (5th century BC) Greek philosopher, contemporary of Socrates. He returned to the notion of Anaximenes that air was the original element of the universe, but developed it under the influence of more recent philosophy, particularly Anaxagoras's theory of Mind, and of medical theory. Diogenes figures behind much of the cosmological and biological speculation attributed to Socrates in Aristophanes's play *Clouds* (423 BC). HT

Diogenes Laertius /daɪ'ɒdʒɪniːz leɪ'ɜːʃəs/ (2nd–3rd century) Little is known about this author of *The Lives of the Philosophers*, which is a compilation from various sources. It contains much that is unreliable, but has lists of works and summaries of the major doctrines. The ten books cover (1) the early sages; (2) the Milesians, Anaxagoras, Socrates and the Socratic schools; (3) Plato; (4) Plato's successors; (5) Aristotle; (6) the Cynics; (7) the Stoics; (8) the Pythagoreans; (9) Heraclitus, the Eleatics, the atomists, etc., Pyrrho and Timon. The tenth book is about Epicurus and contains three important philosophical epistles of his (to Herodotus, to Pythocles, and to Menoeceus) and the *Key Doctrines* (*kyriai doxai*).

Diogenes of Sinope (*c.* 400–*c.* 325 BC) CYNIC philosopher. He was famous, or notorious, for his way of life, carrying with him all his few belongings, making his home in a wine-jar, dressed only in a rough tunic, all in the name of self-sufficiency (*autarkeia*). His advocacy and practice of a 'life according to nature' is said to have overstepped the bounds of propriety. He taught Zeno of Citium, the founder of Stoicism, in which, however, the ideal of a life according to nature is differently understood.

Dionysiac (also Dionysian) *See* APOLLONIAN.

Dionysius Areopagita /daɪə'nɪsɪəs əreɪəpə'dʒiːtə/ In the Middle Ages a number of works were incorrectly attributed to this disciple of St Paul. They were probably written in the fifth century by a theologian whose theories have much in common with the neo-Platonist philosopher Proclus. The extant writings of this pseudo-Dionysius are *Divine Names*, *Mystical Theology*, *Celestial Hierarchy*, *Ecclesiastical Hierarchy* and ten letters. Insight into the divine can be reached by trying to describe what God is (this is the positive or kataphatic way) or by trying to describe what he is not (the negative, apophatic way). Of these, the latter brings us closer to the truth. Evil is characterized as non-existence, a deficiency: something is evil only in so far as it is lacking in some respect. On the doctrine of the Trinity, the orthodoxy of the author is doubtful.

Throughout the Middle Ages these writings were treated as authoritative because of their supposed provenance, and their unknown author became one of the most influential thinkers in the history of Western thought.

Diotima /daɪəʊˈtiːmə/ a priestess and prophetess who had opened Socrates's eyes to the true mysteries of Eros, according to Plato's dialogue *Symposium* 201d–212c.

disambiguate *vb.* **1** to lay bare a hidden ambiguity of an expression. **2** to determine the sense in which an ambiguous expression will be used.

discourse ethics a theory designed to establish the right moral and political principles: the right principles are those that emerge by means of a certain *process* taking place under specified ideal *conditions*. The process in question is communication, i.e. exchange of information and opinion between people. The conditions are: (1) the parties should regard each other as equals; equal regard should be given to the interests of all participants; (2) there should be an absence of direct constraint or force and of indirect, institutionalized or structural pressure; (3) the only admissible form of persuasion should be rational argument; (4) no assumptions should be immune to inquiry; (5) assumptions can be taken as accepted only if all the parties agree; (6) the communication should be open-ended in the sense that no authority could declare an issue settled for ever. The first of these conditions spells out a moral constraint, while the others spell out constraints of rationality.

Actual communication is not ideal, but it is sometimes possible to envisage what the outcome would be if such conditions were fulfilled, wholly or approximately, and this makes it possible to understand what the right principles would be.

The justification for this approach to ethics is that if we communicate at all, the basic principles of discourse ethics are implicitly acknowledged. They are necessary presuppositions for any communication properly so called. This is why its advocates describe the justification as transcendental.

A person who purports to enter into communication but rejects the basic presuppositions would be guilty not of logical inconsistency but of pragmatic inconsistency: i.e. it is not the person's own statements, but his own actions, that are incompatible with what he pretends (as when a person utters 'I am silent' in a loud voice).

This 'transcendental-pragmatic' mode of justifying discourse ethics consists in showing that the very fact that people communicate and seek to reach consensus requires preconditions of the kind set out above. The advocates of this mode of justification contrast it with the 'foundationalist' attempt to establish a basis for morality which in their view must fail, because like other kinds of foundationalism it cannot escape the 'Münchhausen trilemma': dogmatism, question-begging, or infinite regress.

The leading proponents of this approach, which combines impulses from various philosophical traditions, including the linguistic-analytical, are Jürgen Habermas and Karl-Otto Apel. In recent debates, Habermas has noted his affinities with Hare, Rawls, Kohlberg, etc., and has made clear his opposition to many forms of communitarianism and virtue-ethics. Were it not for the fact that 'discourse ethics' has become fairly entrenched, he would prefer to call it a discourse theory of morality, since it deals with the principles for right action, and not with the question of the good life.

discover *vb.* (in older usage) to reveal. In this sense, a person who discovers his identity is not gaining self-knowledge, but lets others know who he is.

discriminate *vb.* to differentiate or distinguish. This is in itself innocuous, and sometimes highly desirable. What is undesirable is discrimination against someone or in favour of someone without adequate justification.

disinterest *n.* **1** A *dis*interested observer *is* interested – though not self-interested. An *un*interested observer *is not* interested. Aesthetic enjoyment has been characterized as disinterested enjoyment, because in the aesthetic enjoyment of a piece of music, a sculpture or a poem, they are enjoyed for their own sake. **2** impartiality, non-partisanship. In this sense, a disinterested party shows impartial concern; an uninterested party shows no concern.

disjunct *n.* a component statement in a disjunction.

disjunction *n.* A compound statement of the form 'p or q' is called a *disjunction*, and the component statements are called *disjuncts*. The term is also used to denote the operation on two statements p, q, which results in the formation of such a compound statement. When understood as a truth-function, a disjunction takes the value *false* if both p and q are false, and otherwise takes the value *true*, so that its truth-table is as Table 8. The symbol '∨', called 'wedge' or 'vel', is commonly used to represent this truth-function.

Table 8 Truth-table for disjunction

p	q	p ∨ q
T	T	T
T	F	T
F	T	T
F	F	F

It has been argued that disjunction, so understood, only covers some uses of 'or', but that in many contexts it would be very odd to regard 'p or q' as true, if both p and q are true. When we say 'p or q' we often mean that *exactly one*, and no more, is the case (e.g. 'either we will go to the beach or we will go to the movies'). This truth-function is called *exclusive disjunction*, in contrast to the former which is also called *inclusive disjunction*.

The truth-table for exclusive disjunction is one in which the disjunction is true if the disjuncts have opposite truth-values, and false if they have the same truth-values. It will therefore be the truth-table of the negated biconditional (see Table 9).

Table 9 Truth-table for exclusive disjunction

p	q	~(p ≡ q)
T	T	F
T	F	T
F	T	T
F	F	F

Some writers use the term *disjunction* for inclusive disjunction alone, and reserve the term *alternation* for exclusive disjunction. Others use *alternation* for (inclusive) disjunction, as defined in Table 8.

Note: The word has other senses. When Hume writes of a 'disjunction of interests' he means that the interests are divergent or opposed. In present-day non-philosophical usage the word can also mean contrast, disjointedness, exclusion, rupture, etc.; but in philosophical contexts, the word is almost exclusively used in the attenuated sense of 'or-statement', as explained above.

disjunctive syllogism an inference *from* a disjunction and the denial of the first disjunct *to* the second disjunct. This is the pattern:

$$\frac{\text{A or B} \quad \text{Not A}}{\text{B}}$$

Note: An inference of the form 'p or q or r; but not p; therefore, q or r; but not q; therefore, r' is a sequence of two disjunctive syllogisms. Chrysippus claimed that even dogs are capable of such reasoning: a hound is in hot pursuit along a path which at one point branches out in three directions. The quarry is out of sight. Having sniffed the first and the second branch without raising a scent, the hound will run along the third *without first sniffing it*!

disquotation *n.* the removal of a pair of quotation marks.

dissective *adj.* a dissective property is one which, if it belongs to a whole, also belongs to every part.

The use of the word in this sense was introduced by Nelson Goodman, in *The Structure of Appearance* 1951. See also DIVISION, FALLACY OF.

dissemination *n.* an important term in Derrida's writings. It figures prominently in *Dissemination* 1972 and in *Positions* 1972. It carries allusion both to the Latin *semen* (seed) and Greek *sēmeion* (sign), but the meaning of the term is such that only those who misunderstand it try to explain it.

distinction *n.* There can be no distinction without a difference, but: (1) distinction is not the same as separation: the redness and the hardness of a surface cannot be prised apart, and yet redness and hardness are not the same; (2) distinction is not the same as non-implication: there is implication from the necessary to the possible, and yet they are distinct notions; (3) distinction is not the same as segregation: it is possible to participate in both the domestic realm and the public realm, and yet there are obvious differences between the two realms.

distribution of terms A term is distributed in a categorical proposition if and only if the proposition implies every other proposition that results from replacing the original term with another term whose extension is part of the extension of the original term.

For example: the extension of *poet* is part of the extension of *human being*; so *Every human being is mortal* implies *Every poet is mortal*. Similarly with any other sub-class of human beings. Accordingly, *human being* is distributed in *Every human being is mortal*.

Generally, the subject of a universal proposition is distributed, and so is the predicate of a negative proposition. Other terms are not distributed. Below, the distributed terms are in bold italics:

Every ***S*** is P	No ***S*** is ***P***
Some S is P	Some S is not ***P***

C. S. Peirce observed that if these statement-forms are paraphrased in terms of identity and non-identity, 'every' is a mark of distribution: (1) *every* S is identical with some P or other; (2) *every* S is distinct from *every* P; (3) some S or other is identical with some P or other; (4) some S or other is distinct from *every* P.

The concept was used in the traditional logic of categorical SYLLOGISMS to formulate criteria of validity: (1) the middle term in a syllogism is distributed in at least one premiss; (2) a term distributed in the conclusion must be distributed in the premisses. A violation of the first rule is known as the fallacy of the undistributed middle.

distributive justice *See* COMMUTATIVE JUSTICE.

distributive law a proposition of this form: a∗ (b#c) is equivalent to (a∗b)#(a∗c).

In a formal system with such a principle, the operator ∗ is said to distribute over the operator #. A well-known example is multiplication: a(b + c) = ab + ac.

divination /dɪvɪˈneɪʃən/ *n.* the art or practice of discovering things future or unknown by paranormal means. Cicero's *De divinatione* is an early discussion of this subject.

division, fallacy of an inference which relies on the invalid principle that whatever is true of a whole is also true of every part.

For instance, if a stone weighs 1 kg, we cannot infer that every part does so too. Or, assume that a committee has reached a wise decision: we cannot infer that every member did.

There *are* properties such that if they belong to a whole they also belong to every part. Nelson Goodman has called them *dissective*.

division, principle of *See* AGGLOMERATION.

docetism /ˈdəʊsɪtɪzm/ (Gr. *dokein* to seem) *n.* a heretical doctrine which maintains that some or all of Christ's human attributes (his body, his suffering) were merely apparent and not real, and that the attributes that truly belong to Christ are divine, not human. At the extreme, Christ's human body is held to be a mere phantasm. Ideas of this kind are hinted at by some of the early Church Fathers, but the full-blown version of the doctrine is part of Gnosticism.

docta ignorantia Lat. learned ignorance. The phrase, not designed to cast a slur on the learned, became established through its use in the title of a book by Nicholas of Cusa. It denotes the rational insight into the incomprehensibility of the divine.

Dodgson /ˈdɒdʒsən/, Charles Lutwidge *See* CARROLL.

dog *See* DISJUNCTIVE SYLLOGISM.

dogma (Gr. *dogma* public decree; belief; scientific principle) *n.* **1** a tenet, a doctrine, regarded as indisputable. **2** a doctrine, or a body of doctrine, authoritatively laid down.

dogmatic *adj.* **1** pertaining to a dogma. **2** pertaining to dogmatism.

dogmatics *n. sing.* the theological study of the dogmas of the church to which the theologian is attached.

dogmatism *n.* **1** The ancient sceptics used this term for non-sceptical theories. They thought that dogmatic philosophers were too audacious in taking certain propositions (in logic, physics or ethics) to be definitely true.

This classical contrast between scepticism and dogmatism can be interpreted as one between fallibilism and foundationalism. For the fallibilist, the body of knowledge-claims is like a ship kept afloat by constantly replacing old parts; for the foundationalist, the body of knowledge-claims is like a building that needs a secure foundation.

2 In Fichte and other post-Kantians, the term was applied especially to the principle that reality is independent of consciousness and that it is the ground of experience: knowledge arises when reality makes an impact on a passive mind. Transcendental idealism was seen as superior, able to put philosophy on a secure path of knowledge. Fichte contrasted dogmatism and idealism: the latter, the view that ultimate reality is self, active and self-conscious, the ground of experience, is the view that alone can bestow validity on our moral values and ideals. A person to whom these things matter will be drawn towards idealism, the other kind of person towards dogmatism. Neither standpoint admits of ultimate proof: your choice of philosophy depends on what kind of person you are (*First Introduction to the Science of Knowledge*, section 5).

3 Currently the term is mainly used in a more or less derogatory sense for the uncritical adherence to a theory.

dolus *n.* This Latin word, together with *culpa* and *casus*, has been used in traditional jurisprudence to signify degrees of an agent's responsibility for an action. *Dolus* is deliberate malicious intent. *Culpa* is fault, but without malicious intent. *Casus* means that what happened was accidental, and that the agent is not to be held responsible.

domain *n.* The *domain* of a function is the set of the individuals which enter into the arguments of the function. The *range* of the function is the set of values of the function. If a function is regarded as a set of ordered pairs of elements ⟨x,y⟩, the values for x belong to the domain, and the values for y belong to the range.

For example, let x and y be paired according to the condition: y = cos x. The *domain* of this function is the set of elements that can replace x, and the *range* of the function is the set of elements that can replace y.

Doppelgänger /ˈdɔpəlgɛŋər/ Gm. 'double-walker' *n.* a ghostly double or counterpart of a living person.

double effect the doctrine or principle of double effect concerns the moral assessment of what a person does, and contains a central distinction between what is *foreseen* by the agent as a likely result of an action and what is *intended.*

In Roman Catholic, especially Thomist, moral theory, the doctrine has been developed especially to deal with moral dilemmas, in which conformity with an absolute moral rule seems to be morally unacceptable.

For example, there is an absolute moral rule prohibiting murder. In the case of ectopic pregnancy, it is not possible with current technology to save the life of both the mother and the foetus, and if the pregnancy continues, both will die. An abortion can in this circumstance be an act *intended* to save the life of the mother, whereas the death of the foetus is a *foreseen*, unintended and unavoidable result of saving the life of the mother.

The moral assessment of this is usually an assessment of the *permissibility* of the act, in this case the abortion. For such seeming transgressions to be permissible, a number of conditions have been formulated: (1) the act (the rescue) must itself be morally good; (2) the agent, foreseeing the bad effect, must not intend it, and should try to find alternative courses of action; (3) the good effect should not be brought about by means of the bad effect; (4) the goodness of the intended good effect must be of sufficient moment to outweigh the foreseen transgression. These conditions have been applied to many moral dilemmas (see TROLLEY PROBLEM) since the contemporary philosophical debate began with Philippa Foot's 'Abortion and the Doctrine of Double Effect', *The Oxford Review* no. 5, 1967, reprinted in her *Virtues and Vices.*

According to many critics, attempts of this kind to formulate the principle so that it would be a useful criterion of moral *permissibility* have not been successful. It has been suggested, however, that the principle should be seen as a criterion not of moral permissibility but of moral *blameworthiness.* This is plausible, given the origin of the distinction in Thomas Aquinas who, as a moral theologian, would be concerned with the imputation of sin.

double negation The law or principle of double negation is to the effect that the negation of the negation of a proposition is always equivalent to that proposition itself; briefly, that: not-not-p is equivalent to p. There are two parts to this principle: (1) that p implies not-not-p; and (2) that not-not-p implies p.

In standard propositional logic, formulae corresponding to (1) and (2) are both theorems. In some systems, however (notably the intuitionistic calculus), the formula corresponding to (1) is a theorem, but that corresponding to (2) is not. At first sight, this may seem strange, but there are a number of interpretations which make (1) seem intuitively more plausible than (2). Examples are as follows.

(A) Suppose we take the negation of p to mean that p is impossible: then (1) amounts to saying that if p is true, it is impossible for it to be impossible, but (2) means that the impossibility of p's being impossible is enough to show that it is true; and the former seems more plausible than the latter.

(B) If we interpret negation as denial, we might then take (1) to mean that asserting that p commits one to denying that one denies that p (which seems plausible), and (2) to mean that denying that one denies that p commits one to asserting that p (which does not seem plausible, since one might have no views about p).

(C) Mathematicians of the intuitionist school reject the principle of proof by *reductio ad absurdum* – they regard a disproof of the negation of p as insufficient to count as a proof of p. They thus reject the inference from not-not-p to p, but accept that from p to not-not-p. GH

Note: Double negation differs from negation repeated for the sake of added emphasis. A court will not take kindly to an assailant's defence that the victim cried 'no' an even number of times.

double truth the view that one and the same statement can be true in philosophy and false in theology (or vice versa), sometimes wrongly attributed to Boethius of Dacia. On the whole, few if any thinkers have endorsed it, but many have been accused of holding it. JM/ed.

doxa Gr. opinion, belief *n.* in ancient philosophy contrasted with *gnosis* or *epistēmē*, i.e. knowledge.

Especially in the Platonic tradition, the view was held that what can be an object of knowledge is of a different nature from that which can be an object of opinion or belief. Aristotle similarly held (*Posterior Analytics* 1, 33 89ª3–5) that *doxa* is about the contingent, *epistēmē* (knowledge) about the necessary.

This is contrary to the modern view that knowledge, opinion, belief and other 'propositional attitudes' do not differ because their object does. JM/ed.

doxastic logic inquiry into, or theory of, the logic of belief-statements.

doxography (Gr. *doxa* + *graphein* to write) *n.* an account of the opinions of a thinker. The word is used chiefly for accounts of past, especially ancient, thought.

doxology *n.* (in religion) a hymn or prayer glorifying God; especially, a certain part of church liturgy.

Driesch /driːʃ/, Hans (Adolf Eduard) (1867–1941) German biologist, a founder of experimental embryology. His researches led him from a mechanistic to a vitalistic (VITALISM) conception of biological life, expounded in *The Science and Philosophy of the Organism* 1908, and later in life he also took a strong interest in parapsychology (*Parapsychologie* 1932, transl. as *Psychical Research*). In his academic work, he switched from science to philosophy in 1912, and then held positions first at Heidelberg, then Cologne, and from 1921 to 1933 at Leipzig. Although best known for his vitalism, Driesch also developed a comprehensive anti-materialist metaphysics.

dual *adj.*, *n.* (in logic and mathematics) A dual formula or the dual of a formula is obtained by replacing one operator with another. For instance, each of the formulae: $\sim (p \mathbin{\&} q) \equiv \sim p \vee \sim q$; and $\sim (p \vee q) \equiv \sim p \mathbin{\&} \sim q$ is a dual of the other.

In certain cases a general proof can establish that what holds for a class of formulae also holds (with appropriate changes) for their duals.

dualism *n.* a theory that has at its basis *two* radically distinct concepts or principles. Examples of dualism are: (1) the religious belief in two opposing principles or divine beings, one good and one evil. It was in this sense that the word was first used about three centuries ago, to describe the ancient Persian religion; (2) in metaphysics, the view that there are two kinds of reality: finite and infinite, matter and form, matter and spirit, relative and absolute, etc.; (3) in the philosophy of mind, psychophysical dualism: the view that human beings are made up of two radically distinct constituents (body, constituted by matter like other natural objects, and an immaterial mind or soul). Another kind of psychophysical dualism, different from this 'substance dualism', is called 'property dualism' or 'attribute dualism', to the effect that there are two radically different kinds of properties, physical and non-physical, belonging to the same brain or human being; (4) in moral philosophy, fact/value dualism: the view that factual statements do not imply any evaluative statement. *Ant.* monism, pluralism.

Note: Dualism is also used in a different sense, as a synonym of *duality*, i.e. two-ness.

du Bois-Reymond /dy bwa ʀɛmɔ̃ (Fr.)/, Emil (1818–96) German scientist and philosopher, professor of physiology in Berlin. He advocated a scientific positivism and held that everything in the natural world is subject to strict deterministic laws. But science, he said, cannot explain everything, and there are fundamental philosophical questions about which we should have the moral strength to recognize that we are and will remain ignorant (summed up in the Latin *ignoramus et ignorabimus*), rather than attempt the impossible quest beyond the limits of human knowledge. His scientific materialism and determinism, combined with metaphysical agnosticism, was articulated in two short pieces: *Über die Grenzen des Naturerkennens* 1872 (The limits of our knowledge of nature) and *Die sieben Welträtsel* 1880 (The seven riddles of the universe), which became widely known and debated. Ernst Haeckel's *The Riddles of the Universe* and Ehrenfels's *Kosmogonie* are among the almost countless responses. The 'seven riddles' are: (1) the nature of matter and energy; (2) the origin of motion; (3) the origin of life; (4) the apparent purposiveness of nature; (5) the origin of simple sensory experience; (6) the origin of language and rational thought; (7) the freedom of the will. Although science might be able to solve some of these riddles, the first three 'transcendental' ones would, in his view, remain beyond the limits of human knowledge.

Duhem-Quine thesis /dyɛm (Fr.)/ the thesis that hypotheses cannot be tested one by one, but only in clusters. If an experiment does not fit the hypothesis, it is not obvious that it is the hypothesis that has to be rejected; perhaps the fault lies elsewhere. For instance, it is perhaps the assumptions concerning the measuring instruments that should be revised! Pierre Duhem's (1861–1916) view, developed in *La Théorie physique, son objet et sa structure* 1906 (transl. as *The Aim and Structure of Physical Theory* 1954), is that what is tested is always a whole set of assumptions. This is adopted and generalized in Quine's holism.

Dummett /ˈdʌmət/, Sir Michael (1925–) Oxford philosopher, fellow of All Souls 1950, Wykeham Professor of Logic 1979–92 and a fellow of New College. Among engagements outside philosophy, his active work against racism deserves special mention.

Dummett's philosophy is to a large extent inspired by the philosophy of Frege and Wittgenstein. Several of his works are directly concerned with Frege, the main ones being the two books *Frege: Philosophy of Language* 1973 and *Frege: Philosophy of Mathematics* 1991. They contain detailed accounts of Frege's various doctrines, as well as Dummett's evaluation of them together with his own contributions. Interpolated between these two volumes Dummett also published *The Interpretation of Frege's Philosophy* 1981, in which he defends his interpretation of Frege against several critics who had advanced divergent interpretations in the lively discussions of Frege's philosophy that followed Dummett's first book.

The most important themes of Dummett's own philosophy concern metaphysics and philosophy of language, and in particular the way in which they are interrelated. The metaphysical issue to which Dummett has especially addressed himself is the question to what extent realism is tenable. Dummett takes an essential ingredient of an anti-realist position to be the rejection of the principle of bivalence of classical logic. Metaphysical issues therefore have consequences for logic. On the other hand, the question of which logic is correct must be a question for the theory of meaning to resolve. Therefore, he maintains, the correct way to approach these interrelated questions is to begin with the theory of meaning, and when this has been set right, we shall also be able to settle the logical and metaphysical questions.

A theory of meaning for a language as conceived by Dummett should explain what it is to know the meaning of the various sentences of the language. In view of the public nature of meaning, the knowledge in question should manifest itself in the use we make of the sentences, and the theory of meaning should describe how the knowledge manifests itself. According to Dummett, those who uphold the principle of bivalence run into difficulties with undecidable sentences. The defenders of bivalence identify the meaning of a sentence with its truth-condition, and must therefore maintain that we can grasp what it is for a truth-condition to obtain even when – as is the case for undecidable sentences – there is no way in which this grasp can be shown. Therefore, he concludes, a tenable theory of meaning must instead identify the meaning of a sentence with some feature of its use, and he considers different ways in which this requirement can be satisfied. One way is to take the meaning of a sentence to be determined by what counts as a verification of the sentence. In this way we arrive at an anti-realism which is a generalization of the intuitionist position in mathematics. Dummett does not commit himself to such a position, but shows much sympathy for it, and urges that further work on the theory of meaning be undertaken in order to obtain a firm basis on which these questions can be resolved.

There is an early but fairly comprehensive presentation of how Dummett sees a theory of meaning and its relation to the dispute between realism and anti-realism in his 'What is a theory of meaning? II', reprinted together with other papers in the volume *The Seas of Language* 1993. The most extensive discussion of the route that Dummett proposes from the theory of meaning to metaphysics is provided in *The Logical Basis of Metaphysics* 1991. He has also contributed to the philosophy of mathematical intuitionism in *Elements of Intuitionism*, which deals extensively with its various philosophical, logical and mathematical aspects. Many of his earlier papers are collected in *Truth and Other Enigmas* 1978. DPR

Duns Scotus /dʌnz ˈskɒtəs/, John (*c.* 1266–1308) probably born at Duns in Scotland; became a Franciscan at an early age. He was ordained priest in 1291, and after that alternated between Oxford and Paris (with a brief spell in Cambridge); he died in Cologne and is buried in the Franciscan church there. His works – lectures and commentaries written at Oxford, Cambridge, and Paris – are voluminous and complex, and were heavily edited by his students; a critical edition is now under way, and will for the first time enable us to distinguish Scotus's own contributions from those of his students.

His work has two distinct foci: theology and metaphysics. Theologically, he emphasized the importance of God's will and, consequently, the contingent nature of both creation and redemption. (He wrote extensively on the theological status of the Virgin Mary, as part of his general interest in the process of redemption.) His metaphysics is his great philosophical achievement; he is the foremost thinker of the later Middle Ages to develop a metaphysics in the Aristotelian sense, that is, a science of being which would be prior to all of the other sciences. But his metaphysics differs radically from Aristotle's by adopting the assumption of creation *ex nihilo*.

His metaphysics starts with the notion of being, which is primary both ontologically and epistemologically. Ontologically, being has two modes (finite and infinite), which exhaust what there is: infinite being (i.e. God) is necessary and uncaused, whereas finite being is dependent and contingent. Scotus has a description of finite being which is basically compositional: that is, he starts from prime matter and says that this prime matter becomes an actual thing by the progressive addition of forms, starting with the form of corporeity which gives the thing whatever physical properties it has, and continuing with the addition of whatever other forms pertain to that thing. These other things would include the common nature, which made it a thing of whatever kind it was, and – if this was a particular thing – there would also be the *haecceitas*, or 'thisness', which was the nature that something had in virtue of being that particular thing. However, this composition is not simply a physical addition, since Scotus had a notion of *formal* identity and formal distinction that was finer-grained than *real* identity and distinction: thus, the various forms added to a thing would be really identical but formally distinct from each other. There has been much argument, then and subsequently, as to whether this notion of formal distinction is even coherent: however, it did give Scotus a complex and subtle way of analysing finite being. He also used it for the description of infinite being: the paradoxical identities and non-identities in the theology of the Trinity could be worked out in terms of formal distinctions and real identities.

Epistemologically, being is also primary: that is, it is the proper object of the human intellect. Scotus has a basically Aristotelian account of knowledge, starting from sense-experience (which includes a primary intuition of being) and abstracting, from that experience, the various forms which actualize the objects known. He emphatically rejected theories which postulated a special divine illumination for infallibly certain knowledge of religious and other truths: such theories (Augustinian in origin) had been put forward by Henry of Ghent among others.

Scotus's argument for God's existence goes through three main stages: he first argues that an uncaused first in each of the three orders of efficient causality, final causality and eminence is possible; then that this first in each order must be already actual (otherwise, if its possibility were due to the possibility of its being caused, it would not be possible, since it could not be uncaused and first); and finally that the first in each order is identical with the first in the others.

His theology also stresses the divine will: this stress is a distinctively Franciscan trait, and it enables him to tie together a number of distinct areas of his thought. Thus, his metaphysics is connected to his doctrine of God by the idea of creation as the actualization of possibilities. In fact, Scotus can analyse the successive divine decisions involved in the process of creation, ordering them according to priority and posteriority; these are correlated with the different forms involved in the actualization of a thing. Scotus needs something analogous to a formal distinction to be able to talk of these successive decisions, because they do not occupy distinct moments of time (the divine will to create is eternal); rather, he talks of them occupying 'moments of nature', which are not temporally distinct but can still be ordered according to priority and posteriority. In a similar way, he describes the divine will as formally (but not really) distinct from the divine essence. In this way, by talking of the relation between divine intellect and will, he can assess the rationality of the created order (a product of the divine will), and also the rationality of the moral law (likewise a product of the divine will). In this way, he was able to reconcile two opposing tendencies in the theology of that period: on the one hand, to stress divine freedom and thus the role of the divine will in creating and in establishing the moral law; on the other hand, to safeguard the rationality both of the created order and of the moral law.

Scotus is important, then, not merely for his metaphysics (impressive though that is) and for certain logical doctrines to do with identity and difference (even though they have been a fruitful source of controversy ever since); what his thought as a whole represents is the integration of the metaphysical and the theological enterprise. This sort of integration is not often achieved at the level that Scotus achieved it, and later thinkers (Ockham in particular), although they might appropriate individual doctrines, did not attempt the same sort of blending of metaphysics and theology that Scotus represents. GW

Durkheim /dyʀkɛm (Fr.)/, Emile (1858–1917) taught at the universities of Bordeaux and Paris, and established sociology as an academic discipline in France. His teaching and writing had a major impact on the intellectual and political life of France and on the subsequent development of sociology and social anthropology.

In *Les Règles de la méthode sociologique* 1895 (The rules of sociological method), Durkheim set out to establish sociology as a positive science dealing with its own distinct reality. It was generally thought that the properties and behaviour of living organisms could not be reduced to those of their chemical and physical components. Similarly, Durkheim insisted, the behaviour and properties of society could not be reduced to those of human individuals. Where the cell was the simplest biological unit capable of life, the horde – a collection of individuals with no internal *social* organization – was the simplest possible society. While Durkheim regarded the horde as a hypothetical construct, unlikely to be found in recorded history, he nevertheless treated tribal societies as having developed out of the simple juxtaposition of hordes. In his view they had rudimentary social structures and little social differentiation. More complex societies, on the other hand, like the higher animals, had highly specialized internal organs and a correspondingly high degree of social differentiation.

Durkheim elaborated on the implications of this evolutionary perspective in other publications, e.g. *La Division du travail social* 1893 (transl. as *The Division of Labor in Society*) and *Le Suicide* 1897 (*Suicide*), focusing on the analysis of social solidarity and the social problems of modern society, the development of modern individualism, and the social character of religion and categories of thought. The conception of society as an organism with a life of its own raises the question of what holds it together. Durkheim argued that simple societies were held together by a mechanical solidarity based on interdependence and the division of labour. On this view, the social problems of modern societies often reflected the weakening of the older ties of solidarity, based on similarity, while complex societies were held together by an organic solidarity before new ties had properly developed. The answer was to strengthen social integration, especially through the promotion of occupational and professional groupings. While simple societies repressed the expression of individuality, Durkheim maintained that the 'cult of the individual' was functional for the integration of modern societies.

Corresponding to this view of society is a perception of the individual as being subject both to biological and psychological exigencies and to the needs of society. Durkheim claimed that while appetites and emotional drives reflected the biological and psychic needs of the human individual, morality, conceptual thought and even the fundamental categories of space, time, number and causality were social in origin. His last major work, *Les Formes élémentaires de la vie religieuse* 1912 (The elementary forms of religious life), argued that the characters of social phenomena were revealed most clearly in the elementary forms which they took in the simplest societies. Religion, he concluded, was the worship of society itself, in the sense that the religious ideas arise from the way that the individual subjectively experiences the powerful influence of social norms and expectations. BHI

Dutch book a combination of bets that is bound to result in an overall loss. The Dutch Book argument is a mathematical proof (first produced by B. de Finetti in 1937) that betting which defies the probability calculus will result in an overall loss. *See also* PROBABILITY.

Note: The first appearance of this part of racetrack argot in discussions of probability theory seems to have been in an article by R. S. Lehman in *Journal of Symbolic Logic 20* (1955).

duty *See* OBLIGATION AND DUTY.

Dworkin /ˈdwɔːkɪn/, Ronald (Myles) (1931–) professor of law and jurisprudence at New York University, Oxford, etc. In his earlier major publications, *Taking Rights Seriously* 1977, 2nd edn 1978, Dworkin rejects the view that the law can be understood as a system of rules laid down by statute and precedent, distinct from the rules or principles of morality. This is the view that he calls legal positivism. One of his objections is that it offers an inadequate account of how courts decide and indeed ought to decide 'hard cases', that is, cases in which the legal rules provide no obvious solution. The inadequate account is essentially that the courts exercise discretion, and ought to do so in a way that supports *policies* which promote the common good.

Dworkin's preferred view is that the law does not merely consist of rules with gaps that have to be filled by discretionary decisions when the need arises, but that it embodies *principles* which safeguard individuals' rights against the collectivity, especially the right to equal concern and respect. In particular, Dworkin's theory of adjudication requires that judges base their decisions on the principles inherent in the 'best theory' of political morality of the legal system they are interpreting. Although his theory is a theory of Anglo-American legal systems, it may have a more general application to legal systems which also recognize principles in the way required by Dworkin's theory.

Later, Dworkin has argued, in *A Matter of Principle* 1985 and *Law's Empire* 1986, that legal decision-making is 'interpretive' and hence can be illuminated through a comparison with literary interpretation. Judges must interpret a body of legal 'data', namely legal texts and court decisions. Dworkin proposes that the interpretation of social practices like law and literature requires interpreters to apply value-judgements. He rejects a common rival view that interpretation requires the discovery of some actual intention. In *Law's Empire* Dworkin also provides a detailed argument for his theory of 'law as integrity'. He claims that adjudication should attempt to bring the principles inherent in a legal system into a coherent whole, thus promoting 'integrity'.

Dworkin has also written extensively in political philosophy, especially on civil liberty and equality, and on US constitutional interpretation, where he advocates liberal ideals when dealing with questions of affirmative action, free speech, pornography, abortion and euthanasia – the last two being discussed at length in his *Life's Dominion* 1993. NS

dyad /'daɪæd/ (Gr. *dyas* a pair) *n.* a group of two.

dyadic relation a two-place relation, e.g. *being to the left of* and *being the father of*. *See also* MONADIC PREDICATE.

dynamis/energeia the Greek words, used by Aristotle and others, that correspond to the later Latin *potentia/actus* and English *potency/act* and POTENTIALITY/*actuality*.

dysgenic /dɪs'dʒɛnɪk/ *adj.* pertaining to the deterioration of inherited qualities in a strain or breed.

dystopia /dɪs'təʊpɪə/ (Gr. *dys-*, signifying badness or difficulty, and *topos* place) *n.* a fictional account of bad political and social conditions; the story is often one of social and political movements or developments which promise utopia and inspire hope, but end up as a utopia in reverse. Examples of the genre are Zamyatin's *We* 1924, Aldous Huxley's *Brave New World* 1932, Karin Boye's *Kallocain* 1940 and George Orwell's *1984* 1948. Cf. UTOPIA.

Note: The word was coined by John Stuart Mill.

E

Eckhart, (Johannes?) Meister (= Master) (*c.* 1260–1327) one of the most important speculative mystics of the Middle Ages. There is uncertainty about his Christian name. He studied and later taught at Cologne and Paris, and held administrative positions within the Dominican order. His lasting fame and influence are due to his sermons and meditations in the vernacular. Their central theme is the union of the soul and God, and they contain, as do his more strictly philosophical writings, important neo-Platonic elements. Distinctive is his concept of *scintilla animae*, the spark of the soul; it is that in man which is uncreated and uncreatable, and it is the basis for the knowledge of God and for the return of the soul to God, together with the rejection of all created things.

Some theories of Eckhart's have a pantheistic ring. He wrote, for instance, that God is immanent in his creatures, but also that they are immanent in God; trying, as pseudo-Dionysius, St Thomas and others had also tried, in his own way to formulate metaphysical truth about an unfathomable ultimate being. Some of his views, about the usefulness for salvation of exterior acts, about the nothingness of creatures and the need for detachment, were considered unorthodox, and his view of God as essentially unity seemed to imply a denial of God's Trinitarian nature. Twenty-eight theses of his were condemned by the Pope in 1329. But Eckhart's views on these theologically controversial matters were not unequivocal, and there are also statements of a more orthodox kind in his works.

YP/ed.

eclectic (Gr. *eklektikos* selective) *adj.*, *n.* An eclectic thinker is one who selectively adopts ideas from different sources and combines them in the development of a new theory. In philosophy the term has on the whole had a pejorative ring since Hegel, suggesting lack of originality and inability to integrate the selected elements into a coherent whole.

Earlier, in the seventeenth and eighteenth centuries, the sense was more favourable. Eclectic thinkers were taken to be commendably undogmatic and to be willing to overcome prejudice, dogmatism, and undue respect for authority, in contrast to those who simply adhered to an established doctrine.

Various writers and schools through the ages have been described as eclectic: Cicero, Hellenistic philosophers (Hume mentions in his essay on the Rise of the Arts and Sciences 'the Eclectics, who arose about the age of Augustus', who professed 'to chuse freely what pleased them from every different sect . . .'), Christian Thomasius, French Enlightenment *philosophes*, Victor Cousin, etc.

ecofeminism *n.* theory of a special, significant relation between women and nature. It rejects past and present theories of women and of nature which take male domination over women and over the natural environment for granted, as being in accord with the natural order of things. It sees a close analogy or indeed affinity between the human domination over nature, and the male domination over women. This implies that various forms of domination cannot be disentangled from each other, and indeed environmentalism is a necessary part both of the resistance against all kinds of oppression and of the promotion of the community of all beings.

ecology *n.* **1** a scientific discipline which has for its object natural systems of biological organisms. It investigates the manner in which the parts of such systems interact, and the impact of external forces on them. **2** the object of the inquiry mentioned under (1).

economic rationalism a term commonly used since the 1980s for two ideas, singly or in combination. One is that economic considerations alone should guide government policies; the other, that market mechanisms are preferable to government intervention. The rationality of these two assumptions has been subject to lively debate.

economics *n. sing.* **1** the study of the production, distribution and exchange of goods and services. **2** household management. This is an older sense, still to be found in seventeenth- and eighteenth-century NATURAL JURISPRUDENCE and political philosophy, where three kinds of 'economic', i.e. domestic, relations are distinguished: marital, parental, master/servant.

economism *n.* **1** (in some Marxist writings) over-simplified crude explanations of all aspects of social and cultural life in terms of economic forces. **2** (in other Marxist writings) the view that workers should primarily struggle to improve their economic condition in the workplace, and that activity with broader moral and political aims is pointless, or at any rate should be left to others.

economy *n.* **1** the production, distribution and exchange of goods and services. **2** cost-reduction; frugality; thrifty management. **3** housekeeping; management. **4** an ordered structure.

economy of thought The principle of least effort, proposed by Galileo and Newton as a law of mechanics, inspired attempts at generalization, so that it would apply not only to physical but also to mental phenomena. For instance, the principle of economy of thought, i.e. of the least intellectual effort, can be included in a theory of evolution: an individual or a species is better adapted if *ceteris paribus* it requires less energy to perform certain functions, including intellectual ones. This principle was also used by Avenarius and Mach as a basis for the formulation of a criterion of adequacy for theories: of two conflicting theories, the one which requires less effort for its formation and verification is the correct one. By this criterion, it was argued, a theory which confines itself to the data of experience is to be preferred over one which recognizes these but adds metaphysical assumptions.

ecosophy *See* DEEP ECOLOGY.

ecthesis (Gr. a setting out, exposition, exemplification) *n.* **1** [usually pronounced ɛk'θiːsɪs] the process of picking an arbitrary individual term to establish a logical thesis, especially in Aristotelian logic. For instance, the thesis 'If no S is P, then no P is S' may be proved by a form of argument that begins: 'Take this s (which is an S), for example . . .' **2** [usually pronounced 'ɛkθəsɪs] the Ecthesis of the Byzantine Emperor Heraclius was an edict promulgated in 628 that Christ has only one will.

ectype /'ɛktaɪp/ *n.* the image or copy of an ARCHETYPE.

Edwards /'ɛdwədz/, Jonathan (1703–58) The most eminent American philosopher of his time, Edwards, a Presbyterian minister, presented his philosophy mainly in writings that are primarily theological. In his idealist theory of knowledge, similar to Berkeley's, he argued that colour is no more *in* a thing than pain is *in* a needle. The same applies to secondary qualities generally, but also, he argued, to primary qualities: they are all definable in terms of physical resistance, which is the way we perceive an actual exertion of God's power. Since absolute nothingness is impossible, being is necessary, and must be identical with God. Edwards also identified it with space, in which everything created exists and has its being. The faculties of will and intellect in man are both passive: they do not have the power of self-determination, which is peculiar to God. This gave scope for Edwards's endorsement of the traditional Calvinist doctrines of innate depravity and predestination.

effability, principle of the principle that every mental content (thought, belief, idea, etc.) can, in principle, be expressed in language.

efficient cause *See* CAUSE.

egalitarianism *n.* an outlook that opposes privilege and favours equality between individuals. The equality is always in some respect which is specified explicitly or understood from the context. For instance, many egalitarians oppose special birthrights for children of the aristocracy or the plutocracy and favour equality of *opportunity*. In another respect, pertaining to the *outcome*, the same egalitarians can without inconsistency tolerate inequality: they accept that those who perform best or have better luck get better rewards. More radical egalitarians may oppose rewards based on luck or skill, and favour equal rewards for everyone.

egocentric particular *See* INDEXICAL.

egocentric predicament The egocentric predicament consists in the supposed impossibility of being aware of anything which goes beyond one's own thoughts and perceptions.

The expression was coined by R. B. Perry (whose paper with that title of 1910 has been described as the most important single study of the neo-realists) to designate the starting-point from which idealism (here taken as the view that nothing can exist unless some mind is aware of it) is erroneously inferred. In later philosophical writings the precise characterization of it can vary.

egoism (Gr. or Lat. *ego* I) *n.* This term is used to designate a *theory* (1–3) or a *disposition* (4).

1 *Ethical egoism* is an ethical theory, to the effect that one *ought* always to act in one's own best interests; that an action *is right* if and only if it benefits the agent; that what is valuable and desirable is that which benefits oneself.

2 *Psychological egoism* is a theory about people's actual motivation and conduct, to the effect that all action *is* self-interested.

Two main varieties can be distinguished. One says that disinterested action is impossible, like an uncaused effect, or an uncaused event. Another less extreme variety does not say that disinterested action is impossible, but takes it to be illusory, always, or for the most part: scratch the surface, and ulterior motives of self-interest, often disguised by pretence or hypocrisy, will be found behind seemingly disinterested actions.

In the modern era, psychological egoism in either of these varieties, or in a confused amalgam of them, found adherents in a large number of theologians, moralizing satirists, and philosophers such as Hobbes and Schopenhauer. The standard anti-egoist objections were articulated by

Hutcheson, Butler and Hume. Today, egoistic assumptions are common among economists, psychologists, politicians, etc. The causal explanations of action offered in the behavioural sciences operate at a different level, and psychological egoism can hardly find support there.

3 the view that nothing exists except one's own self and the contents of its consciousness. This was the original sense of *egoism* when the word was first devised by Christian Wolff in the early eighteenth century. In this sense the word is obsolete, and *solipsism* is currently used instead.

Kant distinguished in lectures between this 'metaphysical egoism' and 'logical egoism'. The 'logical egoist' has a closed mind and is prepared to accept only those opinions that fit his preconceived ideas. This usage had very limited currency.

4 selfishness, the characteristic disposition of a person concerned to satisfy his own appetites, desires and interests with undue disregard of others. When taken in this sense, the antonym is ALTRUISM.

The words egoism and altruism in these senses came into common use in the nineteenth century. Before then, the contrast was expressed by 'self-love/benevolence', 'private affection/public affection', 'selfishness/kindness', etc.

egoist *n.* **1** a person exclusively or excessively concerned with his private advantage. **2** a person who subscribes to a theory of *egoism*; for instance, a psychological egoist is a person who subscribes to psychological egoism.

egology *n.* a term used by Husserl in his *Cartesian Meditations* 1931 for the inquiry into, or theory of, the nature of the transcendental ego. Access is gained to this primordial realm by abstraction from all experienced objects and properties. His accounts of how this is done varied over time.

Note: Egological is occasionally used as a synonym of *egocentric*.

ego, transcendental a self or a mind, whose existence is seen as a necessary presupposition for our knowledge of the world around us. It may be seen to be somehow inherent in, although not identical with, the consciousness of actually existing individuals.

Kant introduced this concept in order to explain the coherence of our knowledge of the world. Fichte went further, by rejecting the notion of a thing-in-itself, and argued that the world that is an object of consciousness springs from a primeval act of 'positing' in which the transcendental ego produces something-other-than-itself. More recently, the concept plays an important part in Husserl's later phenomenology: the transcendental ego or 'pure consciousness' is a mind, distinct from individual minds. To be is to be an object for this consciousness.

Ehrenfels /'eːrənfɛls (Gm.)/, Christian von (1859–1932) one of the many important philosophers who was influenced by Brentano; professor in Prague from 1896. He gave an important impulse to the development of Gestalt psychology by proposing in 1890 ('*Über Gestaltqualitäten*') a theory of gestalt qualities, which are linked to, but not analysable as, complexes of separable mental contents. Along with Meinong, he was one of the first to attempt a *general* philosophical theory of value in his *System der Werttheorie* 1897–8 (System of value theory), which would cover not only values relating to character and conduct, but also the values which are the subject-matter of aesthetics, economics, etc. The leading idea in his analysis is that value is relational. That an object has value means that it is an object of desire. Something can be an object of desire either actually, when a person believes that it exists and desires it, or counterfactually, when a person would desire the object if he believed that it exists.

Later, Ehrenfels became more interested in applied ethics – *Sexualethik* 1907 – and in EUGENICS; but he also developed a speculative metaphysics in his *Kosmogonie* 1916 (*Cosmogony*). He rejected psychophysical dualism and claims that ultimately reality is mind-like, although neither mind nor matter. At the same time he accepted, with mention of Anaxagoras, a metaphysical duality of evil and good: there is a chaotic, formless principle in the universe which the opposite divine principle strives to overcome, and man is able to partake in this noble endeavour.

eidetic /aɪ'dɛtɪk/ *n.*, *adj.* a term devised by Husserl (from *eidos*) for the intuition of essences, which is the method of phenomenological inquiry.

eidos /'aɪdɒs/ (*sing.*) ***eidē*** (*pl.*) Gr. shape, visual appearance *n.* a word in Plato which, like *idea*, used to be translated as 'idea', but is nowadays often translated as 'Form'.

Einfühlung /'ainfyːlʊŋ (Gm.)/ Gm. EMPATHY.

élan vital /elɑ̃ vital (Fr.)/ Fr. *élan* impulse, impetus, urge; in Bergson's (1859–1941) *L'Evolution créatrice* 1907 (Creative evolution), the vital force which underlies various kinds of reality. We can directly grasp it in certain experiences which are neither thoughts nor sense-perceptions. Matter is one manifestation of this force. At the biological level, it manifests itself as a life-force immanent in all organisms, not capable of explanation within the physical sciences. It is also the principle which can explain evolution in general, without creating the problems arising from the assumption of randomness in the Darwinian theory of natural selection. The *élan vital* can also explain discontinuities (in various developmental or historical processes) that science is unable to predict.

Eleatic /ɛlɪ'ætɪk/ *adj.* Eleatic philosophy derives its name from Elea, a town in southern Italy. The founder of the school, which flourished in the fifth century BC, was Parmenides. Other prominent representatives were Zeno of Elea and Melissus.

element /'ɛlɪmənt/ *n.* a fundament; a basic component. There were four elements or basic constituents of the physical world according to Empedocles: fire, earth, air, water; but a much larger number according to modern chemistry.

The textbook most widely used throughout the history of Western culture is probably Euclid's *Elementa*.

In set theory, 'member' and 'element' are used synonymously.

elenchus /ɪ'lɛŋkəs/ (Gr. *elenchos* refutation) *n.* refutation of an opinion (or of an opponent), especially by eliciting self-contradiction or self-refutation within the interlocutor's thought.

elenctic *See* DEICTIC.

elide *See* ELISION.

eliminatism /ɪ'lɪmɪnətɪzm/ *See* ELIMINATIVISM.

eliminativism /ɪ'lɪmɪnətɪvɪzm/ *n.* a type of theory that combines two basic tenets: (1) the entities and properties to which a certain vocabulary or discourse supposedly refers do not exist; (2) the vocabulary or discourse in question ought to be eliminated.

There are many examples of eliminativist theories in the history of philosophy. Various thinkers have denied the existence of time, of matter, of spirit; of angels, witches, demons and other objects of superstition; of phlogiston, vital forces; of rights; and they have argued that an adequate theory can make no use of such concepts.

The word is, however, of recent currency,

and is used mainly in the philosophy of mind, where it designates the view that mentalistic concepts, e.g. belief, intention and thought, can have no place in an adequate theory, and that our ordinary common-sense view of the mind is fundamentally flawed because it uses such concepts. This thesis is often linked with a materialist thesis, that the human behaviour which common-sense psychology tries but fails to explain can only be accounted for by the concepts and theories of neurophysiology, cognitive science and other empirical sciences. The combination of these two theses was appropriately called eliminative materialism; 'eliminativism' was first used by J. Cornman in 1968. It was articulated by Paul Feyerabend in 'Mental Events and the Brain', *Journal of Philosophy 60* (1963) and Richard Rorty, 'Mind–Body Identity . . .', *Review of Metaphysics 29* (1965), and further developed in the 1980s by Paul and Patricia Churchland, Stephen Stich and others.

Eliminativism is not the same as reductionism. Eliminativist theses take the form: 'In reality, there are no tables (mental states, ghosts)'; reductionist theses take the form: 'In reality, tables (mental states, ghosts) are nothing but . . .'

Eliminativism is not the same as non-cognitivism, non-descriptivism, non-factualism, etc. They deny the objective reality of values, modalities, secondary qualities, numbers, universals, etc. That is one thing; to leave scope for or urge a linguistic or conceptual purge is another.

A shorter form, 'eliminatism', has been used in the early 1990s by one author for the view that a certain type of moral discourse (in terms of rules of conduct) should be eliminated (in favour of a virtue-morality).

elision /ɪˈlɪʒən/ *n.* omission, elimination. The word has its main use in grammar, where it denotes omission of a vowel sound or of a syllable, e.g. *don't* and (in French) *l'homme*. The general use of the word is a recent vogue.

ellipsis (Gr. *elleipsis* shortfall; ellipse) *n.* **1** (in grammar and rhetoric) omission of a part of a grammatically complete sentence. The word is also used to denote the three dots – '. . .' – that conventionally symbolize such an omission.

The fallacious argument from a premiss *S is P* to the conclusion *S is* (= S exists) has wittily been called Argument by Ellipsis.

2 (in logic) an ENTHYMEME can be described as an elliptical argument.

emanation *n.* an issuing forth from, an arising out of. It is a key concept in Gnostic and neo-Platonic philosophy. The One, or God, has a fullness, indeed an overflow of being, and other things come into being at various levels as emanations of the divine. This is why, given their present imperfection and the perfection of their source, they have an inner urge towards union with The One.

Emerson /ˈɛməsən/, Ralph Waldo (1803–82) American author, the leading figure in the intellectual movement known as New England transcendentalism. His *Nature* 1836 was an attempt to find meaning in life not from outside, as in traditional religion, but in a life of individual self-realization, a life that may involve a refusal to conform to convention. There is a strong influence from German romantic philosophy, partly mediated by Coleridge and Carlyle. His preferred kind of writing was the non-technical free-flowing essay or secular sermon. The conventional image of Emerson has been that of a solitary serene figure given to vaporous meditation on the Oversoul. In fact, he was energetic, active, uncompromising, and persistent in the struggle to abolish slavery. He was also a critic of modern industrialized mass society, complaining of declining culture, coarsening of taste, and suppression of individuality.

Emile /emil (Fr.)/ One of Rousseau's major works, published 1762. It outlines the way in which the main character, Emile, is educated from his tenderest years until the stage that he marries his betrothed, Sophie. In this work, Rousseau argues with passionate eloquence for principles of a child-centred education, for his faith in the natural goodness of human nature, which would remain uncorrupted were it not for the effects of modern culture, and, in the part entitled 'The profession of faith of the Savoyard Vicar', for his belief in an undogmatic deistic religion.

eminent *adj.* In Aquinas and other scholastic philosophers, an effect is said to be *formally* contained in its cause if the nature of the effect is present in its cause. Thus heat (an effect) is formally contained in fire (its cause) because fire contains heat within itself. An effect is said to be *virtually* contained in its cause if the cause, without containing the nature of the effect, can produce the effect. Thus heat in a human being can be produced by spices or by wine, although these do not contain heat within themselves. The causal relation between a sculptor and a statue is also virtual. An effect is said to be *eminently* contained in its cause if the nature of the effect is present in its cause except for the imperfections of the effect. It is in this sense that God is the cause of what he has created: in their perfect state they are contained in him, but the imperfections they actually possess do not emanate from him.

In the third of Descartes's *Meditations*, three ways are distinguished in which a thing can have reality: (1) *objectively* – being an object of an idea of ours. (This comes close to what in modern terminology would be subjective reality – existing 'in' the mind); (2) *formally* – having actual existence in our world, represented by our idea (i.e. existing 'outside' the mind); (3) *eminently* – having existence without limitation or imperfection, as contained within a higher level of being. From the standpoint of the world in which we exist, that which is eminently real exists potentially, not actually.

emotive meaning An explanation of the meaning of many terms and predicates in a language will be incomplete if nothing is said about the overtones that may colour a particular expression. For instance, to explain the meaning of an abusive term like 'wog' it is not enough to give its sense and reference. That explanation will only give the *descriptive* (factual, propositional) meaning. In order to explain the meaning of 'wog' adequately, the fact that it is a term of abuse must also be mentioned. In other words, this term has an *emotive* meaning.

This contrast between two kinds of meaning was proposed by C. L. Stevenson in chapter 3 of *Ethics and Language* 1944. According to his theory, the meaning of an expression can be analysed as its power to bring forth (in normal circumstances and *ceteris paribus*) a certain reaction in a hearer. The descriptive meaning of an expression is its power to produce an idea or a belief in a hearer. The emotive meaning of an expression is its power to produce a feeling or an attitude in a hearer. Thus, the emotive meaning of an abusive expression is the power of that expression to produce a feeling of dislike, hostility or the like in a hearer.

The concept of emotive meaning was used to give an account of the meaning of ethical terms.

emotivism *n.* also called *the emotive* (better *emotivist*) *theory of ethics*, one form of moral non-cognitivism: the theory that there are no ethical facts, no ethical knowledge, no informative ethical propositions. Ethical statements are neither true nor false but express emotions, desires or attitudes. To affirm, for instance, that an action is morally right is, according to emotivism, to show a favourable attitude towards the action. There can be rational argument about the facts of a case, but the place for rational argument about the moral assessment of these facts is at best a subordinate one: the ultimate appeal can only be to feelings, desires and attitudes. These need not, however, be fixed for ever. Further personal experience, and influence from others who show their attitudes, for instance by making ethical statements, may modify previous attitudes.

Although first proposed by Hägerström, emotivism became more widely debated through the version sketched by Ayer and articulated more fully in Stevenson, who linked it to his theory of different kinds of meaning (descriptive/emotive). Emotivism, and non-cognitivism generally, does not stand or fall with that particular theory of meaning, since there are alternative non-cognitivist accounts of the crucial dichotomies involved, such as fact/value; belief/attitude; theory/practice.

empathy *n.* **1** an important element in aesthetic perception: the unconscious projection of qualities which belong to our own imagination and feeling, into the aesthetic object.

Empathy was introduced as a central concept in the psychological and aesthetic theory of Theodor Lipps (1851–1914) in his *Ästhetik* 1903–6. Aesthetic pleasure is an enjoyment of our own activity *in* an object. It is a central point of this theory that, to take an example, the majestic quality of a building or a natural phenomenon is to be explained by the projection of certain inner states of ours on to the object. Lipps also used this concept, styled *Einfühlung* in the German, to explain the origin of our knowledge of other persons. The English equivalent *empathy* was coined early in the twentieth century by the psychologist E. B. Titchener (1867–1927) and was initially used mainly in aesthetic theory.
2 The word *Einfühlung* ('feeling into') had, however, been used earlier by Herder for the intuitive understanding of a literary tradition, a people, a culture, a *Zeitgeist* (spirit of the times).
3 Once 'empathy' had been coined, it soon came to be used for the ability to share or enter into another person's way of thinking or feeling, and for the sympathetic understanding of others. Previously, especially in the eighteenth century, the word 'sympathy' was used in this sense, e.g. by Hume and Adam Smith. But 'sympathy' is now used in different senses, involving compassion with, benevolence towards, acceptance of, another person, and 'empathy' has filled the gap.

Empedocles /ɛmˈpɛdəkliːz/ (*c.* 495–435 BC) ancient Greek philosopher from Acragas, Sicily, who established the theory of the four elements and was the first thinker to identify independent forces in nature.

Empedocles's thought shows influences from Parmenides and the Pythagorean tradition. Although he accepts Parmenides's argument that nothing can come to be, he nevertheless rejects the consequence Parmenides draws, that there is no change. In order to explain the appearance of change he posits the existence of four basic 'roots' – earth, water, air, and fire – and two forces personified as Love and Strife. The four elements satisfy Parmenides's requirements by neither coming to be nor perishing; but they can arrange themselves in different combinations and thus generate compound substances such as blood and bone as they mix in determinate ratios. The forces of Love and Strife can explain the alternative possibilities of attraction or repulsion between different elements. Empedocles rejected Parmenides's criticism of the senses, arguing that they can give us access to some facts.

Empedocles's Pythagorean heritage appears in his conception of soul. The soul is separated from its divine estate by a kind of original sin, the eating of flesh. Undergoing reincarnation as plants, animals and humans, it can reclaim its divine status by pursuing philosophy. The soul's career somehow reflects cosmic cycles in moving from a state of Love to Strife to Love. In what must have seemed to him a confirmation of his belief in his own spiritual progress, Empedocles seems to have received divine honours as a prophet and healer.

The immediate legacy of Empedocles was a natural philosophy which accorded with Parmenidean restrictions while allowing natural change. The four elements were taken over by virtually all Empedocles's successors and remained the basis of chemical theory down to the early modern period. More important in the long run was his conception of changeless elements entering into chemical combinations, a concept that in its later, more developed form, provided the basis of modern chemistry. Empedocles's conception of animal development, while crude (at one stage in the cosmic cycle, chance combinations of limbs were formed to produce monsters which could not but perish, as well as viable organisms), provided early suggestions of a theory of natural selection. And in general his distinction between basic substances and natural forces offered the first steps towards a categorial distinction between things on the one hand, and qualities, powers and activities on the other. DG

emphasis *n.* (in rhetoric) originally, a figure of speech in which more is implied than is explicitly stated. For example: 'He is human', uttered in a way that implies that he can err. There are various ways in which the speaker can signal that more is implied. Among them is the use of a different tone of voice, e.g. a stronger one; hence the modern sense of stress or vigour of expression.

empiric (Gr. *empeiria* experience) *n.* An empiric is a physician who simply practises, without any theory (Leibniz, *Monadology* 28). The word has been used in this sense since Plato, and for the most part pejoratively, with the suggestion that without any theory, the doctor would be indistinguishable from a quack, having to proceed by trial and error.

In current usage, the words *empiric* and *empiricist* do not mean the same. An empiricist is a person who subscribes to empiricism.

empirical *adj.* pertaining to experience, especially sense-experience. A belief, statement, theory, method, etc. is said to be empirical if it originates in, has a basis in, is derived from, or can be confirmed by, sensory observation. Empirical science has commonly been contrasted with formal or deductive science, such as logic and mathematics, whose theorems are taken to be valid independently of sense-experience. For the same reason, empirical inquiry has also commonly been contrasted with transcendent metaphysics.

Note: The phrase 'empirical experience' is a pleonasm.

empirical philosophy in older usage, empirical science or inquiry; in its present-day sense, a synonym of empiricism.

empiricism *n.* the view that all knowledge is based on or derived from experience. Empiricism has seemed attractive because it holds out the promise of a basis from which irrationality, false profundity, superstition and obscurantism can be firmly rejected. There are, however, important theoretical difficulties, since essential parts of human knowledge seem indeed to be *a priori*. For instance, empiricism has to account for principles of space, time and causality that seem to be necessary presuppositions for empirical knowledge and which therefore cannot themselves be based on experience. Again, an explanation has to be given of the seemingly *a priori* nature of the truths of logic, mathematics, and even ethics. Denying innate knowledge, empiricism has to provide an alternative theory to deal with these problems.

John Locke, David Hume and John Stuart Mill are among the major philosophers regarded as empiricists. In the twentieth century, influential representatives have been Bertrand Russell, A. J. Ayer, Rudolf Carnap, Hans Reichenbach, and other logical positivists.

The use of *empiricism* to denote the method (or, rather, the lack of method) typical of an EMPIRIC is now obsolete, but occurs as recently as in John Stuart Mill, who expresses a low opinion of the vagueness and guesswork typical of 'empiricism and unscientific surmise', *System of Logic* (8th edn 1872) Book 6, chapter 10, the last paragraph.

empiricism, logical a philosophical theory and movement, more commonly called logical positivism (*see* POSITIVISM).

Empiricus *See* SEXTUS EMPIRICUS.

empiriocriticism *n.* the name given by Richard Avenarius (1843–96) to his empiricist philosophy, developed independently of but quite close to that of Ernst Mach (1838–1916). Both were attacked by Lenin in *Materialism and Empiriocriticism* 1908. Among those influenced by Mach was Karl Pearson, and the Vienna Circle consisted initially of the members of the Ernst Mach Society which had been organized by Schlick.

Encyclopaedia *n.* The great French *Encyclopédie* of arts, sciences and trades had a chequered publication history spanning the years 1751–66 (for the text; the last volume of plates came in 1772), during which time Diderot was chief editor. Its 26 large volumes contained a vast number of important articles on metaphysical, religious, moral and political subjects, and were influential in spreading the ideas of the ENLIGHTENMENT. Remarkable also is the great scope given to the various crafts and trades, with detailed descriptions and illustrations of the methods and machinery used. Among eminent philosophers who contributed were Condillac (1715–80), Diderot (1713–84), d'Alembert (1717–83), Helvétius (1715–71), Holbach (1723–89), Montesquieu (1689–1755), Rousseau (1712–78), Turgot (1727–81) and Voltaire (1694–1778).

endogenous /ɛnˈdɒdʒɪnəs/ *adj.* originating from within. *Ant.* exogenous.

endoxon /ˈɛndɒksɒn/ (*sing.*); ***endoxa*** (*pl.*) Gr. (in Aristotle) common, accepted, reputable opinion(s) *n.*

energeia *See* DYNAMIS.

Enlightenment a current in the cultural and intellectual history of Europe that gradually gained influence from the 1680s to the 1780s, characterized by belief in progress, expected to be achieved by a self-reliant use of reason, and by rejection of traditionalism, obscurantism and authoritarianism.

Various traditional ways of thinking were subjected to more insistent criticism than before. In theology, LATITUDINARIAN and neological (NEOLOGY) tendencies gained strength, and so did DEISM: religious doctrine had to be intelligible and rationally acceptable. Even more radical were the atheist opinions that came to public expression, mainly after the 1750s, from a small but growing number of radical thinkers like Holbach and Diderot. There was also an increasing anti-clericalism and resistance to the view that the church should have power independent of secular authorities.

In legal matters, there emerged strong opposition to judicial torture, to prosecutions for witchcraft, to wretched prison conditions, and to many other abuses (Montesquieu, Voltaire, Beccaria). Important reforms followed. In certain respects, success was partial only. For instance, abuses of entrenched privilege in the legal profession were only partially curbed, due to the resistance from vested interests, and even today what Bentham attempted has been only partially accomplished.

Of the natural sciences, some reached a high degree of perfection (Newton), others commenced their growth (Lavoisier, Scheele, Priestley, etc.). In agriculture, trade, commerce, transport and engineering, there was an increasing willingness to try innovations.

The period was also marked by pioneering efforts towards reform at all levels of schooling (Pestalozzi, Basedow).

In politics, great emphasis was given to the principles of natural liberty and equality, and to basic human rights, including religious toleration. The prevailing distinctions of rank and inequalities of wealth came under attack more slowly, and advocacy of universal male suffrage was rare. It was only at the most radical fringe of this intellectual ferment that one could find writers, chiefly in France, who favoured communism.

In philosophy, materialism, determinism and other theories incompatible with traditional religious and moral ones gained support. The traditional assumption of mankind's having a central or at least very special place in the overall scheme of things was undermined, and so were common-sense assumptions about our moral responsibility for our actions.

On the whole, the universities did not play an important part in these developments. But the new ideas found a location in the many academies and learned societies that were founded in the eighteenth century. One of them, founded in Berlin 1736, had as its motto the words from Horace: *sapere aude* – dare to use your reason. These words can serve as the motto for the Enlightenment, Kant wrote in his famous essay 'What is Enlightenment?' 1784. He characterized the Enlightenment as man's mental emancipation from self-incurred *Unmündigkeit* (minority, immaturity, tutelage).

The evaluation of this cultural and intellectual movement has been hotly disputed ever since the French Revolution, with its successes and excesses. The opponents of the Enlightenment have found many faults with it: it was 'superficial', it was 'French in spirit', etc. The negative view is succinctly expressed in the remarkable entry in the *Shorter Oxford English Dictionary*: 'Shallow and pretentious intellectualism, unreasonable contempt for authority and tradition etc.; applied esp. to the spirit and aims of the French philosophers of the 18th c.'

Critics of the Enlightenment accused it of cold-hearted neglect of important values: of tradition, of community, of attachments and commitments which, even if they are non-rational, should not be rejected as irrational. In the 1940s, Horkheimer and Adorno claimed in *Dialectic of Enlightenment* that the Enlightenment ideals of rationality and criticism had their natural conclusion in the cynicism and brutality of de Sade's fantasies. Other objections have come from present-day critics like Michel Foucault, whose attitude to the abolition of the barbaric practices of eighteenth-century criminal justice may seem ambivalent; or from early nineteenth-century writers like Joseph de Maistre, whose praise of the hangman is rapturous. Clerical, Marxist, fascist, Nazi, Maoist and other ideologists have seen in this tradition a natural enemy.

The belief that progress is historically inevitable now has few supporters, but the belief that something can be done to improve the human condition, and the demand that human dignity and human rights be respected, remain part of a living but contested intellectual tradition.

Enneads /'ɛnɪædz/ (Gr. nines) the name given to Plotinus's writings, as edited by his disciple Porphyry in six volumes with *nine* treatises in each.

ens medieval Lat. being *n. being* in the most general sense, whether a substance or an accident. JM

en soi /ɑ̃ swa (Fr.)/ Fr. in itself, in oneself. *See* IN ITSELF.

entailment *n.* As the term is normally used by philosophers nowadays, to say that a proposition p entails a proposition q is simply an alternative (and often more convenient) way of saying that q follows logically from, or is logically deducible from, p.

The question of the precise conditions under which the relation of entailment holds between propositions has been the subject of much controversy. Perhaps the simplest view, and one which has been widely held in both medieval and modern times, is that p entails q if and only if it is logically impossible that both p and not-q.

This view has, however, been objected to, chiefly for the following reason. It seems clear that if a proposition is impossible, so is the conjunction of it and any other proposition; hence if p is impossible, so is (p and not-q), no matter what q may be; thus if the view in question is correct, any impossible proposition entails any and every proposition whatsoever – a result which many philosophers (though by no means all) have thought intuitively unacceptable.

A more restricted result, viz. that every proposition which is self-contradictory – i.e. of the form 'p and not-p' – entails any proposition whatsoever, can be derived by an argument which does not assume the above account of entailment but only the following principles: (A) that any conjunction entails each of its conjuncts; (B) that any proposition entails the disjunction of itself and any other proposition; (C) that a disjunction and the negation of one of its disjuncts together entail the other disjunct (the principle of 'disjunctive syllogism'); (D) that entailment is transitive. The argument runs as follows:

(1) p and not-p
(2) p [from (1) by principle (A)]
(3) p or q [from (2) by principle (B)]
(4) not-p [from (1) by principle (A)]
(5) q [from (3) and (4) by principle (C)]

Hence, by principle (D), (p and not-p) entails q, where q is any arbitrary proposition.

This argument (or some simple variant of it) is found in the works of several medieval logicians. It was revived by C. I. Lewis and C. H. Langford in their *Symbolic Logic* 1932 and has been the subject of much controversy since then. It seems clear that anyone who rejects its conclusion must deny, or at least restrict, one or more of the principles (A)–(D). The most popular candidate for rejection is (C), disjunctive syllogism.

The logical use of 'entail' derives from G. E. Moore's paper 'External and Internal Relations', first published in the *Proceedings of the Aristotelian Society* 1919–20 and reprinted in Moore's *Philosophical Studies*. Moore preferred this word to 'imply', which had been used in a different sense by Bertrand Russell.

entelechy /ɛn'tɛlɪkɪ/ (Gr. *entelecheia* actualization, completion) *n.* a term of art introduced by Aristotle in *Metaphysics* Θ, 8, 11 1050^a20. It can be understood as the state of perfection towards which, by nature, each thing of a certain kind tends. Modern vitalists like Hans Driesch have used the term for a dynamic organic non-material force.

enthusiasm (Gr. *enthousiasmos* divine in-dwelling) *n.* a state of religious exaltation. In its less attractive manifestations, the fervour expresses itself in irrational conduct, zealous intolerance, and the like. This is why in the seventeenth and eighteenth centuries most writers, including Locke (*Essay Concerning Human Understanding* Book 4, chapter 19: it arises from 'the conceits of a heated or over-weening brain'), and Leibniz used the term pejoratively in the manner that we now use the word *fanaticism*. Shaftesbury opposed this in his *Letter Concerning Enthusiasm* 1708, in favour of a positive appreciation of states of inspiration and rapture, and wrote of 'noble enthusiasm'.

enthymeme /'ɛnθɪmiːm/ *n.* an argument with an unstated premiss or an unstated conclusion. This accords with the seventeenth-century definition of an enthymeme as 'a syllogism complete in the mind and incomplete in expression', e.g. 'If it is raining, I will take my umbrella; therefore, I will take my umbrella.' Here, the premiss 'It is raining' is not stated, perhaps because on the particular occasion it will be too obvious for words.

In some enthymemes, it is the conclusion that is not explicitly stated, and again the reason may be that it is obvious. For instance: 'It is raining, and if it is raining I will take my umbrella.' At that point enough has been said for purposes of normal conversation.

It may happen that *both* the conclusion and some premiss is implicit. The statement: 'Either he is a rogue, or I will eat my hat' can be understood as an enthymeme with a suppressed premiss: 'I will not eat my hat' and a suppressed conclusion: 'He is a rogue.'

entity *n.* a thing, a being.

enumerable *adj.* DENUMERABLE.

environmentalism *n.* **1** (in psychology) the view that a person's intellect and character are determined by the social and natural environment, and that heredity does not play a significant part. **2** (in the social sciences) the view that differences between human cultures are due to external factors such as soil, climate, food supplies, etc. **3** (in ethics and politics) the view that the protection of the natural environment is of major practical and moral concern for mankind; the movement based on and promoting that view.

eo ipso *adv.* Lat. by that very fact.

eon /'iːɒn; 'iːən/ (Gr. *aiōn* life-span; age; eternity) *n.* **1** a very long period of time; in Gnosticism: a long period during which the universal Self attains a new spiritual level. **2** AEON.

epagoge /ɛpə'gəʊgɪ/ *n.* Gr. induction.

epexegesis /ɛpɛksɪ'dʒiːsɪs/ (*sing.*) **-es** /-iːz/ (*pl.*) *n.* the addition of a word or words for purposes of elucidation. If in an expression of the form *A or B* the *or* is epexegetic, B should elucidate A.

ephectic /ɪ'fektɪk/ *adj.* pertaining to *epochē*, suspension of judgement.

epicene /'ɛpɪsiːn/ *adj.* (in grammar) non-gendered. In English, the search for an epicene personal pronoun, i.e. one that is indifferent between 'he' and 'she', has been in progress since the nineteenth century and is continuing.

Epictetus /ɛ'pɪktətəs/ (55–*c.* 135) Stoic moral philosopher, originally a slave, whose views have come to us from his pupil Arrian in the form of two works, the *Manual*, a summary of his views, and the *Discourses*, a more extensive record of lectures in eight books, of which four survive. These works, particularly the *Manual*, subsequently influenced Marcus Aurelius and generations of moralists ever since. The emphasis is on humanity's small place in a providentially run universe, and on our inability to change anything except ourselves. We are therefore encouraged to live in harmony and bear the blows of fate as something of no importance, and to strive to maximize our virtue, wherein alone happiness can be found. HT

Epicureanism /ɛpɪ'kjʊərɪənɪzm/, **modern** In the Renaissance, knowledge of ancient Epicureanism was revived through the writings of Lucretius and Diogenes Laertius. The ancient atomic theory was regarded as dangerously irreligious, denying divine providence and the immortality of the soul. In the early seventeenth century Pierre Gassendi made it acceptable as both a scientific and a religious theory. He set out to show that the atomic theory could explain known physical events better than the prevailing Aristotelian natural philosophy or the new physics of Descartes. By offering his 'Epicureanism' as a hypothesis for explaining phenomena, Gassendi avoided any commitment to a metaphysical materialism. As a priest, Gassendi restricted Epicurean atomism to dealing with the natural world; doctrines about the soul and God were to be accepted on faith. Following Gassendi, atomism became a popular scientific model among researchers in England and France. Robert Boyle and others developed a corpuscular theory of the ultimate constituents of matter.

During the eighteenth century scientists sought for the best explanations in materialistic terms, some developing further the atomistic view, others some forms of vitalism. Though 'the hideous hypothesis of Epicurus' still aroused opprobrium, new forms of atomism were offered as the best way of explaining how natural events occurred. Atoms were still conceived as minimal units of matter with rather vague properties. At the beginning of the nineteenth century, John Dalton (1766–1844) connected chemical findings with the atomic theory. For him, atoms were understood not just as smallest physical units, but as units possessing chemical properties. With advances in chemistry, it was possible to see that various elements could be defined in terms of atomic properties. From then on, atomism developed as a scientific theory independent of metaphysical speculation about the nature of things, and independent of the moral and religious implications of classical Epicureanism.

In moral philosophy, Epicurean ideas also became more widely known after the 1650s, when the works of both Lucretius and Gassendi appeared in English and were widely read. But initially the ideal of an Epicurean life of pleasure, serenity, and freedom from religious fears found adherents only among a limited number of freethinkers. On the other hand, the Epicurean theory of motivation, that all action is for the sake of the agent's pleasure or advantage, was widely accepted by writers on moral subjects, including theologians who found it compatible with the doctrine of the corruption and selfishness of fallen man. RPO

Epicurus /ɛpɪ'kjʊərəs/ (341–270 BC) founder of the Epicurean school. Born in Samos, he probably learnt atomist philosophy from the Democritean thinker Nausiphanes. When settling in Athens, he bought a property whose garden was the centre of his school, to which slaves and women were also admitted.

Epicurus favoured a philosophy that would be easily intelligible and expressed in language which ordinary people could understand. Philosophy was divided into three areas: ethics, physics, and canonic. This last was essentially epistemological. It did not include formal logic, the usefulness of which was questioned. Both canonic and physics were seen as ancillary to ethics, the central part of Epicureanism. The aim was to achieve serenity, peace of mind, which is necessary for happiness.

Epicurus was a hedonist: in his view, only pleasure is good in itself. The goal of all action, the Epicurean life, was pleasure, which was held to be naturally and visibly pursued by all creatures and alone good in itself. But pleasure, in this theory, was virtually equivalent to the absence of pain, since there was no neutral state between the two. Epicurus sharply distinguished two types of pleasure: (1) the underlying harmonious state of body or of mind (catastematic pleasures); and (2) alterations of state, activities, etc. of body or of mind (kinetic pleasures). The former type was to be preferred, and indeed provided the only reliable basis for the expectation of the latter. Once the underlying state had been perfected and all pain removed, then there was no possibility of increasing pleasure, only of varying it by different activities. Some kinetic pleasures were to be rejected if they were a threat to one's underlying well-being. The well-being of the mind, or freedom from disturbance (*ataraxia*), was particularly important. The virtues, including justice, were explained in terms of enlightened self-interest on hedonist principles; nobody was thought to be virtuous for any other end except the maximization of pleasure and minimization of pain.

The biggest threat to one's underlying mental well-being was fear, above all fear of the gods and fear of death. The purpose of Epicurean physics is to understand the universe in such a way that these fears are dispelled. Atomic theory demanded that the soul, like all else, was composed of atoms and void – small round atoms which would easily disperse at death, so bringing an end to sensation. 'Death is nothing to us.' Likewise, sensations had to be the product of actual atoms reaching and affecting the mind, and though conglomerations of atoms could become distorted in transmission, recurrent sensations building up a clear picture in the mind must owe their origin to something existent. One such recurrent 'sensation' was our dream-images of the gods, superhuman creatures living in a blessed condition. The tenuous atomic images which built up such pictures of the gods came from another world far away, and their blissful condition meant that the gods had no concern for humans: such concerns would be painful. Thus we have nothing to fear from the gods any more than from death, and there is no divine providence or rationality governing the universe. Epicurean physics differed from Democritus's by introducing the atomic swerve. Such a swerve seems to have been an occurrence of low probability, but was needed to explain how the atoms, originally falling uniformly through the void, should have come to collide in such a way as to generate interactions leading to the formation of a world. The swerve was also used to avoid an inevitable chain of causes and effects (i.e. fate), and so reconcile atomism with mankind's clear concept of free will.

Epicurean epistemology emphasized the importance of three criteria of truth: the five senses, the anticipations or preconceptions (*prolēpseis*), and the affections (*pathē*). All sensations were true, equally valid in their own way and all to be considered in devising the total picture of a thing; only in their interpretation did error arise, since the mind could add to and subtract from the content of an act of sensation when forming an opinion. The preconceptions were mental pictures of things built up naturally (hence without the intrusion of fallible opinion) from repeated acts of sensation. Since opinions, unlike sensations, may be true or false, a method was devised for distinguishing them. True, are those which have some confirmation (*epimartyrēsis*, confirmatory testimony) in our sensations and/or disconfirmation of the contrary (*ouk antimartyrēsis*). False, are those which have disconfirmation and/or confirmation of the contrary.

Epicurean social and political philosophy emphasized the amount of trouble that political and social commitments could bring with them, thus preventing us from achieving the goal of mental well-being. In opposition to the Stoics as well as to established Hellenistic ideals, it advocated the avoidance of political life, marriage and child-raising, having as a motto *lathe biōsas* (get through life unnoticed).

Epicureanism became the second most influential of the Hellenistic philosophies, after Stoicism. Owing to the devotion of later Epicureans to their master, the basics of the philosophy remained more or less unchanged for centuries; but, above all, the theology and the hedonism provoked criticism among the ancients. The other schools were united in their opposition to the Epicureans from the time of Cicero, and it began to lose its appeal in later imperial times, with a change in religious and moral sensibilities.

Among the sources for our knowledge of ancient Epicureanism are the extant works of Epicurus himself, mainly through Diogenes Laertius, who preserves the *Letter to Herodotus* (on natural philosophy), the *Letter to Menoeceus* (on ethical theory), the *Letter to Pythocles* (on heavenly phenomena, of uncertain authenticity), and the forty *Kyriae Doxae* (*Principal Doctrines*), and through works by Lucretius, Cicero and Plutarch. HT

epicycle /ˈɛpɪsaɪkl/ *n.* Epicycles were an invention of ancient Greek astronomers. When the idea that planets moved in circles around an immobile central Earth proved unworkable, some said that planets moved in circles ('epicycles') about points which themselves moved in circles around an immobile central Earth. This was, in fact, a better theory, as a basis for predicting the movements of planets. But it was also false – planets do not go around an immobile central Earth at all.

'Epicycle' and 'epicycling' also have figurative uses for *ad hoc* efforts to rescue a dubious hypothesis. AM

epideictic /ɛpɪˈdaɪktɪk/ *See* RHETORIC.

epigenetic /ɛpɪdʒɪˈnɛtik/ *adj.* **1** pertaining to epigenesis, i.e. the development of an animal or plant by gradual cell differentiation. The contrast is with preformation, the supposed development of organs and parts which are differentiated from the outset. **2** genetically influenced. This is the sense intended when, e.g., sociobiologists such as E. O. Wilson and M. Ruse have argued that morality should be understood as a set of 'epigenetic rules', i.e. as processes or rules which genetically predispose an individual to behave in certain ways.

epigone /ˈɛpɪgəʊn/ (Gr. descendant) *n.* an undistinguished follower (of a great teacher).

Epimenides /ɛpɪˈmɛnədiːz/ ancient philosopher (6th century BC), competing with Eubulides, the Megarian logician, for fame as originator of the LIAR PARADOX – the most renowned of all the logical paradoxes.

epiphany /ɪˈpɪfənɪ/ (Gr. *epi-* on, upon, on

to + *phanein* to show, to manifest) *n.* **1** a manifest appearance of a divine being in the world. **2** a manifestation, revelation or disclosure of an underlying hidden reality.

epiphenomenalism /ɛpɪfɪˈnɒmɪnəlɪzm/ *n.* a theory about the relation between matter and mind, according to which there is some physical basis for every mental occurrence. Mental phenomena are seen as by-products, as it were, of a closed system of physical causes and effects, and they have no causal power of their own. (T. H. Huxley likened them to the whistle on a steam train.) AM

epiphenomenon /ɛpɪfɪˈnɒmɪnən/ (*sing.*); **epiphenomena** (*pl.*) *n.* a secondary phenomenon; a by-product.

episteme /ɛpɪˈstiːmɪ/ (*sing.*); (Gr. *epistēmē* knowledge, science) *n.* Aristotle (*Metaphysics* 1025ᵇ–1026ᵃ) divides it into *praxis* (knowing how to act), *poiēsis* (knowing how to make something) and *theoria* (insight, theoretical knowledge), which in turn has three branches: mathematics, physics (i.e. knowledge of the natural world) and 'theology'. It is made clear also in the *Nicomachean Ethics* (6, 3 1139ᵇ31–33), as it is in Plato, that it is knowledge demonstrable from first principles, in contrast to knowledge of the contingent.

In a different sense, the word has gained currency through the influence of Michel Foucault. He uses it in *Les Mots et les choses* 1966 (*The Order of Things*) for the anonymous, historically emergent structures of thought, which set conditions and boundaries for what can be thought or said within a certain social and intellectual setting. An episteme is a time- and culture-bound framework of discourse. Thus, during the Renaissance, the predominant episteme was a search for resemblances. In the seventeenth century, the search was on for differences and contrasts. Later, the concept of evolution became predominant. The modern episteme, beginning at the end of the French Revolution, gave rise to the concept of a human subject, and so the human sciences emerged. This period is now coming to an end. In *The Archaeology of Knowledge* 1969 Foucault abandoned the terminology of 'knowledges' ('knowledges' is not English, but he cannot be blamed for the solecisms of his translators), modifying the notion of rigid underlying epistemic structures in favour of 'discursive practices'.

Foucault's concept has something in common with the Kuhnian concept of PARADIGM and the Marxist concept of ideology, although an episteme may be a structure at a deeper level which can give rise to different ideologies and paradigms. The word has, however, been used for sets of ideas which can be described simply as a predominant theory or ideology. Thus, Roland Barthes called the materialist dialectic (in the Marxist tradition) and the Freudian dialectic (in psychoanalytic theory) 'the two great epistemes of modernity'.

epistemic *adj.* pertaining to knowledge.

epistemological realism *See* REALISM.

epistemology *n.* theory of knowledge; the branch of philosophy that inquires into the nature and the possibility of knowledge. It deals also with the scope and limits of human knowledge, and with how it is acquired and possessed. It also investigates related notions, such as perception, memory, proof, evidence, belief and certainty.

The traditional investigation from Plato to the twentieth century of the nature of knowledge concentrated on the question of what it is for someone to know that something is so. The traditional assumption was that a person knows that p, if and only if (1) he believes that p, (2) p is true, and (3) he has good grounds for the belief.

Currently, this account has been challenged (*see* GETTIER PROBLEM). One alternative view is that knowledge is simply the ability, based on some non-accidental means, to provide the right answers.

A step away from the traditional concentration on propositional knowledge was made by Bertrand Russell when (influenced, or at least anticipated, by William James and John Grote) he distinguished between our knowledge of truths and our knowledge of things, such as persons and places. Within the latter he distinguished between our knowledge by acquaintance, which those who have actually been to Paris might have – though he himself thought that this knowledge was limited to such things as sense-data and mental images – and our knowledge by description, which might simply be of Paris as the capital of France.

Again, Gilbert Ryle distinguished between our knowledge of truths, what we commonly call 'knowing that', e.g. Paris is the capital of France, and our knowledge of skills, what we commonly call 'knowing how to', e.g. to speak French, both of which he considered to be abilities to get things right.

Throughout the history of philosophy, theories of knowledge have at different times treated it as a mental act, a mental achievement, a mental state, a mental disposition, and a mental ability.

Traditionally, much philosophical attention has also been given to the acquisition of knowledge, to what Locke called 'the original, certainty and extent of human knowledge'. The great historical division has been between the empiricists, such as the British philosophers Locke, Berkeley and Hume, and the rationalists, such as the continental philosophers Descartes, Leibniz and Spinoza. The former held that all our knowledge must ultimately be derived, as it is in the sciences, from our sense-experience, while the latter insisted that knowledge properly so called requires a direct insight or a demonstration, for which our faculty of reason is indispensable.

Pervading all epistemology was a desire to provide a foundation for knowledge which would make it immune to scepticism. There are varieties of scepticism: one is that there can be no knowledge of other persons or other minds, another that there can be no knowledge of the past, another that there can be no knowledge of contingent truths, and, the most radical of them all, that nothing can be known. This made it necessary to examine our notions of belief, of certainty and evidence, both deductive and inductive.

Perception and memory have been repeatedly discussed in epistemology, both for their own intrinsic interest and for their connection with knowledge. Perception is one way in which we acquire knowledge, and memory is the way in which we retain it. In the discussions of both there has been a continuing controversy between realists and representationalists. Realists believe that what we are aware of in perception are the objects, such as chairs and trees, which now exist around us, and in memory the objects, such as chairs and trees, which once did so exist. Representationalists, on the contrary, believe that what we are aware of in perception are merely the appearances of these objects, and in memory merely their images. The usual reason offered in support of the representationalist view is the belief that in perception it is impossible, sometimes in practice and perhaps even in principle, to distinguish between the appearances which we are presented with by actual chairs and trees and the appearances which we are presented with in illusions, hallucinations, reflected images, etc. Similarly, in memory it is impossible, on this view, sometimes in practice, and perhaps even in principle, to distinguish between those mental images which are due to our actual recollection and those which are due to our imagination. On the basis of these appearances and these images we can only infer, according to the representationalists, sometimes rightly and sometimes wrongly, the existence of presently or previously existing chairs and trees. Some representationalists take the further step of saying that, therefore, what we really 'perceive' are those appearances and – though this is a less common step – what we really 'remember' are those images. AW

epizeuxis /ɛpɪ'zjuːksɪs/ (Gr. *epi-* on, upon, on to + *zeugma* a yoking) *n.* (in grammar) repetition of a word for emphasis, e.g. 'yes! yes! yes!'

epochē /ɛpɒ'keɪ/ Gr. a holding back, a pause *n.* **1** suspension of judgement; a refusal to affirm or deny; a central concept for the ancient sceptics, who recommend *epochē* on the ground that certainty is unattainable. *Epochē*, they claim, is necessary for achieving peace of mind (*ataraxia*) which, in turn, is indispensable for happiness or indeed identical with it. **2** Husserl uses the term to describe the bracketing of natural common-sense assumptions (about the existence of an external world, etc.) by which we can focus our mental gaze purely on the structure of the act of consciousness (transcendental reduction) or on the essences inherent in the experienced content (eidetic reduction). This phenomenological *epochē* agrees with the sceptical one in leaving no place for assent or dissent, but differs in that it does not imply doubt, and in that its primary aim is not *ataraxia* but insight (*theoria*). **ephectic** *adj.*

eppur si muove /ɛp'ur si 'muove (It.)/ It. and yet it (the Earth) does move. It is said that these were the words uttered by Galileo in a low voice when condemned by the Inquisition at Rome in 1633 and forced to retract his endorsement of the Copernican theory of the Earth's movement. The story is probably apocryphal.

equipollence /iːkwɪ'pɒləns/ (Lat. equality of strength, from *aequi-* equal + *pollere* to be able, strong) *n.* (in logic) two sets of sentences, e.g. two formal systems, are said to be equipollent, if every sentence in one set can be derived in the other and vice versa. If each of the two sets contains exactly one sentence, equipollence amounts to equivalence.

equivalence /ɪ'kwɪvələns/ *n.* In logical contexts, to say that two propositions are equivalent means that necessarily they have the same truth-value. Two propositions that imply each other are equivalent.

Sentences with the same meaning are equivalent, but equivalent sentences can differ in meaning. *T has three equal sides* and *T has three equal angles* (where T denotes a particular triangle) are equivalent, but do not have the same meaning.

equivalence, material Two propositions with the same truth-value are said in Russellian formal logic to be materially equivalent, i.e. two propositions, each of which materially implies the other, are materially equivalent. In other words, two statements, p and q, that make up a true biconditional, p iff q, are materially equivalent. For instance, *The moon is made of green cheese* and *2 + 2 = 5* are materially equivalent, and so are *A has a heart* and *A has a kidney*.

equivalence relation a relation that is TRANSITIVE, SYMMETRIC, and REFLEXIVE. Identity is an equivalence relation.

equivocal /ɪ'kwɪvəkəl/ *adj.* ambiguous, polysemous. *Ant.* univocal.

Erastianism /ɪ'ræstɪənɪzm/ the doctrine that the state has authority over the church even in matters relating to church doctrine and church discipline.

Richard Hooker (1553–1600), in his *The Laws of Ecclesiastical Polity* 1593, named this general doctrine after Thomas Erastus (1524–83), a Swiss Protestant theologian who advocated that the civil authorities should have jurisdiction in matters of church discipline.

erasure *n.* the crossing out or striking through of a written or printed word. The function is intended to be similar to that of 'scare quotes'. By 'erasing', the author distances himself from the use of the word. Erasure is not the same as deletion: the effect cannot be achieved by using rubber or white-out.

ergo /'ɜːgəʊ/ (Lat. *ergo* consequently) *conj.* indicates, like *consequently*, *therefore* and other illative expressions, that the sentence following is to be understood as the conclusion of an inference.

ergon /'ɜːgɒn/ Gr. work; deed; product; function.

eristic /ɛ'rɪstɪk/ (Gr. *eris* strife, conflict) *adj.*, *n.* (in ancient Greek philosophy) argument aiming at persuasion or victory in debate. It was contrasted with dialectic, which aims at truth.

Eriugena /ɛrɪ'ʊdʒənə/ or **Erigena** /ɛrɪ'dʒiːnə/, Johannes Scotus (before *c.* 825–*c.* 870) an Irishman who spent his working life on the continent, under the patronage of Charles the Bald. A teacher of the liberal arts at Charles's palace school, he was asked (*c.* 855) to write a treatise condemning the view, advocated at the time by Gottschalk, that there is dual predestination, of the blessed to heaven and the damned to hell. But in his *De praedestinatione*, Eriugena went much further, denying that God was at all responsible for the condemnation of the wicked, and insisting that the punishments of hell should not be understood literally. After writing this work, Eriugena learned Greek, and proceeded to translate the works of pseudo-Dionysius (a fifth-century Christian neo-Platonist) and some other philosophically-minded Greek Christian writers. This reading made his masterpiece, the *Periphyseon* (*c.* 862–6), a lengthy, wide-ranging treatise in dialogue form, very different in its concerns from the works of his Western contemporaries.

The *Periphyseon* begins with a four-fold division of universal nature into that which is not created and creates; that which is created and creates; that which is created and does not create, and that which is neither created nor creates. The first of these divisions is God, the creator of the universe. The second is occupied by the 'primordial causes', a cross between Platonic Idcas and Stoic seminal reasons, through which the work of creation is accomplished. The third division is the rest of the created universe; whilst the fourth is, like the first, God – envisaged here as that to which all things return. The contrast between God as the first division and God as the fourth illustrates the juxtaposition within Eriugena's thought of positive and negative theology. Positive theology is the attempt to say something about God, although he is beyond any literal description. Negative theology recognizes God's unknowability. He is beyond all things, even being itself. It is truer to say that 'God is not' than that he is; and, in a daring (if not entirely coherent) move, Eriugena equates the 'nothing' from which, according to Christian belief, God created the world, with God, who is nothing because he is beyond all being. Book I of the *Periphyseon* sets forth negative theology, by showing that none of Aristotle's ten categories applies to God. Books II–V expound positive theology through an exegesis of the beginning of *Genesis*, which is interpreted allegorically as the story both of the Creation and of the return of all things to God at the end of time. The whole created universe, explains Eriugena, is a 'theophany', a manifestation of God. God, therefore, can in a sense be known through his Creation and, especially, through the divinely-inspired biblical account of Creation and return. But it is *only* through theophanies that he can be grasped by the human mind. In himself, God is incomprehensible, not just to the highest created beings, but also to himself. Were he fully knowable, even by himself, God would no longer be beyond every definition and circumscription. JM

Erlangen /'ɛrlaŋən (Gm.)/ **School** a group of German philosophers, located primarily in the universities of Erlangen and Konstanz, whose work centres on epistemology and philosophy of science – in the wide sense of that term, including all areas of systematic inquiry from mathematics to the humanities. They critically analyse the structures and underlying assumptions of these disciplines, and see the task of philosophy as that of giving a rational foundation to the various sciences and thus reconstructing them. Leading representatives are Paul Lorenzen (1915–94), Kuno Lorenz (1932–), Friedrich Kambartel (1935–), Jürgen Mittelstrass (1936–) and Peter Janich (1942–).

Erlebnis /ɛr'lebnɪs (Gm.)/ Gm. an experience *n.*

eros /'ɪərɒs; 'ɛrɒs/ *See* AGAPE; PLATONIC LOVE.

erotematic, erotetic *adjs.* (Gr. *erōtaein* to question) Erotematic teaching methods consist in asking questions of the pupil in order to elicit knowledge. Erotetic logic is the logic of questions, as contrasted with the imperative logic and with the usual logic of indicatives.

error theory the theory that all statements within a certain area are false.

The term has been most frequently applied to the view that all *moral* statements are false. The central argument for this view rests on two premisses. The first premiss, about the meaning of moral statements, is that they all assert that some objective moral property belongs to an action or a state of affairs. For instance, the statement that it is morally obligatory to keep a promise asserts that there is a property of moral obligatoriness that belongs to the keeping of the promise. The second premiss, about what there is, is that there are no objective moral properties. John Mackie is the best-known advocate of this view, which can be found in his 'The Refutation of Morals', *The Australasian Journal of Psychology and Philosophy 23* (1964), and *Ethics: Inventing right and wrong* 1977.

eschatology /ɛskə'tɒlədʒɪ/ (Gr. *eschatos* last (*adj.*)) *n.* religious doctrine of the last things, i.e. the ultimate fate of mankind. Since the nineteenth century, some schools of theology have conceived of eschatology not as a *theory* which predicts what will happen in a more or less distant future, but as an expression of religious *faith* in what the believer may hope for.

esoteric /iːsə'tɛrɪk/ (Gr. *esōterikos* inner) *adj.* rites, doctrines, tastes, etc. described as esoteric are those which are for initiates only, or which belong exclusively to an inner circle.

There is a tradition that Aristotle communicated an esoteric doctrine to a smaller circle of disciples; it is the one that is recorded in the extant writings. The EXOTERIC teaching seems to have been presented in a more popular and easily accessible form, but is now lost, but for a few fragments. Pythagoras and Plato are said to have taught esoteric doctrines. *Ant.* exoteric.

ESP acronym for EXTRASENSORY PERCEPTION.

esse *vb.* Lat. to be. The word is also used as a noun: the *esse* of a thing is its being.

esse est percipi /ˈɛsɪ ɛst ˈpɜːtʃɪpɪ/ Lat. to be is to be perceived. This is an important principle in idealistic theories, and is especially associated with Berkeley, who denied that matter can exist in its own right and maintained that what we think of as matter is nothing but the content of some mind.

essentialism *n.* **1** (in logic and metaphysics) the view that some properties inhere necessarily in the individuals to which they belong.

On an essentialist view, Socrates is human essentially, but Socrates is bald accidentally (i.e. non-essentially). In other words: it is not possible that Socrates is not a human being, but it is possible that Socrates is not bald.

The view that there are *de re* necessary truths, in opposition to the view that all necessity is *de dicto*, is implied by essentialism, and many writers even identify it with essentialism.

With the development of possible-worlds semantics for modal logic (i.e. the logic of necessity and possibility) since the late 1950s, there emerged a framework within which essentialism could be rehabilitated. According to Kripke, the origin of an organism is essential to it; according to Putnam, the fundamental physical properties of a compound, an element, a biological species, are essential to it; according to Wiggins, it is essential to an organism that it is of a certain biological kind; etc.

The word first gained currency through Karl Popper's *The Open Society and Its Enemies* 1945. He uses it for the belief in real essences that underpins Plato's and Aristotle's theories of knowledge, i.e. the view that we can have a direct intellectual intuition into the nature of things, which comes to expression in definitions and constitutes knowledge in the proper sense. Popper vehemently rejects this outlook, taking it to be a major obstacle to political, moral and scientific progress.

2 (in philosophical anthropology) the view that there is a human nature or essence. The use of *essentialism* in this sense, as a contrasting term to existence-philosophy or existentialism, can be traced to a work by Emil Przywara in 1939, and became current through Paul Foulquié's account of Sartre's thought in *L'Existentialisme* 1946.

3 (in feminist philosophy) the view that femininity is determined in central respects by nature, and is not merely the product of contingent social customs and conventions. Much recent feminist theory condemns this view.

esthetic(s) *See* AESTHETICS.

eternal *adj.* **1** timeless, beyond time, nontemporal. **2** everlasting, omnitemporal, sempiternal.

eternal recurrence The doctrine of eternal recurrence asserts that every actual state of affairs must come into being again on infinitely many other occasions.

In ancient times, such a doctrine was adopted by the Stoics, and before them probably also by the Pythagoreans and by Heraclitus. Nietzsche proposed a doctrine of this kind in *Thus Spake Zarathustra* 1883–5. He was probably influenced by some French writers of popular books on philosophical topics, like Blanqui, Le Bon and Guyau. Nietzsche may not have intended this as a scientific hypothesis but as the positive alternative to nihilism, the endorsement of an attitude of life-affirmation and life-celebration: 'so live that you wish to live again'. *Syn.* eternal return.

ether *n.* **1** an invisible all-pervasive substance that fills up 'empty' space in the universe, assumed to exist in classical physics as the medium through which light is propagated. This hypothesis was rendered obsolete by Einstein's theory of special relativity. **2** In Aristotle's *Physics*, the earth is surrounded by layers of water, air, fire, and outermost by a number of shells which carry the heavenly bodies and which consist of a fifth element called ether.

ethical egoism *See* EGOISM.

ethical formalism the view that an ethical norm or standard does not depend for its validity on what it prescribes, i.e. its content, but on its form. Kant's ethics is often said to be formalist(ic).

ethical hedonism *See* HEDONISM.

ethical rationalism theories according to which moral knowledge is based on rational insight, in a manner analogous to rational intuition into the truths of mathematics and logic. There is a suggestion in Locke to this effect. Among ethical rationalists were Cudworth and, in the eighteenth century, Clarke, Wollaston, Balguy and Price; in the twentieth century similar views have been defended by H. Prichard, W. D. Ross and others.

ethical relativism **1** the view that, as a matter of fact, different individuals, groups, societies, cultures, differ in their view of what is good or bad, right or wrong, in relation to character and conduct.
2 the view that whatever is good or bad, right or wrong, in respect of character and conduct, is so only relatively: (a) relative *to a situation*. This can mean (i) that some rules can have exceptions; circumstances sometimes change cases; *or* (ii) that all rules can have exceptions. This is not uncontroversial. Relativism in this sense opposes absolutism, according to which some rules admit of no exceptions, like the rules prohibiting incest, blasphemy, or the deliberate killing of an innocent person; *or* (iii) that different rules are appropriate depending on the situation: water-conserving conduct is right in times of drought. (b) relative *to the judging of a situation*. Moral opinions are true or false, correct or incorrect (i) only relative to the individual whose opinion it is: my statement 'P did the right thing' is true if and only if it is my opinion that P did the right thing; *or* (ii) only relative to the group or society, whose opinion it is: my statement 'P did the right thing' is true if and only if it is the opinion of the group or society that P did the right thing.

To some people, relativist views as defined above have a certain allure because they seem to underpin a 'non-judgemental' approach to morality – one ought not to sit in moral judgement over others, and they seem to underpin a 'non-interventionist' approach to morality – one should not interfere. But there are grave problems with ethical relativism. One of the objections runs parallel to that against TRUTH-RELATIVISM.

ethics *n. sing.* The word is related to the Greek *ēthos* habit, custom. It is used in a number of related senses, which have to be distinguished to avoid confusion.

1 (normative ethics) rational inquiry into, or a theory of, the standards of right and wrong, good and bad, in respect of character and conduct, which *ought to be* accepted by a class of individuals.

This class could be mankind at large, but we can also think of medical ethics, business ethics, etc. as a body of standards that the professionals in question ought to accept and observe.

This kind of inquiry and the theory resulting from it (well-known examples are Kantian ethics and utilitarian ethics) do not describe how people think or behave, but prescribe how people ought to think and behave. This is accordingly called *normative ethics*, since its main aim is to formulate valid norms of conduct and of evaluation of character. The study of what general norms and standards are to be applied in actual problem-situations is also called *applied ethics*.

In recent times, the expression *ethical theory* is often used in this sense. Much of what is called moral philosophy is normative or applied ethics.

2 (social or religious ethics) a body of doctrine concerning what is right and wrong, good and bad, in respect of character and conduct. It makes an implicit claim to general allegiance. In this sense there is, for instance, Confucian ethics, Christian ethics, etc. It is similar to philosophical normative ethics in its claim to general validity, but differs from it in so far as it does not claim to be established merely on the basis of rational inquiry.

3 (positive morality) a body of doctrine that is generally adhered to by a set of individuals, concerning what is right and wrong, good and bad, in respect of character and conduct. The individuals may be the members of a community (e.g. Hopi ethics), of a profession (certain codes of honour), or of some other kind of social group.

Positive morality can be contrasted with critical or ideal morality. The positive morality of a society may tolerate slavery, but slavery may be declared intolerable by appeal to a theory supposed to have the authority of reason (normative ethics) or by appeal to a doctrine that has the authoritative support of tradition or religion (social or religious ethics).

4 (descriptive ethics) The study from outside, as it were, of such a system of beliefs and practices of a social group is also called ethics, and more specifically *descriptive ethics*, since one of its main aims is to describe the ethics of the group. It has also been called ethnoethics, and belongs to the social sciences.

5 (metaethics) A kind of philosophical inquiry or theory, distinct from normative ethics, is called *metaethics* or *analytical ethics*. It is so called because it treats ethical concepts, propositions and belief systems as objects of philosophical inquiry. It analyses concepts of right and wrong, good and bad, in respect of character and conduct, and related concepts, e.g. moral responsibility, virtue, rights. It also includes moral epistemology: the manner in which ethical truth can be known (if at all), and moral ontology: whether there is a moral reality corresponding to our moral beliefs, etc. The questions of whether and in what sense morality is subjective or objective, relative or absolute, fall under this heading.

Note: The Latin *moralis* was first used by Cicero as an equivalent to the Greek *ēthikos*, which explains why in many contexts *moral/ethical*, *morality/ethics*, *moral philosophy/ethics* are pairs of synonyms. However, writers frequently use the two words in different or contrasting senses. *See also* MORAL.

ethics of belief In a famous article entitled 'The ethics of belief', first published in *Contemporary Review*, January 1877, the Cambridge mathematician and essayist W. K. Clifford (1845–79) argued that 'it is wrong always, everywhere, and for everyone, to believe anything on insufficient evidence'. Such belief is condemned as unwise by Hume: 'A wise man proportions his belief to the evidence' (*Enquiry Concerning Human Understanding*, Section X, 'Of Miracles', the 4th para.).

ethnoethics (Gr. *ethnos* race, a people) *n.* the study of the positive morality of a society.

ethnopsychology *See* FOLK PSYCHOLOGY.

ethology *n.* **1** the scientific study of the

behaviour of animals in their natural environment. **2** a science of the laws of formation of the human personality, projected by John Stuart Mill (*System of Logic*, Book 6), who also coined the word, in the hope that it would form a theoretical basis for educational improvements.

ethos *n.* the spirit or character of a culture, a community, or a group. In ancient Greek, *ēthos* meant the character and habits of a person. In ancient rhetoric, the construction of a person's ethos, i.e. the depiction of a character, was an important element.

etiology *n. See* AETIOLOGY.

Eubulides /juːbə'liːdiːz/ a philosopher from Miletus, of the Megarian School, a contemporary of Aristotle. Diogenes Laertius (Bk 2, 108 f.) ascribes to him a number of paradoxes, of which the most important are the SORITES and the LIAR PARADOX.

Eucken /'ɔɪkən (Gm.)/, Rudolf (1846–1926) professor in Jena from 1874. In reaction against predominant naturalistic tendencies, Eucken developed an idealistic philosophy which would help in the quest for meaning in the universe and in the search for meaning in one's own life. The reluctance to accept a merely naturalistic view of man's place in the world is one of the manifestations, in the human mind, of the activity of a universal spiritual principle of life. The rejection of naturalism and the adoption of a higher form of religious faith makes the achievement of spiritual autonomy possible. There were many editions and translations of his works, among them *Die Lebensanschauungen der grossen Denker* 1890 (transl. as *The Problem of Human Life . . .*) and *Der Sinn und Wert des Lebens* 1908 (The meaning and value of life), and for a long time they enjoyed a remarkable international popularity, although academic philosophers remained cool. He was awarded the Nobel Prize for Literature in 1908.

Euclid /'juːklɪd/ (fl. 300 BC) wrote a number of works in mathematics and geometry, and his *Elements* have been used, in more or less revised forms, as a textbook until the present time.

The *Elements* is the first known *axiomatic theory*. Its basis consists of five *axioms* (or 'common notions') concerning wholes and parts, five *postulates* concerning geometrical concepts, and a number of *definitions*. On this basis, a large number of propositions are proved with a high degree of deductive rigour.

Euclidean/non-Euclidean geometry Any geometry different from Euclid's can of course be called non-Euclidean, but the theories so called are chiefly the ones that deviate from Euclid by not including his fifth postulate. The first theories of that kind were devised in the nineteenth century by Lobachevski, Bolyai and Riemann.

Euclid's fifth postulate is: given two lines intersected by a third, if the sum of the two interior angles on the same side is less than two right angles, then the two lines will intersect if drawn out indefinitely.

Euclid of Megara (*c.* 430–*c.* 360 BC) influenced by Parmenides, appears as a participant in Plato's dialogue *Theaetetus*, as a friend of Socrates in the *Phaedo*, and is regarded as the founder of the Megarian School. No writings of his have been preserved.

eudaimonia /juːdaɪ'məʊnɪə/ Gr. well-being happiness *n.*

eudaimonism /juː'diːmənɪzm/ *n.* the view that happiness is the highest good. Some writers take this term to designate the view that *pleasure* is the highest good, but that view is more properly called *hedonism*.

Happiness and pleasure are distinct notions.

Kant was an important opponent of eudaimonism. He rejected the view that happiness is the highest good, and insisted that happiness can be an ingredient in the highest good only if it is deserved.

eugenic /juːˈdʒɛnɪk/ *adj.* pertaining to the improvement of inherited qualities in a strain or breed.

eugenics /juːˈdʒɛnɪks/ (Gr. *eugenēs* well-born) *n. sing*. The word was created by Francis Galton (1822–1911), author of *Hereditary Genius* 1869, for the scientific inquiry into the hereditary factors which determine the quality of offspring, with a view to the general improvement of a human population, and for the social control of human reproduction for that purpose.

In modern times, interest in eugenics grew steadily from the mid-nineteenth century. The belief came to be widely held that the number of persons possessing desirable physical and mental qualities could over time be increased by selective breeding, and especially that the same method would reduce the number of persons with undesirable traits (predisposition for mental or physical illness, anti-social tendencies, etc.). Many of those who accepted this outlook – but not all – also adopted some theory of racial superiority then current. On the question of what practical steps could be taken, if any, there was a considerable diversity of opinion. Many of the ideas of the eugenic movement, especially as it developed in the United States, were taken up by German national socialists or coincided with their racial doctrines. After the defeat of Germany in the Second World War such ideas fell into disrepute. Modern developments in biomedicine, however, have reactivated the debate, particularly in relation to embryo selection and genetic engineering.

euhemerism /juːˈhiːmərɪzm/ *n.* a theory proposed by Euhemerus (*c.* 340–*c.* 270 BC) that the gods are nothing but great kings, warriors, inventors, etc. of a distant past, who in the myth-making imagination of posterity have been promoted to divine status.

Euler /juːlə (Eng.); ˈɔɪlər (Gm.)/ **diagrams** Devised by the Swiss mathematician Leonhard Euler (1707–83), these consist of arrangements of circles representing the terms of categorical propositions. They can be used to test the validity of categorical syllogisms, but when diagrams are used for this purpose, those devised by Venn are now preferred. *See also* VENN DIAGRAMS.

eutaxiology /juːtæksɪˈɒlədʒɪ/ (Gr. *eu-* goodness, well-ness + *taxis* order) *n.* Eutaxiological arguments seek to establish that the *well-ordering* of natural phenomena must be due to a designing, planning mind. The word was coined by G. L. Hicks (*A Critique of Design Arguments* 1883) and used by him to mark the contrast with TELEOLOGICAL arguments which seek to establish *purposiveness*: that the contrivances of nature exist for the sake of some purpose. This pair of terms (eutaxiological/teleological) has lain dormant but reappeared in J. D. Barrow and F. J. Tipler, *The Anthropic Cosmological Principle* 1986.

euthanasia /juːθəˈneɪzɪə/ (Gr. *eu-* goodness, well-ness + *thanatos* death) *n.* 'a good death': the bringing about of a painless or serene death. Its permissibility has been keenly debated in the twentieth century. A distinction should be made between voluntary euthanasia (assisted suicide) and involuntary euthanasia. Again, with involuntary euthanasia, i.e. assisting someone 'out of his misery', a distinction has to be made between actual misery (e.g.

of a terminally ill patient in severe pain) and forecast misery (e.g. of a severely deformed infant and its parents). It is also necessary to distinguish the question of what is morally permissible from the question of what legislation is appropriate.

euthymia /ju'θɪmɪə/ (Gr. equanimity, cheerfulness) *n.* the central element of human well-being, according to Democritus.

Euthyphro /'juːθɪfrəʊ/ **dilemma** In Plato's dialogue *Euthyphro*, Socrates asks: 'Is that which is pious (*hosion*) pious because the gods love it, or do the gods love that which is pious because it is pious?' To call the question a dilemma is to imply that both alternatives are problematic.

Many important philosophical problems have the same structure. They can be generated by substitutions ((1)–(3), and combinations of these): (1) replace *pious* with *morally right*, or *morally good*, etc.; (2) replace *the gods* with *God* or *Society* or *I*, etc.; (3) replace *love* with *approve* or *like* or *command*, etc.

Similar important philosophical problems arise also outside ethics. For instance: is an inference valid because it would be accepted by a perfect thinker, or does a perfect thinker accept a valid inference because it is valid?

event (Lat. *ex* out + *venire* to come) *n.* **1** (in older usage) outcome, result. For instance, when Hobbes writes 'the event of the contention' he means the outcome of the dispute.
2 happening, the occurrence of a state of affairs.

In present-day metaphysics, the analysis of the concept of an event has centred on what it is for something to be *one and the same* event. The problem is, in other words, the individuation of events. A small sample of points arising in these inquiries follows.

One view is that two events are identical if their causes are all identical and their effects are all identical. Against this early proposal of DAVIDSON's, various complaints of circularity have been raised – among them that the causes and effects in question are themselves events. A further problem is this: Jack is annoyed, answers the telephone, and says 'hello' in a loud voice. Is *his saying 'hello'*, and *his saying hello in a loud voice* one event or two? Jack's annoyance causes the second, but not the first. So it seems that, on Davidson's view, there would be two events.

Another view is that two events are identical if they occur at the same time and place. Against this proposal of QUINE's it has been argued that *taking a bath*, *singing in the bath*, and *thinking about Goldbach's conjecture* are three events, but they would count as one if they happen at the same time and place.

evidence *n.* **1** that which provides a ground for a belief or theory. **2** the quality of obviousness, intuitive certainty. In this sense, the word corresponds to the German *Evidenz*.

evil, problem of There is evil in the world: bad things happen to people, and people do bad things. These two are usually called physical (or natural) evil and moral evil, respectively. There is also a third kind of evil, often neglected in modern discussions. It is the evil consisting in a disproportion between virtue and happiness, between vice and misery: an evil exemplified when the wicked prosper and good people meet a grim fate. Given the existence of evil, 'Epicurus's old questions are yet unanswered. Is [God] willing to prevent evil, but not able? then he is impotent. Is he able, but not willing? then he is malevolent. Is he both able and willing? whence then is evil?' (Hume, *Dialogues Concerning Natural Religion*, part X.)

An attempt to show that the problem

need not lead to a denial of God's existence is often called a THEODICY.

The problem of evil arises not only in religious thought, but also for metaphysical theories according to which ultimate reality possesses certain perfections.

evolutionary epistemology an attempt to incorporate Darwinian insights into epistemology. The evolution of biological features proceeds by variation, selection and retention. An organism's cognitive faculties are no exception. Frogs, mice and human beings have developed cognitive faculties that are adaptive. It is, however, a disputed question among evolutionary epistemologists whether the fact that the human sensory system is an evolutionary product shows that it is generally reliable. Some argue that this is indeed the case, or else we would have been eliminated by natural selection, since having true perceptual beliefs is advantageous to us. Against this it has been argued that beliefs that are advantageous may nevertheless be false. Timid mice often run away from nothing at all – might not perceptual beliefs which are often false be advantageous too?

There is also another type of evolutionary theory of knowledge. It explains the development of knowledge in analogy with the biological theory of natural selection. Knowledge arises through a process that involves *variation*, when various more or less fanciful hypotheses are conjectured; *selection*, when they are tested and 'killed' if they fail the test; and *retention* of those that have not failed the test, in memory and documents, as a basis for further inquiry. An influential representative of this view is Karl Popper. AM

evolutionary ethics the view that we need only consider the tendency of evolution in order to discover the direction in which we ought to go. This is G. E. Moore's definition of what he called evolutionistic ethics (*Principia Ethica*, section 34).

Although Hegelian ethics has been called evolutionary, the word is most commonly used for theories of a more naturalistic or scientific kind which came into their own in the nineteenth century. There were two accounts of evolution that could serve as a basis for determining what its tendency might be. Spencer, an evolutionist before Darwin, proposed a general law of evolution from indefinite uncoordinated homogeneity to definite integrated heterogeneity, and held that biological evolution was a special case of this general law. But it was Darwin's theory of natural selection and the survival of the fittest that had a major impact on the common mind.

Some kinds of evolutionary ethics take a 'social Darwinist' stance. They see struggle and competition as both necessary and desirable; assistance to the 'losers', e.g. the poor or the sick, is seen as harmful. Other kinds of evolutionary ethics take an opposite view, arguing that it is by means of cooperation and altruism that overall 'fitness' is enhanced.

An objection to evolutionary ethics is that biological theories may explain why we are born with certain instincts, capacities, tendencies, etc. but cannot indicate whether these should be followed or resisted.

examination paradox *See* PREDICTION PARADOX.

exchange dilemma another name for PRISONER'S DILEMMA.

excluded middle, law of This is the principle that, for any proposition p, either p or not-p; i.e. that there is nothing intermediate, or 'middle', between something's being so and its not being so. This law should not be confused with the law of non-contradiction: not both p and not-p. In 'orthodox' or 'classical' versions of propositional logic, both laws are theorems; but there are systems (e.g. the intuitionist propositional calculus) in which the latter can be proved, but not the former.

The law of excluded middle should also not be confused with the law of bivalence, which is a metalogical principle to the effect that there are two and only two truth-values, 'true' and 'false', and that every proposition has precisely one of these. The exact relation between the laws of excluded middle and bivalence has been a matter of considerable controversy. GH

exegesis /ɛksɪˈdʒiːsɪs/ (*sing.*); **-es** (*pl.*) (Gr. *exegeisthai* to guide, to show the way) *n.* explanation of the meaning of a text; interpretation of a text. The word is commonly used in biblical contexts.

ex falso quodlibet /ɛks ˈfɒlsəʊ ˈkwɒdlɪbɛt/ Lat. from the false, anything (follows). The words are used for the principle that from a (logically) false proposition (e.g. a contradiction), anything follows. This principle is accepted in standard systems of logic, but rejected in PARACONSISTENT systems.

existence *n.* the main subject-matter of metaphysics, especially ontology. Note, however, that some philosophers who sound as if they were concerned with existence generally are in fact preoccupied exclusively with human existence.

existential generalization In predicate logic, given a formula A which contains a free variable x, (∃x)A is the existential generalization of A. For instance, the existential generalization of Wx is (∃x)Wx. In ordinary language, the parallel move is from *Socrates is wise* to *Someone is wise*.

existential import A universal proposition which is held to imply the corresponding particular proposition is said to have existential import. According to traditional syllogistic logic, *Every man is mortal* has existential import because it implies *Some man is mortal*.

In predicate logic, *Every man is mortal* is analysed *For every x, if x is a man then x is mortal*, and *Some man is mortal* is analysed *There is at least one x such that x is a man and x is mortal*. Given this analysis, the universal proposition does not have existential import, since a proposition of that form can be true even if the corresponding particular proposition is false.

existential instantiation In predicate logic, given a formula (∃x)A, in which A is a formula that contains the free variable x, A is the existential instantiation of (∃x)A. For instance, Wx is the existential instantiation of (∃x)Wx.

The inference from (∃x)Wx to Wx can be compared with the inference from *Someone is wise* to *Nero is wise*, which is not valid. But given that someone is wise, there will be at least one wise person to whom, pending further information about his identity, we can assign a dummy name like *x*. Existential instantiation, mirrored by this step from *Someone is wise* to *x is wise*, is valid, given suitable restrictions (not presented here).

existentialism *n.* a philosophical movement that is usually traced back to the nineteenth-century Danish philosopher Søren Kierkegaard. The name itself was coined by Jean-Paul Sartre, although the expression 'existence philosophy' had been used earlier by Karl Jaspers, who belonged to the same tradition. The existentialists differ widely from one another and, given their individualistic emphasis, it is not surprising that many of them have denied involvement in any 'movement' at all. Kierkegaard was a devout Christian; Nietzsche was an atheist; Jean-Paul Sartre was a Marxist and Heidegger, at least briefly, a Nazi. Kierkegaard and Sartre enthusiastically insisted on the freedom of the will; Nietzsche denied it; Heidegger hardly talked about it at all. But one would not go wrong in saying that existentialism represented a certain attitude particularly relevant to modern mass society. The existentialists have a shared concern for the individual and for personal responsibility. They tend to be suspicious of or hostile to the submersion of the individual in larger public groups or forces. Thus, Kierkegaard and Nietzsche both attacked 'the herd', and Heidegger distinguished 'authentic existence' from mere social existence. Sartre emphasized the importance of free individual choice regardless of the power of other people to influence and coerce our desires, beliefs and decisions. Sartre, in particular, stressed the importance of the individual's need to make choices. Here he follows Kierkegaard, for whom passionate, personal choice and commitment are essential for true 'existence'.

Søren Kierkegaard (1813–55) is the chief exponent of religious existentialism, a very personal approach to religion that emphasizes faith, emotion and commitment and tends to minimize theology and the place of reason in religion. Kierkegaard attacked the theologians of his day for attempting to show that Christianity was a thoroughly rational religion, claiming instead that faith is important precisely because Christianity is irrational and even absurd. The important thing, he argued, is not the merely intellectual and ill-conceived challenge to prove that God exists but the 'subjective truth' of one's own existence in the face of objective uncertainty. The very word 'existence', for him, has exciting and adventurous connotations. 'To exist' is to face the uncertainties of the world and to commit oneself passionately to a way of life. It is not, by contrast, simply to adopt certain beliefs or enjoy oneself or 'go along with the crowd'.

Although Kierkegaard's work inspired an influential school of twentieth-century religious existentialists (including Paul Tillich, Martin Buber, Karl Barth and Gabriel Marcel), the existentialist attitude is perhaps more often associated with atheistic thinkers to whom religious belief seems like an act of cowardice or, as Albert Camus calls it, 'philosophical suicide'. Friedrich Nietzsche's (1844–1900) attack on Christianity and Christian morality is based on his accusation that religion provides crutches and weapons for the weak. Religion and morality too are the legacy of a 'slave morality' that prefers safety and security to personal excellence and honour. In contrast to this ideology of weakness and mediocrity, Nietzsche holds up various examples of 'master morality' and 'higher men', who reject and despise weakness and live as exemplars of what he calls the 'will to power', which is best illustrated in artists and other creative geniuses. In one of his most famous images, in his pseudo biblical poem *Thus Spake Zarathustra*, Nietzsche introduces the exciting but obscure ideal of the *Übermensch*. But if the ideal is obscure, Nietzsche's aim is nevertheless clear: to encourage individual aspiration rather than mere mediocrity and conformity.

Twentieth-century existentialism has been greatly influenced by the method known as phenomenology, originated by Edmund Husserl and pursued into the existential realm by his student Martin Heidegger (1889–1976). Husserl's method, simply stated, was to find and examine the essential structure of experience, with the aim of establishing the universal truths necessary to basic consciousness. Husserl's own philosophy was primarily concerned with abstract questions concerning the foundations of mathematics and matters of *a priori* knowledge, but Heidegger borrowed the phenomenological method and applied it to more personal problems – questions about how human beings should live, what they are, and the meaning of life and death. His seminal work *Being and Time* 1927 is nominally concerned with metaphysics, but it has been widely read as a radical reassessment of what it means to exist as a human being. Heidegger rejects the classical Cartesian concept of consciousness ('I think, therefore I am') and replaces it with the concept of *DASEIN*. He rejects the idea of a consciousness separate from the world in which one finds oneself 'abandoned'. The 'ontological' problem of *Dasein* is to find out who one is and what to do with oneself, or, as Nietzsche said, how to become what one is. Phenomenology, for Heidegger, becomes a method for 'disclosing [one's] being'.

Jean-Paul Sartre (1905–80) defined the term existentialism, and following both Husserl and Heidegger, he used the phenomenological method to defend his central thesis that humans are essentially free. Retreating from Heidegger's attack on the Cartesian view of consciousness, Sartre argues that consciousness is such (as 'being-for-itself') that it is always free to choose (though not free not to choose) and free to 'negate' the given features of the world. One may be cowardly or shy, but such behaviour is always a choice and one can always resolve to change. One may be born Jewish or black, French or crippled, but it is an open question what one will make of oneself – whether these will be made into handicaps or advantages, challenges to be overcome or excuses to do nothing. Sartre's colleague Maurice Merleau-Ponty (1908–61) convinced him that he should modify his 'absolute' insistence on freedom in his later works, but the insistence on freedom and responsibility remains central to existentialist philosophy.

Albert Camus (1913–60) borrowed from Heidegger the sense of being abandoned in the world, and he shared with Sartre the sense that the world does not give meaning to individuals. Whereas Sartre surpassed Heidegger in insisting that one must make meaning for oneself, Camus concluded that the world is 'absurd', a term that has (wrongly) come to represent the whole of existentialist thinking. Indeed, one of the persistent errors in the popular understanding of existentialism is to confuse its emphasis on the 'meaninglessness' of the universe with an advocacy of despair or 'existential *Angst*'. But even Camus insists that the Absurd is not licence for despair, and Nietzsche insists on 'cheerfulness'. Kierkegaard writes of 'glad tidings', and for both Heidegger and Sartre the much celebrated emotion of *Angst* is essential to the human condition as a symptom of freedom and self-awareness, not as despair. For Sartre, in particular, the heart of existentialism is not gloom or hopelessness, but a renewed confidence in the significance of being human. RSO

existential proposition a proposition that *there is* (was, will be) such-and-such, or that such-and-such *exists*.

existential quantifier an operator in predicate logic, usually written (∃x). The combination of an existential quantifier and an OPEN SENTENCE containing some free occurrence(s) of the same variable is intended to be interpreted as an existential proposition. *See also* QUANTIFIER.

ex nihilo nihil fit /ɛks ˈniːhɪləʊ ˈniːhɪl fɪt/ Lat. nothing is made out of nothing; nothing emerges out of nothing.

exogenous /ɛkˈsɒdʒɪnəs/ *adj.* originating from outside. *Ant.* endogenous.

exordium /ɛkˈsɔːdɪəm/ *n.* the first part of a speech, in classical rhetoric.

exoteric (Gr. *exōterikos* outer) *adj.* used of teaching which is intended to be generally communicated and understood, in contrast to esoteric teaching. *Ant.* ESOTERIC; ACROAMATIC.

expansive *adj.* An expansive property is one which, if it belongs to every part, also belongs to the whole. The use of the word in this sense was introduced by Nelson Goodman in *The Structure of Appearance* 1951.

expectabilism *See* ACTUALISM.

experiment *n.* **1** a procedure undertaken to test a hypothesis. **2** (in older usage) authors such as Milton and Hume use the word for any empirical observation; and *experimental* simply meant empirical.

explication *n.* In the standard sense, introduced by Rudolf Carnap, an explication consists in replacing a vague or otherwise defective pre-theoretical concept, the *explicandum*, with a better one, the *explicatum*. The new concept must be similar to the old, but more precise or in some other way more adequate for theoretical purposes. Explication differs from analysis in that the aim is not to *lay bare* what is implicit in a given concept, but rather to *lay down* the meaning of a new concept; but explication differs from mere stipulation in that the new concept cannot be arbitrarily chosen, since it is intended to replace the old one.

exportation *n.* the name given to inferences of this form:

$$\frac{\text{If (A and B) then C}}{\text{If A, then (if B then C)}}$$

and to the theorem in standard systems of propositional logic:

$$((p \;\&\; q) \supset r) \supset (p \supset (q \supset r))$$

The converse is known as *importation*.

expressionism *n.* a style, especially in painting (Edvard Munch, Georges Soutine) and in film (especially German) in the early twentieth century, aiming to represent externally the inner world of elemental emotions of fear and loathing, anxiety, love, etc., often by exploiting unconventional techniques.

expressivism *n.* the view that words or statements of a certain kind are typically used by a speaker to *express* a feeling, an attitude, a desire, etc. but not to assert (truly or falsely) that something is the case. Expressivism about moral judgements, for instance, has as a central claim that they do not purport to state facts and cannot, strictly speaking, be evaluated as true or false, but that they serve to express certain attitudes or dispositions.

extension *n.* **1** having spatial dimensions. According to Descartes, there are two created substances, matter and mind. Extension is the essential characteristic of matter, consciousness of mind. The corresponding adjectives are *extended* and *extensive*. **2** The extension of *name* – or, more generally, a singular term – is the object referred to by that name or term; thus the extension of 'Socrates' is Socrates. The extension of a *predicate* is made up of those things to which the predicate applies. Thus the extension of 'horse' is all horses, and of 'red' all things which are red. Similarly, the extension of relational predicates are those pairs, triplets, etc. of particulars between which the relation holds. Extension is also ascribed by some logicians to *sentences* and is then defined as their truth-value. The corresponding adjective is *extensional*. *Syn.* denotation; reference. *See also* INTENSION.

extensional *adj.* pertaining to the extension of an expression.

extensional/intensional context, occurrence Consider the statement: 'Socrates is wise.' Remove 'Socrates'. The remaining open sentence '. . . is wise' is the *context*. Fill the gap with any other expression that has the same extension as 'Socrates', for instance 'the husband of Xanthippe'. We then obtain: 'The husband of Xanthippe is wise.' The two statements are bound to have the same truth-value, and 'Socrates' is then said to *occur* extensionally.

In general, that an *occurrence* of an expression is extensional means that replacing it by another expression which has the same extension does not change the extension of the context in which it occurs; and that a *context* is extensional means that its extension remains unchanged if an expression contained in the context is replaced by a coextensive expression.

Truth-functional contexts are extensional. That is, the truth-value of a truth-functional compound containing a proposition p remains unchanged if p is replaced by another proposition that has the same truth-value as p.

In contrast, consider an intensional context: 'P believes that Socrates is wise.' If 'Socrates' is replaced by another expression that has the same extension, like 'the husband of Xanthippe', we obtain: 'P believes that the husband of Xanthippe is wise.' But these two statements need not have the same truth-value, since P may be ignorant of Socrates's domestic situation. In this context, the occurrence of 'Socrates' is intensional.

In general, that an *occurrence* of an expression is intensional means that replacing it by another expression which has the same extension can change the extension of the context in which it occurs. And that a *context* is intensional means that its extension may change if an expression contained in the context is replaced by a coextensive expression.

Contexts involving propositional attitudes: 'P believes (doubts, is certain) that . . . ,' are intensional, and so are modal contexts: 'It is necessarily (possibly) the case that . . .'

Extensional contexts for names are also said to be referentially transparent (TRANSPARENCY), and intensional contexts are also said to be referentially opaque.

extensionalism *n.* the philosophical approach that adopts the thesis of extensionality (*see* EXTENSIONALITY, THESIS OF).

extensionality, axiom of one of the axioms of set theory: two sets are identical if and only if they have all members in common. This is also called the principle of extensionality.

extensionality, law of a theorem or a rule in systems of formal logic which permits an expression with an extension to be replaced by any other expression which has the same extension.

extensionality, principle of **1** If x and y are identical, they have all their properties in common. The principle is so called because it is valid only for extensional contexts. This is also called Leibniz's law; it is also called the principle of indiscernibility of identicals. **2** axiom of extensionality (*see* EXTENSIONALITY, AXIOM OF).

extensionality, thesis of The thesis asserts that once our language has been purged of nonsense, obscurity and confusion, intensional contexts will be eliminated. The extension of every compound expression will be entirely determined by the extension of its components: especially, the truth-value of every compound statement will be entirely determined by the truth-values of its components.

This thesis was adopted by Frege, Russell, Wittgenstein in his *Tractatus Logico-Philosophicus*, Quine, and many others.

extensive magnitude spatial (size) or temporal (duration). Kant uses these terms in the *Critique of Pure Reason*. The contrast is with intensive magnitude: the degree to which an object of perception influences a sensory organ.

externalism *See* INTERNALISM.

externality *n.* a consequence considered irrelevant in deliberation on evaluation; especially, a cost or a benefit not included in the accounts. Things that have value but no price – e.g. environmental beauty – are, from the standpoint of accountancy, externalities.

external negation *See* NEGATION.

external preference *See* PREFERENCE.

external relations *See* RELATION.

extrasensory perception perception of things, states of affairs, events, etc. not conveyed by the known senses. The main kinds of extrasensory perception are *clairvoyance*, i.e. the direct perception of past or remote phenomena, *precognition*, i.e. the direct perception of future phenomena, and *telepathy*, i.e. the direct communication with another person without the use of known normal pathways. Extrasensory perception, often referred to under its abbreviation ESP, is the main subject-matter of PARAPSYCHOLOGY. No attempt to verify the existence of extrasensory perception has been successful. The expression was coined by J. B. Rhine in the early 1930s.

extrinsic (Lat. *extrinsecus* from outside) *adj.* **1** external, not part of the nature or essence of a thing. **2** belonging to something in virtue of its relation to something else. *Ant.* intrinsic.

F

fact *n.* The word comes from the Latin *factum* a deed, something done. This is the sense of the word in older usage. Current philosophical usage is wider: 'it is a fact that p' is used as a synonym for 'it is the case that p', or 'it is true that p' or '"p" is true'.

fact/value dualism In moral philosophy, fact/value dualism is the view that statements of fact – factual statements – are of a different kind from statements of value – evaluative statements – and that no statement of the second kind can be inferred from statements of the first kind; in other words, that evaluative statements are logically independent of factual statements, so that even if all the facts are given, the question of how to evaluate the situation still remains open.

Fact/value dualism, and related dualisms, for instance fact/ought dualism, have been at the centre of debate in twentieth-century metaethics. Such dualisms are accepted both in objectivist ethical theories like that of G. E. Moore, and in anti-objectivist theories like those of A. J. Ayer, Charles L. Stevenson, Karl Popper, R. M. Hare, John Mackie, etc.

The last paragraph of Book 3, Part 1, Section 1, in Hume's *Treatise of Human Nature* 1740 comments on the 'vulgar [i.e. common] systems of morality' which proceed from 'is'-statements to 'ought'-statements but fail to explain the transition. This much-quoted paragraph has been interpreted as a statement of fact/value and fact/ought dualism.

facticity *n.* the characteristic of being a fact. The writers who use this term seem to apply it mainly to contingent conditions not of our choosing.

Facticity is the name that Heidegger and Sartre give to that aspect of human existence that is defined by the situations in which we find ourselves, the 'fact' we are forced to confront. Facticity includes all of those factual details over which one has no control – one's date and place of birth, one's parents, one's basic attributes and limits – but it also includes the nature and limits of being human as such, for example what Heidegger dramatically called 'Being-unto-death' or the fact that we all must some day die. Facticity is important for these two 'existentialists' because it establishes a necessary grounding for all of our actions. It is only 'in situation', Sartre tells us, over and over again, that we are free. Our freedom of action, our ability to transcend our circumstances – our 'transcendence' – was always against a background of facticity. And it is only in the facticity of society, in terms of an identity and a system of values that we ourselves have not chosen, that we exercise the personal 'resolve' that defines our existence, according to Heidegger. RSO

faction *n.* **1** a sub-group within a society or party. In the seventeenth and eighteenth century, the use of the word in this sense was often pejorative. **2** dissension, strife.

factious *adj.* given to dissension or conflict, within a society or party.

factitious *adj.* artificial, contrived, manufactured. The word is used by Descartes in the Third Meditation, where he distinguishes three kinds of ideas: the innate ones that we are born with, the adventitious ones that we receive, and the factitious ones that we make up ourselves.

Since the mid-twentieth century, the word has been used in the entirely different sense of *having the character of* FACTICITY, i.e. being a contingent fact. Confusion can easily arise. Blame for it rests with the translators of the writings of Heidegger into French, and with the translators of Heidegger, Sartre and others into English. To determine whether the intended sense is the same as that of 'artificial' or that of 'contingent', it is necessary to consider the context, the author, etc.

factitive *adj.*, *n.* (in grammar) verbs or verb-constructions that denote a process by which a result was achieved, e.g. 'They made him their leader'.

factive *adj.*, *n.* **1** a grammatical term used for certain expressions that signify that an embedded clause represents something as a fact. For example: 'He realized that the danger was past.' This statement implies that the danger was past, so 'realized' is factive. This is in contrast to: 'He hoped that the danger was past.' This statement does not imply that the danger was past, so 'hoped' is not factive. The statement: 'He laboured under the illusion that the danger was past' implies that the danger was not past, and is *contrafactive*. **2** Some writers use 'factive' more widely, for any that-clause, in contrast to nominal clauses. For instance, 'He sees that the snow is falling' is said to have an embedded factive, while 'He sees the snowfall' does not.

factual *adj.* a factual statement states a fact – truly or falsely. They are contrasted with statements which are neither true nor false. According to certain theories, value-statements and ought-statements are non-factual, i.e. they are not true or false, but have the force of, e.g., a request or a warning. Factual statements are also defined as statements about matters of fact which are logically contingent, in contrast to statements which are necessarily true or necessarily false.

Note: 'factual' does not mean the same as 'true'.

factualism *n.* Factualism, in respect of a certain kind of statements, is the view that they state facts, truly or falsely. The denial of such a view, usually combined with an alternative account of the linguistic role of such statements, is called *non-factualism.*

faculty *n.* A faculty is that in virtue of which an individual *can* do (or suffer) something. The faculty of recollection, for instance, is that in virtue of which a person can remember things. The word, a near-synonym of *power* and *ability*, may be regarded as a nominalization of the verb 'can', and has, like 'can', a variety of meanings. It is used mainly for non-physical powers or abilities, i.e. mental, moral and legal ones. When the right, power or authority by which a superior commands a subordinate (or a creditor demands payment from his debtor) is called a faculty, it is because the superior 'can' make a claim and create an obligation on the other party.

faculty of arts In the arts faculties of medieval universities, students studied, in addition to grammar, a course in logic, natural science, ethics and metaphysics, based on the reading of Aristotle's works. Only after taking an arts degree (or, for members of religious orders, studying arts in their houses of study) could students enter one of the *higher faculties*: law, medicine or theology. Although the textbooks of the theology faculty were religious (the Bible and the mid-twelfth-century *Sentences* of Peter the Lombard), logical and philosophical problems were often raised in discussing them. Most of what we think of as medieval *philosophy* (the works, for instance, of Thomas AQUINAS and DUNS SCOTUS) was produced by theologians working in the faculty of theology. JM

faculty psychology psychological theory which regards the faculties of the mind (memory, imagination, intellect, will, desire, etc.) (1) as if they are separate parts of the mind; or (2) as if they could be used as genuinely explanatory factors.

This view, ascribed to Christian Wolff et al., was rejected by Herder, Herbart, and many others. The critics insisted on the integrated character of the human individual, arguing that although the faculties can be distinguished – of course memory is not the same as desire – it is a misconception to treat them as separate parts; and to explain a volition by the faculty of willing, a remembrance by the faculty of memory, is like explaining the soporific effect of opium by its dormitive power.

Fall, the Adam's sin caused, or symbolized, a fall from a higher and more blessed kind of existence to a life filled with suffering and labour. In Christian theology Adam's sin confers guilt on all human beings. This original sin makes each of them deserving, from birth, of divine punishment in a future state. The idea of a Fall of mankind is present also in the Platonic tradition, but there it is represented as a descent from a spiritual to a material mode of being, and any individual guilt can be understood to have arisen from the soul's transgressions in an earlier life.

fallacy /ˈfæləsɪ/ (Lat. *fallax* deceptive, deceitful) *n.* **1** (an) error in reasoning. **2** (an) error in reasoning resulting in a false belief.

In philosophical contexts, 'fallacy' is not often used as a mere synonym of 'false belief' but means an error in reasoning.

It is human to err, and since it can be done in a variety of ways, Aristotle and many philosophers since have tried to establish a systematic theory of errors in reasoning. This has turned out to be a difficult task.

Many elementary logic texts distinguish between formal and informal fallacies. One way of characterizing the distinction is as follows.

A *formal fallacy* is an argument which rests on a principle of inference which *seems* to be valid but is not. For example, arguments which AFFIRM THE CONSEQUENT can be regarded as formal fallacies. Another example is *QUATERNIO TERMINORUM*. Again, fallacies of DIVISION and COMPOSITION, fallacies of scope (*see* SCOPE, AMBIGUITY OF), QUANTIFIER SHIFT fallacies, etc. can be counted in this category. So can the GAMBLER'S FALLACY.

An *informal fallacy* is an argument which fails in some other way. For instance, a speaker may present an argument which, though perfectly valid, is irrelevant or begs the question. Many of them have well-known Latin tags, like *IGNORATIO ELENCHI*, *PETITIO PRINCIPII*, etc.

There are also techniques of persuasion which, arguably, are not arguments at all. Suppose that a person is induced to assent not by argument, but by the prospect of certain favours, by respect for the authority of another party, or by fear of the unpleasant consequences of dissent. Persuasion brought about in such ways is not due to error in reasoning, so there is no fallacy. But they are often described as fallacies in texts on informal logic, and are given Latin tags (many of which are of recent origin) like *argumentum ad baculum*, *argumentum ad verecundiam*, *argumentum ad populum*, etc. *See* *ARGUMENTUM AD* . . .

fallibilism /ˈfælɪbɪlɪzm/ *n.* Various philosophical views asserting the possibility of error are called fallibilist. Among them is the view proposed and so named by C. S. Pierce, that while we may hold certain propositions to be *individually* perfectly certain, we ought to think that *on the whole* it is likely that at least some of them are false. Our beliefs about the world are obtained by induction and abduction, so it is *possible* that from true premisses and correct inferences of those kinds, a false conclusion is drawn. The term is also used for similar views of other philosophers (Reichenbach, Popper, Quine, etc.) that all knowledge-claims are provisional and in principle revisable. In another formulation, fallibilism is the view that the possibility of error is ever-present.

false *adj.* 1 Beliefs, opinions, theories, doctrines, statements, etc. – in short, anything which is capable of assertion or denial – can be said to be true or false. For instance, a statement 'snow is white' is true if and only if snow is white, and is false if and only if it is not the case that snow is white. 2 spurious, fake, forged. 3 dishonest, insincere. In logic and epistemology, senses (2) and (3) are not relevant.

false cause In some textbooks, the erroneous inference from *A preceded B* to *A caused B* is called the fallacy of false cause.

falsifiability *n.* A falsifiable hypothesis is one which can be put to a test by which it could conceivably be refuted. The concept is important in Karl Popper's philosophy of science, according to which the distinctive feature of *any* scientific theory is that its hypotheses *can* be put to a test. The distinctive feature of a *good* scientific theory is that its hypotheses *pass* the test. The contrast is with pseudo-science. The adherents of a pseudo-science are able to cling to its hypotheses no matter how events turn out, because the hypotheses are not testable.

falsification *n.* refutation; showing that a hypothesis is false.

fatalism *n.* 1 the doctrine that all human actions and indeed all events are predetermined, so that all attempts to change the course of events are futile. The arguments for fatalism are of three kinds. Some are based on logical principles (*see* e.g. DIODORUS CRONUS), some on the principle of causality (*see* DETERMINISM), and some on the assumption of perfect divine foreknowledge. 2 an attitude of submission to fate.

The arguments for fatalism have been subjected to much criticism. In the past, critics also assailed the doctrine itself, complaining that it encourages ignorance, sloth and vice.

Feigl /ˈfaɪgl/, Herbert (1902–88) an early member of the Vienna Circle. He emigrated in 1930 to the United States, where he taught at various universities. He formulated a materialist theory of mind in an important major essay, 'The "Mental" and the "Physical"' 1st edn 1958, 1967.

felicific /fɪlɪˈsɪfɪk/ (Lat. *felix* happy + *-fic* -making) *adj.* productive of happiness (felicity). The *felicific calculus* is the method for calculating the total value of the consequences of an action, proposed by Bentham, who also created the word, in chapter 4 of *An Introduction to the Principles of Morals and Legislation* 1789. *See also* HEDONIC CALCULUS.

feminine economy a concept in focus in the writings of the French psychoanalytical writer Hélène Cixous. In her *Sorties*, in *Jeune née* 1975 (*The Newly-Born Woman*), for instance, the term 'economy' has reference both to material wealth and to psychological structures. Masculine economy is concerned with private property, 'capitalist acts between consenting adults', and rational manipulation of others. In its psychic basis the desire for domination looms large. In contrast, feminine economy has a different psychic basis, because castration plays a different role. The feminine economy is concerned with community, sharing, and relating to others in a non-mercenary spirit.

feminist epistemology Some feminist writings in the 1980s seek to develop a distinctively feminist theory of knowledge. Some of the views advanced are radical: for instance, that the validity of a theory or a knowledge-claim depends on *by whom* (a male? a female? a feminist? etc.) it is proposed. Some also hold that traditional concepts and ideals of truth, objectivity and value-neutrality are to be rejected on the ground that they are used for purposes of male domination. Other writings are not radical in this way, and draw attention to implicit sex-specific assumptions that have tacitly been taken for granted in the tradition without critical analysis.

Fénelon /fenlɔ̃ (Fr.)/, François de Salignac de la Mothe (1651–1715) bishop of Cambrai, greatly admired for nobility of character, sincerity of religious belief, and for his literary and philosophical work. He wrote on NATURAL RELIGION, he defended the mysticism of Mme Guyon against attacks from the orthodox, foremost among them Bossuet, but is best known for his novel *Télémaque* (*Telemachus*), extremely popular in its time, which conveys a set of political ideals to be observed by rulers of a country.

Towards the end of the century, William Godwin used Fénelon as the paradigm of a great benefactor of mankind in a thought-experiment, as follows. You can save only one person from a burning building. Of the two inside, one is the manservant, a coarse, lazy drunkard given to brawling and dishonesty, the other is Archbishop Fénelon. Whom ought you to save? The answer is obvious: you ought to save the great benefactor of mankind, because, all things considered, this is what is likely to have the best consequences. But there is a sting in the tail of the story: what if the coarse etc. drunkard is your father?

Ferguson /ˈfɜːgəsən/, Adam (1723–1816) professor at Edinburgh, best known for his *Essay on the History of Civil Society* 1767, a pioneering effort to understand history sociologically. He was a liberal-minded eclectic philosopher who tried to formulate a synthesis of the moral theories of his compatriots: Hutcheson, Hume, Smith.

Fermat's /fɛʀma (Fr.); ˈfɜːmæt (Eng.)/ **last theorem** a proposition in number theory, proposed by Pierre de Fermat (1601–65) in the margin of a book where there was too little space for the proof he claimed to have. It states that if $n > 2$, then there are no positive integers x,y,z such that $x^n + y^n = z^n$. No proof or disproof was known until late June 1993, when the Cambridge mathematician Andrew Wiles in a lecture at Princeton University presented a proof. After revision, resulting from joint work between Wiles and the Cambridge mathematician Richard Taylor, and a period of review, there is now consensus that the proof is conclusive.

fetish (Port. *fetiço* factitious, fake) *n.* an object supposed to be inhabited by a spirit or a special magical power, and therefore held in awe; in a transferred sense, an object of excessive devotion.

fetishism *n.* **1** pagan cults that centre on fetishes. **2** animism, animistic cults. **3** blind devotion.

Feuerbach /ˈfɔɪərbax (Gm.)/, Anselm von (1775–1833) In early writings (1794 and

1796), Feuerbach gave an incisive analysis of the concept of a right, trying to give a Kantian account of a subject-matter that Kant himself had not covered at the time. (Kant did so in 1797 with the *Metaphysics of Morals*.) His fame is mainly due to his work to reform the criminal law in Bavaria; however, his ideas were very influential all over Europe. Desiring, like Beccaria, to humanize the criminal law, Feuerbach argued that it ought to be based on the principles of legality: *nullum crimen sine lege* and *nulla poena sine lege* (every crime should be defined by a law, and every penalty specified by a law); that its proper function was not to satisfy feelings of vindictiveness, but solely to discourage people from offending. This purpose, he thought, would be best served if criminal cases were conducted in open court, and not decided by a jury.

Feuerbach /ˈfɔɪərbɑx/ (Gm.), Ludwig (1804–72) Son of Anselm Feuerbach, he was one of the nineteenth-century German philosophers whose radicalism prevented them from holding a university position. His most important work is *Das Wesen des Christentums* 1841 (*The Essence of Christianity*). He argued that there is an essential difference between human and other animals. The latter are driven by instinct alone, whilst human beings also have the power of reflection, which allows them to grasp the essential properties of their species. Among them are love, sympathy, benevolence, intelligence; indeed, all the characteristics that we take to be perfections. It is of course true that we are not perfect, but that only shows that we fall short of the essence of our species, and that we ought to become what we are. To explain the shortfall, Feuerbach uses the Hegelian concept of ALIENATION, and argues that we in our thinking ascribe all the human perfections to an imaginary non-human being, i.e. God, to whom we misdirect the love and concern that we ought to have for our fellow human beings. We impoverish ourselves for the sake of an illusion. The various articles of faith and symbols of Christianity are illusory, but can be understood as truths in disguise, not about God, but about man. 'The secret of theology is anthropology.' Through the insight into the fundamental truth that human perfections do indeed belong to the essence of man, human love and concern will be redirected towards its proper object, i.e. mankind, and the human condition will be radically improved, once the illusions of religion are abolished.

It was this point that in Marx's opinion ought to be reversed: by improving the condition of mankind, the illusions of religion will disappear. But in Marx's early manuscripts he made considerable use of the concept of a species-essence.

Later in life, Feuerbach's philosophy took a more strongly materialistic turn ('*Der Mensch ist, was er isst*'; freely translated: 'You are what you eat'), in which the earlier key concept of a species-essence no longer appears.

Feyerabend /ˈfaɪəraːbənt (Gm.)/, Paul (1924–94) Austrian-born philosopher of science, Feyerabend held university teaching positions at Bristol, London, Berlin, California (Berkeley), Zürich, etc. His thinking was variously influenced by Viktor Kraft, Karl Popper (although Feyerabend sometimes contested this), and the later Wittgenstein (*Science in a Free Society* 1978, *Killing Time* 1995). In his early writings he espoused scientific realism, and criticized inductivism, foundationalism, and logical empiricism. He applied the idea that explanation may involve the correction of theoretical ideas implicit in the description of what we are trying to explain, in order to argue for the possibility of an eliminative reduction of the mental to the physical. He also argued – in his *Philosophical Papers*, vol. 1, 1981 – that a plurality of competing theories is desirable for the progress of science.

Feyerabend's later work criticizes ideas of rationality drawn from the philosophy of science – notably those of Popper – both as an account of the growth of science, and as a social ideology. His own account of the growth of science, which he described in *Against Method* 1974, 3rd rev. edn 1993, as an 'epistemological anarchism', stresses the positive role played by scientists whose actions departed from the methods recommended by philosophers of science. He championed cultural pluralism and the diversity of forms of knowledge against those who claim a privileged position for science, and wrote passionately on the value of minority cultures and alternative forms of medical treatment in *Science in a Free Society* 1978, *Farewell to Reason* 1987, and *Three Dialogues on Knowledge* 1991.

These later writings are seriously playful, and Feyerabend is perhaps best understood as taking up a Socratic role, as being concerned that individuals should make up their own minds, rather than being browbeaten by pedants. His works are consciously written against the very enterprise of a philosophy of science understood as the attempt to lay down rules for scientific method.

Feyerabend has advanced interesting and original criticisms of the views of other people; his writing is lively and provocative and brings an immense range of knowledge and a lively imagination to bear on the subjects under discussion. However, his challenge is taken to the point of disavowing any systematic position. This renders his views difficult to characterize, and may also have the consequence of protecting his substantive views from criticism. JSH

Fichte /'fiçtə/, Johann Gottlieb (1762–1814) As a student in Leipzig, Fichte took an interest in Spinoza's philosophy, but when later he discovered Kant's writings he found them more to his liking. Influenced by them, he wrote *An Attempt at a Critique of all Revelation* 1792, in which he showed scant regard for orthodoxy, and saw morality as the essential content of religion. The work was published anonymously and, being in tune with Kant's philosophy, it was initially supposed to be by Kant himself, from whom a long-awaited book on the philosophy of religion was expected at the time. It attracted favourable attention from the reading public and also from Kant himself.

In 1794 Fichte became professor of philosophy in Jena, where his lectures attracted a large following. At the same time, his strict insistence on a morality of duty, not only in his ethical theory but also in his public criticism of student life (which was characterized by coarseness, drunkenness, lewdness and brawling), provoked hostile reactions. So did also his unorthodox philosophy of religion, and this, in combination with a somewhat unyielding personality, led to his having to vacate his chair in 1799. He removed to Berlin, and became in 1810 the first professor of philosophy in the new university.

More than anything, Fichte wanted to refute 'dogmatism': the doctrine that there exists a world 'out there', independently of us and entirely indifferent to our values. This was the world-view that he had found in Spinoza and in the philosophers of the Enlightenment. In his opinion, it led inevitably to atheism, materialism, and determinism, which in turn would rule out moral values and moral responsibility. This dogmatism implies that our consciousness and its contents are ultimately caused by something objective that has independent existence and imposes itself on us. It leaves no place for freedom. Kant had shown the way to overcome dogmatism in this sense, but had not been entirely successful, since a remnant of it remained in the assumption of a NOUMENON, a realm of primordial being distinct and separate from consciousness. Fichte wanted to restore the conception of human beings as radically autonomous agents. He therefore argued for the alternative to dogmatism: idealism.

Essential to Fichte's conception of idealism is the thesis that it is mind that brings into being all that which we think of as the reality which we inhabit. This outlook alone is compatible with human freedom. One can be aware of freedom, of spontaneous activity, of being more than merely a prey to causal influences, only by reflecting on one's self as something active. Fichte held that this feature of spontaneity presupposes that there is a transcendental self or ego, which is the ultimate reality. It is better understood as pure activity than as an active entity. Ultimate reality is spontaneous activity. This is Fichte's version of Kant's thesis of the primacy of practical reason. A line from Goethe's *Faust* expresses Fichte's view: 'In the beginning was the deed.'

The choice between dogmatism and idealism cannot itself be made on purely theoretical grounds. It depends, Fichte insisted, on what kind of person one is. He believed that persons mature enough to see themselves as free agents would incline towards idealism, whilst those at a lower stage of character-formation would tend to prefer dogmatism.

Fichte gave a statement of his philosophy in *Grundlage der gesamten Wissenschaftslehre* 1794 (Foundation of the science of knowledge), and two Introductions to it a few years later. He tried to present it in untechnical language in *Die Bestimmung des Menschen* 1800 (The vocation of man) which in its three parts, Doubt, Knowledge, and Faith, deals with man's vocation and destiny.

Fichte's work on natural law 1796 spelled out an individualistic rights-theory, but later he brought welfarist elements into his political philosophy. *Der geschlossene Handelsstaat* 1800 (The closed commercial state) advocates government control over foreign trade, in order to ensure the state's economic independence and its ability to resist external pressures.

The *Reden an die deutsche Nation* 1807–8 (Speeches to the German nation) aimed to give theoretical and moral support to the resistance against Napoleon. An important part of the argument is Fichte's diagnosis of the spirit of the age in a work published a year earlier. He condemns resoundingly its complete unconcern for the common good. He accuses it of acknowledging one virtue only: seeking advantage for oneself, and one vice only: missing out on an advantage for oneself. Political misfortune had – fortunately – brought this egoism to bankruptcy. The only way out of the moral nadir was up. Commitment to higher ideals of moral and intellectual endeavour were now both possible and necessary. The Germans, because of their national character and the special excellence of their language, were eminently qualified to rise to the challenge.

Ficino /fi'tʃiːno (It.)/, Marsilio (1433–99) As the founder and central figure of the Academy of Florence, Ficino promoted the Platonic tradition, not only by an annual banquet celebrating Plato's birthday, but, more importantly, by translations from Greek to Latin of hermetic texts and of works by Plato and Plotinus, by his commentary on the *Symposium*, and by his own articulation of a Platonistic worldview. In his speculative metaphysics the concept of Platonic love plays a significant part.

fictionalism *n.* **1** the theory put forward by VAIHINGER that in science, ethics, religion, etc. fictions are useful and indeed indispensable. There are some affinities between this outlook and INSTRUMENTALISM. **2** the view that the talk of possible worlds in modal logic should not be taken literally as referring to a plurality of worlds, but only as a convenient fiction. In the same way as statements about Hamlet are true or false relative to Shakespeare's drama – a piece of fiction – so statements about worlds are true or false relative to the 'story' that there are many worlds. This modal fictionalism opposes David Lewis's version of modal realism.

fictitious entities Fiction (from Latin *fingere* to feign, fashion or form, make) poses problems for philosophy particularly with regard to reference and ontology. Fictitious entities – the invented characters, objects or places associated with novels, myths, fairy tales and legends – often appear vividly real and can be known in intimate detail, yet they do not exist in reality. The question is, must they be ascribed some kind of 'being' to explain the attitudes, cognitive and affective, that people have to them?

Some philosophers, notably Meinong, have wanted to acknowledge such entities as genuine 'objects', claiming that they possess properties but only lack the property of existence. The attraction of this view is that it gives full referential status to names like 'Pegasus' and 'Mr Pickwick' and shows how 'Pegasus flies' can be true and 'Mr Pickwick is thin' false. However, the theory rests on the ontologically problematic conception of a non-existent object.

Other philosophers have tried to show how all talk purportedly about fictitious entities can be reconstructed as being about only what is real. So, for example, talk about Sherlock Holmes is said to be just a shorthand way of talking about sentences in Conan Doyle's stories. One difficulty with this view is that people are able to talk about Sherlock Holmes in spite of knowing little about the stories; also, it is not always clear, e.g. with assertions like 'Sherlock Holmes is cleverer than Poirot', how the paraphrase can be carried out.

A third view about fictitious entities is that no reference at all is involved, only the pretence of reference. Story-tellers pretend to describe actual events and pretend to refer to real people, but in fact their discourse is part of an elaborate game (usually without any intention to deceive). Pretence or 'game' theories of fiction currently have wide support, but they leave as problematic the serious side of fiction and the fact that fictitious entities seem to appear in non-game-playing contexts.

Analytic philosophers of language have characteristically placed reference and truth at the centre of their theories of meaning. If sentences acquire meaning by representing or 'latching on to' states of affairs in the world, then fiction, which by all accounts is perfectly meaningful, poses a deep problem. It is not surprising that those philosophers and literary theorists who seek radically to revise standard assumptions about meaning (and truth) (*see* DECONSTRUCTION) often give prominence to the uses of language in narrative fiction. PL

fideism /ˈfiːdeɪɪzm/ *n.* Fideism is the thesis that religious belief is based on faith and not on either evidence or reasoning. Such a view has been advanced from ancient times in Judaism, Christianity and Islam down to some present neo-orthodox theologians. The fideistic contention is that the fundamental claims of religion cannot be established by either scientific data or rational proofs. In other words, natural theology is declared to be impossible. Montaigne (1533–92), for instance, argued in 'Apologie de Raymond Sébond', *Essais*

II, 12, that Christians are mistaken when they want human reason to give support to beliefs which can be engendered only by faith and by a special gift of divine grace, and that only faith can give a vivid and certain grasp of the profound mysteries of religion. Another important advocate of fideism was Pierre Bayle (1647–1706). F. H. Jacobi (1743–1819) used Hume's philosophy in defence of religious fideism: Hume's philosophy can be understood as having sceptical consequences generally if we take him to be saying that even what he first took to be pure knowledge ultimately turns out to rest on belief.

An extreme form of fideism was advanced in the nineteenth century by the Danish philosopher Kierkegaard (1813–55), who contended that religious truths were not like truths which could be called probable or reasonable. Kierkegaard went further than Bayle in this in saying that the central tenet of Christianity, that God has become incarnate, is not only contrary to reason but self-contradictory, and so impossible on rational standards. Because this tenet is absurd in human terms, it is then totally a matter of belief, requiring a 'leap into faith', that cannot in any way be justified by facts or reasonings. In this sense, extreme fideistic belief is considered to be irrational or anti-rational.

A more moderate form of fideism was set forth by St Augustine and Pascal, who insisted that faith has to come before reason in establishing central religious truths, but nonetheless reason and evidence can have some role both in the quest for these truths and in making them comprehensible. Augustine and his followers had said, 'I believe in order to know'. The act of belief can be preceded by rational inquiry, and followed by philosophical and theological explication. RPO

Filmer /ˈfɪlmə/, Robert (1588–1653) English political writer. His most important work, *Patriarcha, or the Natural Power of Kings*, which circulated in manuscript in the early years of the English Civil War, defends royal authority with scriptural and other arguments. It was first printed in 1680, to support the Crown against the Whig opposition. At the time, Locke drafted a polemical reply, which in the version published after the Glorious Revolution 1688 constituted the first part of his *Two Treatises of Government* 1690.

final cause (Lat. *finis* end; purpose) a purpose or end by which a thing, event or process is explained. In Aristotle, it is one of the four kinds of cause or explanatory factor. Explanations of this kind are called TELEOLOGICAL. Note that in this context 'final' does not mean last or ultimate.

first-order logic the standard predicate logic, which has only individuals as arguments of predicates and which quantifies over individuals only, and not over predicates or classes.

Five Ways Five ways to prove God's existence were proposed by Thomas Aquinas in his *Summa Theologiae* 1a, qu.2, art.3. Each of the five arguments starts from features of the world as we know it. Very briefly, the starting-points are (1) change, (2) efficient causality, (3) contingency, (4) degrees of perfection, (5) purposiveness.

Fodor /ˈfəʊdɔː/, Jerry (Alan) (1935–) professor of philosophy at Rutgers University. Fodor's work in the philosophy of mind and cognitive science has attracted attention to a remarkable degree. After his earliest book, *Psychological Explanation* 1968, which explored the distinctive role played by explanations in the special sciences in general and psychology in particular, he went on to produce *The Language of Thought* 1975.

In this book, Fodor argued that thought

itself must proceed by computational operations on syntactic elements, and that for each primitive concept there is a neural symbol to be found in the human brain. Complex propositions are represented by systematic combinations of these symbols, just as in natural language the meaning of a sentence depends on the meanings of its components, and ultimately on words that are atomic representations. Whether these complex representations are beliefs or desires, however, is said to depend on their functional role: roughly, a *belief* is a representation that causes an individual to behave as though it were true, whereas a *desire* is one that causes an individual to behave so as to make it true. Perhaps the most influential statement of this view is in 'Why there still has to be a language of thought', in his *Psychosemantics* 1987. This language of thought view is still the cornerstone of many approaches to cognitive science and artificial intelligence.

In 1983 Fodor published *The Modularity of Mind*, a work of philosophical psychology which aims to show that many mental processes work independently of each other, sending their results to the rest of the mind while having their internal natures isolated from scrutiny by those other areas.

Fodor's next two works, *Psychosemantics* 1987 and *A Theory of Content and Other Essays* 1990, are among the most influential contributions to the debate about the nature of mental content, i.e. the debate about how thoughts get to be *about* things. The upshot of these works is a view which has become known as the asymmetrical dependence view of content. Its central thesis is that a thought is about A rather than B because the fact that instances of the symbol in the language of thought occur in the presence of Bs depends on the fact that they occur in the presence of As, but not vice versa.

Recently Fodor has become interested in the question of holism about the mind: whether the representational powers of one symbol depend on the representational powers of others or indeed of all of them. This is explored in his book with Ernest LePore, *Holism: A Shopper's Guide* 1992. Fodor is also co-author, with Z. Pylyshyn, of a much cited paper attacking the explanatory pretensions of connectionism: 'Connectionism and cognitive architecture: A critical analysis', in *Cognition 28* (1988). DBM

folk psychology **1** common-sense psychology, i.e. the range of concepts and beliefs about the mind that are common in everyday life. The use of the term in this sense (anticipated already in 1972 by David Lewis, who wrote of 'common-sense psychology – folk science rather than professional science') became common in the 1980s with writers like S. Stich, *From Folk Psychology to Cognitive Science: The case against belief* 1983, Paul M. Churchland, *Matter and Consciousness* 1984, and Patricia A. Churchland, *Neurophilosophy* 1986. They reject the common-sense beliefs about the mind as a radically false theory, comparable to false superstitions, which ought to be replaced by a scientific theory. This radical view has provoked lively debate. **2** Originally, 'folk psychology' (ethnopsychology, from the German *Völkerpsychologie*) did not mean the common theory of the mind, but the theory of the common mind, that is, the study of the mentality of a people as it comes to expression in language, myths and customs. This extension of psychology beyond the individual, and its name, were introduced by M. Lazarus and H. Steinthal in 1860. Their work influenced Wilhelm Wundt, whose *Völkerpsychologie* is a major comparative study of cultures and civilizations from a psychological standpoint.

fond *adj.* (in older usage) foolish; foolishly

cherished. In 1705, for example, Samuel Clarke attacks 'fond, absurd and superstitious practices'.

Fordism *n.* methods of mass production, devised for maximal efficiency; especially assembly-line procedures. More generally, the phenomena of mass production and consumption characteristic of modern society. The term, used mainly in left-wing sociopolitical analysis since Gramsci, alludes to Henry Ford (1863–1947), the automobile manufacturer who founded and led the Ford Motor Company.

Form(s) *See* PLATO.

formal *adj.* pertaining to form. Note, however, that medieval and some later philosophers (Descartes, Leibniz, etc.) used the word in a special sense. *See also* EMINENT.

formal cause one of the four kinds of 'cause' or explanatory factor, in Aristotle. The formal cause is the distinctive properties that belong to a piece of matter. It is in virtue of the formal cause that a statue is something other than a mere block of marble.

formalism *n.* This word has many senses, of which four are listed here. **1** (in philosophy of mathematics) a theory of the nature of mathematics, represented by Hilbert. It was given this name by Brouwer, who rejected it in favour of his own INTUITIONISM. **2** (in literary criticism) an approach to the analysis and criticism of literary texts, inspired by Roman Jakobson. It shuns subjective interpretation, and attends to narrative techniques, relations between phonetic and semantic features, and various structural characteristics. An important assumption is that it is features of this kind that make a text into a work of art (rather than the content, the author's intentions or general circumstances, or other externalities). **3** (in moral philosophy) Kant's moral theory has been called formalist, on the ground that it is the form of the agent's volition, and not its content, that determines whether the action accords with the demands of morality. **4** (in logic) the symbols that come to be used in a formal system can collectively be called the formalism of the system.

formal language Formal languages are used in logic, mathematics, computing, etc. A formal language is specified by its primitive symbols and formation rules. One reason for devising formal languages is to eliminate the ambiguities in natural languages (English, Latin, Chinese, etc.).

formal mode/material mode Many statements can be formulated in these two different modes. For instance, *'"red" is a predicate'* is formulated in the formal mode, but can also be phrased in the material mode: *'red is a property'*. Both statements are really about language. This is made explicit in the formal mode, but the material mode makes it sound as if the statement is not about language but about entities in the world. The use of the material mode can lead to confusions and philosophical pseudo-problems. The remedy consists in giving preference to the formal mode.

All the above is according to Rudolf Carnap, who presented the distinction in *The Logical Syntax of Language* 1934. The shift from the material to the formal mode is an instance of what Quine later called SEMANTIC ASCENT.

formal system A system of formal logic uses a formal language. The language is constituted by its *primitive symbols*, and by *formation rules* which specify what counts as a well-formed formula.

There are two types of systems of formal logic: axiomatic systems, and systems of natural deduction. An axiomatic system consists of a subset of the well-formed formulae. The elements of this subset are the axioms and theorems of the system. Axioms are specified from the outset. Theorems are derived from axioms by means of an application of *transformation rules* specified for the system. (An axiom can also be called a theorem, since it can be derived from itself.)

Such a system can be seen as a set of meaningless symbols and strings of symbols, with rules indicating how to generate new strings from given ones. An interpretation of a system of formal logic consists in assigning meanings to the symbols and the well-formed formulae. Formal systems normally have an intended interpretation such that their theorems become necessarily true statements. The first to articulate clearly this conception of a formal system seems to have been Gottlob Frege (1848–1925).

A natural deduction system is characterized by primitive symbols, formation rules, and basic rules of inference; but there are no axioms. The intended interpretation is such that applications of the basic rules can be understood as valid inferences, and conclusions that depend on no assumptions as necessarily true statements.

Not all formal systems are systems of logic. For instance, in *Grundlagen der Geometrie* 1899 (Foundations of geometry), Hilbert presented a formal system which on interpretation yields geometrical theorems.

formation rules the rules which specify what is to count as a well-formed formula in a formal language.

form, logical *See* LOGICAL FORM.

fortitudo Lat. courage. One of the four CARDINAL VIRTUES.

Foucault /fuko: (Fr.)/, Michel (1926–84) a leading French intellectual, professor at Collège de France from 1970. He characterized his work as a 'history of the present' in the spirit of Hegel, Marx and Nietzsche, i.e. a historical reflection on how we have come to think and act as we do.

Foucault's concern with the present is a critical one. He wants to know how we have come to be 'trapped in our own history', in historically emergent systems of thought and action that determine our most familiar behaviour; and by illuminating the historicity and contingency of our present order of practices, he wants to open up the possibility of changing them, of inventing new forms of thought and action.

For convenience, three phases of Foucault's thought can be distinguished. In his work of the 1960s, represented by *Les Mots et les choses* 1966 (Words and things, transl. as *The Order of Things*) and *L'Archéologie du savoir* 1969 (*The Archaeology of Knowledge*), Foucault reflects on the emergence of our present forms of knowledge. He finds the conditions of knowledge in anonymous, historically emergent 'epistemes', i.e. frameworks and practices of discourse. The modern episteme emerged at the end of the eighteenth century, and makes possible those sciences that take human beings as their theme, the 'human sciences'. In this context Foucault also locates the emergence of the modern notion of the subject. The human sciences construct particular conceptions of human nature, which are then used as a basis for theories about how individuals and society should operate. Foucault's refusal to embrace the idea of a pre-given self or human nature, his location of the self in a historical context, is characteristic of his work as whole.

In the 1970s, in such works as *Surveiller et punir* 1975 (*Discipline and Punish*) and *L'Histoire de la sexualité I* 1976 (*History of Sexuality* vol. I), Foucault moves away from his earlier focus on discursive practices. Discourse is located in a larger context of non-discursive practices, particularly practices of power. Foucault's history of the present becomes a history of the way in which, since the eighteenth century, the modern system of disciplinary power has emerged along with the human sciences. Discipline is a set of techniques for governing human beings which both enhance their capacities and ensure their controllability. Such control requires detailed knowledge of individual behaviour, and human sciences such as psychology and modern medicine are now understood to have been made possible by, and to assist in, the spread of disciplinary power. It is in this context that subjectivity is now located. To discipline people is to turn them into certain kinds of subjects, in the sense of bringing them to act in accordance with disciplinary norms and standards, behavioural ideals which the human sciences define as normal, natural or essentially human. With this account of power as interwoven with forms of knowledge, and as productive of subjects, Foucault departs significantly from the more traditional liberal and Marxist understandings of power.

In the last phase of his work in the 1980s, Foucault supplements his reflections on knowledge and power by developing further his analysis of subjectivity, particularly in terms of what he calls 'practices of the self' – practices carried out by people on themselves, forms of self-relation. In the modern era, we are encouraged to relate to ourselves by discovering and acting in accordance with our essential nature or true self. For Foucault, what we are in fact being encouraged to do here is to attach ourselves to a self that has been made available through psychological and medical discourses, and thereby to participate in our subjection to the disciplinary order. In the second and third volumes of *L'Histoire de la sexualité* 1984, Foucault turns to an examination of ancient Greek and Roman forms of self-relation to suggest that although our present form of self-relation is caught up in the disciplinary order, it is not the only possible way of relating to ourselves.

It is in terms of the possibility of establishing a different way of relating to ourselves that Foucault comes to address the issue of freedom. For Foucault, we are not passively shaped by forms of power. Power always involves a relation of struggle, in which some try to direct the activities of others, who in turn resist and strive to counter these impositions. Systems of power emerge to the extent that resistance is overcome and individuals are rendered docile and predictable. At the same time, the possibility of resistance can never entirely be eliminated. And since modern systems of power involve bringing us to identify with a certain conception of what we essentially are, a key part of resisting such power is to 'refuse what we are'. Foucault suggests that we need a different way of relating to ourselves, not self-discovery but self-detachment and self-creation. We need to detach ourselves from existing ways of being, thinking and acting, and to invent new ways not caught up in the disciplinary order. Foucault refers to this reflective activity as the 'work of freedom', and sees it as including a certain way of doing philosophy – his own effort being to reflect historically on ourselves and our present, to illuminate the contingency of existing forms of life and so promote the possibility of changing them. Thus Foucault fashions a philosophy which in the last analysis is not a philosophy of power but of freedom.

Some critics have accused Foucault of relativism, but whilst he holds that our systems of thought and action are historically specific, he clearly does not think that we are trapped in them. We can escape from their sway through the critical understanding of how they came to be, and the reinvention of our forms of life. Other critics have observed that Foucault offers no road-signs or guide-posts for new ways that we are to invent, and have held that this gives his oppositionism a destructive and nihilistic flavour. Foucault himself argues that his role is not to lay down the law for others, which runs the risk of stifling resistance, but to promote something for which prescriptions cannot be given, the creative work of freedom. CF

foundationalism *n.* the doctrine that knowledge is ultimately based on beliefs that require no further justification. It arises from the recognition that a person's beliefs are in general justified by other beliefs. This produces an infinite regress. The foundationalist response is to claim that this regress can only be stopped if there are basic or foundational beliefs which are self-justifying.

Traditionally, foundational beliefs have been taken to be those which are certain or beyond doubt. Descartes provides a classical example. Starting from his famous *Cogito, ergo sum* (I think, therefore I exist), he argued that he could be certain that he existed as a thinking being, and this certainty was the rock on which he sought to establish further knowledge of the world.

Others have turned to logical truths or to beliefs about one's current sensory experiences or mental states. There are two problems for traditional foundationalism. First, it is argued that the beliefs that are actually proposed as foundations are in fact subject to doubt and therefore are not self-justifying. Secondly, even if they are free from doubt, it is difficult to see how beliefs so slender in content can justify the more full-bodied beliefs about the external world.

A recent response to these problems has been to formulate a fallibilist foundationalism. It is claimed that beliefs need not be certain in order to be self-justifying. A belief arising from a direct sensory perception, for instance my belief that I am seeing a green Ford, is justified so long as I have no reason to suppose that in this instance my senses mislead.

The main alternative – first proposed by pragmatists like Peirce and Dewey – to the foundationalist approach is coherentism, according to which a belief is justified so long as it forms part of a coherent *total* set of beliefs. Another alternative is sometimes called contextualism. According to it, a belief is justified so long as it forms part of a coherent *particular* set of beliefs. This seems to open up the possibility that a belief is justified within one context but not within another.

The method of REFLECTIVE EQUILIBRIUM has often been identified with coherentism, but this has recently been questioned. CC

four causes Aristotle distinguished four kinds of explanatory factors or 'causes': material, formal, efficient and final. *See also* ARISTOTLE; CAUSE.

four elements in ancient Greek philosophy, fire, water, earth and air. *See also* EMPEDOCLES.

four humours Galen (129–99), the authority on medicine until the rise of modern science, distinguished four kinds of humours, i.e. bodily fluids: blood, black bile, yellow bile and phlegm. Correlated to these are four basic kinds of temperament: sanguine, melancholic, choleric and phlegmatic (joyful, sad, temperamental, calm).

Fourier /ˈfʊərɪeɪ (Eng.); fuʀje (Fr.)/, Charles (1772–1837) French political thinker. A strong critic of the repression and hypocrisy of civilization as we know it, he advocated in *Le nouveau Monde industriel* 1829 (The new industrial world) a utopian social system based on cooperative associations, which he called phalanxes, each with approximately 1800 members. Within these organizations, it would be possible for an individual to undertake a variety of tasks, so as to avoid the warping effect of narrow specialization in one occupation only. It would also become possible to indulge the natural passions without harm to others.

four-term fallacy *See* QUATERNIO TERMINORUM.

Frank /fraŋk (Gm.)/, Philipp (1884–1966) physicist and philosopher of science, a leading member of the Vienna Circle. Forced into exile, he was a professor at Harvard University; author of *Philosophy of Science* 1957.

Frankfurt School a group of intellectuals with links to the *Institut für Sozialforschung* (Institute for Social Research) set up in Frankfurt am Main in 1923, by means of a private endowment by Felix Weil, but also partly supported by the Frankfurt University. During exile due to the rise of Nazism, an International Institute of Social Research was created in association with Columbia University 1933–47. Two of the leading members of the school, Max Horkheimer (1895–1973) and Theodor Adorno (1903–69), returned to Frankfurt in the late 1940s, and resumed teaching and writing there. Other members of the school were Walter Benjamin (1892–1940), Herbert Marcuse (1898–1979), Erich Fromm (1900–1980) and Karl Wittfogel (1896–1988). In a second generation, Jürgen Habermas (1929–) is most prominent.

Although its sympathies were on the Left, the school had no allegiance to any political party, and was very critical of communist parties (for obvious reasons) but also of social democratic parties, whose reformism was thought to be insufficient to transcend present society. Nor was the class-consciousness of the proletariat taken as the ultimate instance of appeal, since it was itself distorted by the reifying and alienating influences of modern society. At the same time, however, attempts to design utopias were rejected. In the late 1960s, Herbert Marcuse's critique of the established order greatly influenced the leaders of the student unrest in the United States, but on the whole the members of the school did not see themselves as the leaders of any revolution. They saw their task as one of theory, although a critical theory whose insights would raise awareness and lead to social change.

The theorizing made use of the concepts of reification and alienation, taken over from Marx, Korsch and Lukács. Important theoretical influences came also from psychoanalytic theory, and from Max Weber. Many kinds of empirical sociological research into mass media, bureaucracy and technocracy were first undertaken by members of this school.

The Critical Theory of this school was a critique of modern society, exhibiting its oppressive and exploitative mechanisms. In contemporary society these mechanisms are insidious – people are not even aware of their unfreedom, brought about by the manipulation of individuals through modern mass media. Indeed, the mass media are bringing about a degradation of all kinds of aesthetic and intellectual culture, and are used by public bureaucracies and commercial organizations to manipulate and distort public awareness of social and political matters. Cultural and personal values are neglected, having been made prey to market forces. Material wealth, and not overall well-being, is presented as the highest good. This can be seen as a result of 'the Enlightenment project': it involved what Max Weber described as rationalization, a process that has resulted in modern bureaucracies and markets. This 'project' is described as one which takes for granted that all rationality is instrumental: reason cannot establish any ends, but can only indicate means to ends.

The function of critical social theory is to explore, analyse and explain these phenomena. This can in turn be used to raise critical awareness generally in society. The outcome hoped for is emancipation, and a society in which individuals can be truly autonomous and freely cooperate.

The members of the school were hostile to positivist and scientistic philosophies. The main objection was that when these take human knowledge, including knowledge established in the natural and social sciences, to be independent of our interests and value-free, they promote a misconception which is not only false but also harmful, since they reduce social science to a technology of satisfying people's preferences and also a technology aimed at shaping those preferences, but are unable to legitimize any basic values.

Underlying the emancipatory concern was the assumption that progress is possible. Leading theorists such as Horkheimer and Adorno, however, became increasingly pessimistic. It seemed to them increasingly unlikely that individuals in present-day society could possibly develop a critical perspective on their society – a necessary precondition for change. Habermas is less despondent: the rationalization of life introduced by the Enlightenment is a precondition, rather than an obstacle, to progress. Moreover, the Enlightenment view of reason contains not only a merely instrumental conception; it also includes a richer emancipatory conception of communicative rationality, by communicative interaction, as people come closer to an 'ideal speech situation'. This is a situation in which distorting influences on interpersonal communication are overcome, and the participants reach that autonomy which was the aim of Enlightenment emancipatory aspirations. So, Habermas argues that while the emphasis on *instrumental* reason is indeed problematic, the Enlightenment also contains a richer, emancipatory conception of reason which critics of modern society must not discard in an indiscriminate critique of reason as such.

free choice permission a permission to do this or that which implies a permission to do this and a permission to do that (i.e. $P(p \vee q)$ implies Pp & Pq). This is a natural way of interpreting permissions, but together with the principle that whatever is obligatory is also permitted, it generates ROSS'S PARADOX.

freedom *n.* I am not free to pick an apple from this tree if an angel with a flaming sword blocks my path. Again, in a different setting, I am not free to do so, this time because there is no apple. In the first instance, there is interference, in the second, absence of opportunity. Already this simple example indicates that distinctions are needed when we reflect on freedom – in fact, many different ones. An important distinction is that between positive and NEGATIVE FREEDOM.

free logics so called because they are free of existence-assumptions.

Traditional logic, such as Aristotle's syllogistics, assumes that general terms are not empty: *every S is P* is taken to imply that an S exists. Most modern logic since the time of Venn, Frege and Russell rejects that assumption, but accepts that singular terms refer, and hence permits inferences of this form:

$$\frac{Fa}{(\exists x)Fx}$$

Free logics reject this rule of inference. The closest acceptable rule is:

$$\frac{Fa \quad a \text{ exists}}{(\exists x)Fx}$$

Systems of free logic were first proposed in the mid-1950s by H. S. Leonard, soon followed by H. Leblanc, J. Hintikka, K. Lambert, B. van Fraassen *et al.*

free rider Fare evasion and tax evasion are examples of free-riding. The free rider enjoys a benefit which would be unavailable if everyone likewise evaded paying. Free-riding is an important problem for ethics and decision theory. It seems perfectly rational for people to take a free ride, if they can get away with it: the pay rise negotiated by a trade union may also flow on to non-members. Fare and tax evasion is to the individual evader's advantage, and the collective disadvantage is utterly insignificant. And yet, decisions to take a free ride seem irrational, since they tend towards an outcome – the disappearance of a collective good – that is not desired.

free variable A variable within the scope of a quantifier containing that variable is *bound*; a variable not within the scope of such a quantifier is *free*.

Examples: in the expression Fx (intended to be read as 'x has the property F'), x is a free variable, but in the expression (∀x)Fx (intended to be read as 'for every x, x has the property F', i.e. 'everything is F'), x is a bound variable.

In the expression (∃y)Rxy (intended to be read as 'there is something to which x stands in the relation R'), x is a free variable, but in the expression (∃y)(∀x)Rxy (intended to be read as 'there is something to which everything stands in the relation R'), x is a bound variable.

free-will defence One solution proposed for the problem of evil is that evil is due to free created agents and that God cannot be held responsible. One of the objections to this solution is that, at best, it would apply to evils caused by agency, but would not apply to evils due to natural causes, for instance the suffering caused by a natural disaster or by an illness. In reply to this, Alvin Plantinga has argued that although it is extremely unlikely that free agents (demons) are responsible for all these natural evils – he does not propose it as a hypothesis to be seriously entertained – it is not absolutely impossible. It is, then, *possible* that all evils are due to the actions of free agents. This invalidates the atheist view that it is *impossible* for God and the actual evils in the world to coexist. It is this argument of Plantinga's that is usually called the free-will defence.

Frege /'fre:gə/, Gottlob (1848–1925) German logician, professor of mathematics at Jena. Frege, the greatest innovator in logic since Aristotle, came to logic and philosophy from mathematics. He regarded Kant's theory that arithmetical truth is synthetic as fundamentally mistaken, and proposed a logicist reduction programme: (1) the concepts of mathematics had to be defined in terms of pure logic, and (2) the theorems of mathematics thus transformed had to be shown to be truths of logic. In this way arithmetic would be reduced to logic. (Frege did not, however, think that the same applied to geometry: he agreed with the Kantian view that there are synthetic truths of geometry.) In place of the traditional two-term form of judgement 'S is P', Frege uses a unary form ascribing truth to a simple propositional content. Such a simple content or 'thought' has the form Fa, that is, it is treated by him as a mathematical function/argument structure. Thus, for instance, 'Socrates is mortal' is analysed as 'the function ξ *is mortal* is applied to the argument *Socrates*'. Using this novel form of judgement in his *Begriffsschrift* 1879 (Conceptual notation), Frege was able to give a simple and satisfactory treatment of the logic of generality-words such as 'all' and 'there is' by means of his theory of quantification. Also, the quantifier-phrases 'all' etc. stand for (higher-level) functions (of functions). For instance, 'all men are mortal' is analysed: 'the higher-level function *all* applied to the function "if ξ is a man, then ξ is mortal"'. The importance of this insight can hardly be overestimated: essentially this Fregean treatment is still current today.

The logicist reduction programme, as well as incisive work in the philosophy of mathematics, is contained in the non-technical *Grundlagen der Arithmetik* 1884 (Foundations of arithmetic). Particularly important here are the emerging anti-psychologism – the laws of thought are not empirical, descriptive-psychological laws – and the *context principle*: never ask for the meaning of a word in isolation, but only in the context of a sentence. The technical elaboration of logicism took place in the two-volume *Grundgesetze der Arithmetik* 1893, 1903 (Basic laws of arithmetic). The logic of this work contains the assumption that (roughly) *every predicate determines a class*, and this assumption is needed for Frege's purpose of deducing arithmetic. But in 1902 Bertrand Russell wrote to Frege with a proof that the assumption is inconsistent, since it leads to the paradox concerning the class of classes that do not contain themselves as elements.

Frege's logicism is no longer a viable option in the philosophy of mathematics, and his current fame rests on his logical achievements and on his work in the philosophy of language. This was mainly carried out in three classical essays, '*Funktion und Begriff*' (Function and concept), '*Über Begriff und Gegenstand*' (On concept and object) and, especially, '*Über Sinn und Bedeutung*' (On sense and reference), just prior to the appearance of the first volume of the *Grundgesetze*. Here Frege had occasion to reflect on the linguistic devices used, and on the ontology of his semantical apparatus. In '*Über Sinn und Bedeutung*' Frege noted that true identity statements are puzzling, because they are true and informative. His famous example concerning the planet Venus illustrates the point well. When told that Venus is Venus, it does not seem that I get to know something very novel or interesting, whereas the step to the truth of 'the Morning Star is the Evening Star' was a major advance in Babylonian astronomy. In order to resolve this 'paradox of informativeness' Frege introduced the distinction between the *Sinn* and the *Bedeutung* of an expression. The latter is the entity designated by the expression; the *Bedeutung* of 'the Morning Star' is the planet Venus. The *Sinn* of 'the Morning Star', on the other hand, is not the planet, but rather the way in which the planet is presented by the term (namely as a very bright star visible in the eastern sky shortly before sunrise). Furthermore, he noted that indirect discourse and other that-contexts need special treatment. It seems that the step from 'It is not informative that the Morning Star is the Morning Star' to 'It is not informative that the Morning Star is the Evening Star' does not preserve truth. Therefore, in such contexts the rule that allows the interchange of different names for the same object does not seem to preserve truth. Frege saves the principle by remarking that no substitution of equals takes place, since in the relevant that-context, 'the Morning Star' does not stand for Venus, but for its *Sinn*, and similarly for 'the Evening Star'. Accordingly, since the terms stand for their respective *Sinn*, which are different, there is no question of a failure of logical laws. The *Sinn*/*Bedeutung* distinction, in one version or other, and the uses to which it can be put, has been the cornerstone around which much of contemporary philosophy of language has been built. Invariably it returns in most of the systems currently proposed.

Frege was a masterly writer, but a poor classroom teacher. His talent for polemical philosophical writing is unrivalled and his powerful expository prose is a pleasure to read. Through his contributions to logic, and to the philosophies of language and mathematics, Frege steps to the foreground as one of the major thinkers of the nineteenth century. GS

Fries' trilemma an anti-foundationalist argument (also known as the Münchhausen trilemma) formulated by Jakob Friedrich Fries (1773–1846): any argument purporting to establish an ultimate basis must be defective, since it is bound to lead to an infinite *regress* or to a logically vicious *circle*. But to assume an ultimate foundation without argument is *arbitrary*.

function *n.* **1** When considering the function of a thing it is important to distinguish: (a) what the thing *does* in the normal course of events (an activity); (b) what the thing *brings about* in the normal course of events (the result, the outcome of an activity). In the first sense, the function of a heart is to pump blood: that is how the heart works. In the second sense, the function of a heart is to keep the organism alive by supplying oxygen etc. through the bloodstream.

To this should be added that when a function is ascribed to something, it is usually implied that a certain purpose is served. The purpose may be the maintenance or preservation of a biological or social entity, or it may be a purpose adopted by an agent. **2** a particular kind of relation between the first and the second term in an ordered pair. What distinguishes a function from two-term relations generally is that for any given first term there is *exactly one* second term. In other words, if Rxy and Rxz imply y = z, then R is a function.

The constituent(s) of the first term are called the *argument(s)* of the function, and of the second, the *value* of the function.

The set to which the arguments belong is called the *domain* of the function, and the set of values is called the *range* of the function. Examples: (a) multiplication of numbers by a constant is a function. For instance, 5x = y. Here, x stands for an argument, y for a value of the function. Whatever can replace x belongs to the domain of the function; whatever can replace y belongs to the range of the function; (b) multiplication of any two numbers is also a function. It can be written 'xy = z'. Here again, for any particular arguments replacing x and y, there is *exactly one* value that can replace z; (c) in propositional logic, the so-called truth-functions are indeed functions, as can be seen by inspecting the way they are represented in a truth-table.

functional calculus another name for predicate logic, due to the fact that the OPEN SENTENCES it deals with are also called propositional functions.

functional explanation One way of explaining why a certain phenomenon occurs, or why something acts in a certain way, is by showing that it is a component of a structure within which it contributes to a particular kind of outcome, i.e. the continuing stability or preservation of the system. Such an explanation suggests that a certain purpose is served. This is how biological phenomena are commonly explained. Functional explanations have been given for social customs and institutions, for dreams (by psychoanalysts), for economic phenomena, etc. Rain-making ceremonies, for instance, are explained by their function of maintaining social cohesion in times of drought.

If the continuing stability or preservation of a system is regarded as a purpose, there is a problem in that such an assumption cannot be verified by observation. This is why explanations in terms of functions became suspect with the rise of modern science and its rejection of the Aristotelian assumptions of FINAL CAUSES, and were regarded as non-empirical pseudo-explanations. They have, however, been to some extent rehabilitated in recent philosophy of science.

functionalism *n.* The term is used in many contexts in which functions or the concept of a function figure importantly.

1 (in the social sciences) Functionalist analysis of social phenomena, promoted especially by Malinowski and Radcliffe-Brown, and refined by Robert K. Merton, investigates the *function* of a social institution or practice, that is, the contribution it makes to the preservation of a greater social whole of which it is a part. This method was developed in opposition to theories which seek to explain social phenomena on the basis of an investigation into their *origins*.

An example is rain-making ceremonies. If they could succeed in making rain, their function would be clear; but such ceremonies do not succeed in making rain. A functionalist analysis will investigate what other social function they may have, and may show that the ceremony helps to relieve anxiety, brings the members of the society together, and reinforces social cohesion. Functions of which the parties involved are unaware are called *latent*, in contrast to the *manifest* ones.

Among social theorists who adopt this method, some have also postulated one or both of the following: that every social practice has a function, and serves in one way or another the preservation of the society; and that it is the functionalist approach that distinguishes sociology from other social sciences. The first tends to favour conservatism, to give 'an overall endorsement of current practices and norms', and reveals 'a pro-attitude to stability'; and the second tends to restrict inquiry. Both are problematic, but neither is essential to a functionalist approach.

2 (in design and architecture) (a) the theory that design should be true to the material, and should exclusively serve the function of the object or structure designed. It is in direct opposition to designs which include merely decorative elements; (b) the style of designs made in accordance with this outlook.

The functionalist theory and style, which began to flourish from the 1920s, is often described as modern, and the subsequent movement away from it, especially in architecture, is sometimes called post-modern.

3 (in philosophy of mind) the view that what makes a mental state what it is (an experience of pain, a desire to drink, a belief that p), is the functional role it occupies. The view is usually associated with materialism about the states that have these functional roles.

We are familiar with such functional concepts. What makes a certain thing a mouse-trap is what a mouse-trap does. Many different physical devices are mouse-traps simply because they have the same function. So understood, a mouse-trap *is* what a mouse-trap *does*. The same applies to calculators and computers. They are constructed and programmed in a variety of ways. What is common to them is not certain physical features, but the fact that they can all do sums. What we think of as a mental state, functionalists argue, can be analysed in the same way: very different physical bases in different organisms may work in the same way. Being hungry is a case in point. The physical basis for hunger need not be the same in human beings, tigers and octopuses. What is common to these states of hunger is not a certain physical state, but the manner of operation, the 'program', so to speak.

This view was proposed to overcome problems in materialist theories of mind, and especially the identity theory of mind, which seek to identify a certain kind of mental state with a certain kind of physical state. One problem for such theories is that mental states of the same kind seem to be bound up with very different physical conditions. Men and dogs alike feel pain, but their brains and nervous systems may be very different.

A significant early advocate of functionalism was Hilary Putnam, whose view has remained very influential, in spite of his own later recantation and strong denunciation (in *Representation and Reality* 1988) of the theory which continues to occupy a central place in the current debates in the philosophy of mind. Other important representatives are Jerry Fodor in his *Psychological Explanation* 1968 and David Lewis in his *Philosophical Papers* 1983–6.

4 (in psychology) the view that behaviour and mental phenomena can be explained as an organism's strategies for adapting to its biological or social environment. The foremost representative of this theoretical approach, which owed something to William James and John Dewey and which flourished in the early decades of the twentieth century, was the American psychologist J. R. Angell.

5 The word *functionalism* is also used in various other contexts. For instance, Susan Moller Okin uses the word in her *Women in Western Political Thought* 1979, 2nd rev. edn 1992, for the view that women by nature have specific functions, especially child-bearing and housekeeping, a view usually combined with assumptions about the secondary role, if any, that women can play in other fields of endeavour (intellectual, professional, political, etc.).

functor *n.* (in formal logic) an expression that is neither a singular term nor a sentence. Among the different kinds of functors are: (1) propositional connectives that turn one or more sentences into a sentence ($\sim$p, p $\supset$ q); (2) predicates which, when applied to a singular term, turn out a sentence; (3) operators that turn one or more singular terms into a singular term: 'father of ...' is a one-place functor, '... + ...' is a two-place functor; (4) subnectors, which turn a sentence p into a singular term: that p; (5) the IOTA-operator, which turns an open sentence into a definite description.

future contingents Is it true that there will be a sea-battle tomorrow? Or is it false?

It is natural to assume that it must be one or the other, and that the statement 'There will be a sea-battle tomorrow' is either true or false. The problem is that if it is true, then there will be a sea-battle tomorrow, no matter what we do today. And if it is false, there will be none, no matter what we do today. This is fatalism.

It seems, then, that if we are not prepared to accept fatalism, we have to admit that the prediction is neither true nor false. But that does not seem right either. Our prediction today is true if there is a sea-battle the day after, and otherwise false.

This dilemma, set out in chapter 9 of Aristotle's *De interpretatione*, illustrates the general problem of contingent propositions about future events. His own response, as interpreted by Ockham and by present-day philosophers, was to accept the law of the excluded middle, i.e. the truth of every disjunction of the form *p or not p* (which does not seem to imply fatalism), but to reject the principle of bivalence, i.e. the principle that every statement *p* is true or false (which does seem to imply fatalism). The problem is relevant to questions of determinism, free will, foreknowledge, predestination, etc. It also gave the impulse to Łukasiewicz's devising a three-valued logic. *See also* DIODORUS.

futurism, moral *See* MORAL.

futurology *n.* inquiry into the methods of forecasting, and into what the future will hold. Prediction is an integral part of the scientific enterprise, but the idea of futurology as an independent academic discipline, widely touted in the 1960s, seems to have sunk into oblivion.

fuzzy logic the name commonly given to a class of non-classical logics that may be characterized by their abandonment of the classical, exhaustive categorization of propositions into the 'true' or the 'false' in favour of 'degrees of truth'. Fuzzy logic is based upon fuzzy set-theory, in which the simple notion of membership of a set is replaced by a notion of membership to some degree. Again, the basic (or atomic) formulae of a system of fuzzy logic are no longer evaluated as simply 'true' or 'false', but evaluated as true (or false) to degree x, where x ranges continuously from 0 to 1. Instead of merely two truth-values (i.e. true and false), there are uncountably many.

The truth-value of a complex propositional formula depends, in fuzzy logic as in classical logic, entirely on the truth-values of the components of the complex. But the way in which, for example, the truth-value of the components p and q determines the truth-value of the complex (p & q) can be defined in more than one way. Suppose that p has truth-value a and q has truth-value b. What, then, is the value of (p & q)? We may say that it is the minimum of a and b; or we can say that it is a × b; and other proposals are of course also possible. In this way, there can be many different fuzzy systems of logic.

The reason for the invention of fuzzy logic was to accommodate vague or imprecise terms within the scope of logic. This was in opposition to writers such as Frege, Russell and Carnap, who saw vagueness as a defect of natural languages and therefore a reason for creating an artificial logical language. Its development in the 1960s by the engineer Lofti Zadeh was specifically for the purpose of modelling vague concepts, whose presence in reasoning is seen as the source of an important paradox, the ancient SORITES.

To assert that a statement p is *true to degree x* is distinct from saying that p is probably (with a degree of probability x) *true* (simpliciter). Probability logic does not operate with 'degrees of truth'; fuzzy logic does. DH

G

Gadamer /'gædəmə (Eng.); 'gaːdamər (Gm.)/, Hans-Georg (1900–) German philosopher, professor in Leipzig, and after the war in Heidelberg. In *Wahrheit und Methode* 1960 (Truth and method), Gadamer elaborates Heidegger's idea that all knowing and doing involves understanding and interpretation. His project is to develop a philosophical hermeneutics, i.e. a general theory of understanding and interpretation which shows that these are by no means rule-governed procedures or methods for ensuring the objectivity of the 'human' (as opposed to the 'natural') sciences. In fact, they are not methods or procedures at all, but fundamental skills manifest in everything that human beings, as self-conscious linguistic animals, do. In particular, understanding and interpretation are not restricted to the comprehension of written texts, past and present; they are just as much involved in the aesthetic appreciation of art, the juridical application of law and the historical interpretation of past events. Indeed, Gadamer sees this skill, or rather its exercise, as what gives human existence its essentially historical character.

Gadamer can only make these strong claims for understanding and interpretation because he rejects older notions of hermeneutics and understanding. The nineteenth-century theorists of understanding, notably Schleiermacher and Dilthey, saw understanding the meaning of texts and historical events as a matter of understanding how the authors and actors of these texts and events understood them. But, according to Gadamer, we are so radically conditioned by our position in history that it is not at all possible to return to the perspective of past authors and actors. This, however, does so little to render understanding impossible that it actually facilitates it. To understand the meaning of a text or event is, in his view, always to relate it to one's own concepts, preconceptions and prejudices; it thus lies in the nature of meaning that it should be spelt out in the light of the interpreter's own historical situation. In opening up a text or event from the past, we necessarily make the (defeasible) presumption that the text constitutes a good answer to a question which we ourselves, from our historical perspective, could put. This is not the question the author took him- or herself to be addressing – or if it is, it is so only in the sense that it is that question which, in the light of the text's *Wirkungsgeschichte* (the history of the text's influence), the author would regard the text as addressing. It is for this reason that Gadamer sees interpretation as a virtual dialogue. In a true dialogue no one party determines its course in advance. Rather, each is open to the unexpected insights and changes of direction which the other might contribute. The same applies to interpretation across the ages: neither author/actor nor interpreter has special privilege. The interpreter, with the benefit of hindsight, can disclose aspects of meaning which were hidden to the author or actor. At the same time, the text or event can always disclose aspects which previous interpretation had missed. If this is right, then it is to misconstrue the nature of meaning itself to see it as something we can access only by methodically purging ourselves of our own historically conditioned preconceptions in order to see things as the author or actor once did. Relatedly, it is mistaken to think that it is possible to grasp the meaning of a text or event without judging its truth or rationality. It is only if we can make no sense of it as true or false, rational or irrational, that we look for explanations: perhaps there were errors in observation or in transmission, perhaps the statement was made in jest, etc. And only when such explanations are unavailable do we try to probe the author's or actor's state of mind to discover the source of what we take to be his error.

Gadamer disclaims relativism, but does maintain that there is no timeless truth, since there is no interpretation valid for all times: from epoch to epoch we only understand differently. This notwithstanding, the historical process of interpreting texts and events ever anew is immensely productive: in reading the text or event in the light of the present, in seeing what question of ours it addresses, we do not leave the present and ourselves unchanged. Understanding involves what Gadamer calls a fusion of the horizons of past and present. In it, the perspectives of the author and the interpreter fuse to produce a new perspective, in being integrated into the world of the interpreter. In this way, the interpretation of texts enriches and changes history at the same time. Underlying this notion of the fusion of horizons is a conception of texts, and even events from the past, as having meaning in the manner in which works of art have meaning. The work of art is often said to have an inexhaustible meaning which generation upon generation must appropriate for itself in its own way. And it is often said that in being appropriated into the present world the great work of art can also change it – through changing the persons who appropriate it. Gadamer sees something similar applying to texts and events from the past. This is why he claims that the dimension of hermeneutics is wider than previously held, in that it encompasses the aesthetic. At the same time, it indicates that this assimilation of the work of art to the text is achieved on the basis of a prior assimilation of the text to the work of art. BC

Gaia /ˈgaɪə/ **hypothesis** the theory that the Earth as a whole, including the biosphere, atmosphere, oceans and soil, and the interaction of their living and their inorganic parts, can be regarded as a living being, as an organism which strives to maintain an equilibrium by feedback mechanisms.

The theory was proposed by the English biochemist James E. Lovelock. Following a suggestion by the novelist William Golding, he named it after the Greek earth-goddess Gaia (other spellings are Gaea or Ge). It is developed in his *Gaia* 1979 and *The Ages of Gaia* 1988.

Further ideas, proposed by Lovelock and others, can be regarded either as parts of the Gaia hypothesis or as additional hypotheses. Among them is the belief that the Earth works for some purpose, such as the promotion of organic life or of spiritual values; and that the Earth as a whole is not only alive but also conscious. Appeals to the Gaia hypothesis also occur in some varieties of modern paganism.

Galen /ˈgeɪlən/ (129–99) Greek philosopher and physician, of Pergamon, whose vast written output covered logic, physics, ethics, medicine and linguistics. His fame rested primarily on his medical theories, which were dominant until the modern era. His name is particularly associated with his theory of the FOUR HUMOURS and temperaments. The fourth ('Galenian') figure of the syllogism was named after him, but it may have been devised earlier. It is only in the 1990s that the great significance of his *Institutio logica* in the history of logic has been properly recognized. His reputation as a philosopher (rather than as a physician) is now rising.

Galilei /gælɪ'lei/, Galileo (1564–1642) Italian astronomer, physicist and mathematician, professor at Padua, advocate of the Copernican theory that the Earth rotates around the sun. He saw nature as lending itself to geometrical analysis. 'The book of nature is written in the language of mathematics. The letters of its alphabet are triangles, circles, and other geometrical shapes.' He proposed a distinction between primary and secondary qualities, later adopted by Boyle, Locke, Berkeley and others up to the present day. He was one of the earliest representatives of the modern scientific world-view: Aristotelian philosophy was rejected, physics was to be separated from philosophy, knowledge was to be gained by observation and experiment. His *Dialogue concerning the two chief world systems* 1632 (i.e. the Copernican and the Ptolemaic) stirred the Roman Inquisition into action, and he was condemned to life imprisonment (served in house arrest) in 1633, but posthumously rehabilitated in 1992.

Gall /gɔːl (Eng.); gal (Gm.)/, F(ranz) J(oseph) (1758–1828) *See* PHRENOLOGY.

gambler's fallacy This is an example of the gambler's fallacy: on tossing a fair coin, heads have now come up 15 times in succession. But runs of 16 are extremely improbable. Therefore, it is now extremely probable that the next toss will come up tails.

This fallacious reasoning has an air of plausibility which makes it easy to separate an incautious gambler from his money. That the reasoning is fallacious becomes clear on considering that the coin has no memory. In the sixteenth toss, as in any other, the probability of tails is the same as in any other toss.

Gassendi /gasɛ̃ndɪ (Fr.)/, Pierre (1592–1655) Provost of the Cathedral of Digne, a Roman Catholic priest, and for a brief time professor of mathematics at the Collège Royal, Pierre Gassendi was one of many in the early seventeenth century who struggled to extricate themselves from Aristotelianism as they embraced the new scientific movement. He was a pioneer of modern atomic theory.

Gassendi was a humanist steeped in the learning of the classical authors. His project was to present the ancient Epicurean atomism, revived and Christianized, as a replacement for the decadent Aristotelian philosophy of the universities. His most influential work was his *Syntagma philosophicum* 1658, an eclectic synthesis of Epicurean and Stoic natural philosophy which included logic, physics, astronomy, earth sciences, biology, physiology, psychology and ethics. He intended to present a completely mechanistic-scientific account of all natural phenomena. The only immaterial entities to be admitted were God, the creator of the vast machine we call the world, and the rational part of the human soul.

In opposition to what he termed the 'dogmatism' of the Aristotelians, he proclaimed himself a philosophical sceptic: he claimed that we cannot have knowledge of the essences of things and of the inner causes of phenomena, but must be content with an empirical and probabilistic knowledge: the only certainties we have are those of Christian revelation and faith. His ideas on these questions influenced the development of modern empirical science.

He emphasized the authority of tradition, usually the tradition of the classical philosophers. Consequently, he is less of a modern than his more famous contemporary, Descartes, who dismissed all arguments from tradition. The two philosophers clashed when Descartes did not take kindly to Gassendi's 'Fifth set of objections' against the *Meditations*. Nor were Gassendi's views on mathematics in harmony with those of Descartes and other leaders of the scientific movement: mathematics for him was merely a tool for ordering the data of experience; it did not enable one to see into the intimate causes or inner natures of things.

Gassendi was an accomplished astronomer. He was the only person to make a properly scientific observation of the transit of Mercury across the sun on 7 November 1631, a phenomenon that had been predicted by Kepler. He was an enthusiastic Copernican until Galileo's *Dialogue concerning the two chief world systems* was condemned by the Holy Office in 1633. Shocked and frustrated by that authoritative decision, Gassendi felt bound to cease his public support for heliocentrism: he rewrote sections of his philosophical writings, and thereafter supported the compromise geocentric system of Tycho Brahe.

In ethics Gassendi made a sharp break with received and current theories. He argued that our natural reason gives us access to the moral truths we need to know, independently of revelation; that these truths are in the main those that Epicurus had discovered; and that the bad reputation of Epicurean ethics for being gross and impious was entirely undeserved. Happiness consists in ease of the body and tranquillity of the mind; those thoughts and actions which are conducive to that end, are right.

Much acclaimed during his lifetime, when his system of philosophy was regarded as the principal rival to that of Descartes, his star waned soon after his death. History has accorded him a place on the edge of the inner circle of genius in the seventeenth century. BB

Gay /geɪ/, John (1699–1745) English clergyman. His short 'Dissertation concerning the fundamental principle of virtue or morality', published as a preface to another work, Edmund Law's English translation of William King's *Essay on the origin of evil* 1731, put forward an important element of utilitarianism, arguing that the competing moral theories agreed that the pursuit of general happiness is the essence of virtue. In response to Hutcheson's and Butler's objections to psychological egoism he proposed a causal theory: benevolence is not innate, but we learn that it has its rewards, and through this learning process we become genuinely benevolent, and learn also to reward others so as to encourage benevolence in them.

Gedankenexperiment /gə'daŋkənɛksperɪmɛnt (Gm.)/ Gm. thought-experiment *n.*

Gehlen /'geːlən (Gm.)/, Arnold (1904–76) German philosopher, professor in Leipzig (after Driesch) 1933, Königsberg 1938, Vienna 1940, but in more modest stations in academic life after the war. Gehlen is mainly known for his philosophical anthropology and his critique of modern culture. Man cannot be understood as a member of the animal kingdom, but, as already pointed out by Herder, is unique in nature because of the lack of inborn survival instincts and techniques. In fact, human beings are by nature cultural beings: work, technology, culture and language pertain to their nature. Gehlen believed that the development of culture requires social formations and institutions, whose function replaces that of instinct in other species, and in which leadership is of crucial importance. These institutions, and the traditional cultural and personal values associated with them, are undermined by modern individualism and subjectivism. Further, our time suffers from the rejection and loss of traditional non-rational certainties. The organic farming village is gone, and the modern world is ailing from loss of confidence, increased aggressiveness, and hectic pleasure-seeking amongst the masses. Another troubling feature is the widespread universalistic humanitarianism and egalitarianism, especially among the educated. This moral outlook is in Gehlen's view not a slave-morality, as Nietzsche thought. It is a morality of concern for others that is fully valid within its primary sphere, the family. What has gone wrong in modern morality is the extension of this primary morality beyond its proper sphere. This moral excess, this 'hypermorality', comes to expression in many forms: universalism, pacifism, feminism, etc.

The malaise of our times, Gehlen maintained, can be overcome only if individuals again become able and willing to sacrifice themselves for higher ends, and only if social structures once more become dominated by an elite.

There is in Gehlen a synthesis of biological theorizing and political elitism that has certain affinities with the ideas of the Nazi Party, of which he was an active member. His major work is *Der Mensch* 1940 (*Man*). Later editions were revised; the changes are recorded and discussed by the editor of part 3 (1993) of the *Gesamtausgabe* (Collected works).

Geist /gaɪst (Gm.)/ Gm. ghost; spirit *n.*

Geisteswissenschaft /gaɪstəs'wɪsənʃaft (Gm.)/ (Gm. *Geist* + *Wissenschaft* science; rational inquiry) *n.* cultural science, human science; often compared or contrasted with the natural sciences.

Gemeinschaft/Gesellschaft /gə'maɪnʃaft; gə'zɛlʃaft (Gm.)/ Gm. community/society *n.* This pair of contrasting terms became established through *Gemeinschaft und Gesellschaft* 1887 (Community and association) by the German social theorist Friedrich Tönnies. He argued that the growth of capitalism since the Middle Ages had led to the gradual disappearance of traditional community, based on custom and tradition and a sense of belonging. Instead, modern society was emerging, and with it individualism, competition, and relationships merely contractual and impersonal.

gender *n.* **1** (in grammar) In many languages, nouns and other words belong to one of a usually very small number of classes, called genders, with differing patterns of inflection. German, Latin and ancient Greek have three: masculine, feminine and neuter. Romance languages have the first two. In English, gender differences have almost entirely disappeared. **2** (in feminist theory) *gender* designates the aspects of masculinity and femininity that are socioculturally determined, in contrast to *sex*, which is biologically determined. This distinction became established in the early 1970s.

genealogy *n.* inquiry into, or account of, ancestry and descent.

generalization *See* EXISTENTIAL; UNIVERSAL.

general will a central concept in ROUSSEAU'S *Contrat Social* 1762 (*The social contract*). In his ultra-democratic theory, the citizenry decides on legislation by a collective deliberation, which results in an expression of the general will (*la volonté générale*). There can be no appeal against it, since sovereignty rests inalienably with the citizenry. The general will is by its very nature directed towards the common good and therefore unaffected by particular interests that would be contrary to the common good. The general will cannot err – it is infallible. Against the objection that the citizenry assembled may legislate unwisely or unjustly, Rousseau's answer is that such a decision is produced not by the general will, but merely by the will of all (*la volonté de tous*) which, like most things human, is fallible.

genesis *n.* birth, coming into being; origin.

genetic fallacy inference of the form 'the origin of x is F, therefore x is F'. This form of argument is fallacious. A water-lily has its roots in mud and slime; but it would be wrong to infer from this that it lacks beauty.

Geneva Swiss city and canton. Its name was used metonymically for (Calvinist) Protestantism, as 'Rome' was used for Roman Catholicism.

genius *n.* **1** the distinctive mental or spiritual character of a personality or nationality. **2** in pre-Romantic and Romantic aesthetics, the free, spontaneous, creative self-expression and self-assertion of the poet, painter, sculptor or composer, which alone makes for true art. An individual with this special gift, which elevates him above the common run of men, is said to *have* genius, but can also be said to *be* a genius. Kant defined genius as the ability to create works of art according to new rules laid down by the artist.

The modern idea of artistic genius can be traced to Edward Young's (author of *Night Thoughts*) *Conjectures on Original Composition* 1759 and the writings of Hamann, enthusiastically adopted by the German *Sturm und Drang* literary movement of the 1770s and 1780s. The adoration of artistic genius can be seen as a secularized counterpart to the veneration of inspired men in various religious cults. In both cases, devotees are prepared to tolerate even major faults, ranging from dishonesty to uncleanliness, in their revered guru or artist.

Gentile /dʒɛn'tilɛ (It.)/, Giovanni (1875–1944) professor of philosophy at Palermo, Pisa and Rome. From the early 1920s he held high positions in Mussolini's government. His support of fascism led to a break with Benedetto Croce, his close colleague. His neo-Hegelian philosophy was predominant in Italy between the wars, and has retained some influence since.

Gentzen /'gɛntsən/, Gerhard (1909–45) German logician, best known as the originator of NATURAL DEDUCTION systems of formal logic.

genus (*sing.*); **genera** (*pl.*) (Lat. a kind) *n.* often contrasted with a species. In Aristotelian and medieval philosophy, the essence of a thing is given by its definition, and the definition states what kind the thing is in the first instance (*genus proximum*), and its specific difference (*differentia specifica*). A standard example is the definition of human being as a rational (specific difference) animal (the nearest kind). *See also* SUBSTANCE.

geocentric theory (Gr. *gē* Earth) the theory that the sun (and other heavenly bodies) rotate around the Earth.

geometric method in philosophy In order to attain the clarity and distinctness that for Descartes was the mark of genuine knowledge, attempts have been made to demonstrate philosophical propositions in the manner of Euclid's geometry. That is, all key concepts are defined, certain principles are laid down as indubitable axioms and postulates, and propositions are then deduced by rigorous logical inferences. The best-known attempt of this kind is Spinoza's *Ethics*, '*more geometrico demonstrata*', i.e. demonstrated in the geometric manner.

Gerson /ʒɛʀsɔ̃ (Fr.)/, Jean (1363–1429) French theologian. In his writings he opposed what he saw as arid scholastic speculation, and developed a philosophical and theological outlook that would, in contrast, be relevant to genuine piety. His main sources of inspiration were pseudo-Dionysius and St Bonaventure.

Gersonides (Levi ben Gershom) (1288–1344) Provençal Jewish scientist, philosopher and theologian. He followed Maimonides in many respects, but rejected the doctrine that God had created the world out of nothing and asserted the eternity of matter. He held that God can be known by his positive attributes, and found a place for genuine free will through the assumption that knowledge properly so called is about universals and that therefore God's prescience does not extend to a particular human action.

Gesellschaft *See* GEMEINSCHAFT.

Gestalt /gə'ʃtalt (Gm.)/ Gm. shape, form, configuration.

Gettier problem This is a problem of finding the correct analysis of the concept of knowledge. A plausible analysis is this: knowledge is justified true belief. But in an article 'Is justified true belief knowledge?', *Analysis 23* (1963), pp. 121–3, the American philosopher Edmund Gettier gave persuasive counter-examples which show that one can have *justified true belief that p* without *knowing that p*. The Gettier problem is that of finding an adequate additional clause to the analysis.

Geulincx /ʒøːlɛ̃ːks (Fr.)/, Arnold (1624–69) an early adherent of Cartesianism. He opposed the Aristotelian philosophy cultivated at Louvain, and when he converted to the reformed faith in 1658 he left for Leiden, where he held a chair. Descartes's answer to the question of how mind and body, two radically distinct and separate substances, can interact, had satisfied neither opponents nor adherents. Geulincx was the first to propose the occasionalist solution: there is no interaction at all, but God has preordained that every mental occurrence is the occasion for a bodily one, and vice versa. In a logic textbook published in 1662 he gave an early formulation of the laws now known as de Morgan's.

ghost *See* SPIRIT.

ghost in the machine an expression used by Gilbert Ryle in his *The Concept of Mind* 1949, in his attack on what he called Descartes's Myth, the dualist view that the mind is, as it were, a ghost mysteriously ensconced in a machine, the body, and the related assumptions that there are two realms of existence, that there is privileged subjective access to one's own mind, etc. Ryle maintained that the errors are (or are due to) what he called category-mistakes.

Giles of Rome (1243–1316) (Latin name-form: Aegidius Romanus). A member of the order of St Augustine, author of works in political philosophy, e.g. *De regimine principum* (On the government of kings). His *Apologia* was discovered only recently and first published in 1985. It has been identified as the document that Giles was known to have submitted in his defence at the University of Paris in 1277 against the accusation of Aristotelianism. In his ontology he maintained that essence and existence are not merely distinct, but indeed separable, entities. His main opponent was Henry of Ghent.

Gilligan /'gɪlɪgən/, Carol (1936–) professor of education at Harvard University. *In a Different Voice* 1982, 2nd edn 1993 draws a contrast between two kinds of morality. One is formulated in terms of rules, rights and justice. Among contemporary writers who understand morality in this way are Hare, Rawls and Kohlberg (whom Gilligan had initially assisted in his research into

Table 10 Two kinds of ethics (Gilligan)

	Ethic of justice (masculine)	*Ethic of care (feminine)*
1. learning	moral principles	moral dispositions
2. key concepts	rights and justice	responsibilities and particular relationships
3. reasoning	from general principles	from the particular context

moral development). Gilligan argues that their 'ethic of justice' – typically masculine – neglects important moral dimensions of care and sense of personal responsibility which characterize the female ethic, an ethic in which questions of context and particular circumstances are taken to be legitimately involved in the formation of a moral judgement.

The two kinds of ethic differ in three important respects as shown in Table 10.

In the justice perspective the moral agent is an autonomous rational individual. The authentic female moral perspective sees moral agents as interdependent, more responsive to the needs of others than to the demands of abstract rules.

Gilson /ˈgɪlsən (Eng.); ʒilsɔ̃ (Fr.)/, Etienne Henri (1884–1978) French historian of medieval philosophy, and a prominent representative of neo-Thomism. His account of Descartes's philosophy (*Etudes sur le role de la pensée médiévale dans la formation du système cartésien* 1930 (Studies on the influence of medieval thought on the development of the Cartesian system)) was influential in showing that Descartes was heavily indebted to his medieval predecessors and did not start from a theoretical *tabula rasa*.

Glanvill /ˈglænvɪl/, **Joseph** (1636–1680) English philosopher, an early member of the Royal Society. He opposed the Aristotelian philosophy taught at his university, Oxford, being to some degree influenced by the Cambridge Platonists. In *The Vanity of Dogmatizing* 1661 he pleaded for an empirical science which could attain relative certainty but not infallibility. He anticipated the Humean view that in the relation of cause and effect, *propter hoc* is nothing but a repeated *post hoc*. In opposing materialism and atheism, he defended (*Philosophical Considerations Touching Witches and Witchcraft* 1666, retitled *Sadducismus triumphatus* in 1681, with allusion to the secular world-view traditionally attributed to the Sadducees) not only belief in God but also belief in witchcraft, to the detriment of his posthumous reputation.

Glucksmann /ˈglʌksmən (Eng.); glyksman (Fr.)/, André (1937–) French intellectual prominent among the *Nouveaux philosophes* (new philosophers) who came to the fore in the late 1970s in emphatic reaction against the hegemony of Marxist and other left-wing philosophy in post-war France. (Glucksmann himself drafted a Maoist-anarchist manifesto in 1968!) The mission of philosophy is for Glucksmann the defence against stupidity. No theory can be formulated for this: a tradition represented by the Cynics, Montaigne, Descartes, etc., but above all by Socrates, can inspire critical reflection capable of subverting all-encompassing theories of man and society, and especially those which in the name of human emancipation or other abstract ideals demand human sacrifice.

gnomic /ˈnəʊmɪk; ˈnɒmɪk/ *adj.* having the

style of a proverb. A gnome is a proverb, aphorism, or maxim of popular wisdom.

gnoseology /nəʊsɪˈɒlədʒɪ/ *n.* theory of knowledge, epistemology. The word is not often used, but occurs in this sense in Baumgarten and N. Hartmann.

gnōsis /ˈnəʊsɪs/ Gr. knowledge *n.* This was the common term for knowledge in ancient Greek. Later, with the rise of Gnosticism, it was given the special sense of a higher spiritual insight that leads to salvation.

Gnosticism /ˈnɒstɪsɪzm/ an esoteric religious movement which emerged early in the Christian era, was suppressed by the Christian church as a heresy, but has periodically reappeared under different names, within or on the fringes of Christianity. Its name is derived from *GNOSIS* and its followers claimed to know 'who we were, and what we have become, where we were, where we were placed, where we are hurrying to, what we were redeemed from, what birth is, and what rebirth is', as one second-century Gnostic put it.

Until recently, Gnosticism was known mainly from the polemics of the Church Fathers against it, which included only a few direct quotations from Gnostic teachers. Some original Gnostic texts have now been recovered, however, including a library of 13 codices of texts discovered at Nag Hammadi in Egypt in 1945. These texts include the *Gospel of Thomas*, a collection of sayings of Jesus partly parallel to those in the New Testament gospels, and partly different, but all modified by Gnostic spiritualizing. The texts also suggest influence from esoteric Judaism, Greek and Egyptian mythology, and Platonism.

Typical Gnostic beliefs include: the notion that the physical world is an imperfect creation by a lower god; a revelation from a higher world (often, but not always, said to have been brought by Jesus); the distinction of human beings into 'spiritual' and 'material'; and the claim that only the 'spiritual' are able to hear the revelation, as only they belong to the higher world. Salvation is thought of as a liberation of the spirit from the bondage of matter. These beliefs are often presented in mythological form, and some readers find the interest of Gnosticism precisely in its 'remythologizing' of religious and philosophical ideas. RB

gnōthi seauton /ˈnəʊθɪ sɪˈaʊtɔn/ Gr. know thyself – an inscription on the temple of Delphi in ancient Greece.

God (in philosophy) a unique entity, in some or all respects perfect and absolute, whose existence can supply answers to fundamental questions in metaphysics and ethics. This is not necessarily the same as the religious concept of a personal being who ought to be worshipped, obeyed, etc.

God, arguments for the existence of *See* COSMOLOGICAL ARGUMENT; DESIGN, ARGUMENTS(S) FROM; ONTOLOGICAL ARGUMENT; PHYSICO-THEOLOGY; MORAL ARGUMENTS.

God, death of the phrase occurs in Nietzsche's *Thus Spake Zarathustra* 1883–5 and has been adopted by many writers to refer portentously to the waning of belief in God.

Gödel /ˈgøːdəl (Gm.)/ **number** In order to prove the theorem described below, Gödel devised an ingenious method of correlating the formulae of first-order logic with positive integers, so that every different formula corresponds to a different number.

Gödel's theorem a mathematical theorem proved by Kurt Gödel (1906–78) in his 1931 article entitled 'On formally undecidable propositions in *Principia Mathematica* and related systems'. The theorem asserts that every formal arithmetic is incomplete in the sense that there exists a sentence (in the language of the first-order predicate calculus) which expresses an arithmetical truth and yet is not provable within the system.

A formal system consists of a set of axioms and a range of rules whereby theorems can be derived from the axioms in a purely formal fashion, i.e. without reference to meaning. The only requirement is that the definitions of the axiom set and of the rules be *effective*. In other words, there must be a feasible mechanical procedure for deciding membership of the set and a similar procedure for deciding in any particular case whether the rules have been correctly applied. The class of formulas derivable within such a system is then effectively enumerable: it is in principle possible to build a computer which will generate all and only the derivable formulas, any one of them in a finite amount of time. Gödel invented a method whereby, given any consistent system of this sort, an arithmetically true sentence can be found which cannot be derived within that system.

Gödel's proof put paid to the hope harboured by Hilbert and other formalists that the class of arithmetical truths can be circumscribed purely syntactically and that the notion of arithmetical truth can therefore be supplanted by that of derivability in a formal system. PTI

God of the philosophers Pascal recorded an intense religious experience on the night of 23 November 1654 on a slip of paper, found inside the lining of his coat after his death: 'Fire. God of Abraham, God of Isaac, God of Jacob, not of the philosophers or of the learned. Certitude, feeling, joy, peace' etc. The allusion is to Exodus 3,15. A transcendent personal God is contrasted with a depersonalized ultimate reality.

Godwin /ˈgɔdwɪn/, William (1756–1836) English novelist (author of *Caleb Williams*) and political writer, author of *Enquiry Concerning Political Justice* 1793 (3rd rev. edn 1798), the basic text for the political theory known as anarchism. Godwin's radical political theory is uncompromisingly utilitarian and anarchist in a liberal-individualist vein. His compelling attack on abuses in society, on the oppression and exploitation in political society, leads him to the general thesis that it has a corrupting influence and violates the rights of the individual.

He married Mary Wollstonecraft (1759–97). Their daughter Mary (1797–1851) married Shelley, and was herself an author, best known for her *Frankenstein, or the Modern Prometheus* 1818, a work often cited by critics of modern science and technology.

Goethe /ˈgøːtə (Gm.)/, Johann Wolfgang von (1749–1832) In the history of German literature, Goethe ranks foremost. Although philosophy was not a major interest of his, he wrote extensively in the area of nature-philosophy, opposing his own theory of colours to Newton's *Optics*. A motivating factor was the dislike of theories that reduced qualitative phenomena to something purely mathematical and mechanical, leaving the subjectively experienced aspects out of account.

Goldbach's conjecture /ˈgəʊldbaːx (Eng.); ˈgɔltbax (Gm.)/ This is the conjecture that every even number greater than 4 is the sum of two odd prime numbers. It was proposed by the German mathematician Christian Goldbach (1690–1764); it has not been proved or refuted.

golden rule Matthew 7,12: 'Whatsoever you would that men should do to you, do you even so to them' (*King James Bible*). 'So treat others as you would like them to treat you' (*Jerusalem Bible*). Luke 6,31: 'And as ye would that men should do to you, do ye also to them likewise' (*King James Bible*).

'Treat others as you would like people to treat you' (*Jerusalem Bible*).

Goodman /ˈgʊdmən/, Nelson (1906–98) American philosopher, professor at Pennsylvania (1946), Brandeis (1964) and Harvard (1967). In Goodman's view, we operate in our beliefs with certain initial data in which we have faith. These are of course finite in number, and allow of a variety of extrapolations, i.e. for the making of different worlds (which perhaps means: for different ways of viewing the world), none of which can be said to be *the* real world. We are free to adopt any world-view that is consistent and fits what we take to be initially credible. They are all equally valid. Goodman does, however, hold that we should have a presumption in favour of what is currently adopted, in favour of entrenched concepts, but they should not be regarded as immune to revision. These views are developed in *The Structure of Appearance* 1951, *Fact, Fiction and Forecast* 1954, *Ways of Worldmaking* 1978, and (with C. Z. Elgin) *Reconceptions* 1988. Goodman has also written on aesthetics. In *Languages of Art* 1968 he maintains that art forms are symbol-systems which, like language, have syntax (structural principles) and meaning. This is why works of art can be *understood*, i.e. interpreted correctly, as distinct from being enjoyed, appreciated, etc. He rejects the view that art represents reality by resembling it.

Goodman's paradox It is natural to suppose that if we have observed many emeralds and found them all to be green, we have good reason to adopt the hypothesis that all emeralds are green and good reason to predict that the next emerald we observe will also be green. But consider the alternative hypothesis that all emeralds are *grue*, where 'grue' is a technical term which means 'green if observed up to a certain future time T, otherwise blue'. Does not the observation of many green emeralds give us equally good reason to adopt this hypothesis and to predict that the emeralds we observe after T will be blue? And if for some reason (or for no reason at all) we prefer to predict that the emeralds observed after T will be black or purple, then we can coin other technical terms ('grack' and 'grurple') in order to fashion hypotheses which will do just that.

This 'new riddle of induction' is due to Nelson Goodman (*Fact, Fiction and Forecast* 1954). It extends to qualitative hypotheses like 'Emeralds are green' a well-known fact regarding quantitative hypotheses. Given any finite number of points in a coordinate system representing pairs of values of two measurable quantities, infinitely many curves can be drawn which pass through all the points and which yield differing predictions about unmeasured values of those quantities. Goodman's paradox extends this 'curve-fitting problem' to qualitative hypotheses also.

These reflections lead to a general sceptical claim: no prediction about the future is more reasonable than any other. For given any body of evidence E and any 'natural' hypothesis H which yields the 'natural' prediction P, one can concoct an unnatural or 'gruesome' hypothesis H* which is equally consistent with the evidence E and which yields the unnatural prediction P*.

The challenge is somehow to discriminate natural hypotheses and their predictions from 'gruesome' ones. Goodman himself simply said that words such as 'green' are 'entrenched' in language and 'projected' into the future, while words such as 'grue' are not. But why should the fact that a word is 'entrenched' and 'projected' be decisive? Others point out that gruesome hypotheses (and 'funny' curves drawn through data points) are less simple than natural ones. But why should lack of simplicity (supposing that it can be demonstrated) tell against gruesome hypotheses and their predictions? Why assume that nature is simple, so that the simpler of two hypotheses is more likely to be true?

Others argue that although gruesome hypotheses are designed to be consistent with the available evidence, mere consistency is not sufficient for evidence genuinely to support a hypothesis. They hope to work out a theory of evidential support which will show that gruesome hypotheses are not so well-supported as natural ones.

It has been noted, however, that if 'grue' (green if observed before T, otherwise blue) and 'bleen' (blue if observed before T, otherwise green) had happened to be our entrenched predicates, then they would have been taken as simple, and the ordinary predicate *green* would then be considered as an artificial complex construction, since green would be identical with 'grue if observed before T, otherwise bleen'. AM

Gorgias /ˈɡɔːɡɪəs/ (*c*. 483–*c*. 376 BC) Gorgias (of Leontini, in Sicily) is usually described as one of the ancient Sophists. Our knowledge of him is very limited. He seems to have stressed the subjective and relative aspects of opinion and knowledge, and to have been a follower of Empedocles in physics and metaphysics. He is an important figure in the history of rhetoric. One of Plato's dialogues is named after him.

grace *n.* **1** (in philosophy) Friedrich SCHILLER'S essay *Über Anmuth und Würde* 1793 (On grace and dignity) explains the contrast between the two concepts, and assigns to grace a fundamental role both in aesthetics and in ethics. He argued that Kant's ethics overemphasizes dignity at the expense of grace. **2** (in theology) According to some statements of St Paul and according to many theologians, including Augustine, Luther, Calvin and Pascal, man is thoroughly sinful and incapable of salvation through any efforts of his own; only grace, a free gift freely bestowed by God, can save the sinner. It was against this doctrine of justification through grace that Pelagius argued that man is capable of good works through which favour can be found with God.

grammar *n.* the systematic description of the way a language is structured, in contrast to its lexicon, which is the inventory of words in the language and the meanings assigned to them. Traditionally, grammar is divided into two major parts: *morphology*, which describes word-formation, word-classes, declensions, conjugations, etc., and *syntax*, which describes features relating to sentence-formation.

grammatology *n.* the kind of inquiry undertaken by Derrida in his *De la Grammatologie* 1967 (*Of Grammatology*), where it is characterized as a 'science of writing'; but it is to be noted that 'writing' is not used in its ordinary sense.

Gramsci /ˈɡræmʃɪ/, Antonio (1891–1937) Italian Marxist thinker. He was politically active and held leading positions in the Italian Communist Party, but was imprisoned by the fascist authorities from 1926. They allowed him access to books and periodicals, and permitted him to write. His *Quaderni del carcere* (Prison notebooks) are of central significance for a study of his thought. Gramsci's general philosophical outlook, influenced by Croce, is in many respects relativist. He rejected many of the 'materialist' tenets proclaimed by Engels and Lenin, including objectivism: the view that a certain reality would exist even if man did not. The idea that there can be an objective standpoint is, for Gramsci, the remnant of the illusory religious assumption of a God's-eye point of view, and we find the idea plausible only because of the long-term influence of religious doctrine on common sense. In his political theory, he rejected parliamentary democracy, which in his view could not adequately meet the interests and needs of society at large. He also condemned bureaucratic centralism (Lenin, Trotsky, Stalin) because its main characteristic, in his view, was the brutal exercise of force. The alternative, at least in his early writings, was workers' councils which would manage not only the productive but also the political and cultural life of society. In his later thought, he developed a theory of hegemony to explain why the exploited classes accept the existing social order, when according to Marxist theory they would not do so. Gramsci argued that the domination of a class depends not so much on the repressive machinery of the state, but on the fact that a prevailing mode of thought shields the existing social order, by persuasively defining for the whole of society what is to be regarded as natural and normal. A predominant ideology is not a mere side-effect of economic and political realities. Therefore, the struggle for cultural and intellectual hegemony, for a position of influence on the public mind, is a necessary step for making a new way of thinking hold sway, and this is in turn a necessary condition for revolutionary change.

greatest happiness principle 'The greatest happiness for the greatest number' was a formulation used by Bentham to explain his principle of utility. His source was Helvétius or Beccaria. The earliest well-known formulation is that of Hutcheson (1725): 'that action is best, which procures the greatest happiness for the greatest numbers; and that worst, which in the like manner occasions misery.' Bentham abandoned the phrase in later writings, since it is possible to maximize happiness even if happy individuals are in a small minority, and it is possible to maximize the number of happy individuals without maximizing happiness.

Green, T(homas) H(ill) (1836–82) Oxford philosopher, fellow of Balliol College, a leading representative of Hegelian idealism. He rejected the scientific materialism and utilitarianism popular at the time, and wrote an important critique of empiricism in the introduction to his edition (jointly with Grose) of Hume's works. Green's political philosophy, as developed in his *Lectures on the Principles of Political Obligation* 1885, was liberal, but his objections to *laissez-faire* principles show the influence of Hegel.

Greimas /gʀæmas (Fr.)/, A(lgirdas) J(ulien) (1917–92) born in Lithuania; studied in France 1936–9; held teaching positions in Alexandria and Ankara 1949–65, and subsequently in France, where at the time of retirement in 1985 he held a chair of general semantics in Paris. In *Sémantique structurale* 1966 (Structural semantics), he emphasized that it is certain elementary structural features, above all relations of opposites, that give rise to meaningful language. Thus, 'dark' makes sense only because it has an opposite, 'light'. In the same way that others had claimed that it is a sentence, not a word, that is the primary bearer of meaning, so Greimas proposed that it is a whole discourse, rather than a sentence, that plays that part. He also emphasized that it is structural features that make narratives make sense. Important concepts are three pairs of opposed ACTANTS: subject/object; sender/receiver; helper/opponent. From that basis, a 'grammar' of narrative, analogous to the grammar of a language, is constructed. Initially, Greimas's analysis concerned the structure of narrative, but was generalized in *Du Sens* 1970 (partly transl. in *On Meaning*) to apply to discourse in general, indeed, to the structures of the workings of the human mind. Greimasian analysis has also been tried in other areas, including jurisprudence. An important source is an encyclopedic work by Greimas and Courtés: *Sémiotique* 1979, 1986 (in part transl. in *Semiotics and Language* 1982). *The Social Sciences: a Semiotic View* 1990 (alternatively entitled *Narrative, Semiotics and Cognitive Discourses*) contains selections from his works.

Grelling's paradox /ˈgrɛlɪŋ/ Some words have the property they designate. For instance, 'short' is a short word, 'English' is an English word. Such self-describing words are said to be *autological*. Other words do not have the property they designate. For instance, 'long' is not a long word, 'French' is not a French word. Such non-self-describing words are said to be *heterological*.

Consider now the word 'heterological'. There are exactly two possibilities. One, that 'heterological' is a heterological word. The other, that 'heterological' is an autological word.

First, if 'heterological' is a heterological word, then it is clearly autological (by definition). On the other hand, it is not autological (by assumption).

Second, if 'heterological' is an autological word, then it is clearly heterological (by definition). On the other hand, it is not heterological (by assumption).

In either case, a contradiction arises. This gives rise to a paradox: an apparently sound proof of an unacceptable conclusion. It was first presented in a paper co-authored by Kurt Grelling (1886–1942) and Leonard Nelson in 1908.

Grice /graɪs/, (H.) Paul (1913–88) British philosopher. Grice taught at Oxford until 1967, and then at Berkeley. Particularly notable is his contribution to the philosophy of language, where he has drawn attention to features which are essential to an understanding of linguistic meaning, but which are not captured in the standard patterns of analysis. His concept of *conversational implicature* has proved fruitful. A conversational implicature is something that can be inferred from the fact that a speaker uses a particular kind of utterance on a particular occasion.

Grice gives basic principles for conversational cooperation: (1) be as informative as required; (2) do not be more informative than required; (3) do not state what you know to be false; (4) do not state what you cannot back by adequate evidence; (5) be relevant; (6) do not be obscure; (7) do not be ambiguous; (8) do not be prolix; (9) do not be messy, but observe some order. Such principles can explain many aspects of communication. To give one example: a speaker can convey meaning by being irrelevant (i.e. violating rule 5 above), if he evaluates a musical performance by saying 'the singer is very handsome'. The utterance *logically* implies nothing about the performance, but certainly does so *conversationally*, suggesting a negative view of the singer's performance.

Together with P. F. Strawson, Grice wrote 'In Defence of a Dogma' *Philosophical Review 65* (1956), defending the analytic/synthetic distinction against Quine's objections in 'Two Dogmas of Empiricism', *Philosophical Review 60* (1951). Grice also defended an objectivist theory of value, adopting a view with Kantian affinities that personhood, as a basis for absolute value, cannot be reduced to naturalistic, in particular biological, concepts.

Many of Grice's writings are published (or re-published) in *Studies in the Ways of Words* 1989. R. Grandy and R. Warner (eds), *Philosophical Grounds of Rationality* 1986 contains papers by Grice and others who discuss his work.

Grosseteste /ˈgrəʊstɛst/, Robert (*c.* 1165–1253) taught theology, metaphysics and physics at Oxford, and probably also elsewhere; later, he was bishop of Lincoln. He was receptive to the rediscovered theories of Aristotle, whose ethics he translated about 1240, and those of his Jewish and Muslim near-contemporaries. In his own physics and metaphysics the concept of light plays a central role as an explanatory factor.

Grotius /ˈgrəʊtɪəs; grəʊʃɪəs/, Hugo (1583–1645) Dutch lawyer, theologian, poet and statesman, in exile, mainly in France, from 1621. In the work that established his fame as the father of international law, *De jure belli ac pacis libri tres* 1625 (Three books on the law of war and peace), Grotius set out to explain what is right and wrong in the conduct of a war, and to show what are the grounds for a just war.

In the *Prolegomena* to the work there is a famous statement that the moral principles laid down in the work would have some degree of validity even if there was no God commanding obedience.

The main principle of Grotius's theory is that there are as many grounds for a just war as there are grounds for bringing a civil action or a criminal prosecution before a court. The kind of court that he has in mind is one that decides rationally, in accordance with natural law. There is, in general, only one kind of ground for bringing an action: that *a wrong* has been committed. It is therefore important to know what counts as wrongs, as injuries. He lists attacks on life, health, liberty, possessions, reputation, honour, or sexual modesty. Violations of rights arising from agreements also count as wrongs. If an individual in civil society is wronged and recourse to courts of justice is possible, then it is not permissible to take the law into one's own hands. In a state of nature, where there is no civil authority, one may take the law into one's own hands.

At the international level, the list of wrongs that states can commit or suffer is similar, though not identical. But there is no common law-enforcing agency, and states are therefore entitled to take the law into their own hands and react against wrongs done. They may also act preventively against wrongs that are about to be done.

Grotius wished to prevent war, or at least limit the frequency and viciousness of the wars of religion and wars of conquest so prevalent in the history of medieval and modern Europe. Since he wanted his work to have practical application, he discussed not only what was right according to nature or reason, but also what was right according to the common custom of all nations, or at least of the more civilized ones. This he called *ius gentium* (the law of nations), in contrast to *ius naturale* (natural law) or *ius naturae* (the law of nature).

It is sometimes said that Grotius employed a geometric method in developing his theory; this is incorrect. His manner of writing was that of an erudite humanist, with an abundance of quotations from ancient poets and philosophers.

Some ideas whose historical life began with Grotius have exercised a great influence. The idea of a law of nations became more firmly established. The individualist perspective provided by the list of wrongs, together with the principle that one may react with violence against any of them, is at the centre of many subsequent analyses of rights and of rights-based moral theories.

In theology, Grotius represented the Arminian (ARMINIANISM) standpoint. He wished for an end to the conflict between various churches and sects, as can be seen from his widely read *De veritate religionis Christianae* 1627 (On the truth of the Christian religion).

Method of citation: The Prolegomena of *De jure* . . . , by paragraph number. The main text, by number of book, number of chapter, number of section, number of subsection. For instance, 2,40,5,1 refers to Book 2, chapter 40, section 5, subsection 1.

grue *See* GOODMAN'S PARADOX.

Guyau /gyɪo (Fr.)/, Jean (1854–88) French philosophical writer who played an important part in introducing the thought of John Stuart Mill and Herbert Spencer in France. His works were very popular with the reading public in France and abroad. The tenor of his thought is well indicated by the titles of two of them: *L'Irreligion de l'avenir* 1887 (The irreligion of the future) and *Esquisse d'une morale sans obligation ni sanction* 1885 (Outline of a morality without obligation or sanction).

Gyges /ˈgaɪdʒiːz/ According to a story told in Book II of Plato's *Republic*, a Lydian shepherd (known from other sources to have been a coarse but shrewd fellow) found a miraculous ring which, when being turned, made its bearer invisible. Being a member of a deputation to the king of Lydia, he took the opportunity to seduce the queen, murder the king with her help, and usurp the throne. His reign (in the first half of the seventh century BC) was lasting and glorious. In the *Republic*, Glaucon uses the story as a challenge to Socrates to explain why one should not act unjustly if one can get away with it, for instance by making oneself invisible. Much of the *Republic* is taken up with Plato's answer to the question.

gynocentrism /dʒaɪnəʊˈsɛntrɪzm/ (Gr. *gynē* woman) *n.* female-centred bias; emphasis on feminine interests or point of view. Cf. ANDROCENTRISM.

gynocracy /dʒaɪˈnɒkrəsɪ/ (Gr. *gynē* woman) *n.* **1** a form of social organization in which women have ruling power. **2** a society in which women have ruling power.

H

Habermas /ˈhaːbərmas (Gm.)/, Jürgen (1929–) German philosopher, professor at Frankfurt 1964–71, and again 1983–94; at the Max Planck Institute in Starnberg in between. He is the major contemporary representative of the 'second-generation' Frankfurt School. He takes up the project of reformulating Marxism as a critical social theory, concerned with identifying and dissolving all oppressive and exploitative power-relations in order that human beings will be able to organize society consciously and deliberately.

Habermas also resumed the critique of the view that social theory can and ought to be objective, disinterested and value-free. In *Erkenntnis und Interesse* 1968 (*Knowledge and Human Interests*), he argues that the Kantian problem of how reason can provide a motive for action can only be solved by taking knowledge itself to be grounded in fundamental human interests, in deep-seated needs. Human beings seek to master nature through labour, and the interest in technical control inherent in labour underpins the natural sciences. Moreover, human beings also interact and communicate with one another, and the interest in this generates another kind of inquiry, that of the historical and hermeneutic disciplines (history, social anthropology, cultural and literary studies, etc.). A third type of interest is emancipatory. It underpins inquiries with a critical orientation such as philosophy, psychoanalysis, and critical social theory, which analyses and seeks to overcome the distortions imposed by the workings of power and domination in society. Its aim is to realize human freedom and responsibility, and its ideal is a society in which social arrangements are those that would result from an unconstrained consensus achieved in open and well-informed dialogue.

Habermas's work in the 1970s (e.g. *Legitimationsprobleme im Spätkapitalismus* 1973 (transl. as *Legitimation Crisis*) and *Zur Rekonstruktion des historischen Materialismus* 1976 (some of these essays also in *Communication and the Evolution of Society*) has in focus the elaboration of the idea that all critical evaluation of moral, social and political matters must have an ultimate basis in the very nature of human communication. Through an analysis of the conditions of possible communicative understanding, an analysis influenced by linguistic philosophers like Austin, Searle and Grice, he argues that understanding, the *telos* of language, is a matter of genuine, unforced consensus, and that such consensus is only possible if discussion is entirely open and unconstrained. Hence, with every communicative act we necessarily presuppose – even if counterfactually – that we are in an 'ideal speech situation' of open, uninhibited dialogue. Habermas goes on to argue that communication, with its presupposition of this ideal speech situation, thus anticipates the realization of a form of social life in which social and political institutions permit open, unconstrained dialogue and consensus. And this provides the standpoint against which to measure actual forms of social life.

In his two-volume magnum opus, *Theorie des kommunikativen Handelns I-II* 1982 (*Theory of Communicative Action*),

Habermas modifies his position somewhat. He no longer thinks that we can derive a concrete conception of social life from an abstract, formal notion like the ideal speech situation. Indeed, that notion no longer appears. Habermas continues to argue, however, that there is an orientation towards understanding and consensus inherent in communicative action, an orientation which can serve as a basis for the diagnosis and remedy of particular social pathologies. What Habermas has consistently sought is, then, a normative foundation for social critique in the dimension of human communication.

In recent years, especially in *Der philosophische Diskurs der Moderne* 1985 (*The Philosophical Discourse of Modernity*), he has engaged in a vigorous debate with French post-structuralists, e.g. Foucault and Lyotard, arguing that their radical rejection of any notion of foundations destroys the very possibility of social critique. Other writings since the late 1980s, e.g. *Moral Consciousness and Communicative Action* 1990 and *Justification and Application* 1993, have further elaborated and modified the theory of DISCOURSE ETHICS, making clear its affinities in certain respects with the views of writers such as Rawls and Kohlberg, and acknowledging impulses from them. Habermas takes the concepts of justice and of right and wrong action to be fundamental moral categories, and states that were it not for the fact that 'discourse ethics' has become entrenched, he would prefer to call it a 'discourse theory of morality'. RCA

Hades /'heɪdiːz/ (in ancient Greek mythology) **1** the realm of the dead. **2** the ruler of that realm, i.e. Pluto.

haecceity /hek'siːɪtɪ/ (Lat. *haecceitas* thisness) *n.* **1** that by which, according to the followers of Duns Scotus (who coined the word), each single instance of the same species is distinguished from other members of the species. In the twentieth century, *haecceitism* is used similarly, for the view that simple individuals have individual essences, that is, properties which are not only essential but also unique to the objects which possess them. **2** In another sense, the term has been used since the 1970s in the context of possible-worlds interpretations of modal concepts: haecceitism is the thesis of transworld identity of individuals. The thesis implies that the sitting Socrates (in the actual world) is identical with the Socrates who is standing (in a possible world). This is similar to the way we think that the Socrates who defends his city (at one time, at war) is identical with the Socrates who defends himself (at another time, in court). Some writers, most notably David Lewis, see difficulties in the idea of transworld identity and subscribe to anti-haecceitism. *See also* QUIDDITY.

Haeckel /'hɛkəl/, Ernst (1834–1919) German biologist and philosopher, and the first major advocate of Darwinism in Germany. He formulated the law of biological recapitulation: that ontogeny (the development of an individual) recapitulates phylogeny (the development of the species). His bestseller *Die Welträtsel* 1899 (*The Riddles of the Universe*) contains an emphatic rejection of traditional religious beliefs and practices. His neutral monism, which has affinities with Spinoza's metaphysics, is an attempt to avoid the difficulties of idealism and materialism. Haeckel founded the *Monistenbund* (Monist League) in order to promote the new scientific metaphysics and ethics.

Hägerström /'hæːgerstrœm (Sw.)/, Axel (1868–1939) the senior representative of the Uppsala School which flourished in the first half of the twentieth century. It had an anti-metaphysical orientation and took the task of philosophy to be conceptual analysis and clarification.

In his inaugural lecture 'On the truth of moral ideas' 1911 Hägerström argued that moral judgements, i.e. judgements that involve the concepts of a categorical ought or a supreme value, are neither true nor false. This seems to have been the first unequivocal statement of moral NON-COGNITIVISM. There are, however, in his writings also suggestions of an ERROR THEORY, according to which certain kinds of normative statements are all false (rather than neither true nor false).

Metaphysics was rejected as absurd or nonsensical because it has to assume that expressions such as 'reality', 'being', etc. themselves designate something real, something which *is*; this, however, can be shown to lead to absurdity. There is no transcendent reality: everything that exists must belong to one and the same all-encompassing context of space and time. Hägerström held the view that metaphysical assumptions had infested not only traditional philosophy but also common sense, religion, morality, the human sciences and the natural sciences. In legal science, a close analysis and critical revision of legal conceptions would be needed to obtain a realistic jurisprudence (*Inquiries into the Nature of Law and Morals* 1953), and, more generally, in most areas of inquiry, a radical revision of traditional modes of thought would be needed to remove the illusions of metaphysics.

Hamann /'haːman (Gm.)/, Johann Georg (1730–88) German thinker. His powerful, albeit oracular, writings challenged the prevalent eighteenth-century faith in rationality. Analysis distorts reality; to dissect is to murder; rationality, both in thinking and in social practice, is dehumanizing. He wrote on behalf of artistic GENIUS and simple piety, using Hume's anti-rationalist arguments in support, and turning Hume's view that belief belongs to the sensitive, not the cogitative, part of our nature to unexpected use. Perhaps this was facilitated by the fact that the German *Glaube* can be used to translate both *belief* and *faith*. Hamann insisted that not everything can be proved, but in the same way that we cannot ultimately reject our sensory experience, so we should accept poetic feeling and religious faith. He accused in particular the French Enlightenment writers of arrogant disregard of vast areas of human experience and values. J. G. Herder and F. H. Jacobi were among those influenced by him.

Hamilton /'hæmɪltən/, Sir William (1788–1856) Scottish philosopher, professor at Edinburgh, a man of great learning. His intuitionist philosophy, influenced by Reid and Kant, was the subject of a major critical examination (1865) by John Stuart Mill. In logic, Hamilton proposed that the basic categorical propositions (All S is P, etc.) should be replaced with forms like All S is all P, All S is some P, No S is all P, etc., in which both subject and predicate are quantified, but this theory did not gain general acceptance.

Hampshire /'hæmpʃə/, Sir Stuart (Newton) (1914–) Oxford philosopher. *Thought and Action* (1959, rev. edn 1982) and other writings (e.g. *Morality and Conflict* 1983) explore the differences between actions and mere events, between statements of one's intentions and mere predictions of one's future conduct, and the closely related questions of freedom and causal determination.

Hanslick /'hanslik (Gm.)/, Eduard (1825–1904) Austrian music critic. In his *Vom Musikalisch-Schönen* 1854 (The beautiful in music), he argued for a pure theory of music. Music does not depict scenery or events, and its function is not to represent feelings or emotions. Nor is it the function of music to arouse particular emotions. What gives music value are qualities intrinsic to it.

hapax legomenon /'hæpæks lə'gɒmɪnɒn/ Gr. something said once only; a nonce-word, i.e. a word used only on a single occasion, or of which only a single occurrence is known.

Hare /hɛə/, R(ichard) M(ervyn) (1919–)

A philosophical self-portrait: My parentage was English. After studies at Balliol College, Oxford, which were interrupted by war service in the East and by being held prisoner of war by the Japanese, I taught at Oxford 1947–83, and after retiring from my chair there, I served at the University of Florida until 1994.

Theoretical and applied ethics have been my main interests. I have insisted on a distinction between descriptive and prescriptive elements in the meaning of moral statements. Their descriptive meaning is the properties (themselves non-moral – e.g. *being an act of promise-breaking*, or *marrying a person of another race*) which are the reasons for making moral statements about actions or people. The reasons for the moral statements vary from culture to culture, so that if their descriptive meaning were the only element in their meaning, the consequence would be relativism. Objectivity is attained only because of the prescriptive element, common to different cultures which share a moral language, and the logic governing this. The logic of the prescriptive element requires moral prescriptions to be applied universally to all similar cases, and hence constrains them to be impartial.

Moral thinking takes place at two levels. At the lower, or intuitive, level we simply apply principles that we have learnt, without questioning them. At this level descriptivism (the view that moral judgements are purely descriptive) can seem plausible, and so can intuitionism, which is one of its main versions. We do, at this level, have moral convictions which we cannot easily doubt. However, these convictions support rather simple general principles, which can conflict in awkward cases. For this reason, and because we need to be sure that the convictions are the right ones to have (many people are completely convinced of the most deplorable moral principles), a higher level of thinking is required, to justify them and decide conflicts between them. This higher or critical level of thinking will be rational if we take seriously the requirement of universalizability mentioned above: that is, that we accept only those moral prescriptions which we are prepared to prescribe for all similar cases, no matter what position we ourselves occupy in them. This is a version of Kant's Categorical Imperative, but it leads to a morality, at the critical level, similar to one kind of utilitarianism; for this method makes us treat all others on equal terms with ourselves and seek the good of all equally. Apparent conflicts between utilitarianism and intuition can be resolved by showing that the conflicting intuitions are generated at the lower, or intuitive, level, and will not necessarily yield the right answers in unusual cases with which this level is not suited to deal. Sound critical thinking at the higher level will, however, recommend the cultivation of these good intuitions for use in all ordinary cases that we are likely to meet.

In applied ethics, I have used this theory to illuminate questions in many fields, including bioethics, political philosophy (especially questions about rights), environmental ethics, education and philosophy of religion.

Books that I have published are *The Language of Morals* 1952, *Freedom and Reason* 1963, *Moral Thinking* 1981, and collections of my essays on various topics in analytical and applied moral philosophy. RH

harmony, pre-established an important principle in Leibniz's metaphysics: the MONADS cannot interact; but God has so arranged the world that any change in one of these substances is perfectly correlated with change in the others. For instance, in an aggregate of monads which constitute a person, body and mind do not causally affect each other, but their respective changes have been synchronized once and for all by God. This is in opposition to the occasionalist (OCCASIONALISM) idea of *ad hoc* divine intervention and to the Cartesian idea of direct interaction.

Leibniz illustrated his point by a simile: if in a clock-tower two clocks always show the same time, three hypotheses can be formed: that they influence each other (Descartes), that God intervenes on occasion to ensure their agreement (Malebranche), or that God constructed and started them so that they function in harmony. (A fourth way would be Spinoza's: that the two are driven by one and the same mechanism.)

Harrington /'hærɪŋtən/, James (1611–77) English political philosopher. *The Commonwealth of Oceana* 1656 argues that the exclusion of the property-owning middle classes from political influence leads to political instability. As an advocate of a moderate democracy, he was well regarded by eighteenth-century Whigs and by the authors of the American constitution.

Hart /hɑːt/, Herbert Lionel Adolphus (1907–92) Hart studied philosophy at Oxford, and continued with law to become a barrister. After the war he taught philosophy at Oxford, and was professor of jurisprudence there from 1952 until 1968 (when he was succeeded by Ronald Dworkin). Influenced first by his teachers, especially H. W. B. Joseph, and later by linguistically and analytically orientated philosophers among his contemporaries (Ryle, Hampshire, Austin, Waismann), Hart developed an approach to legal philosophy that was to establish him as the leading philosopher of law in the anglophone world, and at the same time enhance the standing of that branch of philosophy.

In his best-known work, *The Concept of Law* 1961, Hart argued against the prevailing theory of legal positivism, derived from the writings of John Austin (1790–1859), that the law is ultimately a collection of rules of conduct backed by threats. Such a theory cannot account for legal powers, nor can it do justice to the core of truth present in traditional ideas of natural law, i.e. that there are natural limits, imposed by basic features of the human condition, to what can count as law. He did not, however, believe that in every 'hard case' before a court there is a right answer for the judge(s) to discover. In Hart's view, there has to be such a thing as judicial discretion and judge-made law.

Other writings of Hart's deal with causation, responsibility, utilitarianism, and a series of essays on problems related to Bentham's thought. His name became more widely known through the debate with Lord Devlin on law and morality. Hart defended, in *Law, Liberty and Morality* 1963 and other writings, the view of the Wolfenden report (1957) that the law should not be concerned with the private sexual conduct of consenting adults, against Devlin's view that the law may properly be used to protect existing social morality.

Hartley /'hɑːtlɪ/, David (1705–57) English physician and philosopher. In his *Observations on Man* 1749 he developed an associationist theory of the human mind, along lines consonant with materialism. His theory became very influential. Priestley adopted and promoted his associationism, as did James Mill, and his classification of various kinds of pleasures and pains was echoed by Bentham.

Hartmann /'hartman (Gm.)/, Eduard von (1842–1906) German philosopher. The best-known of Hartmann's many works was his *Philosophie des Unbewussten* (3 vols) 1869 (The philosophy of the unconscious). In the last volume he developed a pessimistic world-view: this world is the best possible, but it is not good enough. We can escape it only by making an end to willing, with its concomitant misery. At the metaphysical level our hope should be that God (philosophically conceived) should overcome his creative urge, with ultimate total annihilation of everything as the final outcome. This world-weary message made his philosophy immensely popular. The pessimism was, however, only one part of his whole philosophical system, which combined elements from Kant, Schelling, Hegel, Schopenhauer, and from the scientific theories of the time. In other writings he discussed problems in early Darwinism, criticized Christian belief, and agitated in the cause of anti-semitism.

Hartmann /'hartman (Gm.)/, Nicolai (1882–1950) German philosopher. He held chairs in Marburg, Cologne, Berlin and from 1945 in Göttingen. Initially influenced by the neo-Kantianism of the Marburg School (Cohen, Natorp), he later turned against its latent subjective idealism and against the tradition which since Descartes had regarded the subject as the starting-point of philosophical reflection. Instead, he developed, in *Zur Grundlegung der Ontologie* 1935 (Foundation of ontology), *Möglichkeit und Wirklichkeit* 1938 (Possibility and actuality) and *Der Aufbau der realen Welt* 1940 (The construction of the real world), a theory with monist and realist elements, insisting that ontology, not epistemology, is the fundamental philosophical discipline. In his theory of values and morals, which is intended to overcome Kant's ethical formalism, he distinguished two basic types of valuation of situations, and of agents. What is valued in agents are virtues. Hartmann gives detailed accounts of them. He held that freedom is presupposed in moral value-judgements and that this freedom implies independence of natural causality. Kant's explanation of freedom in terms of autonomy did not, however, satisfy Hartmann, but he did agree with Kant that this freedom ultimately defies understanding.

Hayek /'hajɛk (Gm.)/, F(riedrich) A(ugust) von (1899–1993) Austrian/British economist and political philosopher, who taught in Vienna 1921–31, then in London (1931–50), Chicago (1950–62), Freiburg (1962–8) and Salzburg (1968–77). Hayek is best known for his critique of socialism and the welfare state from a classical liberal perspective. A leading economic theorist of the 1930s, his reputation and influence declined with the rise of Keynesian economics. Interest in his work revived with the award of the 1974 Nobel Prize in Economics.

Hayek made important contributions in the fields of philosophy, economics, jurisprudence and the history of ideas. In his philosophy of science he is best known for his defence of 'methodological individualism', sharing some of the ideas of Karl Popper. His economic theory may be viewed as an attempt to see economics as a coordination problem: the economic problem of society is not how to allocate given resources but rather 'how to secure the best use of resources known to any of the members of society, for ends whose relative importance only those individuals know'. His work in capital, trade cycle and monetary theory attempts to explain failures in economic coordination, particularly over time. Hayek's critique of Keynesian economics stemmed from these concerns, since he thought that Keynes ignored the temporal character of economic production and so failed to see how market processes facilitated economic coordination over time.

Hayek's economics is the starting point for his social philosophy, which views society as a 'spontaneous order'. Most of society's important institutions, he argued, were not the result of design, but spontaneous developments. Economic order, no less than language and law, is best understood as the product of evolution. The threat to order – and to civilization – comes from man's mistaken confidence in the capacity of reason to take control of these processes to shape society's development. Socialism is the noblest and most sophisticated example of this mistake. Most of Hayek's work, both as economist and political philosopher, has been devoted to a critique of socialism. This is presented in a number of works, of which some of the most important are: *The Road to Serfdom* 1944, *Individualism and Economic Order* 1949, *The Counter-Revolution of Science* 1952, *The Constitution of Liberty* 1960, and *Law, Legislation and Liberty* 1973–8. CK

heap *See* SORITES.

hedonic calculus (Gr. *hēdonē* pleasure) a method of working out the sum total of pleasure and pain produced by an act, and thus the total value of its consequences; also called the felicific calculus; sketched by Bentham in chapter 4 of his *Introduction to the Principles of Morals and Legislation* 1789. When determining what action is right in a given situation, we should consider the pleasures and pains resulting from it, in respect of their *intensity*, *duration*, *certainty*, *propinquity*, *fecundity* (the chance that a pleasure is followed by other ones, a pain by further pains), *purity* (the chance that pleasure is followed by pains and vice versa), and *extent* (the number of persons affected). We should next consider the alternative courses of action; ideally, this method will determine which act has the best tendency, and therefore is right. Bentham envisaged that the calculus could be used for purposes of criminal law reform: given a crime of a certain kind it would be possible to work out the minimum penalty necessary for its prevention.

hedonism (Gr. *hēdonē* pleasure) *n.* **1** the thesis that pleasure is the highest good: that only pleasure has value in itself and that all pleasure has value in itself. Among philosophers held to have advocated this view are Aristippus, Epicurus and Bentham. It is sometimes called ethical hedonism, to distinguish it from PSYCHOLOGICAL HEDONISM.

Note: Pleasure is not the same as happiness, so hedonism is not the same as eudaimonism, the thesis that happiness is the highest good.

2 devotion to pleasure-seeking.

hedonism, paradox of The impulse towards pleasure can be self-defeating. We fail to attain pleasures if we deliberately seek them. This is what Sidgwick (*The Methods of Ethics* 1874) called the paradox of hedonism.

There is a similar paradox concerning happiness. In order to be happy, an agent must aim at things other than his own happiness. Some writers use the same label for this paradox, somewhat inaccurately, since pleasure is not the same as happiness.

hedonistic utilitarianism *See* UTILITARIANISM, HEDONISTIC.

Hegel /ˈheɪgəl (Eng.); ˈheːgəl (Gm.)/, George Wilhelm Friedrich (1770–1831)

Born in Stuttgart in southern Germany, Hegel was educated at the Tübingen theological seminary, where he formed friendships with Schelling and the poet Hölderlin and, like them, was excited by the French revolution and by the works of Kant. On leaving the seminary, he was employed as a house-tutor, first in Bern and later in Frankfurt. He studied the British economists and Kant's ethical works, but those of his writings that survive from this period, the so-called 'Early Theological Writings' (first published in 1907), deal mainly with religious questions, such as 'Why did Christianity, whose founder proclaimed a message of love, become a POSITIVE religion, a religion based on institutionalized rules and dogmas?' and 'Can philosophy, with its hard and fast conceptual thought, do justice to the fluidity and apparent contradictoriness of religious faith?' At this stage, he inclined to the view that philosophy was inadequate to this task, but his later works are motivated in part by a desire to forge a philosophy that will bring conceptual thought, in the form of fluid reason (*Vernunft*) rather than rigid understanding (*Verstand*), into convergence with religion. In 1801, Schelling found him a post at the University of Jena; here he developed, in lectures, the germ of his later system. Napoleon's victory at Jena in 1806 closed the university, and Hegel went to Bamberg in Bavaria (where he edited a Napoleonic newspaper) and in 1808 to Nuremberg, where he was headmaster of a high school. In 1807 he published his first major work, the *Phänomenologie des Geistes* (*Phenomenology of Spirit*). Between 1812 and 1816, he published the *Wissenschaft der Logik* (*Science of Logic*), which won him, in 1816, a professorship at Heidelberg. There he produced his *Encyklopädie der philosophischen Wissenschaften im Grundrisse* 1817 (Encyclopedia of the philosophical sciences in outline) with expanded editions in 1827, 1830 and 1840–45. From 1818 until his death he was professor at Berlin. His last major work, *Grundlinien der Philosophie des Rechts oder Naturrecht und Staatswissenschaft im Grundrisse* (*Foundations of the Philosophy of Right: Natural Right and Political Science in Outline*), appeared in 1821. He lectured at Berlin on the whole range of philosophy; his lectures on aesthetics, on the philosophy of history, on the history of philosophy, and on the philosophy of religion were posthumously edited from his own and students' notes.

Hegel's works are notoriously difficult. Much of their difficulty stems from the wide range of problems which they attempt to solve. Hegel faced a variety of epistemological problems. How can we be sure that we know things as they are in themselves and not simply (as Kant had argued) as they appear to us? Given the many competing, but internally coherent, philosophies, how can we know which is true? How can a philosophy be constructed which does not depend on unproven and controversial presuppositions? Hegel also took seriously the fact that man (but not, on his view, nature) has a history. We cannot suppose (as Kant had done) that all men at all times share essentially the same thoughts or categories. A philosophical system must do justice to the fact that human thought, as well as human life, develops over time. Again, Hegel, a devout if somewhat unorthodox Lutheran, held that philosophy must be not only compatible with religion, but able to give a rational account of it. Hegel's age was also faced with immense practical problems. How could a stable social order be restored after the overthrow of the old autocracies by the French revolution? How can individual freedom and autonomy be reconciled with a cohesive political community? Finally, philosophy must, in Hegel's view, form a single system, in which not only the answers to such problems as these, but all human knowledge, has a place. The motivation for this belief is in part epistemological – only systematized knowledge can be secure against sceptical attack; and in part ontological – the nature of things itself forms a system, and only systematic knowledge can do justice to it.

In the face of these problems, it is not surprising that one of Hegel's main difficulties is to know how to begin. Descartes supposedly began with the *cogito*, Spinoza with axioms and definitions (e.g. of substance and attribute) from which he then derived the nature of things *more geometrico*, Fichte with the pure I or ego. In a similar way, Hegel begins with logic, and, in logic, with pure being. But, he argues, no such philosophical beginning is ever wholly 'unmediated'. Descartes's introduction of the *cogito*, for example, is preceded by an account of his previous beliefs and of his reasons for doubting them; it also presupposes a prior historical development of humanity, since not all men in all periods had, or could have, the thought 'I think'. But such historical and intellectual mediations cannot be excluded from our philosophical system, if that system is to be complete. Thus Hegel prefaces the system or 'science' proper with an introduction that is an integral part of it: the *Phenomenology of Spirit*. Corresponding to the variety of mediations (historical, epistemological, etc.) to which a beginning is subject, as well as to the diversity of Hegel's problems, the *Phenomenology* begins as an exercise in epistemology, concerned with the question 'How can we surmount, or circumvent, the gulf that apparently separates us from things in themselves?'; but soon becomes a philosophical history, recording the ascent of humanity through a variety of cognitive, moral, political, religious, etc. 'forms of consciousness' to 'absolute knowledge', that is, philosophical science. The *Phenomenology* has several features that persist in Hegel's later works. Each form of consciousness, starting with the first ('immediate knowledge'), finds itself to be inadequate or 'contradictory' and, as a result of its own inner 'dialectic', turns into another form. Hegel himself purports simply to watch this process from a superior vantage-point which consciousness itself attains only at the end of its journey, in 'absolute knowledge'. True dialectic is not a dialogue with another person or with the subject-matter, but the intrinsic development of the subject-matter.

When humanity (and Hegel's reader) has attained to absolute knowledge, they are now in a position to turn to science proper, beginning with logic, presented in the *Science of Logic* and, in an abbreviated form, in the first volume of the *Encyclopaedia*. Hegel's logic attempts to unite, systematize and develop *both* Kant's transcendental logic of the categories involved in our experience of the world *and* Aristotle's logic of the forms of our thought about the world. It displays the repeated triadic structure that is characteristic of his mature works. It is divided into three parts, the doctrines of being, essence and concept, and each of these parts is in turn divided and subdivided etc. into three. The doctrine of being examines one-dimensional categories, beginning with pure being and ending with 'measure' (*Mass*), the union of quality and quantity which leads into the dyadic categories of the doctrine of essence, e.g. thing/properties, cause/effect, whole/parts. The doctrine of the concept restores unity at a higher level by introducing categories that are explicitly conceptual and teleological, such as life. This part also includes an account of concepts, judgements and syllogisms (the subject-matter of traditional formal logic), which inform, in Hegel's view, not only our thought about things, but also things themselves. Throughout the logic, categories 'pass over' into each other by their inner dialectic, and the whole conceptual system is welded together by the contradictions in any given category which require resolution by its successor. The logic concludes with the absolute idea, which 'freely releases itself' into nature.

Logic is the centre of Hegel's system. The thoughts or categories are, firstly, embedded in nature: lower entities, such as space, embody lower categories (e.g. being); higher entities, such as living organisms, embody higher categories, such as the concept, purpose and life itself. Thus logic provides a framework for the account of the levels of nature in *Encyclopaedia II*. The claim that natural entities actually embody thoughts, and are not (as Kant held) simply constituted by our imposition of thoughts on our sensory intuitions, is a central feature of Hegel's idealism; for these thoughts or categories also form the central core of the human mind or spirit (*Geist*). But the thoughts are not explicitly available at every stage of the development either of the individual or of humanity as a whole: the system of categories is gradually unravelled both over history and in the life of the individual. This logico-historical process is recorded in *Encyclopaedia III*, the *Philosophy of Spirit*. Spirit appears in three ascending forms: subjective spirit (i.e. individual psychology), objective spirit (the interpersonal norms and institutions that govern our moral, social and political life), and absolute spirit (art, religion and philosophy). Spirit is essentially activity: it takes over, moulds and comprehends its other (nature), and thereby develops and comprehends itself, rising to ever greater heights of 'freedom' and 'self-consciousness'. The view that the world-process culminates in spirit and that spirit 'sublates' (i.e. preserves, destroys and elevates) what is other than spirit is also a central feature of Hegel's idealism. An expanded account of objective spirit is given in the *Philosophy of Right*, and also in the lectures on world history. Absolute spirit is considered in its historical development in the lectures on art, religion and philosophy. Hegel's view of the state, the culmination of objective spirit and of law (*Recht*), mirrors his view of the universe as a whole. The modern state is neither a homogeneous substance, like the Greek city-state, nor a collection of independent individuals, as social contract theorists viewed it, but a unified whole that informs its individual members, yet gives free play to their self-seeking and moral individuality; if they stray too far, they are brought back to unity by wars against other states. Analogously, Hegel is neither a monist, like Spinoza, nor a pluralist, like Leibniz: the unifying logical structure of the world allows free play to the individuality and development of finite entities, and their unity is restored by the comprehending activity of the human spirit: 'the absolute is subject, as well as substance'.

A central factor in the development of spirit over history is this: spirit, in the person of the historian, artist or philosopher, essentially reflects on its present state; but it thereby transcends its present state, developing thoughts that it did not previously have explicitly, thus providing new material for further reflection and development. Later phases of spirit preserve, as well as cancel, its earlier phases. Thus Hegel's own philosophy contains, and does not simply compete with, earlier philosophies: it is the universal philosophy, an *all-comprehensive* system. Hegelian idealism does not *exclude* materialism or realism, but sublates or embraces them. Thus, one of Hegel's responses to scepticism is that his system is not one position among others, but the integration of all positions. Another response is that the system forms a circle, rather than a unilinear progression from presupposed premisses: beginning with logic, it concludes with the highest phase of absolute spirit, philosophy itself – which returns us to logic.

Hegel saw his philosophy as the presentation in conceptual form of the pictorial imagery of Christianity. The logical structure of the world represents God the father; nature God the son; and spirit the Holy Spirit. God is not distinct from the world and independent of it – he would not in that case be infinite, but finite, *bounded* by the world – but God 'alienates' himself into nature and then reclaims himself in the cognitive and practical activity of spirit. Man is not sharply distinct from God, but 'rises to God' over the course of history.

When opposites reach their extreme points, Hegel argued, they turn into each other. For this reason, among others, his thought is often ambiguous: extreme theism, for example, can easily veer into extreme atheism. Such ambiguity gave rise to a division among his followers between the right Hegelians, who held that, in Hegel's view, history had reached a rational climax in the Prussian state and in the reconciliation of philosophy with Christianity; and the left Hegelians, who saw atheistic and revolutionary implications in his thought.

Hegelianism declined in Germany soon after Hegel's death, both because of advances in the natural sciences and because the more talented left Hegelians, such as Feuerbach and Marx, were excluded from university posts. But Hegel's influence extended throughout Europe – the British idealists (Bradley, Bosanquet and McTaggart), Gentile and Croce in Italy, and Kojève and Sartre in France – and also the United States (William Torrey Harris, Peirce, Royce). He exerts a continuing influence not only on philosophy, but also on such disciplines as theology and political theory. MI

hegemony /hɪˈgɛmənɪ/ *n.* preponderance; holding sway. *See also* GRAMSCI.

Hegesias of Cyrene (3rd century BC) The hedonism of Hegesias was negative: the good consists primarily in absence of pain and misery, rather than the presence of pleasurable states. But, he argued, the good is not attainable even on this more limited conception. That is, misery is inevitable. He convinced many of his hearers, and quite a number of them are reported to have committed suicide; hence his by-name *peisithanatos*, 'death-persuader'.

Heidegger /ˈhaɪdɛgər (Gm.)/, Martin (1889–1976) German philosopher; professor at the universities of Marburg (1923–8) and Freiburg (1928–51), famous for his theories of being and human nature and for his unique interpretations of traditional metaphysics. His work has influenced such varied fields as theology (Rudolf Bultmann, Karl Rahner), existentialism (Jean-Paul Sartre), contemporary hermeneutics (Hans-Georg Gadamer), and literary theory and deconstruction (Jacques Derrida). He served briefly as rector of Freiburg University (1933–4), and his outspoken support for Hitler and Nazism during that period continues to haunt his otherwise considerable reputation as one of the most original philosophers of the twentieth century.

All his major works have been translated into English. Among them are (given here with the date of the first German editions): *Being and Time* 1927, *Kant and the Problem of Metaphysics* 1929, *Introduction to Metaphysics* 1953, *What is Called Thinking?* 1954, *On the Way to Language* 1959, *Nietzsche* 1961, and *What is a Thing?* 1962. Some of his shorter works are translated in *Basic Writings*; *Poetry, Language, Thought*; *The Question of Technology*, and elsewhere. The collected edition of his works, including his university lecture courses, began appearing in 1975 and will run to 100 volumes, some of which (for example *The Basic Problems of Phenomenology* and *History of the Concept of Time*) have already been translated into English.

Trained in Catholic theology and scholastic philosophy before the First World War, Heidegger emerged after the war as a creative proponent of the phenomenology of Edmund Husserl. However, Heidegger's radical reformulation of the method and tasks of phenomenology led to a break with Husserl.

Fame came in 1927 when he published *Sein und Zeit* (*Being and Time*). It was published as the first two parts of a projected six-part work of what he called 'fundamental ontology' which would explore the question of what it means *to be*. He held that Western metaphysics since Plato had lost sight of this question as a significant one. Heidegger's idea was to start with the kind of being that each of us manifests, in order to open up the more general question, and to adapt Husserl's phenomenology as the method to be used for the inquiry. He also wanted to prevent misunderstandings that would arise from using the terminology of traditional metaphysics – instead, he showed a strong predilection for homely expressions, colloquial phrases, and evocative neologisms. His use of language is one reason why many readers have found him obscure.

In Heidegger's view, the point of departure of modern philosophy was Descartes's notion that a human being is essentially a *res cogitans* – a thinking thing – and that there is nothing to which we have more immediate access than to our own mind and its contents. This view leaves aside as inessential the fact that we are conscious self-interpreting selves embodied in material, social and historical contexts and above all constrained by our mortality. In the Cartesian framework, I can establish conclusively that I exist – but Descartes never stopped to inquire into the nature of the existence of that entity which I am. This inquiry Heidegger proposed to undertake, by investigating how this kind of existence (he called it *DASEIN*) is revealed in our actual existence and experience.

Dasein, this particular way of existing, is different from the ordinary existence of things in the world around us. The difference is that things are determinate and have their distinctive properties. That is their kind of being. But the sort of being that *I* manifest is not that of a thing-with-properties. It is a range of possible ways to be. I define the individual I become by projecting myself into those possibilities which I choose, or which I allow to be chosen for me. Who I become is a matter of how I act in the contexts in which I find myself. My existence is always an issue for me, and I determine by my actions what it will be. Human existence is always a projecting of oneself into the future: it is at any moment being essentially 'on the way' from what we were and sought to be, towards what we will be.

Our existence is thus essentially temporal, in the sense that we have a past experienced in guilt, and a future anticipated in dread. Time is not here conceived as stretching towards an unlimited future; on the contrary, it stretches towards an indefinite future limited by death. So our way of being is essentially finite, an ineluctable movement towards ceasing to be. The awareness of mortality is an essential part of *Dasein*.

The ways individuals exist, vary. Some engage with the world in awareness of their mortality; they live in a way that is genuinely self-determining and self-revising. Their existence is more authentic: it is in keeping with their ontological nature. In contrast, there are those who lead a life of superficiality and idle chatter, and let their lives be determined by social convention and conformism: their existence is inauthentic.

Another basic feature of the kind of existence we have is that we exist in the world. We experience that we belong to a world: indeed, we find ourselves 'thrown' into it, for no discernible reason. We are immersed in this world and deal with the things in it (not, as required by traditional epistemology, by bridging the gap, in fact unbridgeable, between a self-enclosed consciousness and an external object, but by relating objects to our practical concerns: as tools, as something at hand, or missing). It is only by subsequent abstraction that we develop our theoretical concepts and regard things with their essential and accidental properties as objects of theoretical knowledge, and this in turn makes it possible to think, erroneously, of our existence as if it is of the same kind as that of objects.

It is by revealing the fundamental features of *Dasein* – of the kind of existence we have – that we can come to understand other kinds of existence, i.e. other senses of 'being', and thus answer what Heidegger calls 'the question of being'.

By finding the right way of dealing with this question, Heidegger hoped to overcome the tradition of Western metaphysics that began with Plato. Its main shortcoming is its 'forgetfulness of being'. Traditional metaphysics tends to single out certain privileged entities (the Forms, God, a transcendental Self, Spirit, etc.), thereby forgetting the fact that our understanding of being is based on the way we are in the world and relate to entities in it. This defect in traditional metaphysics leads to the misguided quest for a definitive theory of everything: a total account, once and for all, of why things are as they are.

It is not only inner states (the sense of dread, of being 'thrown', of boredom, of guilt, etc.) that philosophy can understand as disclosures of being, but also certain social and cultural conditions. The modern cult of 'technology' – a way of relating to the world that treats things only as objects of domination and consumption, without insight into its own limitations – is itself an expression of nihilism, the only philosophy left for a metaphysical ambition that has come to grief. It is a mentality that can be overcome with a better insight into the true meaning of what it is to be, and with the rejection of what Heidegger called 'humanism', reason's claim to be able to know the world exhaustively and to put it entirely to human use. The calculative thinking of modern science and the resulting technology cannot sensibly be resisted (though some things in Heidegger suggest a yearning for the pre-modern rural life), but it can be transcended by a kind of 'inner emigration' away from the intrusiveness and superficiality of modern life towards *Gelassenheit* (a word borrowed from Meister Eckhart, which connotes detachment – 'leaving things be' – and serenity), in which one has come to terms with one's own mortality.

There has been heated controversy around Heidegger's thought. Admirers have found in him penetrating insights into the deeper truths about the human condition and the nature of man. Critics have complained of obscure language, weak arguments and dubious etymologies; and there has been much debate as to whether his political stance reveals a deep flaw in his philosophy. RCA/BC/ed.

Heisenberg /'haɪzənbɜːg (Eng.); 'haɪzənbɛrk (Gm.)/, Werner (1901–76) German physicist, professor in Leipzig, Berlin and Göttingen. He was one of the principal creators of the theory of quantum mechanics, and one of the authors of the so-called Copenhagen interpretation of the theory. This is that the state-descriptions of the physical system do not provide information about the actual physical quantities possessed by the system, but about the probabilities of the possible measurement results of those quantities. Applied to the uncertainty principle, this means that the position and the momentum of a particle cannot be determined simultaneously with absolute precision. The product of the average uncertainty in the measured value of the position of a particle and the average uncertainty in the simultaneously measured value of its momentum cannot be less in order of magnitude than Planck's constant (6.63×10^{-27} erg sec) divided by 4π.

heliocentric theory (Gr. *hēlios* sun) the theory that the Earth (and other planets) rotate around the sun. It was proposed by Aristarchus of Samos (*c.* 310–230 BC), and again by Copernicus and Galileo.

Helmholtz /'hɛlmhɔlts (Gm.)/, Hermann von (1821–94) German physiologist, physicist and philosopher of science. He formulated the principle of conservation of energy for the physical universe. He advocated a scientific empiricism which took the form of physicalistic reductionism, and firmly rejected speculative *Naturphilosophie* and vitalistic biology. His discoveries supported this; for instance, he showed that nerve impulses can be accounted for in physical terms, without recourse to any notion of vital forces.

Helvétius /hɛl'viːsɪəs (Eng.); ɛlvesjys (Fr.)/, Claude-Adrien (1715–71) French Enlightenment philosopher, best known for his *De l'Esprit* 1758 (On the mind), the main ideas of which were further developed in *De l'Homme* 1772 (On man). On the question of 'nature v. nurture' he advanced the view that all human beings are born with equal mental faculties and that the differences between individuals are all due to environment and education, and not to hereditary factors. 'Education is everything. It teaches bears to dance.' Helvétius rejected the traditional theories and institutions maintained by the *ancien régime* and the church, and advocated radical reform for the improvement of man and society. Since the ultimate factors motivating human conduct are pain and pleasure, he envisaged that such reform would be brought about by assigning rewards and penalties rationally. The overall character of his views is empiricist and materialist. They provoked strong opposition.

Hempel /'hɛmpəl/, Carl (Gustav) (1905–97) German philosopher. In exile in the United States from 1937, Hempel held chairs at Yale, Pittsburgh and Princeton. He proposed an improved version of the logical positivist criterion of meaning (*see* VERIFIABILITY PRINCIPLE), arguing that *verifiability* could not serve as a criterion, and ought to be replaced by *translatability into an empiricist language* (adequately specified). His account of scientific explanation has been very influential. The principal idea is that an event is explained by being subsumed under a covering law. When discussing the relation between a hypothesis and the evidence supposed to confirm it, he formulated in 1945 the paradox of confirmation (CONFIRMATION, PARADOX OF) also known as the raven paradox. Among his writings are *Aspects of Scientific Explanation* 1965 and *Philosophy of Natural Science* 1966. GC

henotheism /'hɛnəʊθiːɪzm/ (Gr. *heis* one + *theos* god) *n.* the belief that there are many gods but that only one ought to be worshipped. The term was coined by Max Müller in 1880.

Henry of Ghent (*c.* 1217–93) studied and taught at the University of Paris. His theological orientation was conservative: in particular, he was opposed to the influence of Aristotle on the theology of the time, and he was one of the leading figures behind the condemnation of Aristotelian doctrines promulgated by the University of Paris in 1277. Opposed to Aristotle, he relied for his theological orientation on Augustine, Plato and Avicenna.

Theologically, he denied the radical Aristotelian doctrine that the world was a necessary and eternal emanation from God; instead, he saw the world as created in time by a free divine decision. Philosophically, he held several innovative doctrines. On the basis of his account of the ontology of relations he reformulated the Augustinian-Platonic theory of divine ideas. These are usually supposed to be ideas in the mind of God which serve as archetypes for creation, but Henry described them as relations between God and the objects in question, thus avoiding the need to postulate the real existence of Platonic universals. He also formulated a theory of knowledge which blends the Aristotelian account of knowledge as a process of abstraction from sensory experience with the Augustinian claim that divine illumination is needed.

GW

Heraclitus /hɛrə'klaɪtəs/ (*fl. c.* 500 BC) ancient Greek philosopher of Ephesus in Asia Minor. Writing in riddling prose epigrams, he announced that he would expound the nature of things according to the *Logos*, the objective principle of order in the world. Although the Logos is available to all, most mortals ignore it, living like sleep-walkers, in a dream world of their own. The philosopher's task, Heraclitus implies, is to express everyday truths in such a way that their underlying meaning can leap to one's attention – like the solution of a riddle. Thus Heraclitus presents paradoxical truths: The way up and the way down are one and the same. Justice is strife. Living and dead, waking and sleeping, young and old, are the same. This doctrine of flux is probably not that ultimate reality *is* change, but that change is the manner in which ultimate reality, Logos, manifests itself.

At one level Heraclitus presents a physical theory very much in the spirit of the philosophers of Miletus (Thales, Anaximander, Anaximenes): there is an original substance, in Heraclitus's case fire, which is transformed into other substances in a cyclical process that maintains the world as we know it. Fire changes into water and water into earth. The proportions of each resulting substance are equivalent to the corresponding amount of fire.

But there is an implicit critique of the tradition in Heraclitus's version. His original substance is the least substantial of all things. And instead of stressing its priority to other substances, Heraclitus points out its unity with the other substances of the cycle of transformations. Hot becomes cold, dry becomes wet, and thus all opposites are one. The opposites would not exist without each other, and thus 'strife' is responsible for the existence of the world; but opposites are held together in a unity which is more fundamental than the surface manifestations of difference. Moreover, there is a single process of transformation: the way up and the way down are one and the same. Thus the several substances of the cosmic cycle are related as opposites to one another – but the opposites presuppose a deeper unity embodied in the tension between them or the process that transforms them into one another. For Heraclitus, the ultimate reality is not any substance, for substances are not permanent; but the process of change, the law of transformation, which is perhaps to be identified with the Logos itself.

Heraclitus further differs from his predecessors in insisting that the world-order did not come to be out of chaos, but is an everlasting process of fiery transformations. He emphasizes the importance of soul, which is rational and virtuous when it is dry, but helpless when it is wet – as when one becomes drunk. In analogies Heraclitus stresses the place of humans as intermediate between the divine and animal worlds, between life and death, knowledge and ignorance, waking and sleeping. Only the philosopher is fully alive.

Plato and Aristotle criticized Heraclitus for violating the law of non-contradiction in identifying opposites, and for introducing a radical kind of change which makes knowledge impossible. In this interpretation they seem to be following a later Heraclitean, Cratylus of Athens, whose lectures Plato heard. But Heraclitus never asserts the simple identity of opposites, nor does he postulate change without an underlying unity. Nevertheless, the radical interpretation inspired Plato's account of the sensory world, and it may earlier have stirred Parmenides to react against physical theories based on opposites. Later the Stoics built their physical theory on Heraclitean principles. DG

Herbart /'hɛrbart (Gm.)/, Johann Friedrich (1776–1841) professor in Königsberg from 1809 and in Göttingen from 1833. In opposition to the idealism of his time, Herbart advanced an ontology of ultimately simple 'reals' which have often been compared with Leibniz's monads. Herbart developed a mathematical theory of psychological statics and dynamics, in analogy with the branches of physics so named. Aesthetics was the name he gave to the general theory of value, and ethics is that part of the theory which deals with approvals and disapprovals of volitions. There are five basic relations involving volitions (i.e. five basic ethical categories): authenticity, consistency, benevolence, justice, and requital. On the whole, Herbart's sober, even prosaic intellectual style was out of fashion in his time, and it was only through his writings in the philosophy of education that he posthumously came to exercise a notable influence. His writings were, however, closely studied by Bradley, who found much of value in the method, but much to contradict in the conclusions, e.g. on the nature of judgement. Herbart seems to have been the first to conceive of philosophy as conceptual analysis: this activity will, for certain concepts, result in clarification. For other concepts, analysis reveals internal contradictions and shows that the concept has to be radically revised or entirely discarded. Such are the concepts of self-consciousness, and of an identical thing with shifting qualities.

Herbert of Cherbury /'hɜːbət əv 'ʃɑːbərɪ/ (Edward Herbert, first Baron Herbert of Cherbury) (1583–1648) commonly regarded as the originator of DEISM. He held that there are five basic tenets, or Common Notions, of natural religion: (1) there is one supreme God; (2) God ought to be worshipped; (3) worship consists in virtue and piety; (4) wrongdoing should be repented; (5) there are divine rewards and punishments in this life and the next. These tenets are rationally knowable and constitute the basis for a true universal religion and for religious tolerance.

His major philosophical works are *De veritate* 1624, 2nd rev. edn 1633 (On truth), *De causis errorum* (On the causes of errors) including *De religione laici* 1645 (The layman's religion), and *De religione gentilium* 1663 (The ancient religion of the Gentiles).

Locke gives a summary of the five principles in *Essay Concerning Human Understanding* (Bk 1, Ch. 3, §15), where he discusses and rejects Herbert's view that they are innate.

Herder /'hɛrdər (Gm.)/, Johann Gottfried (1744–1803) received early influences from Kant, Hamann and Goethe. He held teaching and preaching positions in Riga,

Strasbourg, Bückeburg, etc. In 1776 he became a senior church administrator in Weimar. It was there that he published his *Ideen zur Philosophie der Geschichte der Menschheit* 1784–91 (Ideas for a philosophy of the history of mankind), putting forward a conception of natural and human history as the evolution to higher levels of one organic unity – mankind. He held that different cultures belonging to different times and places should not all be evaluated by some supposedly universal standard, but in relation to the conditions in which they exist, in the same way that different standards apply to children, adolescents, women and men. This view is not relativist in the sense that it rejects the objectivity of standards. Herder's cultural pluralism is in striking contrast, however, to the prevailing Enlightenment attitude, expressed, for instance, in Voltaire's *Essai sur les mœurs*, which presupposes a universal moral standard and accordingly presents human history as a chronicle of folly, force and fraud.

Herder's translations of folk poetry made him aware of the rich variety hidden in local and national traditions. These cultural treasures, the expressions of the soul of a people, had been neglected in a period of Enlightenment that valued above all the rational and the universal. He held that language expresses the culture and essential character of a nation. Language is more than a set of signs for objects and states of affairs; it expresses a whole way of seeing the world, so that the content of a thought and the language expressing it cannot be sharply separated.

Herder insisted that an individual actualizes his potential only as a member of a people with shared customs, traditions, language. He rejected the view that there was one ideal way to human fulfilment, the same for all individuals, cultures and historical periods, and condemned the imposition of an alien culture on an indigenous one: the British did wrong in imposing their way of life on the Indians; even the Church had been wrong when it brought about the conversion of the Balts in the Middle Ages, and likewise the Romans when they liquidated native civilizations.

Herder's writings were an important source of inspiration for the rise of nationalism within the Russian, Austrian and Turkish empires, and elsewhere in Europe, and were particularly influential in the Balkans. However, there was no doubt in his mind that different national cultures could harmoniously flourish together in peace, like a variety of flowers in one garden.

Herder's varied and prolific literary output includes a *Metakritik* 1799 of Kant's theory of knowledge and a critique of Kant's aesthetics in *Kalligone* 1800.

hereditarianism *n.* the theory that certain characteristics are genetically transmitted. *See also* ENVIRONMENTALISM.

hermeneutic circle The hermeneutic circle consists in the fact that in the search for meaning of a *text*, of an *action*, of *a set of ideas*, etc., the interpretation of a part requires a prior understanding of the whole to which the part belongs, and the interpretation of a whole requires a prior understanding of its parts. Written texts are a case in point. The understanding of the parts, down to the words and sentences, requires a grasp of the larger work constituted by them, and of the literary or cultural tradition to which that work belongs. Also, the grasp of the larger work may require an understanding of the genre, and the literary and cultural tradition to which it belongs, and again the genre is understood through the works that belong to it. In a third form, there is a circle in that a work can be properly understood only by a grasp of what the author had in mind, and vice versa. In general, the hermeneutic circle (the expression was used by Dilthey and may have been created by him) presents the problem of getting beyond the letter to the spirit, although we cannot interpret the letter unless we understand the spirit.

hermeneutics /hɜːmɪˈnjuːtɪks/ (Gr. *hermēneuein* to translate, interpret, make intelligible) *n. sing.* **1** interpretation. **2** inquiry into, or theory of, the nature or methods of interpretation.

There has been reflection on the art of interpreting texts since ancient times, but the word 'hermeneutics' was first used by J. C. Dannhauer in the mid-seventeenth century. He noted that texts for which a theory of interpretation was needed fell into three classes: Holy Scripture, legal texts (statutes, precedents, treaties, etc.), and the literature of classical antiquity.

One important problem for traditional hermeneutics was that it had two radically different aims in its main areas: theology and jurisprudence. One aim was to provide a *correct* interpretation, the other to establish an *authoritative* statement of dogma or of law. It can at times be difficult to satisfy both requirements, and this is why it has been said that hermeneutics is the art of finding something in a text that is not there.

The first major thinker to propose a general theory of interpretation was Friedrich Schleiermacher (1768–1834). He went beyond the traditional view, in his proposal that interpretation requires not only a proper grasp of the relevant linguistic and historical facts, but also a mental retracing, an imaginative reconstruction, of the way in which a text came into being. An interpreter of a text may be in a position to see the author's life and work as a whole, and to place it in a historical setting. Such knowledge, unattainable to the author, can enable an interpreter to understand the text better than the author.

From Schleiermacher and on, the field of hermeneutics was extended to include texts generally, and not only those of scripture, law and ancient classics. The historian J. G. Droysen (1808–84) stressed that knowledge gained by interpretation – he had historical knowledge especially in mind – is entirely different from scientific knowledge. This contrast became well-established through Wilhelm Dilthey (1833–1911). He explained it as a contrast between understanding (*Verstehen*) and explanation (*Erklären*). Our knowledge of historical, social and cultural facts – the realm of the *Geisteswissenschaften* (the human, or cultural, sciences) – essentially involves interpretation. This is why it is radically different from the knowledge gained by application of scientific method in the *Naturwissenschaften* (the natural sciences). Hermeneutics has since been regarded as a theory of interpretation of *all* bearers of meaning: not only texts but also human action and the various features of human culture and society.

Hermeneutics can be seen as a part of a theory of knowledge, since it is a study of the principles by which certain kinds of knowledge are obtained. But the claim that interpretation provides knowledge seems incompatible with three fundamental tenets in positivist (POSITIVISM) thought which have enjoyed wide acceptance: (1) that in principle, scientific method can and must be applied in all fields of inquiry in order to gain knowledge; (2) that the method of the physical sciences is the ideal paradigm; (3) that facts are to be explained causally, and that such an explanation consists in subsuming individual cases under general laws.

Paul Ricoeur has distinguished between a hermeneutics of tradition and a hermeneutics of suspicion. The former aims to listen intently to what is communicated in order to gain insight from, or become aware of, a message hidden under the surface. A representative of this tendency is Gadamer. The latter is 'subversive', attempting to show that, properly understood, texts and human action are not as innocuous as they may seem to be, but may be reflections of hidden drives, class interests, etc. Representatives of this tendency are Nietzsche, Freud, Foucault. There are affinities between these and the so-called critical hermeneutics represented by Apel and Habermas, which continue a tradition of critique of ideologies that goes back, via Marx, to the eighteenth century. The aim of this approach is to criticize existing social, political and cultural conditions by interpretations that are at the same time demystifications.

The so-called HERMENEUTIC CIRCLE presents a problem for interpretation.

'Hermeneutics' has also been used to denote an ontological inquiry, or theory, which explores the kind of existence had by beings who are able to understand meanings, and to whom the world is primarily an object of understanding (rather than, say, of sense-perceptions). Heidegger's philosophy can be described as hermeneutical in this sense.

hermeticism *n.* the tradition associated with a set of seventeen treatises collectively known as the *Corpus Hermeticum.* They deal mainly with occult matters (including astrology, magic and alchemy), but also have philosophical content of a Gnostic and neo-Platonic kind. The name derives from Hermes Trismegistus, the supposed, though fictitious, author. For a long time these writings were thought to be very ancient, predating the Greek philosophers, and to embody the wisdom of the ancient Egyptian priesthood; this contributed to their influence on many Renaissance thinkers, including Marsilio Ficino, Pico della Mirandola, and Giordano Bruno. In 1614, the eminent philologist Isaac Casaubon established that the writings date from the early centuries of the Christian era, and this has since been the accepted view.

The term has also been used for a certain style of French and Italian poetry around the turn of the twentieth century.

Herrenmoral /ˈhɛrənmɔraːl (Gm.)/ Gm. master-morality *n.* The morality of the aristocrats, of the powerful. Its values are courage, self-discipline, truthfulness, respect for age and ancestry, and cruelty towards inferiors. It is outlined by Nietzsche in *Jenseits von Gut und Böse* 1886 (*Beyond Good and Evil*). He contrasts it with slave-morality in *Zur Genealogie der Moral* 1887 (The genealogy of morality).

heterodoxy /ˈhɛtərəʊdɔksɪ/ (Gr. *hetero-* other + *doxa* opinion, belief) *n.* deviation from a doctrine (especially religious or political) authoritatively defined. **heterodox** *adj. Ant.* orthodoxy.

heterological *adj.* non-self-describing. *See* GRELLING'S PARADOX.

heteronomy /hɛtəˈrɒnəmɪ/ (Gr. *hetero-* other + *nomos* law, rule) *n.* literally, 'other-legislation'. Kant uses the term for willing inspired by hope or fear. An action undertaken out of fear of disadvantage or out of hope for benefit may be right, but is heteronomous and it therefore lacks moral worth. Kant contrasts this with AUTONOMY, 'self-legislation'. Autonomous willing alone has moral worth. He uses the terms in *Grundlegung* . . . 1785 (*Foundations of the Metaphysics of Morals*) and *Critique of Practical Reason* 1788.

heteronymy *See* AUTONYMY.

heuristic /hjʊˈrɪstik/ (Gr. *heuriskein* to find out, discover) **1** *adj.* pertaining to an experimental, trial-and-error kind of procedure. **2** *n.* the art of discovery.

hiatus /haɪ'eɪtəs/ *n.* **1** a break in pronunciation, in contrast to elision, for instance when we say '*the example*' with a short break, rather than '*th'example*'. **2** a gap (in a sentence, in an argument, or in a discourse).

Higher Criticism *See* CRITICISM, HIGHER.

higher faculties *See* FACULTY OF ARTS.

higher-order logic predicate logic in which there are not only individual variables with quantifiers to bind them, but also predicate variables with other quantifiers to bind them.

Hilbert /'hilbərt/ (Gm.)/, David (1862–1943) professor of mathematics at Göttingen 1895–1930; an eminent mathematician, who also made important contributions to the philosophy of mathematics. His *Grundlagen der Geometrie* 1899 (Foundations of geometry) laid the foundations for the modern notion of an axiomatized formal system.

Hipparchia /hɪ'pɑːkɪə/ (*fl.* 300 BC) Influenced by the teaching of Crates, her works, now lost, belong to the Cynical tradition. She broke away from her comfortable social position to marry Crates, despite her wealthy parents' – and his own – attempts to dissuade her. As befits CYNICS, they lived frugally, 'according to nature', and despised convention, including (according to ancient sources) normal standards of modesty, on the principle that nothing natural is shameful.

Hippias /'hɪpɪæs/ of Elis (*c.* 460–*c.* 415? BC) ancient Sophist, greatly admired as a polymath. Little is known about him. He is thought to have advocated moral universalism, opposing nature to convention. Two of Plato's dialogues are named after him.

historical materialism *See* MATERIALISM.

historicism *n.* Central to historicism – the term is used in a number of different senses – is the insistence that a particular language, culture, religion, etc. can be properly understood, explained, or evaluated only by relating it to a historical context. Historicism rejects appeals to timeless standards of rationality or morality. Such appeals are seen as invalid, because there are no timeless universal standards; or as futile, because such appeals can make no difference to the relentless unfolding of history.

One strand in historicism stresses the uniqueness of individuals, events, cultural phenomena, etc. in opposition to what is seen as a distortingly abstract rationalist search for timeless truths about man and history. Vico, Croce and Collingwood are among those who, in different ways, represent this outlook.

Another strand in historicism stresses the assumption that the course of history is governed by general laws. Knowledge of these makes it possible to predict the future of a society, of Western civilization, etc. These laws are held to be inexorable, so that resistance on moral grounds is pointless. Views of this kind can be found in Hegel, Comte, Marx, Spencer, Spengler and Toynbee. It is against such a view that Popper argued in *The Poverty of Historicism* 1944.

Althusser's rejection of the historicism he ascribed to Marxists like Lukács and Gramsci is a part of his own rival structuralist interpretation of Marx.

historism *n.* The word is sometimes used in the same sense(s) as HISTORICISM; but in *The Open Society and Its Enemies* 1945, Popper distinguishes historism from historicism. Historism, or historical relativism, is defined as the view that all our opinions are determined by our historical situation.

history *n.* Note the ambiguity: an account of certain events, or the events themselves. *See also* PHILOSOPHY OF . . .

Hobbes /hɒbz/, Thomas (1588–1679) Perhaps the best-known English political philosopher, Hobbes arrived at his argument for absolute submission to an undivided sovereign power in the period of civil war in England that began with parliamentary difficulties for Charles I and ended in victory for Cromwell's forces. He was a member of the household of an aristocratic family for most of his adult life, and the earliest statement of his political theory was a privately circulated treatise, *The Elements of Law*, completed in 1640, that royalists could use in parliamentary debates. Although Hobbes came to believe that his theory justified obedience to any strong sovereign power, whether royalist or not, it was originally put forward by a man who preferred rule by kings to government by representative assemblies.

The Elements of Law is one of the three major sources of Hobbes's political philosophy. The other two are *De cive* 1642 (On the citizen) and *Leviathan* 1651. The readership of *De cive* (known in the English translation, first published in 1651, as *Philosophical Rudiments concerning Government and Society*) has always been smaller than that of *Leviathan*, but Hobbes regarded this second statement of his political theory as the most genuinely scientific of the three, and when he credited himself with having achieved something in political philosophy, it was as the founder of a true *science* of politics. Besides, *De cive* concentrates on the rights of rulers and the duties of citizens, which are plausibly held to be at the centre of political philosophy, whereas *Leviathan* first states this theory of rights and duties and then applies it at length to Church–state relations. It is as much a book about the nature of a Christian commonwealth as about the nature of the state in general.

De cive opens with a strong denial of the Aristotelian maxim that man is by nature fit for life in the polity. Life in the state does *not* come naturally to human beings, according to Hobbes, and once government is established, it is always at risk from the 'manners' of some human beings and the natural situation of all human beings. *Leviathan* is not as explicit as *De cive* and the *Elements of Law* are about the anti-Aristotelian character of Hobbes's political philosophy, but the message is much the same in all three books: Aristotle is wrong about the natural situation of man, about the highest good of man, and about the place of the political in life when the highest good is realized.

The natural situation of human beings – 'the state of nature', as Hobbes calls it – is one in which everyone pursues felicity as they understand it. There is no single conception of felicity that all human beings share, for felicity is a matter of the continual satisfaction of desire or appetite, and individuals differ in their particular wants or appetites. In pursuing felicity as they see it, people naturally exercise the right – the 'right of nature', Hobbes calls it – of judging for themselves how best to get what they want. Problems arise when individuals want the same thing, or when greedy or vainglorious individuals – they need only be a minority – act in character and want more goods or esteem than their neighbours. In all of these cases, commonplace in the nature of things, people are anti-social. They come into conflict. The conflict need not manifest itself in outright fighting, but there is always a danger that it will. Indeed, the right of nature entitles people to use violence in pursuit of their aims if they judge it to be appropriate. Even extreme violence may be justified by the right of nature. In this way the state of nature can amount to a state of war, and indeed is likely to. Either violence will be resorted to gratuitously by the greedy and vainglorious; or it will be resorted to reluctantly and reasonably by moderates intent on protecting their lives and goods from those who are immoderate.

The establishment of a strong state is a solution to the problem of war, an antidote to the threat of conflict latent in the human situation and the manners of particular men. The key to the establishment of the state is the abandonment of the right of nature. People have to agree to entrust judgements about their safety and well-being to an agreed man or body of men who, in return for coming up with effective security and a modicum of commodious living through the civil law and other institutions, is entitled to expect obedience from the many. The device that Hobbes used to explain the establishment of a state on these terms was a fictional covenant between individuals in the state of nature, the effect of which was to make those individuals subjects of a sovereign – either a sovereign individual or a sovereign assembly. Hobbes invited his readers to view existing monarchies as potential providers of security, albeit ones that were unlikely to succeed in doing so until sovereigns were recognized as having, and exercised, more extensive rights than had previously been acknowledged.

The secure life that the many could exchange for the savage free-for-all of the state of nature was not supposed to be a paradise. But it would be better than the natural life of man, which was 'solitary, poor, nasty, brutish and short'. If the sovereign played his part, people would be free to trade, farm, travel and form associations within limits; they would not just be protected from violent attack. But they would not be involved in the political life in the manner of an Aristotelian citizen – a man of virtue who would make his virtue rub off on the many through participation in law-making and magistracy. They would be involved in political life primarily through obedience, although some subjects would of course assist the sovereign in exercising the functions of sovereignty, and by giving expert advice, etc.

Just as Hobbes's political philosophy is strongly anti-Aristotelian, so his metaphysics and natural philosophy belong to the movement of ideas – so-called modern philosophy – that began to supersede Aristotle and the scholastics in the seventeenth century. From 1640 to 1650, a time spent in exile in Paris, Hobbes became a member of a group of self-consciously 'modern' philosophers and scientists centred on Marin Mersenne in Paris. One of the earliest indications in print of Hobbes's metaphysical leanings came in his Objections to Descartes's *Meditations* (1641), the third of seven sets of comments collected by Mersenne. Hobbes railed against Descartes's immaterialism; not only the immaterialism of his theory of the self (Hobbes thought that 'I' could name a body) but also the immaterialism of Descartes's theory of thought and cognition (Hobbes believed that thought was a matter of images associated with names).

Hobbes's own positive views in metaphysics and natural philosophy were stated in a treatise entitled *De corpore* 1655 (On body) which, with *De homine* 1658 (On man) and *De cive*, was supposed to constitute a survey of the elements of philosophy as a whole. *De corpore* attempts to show how the whole range of natural sciences, from geometry to physics and psychology, can be understood to be concerned with effects of different types of corporeal motion. Aristotle's trichotomy of theoretical, practical and productive sciences is done away with, and within Aristotle's theoretical sciences the apparatus of form, matter, substance, attribute, species and genus is subjected to redefinition in mechanistic terms. TSO

Høffding /'hœfdɪŋ/, Harald (1843–1931) Danish philosopher, professor at Copenhagen from 1883, a prominent European intellectual. On questions of ethics he adopted a liberal humanism, and the essence of religion was, in his view, a faith in the permanence of our highest values. Among his many books is *A History of Modern Philosophy* 1900.

Holbach /dɔlbak (Fr.); ˈhɔlbax (Gm.)/, Paul Henri Thiry, Baron d' (1723–89) a naturalized Frenchman of German origin, who translated scientific works, contributed to the *Encyclopédie*, and wrote, adapted or translated numerous anti-religious books. *Le Christianisme dévoilé* 1756/61 (Christianity unmasked) exposes the fraudulent practices and contradictory doctrines of Christianity. His works on society and politics, *Système social* 1773, *Politique naturelle* 1773 and *Morale naturelle* 1776, denounce the injustices and inefficiencies of absolute monarchy. They do not, however, advocate or envisage any radical changes in the existing social and political structures, but urge reform by an enlightened ruler, who would render citizens virtuous and content with their lot by means of state-organized behaviour-modification.

Holbach is, however, remembered above all for his *Système de la nature* (2 vols) 1770. The notoriety of this work rests on the fact that for the first time all the available arguments for materialism and atheism emerged from their earlier clandestinity and were brought together in full public view. It not only challenged traditional religion, but attacked also the various forms of deism or 'natural religion' much in fashion at the time. Holbach argued that both reason and experience lead to the conclusion that nature as a whole is an eternal, infinite being. It is made up of basic material elements ceaselessly rearranged and subject in all its operations to strictly deterministic laws. Even the existence of life is merely the product of the working of blindly mechanical natural forces. There is no such thing as free will, but scientific inquiry can discover the methods by which human beings can be caused to become useful and well-adjusted members of society.

Many of the important figures of the Enlightenment, including Voltaire, Frederick the Great and Rousseau, joined Christians in their rejection of Holbach's completely secular philosophical outlook with its latent subversive tendencies.

Supporters of Marxism, liberalism, secular humanism and behaviourism can all legitimately claim Holbach, and his *Système de la nature* in particular, as an influential precursor. KM

Hölderlin /ˈhøldərliːn (Gm.)/, Friedrich (1770–1843) German poet, a close friend of Schelling and Hegel. He rejected Fichte's theory of an absolute self, arguing that love is the principle by which opposition and difference are overcome. A central theme in his work is that of emancipation and self-actualization. His influence on the thought of Hegel, Nietzsche and Heidegger is considerable.

holism (Gr. *holos* whole, entire) *n.* **1** the view that an account of all the parts of a whole and of their interrelations is inadequate as an account of the whole. For example, an account of the parts of a watch and of their interaction would necessarily be incomplete as long as nothing is said of the action of a watch as a whole. **2** the view that an account or an interpretation of a part is impossible or at least inadequate without reference to the whole to which it belongs.

In the philosophy of science, holism is a name given to views like the Duhem–Quine thesis, according to which it is whole theories rather than single hypotheses that are accepted or rejected. For instance, the single hypothesis that the Earth is round is confirmed if a ship disappears from view at the horizon. But this presupposes a whole theory – one, say, which includes the assumption that light travels in straight lines. The disappearance of the ship, together with a theory that light-rays are curved, can also be taken to confirm that the Earth is flat. The Duhem–Quine thesis implies that a failed prediction does not necessarily refute the hypothesis from which it is derived, since it may be preferable to maintain the hypothesis and instead revise some background assumption.

In the social sciences, holism is the view that the proper object of these sciences are systems and structures which cannot be reduced to individual social agents. Among proponents of this view are Comte, Durkheim, Parsons, Lévi-Strauss. It is often contrasted with (methodological) individualism.

In the philosophy of language, semantic holism or meaning-holism is the view that the meaning of any term or sentence depends on the meaning of every term or sentence in the language. Leading advocates of semantic holism are Quine, Davidson and Putnam.

In environmental ethics, holism is the view that the entire ecosystem forms a unity and that all its parts are interdependent. It is often associated with the view that human interests do not have a privileged position.

The term was created by Jan Smuts (1870–1950), the South African statesman and philosopher, and used in the title of his *Holism and Evolution* 1926. His holism is a thesis which, in opposition to mechanism and materialism, affirms that natural wholes are more than the sum or mere aggregate of their parts. This is due to an inherent non-material integrating dynamic principle in the universe, without which there would have been no evolution and no emergence of consciousness. **holistic** *adj.*

Note: Among contrasting terms, depending on context, are individualism, particularism, reductionism, and (rarely) merism. Some holisms are prosaic, some are poetical or mystical. When mis-spelt ('wholism'), it is the latter kind.

Home /hjuːm/, Henry, Lord Kames /keɪmz/ (1696–1782) Scottish judge, legal historian, legal theorist and man of letters. Kames was the complete Enlightenment figure, writing on a large variety of topics, engaging in schemes for economic and social improvement, active in learned and reforming societies. Philosophically he was eclectic, combining in his *Essays on the Principles of Morality and Natural Religion* 1751 a realist theory of primary qualities with a moral-sense theory derived largely from Shaftesbury and Hutcheson. His anti-sceptical arguments anticipated those soon to be developed properly by Thomas Reid. But he subscribed to a determinist view of human action, the idea of freedom being akin to the ideas of secondary qualities. In his aesthetics (*Elements of Criticism* (3 vols) 1762) and his large-scale conjectural histories of humanity's moral institutions (*Sketches of the History of Man* 1774), the basic formula is the balance between the universal elements of human nature and their historically variable expressions. Thus he saw basic legal phenomena, such as property and punishment, as rooted in constant patterns of natural feelings which lead to different institutional forms in different stages of society. This allowed him to operate with a notion of natural justice which again inspired original work on equity. KHA

homeostasis /həʊmɪəʊˈsteɪsɪs/ *n.* the tendency of an organism to maintain stability in changing conditions.

homo /ˈhəʊməʊ/ (*sing.*); ***homines*** (*pl.*) *n.* Lat. man, human being.

homograph /ˈhɒməgraːf/ (Gr. *homo-* the same + *graphein* to write) *n.* Two or more words which are the same in spelling but not in meaning or pronunciation are homographs. For instance, *lead* (*vb.*) and *lead* (*n.*).

homo homini lupus Lat. man is a wolf to man (from Plautus, ancient Roman playwright).

homonym /hɒˈmənɪm/ (Gr. *homo-* the same + *onoma* name, word) *n.* Two or more words which are the same in pronunciation or spelling but have different meanings are homonyms. For instance, *flower* and *flour*.

If one word has different meanings, it is said to be ambiguous, equivocal, polysemic, etc.

Different words which have the same meaning are said to be SYNONYMS.

homophone /ˈhɒməfəʊn/ (Gr. *homo-* the same + *phōnē* sound) *n.* Two or more words which agree in pronunciation but not in meaning are homophones. For example, *read* (present tense) and *reed* are homophones, and so are *read* (past tense) and *red*.

Horkheimer /ˈhɔːkhaɪmə (Eng.); ˈhɔrkhaɪmər (Gm.)/, Max (1895–1973) Horkheimer was the leading figure of the FRANKFURT SCHOOL. The 1930s and 1940s were spent in exile, mainly in the United States. His main interests were in social philosophy and the analysis of contemporary culture. Setting as an ideal the free and undistorted understanding of man and society – a necessary precondition for bringing about social justice – he found that it is nowhere realized, and that (contrary to the Marxist view, with which he had otherwise much in common), no social class is immune to the distorting influences of social mechanisms, whether in the form of open repression, economic structures, or hidden manipulation. The main argument of *Dialektik der Aufklärung* 1947 (The dialectic of enlightenment), co-authored with Adorno, is that the progress sought by the Enlightenment was illusory and that it was bound to end up in totalitarian barbarity or commercialized vulgarity. This theme was followed up in his collection of essays, *Zur Kritik der instrumentellen Vernunft* 1967 (*Critique of Instrumental Reason*). Horkheimer's later writings, many of them in the form of aphorisms or short essays, show an increasing pessimism and resignation: the good in the individual and social sphere cannot be identified, but evil can. If we aim to realize the good, we will fail; all we can do is to struggle against evil.

horme /ˈhɔːmɪ/ (Gr. *hormē* impulse) *n.* (in Jung's psychology) vital or purposeful energy. **hormic** *adj.*

Hügel /ˈhuːgəl (Eng.); ˈhyːgəl (Gm.)/, Friedrich von (1852–1925) Roman Catholic religious philosopher, of Italo-Austrian origin. He spent most of his life in England. Characteristic of his thought is the emphasis on direct religious experience, which reveals a reality beyond that known to common sense or science. He was condemned by the Church for his modernist (MODERNISM) leanings.

Huguenot /ˈhjuːgənəʊ/ *n., adj.* a designation in general use from the sixteenth to the eighteenth century for the Protestants in France. They were persecuted in the decades around 1685, the year when Louis XIV revoked the Edict of Nantes of 1598 which had granted them protection, and the word refugee (*refugié*) was then first used for the many who fled to Switzerland, Prussia, the Dutch Republic, Great Britain and elsewhere.

Their fate, and the contact with many of them, had a perceptible impact on the thought of John Locke (1632–1704) and other major philosophers. In their ranks were a number of influential thinkers and journalists, e.g. Pierre Bayle (1647–1706), Jean Le Clerc (1657–1736) and Jean Barbeyrac (1674–1744).

humanism *n.* **1** an intellectual and cultural movement, linked to the revival of classical learning in the Renaissance (Petrarch, Lorenzo Valla, Pico della Mirandola, Erasmus, Thomas More, etc.), which adopted an ideal of the full development of the individual, rejecting religious asceticism, narrow scholasticism and humble piety alike. The ideal of a rich flourishing of individual potentiality, enhanced by the study of classical languages and literature, was revived towards the end of the eighteenth century by neo-humanists in Germany: Goethe, Schiller, Wilhelm von Humboldt. **2** Especially in the English-speaking world, *humanism* has since the nineteenth century come to designate a non-religious or anti-religious world-view, usually based on a belief in man's capacity for self-cultivation and self-improvement, and in the progress of mankind. **3** In contemporary French philosophy, humanism is the conception of man as an autonomous being, capable of self-determination, together with the assumption that an individual's choices can make a real difference to a society, or to the course of history. Against this, anti-humanists (Lévi-Strauss, Lacan, Althusser, Foucault) point to the decisive influences of social, economic and psychological structures. These determine the ways in which individuals act; the self-determination of the individual is an illusion; all consciousness is causally or structurally determined. The anti-humanist view is that man can only be a pawn in the game of life, while the humanist view is that man can be a player. **4** There are various other senses of 'humanism', for instance F. C. S. Schiller's version of pragmatism.

humanities *n. pl.* **1** (the study of) ancient Greek and Latin language and literature. **2** (the study of) philosophy, history, languages and literatures. In general, the humanities can be described as the study of man as a cultural being, in contrast to man as a physical and biological entity. They are often thought to involve understanding and interpretation of a kind distinct from observation and explanation in the sciences.

humanity *n.* **1** the quality of being human. **2** mankind. **3** the quality of being humane: kindness, benevolence; beneficence. **4** (in Scotland) Latin language and literature.

humanity, principle of speakers of a language should be so interpreted that what they say about the world is by and large reasonable. This is Donald Davidson's amended version of his principle of charity (CHARITY, PRINCIPLE OF).

Humboldt /'hʌmbəult (Eng.); 'hʊmbɔlt (Gm.)/, Wilhelm von (1767–1835) German thinker, educational reformer, diplomat and philologist. One of the founders of Indo-European philology, Humboldt stressed the importance of language and linguistics for the gaining of historical and cultural understanding. A language is more than a grammar and a vocabulary – it embodies a distinctive world-view, and it is that which constitutes the common element and which expresses the common culture underlying the diversity of individuals within a nation. He believed that the study of classical, especially ancient Greek, language and culture had a crucial role to play in the development of a rich and harmonious personality. As a top-ranking civil servant he proposed reforms in higher education along these lines, which were adopted in nineteenth-century Prussia and in other parts of Germany.

In *Ideen zu einem Versuch, die Grenzen der Wirksamkeit des Staats zu bestimmen* (transl. as *The Limits of State Action*), written in 1791 but not published in full until 1851, Humboldt established as the highest good for man the free unfolding of the individual's potential to a rich and many-sided flourishing. This would best be achieved by limiting the role of government to the protection of personal security and property, thus giving maximal scope to individual initiative and choice in all realms of activity: religion, education, trade and commerce, domestic arrangements including marriage, etc. The influence of this work is everywhere perceptible in John Stuart Mill's classic *On Liberty*.

Hume /hjuːm/, David (1711–76) Scottish empiricist philosopher and historian, commonly considered the greatest philosopher to have written in English, born near Berwick. He studied law at Edinburgh University, but determined early on a literary career, in preference to law. He abandoned his family's Presbyterian convictions in youth, and his moral and philosophical attitudes were shaped by his reading of the classics, especially Cicero.

While still a very young man, Hume conceived a project for the reform of philosophy, pushing his studies to the point of exhaustion and near breakdown. After a brief detour into commerce, he went to La Flèche in France in 1734, returning in 1737 to arrange for the publication of *A Treatise of Human Nature*, which appeared in 1739 and 1740. He was disappointed by its reception, saying with some exaggeration that 'it fell dead-born from the press'. He presented some of its main epistemological arguments again in the *Enquiry Concerning Human Understanding* 1748 and did the same for its ethical arguments in the *Enquiry Concerning the Principles of Morals* 1751. While his fame gradually grew, this was largely due to his *History of England* 1754–62, and his philosophical acceptability was always clouded by a reputation for scepticism and irreligion, which prevented his selection for chairs of philosophy in both Edinburgh (1745) and Glasgow (1752). Until his fame made him wealthy, Hume had to live as a tutor and librarian, and he had some success as a diplomat; but his final years were spent in comfort and relative quiet in Edinburgh. On the advice of his friends, he did not publish his last great philosophical work, the *Dialogues concerning Natural Religion*, in his lifetime; it appeared in 1779.

In his own day and since, Hume has been classified as an empiricist, a sceptic and a secularizer, but he is most fundamentally a *naturalist*: his primary philosophical objective is to present us to ourselves as part of the natural order. He pursues the classic Socratic objective of self-knowledge, but believes it can come about through a scientific understanding of human nature that parallels Newtonian physical science. Such an understanding, developed in the *Treatise*, reveals that we are fundamentally creatures of instinct and habit whose mental lives are dominated by passion rather than reason, whose beliefs are formed by mechanisms of association and custom rather than by *a priori* reflection, and whose moral lives are the product of feeling trained by convention. That we are like this is a fact we must accept, and cannot change or explain. Rationalist systems misrepresent our natures profoundly, and suggest that the human soul is alien to the world in which it finds itself; the same is true of the Christian religion, which generates life-denying ethical objectives that hinder the socialization necessary for the growth of moral virtue.

Hume's theory of knowledge is a detailed application of his claim that belief is 'more properly an act of the sensitive, than of the cogitative part of our natures'. The contents of the mind he calls 'perceptions', and he divides them into impressions (sensations and feelings) and ideas (the copies or images of these). The mind has its own laws, namely those of association, where ideas lead on from one another and are called forth by impressions, and where the feelings (or passions) lead from one to another, as when pleasure leads to love and love to benevolence. Our key beliefs are the products of these associative laws of the imagination, not of reasoning as rationalist philosophers suppose.

Hume tries to show this in three key areas: (1) in his celebrated analysis of induction and causation, he argues that our belief in the causal regularity of the world is a product of custom: we are habituated by experience to expect natural sequences to repeat themselves. The impression of a familiar cause calls up the idea of the usual effect, and we then project the inner inevitability of this expectation on to the world, ascribing a necessity to nature that is only psychological; (2) in spite of the momentary and fragmentary nature of our impressions, we ascribe a distinct and continued existence to them, and thus generate the belief in an external world of continuing objects. The belief is a product of our indolent preference for smooth sequences of related impressions, whose separateness we elect to ignore; (3) we similarly allow ourselves to ascribe identity to the successive changing perceptions that make up the mind, treating a related series of perceptions as though its members were one and the same; we thus create the 'fiction' of personal identity.

These three natural beliefs are inescapable, but cannot be given the justification in reason that epistemologists since Descartes have sought for them. Hume is, therefore, a sceptic in denying that our key natural beliefs can be intellectually supported; but he parts company with the sceptics of antiquity in maintaining that we are unable to suspend judgement on them, except for the briefest of periods in the course of philosophizing. In the language of our time, he suggests that we are biologically programmed to believe. In this we are fortunate: if we were rational in the way scepticism required, we would be reduced to inaction and confusion. Reason must serve these life-giving instincts, and not try to supplant them.

The same subordination of reason to instinct is at the core of Hume's moral theory. Near the close of his account of the passions in Book 2 of the *Treatise*, Hume insists that it is only the passions, including particularly the desires, that can move us to action, and that reason must be their 'slave', operating in their interest. Our passionate nature includes an ability to share in the emotions we can infer to be present in others; this ability, which Hume calls sympathy, enables us to share in the pleasures and sufferings of those who are affected by the states of character of ourselves and our fellows.

When we discern that a character trait or mental quality is agreeable to its possessor (e.g. peace of mind); useful to its possessor (e.g. frugality); agreeable to others (e.g. affable wit); useful to others (e.g. honesty), we approve, and call it a virtue. If we find that it is disagreeable or harmful, we disapprove and call it a vice. But Hume stresses that the approval is moral only if it is from a general standpoint, and not a merely personal like or dislike. We may admire and regard as a virtue the courage of a person whom we detest as a personal enemy.

Of special interest is Hume's treatment of the rules of justice, which enjoin us to respect property, keep promises, obey the laws, etc. He argued that they are merely conventional, and have no intrinsic merit. There is no intrinsic rational necessity that binds us to these rules. This is contrary to the Modern Natural Law Theory, which was the current view at the time. Hume argued that the observance of the rules of justice, like that of other conventions (e.g. the rules of modesty and chastity), is virtuous only because of its general usefulness. The rules of property and promise-keeping have their merit only because of contingent factors: that we, for the most part, live in conditions of limited mutual benevolence, and moderate scarcity of resources. If conditions were different the rules would serve no useful purpose. And in the absence of a useful purpose, they would have no point.

Hume's system accords reason a much humbler role in human life than is ascribed to it by rationalists or most empiricists; but that role is still essential. Our belief in the causal regularity of nature generates the whole apparatus of natural science, wherein reason forms rules for predicting the course of natural sequences. This subordinate but vital function is threatened by faction and superstition, and Hume considers that most religious beliefs threaten it in this way. In section X of the first *Enquiry*, Hume argues that testimony to miracles runs counter to our commitment to natural regularity, and that we should never yield it acceptance. In the *Natural History of Religion* 1757 he claims that religious beliefs arise from a propensity to ascribe natural calamities to invisible personal forces, rather than to explain them scientifically. In the *Dialogues Concerning Natural Religion* he shows in detail that the influential Argument from Design, which ascribes the mechanical order of nature to a divine mind, cannot survive careful application of the standards we use in scientific thinking. This last work, in spite of its polite and careful ambiguities, is the most powerful anti-theistic work of modern times.

Hume's influence has been immense, but has often hindered the understanding of his actual opinions. Thomas Reid and his followers emphasized his scepticism, and attempted to counter it by stressing the very common-sense beliefs Hume himself had held to be natural to us. Kant, following Hume in recognizing the mind's own contributions to knowledge, attempted to restore reason to a more central place in the genesis of science, but still maintained that things-in-themselves are unknown to us. Positivists have welcomed the limits he places on the capacity of reason to understand nature, but have not followed him in the detailed exposure of rationalist pretensions. Ethical emotivists and utilitarians have seen their views prefigured in his, but have neglected the subtle moral psychology and political conservatism with which he states them. Only in recent years has the systematic subtlety of his philosophy been widely appreciated.

Method of citation: Hume's *Treatise* is cited by number of book, number of part, number of section, for example, '*Treatise of Human Nature* 3,2,5'. Since many sections are lengthy, reference by page number is sometimes useful. The edition most often used is the one published by Oxford University Press. TP

Hume's fork Hume's dichotomy between relations of ideas and matters of fact.

Hume's law The principle that factual premisses alone cannot imply an ought-statement. Hume is usually taken to have subscribed to this principle (although there are dissenting interpretations) on the strength of the well-known 'is–ought' passage at the end of *Treatise* 3,1,1.

Husserl /'hʊsərl (Gm.)/, Edmund (1859–1938) born in Moravia; studied mathematics and philosophy in Berlin, Vienna and Halle. He taught at Halle 1887–1901, Göttingen 1901–16, and Freiburg 1916–29. He is the founder of the phenomenological movement in modern philosophy.

As a mathematician, Husserl became interested in the foundations of arithmetic, and published his *Philosophie der Arithmetik* 1891 (*Philosophy of Arithmetic*). At the time, experimental and philosophical psychology were coming into their own, and Husserl's work reflects this psychologism.

On mature reflection, to which Frege's criticism of this work may have contributed, Husserl gave a new account of logic (and mathematics) in *Logische Untersuchungen* 1900–1901 (*Logical Investigations*). The account was anti-psychologistic: the laws of logic and mathematics are not empirical laws that describe the workings of the mind, but ideal laws, whose necessity we intuit, i.e. see, *a priori*. In *The Idea of Phenomenology* 1907 Husserl gave a clear and concise account of his new approach, and in *Ideen* 1913 (*Ideas*) he defended phenomenology as a 'presuppositionless' and pure description of the *content* of consciousness, i.e. what is before our mind when we have a thought. Husserl's phenomenology adopts Brentano's thesis that consciousness is *intentional*. That is, every act of consciousness is directed at some object or other, perhaps a material object, perhaps an ideal object – as in mathematics. The phenomenologist distinguishes and describes the various kinds of intentional acts and the intentional objects of consciousness, which are determined through the content of consciousness. The description of the content of consciousness does not carry with it any commitment to the reality or unreality of the object. One can describe the content of a dream in much the same terms as one describes the view from a window or a scene from a novel. What interests the phenomenologist are the contents of consciousness, not things in the world. Thus in *Ideas*, Husserl distinguishes between the natural and the phenomenological standpoint. The former is the ordinary everyday viewpoint and the ordinary stance of the natural sciences, describing things and states-of-affairs. The latter is the special viewpoint achieved by the phenomenologist who focuses not on things but on our consciousness of things.

The ultimate aim is for Husserl to overcome the preconceptions of science and common sense, and the colouring that our interests bestow on the world around us as we experience it, and thus to reach an ultimate, primordial level. Steps towards this standpoint are taken by means of a series of methodical procedures called 'reductions'. Husserl distinguished several kinds of reduction and shifted his emphasis throughout his career, but two deserve special mention. The first and best-known is the *epochē* or 'suspension', described in *Ideas*, in which the phenomenologist leaves behind the ordinary natural world, 'brackets' all questions of truth or reality and simply describes the contents of consciousness. When this establishes an insight into the essential nature of a content, it is the result of what he calls an *eidetic* reduction. A different kind of reduction (or set of reductions) focuses on the essential features of various *acts* of consciousness.

In *Ideas* Husserl defended a strong realist position: the things perceived in consciousness are not merely contents but things themselves. In his later philosophy he abandoned this realism, and moved towards an idealist view that the world must always be *for* a mind.

While the rejection of psychologism and the conceptual analyses of Husserl's early phenomenology have many affinities with the analytic tradition, critics have objected to the more speculative turn of his later philosophy which, nevertheless, attracted a considerable following. RSO/ed.

Hutcheson /ˈhʌtʃɪsən/, Francis (1694–1746) came from the Presbyterian community in Ulster. After studies at Glasgow he lived in Dublin in the 1720s, where he wrote and published the works that established his reputation and led to his appointment in 1730 as professor of moral philosophy in Glasgow. He was the first major participant in the cultural and intellectual movement that has become known as the Scottish Enlightenment, which counted Hume, Adam Smith, Kames, Reid and Ferguson among its philosophical luminaries.

Hutcheson strongly opposed a number of views that had wide currency at the time. They all sprang from PSYCHOLOGICAL EGOISM, the doctrine that human nature is incurably selfish. For theologians, this meant that only a miracle can bring about anything that is genuinely meritorious. For satirists, it gave ample opportunity to reveal pretence and hypocrisy. Ultimately, the only reason the theory could offer in favour of honesty was that it pays.

Influenced mainly by Shaftesbury, Hutcheson developed, in *An Inquiry into the Original of our Ideas of Beauty and Virtue* 1725, an alternative to this prudential, or indeed mercenary, theory of morals. This had already been tried by rationalist ethical theories according to which moral goodness or rightness is inherent in actions and situations and perceivable by direct rational intuition, in a manner similar to the way in which, aided by the light of reason, we immediately grasp the truth of the axioms of geometry. Hutcheson, however, rejected that approach, and in his *Illustrations on the Moral Sense* 1728 he raised objections subsequently adopted by Hume in the famous critique of ethical rationalism (in Book 3, Part 1 of Hume's *Treatise of Human Nature*). Instead he argued that in addition to our ordinary five senses we have many more, and important among them are the sense of beauty and the moral sense. We are immediately pleased by objects perceived by us to be beautiful through our sense of beauty and, in a similar way, we are immediately pleased (without any reference to private advantage) by character and conduct perceived by us to be virtuous through our moral sense. An interesting consequence of this is that in the same way as there can be no aesthetic education of a person who lacks any sense of beauty, so a moral sense is presupposed in all moral education.

Hutcheson can then respond to the question why we should be moral. The response is that the question does not arise, unless our moral sense is defective, or unless we are in some way misinformed about the facts of the situation. When we consider a prospect or a situation to be agreeable, we spontaneously take a favourable interest in it.

Which kinds of conduct and character do we perceive as virtuous? In some places, Hutcheson seems to allow for a plurality of virtues. However, he is usually taken to admit only one: benevolence, i.e. concern for the happiness of others. The virtuous person is the one who tries to be maximally benevolent. Hutcheson is thus led to a utilitarian theory, and originated the phrase 'the greatest happiness for the greatest number'.

A System of Moral Philosophy 1755 also contains an attempt to give a utilitarian interpretation of the current ideas of natural law and natural rights, and rejects Hobbes's view of man's unsocial nature.

hylē /ˈhaɪliː/ Gr. timber, wood; stuff, matter *n.*; contrasted by Aristotle (*Physics*, Book 1) with form (*eidos*; *morphē*). An individual substance is a combination of matter and form.

hylolatry /haɪˈlɒlətrɪ/ (Gr. *hylē* + *latreia* service, worship) *n.* worship of matter.

hylomorphism /haɪləʊˈmɔːfɪzm/ (Gr. *hylē* + *morphē* form, shape) *n.* a neo-scholastic term for the theory, in Aristotle's *Physics* and *Metaphysics* (Book Z, 1033^{a}24–^{b}19), that every material object is constituted by two principles: matter, which is by itself something potential only, and the form, that in virtue of which an object becomes actualized. The difference between change in one object, and a mere succession of one object by another, is that in the first case the matter (something indeterminate) remains.

hylozoism /haɪləʊ'zəʊɪzm/ (Gr. *hylē* + *zoē* life) *n.* the theory that life is inherent in all matter. The term was first used by Cudworth.

Hypatia /haɪ'peɪʃɪə/ (370–415) a woman much admired for her remarkable intellectual gifts and wide learning, and held in high esteem also for her excellent personal qualities. She was head of the neo-Platonist Alexandrian school. While little is known about her philosophy, she is known to have written extensively on mathematical topics. She was brutally murdered by a fanatical Christian mob at the instigation of their clergy.

hyperbole /haɪ'pɜːbəlɪ/ (Gr. *hyper-* over, above + *bolē* a throw) *n.* a figure of speech in which something is 'praised to the skies', or otherwise described in a manner exaggerated or extravagant. *Ant.* MEIOSIS.

hypodiegetic *See* DIEGESIS.

hypostasis /haɪ'pɒstəsɪs/ (*sing*); **hypostases** /haɪ'pɒstəsiːz/ (*pl.*) Gr. basis; substance *n.* 1 In present-day usage, which began with the Middle Stoa (Chrysippus, Posidonius), to *hypostatize* is to regard or treat something that is not a 'thing' or an object as if it were one. Alternatively, in Carnap's account (using the 'formal mode' instead of the 'material mode' above), hypostatization consists in treating as a name an expression that is not a name. *Syn.* reification. 2 In neo-Platonism each of the three levels of intelligible reality – the One, Mind, Soul – is called a hypostasis. 3 person (of the Trinity) in the Greek formulation: one *ousia* (essence) and three *hypostaseis*. **hypostatize** *vb.*; **hypostatization** *n.*

hypotaxis /haɪpəʊ'tæksɪs/ *n.* (in grammar) syntactic subordination. *Ant.* PARATAXIS. **hypotactic** *adj.*

hypothesis /haɪ'pɒθəsɪs/ (*sing.*); **hypotheses** /haɪ'pɒθəsiːz/ (*pl.*) *n.* 1 a supposition or conjecture. 2 a supposition or conjecture, to be subject to further inquiry or tests. 3 a premiss which is merely assumed but not asserted.

hypothetical /haɪpə'θɛtɪkəl/ **imperative** (in Kant's ethics) an ought-statement which describes an action necessary to achieve a certain end and which is valid only if the end is desired by the agent.

For example, the statement 'you ought to practise your scales', made on the assumption that it is your wish to improve your piano-playing, and that practice will help, is a hypothetical imperative. But if you are not concerned about your piano-playing, the ground for accepting the ought-statement is removed.

Kant stressed that the imperatives of morality are not hypothetical, but categorical. They apply independently of the agent's desires. Previous moral theories, in his opinion, had failed to do justice to this fundamental point.

hypothetical syllogism an inference of this form:

$$\frac{\text{If p then q} \quad \text{If q then r}}{\text{If p then r}}$$

In older logic, MODUS PONENDO PONENS and MODUS TOLLENDO TOLLENS, which each contain a conditional statement, were sometimes called hypothetical (or conditional) syllogisms. This usage is no longer current.

hypothetico-deductive method The scientific procedure by which (1) a general hypothesis is formulated; (2) a particular statement is deduced from it; (3) the statement is checked by experiments or observations. If the result is negative, the general hypothesis has to be abandoned. In some situations, however, it may seem more reasonable to retain the hypothesis and explain (or 'explain away') the negative result in other ways.

Hyppolite /ipɔlit (Fr.)/, Jean (1907–68) French philosopher, best known for his Marxist-influenced translations and interpretations of Hegel, which in the early post-war years did much to draw attention to Hegel in France.

hysteron proteron /ˈhɪstərɒn ˈprɒtərɒn/ Gr. the later (the consequent); the earlier (the antecedent). In general, getting things back-to-front; especially, the defect in an argument also known as *petitio principii* or begging the question.

I

Ibn Rushd /'ɪbn rʊʃt/ *See* AVERROES.

Ibn Sina /'ɪbn siːnə/ *See* AVICENNA.

iconoclasm /aɪ'kɒnəklæzm/ Gr. destruction of icons, of images *n.* Christian iconoclasts in the eighth and ninth centuries regarded the use of images in worship as idolatry, and did their best to have them destroyed. Their opponents, the iconophiles, prevailed, and iconoclasm was condemned at an ecumenical council in Nicaea in 787, and reaffirmed in 842. In the early stages of the Protestant reformation some groups revived iconoclasm in their zeal to purify religious doctrine and practice, and many works of art were lost.

idea *n.* This word has been used throughout the history of philosophy in different, although related, senses. Here follow two of the most important ones. **1** In Plato, the concept of an idea or form is given various theoretical functions and it cannot be taken for granted that it is the same in all of the dialogues. The idea or form of beauty, for instance, is a *universal*, that which all beautiful things have in common, and is that which through its presence in a beautiful thing makes it beautiful. It is also a perfect *paradigm*, something which is itself more beautiful than anything else. It can also be conceived as an *end* or *purpose*, which pulls towards its more perfect actualization. **2** In the modern era, beginning with Descartes, Locke, Berkeley, Hume and many others, the term is primarily used to signify something that exists in the mind. An idea is a *mental content*, a *mental representation*.

ideal **1** *adj.* perfect, optimal. **2** *n.* A model or standard of perfection. For instance, the wise man (of the Stoics) is an individual that instantiates the concept of perfect wisdom. **3** *adj.* Imaginary, fictitious. *Ant.* real, actual. **4** *n.* (in mathematics) a sub-ring of a ring.

idealism *n.* **1** the Platonist view that the ideas or forms (in Plato's sense) alone possess genuine reality. The word was first used by Leibniz, for Plato's ontology, to contrast it with Epicurus's materialism. **2** a view which rejects materialism and naturalism in favour of a religious or otherwise value-orientated world-view. **3** the view that only minds and mental representations exist; there is no independently existing external material world. Berkeley's metaphysics is idealistic in this sense. **4** (in the popular sense) having ideals to guide one's life. *See also* ABSOLUTE; BRADLEY; TRANSCENDENTAL IDEALISM.

ideal observer As a theory of normative ethics, an ideal observer theory maintains that a situation or an action is good or right if and only if an ideal observer would approve of it. Here the approval serves as a criterion. As a theory of analytical ethics, an ideal observer theory maintains that the rightness of an action (or the goodness of an agent) consists in being of such kind that an ideal observer would approve of the action or the agent. Rightness and goodness can be defined in terms of such approval.

Theorists who use the concept agree that the ideal observer must be rational, impartial and sympathetic. Opinions vary on what is implied by these qualities, and on whether any further ones should be added.

In ethical theory an ideal observer was first explicitly introduced by Adam Smith in his *Theory of Moral Sentiments* 1759.

An ideal observer theory of truth could be a theory that P is true if and only if S (an ideal observer) believes that P. The problem with this, and indeed all ideal observer theories, is how to characterize S so that the theory is both plausible and non-circular. *Syn.* ideal spectator.

Ideal of Pure Reason a technical term in Kant's philosophy. In one sense, *ideal* denotes an individual perfect being; but Kant also uses the word to denote a piece of reasoning which has as its conclusion the existence of such a being. In his terminology, then, 'ideal of pure reason' designates (1) the individual being (God) which instantiates one of the Ideas of reason (the Idea of ultimate and complete reality) or (2) the pseudo-rational reasoning supposed to establish the existence of God.

Kant's usage suggests that *ideal* relates to God's existence in the same way that the terms *paralogism* and *antinomy* relate, respectively, to the other two Ideas of reason, i.e. immortality and freedom. He uses 'paralogism' to designate the invalid reasoning that makes us think that we can have knowledge of a simple continuous self, and the position of reason when trying to conceive the absolute totality of a series of conditions is the *antinomy* of pure reason. These are the three types of dialectical inference undertaken by pure reason.

ideal utilitarianism *See* UTILITARIANISM, IDEAL.

Idea of (Pure) Reason Kant used this term in a special, technical, sense: an Idea is a concept which is formed from pure concepts of the understanding and which transcends all possible experience. There are three transcendental Ideas of reason: God, freedom and immortality. To think that there can be any knowledge of these is an illusion. Their only legitimate use is in relation to our moral endeavour.

Kant explains this concept, for which he uses the German word *Idee*, in Book 1, Section 1 of the Transcendental Dialectic in his *Critique of Pure Reason* (pp. B368–B377). It is often translated with a capital I, to distinguish it from *idea*, used to translate *Vorstellung*, i.e. mental representation.

idempotence / ˈaɪdəmˈpəʊtəns/ *n.* a property of a binary operation. For instance, CONJUNCTION is idempotent, because *p&p* and *p* have the same truth-value. In general, that an operation $*$ is idempotent means that for all x in the relevant domain, $x*x = x$.

identity, law of 1 (in traditional logic) A = A; everything is what it is. **2** (in propositional logic) the formula $p \supset p$.

identity of indiscernibles a logical principle which states that two things a and b are identical if every property that belongs to one of them also belongs to the other. It is also called Leibniz's law. In *Discourse on Metaphysics*, he wrote that two substances cannot be exactly alike and differ only numerically. The converse of this is the principle of the INDISCERNIBILITY OF IDENTICALS.

identity theory of mind The identity theory of mind is the theory that mental states and events, such as dreaming, believing, hoping, fearing, feeling pain, etc. are identical with certain states or processes in the central nervous system.

This is not to say that a statement about a belief has the same meaning as a statement about, say, a brain state. The theory is that two such statements refer to the same phenomenon, although they have different meanings, in the same way that 'Lightning struck' and 'There was an electric discharge' can refer to the same event and yet differ in meaning.

Note that it was by means of scientific research that the well-known phenomenon of lightning was found to be an electric discharge. Similarly, identity theorists argue, it is by means of research that identities between mental events, like an experience of pain, and processes in the central nervous system, can be discovered.

The theory was proposed in a seminal essay by U. T. Place, 'Is consciousness a brain process?' (1956). Its best-known representatives are J. J. C. Smart and David Armstrong.

One version of the theory is the type–type identity theory: every type (i.e. kind) of mental state is identical with some type of bodily (primarily neurophysiological) state. For instance, every pain is identical with a C-fibre stimulation. In other versions, such as Davidson's anomalous monism, this is rejected, and instead it is proposed that every token (i.e. particular instance) of a mental state is identical with some token of a bodily state.

There are two main lines of objection to the theory. One, urged by Kripke and others, rejects the adoption of the notion of contingent identity, in this instance between mental and bodily occurrences. The other, urged by Kathleen Wilkes and others, is that there are great problems in specifying what is to count as one mental item: how does one tell whether two thoughts are the same, or different? In the course of the continued debate, some materialist sympathizers with the theory have come to consider functionalism a plausible alternative. *Syn.* the mind–brain identity theory; central-state materialism.

ideology /aɪdɪ'ɒlədʒɪ/ *n.* The term was first used by Destutt de Tracy in *Eléments d'idéologie* 1796 to designate a projected science of ideas, which he described as a branch of zoology devoted to empirical investigation of the origins of ideas and the relations between them. The practical objective of this science was to provide a new basis for education, free from any religious and metaphysical prejudices.

While that 'scientific' usage continued into the nineteenth century, it was soon displaced by the widespread use of the term to refer to a kind of obstacle to rational thought and clear perception that is supposed to affect the thinking of others, and especially of one's political opponents. Here ideology is regarded not just as a set of errors of reasoning, but rather as a systematically distorting factor that causes the errors in the thought of its victims. An early example appears in *The German Ideology* 1845–6 where the authors, Marx and Engels, describe ideology as making 'men and their circumstances appear upside down as in a *camera obscura*'. This usage suggests that the distorting effects of ideology can be reliably identified only by those who do not suffer from them. Ideological thinking is therefore usually regarded as something that can and should be avoided, at least in principle – although Althusser's treatment of ideology as both misleading and inescapable is a notable exception.

A second contemporary usage regards ideologies as sets of ideas associated with distinctive political standpoints – conservatism, environmentalism, feminism and socialism. In this usage, ideologies are sometimes said to represent the interests of classes or other collectivities. Marx's preface to *A Contribution to the Critique of Political Economy*, for example, presents ideology as the form in which 'men become conscious' of their competing interests. An ideology in this sense might also be regarded as misleading, but this usage often appears in a purely descriptive sense. BHI

idiographic /ɪdɪə'græfɪk/ (Gr. *idios* one's

own; private; peculiar + *graphein* to write, to describe) *adj.* History, and in general the human sciences, are sometimes said to be idiographic, i.e. what they describe is taken to be particular and non-recurrent. It is in this that they differ from the natural sciences, which are NOMOTHETIC. This analysis and this pair of terms were introduced by Windelband in an address given in 1894. He did observe that the same subject-matter can be the object of both types of inquiry.

idiolect /ˈɪdɪəlɛkt/ *n.* an individual's variety of a common language, with particular distinctive features.

idol /ˈaɪdəl/ (Gr. *eidōlon*; Lat. *idolum* image) *n.* **1** an object (image or material object) of religious worship. **2** an improper object of worship; a false god. **3** in his *Novum Organum* I, 39–51 (1620) which, as the title suggests, was intended to replace Aristotle's *Organon*, Francis Bacon presented a theory of four kinds of 'idols' of the mind: they are false preconceptions that lead us astray in our thinking. They arise from four important kinds of error-inducing tendencies in the human mind: (1) people tend to think anthropomorphically (*idola tribus*: the idols of the tribe); (2) they tend to be unduly influenced by their personal habits and prejudices (*idola specus*: the idols of the cave); (3) they tend to be misled by language (*idola fori*: the idols of the marketplace); (4) they tend to be misled by established theological, philosophical and scientific opinion (*idola theatri*: the idols of the theatre).

idolatry /aɪˈdɒlətrɪ/ *n.* worship of an image or a material object; strongly condemned in Judaism, Christianity and Islam. Cf. Exodus 20,3; Leviticus 19,4; Deuteronomy 20,15–20. *Syn.* idololatry.

iff *conj.* an abbreviation, used mainly by logicians, for 'if and only if'.

In definitions in mathematics, logic, etc., 'if and only if' or 'iff' is often used to join definiendum and definiens; but, strangely, by tacit convention in these disciplines, 'if' has often been used in definitions instead of 'if and only if'.

ignoramus; ignorabimus Lat. we do not know; we shall not know. These words were used as a motto in a famous lecture on the limits of scientific knowledge, delivered by the German physiologist E. du Bois-Reymond in 1872, in which he defended an agnostic metaphysical position against the dogmatic scientific materialism of his time.

ignoratio elenchi /ɪgnəˈreɪʃɪəʊ ɪˈlɛŋkaɪ/ Lat. 'misconception of the refutation'; missing the point, by arguing against something that the other party has not proposed.

illation *n.* inference (now rare).

illative (Lat. *in-* + *latum* carried) *n.*, *adj.* **1** Illatives, or illative expressions, are words like *so*, *ergo*, *therefore*, *consequently*, *it follows that*, which are used to indicate that a statement is a conclusion from given premisses. **2** (in grammar) the illative case, e.g. in Finnish, signifies motion towards.

illatum (*sing.*); **illata** (*pl.*) *n.* something whose occurrence is inferred but cannot be directly observed. For instance, inner mental processes and activities which we ordinarily take for granted in order to make sense of observed external behaviour have been described as 'illata of folk psychology'.

illocutionary act an act performed *in* saying something. Examples of illocutionary acts are naming, laying a bet, promising, commanding, warning, asking, etc. This is a central concept in J. L. Austin's theory of speech-acts. It is contrasted with the locutionary and perlocutionary acts involved in a speech-act. To ask for the (illocutionary) force of an utterance is to ask what kind of illocutionary act is being performed. For instance: 'Was what P said a promise or a threat?' *See also* SPEECH ACTS.

illuminism *n.* the name given to an eighteenth-century esoteric doctrine and movement, similar to freemasonry. It was founded by Adam Weishaupt, professor in Ingolstadt, in 1776 and flourished in Bavaria, but was suppressed eight years later because of its political activities. It urged resistance to the influence on state and Church exercised by the Jesuits, and advocated secular and liberal ideals of natural rights, religious toleration and human progress. Similar groups sprang up in early nineteenth-century Italy.

The term has also been used for other religious-mystical groupings, e.g. the Spanish *aluminados* (finally suppressed by the Inquisition in the sixteenth century), certain Rosicrucians, and followers of the French mystic L.-C. de Saint-Martin (1743–1803).

illusion, argument from From the fact that there are perceptual illusions and hallucinations it is clear that some sensory perceptions do not present to us the actual qualities of an external object. In such cases, all that is presented is a sense-datum or a complex of sense-data (i.e. items directly 'given' to our senses). But our sensory perceptions contain no distinguishing marks between the illusory and the veridical ones. Therefore, the argument goes, the qualities we perceive are not inherent in objects, but are merely data presented to us in our sensory experience, i.e. sense-data. Generalized, the argument leads to the conclusion that we never perceive reality, but only appearance.

The argument was known to the ancients, and so were the closely related arguments from the fact that a thing with the same qualities can appear different at different times, or to different observers. They were persuasively stated by Berkeley in the first of his *Three Dialogues* 1713 and by A. J. Ayer in his *The Foundations of Empirical Knowledge* 1940, and used to underpin phenomenalism.

illusion, transcendental According to Kant, reason has a natural tendency to go beyond its boundaries by applying the categories (the concepts of the understanding) beyond their proper range of application, i.e. the empirical realm. This gives rise to the illusions that we can have knowledge of the soul, freedom of the will, and God. Kant examines them in the part of the *Critique of Pure Reason* called Transcendental Dialectic. In his view, they are natural, like certain optical illusions, and do not go away, but we can come to realize that they are misleading.

imaginary **1** *adj.* pertaining to the imagination; fictitious.

2 *n.* As a noun, the word is a recent import from the French and bears the traces of a long history of theorization about *the imaginary* within French philosophy, aesthetics, literary theory, cultural anthropology and psychoanalysis.

The term has been in common use at least since the Surrealists, with reference to all kinds of imagined or invented meanings. It is a key concept in work as diverse as that of cultural anthropologist Gilbert Durand and that of the philosopher Michèle Le Doeuff. Its recent history also owes much to the work of the French psychoanalyst Jacques Lacan and critics such as Luce Irigaray and Cornelius Castoriadis.

Sartre uses the term in his *L'Imaginaire* 1940 (transl. as *The Psychology of the Imagination*) to refer to the intentional objects of the imagining consciousness, as opposed to the perceptual or rational consciousness. These may be external, in the form of art works, or internal, as in the case of fantasies and daydreams. Gaston Bachelard uses it similarly in his poetics, but in his epistemological studies (e.g. *La Formation de l'esprit scientifique: contribution à une psychanalyse de la connaissance objective* Paris 1957 (*The development of the scientific spirit: contribution towards a psychoanalysis of objective knowledge*)) he also uses it to refer to the distorted products of perceptual experience, the imaginary elements of scientific reports, in so far as these may constitute an obstacle to knowledge. Gilbert Durand, a disciple of Bachelard, adopts an anthropological point of view in order to undertake a systematic classification of the human imaginary (*Les Structures anthropologiques de l'imaginaire* 1st edn 1969, 1992 (*The anthropological structures of the imaginary*)).

For Lacan, the Imaginary is a key theoretical concept in his reformulation of Freud's theory, drawing upon his account of the ego and its relation to narcissism. It refers primarily to the stage in the formation of the ego at which the child acquires a coherent self- or body-image. (Cf. 'The Mirror Stage as Formative in the Function of the I as revealed in Psychoanalytic Experience' in *Ecrits*.) Social theorists such as Castoriadis (*The Imaginary Institution of Society* 1987) broaden the concept so that it refers to a dimension of particular forms of society, something closer to Marx's realm of ideology or what Hegel called 'the spirit of a people'. Luce Irigaray also uses the term in a broad sense to refer to a pre-discursive level of experience which underpins culture as well as individual psychic development. Importantly, she advances the claim that the Imaginary is sexed, and argues that the dominant figures of Western thought and rationality develop the form of male morphology: the male imaginary is characterized by unity, individuation, stable form and identity, while the female imaginary is characterized by plurality, fluidity and mobility or formlessness.

Michèle Le Doeuff (*The Philosophical Imaginary* 1989) uses the term in a much less strictly psychoanalytic sense and in a manner closer to earlier philosophers such as Bachelard. For her, the philosophical imaginary refers primarily to the stock of images deployed in philosophical texts. Her view is that these are cultural products, in part the effects of unconscious fantasies which structure the subjectivity and projects of the philosophers, but also peculiar to the philosophical domain of culture. Contrary to the view which treats imagery as inessential to philosophical discourse, Le Doeuff regards it as inevitable. Typically, images such as Descartes's famous 'tree of knowledge' or Kant's 'island of truth' represent, in her view, points of tension or even contradiction within a philosophical system, papering over cracks in the edifice or holding out the hope of more than the system can provide. PP

immanent /ˈɪmənɛnt/ (Lat. *in-* in + *manere* to stay, to remain, to reside) *adj.* being within or inside, in contrast to *transcendent*, i.e. being beyond or outside.

In traditional theism, God is seen as a transcendent being, i.e. not part of the world he created, whilst in other religious traditions and especially in pantheism, God is thought of as immanent.

Immanent criticism of a theory is based on the theory's own assumptions, in contrast to transcendent criticism.

immaterialism *n.* the view that matter does not exist; that there are no material objects, but that to exist is to perceive or to be perceived. The best-known representative of this view is Berkeley, who also coined the word.

immediate inference in traditional logic, an inference (e.g. subalternation, conversion) from *one* premiss, in contrast to a syllogistic inference, which has more than one premiss.

impartial observer, impartial spectator *See* IDEAL OBSERVER.

implication *n. p implies that q* (where p and q are propositions) means that q can be correctly inferred from p. *See also* ENTAILMENT; CONDITIONAL.

Note: 'p infers (that) q' (where p and q are propositions) is an obsolete usage, no longer considered acceptable. Inferring is the drawing of a conclusion.

Inferring and implying are not the same. A person who *infers that q* draws the conclusion that q. A person who *implies that q* leaves it to the audience to infer that q.

implication, material Where p and q are propositions, 'p materially implies q' means that the conjunction of p and not-q is false. It is often symbolized by a horseshoe (or 'hook'): p ⊃ q. This formula is often read as 'if p then q', but must then be understood only to mean the same as 'not both p and not-q'. *See* CONDITIONAL.

The term was introduced by Bertrand Russell. It can easily mislead, because 'p materially implies q' carries a strong suggestion that p somehow implies q, and hence that there must be some kind of connection between p and q. And yet, as defined, there need not be any. Statements of the form 'if p then q' are better called Conditionals, and 'material conditional' is certainly preferable to 'material implication'.

implication, paradoxes of In standard systems of logic, *A materially implies B* if and only if it is not the case both that A is true and B is false. This gives rise to the paradoxes of material implication: a false proposition materially implies any proposition, and a true proposition is materially implied by any proposition.

Again, in standard systems of logic, *A strictly implies B* if and only if it is necessarily not the case both that A is true and B is false. This gives rise to paradoxes of strict implication: a necessarily false proposition (e.g. a contradiction) strictly implies any proposition, and a necessarily true proposition (e.g. a tautology) is strictly implied by any proposition.

These are paradoxes only in the wider sense that what sounds strange and surprising seems to be true, but not in the narrow sense that a genuine absurdity is generated. It may be argued that the problems arise only because logicians have not taken sufficient care in their use of the word 'implication'.

implication, strict Where p and q are propositions, 'p strictly implies q' means that the conjunction of p and not-q is logically impossible. Strict implication is thus a stronger relation than material implication, since p materially implies q whenever it is not the case that (p and not-q), irrespective of whether or not this conjunction is impossible. Whether strict implication is as strong a relation as *entailment* is a controversial matter. GH

implicature, conversational A conversational implicature is a proposition that is conversationally implied; that is, a proposition that can be inferred from *the fact that* something was said, or from *the manner* in which it was said, or from *the context* in which it was said. For example, if a person P says '*that book was written by Austin or by Ryle*' we may infer from that utterance that *P is uncertain about the authorship of that book*. The utterance of the first implies the second conversationally, not logically. If person P says 'her dress is most elegant' we may infer from that utterance *that P has a low opinion of her singing* – if the utterance is in response to the question 'What did you think of her singing?'

This can be distinguished from conversational *impliciture*, which is a matter of saying one thing and communicating not it, but something else instead. For instance, in appropriate circumstances the utterance 'you are not going to die' does not communicate that you are immortal, but something else, e.g. that your toothache is not going to kill you. The term 'impliciture' was first used by Kent Bach in an article in *Mind and Language 9* (1994). *See also* GRICE.

importation *n.* the name given to inferences of this form:

$$\frac{\text{If A, then (if B then C)}}{\text{If (A and B) then C}}$$

and to the theorem in standard systems of propositional logic:

$$(p \supset (q \supset r)) \supset ((p \,\&\, q) \supset r).$$

The converse is known as EXPORTATION.

impredicative definition The term was introduced by Bertrand Russell. He wanted every predicate to define a set; but Russell's paradox showed that there are definitions that do not generate a set. This is why such definitions were called impredicative. The definitions that are impredicative violate the principle that 'whatever involves all of a collection must not be one of the collection'. They offend against what Russell called 'the vicious circle principle'.

An example of a concept that requires an impredicative definition is *having all the properties of a great general.*

improper part, improper subset P is an *improper part* of a whole W if and only if P is identical with W. P is an *improper subset* of W if and only if P and W have the same membership.

imputation *n.* ascription of responsibility to a person: holding a person responsible for an act.

incommensurability *n.* having no common measure. Two things are said to be incommensurable if they cannot be compared with one another. The term was first used by the ancient Greeks in relation to the irrational magnitudes they discovered. A simple example is the length of the diagonal of a square whose sides have length 1. By Pythagoras's theorem, it is $\sqrt{2}$. The ancient Greeks proved (the proof is preserved for us in Euclid's *Elements*) that $\sqrt{2}$ cannot be a rational number. Irrational numbers were said to be incommensurable with rational numbers.

Some modern philosophers of science (Kuhn, Feyerabend et al.) have argued that different scientific theories are incommensurable in the sense that, on the usual criteria for comparing and ranking theories, neither of the two theories comes out better than the other. This 'incommensurability thesis' has been hotly disputed, because it calls into question the idea that science may make progress by abandoning one theory in favour of a better one. AM

incompatibilism *n.* This term is mainly used for the view that free agency is incompatible with the principle that every event is determined by efficient causes. (It can of course be used for any view that two things are incompatible.)

incompatible *adj.* not COMPATIBLE.

inconsistent *adj.* not consistent (*see* CONSISTENCY).

inconsistent triad a set of three propositions which cannot be true together.

Why is it that inconsistent sets of propositions which have exactly *three* members are singled out and given a name? After all, inconsistent monads, dyads, tetrads, pentads, etc. are rarely heard of. One reason is that many basic patterns of inference, like the categorical syllogisms, contain three propositions, and a standard criterion of their validity is that the two premisses, together with the negation of the conclusion, form an inconsistent triad. Cf. ANTILOGISM.

incontinence *n.* lack of self-control; weakness of will. *See also* AKRASIA.

indeterminacy of translation *See* RADICAL TRANSLATION.

indeterminism *n.* the view that some events are not causally determined.

Some writers use the term for the view that some future events are in principle unpredictable. In literary theory, 'indeterminism' has been used for the view that literary texts have no determinate meaning.

Index short for *Index librorum prohibitorum* (Lat. Index of prohibited books), a list of books to which, by decree of the Holy See, lay readers should have no access except by permission specially granted by Church authorities. The first Index was issued in 1557, the last was abolished about four centuries later, in 1966. The lists included books by Copernicus, Montaigne, Bacon, Galileo, Milton, Descartes, Hobbes, Spinoza, Locke, Bayle, Voltaire, Kant, etc. – indeed many of the philosophical, scientific and literary works now regarded as classics.

indexical *adj.*, *n.* expressions whose references depend on the circumstances of their utterance. Examples are words like *here*, *over there*, *now*, *last month*, *I*, *you*, which refer to different persons, places and times depending on the situation in which they are uttered. The term was introduced in this sense by Peirce. Reichenbach used the term *token-reflexive*; Russell preferred *egocentric particular*.

indifference *n.* (in older usage) impartiality.

indirect proof An *indirect proof* of a proposition p consists in deriving a false proposition either from not-p alone, or from not-p together with other true premisses. *See also* *REDUCTIO AD ABSURDUM*.

indirect utilitarianism *See* UTILITARIANISM, INDIRECT.

indiscernibility of identicals a logical principle which states that if A and B are identical, every property that belongs to one of them also belongs to the other.

Quine formulates the principle as follows (in his essay 'Reference and Modality', included in his *From a Logical Point of View* 1953): 'given a true statement of identity, one of its two terms may be substituted for the other in any true statement and the result will be true'. As Quine points out, there appear to be many exceptions to this principle. The contexts for which the principle is valid are called extensional contexts. *See also* TRANSPARENCY; EXTENSIONAL.

The converse of this is the principle of IDENTITY OF INDISCERNIBLES.

individual *n.* **1** anything regarded as something single, as a unit. **2** especially: a person, a human being.

In Mounier's personalism, 'individual' is used pejoratively, in contrast to 'person'. An individual is shallow, egocentric, inauthentic, materialistic, with no sense of values or vocation in life. A person is the opposite, adopts freely values by which to live, and relates to others in a spirit of community.

The word derives from the Latin *individuum*, which was used by Boethius to translate the Greek *atomon*; both words signify undividedness.

individualism *n.* an outlook which assigns primacy to individual human beings. There can be primacy in different respects: (1) (in ontology) only individuals are real, but the wholes of which they are parts, such as social groups, political societies and the like, have no independent reality over and above that of their components and the interrelations and interactions amongst these; (2) (in methodology) social inquiry and theory should proceed as if individuals alone have real existence. The doctrine that explanations of what happens in society must appeal only to the characteristics, particularly the psychological characteristics, of individual people is called 'methodological, because it is a piece of advice about how to proceed with inquiry, rather than an assertion about the nature of the world. If the doctrine offers good advice, however, it is probably because the social world is in some very broad sense composed entirely out of individual people, but what this sense is has not been made clear by the advocates of methodological individualism. The doctrine stands opposed to HOLISM, according to which explanations of society would sometimes be incomplete without reference to social forces, institutions or other non-individual wholes; (3) (in axiology) intrinsic value is to be found in that which is essential for the individuality of a human being. The individual can be valued in different ways: for his achievements, for his unique personality, for his self-determination, for his independence of others: (i) *achievement*: an individual can be valued for winning a race. The value of a collective achievement (a win by a football team; a successful performance by a theatre company; a country's successful national effort) depends on the value of the component individual achievements; (ii) *uniqueness*: in the age of romanticism, writers like J. G. Herder, W. von Humboldt, F. Schlegel and F. Schleiermacher put their emphasis on individuality, on that which distinguishes one individual from another, on that which makes an individual unique. This is also an important ingredient in the thought of John Stuart Mill. Some of these writers also ascribed value to the unique individuality of nations and cultures; (iii) *self-determination*: the ideal individual is self-determining, makes decision independently of external influences; (iv) *self-reliance*: the ideal individual strives for the greatest possible independence of the assistance or support of others; (4) (in philosophy of language and mind) *see* INTERNALISM.

GC/ed.

induction *n.* inference from a finite number of particular cases to a further case or to a general conclusion.

For instance, if a number of ravens have been observed, all of which are black, and if no raven has been encountered that is not black, the inferences to the conclusion that the next observed raven will be black or to the general conclusion that all ravens are black are inductive inferences.

Many inductive inferences seem plausible, some indeed seem extremely plausible, but the truth of all the premisses can never guarantee the truth of the conclusion, since the conclusion goes beyond what is given in the premisses. In this respect, they are contrasted with deductive inferences, in which the truth of all the premisses guarantees the truth of the conclusion.

Aristotle introduced the concept of induction in the *Posterior Analytics*. It has been claimed, however, that there, 'induction' does not mean a process of reasoning, but the examination of instances that results in a common feature coming to view.

induction, mathematical a method of proof in mathematics and formal logic. A proof by mathematical induction consists of two sub-proofs. One is a proof of the basis clause, the other of the induction clause. Once the two proofs are given, the conclusion can be drawn:

basis clause	o has the property F.
induction clause	If the natural number k has F, so does k + 1.
conclusion	Every natural number n has F.

There is a variant of this pattern, called strong induction:

basis clause	o has the property F.
induction clause	If every natural number less than k has F, so does k.
conclusion	Every natural number n has F.

For propositional logic, the usual patterns are:

basis clause	Each atomic formula (p, q, . . .) has the property F.
induction clause	If the formula A has F, so does ~A. If the formulae A and B each has F, so do (A & B) and (A ∨ B) and (A ⊃ B).
conclusion	Every formula has F.

and for strong induction:

basis clause	Each atomic formula (p,q, . . .) has the property F.
induction clause	If every formula of length less than A has F, so does A.
conclusion	Every formula has F.

Note that in proofs by induction, the conclusion is a necessary, not merely a probable, consequence of the premisses. One of the earliest authors to give an explicit formulation of this method of proof was Pascal, in his treatise (1665) on the arithmetic triangle.

induction, new riddle of this is how GOODMAN'S PARADOX is described by its author.

induction, problem of What can justify our reliance on inductive inferences? The answer that they have worked well in the past will not do, because that answer itself relies on induction, and hence begs the question: we would justify our reliance on induction by relying on induction. The first to give this problem a sharp formulation was David Hume, in his *Treatise of Human Nature* 1739.

The discussions of this problem have been wide-ranging. One interesting contribution to the debate is that of Karl Popper, who has argued that the concern over the problem is misplaced, since the regular method of science is not, as Bacon thought, inductive, but rather hypothetico-deductive. In his view, we do not start with particular observations and then generalize; rather, we start with generalizations and then subject them to tests.

inductive logic inquiry into, or theory of, the principles of sound inductive inferences.

inductivism *n.* the view that induction is the basis of proper scientific inquiry.

ineffable (Lat. *fari* to speak) *adj.* unsayable, inexpressible in words.

inference *n.* the drawing of a conclusion. The activities of inferring and implying are not the same. A person who *infers that q* draws the conclusion that q. A person who *implies that q* leaves it to the audience to infer that q.

inference, immediate *See* IMMEDIATE INFERENCE.

inference, rule of Within an axiom system, rules of inference permit the generation of theorems from the axioms. Typical rules are the rule of uniform substitution (that a given expression may everywhere be replaced by another one, so that if, for instance, $p \supset p$ is a theorem, so is $q \supset q$), and the rule of detachment (or modus ponens): if A and A ⊃ B are theorems, so is B.

NATURAL DEDUCTION systems of logic do not need any axioms, but have at their basis a set of rules of inference from well-formed formulas to other well-formed formulas.

inference to the best explanation a kind of non-deductive reasoning that divides into two stages. The first is an abduction in Peirce's sense, i.e. an argument to this effect:

B has been observed.
If A had been the case, B would have been observed.

Therefore, A was the case.

The second stage consists in considering alternatives to A in the second premiss, i.e. rival explanatory hypotheses. To illustrate:

Bootprints in the sand have been observed.
If a person wearing boots had walked on the sand, there would have been bootprints.

Therefore, a person wearing boots walked on the sand.

Compare this with:

Bootprints in the sand have been observed.
If a cow wearing boots had walked on the sand, there would have been bootprints.

Therefore, a cow wearing boots walked on the sand.

We would of course find that less plausible, and consider the first explanation a better one. The question is what criteria there are for judging one explanation better than another, so that one is in a position to infer to the best explanation. This is a question much debated. The contemporary discussion began with an article by Gilbert Harman, 'The inference to the best explanation', *Philosophical Review 74* (1965).

infinite /ˈɪnfɪnɪt/ (Lat. *finis* end, boundary, limit) *adj.* indefinite, indeterminate, endless. Endlessness, absence of a boundary, in time or space is one kind of infinitude, but in philosophical usage, it is not the only kind.

infinite set a set containing a number of members greater than any natural number. An equivalent definition was given by Georg Cantor: an infinite set is one whose members can be paired off with the members of a proper subset, without any members omitted. For instance, the natural numbers 1,2,3 . . . n . . . can be paired off with the numbers 3,6,9,12 . . . 3n, . . . , which are the members of a proper subset of the natural numbers.

infinitesimal *adj.*, *n.* a very small non-zero number, for certain purposes regarded as equal to zero in the early formulations of the differential and integral calculus (which used to be called the infinitesimal calculus). Berkeley exploited with great acuteness this theoretical weakness, in *The Analyst* 1734. The problem was overcome about a century later, when Cauchy and Weierstrass developed the concept of infinite sequences tending towards a limit. This eliminated the need for infinitesimals. In Abraham Robinson's non-standard analysis, developed in the mid-twentieth century, infinitesimals have in a certain sense been theoretically rehabilitated.

infinity, axiom of an axiom in set theory which lays down a condition that ensures that the domain of the theory has infinitely many members.

infinity, bad bad infinity, an expression used by Hegel, is infinity incorrectly understood. He distinguishes two ways of being mistaken about infinity. One is to have a surreptitiously finite conception of the infinite. Hegel uses as an example ancient Judaism, where God, the infinite, is objectified, taken to be something outside, separate from the finite, as something transcendent. In contrast, the infinite, or God, should according to Hegel be conceived as something that is immanent in, and at the same time contains within itself, everything finite and unfolds itself in it. The other way of erring is by conceiving infinity as open-ended (like an endless straight line); in contrast to such bad infinity, genuine infinity is self-enclosed (like a circular line).

infralapsarianism /ɪnfrəlæp'sɛərɪənɪzm/ (Lat. *infra* below; *lapsus* slip, fall) *n.* the Calvinist doctrine that God (foreseeing it all) elected some to be saved, others to be damned for ever, after the Fall which made them all sinners. This doctrine is in contrast to SUPRALAPSARIANISM. The terms date from the seventeenth century. *Syn.* sublapsarianism.

Ingarden /ɪn'gaːdən/, Roman (1893–1970) Polish philosopher, who taught at Lwow and Cracow, decisively influenced by Husserl's phenomenology, but resisting the later Husserl's move in an idealist direction. Against this he elaborated a realist ontology. Ingarden is best known for his writings on aesthetics. *Das literarische Kunstwerk* 1931 (The literary work of art) and later writings (*Selected Papers in Aesthetics* 1985) discuss the ontology of literature: what is it for a literary work to *exist*?

in itself/for itself (Gm. *an sich/für sich*; Fr. *en soi/pour soi*). The contrast between what a thing is in itself and how it is in relation to a consciousness is a common one in philosophy. Kant distinguishes between *the thing-in-itself*, and *the thing for us*, i.e. as it is perceived or known.

In twentieth-century philosophy influenced by Hegel, this pair of concepts has been used to characterize the contrast between consciousness, which is said to be *for itself* by its very nature, free and not bound by the laws of causality, and a thing, which can only be *in itself* and as a mere object completely subject to causal determination from outside. Indeed, Merleau-Ponty uses 'the in-itself' as a general label for nature, in contrast to humanity, where alone 'the for-itself' is present.

This pair of concepts is also used to explain bad faith and inauthenticity in Sartre and, before him, Heidegger. This is the human tendency to regard an individual, especially oneself, as an unfree object and not as a free agent, or, in other words, to see one's own existence as factitious (i.e. as nothing but a contingent matter of fact). This, they moralize, is to shun arduous responsibility. Sartre also holds that only that which exists *in* itself has full reality, whilst that which is *for* something is lacking in that respect and accordingly has in it an element of nothingness, which is subjectively experienced with a sense of anguish or nausea. 'It is what it is not.'

In medieval philosophy, substances are said to exist in themselves (*in se*), i.e. independently, in contrast to accidents, which exist in something else (*in alio*). RSO/ed.

in medias res /ɪn 'miːdɪæs reɪs/ Lat. in or into the middle of things; with omission of preambles and preliminaries.

innatism *n.* a theory according to which certain human characteristics are innate. The term is most frequently used for (1) the Platonic and Cartesian view that some of our knowledge is innate; (2) the view proposed by Noam Chomsky that certain grammatical structures are genetically inherited.

The term is used less frequently for other theories of this kind. The view that certain intellectual or behavioural tendencies are inherited, and so innate, is sometimes called innatism, but often the word hereditarianism is used instead.

inquisition *n.* a mode of criminal procedure in which the court itself conducts the investigation into the crime. This inquisitorial procedure is contrasted with the accusatory, in which all the evidence is brought before the court by a prosecutor (a private citizen or an official).

Inquisition Within the Roman Catholic Church, there have been various Tribunals of Inquisition. They reached their first flourish after being instituted in 1232 by Pope Gregory IX against heretics. The task of the Spanish royal Inquisition from 1479 was to persecute relapsed Jews and Muslims. The Holy Office in Rome was set up in 1542 to crush the Reformation; it was also responsible for the Index. It took many centuries before these bodies had to discontinue their activities.

in se /ɪn seɪ/ Lat. in itself.

insolubile (*sing.*); ***insolubilia*** (*pl.*) Lat. unsolvable(s) *n.* A medieval term for logical paradoxes, especially the variants of the Liar paradox. One example is this: if a person swears that he swears falsely, then, if his oath is false, i.e. if he does swear falsely, he does not swear falsely; but if his oath is true, i.e. if he does not swear falsely, then he does swear falsely.

Again, is the following statement true? 'Socrates will not cross the bridge.' The conditions are that there is a bridge, and Socrates comes to the bridge and (1) anyone who speaks the truth will cross the bridge; (2) anyone who speaks a falsehood will not cross the bridge; (3) there is only one Socrates; (4) this Socrates says: 'Socrates will not cross the bridge'.

instantiation *See* EXISTENTIAL INSTANTIATION; UNIVERSAL INSTANTIATION.

institution, institutes *n.* (in older usage) the elements of a discipline; a text containing the elements of a discipline.

institutional fact *See* BRUTE FACT/INSTITUTIONAL FACT.

instrumentalism *n.* **1** the view that theories, especially in the sciences, are not strictly speaking true or false but are to be regarded as tools. Their main use is to assist in predictions, in making the transition from one set of data to another. Some theories prove more useful for this purpose than other ones and this, rather than their supposed truth, is why they can justifiably be accepted. This is a view of science adopted by many pragmatists, e.g. Peirce, Dewey, James, and by some positivists, e.g. Mach, Schlick. **2** the view that statements about a certain kind of entities M can be true, although strictly speaking there are no Ms. For instance, statements describing the functioning of a perfect market can be true, and useful, although no market is perfect. Another example is the view that a statement attributing a belief or a desire to a person can be perfectly true, although there are no real 'inner states' of that nature. The suggestion is that the truth of such statements consists in their usefulness as instruments for predictions.

Of these two views, the first seems to reject truth in favour of usefulness, whilst the second seems to identify truth with usefulness.

insult *n.*, *vb.* (in older usage) an attack; to attack. The word is used in this sense by Hume.

integrity *n.* (in ethics) The term has been used in a special sense by Bernard Williams (1929–) to describe what is lacking in a person who, in a self-detached manner, views his own desires, interests or beliefs on a par with those of any other person. A consistent utilitarian, Williams contends, is bound to lack integrity in this sense. He is bound to be too self-effacing, ready to abandon any project or commitment, no matter how significant it is for him, if this seems to enhance overall universal happiness. This subtle form of depersonalization is the opposite to integrity.

intellectual virtues The intellectual excellences are distinguished from the excellences of character, the 'moral virtues', in Aristotle's *Nicomachean Ethics*, Book 6. There are four main intellectual faculties which can be employed more or less well: *epistēmē* ('scientific' knowledge of what is non-contingent, acquired by demonstration); *nous* (intelligence: intuitive reason); *phronēsis* (practical wisdom, the ability to deliberate well on matters concerning human welfare); and *technē* (skill, art). *Sophia* (wisdom, theoretical excellence) combines *epistēmē* and *nous*. There are accordingly five kinds of intellectual virtue.

intelligible *adj.* **1** understandable.
2 In Plato, the Forms are mentally grasped through *nous*, the intellect, and not through the senses: they are intelligible but not sensible, and so is the realm to which they belong.

Kant makes use of this terminological contrast when he distinguishes the sensible, empirical world from the intelligible world, which is the realm of the noumenon. The latter is beyond human knowledge, for all knowledge is based on direct intuition, and we have no non-sensory intuition. This means that the intelligible realm is unknowable! Kant was aware of this terminological paradox and commented on it in a note in section 34 of his *Prolegomena*.

intension *n.* the meaning of a term or of a predicate: the characteristic(s) determining its applicability; correlated term: *extension*, i.e. that to which the expression applies; that which falls under a concept. For example: 'animal with a heart' and 'animal with kidneys' have different intensions but the same extension. Similarly, 'unicorn' and 'centaur' have different intensions but the same extension – i.e. none, since there are no animals of that kind. *Syn.* connotation; sense.

Note: Intension and *intention* differ in meaning.

intensional context *See* EXTENSIONAL/INTENSIONAL CONTEXT.

intensional logic *See* MODAL LOGIC.

intensive magnitude the degree to which an object of perception influences a sensory organ. The contrast is with extensive magnitude, which is spatial (size) or temporal (duration). Kant uses these terms in the *Critique of Pure Reason*.

intentional fallacy the interpretation or evaluation of a work of art, especially a literary work, in the light of the author's intention in creating the work. The term is mainly used in the theory of literary criticism, where it was introduced in 1946 as the heading of an article by W. K. Wimsatt and M. C. Beardsley.

intentionality *n.* the property of mental phenomena whereby the mind can contemplate non-existent objects and states of affairs.

The relation between the mind and that which is *believed*, feared, *hoped for*, etc. is very different from ordinary relations. Ordinary relations cannot hold between something that exists and something else that does not exist. But the intentionality of the mind is not like that: the paranoid fear of a conspiracy, or the hope for an inheritance from a fairy godmother, are examples of mental attitudes with non-existent objects.

According to Brentano, intentionality is the distinctive characteristic of mental phenomena.

interactionism *n.* It is a common-sense view that what happens in one's mind can affect one's body, and vice versa. The term *interactionism* is mainly used when this view is combined with psychophysical dualism, typically represented by Descartes, according to which body and mind are utterly dissimilar, the mind being essentially consciousness, something immaterial and non-spatial, in complete contrast to bodies. This dualism *seems* to rule out all interaction, but interactionism tries to establish that this need not be so.

inter alia /ˈɪntə ˈeɪlɪə/, ***inter alios*** /ˈɪntə ˈeɪlɪəʊs/ Lat. among other things; among other people.

interest *n.* In contemporary usage, 'interest' normally means interest, but sometimes has the narrower sense of self-interest. A person who *is* interested, but not self-interested, is said to be *disinterested.* A person who *is not* interested is said to be *uninterested.*

interlocutor /ɪntəˈlɒkjʊtə/ *n.* a participant in a conversation.

internalism/externalism The use of this pair of terms for various philosophical positions is fairly recent. The main current uses are as follows.

1 (in moral philosophy) Internalism is the view that there is an internal connection between one's *opinion* about moral right and wrong and one's *motivation*. Richard Price's view (*Review of the principal question* ... 1787, p. 194) is internalist: 'When we are conscious that an action ... *ought* to be done, it is not conceivable that we can remain *uninfluenced*, or want [= lack] a *motive* to action.' (In a related sense, internalism is the view that when we are conscious that an action ought to be done it is conceivable that we remain uninfluenced – but only if we are irrational.)

Externalism, in contrast, denies that moral beliefs have in themselves a motivating dimension, and allows that, without being irrational, one can think that an action is wrong without being in any way moved not to do it.

In moral philosophy, this pair of terms can be traced to W. D. Falk, 'Ought and Motivation', *Proceedings of the Aristotelian Society* 1947–8, but it was Thomas Nagel's *The Possibility of Altruism* 1970 that brought the term into wider use.

2 The view, also called *internal realism*, that standards of truth are internal to an area of inquiry.

The contrasting internalist and externalist perspectives were outlined by Hilary Putnam in *Reason, Truth and History* 1981. The externalist perspective is that of metaphysical realism: the world consists of a totality of mind-independent objects, and truth involves a correspondence between what we think or say and the way things are. From the internalist perspective (the one favoured by Putnam), questions about the world and what it contains make sense only within a theory or description. Truth involves a coherence between our beliefs and experiences, and between our beliefs and those of other truth-seekers, but the experiences are already represented in a particular way within our belief-system, and there is no independent 'God's-eye point of view', nor a 'no-eye point of view', i.e. truth independent of any observer.

One of Putnam's arguments in favour of internal realism is a thought-experiment involving brains in VATS.

Views of an internalist kind have affinities with coherence theories of truth. *See also* VERIFICATIONISM and PRAGMATISM.

3 (in epistemology) In the 1980s, the pair internalism/externalism gained currency in epistemological contexts, where it is applied, though not without terminological confusion, to the analysis of knowledge and of justified true belief.

Internalism is the view that what justifies

a person's belief depends entirely on internal states, for instance a perception or a thought-process that soundly establishes the belief, in contrast, say, to wishful thinking. A justified belief is one for which one has good reasons. If a belief is justified, the believer is aware that it is.

In contrast, externalism is the view that factors other than the internal states of the believer are relevant. Reliabilism is one kind of externalism: what matters for knowledge is that the true belief is produced by a reliable process. Another externalist theory is the causal theory of knowledge: a justified true belief that p is one which is caused by the state of affairs p. A young child's belief may *be* justified even if the child does not *have* good reasons for adopting it. The conditions necessary for a belief to be justified can be fulfilled even if the believer is unaware of the fact. Externalism allows for the possibility that no conscious states enter into the justification.

4 (in philosophy of mind) Internalism is the view that the nature of any given mental state, such as a belief, is fixed solely by considerations about the individual alone – i.e. internal considerations. Externalism, on the other hand, is the view that the nature of mental states may depend upon considerations that are external to the individual – for example, facts about the environment.

When the words internalism and externalism are used in the philosophy of mind, it is most commonly in connection with debates about the *meaning* or *content* of mental states. According to externalism, what I really 'have in mind' when I believe that aluminium is a light metal is not entirely up to me; it depends also on such 'external' things as the nature of aluminium and the way my society uses its words. Thus, suppose that there is another world, as in the 'TWIN EARTH' thought-experiment, identical to this world in all ways except that some of these external features were changed. What is called aluminium in that world is a different substance, although its appearance, its use, etc. is the same as in our world. My counterpart in that world would have something else in mind when believing that aluminium is a light metal. The two beliefs, although expressible in the same words, would differ in content because of external circumstances.

An extreme version of internalism, by contrast, is Descartes's picture of the mind, according to which it makes sense to suppose that I might have exactly the same mental states as I now have even if there is no external world at all corresponding to my beliefs, perceptions, etc.

The '*narrow content*' of an individual's mental state is that portion of its content which is fixed solely by internal factors. The '*wide content*' is its full content, i.e., as fixed by both internal and external factors.

TVG/ed.

internal negation *See* NEGATION.

internal relation *See* RELATION.

interpretation *n.* In propositional logic, an interpretation assigns a truth-value to each propositional variable. In predicate logic, an interpretation also assigns an object (or a name) to each individual variable, a pair of objects (or names) to each pair of variables, etc. In standard interpretations, the meaning of the logical operators remains constant.

Given an interpretation of the basic components in a formula, a valuation of the formula can be made, by applying the rules laid down for the semantics of the system to which the formula belongs. A formula in a system is logically true if and only if it is true under all standard interpretations.

In contemporary discussions of problems of semantics, a distinction is often made between interpretation and translation. An interpretation explains what an expression means. A translation presents two expressions, together with the claim that they have the *same* meaning, which can be done without telling what the meaning is.

intertextuality *n.* The relationship of a given text to other texts by echo, allusion, acceptance, rejection, etc. This is a key concept in the semiotics of Julia Kristeva. In her view, a text cannot be regarded as something given, with a definite meaning. It is nothing but a mosaic which can be understood only through its absorption and transformation of the other writings to which it is related. No text can ever be free of other texts. A particular text is a confluence of many writings: by the author, the reader, the cultural and historical contexts, etc. This concept of intertextuality is applied not only to texts in the everyday sense, but to everything capable of signifying.

intransitive *See* TRANSITIVE.

intrinsic (Lat. *intrinsecus* from inside) *adj.* **1** belonging to the nature or essence of a thing. **2** belonging to something independently of its relation to other things. *Ant.* extrinsic.

intuition (Lat. *intueri* to gaze at, to behold, to look at) *n.* **1** immediate insight or knowledge, in contrast to insight or knowledge arrived at discursively, by means of analysis or proof. This is how the term is used by Descartes, Locke, Leibniz and Hume. Husserl saw the intuiting of essences as the task of phenomenology.

The contrasting term used by Descartes for knowledge by way of analysis or proof was *deduction*, whereas Locke and Hume used *demonstration*.

As with other epistemic terms there is an act/content ambiguity: 'intuition' can denote the manner in which something is known, or that which is known in a certain manner.

2 direct perception of an object. This is roughly the meaning of 'intuition' when used to translate the German *Anschauung* in Kant and others. According to him we have sensory intuitions, but no non-sensory, intellectual intuitions, and therefore no knowledge of superempirical facts. On this last point, Fichte and Schelling took an opposite stand. The direct awareness of an object has also been called *acquaintance*, e.g. by Bertrand Russell.

3 immediate, unreflected belief 'that we find ready in ourselves as soon as we begin to reflect' (Bertrand Russell). Intuitions, in this sense of the word, are simply non-inferential beliefs. But the term is sometimes reserved for non-inferential beliefs which are highly resistant, although not immune, to revision or rejection.

This usage, which can be traced back to the 1940s, is now adopted by many contemporary philosophers in the analytical tradition. In this tradition it has also become common to appeal to intuitions as the data against which philosophical theories must ultimately be tested.

Expressions like 'intuitive knowledge' are ambiguous between (1) knowledge which is not immediate but has its basis in intuition(s) of objects, and (2) immediate knowledge that such-and-such is the case.

intuitionism *n.* **1** The term was used by John Stuart Mill to characterize the anti-empiricist philosophy represented in his time by Hamilton, Whewell et al. He considered their theories of logic, science and ethics not only to be in error, but also to be obstacles to scientific and moral progress. **2** a theory of moral knowledge according to which we have immediate knowledge of the rightness or wrongness of certain actions. Twentieth-century British proponents of such a view are H. A. Prichard, W. D. Ross and A. C. Ewing. Their outlook has sometimes been described as neo-intuitionist, to distinguish it from the one debated by Mill.

3 a theory of moral knowledge according to which we have immediate knowledge of the intrinsic goodness of certain kinds of things or states of affairs. G. E. Moore advocated this view in *Principia Ethica* 1903. The term is sometimes used loosely to denote the whole of Moore's theory of intrinsic goodness (that intrinsic goodness is simple, indefinable, non-natural, etc.), but strictly speaking it should be used solely for Moore's view of how intrinsic goodness is *known*.

4 a theory of mathematical knowledge, advocated in opposition to the theories of Cantor, Hilbert, Frege and Russell by L. E. J. Brouwer (1881–1966). His basic outlook had a Kantian inspiration. The natural numbers are the primary object of mathematical knowledge: they are concepts formed from the immediate experience (i.e. intuition) of the flow of time. In his view, mathematicians and logicians had been too permissive in their adoption of infinite domains, and he wanted to reject proofs which contain a survey (albeit idealized) of an infinite domain. Instead, theorems are to be accepted only on the basis of finite 'construction'. Initially he insisted that mathematical insight is *sui generis* and that mathematical proofs are different in kind from what can be obtained simply by a mechanical application of logical rules. Later, he modified this view, and accepted the intuitionistic logic developed by Heyting.

intuitionistic logic a system of logic which, like relevance logic, quantum logic, etc. is obtained by excising a part from standard propositional logic. Notably absent are the theorems p ∨ ~p (the law of excluded middle) and ~~p ⊃ p (i.e. one half of the law of double negation).

A consequence of this restriction is proofs that combine *reductio ad absurdum* with double negation are not accepted, and mathematical theorems that cannot be proved by other means have to be abandoned. That is, two derivations of the form

$$\frac{A \quad {\sim}B}{C} \qquad \frac{A \quad {\sim}B}{{\sim}C}$$

together justify the inference from A to ~~B, but not the inference from A to B.

Intuitionistic logic was so called because it was designed to admit only those logical principles that are countenanced by intuitionism as a theory of mathematical knowledge.

The first formalized system of intuitionistic logic was devised by Arend Heyting in 1930. In his formulation, conjunction (&), disjunction (∨), implication (⊃) and negation (~) are all taken as primitive. His system has eleven axioms, and two rules of inference: uniform substitution of variables and modus ponens for implication. Subsequently, simplified bases for this logic have been developed. GH

invalid /ɪn'vælɪd/ *adj.* not VALID.

inverse, inversion *n.* an immediate inference in systems of syllogistic logic which admit negative terms:

$$\frac{\text{every S is P}}{\text{some not-S is not-P}}$$

In propositional logic the inverse of a conditional is obtained by negating its components: the inverse of p ⊃ q is ~p ⊃ ~q. A conditional does not imply its inverse.

Ionian /aɪ'əʊnɪən/ **School** the collective designation for the pre-Socratic philosophers Thales, Anaximander and Anaximenes, who all came from Miletos, an Ionian city situated on the west coast of Asia Minor. *Syn.* Milesian School.

iota /aɪˈəʊtə/ the Greek letter ι was introduced by Russell as an operator which turns an open sentence Fx into a definite description (ιx)Fx. For example, if Fx stands for 'x is King of France', (ιx)Fx is to be read as 'the King of France'.

ipso facto /ˈɪpsəʊ ˈfæktəʊ/ Lat. by the fact itself; by that very fact.

irenic /aɪˈriːnɪk/ (Gr. *eirene* peace) *adj.* peace-loving; tending towards conciliation and concord. The term came into use especially in theological contexts at the time of the Reformation. **irenicism** *n.*

Irigaray /ɪˈrɪgəraɪ/, Luce (1930 or 1932–) Irigaray came from her native Belgium to France in the 1960s, when she trained as an analyst with the Lacanian Freudian School of Paris and prepared her doctoral thesis in philosophy, published under the title *Speculum* 1974. She has held various academic positions in Paris, most recently at the Collège International de Philosophie. The feminist critique of Lacan implicit in *Speculum* led to her expulsion from the Lacanian School of Psychoanalysis at the University of Paris VIII (Vincennes) and launched her on a public career as a feminist and philosopher of sexual difference. One can distinguish four distinct strands in her work: linguistics, psychoanalysis, philosophy, and social critique. In *This Sex Which is Not One* 1977, she posited that there might be significant differences between the language spoken by women and that spoken by men. Subsequently she has developed more fully the notion of a sexuate discourse in a number of publications in the late 1980s. In *Speculum*, she joins a psychoanalytic attention to what is repressed by culture to a Derridean-inspired account of the repressions required by metaphysics, to produce a far-reaching critique of Western culture for its exclusion of the feminine. One case in point is the traditional Western conception of knowledge as something that ideally presupposes a disinterested standpoint. In her view, there is inherent in this conception a desire for control that is essentially phallic; masculinism, however, also imbues the best-known recent 'post-modernist' attacks on objectivity.

Irigaray's engagement with the history of philosophy is continued in a number of books from the period 1980–84, which constitute a series of readings of Plato, Aristotle, Descartes, Spinoza, Merleau-Ponty and Levinas.

Subsequently, her activities have become increasingly directed towards social change. A number of books published by her since the mid-1980s, beginning with *Sexes and Genealogies* 1987 and *Time for Change* 1989, all display a more direct focus on women's civil status, their position as a sex before the law, the need for *woman*kind to be recognized as a genre distinct from *man*kind, and the importance of translating sexual difference into specific social forms (*Je, tu, nous: Toward a Culture of Difference* 1993). She has since explored further the question of women and the divine, already raised in the essay 'Divine Women' (1986) (in *Sexes and Genealogies*). Various writings are translated in M. Whitford (ed.), *The Irigaray Reader* 1991.

irony /ˈaɪrənɪ/ (Gr. *eirōneia* dissembling; understatement) *n.* **1** the mocking or complaining use of words to convey the opposite of their literal meaning. E.g. 'That was brilliant' said about an unjustifiably poor performance. **2** more generally, distancing oneself from the message one conveys. **3** in a wider sense, the irony of a situation, or in a sequence of events, consists in there being a striking contrast between two of its salient features.

irony, romantic the artist's distancing himself from the work, by expressing his awareness of the inevitable limitations of all artistic endeavour. It can express itself by the surprise intrusion by the author into the work, breaking the illusion the work is supposed to sustain. Examples are Sterne's *Tristram Shandy* and Byron's *Don Juan*. Friedrich Schlegel (1772–1827) formulated the concept. Artistic earnestness stands in contrast to the detachment and playfulness of romantic irony.

irony, Socratic self-depreciation through pretended ignorance in a discussion, feigned in order to advance the search for truth.

irrationalism *n.* **1** rejection of reason. As a philosophical theory or attitude, irrationalism is exposed to a dilemma. If it is not supported by rational argument, why should it be accepted? But if it is supported by rational argument, then the rejection of the use of reason is in effect abandoned.

Many irrationalist doctrines do not actually reject the use of reason entirely, but assign to reason a reduced, subordinate role. Instead, unreflective intuition, instinctive feeling and spontaneity are extolled, and the controlling influence of moral principles and factual knowledge is scorned. Ludwig Klages and Oswald Spengler are often taken to represent this outlook.
2 (in philosophy of religion) fideism.
3 (in philosophical anthropology) rejection of the view that man is a rational animal.
4 (in metaphysics) denial of the view that ultimate reality has a rational character.

irrational number a real number which cannot be expressed as a fraction of two integers. $\sqrt{2}$ is irrational and, as proved by Lambert, so is π. Most real numbers are irrational. In comparison, integers and fractions are exceedingly rare.

irrealism *n.* **1** a theory rejecting the idea of an objective reality. The use of the word in this sense is recent. Nelson Goodman uses it in *Ways of Worldmaking* 1978, to designate his rejection of the idea of an objective reality and of the idea of truth; his radical relativism does nevertheless acknowledge that there can be standards of correctness.
2 a theory rejecting the view that entities of a certain kind are real. For instance, moral irrealism denies the reality of moral properties. The use of the term in this sense dates from the mid-1980s.

irreflexive *See* REFLEXIVE.

Islam monotheistic religion, founded by the prophet Muhammad in the seventh century. Its adherents are called Muslims (or Moslems); its sacred book is the Koran. In the Middle Ages, especially from the tenth to the thirteenth centuries, the main flourish of higher learning took place in Islamic countries, from Spain to Persia.

-ism, -ist (from Greek *-ismos*, a noun-forming suffix. Among its many functions is that of signifying a theory, or a practical disposition.) Many ism-words used by philosophers have two different senses, one theoretical and one practical. That is, these words may signify a *belief* (a doctrine, a theory), and they may signify an *attitude* (a trait of character, a mode of conduct).

For example, egoism is a theory, but the word is also used to describe a person's character and actions. In one sense, an egoist subscribes to the theory that all motivation is ultimately self-interested; in the other sense, an egoist shows concern for others only if it benefits himself. There is no inconsistency in being an egoist in one sense but not the other. Similarly with realism: in one sense, a realist is an adherent of a theory of realism, but is, in another sense, a person not given to illusions, hard-headed, with both feet on the ground.

Note: There are different ways of referring to a theory. One way is by stating it in a that-clause: e.g. 'the belief that God exists'. Another way is by naming it, e.g. 'theism'. Naming a theory, by means of an ism-word has the virtue of brevity. But only too often the same ism-word acquires more than one sense. This confuses matters, creates the need for further clarification, and what was gained in brevity is lost in explanation. The great classical philosophers hardly ever used ism-words.

iteration *n.* repetition.

ius /jʊs/ (*sing.*); ***iura*** (*pl.*) *n.* Lat. a right; a legal system **1** a legal system; thus, *ius commune* = Common Law; *ius romanum* = Roman Law; *ius naturale* = Natural Law; *ius naturae* = the Law of Nature. The Latin word for a legal rule or an enacted piece of legislation is *lex*. **2** a right, i.e. an attribute of a person, a legal/moral power that a person has. *Ius naturae* can mean either law of nature or right of nature; *ius naturale* can mean either natural law or natural right. Also written *jus, jura*.

J

Jacobi /dʒəˈkəʊbɪ (Eng.); jaˈkoːbi (Gm.)/, F(riedrich) H(einrich) (1743–1819) German philosopher. Like his friend Hamann, he opposed determinism (of which he saw Spinoza as the typical representative) and in general what he saw as the soullessness of the eighteenth-century reliance on reason. He rejected much of the contemporary critique of religious belief, arguing that immediate feeling and faith must be recognized as the ultimate basis for all our beliefs. He invoked Hume in support: *David Hume über den Glauben* 1787 (David Hume on belief), and in later writings he defended the authority of feeling against Kant's insistence that our beliefs must be confined within boundaries that our reason and intellect cannot overstep. His political sympathies were democratic, and he attacked the paternalist and conservative theories commonly used to defend the monarchies of his time. Among his writings are two philosophical novels, *Eduard Allwills Briefsammlung* 1776 (Edward Allwill's collected letters) and *Woldemar* 1779.

James /dʒeɪmz/, William (1842–1910) Born in New York, the oldest son of a Swedenborgian father of independent means, and brother of Henry, the novelist, James was educated in the United States and Europe, sometimes in schools, sometimes by private tutors. He received his MD from Harvard in 1869 and taught at Harvard (first physiology, later psychology and philosophy) from 1872 until 1907.

Together with Charles S. Peirce (1839–1914), James developed Pragmatism, North America's unique contribution to world philosophy. He credits Peirce with the Pragmatic Maxim, 'to attain perfect clearness in our thoughts of an object, then, we need only consider what conceivable effects of a practical kind the object may involve – what sensations we are to expect from it, and what reactions we must prepare. Our conception of these effects . . . is then for us the whole of our conception of the object' (*Pragmatism* 1907, second lecture). Applying this principle to the conception of truth, i.e. to a belief's agreement with reality, James points out that what counts as 'agreement with reality' depends on the sort of belief in question. Thus, common-sense beliefs are true if, when acted upon, they do not lead to unpleasant surprises. But truth, especially scientific truth, evolves; new truths emerge when new facts clash with old beliefs and must be accommodated in a coherent system. Values exist where and only where sentient beings have feelings and desires and make demands. Values, and hence value-judgements, become objective if these beings care for one another, thereby constituting and accepting an interpersonal standard. Indeed, a community of thinkers is required for all objective truth. In his *Essays in Radical Empiricism* 1912, James rejects the assumption of classical epistemology that one knows directly only one's own sense-data, for out of a collection of private worlds no common world can be constructed. In contrast, James holds with common sense that external things are directly perceived. Several minds can know one thing as several lines can intersect in one point; the point ('pure experience'), e.g. Bob's and Jane's seeing the moon, is an event in the histories of Bob, of Jane, and of the moon.

Some important issues, e.g. whether to trust a person one has just met, or whether to believe in a god, cannot be settled by the rational procedures of common sense or science, nor by the kind of agreement that evolves in ethics, yet suspension of belief has in these cases the practical effect of settling the question one way rather than another. In such situations, and only in these, James exhorts us to 'will to believe', i.e. he asserts that we have a right to believe ahead of the evidence. James exercises that right when he affirms that we have free will, that there are objective values, that we can make a difference to the way the world will be, and that the world's salvation requires both our help and God's. James studied the phenomenon of faith in his most widely read book, *The Varieties of Religious Experience* 1902.

Moral concerns are the ultimate motivation for James's philosophizing. He affirms free will because only actions chosen from equally possible alternatives have a moral quality. Moral choice involves choosing what character to become. Hence we must seize every opportunity to act in ways that will develop and maintain good habits. While many of our ideals are connected to simple bodily pleasures and pains, we also feel directly a fitness between certain forms of actions and certain types of experience. Our higher, more revolutionary ideals are not learnt from experience; rather, they are a guide to future experience and corrigible by it. Actions have real value only if they make a real difference; and only if belief that this is so can motivate strenuous moral effort. All obligations are grounded in the multifarious actual claims of actual persons, but not all claims are co-satisfiable. Since values do not have a common measure, we must seek ideals that can be realized at least cost in terms of frustration of other ideals. Human moral progress consists in replacing less inclusive ideals by more inclusive ones, e.g. votes for men by votes for men *and* women. While there is a presumption in favour of the established order, one is free to attempt to realize a new (presumed to be more inclusive) ideal, provided one is willing to risk one's life and character in the attempt, and is sensitive to 'the cries of the wounded', for ideals, as well as scientific hypotheses, are provisional.

In his two-volume *Principles of Psychology* 1890, James conceives psychology as the theory of the relations between mental events and physiological changes. Thus, according to the James–Lange theory, emotions are feelings of bodily changes caused by the perception of the fact that is commonly said to cause the emotion. Purposeful behaviour indicates the presence of consciousness or thought; it consists in an introspectively continuous stream. Though psychology, as a science, presupposes an order of uniform causation, James, as noted above, held that this is included in a wider order that leaves room for free will.

Among James's writings is also *The Will to Believe and Other Essays in Popular Philosophy* 1897. See also Jacques Barzun, *A Stroll with William James* 1983. RPU

Jansenism /ˈdʒænsənɪzm/ *n.* a doctrine named after Cornelius Jansen (1585–1638), rector of Louvain, bishop of Ypres. His *Augustinus* 1640 interpreted Augustine as holding that God efficaciously gives his grace only to those whom he has chosen. This is contrary to the view of Luis de Molina (1535–1600) that God gives his grace to all, although it becomes efficacious only to those who accept it. The debate is relevant to philosophy because of the close connection with the problems of evil, free will, determinism, etc.

Jansenism became known and influential through the Port-Royal circle: St Cyran (Prosper du Verger de Hauranne) (1581–1643), Antoine Arnauld (1612–94), Blaise Pascal (1623–63) and Pierre Nicole (1625–95).

Its main enemies, theologically and politically, were the Jesuits. Although condemned by Church and state authorities, Jansenism maintained a strong presence in France from the mid-seventeenth century, but in the latter half of the eighteenth century the conflict between Jansenists and Jesuits faded into the background, as the rise of anti-religious free-thought equally challenged them both; and at the political level their conflict was overshadowed by the financial crisis and social fermentation that resulted in the events of 1789.

Jaspers /ˈjaspɛrs/, Karl (1883–1969) German philosopher, professor at Heidelberg, from 1916 in psychiatry, from 1922 in philosophy, until 1937 when he had to resign for political reasons, professor at Basel from 1948. He saw the task of philosophy to consist not primarily in the discovery of theoretical truths, but in assisting the individual in the process of self-discovery and insight. His writings, however, are not sermons, but wide-ranging syntheses of history, psychology, literary theory, etc. The aim is to help the individual towards *Existenz* (being genuinely oneself and making sense of one's life). This authentic way of living is something to be achieved. Ultimately, it is reached by one's own free decision. Jaspers contrasts it with *Dasein*, existence in the ordinary sense, common to all existing individuals. His outlook, usually described as existentialist, sometimes criticized as irrationalist, has many religious resonances, although he distanced himself from traditional theology. His main work is *Philosophie* (3 vols) 1932; among his numerous writings are *Vom Ursprung und Ziel der Geschichte* 1949 (On the origin and goal of history) and *Einführung in die Philosophie* 1950 (Introduction to philosophy, transl. as *Way to Wisdom*).

Joachim a Fiore /ˈdʒəʊəkɪm æ ˈfiɔːreɪ/ (*c.* 1135–1202) Calabrian monk and saint; his writings contain a visionary philosophy of history. As there are three persons in the Trinity, so there are three main stages of history. The third age, that of the Holy Spirit, was about to begin. It would emerge by an inner logic of historical development, bringing to fruition tendencies already latent. In that stage, all mankind would reach a higher level of perfection, characterized by freedom, love and holiness.

The view that history has a predetermined necessary course – along an upward path – in which latent tendencies become actualized, has since been developed in various directions by many other religious visionaries, but also by Enlightenment thinkers (Lessing), romantic thinkers (Schelling), positivists (Comte), and of course Hegelians and Marxists. In all its varieties, it raises the problem of whether people should sit back and let history take its course, or intervene in order to help it along.

jus /jʊs/ alternative spelling of IUS.

jusnaturalism *n.* natural law theory.

just, justice Justice is an attribute of *political systems*, *relations between individuals*, *actions*, and we also say of *persons* that they are just.

In the history of philosophy, some conceptions of justice have been wider, others narrower. Plato's *Republic* Book 4 (432a ff) takes the *dikaiosynē* (traditionally translated as 'justice', although 'morality' may be preferable) of a person to be the overarching virtue of a person which consists

Figure 2 Concepts of justice (Aristotle)

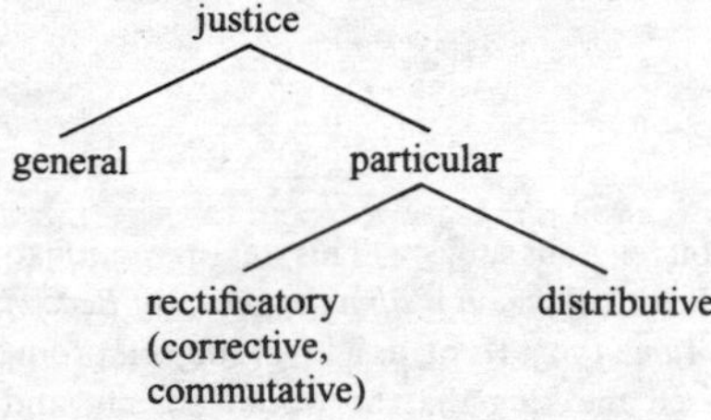

in the three parts of the soul each fulfilling its proper function and, analogously, justice of the body politic consists in each of its three parts doing likewise.

In Book 5 of the *Nicomachean Ethics*, Aristotle distinguishes concepts of justice in the pattern of Figure 2.

In the *general* sense, justice includes all the habits and dispositions of a good citizen: not only courage, honesty and loyalty, but also virtues like sobriety. If, as in Stoicism and later systems, human beings are regarded as citizens of the world and not only of a city-state, justice will include all the habits and dispositions of a good human being.

In the *particular* sense, in contrast, justice is only one of the virtues. There are two kinds of particular justice: one is distributive justice (*dianemētikon dikaion*), which operates in a society and allocates benefits and burdens fairly; the other is rectificatory justice (*diorthōtikon dikaion*), also called corrective justice or commutative justice, which operates between two parties, and which maintains or restores a balance. It is further subdivided: one kind covers voluntary transactions in which each party keeps his part of a bargain; the other kind covers involuntary transactions, especially damages and penalties that make up for a tort or a crime.

In the modern era, moral philosophy has often operated with a dichotomy. On one side is justice, on the other side lie humanity, benevolence, charity, generosity, hospitality, etc. The dichotomy between the two branches of moral philosophy has been variously explained. The duties of justice are often said to be perfect, the duties of humanity imperfect. *See also* PERFECT DUTY.

Utilitarian or consequentialist theories are less accommodating to this dichotomy, since according to them all duties are, in principle, equal. What counts as a duty depends entirely on the value of the consequences of actions. John Stuart Mill tried to distinguish duties of justice from other moral duties, in the last chapter of *Utilitarianism* (1861), in terms of rights: we have a duty of justice to do x if and only if someone else has a right to our performance of x; and to have a right to something means that society has a duty to assist or protect us so that we are not without it. Whether Mill succeeded in accommodating justice within a utilitarian theory is a matter of controversy.

The starting-point of the present-day discussion of justice has been John RAWLS'S *A Theory of Justice* 1971. *See also* COMMUTATIVE JUSTICE.

Note: In older usage (Locke, Hume, etc.) *just* is often used to mean 'correct': a 'just sentiment' is simply a correct opinion.

justice, precepts of *See* PRECEPTS OF JUSTICE.

just in case *See* CASE, JUST IN.

K

kabbala /kə'baːlə/ (Heb. tradition) *n.* a kind of Jewish mysticism which reached its flowering in the Middle Ages. Christianized varieties also emerged during the Renaissance (Pico della Mirandola 1486; Johann Reuchlin 1516). The tradition is in essence religious, but in its various manifestations it can include both esoteric doctrines and magical practices, such as alchemy, allegorical interpretation of sacred writings, astrology, communication with spirits, numerology, etc.

Kallikles *See* CALLICLES.

Kames *See* HOME.

Kant /kænt (Eng.); kant (Gm.)/, Immanuel (1724–1804). One of the most influential philosophers of modern times, Kant was born in Königsberg (East Prussia) and grew up and received his education there. From 1747 to 1755 he was a private tutor for a number of families in the area. When he began to teach at the University of Königsberg in 1755 he appears to have been successful as an academic teacher from the very beginning. Herder was later to praise him highly as his only true teacher. Kant was appointed to a chair in philosophy in 1770. He never left the environs of Königsberg, and remained unmarried, living the uneventful life of a scholar. His teaching covered logic, metaphysics, mathematics, physical geography, anthropology, ethics, natural jurisprudence, natural theology, etc. On one occasion he was subject to political interference. In 1794 the Prussian censor, in the name of Frederick William II, King of Prussia, forbade him to write on religious subjects. This was in reaction to Kant's *Religion Within the Limits of Reason Alone* 1793. Kant, as a loyal subject, promised the king that he would refrain, and kept his promise until the obligation lapsed with the death of the king.

Kant's intellectual life is usually divided into two periods: the so-called 'Pre-Critical' period up to 1770, followed by the 'Critical' period. During the first of these periods he published a number of works in the style of philosophizing then current. These works show that while Kant was deeply influenced by the philosophical thought of Leibniz, Wolff and their followers, he was also open to the ideas of such philosophers as Locke, Hume and Rousseau who, in the 1760s, began to have an influence in Germany. It would be a mistake to characterize Kant's view during this period as either a thoroughgoing rationalism or as a traditional form of empiricism. Though he was convinced of the truth of Newton's physics, he was far from clear as to how this science of phenomena was to be founded in a metaphysical system. Like most of his contemporaries, Kant was during the 1750s and 1760s an eclectic who did not dogmatically accept one fixed metaphysical system as the only possible explanation of the world. He was at the time much more of a sceptic in metaphysical matters than is commonly realized. The most important works of this period are *Der einzig mögliche Beweisgrund zu einer Demonstration des Daseins Gottes* 1763 (The only possible basis for a proof of God's existence), *Untersuchung über die Deutlichkeit der Grundsätze der natürlichen Theologie und der*

Moral 1764 (An enquiry into the distinctness of the fundamental principles of natural theology and morals), *Beobachtungen über das Gefühl des Schönen und Erhabenen* 1764 (Observations on the feeling of the beautiful and the sublime) and *Träume eines Geistersehers* 1766 (Dreams of a spirit-seer).

Kant's Critical period begins with his so-called Inaugural Dissertation entitled *De mundi sensibilis atque intelligibilis forma et principiis* 1770 (On the form and principles of the sensible and the intelligible world). From then until 1781 Kant published almost nothing. These 'silent years' saw him working out the basic outlines of his later 'Critical' philosophy. Though he was well known to the educated Germans of his time for his early works, he became and remains truly famous on the basis of the works he published during his second period. The most important of these are the *Kritik der reinen Vernunft* 1781 (Critique of pure reason; 2nd edn, with some important revisions, 1787); *Prolegomena* . . . 1783; *Grundlegung zur Metaphysik der Sitten* 1785 (Foundations of the metaphysics of morals); *Metaphysische Anfangsgründe der Naturwissenschaft* 1786 (Metaphysical elements of natural science); *Kritik der praktischen Vernunft* 1788 (Critique of practical reason); *Kritik der Urteilskraft* 1790 (Critique of judgement); *Die Religion innerhalb der Grenzen der blossen Vernunft* 1793 (Religion within the limits of reason alone); and *Metaphysik der Sitten* 1797 (Metaphysics of morals).

Kant's philosophy can be characterized as an attempt to answer three fundamental questions: 'What can I know? What ought I to do? What may I hope for?' He addresses the first of these questions in his *Critique of Pure Reason*, which is often simply referred to as his 'first Critique'. In it, Kant attempts to show that traditional metaphysics rests on a fundamental mistake: it presupposes that we can make substantive knowledge claims about the world independently of experience. Kant characterizes such claims as 'synthetic *a priori*', and he argues that it is impossible to know anything *a priori* about the world as it is, independently of our cognitive apparatus. Though we can make certain synthetic *a priori* claims, these claims are not about reality *per se*, but only about reality as it is experienced by beings such as ourselves. It is only because we possess certain cognitive principles enabling us to experience the world that we can make certain claims *a priori* about the world as it appears. Thus metaphysics can only be concerned with the presuppositions of experience, or with the conditions that must be fulfilled before any experience whatsoever. These *a priori* epistemic conditions are described by Kant as different 'forms' that knowledge is necessarily subject to. He distinguishes three such forms, namely (1) the forms of sensibility, (2) the forms of the understanding, and (3) the forms of reason.

(1) The forms of sensibility are space and time. They are not characteristics of 'things in themselves', but are only subjective conditions for our knowledge of the world. However, because we cannot but view the world as spatial and temporal, things in space and time, or 'the appearances', are objective for us. Kant says that they are 'empirically real but transcendentally ideal'.

(2) Our knowledge is further dependent on the forms of the understanding, i.e. on a number of basic *a priori* concepts. Kant, borrowing a term from Aristotle, calls these basic concepts 'categories'. They include for him basic concepts of quantity (unity, plurality and totality), quality (reality, negation and limitation), relation (inherence, causality and reciprocity), and modality (possibility/impossibility, existence/non-existence, and necessity/contingency). They appear to have a more

extended application than space and time because we seem to be able to make claims about things that are not part of our spatiotemporal world. Many philosophers, for instance, use the concept of causality in talking and devising proofs about God who, as they also claim, is neither in space nor in time. Kant believes that this is a mistake. He argues that the use of the categories is restricted to spatiotemporal objects, or appearances. His complex Transcendental Deduction in the first *Critique* is essentially an attempt to establish this restriction on our use of the categories. One of the most important consequences of this part of Kant's view is that the traditional proofs concerning the nature of the soul, the world and God must be unsound. They cannot establish knowledge in any sense. If they are taken as establishing knowledge, they inevitably lead to contradictions. Indeed, the dialectical parts of Kant's first *Critique*, namely The Paralogism of Pure Reason, The Antinomy of Pure Reason, and the Ideal of Pure Reason, are attempts to expose the fallacious character of traditional metaphysics.

(3) This does not mean that Kant believed that the proofs are entirely useless. They address fundamental questions that are unavoidable for us. He believed that they are expressions of deep 'interests' of reason that cannot simply be dismissed. Metaphysical speculation is as inevitable for us as is breathing. Indeed, it is part of the human condition that our 'reason has this particular fate that in one species of its knowledge it is burdened by questions which, as prescribed by the very nature of reason itself, it is not able to ignore, but which, as transcending all its powers, it is also not able to answer'. These questions concern the forms of reason – what Kant calls the 'transcendental Ideas'. The Ideas – there are three, according to Kant – are those of God, freedom and immortality. They do not afford any kind of knowledge beyond that which is possible through space and time and the categories. They can give rise only to a kind of rational faith.

In *Prolegomena* 1783 Kant tried to present the main doctrines of the *Critique of Pure Reason* in a manner more digestible to a wider readership. The *Foundations of the Metaphysics of Morals*, published two years later, contained a provisional statement of the position stated more fully in the *Critique of Practical Reason* 1788. Those two works deal with morality. Kant analyses the common-sense conception of morality, which he takes to be valid. He takes for granted that the concept of something that is good without qualification is present in our conception of morality, and argues at the beginning of the *Foundations* that there is one and only one such thing: a good will. Kant finds that a good will is present in a human rational agent if and only if the agent's reason for doing the right thing is that it is the right thing to do, or, in his formulation, that it is one's duty. This motive of duty is described by Kant as reverence for a (moral) law. Kant's analysis of the way we think about morality results in the assertion that we assign moral worth, i.e. goodness-without-qualification, to an act if and only if we take the motive to be of this special kind. If a person merely acts according to inclination, we do not assign moral worth to the action, even if it is most commendable. Moral baseness consists in disregarding the principles one has, or at least ought to have, as a moral agent. The slogan often used by politicians that 'principle must be balanced by pragmatism' would in Kant's opinion be a paradigm of immorality.

Not every rule of action can yield a moral motive. We can determine what is willing in the right way by applying a principle that Kant calls the 'categorical imperative'. He offers several formulations of this categorical imperative; the one that has received perhaps the most attention is a principle of universalization, which states that I should always act in such a way that I am able at the same time to will that the maxim of my action be a universal law of nature. According to the second formulation I should treat humanity, whether in my own person or that of anybody else, never merely as a means but always also as an end. This implies respect for persons, but also self-respect; it rules out slavery and servility alike. A third formulation of the categorical imperative, claimed by Kant to follow from the two earlier ones, is that we are not only bound by the moral law, but can also regard ourselves as the authors of this law. In so far as morality has any validity at all, we must regard ourselves as truly autonomous. This concept of autonomy, according to Kant, is coextensive with the concept of freedom, so morality requires freedom. Therefore we must assume that we are free in so far as we are moral or rational beings.

Since freedom is also one of the Ideas to which theoretical reason leads us, it forms the point at which the two *Critiques* come together. Kant believes that the second *Critique* shows that freedom is a genuine concept, i.e. not a mere thought, but something that has a genuine foundation in morality. Nevertheless, Kant insists that we cannot *know* ourselves to be free in any strict sense. It is our moral experience, or perhaps better the experience of our morality, that gives us the right to believe in the reality of freedom.

Furthermore, morality and freedom also give us the right to believe in the reality of two other Ideas of reason, namely those of God and immortality. He argues that we must postulate the reality of these Ideas in order to be able to act as moral beings in this world. Without immortality and God we would be condemned to moral despair. Moral action makes us deserving of happiness but frequently does not lead to happiness in this world. If we want to establish a connection between the two, we must assume that they will be made to coincide by God in the long run. In this way, the notions of God and immortality, as prerequisites for the realization of the *summum bonum* or the highest good, make possible the moral enterprise for Kant, and therefore we must believe in their reality.

Belief in these three concepts is central in Kant's so-called moral faith. Though Kant himself was not religious and was indifferent to forms of external religious worship, he did believe that morality inevitably leads us to the acceptance of certain tenets of traditional theism. In his essays on religious matters and especially in his *Religion within the Limits of Reason Alone* of 1793, Kant attempts to develop the parallels between revealed religion and philosophical theology. He claims, in true Enlightenment fashion, that all that is essential in religion can be reduced to morality. Accordingly, he criticizes established religion severely as engaging in mere idolatry in its insistence on merely formal requirements. According to Kant, then, what we may hope is that our moral actions ultimately do make a difference.

Kant's *Critique of Judgement* of 1790, the third *Critique*, is often simply read as a treatise in aesthetics; and its first part, the Critique of Aesthetic Judgement, deals essentially with aesthetic problems. Kant argues that although aesthetic judgements are based on feeling, their claim to objective validity is not based on these feelings themselves but upon *a priori* principles of judgement that are preconditions for such feelings. However, apart from addressing the problem concerning the validity and characteristics of aesthetic judgements, Kant also deals in this work with the problem of the unity of his own system, the general problem of the apparent purposiveness of nature, and the problems arising from a presumed necessity of applying teleological concepts in biology.

Kant's works had a strong influence on German idealism. Fichte, Schelling and Hegel cannot be understood without reference to Kant. Yet their philosophy soon began to overshadow that of Kant. Late in the nineteenth century Kant's ideas experienced a renaissance. The neo-Kantians, under the motto 'back to Kant', argued that the idealists had misunderstood Kant, and that his epistemology and his ethics provided the best models for philosophizing in a scientific age. Many recent philosophers in English-speaking countries would seem to agree with this sentiment. While the old adage that 'You can philosophize with Kant, or philosophize against him, but you cannot philosophize without him' is perhaps an exaggeration, it would be difficult to overestimate the importance of these works for the subsequent history of Western thought.

Method of citation: (1) the page-numbers of the first edition of *Critique of Pure Reason* 1781 are standardly prefixed by 'A', of the second edition by 'B'. (2) title, volume number and page number in the Academy edition (often designated 'AA', short for 'Akademie-Ausgabe') of Kant's collected works. MK

Kant–Laplace hypothesis Proposed by Immanuel Kant in 1755 and (probably independently) by the French astronomer and mathematician Pierre Simon de Laplace (1749–1827) in 1796, this states that the solar system evolved from a whirling mass of gas. The sun and planets were formed as the mass cooled and contracted. This explains why the planets all move in the same direction around the sun, like tea-leaves in a stirred cup of tea. AM

katalepsis (*sing.*); **katalepses** (*pl.*) /ˈkætəˈlɛpsɪs, -iːz/ (Gr. *katalēpsis* (having) a firm grasp) *n.* The term was used, especially in Stoicism, for certain impressions and propositions: those so grasped had indubitable certainty. Science – genuine knowledge – was described as a system of katalepses.

kataphasis /kəˈtæfəsɪs/ Gr. affirmation; affirmative *n.* Aristotle's term for an affirmative categorical proposition.

Kelsen /ˈkɛlzən/ (Gm.), Hans (1881–1973) the main author of the 1920 Austrian constitution, professor of jurisprudence in Vienna until 1930. He subsequently taught at Cologne, Geneva and Prague, but had to leave Europe in 1940 and held a chair at Berkeley 1942–52. As a legal philosopher, he developed a 'pure theory of law' in *Die reine Rechtslehre* 1st edn 1934 (transl. as *Introduction to the Problems of Legal Theory*), rejecting attempts to reduce law to morality; hence his opposition to natural-law theories. But he also rejected the attempt to regard law simply as a social fact; hence his opposition to the kind of legal positivism which reduces law to mere power-relations. Legal norms direct human conduct, ultimately by the use of sanctions. Laws differ from other general commands to which an individual may be exposed, by being valid. Their validity derives not from moral or political principles, nor from historical or social facts, but from a higher legal norm. For instance, the decision of a court that D is to pay C a sum of money has its validity by virtue of norms that give the court certain powers. These norms, in turn, must have been validly enacted, in accordance with higher norms. At the apex of such a derivation is a basic legal norm (*Grundnorm*). Its validity is underived and must be postulated. In this way, the normativity (i.e. the 'ought-ness') of laws can be accounted for, without blurring the distinction between law and morality. A final formulation of his legal theory was given in his posthumous *Allgemeine Theorie der Normen* (General theory of norms).

kenosis /kɪˈnəʊsɪs/ (Gr. *kenōsis* emptying, shedding) *n.* (in theology) Christ's relinquishing of his divine attributes in order that he could fully experience the human condition. **kenotic** /kɪˈnɒtɪk/ *adj.*

kenoticism *n.* a theory of the incarnation of Christ which puts stress on his human attributes. Cf. DOCETISM.

Kepler /ˈkɛplər (Gm.)/, Johannes (1571–1630) German mathematician and astronomer after whom were named the three laws of planetary motion which he discovered.

kerygma /ˈkɛrɪgmə/ (Gr. proclamation, promulgation) *n.* The word is often used in New Testament theology. In the twentieth century, it has been used in a special sense in the theology of BULTMANN. He contrasts kerygma, the significant message, from myth – accounts of doubtful historical validity – which are not now essential to faith.

Keynes /keɪnz/, John Maynard (1883–1946) Keynes exercised a decisive influence on twentieth-century economic theory and practice through his *The General Theory of Employment, Interest and Money* 1936. He wrote one philosophical work, *A Treatise on Probability* 1921.

Keynes, John Neville (1852–1949) Cambridge economist and logician, father of John Maynard Keynes. He wrote a treatise on logic, which revised traditional logic by incorporating BOOLE's approach.

Kierkegaard /ˈkɪəkəgaːd (Eng.); ˈkirgəgɔːr (Dan.)/, Søren (1813–55) Kierkegaard is often called the first 'existentialist'. He gave a rather spectacular interpretation to the otherwise banal concept of 'existence' and insisted on the importance of passion, free choice and self-definition in opposition to the rationalist philosophies then popular in Copenhagen (where he lived), in particular Hegelianism. Existence, according to Kierkegaard, is not just 'being there' but living passionately, choosing one's own existence and committing oneself to a certain way of life. Such existence is rare, he says, for most people simply form part of an anonymous 'public' in which conformity and 'being reasonable' are the rule, passion and commitment the exceptions. In his *Concluding Unscientific Postcript*, he compares existence with riding a wild stallion, and 'so-called existence' with falling asleep in a hay wagon. Kierkegaard's own chosen way of life was Christianity, which he distinguished with great irony and frequent sarcasm from the watered-down beliefs and mutual social hand-holding of 'Christendom'. To be or become a Christian, according to Kierkegaard, it is necessary to passionately commit oneself, to make a 'leap of faith' in the face of an 'objective uncertainty'. One cannot know or prove that there is a God; one must simply choose to believe.

At the heart of Kierkegaard's philosophy in his emphasis on the individual and his related notion of 'subjective truth'. The main targets of his attack included Hegelian philosophy and the Lutheran Church of Denmark, both of which emphasized the importance of rationality and collective spirit. Against this, Kierkegaard urged attention to the individual human being and his or her particular life-defining decisions. Thus he criticized Hegel with his long view of history and his all-encompassing concept of 'spirit' as 'an abstract thinker' who completely ignored 'the existing, ethical individual'. Whereas Hegel had formulated a 'dialectic' which defined the course of history and human thought and resolved the various tensions and conflicts therein, Kierkegaard emphasized the personal importance of concrete choices such as whether or not one should get married – a decision which played a dramatic and continuing role in his own life. Whereas Hegel had developed what Kierkegaard called a 'both/and' philosophy in his dialectic, a philosophy of reconciliation and synthesis, Kierkegaard urged the necessity of an 'either/or' philosophy and an 'existential dialectic', one that emphasized choices and personal responsibility rather than overall rationality. So, too, his notion of subjective truth was polemically formulated in opposition to the idea that all such choices have a rational or 'objective' resolution. In choosing the religious life, for example, Kierkegaard insists that there are no ultimately rational reasons for doing so, only subjective or personal necessity and passionate commitment. Similarly, choosing to be ethical, which is to say, choosing to act according to practical reason, is itself a choice which is not rational. The notion of subjective truth does not mean, as it may seem to mean, a truth that is true 'for me'. It is rather a resolution in the face of an objective uncertainty – for example, the existence of God, or, as in Kant, the ultimate commensuration of virtue and happiness – for which there is no adequate argument or evidence. *See also* EXISTENTIALISM; FIDEISM. RSO

kinēsis /kɪˈniːsɪs/ Gr. movement.

kingdom of ends a system of persons, all of whom are ends-in-themselves and each a moral legislator for all. Kant introduced this metaphor in *Foundations of the Metaphysics of Morals* 1785, chapter 2. The German is *Reich der Zwecke*, also translated as *realm of ends*.

Klages /klaːgəs (Gm.)/, Ludwig (1872–1956) German philosopher, a leading representative of vitalism and irrationalism, influenced by Romantic philosophy and Nietzsche. He maintained in his main work, *Der Geist als Widersacher der Seele* 1929–32 (The mind as adversary of the soul) that our culture had suffered a major loss because the essentially male rationality of Western philosophy had suppressed the soul, something vital, vibrant, essentially female. An anti-semitic tendency is discernible in his writings. In 1905 he founded an institute for characterology in Munich, which removed to Zürich in 1919. He laid great emphasis on graphology as a means of determining a person's character. *See also* LOGOCENTRISM; MATRIARCHY.

know, knowledge Knowledge is not the same as belief or opinion. To say that a person *knows* that p implies that p, but to say that he *believes* that p does not imply that p.

The two statements *A knows that p* and *B knows that not-p* cannot be true together, for the first implies that p and the second implies that not-p. People can know different things, but they cannot know incompatible things.

knowledge argument an argument designed to refute physicalist theories of consciousness. According to physicalism, all there is to know about a certain mental, subjective state or event *is* known by a person who knows all about what goes on in the relevant nervous system. Against this, the objection raised by the 'knowledge argument' is that on this physicalist view, it would be possible for a colour-blind person to know what it is to see red. But this is not the case, for if the colour-blindness is cured, the observer who sees red for the first time will learn something that he did not know before. The argument was so named by the Australian philosopher Frank Jackson in the article 'Epiphenomenal Qualia', *Philosophical Quarterly 32* (1982), and has been much discussed since.

knowledge-relativism *n.* This is the view that an unqualified concept of knowledge does not make sense and that there is nothing beyond various perspectives. This view is implied in the current use of the barbarism 'knowledges'. It is also implied in talk of 'bourgeois knowledge', 'proletarian knowledge' and the like. Such talk does not simply make the point that different people know different things. It makes the point that there is no cognitive justification over and above a class perspective. Since *it is known that p* implies that *p is true*, knowledge-relativism implies truth-relativism.

knowledge, theory of philosophical inquiry into, or theory of, the nature, possibility, scope and limits of human knowledge. *Syn.* EPISTEMOLOGY.

Kohlberg /ˈkəʊlbɜːg/, Lawrence (1928–87) American psychologist, professor of education at Harvard University from 1968. He specialized in studying the development of moral knowledge and moral judgement. His work was a development and refinement of that of the Swiss structuralist psychologist Jean Piaget (1896–1980). Piaget's research was designed to show that in many areas of knowledge – including language acquisition and mathematical and logical knowledge, as well as in the formation of moral judgement – children pass through an invariant sequence of stages of knowledge, from the more concrete to the more abstract. Stages cannot be bypassed, although not all human beings will progress to the later or 'higher' stages. Kohlberg sought to show (e.g. in *Essays in Moral Development* I–II, 1981, 1984) that moral development was more complex than Piaget had supposed and that there were in fact three levels: pre-conventional, conventional, and post-conventional or principled, each with two stages – a total of six stages. They are: (1) stage of a heteronomous morality – responding to punishment and reward; (2) stage of acceptance of rules as personally advantageous; (3) stage of mutual interpersonal expectations; (4) stage of conscience and acceptance of social order; (5) stage of social contract or utility; (6) stage of universal principles.

According to the theory, the sequence of stages is culture-invariant, although the number of persons who reach a certain stage may differ between societies.

Towards the end of his life, Kohlberg speculated that there might be a seventh stage, consisting of something more like mystical insight, but this was never incorporated into the theory.

Kohlberg's work was empirical. Subjects were presented with moral dilemmas in order to elicit their opinion. Of particular importance was the 'Heinz dilemma': would it be right for a man, Heinz, to steal a drug in order to save the life of his dying wife? Investigators recorded the reasons children and adults gave for their answers to this question, and estimated their level of moral development on this basis.

Both Piaget and Kohlberg had based much of their research on the replies of male subjects. Carol Gilligan, in conducting research into female respondents, some of it relating to the peculiarly female problem of an abortion decision, formed the view that their replies, which in Kohlberg's terms placed them at a 'low' stage of moral development, in fact revealed a distinctively different, rather than inferior, approach to morality – 'a different voice'. This led her to a fundamental critique and reappraisal of Kohlberg's theoretical assumptions, which had presupposed a Kantian approach to morality and a universalistic ethic based on an abstract conception of justice and rights. BA

Kojève /kɔʒɛv/, Alexandre (1902–68) Of upper-class Russian origin, born Aleksander Vladimirovitch Kojevnikov, he fled after the Revolution but remained sympathetic to communist ideas. After further study in Germany, he settled in Paris where from 1933 he gave a lecture course (published in English as *Introduction to the Reading of Hegel*) on Hegel's *Phenomenology of Spirit*, offering a new interpretation of Hegel's account of the dialectic between 'master' and 'slave', as representing the dynamics of the relation between classes in society and being at the core of the historical process. However, this process (i.e. history) was coming to an end as mankind, since the early nineteenth century, was gradually moving towards becoming organized in a universal state. His interpretation markedly influenced his audience, among whom many became leading intellectuals in post-war France: R. Aron, E. Weil, M. Merleau-Ponty, G. Bataille, R. Queneau, J. Lacan. After the war, he became a high-ranking civil servant, but maintained his philosophical interests; and a considerable number of writings, centred around the themes of the 'end of history' and 'end of philosophy', have been published posthumously.

Kolakowski /kowa'kofskɪ (Po.)/, Leszek (1927–) Polish philosopher, in exile since the late 1960s, fellow of All Souls College in Oxford. He was an early advocate of a Marxist humanism, but was later to reject many of the main tenets of the Marxist tradition, especially in his major work *Main Currents of Marxism* 1978, and to develop a philosophy with greater openness towards religion.

Koran, the the authoritative text of Islam, containing the teachings of the prophet.

Kripke /'krɪpkə/, Saul (1940–) American philosopher, professor at Princeton University since 1977. One of his major contributions to logic has been his construction of a semantics for modal logic in terms of possible worlds.

In a major article published in 1972, and later in a book with the same title, *Naming and Necessity* 1980, Kripke challenged the view prevalent since Frege which assimilates names to definite descriptions. According to that view, the name 'Seneca' means: the author of the letter to Lucilius and the teacher of Nero, or . . . But if historians were to discover that Seneca did not write those letters, we should not infer that Seneca was not Seneca. We can refer to Seneca even if a great deal of the information about him were to be found incorrect. He might not have written those letters, he might not in fact have taught Nero, he might not have been Iberian but in fact Numidian. But there are limits to what Seneca might not have been. We could not make sense of thinking that he might not have been a human being. Some properties are essential – the ones whose absence would imply that Seneca did not exist, but was merely the figment of the historians' imagination.

Something similar applies to names of natural kinds, like 'gold'. It is possible that gold might have had another colour, but again, there are limits to what gold might have been without ceasing to be gold. These are the essential properties of gold, discovered by scientific research. What is then discovered is a necessary truth about gold, but it is not *a priori*. Thus Kripke's work on reference implies that there is a sharp distinction between what is necessary and what is knowable *a priori* – contrary to empiricist philosophy.

Names and natural kind terms can function the way they do because they become attached to their bearers by an act of naming or some other process that has the same result. This makes such terms 'rigid designators'.

This analysis has been applied by Kripke

against the identity theory of mind: the theory that every mental state is identical with some brain-state. The theory takes such identities to be contingent. Kripke's objection is that the terms used to refer to mental states and brain-states are natural-kind terms; therefore, if there are such identities, they cannot be contingent.

Wittgenstein on Rules and Private Language 1982 presents the later Wittgenstein as a sceptic about the existence of a definite meaning for a linguistic expression.

Kripke's work has been widely acclaimed for its remarkable clarity and originality, and has since the 1970s been at the centre of attention in analytical philosophy.

Kristeva /kristɛva (Fr.)/, Julia (1941–) born in Bulgaria, educated by French nuns; arrived in Paris as a student in 1965 and stayed there. As her intellectual work has been constantly evolving, it is appropriate to focus on this in a general survey of her work.

Kristeva's first major writing was on 'carnival' and 'dialogue', as these appeared in the work of the Russian literary theorist Mikhail Bakhtin. Carnival, Kristeva shows, transcends the binary logic of science, for it includes otherness within itself, while 'dialogism', as found in Dostoyevsky's writing, introduces the polyphonic voice into the novel: narrative and intrigue unfold through a 'polyphony' of voices or positions; and these voices relate to each other on a strictly horizontal – that is, equal basis.

Bakhtin enabled Kristeva to develop conceptual tools for formalizing what, in the late 1960s, she came to call 'poetic language'. The limit to formalization which affected poetic language was not a real limit, she maintained, but the result of a narrow view of logic as essentially binary – based on the 0–1 (Other and One) paradigm, where 0 excludes 1, and vice versa. Here, there must be 0 *or* 1, but not both. Of course, this logic is widespread and quite familiar. It comes into play in dealing with (or in attempting to exclude) contradiction. Poetic logic accepts contradiction – the notion of the One *and* the Other existing simultaneously. More practically, Kristeva aimed at this time to give voice to the 'musicality' of language – to its sounds, rhythms and graphic disposition (its material side) as much as to its symbolic or communicative side (grammar, syntax, sign, or meaning structure).

In *Sémanalyse* 1969, Kristeva coins a number of terms germane to her mode of analysing texts: 'semanalysis' designates a project of textual analysis which includes the 'poetic' or material aspect of language within its ambit; 'genotext' and 'phenotext' refer, respectively, to the process of the text's generation, and to the text as a medium of communication.

While semiotics and linguistics form the basis of Kristeva's theoretical framework between 1965 and 1970, in the early 1970s psychoanalysis provides her with her framework of coherence, with emphasis being given to the formation of the subject. Two terms which assume an extraordinary importance here are 'the semiotic' and 'the symbolic', both first elaborated in her doctoral thesis, *La Révolution du langage poétique* 1974 (partially transl. as *Revolution in Poetic Language*). Here, the semiotic is not simply the study of signs and significations, but is linked to the drive dimension of subjectivity observable in the musicality (rhythm and timbre) of utterances – the dimension which opens the subject up to change and renewal. The semiotic is in many ways a revised version of her earlier conceptions of poetic language and the genotext; only now, these become factors in the formation of subjectivity and are linked to Freud and Lacan's theories of sexual difference. For its part, the symbolic, which is now connected to the formation of identity, corresponds to the earlier concept of the phenotext.

From 1980 onward, Kristeva has engaged in a series of studies which have combined her linguistic and psychoanalytic orientations. Among them are studies of abjection in *Pouvoirs de l'horreur* 1980 (Powers of horror); of love and idealization in *Histoires d'amour* 1983 (Tales of love); of depression and melancholia in *Soleil noir* 1987 (Black sun). She has also taken up the discussion of nationalism and the other in *Etrangers à nous-même* 1988 (Strangers to ourselves) and she has produced a work on Proust – *Le Temps sensible* 1994 (*The Experience of Time*). In all cases, psychoanalytic concepts are close at hand in analyses of the unnameable and the symbolizable. JL

Kropotkin /kra'pɔtkɪn (Rus.)/, Peter Alexeyevich (1842–1921) Russian anarchist thinker and political activist. In his influential work *Mutual Aid* 1902 he argued, against the social-Darwinist view, that the necessary and desirable road to progress is by means of conflict in which the 'fittest' win and the weak are destroyed; that cooperation is an essential feature in evolutionary processes; and that society could be organized along principles of mutual aid, without subjection to a coercive authority.

Kuhn /kuːn/, Thomas S. (1922–96) American philosopher and historian of science, professor at Berkeley, Princeton and, from 1978, at the Massachusetts Institute of Technology. His *The Structure of Scientific Revolutions* 1962, 2nd rev. edn 1970, was very widely read and discussed because it presented a view of science very different from those current among philosophers and scientists. Earlier views were that science is cumulative: scientists discover more and more truths about the world. The realization that this is naive, and that sometimes scientists abandon earlier views as mistaken, did not really alter the basic optimism: it was said that an earlier scientific theory is only abandoned in order to put a better theory in its place.

All this seemed threatened by Kuhn, who took a more historical and/or sociological look at science. A science or branch of science is the preserve of a particular community of scientists. These scientists, by virtue of their common education (or, rather, dogmatic initiation) all take for granted a 'paradigm', a way of viewing the world and of practising science in it. In an attempt to force nature to fit their paradigm, they try to solve puzzles defined by the paradigm. If a scientist solves a puzzle, the scientist is congratulated and rewarded. If a scientist fails to solve a puzzle, the scientist is blamed and the puzzle reserved for other, better scientists. Thus, 'normal science', which as its name suggests is the norm, is puzzle-solving under the aegis of an unquestioned paradigm. However, every paradigm has its day. Unsolved puzzles accumulate; scientists begin to lose confidence in their paradigm. The community plunges into a 'crisis state', into a period of 'extraordinary or revolutionary science': nothing is taken for granted any more, alternative paradigms are canvassed. One of these will solve one or two of the unsolved puzzles that the earlier paradigm could not solve. Seeing its promise, more and more scientists will 'convert' to the new paradigm. Usually these are the younger scientists: older ones will simply die out, exemplifying the dictum 'You cannot teach an old dog new tricks'. A new generation of scientists is taught to recognize the virtues of the new paradigm; a new period of 'normal science' begins.

Does science make progress through scientific revolutions? Are later paradigms better than earlier ones? No, Kuhn suggests, they are just different. The scientific revolutions which supplant one paradigm with another do not take us closer to the truth about the way the world is. Successive paradigms are INCOMMENSURABLE. Kuhn says that a later paradigm may be a better instrument for solving puzzles than an earlier one. But if each paradigm defines its own puzzles, what is a puzzle for one paradigm may be no puzzle at all for another. So why is it progress to replace one paradigm with another which solves puzzles that the earlier paradigm does not even recognize?

Many philosophers thought that Kuhn was impugning the rationality, objectivity and progress of science. In his later writings (especially the 'Postscript' to the second edition of his book) Kuhn tried to reassure them that this was not so. On the other hand, sociologists of science and others anxious to debunk science responded to Kuhn's ideas with enthusiasm. So did some social thinkers who took Kuhn to be saying that the way to become truly scientific is to become dogmatically committed to some 'paradigm'. AM

L

Labriola /labri'ola (It.)/, Antonio (1843–1904) professor of moral philosophy at the University of Rome from 1874. Croce was one of his disciples. A liberal and radical in his youth, Labriola developed an interest in the theories of Karl Marx, and stands as the main founding thinker of Italian Marxism. He wrote *Essays on the Materialist Conception of History* 1896, 2nd edn 1902. He rejected historical determinism and favoured a humanist Marxism.

La Bruyère /la bʀyjɛːʀ (Fr.)/, Jean de (1645–96) French moralist. His *Caractères* were modelled on those of Theophrastus and on first publication 1688 were appended to his translations of them. He was a penetrating observer of human affairs, probing pride, pretence and other moral failings in brilliant character sketches.

Lacan /lakã (Fr.)/, Jacques (1901–81) French psychoanalyst. He developed an analysis of psychoanalytic practice which influenced a generation of French structuralist, post-structuralist and feminist thinkers. His psychoanalytic theory remains controversial: he was barred from the International Psychoanalytic Association in 1960, but his influence continues to spread internationally in both psychoanalytic and intellectual circles.

Lacan's central thesis is that the unconscious is structured like a language; a thesis that he locates in Freud's discovery that condensation and displacement (and their prototypes, METAPHOR and METONYMY) are the primary mechanisms of the unconscious. It follows from this that the capacity of the psychoanalyst to affect the symptom is located purely at the level of speech. Formations of the unconscious (slips of the tongue, memory lapses, dreams, etc.) are understood by Lacan as instances of failed communication. The neurotic symptom, in this sense, is understood as an encoded message that has been excluded from the circuit of discourse and can only be communicated in a disguised form. By means of the transference, the analyst becomes the addressee of the symptom's hidden message and, through interpretation, inserts the communication back into discourse.

Lacan's early work, 1936 to the early 1950s, focused on what he would later call the register of *the imaginary*. The mirror stage refers to the joy expressed by the child of six to eighteen months, when faced with its image in the mirror. This joy, according to Lacan, results from an anticipation of the bodily unity of the mirror image, in contrast with the physical immaturity of the child's own motor development. Fundamental to the theory of the mirror stage is the view that the 'self' constitutes both itself and the other, its counterpart, through an identification with an image of itself as other. The intersubjective relationship is therefore essentially dual, characterized by imaginary identification and alienation, and marked by an ambivalent relationship of aggressive rivalry with and erotic attachment to the other. The ego, according to Lacan, is the outcome of a series of such imaginary identifications and therefore does not have the function of synthesis and unity assigned to it by ego-psychology (Kris, Lowenstein, Hartmann).

In the 1950s, Lacan introduced the distinction between the imaginary and *the symbolic*. Following Saussure, Lacan divides the symbolic into two dimensions, speech and language. The psychoanalytic cure is located at the level of speech. Combining the linguistic concept of speech with Hegel's master–slave dialectic, Lacan argues that speech establishes a social bond, or symbolic pact, which overcomes the erotic-aggressive relationship of ego to ego ('small other'). Language, on the other hand, consists of a network of signifiers that can only be defined in relation to each other and are themselves meaningless. It is at this purely formal level of language, conceived as a network of signifiers, that Lacan locates the Other. A place, rather than a subject, Lacan's concept of the Other can be given no singular or positive definition. For Lacan, the Other is other to the subject, speech and language. It exists prior to the subject's entry into language, and is fundamentally alien to the subject. It is the place from which dreams, as the discourse of the desire of the Other, are spoken. In psychoanalysis it is the guarantor of the subject's truth. It is the third element in every dialogue, the discourse that the analysand enters into through the process of analysis. In Freudian terms it is the unconscious.

For Lacan, the symbolic relationship to the Other takes precedence over the imaginary relation to the small other. However, both the other and the subject contain a fundamental lack, and it is this lack or 'want to be' that gives rise to a chain of desire which can never be satisfied. That is, the continuing search for a lost object that the subject has never possessed and that the other cannot provide.

In the 1960s Lacan began to develop his concept of *the real*. The real is excluded both from the symbolic and the imaginary. It can only be reconstructed on the basis of the structural distortion it produces in the symbolic order of the subject. Based on the concept of trauma that Freud initially regarded as the ultimate origin of all neurotic disorders, the real is an 'APORIA' internal to the symbolic which progressively reveals itself to be at the centre of the analytic experience.

Lacan's *Ecrits* 1966 is a selection of writings, some of which are translated as *Ecrits: a Selection* 1977 and *The Language of the Self* 1978. Edited transcripts of his *Séminaires* are published as *The Seminar of Jacques Lacan* Book I, Book II, Book III, Book VII. JR

Ladd-Franklin /læd 'fræŋklɪn/, Christine (née Ladd) (1847–1930) American academic, who taught at Johns Hopkins University from 1904 and at Columbia University in New York from 1910. In 'The algebra of logic' 1883 she introduced the concept of ANTILOGISM for the analysis of syllogisms. Her main work, however, was in mathematics. In the theory of vision, she proposed in 1892 an evolutionary account of colour perception.

laissez faire, laisser faire /'leɪseɪ fɛə; lɛseɪ fɛə (Eng.); lɛse fɛːr (Fr.)/ (Fr. *laisser* to let, to allow; *laissez* let!, allow! + *faire* to do) Leave things alone, allow things to look after themselves. This was a maxim of the eighteenth-century French physiocrats (Quesnay et al.), who were the first to develop a scientific theory of economics. As the term suggests, their view was that nature (Gr. *physis*) should rule (Gr. *kratein*). The natural order of a society and its economy, as elaborated in their theories, should not be interfered with. Consequently, they opposed restrictions and imposts on trade and commerce, and especially those imposed by governments. Turgot tried to implement some reforms in this spirit, but was soon removed from office, in 1776. Many of the physiocrat ideas were accepted by later economists (Adam Smith, Ricardo, James Mill, and even Keynes).

The motto *laissez faire* has come to be associated with economic liberalism and opposition to governmental intervention in economic activity.

Lakatos /ˈlækətɒs/, Imre (né Lipschitz) (1922–74) Hungarian-born philosopher of mathematics and science; taught at the London School of Economics. Influenced by the work of George Polya on mathematical heuristics and by Karl Popper's philosophy of science, Lakatos's early work, written as a PhD dissertation at Cambridge, included a lively reconstruction in dialogue form of episodes from the growth of mathematical knowledge, arguing that it conformed to a pattern of 'proofs and refutations', akin to Popper's ideas about the growth of science (*Proofs and Refutations* 1976). A 'proof', rather than establishing the thesis proved, furnished an opportunity for criticism, or for the discovery of objections. Lakatos imaginatively explored the dialectic of argument in the history of mathematics, and developed many ideas which he subsequently used in other contexts. While Lakatos wrote several other papers (*Philosophical Papers*, vol. 2, 1978) on the character of mathematical knowledge, suggesting that the dialectical character of the growth of mathematical knowledge could be understood as a form of empiricism, his efforts turned gradually to the philosophy of science.

Thus, he initially used ideas developed in his work on the growth of mathematics to criticize Carnap's programme for the development of inductive logic as degenerative over time. Subsequently, he offered a complex reconstruction of Popper's views to meet problems about the continuity of science and the resilience of theories against falsification raised by Thomas Kuhn and Michael Polanyi. Lakatos increasingly came to differentiate between his ideas and those of Popper. He argued that Popper had not successfully solved the problem of induction, and that his own ideas about science, which stressed the role of rational heuristic and the benefits of making methodological decisions to protect theories from refutation in the face of empirically-generated problems, were to be preferred to those of Popper. He also argued (*Philosophical Papers*, vol. 1, 1978) that normative conceptions of science were to be evaluated on the basis of their ability to offer a reconstruction of the judgements of leading scientists in the history of science. He had for a long time projected a work on the changing logic of scientific discovery, but this was not brought to completion before his premature death. Lakatos inspired his followers to undertake several case-studies, applying his ideas to the reconstruction of the history of natural science, and especially to economics. Since Lakatos's death, his work has come in for criticism, in part for problems of its own, in part for problems it shares with Popper's views, of which much of his work is an extension. JSH

lambda operator, lambda calculus an operator, originally defined by Alonzo Church, which turns an open sentence into a predicate. If p is an open sentence that contains a free variable x, then λx[p] is its lambda transform; for instance, the proposition ∃x(Fx ∨ Gx) which can be read 'something is F or G', contains the open sentence (Fx ∨ Gx) and it has the lambda transform λx(Fx ∨ Gx) which can be read 'the property of being F or G'.

Lambert /ˈlambɛrt (Gm.)/, Johann Heinrich (1728–77) Swiss-German mathematician, scientist and philosopher. He was the first to prove that the number π is irrational. The title of his major philosophical work *Neues Organon* 1764 (The new Organon) alludes to Aristotle and Bacon: it deals with the principles for discovering truths. This work, and a later one on philosophical 'architectonic' 1771 which, like the earlier one, had a marked anti-metaphysical tendency, broke a path away from the dominant Wolffian philosophy. At the time, Lambert's influence was limited, but can be seen in Mendelssohn and above all in Kant, with whom he corresponded and who held him in great regard.

La Mettrie /la metʀi (Fr.)/, Julien Offray de (1709–51) French physician and radical Enlightenment philosopher, an advocate of materialism and atheism. He published his *Natural History of the Soul* in 1745, but the work that made him famous is *L'Homme machine* 1748 (Man a machine). The reaction caused by these publications, and other ones in which he satirized the medical profession, created a need for protection, met by Frederick II of Prussia, and La Mettrie spent his last five years in Berlin.

His theory of man is naturalistic, materialistic and anti-dualist. Drawing on recent scientific observations, he was also able to assume that matter is not in its essence inert, so that it is not necessary to assume some non-material principle to explain motion. Mental processes can be scientifically explained in physiological terms; they may be more complex, but not in principle different from other processes in nature. Human conduct, like other natural processes, is determined by natural causes, and there is no place for free will. One consequence that La Mettrie drew from this was that remorse is irrational. Many details of La Mettrie's work, especially the physiology, have been superseded, but the spirit of his metaphysical materialism is present in much of twentieth-century analytic philosophy.

La Mothe Le Vayer /la mɔt lə vaje (Fr.)/, François de (1588–1672) French sceptical philosopher, a great admirer of Sextus Empiricus and Montaigne. In his writings, he elaborated on the vast diversity of social customs, moral opinions, scientific theories, religious beliefs, etc., all of which show that little can be known with certainty. Religious dogmas, on the other hand, are accepted through faith, and not by ways open to sceptical doubts. As in the case of Bayle, opinions differ on whether he accepted Christian doctrine as a non-rational matter of faith, or rejected it because of its irrationality.

Lange /ˈlaŋə (Gm.)/, Friedrich Albert (1828–75) German philosopher. He wrote in favour of democratic socialism. His best-known philosophical work is his *Geschichte des Materialismus und Kritik seiner Bedeutung in der Gegenwart* 1866; 2nd edn 1873–5 (History of materialism, with an examination of its contemporary significance). He argued that at the level of scientific method, materialism is the only legitimate assumption, but that as a metaphysical theory it is as faulty as the idealism it opposes. Metaphysics is comparable to poetry or religion, but can yield no genuine knowledge. Lange followed Kant in developing a theory of limits to human knowledge that metaphysical theories try to overstep. He initiated the neo-Kantian revival, although other neo-Kantians were soon to reject his psychologistic (*see* PSYCHOLOGISM) reading of Kant.

Langer /ˈlæŋə/, Susanne (née Knauth) (1895–1985) American philosopher who taught at Radcliffe College from 1927, at Columbia University from 1945, and at Connecticut College from 1954. The analysis of the arts was her major interest. They hold a central place in the human world and give a key to the understanding of human nature and the human condition (*Philosophy in a New Key* 1942; *Feeling and Form* 1953). Since they contain a symbolic transformation of reality, the nature of symbolism is at the core of philosophical inquiry. An important influence on her thought was that of Ernst Cassirer.

language-game *n.* a concept in the philosophy of the later Wittgenstein. Language-games are linguistic practices, governed by certain rules and conventions. In *Philosophical Investigations* 1953 he argued, using striking examples, that there is a great variety of language-games. It follows that the project of a general theory of language, of the kind proposed in his *Tractatus*, is misconceived. There, the assumption was that all language is used to play *one* kind of game only: picturing facts.

Laplace /laplas (Fr.)/, Pierre Simon de (1749–1827) French astronomer and probability theorist. On the basis of Newtonian physics, he held the view that the total course of events in the universe would be perfectly predictable to an intelligence who knew the position of every particle in the universe and the forces acting upon it. In the absence of such perfect knowledge, however, we should be guided by a rational estimate of probabilities.

La Rochefoucauld /la ʀɔʃfuko (Fr.)/, François de (1613–80) French moralist. His *Maxims and Reflections* offer penetrating insights into the predominance of pride and self-interest in human character and conduct, and unmask deception and self-deception in a sustained quest for honesty and lucidity. It is not clear whether his emphasis on the prevalence of self-love amounts to an endorsement of the theory that all motivation is bound to be self-interested, i.e. psychological egoism.

Lassalle /lasal (Gm.)/, Ferdinand (né Lasal) (1825–64) German political thinker and organizer of working-class political parties. In his critique of the bourgeois-liberal preference for minimal government intervention, he coined the metaphor of 'the nightwatchman state'. Some of his writings are Hegelian in inspiration and show an affinity with Marx's view of history. He also wrote a major study of Heraclitus's thought.

last-person argument 'Even if P were the last human being (or sentient being) ever to exist, it would still be worse if P caused the destruction of a great work of art (a rainforest, etc.) than if he did not.' This is the main premiss in one kind of argument to establish non-anthropocentric values. It appeals to intuition. The contrary intuition is that the alternatives do not differ in value.

latitudinarianism *n.* (in the Church of England) the view that great latitude ought to be allowed within the Church to differences in doctrine and liturgy.

Among its early advocates in the seventeenth century were William Chillingworth, John Hales, the Cambridge Platonists, John Tillotson, etc. Their view developed in reaction against the dogmatism and intemperate antagonism displayed in the religious and political conflicts in England from the 1640s and on. Ideas of this kind persisted, e.g. in the Broad Church opposition to High Anglicanism in nineteenth-century England.

The word was initially used derogatorily by opponents to this undogmatic view.

Lavater /ˈlaːvaːtər (Gm.)/, Johann Caspar (1741–1801) German-Swiss popular philosopher, whose *Physionomische Fragmente* 1775–8 presented a new theory of physiognomy, trying to establish correlations between body-types and character-types. Also influential were the sentimental piety and the extolling of subjectivity and feeling in his poetry, which enjoyed a remarkable popularity.

laws of nature It has long been recognized that the universe is, at least to some extent, orderly. The ancient Greeks expressed this thought in the claim that our world is not a chaos but a cosmos. During the scientific advances of the sixteenth and seventeenth centuries, and especially following the successes of Isaac Newton, the idea took hold that the order in the world consisted in, and could be expressed through, exact quantitative relationships among physical quantities. Such relationships, when discovered, took the name of laws: Newton's Law of Gravitation and Boyle's Law for gases are among the more familiar examples. As psychology and other human sciences developed, the idea of laws was extended to them also.

Some of the principal issues regarding laws are whether there really are any, and, if so, whether all that happens is governed by them. These questions are of great importance to natural theology, the problem of free will, and the respective roles of cause and of chance in the unfolding of the natural world.

Other questions which have concerned philosophers include whether laws could be merely local, or must embrace all of space and time; whether they might admit of occasional exceptions; and whether they might alter. On all these issues, the course of scientific development needs to be taken into account.

In debates on these matters the character of laws themselves is usually taken for granted, yet the question of the true logical form of laws of nature is a warmly debated one. The simplest proposal is that a law of nature is a true universal statement of the form (in the standard symbols of predicate logic):

$(\forall x)\ (Fx \supset Gx)$, i.e. every F is a G

or of the slightly more complex form:

$(\forall x)\ (\exists y)\ (Fx \supset Gy)$, i.e. for every F there is a G.

Setting aside the technical objection that in standard modern logic, every conditional with a false antecedent is true, so that if there are no Fs at all, every universal statement about Fs counts as a law of nature, this simple proposal seems neither necessary nor sufficient.

It is not necessary, since in quantum theory we now recognize as laws of nature merely probable, not universal, links among physical quantities. Nor is it sufficient, since not every true universal statement is a law. Some concern merely accidental or coincidental links. Contrast, for example: 'All molecules of water have the same mass' with 'All United States banknotes are the same size.' The difference between a law and an accidental generalization is often expressed in the idea that only a law supports counterfactuals – if some molecule of some other substance had been water, it could not but have the same mass as all the others. But if a larger denomination banknote were to be adopted by the United States, it is not the case that it could not but have the same dimensions as all the others.

Many philosophers, inspired by Hume's discussion of causality, take the objective content of a law of nature to involve no more than a regularity of sequence or coexistence. They ('Humeans') claim that the difference between a law and an accidental universal statement does not lie in any necessary link among physical quantities involved, but in how we humans treat the universal statement. We regard it as especially well-credentialled, reliable, or basic.

The opposite 'anti-Humean' view is that the tie between the quantities related by a genuine law is closer than mere regularity of combination, involving some kind of *necessity*. A genuine law tells us not merely what does, as a matter of fact, always happen, but what *must* occur. The most important current anti-Humean view holds that a law is not a generalization about particular cases, but concerns the very physical quantities (universal properties or relations) of which the law treats. A law asserts a necessitating relation between these universals, the precise nature of which is still being debated. These discussions will need to accommodate the possibility, foreshadowed in quantum physics, that all the basic laws of nature prove to be probabilistic, rather than strictly necessary. *See also* NATURAL LAW. KC

laws of thought The truths of logic are sometimes called laws of thought. It is, however, generally agreed that they are not to be understood as descriptions of our thinking processes: logic is not a branch of psychology.

The expression 'laws of thought' was traditionally reserved for three logical principles: (1) the law of identity, A = A, i.e. everything is what it is; (2) the law of non-contradiction, i.e. not both p and not-p; (3) the law of the excluded middle: p or not-p. The view that these three laws of thought are more fundamental than other logical laws was common in the past, but has fallen out of favour with modern logicians.

These laws are sometimes misunderstood. The first does *not* imply that nothing ever changes. The second does *not* imply that a thing can have only one property. The third does *not* imply that everything is black or white; it implies only that either everything is black or something is not black.

lazy argument, lazy sophism an argument for fatalism proposed by Chrysippus and criticized by Cicero in *De fato* (On fate). The argument has as a premiss that whatever will be, will be. For instance: 'If fate has decreed that you will recover, then you will recover whether or not you consult a physician. If fate has decreed that you will not recover, then you will not recover whether or not you consult a physician. Fate has decreed one or the other. Therefore, it is pointless to consult a physician.' The argument is called 'lazy' because its conclusion encourages inaction.

Lecomte du Noüy /ləkɔ̃t dy nwi (Fr.)/, Pierre André (1883–1947) French biophysicist and religious philosopher. His best-known work, *Human Destiny* 1947, was an attempt to defend a theistic world-view from a scientific standpoint. One line of argument was that the emergence of organic life was too improbable to be due to chance; another that the evolutionary process does not conform to the Second Law of Thermodynamics.

Le Doeuff /lə dɜːf/, Michèle (1948–) Le Doeuff's book *L'Étude et le rouet* 1990 (transl. as *Hipparchia's Choice*) takes its title from the sentence quoted in the frontispiece in which HIPPARCHIA summed up the relation of women to philosophy: 'I have used for the getting of knowledge all the time which, because of my sex, I was supposed to waste at the loom.' The question of women's relation to philosophy has been a constant theme of Le Doeuff's work, and her essay 'Women and Philosophy' in *Radical Philosophy 17* (1977) was an influential contribution to the recent development of feminist philosophical thought in the English-speaking world. This theme is pursued in *Hipparchia's Choice*, along with reflection upon the likely effects upon philosophy of the encounter with post-war feminism, the particular case of Sartre and de Beauvoir, and broader questions of ethics and politics.

Le Doeuff's work has always included a strong element of reflexive questioning of the nature of philosophy itself, with particular reference to its own self-conception and the ideal of a pure, self-contained rationality. Against this, she points to the role played in philosophical texts by recourse to imagery: 'My work is about the stock of images you can find in philosophical works, whatever they refer to: insects, clocks, women, or islands' (*French Philosophers in Conversation*, ed. R. Mortley, 1990). Her earlier work pursues the question of the function of images in a variety of cases, drawn from philosophers such as Thomas More, Descartes, Rousseau and Kant. Le Doeuff argues both that there is a necessary recourse to images on the part of the most rational of philosophers, and that there is a specifically philosophical stock of images which she calls 'the philosophical imaginary'. Given the frequency of recourse to sexually coded imagery throughout the history of philosophy, she suggests that it is not surprising that someone interested in the figures of 'woman' and the roles that these play within philosophy should have been led to investigate the nature and function of this normally overlooked dimension of philosophy.

Le Doeuff is also known in France for her work on Renaissance English thought. She has translated Bacon's *New Atlantis* into French, published along with an essay on Bacon ('Voyage dans la pensée baroque' with M. Lasa) in 1983, and has also translated one of Shakespeare's longer poems published with an essay 'Genèse d'une catastrophe': *Shakespeare: Vénus et Adonis* 1986. PP

Lefebvre /ləfɛːvʀ (Fr.)/, Henri (1901–91) French Marxist philosopher, a prolific writer of vast erudition. In his younger days a communist activist, he later met with party disapproval and left in 1958. His undogmatic Marxism, in which the theory of alienation and the critique of state power play an important part, was perhaps the most significant intellectual influence behind the student revolt in France in May 1968. His Marxist humanism was also the framework for a sustained critique of consumer society and the standardization, conformism and bureaucratization of our times.

legalism *n.* **1** the moral evaluation of an act by reference only to its conformity to a moral rule, without regard to the agent's motives. **2** a theory that sees morality as being analogous to a legal code, i.e. as a set of rules of conduct, backed by sanctions (more or less vaguely conceived) which provide a motive for conforming to the rules.

legal positivism *See* POSITIVISM.

legal realism *See* REALISM.

Leibniz /ˈlaɪbnɪts (Eng.); ˈlaɪpnɪts (Gm.)/, Gottfried Wilhelm (1646–1716) the most important figure of seventeenth-century rationalism. He was born in Leipzig and died in Hanover. Leibniz was well informed about almost all the scientific developments of his time and corresponded with almost every important contemporary scientist and philosopher. After studying philosophy in Leipzig and Jena, and law in Altdorf near Nuremberg, he held court appointments throughout his life. Like Descartes, Spinoza and Locke he was never a professor of philosophy.

Leibniz wrote on philosophy, theology, mathematics, physics, linguistics, etymology, genealogy, history, politics, medicine and economy, and was in all these disciplines influential, in some of them creative and even pioneering. Thus he is rightly called 'the Aristotle of the modern era'. He wrote in Latin, using post-medieval scholastic Latin, and in French. The scholastic background of his thought means that he can be characterized also as a representative of German Protestant university philosophy, which in Leibniz's day was dominated by Aristotelianism.

Leibniz was also influenced by non-scholastic thinkers of his time, above all by the German physician and logician Joachim Jungius (1587–1657), the French philosopher and theologian Antoine Arnauld (1612–94) and the Dutch scientist Christian Huygens (1620–99). No doubt there was also an influence from Descartes, and from Spinoza, whom he once met in Amsterdam, but his treatment of their work is generally critical.

The most important works by Leibniz are the *Dissertatio de arte combinatoria* 1666; the *Discours de métaphysique* (Discourse on metaphysics) and the *Generales inquisitiones* 1686 (General inquiries); the *Nouveaux essais sur l'entendement humain* 1703–5 but not published until 1765 (New essays on human understanding); the *Theodicy* of 1710; and the *Monadology* of 1714. There is also the correspondence with Arnauld, with Bartholomaeus des Bosses (1688–1738), with Burcher de Volder (1643–1709) and with Samuel Clarke (1675–1729). But a large number of manuscripts were published much later: Couturat brought out important logic manuscripts in 1901, and the publication of the collected works is still in progress.

Two pairs of concepts (formulated in *Monadology* 31–36) are everywhere significant in Leibniz's thought. One is that of *truths of reason*, which are necessary, and *truths of fact*, which are contingent. This distinction is associated with two principles: the *law of non-contradiction*, which applies to both kinds of truth and states that what involves a contradiction is false, and the *principle of sufficient reason*, which applies to truths of fact and states that no fact can obtain and no proposition can be true unless there is a sufficient reason why it should be thus and not otherwise. Leibniz conceives of such reasons as explanatory factors, which are either efficient causes or final causes.

Philosophy of language: one of Leibniz's desiderata, which he shared with many philosophers and scientists of his time, is the development of a *characteristica universalis*, a general theory and a system of signs which comprehends both logic and grammar as parts. This characteristic is for Leibniz on the one hand an art, skill or capacity, the art of finding the right signs and of manipulating them in an appropriate way. On the other hand it is also a science, and as such a branch of metaphysics. The characteristic has a syntactical, semantic and a pragmatic aspect, corresponding to the syntax, semantics and pragmatics of modern logic.

The Leibnizian idea of a characteristic was based on a combinatorial approach to simple concepts; he wanted to construct a language on the basis of a one-to-one relation between signs and simple concepts. This programme, although never realized, was historically very influential, and among the philosophers who have adopted Leibniz's idea of a *characteristica universalis* are Peirce, Husserl, Frege and Wittgenstein.

Logic: Leibniz's main contribution to logic is the development of the first logical calculi. Between the years 1679 and 1690 he developed different algebraic calculi and one arithmetical calculus. He was successful also in his main aim, namely that of embedding the reconstructed traditional Aristotelian-scholastic syllogistic within the framework of his own logical system. In his treatment of the arithmetical calculus from 1679 we even find the first formulation of a general concept of logical validity.

Another Leibnizian project was that of developing a geometrical calculus which would allow him to express geometrical relations directly and not via rational numbers as in Descartes's analytical geometry. This project was never realized, but it nonetheless influenced later developments in the field of topology.

Leibniz's logic was of terms or concepts,

not of propositions or sentences. Via an analysis of the elementary sentence 'A is B' (e.g. 'Socrates is a human being'), Leibniz shows that we can always proceed to the form 'A B is', which he reads as meaning the composite concept 'AB (Socrates-human being)' is possible (consistent) in virtue of the fact that the individual concept of Socrates contains the concept of human being.

Using this same syntactical relation Leibniz was able to reformulate the universal categorical sentence 'All A are B' as: 'It is not possible that A and not B'. On this basis he developed the structure of a rudimentary Boolean algebra, a fact well known to and explicitly acknowledged by Frege.

Metaphysics and ontology: Leibniz was a metaphysician from the beginning, and his first publication was on metaphysics: a dissertation of 1662 on the principle of individuation. He was one of the first philosophers who made use of the word 'ontology', which deals with four relations: (1) the inherence of accidents in their substance; (2) the relation of part to whole (mereology); (3) the relation of cause and effect; and (4) the relation of means and end (teleology).

The most important ingredient of Leibniz's ontology or metaphysics is the individual substance or the 'monad', as he calls it in his mature philosophy. Leibniz takes the concept of substance from the Aristotelian tradition, but he develops it in two ways. First, he introduces the notion of an individual concept. Every individual substance, he holds, has one and only one individual concept. This concept is complete, i.e. every accident of the substance falls under a part-concept of its individual concept; and it is also maximally consistent, i.e. it contains every concept consistent with it, and any additional concept would make it inconsistent.

A second important feature of the individual substance as Leibniz conceives it, is that it has no parts. But it does have 'accidents' (mental qualities and dispositions). Monads are spiritual substances and, as such, primitive in relation to the part-whole analysis and very complex in relation to the substance-accident analysis.

Leibniz distinguishes two kinds of attributes of monads: perceptions and apperceptions. Perceptions are passive and non-reflexive; they constitute the relation to other monads and their attributes. Apperceptions are active; they include reflexive mental acts like thinking and knowing which are peculiar to human beings, whereas we share perceiving and memory with animals.

There is no causal relation between monads, but only between different states of a monad. Every monad is a microcosmos or a world apart, however, and reflects the whole macrocosmos (i.e. every other monad and its attributes). By this we do have a sort of derivative causality in the world.

The fourth or teleological relation, that of means and end, has to do with human action and also with that of God. God creates the best of all possible worlds because of his goodness, and this creation is not dominated by metaphysical, geometrical or logical necessity but by moral necessity. The difference is that in the former case the contrary is impossible; in the case of moral necessity, however, it is possible but very improbable. God creates the best of all possible worlds with moral necessity, and one consequence of this is that physical necessity, too, in depending on moral necessity, is not absolute necessity at all, but only a degree of contingency approaching absolute necessity. Thus the laws of nature for Leibniz, in contradistinction to Descartes, are not necessary but have only a very high degree of probability.

Mereology: like the tradition before him, Leibniz knows and uses three kinds of whole: essential wholes, integral wholes, and aggregates. In the first case no part is separable; in the second case some parts are separable and some not; and in the third case every part is separable. As examples of essential wholes Leibniz offers God, angel and soul, but also geometrical entities like triangles. As examples of integral wholes he mentions composed substances like human beings, but also artefacts like machines. As examples of aggregates he generally uses a contingent set of substances or a body.

Mind and body: Leibniz uses the term 'corporeal substance' to mean a composed substance unified by a dominating monad. This dominating monad is a soul or a spiritual substance. All living substances, including human beings, are corporeal substances. Bodies are only aggregates or heaps in a mereological sense. Aggregates are phenomenal, and Leibniz discriminates between three kinds of phenomena: first, illusory phenomena like rainbows; secondly, mental phenomena, appearances whose unity is only apparent since it is manufactured by the mind or by concepts; and thirdly, derivative phenomena, appearances of aggregates whose reality is completely derived from that of their constituents. These constituents can be monads or corporeal substances. Aggregates have a borrowed reality and are founded in individual substances or individual accidents. Thus the ontological status of bodies is very weak.

Since Descartes the relations between soul and body have been intensively discussed. Leibniz thinks that there is no causal relation between soul and body, but there is what he calls a 'pre-established harmony'. This harmony is founded in the relations of representation between the soul and its body. Perceptions between the dominating monad and its corporeal counterpart are regulated by the in-built law of series which produces the different states of monads. Leibniz characterizes representation as constant and regulated. The difference between the monads lies in the degree of regulation. Higher monads are better regulated and represent their body and the world in a clearer way than monads on a lower level. Thus Leibniz subscribes to a kind of psychophysical parallelism.

Individuation: Leibniz accepts only the *entitas tota* as a principle of individuation, i.e. all the attributes of an individual – and his view of individuals as unique, non-divisible, non-material entities, individuated by their whole entity, has its roots in later scholasticism, especially in nominalists like Suárez. In a letter to Arnauld, Leibniz speaks of an Adam who is characterized by only four attributes, and he says that this Adam could live in several possible worlds. Leibniz creates through this theory a new genus, namely that of a general Adam, who could exist in different possible worlds. But in fact this Adam is not a genus but only an incomplete concept of the individual Adam. Incomplete concepts do not belong to a single possible world, only individuals do, and Leibniz stresses further that every property must be present or known in order for that individual to be identified.

Identity: Leibniz gave prominence to a principle of identity, now called Leibniz's law, which states that if A and B are identical, they have all their properties in common. This principle, already formulated by Aristotle and Thomas Aquinas, is not valid for intensional contexts, as Leibniz showed. Because of this it is also called 'the principle of extensionality'. The reverse formulation of this principle, viz., if A and B have all their properties in common they are identical, is called by Leibniz 'the principle of the identity of indiscernibles'.

Possible worlds: a central concept in

Leibniz's philosophy is that of possible worlds. Leibniz stresses that God's thinking contains an infinity of possible worlds, which he constructs by combining *prima possibilia*, i.e. first or simple concepts, in different ways. All these worlds are composed of substances and accidents and have a certain tendency to exist. But only the best of them is realized, i.e. the most perfect composition. The competition between possible worlds is decided by the principle of the best, the principle which favours the world best fulfilling the minimax principle, i.e. a world with a minimum of rules or laws and a maximum of states of affairs, or, as Leibniz also puts it, a minimum of causes and a maximum of effects, or a minimum of means and a maximum of ends.

Our world, the best of all possible worlds, is a maximally consistent set of monads, i.e. of substances and their accidents, fulfilling the minimax principle. But there is metaphysical, physical and moral evil in our world. Only a mereological analysis can show the cause of these evils. The property 'to be the best' is not DISSECTIVE from the whole of the world to its parts. In the best of all possible worlds not every part is the best. There could be a better part in a world which is not the best.

Leibniz argues in his correspondence with Clarke against the Barrow-Newton theory of space, which holds that there exists an absolute space into which God has placed the world. Leibniz holds that space and time are dependent on the things. Space for him is the order of coexistent things, and time the order of successions. Time is dependent on the different states of monads, states which are connected by causality. Leibniz hereby develops the first causal theory of time: 'If one of two states which are not simultaneous involves a reason for the other, the former is held to be prior, the latter posterior.'

Space and time for Leibniz are relational entities, having their foundation in the accidents of things, and Leibniz is convinced that these accidents are individual. Space and time are not purely mental entities, but mental entities with a foundation in reality, i.e. a fundament in individual accidents of substances. Thus place has its foundation in the individual situation of each body, and time has its foundation in the successive states of monads. HB

Leibniz's law the principle of INDISCERNIBILITY OF IDENTICALS.

lemma (*sing.*); **lemmas**, **lemmata** (*pl.*) Gr. *lēmma* something to take for granted; a premiss *n.* **1** (in mathematics and logic) an intermediate conclusion, derived to make it easier to follow the proof of the main proposition. **2** (in critical editions of classical texts) a headword; an expression provided with a gloss.

The ancient sense of the word, to mean an assumption or premiss, rather than an intermediate conclusion, is now obsolete.

Leninism *n.* a theory in the Marxist tradition, outlined in the writings of V. I. Lenin (1870–1924), of the conditions for a revolutionary change from existing economic and political structures to a communist dictatorship. Such a dictatorship, according to the theory, will in turn be replaced eventually by a free, cooperative and happy socialist society where for the first time in history the free unfolding of the creative potentiality of every individual will be possible. The theory has two related components: an analysis of social and political structures and events, and recommendations for the strategy and tactics of the revolutionary struggle of workers and peasants. Critics have complained that in conflicts between morality and expediency, morality is always the loser in Leninist theory and practice.

Lesniewski /lɛʃ'njɛvskɪ (Po.)/, Stanislaw

(1886–1939) Polish logician and philosopher, professor of mathematics at Warsaw 1919–39, author of a general theory that combines logic and metaphysics. In logic, he is best known for his development of MEREOLOGY.

Lessing /ˈlɛsɪŋ/, Gotthold Ephraim (1729–81) the leading dramatist and literary theorist of the German Enlightenment, particularly noted for his *Laokoon* 1766 in which he discusses the relation between poetry and the plastic arts. In his aesthetic writings, he opposed the constraints of convention implicit both in the ideals of French classicism and in neo-classical idealization of the art of ancient Greece. In his theological writings, he rejected orthodox theology, arguing that historical events (like those narrated in the gospels) are contingent and that the accounts of them cannot be absolutely reliable. For these reasons they cannot form an adequate basis for faith. Unlike his friend Moses Mendelssohn, he believed in the overall progress of mankind and, taking up a theme anticipated by Tertullian and Joachim a Fiore, he saw the history of mankind as an educational process towards an ideal limit of perfection. *Die Erziehung des Menschengeschlechts* 1777–80 (The education of the human race) is a brief statement of this outlook. Interpreted in this way, the hope of religious believers had a foundation. His eloquent attacks on narrow-minded orthodoxy, inspired in part by his reading (and translation) of theologically undogmatic British writers like Shaftesbury and Hutcheson, exerted a powerful influence, and so did his fervent plea for religious toleration and the universal brotherhood of man in his play *Nathan the Wise* (1779) and other writings.

Leucippus /ljuːˈkɪpəs/ (*fl.* 450–420 BC) Leucippus was the first to propose a materialistic, atomistic metaphysics. Little is known about him. His ideas were taken up by Democritus and later by Epicurus and his school.

Leviathan /lɪˈvaɪəθən/ a monster, mentioned in a number of places in the Old Testament: Job 41,1–34; Psalms 74,14; 104,26; Isaiah 27,1; 51,9; Amos, 9,3. Hobbes used the name, alluding to Job, in the title to his major work (1651) to designate the 'mortal god' who is the sovereign in a state.

Levinas /levinas (Fr.)/, Emmanuel (1905–95) French-Jewish philosopher of Lithuanian origin, professor of philosophy at the Sorbonne. He placed ethical concerns and the inquiry into their transcendental presuppositions at the very centre of philosophy. A central point in his writings, among which are *Totalité et infini* 1961 (Totality and infinity) and *Autrement qu'être, ou au-delà de l'essence* 1974 (Otherwise than being, or beyond essence), is the revision of the idea of intersubjectivity, as shaped in a tradition that stretches from Descartes to Husserl, whose philosophy had a strong influence on Levinas. In that tradition, the basic concept is that of a subject: a mind which grasps what it confronts in experience and turns it into its (mental) content. In this picture of the mind, everything given to the mind is both something other than the mind but also the mind's own, something of which the mind takes possession. Levinas questions the assumption behind this picture, that everything is 'given' as a representation, as an intentional content. Instead, he is proposing another conception of the way a subject can stand in relations, a more direct way of relating, which has an obvious ethical dimension: the face-to-face relation to the other person. Such a relation is an ultimate fact which defies reduction. It is essentially something concrete, and cannot be described or prescribed by general statements or rules of conduct which are in their nature impersonal and abstract.

Lévi-Strauss /ˈlɛviˈstraʊs (Eng.); levistʀos (Fr.)/, Claude (1908–) French social anthropologist. In his pioneering theoretical works, e.g. *Les Structures élémentaires de la parenté* 1949 (The elementary structures of kinship) and *La Pensée sauvage* 1962 (The savage mind) he adopted from the linguistics of Saussure and Jakobson a structuralist approach, applying it to social relations rather than grammatical ones, and he used this to analyse how people are able to deal with and make sense of complicated relationships in their social life, e.g. kinship relations, conventions of social interaction, totemism, etc. There are also searching analyses in his writings, e.g. *Tristes Tropiques* 1955, of the very project of social anthropology and the aspects of contemporary Western society that lie behind it. He has exercised a major intellectual and cultural influence in post-war France and abroad.

Lévy-Bruhl /levibʀyl; levibʀul (Fr.)/, Lucien (1857–1939) French philosopher and social anthropologist. His early writings dealt with philosophy and its history. In *La Morale et la science des mœurs* 1903; rev edn 1910 (Morals and moral science) he argued, in the spirit of Comte, against traditional ethical theories, especially those with a theological or metaphysical slant, and in favour of a moral science that would engage in an empirical examination of social and psychological data. This would produce a proper basis for the general formulation and application of moral norms.

Inspired in part by Kant and Jacobi, he held the view that emotional-affective components can often be inextricably part of our cognitive states. It is only at a higher stage of theoretical reflection that we are able to analyse and clearly distinguish the different aspects. This stage is not reached in primitive society, and in this sense the primitive mind is 'pre-logical'. The difference is not innate, however, but due to the social structures that shape the individual's mind. Lévy-Bruhl's initial formulations about the primitive mind, daring in their generality, were revised in later writings: the emotional and non-rational character of certain experiences and beliefs is not confined to primitive peoples and does not characterize all their thought. In effect his theory is about mystical and magical thinking, no matter in what type of society it occurs.

Lewis /ˈluːɪs/, C(larence) I(rving) (1883–1964) American philosopher, who taught at Berkeley from 1911, and was professor at Harvard University 1920–53. He wrote major works in epistemology and ethics, e.g. *An Analysis of Knowledge and Valuation* 1946. His philosophy has a pragmatist tendency: the ultimate reasons for adopting a set of basic concepts or categories is convenience and usefulness. This also applies to the adoption of a system of logic. Lewis laid the basis for the modern study of MODAL LOGIC, first in a series of articles from 1911, and in *Symbolic Logic* (with C. H. Langford) 1932. His modal logic uses a concept of strict implication, which he defined in order to avoid the difficulties he saw as inherent in Russell's concept of material implication.

Lewis, David (1941–) professor at Princeton University, famed for his analytical work on convention, on counterfactuals, and on other topics in metaphysics, philosophy of mind and philosophy of language. In each of these areas it is frequently his ideas, presented with great clarity and elegance, that have originated new lines of inquiry. He is most widely known for his modal realism, according to which there is an infinite number of possible worlds, none of which causally influences any other. The actual world, our world, differs from the ones that we call 'possible worlds' only in that it is the one where we are. The concept of COUNTERPARTS is important in this theory, and so is that of similarity or closeness, since his basic analysis of counterfactuals, i.e. statements like 'If A had been the case, then B would also have been the case', is that such a statement is true if and only if some world where A and B are the case is more similar to our world than any world where A and not-B are the case. Lewis analyses chance in terms of counterfactual dependence. In the philosophy of mind he advocates a functionalist kind of materialism. Among his writings are *Philosophical Papers I–II* 1983, 1986 and *On the Plurality of Worlds* 1986. FJ

lex (*sing.*); ***leges*** (*pl.*) Lat. a law; a legal system *n.*

lex talionis Lat. law of retaliation; a law that prescribes equality between crime and punishment: 'an eye for an eye, a tooth for a tooth'. Cf. Lev. 24:17–23.

liar paradox a paradox generated by a sentence which, actually or apparently, directly or indirectly, asserts its own falsity. Many examples have been discussed. The simplest are: (1) *This sentence is false*; and (2) the case in which someone says: '*What I am now saying is false*'. More complex examples are: (3) a card on one side of which is written '*The sentence on the other side of this card is false*' and on the other side of which is written '*The sentence on the other side of this card is true*'; and (4) the sentence '*There are exactly the same number of true and false sentences*', said when the only sentences that exist are this one itself, and three more: two that are uncontroversially true, and one that is uncontroversially false.

In each case the paradox arises because it seems possible to prove that the sentence in question is true if and only if it is false. In the case of (1), e.g., the argument runs: suppose that (1) is true; then what it asserts is so; but what it asserts is that (1) is false, hence (1) is false. Suppose now that (1) is false; then what it asserts is not so; but what it asserts is that (1) is false; hence (1) is not false, and so must be true.

Many purported solutions of the liar paradoxes have been offered. Most of them are of one or other of three types: (a) some hold that the 'liar sentences' are meaningless, on the ground that it makes no sense to suppose that one part of a sentence refers to the sentence of which it is a part; (b) others hold that the sentences are meaningful but are neither true nor false; (c) others again hold that they are false, and attempt to refute the arguments designed to show that if they are false they are true.

Liar paradoxes in one form or another have been discussed in ancient, medieval and modern times. An early version starts with: 'Epimenides the Cretan said that all Cretans are liars.' At no time has there been any consensus about how they should be solved. GH

liberal arts the three verbal arts of the TRIVIUM: grammar, logic (or dialectic) and rhetoric, and the four mathematical arts of the QUADRIVIUM: arithmetic, geometry, astronomy and music. Together they made up the school curriculum which by the ninth century had become widely adopted. JM

liberalism *n.* a set of ideas in social and political thought which emphasizes the value of individuals' rights, and individual freedom of choice and freedom from interference. The role of the state is primarily to protect these rights. This presupposes the rule of law and legal provisions for freedom of association, freedom of the press, freedom of religion, freedom to travel, freedom to choose a gainful occupation, etc.

Liberals have traditionally sought to *limit* the scope of state action and to prefer non-governmental initiatives to governmental ones, where this is feasible. An early application of liberal principles was the insistence on a separation of Church from state: religious affairs should be non-governmental. Liberals tend to prefer an educational system in which non-governmental schools and universities play an important part. Similarly, they tend to prefer letting non-governmental agencies assume responsibility, partly or wholly, for health care and social welfare.

Locke, Montesquieu, Adam Smith and Kant can be regarded as precursors or early representatives of liberalism. The word began to be used in the late 1790s. Among early liberal thinkers who advocated very narrow limits to state action were Wilhelm von Humboldt and Herbert Spencer. A more moderate line was taken by Benjamin Constant and John Stuart Mill.

In contemporary usage in the United States, 'liberalism' and its cognates are frequently used for political views which favour an increased scope for state action in areas such as education, health care, and social welfare. This is a consequence of the liberal principle that the protection of individuals' rights is an essential function of government, in combination with an increase in the number of goods and services that are thought of as rights, and an increase in the number of ills and impositions (poverty, illness, negative discrimination, lack of education) that have come to be regarded as violations of rights.

A shift of this kind was noted by Herbert Spencer already in *The Man Versus the State* 1884, which makes a case for individualistic liberalism and minimal government. He complained that the Liberal Party in Britain increasingly supported government intervention, and that it was their Tory conservative opponents, traditionally in favour of state power, who had turned round to be the driving force in the 'Liberty and Property Defence League'.

libertarianism *n.* **1** the view which, in opposition to determinism, asserts that it is possible for human agents to act freely, independently of necessitating causes. **2** an extreme liberal view, which favours very narrow limits to state action and assumes that needs are best satisfied and conflicts best resolved by market mechanisms. **3** an outlook prevalent in circles influenced by John Anderson, politically radical, anti-bourgeois, anti-Marxist, and anti-philistine. It mainly flourished in Sydney from the late 1930s until the late 1960s.

libertinism *n.* free-thinking. The term was first used in seventeenth-century France, to designate deism and materialism. It was, however, often used polemically, with the clear implication that free-thinkers were irreligious and that (according to Cotgrave's dictionary of 1611) they favoured 'epicurism, sensualitie, licentiousnesse, dissolutenesse'.

libido /lɪˈbiːdəʊ/ (Lat. desire; lust) *n.* sexual desire. In Freudian and Jungian theory, the term covers all psychic energy, drives and desires at the instinctual level.

Lichtenberg /ˈlɪçtənbɛrk (Gm.)/, Georg Christoph (1742–99) German physicist, mathematician and philosopher, professor in Göttingen from 1767. He displayed brilliant wit in his philosophical aphorisms and in his satirical writings against pretentiousness and theoretical flights of fancy (e.g. against Lavater). His writings contain interesting anticipations of the linguistic turn in philosophy.

linear order(ing) a binary relation which is REFLEXIVE, ANTI-SYMMETRICAL, TRANSITIVE, and CONNECTED. A **strict linear order** is asymmetrical, transitive, and connected. For example, among the integers, the relation $\leq$ is a linear order, and the relation $<$ is a strict linear order.

linguistic philosophy an approach to philosophical inquiry which gives careful attention to actual linguistic usage as a method of dealing with the problems of philosophy. The result may be that the problem is solved, or that it is dissolved. This approach flourished in Britain in the post-war period, notably in Oxford. Among its leading practitioners can be mentioned John Wisdom, Gilbert Ryle, J. L. Austin, Paul Grice, P. F. Strawson and Alan White. The challenge to it in E. Gellner, *Words and Things* 1959 (rev. edn 1979) provoked controversy.

Lipps, Theodor (1851–1914) German philosopher, particularly interested in psychology and aesthetics. He taught in Bonn, Breslau and, from 1894, Munich. He is best known for his concept of EMPATHY which he used in his theory of knowledge and which played a central part in his aesthetics.

litotes /ˈlaɪtəʊtiːz; lɪˈtəʊtiːz/ (Gr. *litos* small) *n. sing.* a figure of speech: understatement by way of negation. For example, creating this new dictionary of philosophy is 'not a bad idea' – this may be a way of saying that it is indeed an excellent initiative.

Some writers restrict the use of the term to understatements of a particular form: a superlative is replaced by the negation of a contrary positive, or a positive is replaced by the negation of a contrary superlative. For example: describing a *most impressive* performance as a performance *not to be scoffed at*, or describing an *indifferent* performance as *not being the most outstanding*.

Lobachevsky /ləbəˈtʃɛfskij (Rus.)/, Nikolai Ivanovich (1792–1856) Russian mathematician, professor in Kazan. He was the first to develop a non-Euclidean geometry in which Euclid's parallel postulate is not included.

Locke, John (1632–1704) one of the most influential philosophers in the history of modern thought. His main philosophical works are *An Essay Concerning Human Understanding* 1690 which is mainly, although not exclusively, concerned with the theory of knowledge and philosophy of science, and the *Two Treatises of Government* 1689 which contains his political theory. Locke also made major contributions in a number of other areas, including educational theory, philosophy of religion, and economics.

Locke studied scholastic metaphysics and logic at Christ Church, Oxford, but took a keen interest in contemporary French philosophers like Descartes and his critic Gassendi. He was interested, too, in the developing experimental sciences and worked with Robert Boyle. Locke's conservative political views changed during his association with the first Earl of Shaftesbury, who led the opposition against Charles II in the early 1680s and founded the Whig party. After the Glorious Revolution 1688 Locke returned from Holland, where he had lived since 1683 for political reasons.

By the mid-1690s Locke had gained fame as a philosopher. In addition to his *Two Treatises* and *Essay*, he had published *A Letter Concerning Toleration* 1689, the influential *Some Thoughts Concerning Education* 1693, and a theological work entitled *The Reasonableness of Christianity* 1695. He continued to revise and make substantial additions to his main work, the *Essay*, of which the fourth edition appeared in 1700.

Although the *Essay* is mainly concerned with what is now called epistemology (theory of knowledge) and philosophy of science, it discusses a number of other issues, e.g. questions in ethics and what is known today as philosophy of mind. Apart from various original theories on particular topics, the originality of the *Essay* as a whole consists in the very project of a critical epistemology and in the realization of this project. Philosophers before Locke, especially Descartes, had asked questions about knowledge, but Locke was the first in the modern period to commit himself programmatically to the question of the possibility of knowledge and to set out to answer this question systematically and in detail.

The *Essay* consists of four main parts or 'books'. In the first, Locke criticizes and rejects the then widely held view about the origin of our knowledge, according to which fundamental theoretical and practical principles and ideas are innate. For Locke, knowledge must be acquired. Our mental faculties (perception, reason, etc.) are natural to us and may be said to be innate; however, it is only through the proper application of these faculties that we can acquire knowledge itself. Locke expounds his own theory of knowledge in Books II to IV. Book II deals with the origin of our 'ideas' (i.e. mental contents); these are the 'materials of Reason and Knowledge'. Locke argues that all ideas are ultimately derived from experience; and experience is twofold: external experience ('sensation') and inner experience ('reflection'). Through sensation we receive ideas of the sensible qualities of physical objects. Through reflection we receive ideas of the operations of the mind, such as 'perceiving', 'thinking', 'doubting', 'willing', and so on. However, our ideas are not restricted to what we receive directly from those two sources. The human understanding can operate on the original material given through sensation and reflection: it can apply operations such as comparing, combining, and abstracting and thereby form new ideas – 'infinitely beyond what *Sensation* or *Reflection* furnished it with'.

According to Locke, the ideas we receive directly through sensation and reflection are simple ideas, i.e. they are not further analysable units of thought. Those ideas which we form by applying mental operations such as combining, comparing, etc. Locke terms *complex* ideas. He further distinguishes between different kinds of complex ideas: between ideas of substances, of relations, and ideas which he calls 'modes' (which unlike ideas of substances are not meant to copy external reality, e.g. mathematical ideas and moral ideas).

In Book IV Locke deals with the question of how the understanding constructs knowledge out of its ideas. Here he distinguishes between intuitive, demonstrative and sensitive knowledge: (1) intuitive knowledge is immediate and does not require proof or mediation of other ideas; it is characterized by the highest degree of certainty. Thus, we know intuitively that each particular idea in our mind is what it is and that it is distinct from all other ideas. Locke also holds that we have intuitive knowledge of the existence of the self; (2) demonstrative knowledge is, by contrast, mediate knowledge. The capacity of the mind to acquire demonstrative knowledge is reason. Locke's prime example of demonstrative knowledge is mathematics. Through (3) sensitive knowledge we are assured of the existence of particular external objects. However, although Locke argues that there is no reason to doubt the *existence* of the external world, he is more sceptical about our knowledge of the nature or *essence* of the external world.

We have ideas of the *qualities* of external objects through sensation; but not all of these ideas are copies of something that exists in the objects themselves. In Book II Locke distinguishes between *primary* and *secondary qualities*. This distinction is part of a larger hypothesis about the nature of matter: the atomist or *'corpuscular' hypothesis*. Locke took over atomism and the distinction between primary and secondary qualities from his friend Robert Boyle. According to this hypothesis, there is one universal matter which is common to all bodies. This universal matter consists of tiny imperceptible particles ('corpuscles' or 'atoms'), and the properties of the various bodies are caused by the interaction of these particles or corpuscles.

Primary qualities are qualities such as solidity, extension, figure and mobility: these qualities are essential to all bodies as such (including atoms); and they can cause ideas in our mind which represent them. Thus, there is solidity in the object itself which corresponds to our idea of solidity. Ideas of secondary qualities, in contrast, do not represent something that exists in the object itself, although they are caused by powers inherent in the internal corpuscular structures of bodies. These ideas are, e.g. colour- and sound-perceptions, and tastes and smells. There is no blueness in the object which corresponds to our perception of blue. What corresponds to our perception of blue in the object is the internal 'corpuscular' structure of the object which has the power to cause, or at least contribute to the causation of, the perception of blue in our mind. Thus, Locke explains the cause of ideas of secondary qualities, such as colour-ideas, in terms of an imperceptible ('corpuscular') cause in the external world. Ideas of both primary and secondary qualities are elements of our complex ideas of physical substances such as horse, stone, iron, gold. According to Locke, we form ideas of particular kinds of substances by combining various ideas of qualities, behaviour, etc. into a complex idea. For example, we form our ordinary idea of iron as the idea of a body of a particular colour, weight and hardness, by combining these ideas (of colour, weight, etc.) into a complex idea and attaching to it the name 'iron'. Words or 'names' are important here: the term 'iron', for instance, unites the various simple ideas into a permanent unity. It is only through words that we are able to refer to the same idea at different times. Locke emphasizes the importance of precision and clarity in language, and in Book III he discusses the function that language fulfils for the constitution of knowledge.

Locke terms the nature of a thing as represented in our complex idea its *nominal essence*. He distinguishes between nominal and *real essence*: a real essence is the inner constitution of a thing which gives rise to its observable qualities. He interprets the real essence of physical substances in terms of the corpuscular hypothesis: the cause of the observable qualities of physical substances is to be understood in terms of its corpuscular structure. However, the real essence of any given physical object is not known to us since the internal corpuscular structure is beyond our experience, which is confined to observable qualities: neither reason nor experience can discover the real essence of bodies. Our ideas (nominal essences) do not reach the real essences. Locke concludes that we cannot have general and absolutely certain knowledge of physical substances. Yet he holds that although we cannot attain absolute certainty here, there are nevertheless good reasons for studying nature as long as this study is experience-based. Through 'rational and regular experiments' we may make progress and arrive at an increasingly precise description of natural phenomena and processes. On the basis of our experiential study we are justified in forming hypotheses, i.e. explanatory models which in turn may guide our further research and lead to new discoveries. Locke also believes that the experience-based study of nature is useful for mankind: he cites the invention of printing and the discovery of the use of the compass as examples. However, he emphasizes that our statements about nature are only ever probable and can never attain the status of absolute certainty.

Locke believes that absolute certainty *is* possible in mathematics and ethics. Mathematical ideas and moral ideas (Locke's 'modes') are not meant to be copies of things existing independently of us: what a triangle is, does not lie in the inaccessible constitution of external reality. For example, reason can discover the properties of a triangle on the basis of *our idea* of a triangle (a figure which contains space within three straight lines): reason can show with absolute certainty that the internal angles of such a figure equal two right angles. Here our idea contains the real as well as the nominal essence; and that is why we can attain demonstrative and absolutely certain knowledge in this area. Since moral ideas (such as obligation, theft, murder, justice) are also 'modes', Locke argues that it must be possible to establish a purely rational system of ethics.

Thus, Locke's position in epistemology lies between that of the Cartesians and the scholastics on the one hand, and the radical sceptics on the other. He rejects the former's overconfidence in the power of human reason as well as the latter's claim that we cannot know anything. His position is often (and appropriately) described as moderate or mitigated scepticism. Locke's frequent appeal to experience as a source of our ideas is the reason why he is often called an empiricist. This label can be misleading, since he does not believe that knowledge is directly derived from experience; rather, he believes that knowledge is constituted through the understanding which makes use of the experience-based ideas.

As indicated above, Locke argues that demonstrative knowledge is possible in ethics as well as in mathematics. His views and arguments on ethics occur in various places in the *Essay* and in a number of tracts and notes published posthumously. As understood by Locke, ethics is concerned with giving a systematic account of absolutely valid and universally binding normative principles of right action. Human reason can, in principle, discover these moral principles; but it cannot itself be the source of these principles: objective and universally binding principles must be of divine origin. Therefore, Locke refers to the moral law as divine law; and it follows from this that reason is not the only means of discovering moral laws. The system of moral laws which can, in principle, be known through reason can also be known through revelation: the Gospel contains such a body of moral principles.

In his theological work, *The Reasonableness of Christianity*, Locke emphasizes the ethical aspect of Christianity. He holds that, on examination, those moral rules which may be found in the Bible agree with what reason discovers. Locke develops his thoughts about the relationship between reason and revelation, i.e. the fundamental ideas of his *philosophy of religion*, in the *Essay*: there are truths which can be discovered through both reason and revelation (e.g. moral laws, and the existence of God). Statements which contradict reason must not be accepted, even if someone claims that revelation is their source (for example, the statement that one and the same body is at two different places at the same time contradicts reason and, therefore, cannot be part of divine revelation). Locke holds that those beliefs which neither coincide with nor contradict reason, but are *above* reason, constitute religious faith proper (e.g. the belief in resurrection of the dead). However, even here reason fulfils an indispensable function: reason must decide whether something is a revelation, and examine the meaning of the words in which the revelation is expressed. As Locke declares: 'Reason must be our last judge and guide in everything.'

In *The Reasonableness of Christianity* Locke argues that only a few beliefs are essential to Christianity (such as belief in God and in Jesus as God's son and the Messiah). And since a Christian need subscribe to a few fundamental articles of faith only, Locke can argue for the toleration of those Protestants who dissent from the Anglican state church. This he does in the *Letter Concerning Toleration*. Here, Locke sharply distinguishes 'the business of civil government from that of religion'; religion has to do 'with the care of the soul'; the function of civil society is to protect the individual's right to life, liberty and property. The latter is explained in more detail in the *Two Treatises of Government* (see below).

Locke argues that knowledge of the moral law through reason and revelation does not, on its own, motivate us to *act* in accordance with that law. He points out that people's convictions and motives are formed by 'education, company, and customs of their country'. We are by nature rational beings: that is, in principle, we are capable of acting in accordance with what reason tells us; but in order to be able to exercise this capacity we need to be educated appropriately, so that we develop the motivation to live virtuously. Locke connects his views on ethics and education in *Some Thoughts Concerning Education*. The main aims of education are 'virtue, wisdom, breeding, and learning'. The most important of these is virtue: the aim is to educate the child so that 'it may be disposed to consent to nothing, but what may be suitable to the dignity and excellency of a rational creature'. This aim can be achieved by making use of concrete examples, and by giving reasons for evaluating the actions of others. Locke says that the parents, too, should 'consult their own reason, in the education of their children, rather than wholly . . . rely upon old custom'.

In 1680–82 (there is some dispute about the date) Locke composed, but did not publish, his *Two Treatises of Government*. He wrote this book against the background of the attempt (in the event unsuccessful) by Shaftesbury and his party to exclude James, Charles's Catholic brother (and indeed any Catholic), from succeeding to the throne. However, the importance of the *Two Treatises* goes beyond this historical context. The work contains a number of original doctrines on particular topics, such as Locke's now famous theory that the origin of private property is in the mixing of one's labour with the object, independently of agreements with others. The fundamental, related questions that Locke addresses in the book are these: what legitimizes *political authority*? and what function does political authority have to fulfil? Locke puts forward his own answer in the *Second Treatise*. In the *First Treatise* he discusses and criticizes the theory according to which monarchs have political authority by 'divine right', proposed in Filmer's *Patriarcha*, which had been published in 1680 to promote the Stuart cause. In the *Second Treatise* Locke's concern is 'the true original, extent and end of civil government'. In order to show what the function of political authority is, he first explains what rights and duties human beings 'naturally' have, independently of and prior to all positive law'. About this 'law of nature' he says: 'reason, which is that law, teaches all mankind . . . that being all equal and independent, no one ought to harm another in his life, health, liberty, or possessions'. In other words, each individual has a right to life, liberty and property, and it is the job of the political authority to protect these rights of the individual: this is what legitimizes political authority.

Locke's argument that the people have a right of resistance against unjust authority is crucial to his theory. He defines the relationship between the people and political authority in terms of the notion of *trust*. Whenever the political authority breaks that trust and tries to 'reduce [the people] . . . to slavery under arbitrary power', it forfeits the power the people had put in its hands, 'and it devolves to the people, who have a right to resume their original liberty, and, by the establishment of a new legislative . . . provide for their own safety and security, which is the end for which they are in society'. The people have a right of resistance and even revolution when the political authority no longer fulfils its proper function, that is, protecting the rights of individual citizens to life, liberty and property.

The impact of Locke's thought on subsequent philosophy has been immense. In the eighteenth century, Locke's thought was at the centre of philosophical discussions. By emphasizing the primacy of critical reason in all areas, Locke became one of the first and leading figures of the Enlightenment. He influenced not only philosophical debates, but also developing disciplines like psychology and educational theory. Further, Locke's philosophy had a strong effect on academic thought as well as on the educated public. Even today, Locke's views and arguments are often the starting point of debates concerning a number of central philosophical issues.

Locke's writings are available in many different editions. The best edition of the *Essay* is that of Nidditch, of the *Two Treatises* that of Laslett. UT

locutionary acts *See* SPEECH ACTS.

logic *n.* **1** the inquiry which has for its object the principles of correct reasoning. **2** In current usage, *logic* is chiefly the inquiry into *deductive* reasoning, i.e. into inferences in which the conclusion follows *necessarily* from the premisses. **3** In the nineteenth century *logic* was given quite a wide signification. Works on logic by Mill, Lotze and others dealt at length with epistemology and scientific methodology.

In common parlance, *logic* is often used as a synonym to *reasoning* or *argument*. For instance, 'I disagree with his logic' simply means that I reject his reasoning. This usage is avoided in philosophical contexts.

logic, deductive *See* DEDUCTION.

logic, deontic *See* DEONTIC LOGIC.

logic, dialectical The concept of a dialectical logic was developed by Friedrich Engels on the basis of Hegelianism. He argued that it was superior to standard logic, which, he alleged, was static and one-sided. The proposed laws of dialectical logic were supposed to be both rules for valid reasoning and general laws of development and change. *See also* MATERIALISM, DIALECTICAL AND HISTORICAL.

logic, dialethic *See* DIALETHIC LOGIC.

logic, inductive *See* INDUCTION; INDUCTIVE LOGIC.

logic, many-valued general name for systems of logic in which the values which propositions can have include not only the 'classical' values *true* and *false* but one or more others as well. The usual way of constructing such a system involves (1) specifying a set of such values; (2) giving for each operator a *matrix* (a truth-table) stating the value of a formula formed by means of it, given the value(s) of its arguments; and (3) defining validity by *designating* one or more of the values and ruling that a formula is to count as valid if and only if it has a designated value for every possible assignment of values to the variables in it.

An example of a *three-valued* logic, due to Łukasiewicz, may be sketched as follows: (a) the values are 1, ½ and 0 ('1' and '0' are thought of as meaning 'true' and 'false' respectively); (b) matrices: for negation (~):

~A has the value 0 if A has the value 1, 1 if A has 0, and ½ if A has ½. For conjunction (&): A & B has the value of A or that of B, whichever is the less. For disjunction (∨): A ∨ B has the value of A or that of B, whichever is the greater. For implication: A ⊃ B has the value 0 if A has 1 and B has 0, the value ½ if either A has 1 and B has ½ or A has ½ and B has 0, and the value 1 in all other cases. *See* Table 11; (c) the sole designated value is 1. (In this logic, neither p ∨ ~p nor ~(p & ~p) is valid, but p ⊃ p is valid.) A number of other three-valued systems have been constructed, usually differing from the above by modifying the matrices in various ways.

In a many-valued logic the value or values other than those interpreted as *true* or *false* have been interpreted in various ways; e.g. in a three-valued logic the intermediate value may be taken to mean 'half true', 'indeterminate', 'undecidable', or in other ways. The matrices given are likely to be intended to reflect the interpretation the author has in mind.

Table 11 Truth-tables for a three-valued logic

A	B	~A	A & B	A ∨ B	A ⊃ B
1	1	0	1	1	1
1	½	0	½	1	½
1	0	0	0	1	0
½	1	½	½	1	1
½	½	½	½	½	1
½	0	½	0	½	½
0	1	1	0	1	1
0	½	1	0	½	1
0	0	1	0	0	1

An infinite-valued logic, designed to express the idea that propositions can have any degree of truth ranging from completely true to completely false, can be obtained by generalizing Łukasiewicz's rules as follows: (1) the values are to consist of all fractions from 1 to 0 inclusive; (2) where the value of A is x, that of ~A is 1 − x. The matrices for & and ∨ are as in Łukasiewicz's system above. For A ⊃ B: let the values of A and B be x and y respectively; then the value of A ⊃ B is 1 if x < y and 1 − x + y if x > y; (3) as before, the sole designated value is 1. GH

logic, modal *See* MODAL LOGIC.

logic, paraconsistent *See* PARACONSISTENT LOGIC.

logic, quantum *See* QUANTUM LOGIC.

logic, relevance/relevant *See* RELEVANCE LOGIC.

logical atomism an ontological theory, according to which reality is ultimately composed of atomic facts. The existence of one atomic fact does not logically imply the existence of any other atomic fact. The theory was articulated by Bertrand Russell in the 1910s and 1920s (although developed in manuscripts as early as 1901), by Wittgenstein in the *Tractatus Logico-Philosophicus*, by G. E. Moore, John Wisdom, etc.

Most logical atomists took atomic facts to be simple empirical data, and the manner in which they combined to form molecular facts was taken to be truth-functional. That is, atomic facts are represented by atomic propositions, and molecular facts by truth-functional compounds of atomic propositions.

Philosophy would naturally have analysis as its method: analysis in the sense that the atomic constituents of the object of a philosophical inquiry, and the way they combined, would be put on display. The theory was given its name by Russell in 1918, to underscore the contrast with what may be called 'logical holism'; i.e. the view that the world is such that no part is genuinely known unless the whole is.

logical consequence In general, to say that B is a logical consequence of A is another way of saying that B logically follows from A. In relation to systems of logic, however, consequence is given more precise definitions: **1** syntactic consequence (often symbolized by a single turnstile): $A_1, A_2 \ldots, A_n \vdash B$ means that the rules of the formal system in question allow a derivation of the formula B from the formulae $A_1, A_2 \ldots, A_n$. **2** semantic consequence (often symbolized by a double turnstile): $A_1, A_2 \ldots, A_n \vDash B$ means that there is no interpretation of the formulae such that all the A's are true and B is false.

In the usual systems of elementary logic these two consequence-relations apply jointly. In other words, $A \vdash B$ if and only if $A \vDash B$. But in more advanced systems this is not possible. (This is a corollary of Gödel's incompleteness theorem for arithmetic.)

logical constant Logical constants are words like 'not', 'and', 'or', 'all', 'necessarily' and their symbolic counterparts, which represent a feature of an expression's form, in contrast to its variable content. For example, in an expression that has the logical form ($p \vee q$), '$\vee$' is a constant expressing the disjunction of two propositions.

Although we seem to have an intuitive grasp of this notion, it is difficult to provide an uncontroversial explicit definition.

logical construction The concept of a logical construction plays an important part in logical atomism, logical positivism, behaviourism, and other kinds of reductionist theory. If statements about M can be reduced to a set of atomic statements about $A_1, A_2 \ldots A_n$, then M is said to be a logical construction out of the A's. Thus, tables and chairs might be constructions out of simple sensory experiences; nations might be constructions out of individuals and legal norms (which in turn might be constructions out of simpler elements); and the statement that the average family has 2.2 children should not normally be taken at face value.

logical empiricism another name for logical POSITIVISM.

logical falsity *See* LOGICAL TRUTH.

logical form A distinction can be made between form and content of propositions. For instance, *All swans are white* and *All ravens are black* share a form that can be represented as *All S is P*. Similarly for arguments:

$$\frac{\text{No raven is a white bird}}{\text{No white bird is a raven}}$$

has a form

$$\frac{\text{No S is P}}{\text{No P is S}}$$

Two propositions A and B have a form in common if B can be obtained from A by replacing some part of A that is not a logical constant with another expression of the same logical category (i.e. replacement of singular terms with singular terms, predicates with predicates, propositional letters with propositional letters, etc.).

It can be misleading to talk of *the* form of a proposition or of an argument. There can be more than one. For instance, *All swans are white* has the form *All S is P*, but also the form *p*. And the statement: 'if someone laughs, everyone will laugh' has the forms:

p;
if p, then q;
if $\exists xFx$ *then* $\forall xFx$*;*

(and by considering the tenses of the verbs)

$(\forall t)(t \text{ after now} \supset ((\exists x)(Lxt) \supset (\exists t')(\forall x)(Lxt' \mathbin{\&} t' \text{ coincides with or is shortly after } t)))$.

This shows that if one is to talk of 'the' logical form of a proposition at all, additional assumptions are needed, and the same applies to argument forms. It is worth noting that an argument is not invalid just because it has *some* invalid form. It is invalid only if it has *no* valid form.

In the examples above it is easy to grasp the difference between form and content intuitively, but to give a general characterization of the difference has proved difficult.

Analytical philosophers such as Bertrand Russell, Rudolf Carnap, Gilbert Ryle, etc. distinguished the *grammatical* form of a sentence from its *logical* form, claiming that many philosophical problems arise because we are deceived by the grammatical form of sentences, and are solved by discerning the logical form of the proposition expressed by the sentence. An illustration of this is provided by Russell's theory of definite descriptions. In making this distinction they were re-stating a point often made in the Middle Ages.

logically proper name Names like 'Socrates', 'Napoleon', 'Pegasus' are commonly regarded as proper names, but as analysed by Bertrand Russell they are disguised descriptions; he suggested that only indexicals like 'I' and 'this' can be logically proper names, in the sense that they refer to something directly without any implicit description.

logical positivism *See* POSITIVISM; VIENNA CIRCLE.

logical semantics, logical syntax The syntax of a formal system consists of the rules that specify what is to count as a well-formed formula and what is to count as a sentence, together with rules of inference, specifying which formulae are theorems of the system.

The semantics of a formal system consists of the rules specifying when a formula or sentence counts as true (or true-in-an-interpretation).

logical truth The statement 'Either it is raining or it is not raining', to take an example, is *logically true* because it has the form 'p or not-p', which is a valid principle of logic. In general, a statement S is logically true if and only if S is a substitution-instance of a valid principle of logic. It follows that if a statement is logically true then it is necessarily true.

On the other hand, to take an example, the statement 'it is not the case that either it is raining or it is not raining' is *logically false* because it has the form 'Not (p or not-p)' which is the negation of a valid principle of logic (and is indeed equivalent to the contradiction 'p and not-p'). In general, a statement S is logically false if and only if S is a substitution-instance of a negation of a valid principle of logic. It follows that if a statement is logically false then it is necessarily false.

Contingent statements are neither logically true nor logically false. But are all non-contingent statements logically true or logically false? Examples like *All brothers are male* suggest that this is not the case.

There is in older writers a usage, now obsolete, which contrasts logical truth or falsity with moral (or ethical) truth or falsity. In this sense, a logically true statement presents the facts as they are, while a logically false statement misrepresents them; a morally (or ethically) true statement is sincerely made, while a false statement of that kind misrepresents what the speaker thinks.

logica vetus, logica nova, logica modernorum The *logica vetus* (old logic) included only the logical texts which alone were available up to *c.* 1130: Porphyry's *Isagoge*, Aristotle's *Categories* and *De interpretatione*, and the logical textbooks and commentaries of Boethius. The rest of Aristotle's logic – the *De sophisticis elenchis*, *Topics* and *Prior* and *Posterior Analytics* – which came into use gradually from *c.* 1130 was known as the *logica nova* (new logic). The new branches of logic, unknown in ancient times, which were elaborated from the twelfth century onwards, were called the *logica modernorum* (contemporary logic): among them were the theory of the properties of terms, which examines the 'supposition' of terms and the theory of *consequentiae* (entailments). JM

logicism *n.* **1** (in philosophy of mathematics) Frege's view, subsequently adopted by Russell, Carnap and others, that arithmetic can be reduced to logic. **2** anti-PSYCHOLOGISM, in the interpretation of the nature of logic; or in the interpretation of Kant's theory of knowledge.

logistic(s) *n. sing.* formal logic. This sense was common in the early twentieth century, but has since become obsolete. The current sense of *logistics* is different: organization of the provision of goods and facilities (especially in military or business administration).

logocentrism *n.* **1** In Ludwig Klages's irrationalist philosophy, logocentrism is the shallow, mechanistic, rational, scientific attitude, which is indifferent or hostile to everything living and vibrant. **2** In Jacques Derrida's philosophy, logocentrism is the pervasive but profoundly mistaken assumption that speech is prior to writing. He complains that writing is repressed in Western thought. The mistake is said to consist in the assumption that there is something outside 'the text' that gives it a fixed meaning – an assumption said to be common to all forms of idealism.

logomachy /lɒ'gɒməkɪ/ (Gr. *logomachia* battle of words) *n.* a merely verbal dispute.

logorrhea /lɒgə'rɪə/ (Gr. *logos-* + *rhein* to flow) *n.* inability to stem one's flow of words; excessive verbosity.

logos Gr. an utterance, an account, a discourse, a thought, a reason why, the faculty of reason, etc. *n.*

-logy a word-element derived from the Greek *LOGOS*. Words ending in -logy usually denote inquiry into, or theory of, a particular subject-matter. Epistemology is theory of knowledge; anthropology is the study of human beings; sociology is the study of human society. Methodology is the study of method, but note that scientific methodology is not the scientific study of method, but the study of scientific method.

Sometimes 'methodology' is used where 'method' would be preferable. Similarly, 'psychology' is used where in fact 'psyche', 'mind' or 'mental life' is meant. There is a distinction between an inquiry and the object of inquiry.

lottery paradox In a lottery with, say, 1000 tickets and one prize,

> it is unlikely that ticket No. 1 will win
> it is unlikely that ticket No. 2 will win
> it is unlikely that ticket No. 3 will win
> . . . .
> . . . .
> it is unlikely that ticket No. 999 will win
> it is unlikely that ticket No. 1000 will win

Therefore, for any ticket it is unlikely that it will win. And yet, it is certain that one ticket will win the prize!

There has been a lively discussion of this paradox since it was first formulated by

Henry Kyburg in *Probability and the Logic of Rational Belief* 1961.

Lotze /ˈlɔtsə (Gm.)/, Rudolf Hermann (1817–81) German philosopher who held the philosophy chair in Göttingen after Herbart from 1844 to 1879. He protested against the contemporary emphasis on epistemology, because its preoccupation with the possibility of knowledge led to a neglect of the search for actual knowledge. 'The constant whetting of the knife is tedious if it is not proposed to cut anything with it', he wrote in his *Metaphysics* 1879. He rejected vitalism, and defended a mechanistic conception of nature as a basis for science. He did, however, combine this with a teleological metaphysics: nature as a whole can be understood in purely mechanical terms, but it is part of a wider system which is imbued with higher values and purposes. This cannot be strictly argued for, but 'I am still convinced that I am on the right track in seeking the ground of that which *is* in that which *ought to be*'. This is why the existence of the world can become meaningful to us. Within this metaphysics, religious and moral beliefs could also be accommodated. The assumption of an underlying, non-material, absolute being is also, he thought, necessary to explain the possibility of change and causation in the world. In aesthetics, he anticipated Lipps's theory of empathy. His *Microcosmos* 1856, written in a popular style, was very widely read in its time.

Lovejoy /ˈlʌvdʒɒɪ/, Arthur O(ncken) (1873–1962) American philosopher, historian of ideas, first editor of the *Journal of History of Ideas*. He initiated a new approach to intellectual history, by avoiding broad classifications, for instance in terms of major '-isms'. Instead, he gave close attention to 'root ideas' and to their thematic recurrence over time. This also meant that the excessive focusing on a handful of great thinkers was rejected, in favour of an analysis of broader currents of thought. His best-known works are *The Great Chain of Being* 1936 and *Essays in the History of Ideas* 1948.

Lovelock /ˈlʌvlɒk/, James *See* GAIA HYPOTHESIS.

Löwenheim-Skolem theorem The theorem says that any set of statements in a first-order language which has an infinite model also has a denumerably infinite model.

One application of the theorem is to set theory, which is a theory in a first-order language.

Lucretius /luːˈkriːʃəs/ (*c.* 95–*c.* 54 BC) Titus Lucretius Carus, Roman philosopher, was the author of *De rerum natura* (On the nature of things), a major philosophical treatise written in Latin hexameters. It is an exposition of the materialistic philosophy of Epicurus. Various natural phenomena are explained by their natural causes, in opposition to explanations of a mythical or superstitious kind, favoured by the credulous. An important theme is the critique of religion, summed up in the famous line (Book I, V.101): '*tantum religio potuit suadere malorum*' (so powerful was religion in persuading to evil deeds). Epicurus is hailed as a benefactor of mankind, a liberator from the anguish and misery caused by superstitious terror of divine powers.

ludic (Lat. *ludus* play) *adj.* playful; pertaining to playing.

Lukács /ˈluːkætʃ/, Georg (1885–1971) Hungarian Marxist philosopher and aesthetic theorist. His *Geschichte und Klassenbewusstsein* 1923 (History and class consciousness) has been regarded as a major contribution to Marxist theory, although he disavowed much of it in the early 1930s when it encountered Stalinist criticism. Instead of the basis/superstructure model of analysis, Lukács gave a Hegelianizing interpretation of Marx, in which an important role is played by the concepts of reification and alienation. This interpretation turned out to be in tune with Marx's *Economic-Philosophical Manuscripts* of 1844, which were then unknown and not published until the early 1930s. In this sense Lukács anticipated a version of Marxist humanism that subsequently gained a considerable following. His formulation and lifelong defence of the doctrine of socialist realism in literature and the arts was widely influential in the cultural politics of the countries of the Soviet bloc.

Łukasiewicz /luːkə'sɛvɪtʃ (Eng.); wuka'ʃevit-ʃ (Po.)/, Jan (1878–1956) Polish logician, professor at Warsaw; he spent the post-war years in Dublin. He created (in 1917) the first many-valued logic (LOGIC, MANY-VALUED) and was also the inventor of the bracket-free notation in formal logic, known as the POLISH NOTATION. He was the first to subject the writings of ancient and medieval logicians to investigation informed by modern logic, bringing to light theories of great interest and showing up shortcomings in the standard treatises on the history of logic. Thus, he discovered that the Stoics had in fact anticipated modern propositional logic. His pioneering treatise on Aristotle's syllogistics presented it as a consistent and complete axiomatized system in which the syllogistic forms occur as theorems.

Lullus, Raymundus (*c.* 1235–1315) Franciscan scholar. He devoted himself to the conversion of Muslims, and to the struggle against Islam and Averroism, attacking the doctrine of double truth which he attributed also to Siger of Brabant and Boethius of Dacia. Among his many learned works, his *Ars Magna* attracted attention for many centuries. It outlines a series of basic categories and concepts, which in turn allow for a vast number of combinations. This may have been a way of systematizing existing knowledge, although there are occasional hints that it could also be used as a method of acquiring new knowledge. It has been argued, however, that the aim was only to serve purposes of memorization and exposition, and not the same as Leibniz's, i.e. to establish a basis for deductions.

Luther, Martin (1483–1546) A monk in the order of St Augustine, and a professor of theology at the University of Wittenberg, Luther stressed in his theology the doctrine of justification by faith alone. He was also critical of certain practices in the Church, e.g. the trading in indulgences. On All Saints' Eve 1517 he spiked on the door of the Castle Church at Wittenberg 95 theses, i.e. propositions put up for disputation. These were soon widely circulated and triggered the chain of events through which he became the instigator of the Protestant Reformation.

Lyceum (Gr. *Lykeion*) the place in Athens where Aristotle taught. According to Aulus Gellius (*Noctes Atticae* 20,5), the more advanced teaching was acroamatic and took place in the mornings. Later in the day, the instruction was exoteric, dealing with rhetoric, ethics and politics.

Lycophron (*fl.* early in the 4th century BC) ancient Sophist, known only from a few extant fragments. He believed in the natural equality of all human beings, rejecting the Platonic-Aristotelian view that some are born to rule, others to obey, and proposed a social contract theory.

Lydian shepherd *See* GYGES.

Lyotard /liɔtaʀ (Fr.)/, Jean-François (1924–98) lecturer and professor at institutes of higher learning in Paris since the

1960s until retirement in 1987. For many years, until 1966, Lyotard was a member of the strongly Marxist group 'Socialisme ou barbarie'. His writings in the 1970s broke away from dogmatic Marxism, and from his earlier dogmatic adherence to the theories of Freud and Lacan. He continued, however, to combine philosophical and political concerns.

A major theme in Lyotard's work is the opposition to the ambition, attributed with 'modernity', to establish wide-ranging, coherent, definitive theories and interpretations which ideally answer all our questions.

The general rejection of 'grand theory' came in *La Condition postmoderne* 1979 (The post-modern condition). What characterizes post-modernity is the rejection of 'grand narratives', i.e. the major systems of religious, political or cultural ideas (Christianity, emancipation, capitalism, socialism, technological progress) which have been used to underpin social and political institutions and practices and intellectual styles. A further characteristic of post-modernity is the incommensurability of various forms of discourse, which means that a consensus which can serve as an objective basis for conceptions of justice and truth is not even ideally attainable. In this post-modern condition, however, people are becoming more sensitive to these breakdowns in communication and are developing a better understanding of them.

Le Différend 1983 (*The Differend*) presents a theory of 'differends': points of incommensurability between 'language games'. They are incommensurable, and yet their coexistence does imply dispute and conflict. To engage in one is to do injustice to the other. Auschwitz is emblematic in this regard – it is an event which cannot be bypassed, but cannot be described by a historian as one event among others. There is a discrepancy between the horror of the event and any attempt to describe it. In a 'normal' conflict or difference of opinion there is a certain equality between the parties, they are able to communicate, and their conflict can in principle be impartially adjudicated. In contrast, differends are intractable: it is impossible to do justice both to the spider and to the fly. Respect for justice involves keeping the question open. The idea, developed by Habermas and Apel, of a consensus that can ideally be reached in the long run is explicitly rejected by Lyotard, who argues that one would do an injustice to a genuine 'differend' in the attempt to do justice to the conflicting parties. One does justice to such a conflict by not trying to bridge the gap. This prevents the discussion from coming to a close.

Lyotard's concept of a differend is quite wide, and also includes intractable situations of a different kind, like those arising from paradoxes like the LIAR PARADOX.

The recognition of intractable *différends* is, for Lyotard, an act of resistance to capitalism, which tries to bring uniformity to all kinds of discourse by exploiting the capabilities of modern information technology. This technology can be used, however, to promote post-modern pluralism.

In post-modern art, the task is to represent the unrepresentable and bear witness where discursive ways of representation break down. BR/ed.

M

Mably /'mæblɪ (Eng.); mabli (Fr.)/, Gabriel Bonnot de (1709–85) In a number of historical and political works, Mably, an elder brother of Condillac, strongly criticized the social and political conditions of his time. He argued against private property, and advocated radical reform along socialist and egalitarian lines. *De la législation* 1776 (On legislation) contains a comparison between the two countries that in his opinion had the best political systems, England and Sweden, and finds in favour of the latter: the English had yielded too much to greed and ambition.

Mach /max (Gm.)/, Ernst (1838–1916) Austrian physicist, and historian and philosopher of science, who taught at the universities of Graz, Prague (for almost 30 years) and Vienna. His ideas inspired Bertrand Russell, William James and the Vienna Circle early in the twentieth century. Mach played an important part in the revival of empiricism in the late nineteenth century, opposing in *Die Analyse der Empfindungen* 1886, 5th edn 1906 (The analysis of sensations) the 'metaphysical' assumptions, in science, of entities which we cannot directly experience. Thus he criticized Newton's doctrines of absolute space and time, never accepted the existence of atoms, and was reluctant to accept new developments in physics such as relativity theory and the idea of sub-atomic particles. (The new preface to the 1913 edition of his *Principles of Physical Objects* contained a vehement denunciation of Einstein's special relativity theory, but it has been argued that this was written and inserted by his son without the author's approval.) In *Erkenntnis und Irrtum* 1905 (Knowledge and error) Mach fashioned a metaphysics and philosophy of science congenial to this scepticism and akin to Berkeley's phenomenalism. According to this metaphysics, sensations are all that really exists. Talk of atoms and molecules, not to mention talk of tables and chairs, is never literally true. However, such talk might be useful in enabling us to predict future sensations. It might effect an 'economy of thought', and that is its only virtue. The principle of economy of thought, a variant of Ockham's razor, was formulated by Mach. He dealt with the mind–body problem by means of a monistic theory: mind and body are different types of clusters of sensations.

Mach was in sympathy with the political aspirations of the working classes and supported the social-democratic movement in Austria. His subjectivist theory of knowledge earned him the wrath of Lenin, who attacked him and his Russian followers in *Materialism and Empirio-Criticism* 1908. AM

Machiavelli /mækɪə'vɛlɪ (Eng.); makia'vɛli (It.)/, Niccolò di Bernardo (1469–1527) Florentine historian, playwright, but chiefly a political thinker. His theory of statecraft, as presented in *Il principe* (The prince), written in 1513 and first published in 1532, by condoning the ruler's use of force and fraud seemed indifferent or even hostile to accepted moral standards. The laudable ends, for which immoral means could be permissible, were to protect the state from internal disruption and external aggression, and to promote the welfare of the citizens. In his *Discorsi sopra la prima deca di Tito Livio* (Discourses on the first ten books of Livy), written *c.* 1517 and first published in 1531, Machiavelli stressed the importance of 'civic virtue' in states that were in good order: public-spirited citizens would put the common good above the exclusive pursuit of selfish interests, with its inherent corruption and venality. In Isaiah Berlin's interpretation, the recourse to immoral means is not for Machiavelli a regrettable deviation in exceptional cases from Christian principles. Rather, his outlook can be described as non-Christian, secular, indeed pagan. His ideal of the good life included vitality, genius, pride, variety and success, and for him, virtues are those qualities that accord with that ideal; they are different from the Christian virtues. This brings to our attention the irreconcilable plurality of our values.

MacIntyre /ˈmækɪntaɪə/, Alasdair (1929–)

A philosophical self-portrait: My ancestry is Scots and Irish. I have taught in British universities and, from 1970, in American ones, most recently at Notre Dame 1988–94, and from 1995 at Duke University. My philosophical development has had three stages. Until 1970 my work had an eclectic quality, sometimes fruitfully, sometimes less so. My interest in questions about the truth of the tenets of orthodox Christianity and of Marxism was in tension with what I had learnt – often inadequately – from Frege and Wittgenstein. I thought it philosophically important to study concepts in context as socially and historically embodied in activities and practices. My work in this period was published in *A Short History of Ethics* 1966 and the essays in *Against the Self-images of the Age* 1971.

In an interim period I became aware of the defects of the *Short History*, while also working out further the critique which had underpinned my rejection of Marxism. This rejection did not entail any change in my negative view of late twentieth-century bureaucratized consumer capitalism and the liberal individualism which is its dominant ideology. What did change was my view of how the moral philosophy which informs that ideology had been generated by the fragmentation of an older moral tradition concerning human goods, virtues and the social relationships in and through which goods can be pursued, of which the classical expression is the ethics of Aristotle. I also returned to the problems of rational theology, both in metaphysics and in discussion of the relation between Christian theism and modern secular societies.

The first of these lines of inquiry resulted in *After Virtue* 1981 (2nd edn 1984). The two lines of inquiry together resulted in a recognition that it is from the standpoint of a Thomistic Aristotelianism which is able to learn from the central debates of recent philosophy, that the issues confronting contemporary moral philosophy can best be understood. I have continued the project initiated in *After Virtue* by considering how one particular tradition of moral inquiry may succeed or fail in vindicating its claims to rational superiority over its rivals, both in *Whose Justice? Which Rationality?* 1988 and in *Three Rival Versions of Moral Enquiry* 1990. This made it necessary for me to pay particular attention to the adequacy or otherwise of different conceptions of rationality, incommensurability and, especially, truth. My work in progress focuses on these issues in two very different contexts: that of Aquinas's treatment of truthfulness; and that provided by a study of Edith Stein and Heidegger.

Mackie /ˈmækɪ/, John (1917–81) a leading representative of Australian analytical philosophy, notable for its dislike of obfuscation and obscurantism and for its quest for clarity and precision. Mackie, a pupil of John Anderson, taught at Otago, Sydney, York and Oxford. In *The Cement of the Universe* 1974, 2nd edn 1980 he gave an important analysis of causality, and in *The Miracle of Theism* 1982 he stated a powerful case against the arguments for God's existence. His article 'Evil and Omnipotence', *Mind 64* (1955) had by then already become an established point of reference in the philosophical discussion of the problem of evil. 'A Refutation of Morals', *Australasian Journal of Philosophy and Psychology 24* (1946) defends a metaethical ERROR THEORY, restated and further articulated in *Ethics: Inventing Right and Wrong* 1977. The theory is that when people make moral judgements, they ascribe a moral quality, which they take to exist objectively, to an object or state of affairs. But, Mackie argued, since there can be no objective qualities of that kind, the moral judgements that people ordinarily make are all of them false. In his view it is, however, possible to develop a moral theory and to deal with moral problems without lapsing into error.

MacPherson /mək'fɜːsən/, C(rawford) B(rough) (1911–87) taught at the University of Toronto from 1935. A central theme in his writings is the critique of existing forms of capitalist liberal democracies from the standpoint of a Marxism combined with the humanist elements in nineteenth-century liberal theory. He attacked the fixation on the market in current political thought, and the narrow conception of human nature that goes with it. In *The Political Theory of Possessive Individualism* 1962 and in his introduction to the Penguin edition of Hobbes's *Leviathan* he argued that such an outlook is present in the classical political writings of Hobbes and Locke who, according to MacPherson, were early ideologists of the rising bourgeoisie. That outlook, he urges, ought now to be superseded: instead of private utility-maximization the overriding ideal should be one of the full actualization of human potentiality in cooperation with others. Other writings on this theme are *The Real World of Democracy* 1965, and *The Life and Times of Liberal Democracy* 1977. Critics found these analyses of classical political thought implausible, and the social and political theory unrealistic for about two decades from the mid-1960s, but his ideas had a marked influence in English-speaking countries and elsewhere, not least in Germany.

macrocosm (Gr. *makros* large + *kosmos* order; world-order) *n.* This term and **microcosm** (Gr. *mikros* small) are used to draw contrasts or analogies between a large world, or order of things, and a smaller. The concepts can be traced back to Plato (*Timaeus* 30b), Aristotle (*On the Heavens* 2,12) and Democritus.

maieutic /meɪ'juːtɪk/ *adj.* **maieutics** *n.* (Gr. *maieutikē* (*technē*) (the art of) mid-wifery) Socrates's dialectical method, which helps to bring to light knowledge already latent in a person's mind, is likened to the art of midwifery in Plato's *Theaetetus* 149a–151d; 184b; 210b–d.

Maimon /'maɪmɔn (Gm.)/, Salomon (*c.* 1752–1800) German philosopher, of Lithuanian-Jewish origin. Kant greatly respected his keen intellect. In his first published work, *Versuch über die Transcendental-philosophie* 1790 (An essay on transcendental philosophy) he emerged as an incisive early critic of Kant's critical philosophy. He raised the question how the understanding (active and non-temporal) could mesh with sensibility (passive and temporal). He also argued that Kant had provided no clear way of distinguishing causal sequences of events from non-causal ones. Of special interest is his view, anticipating Fichte's, that Kant was inconsistent in retaining a notion of an unknowable thing-in-itself which underlies the world as it is known to us.

Maimonides /maɪ'mɒnɪdiːz; maɪmə'niːdɪs/, Moses (1135–1204) Jewish philosopher, physician, jurist and theologian, born in Spain; escaped persecution and settled eventually in Cairo in 1165, where he soon came to have a leading position in the Jewish community. Many of his works were written in Arabic. His metaphysics is influenced by the Islamic Aristotelians, especially Alfarabi (*c.* 870–950) and, to some extent, Avicenna (980–1037), but he also held his contemporary Averroës (1126–98) in high esteem, and agreed with him in deviating from the dogma of individual immortality. Of his works, his *Guide for the Perplexed* (*c.* 1190) is the most interesting philosophically. The perplexity alluded to in the title arises from the challenge of rational inquiry, i.e. Aristotelian philosophy and science, to traditional (Jewish) faith. For the most part, he argued that seeming inconsistencies between the two could be resolved, and that the two ways to knowledge complement one another. One discrepancy seemed impossible to bridge: that concerning the eternity of the world, a doctrine unacceptable to Jews and Christians alike. At this point, Maimonides held that since the rational arguments were inconclusive, the doctrines of divine creation (and of miracles) could still be accepted as a matter of faith alone. Among Jewish scholars, Maimonides became the standard theological and philosophical point of reference, but he was also regarded as an important authority by Aquinas, Eckhart, and other Christian thinkers. He adopted the principle, which he ascribed to Aristotle, that every genuine possibility is actualized at some time, for an argument for God's existence which anticipates the third of Aquinas's Five Ways.

Maine de Biran /mɛn də birɑ̃ (Fr.)/, François Pierre (1766–1824) French politician and philosopher. In his mature philosophy, as presented in his *Essai sur les fondements de psychologie* 1812 (Essay on the foundations of psychology) in which the tenor is anti-materialist and anti-determinist, he emphasized the central role of inner experience. It differs from mere sense-experience in that it is an experience not of objects, but of facts, i.e. an experience *that* such-and-such is the case. In inner experience of our willed efforts we discern activity: this is the primary experience. Maine de Biran replaces Descartes's *cogito, ergo sum* with a *volo, ergo sum* (I will, therefore I am). Self-consciousness arises from the experience of the relation between one's will and one's body; we find ourselves as free agents. Consequently, he rejected Hume's assertion that we have no impression of a necessary connection between cause and effect (and hence no idea of it either), arguing against Hume that we do directly experience this in the inner experience of willed effort. Our knowledge of other persons, he also held, is not a part of our knowledge of the external world, but arises directly in personal relations.

Maistre *See* DE MAISTRE.

major premiss the premiss in a categorical syllogism which contains the major term.

major term the term in a categorical syllogism which is the predicate in the conclusion (Aristotle, *Prior Analytics*).

mala fide; mala fides /'mælə 'faɪdɪ; -iːz/ Lat. in bad faith, deceitfully; bad faith.

Malcolm /'mælkəm/, Norman (1911–90) American philosopher who taught at Cornell University 1947–79. Influenced by Moore and Wittgenstein, he held the view that philosophical analyses that end up in opposition to ordinary language must be defective. He proposed an interpretation of Anselm's ontological argument for the existence of God, designed to bypass the classical objections. In this version of the argument, as presented in *Knowledge and Certainty* 1963, the conclusion that God exists is derived from premisses, among which are: (1) it is not impossible for a perfect being (like God) to exist; and (2) the existence of a perfect being (like God) is non-contingent, i.e. necessary. Other writings are *Dreaming* 1959, where he accepts in earnest Wittgenstein's dictum that an 'inner process' stands in need of outward criteria, and argues that since we usually talk and think of our dreams as inner processes, many of the things we say or think about the nature of dreams should be rejected. Among other writings is *Memory and Mind* 1977.

Malebranche /malbrɑ̃ːʃ (Fr.)/, Nicolas (1638–1715) Born in Paris. He studied philosophy and theology at the Sorbonne, and then entered the religious Oratory, where he was ordained a priest. He first encountered one of Descartes's works in 1664, and devoted the next ten years to examining his philosophy. In 1674–5 he published the fruits of his labours, *De la recherche de la verité* (On the search after truth), in which he developed a metaphysical system to overcome some of the difficulties in Descartes's theory. Malebranche insisted that all that we are aware of are ideas and feelings. Ideas are truths that exist independently of us, and are seen in God. We are illuminated by divine ideas. Mathematical ideas are of intelligible extension, which co-exists and is co-eternal with God. We do not and cannot have any knowledge of a physical external reality, since such knowledge would be different from our ideas. Malebranche put forward a distinctive theory of causality, known as occasionalism. He argued that in inspecting our ideas and our feelings, we cannot discover any necessary connections between them. God, and God alone, is the cause of all events. So, when we see one event followed by another, such as one billiard ball striking another, and then the second one moving, we do not see the necessary connection or power that makes the second move. Malebranche's explanation is that God causes each and every event. What we take to be causal sequences are in fact just independent occasions of God's acting. God acts by general rules, so that we are able to formulate scientific laws, which describe the sequences of God's activities. Apart from God, there are no efficient or secondary causes. There is no connection between mind and matter, but on the occasion of God causing a mental event, he also causes a physical event. We do not see or know the physical world, but know by revelation that God has created it.

Malebranche's occasionalism was seen as a way of making Cartesianism consistent, by eliminating the difficulty of explaining mind–body interaction. Neither mind nor body has causal power and hence they do not interact. God affects one on the occasion of his affecting the other. However, whilst this solves one problem for Cartesianism, it creates another: whether God is the cause of immoral events, which Malebranche struggled to resolve in his *Traité de la nature et de la grâce* 1680 (Treatise on nature and grace).

Malebranche was seen as one of the great metaphysicians of his time, although his theory was strongly opposed by Arnauld, Bayle, Leibniz and Locke. It greatly influenced both Berkeley's idealism and Hume's analysis of causality.

The Search after Truth 1980 is a translation of his major work. Among other translated works is *Dialogues on Metaphysics* 1980. RPO

maleficence /mə'lɛfɪsəns/ *n.* ill-doing; the activity of doing evil to others.

malevolence /mə'lɛvələns/ *n.* ill-will; the disposition to do evil to others.

Malthus /'mælθəs/, Thomas Robert (1776–1834) An English clergyman, with a background of study in mathematics and economics as well as theology, Malthus developed a theory of population growth in his *Essay on the Principle of Population* 1798, significantly revised in the second (1803) and later editions. An important aim was to refute the radical theories of Condorcet and Godwin, which assume that progress and an increase in general happiness is possible. Malthus argued that there is always a natural tendency towards over-population. Population growth will tend to outstrip growth of resources. This tendency is only kept in check by physical evils (famine, disease, wars, natural disasters, etc.) or by moral evils (contraception, abortion, etc.). In short, mankind's tendency to go forth and multiply leads to misery. Malthus recommended sexual restraint and late marriages to limit population growth.

Mandeville /'mændəvɪl/, Bernard (1670–1733) Mandeville's main work, *The Fable of the Bees* (early versions 1705 and 1714; more complete versions from 1723), contains both a moral and an economic theory. Against Shaftesbury, he asserted that all our actions are self-interested. He also argued that self-denial, commonly regarded as virtuous, does little good, but tends to reduce society to stagnation, unemployment, poverty and misery. His view, in present-day terms, was that if there were no crimes against property, most police, accountants, auditors, bank employees, locksmiths, security guards and all those assisting them would be unemployed. If there is no luxury, but everyone lives frugally, all those involved in the manufacturing and trade of luxury goods will be unemployed. Cultivate virtue, and 'The Economy' will suffer. Prosperity and the absence of material want are largely due to vice, i.e. to conduct which moralists of all ages have condemned. Mandeville anticipated Adam Smith's theory of an 'invisible hand' by whose guidance self-interested seekers of pleasure or profit unwittingly promote the common good. The invisible hand does not always suffice to create the coordination and non-selfish action needed in a society. How can selfishly motivated agents come to act non-selfishly? Mandeville gives an interesting psychological analysis: we have an innate sense of pride or honour. This sense is susceptible to flattery, which skilful politicians will use. The result is that selfish agents will feel pleased with themselves when toeing the line and doing 'the right thing'. Non-selfish action thus has a reward: the sense of self-satisfaction that flattery has begotten upon pride. The prospect of such a reward can motivate a selfish agent.

Hutcheson criticized Mandeville in his *Inquiry* 1725; Berkeley did so in his *Alciphron* 1732.

Manich(a)eism /mænɪ'kiːɪzm/ *n.* a religious belief-system named after its founder, a Persian called Mani or Manes (AD 216–*c.* 275). Its doctrine and discipline were ascetic, and its organization that of a church. A central tenet was that there are two ultimate principles of being: one good, the other evil. On the good side is light, God, and the soul; on the evil side, darkness, Satan, and the body. The aim of the ascetic exercises was to release the light that had become trapped in the body. This metaphysical dualism was regarded as a heresy and firmly condemned in mainstream Christianity, e.g. by Augustine in his *Contra Faustum* (*Against Faustus*). It re-emerged in later cults, such as catharism. In a famous article in his dictionary, 'Manichaeans', Bayle argued that the answer to the problem of evil offered in this false belief-system was more rational than that of the Christian theologians, and used this in support of his thesis that rationality and true religion are incompatible.

Mannheim /'manhaɪm (Gm.)/, Karl (1893–1947) Social theorist of Hungarian-German-Jewish descent, professor in Frankfurt 1930, but driven into exile in 1933, he taught at the London School of Economics from 1933. In his major work, *Ideology and Utopia* 1936 (a work different from his earlier *Ideologie und Utopie* 1929, which is of interest in its own right) he argued that traditional epistemology should be replaced by the sociology of knowledge, in which the links between the social and historical situation of a theorist and the content of the theory are explored. To conceive of the truth of a theory in an absolute sense is futile: a theory can only be adequate in relation to its own social background. This view has obvious relativist implications. Mannheim tried to mitigate them by his theory of the free-floating intellectual who has become detached from a particular social class and whose theories therefore do not suffer from class bias.

many-valued logic *See* LOGIC, MANY-VALUED.

Maoism /'maʊɪzm/ *n.* the thought of Mao Zedong (Tse-tung), communist dictator of China from 1949 to his death 1978. It is chiefly an application to current politics of ideas derived from Marx, Lenin, Trotsky, folklore, etc., and has no independent philosophical merit. A sample of Maoism can be found in Mao's *Little Red Book*, published in hundreds of millions of copies. It is no longer a state ideology in China or Albania, but some extreme-left political groupings in France, Peru, Cambodia, etc. have continued to profess allegiance to this ideology.

Marburg School a neo-Kantian school, whose main representatives, Hermann Cohen (1842–1918), Paul Natorp (1854–1924) and Ernst Cassirer (1874–1945) were associated with the University of Marburg (Germany).

Marcel /maʀsɛl (Fr.)/, Gabriel (1889–1973) French philosopher and playwright. In his philosophical reflections on the human condition, he emphasized the role of interpersonal relations and of community for the understanding of various modes of human experience. In this respect his thought shows affinities with Kierkegaard and Buber. The basis of thought and being cannot be an 'I am' but rather 'we are'. Influenced by Bergson and other idealist philosophers, his own outlook had a strong religious component. He rejected the empiricist and analytical conceptions of philosophy, which he found too narrow.

Marcus, Ruth Barcan *See* BARCAN MARCUS, RUTH.

Marcus Aurelius (Antoninus) /'maːkəs ɔː'riːlɪəs æntə'naɪnəs *See* STOICISM.

Marcuse /mɑː'kuːzə/, Herbert (1898–1979) German-Jewish philosopher and social critic, associated with the FRANKFURT SCHOOL. Forced into exile in 1933, he moved to the United States, where in the 1960s his thought was taken up by the radical left. Early sources of philosophical inspiration were Hegel and Marx. In Marcuse's view, the need for philosophy is a need for emancipation from a stagnant and oppressive political reality. This was the aim of Marxist communists, but it was not achieved. To explain this, Marcuse turns to Nietzsche and Freud. The rationality that was to have a liberating effect comes into conflict with our natural libidinal tendencies. In Freudian terms, the pleasure principle rebels against the reality principle. In ideal social conditions reality need not conflict with the innate pleasure principle. Marcuse is not very specific about what these ideal conditions would be like. His emphasis is more on the critique of present-day conditions, in works such as *Eros and Civilization* 1955 and *One-Dimensional Man* 1964. In his view, it is an essential part of the Enlightenment belief in reason, science and progress, that people are seen merely as manipulable tools to be used for the purposes of those who hold positions of power. As this scientific outlook has come to dominate modern societies, individuals become more and more neurotic, the societies themselves are becoming increasingly coarse, violent and crime-ridden, and wars and genocide are the natural outcome. Individual freedom – a central value for Marcuse – is destroyed in the modern world. In fascist and communist systems this is done openly, by direct oppression: in capitalist countries, more insidiously. Whilst in the past genuine protest could find authentic expression in works of art (Beethoven, Schiller, Hölderlin), it has been stifled by modern mass culture which commercializes and trivializes every cultural product into mere entertainment. Genuine freedom is also destroyed by modern schooling. It is designed to make individuals useful in the production of goods and services. The pervasive conformism and acceptance of the status quo, imposed by modern society, is totalitarian. It is impossible for individuals to develop a critical distance to it: in this sense, they become one-dimensional. In Marcuse's view, this repression was essentially the same in communist dictatorships and Western democracies: only the repressive techniques differed.

Marcuse's critics have complained that he singled out the West for most of his attacks. He regarded democratic pluralism as a cloak for the imposition of conformity, and argued against freedom of opinion which in practice favours the defenders of the established order and so benefits the cause of oppression (R. P. Wolff, Barrington Moore Jr & H. Marcuse, *A Critique of Pure Tolerance* 1969). It is a repressive tolerance, which permits expressions of dissent but ensures that they are ineffectual. Marcuse's radical rejection of most aspects of contemporary social and political life in industrialized democratic countries gained a wide following but also gave rise to bitter controversy.

Maritain /maʀitɛ̃ (Fr.)/, Jacques (1882–1973) French neo-Thomist philosopher. Maritain taught in France, Canada and the United States. He was a prolific and influential author who participated in drafting the United Nations' Universal Declaration of Human Rights. His views of political philosophy are presented in *Man and the State* 1951 (revised in later editions), and there, as in his other philosophical works, he tried to give a modern rendering of Thomistic principles. He presented modernized versions of the FIVE WAYS of proving God's existence in *Approaches de Dieu* 1953 (*Approaches to God*), adding to them a sixth. It starts from two assumptions: (1) I, the self, cannot be thought of as not existing; (2) this particular person, like any other finite existing thing, can be thought of as not existing. By further steps of reasoning, the conclusion is inferred that some personal being (of a divine nature) must exist. *Distinguer pour unir* 1932 (transl. as *The Degrees of Knowledge*) outlines his theory of knowledge. He argued that sense-experience, conceptual thought and scientific method are not the only ways of gaining knowledge. There are also other, more direct ways. One of these is 'knowledge by inclination'. By becoming intuitively aware of tendencies within ourselves which express our true nature, we gain access to the basis for moral knowledge. Moral philosophy articulates this knowledge at a more reflective, rational level. In his aesthetic theory, the arts – for instance, poetry – are also seen as expressing direct, intuitive, non-conceptual knowledge.

Marsilio Ficino *See* FICINO.

Marsilio of Padua (*c.*1275–1342) His best-known work is *Defensor Pacis* (The defender of peace). It was completed in Paris in 1324 and dedicated to Louis of Bavaria, the main opponent of Pope John XXII. Marsilio objected to the papal claims to political supremacy over kings, princes and nations, arguing that political authority and legislative power belong to the secular rulers, and that secular power should have ultimate authority also in church government. Of special interest is the new emphasis given to the view that political authority in turn is derived from and depends on the will and consent of the people.

Martineau /ˈmɑːtɪnəʊ/, James (1805–1900) prominent Unitarian, brother of the eminent writer Harriet Martineau, author of *Types of Ethical Theory* 1885, 3rd edn 1891. His standpoint can be described as intuitionist, opposed to the contemporary utilitarian theories outlined by John Stuart Mill and Henry Sidgwick. One important point of difference concerns the central subject-matter of ethics. For the utilitarians it is the rightness of an agent's choices; for Martineau, it is the goodness of the agent's character.

Marx /mɑːks (Eng.); marks (Gm.)/, Karl (Heinrich) (1818–83) Marx was both a revolutionary and a scholar. He studied at the University of Berlin where he was involved with the Young Hegelian movement, and then became editor of the liberal newspaper *Rheinische Zeitung* in Cologne. The paper was suppressed in 1843 and Marx moved first to Paris, where he met Friedrich Engels and made contact with French socialists, and later to Brussels. He returned to Germany following the outbreak of the revolution of 1848 to found the *Neue Rheinische Zeitung*. After the revolution was defeated he moved to London where he lived for the rest of his life.

By the time of his death Marx was known chiefly as the author of *The Communist Manifesto* (written jointly with Engels in 1848), the first volume of *Das Kapital* 1867 (*Capital*), numerous newspaper articles and several longer pieces of political analysis. With the exception of an extended critique of Proudhon (*The Poverty of Philosophy* 1847), the most important of Marx's directly philosophical writings were not published until many years after his death. The *Economic and Philosophical Manuscripts* (written in 1844) and the full text of *The German Ideology* (written with Engels in 1845–6) did not become available until the 1930s, while the *Grundrisse* 1857–8, a draft to Outline for a Critique of Political Economy, did not become generally available until 1953. BHI

Marxism *n.* As a political doctrine, Marxism emerged as one of several doctrines competing for support within the growing working-class movement. The process of popularizing Marx's ideas began with Engels' *Anti-Dühring* 1878 – the first part of which appeared as a widely read pamphlet under the title *Socialism: utopian and scientific* – and was continued in the socialist parties of the Second International and later in the Russian and other communist parties that emerged after the Russian revolution of 1917. Engels presented Marxism as a distinctive body of social and political theory constructed out of the most advanced developments in philosophy, political economy and socialism. This Marxism promised to provide an effective guide to socialist political practice based not on utopian ideals, but rather on a scientific understanding both of history in general and of modern capitalist societies in particular. The point of Engels's pamphlet, then, was to help educate the working class and its bourgeois sympathizers in the science that would serve their interests.

Almost from its beginning, then, Marxism has been structured both by pedagogic and by political imperatives: the one promoting a doctrine that could be presented in party classes and pamphlets to audiences of varying degrees of sophistication, and the other allowing political disagreement and doctrinal error to be seen as two sides of the same coin. The first important Marxist orthodoxy appeared in the German Social Democratic Party towards the end of the nineteenth century. It was soon to be disputed: by revisionists, who rejected the very idea of orthodoxy in a theory with scientific pretensions; and by competing versions claiming to be orthodox, of which communism (under the leadership – later disputed by the Chinese and other parties – of the Communist Party of the Soviet Union) has been by far the most influential.

These orthodoxies have generally presented Marxism as combining a philosophy and a science of history (MATERIALISM, DIALECTICAL AND HISTORICAL). The former derives largely from the work of Engels, while the latter is based on the outline of his historical method presented in Marx's Preface to *A Contribution to a Critique of Political Economy*, selective readings of *The Communist Manifesto*, vol. 1 of *Das Kapital* and other writings of Marx that were available at the time of his death, and the more general historical and political works of Engels. Marx's Preface sketches a view of society as consisting of an economic foundation, 'upon which rises' a political and legal superstructure, and 'to which correspond . . . forms of social thought'. While the precise relationships indicated by these phrases remain somewhat obscure, the Preface clearly locates the fundamental source of social change in transformations of economic relations which themselves result from the development of productive forces – unlike *The Communist Manifesto* which presents class struggle as the most important cause. Orthodox Marxisms differ in their elaborations on these basic ideas, and some add further elements from the work of later political leaders. Marxism-Leninism, for example, is a Marxism that incorporates Lenin's analysis of imperialism as well as ideas taken from his philosophical polemics against socialist followers of Mach and conventionalist philosophy of science, in *Materialism and Empirio-Criticism* 1908.

A careful reading of *Das Kapital* would suggest that Marx's own views could not easily be fitted into the frameworks provided either by his much-quoted Preface or by these official Marxisms. While this point had sometimes been made by Marxist scholars, more serious intellectual challenges to Marxist orthodoxy followed the publications of Marx's philosophical writings. The most influential of these writings were contained in the *Economic and Philosophical Manuscripts* written in 1844 and finally published in 1932. The immediate effect of their publication was to present Marx as a considerably more sophisticated philosopher than orthodox readings of his published works or any version of dialectical materialism might suggest.

In the *Manuscripts* Marx engages with the work of Hegel, Feuerbach and other Young Hegelians to argue that productive activity, i.e. labour, should be seen as an essential component of man's being. Private property represents the products of labour as if they were things: it is the alienation of labour from itself. Capitalism, in which labour is treated as a commodity, further intensifies that alienation and generalizes it throughout all levels of society. The end of alienation therefore requires communism: the abolition of private property in general and wage labour in particular. Capitalism also creates an ever-growing class of persons with no private property and with nothing to sell but their labour – and who therefore have an interest in the abolition of private property. On this view, the social forces that will finally put an end to alienation are themselves the product of alienation in its most extreme and most extensive form.

Marx's account of the process whereby labour finally overcomes its own alienation has obvious parallels with some of Hegel's arguments. Indeed, Engels maintained that Marx's approach stood Hegel's dialectic on its head. The most important consequences of the publication of Marx's philosophical writings for the subsequent history of Marxism were twofold. First, it became possible for dissident Marxists to quote Marx the philosopher against the orthodoxies of their day, a development that soon led to the growth of an alternative, humanistic Marxism – especially in the West, where defenders of the orthodoxies had limited access to political power. Secondly, the appearance of Marx's philosophical writings raised a host of questions about the relationships between the younger, more philosophical Marx and the later, more 'scientific' figure. When Marxist humanists argued that the earlier writings held the key to the later texts, their opponents, e.g. ALTHUSSER, maintained that there was a discontinuity or 'epistemological break' between them. These disputes persisted until the collapse of Western Marxism in the 1980s. BHI

mass noun 'Water', 'gold', etc. are mass nouns, in contrast to *count nouns*, like 'lake' or 'bracelet'. A count noun denotes an individual, a mass noun does not. Count nouns have singular and plural forms, mass nouns do not. In standard predicate logic, variables for individuals are replaceable by count nouns, but not by mass nouns, which require a different logical theory. *Syn.* (in grammar) uncount noun.

master argument *See* DIODORUS.

material cause *See* CAUSE.

material implication *p materially implies q* means only that *it is not the case that both p and not-q*. Once the truth-values of p and q are given, the truth-value of *p materially implies q* is also determined; in other words, material implication is a truth-function. In standard symbolism, the ⊃ (horseshoe) or the → (arrow) is used. Table 12 is the truth-table.

It was Bertrand Russell who gave this truth-function the name *material implication*, but since there does not have to be any implication, indeed any connection at all, between p and q, the expression (*material*) *conditional* is preferable.

Table 12 Truth-table for material implication

p	q	p ⊃ q
T	T	T
T	F	F
F	T	T
F	F	T

material implication, paradoxes of *See* IMPLICATION.

materialism *n.* the theory that matter alone exists. It immediately implies a denial of the existence of minds, spirits, divine beings, etc., in so far as these are taken to be non-material. It was proposed by the ancient atomists (Democritus, Epicurus) and in the modern era by Gassendi, Hobbes, Meslier, La Mettrie, Helvétius, Holbach, etc. Its current versions, formulated with greater conceptual refinement, are often called PHYSICALISM. It has been said that during the 1960s (and since), materialism became one of the few orthodoxies of American academic philosophy, and analytic philosophy elsewhere has shown a similar tendency. The doctrine is older than the word, of which the earliest use can be traced to the 1660s.

materialism, dialectical and historical a philosophical theory of nature and of history, respectively, that became established as a part of the Marxist tradition through the later works of Engels, notably his *Anti-Dühring* 1878 and *Ludwig Feuerbach and the End of Classical German Philosophy* 1889. Engels maintained that Marx had, rightly, preserved Hegel's dialectical method but supplied a materialistic basis for it. There are, in Engels's view, contradictions in the material world, not only in thought. Natural phenomena can be properly understood and explained only in a dialectical framework which, he maintained in *The Dialectics of Nature* (a manuscript draft, first published in 1925), contains three basic laws of universal application: (1) the transformation of quantity into quality, so that under certain conditions there is a 'revolutionary' leap from a difference in degree to a difference in kind; (2) the interpenetration of opposites; (3) the law of the negation of the negation, which does not lead back to the starting point, but spirals towards a new synthesis. The theory has a polemical edge against so-called mechanical materialism, advocated by popular philosophers like Büchner and Dühring, and of course against various idealist schools. Lenin adopted this outlook, on which his philosophical mentor Plekhanov had bestowed the name 'dialectical materialism', and it became the orthodoxy in the countries under communist rule, achieving its canonical expression in Stalin's *Dialectical and Historical Materialism* 1938. Historical materialism is an interpretation along similar lines of Marx's analysis of history and of capitalist society. Anti-Marxists found little merit in this philosophy, and many Marxist intellectuals also rejected what they saw as simplistic philosophical dogma, especially after the publication in 1932 of Marx's *Economic and Philosophical Manuscripts*. BHI/ed.

material mode *See* FORMAL MODE.

mathematical induction *See* INDUCTION, MATHEMATICAL.

mathematical logic inquiry into, or theory of, the logical principles underlying mathematical concepts and proofs.

matriarchy /ˈmeɪtrɪaːkɪ/ *n.* (Lat. *mater* mother + Gr. *-archia* rule) **1** a form of social organization in which control, power and authority are in the hands of mothers or adult women generally. **2** a society organized in this way. Matriarchy is the central concept in *Das Mutterrecht* 1861, by the Swiss social anthropologist J. J. Bachofen (1815–87). He regarded matriarchy as an early stage in the evolution of mankind. At that stage, sharp distinctions and lines of demarcation and exclusion are absent. The customs and the mentality of society are generously open and promiscuous, and there is a closeness to the soil. All this is lost when the male principle, more intellectual and spiritual, takes over. Ludwig Klages drew a similar contrast, assigning positive value to GYNOCRACY: spirit is the male principle, soul and nature the female, which we have lost but should try to regain. *Ant.* PATRIARCHY.

matter of fact a concept in Hume's theory

of knowledge, contrasted with relations of ideas. Matters of fact are contingent, and our knowledge of them is *a posteriori*. Relations of ideas are non-contingent, and are known *a priori*.

Mauthner /ˈmaʊtnər (Gm.)/, Fritz (1849–1923) journalist and author of essays, satires, poetry, novels (e.g. *Hypatia* 1892), and philosophical works, first in Prague, from 1876 in Berlin, and from the early 1900s in the south of Germany. Philosophically he was most strongly influenced by Mach and Nietzsche. His major philosophical works are *Beiträge zu einer Kritik der Sprache* (1901) 1923 (Contributions to a critique of language), *Wörterbuch der Philosophie* 1910 (Dictionary of philosophy), and *Der Atheismus und seine Geschichte im Abendlande* 1920–23 (Atheism and its history in the Western world). In his view there can be no knowledge without language. And yet language constitutes a veil which prevents access to reality, so that genuine knowledge cannot be gained through language which can only reflect our subjective experiences and is determined by its social functions. Thus, linguistic structures (subject/predicate, for instance) do not mirror ontological structures (e.g. thing/property) although they seem to do so. Later, he combined his radical scepticism with a theory of mystical intuition.

mauvaise foi /movɛz fwa (Fr.)/ Fr. bad faith; intention to deceive; dishonesty. In Sartre's existentialism, self-deception, especially in disclaiming responsibility for the way one leads one's life.

maxim *n.* (Lat. *maxima (propositio)* a 'greatest' or 'highest' proposition, i.e. one taken as a starting point) **1** a general proposition or rule. Most writers use the term primarily for statements which relate to practical matters or are useful for the conduct of life, and which are expressed in aphoristic form, like proverbs and adages. A famous collection of maxims and reflections is that of La Rochefoucauld. Locke, however, uses the word in a more general sense as a synonym for 'axiom', a truth taken to be basic and self-evident (*Essay Concerning Human Understanding* Bk 4, ch. 7; Bk 4, ch. 12). **2** In some eighteenth-century philosophers, including Kant, a maxim is a rule of action adopted by the agent, a 'subjective principle of volition'.

maximin principle a rule for decision-making. It recommends that when deciding between policies, we should consider only the worst possible outcome for each policy, and opt for the one of which the worst outcome is least bad.

A simple example is this: suppose we can envisage that deciding *one* way will result in a gain of 5 units at worst, and 50 units at best, and that deciding *another* way will yield 3 units at worst and 500 units at best. The rule recommends *maxi*mizing the *min*imum gain and will therefore favour the first policy. It suits a pessimist: it is reasonable to favour the first, if you see yourself as a potential loser.

In *A Theory of Justice* 1971, John Rawls argues that the maximin principle is the one that a rational agent would adopt in the 'original position' when agreeing on a social structure without knowing what place he might occupy within it.

Maximizing the minimum gain and minimizing the maximum loss comes to the same in this context, and some writers like John von Neumann and Robert Nozick have called it the *minimax* principle.

Mazdaism *See* ZARATHUSTRA.

McTaggart /mək'tægət/, John McTaggart Ellis (1866–1925) Cambridge philosopher, fellow of Trinity College. Much of his work was devoted to close critical studies of

Hegel's philosophy. His metaphysics, presented with clarity and rigour in *The Nature of Existence*, 2 vols, 1921, 1927 is at considerable variance with common sense. The only existing entities are minds, and the essential relation between them, as yet very imperfectly realized, is one of love. Love has intrinsic value: this is a simple, unanalysable property. The existence of a mind has a timeless aspect, indeed time is, strictly speaking, unreal: hence, souls are immortal. McTaggart did not, however, believe that there could be an over-arching mind, i.e. God. Various mental contents, e.g. sense-data, judgements and inferences, do not exist; nor do material objects, space and time.

Because of the careful and lucid argumentation, especially as regards the nature and non-existence of time, McTaggart's views have remained on the philosophical agenda.

Mead, George Herbert (1863–1931) American philosopher, professor at the University of Chicago from 1892. His most important writings were collected posthumously in *Mind, Self and Society* 1934. He developed a theory of the social constitution of the self, in which communication with others is seen as essential for self-awareness and all higher forms of mental activity. The ability to adopt more than one vantage point, which can come into being only by means of social interaction, is an essential characteristic of the mind.

mean, doctrine of the A virtue is a mean between two extremes, according to Aristotle's *Nicomachean Ethics*, Book 2, 6 (1106^{a}ff). For instance, courage lies between the excesses of timidity and rashness, generosity between stinginess and extravagance, gentleness between stolidity and irascibility.

Megarian School a number of ancient philosophers who, according to tradition, formed a group named after Euclid of Megara (d. *c.* 366 BC), a disciple of Socrates. Among its members, known for their interest in logic and dialectic, are counted Eubulides, Diodorus and Stilpo.

Meinong /'maɪnɔŋ (Gm.)/, Alexius (1853–1920) Austrian philosopher, who studied under and was heavily influenced by Brentano. From 1889 he was professor at Graz, where he established an influential institute of psychology and an important school of philosophy.

Meinong's main investigations all begin from his philosophy of mind, where he put forward a general tripartite analysis of mental experience, comprising act, content and object. It is a distinguishing mark of the *mental* that mental experiences and states are always directed to an object. Such universal direction of mental experience to objects is sometimes dignified as the 'thesis of intentionality'. Much of Meinong's highly original systematization grows out of further investigation of the *objects* involved; this soon turns out to go far beyond the experiencing subject. In the full relational analysis of basic mental experience, subject-directed-to-object, the further elements give the two dimensions of direction and focus. The 'act element' signifies the manner in which the given subject is directed to the object concerned, while the 'content element' gives focus; it is that which swings the direction to one object rather than another. For example, the difference between thinking of a god and believing in a god is a difference in act; that between thinking of a god and thinking of a unicorn a difference in content. Roughly, in judging that Pegasus is winged, the *act* is judging, the *object* is the proposition (or objective) that Pegasus is winged, and the *content* is what directs that judging to that proposition. In act–content terms, a detailed classification of mental phenomena can be reached. Broadly, these divide into three types: (1) presentations, (2) assumptions and judgements, and (3) affective and desiderative attitudes. To these correspond, roughly, three prime divisions of Meinong's philosophical theory: object theory, complex theory and value theory.

Object theory. Object theory represents an enormous expansion of ontology, the theory of what exists, to encompass as well what does not exist, including both objects that are merely possible and objects that are impossible, and perhaps also objects that are defective. By contrast, the whole of traditional metaphysics, of which ontology is the centrepiece, exhibits a heavy 'prejudice in favour of the actual', and tends to neglect and denature what does not steadfastly exist – not merely objects that exist only marginally or flickeringly, but, above all, objects that may have no kind of being at all.

According to Meinong's general object theory, very many objects do not exist, yet these objects are constituted in some way or other, through features they have, and so may be made subjects of true predication. First, every object has a character (a *Sosein*). This character is given through a set of characterizing (or nuclear) features. Secondly, objects truly possess their characterizing features. For example, the round square is both round and square; the statements 'the round square is round' and 'the golden mountain I am thinking of is golden' are true statements, although about non-existent objects. Thus thirdly, how they are, as given through their characterizing features, is substantially independent of whether they exist. The point is elevated in the thesis of independence of *Sosein* from *Sein* (being), of make-up from existence. This thesis forms part of Meinong's doctrine of *Aussersein* (being beyond) concerning a class of objects beyond being of any kind, subsistence or existence.

Objects divide into a wondrous variety of types. A major division separates (basic) objects from higher-order objects, which are founded on objects of lower order. Among objects, an important division among non-existent objects is between merely possible objects, including incomplete objects, and impossible objects, whose features prove very perplexing for standard logical theory. We refer to a golden mountain although it does not exist; incomplete objects, such as 'something blue', having no definite shape features, violate the usual law of excluded middle; impossible objects, such as the round square, infringe the usual law of non-contradiction.

Although Meinong's theory itself remains incomplete on several issues of importance, such as just which features are nuclear and which features non-existent objects lack, Meinong does indicate several further principles of prime logical importance. These include: (1) an object abstraction axiom: for every *Sosein* there is a corresponding object; (2) freedom of thought and assumption: every object can be thought of, and (at a higher order) any proposition can be assumed; (3) the signification principle: the signification (*Bedeutung*) of every subject term is an object. These principles vastly simplify and smooth general logical theory. For example, they facilitate a uniform semantic theory, since every subject term initially functions in the same way, and they enable a uniform treatment of fact and fiction, as there is no initial qualitative difference between characters of objects, whether they exist or not.

Complex theory. Among complex objects, those composed of other items are wholes, relational clusters, and higher-order objects (those that contain objects as constituents). Among the latter are objectives, the objects of assumption and judgements. Such an assumption as that 'flying saucers are illusory' signifies neither a basic nor a concrete object, but an objective, the illusory being of flying saucers, an object of higher order containing flying saucers as a constituent. That is, assumptions, like judgements, take objectives as their objects. In fact, an objective is what philosophers more usually call a proposition or a complex fact. In the same way that there are objects which do not exist, so there are objectives which do not obtain, i.e. false propositions. Such objectives are genuine objects also, with a make-up that is independent of thought or expression. This theory of objectives helps immediately in dislodging traditional puzzles, such as how it is that one can express, or believe, what does not obtain. Meinong argues, more generally, that the theory of assumptions and their signification alone can explain properly such phenomena as apprehension of negative facts; the nature of inference, of dialogue and communication in general; and even the nature of play and of games, and art.

Evidence theory and object apprehension. Objects which do not exist play a major mediating role in apprehension of those which exist and in acquisition of knowledge. Incomplete objects, indeterminate in many respects, are the means by which we have mental access to objects which do exist and are fully determinate in their traits. For example we perceive the speckled hen by way of an object, datum, with no determinate number of speckles. In epistemology, Meinong adjusts Brentano's theory of evidence and self-evidence (*a priori* judgements are not affected by whether their objects exist or not) and, more daringly, introduces a notion of *surmise-evidence* (*Vermutungsevidenz*) which is needed to understand, and justify, perception, memory and induction. We discover the misleading elements by their lack of coherence with our overall body of knowledge. Thus, evident prescriptions may be directly evident, but not certain, and indeed occasionally false. Meinong resolves in a holistic fashion the problems that this unusual consequence appears to generate (anticipating the later conception, e.g. in John Rawls, of reflective equilibrium). For example, such pieces of knowledge may be compared with cards in a pack, no one of which can stand up by itself but several of which placed together can hold one another up successfully.

Value theory. In Meinong's mature theory of (impersonal) value, there are features or forms of objects, including value features and value universals, which are discerned *through* our emotions and desires, by emotional presentation. (Meinong's earlier theory of personal value is significantly different, being much more psychological.) That is, emotions and desires, like sense-perceptions, have subsidiary cognitive functions. The theory is neither a subjective nor an emotive one, nor a moral sense one, as there is no special sense, only a feeling-basis for value data and like information. For example, the feeling of awe upon entering the closed forest *directs* us to the splendour of the forest. The splendour so emotionally presented is no doubt *based* on natural features of the forest such as its many layerings, its variety of habitats, and the variety and huge dimensions of the trees in it. But once again the value concerned, splendour, does not reduce to some sum of these natural features, any more than it does to features of its presentation, to aspects of its methods of verification. Meinong is not aiming for a reductive analysis of value, which would be inappropriate for distinctive value objects 'out there' independent of us; rather, he is working his way to a full phenomenological theory of value.

The process of valuation also discloses various sorts of higher-order valuational objects, value universals; disclosed (by abstractions), along with the good and the beautiful, are the agreeable, the desirable, and the obligatory (of this or that type), and so on. This leads Meinong into a detailed classification and investigation of *dignitatives*, corresponding to axiological concepts, and *desideratives*, corresponding to deontic concepts.

Few of Meinong's writings have been translated into English, but J. N. Findlay, in *Meinong's Theory of Objects and Values*, offers a reliable account. RSY

meiosis /maɪ'əʊsɪs/ (Gr. *meiōsis* diminution) *n.* **1** (in rhetoric) a figure of speech in which the importance of what is said is transparently played down; an understatement. *Ant.* hyperbole. **2** (in biology) a kind of cell division, in which the new cells each have only one chromosome from each pair of chromosomes in the parent cell.

meliorism /'miːlɪərɪzm/ (Lat. *melior* better) *n.* the view that the human condition is improving, or, in particular, the view that social conditions are improving or can be improved as a result of human effort.

Melissus /mə'lɪsəs/ (*fl.* 440 BC) of Samos. He adopted the monism of the Eleatic school, with its rejection of the possibility of change and motion. Of his writings, only fragments are extant.

meme /miːm/ *n.* a unit of cultural replication. The concept was introduced by Richard Dawkins in his *The Selfish Gene* 1976 in analogy with the concept of a gene, the unit of biological replication. Memes, such as tunes, fashions, traditions, moral rules or theories, are transmitted from one generation to another culturally (by social influences on the individual), in contrast to genes, which are transmitted biologically; but memes are similar to genes in being subject to processes of mutation and selection.

Mendelssohn /'mɛndlsən (Eng.); 'mɛndəlzoːn (Gm.)/, Moses (1729–86) German-Jewish philosopher, whose first languages were Yiddish and Hebrew; he learnt German, French, English, Latin and Greek later in life. It was with him that Jewish intellectual life again began to flourish. It had for centuries been largely isolated from the rise of humanism and the growth of modern science and philosophy represented by Bacon, Galileo and Descartes.

Mendelssohn was one of the leading representatives of Enlightenment philosophy. His friendship with some of the leading writers of his time was close and lasting. When German dramatic art reached full maturity with the drama *Nathan der Weise* 1779 (Nathan the wise), written by his friend G. E. Lessing (1729–81), the main character was modelled on him.

Mendelssohn joined the efforts of other German 'popular philosophers' to introduce philosophical ideas to a wider reading public. His style set a new standard of simplicity, elegance and clarity.

In aesthetics, he introduced a distinction between two kinds of perfection: metaphysical and aesthetic. To suggest that beauty consists of unity amidst variety (as Hutcheson had done) would be to confuse the two. The beautiful pleases subjectively, even though something aesthetically pleasing may be objectively imperfect: tragedy is an obvious case in point.

In 1764 the Royal Prussian Academy awarded him its prize (ahead of Kant, Lambert and Thomas Abbt) for an essay on the question of what kind of evidence there can be for metaphysical theories. His *Phädon* 1767, an adaptation of Plato's *Phaedo*, gives arguments for the indivisibility, indestructibility and hence immortality of the soul. He believed that other basic doctrines of religion and metaphysics can also be established by reason alone, and was not persuaded by the opposing theory of Kant's *Critique of Pure Reason* 1781, as can be seen in his *Morgenstunden* 1785 (Morning hours), which presented arguments for the existence of God. It also rejected idealism of the Berkeleian kind.

In *Jerusalem* 1783 he advocated religious toleration, making use of Modern Natural Law Theory. He argued that the diversity of religions ought not to prevent them from coexisting peacefully, since they all agree on the basic principles of morals and metaphysics, principles which are capable of rational demonstration. All enforcement, not only of civil laws but also of the rules of a religious body, belongs to the secular authority. If this is accepted, toleration becomes practicable.

mentalism *n.* the view that the causal explanation of behaviour cannot be satisfactory if it is expressed exclusively in non-mental terms. *Ant.* behaviourism; physicalism.

mention *See* USE.

mereology (Gr. *meros* part) *n.* the theory of the relation between parts and wholes.

merism (Gr. *meros* part) *n.* a theory which explains a whole through the nature or functioning of its parts. *Ant.* holism.

Merleau-Ponty /mɛʀlopɔ̃ti (Fr.)/, Maurice (1908–61) French philosopher. In works such as *La phénoménologie de la perception* 1945 (Phenomenology of perception) and *Le visible et l'invisible* 1964 (The visible and the invisible) he offered an analysis of perception, action, the self, and their interplay in human experience and reflection. The aim was to construct an anti-sceptical account of knowledge and reality that is neither monist nor dualist, and which has at its basis the world of perceptual experience. The originality of his description of this experienced world, called *Lebenswelt* ('life-world') by Husserl, is due to the attention given to the role of the body in the construction of a spatiotemporal world.

In the early post-war years he was the driving force, together with Jean-Paul Sartre and Simone de Beauvoir, behind the influential journal *Les Temps Modernes*, but in the early 1950s he fell out with them as his sympathy with the Soviet political system waned more rapidly than theirs.

Mersenne /mɛʀsɛn (Fr.)/, Marin (1588–1648) French man of learning. He criticized the shortcomings of Aristotelian science, but was also hostile to cabbalism, astrology, alchemy, belief in sorcery and witchcraft, and other forms of occultism, which had been cultivated by some anti-Aristotelian renaissance humanists. Mersenne's sympathies were with the new scientific outlook. In his view, the physical universe points to a mathematician-God. He maintained friendly contact with Protestants and Socinians, and was on good terms with Gassendi, Descartes, and many other philosophers and scientists. By conversation and by maintaining a vast correspondence, he was a central figure in the rise of modern philosophy and science, 'the secretary of the learned Europe'.

Meslier /mɛlje (Fr.)/, Jean (1664–1729) Occupying a modest station in life as a priest (*curé*) in a small parish in northern France, Meslier prudently kept his extremely radical opinions to himself but, after his death, a major manuscript, known as his *Testament*, was found. It had a wide clandestine circulation in manuscript copies, and influenced the radical writers of the French Enlightenment. Voltaire published extracts from this manuscript, but it was not published in full until the 1860s, and the only complete and authoritative edition is the one published in Paris 1970–72.

In Meslier's view, all revealed religion is nothing but fraud and imposture maintained by cunning priests and princes. He also raised persuasive objections against the standard arguments (from motion, from design, etc.) for natural religion and rejected mind–matter dualism. His own standpoint was uncompromisingly atheist and materialist. This outlook would not, he argued, have an adverse effect on morality, since all of us can directly grasp the truths of morality by the light of natural reason. On the basis of this natural morality, of which natural justice is a part, he condemned the spiritual and material oppression and exploitation of the numerous poor by the powerful few, describing vividly but accurately the vast amount of human misery caused by it. This was the misery of poverty, hunger and illness, but also the suffering resulting from the inculcation and enforcement of a repressive sexual morality.

His vehement condemnation of all-prevailing injustice also inspired his call to the common people to rise and violently overthrow their rich and powerful oppressors, and to set up a different kind of society, along communitarian lines, in which all could live in cooperation and harmony.

For his time, Meslier's combination of materialism, atheism and revolutionary communism is most remarkable.

Meslier's reputation preceded publication. Holbach took advantage of this, and wrote and published anonymously *Le Bon sens du curé Meslier, c.* 1772 (transl. as *Superstition in All Ages* 1878). It contains radical views, but Meslier is not the author.

Mesmer /'mɛsmər (Gm.)/, Franz Anton (1734–1815) Mesmer became a celebrity through public performances of many curious tricks, including hypnotic phenomena. These were explained in terms of a previously unexplored force called animal magnetism; this theory found favour among romantic philosophers because of its seemingly anti-mechanistic implications. An official contemporary inquiry into Mesmer's claims resulted in a negative report. Kant thought that Mesmer was essentially an entertainer comparable to ventriloquists and conjurors. His activities did, however, stimulate subsequent research into hypnotism.

meta- a Greek word-element, meaning *beyond* or *above*. In twentieth-century philosophy this prefix signifies 'aboutness' and is used to form new terms which signify a discourse, theory or field of inquiry one level above its object, which is also a discourse, theory or field of inquiry. Accordingly, *metaethics* is the analysis of moral concepts and arguments, *metamathematics* is the theory of mathematical concepts and proofs, etc.

metabasis /mɪ'tæbəsɪs/ Gr. change, a taking beyond, transition *n.* The word is now used chiefly in the phrase *metabasis eis allo genos*, an (impermissible) transition to another kind – e.g. a category mistake.

metadiegetic /mɛtədaɪɪ'dʒiːtɪk/ (Gr. *meta-* + *diēgēsis* narrative) *adj.* (in literary theory) a metadiegetic narrative is an embedded narrative, a story told by a character in the main story. This neologism, as used by the literary theorist G. Genette in his *Narrative Discourse* 1980, can be confusing, since 'meta-' normally would suggest a framing rather than a framed level. Other theorists have preferred *hypodiegetic*.

metaethics /mɛtə'ɛθɪks/ *n.* the philosophical analysis of moral concepts, judgements and arguments. Among the questions that fall within the purview of metaethics are: (1) semantic questions: What is the meaning of moral terms like 'good', 'ought', and 'right'?; (2) logical questions: What are the conditions of validity of moral arguments?; (3) ontological questions: In what sense are there moral facts?; (4) epistemological questions: Is there such a thing as moral knowledge, and, if so, what are its scope and limits?

In contrast, the inquiry which has the evaluation of human character and conduct as its subject-matter is called ethics, or, to mark the contrast, normative ethics.

The sharp division between metaethics, also called analytical ethics, and normative or substantive ethics was not much observed before the twentieth century.

Note: Mary Daly's 'metaethics of radical feminism' in her *Gyn/Ecology* 1978 is a deviant use of the term, intended to suggest a type of inquiry more profound and intuitive and in that sense 'beyond' ethics.

metalanguage *n.* a language used to talk *about* a natural language (e.g. English, French, Latin, Mandarin) or *about* a formal language (e.g. formalized propositional logic). The language talked about is called the object-language. For example, the statement ' "(p & q)" is a well-formed formula' says something about an expression in the formal language of propositional logic. The statement is in the metalanguage, and the part enclosed by double quotation marks is in the object-language.

metalepsis (*sing.*); **metalepses** (*pl.*) /mɛtə'lɛpsɪs; -iːz/ (Gr. a taking beyond) *n.* **1** (in rhetoric) the use of metonymy to replace an expression that is already used figuratively. **2** (in literature) a statement that conveys a message indirectly, for example, the courteous 'I have got some letters to write' when the fact is that I do not want company. **3** (in semiotics) transgression of narrative levels, as when a narrator breaks into the story to address the reader directly.

metalogic *n.* the inquiry which has for its object systems of formal logic. The consistency and the completeness of a system are among the topics that belong to this field of inquiry.

metamathematics *n.* the inquiry which has for its object a formalized mathematical theory. The derivability, provability, computability and decidability of the statements of a mathematical theory are among the topics belonging to this field of inquiry.

metanarrative *n.* stories that underpin the legitimacy of a commitment or activity. The concept was introduced by LYOTARD. Examples of such stories are: that society exists for the good of its members; that society is divided into two opposing classes; that knowledge is worth seeking for its own sake; etc. Some metanarratives are described as 'grand narratives'. These are general accounts of human society and its history, as provided by Christianity, Hegelianism or Marxism. The view that history is a process of human emancipation (Condorcet, Kant) is another 'grand narrative'. Lyotard takes the adherence to some metanarrative to be characteristically 'modern' and argues against it in favour of the 'post-modern' pluralistic insight that human affairs are more fragmented and less neatly structured than such metanarratives allow.

In literary theory, the word has been used in an entirely different sense by G. Genette, for a METADIEGETIC narrative.

metanoia /mɛtə'nɔɪə/ (Gr. *metanoia* change of mind) *n.* spiritual or intellectual conversion; a radical 'change of heart'.

metaphilosophy *n.* inquiry into, or theory about, the nature of philosophy.

Asserting that philosophy has come (or ought to come, or will soon come) to an end, some French writers (H. Lefebvre, *Métaphilosophie* 1965; K. Axelos) have used the word in an entirely different sense, to denote the theoretical or practical activity that remains available *after* the demise of philosophy.

metaphor /ˈmɛtəfɔː; ˈmɛtəfə/ (Gr. *metaphora* a transfer) *n.* a figure of speech in which one linguistic expression is used instead of another, in order to suggest some similarity, for example 'the river of time'; 'A mighty fortress is our God'; 'A woman is a rose'. Unlike a simile, there is no 'as' or 'like' to point to the similarity.

The analysis of metaphor and the distinction between metaphorical and literal meaning are widely debated in contemporary philosophy.

Note: A *metaphor* is not the same as a *symbol* or a *symptom* or a *sign*. It is not correct to say that Madonna (a stage performer) is a 'metaphor' for post-modernity. She may be said to *symbolize* it. An undue delay in offering service can be a symptom of weakness in a bureaucracy but is not properly called a metaphor of the weakness.

metaphysics /mɛtəˈfɪzɪks/ *n.* (Gr. *ta meta ta physika* what comes after the Physics; but it can also mean 'what lies beyond nature')

When Andronicus of Rhodes (first century BC), the tenth head of the Lyceum, edited Aristotle's works, the fourteen books dealing with 'The First Philosophy' were placed *after* the books on *physics* (*meta ta physika*) and were accordingly called metaphysics. They deal with the most fundamental concepts: reality, existence, substance, causality, etc.

Such an inquiry would lead to an understanding of the ultimate reality which lies behind that which we confront in sensory experience. This understanding is not itself based on sensory experience, but on rational analysis or insight. It was then only a short step to interpret *ta meta ta physika* as the inquiry into or theory of that which lies *beyond nature* and transcends the limits of ordinary knowledge and experience.

Metaphysical inquiry has a continuous history as much as philosophy itself. One influential division of its subject-matter was codified by Christian Wolff (1679–1754). He took metaphysics to have four major parts: ontology (the general doctrine of being or existence), rational theology (the doctrine of God's existence and attributes); rational cosmology (the doctrine of the world); and rational psychology (the doctrine of the existence and attributes of the soul).

Kant used the word *metaphysics* in various ways. In one sense, he took *metaphysics of nature* and *metaphysics of morals* to consist of what can be known *a priori* within these areas, and his books with those words in their titles attempt to give a systematic account of this. But Kant also used the term *metaphysics* to signify the traditional attempt to establish knowledge about a realm lying beyond our natural world, a transcendent realm. Like Hume before him, though for different reasons, he considered metaphysics in this sense an impossible task.

Hume and Kant were not, however, the first to reject metaphysics. Concurrent with the cultivation of metaphysics through the ages there have regularly emerged strong doubts or outright rejection. Especially since the rise of modern science it has been regarded as useless speculation. Many empiricists and positivists (Hume, Comte, Carnap) have strongly rejected the assumption that there is a reality beyond the natural and empirical world, and that something can be known about it. This rejection of *transcendent* metaphysics does not rule out philosophical inquiry into the concepts of reality, existence, substance, etc.

metaphysics of presence an expression used

by Derrida for an assumption which is said to underlie the Western philosophical tradition, viz. that ultimately reality is a unity, and that differences are not ultimately real. This view, which implies that (ultimately) everything is identical with everything else, is rejected by Derrida. But his rejection of this view seems also to include a rejection of the entirely different and extremely plausible view that everything is identical with itself. The two views are not equivalent. *See* DIFFERENCE, METAPHYSICS OF.

metapsychology /mɛtəsaɪˈkɒlədʒɪ/ *n.* (in psychological theory) a term introduced by Freud for his own theory of the unconscious, by which he indicated that it went *beyond* the standard object of psychological investigation, i.e. the conscious mind.

metatheory *n.* A metatheory has for its subject-matter the inquiry into, or theory of, a certain subject-matter; it is a second-order inquiry or theory.

metempsychosis /mɛtəmsaɪˈkəʊsɪs/ (Gr. *meta-* + *en-* in, within + *psychē* soul) *n.* transmigration of the soul.

meteorology *n.* Until Aristotle, the term was used for the study of *all* the things 'up there': stars, planets, comets, clouds, etc.

methexis /məˈθɛksɪs/ (Gr. partaking, participation) *n.* the relation between a particular and a form (in Plato's sense), e.g. a beautiful object is said to partake of the form of beauty.

methodological individualism *See* INDIVIDUALISM.

methodology *n.* **1** the discipline which investigates and evaluates methods of inquiry, of validation, of teaching, etc. **2** a theory within that discipline. Note that methodology is *about* method, and not the same as method.

metonymy /mɪˈtɒnɪmɪ/ (Gr. *metonymia* a renaming) *n.* the substitution of one linguistic expression by another, when there is a significant association between the two, e.g. the use of *Washington* to mean the United States government, of *Bush House* to mean the British Broadcasting Corporation, or of *heart* to mean a person's feelings.

Metaphor, in which the link between the two expressions is one of similarity, is a kind of metonymy.

microcosm *See* MACROCOSM.

micrology *n.* excessive attention to petty detail.

middle knowledge *See* MOLINA.

middle term the term common to the two premisses in a categorical syllogism.

Milesian *adj.* pertaining to Miletus.

Miletus a Greek city-state on the Ionian west coast of Asia Minor (today's Turkey), home to the first philosophers, Thales Anaximander and Anaximenes, in the sixth century BC.

Mill, John Stuart (1806–73) born in London in 1806, son of James Mill, philosopher, economist and senior official in the East India Company. Mill gave a vivid and moving account of his life, and especially of his extraordinary education, in the *Autobiography* 1873 that he wrote towards the end of his life. Mill led an active career as an administrator in the East India Company, from which he retired only when the Company's administrative functions in India were taken over by the British government following the Mutiny of 1857. In addition, he was Liberal MP for Westminster 1865–8, and as a young man in the 1830s edited the *London and Westminster Review*, a radical quarterly journal. He died at Aix-en-Provence in 1873.

Mill was educated by his father, with the advice and assistance of Jeremy Bentham and Francis Place. He learned Greek at three, Latin a little later; by the age of 12, he was a competent logician and by 16 a well-trained economist. At 20 he suffered a nervous breakdown that persuaded him that more was needed in life than devotion to the public good and an analytically sharp intellect. Having grown up a utilitarian, he now turned to Coleridge, Wordsworth and Goethe to cultivate his aesthetic sensibilities. From 1830 to his death, he tried to persuade the British public of the necessity of a scientific approach to understanding social, political and economic change while not neglecting the insights of poets and other imaginative writers.

His *System of Logic* 1843 was an ambitious attempt to give an account not only of logic, as the title suggests, but of the methods of science and their applicability to social as well as purely natural phenomena. Mill's conception of logic was not entirely that of modern logicians; besides formal logic, what he called 'the logic of consistency', he thought that there was a logic of proof, that is, a logic that would show how evidence proved or tended to prove the conclusions we draw from the evidence. That led him to the analysis of causation, and to an account of inductive reasoning that remains the starting point of most modern discussions. Mill's account of explanation in science was broadly that explanation seeks the causes of events where it is events in which we are interested; or seeks more general laws where we are concerned to explain less general laws as special cases of those laws. Mill's discussion of the possibility of finding a scientific explanation of social events has worn equally well; Mill was as unwilling to suppose that the social sciences would become omniscient about human behaviour as to suppose that there was no prospect of explaining social affairs at any deeper level than that of common sense. Throughout the *System of Logic* Mill attacked the 'intuitionist' philosophy of William Whewell and Sir William Hamilton. This was the view that explanations rested on intuitively compelling principles rather than on general, causal laws, and that ultimately the search for such intuitively compelling principles rested on understanding the universe as a divine creation governed by principles that a rational deity must choose. Mill thought that intuitionism was bad philosophy, and a comfort to political conservatism into the bargain. His *Examination of Sir William Hamilton's Philosophy* 1865 carried the war into the enemy camp with a vengeance; it provoked vigorous controversy for some twenty years or so, but is now the least readable of Mill's works.

To the public at large, Mill was better known as the author of *Principles of Political Economy* 1848, a work that tried to show that economics was not the 'dismal science' that its radical and literary critics had supposed. Its philosophical interest lay in Mill's reflections on the difference between what economics measured and what human beings really valued: leading Mill to argue that we should sacrifice economic growth for the sake of the environment, and should limit population as much to give ourselves breathing space as in order to fend off the risk of starvation for the overburdened poor. Mill also allowed that conventional economic analysis could not show that socialism was unworkable, and suggested as his own ideal an economy of worker-owned cooperatives. Commentators have argued inconclusively over whether this is a form of socialism or merely 'workers' capitalism'.

Mill remains most nearly our contemporary in the area of moral and political philosophy, however. His *Utilitarianism* 1861 remains the classic defence of the view that we ought to aim at maximizing the welfare of all sentient creatures, and that that welfare consists of their happiness. Mill's defence of the view that we ought to pursue happiness because we do pursue happiness, has been the object of savage attack by, among others, F. H. Bradley in his *Ethical Studies* 1874 and G. E. Moore in *Principia Ethica* 1903. But others have argued that on this particular point, Mill was misinterpreted by his critics. His insistence that happiness was to be assessed not merely by quantity but by quality – the doctrine that a dissatisfied Socrates is not only better than a satisfied fool, but somehow happier, too – has puzzled generations of commentators. And his attempt to show that justice can be accounted for in utilitarian terms is still important as a riposte to such writers as John Rawls (*A Theory of Justice* 1971).

During his lifetime, it was his essay *On Liberty* 1859 that aroused the greatest controversy, and the most violent expressions of approval and disapproval. The essay was sparked by the feeling that Mill and his wife, Harriet Taylor, constantly expressed in their letters to one another: that they lived in a society where bold and adventurous individuals were becoming all too rare. Critics have sometimes thought that Mill was frightened by the prospect of a mass democracy in which working-class opinion would be oppressive and perhaps violent. The truth is that Mill was frightened by middle-class conformism much more than by anything to be looked for from an enfranchised working class. It was a fear he had picked up from reading Alexis de Tocquevillé's *Democracy in America* 1836, 1840; America was a prosperous middle-class society, and Mill feared that it was also a society that cared nothing for individual liberty.

Mill lays down 'one very simple principle' to govern the use of coercion in society – and by coercion he means both legal penalties and the operation of public opinion; it is that we may only coerce others in self-defence – either to defend ourselves, or to defend others from harm. Crucially, this rules out paternalistic interventions to save people from themselves, and ideal interventions to make people behave 'better'. It has long exercised critics to explain how a utilitarian can subscribe to such a principle of self-restraint; a utilitarian is obliged to support the principle that we should coerce people whenever it does more good than harm. Mill saw this, and argued that it was because human beings were 'progressive' creatures that utility itself required such self-restraint. In essence, Mill argues that only by adopting the self-restraint principle can we seek out the truth, experience the truth as 'our own', and fully develop individual selves.

Of Mill's shorter works, two others deserve mention. *The Subjection of Women* 1869 was thought to be excessively radical in Mill's time but is now seen as a classic statement of liberal feminism. Its essential case is that if freedom is a good for men, it is for women, and that every argument against this view drawn from the supposedly different 'nature' of men and women has been superstitious special pleading. If women have different natures, the only way to discover what they are is by experiment, and that requires that women should have access to everything to which men have access. Only after as many centuries of freedom as there have been centuries of oppression will we really know what our natures are. Mill published *The Subjection of Women* late in life to avoid controversies that would lessen the impact of his other work. He chose not to have his *Three Essays on Religion* 1874 published until after his death. They argued, among other things, that it is impossible that the universe is governed by an omnipotent and loving God, but not unlikely that a less than omnipotent benign force is at work in the world. They thus tended to disappoint those of Mill's admirers who looked for a tougher and more abrasive agnosticism, while doing nothing to appease critics who deplored the fact that he was any kind of agnostic. But they remain models of the calm discussion of contentious topics, and highly readable to this day. AR

millet seed paradox one of ZENO OF ELEA'S paradoxes. A single grain of millet makes no sound when it falls. A bushel of millet makes a sound when it falls.

One interpretation of this is that Zeno wanted to argue simply that our sense of hearing is not very acute. But it can also be interpreted as a case in which, so to speak, something seems to be produced by a finite number of nothings: an audible sound from a finite number of inaudible sounds. Reason tells us it cannot be done; our senses contradict this, and therefore they cannot be trusted.

mimesis /mɪˈmiːsɪs/ (Gr. imitation) *n.* an important concept in ancient aesthetics: Aristotle held that art imitates nature and, by representing the character, actions and destinies of persons, brings out the universal (*Poetics*, chapter 9). Plato had a low opinion of most art forms because of their imitative nature, which makes them far removed from truth, from 'the real thing'. In the *Republic*, Book 3, 395c, he also warns that bad qualities may rub off on the artist who imitates a bad character. He contrasts *mimesis* with *diegesis* (narrative), where there is more of a distance between the story-teller and the story told. **mimetic** *adj.*

mind–brain identity theory *See* IDENTITY THEORY OF MIND.

minimalism *n.* a theory which works from a reduced or limited number of assumptions.

This usage seems to have become fashionable among philosophers since the late 1980s. For example, a redundancy theory of truth can be described as minimalist, and the view that it is possible to do without metaphysical assumptions when settling the question whether persons can be held responsible for their actions has also been so described.

minimax principle *See* MAXIMIN PRINCIPLE.

minor premiss The minor premiss in a categorical syllogism is the premiss which contains the minor term.

minor term The minor term in a categorical syllogism is the term which is the subject of the conclusion.

miracle /ˈmɪrəkl/ (Lat. *mirari* to be astonished, to wonder, to admire) *n.* an event which could not or would not have occurred in the ordinary course of nature but is brought about through the deliberate intervention of a supernatural being.

It was in this vein that Hume defined a miracle as 'a transgression of a law of nature by a particular volition of the Deity, or by the interposition of some invisible agent' (*Enquiry Concerning Human Understanding* 1748, section X 'Of Miracles', Part 1, footnote).

Judaism, Christianity and Islam have at their foundation certain alleged miracles. Because of this, questions concerning the nature and possibility of miracles were taken to be of central significance. Without miracles these religions, or at least central doctrines in them, must be rejected or else radically re-interpreted.

In the modern era, virtually all the great philosophers have rejected the belief in miracles. Spinoza held that miracles are impossible and belief in them a mere superstition. Miracle stories could, however, benefit and edify the ignorant. Hume argued that it is always more likely that the testimonies and other evidence for a miracle are fraudulent or at least mistaken, than that it actually took place.

misandry /'mɪzændrɪ/ *n.* dislike or hatred of men. (Also *misandrism.*)

misanthropy /mɪz'ænθrəpɪ/ *n.* dislike or hatred of mankind.

misogyny /mɪ'sɒdʒɪnɪ/ *n.* dislike or hatred of women.

misology /mɪ'sɒlədʒɪ/ *n.* 'hatred of reason'; an anti-intellectual attitude. The word occurs in Plato, *Phaedo*, 89d, whom Kant echoes in *Critique of Pure Reason*, B883 and in *Foundations of the Metaphysics of Morals*, chapter 1, AA 395.

misoneism /mɪsəʊ'niːɪzm/ *n.* dislike or hatred of innovations.

mitosis /mɪ'təʊsɪs; maɪ'təʊsɪs/ *n.* (in biology) cell division.

modal *adj.* **1** of or pertaining to a MODE. **2** of or pertaining to MODALITIES.

modalities *n.* modal concepts, propositions, terms or verbs. **1** According to classical logic, there are three modalities: necessity, actuality and possibility. Propositions can be true necessarily, actually or possibly. Two important logical principles involving modalities are: (a) *Necessarily p* implies *Actually p* (Lat. *a necesse ad esse valet consequentia*); (b) *Actually p* implies *Possibly p* (Lat. *ab esse ad posse valet consequentia*). **2** In present-day philosophy, it is primarily necessity and possibility that are counted as modal concepts. These can be expressed in a variety of idioms, using words like 'necessarily', 'possibly', 'must', 'may', 'can', etc.

The usual basic logical relations can be easily surveyed in a modal hexagon (Figure 3), which also shows that (together with negation) only one of *necessarily* and *possibly* is needed to define the rest. Arrows signify implication, forks contradiction.

These concepts are primarily ascribed to *states of affairs* or *propositions*, rather than to objects or individuals. This means that they are most naturally construed with 'that'-clauses ('It is necessarily the case that p'; 'it is possibly true that p', and the like). Other groups of concepts resemble them in this respect, and can therefore also be called modal in a wider sense. The ones presented above are then called *alethic* modalities, to distinguish them from e.g. *epistemic* modalities ('it is believed that p', 'it is known that p'), from *deontic* modalities ('it is obligatory that p', 'it is permissible that p'), etc.

modal logic a branch of logic which studies and attempts to systematize those logical relations between propositions which hold by virtue of containing (alethic) modal terms, typically such terms as 'necessarily', 'possibly' and 'contingently'. Sometimes the term 'modal logic' is used more widely, to cover in addition the study of propositions containing epistemic terms such as 'known' or 'believed', or deontic terms such as 'obligatory' or 'permissible'. Sometimes the term 'intensional logic' is used in this wider sense.

Modal logic was investigated in ancient Greece, chiefly by Aristotle, whose main achievement in this field was the study of the effect of introducing modal terms into the premisses and conclusions of syllogisms. Work in this tradition was considerably extended and elaborated by medieval logicians; but after the end of the medieval period and until the early twentieth century, little if any original work appears to have been done in this area. Since then, however, the subject has developed rapidly and vigorously.

Modern modal logic has developed

Figure 3 Logical relations between modal statements

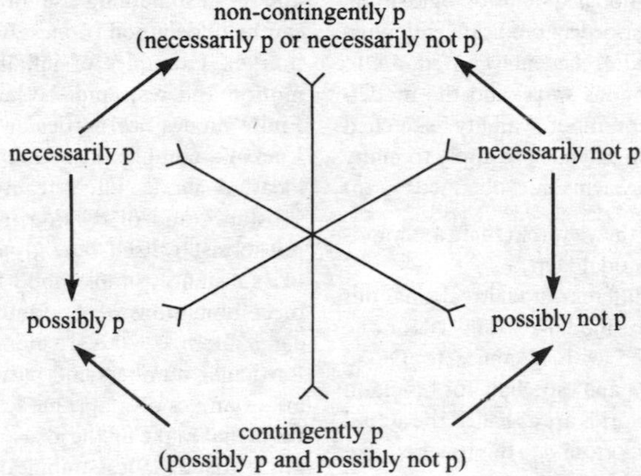

mainly, though not exclusively, in two directions: by the setting up of axiomatic systems, and by the construction of semantic definitions of validity.

Typically (though not invariably), an axiomatic system of modal logic is constructed by adding some new elements to some system of non-modal logic, such as one of the standard axiomatizations of the two-valued propositional calculus. For this purpose, one or more operators intended to be given a modal interpretation are added to the standard notation; often, one (written 'L' or □ for 'necessarily', and another (written 'M' or ◇, defined as '∼L∼' or ∼□∼ for 'possibly', are used. Some new axioms and/or transformation rules, involving these modal operators, are then added to the non-modal axiomatic basis. Some of the best-known systems have been produced by adding to orthodox propositional calculus the extra transformation rule that if α is a theorem so is $L\alpha$, and as extra axioms the formula $L(p \supset q) \supset (Lp \supset Lq)$ together with one or more of the formulae $Lp \supset p$, $Lp \supset LLp$, $p \supset LMp$, $Mp \supset LMp$.

The commonest type of validity definition for modal formulae starts from the notion of a model, which consists of (1) a non-empty set of elements ('points', 'possible worlds'), (2) a dyadic relation ('accessibility') which is defined over these elements (i.e. it is specified which worlds are to be taken as accessible from which), and (3) a specification, for each point, of which propositional variables are taken to be true at that point. Any modal formula can then be evaluated as true or false in any given world by applying the ordinary rules for truth-functional operators, together with the rule that $L\alpha$ is true at every point accessible from that point. If we now take some definable class of models (e.g. all those in which the accessibility relation is transitive), validity with respect to that class is defined by saying that a formula is valid if and only if it is true at every point in every model in that class. It has proved possible in a great many cases to show that the formulae are valid with respect to a certain class of models (notably when this class is defined by some condition on the accessibility relation) coincide exactly with the theorems of some axiomatic modal system.

Other non-modal systems of logic (especially the first-order predicate calculus) have had modal elements grafted on to them in analogous ways, and the model-theoretic account of validity sketched above has been extended to apply to many of the modal systems thus obtained. GH

modal realism the view that there are mind-independent modal facts.

There are different modal realisms, but the expression 'modal realism' is for the most part used with reference to David Lewis's theory, and especially for his claim that possible worlds are as real as the actual world. The background to this is in Leibniz, who inspired this account: '"p" is true if and only if in *this* world, p. "Necessarily p" is true if and only if in *every possible* world, p. "Possibly p" is true if and only if in *some possible* world, p.'

There are advantages in this analysis, in that much of modal logic can, as it were, be analysed in terms of the logic of 'every' and 'some', i.e. predicate logic. A problem with the analysis, however, is that it refers to *possible worlds*. Do they exist? If they do not, nothing is explained, but if they do, they seem to be actual rather than not.

According to David Lewis's version of modal realism, possible worlds do exist. They are as real as this world, the actual world. The only difference between the actual and the other real worlds is that the actual world is the one in which we are. There is, however, no interaction of any kind between worlds. An individual is actual in exactly one world. So, for instance, my concern about what *might* have happened to me but did not actually happen is a concern about what *did* happen to another individual, viz. my COUNTERPART in a possible world.

mode *n.* **1** (in Descartes) an accident or quality (of a thing). **2** (in Spinoza) an affection of the substance; something that inheres in something else through which it can be understood (*Ethics*, Book 1, definition 5). Examples of infinite modes are motion and rest, and the laws of nature. Finite modes are particular things. **3** (in Locke) a complex idea, a combination of ideas. A mode differs from the ideas of substance and of relation in that it does not subsist by itself, but only as an affection of a substance. Simple modes are variations or combinations of the same simple idea, e.g. *a dozen*, *a score* are modes of *number*. Particular numbers and particular shapes are examples of simple modes, because the parts that make up the idea are of the same kind. Mixed modes combine different ideas. Beauty is a mixed mode, composed of colour and figure. Ideas relating to conduct are very mixed: inebriation, gratitude, theft, etc. (*Essay Concerning Human Understanding*, 2, 12, 4–5; 2, 13ff). **4** In older usage, e.g. in Locke, the moods of the syllogism are called modes. **5** Twentieth-century writers like Collingwood and Oakeshott have used the term to designate distinct realms of thought or action, each with its own 'truth'. **6** Fashion: the current prevailing taste in dress, manners, style, etc.

model *n.* (in logical theory) a model *of a formula* of a (formal) language is an interpretation of the language such that the formula comes out true. A model *of a formal system* is an interpretation of the formal language of that system such that all formulae that are theorems of the system come out true.

modern *adj.* This is a relative term, and can indeed be used to designate many different periods, doctrines, styles, etc. Generally, the word implies a contrast between a recent (late Lat. *modo*) and an earlier period. One example is the literary 'battle between the ancients and the moderns' in France and

England in the late seventeenth century. Depending on how the recent period is delimited, and which characteristics are seen as significant, the word can be given a variety of meanings.

In the history of philosophy, 'modern philosophy' is the label often assigned to the new philosophy that emerged early in the modern era, and which had as its first major representatives Bacon and Descartes in the early seventeenth century.

Bacon, Locke, Berkeley, Hume, etc. can be described as 'modern empiricists', but that description can also be reserved for twentieth-century philosophers like Mach, Schlick, Carnap, Reichenbach, etc. Similarly, Grotius and Pufendorf are often described as founders of 'modern natural law theory', but sometimes that designation is reserved for more recent writers on natural law.

This is a case in which definition must precede any meaningful discussion. The same applies also to *pre-modern* and *post-modern*.

modernism *n.* a doctrine, or a certain style of thought, or a certain style in the arts. **1** the nominalist *via moderna* of logic, deriving from William of Ockham. The term was used from the fourteenth to the sixteenth century. The implied contrast is with the *via antiqua* of earlier scholastics. **2** a movement within the Roman Catholic Church in the late nineteenth century. Its main representatives were Alfred Loisy (1857–1940) and George Tyrrell (1861–1909). A prominent sympathizer was Friedrich von Hügel (1852–1925). The aim was to adapt the theological and social teachings of the Church to changed conditions. These included the changing social and political conditions due to urbanization and industrialization, the decline of traditional authority, the rise of liberal, democratic and socialist ideas, the changes in world-view due to the influence of modern science, and the scientific and historical approach to Scripture. Although influential, the outlook it represented was entirely rejected in papal encyclicals, especially the *Quanta cura* of 1864 and the *Pascendi dominici gregis* 1907, and its leading representatives were excommunicated or dismissed. **3** a tendency and a movement in the creative and the performing arts, the beginnings of which can be traced to the mid-nineteenth century. It has two distinctive features. One is the probing beneath the surface: showing that things are not what they seem to be or are made out to be; the works of Freud, Nietzsche and Proust exemplify this. The other is the rejection of traditional styles and theories. Modernists wanted to be the avant-garde of an adversary culture, using various techniques to defy and challenge established conventions, in opposition to the complacency of bourgeois philistinism and the vulgarity of a commercialized society; many of them felt keenly the loss of a sense of community in modern life. In literature, among the leading representatives were Ezra Pound, Franz Kafka, T. S. Eliot and James Joyce; in music, Schönberg, Satie and Stravinsky. **4** The word is also used more broadly for the ideals and assumptions often associated with the Enlightenment.

modernity *n.* **1** a certain historical period to which a 'modern' character is ascribed. The period is variously specified. At the core of this conception is the nineteenth- and twentieth-century world of nation-states, political democracy, capitalism, urbanization, mass literacy, mass media, mass culture, rationality, anti-traditionalism, secularization, faith in science, large-scale industrial enterprise, individualism, enlightenment ideals and a public ideology in which liberal, progressive, humanitarian ideals are prominent. Many different combinations of these can be regarded as essential to modernity and used to define it. **2** the character of the period described above.

modulo /ˈmɒdjʊləʊ/ *prep.* **1** Two integers are said to be *congruent modulo n* if they have the same remainder when divided by the integer *n*, or (equivalently) if their difference is a multiple of *n.* For example, 5 and 17 are congruent modulo 3. A clock shows the time modulo 12, and an odometer in a car shows the number of kilometres travelled modulo 100,000. **2** Derived from this usage, some writers use expressions of the form *p, modulo N* to qualify an assertion that p. Synonymous expressions are *p, setting aside N*; *p, bracketing N*; *p, leaving out of account whatever difference there may be in respect of N.*

modus *n.* Lat. a manner, a mode, a mood.

modus ponendo ponens *See* MODUS PONENS.

modus ponendo tollens an inference *from* the negation of a conjunction, together with the first conjunct, *to* the negation of the second conjunct. This is the pattern:

$$\frac{\text{Not both A and B} \qquad \text{A}}{\text{not B}}$$

modus ponens (Lat. *ponere* to lay down, to affirm) 'the positing mode': an inference *from* a conditional statement, together with its antecedent, *to* its consequent. This is the pattern:

$$\frac{\text{If A then B} \qquad \text{A}}{\text{B}}$$

An inference of this form conforms to a rule sometimes called '(the rule of) affirming the antecedent', also called '(the rule of) detachment'.

In the past, this form of inference was called *modus ponendo ponens.*

modus tollendo ponens *See* DISJUNCTIVE SYLLOGISM.

modus tollendo tollens *See* MODUS TOLLENS.

modus tollens (Lat. *tollere* to remove) 'the removing mode': an inference *from* a conditional statement, together with the denial of its consequent, *to* the denial of its antecedent. This is the pattern:

$$\frac{\text{If A then B} \qquad \text{not B}}{\text{not A}}$$

An inference of this form conforms to a rule sometimes called '(the rule of) denying the consequent'.

In the past, this form of inference was called *modus tollendo tollens.*

Moira /ˈmɔɪrə/ (Gr. fate, necessity) a religious-mythical concept in ancient Greek thought. Also personified in the three *Moirai* (Fates): Clotho, who spins the thread of life; Lachesis, who determines its length; and Atropos, who cuts it off.

Moleschott /ˈmoːləʃɔt (Gm.)/, Jakob (1822–93) Dutch-German physiologist, who taught at Heidelberg, Zürich and Rome. He was a leading representative of nineteenth-century popular scientific materialism.

Molina /mɔˈliːna (Sp.)/, Luis de (1535–1600) Spanish Jesuit, who taught at Coimbra and Evora in Portugal. In order to resolve the tension between human freedom and divine foreknowledge, he proposed (as also did Suárez) that in addition to the two kinds of divine knowledge distinguished by Aquinas, there is a third kind, 'middle knowledge' (*scientia media*), which falls between God's knowledge of the actual and his knowledge of what is possible – namely, knowledge of what *would* have been actual had certain counterfactual conditions obtained (e.g. what Kennedy would have freely chosen to do about Vietnam had he not been assassinated). This knowledge is also between God's knowledge of what is necessary and his knowledge of what he himself causes to be. The objects of middle knowledge are counterfactual truths of the following form (where P is a possible free agent, and A is a possible free action or omission): 'If a person P were in conditions C, then P would freely do A.' A fact of that kind is not logically necessary, because then P would not be free to do A. Nor is it brought about by God, because again P would not be free. So, God's knowledge of a fact of that kind is a third kind of knowledge, 'middle' knowledge.

Molina thought that by means of this concept, human freedom could be explained, and there would be no need to accept the doctrine of predestination adopted by Augustine, by the Protestant reformers, and by Dominican opponents, foremost among them Domingo Bañez (1528–1604). The concept of middle knowledge has been revived by A. Plantinga and others in modern discussion of the problem of evil, to explain why God did not create a world in which everyone always and freely does the right thing.

Molyneux /ˈmɒlinəʊ/, William (1656–98) As a political writer, Molyneux advocated political autonomy for Ireland within a United Kingdom, but he was primarily a scientist and is now best known as the proposer of the famous 'Molyneux problem': would a blind person, able to distinguish a cube from a sphere only by the sense of touch, who suddenly gained sight, be able immediately to distinguish the two objects by sight alone? The problem was first proposed in a letter to the journal *Bibliothèque Universelle* in 1688, and later to Locke in 1693. Molyneux's own answer was negative. So was Locke's, in the second (1694) and later editions of the *Essay Concerning Human Understanding* (2,9,8), and Berkeley's in his *New Theory of Vision* 1709. Leibniz (in *Nouveaux Essais*, 2,10) took a different view.

moment *n.* **1** a part, an aspect; an element; a constituent; a stage (of a process). The use of the word in this philosophical sense can be traced to Hegel. **2** a point or period of time. **3** significance or importance, as in 'of great moment'.

monad /ˈmɒnæd; ˈməʊnæd/ (Gr. *monas* unit) *n.* This word was first used by Leibniz in 1695 in a letter, where he defined a monad as a simple substance. That it is simple means that it has no parts.

In Leibniz's view, the ultimately real, something which depends on nothing else for its existence, cannot have parts. If it had parts, its existence would depend on them. But whatever has spatial extension has parts. It follows that what is ultimately real cannot have spatial extension, and that atomism and materialism must be rejected. The monads are ultimately real. Each of them is an indivisible and immaterial substance. Their number is infinite, and they are all different from each other. None of them interacts with any other, but the state of each and the development of each reflects, more or less obscurely, the state and development of any other. The underlying model for this conception is that of a self, capable of awareness. This concept of a primary substance occurs in many of Leibniz's writings after 1695 and is most fully discussed in a work published in 1714, entitled *MONADOLOGY*.

monadic operator an operator which yields a well-formed formula when applied to exactly one argument. In propositional logic, the negation sign is a monadic operator, because when applied to exactly one (simple or complex) well-formed propositional formula, it yields a well-formed formula. The same holds for the necessity operator in modal logic. A non-monadic operator, e.g. the disjunction sign, is *polyadic*. *See also* MONADIC PREDICATE.

monadic predicate In an open sentence of the form Fx, where the property F is predicated of *one* individual x, F can be called a monadic (one-place) predicate.

The contrast is with relational predicates, also known as polyadic or many-place predicates: they are two-place (dyadic), three-place (triadic), four-place (tetradic), five-place (pentadic), six-place (hexadic), seven-place (heptadic), etc. (These terms are all derived from ancient Greek.)

Examples: in the open sentence *x is to the left of y* the dyadic (two-place) predicate 'is to the left of' has x and y as its arguments. Its form can be represented by Fxy.

In the open sentence *x is situated between y and the mid-point of z and u* a tetradic (four-place) predicate has x, y, z, u as its arguments. Its form can be represented by Fxyzu.

Note: 'singulary', 'binary', 'ternary', and 'quaternary', which stem from the Latin distributive numerals, are also used for one-, two-, three- and four-place predicates, respectively. The next words in this sequence are 'quinary', 'senary', 'septenary', etc. From a linguistic point of view, 'unary' is suspect and 'biadic' does not exist.

Monadology One of Leibniz's works, first published in 1714. It sets out his theory of MONADS. The word '*Monadologie*' first occurs on the title-page of Heinrich Köhler's German translation of 1720, and this title has since become established.

monism *n.* in general, any doctrine affirming the unity or the uniqueness of its subject-matter, in contrast to dualism or pluralism. In moral philosophy, for instance, some writers use *monism* for the view that there is exactly one basic moral principle or exactly one basic value. In metaphysics, where the term is used most frequently, it stands for the doctrine that there is exactly one substance, or exactly one kind of reality.

Towards the end of the nineteenth century, *monism* was used for the doctrine that there is only one truth: nothing is true except the whole truth about the Whole. In this sense, the systems of Hegel, Lotze and Bradley were described as monistic; but at that time *monism* was also used for a different philosophical outlook and movement with secularist and social reformist aims, which rejected traditional religion and speculative philosophy, proposing NEUTRAL MONISM as the ontology appropriate to the modern, scientific world-view. Leading representatives were Ernst Haeckel and Wilhelm Ostwald in Germany. A less confrontational stance, which nevertheless stressed a unitary conception of the world, was taken by Paul Carus, who founded the journal *The Monist* in 1888. *See also* ANOMALOUS MONISM.

monotheism *n.* The doctrine that there is exactly one personal God and that he ought to be worshipped. Monotheism can be contrasted with *atheism*, *polytheism*, *henotheism*, etc. The word seems first to have been used by Henry More around 1660, and gained wider currency through writers such as Bolingbroke, Hume and Kant.

Montague /'mɒntəgjuː/, Richard (1930–71) American philosopher, professor at the University of California, Los Angeles, from 1963. His central project was to develop formal methods that would apply to the study of natural languages. This would involve the construction of a universal grammar in which the syntax and semantics would apply both to the formalized languages of logic and to natural languages. Thereby, the formalizations of everyday language would no longer be based on mere intuition, but systematically on the basis of a theory.

Montague, William Pepperell (1873–1953) American philosopher, professor at Columbia University. A leading representative of the NEW REALIST movement.

Montaigne /mɔ̃tɛɲ (Fr.)/, Michel de (1533–92) French thinker. He invented the 'essay' as a literary form; his own contain incisive observations presented in a deceptively rambling manner. Together they constitute an extended plea for scepticism and tolerance. His motto was '*Que sais-je?*' ('What do I know?'). Reviving the ancient tradition, especially as presented by Sextus Empiricus, his scepticism was essentially a recognition of the variety and fallibility of belief. Accordingly, Montaigne saw no conclusive reason for breaking with custom in matters of religious doctrine, and had no sympathy for the religious fervour of his time that regularly led to persecution and bloodshed. These sceptical essays exercised an important influence on many philosophers, including Descartes, Pascal, Bayle and Hume. *See also* SCEPTICISM.

Montanism *n.* a Christian movement and doctrine, named after its founder, Montanus, in the latter half of the second century. In its earliest stages it cultivated ecstasy and prophecy; later, it was mainly distinguished by its ascetic orientation. Its most prominent adherent was TERTULLIAN.

Montesquieu /mɔ̃tɛskjø (Fr.)/ (1689–1755) Charles-Louis de Secondat, later Baron de la Brède et de Montesquieu, was the leading political thinker of the French Enlightenment. His early *Lettres Persanes* 1721 (Persian letters) are an entertaining, perceptive and incisive critique of French social conventions and political institutions, in the form of letters written by two astonished Persian travellers. His main work was *De l'Esprit des lois* 1748 (The spirit of the laws). He favoured political institutions that protect individual liberty and respect for the rights of the individual and believed that this could be achieved by letting different bodies exercise the legislative, executive and judicial powers. In his view, the constitution of England was an excellent example of this. Montesquieu differed from other natural-law writers by not merely describing what good political institutions would be like, but also pioneering an extensive empirical analysis of the geographical, sociological and historical conditions under which political institutions exist.

Like other Enlightenment thinkers, Montesquieu advocated religious toleration, condemned the bloodthirsty fanaticism of religious persecutors in Spain, France and elsewhere, and his writings were put on the INDEX.

mood *See* SYLLOGISM.

Moore /mʊə; mɔː/, G(eorge) E(dward) (1873–1958) fellow of Trinity College, Cambridge 1898–1904. After some years at Edinburgh, Moore taught in Cambridge 1911–39, as a professor of philosophy from 1925. He edited the philosophical journal *Mind* 1921–47. Outside academic circles Moore was best known as an inspiration to the Bloomsbury group of writers and artists, who took as a model of their way of life what he had declared in his *Principia Ethica* 1903 (2nd rev. edn 1993) to be the two things that are intrinsically good, namely 'the pleasures of human intercourse and the enjoyment of beautiful objects'. There are, he argued, no absolute rules of conduct: right action is that which promotes what is intrinsically good, and prevents intrinsic evils, which, in Moore's view, fall into three main classes: consciousness of pain, hatred or contempt of what is good or beautiful, and the love, admiration or enjoyment of what is evil or ugly. It was also in this book that Moore defined and rejected the NATURALISTIC FALLACY – a conceptual point of little interest to Bloomsbury but of signal importance for twentieth-century metaethics.

In philosophy his reputation otherwise mainly rests on the 'appeal to common sense', by which he drew a contrast between his puzzlement and doubts about the truth and meaning of what philosophers say, and his clarity and certainty as to what, as non-philosophers, most of us commonly and ordinarily mean and believe. He was interested in what he called the analysis of this meaning. The object of analysis was an entity, often called a concept. A person who knows the meaning of a word, e.g. of 'good' (or of the French 'bon' or of any other synonymous word), has the concept. In an analysis, one puts the concept before one's mind, and the correct analysis is established by working out how this concept is related to and differentiated from other concepts.

It is his attempts to arrive at correct analyses of what we say when we talk, for example in morals about something being 'good' or 'right', in perceptions about something being 'seen' or 'heard', and in epistemology about something being 'known' or 'certain', which constitute his major philosophical conclusions. Because the first dubious philosophical thesis that Moore encountered was the prevailing Idealism, orginating from Berkeley and Hegel, and dominant at the time in England through Bradley at Oxford and McTaggart at Cambridge, his method found its first claim to fame in his article 'The Refutation of Idealism' *Mind 12* (1903). In the same year he exposed what he called the 'naturalistic fallacy', which confuses the criteria of goodness, especially those in naturalistic terms, with the meaning of 'good'.

In general, however, it is his method of analysis, not his actual conclusions, which has proved of lasting value. He impressed generations of philosophers through his constant quest for accuracy and clarity of thought and expression. Neither the distinctive form of 'ideal utilitarianism' which he advocated and the indefinability of 'good' which he argued for in his *Principia Ethica*; nor the existence of sense-data as objects which we directly see, which he put as the basis of most of his writings on perception; nor his famous 'proof' of the external world which he offered in his British Academy lecture of 1939, have stood the test of time. But his position beside Bertrand Russell as a founder of twentieth-century analytic philosophy is secure. AW

Moore's paradox A person, A, who says 'p, but I do not believe that p' has asserted that p, and that implies *that he believes that p*. But he has also asserted *that he does not believe that p*. So what he says implies a contradiction. But, on the other hand, what he says clearly does not imply a contradiction, since *p* need not contradict a statement to the effect that *A does not believe that p*.

This is a paradox: an absurd conclusion derived by apparently sound reasoning from true premisses.

The problem was first raised by G. E. Moore in his *Ethics* 1912, and he returned to it in P. Schilpp (ed.), *The Philosophy of G. E. Moore* 1942, pp. 540–43.

There is a similar problem with the person who says 'not-p, but I believe that p'. Moore discussed it in P. Schilpp (ed.), *The Philosophy of Bertrand Russell* 1944, p. 204. But there are differences between the two formulations, so a solution to one of the problems may not do for the other.

moral *adj., n.* This word and its cognates refer to what is good or bad, right or wrong, in human character or conduct. But moral goodness (etc.) is not the only kind of goodness, so the question is how to distinguish between the moral and the non-moral. This is a disputed question. Some answers are in terms of *content*. One opinion is that moral concerns are those that relate to sex, and those only. More plausible is the suggestion that moral concerns are those, and those only, that affect other persons. But there are theories (Aristotle, Hume) which would consider even this demarcation too narrow. Other answers provide a *formal* criterion: for instance, that moral demands are those demands that come from God, or that moral demands are those that override all other kinds of demands, or, again, that moral judgements are universalizable.

The Latin word *moralis*, from which the English word originates, was created by Cicero from *mos* (*pl. mores*), meaning custom(s), which corresponds to the Greek *ēthos* (custom). This is why in many contexts, though not always, moral/ethical, morals/ethics, moral philosophy/ethics etc. are interchangeable. But the two words have also been used to mark various distinctions. *See also* MORALITY.

moral act(ion) **1** an act which can be morally evaluated, in contrast to a merely physical event. *Ant.* non-moral act. **2** an act which is morally right or good, in contrast to an immoral one; one which is not morally right or good. *Ant.* immoral act.

moral arguments for God's existence Many arguments for God's existence invoke morality. They may rely on assumptions like the following: (1) that moral conscience can only be explained as the voice of God; (2) that moral concepts (duty, rightness, justice, etc.) make no sense unless defined in terms of God's will; (3) that morality derives its binding force from rewards and punishments in a future state, administered by God; (4) (in Kant) that it is a demand of reason that at least in the long run there be a due proportion between the moral worth and the happiness of a person, and that therefore as agents we are rationally entitled to accept God's existence (and the immortality of the soul) as a 'practical postulate'.

moral certainty virtual certainty; a high degree of probability.

This old expression is often misunderstood; the certainty is called moral because it is the kind of certainty attainable in relation to human affairs. Such certainty is taken to be less than demonstrative certainty, attainable in the exact sciences. Aristotle notes (*Nicomachean Ethics*, 1,1 1094^{b}10ff and 1,7 1098^{a}25ff) that there can be no demonstrative certainty in human affairs, which are of a contingent nature. The degree of certainty related to practical concerns was called 'probable certainty' by Aquinas (*Summa Theologiae* 2a 2ae, q.70, ad 2), who refers to Aristotle. The expression is now rare, but is common in older texts. Descartes wrote: 'moral certainty is sufficient to regulate the conduct of one's life even if it is in principle possible that we can be mistaken' (*Principles of Philosophy*, §4). Hume wrote: 'All reasonings may be divided into two kinds, namely, demonstrative reasoning, or that concerning relations of ideas, and moral reasoning, or that concerning matter of fact and existence' (*Enquiry Concerning Human Understanding* section 4, part 2). When he calls the second kind of reasoning moral, it is because it is merely probable, in contrast to demonstrative reasoning, which is certain.

moral entities (Lat. *ens morale*, (*pl.*) *entia moralia*) the name given by Pufendorf (*The Law of Nature and Nations* 1672, Book 1, chapter 1) to qualities, relations, etc. which depend for their existence on 'imposition', i.e. on a decision or enactment, human or divine. They are contrasted with physical entities, which can exist independently of any volition. According to this theory, *being* *red-haired* is a physical quality, *being a servant* is a moral quality. Rights and obligations are moral entities. The obligation to keep a promise, for instance, arises from an act of will, known as promising.

moral futurism the view that what will be is right. The expression was introduced by Karl Popper in *The Open Society and Its Enemies* 1945.

moralism *n.* This word is commonly used in a derogatory sense for the excessive tendency to pass moral judgement.

moralist *n.* **1** a person given to moralism. **2** a person who employs keen and discerning powers of observation in describing and reflecting on human character and conduct. Many novelists can be so described, but the term has especially been used for authors of essays, character sketches or aphorisms, such as Plutarch, Montaigne, Gracián, La Bruyère, La Rochefoucauld, Chamfort, Lichtenberg and Schopenhauer.

morality *n.* The word is used in a variety of ways:

1 *Profession v. practice.* Talk of the *morality* of a person or of a society can refer to what they *profess*, or to what they actually *do*. The acknowledged standards applied to character and conduct may be different from what is commonly countenanced. We may, for instance, imagine a society which preaches an ideal of female submissiveness, although in practice women in that society are assertive and independent. Or the people in a society may profess a morality dominated by charity, but their actions may belie their words.

2 *Positive v. critical.* Another distinction is that between the *actual* practices and opinions in a society and those that *ought to* obtain. The distinction is sometimes expressed in terms of a contrast between *positive* and *critical* (or *ideal*) morality. Thus, the inferior status of women in a society could conform to the positive morality of that society (i.e. its prevalent practices, opinions or customs) but could nevertheless be morally wrong, that is, contrary to critical or ideal morality.

3 *Positive v. natural.* Related to the preceding is the contrast between the norms and standards which are valid merely because of an act of divine or human *legislation*, and those whose validity is independent of that. It was in this sense that the relation between *positive* duties, i.e. those posited by God's commands, and *moral* duties, i.e. those which have their validity independently of any legislative act, was debated in the eighteenth century.

4 *The ethical v. the moral.* The two words are used to mark various contrasts. For instance: (a) Hegel contrasts *Moralität* (morality) with *Sittlichkeit* ('ethicality', the ethical life). According to him, morality, which originated with Socrates and was reinforced with the rise of Christianity, the Reformation and Kant, is the concern of the autonomous individual. Although morality involves a concern for the welfare not only of self but also of others, it falls short because of its potential incompatibility with shared established social values and with the customs and institutions which embody and maintain these values. To live in unforced harmony with these is *Sittlichkeit*, within which the autonomy of the individual, the rights of the individual's conscience, are acknowledged but kept within due bounds; (b) In a similar vein, some more recent writers use the word *morality* to designate a special kind of ethics. Bernard Williams (*Ethics and the Limits of Philosophy*, 1985), for instance, argues that 'the institution of morality' takes ethical standards and norms to resemble legal rules, and that therefore obedience to the call of duty becomes the only genuine virtue. This is an outlook

which in his view should be abandoned in favour of a less moralistic and more humane and unconstrained approach to ethical life; (c) Habermas, on the other hand, makes a distinction which is also implicit in Rawls's *Theory of Justice* between ethics, which relates to the good life (which is not the same for everyone), and morality, which is concerned with the social dimension of human life and hence with principles of conduct that can have universal application. Ethics is concerned with the good life, morality with right conduct.
5 *Legality v. morality* (i) A contrast is often drawn between a theory of justice and a theory of virtue. The former includes the PERFECT DUTIES, the latter the imperfect ones. A person has a perfect duty, a duty of justice, to pay a creditor; and an imperfect duty, a duty of virtue, to give to charity. This contrast is also expressed in terms of *legal* and *moral*. In this terminology, the duties of justice are of a kind different from moral duties, as is obvious from the possible discrepancies between them (a)–(d):

(a) Positive law v. positive morality: for instance, the law of the state may impose universal primary education for all, although the bulk of the society considers it wrong to include girls;

(b) Positive law v. ideal morality: for instance, the law of the state may exclude girls from the primary education system, although this is morally wrong;

(c) Ideal law v. positive morality: for instance, good laws prohibit cruel and unusual punishments, even if positive morality favours them;

(d) Ideal law v. ideal morality: good laws do not prohibit all moral wrongs, but ideal morality does.
6 *Legality v. morality* (ii) In Kant's terminology, the morality or moral worth of an action (which depends on the agent's motivation) is distinct from the legality or the mere rightness of the action.

moral law a rule which lays down what conduct is morally right. The term is also used by Kant for his supreme rule of morality, 'the categorical imperative'.

Note: A 'moral law' is not the same as a 'just law', a morally acceptable legal rule.

moral person **1** a person whose character and conduct conform to moral standards. **2** any individual being or composite being (e.g. a society) capable of having rights.

moral philosophy *Moral philosophy*, also called ETHICS, designates two distinct but related kinds of inquiry: substantive and analytical.

Substantive ethics deals with the questions of what is right and wrong, good and bad, in respect of character and conduct. Its aim is to formulate standards of correctness for evaluation and decision. It is also called *normative ethics*, since it can be said to deal with norms of evaluation and norms of conduct. *Moral theory* is the term frequently used in the second half of the twentieth century for a theory of substantive ethics which aims to be comprehensive and systematic. The ambition is that such a theory, usually conceived as a theory of what is right and wrong, would ideally have the virtues of a good scientific theory: simplicity, unity, explanatory power, etc. An adequate moral theory is often also expected to provide a procedure for finding the right answer to all moral questions about what to do.

Analytical ethics, also known as *metaethics*, is the enquiry into moral concepts and their logic, but does not itself aim at providing standards of correctness for evaluation and decision.

moral positivism the view that what makes moral standards right is that they are the ones actually adopted (by a society, by an authority).

The label is infrequently used, but theories of this kind are not uncommon. Moral positivism of the sociological variety is relativist, and rules out any moral challenge to an established social morality. Moral positivism of the theological variety is often called the divine command theory.

Moral positivism must not be confused with positivist moral philosophy, i.e. the moral theory that may be part of a system of positivist philosophy.

moral realism *See* REALISM.

moral sense The moral sense is conceived in analogy with our sense of beauty in the writings of Shaftesbury (1671–1713) and Hutcheson (1694–1746). In the same way as the sense of beauty enables us to discern beauty in an object and produces a special kind of pleasure at the sight of a beautiful object, so the moral sense enables us to discern virtue at the sight or thought of an action or character and produces a special kind of pleasure at the sight or thought of a virtuous action or character.

The approval and pleasure is in both instances disinterested. In this respect the theory differed from the mainstream contemporary theories which gave an account of morality in terms of self-interest. The theory also differed from rationalist accounts of moral knowledge as an immediate rational insight, analogous to geometrical intuition. Hutcheson and Hume objected that such insight involves only 'the cool assent of the intellect', so the rationalist theory cannot explain why moral insight would move us to action.

moral theory *See* MORAL PHILOSOPHY.

more geometrico /ˈmɔːreɪ dʒɪəˈmɛtrɪkəʊ/ Lat. in the manner of geometry. Euclid's manner of exposition. It was admired and adopted by some modern philosophers: Descartes, Spinoza, Christian Wolff, etc. Descartes uses it in his 'Replies to the Second Set of Objections' (to his *Meditations*), but the best-known example is Spinoza's *Ethics*.

More, Henry (1614–87) fellow of Christ's College, Cambridge, a leading representative of Cambridge Platonism. His thinking shows influences of neo-Platonism and cabalistic mysticism, which he tried to incorporate in a Christian world-view. In his writings, he defended the authority of reason both against atheists and against religious enthusiasts who regarded the use of reason as carnal and hence sinful. Although he had initially found much of value in Descartes's philosophy, he insisted that mind and body alike have extension, immaterial and material respectively, and he rejected Descartes's NULLIBISM because he saw it as implying mechanistic materialism. In his epistemology he followed Plato in adopting a theory of innate ideas. Like Cudworth, he proposed a theory of 'plastic natures', i.e. active, although not conscious, forces which can explain natural phenomena that a purely mechanistic theory cannot account for.

More, Thomas (1478–1535) a leading humanist (HUMANISM), author of *Utopia* 1516, which was the first in a long line of imaginary ideal societies. In More's Utopia there is no private property and there is sexual equality in the division of tasks. These are among the conditions for a pleasurable life, which More, in the spirit of an Epicureanized Christianity, regarded as the highest good. *See also* UTOPIA.

Morelly /mɔʀɛli (Fr.)/ (first name unknown) (1716–81) French political thinker, best known for his *Code de la Nature* 1755–60 (The code of nature), in which he advocated a utopian humanitarian socialism. A better society could be created by abolishing the institution of private property and the egoism on which it is founded. This would leave scope for the benevolent impulses inherent in human nature. He gave a detailed outline of how life in the uniform small communes would be regulated, anticipating Fourier. In the early 1790s, Baboeuf was influenced by this egalitarian communism.

morphology *n.* within a discipline, the inquiry into, or account of, shapes or forms. The term was coined by Goethe and used in his work on the physiology of plants. In grammar, morphology is the branch that deals with word-formation and inflections.

Morris, Charles (1901–79) American philosopher, at the University of Chicago from 1931 to 1971. He played an active part in establishing communication between the logical positivists and American philosophers. Morris is best known for his attempt, first formulated in *Foundations of the Theory of Signs* 1938, to create a general theory of signs, which he called semiotic, borrowing the term from Locke's *Essay Concerning Human Understanding*. He envisaged that semiotic could serve as a general theory for the various disciplines in humanities and social sciences, and that it could ultimately be formulated in biological and behaviouristic terms. In the study of language, Morris's Peirce-inspired structuring of semiotic has gained wide acceptance: he conceived it as having three main branches, syntactics, semantics and pragmatics. Syntax deals with relations between various signs within a language: the grammar of a language. Semantics deals with the relation between signs and that which is signified: it is a theory of the meaning of signs. Pragmatics concerns the way signs are used in communication and social contexts.

mos geometricus /mɔs dʒɪə'mɛtrɪkəs/ Lat. geometrical manner.

Mounier /munje (Fr.)/, Emmanuel (1905–50) The autonomy and value of the person is at the centre of Mounier's philosophical outlook, known as personalism. To be a *person* involves having a set of values freely adopted. It involves creativity and communion with others. In contrast, to be an *individual* is to lead an egoistic, materialistic, inauthentic life; the individual is shallow, a mere member of the crowd. Personalism opposes the dehumanizing tendencies of communism and capitalism alike, and resists their common tendency to see human beings as no more than objects of scientific study and as means to economic ends, and to neglect the need for community and personal relations, necessary for the flourishing of personhood. The journal *Esprit*, founded in 1932, and the movement associated with Mounier and his philosophy have seen themselves involved in a struggle against social injustice, against 'the established disorder', and against the depersonalizing forces in the modern world.

multiple realization the fact that something can come about in more than one way. The expression is used mainly in the philosophy of mind. According to functionalism, for instance, the same kind of mental occurrence, e.g. a pain, may be multiply realized (may have different physical realizations) in that its physiological basis may differ between species. An illustration (inspired by David Lewis) is this: a theory tells us that some poison kills mice. If there is exactly one such poison, the theory has a unique realization. If there is no such poison, the theory is false. If there is more than one, the theory is multiply realized. Similarly, the performances of the same Bach fugue on a harpsichord, an organ, or a piano would count as three realizations of the same work.

Münchhausen /mynçhaʊzən/ **trilemma** This trilemma (three mutually exclusive and jointly exhaustive options, each of them unwelcome) is designed to show that there can be no ultimate foundation for human knowledge. Every foundational claim either starts an infinite regress, or begs the question, or arbitrarily cuts off further questions. The conclusion is anti-foundationalist: there is no Archimedean point. The trilemma was so named by Hans Albert. The allusion is to a late eighteenth-century collection of tall stories, the semi-fictitious memoirs of Baron Münchhausen (by G. A. Bürger), who relates how he once went riding, got into deep water, but saved himself and the horse by holding the horse firmly with his legs, and lifting both horse and rider by his hair.

Also known as Fries's trilemma.

mundus intelligibilis; mundus sensibilis /ˈmʌndəs ɪntɛlɪˈdʒiːbɪlɪs/ˈmʌndəs senˈsiːbɪlɪs/ Lat. the intelligible world; the sensible world. Plato introduced this pair of concepts to distinguish true reality, accessible by the faculty of reason, from the world of sensory experience which provides only an imperfect reflection, shadow or imitation of the real thing. The former is the proper object of knowledge; the latter is the realm of mere opinion and uncertain conjecture. Kant makes use of these terms for his distinction between noumena and phenomena, between the thing-in-itself and the things-for-us. The thing-in-itself, the intelligible world, is of course beyond the limits of our cognitive faculties. (At the terminological level, a paradox arises in that the intelligible world is unintelligible in the sense that we can know nothing about it.)

mutatis mutandis /mjuːˈtɑːtɪs mjuːˈtændɪs/ Lat. with appropriate changes.

N

Naess /nɛs/, Arne (1912–) Norwegian philosopher. After studies at Oslo, Paris, Vienna and Berkeley, Naess held the chair of philosophy at the University of Oslo from 1939 to 1970, when he resigned to devote himself to environmental problems. He was the founder and editor of the journal *Inquiry*. His early work was characterized by empiricism and behaviourism, and included an empirical study of how non-philosophers understand 'truth' and related concepts. He also wrote on the analysis of arguments. From the 1960s, he worked towards a synthesis of Spinozistic and Gandhian ethics. Its leading themes are non-violence and solidarity, both taken to include mankind although extending much further. This is developed in the theory which he originated and for which he is probably best known, i.e. Deep Ecology and its philosophical core, ecosophy. Ecosophy is a total view inspired by ecology and emphasizing basic ecocentric norms relating humans to their environment, which ultimately comprises the cosmos as a whole. His major works include *Scepticism* 1968, *The Pluralist and Possibilist Aspect of the Scientific Enterprise* 1972, *Freedom, Emotion and Self-subsistence* 1975, *Ecology, Community, and Lifestyle* 1989. DB/ed.

Nagel /ˈneɪgəl/, Ernest (1901–85) American philosopher, who taught at Columbia University from 1931 to 1970. In the theory of knowledge and in the philosophy of science, Nagel advocated a moderate empiricism. In his view, genuine science is hypothetico-deductive: its general statements have particular, testable consequences, and are accepted or rejected depending on the outcome of the tests. There is progress in science, but when, for instance, Newton's theory is replaced by Einstein's, it is not because the former is directly refuted, but because it can be incorporated within the latter and taken to cover special cases within a more general theory. There are, then, rational grounds for preferring the new theory to the old. (It was this view that was challenged in the 1960s by Thomas Kuhn, who argued that competing scientific paradigms may be incommensurable, and their success or failure significantly influenced by non-rational factors.) In his discussion of biological theories and concepts, Nagel noted that they cannot easily do without teleology (purposiveness). This is a problem for empiricism, since such concepts seem to take us beyond sense-experience. The same problem arises in the social sciences, where concepts of social wholes (groups, classes, societies, mentalities) seem to take us beyond anything that can ultimately be an object of sensory observation. A further problem in respect of the social sciences is that they can hardly do without value-judgements, and yet from an empiricist standpoint all science properly so called should be independent of value-assumptions, and in that sense value-free. All these questions were dealt with in Nagel's *The Structure of Science* 1961, where he argued that they can be resolved within an empiricist framework. Among other works of his are *An Introduction to Logic and Scientific Method* (jointly with Morris R. Cohen) 1934 and *Sovereign Reason* 1954.

Nagel, Thomas (1937–) American philosopher, who has taught at Berkeley and Princeton, and since 1980 at New York University. The reflection over intractable dualities is a thematic counterpoint in his philosophy. In opposition to Hume's influential theory of motivation, Nagel draws a close parallel between prudence and morality. We see ourselves as the same person over time, and this is why prudence makes sense. Similarly, we see ourselves as one person among others, and this is why morality makes sense. From a rational standpoint, the question 'Why should I be moral?' is like the question 'Why should I be prudent?' In *The View from Nowhere* 1986, Nagel gives a diagnosis of philosophical troublespots by locating them in an irreducible duality between a subjective and an objective standpoint. Human beings *are* parts of nature, and yet an account from that perspective omits the subjective elements: experience, thought, decision, action. To insist that only one of these two standpoints is valid results in theoretical distortions and practical perplexity: as a natural object I (or rather, this person) neither think nor act – merely, certain things happen to this person, who is a link in a chain of causes. Related intractable dualities, including that between one's impartial moral concern for human welfare and one's special concern for particular people (self, family, friends, people with common interests), enter into the discussion of social justice in *Equality and Impartiality* 1991. Many of Nagel's essays have come to be widely known and discussed, e.g. 'Moral luck' and 'What is it like to be a bat?'

narrative *n.*, *adj.* a story; an account of a sequence of events.

narrow *See* BROAD.

narrow content In recent philosophy of mind, properties and contents (of a belief, say) are called narrow if they are entirely determined by a subject's internal physical condition, and wide if not entirely so determined. *See also* INTERNALISM.

nativism *n.* a theory of innate ideas (Descartes, Chomsky). *Syn.* INNATISM.

Natorp /ˈnaːtɔrp (Gm.)/, Paul (1854–1924) German philosopher, prominent in the neo-Kantian Marburg School. His writings covered most areas of philosophy, from the exact sciences, in *Die logischen Grundlagen der exakten Wissenschaften* 1910 (The logical foundations of the exact sciences), to social philosophy and philosophy of education, in his influential *Sozialpädagogik* 1899 (Social education). His interpretation in *Platons Ideenlehre* 1902, 1921 of Plato's theory of forms as an anticipation of Kant's transcendental philosophy gave rise to a lively debate.

natural *adj.* This and related words, especially *nature*, are used in a variety of senses.

Hume, when discussing in *Treatise of Human Nature* 3,1,2 whether virtue and vice are natural, notes that, depending on the sense of the word, the natural can be contrasted with what is *miraculous*, *unusual* or *artificial*. Elsewhere in the same work he contrasts it with *civil* (i.e. originating in social and political institutions or conventions), *mental* (i.e. in our mind, in contrast to physical nature outside ourselves), *supernatural*, etc. Another contrast is that between nature and *culture*.

In the Aristotelian tradition, the nature of a thing is internal to it, its essence, but accounts also for its characteristic functioning or development.

natural deduction Natural deduction systems are systems of formal logic, first published in 1934 by the German logician Gerhard GENTZEN and by the Polish logician S. Jaskowski. They differ from axiomatic systems of the kind developed by

Hilbert, Peano, Russell, et al., which have as their basis (a small number of) axioms or axiom schemata, and transformation rules (rules of inference). Natural deduction systems do not require axioms: their basis consists of (a small number of) rules by which inferences can be made from assumptions. These rules indicate how to derive formulae from formulae, whilst in axiomatic systems the rules indicate how to derive logical truths from logical truths.

The rules of inference in natural deduction systems can be framed as introduction and elimination rules for each of the propositional operators ~ (negation), & (conjunction), ∨ (disjunction) and ⊃ (material conditional), and in predicate logic for each of the quantifiers.

Examples: the introduction rule for negation says that if A is among the assumptions from which a contradiction is derived, then ~A may be inferred from the other assumptions. The introduction rule for conjunction says that from two assumptions A and B, A & B may be inferred. The elimination rule for the material conditional says that from two assumptions A and A ⊃ B, B may be inferred. The elimination rule for the universal quantifier says that from the assumption (∀x)Fx, Fa may be inferred. The formulation of some of the other rules is only slightly more complicated.

The first textbook to introduce natural deduction was J. C. Cooley's *Primer of Formal Logic* 1942. Since then, the approach has gradually become widely adopted.

naturalism *n.* **1** (in modern metaphysics) the view that everything (objects and events) is a part of nature, an all-encompassing world of space and time. It implies a rejection of traditional beliefs in supernatural beings or other entities supposedly beyond the ken of science. Human beings and their mental powers are also regarded as normal parts of the natural world describable by science.

In the early modern period, naturalism was the view (proposed by Vanini, Campanella, Cambridge Platonists, etc.) that the material world contains among its constituents active powers which may be hidden ('occult'). This obviates the need to postulate entities outside the material world. Opposed to this was mechanism (Mersenne, Descartes, etc.): the material world is by itself inert; it operates on purely mechanical principles, and does not contain the active powers needed to explain the way things work. They have to be found elsewhere.

2 (in logic) the view, usually called psychologism, that the validity of logical laws is not *a priori* but based on certain empirical facts about the human mind.

3 (in epistemology) the view that the theory of knowledge is not *a priori* but a part of empirical science. This view opposes the anti-psychologism of Kant, Frege, Husserl and earlier analytical philosophers. In Quine's formulation in 'Epistemology naturalized' in *Ontological Relativity and Other Essays* 1969, the theory of knowledge is the empirical study of the relation between sensory input and cognitive output. Not only psychology, but also evolutionary biology, sociology, etc. have been seen as relevant disciplines.

4 (in philosophy of mind) physicalism, i.e. materialism in combination with the view that mentalistic discourse should be reduced, explained or eliminated in favour of non-mentalistic scientifically acceptable discourse.

5 (in normative ethics) the view that the only way of finding out what conduct is right is by empirical inquiry, mainly in the human, social and biological sciences. Evolutionary ethics is an example.

6 (in metaethics) a naturalistic ethical theory is one in which moral concepts are analysed entirely in terms of natural facts or properties.

7 (in metaethics) a naturalistic ethical theory is one which commits the NATURALISTIC FALLACY.

This is a confusing usage. Moore argued in *Principia Ethica* 1903 that theological, metaphysical and supranaturalistic theories also commit the fallacy which he had already labelled naturalistic. So on the present definition supranaturalism becomes a kind of naturalism, which sounds odd.

8 (in religion) in the seventeenth century deists, who believed that natural religion was enough, were called naturalists. This usage is now obsolete.

9 (in legal philosophy) some writers use *naturalism* as a synonym of natural law theory, and usually contrast it with legal positivism.

10 (in literature) *naturalism* signifies a kind of writing, mainly in prose fiction, in which human beings are observed in a strictly scientific manner; they are seen as determined by factors beyond their control and driven to their fate by heredity and the social environment. Human characters are often, though not necessarily, represented in an unflattering way, with an emphasis on the more brutish aspects of their way of life. Well-known representatives of this movement are Emile Zola and Theodore Dreiser.

naturalist *n.* **1** a person who accepts naturalism. **2** a person who studies animals and plants by observation of them in their natural setting.

naturalistic fallacy This expression was introduced by G. E. Moore at the end of §10 of his *Principia Ethica* 1903 and gained wide currency in moral philosophy. He used it to designate a fallacy which, he argued, was committed by all those who accept ethical naturalism.

In Moore's account it is a fallacy that relates to the analysis of the concept of intrinsic good. He suggested that it is the same mistake as that which occurs when, say, a colour like yellow is identified with light of a certain wavelength. Although, in normal circumstances, the colour and the wavelength occur *together*, they are *not identical*. Similarly, even if it were true that whatever is good is pleasure-giving and vice versa, we would not be entitled to identify *being good* and *giving pleasure*, because two properties can belong to the same thing without being identical.

Moore also wrote that the fallacy consists in the mistaken inference from a purported *definition* of intrinsic value (x is good $=_{df}$ x is F) to a *value-judgement* ascribing intrinsic value to something (all things that are F, and they alone, are good). In a different formulation, he proposed that it consists in a confusion of two different senses of 'is': the 'is' of attribution (or predication) from the 'is' of identity. That is, 'S is good' can mean either (1) the property goodness belongs to S; or (2) the property goodness is identical with S.

Moore's arguments against the naturalistic fallacy, among which the OPEN-QUESTION ARGUMENT plays a significant part, imply that the reduction of ethics to any natural or social science is impossible. All ethical statements presuppose statements about intrinsic value; but statements about intrinsic value are not identical in meaning with any statements about any natural (including social and psychological) facts.

This rejection of ethical naturalism was not advanced on behalf of religious or metaphysical theories. Moore held that they suffer from the same defect as the naturalistic ones. Ethics cannot be based on metaphysics: 'To hold that from any proposition asserting "Reality is of this nature" we can infer, or obtain confirmation for, any proposition asserting "This is good in itself" is to commit the naturalistic fallacy.'

Ethical knowledge is not, then, knowledge of natural or supernatural facts. Moore advocated an ethical intuitionism: on careful reflection, we can directly discern what kinds of things have the distinctive, unanalysable, non-natural property of intrinsic value. Moore held that what we will discern is that personal affection and aesthetic enjoyment have this property. We will also discern that the property of being intrinsically bad belongs to (1) the love, admiration and enjoyment of what is evil or ugly; (2) hatred or contempt of what is good or beautiful; (3) consciousness of pain. The actions we ought to do are those which, all in all, will have the best consequences.

natural jurisprudence especially in eighteenth-century usage, inquiry into, or theory of, natural justice; in modern parlance, natural law theory.

natural kinds a kind of thing that is distinguished by nature itself. Thus *gold*, *tiger* and *water* are natural kinds – they are marked out by, respectively, an atomic, a genetic and a molecular structure – while *telephone*, *chess* and *yellow kind of thing* are not – they are distinguished from other kinds by, respectively, a function, a set of rules and a way of appearing to us. The features of one kind that distinguish it from other kinds constitute its *essence*.

The concept of natural kinds moved to the centre of philosophical attention in the 1970s because of the new analysis proposed by Kripke and Putnam, who rejected the prevailing view that proper names connote. The case is the same with natural-kind terms. Neither these nor names can be defined in terms of a set of defining properties, but refer to their bearer in a more direct way. Kripke and Putnam further maintained that science can discover the essential properties of a natural kind. For instance, science can discover that what has come to be named 'water' is H_2O. This, being an essential property, is true of water not only in our actual world but also in every possible world. But it is a truth known *a posteriori*. Therefore there are – according to this theory – necessary truths *a posteriori*. GC

natural language language actually used by a community. It differs from artificial and formal languages, in which the vocabulary and the well-formed expressions are defined stipulatively. This is not the case with natural languages, where there is scope for disagreement about meaning, grammar, pronunciation and spelling.

natural law Two senses can be distinguished. In the *prescriptive* sense a natural law is a rule of conduct, a general command, permission or prohibition, or a general statement assigning rights or obligations. A law of nature in this sense does not depend for its validity on the will of any legislator. In the *descriptive*, scientific sense a law of nature is a statement that in the natural world events occur in a regular sequence: the law of gravity, Kepler's laws, Mendel's laws.

The difference between these two senses was well explained in Berkeley's *Passive Obedience* 1712:

> We ought to distinguish between a twofold signification of the terms of law of nature; which words do either denote a rule or precept for the direction of the voluntary actions of reasonable agents, and in that sense they imply a duty; or else they are used to signify any general rule which we observe to obtain in the works of nature, independently of the wills of men; in which sense no duty is implied.

The expression *leges naturae* (laws of nature) occurs in Lucretius, but became established in the modern era, since Francis Bacon.

When the prescriptive sense is intended, *natural law* seems to be used more frequently. In the descriptive sense, *law of nature* is more common. *See also* LAWS OF NATURE; NATURAL LAW THEORIES.

natural law theories The origin of the belief in a law of nature as a system of justice common to all human beings can be traced to the ancient Greeks (especially the Stoics – see STOICISM). In contrast to the laws of particular societies, the law of nature applies universally, and is not based on custom, convention or decision. It was sometimes held to be the expression of divine universal force.

All the leading medieval thinkers, including Augustine, Aquinas and Suárez, adopted a natural law theory, trying to work out the relation between the inherent constraints on human conduct that God has induced in his creation, and the constraints that he has imposed through his legislative will.

Two main varieties of natural law theory can be distinguished. One is often called classical, the other modern. The first is *teleological* and can be traced back to Aristotle. It has a basis in the contrast between nature and convention. The law of nature expresses the ends or purposes that by nature belong to a particular kind of living being. These ends form a harmonious system. Human conventions, laws and actions are right if they accord with the purposes of nature; if they do not, they are wrong. Since man, as Aristotle observed, is a social animal, the law of nature enjoins conduct that makes social life possible and enables the individual to flourish within it. This kind of natural law theory was combined, especially in Christian thought, with a theological view, for instance that the purposive structure of nature is an expression of divine will, and that God therefore commands that our conduct be according to nature and prohibits perversions precisely because they are against nature.

The second variety, of which Grotius and Pufendorf are regarded as the founding fathers, is often called 'modern natural law theory'. Among its central tenets are the natural freedom and equality of all human beings, reaffirmed by Locke in his *Two Treatises of Government* 1690, by Rousseau in his *Contrat social* 1762 (Social contract), and by the American and French declarations of rights. On this view, individuals are regarded as entities sovereign by nature, and their integrity and freedom have to be respected, in the same way as that of sovereign states in international law. Inequality can be ultimately justified only by agreements, which create rights and correlative obligations, voluntarily entered into by the parties concerned. An action is right if everyone's innate individual realm and acquired rights are respected; if not, it is wrong. So within the framework of this theory, all wrong conduct consists in the commission of a wrong, an injury; and the law of nature dictates, primarily, respect for each person's integrity and freedom. This kind of natural law theory can also be combined with a theological view, for instance that God commands us to respect the natural freedom and equality of all persons.

Natural law theories that include religious assumptions have of course been rejected by anti-religious or non-religious theorists. Apart from that, the objections to natural law theories are partly moral, partly theoretical.

A moral objection to teleology is that what happens 'naturally' is not necessarily for the best. A moral objection to the emphasis on natural freedom and natural rights is that it is too individualistic and incompatible with the values of community. Other moral objections to natural law theories are as follows: Appeals have been made to natural law to condemn artificial birth control and thereby oppose the efforts to thwart poverty and over-population. Unfair distribution of wealth has been condoned, again by appeal to principles of natural justice. The excesses of the French Revolution were in the name of universal human rights.

The theoretical objections allege that claims to knowledge of natural purposes are spurious, and that natural rights are mysterious entities about which there can be no knowledge.

Among the critics of natural law theories are Bentham, Austin and other utilitarians, as well as some more recent schools of legal philosophy (Kelsen, legal realism). The attacks have often had a political dimension, being prompted by a wish for legal reform. It was argued that the criterion of a good law could not be conformity with a supposed natural law, but rather conformity with the principle of utility or some other principle of general welfare. Other critics – Rousseau, romantic philosophers, the historical school of jurisprudence – rejected the idea that the law could embody timeless principles, insisting that the law was, or ought to be, the expression of the will of those subject to the law, of the people. The authority behind the law could not be a set of valid abstract principles, but should be the genuine will of the nation.

Although its influence was waning since the early nineteenth century, natural law theory retained adherents, especially among neo-Thomists (e.g. Maritain), and regained ground especially since the Second World War. In Germany and Austria it was often regarded as inseparable from religion. In Britain and North America, a number of writers such as G. E. M. Anscombe, G. Grisez and J. Finnis have given new variations to classical themes in Aristotle and Aquinas. Rights-theories have also remained on the agenda. In the 1970s, R. Nozick (*Anarchy, State and Utopia*) and others following him used a theory of natural rights to advocate an ideal of minimal state action.

natural number The positive integers 1, 2, 3, etc. are called natural numbers. Some writers include 0, others do not. There are, then, two different terminologies: (a) the set of natural numbers is {0, 1, 2, 3, 4, . . .}. The set {1, 2, 3, 4, . . .} is called the set of positive integers; (b) the set of natural numbers is {1, 2, 3, 4, . . .}. The set {0, 1, 2, 3, 4, . . .} is called the set of non-negative integers.

natural object On the whole, this term, and *natural property*, are used to indicate that the object or property belongs to the world of experience.

In his discussion of the naturalistic fallacy, G. E. Moore distinguished natural from metaphysical objects. We *experience* the existence of a natural object. We *infer* the existence, in a supersensible real world, of a metaphysical object (*Principia Ethica*, §25, p. 38). In his view, 'good' denotes a non-natural property that is neither natural nor metaphysical. What makes an object natural is its existence in time. Its natural properties can be regarded as its constituents and also as existing in time (*Principia Ethica*, §26, pp. 40ff). The problem of how to adequately characterize 'natural' was one to which Moore kept returning.

natural philosophy an older designation for the natural sciences. For instance, the title of Newton's major work, published in 1687, is in English 'The Mathematical Principles of Natural Philosophy'. Also, some science chairs in the older universities are still so styled.

Note: This is not the same as NATURE-PHILOSOPHY.

natural property *See* NATURAL OBJECT.

natural religion religious or theological doctrine based on reason alone; also known as *natural theology*.

Natural theology was contrasted by Suárez with what he called supernatural theology (*Disputationes metaphysicae* 1597, I, 1), but which is more commonly called revealed religion, based directly or indirectly on communication from God.

An early formulation of a theology that does not depend on revelation is the Stoic theory presented in Cicero's *De Natura Deorum c.* 45 BC (On the nature of the gods). Many ingredients in this theory were adopted by most Christian theologians, who agreed that a part, though not the whole, of Christian doctrine would be known without any special revelation. In the seventeenth century, a number of writers later known as DEISTS argued that a religion within the limits of reason alone contained everything that is essential to true religion, and in the eighteenth century this view became influential. The more radical wing rejected revelation; more popular was the moderate view, proposed e.g. in William Wollaston's *The Religion of Nature Delineated* 1722, 1724, that revelation was a 'republication' of truths attainable by natural means, useful for weaker minds but not essential.

The idea of natural religion was attractive, for being based on reason it could in principle command universal assent and put an end to the disputes and bloody conflicts that had raged for centuries. Another feature found attractive was that it could serve as a refutation of atheism and materialism.

The most important classical criticisms of the project are those of David Hume in his posthumously published *Dialogues Concerning Natural Religion* 1779 and of Immanuel Kant in his *Critique of Pure Reason* 1781, in the Transcendental Dialectic.

The full strength of these criticisms was not immediately grasped. They were disregarded by William Paley in his *Natural Theology, or evidences of the existence and attributes of the Deity, collected from the appearance of nature* 1802, a book that came to be widely used as a text in the English universities in the nineteenth century; and the classical objections are often ignored even in the late twentieth century.

natural theology *See* NATURAL RELIGION.

nature *See* NATURAL.

nature-philosophy (Gm. *Naturphilosophie*) This is a term mainly used for the speculative theorizing about the phenomena of nature which had its principal flourish when Romantic criticism of science was at its peak (1780–1830). Its best-known proponents were Schelling (1775–1854) and Lorenz Oken (1779–1851). Goethe's theory of colours (1795), proposed as a competitor to Newton's *Optics*, and his plant physiology, also represent this trend. Its underlying motivation can be found in the reluctance to accept the view of nature predominant in modern science, a view that rejects anthropomorphism, anthropocentrism, and which does not ascribe any symbolic dimension to the phenomena of nature: its picture of nature is materialistic, mechanistic, meaningless.

Nature-philosophers saw nature as infused with poetry; normal science does not and, hence, they wanted a different approach. They wanted nature to make sense. They looked for symbolic or semantic elements inherent in nature: the phenomena of nature constitute a language that carries a message that we may wish to understand. They felt that it should be possible to grasp the phenomena of nature in an intuitive way, and even by communing with them, rather than by external observation and experiment. The assumption is that the phenomena of nature all have an affinity to, and are expressions of, life or mind. When we contemplate the full moon on a still night, or a rare orchid in its natural habitat, we see that there are aspects of these phenomena that normal science neglects. Nature-philosophy is an attempt to develop or to legitimize theories which at one and the same time do justice to those aspects, *and* provide what we expect from science.

Naturphilosophie Gm. NATURE-PHILOSOPHY.

negation *n.* In ordinary language, negation (or denial) is expressed by *not*, *it is not the case that*, etc.

If a statement p is true, its negation, not p (it is not the case that p), is false. If a statement p is false, its negation is true.

The word 'negation' is used both for the act of negating a given statement, and for the result of that act. This process/product ambiguity is for the most part innocuous.

Negation is not the same as *contradiction*. A negation involves *one* proposition. A person who believes a negation – for example, the proposition that *it is not the case that the Earth is flat* – may be right; indeed, he is! A contradiction involves *two* propositions, which cannot be true together and which cannot be false together. A person who believes a contradiction – for instance, both that *the Earth is flat* and *it is not the case that the Earth is flat* – cannot be right.

Negation and *denial* are often used interchangeably; however, sometimes *denial* is reserved for sentences only, and *negation* used more generally to apply to sentences or to other expressions (e.g. predicates).

In statements of a certain complexity, negation can occur in more than one place. Compare, for instance: It is not possible that pigs fly ($\sim\Diamond p$); and It is possible that pigs do not fly ($\Diamond\sim p$). In the first, the negation is *external*; in the second, *internal*. Of course, a statement can contain both: $\sim\Diamond\sim p$.

Another example is: You are not obliged to drink when on duty ($\sim Op$); and You are obliged not to drink when on duty ($O\sim p$). Again, the difference between external and internal negation is obvious.

See also DOUBLE NEGATION.

negative freedom/positive freedom *Negative freedom*, 'independence of determination by alien causes', and *positive freedom*, which is the same as self-determination or autonomy, were distinguished by Kant in chapter 3 of *Foundations of the Metaphysics of Morals* 1785.

The contrast between these two concepts, especially as they apply in social and political contexts, was elaborated by Isaiah Berlin in 'Two Concepts of Liberty', originally delivered as an inaugural lecture at Oxford in 1958. Negative freedom consists in the absence of coercion, the absence of interference from other people. Liberty in this negative sense means liberty *from*. Positive freedom consists in self-determination, in being one's own master, being in charge of the fulfilment of one's aspirations. At first sight it seems the two kinds of freedom complement each other. But, Berlin argued, in the history of political thought positive freedom has regularly been taken to mean that the individual should be determined by his true, genuine self and not by his actual self, which is imperfect because of innate shortcomings (like original sin) or the bad influence of society. Since individuals are often seen as being blind, ignorant or corrupt, the ideal of positive freedom will normally imply coercion: the unenlightened individuals must in Rousseau's words 'be forced to be free'. It is an ideal that has served to justify much political oppression in the twentieth century: the state acts to protect the individual from himself and to help him to get what is good for him, rather than what he wants. Since it is the individual's own real interests that are being promoted, what looks like coercion is claimed to be liberation.

negative proposition **1** (in syllogistic logic) a proposition of the form *No S is P* or of the form *Some S is not P*. **2** a proposition of the form not-p.

negative theology the view that every affirmative proposition about God's nature is false: God can be understood only by propositions about what he is not. In a formulation by the fourth-century Church Father Gregory of Nyssa: God can be grasped neither by name, nor by any thought, nor any other conception. He is indescribable, unutterable, and above all signification. *Syn.* apophatic theology.

negative utilitarianism *See* UTILITARIANISM, NEGATIVE/POSITIVE

Nelson, Leonard (1882–1924) German philosopher, professor at Göttingen from 1909. His neo-Kantian philosophy was influenced by that of J. F. Fries (1773–1843); he was reluctant to adopt the anti-psychologism of other Kant interpreters. A colleague and friend of Hilbert, Nelson also wrote on the philosophy of mathematics. In ethics he emphasized universalizability in a way that shows some similarity with R. M. Hare.

neo-Kantianism *n.* a philosophical movement in Germany, which arose in reaction against the two tendencies that held sway in the mid-nineteenth century: speculative metaphysics and dogmatic scientific materialism. Against this the philosopher Otto Liebmann (1840–1912) urged the slogan 'Back to Kant!' in his *Kant und die Epigonen* 1865 (Kant and the epigones). The aim was to encourage a sense of intellectual responsibility and a renewed recognition of the limits of human knowledge, in a Kantian spirit. The neo-Kantians characteristically showed antipathy to fashionable pessimism (Schopenhauer, von Hartmann) and to the political and cultural conservatism of the Church. By the turn of the century, this tendency had become predominant in German academic philosophy. Important representatives were F. A. Lange (1828–75), Alois Riehl (1844–1924) and the philosophers of the Marburg School and the Baden (or South-West German) School.

neologism /niːˈɒlədʒɪzm/ *n.* a newly created word or expression.

neology /niːˈɒlədʒɪ/ *n.* a new theory, a doctrinal innovation. **1** (in theology) the tendency, especially among eighteenth-century German Protestant theologians, to replace orthodox interpretations of Christianity with one more accommodating to the demands of natural reason and feeling. **2** (in lexicography) the study of neologisms.

neo-Malthusianism *n.* a theory first proposed around the mid-nineteenth century which, in agreement with Malthus, recognizes the potentially disastrous effects of unrestricted population growth but which, in disagreement with him, advocates family planning by means of artificial birth control (contraception) as an alternative preferable to poverty, epidemics, wars, etc. The early neo-Malthusians were primarily concerned with the condition of the working-class poor, while in the second half of the twentieth century the consequences of a world-wide population growth have been in focus, through the writings of G. Borgström, D. Meadows, P. Ehrlich et al.

Note: Artificial birth control remains unacceptable to some religious authorities. In the twentieth century, it has been condemned in three papal encyclicals (*Casti connubii* 1930; *Humanae vitae* 1968 and

Veritatis splendor 1993). It is held to be contrary to natural law.

neo-Platonism *n.* This term is used for the Platonist movement from the third century AD. Its most important thinkers were Plotinus (205–70), Iamblichus (*c.* 245–*c.* 326), and Proclus (412–85). There is also a noticeable neo-Platonic influence in the writings of Augustine and pseudo-Dionysius. In general, the aim was to reach a personal understanding of higher realities. Little attention was given to social and political philosophy; the principal interest was in theology, metaphysics and logic. Of Plato's dialogues, *Timaeus* and *Parmenides* were given a central place.

Details vary, but there are certain common themes. Ultimate reality is the One, identified with the Good and the highest God. There are then various 'hypostases' in Plotinus's sense: One; Mind; Soul. Matter has no independent reality, nor has evil – indeed, in a deeper sense, neither is real. Whatever derives from a higher principle will *resemble* it and will ultimately *return* to it. The movement is from the more unified to the less unified, and back again. Higher principles have potencies actualized by the lower ones.

The neo-Platonists regarded themselves as followers and developers of Plato's thought. Even after the rediscovery of many of Plato's lost dialogues a thousand years later, they were regarded as such by the Renaissance humanists and by the seventeenth-century Cambridge Platonists. There are of course continuities between Platonism and neo-Platonism, but the need to make a clear distinction between them was not recognized before the eighteenth century, when the earliest histories of philosophy in the modern sense treated neo-Platonism adversely, regarding it as a degenerate form of classical Greek philosophy. Since Hegel its reputation has improved. HT/ed.

neo-positivism *n.* logical POSITIVISM.

neo-realism *See* NEW REALISM.

neo-Stoicism a philosophical movement reviving the ethical theories of ancient Stoicism. Its earliest major representative was the Dutch scholar Justus Lipsius (1547–1606). He appealed to the Stoic concept of 'right reason' as a basis for ethics, developing a synthesis of Stoic and Christian ethics. This synthesis omitted appeals to revealed religion, but it also omitted some Stoic doctrines difficult to reconcile with Christian teaching (e.g. that the wise man is god-like; that compassion is not a virtue; that suicide is not wrong). It included many of the teachings of the ancient Stoics – Epictetus, Seneca and Marcus Aurelius – which resemble Christian ones, especially ethical universalism, i.e. the doctrine that all human beings are equal, independently of race, religion, nationality, etc.

The aim was to develop a theory that could gain general agreement and help to put an end to the religious controversies and violent conflicts of the time, alluded to by the title of a work by the Frenchman G. du Vair (1556–1621): *Traité de la constance et consolation ès calamitez publiques* 1595 (A treatise of constancy and consolation amidst public calamities). Other important neo-Stoics were Gaspar Scioppius (1576–1649) in Germany, Fr. de Quevedo (1580–1645) in Spain, and Th. Gataker (1574–1654) in England.

neo-Thomism *n.* a philosophy based on the teachings of Thomas Aquinas, who was officially sanctioned as the foremost authority on philosophical matters through Pope Leo XIII's encyclical *Aeterni Patris* 1879. Leading representatives were Cardinal Mercier (1851–1926), Jacques Maritain (1882–1973) and Etienne Gilson (1884–1978).

ne quid nimis Lat. nothing to excess.

nescience /ˈnɛsɪəns/ *n.* ignorance.

Neurath /ˈnɔiraːt (Gm.)/, Otto (von) (1882–1945) Austrian sociologist and philosopher. He played a central part in the development of logical positivism and was a core member of the Vienna Circle. Where Carnap had introduced the concept of protocol sentences for foundational sentences which incorrigibly report immediate sense-experiences and constitute a basis for all other knowledge, Neurath, in contrast, used the concept to characterize reports of particular observations of the physical world which, in his view, form the set of basic, but not incorrigible, sentences. By this means the phenomenalism implicit in Carnap's view could be abandoned in favour of physicalism. His example of a protocol sentence is 'Otto's protocol at 3:17 o'clock: [At 3:16 o'clock Otto said to himself: (at 3:15 o'clock there was a table in the room perceived by Otto)]'. Such reports are not incorrigible: 'No sentence enjoys the *noli me tangere* that Carnap ordains for protocol sentences'. What makes for our accepting some of them as true is that they cohere with the class of sentences to which they are adjoined. Neurath advocated the ideal of unified science, and protocol sentences are part of its language, a language free of metaphysics. Implicit in this ideal was the unity of method: the same methods are in principle applicable in any intellectually respectable kind of inquiry, be it ancient history or modern physics.

Politically, most logical positivists were on the Left, and Neurath very much so. He was a civil servant in the short-lived socialist government in Bavaria in 1919 and actively involved in the democratic working-class movements in Vienna in the 1920s. Later, Neurath also devoted much energy to the creation of an internationally usable picture language, anticipating the widespread use of icons in travel centres, on computer screens, etc.

neustic /ˈnjuːstɪk/, **phrastic** /ˈfræstik/ (Gr. *neuein* to nod; *phrazein* to show; to say) *n.* These terms are used to mark the distinction between the different aspects of a sentence. The phrastic is that which is common to 'you are closing the door' and 'close the door, you!', i.e. your closing the door. But the two sentences have different neustic components: the first sentence can be paraphrased 'your closing the door, yes', and the second 'your closing the door, please'. The first sentence expresses a statement, the second an imperative.

This pair of terms was introduced by R. M. Hare in *The Language of Morals* 1952. He used it to explain how imperatives, which lack truth-value, can stand in logical relations, arguing that this is possible since on analysis it becomes clear that it is the phrastics that stand in logical relations. To deal with objections raised by Peter Geach, John Searle and others against his analysis of imperatives, Hare subsequently refined his analysis, in an article in *Mind* 1989, by the introduction of two further concepts, *clistic* (Gr. *kleiein* to separate, to conclude) and *tropic* (Gr. *tropos* turn, manner, mode). The revised analysis of 'your closing the door, please' is:

Clistic:	Message begins
Phrastic:	Your closing the door (the descriptive content of the message)
Tropic:	Please (the manner in which the message is put forward)
Neustic:	Signed R. M. Hare (the assertive nod to the message)
Clistic:	Message ends

The neustic, redefined, gives the assertive nod to the message. The message itself is analysable into a descriptive content, the phrastic, and the manner in which it is put forward, the tropic.

neutral monism the theory that mental and physical phenomena alike are constructed from more ultimate constituents which are neither. This is the view of William James in 'Does "Consciousness" Exist?' 1904, of some of the New Realists, and it was also argued for by Bertrand Russell in *The Analysis of Mind* 1921. *See also* MONISM.

Newcomb's paradox There are two closed, opaque boxes in front of you, A and B. You must choose between either (a) opening and taking the contents of both A and B, or (b) opening and taking the contents of B alone. A person, called 'Predictor' (or 'God', in some versions of the story), is known to have put $1,000 in A and to have put either: (i) $1,000,000 in B if he has predicted that you will take the contents of B alone; or (ii) nothing in B, if he has predicted that you will take the contents of both boxes.

Also, Predictor is known to have a faultless record in predicting whether a subject will take B alone or will opt to take the contents of both boxes. Furthermore, the choice you make will not make any change to the contents of the boxes.

There is a strong case for saying that you ought to choose to take the contents of B alone; for it is all but certain, given Predictor's faultless record, that if you take the contents of B alone, you will end up with $1,000,000, whereas if you take the contents of both boxes, you will end up with only $1,000.

The paradox is constituted by the fact that there is also a strong case for saying that you ought to make the alternative choice of taking the contents of both boxes. The money was placed in the boxes in the past, and the choice you make will not make any change to what is in them. This means that taking the contents of both boxes is bound to leave you better off than taking the contents of B alone. For if the Predictor has put $1,000,000 in B, you will end up with $1,001,000; and if he has not, you will end up with $1,000 rather than nothing. In either case taking the contents of both leaves you $1,000 better off than taking the contents of B alone.

The paradox was formulated by the American physicist William Newcomb, and was brought to the notice of philosophers by Robert Nozick in 1969. FJ

New Criticism a movement in literary criticism. Its approach to a literary work is textual rather than contextual. The historical contexts of the work or the biographical data about the author are considered to be of secondary importance or none at all. The work itself is in focus and subjected to a close reading and explication, which centres on the literary devices employed: symbols, ambiguities, figures of speech, structures of discourse.

The movement derived inspiration from the writings of I. A. Richards, William Empson and T. S. Eliot in the 1920s and 1930s. Among well-known representatives are the American critics Cleanth Brooks, Robert Penn Warren and W. K. Wimsatt. In the United States, it began to fall out of favour in 1957, and has been gradually superseded since the 1960s.

New Left an intellectual and political movement that reached its peak in the late 1960s, inspired by Marxist traditions (Trotsky, Gramsci, Marcuse, Mao Tse-tung, etc.), strongly critical of the political system of the Western democracies, but also deeply disaffected with the official Marxist ideology and policy of the communist parties in eastern and western Europe.

New Philosophers a group of French intellectuals (*les nouveaux philosophes*) who in 1976–7 became widely known for their energetic attacks on the leftism that had dominated intellectual life in post-war France. They saw a close connection between Marxist theory and Soviet practice: from the moral and material shabbiness of everyday life to the labour camps and mass murder. Best known among them are André Glucksmann and Bernard-Henri Lévy (1948–), author of *La Barbarie à visage humain* 1977 (Barbarism with a human face).

New Realism This term has sometimes been used for the realistic opposition to the idealistic philosophies, current especially in Britain and the United States in the first two decades of the twentieth century. However, it has been used more specifically for the views of a group of philosophers in the United States, who formed part of the movement. In 1910, six of these published in the *Journal of Philosophy* a short statement entitled 'The Program and First Platform of Six Realists'. These were Edwin B. Holt, Walter T. Marvin, W. P. Montague, Ralph Barton Perry, Walter B. Pitkin and E. G. Spalding. Their views were subsequently developed and expounded more fully in a cooperative volume entitled *The New Realism* 1912. Their central theme was the independence of what is known from the knower, and the starting point of their polemic was that idealists made illicit use of the fact of our egocentric predicament to argue fallaciously from the tautology that everything that is known is known to the conclusion that everything that is is known.

Before long the New Realism was itself criticized for its failure to deal effectively with the phenomena of error and illusion by R. W. Sellars and other CRITICAL REALISTS who rejected both phenomenalism and the 'direct realism' of the New Realists. QG

new riddle of induction *See* GOODMAN'S PARADOX.

Newton /ˈnjuːtən/, Isaac (1642–1727) One of the greatest of scientists, Newton's theory of mechanics and gravitation in *Philosophiae naturalis principia mathematica* 1687 (The mathematical principles of natural philosophy) established physics as a systematic form of inquiry. That theory is: every body continues in its state of rest or uniform motion unless compelled to change that state by some force impressed upon it; the change of motion is proportional to the impressed force; to every action of a force there is an equal and opposite reaction; between every two bodies there is a gravitational force which is directly proportional to the product of their masses and inversely proportional to the square of the distance between them.

The theory explained Galileo's law that freely falling bodies fall with constant acceleration, and Kepler's three laws concerning the motions of the planets. It also 'corrected' these laws by showing that they only hold if certain simplifying assumptions are made. The theory also made numerous surprising predictions (for example, it predicted the periodic return of Halley's comet many years after Newton's death), and almost all of these predictions eventually proved to be correct. The theory even predicted that if we could throw an object from a high enough point we would have an artificial satellite which would continually orbit the earth. To develop these consequences of the theory, a new mathematics was required, the differential and integral calculus; Newton invented this also. (So did Leibniz at about the same time, independently.) He also discovered from experiments with prisms the composite nature of sunlight and advocated the view that a ray of light is a stream of light particles. He devoted much energy, also, to working out the age of the universe from biblical chronologies and to alchemical speculations about the possibility of converting lead into gold. AM

Note: Pope wrote

Nature and nature's laws lay hid in night:
God said, 'Let Newton be!' and all was light.

Much later, there was a sequel:

It did not last; the Devil, howling 'Ho!
Let Einstein be!', restored the status quo.

And here is a recent continuation:

God rolled His dice, to Einstein's great dismay:
'Let Feynman be!', and all was clear as day.

The second couplet was by J. C. Squire (1884–1958, literary anthologist and critic), and the third by Stephen G. Brush (historian of science) in 1996, in a review of a book about the physicist Richard Feynman. ed.

nice *adj.* (in older usage) fine, subtle, precise.

Nicholas of Autrecourt (*c.* 1300–?) attended the University of Paris. He opposed the Aristotelianism current at the time, arguing that its reliance on reason in religious and other areas went too far. The extent of his own scepticism is subject to conflicting interpretations. Of interest is his apparent anticipation of Hume's critique of the concepts of necessity and causality. GW/ed.

Nicholas of Cusa (1401–64) Born at Kues, in the Rhineland, near Trier, Nicholas rose to eminence in the Church, and equally in the theology and philosophy of his time. Among the many works of this Renaissance thinker the best-known is *De docta ignorantia* 1440 (On learned ignorance). The concept of learned ignorance is central, together with that of the coincidence of opposites, to his theory of religious and secular knowledge. The main theme of the book is the inherent limitations of our intellect. In line with the Platonic tradition it is argued that we can have no knowledge of God: the best we can achieve is some insight into what he is not. Nor can the intellect reach truth about other matters, even if we can get close, in the same way that a polygon can approximate but not coincide with a circle. The doctrine of the coincidence of opposites, formulated in opposition to the Aristotelian principle of non-contradiction, was in his view a necessary part for an understanding of reality, and especially of the divine nature. Opposites exist in God, who transcends them in a way unfathomable to us.

It was in this spirit that he argued that the universe has no centre and no periphery. Whether this break with tradition anticipates the new scientific cosmologies with their rejection of the heliocentric world-view is a debated question.

Nicole /nɪˈkɔl (Fr.)/, Pierre (1625–95) French theologian and philosopher, associated with the PORT-ROYAL circle. He was a friend of Arnauld, and co-author with him of several works, including the *Port-Royal Logic* 1662. Engaged in theological controversies, he wrote against the Jesuits and against the Huguenots. His *Essais de morale* 1671–8 (Moral essays) emphasize the egoism inherent in human nature. Some of them were translated into English by John Locke.

Nicomachean /nɪkəməˈkeɪən/ ***Ethics*** Aristotle's principal work on ethics. According to tradition, he dedicated it to his son Nicomachus.

Nietzsche /ˈniːtʃə/, Friedrich (1844–1900) German philosopher, best known as a radical critic of the Western tradition, with its beliefs in truth, morality and God. He is famed for his claim that 'God is dead' and his theories of the superman (or the overman) and the will-to-power.

Nietzsche's home environment was dominated by women – his father, a Lutheran clergyman, died when he was five. His university studies in Bonn and, later,

Leipzig centred on classical antiquity. While at Leipzig, Nietzsche first read Schopenhauer's *The World as Will and Representation*, which had a marked impact on his later thought despite his eventual rejection of Schopenhauer's pessimism.

Nietzsche had the distinction of being appointed to a chair in classical philology at the University of Basel in 1869 at the early age of 24, without having written his dissertation. His first work, *The Birth of Tragedy* 1872, was therefore met with special interest by the scholarly community. The work proved, however, to be more imaginative and psychological than scholarly, and was not well received by contemporary classical scholars. Nietzsche's account of tragedy draws on the images of the Greek deities Apollo and Dionysus: Apollo, who represents beauty and aesthetic order, contrasts with Dionysus, who is associated with sex, frenzy, wine and music. Nietzsche argued that Greek tragedy reconciled the two principles represented by these gods, principles which are central to the human psyche as well as to aesthetics.

The work was dedicated to Richard Wagner, whom Nietzsche had first met in Leipzig, and his wife Cosima. Although their friendship came to an end, Nietzsche's preoccupation with Wagner remains evident in works spanning his creative life.

Partly in response to the poor reception his first book received, Nietzsche next published four major critical studies, *Unzeitgemässe Betrachtungen* (*Untimely Meditations* or *Unfashionable Reflections*). One important theme in these works – 'David Strauss: Writer and Confessor' 1873, 'On the Advantages and Disadvantages of History for Life' 1873, 'Schopenhauer as Educator' 1874 and 'Richard Wagner in Bayreuth' 1876 – is the condemnation of the philistinism of contemporary intellectual, cultural and political attitudes.

Next came the works of Nietzsche's 'positivistic' period, in which he attacked many traditional religious and metaphysical assumptions, showing a preference for more naturalistic accounts. The first of these works, dedicated to the memory of Voltaire, was *Menschliches, Allzumenschliches* (2 vols, 1878, 1880; *Human, All-Too-Human*) and *Morgenröte* 1881 (Daybreak). They are made up of aphorisms, varying in length from one-line maxims to reflections a few pages long, subtly juxtaposed.

Although strength and health are among Nietzsche's positive values, his own health was never good. It had deteriorated during the positivistic period to the point that he had to resign from his university position in 1879. His unrequited love for Lou Salomé and his disillusion with Wagner, who died in 1883, also marred his personal life. His works of this era, however, are in many ways his most positive. *Die fröhliche Wissenschaft* 1882 (*The Gay Science* or *The Joyous Science*) is an aphoristic work in which Nietzsche defends a light-hearted, life-orientated approach to scholarship. It is also the work in which he first proposes his famous doctrine of 'eternal recurrence', the doctrine that time is cyclical, repeating itself over and over again. This doctrine, although apparently cosmological, is taken by Nietzsche as a criterion for judging the value of one's life. If one is really living a good life, he argues, one would be happy to repeat it over and over. The doctrine of eternal recurrence also provides a basis for a more positive approach to life than Nietzsche finds available through the Christian world-view, which judges a life on the basis of its end – either in heaven or in hell. By contrast, eternal recurrence posits that every moment is integral to the whole. It also implies that no moment is more important than the present, in which one has the opportunity to make active choices that influence the character of the whole.

Also sprach Zarathustra 1883–5 (*Thus spoke Zarathustra*) is Nietzsche's only work with a basically fictional format. Its hero is a modernized Zarathustra (the Persian founder of Zoroastrianism). Nietzsche's Zarathustra preaches a new, atheistic gospel of aspiration towards greatness. This aspiration is embodied in the figure of the *Übermensch* (superman), a new and superior type of human being who rejects existing morality, who overturns existing values by affirming the positive value of earthly life and of the active, creative individual, and who undertakes the creation of his own life in the way the artist creates his works. *Jenseits von Gut und Böse* 1886 (*Beyond Good and Evil*) and *Zur Genealogie der Moral* 1887 (On the genealogy of morals) are perhaps the best known of Nietzsche's works. These are primarily critical works, which aim to undermine Christian morality through an unattractive account of its origins and through an analysis that shows it to be psychologically pernicious: it is an unhealthy slave morality, in contrast to a healthy aristocratic master morality. Nietzsche's main examples of master morality are provided by the 'warrior-nobles' of the Greek, Norse and Indian epics. Master morality makes the primary judgement that the masters' own way of life is good, and it derivatively judges contrasting ways of life as 'bad'. Slave morality, on the contrary, develops among those who are subjugated by the masters. The slaves turn the tables on the masters by internally judging them to be 'evil'. The slaves boost their own self-esteem by judging themselves, derivatively, as 'good'.

While a slave morality is suited to those with a slavish, 'botched and bungled' nature, its message of humility and pity emasculates those 'higher men' who are capable of rising above what Nietzsche calls 'the herd'. For one thing, slave morality also makes self-evaluation a function of traits which one lacks, not traits that one possesses. The slave feels 'good' to the extent that he or she lacks pride, arrogance, assertiveness, and other traits belonging to the masters. The result is that the slave's values, though they secure an imaginary victory over the masters, actually reinforce the slave's relative impotence in the world. Nietzsche goes on to argue that the average Christian conforms to these patterns. The Christian gains self-esteem by means of judging others as sinful and by aspiring, not to an active, creative life, but to an insipid and mediocre life which glorifies his or her own incapacities as 'restraint'.

Nietzsche also makes use of his concept 'the will to power' in his criticism of Christianity. Human beings (and all of life) essentially seek to enhance their power. Even the alleged selflessness of religious individuals is mere camouflage for selfish pursuits. Christianity is also unhealthy because it encourages extirpation of the passions, attacking, in effect, the wilfulness which is essential to human vitality.

A wider target is the belief – Plato's and Kant's, as well as Christian – that there exists a real external world which transcends the world of experience. For Nietzsche, the only world is a Heraclitean one of flux, upon which we impose, through the will to power, our particular perspectives and orderings. Belief in another world is due, in part, to a refusal (due to weakness) to face up to this task of imposing one's individual perspective and, in part, to seduction by language, whose grammar encourages us to look for enduring, fixed realities behind the flux of experience. 'We shall not be rid of God until we are rid of grammar.'

Der Wille zur Macht (The will to power), published posthumously (the first version in 1901, a larger one in 1906), is actually a haphazard collection from Nietzsche's notebooks, compiled by his sister and a devout disciple of his, Peter Gast (pseudonym for Heinrich Köselitz). Scholarly efforts to undo the editorial damage have resulted in several different editions of *The Will to Power*. The appropriateness of relying on this book is still hotly debated by Nietzsche scholars.

Nietzsche's output during 1888, his final productive year, included *Der Fall Wagner* 1888 (The Wagner case), *Götzen-Dämmerung* 1889 (Twilight of the Idols), *Der Antichrist* 1895, *Nietzsche contra Wagner* 1895, and an unorthodox review of his life and writings, *Ecce Homo* 1908. Early in January 1889 insanity set in, and he was hospitalized after collapsing in the street. He never recovered, and died on 25 August 1900. KHI

nihilism /ˈnaɪɪlɪzm/ (Lat. *nihil* nothing) *n.* Any view which contains a significant denial can be described as nihilistic, but when the term is used there is often a suggestion of loss or despair. Among the views so labelled are those which deny the existence of a God, the immortality of the soul, the freedom of the will, the authority of reason, the possibility of knowledge, the objectivity of morals, or the ultimate happy ending of human history. The term has been applied to various negative theses or attitudes. The following short list gives only a sample of what has been understood by 'nihilist':
(i) a radical revolutionary (especially in nineteenth-century Russia), who rejects the existing social order and accepts terrorist activism in order to destroy it. This is how the word was first used in Russia in the late 1850s. It gained currency through Turgenev's novel *Fathers and Sons* 1862;
(ii) a person who rejects all moral restraints;
(iii) a person who does not seriously care about anything;
(iv) an adherent of the theory that nothing is true;
(v) an adherent of moral NON-COGNITIVISM;
(vi) an adherent of eliminativism in the philosophy of mind.

nisus Lat. inclination, tendency, endeavour, urge, motive power.

Nobel Prize winners The Nobel Prize in literature has been awarded to these philosophers: Rudolf Eucken (1908); Henri Bergson (1927; awarded in 1928); Bertrand Russell (1950); Albert Camus (1957); Jean-Paul Sartre (1964; declined).

noble lie (Gr. *gennaion pseudos*, also translated 'royal lie', 'magnificent myth') In Plato's *Republic* 414–15, a myth promoted by the wise rulers of the state is so described. Belief in this myth will produce social harmony by keeping the citizens contented with their station in life.

noema /nəʊˈiːmə/ (*sing.*); **noemata** /nəʊˈiːmətə/ (*pl.*) (Gr. *noēma* something thought) *n.* This term, and *noesis*, were used by Husserl in his analysis of mental acts in *Ideas* 1913 p. 190. Noesis is the particular intentional (i.e. 'directed') act itself; a noema comprises all that which makes the act be as if it were of an object experienced in a certain way. The respective adjectives from these terms are *noematic* /nəʊɪˈmætɪk/ and *noetic* /nəʊˈetɪk/.

noesis /nəʊˈiːsɪs/ (Gr. *noēsis* an act of thought) *n. See* NOEMA.

nomic /ˈnəʊmɪk/ (Gr. *nomos* custom, convention; law, rule) *adj.* of or pertaining to a law of nature.

nominal definition a statement giving the meaning of a linguistic expression. Traditionally this is contrasted with *real* definition: a statement giving the essence of the thing designated by the expression.

nominalism (Lat. *nomen* name) *n.* the view that only individuals are real, i.e. exist independently of a mind, and that words cannot refer to something real unless they refer to an individual. Consequently, universals, i.e. concepts that can be predicated of different individuals, are not real. The same applies to properties, classes, numbers and other abstract entities; any reference to such entities is legitimate only if it can be reduced to talk about individuals. One variant, conceptualism, holds that universals, although not real, exist 'in the mind'; others, like Roscelinus (1050–*c.* 1125), the first major mediaeval nominalist, gave the formulation 'a universal is only a word'. Whether William of Ockham (1285–1347) is correctly described as a nominalist is a matter of dispute. It was, however, his view that only individually existing things and their individual sensible properties (e.g. the snub-nosedness of Socrates) are real. *See* UNIVERSALS.

Later nominalists are Hobbes (1588–1679), in *Leviathan*, chapter 4, and Berkeley (1685–1753), who attacked abstract ideas in paragraph 18 of the Introduction to *Principles of Human Knowledge*. In the twentieth century, more refined modern formulations have been proposed by Rudolf Carnap, Nelson Goodman et al. In close sympathy with nominalism is also W. V. O. Quine, who favours ontological frugality, but may not be regarded as a nominalist in the strictest sense since he countenances the reality of one kind of abstract objects, i.e. classes.

nomological dangler **1** a relation or law that would be a loose end dangling from a network of scientific laws. Herbert Feigl used this expression to describe a relation or a law that connects something that is inter-subjectively observable (for instance, certain brain-states) with something that is not (for instance, the experience of a sensory quality like redness) (H. Feigl, 'The "Mental" and the "Physical"', *Minnesota Studies in the Philosophy of Science*, vol. 2, 1958, p. 428; also in his *The 'Mental' and the 'Physical'* 1967). **2** an entity or a property which cannot properly enter into the formulation of scientific laws. J. J. C. Smart used the expression in this sense, which is different from Feigl's, in *Philosophy and Scientific Realism* 1963.

nomological statement statement of a scientific law. The term was used by Hans Reichenbach (1891–1953), who proposed a set of conditions under which a conditional statement, i.e. a statement of the form *if p, then q*, is to count as a scientific law.

nomos /ˈnɒmɒs/ Gr. custom, convention; law, rule *n.*

nomothetic (Gr. *nomothetein* to lay down a law) *adj.* Sciences that seek to discover general laws for indefinitely repeatable events and processes are nomothetic, in contrast to sciences which are IDIOGRAPHIC in that they describe what is particular and non-recurrent. This characterization and the pair of terms were introduced by Windelband in 1894. To be noted is that the contrast does not by itself concern the object but only the aim of the inquiry, so it is not ruled out that the same area can allow for both kinds of theory. Most human sciences and some natural sciences are idiographic.

non-cognitivism *n.* the theory that there is nothing to be known, and hence that there can be no knowledge, in the area under consideration.

In moral philosophy, where in the late 1940s the term was first used, non-cognitivism is the metaethical thesis that there are no 'moral facts' and hence no moral knowledge. This negative thesis is accepted in existentialist, emotivist, prescriptivist and other theories of ethics. It is usually supplemented with a positive account of the nature of moral beliefs and moral statements.

Other words with the same or closely related meaning are: *anti-objectivism*, *anti-realism*, *irrealism*, *non-descriptivism* and *non-factualism*. The variety of terms can, however, be used to mark certain distinctions. *See also* COGNITIVISM.

non-contradiction, law of in classical logic, the principle that contradictories cannot be true together and cannot be false together. In modern logic, the principle that no statement of the form (p and not-p) can be true. The classical defence of the law of non-contradiction is in Aristotle's *Metaphysics*, Book Γ 4f.

non-Euclidean geometry *See* EUCLIDEAN GEOMETRY.

non-factive *See* FACTIVE.

non-factualism *See* FACTUALISM.

non-naturalistic ethics metaethical theories that reject ethical naturalism and take the fundamental moral properties to be non-natural. The main representative of ethical non-naturalism is G. E. Moore.

non-natural properties In his rejection of the NATURALISTIC FALLACY, G. E. Moore argued that intrinsic goodness cannot be identified with any natural property of an object or a state of affairs, and that it cannot be identified with any supernatural or metaphysical property either. But, he argued, 'intrinsically good' certainly denotes some quality, which he described as non-natural.

non sequitur /nɒn 'sɛkwɪtə/ Lat. it does not follow. A *non sequitur* is an invalid argument, i.e. an argument in which the conclusion does not follow from the premisses.

non(-)tuism *n.* motivation which is neither altruistic nor egoistic. For example, a player who tries to protect his king in a game of chess is actuated neither by egoistic nor by altruistic motives: the question of egoism or altruism is irrelevant. The economist P. H. Wicksteed (1844–1927) invented this word (1910). He argued that the specific characteristic of an economic relationship is not its egoism, nor indeed its altruism, but its 'non-tuism'. The term has only been used occasionally, e.g. in David Gauthier's *Morals by Agreement* 1986.

noosphere /'nəʊəsfɪə/ *See* TEILHARD DE CHARDIN.

norm *n.* a standard or rule (grammatical, legal, moral, etc.).

normative ethics inquiry into, or theory of, what is good and bad, right and wrong, in respect of character and conduct. It can be contrasted with METAETHICS.

nosce teipsum /'nɔskeɪ teɪ'ɪpsəm/ Lat. know thyself. *See* *GNOTHI SEAUTON*.

nosology (Gr. *nosos* sickness) *n.* the classification of diseases.

nothing *n.* 'Nothing requires more space than is available here'.

The preceding sentence is ambiguous. In one sense, it means that there is enough space; in another sense, that there is not.

Ulysses exploited this ambiguity, giving his name to the man-eating cyclops Polyphemus as Nobody (*Outis*). Later he escaped, after having injured Polyphemus. When Polyphemus complained to his fellow cyclopes, they asked him who had done it, and he replied: 'Nobody did it.' He got more laughs than sympathy.

Some critics of Heidegger complain that in his writings the necessary distinctions relating to *nothing* are blurred or neglected.

To associate *nothing* with death, dismay or despair seems as far-fetched as it would be to associate *something* with life, joy or exuberance. There are many bad things we are glad to miss and sad to have.

It is also doubtful whether a dark mystery or a gaping abyss is lurking: for all its seeming elusiveness, *nothing* is explained in every modern logic text in terms of quantifiers.

noumenon /ˈnuːmɪnən/ (*sing.*); **noumena** (*pl.*) (Gr. *noein* to think) *n.* an object of reason. In Kant's critical philosophy, the noumenon is contrasted with the *phenomenon (pl. phenomena)*, i.e. the object(s) of empirical knowledge. Kant gives a negative definition: a noumenon is an object of awareness not produced by sensory experience.

According to Kant we have no faculty of non-sensory intuition. Indeed, we cannot even conceive of what such a faculty would be like. Hence, we can have no noumenal knowledge. All knowledge of objects requires a basis in sense-experience and relates to the realm of phenomena.

There is another concept, the *thing-in-itself*, that Kant also contrasts with the phenomenon. For the most part, e.g. *Prolegomena* §33, Kant identifies the noumenon and the thing-in-itself. That is, he identifies that which would be given for non-sensory rational intuition (if we were endowed with such a faculty) with the object underlying the phenomenon.

nous /naʊs/ Gr. reason, intellect, mind *n.* In Aristotle, *nous* is the mental faculty by which first principles are grasped. When Anaxagoras, Aristotle and other classical philosophers have 'reason' as a force or as an organizing principle for the world as a whole, *nous* is the word used.

Nozick /ˈnəʊzɪk/, Robert (1938–) American philosopher, professor at Princeton 1962 and at Harvard since 1969. His first major work, *Anarchy, State and Utopia* 1974, uses the conception of natural individual rights to set narrow limits on state action. If the changes from an initially just position have come about by just means, then the outcome is just; taxation without consent of the taxed is equivalent to forced labour, and re-distribution of goods is justified only to rectify past injustice.

In the remarkably wide-ranging *Philosophical Explanations* 1981, the account of identity through time of material objects, ships, clubs – and persons – has attracted much attention. Nozick defends a 'closest continuer' theory, which points to the fact that much of our thinking commits us to the extrinsicness of identity. To illustrate: if it was thought that the exiled members of the Vienna Circle were all in Istanbul, one would say that they now constituted the Vienna Circle; but one would retract that claim if the *extrinsic* fact became known that a considerable number of other exiled members had made it to the United States. There are similar assumptions of extrinsicness also in the case of object-identity (cf. the ship of THESEUS) and personal identity.

In epistemology, Nozick has taken up the challenge posed by the GETTIER PROBLEM. His theory is intended to rule out cases in which it is merely a matter of coincidence that S's belief happens to be true. In such cases, we do not say that S knows that p. The basis of his theory, elaborated with great ingenuity, is that S knows that p if and only if: (i) p is true; (ii) S believes that p; (iii) if p were not true, S would not believe that p; (iv) if p were true, S would believe that p.

On this theory, a proposition is known if and only if S's belief in it varies appropriately with the facts across a range of possible circumstances. That is, 'to know is to have a belief that *tracks* the truth'.

Nozick's conception of the nature of philosophy, as reflection different in nature from scientific theorizing, is further developed in *The Examined Life* 1990.

BG/ed.

nullibism /ˈnʌlɪbɪzm/ (Lat. *nullibi* nowhere) *n.* the view that spirits (including God) have no location in space. The term seems to have been created by Henry More.

number theory (also *theory of numbers*) the branch of mathematics that studies the properties of integers (e.g. factorizations, partitions, diophantine equations).

numerology *n.* a superstitious theory and practice. Calculations are made on the basis of numerical data, for instance, a person's birth-date, or on the basis of non-numerical data like the words in a sacred or profane text which are interpreted as a code for certain numbers. The result of the calculation is assigned a special significance by the numerologist, and on this basis predictions are made.

numinous /ˈnjuːmɪnəs/ (Lat. *numen* divine power or spirit) *adj.* of a spiritual, supernatural or divine character.

Nussbaum, Martha (1947–) American philosopher, professor at Brown University. The centre of gravity in Nussbaum's thought is ethics – in both its personal and political dimensions. A distinctive feature in her work is the close integration of literature and philosophy, both ancient and modern. This comes clearly to view in *The Fragility of Goodness* 1986. In her view, many literary works *are* works of moral philosophy. She rejects the usual ways of framing the contrasting concepts of reason and emotion, arguing, in *Love's Knowledge* 1990, that emotions are necessary for insight – indeed, that they *are* themselves cognitions, a theory which in her interpretation of the Hellenistic philosophers (Stoics, Epicureans, sceptics) was held by them. These schools, and their ambition to let philosophy lead to truth but also to individual harmony and well-being, are discussed in depth in *The Therapy of Desire* 1994. In a number of essays, she has attacked the relativism of Foucault and Derrida, of literary theorists such as Stanley Fish and Barbara Herrnstein Smith, and of some feminist epistemology. According to this relativism, the common notion of truth is untenable, and so is the idea that interpretations of legal texts, as well as literary ones, can be said to be correct or incorrect. Inspired, like other antirelativists, by Plato's and Aristotle's ways of dealing with sophistry, Nussbaum points to the ostensibly self-defeating nature of relativism. She also argues that there is a tension between the leftism professed by the authors she criticizes and the illiberal populism which, in her view, is implied by their relativism. Her preferred alternative to relativism is an 'internal realism' in the spirit of Kant and Putnam.

O

Oakeshott /'əʊkʃɒt/, Michael (Joseph) (1901–90) Best known as a conservative political philosopher, Oakeshott was educated at Cambridge as a historian but developed an interest in the philosophy of McTaggart, which he further extended by study in Marburg and Tübingen. His first and only continuous book, *Experience and its Modes* 1933, was almost totally ignored at a time when British philosophy was predominantly analytic, but provides the philosophical structure for the later volumes of essays in which he develops educational and political themes in a manner deeply influenced by Montaigne's scepticism and the political philosophies of Hobbes and Burke.

His central concern is 'human experience recognized as a variety of independent worlds of discourse'. These worlds he at first takes to be history, science and practical experience; he later adds aesthetic experience. Philosophy is not another such discourse; rather it listens to the 'voices' of these discourses, the conversations which take place within them, in the light of experience as a whole. In the essays collected as *The Voice of Liberal Learning* 1989 he takes learning how to listen to these voices in conversation as the point of education proper as distinct from training, professional or otherwise, in which only one voice is heard. In the course of such an education it becomes apparent both that the modes are totally distinct and that each of them has limitations which its self-sufficiency prevents it from recognizing, so that it cannot be taken to provide a satisfactory picture of experience as a whole.

Oakeshott exerted his very considerable influence as a professor of political philosophy at the London School of Economics from 1950, going there, after a brief period at Nuffield College, from a lectureship in history at Cambridge. Like his predecessor Harold Laski, to whose socialist political philosophy he was diametrically opposed, he secured through his large London undergraduate classes and seminars the influence and the disciples which he condemned academics for seeking. Against on the one side the concept of centralized rational planning and on the other side the anarchism sometimes set against it, he emphasized the crucial importance of moral and political traditions within a society admitting the reign of law. These views were central to such essay collections as *Rationalism in Politics* 1962. Politics he saw as an 'art of repair', its object being to keep us afloat in our voyage on a 'boundless and bottomless sea' where 'there is neither harbour for shelter nor floor for anchorage, neither starting point nor point of departure'. To try to use it as a road to perfection is to risk sinking the ship, or at least making it more vulnerable to storms and tempest. Politics by no means lies at the centre of human creativity, and neither can it of itself bring creativity into being; what a politician needs is a keen ear for 'intimations' of change. In other essay collections Oakeshott advanced the central claims of history as a mode of discourse and closely analysed the moral and political teachings of Hobbes. JP

obiter dictum /'ɒbɪtə 'dɪktəm; 'əʊbɪtə/

(*sing.*); ***obiter dicta*** /ˈdɪktə/ (*pl.*) Lat. said in passing; an incidental remark. The expression has a technical sense in jurisprudence, where the reason for a decision (the *ratio decidendi*), but not the *obiter dicta*, is relevant for the formation of precedent.

object *n.* *See* EMINENT; SUBJECT.

objective *n.* *See* MEINONG; *adj.* *See* SUBJECTIVE.

objective idealism **1** Plato's theory that the Forms (or Ideas) are the ultimate reality. **2** absolute idealism. *See* ABSOLUTE; BRADLEY.

objective right the law (i.e. the legal order in a society). In French, *droit* is ambiguous. It is convenient to disambiguate, using *droit subjectif* for a right, something that belongs to a person, and *droit objectif* for law, a system of rules and practices. Similarly in Italian, German, etc. In English, there is no similar ambiguity, and therefore no need for these expressions. *See also* RIGHT.

objectivity *n.* This word has a large number of interrelated senses. Here is a small selection: **1** independence of awareness. The objective existence of atoms and mountains implies that they can exist even if nobody is aware of the fact. But can a pain exist if it is felt by nobody? If it cannot, pain is not objective in this sense. **2** independence of opinion. If we think that a person can deserve admiration even if others have a low opinion of him, we assume that his worth does not depend on how he is thought of. **3** impartiality of judgement. A judgement determined by relevant factors, and not by irrelevant factors such as personal bias, is taken to be objective. **objective** *adj.*

object-language *See* METALANGUAGE.

objectual v. substitutional quantification There are two different ways of explaining what is to be meant by the 'value of a variable' in quantified sentences. The first takes *objects* to be values of a variable, the second *linguistic expressions* (names of objects). More generally: *objectual* interpretation takes the values to be every object x in the chosen domain; the *substitutional* interpretation, every substitution of 'x' that is grammatically admissible.

Suppose that we have a discourse exclusively about tomatoes. We can have open sentences such as 'x is ripe', 'x is hard'. Here, 'x' is a variable (a linguistic entity) and the objectualist will say that the tomatoes are the values of this variable. So '(∃x)Fx' is true if and only if 'F' is true of some tomato or other, and '(∀x)Fx' is true if and only if 'F' is true of all the tomatoes. (In metaphysics, replace 'all tomatoes' by 'all objects'.)

By contrast, the defender of *substitutional quantification* will take the value of a variable as that which can linguistically be substituted for the variable. This is essentially what Wittgenstein did in the *Tractatus Logico-Philosophicus* where '(∃x)Fx' is elucidated as a disjunction 'Fa ∨ Fb ∨ Fc . . .', '(∀x)Fx' as a conjunction 'Fa & Fb & Fc . . .', where 'a', 'b', 'c' . . . are the *names* of all the objects.

One objection to the substitutional interpretation of quantified sentences is that we do not have names even for all tomatoes or all rabbits, and it is in principle impossible that we should have names for all members of an uncountable set, such as that of the real numbers. But, as is clear from the ongoing debate, there are philosophers who do not regard this as a conclusive objection. Sometimes a quantified sentence has to be interpreted substitutionally, as in 'for every sentence p, either p or not-p': '(∀p)(p ∨ ~p)', where 'p' is not in a name-position. Similarly for 'there is some property that Socrates has and Plato lacks': '(∃F)[F(Socrates) & ~F(Plato)]' where again 'F' is not in a name-position. In the one case, a sentence has to be substituted for the variable, in the other case a predicate, and neither of these name objects. W. V. O. Quine, who favours the objectual view, gives an easy introduction to this question in his 'Reply to Professor Marcus' in *The Ways of Paradox* 1966.

JSM

obligation *n.* Having an obligation to do something implies that one ought to do it. But the converse statement is not valid: there are things one ought to do even without an obligation. Obligations provide *one* kind of reason for doing, or forbearing, but not the only one.

There are different views about the nature of obligation. On one view, to be under an obligation is to be liable, in case of non-fulfilment, to some penalty (other than that which may result from the natural course of events). In primitive thought, the liability is like being under a curse: the non-fulfilment of an obligation is risky, since it can provoke invisible powers to act to one's detriment. It is also risky according to the more modern theories of Bentham and Austin: to have a duty or obligation consists simply in being subject to the will of another person who has the requisite *coercive power* which can be actualized in case of non-fulfilment.

Another conception of obligation, regularly adopted by philosophers in the modern era, is that of being subject to the will of another person (a creditor, a claimant, a ruler, God) who has not only the ability, but also the requisite *authority* or *right*, to impose (directly or by an agent) a penalty in case of non-fulfilment. This authority or right that a person has cannot be identified with physical strength or with some kind of mental ability. It belongs to a different category: a moral quality or disposition conceived, like the physical and the mental ones, as an attribute of a person.

In contrast to both of these conceptions, Kant defines obligation as the necessity to act in a certain way. However, this necessity is one that springs neither from mere threats nor from threats based on external authority. Instead, according to Kant, this necessity in respect of action is analogous to being 'compelled' by the standards of valid reasoning in the area of thought.

These three conceptions can be summed up as follows. The first tends to identify obligation with the pressure arising from demands that are joined with threats backed by *brute force*; the second, with the pressure arising from demands (backed by threats) from an *authority*; the third, with pressure arising from the implacable demands of *reason*.

Different from these are conceptions of obligation as pressure subjectively experienced, as something that one feels. Hume's identification of obligation with a kind of sentiment is a case in point.

obligation, active and passive In older usage, an active obligation was understood as power (binding force, authority) by which a person's will becomes bound; a passive obligation was understood as subjection of a person's will. For instance, in the active sense, the obligation of a person's conscience consists in the authoritative character of the person's conscience when deciding or passing judgement on his own actions and omissions; in the passive sense the obligation of conscience consists in the subjection of conscience to a higher law. This usage seems to have become obsolete during the eighteenth century.

obligation, perfect and imperfect *See* PERFECT DUTY; PERFECT OBLIGATION.

obligation and duty The words, like their Latin equivalents *obligatio* and *officium*, were traditionally used in different senses. The word *duty* was used for an *action* that one is bound to do; the word *obligation* signified the *'bond'* by which one is bound to perform the action which is one's duty.

obligations The game of *obligationes* was an argument-game used as an exercise in the arts faculties of medieval universities from the early thirteenth century onwards, in which one player had to manoeuvre his opponent into contradicting himself. JM

obnoxious /ɒb'nɒkʃəs/ *adj.* For a person to be *obnoxious* to something means that he is exposed to (subject to, liable to, open to) something disagreeable (injury, punishment, censure, etc.). For instance, an offender is obnoxious to punishment. This is the standard sense of the word in older texts.

obscurantism /ɒbskjʊ'ræntɪzm/ (Lat. *obscurus* dark) *n.* aversion to clarity or enlightenment. The term was coined in the eighteenth century and used polemically against the romantic-reactionary enemies of Enlightenment ideals.

obscurum per obscurius /ɒb'skjʊərəm pɜːr ab'skjʊərɪəs/ Lat. something obscure by something more obscure. The phrase designates a defect in explanation.

obversion *n.* consists in negating the predicate and changing the quality of a categorical proposition: see Table 13.

Table 13 Obversion

Categorical propositions	Obverses of categorical propositions
every S is P	no S is non-P
no S is P	every S is non-P
some S is P	some S is not non-P
some S is not P	some S is non-P

Each of the pairs is an equivalence. In each pair, one proposition is the obverse of the other. The term first occurred in 1870, in writings by A. Bain and W. S. Jevons.

Occam *See* OCKHAM.

occasionalism *n.* Occasionalism, proposed by Geulincx (1624–69) and Malebranche (1638–1715), assumes that causes are creative and produce their effects, and that this is why there is a necessary connection between cause and effect. And yet, the mere impact of one billiard ball on another is not a creative act. So what accounts for the necessary connection must be something else. In fact, in this view, the impact of one billiard ball on another does not genuinely cause the other to move, but gives God an occasion for causing the other to move.

Interaction between mental and bodily events can be similarly analysed. Here, the possibility of an act of mind causing a bodily movement is even more remote, since body and mind are two distinct substances, inherently incapable of affecting each other. But an event in one's body can be the occasion for God to produce a corresponding mental event, and a mental event an occasion for God to affect the body.

It follows that there can be no genuine causal relations between created things. This need not imply that God intervenes with a particular decision on each occasion. According to Malebranche, God's operations conform to his general immutable decrees. But even with regular combinations of so-called causes and effects, only God can give the push, so to speak. He is the only cause properly so called.

occult quality (Lat. *qualitas occulta*; *pl. qualitates occultae*) The term was originally used to denote an unknown quality not reducible to any of the FOUR ELEMENTS. From the Renaissance onwards, its use for explanatory purposes was denounced as an *asylum ignorantiae*: to explain a natural phenomenon in terms of an occult quality is the same as failing to explain it. Francis Bacon complained that this 'idol of the theatre' leads the learned to 'make the quiescent principles, *wherefrom*, and not the moving principles, *whereby*, things are produced, the object of their contemplation and inquiry' (*Novum Organum* I, 66). Gassendi (*Physica* 1, 4, 14) and Descartes (*Regulae* 9; 12) agreed, and advocated a different kind of scientific explanation.

occultism *n.* belief in hidden and mysterious powers, linked with efforts to control them.

ochlocracy /ɒk'lɒkrəsɪ/ (Gr. *ochlokratia*, from *ochlos* mob, rabble + *-kratia* ruling power) *n.* 'mob rule': the degenerate form of democracy, where a popular government acts without respect for legal or moral constraints. This degenerate form is analysed in Aristotle's *Politics*, but the term was first used by the historian Polybius (*c.* 200–120 BC) and other Hellenistic writers.

Ockham /'ɒkəm/, William of (*c.* 1285–1347) an English theologian and philosopher and a member of the Franciscan order. After studies in theology at Oxford he taught for several years in a Franciscan school, probably in England. During this time he wrote a number of philosophical works, including a *Sum of Logic*, and revised his Oxford disputations on the *Sentences* of Peter Lombard. In 1324 he went to the papal court at Avignon, where his Oxford disputations were examined for heresy by a committee of theologians. In 1328, at the behest of the head of his order, Michael of Cesena, he read the constitutions that Pope John XXII had issued in an attempt to settle controversies about the practice of poverty in the Franciscan order. Ockham decided that in these documents John XXII had taught heresy, and with brother Michael and a few others he left Avignon and joined Ludwig of Bavaria, who was also in conflict with the pope over his election as Emperor. Ockham lived the rest of his life in Ludwig's capital, Munich, sending out pamphlets and books to show that John XXII and later his successor Benedict XII should be removed from the papal office. Ockham's writings thus fall into two groups: academic writings produced before 1324 and polemical writings produced after 1328.

Ockham's academic work has a distinctive character and connecting themes, but it is unlikely that he set out to create a system; like other academics, he took up a selection of the questions debated by his predecessors and contemporaries and tried to give better answers. Usual targets of his criticisms were Henry of Ghent and Duns Scotus. He rejects Scotus's formal distinction (except in the Deity), maintaining that the only distinctions are between thing and thing, concept and concept, and thing and concept. He also rejects Scotus's doctrine of individuation, according to which an individual is a common nature contracted to singularity by an individuating difference formally distinct from it; according to Ockham, every existent is individual through itself and does not need to be individuated.

On universals, Ockham maintains that a universal is a sign (physical object, spoken word or concept) able to stand for any one of an indefinite number of similar objects; this is Ockham's 'nominalism' – a term that he did not himself use. But he did not hold that classification is imposed arbitrarily by the human mind: apart from any mental act, Socrates and Plato are more alike than either is like a donkey, which is why the one sign, 'man', can stand for either of them. Besides Socrates and Plato there is no third entity that is their similarity; except in the Deity, relative terms signify not relative entities, but absolute entities, connoting certain propositions about them. In fact, only terms in the categories of substance and quality name entities, and all the terms and concepts included in the other eight of Aristotle's ten categories are connotative. Ockham also rejects 'species' (in the sense of a likeness of the thing transmitted through the medium and the senses to the mind or produced in the mind as a means of knowing). Ockham's evident desire for a frugal ontology explains the ascription to him of 'Ockham's razor', although he did not invent it and rarely invoked it. He developed specific arguments against each kind of entity that he rejected.

In natural theology, Ockham rejects many of the philosophical arguments then offered as proofs of various points of Christian belief, but he does not draw the general conclusion that Christianity cannot be supported by argument. In ethics, he holds that the precepts of natural law can be overridden by a command of God, but this does not imply (as is often supposed) that morality rests on divine command. In epistemology, he seems to anticipate Descartes's 'evil demon' hypothesis in maintaining that God, by his absolute power (that is, setting aside his goodness and will), can cause in us a false 'creditive' act indistinguishable from an intuitive cognition; however, Ockham does not assume that knowledge is impossible unless we can know whether a seeming intuition is genuine. His philosophy does not seem to lead to scepticism in any sense.

Ockham's polemical writings are usually referred to as his 'political' writings because they deal in detail with many important questions of political philosophy. On property, Ockham rejects John XXII's doctrine that property exists by divine law; according to Ockham it exists by human convention and law, established to control greed and quarrelling. He rejects John's claim that no one can justly consume anything he does not own; their disagreement over property is referred to by Grotius, who attempts to harmonize the two sides. On Church government, although he acknowledges that the pope has 'fullness of power' in a certain sense, Ockham rejects the doctrine that a pope can do anything not immoral and not forbidden by God; popes must respect rights, including the rights of unbelievers, under human law. (Ockham seems to have been one of the first to introduce into philosophy and theology the lawyers' notion of a right.) 'Regularly', the pope cannot be judged by anyone lower in the Church, but 'on occasion' he can, for example if he is suspected of heresy. Ockham rejects the doctrine of papal infallibility. A pope suspected of heresy or serious crime can be tried by a human court; if he is guilty of heresy he has already, by that fact, ceased to be pope, and if he is guilty of crime he may be corrected or deposed. The 'regularly'/'occasionally' contrast is characteristic of Ockham's political thought: he does not believe that any constitution or other legislation can provide for every possible situation; individuals must be prepared to improvise means for dealing with unforeseen occasions. On secular government, Ockham holds that power derives from the people, not from the Church; the Emperor and other rulers do not need to have their election confirmed by the pope and cannot be deposed by the pope (except that on occasion a pope, or anyone else, acting for the people, may depose an unjust or useless ruler). Rulers must respect their subjects' rights, for example to property, though a right can be overridden for the common good. Ockham often criticized Marsilius, whose conception of sovereignty was foreign to Ockham's thinking. He rejected, for example, Marsilius's doctrine that all coercive power must be concentrated in the hands of one ruler; in Ockham's view subjects must be able on occasion to mobilize enough power to correct or depose a ruler who has become a tyrant. Ockham supported the Empire (i.e. the Holy Roman Empire) because of the need for a world government to keep the peace; he held, however, that the Emperor must regularly respect the established independence of kingdoms and free cities. In most of these matters Ockham was reaffirming, defending and developing the ideas of older canonists and theologians; he was one of the channels through which these ideas came to later liberal thinkers. JK

Ockham's razor The name commonly given to a principle usually formulated (in Latin) as *Entia non sunt multiplicanda praeter necessitatem* ('Entities are not to be multiplied beyond necessity'). This formulation is often attributed to William of Ockham, but has not been traced in any of his known writings. Perhaps the remark in his works which comes nearest to it is *Frustra fit per plura quod potest fieri per pauciora* ('It is pointless to do with more [things] what can be done with fewer'); though he may here be quoting a well-known saying rather than saying something original.

Ockham's razor is sometimes interpreted as a metaphysical or ontological principle to the effect that one should believe in the existence of the smallest possible number of kinds of objects; sometimes, as a methodological principle to the effect that one's explanation of any given fact should appeal to the smallest number of factors required to explain the fact in question. GH

Oedipus /ˈiːdɪpəs/ According to the ancient Greek tale that forms the basis for the versions in Homer and Sophocles, Oedipus killed a man in a roadside quarrel, not knowing that he was King Laius of Thebes, nor that the man was in fact his father. Having arrived in Thebes, he married the widowed Queen Iocasta, not knowing that she was his mother. They had four children (Eteocles, Polyneices, Antigone and Ismene). Eventually, the truth was revealed. Iocasta committed suicide, and Oedipus blinded himself, abdicated, and went into exile. His misfortunes had been foretold by the oracle at the time of his birth, but in spite of attempts at that time to prevent them they came to pass, having been ordained by inexorable fate.

Oedipus complex Freud proposed in *Die Traumdeutung* 1900 (The interpretation of dreams) that boys, at about the age of three, become sexually attracted to their mothers and sexually jealous of their fathers. In the normal course of events, the parents do not tolerate this, and feelings of fear and guilt arise in the child, who develops a superego in the process of overcoming them.

The relation between this theory and the Oedipus story is tenuous and, in the opinion of critics, the relation between the theory and reality is even more so.

oligarchy /ˈɒlɪgaːkɪ/ (Gr. *oligarchia*, from *oligoi* few + *-archia* rule) *n.* rule by the (usually wealthy) few. The degenerate form of aristocracy (rule by the best) in Plato's *Republic* (8,3–9,3) and Aristotle's *Politics* (3,7 1279^{a}35, ^{b}4).

Early twentieth-century political analysts like Gaetano Mosca, Vilfredo Pareto and Robert Michels formulated an 'iron law of oligarchy': in all large organizations, be they voluntary associations, business enterprises or political bodies, there inevitably emerges a relatively small and stable group of persons who control the organization.

omega *n.* the last letter in the Greek alphabet: Ω, ω. 1 The word *Omega* is used symbolically in the New Testament, Revelations 1,8 and 22,13, where the Lord says, 'I am Alpha and Omega,' i.e. the beginning and the end. In the mystical-metaphysical speculations of Teilhard de Chardin, the word is used to signify the end-point of history, at which individual minds are all fused together in a cosmic-divine consciousness. J. D. Barrow and F. J. Tipler adopt the term for a final state of the universe in which life has engulfed absolutely everything. **2** (in transfinite mathematics) the smallest infinite ordinal, i.e. the order-type associated with the natural numbers in their natural order.

omnipotence /ɒm'nɪpətəns/ *n.* all-powerfulness. *See also* PARADOX OF OMNIPOTENCE.

omniscience /ɒm'nɪsɪəns/ *n.* complete knowledge of everything.

ontogenesis /ɒntə'dʒenɪsɪs/ *n.* the formation and development of an individual member of a biological species.

ontological argument An ontological argument for God's existence is an attempt to prove rationally that God exists, without appeal to revelation through Scripture or otherwise. It differs from other arguments of that kind by taking as its starting point nothing but the concept of God.

An argument of this kind was first proposed by Anselm of Canterbury (1033–1109) in his *Proslogion c.* 1077 (Allocution). Its three main premisses are that (1) God is a being greater than which none can be conceived and (2) either such a being exists both in one's imagination and in reality, or it exists only in one's imagination; (3) a being that exists in both is greater than one that exists only in one's imagination. Therefore the greatest conceivable being exists in both, and hence exists in reality.

Another argument starting from the very concept of God was proposed by Descartes. Its two main premisses are (1) God is a being with every positive perfection, i.e. God lacks nothing; (2) a being that does not have existence lacks something. Therefore, God exists.

In the twentieth century, Norman Malcolm and Charles Hartshorne have formulated modal variants of the argument, arguing from a concept of God to God's necessary existence.

The best-known classical objections are those of Hume and Kant. Hume appeals to the principle that all propositions affirming that something exists are contingent. Kant argues that existence is not a 'real predicate': once a concept has been defined (in terms of 'real predicates') the question whether the concept applies to something that exists is still open.

ontological commitment The ontological commitment of a theory is made up of its assumptions about what there is, what kinds of entities can be said to exist. The existence of individual objects is usually taken for granted, but opinions differ more about genes and quarks, and about abstract entities such as classes, properties or numbers. If the statements of a theory are paraphrased into a canonical form in predicate logic, the ontological commitment of the theory will be the domains over which its bound variables range. This is expressed in Quine's dictum, 'To be is to be the value of a variable.' He introduced and explicated the expression in 'Designation and existence' *Journal of Philosophy 36* (1939).

ontological realism *See* REALISM.

ontologism *n.* a religious philosophy with a tendency towards rationalism and pantheism that emerged in the nineteenth century. Its main representatives were Antonio Rosmini (1797–1855) and Vicenzo Gioberti (1801–52) in Italy, Casimir Ubaghs (1808–75) at Louvain, and Orestes Brownson (1803–73) in the United States. It had affinities with Hegel and even with more radical left-wing Hegelians such as Ludwig Feuerbach. Church authorities disapproved and gave preference to neo-Thomism.

ontology /ɒn'tɒlədʒɪ/ (Gr. *on* being) *n.* inquiry into, or theory of, being *qua* being. This is the central subject-matter of Aristotle's *Metaphysics*, as stated there in Book Γ 1 1003^a21. The *word* ontology was coined in the early seventeenth century to avoid some of the ambiguities of 'metaphysics'; Leibniz was the first major philosopher to adopt the word. The terminology introduced by Christian Wolff in the early eighteenth century came to be widely adopted: ontology is the general theory of being as such, and forms the general part of metaphysics, or theoretical philosophy. The three special parts are general cosmology, rational psychology, and natural theology, i.e. the theory of the world, the soul, and God.

In the usage of twentieth-century analytical philosophy, ontology is the general theory of what there is. For instance, questions about the mode of existence of abstract entities such as numbers, imagined entities such as golden mountains, and impossible entities such as square circles, are ontological questions. And it is on an ontological question that modern materialism, physicalism and naturalism differ sharply from their opponents: the question of what there is.

opacity /əʊ'pæsɪtɪ/ *See* TRANSPARENCY.

opaqueness *See* TRANSPARENCY.

open-question argument This is a kind of argument introduced by G. E. Moore in section 13 of his *Principia Ethica* 1903 to prove an important point about the definition of good: i.e. that every proposed definition of good is bound to fail. In brief, it can be rendered as follows. Suppose that a kind of thing is said to be good, as, for instance, in the value-judgement that pleasure is good. To wonder whether this is so, and ask whether pleasure is good, is to ask a significant question. It is to ask an *open* question, quite different from asking the self-answering question whether pleasure is pleasure.

Suppose, however, that someone – a philosopher, perhaps – were to propose this definition of good:

x is good $=_{df}$ x is pleasure

On this proposed definition, the question whether pleasure is good would not be an open question, since it would reduce to the self-answering question whether pleasure is pleasure. It follows that this proposed definition is incorrect.

Any similar proposed definition can be given the same treatment by using this open-question argument. The upshot is, for Moore, that no definition of good is possible, and that good cannot be identified with any natural or metaphysical object or property.

The argument gets whatever force it has from a simple underlying principle: all genuine value-judgements are synthetic and can be denied without self-contradiction.

open sentence a sentence in which the place of an expression is filled by a variable. Take, for instance, the sentence 'The golden tree of life is green.' If the referring expression 'the golden tree of life' is replaced by a variable, e.g. 'x', the result is an open sentence 'x is green.' If 'green' is replaced by a variable, e.g. 'F', the result is also an open sentence: 'The golden tree of life is F.'

Similarly, for the sentence 'Socrates is wise' there is a corresponding open sentence 'x is wise', and 'F(Socrates)' and 'Fx' also represent open sentences.

Open sentences can be turned into genuine sentences in two different ways. One is by replacing any variable with an expression of the appropriate category. For example, by replacing 'x' with the name of some person, e.g. 'Socrates', the open sentence 'x is wise' becomes a genuine sentence 'Socrates is wise.' The other method is by prefixing a quantifying expression: for instance, insert before 'x is wise' the words 'There is an x such that'. The result is 'There is an x such that x is wise', or in common parlance 'Someone is wise', which is a genuine sentence. *Syn.* propositional function (Russell), sentential function (Tarski).

open society The concept is outlined, in contrast to a *closed society*, by Henri Bergson in *Les deux Sources de la morale et de la religion* 1932 (The two sources of morality and religion). Closed societies, like closed minds, closed systems of law or closed religions, are static; the open ones are dynamic. The members of a closed society are determined by group attachments in the form of tribalism or patriotism, and outsiders are excluded. In contrast, an open society accepts the ideal of moral universalism. The distinction was adopted by Karl Popper in his influential *The Open Society and its Enemies* 1945 (5th rev. edn 1966).

operation *See* OPERATOR.

operationalism *n.* the idea of Nobel-prize-winning physicist P. W. Bridgman (1882–1962), first presented in his *The Logic of Modern Physics* 1927, that a word or concept must be defined by the operation we carry out to find out whether the word or concept applies. For example, to say that something has a length of 3 feet is to say that if we successively place a one-foot ruler against it we will be able to do so three times. Bridgman hoped that if scientists stuck to operationally defined concepts they would avoid making mistakes. He hoped to 'render unnecessary the services of the unborn Einsteins'. One objection to this is that there are several different ways of measuring lengths. If operation A measures a length as a, and operation B measures it as b, we would like to think that there is a question as to which operation best measures the length. But according to operationalism there is no such question: there are just different operations and therefore different 'lengths'. AM

operator *n.* (in formal logic and in mathematics) an operator is a symbol for a certain procedure, an *operation*. In the expression 2 + 3, the plus sign is an operator signifying the operation known as addition. In ◇p, the diamond (symbolizing 'possibly') is applied to the proposition p.

operator shift fallacy *See* QUANTIFIER SHIFT FALLACY.

ophelimity /ɒfə'lɪmɪtɪ/ (Gr. *ōphelimos* useful, advantageous) *n.* the capacity of

Table 14 The parts of Aristotle's *Organon*

English	Latin	Greek
Categories	*Categoriae*	*Peri tōn kategoriōn*
On Interpretation	*De interpretatione*	*Peri tēs hermēneias*
Prior Analytics	*Analytica priora*	*Analytika protera*
Posterior Analytics	*Analytica posteriora*	*Analytika hystera*
Topics	*Topicae*	*Topika*
Sophistical Refutations	*De sophisticis elenchis*	*Peri tōn sophistikōn elenchōn*

an object or service to satisfy a person's subjective preference. The term was introduced by Pareto, who wanted a clear terminological distinction between preferred (ophelimity) and the preferable (utility).

opposition, square of *See* SQUARE OF OPPOSITION.

optative /'ɒptətɪv/ *adj.*, *n.* (grammar) a verb mood whose primary function is to express a wish; a sentence expressing a wish.

optimific /ɒptɪ'mɪfɪk/ (Lat. *optimus* best + *-fic*, from *facere* to make) *adj.* productive of the best outcome. According to most varieties of utilitarianism, including Bentham's, an action is right, and ought to be done, if and only if it has an optimific tendency, i.e. tends to produce the best consequences, all things considered.

optimism *n.* **1** the view that on the whole and in the long run, good prevails over evil in our world. **2** expectation of success, hopefulness. **3** giving one's main attention to the bright(er) side of a situation. The word was first used by a reviewer in *Journal de Trévoux*, an important French eighteenth-century periodical, to describe the view, advanced by Leibniz in the *Theodicy* 1710, that our world is the best possible world. The word gained currency through Voltaire's *Candide, ou l'optimisme* 1759.

order relations LINEAR, PARTIAL, QUASI- and WEAK orderings are among the different kinds of order relations.

orexis /ɒ'rɛksɪs/ (*sing.*) **orexes** /-iːz/ (*pl.*) Gr. desire, inclination, appetite *n.* **orectic** *adj.*

Organon /'ɔːgənɔn/ (Gr. tool, instrument) the collective title assigned to Aristotle's logical works by Andronicus of Rhodes. Table 14 gives their names in English, Latin and Greek.

Francis Bacon called the work in which he advocated an empiricist approach to science *Novum Organum* in order to imply that it ought to supersede the Aristotelian tradition. A similar title was used by Lambert.

Origen /'ɒrɪdʒən/ (*c.* 185–*c.* 254) One of the leading figures of the ancient Church. He was from Alexandria, where he spent much of his early life, teaching and writing. Later he continued these activities in Caesarea. One of his many works is *Contra Celsum* (Against Celsus), a defence of Christianity against a critical neo-Platonist philosopher. He developed a hermeneutics (method of interpretation) for the explanation and defence of Christian beliefs, according to which Scripture can be understood in three ways. A given text can at the same time have (1) a historical message, by telling a story, (2) a moral message, and (3) a spiritual message of which the story is an allegory. The fact that there is literal, moral and allegorical meaning explains why it is possible to find a deeper spiritual meaning in all parts of Scripture, even the seemingly unedifying ones. Allegorical interpretation is based on the fact that all things have a double aspect: one is physical and sensible, available to all; the other is mystical and spiritual, and only a few have a direct insight into it. In tune with the new neo-Platonic ideas was also Origen's belief in the pre-existence of souls and in the freedom of the will. He believed that the punishments in an afterlife had a corrective function and were therefore not everlasting. At the end of time everyone would be redeemed, with the final restoration of all things (*apokatastasis pantōn*). His view on this and many other matters was firmly rejected by mainstream Christian theology from the early sixth century, although for a long time his method of allegorical interpretation was widely accepted. Much later, in the seventeenth century and onwards, Origen's rejection of the doctrine of the eternity of hell gained increasing acceptance.

Orphism /'ɔːfɪzm/ *n.* a Greek mystery cult centred on the figure of Orpheus, a semi-divine hero of great musical talent, indeed, a personification of the power of music. Death and resurrection, and the liberation of the soul, in itself immortal, from the body (its mortal coil) are important themes in this cult. Traces of these doctrines can be found in Plato's philosophy, and the influence on Gnosticism and neo-Platonism is clear. Recent papyri discoveries, published in the 1970s and 1980s, suggest affinities between Orphic and Heraclitean fragments.

Ortega y Gasset, José /ɔr'teɣa i ga'sɛt, xo'se (Sp.)/ (1883–1955) Spanish author and philosopher. As an essayist and a professor of metaphysics in Madrid from 1910 to 1936, he saw it as his task to help to bring Spain into the mainstream of European culture and to introduce the idea of philosophy as an exercise in intellectual rigour. He is best known for his critique of modern mass society as being dominated by vulgarity and complacency. There is an existentialist element in his belief that it is possible for individuals to break away and adopt higher standards.

orthodoxy (Gr. *orthos* right + *doxa* opinion, belief) *n.* (adherence to) a doctrine authoritatively defined. When spelt with a capital O the term is often used for the theology of the Eastern Church. **orthodox** *adj. Ant.* heterodoxy.

ostensive definition An ostensive definition of an expression explains the meaning of the expression by pointing to that which the expression denotes.

The phrase was introduced by the Cambridge logician W. E. Johnson (1858–1931) in his *Logic* 1921 to describe the way we explain the meaning of a proper name, but the idea is older: Wittgenstein, who discusses it in depth, finds it already in Augustine.

An idea attractive to empiricist philosophers is that ostensive definitions could form the *basis* of linguistic understanding. However, as noted by Wittgenstein, if, for instance, we explain the meaning of 'red' by pointing to a red object which happens to be round, the learner, presumed ignorant, will not know whether we are naming the colour, the shape, or some other feature.

Ostwald /'ɔstvalt (Gm.)/, Wilhelm (1853–1932) Baltic-German Nobel Prize winner for Chemistry (in 1909), he attempted to build up a philosophical theory on a scientific basis. His neutral monism takes ultimate reality to be energy, which can manifest itself as mind or as matter.

other *n.* 'the other of X' is a phrase used to refer to something that is not X: something antithetical, opposite, contrary or contradictory to X; something different or separated from X; etc. Its use is due to continental influences.

overman *See* SUPERMAN.

overridingness thesis (in moral philosophy) the thesis that, in deliberation and evaluation, moral considerations are those that take precedence over considerations of all other kinds.

Owen /'əʊɪn/, Robert (1771–1858) industrialist, social theorist and social reformer. His *A New View of Society* 1813 advocated cooperative forms of ownership and employment to overcome mass pauperization and other evils of industrialization. He tried to put his theories into practice, in some instances successfully (New Lanark). His initiative to establish consumers' cooperatives failed, but was a direct inspiration for the Rochdale pioneers who started the Co-Operative Movement in 1844.

Owen rejected Malthus's theory of population. He argued that if the population were to increase as envisaged by Malthus, the increase in total needs requiring satisfaction would be more than offset by increased productivity.

own *vb.* **1** to admit, concede, acknowledge, confess. To own an action is to admit to having done it, to accept responsibility for it. This is standard usage in authors such as Hobbes, Locke, Hume, etc. **2** to possess legitimately; to have a right of ownership to something.

Oxford philosophy a label frequently used for a kind of analytical philosophy with a distinctively linguistic orientation, which from the mid-twentieth century set the tone for much academic philosophy internationally. Among its leading exponents were Gilbert Ryle, P. F. Strawson, J. L. Austin and H. P. Grice.

It is entirely different from and has only the name in common with the so-called Oxford Movement in the nineteenth century (*see* TRACTARIAN), and with the Oxford Group of the 1930s, led by Frank Buchman and later renamed Moral Re-Armament.

oxonian *adj.* pertaining to Oxford.

oxymoron /ɒksiːˈmɒːrɔn/ (*sing.*); **oxymora** (*pl.*) (Gr. *oxys* sharp, acute + *mōros* dull, foolish) *n.* a paradoxical or contradictory figure of speech, for instance 'a living death', 'a mortal god', 'an eloquent silence'.

P

pace /ˈpeɪsɪ; ˈpɑːtʃeɪ (Eng.); paːkɛ (Lat.)/ from Lat. *pax* peace *prep*. A clause of the form '*pace* Dr Bloggs' means 'may Dr Bloggs hold his peace'. It is used politely to indicate awareness of Dr Bloggs's contrary opinion, when one does not wish to enter into argument over it.

Paine /peɪn/, Thomas (1737–1809) British-born, Paine emigrated to Philadelphia in 1774. *Common Sense* 1776 was an eloquent plea for American independence, which he followed up with spirited defences of the ensuing revolution. Leaving for France, he wrote *The Rights of Man* 1791–2, defending the ideals of the French Revolution and advocating a remarkably modern welfare-state programme, whose primary aim was the abolition of poverty. Excessive disparities of wealth would disappear; there would be work opportunities for the unemployed, relief for the poor, old-age pensions, allowances for every marriage and every birth, universal schooling, etc. He also believed that democracy would remove the motives for wars of conquest and lead to universal peace. *The Age of Reason* 1794 accuses dogmatic Christian orthodoxy of superstitious reliance on mystery, miracle and prophecy, and advocates a rational and enlightened deism.

Paley /ˈpeɪlɪ/, William (1743–1805) studied and taught at Cambridge, and later served as a clergyman in the Church of England. In his *Principles of Moral and Political Philosophy* 1785, Paley formulated a theological utilitarianism whose basis is the moral duty to obey God's commands. We know what these commands are, since we know God's will, both through Scripture and natural reason: God wills the greatest possible happiness for all. It is therefore our moral duty to act so as to maximize happiness.

Paley's two other major works were written in defence of religion. In *A View of the Evidences of Christianity* 1794 he gave a measured defence of belief in miracles, especially those on which the Christian religion is founded, and discussed *inter alia* Hume's famous essay on this topic. His *Natural Theology* 1802 was an influential work. It contains a persuasive statement of the argument from DESIGN for the existence of God. The reader is invited to consider what to infer if an intricate piece of machinery, like a watch, is found on a deserted beach: it is difficult to deny that very probably a watchmaker has been involved.

Paley was certainly not the first to propose an argument from design, nor was his version particularly original; yet it is the version most frequently cited. At least part of the explanation is that throughout the nineteenth century his writings, like those of Butler, were frequently prescribed reading in the English universities.

palingenesis /pælɪnˈdʒenɪsɪs/ (Gr. *palin* again + *genesis* birth) *n.* **1** rebirth, regeneration. **2** the doctrine of transmigration of souls.

Panaetius /pæˈnaɪtɪəs/ (*c.* 185–*c.* 110 BC) born at Rhodes, head of the Stoic school after 129 BC. None of his writings is extant. He introduced Stoicism in Rome, but seems to have abandoned many of the more extreme theses of Stoicism, such as the doctrine of eternal recurrence, and the doctrine of the radical difference between virtue and merely acting rightly (i.e. in accordance with nature). He also differed from many other leading Stoics by his rejection of soothsaying, and especially astrology.

panegyric /pænɪˈdʒɪrɪk/ *n.* a public oration of sustained high praise; an important branch of ancient rhetoric.

panentheism /pæˈnɛnθiɪzm/ (Gr. *pan-* all + *en* in + *theos* god) *n.* the doctrine that all things are in God (cf. Acts 17,28). In contrast to pantheism, the world is not identified with God, but is seen as intimately dependent on God.

The term was created by C. F. Krause in 1828, and later used in the 'process theology' of A. N. Whitehead and C. Hartshorne.

Pangloss /ˈpænglɒs/ the tutor of CANDIDE in Voltaire's philosophical novel. The fictional Dr Pangloss adopts Leibniz's optimistic view that ours is the best of all possible worlds.

panlogism /ˈpænlədʒɪzm/ (Gr. *pan-* all + *logos*) *n.* the thesis that whatever is real is rational and that whatever is rational is real.

The term was first used by J. E. Erdmann in the 1850s to characterize Hegel's philosophy.

panpsychism /pænˈsaɪkɪzm/ (Gr. *pan-* all + *psychē* soul, mind) *n.* This term applies to views according to which a mental element is present in everything that exists.

Philosophical theories of this kind have been proposed through the ages, e.g. by many pre-Socratics, by many Renaissance philosophers, by Leibniz, and by quite a number of philosophers and scientists in the nineteenth century, e.g. Schelling, Schopenhauer, Lotze, Fechner (1801–77), Ernst Haeckel (1834–1919), Friedrich Paulsen (1846–1908), and in the twentieth century, e.g. Samuel Alexander, A. N. Whitehead, Charles Hartshorne, Pierre Teilhard de Chardin, C. H. Waddington.

Note: 'Panpsychism' has also been used as a synonym of IMMATERIALISM.

pantheism /ˈpænθiɪzm/ (Gr. *pan-* all + *theos* god) *n.* the doctrine that the world as a whole, nature in the widest sense, is identical with God.

This identity thesis can be read in two ways. In one way, it can be understood as a religious doctrine to the effect that the world is divine. Many great religious mystics have been pantheists in this sense. In another way, it says that there is no God over and above the world as a whole, and it can be understood as an atheistic doctrine. Spinoza and Hegel have been so interpreted.

The term was created by John Toland and first used in his *Socinianism Truly Stated* 1705.

pantisocracy /pæntɪˈsɒkrəsɪ/ *See* COLERIDGE.

paraconsistent logic any system of logic which, in contrast to standard systems, does not include the principle *ex falso quodlibet*, i.e. that any well-formed formula of the system can be logically derived from a contradiction.

In other words, a paraconsistent logic provides the basis for theories that are inconsistent but non-trivial; that is, a contradiction may, in a paraconsistent system, be derivable from a set of statements without the set being trivial in the sense that any statement whatever is derivable. By contrast, theories based on standard systems are trivialized and so totally wrecked when inconsistency arises, since then everything is derivable and nothing ruled out.

There are different kinds of paraconsistent logic. Particularly radical are the so-called *dialethic* logics which do not merely admit contradictions non-trivially, but actually contain specific contradictions, that is, statements of the form *A and not-A*, such as certain set-theoretic paradoxes. Some dialethic logics *also* contain the law of non-contradiction (for every A, not both A and not-A), some do not.

The earliest attempts to develop paraconsistent systems can be traced to the 1960s. A survey is available in G. Priest et al. (eds), *Paraconsistent Logic* 1989. *See also* RELEVANCE LOGIC. RSY/ed.

paradigm /ˈpærədaɪm/ (Gr. *paradeigma* model, pattern) *n.* **1** (in grammar) a pattern exemplifying, in a conventionally fixed arrangement, the declension or the conjugation of a word.
2 (in philosophy of science) a pattern of thinking, a set of background assumptions taken for granted.

The term came to be frequently used in this sense because of the influence of T. Kuhn's *The Structure of Scientific Revolutions* 1962 (2nd rev. edn 1970): a paradigm consists of the general theoretical assumptions and laws and techniques for their application that the members of a particular scientific community are taught to adopt and sets the standard for the normal way in which inquiry is conducted.
3 the word is also used vaguely for a set of assumptions and attitudes present in a culture, in a society, etc.

paradigm-case argument an argument from the fact that we have learnt to use certain words by reference to actual cases, to the conclusion that such words make good sense. This type of argument has been used to remove doubts about the existence of time, of free will, of secure knowledge, and much else.

A paradigmatic paradigm-case argument is the one set out by Antony Flew in his article 'Philosophy and language' (in A. Flew (ed.), *Essays in Conceptual Analysis* 1956): 'We have all learnt how correctly to use the expression "of one's own free will" and we did so by being confronted with obvious instances, paradigm-cases, of such situations. Therefore, philosophers and others who have denied that there is free will are mistaken.'

Arguments of this kind had a strong appeal to many philosophers in the 1950s and 1960s who were influenced by the later Wittgenstein (*Philosophical Investigations* I. 50–57; 215), but they soon attracted criticism. One objection is that conformity with linguistic norms is not sufficient to guarantee truth. It has also been pointed out that the argument is applicable only to expressions that we learn by having presented to us genuine examples of what the expression refers to; however, many expressions are taught in other ways.

A similar argument appears in Cicero's *De divinatione* I, 65: the use of the word *praesagire* (to pre-cognize) would not have become established if there were no such thing.

paradox (Gr. *paradoxos* beyond belief) *n.* **1** an apparently sound proof of an unacceptable conclusion. **2** an unacceptable conclusion of an apparently sound proof.

These are the two closely related senses in which the word is used in more strictly philosophical contexts. Many paradoxes are of great philosophical interest, and are recorded in this dictionary under their particular names. A near-synonym, used mainly in logical contexts, is ANTINOMY.

In more general and non-philosophical usage paradox is a statement that seems strikingly implausible, but which in fact conveys an interesting or important truth. It is in this sense that the witty *bons mots* in Bernard Shaw and Oscar Wilde count as paradoxes.

paradox of omnipotence An omnipotent being (God) can create any object that can be described without self-contradiction. A stone so heavy that nobody can lift it is such an object. Hence, an omnipotent being can create such a stone. But since an omnipotent being cannot lift such a stone, he is not omnipotent. It follows that an omnipotent being is not omnipotent.

parallelism *See* PSYCHOPHYSICAL PARALLELISM.

paralogism /pə'rælədʒɪzm/ (Gr. *paralogismos* fallacy) *n.* a fallacy. The word is used in this general sense in Aristotle's *Sophistical Refutations*. Kant, in the *Critique of Pure Reason*, reserved the word for those errors of reasoning which give rise to the theory of the incorruptibility and substantiality of the soul (B399; B410 ff.). The Paralogism(s), together with the Antinomy(-ies) and the Ideal of Pure Reason, are the three kinds of dialectical reasoning to which our reason has a natural propensity, according to Kant.

parameter /pə'ræmɪtə/ *n.* a factor or term which is assumed to be constant in a given context. In a different context, the same factor or term may be treated as a variable.

paranormal *adj.*, *n.* There are many things which science cannot explain *at present*, and this is indeed why scientific research is continuing. The paranormal, in contrast, is something which science cannot explain *at all*, because it defies the basic scientific and common-sense assumptions about space, time and causality. In order to account for paranormal events, therefore, a radical revision of these basic limiting principles would be required.

Precognition may serve as an example of a paranormal event: knowing (not just guessing) before the draw which lottery ticket will win. In contrast, out-of-body experiences are not paranormal; such experiences occur. This is not to say that persons *are* outside their bodies – only that it seems that way to them; similarly for *déjà-vu* experiences.

The main kinds of paranormal events are telekinesis, telepathy, clairvoyance and precognition. The inquiry into alleged paranormal events is called PARAPSYCHOLOGY. Physical events are not considered, as such, to be paranormal. There is nothing paranormal about a flying saucer that leaves a saucer-shaped imprint when landing in a field. On the contrary, that is exactly what one would expect a heavy saucer-shaped object to do. (Or again, this is what one might suspect hoaxers to have done under the cover of darkness.)

The existence of genuinely paranormal phenomena is strongly contested and the doubts seem well-founded.

Note: The use of this term is due to the American philosopher C. J. Ducasse (1881–1969).

parapraxis (*sing.*); **parapraxes** (*pl.*) *n.* a faulty act, a lapse; for instance, a slip of the tongue. The word came into use in psychoanalytical writings in the 1930s.

parapsychology *n.* The inquiry into paranormal phenomena is called parapsychology, since they are always supposed to involve the mind. They can be divided into telekinesis and extrasensory perception, and the latter in turn into telepathy, clairvoyance and precognition.

Although the impulse for much parapsychological research is often connected with some religious or spiritualist *Weltanschauung*, there is no necessary connection.

The word was introduced in 1889 by the German philosopher Max Dessoir (1867–1947). At that time, the standard English term was *psychical research*. Among those who took a favourable interest in it were some eminent philosophers, such as H.

Sidgwick, C. D. Broad and H. H. Price.

parataxis /pærə'tæksɪs/ (Gr. *parataxis* placing side by side) *n.* (in grammar) juxtaposition, in which a linking word or clause is omitted, e.g. Julius Caesar's *veni, vidi, vici* – I came, I saw, I conquered.

D. Davidson's analysis of 'G said that p' as deriving from two juxtaposed sentences 'G said *that*. p' has been described as a paratactic theory. **paratactic(al)** *adj.*

Parerga and Paralipomena /pə'rɜːgə; pærəlaɪ'pɒmɪnə/ Gr. (things) additional and supplementary. This is the title of a collection of shorter philosophical writings by Schopenhauer in two volumes (1851). They gained him wide popularity and established his reputation as a philosopher with the reading public.

Pareto /pa'reto (It.)/, Vilfredo (1848–1923) Italian engineer, economist and sociologist. He studied the non-rational roots of social action, making a distinction between 'residues', sentiments and impulses that fall outside the scope of rational justification by the agent, and 'derivations', i.e. ideological belief-systems which have the function of rationalizing the non-rational residues. He argued that a political movement is essentially the attempt of a rising elite to replace a ruling one, and that the ideology underpinning such an attempt is perhaps useful but not valid. His major sociological work is *Trattato di sociologia generale* 1916 (transl. as *The Mind and Society*).

pareto-optimality *n.* a condition of the economy is pareto-optimal if no one can become better off without someone becoming worse off. A principle, named after Vilfredo Pareto, states that a change or a reform promotes social welfare overall if someone becomes better off and no one becomes worse off.

Parfit, Derek (1942–) Oxford philosopher, fellow of All Souls College. His major work, *Reasons and Persons* 1984, has had a considerable influence on the philosophical exploration of our concepts of rationality, morality and personal identity. Indeed, the linking of these questions is a distinctive and original feature of this work. Many of the arguments are designed to show that what we ordinarily believe is false. Thus, the common view that it is rational to act prudently (i.e. in one's own self-interest) is undermined, and pure self-interested concern, often supposed to be morally objectionable but rationally sound, is in fact irrational. These points are connected with Parfit's view that personal identity, over time, matters much less than is commonly assumed. Again, the way we think about and are concerned with the consequences of our actions, and about the welfare of future generations, is riddled with paradox. The thrust of Parfit's work is towards what may be described as a less self-centred, and in that sense a more 'impersonal' but also more universalistic, moral outlook. BG/ed.

pari passu /'pærɪ 'pæsuː; 'pɑːrɪ/ Lat. with equal step. At an equal rate; side by side.

Parmenides /pɑː'mɛnɪdiːz/ (*c.* 515–*c.* 445 BC) ancient Greek philosopher of Elea in Italy who changed the course of Greek philosophy. Writing in response to early pre-Socratic philosophers, perhaps including Heraclitus, he opposed philosophical explanations that showed how the world came to be out of some substance or set of opposites. Rather, he insisted, there is no real change in the world.

Parmenides's surviving writings are fragments of a narrative philosophical poem in epic style. The poem's narrator is represented as being driven in a chariot to a place beyond the gates of night and day, where a goddess expounds to him philosophical doctrines. But rather than invoking her divine authority, the goddess bids the narrator to judge her argument by reason, and indeed the poem constitutes the first sustained philosophical argument in Western philosophy.

The poem falls into two parts, a critical argument and a constructive cosmology, traditionally known as the Way of Truth and the Way of Opinion, respectively. In the first part, the goddess distinguishes two 'paths of inquiry', the path of Is and the path of Is-not, and rejects the latter on the grounds that one cannot know or express what-is-not. She further warns against the path followed by ignorant mortals that confounds being with not-being; sense-experience cannot justify this path. The path of Is is marked by signposts declaring that what-is is (1) not generated or destroyed, (2) all alike, (3) unmoved and (4) complete. In a series of interconnected arguments, the goddess shows that generation, differentiation, and motion involve not-being, which of course cannot be known. For instance, generation is coming to be from not-being, while differentiation presupposes having more or less being. The goddess argues that all change is ruled out by this argument, and that changes and differences are mere names made up by mortals. But in order to forestall the temptation to cosmological thought, she goes on in the second part of the poem to construct a deceptive cosmology based on opposite substances or powers, fire and night, which she warns should not be posited as separate beings.

Clearly Parmenides wishes his critique to undermine the style of natural philosophy common among earlier philosophers. What is not clear is precisely how his own arguments work. One crucial problem is how he understands the grammar and meaning of 'is' and 'is not': does he have in mind a definite subject of the verb? Does he have in mind a complement? Is he confusing the 'is' of predication with the 'is' of existence? Or does he have in mind some 'fused' concept of being, which joins several of the senses we now distinguish? Furthermore, what are we to infer from his rejection of cosmology? Is he presenting a static cosmology of changeless being, or simply marking out a method that must be followed if philosophy is to describe being?

Whatever Parmenides's precise argument and conclusions were, his method of close argument set a new standard of philosophical rigour. The next generation of philosophers felt constrained by his argument to deny generation to the basic entities of the world, but they allowed for change by positing a plurality of Parmenidean substances. Parmenides's followers in the so-called Eleatic school, Melissus and Zeno, raised further objections to theories which allowed for change and plurality. Not until Plato and Aristotle would any philosopher be able directly to challenge the logical and metaphysical assumptions of Parmenides's argument. DG

parousia /pæˈruːsɪə/ Gr. presence *n.* The second coming of Christ, i.e. his final return at the end of time; cf., e.g., 1 Corinthians 15,23.

In its general sense, the word is used by Plato for the presence of a form in an object.

parsimony /ˈpɑːsɪmənɪ/, **law of** states that entities are not to be posited unless it is necessary to do so; also known as 'the principle of economy of thought' and 'Ockham's razor'. JM

partial order(ing) a binary relation which is REFLEXIVE, ANTI-SYMMETRICAL, and TRANSITIVE. A relation with these properties which is also CONNECTED is called a linear ordering. A **strict partial ordering** is ASYMMETRICAL and transitive. A relation with these properties which is also connected is called a strict linear ordering.

particularism *n.* 1 (in ethics) the view that limits moral concerns to a particular group, class, society or nation, with the implicit rejection of universalism, the view that moral concerns in principle extend to the whole of the human race. Tribalism is a kind of particularism.

In ethics, the word has also been used in an entirely different sense, for the view that the particular features of a situation, and not some general principle or rule, determine what conduct is morally right. The details make all the difference. SITUATION ETHICS, which does not accept universal rules of conduct as strictly binding, is sometimes called particularism.

2 (in theology) the view that not everyone will be saved. The doctrine that there is no salvation outside the Church (*extra ecclesiam nulla salus*) is particularist. *Ant.* UNIVERSALISM.

particular proposition in syllogistic logic, a proposition of the form *Some S is P* or of the form *Some S is not P*.

Pascal /paskal/, Blaise (1623–62) French mathematician, physicist, religious thinker and philosopher. His *Lettres provinciales* 1656–7 accused the Jesuits of moral laxity in their theory and application of PROBABILISM. Pascal's sterner outlook was in harmony with the Jansenism adopted by the Port-Royal group with which he was associated. His *Penseés* (*Thoughts*), published posthumously, contain reflections on religion. A recurrent theme is the wretchedness of human nature and the human condition. He also wrote shorter essays on logic and rhetoric. His essay on the geometric spirit is a model of clarity. In his treatise on the arithmetic triangle ('Pascal's triangle') he gave an explicit formulation of the method of proof known as mathematical induction (INDUCTION, MATHEMATICAL). The classical style of his writings is remarkable for its lucidity and precision. Its elegance and purity had the unqualified admiration even of those who, like the arch-orthodox Bossuet and the free-thinking Voltaire, repudiated his religious outlook.

Pascal's wager If God exists, he is infinitely incomprehensible. So human reason has no way of determining whether or not he exists. We cannot make up our minds on the basis of reasoning. But we must make up our minds. How can it be done? Pascal suggests that adopting belief in God, and leading a Christian life, is the soundest bet. In the event of winning the bet, an eternity of bliss is gained. In the event of losing the bet, the loss incurred is utterly insignificant. The alternative, i.e. unbelief, can at best incur an insignificant gain, at worst an immense loss.

To the objection that one cannot simply decide to make up one's mind and begin to believe in something, Pascal's reply is that if one wishes to believe, then changing one's mode of life, subduing one's passions, praying, going to mass, etc. may cause belief to arise.

Passmore /ˈpaːsmɔː/, John (1914–)

A philosophical self-portrait: Born and educated in Sydney, I came under the influence of John Anderson, whose teachings still, in some but not all respects, give shape to my thinking. I taught in Sydney University 1935–49 except for a year in London 1948, particularly at the London School of Economics. From a professorship in Dunedin, New Zealand, 1950–54 I returned after a year in Oxford to Australia, taking up a research post in the Australian National University, where I have ever since remained, although with considerable interludes in Europe, North America and Japan.

At university I divided my attention between philosophy, literature, history, economics, education, and a good deal of discussion with scientists. I have never learnt to specialize, which makes it impossible to summarize my views. From my earliest writings, largely in the *Australasian Journal of Psychology and Philosophy*, I also had a tendency to undertake work in fields which were then largely neglected. My first three books, *Ralph Cudworth* 1951, *Hume's Intentions* 1952 and *A Hundred Years of Philosophy* 1957, were written at a time when the history of philosophy was largely spurned. As with *Recent Philosophers* 1985, they were unorthodox in describing philosophers not so much as coming to particular conclusions but rather as participating in particular controversies and, in the process, struggling to reconcile opposing tendencies in their own thinking in relation to intellectual movements in the society around them. My other writings always have a substantial historical background, but more directly confront neglected issues. They are often concerned with the distinctive characteristics of particular intellectual activities, along with their interrelatedness. That is true of *Philosophical Reasoning* 1961 and of many articles on history, science and philosophy. *The Perfectibility of Man* 1970 is primarily historical but it by no means confines its attention to philosophy: it is a running critique of utopianism and mysticism which is at the same time a defence of moral outlooks which are neither rigorous nor antinomian. *Man's Responsibility for Nature* 1974, which some see as initiating the revival of 'applied philosophy', is similar in its attempt at once to defend a rational environmentalism and to free it from mystical and deontological entanglements, emphasizing that other people, as well as plants and animals, form part of our environment. In a similar spirit *The Philosophy of Teaching* 1980, rejecting the view that there is some single aim of education, tries to mediate between a Romantic, 'self-expression' view of education and a purely disciplinary concept of teaching, and *Serious Art* 1991 is both a critique of certain tendencies in contemporary art and art-criticism, and a rejection of the kind of traditionalism which is often directed against them.

If I cannot summarize my multifarious views, I can point to certain attitudes of mind which run through all my writings. One can most briefly describe my work as a defence of rationality which is at the same time critical of both philosophical and economic rationalism; a humanism which by no means treats human beings as being either actually or potentially god-like; a rejection of both atomism and holism in favour of a consistent pluralism; a preference for diversity as against simplicity and uniformity; praise of imaginativeness which is yet a praise of the critical spirit.

JP

pathetic fallacy The pathetic fallacy consists in ascribing subjective, especially emotional, qualities to inanimate objects – 'the angry sea', for instance. The expression is mainly used in literary and art criticism. It was introduced as a term of disapproval by John Ruskin in *Modern Painters*, vol. 3 (1856), but some of the figures so called can be defended as instances of poetic licence.

pathological *adj.* **1** emotional, pertaining to feelings. Used in this older sense by Baumgarten, Kant and Bentham, but rarely today. Bentham uses 'mental pathology' in the sense of susceptibility to pleasure and pain. Kant's contrast between pathological love and practical love in *Foundations of the Metaphysics of Morals* 1785 is the contrast between benevolence (love as a feeling, a subjective state) and beneficence (love in action).
2 diseased, abnormal. This is the standard present-day sense.

pathos /ˈpeɪθɒs/ *n.* (in rhetoric) the feeling that the speaker should inspire in his hearers, discussed at length in Aristotle's *Rhetoric*.

patriarchalism /peɪtrɪˈaːkəlɪzm/ *n.* a political theory according to which the authority of a ruler and the obligations of his subjects are of the same kind as those of the (male) head and the other members of a household. Theories of this kind were articulated by e.g. FILMER and BOSSUET.

patriarchy /ˈpeitrɪaːkɪ/ (Gr. *patēr* father + *-archia* rule, governance) *n.* **1** a system of domestic or political government in which the authority of the ruler is that of a father, husband, and head of household. **2** a society under such a government. **3** (in feminist theory) the exploitative dominance of men over women, common in most human societies to date.

patristics /pəˈtrɪstɪks/ *n.* the study of the thought and writings of the Church Fathers.

Paul of Venice (1369–1429) a prolific writer, who combined Aristotelian and 'modern' scholastic doctrine in his logic textbooks and other works. They were widely used in the universities, and were a favoured target of Renaissance humanist attacks on scholastic learning.

Peano /pɪˈænəʊ (Eng.); peˈaːno (It.)/, Giuseppe (1858–1932) Italian mathematician, professor in Turin. His insistence on formal rigour in the foundations of mathematics influenced Russell, who together with Whitehead wrote *Principia Mathematica* 1910–13 in which Peano's logical symbolism was also used. A set of five axioms that form a basis for the arithmetic of the natural numbers is named after him.

Pearson /ˈpɪəsən/, Karl (1857–1936) taught mathematical sciences at the University of London, and was the inventor of the chi-squared test. His general outlook was socialist, humanist and positivist. It was in this spirit that he criticized religious and metaphysical beliefs and advocated, *inter alia*, eugenics as one means to improve society. His major philosophical work is *The Grammar of Science* 1892 (rev. edn 1937), in which he presents a phenomenalist theory of knowledge similar to Mach's.

Peirce /pɜːs/, C(harles) S(anders) (1839–1914) American scientist, philosopher and logician of great originality. He is best known for his pragmatism, and for his theories of logic and language. Interest in them has been growing throughout the twentieth century.

Peirce called his general philosophy pragmatist because it relates belief to action. A belief that p is a disposition to act in certain ways, and the meaning of a conception is determined by experiences that arise from acting in various ways. This renders much of metaphysics absurd or meaningless, since rival metaphysical theories do not generate practical differences. Peirce also held that truth, knowledge and reality are to be found at the points towards which our attempts to reach them tend to converge in the long run. To believe that p is true is to believe that anyone who inquires about p well enough and long enough will believe that p. In his later period, however, Peirce did insist on realism: the reality of a world out there is something over and above being a point-of-convergence-of-belief-in-the-long-run. Ultimate reality is mental; matter is nothing but 'effete mind', and the physical laws are the expressions of ingrained mental habits. The right method of inquiry is that of science; it employs abduction (also known as retroduction), deduction and induction.

Many of the characteristic elements of modern logic were introduced by Peirce: the use of inclusive rather than exclusive disjunction, the use of truth-tables, the treatment of 'all' and 'some' as quantifiers, and the treatment of relations as classes of ordered pairs, ordered triples, and in general ordered n-tuples.

Peirce's law a theorem in standard propositional logic: $((p \supset q) \supset p) \supset p$. C. S. Peirce used it as an axiom in his first axiomatization of propositional logic in 1885.

Pelagianism *n.* the doctrine that man's will is free to choose between good and evil, and that there is a natural human capacity for good. This implies a denial of the dogma of original sin, and reduces or eliminates the need for the incarnation. It was proposed by the British monk Pelagius (*c.* 354–*c.* 418), in opposition to the theology of St Paul with its emphasis on justification through divine grace, which in the opinion of Pelagius discouraged believers from making a moral effort and resulted in moral slackness. Augustine, a contemporary of Pelagius, vehemently opposed Pelagianism, and in the early fifth century it was condemned by the Church and has been rejected in mainstream theology since then, although it has attracted many Christian thinkers.

Pentateuch the first five books of the Bible.

peras Gr. end, limit, boundary.

perception, extrasensory *See* EXTRASENSORY PERCEPTION.

perfect *adj.* not lacking in any respect, complete. *Ant.* imperfect.

perfect duty The non-fulfilment of a perfect duty makes coercive measures against the offender permissible; the non-fulfilment of an imperfect duty does not.

The duty to pay a debt is commonly considered to be perfect, the duty to give to charity imperfect. In the Modern Natural Law tradition the perfect duties are identified with the duties of justice while the imperfect duties are the duties of humanity (also called duties of benevolence, of charity, or of virtue). Linked with this is often the view that the perfect duties constitute a moral minimum; the imperfect ones take us to higher levels.

Which duties are perfect, which imperfect? Various answers have been proposed since the seventeenth century. One answer, proposed by Pufendorf, is that the perfect duties are those that are necessary for society; the imperfect ones are those that are desirable without being necessary. Another answer is that perfect duties are those that can be externally enforced, while imperfect ones cannot. Yet another answer is that perfect duties are those that are fulfilled by *not doing* something (e.g. by not taking something that belongs to another), and imperfect ones are those whose fulfilment consists of *doing* something. On this view, if the duty to pay a debt is considered perfect, it must be construed, somewhat awkwardly, as a duty fulfilled by not doing something – in this case by not violating the creditor's right to be paid. A further answer, suggested by Mendelssohn, Kant and others, is that a perfect duty is determinate, whilst an imperfect duty can be fulfilled in a number of different ways as the agent sees fit. In Kant's *Metaphysics of Morals* 1797, perfect duties, the duties of justice, are determinate because they are specified by a law; imperfect duties, the duties of virtue, are indeterminate because what is called for is the realization of morally desirable ends – no law specifies the particular means by which the end is to be achieved.

perfectionism *n.* 1 (in moral theory) perfectionism is a variety of consequentialism. It takes right action to be action which tends to promote the good, but differs from other kinds of consequentialism by taking the good to consist of the realization of human excellence in art, science and culture.

The word is used in this sense in John Rawls's *A Theory of Justice* 1971. His account envisages the varieties of consequentialist (in his terminology 'teleological') theories set out in the table below.

according to	*the good consists in*
hedonism	pleasure
eudaimonism	happiness
(classical) utilitarianism	rational desire-satisfaction
intuitionism	various basic goods
perfectionism	realization of human excellence in art, science and culture

2 (in political theory) the view that a government ought positively to promote the genuine individual and collective goods of the governed. Accordingly, anti-perfectionism is the view that implementation and promotion of ideals of the good life, though worthy in themselves, are not a legitimate matter for governmental action, which should be neutral regarding ideals of the good life.

3 (in theology) the doctrine that once 'saved', the believer is in a state of sinless perfection.

perfect obligation In present-day usage, the words 'obligation' and 'duty' are often used interchangeably. However, traces remain of a traditional distinction between duty and obligation: *duty* signifies the action itself which one is under an obligation (perfect or imperfect) to perform; *obligation* signifies the moral necessity of performing the action – that quality of bindingness that attaches to the performance of it. This is why expressions like 'duties of perfect obligation' and 'duties of imperfect obligation' (in John Stuart Mill's *Utilitarianism*, chapter 5) make good sense.

perfect right Pufendorf (1632–94) introduced this concept. The person who 'can demand' performance of a perfect duty has a perfect right. The person who deserves or merits the performance of an imperfect duty 'cannot demand' it, but has an imperfect right. Before Pufendorf, Grotius and others held that all rights are correlated to perfect duties. The correlate to an imperfect duty was called 'desert' or 'merit': a needy person may deserve to be helped, but 'cannot demand' it.

performative *n.*, *adj.* A performative, or a performative utterance, is one which does what it says it does. For instance, my utterance of the type 'I promise to do A' *is*, in normal circumstances, a promise of mine to do A. My utterance of the type 'I apologize' *is*, in normal circumstances, an apology proffered by me.

J. L. Austin, who introduced the concept, contrasted performatives with constatives. Constatives state facts, performatives do not; constatives are true or false, performatives are not.

Other examples of performatives are utterances of the type 'I hereby declare this bridge opened' (said by an appropriately appointed official when cutting the ribbon); 'I hereby acquit the accused' (said by a judge), etc. These utterances bring it about that the bridge *is* opened, and the accused *is* acquitted.

By extension it is not, however, strictly necessary that the words name or describe the act. The essential feature is that the words are used to perform an act. 'I apologize' can be used to perform the act of apologizing, but so can 'I am sorry.' Both utterances are performatives.

The complications arising at this – and other – points inspired J. L. Austin to a revision of the original distinctions and led to his later speech-act theory (SPEECH ACTS).

per impossibile /pɜː ɪmpɒ'siːbɪleɪ/ Lat. by (assuming) something (which is admittedly) impossible.

peripatetic /pɛrɪpə'tɛtɪk/ (Gr. *peripatein* to walk about) *adj.*, *n.* The Aristotelian philosophy was often called peripatetic because, according to the tradition, Aristotle and his disciples pursued their inquiries and discussions *walking* in the garden and porch of the Lyceum.

The peripatetic philosophy was traditionally counted as one of the four major schools of ancient philosophy, the other three being the academic, the Stoic and the Epicurean.

peripety /pə'rɪpətɪ/ (Gr. *peripeteia* sudden change) *n.* (in literature and drama) a sudden reversal of fortune. The classical discussion of this topic is found in chapter 10 of Aristotle's *Poetics*.

perlocutionary act *See* SPEECH ACTS.

peroration *n.* (in rhetoric) the concluding part of a speech, in which its main points are summed up, with a forceful appeal to the audience.

Perry, Ralph Barton (1876–1957) American philosopher, at Harvard University from 1902 and professor there from 1930 to 1946. He is mainly noted for three things: his participation in the realist movement of the early part of the twentieth century; his elaborately worked-out naturalistic and subjective theory of value; and being an authority on William James. In 1910, he wrote an influential article in the *Journal of Philosophy*, entitled 'The Egocentric Predicament', designed to expose a simple fallacy committed by idealists. In the same year, he combined with five others in the cooperative announcement of 'The Program and First Platform of Six Realists', followed by the publication in 1912 of a book of essays by the same group entitled *The New Realism*. In this volume, he made an important analysis of the concept of independence, using this in support of the realist thesis of the independence of objects from the knowledge of them. While he retained an epistemological realism, his theory of value, set out in *The General Theory of Value* 1926, was one which defined value in terms of object of interest. In 600 pages, he stated his theory with care and detail, concluding that the greatest value, according to the theory, lay in the object of an all-benevolent will. QG

personal identity What is it for the *same* person to exist over time? This is a question of perennial human concern: will we survive our bodily death, or is death the end?

According to one view, bodily death is not the end of one's personal existence. This dualist view, endorsed by Plato, Descartes and many others, is that we are a union of material body and immaterial soul. The body and the soul are different substances, one physical, the other mental, and each can exist without the other. It is the soul which gives us our distinctive identity, and it does not perish when the body dies. We continue to exist, in some immaterial realm.

This view is increasingly being rejected, since we can explain mental functioning in terms of the function of the brain and the central nervous system. This would be surprising if body and soul were distinct substances. At the very least, it shows that belief in the soul is not needed for explaining the character of our mental lives.

Other views fall into two broad categories, physical and psychological. There are physical theories which identify a person with some biological item – typically the brain or the body. One reason for preferring the brain version is the plausibility of the intuition that a person would survive if his brain were successfully transplanted into a new body and his old body destroyed.

Psychological theories refuse to make any identification of the kind 'same brain – same person'. Instead, they take the identity of a person over time to be determined by the continuation of his distinctive stream of mental life. This stream could, in principle, continue in some non-biological item, a silicon brain, for example. What matters, on this view, is that one's mental life continue, not that some particular biological item continue to exit. On such a view, a person survives TELETRANSPORTATION, a thought-experiment in which there is psychological continuity but no material continuity.

This latter view may provoke the question whether persons should be thought of as substances of any sort, biological or otherwise. Perhaps, as Hume believed, persons are not substances, but 'bundles' of interconnected mental events. It is a matter of current debate whether such a view is tenable. *See also* PARFIT. BG

personalism *n.* a view which emphasizes the importance of personhood. Personhood is seen as an ultimate fact. This is in opposition to the naturalist reduction of the person to physical processes, but also to the idealist account of the person as merely a transitory less-than-real manifestation of the Absolute. Especially: **1** a tradition in American philosophy, influenced by H. Lotze and represented by B. P. Bowne (1847–1910), J. Royce (1855–1916) and E. S. Brightman (1884–1953). **2** the thought of Emmanuel Mounier (1905–50) and the philosophical movement which it has inspired.

perspectivism *n.* Perspectivism is the name that has been given to Nietzsche's view, defended through a variety of metaphors, that there is no escaping the partial or perspectival restrictions of experience and knowledge. 'Facts are precisely what there is not, only interpretations.' What is denied in this claim is the possibility of a 'god's-eye view' of the world, which would incorporate every possible perspective and not be perspectival itself. Nietzsche also denies the existence of any *moral* facts, and he rejects any suggestion of a thing-in-itself and so too all of metaphysics. The truth of certain scientific theories is not denied; what *is* denied is the view that science is the only perspective. Science serves certain purposes, but does not serve every purpose.

In his more experimental and anti-dogmatic moods, Nietzsche encouraged us to try a variety of perspectives, to look 'now through this window, now through that one'. In his harsh analysis of morality and Christianity, however, he used the notion of perspectives to insist that some ways of looking at the world were distinctively inferior to others, for example the 'slave' or the 'herd' vision of the world in contrast to the 'masterly' perspective of what Nietzsche called the *Übermensch* (superman).

Nietzsche's perspectivism has been taken to absurd extremes, for instance by those who claim that Nietzsche rejected the very idea that any one perspective or 'interpretation' is better than any other, which he surely did not believe. It is also criticized as inconsistent, in that the view that truth is perspectival must itself be either perspectival or not. In the first case, according to this argument, the view is 'only a perspective' and not to be taken seriously, while in the second case it is self-refuting. But if one sees perspectivism as a statement of limits rather than a metaphysical claim as such, then there is no inconsistency, and Nietzsche's response to the charge is, 'So you want to insist that this too is only an interpretation; well so much the better!'

In the twentieth century, many kindred anti-objectivist theories have been proposed. RSO

persuasive definition a statement which has the form of a definition but the force of a value-judgement. The expression 'defined' keeps its evaluative character, but is given a different denotation.

In this example of a persuasive definition, 'violence' keeps its negative evaluative character, but is given an extended denotation: a speaker asserts that all societies in which wealth is unequally distributed are violent. His interlocutor is unconvinced, pointing to an unequal but non-violent society. The speaker retorts that such a society *is* violent in a subtle way, and adds as his reason that *every condition in which there are great inequalities of wealth is a condition of violence*. This added statement is a persuasive definition. The intention is to extend the denotation of 'violence' to include also situations of economic inequality, in order that the negative evaluation that attaches to violence will be extended to such inequalities.

The concept was introduced by C. L. Stevenson in an article in *Mind* 47 (1938) and used in his *Ethics and Language* 1944. In his account, which presupposes his emotivist theory of value-judgements, the salient features of a persuasive definition are constant emotive tone with a change in descriptive meaning.

pessimism (Lat. *pessimum* worst, the worst) **1** a view of human nature, of the human condition, or of the world as a whole, as being very bad indeed. (The word is sometimes, but rarely, used more specifically for the view that this is the worst possible world.)

The word came into use in the latter half of the eighteenth century, together with its antonym OPTIMISM. But as a designation of a fully articulated metaphysical theory, 'pessimism' seems first to have been used by Schopenhauer in the second edition (1844) of his *The World as Will and Representation* for his own world-view. Not much later, Eduard von Hartmann described his own philosophical outlook as a scientifically based pessimism.

Any sufficiently radical pessimism is prone to pragmatic paradox: if everything is as hopeless as the radical pessimist thinks, what good can he hope to achieve by publishing his views?
2 a mood of despondency.
3 concentrating one's attention on the unfavourable aspects of a situation.

Pestalozzi /pɛsta'lɔtsi/, Johann Heinrich (1746–1827) Swiss social reformer. He advocated wide-ranging educational reform, especially at elementary levels. His guiding idea, influenced by Rousseau, was to let instruction keep pace with the natural development of the child.

Peter Aureoli (*c.* 1275–1322) French scholastic philosopher, of the Franciscan order, he taught in Paris from 1316. He used the argument from illusion (ILLUSION, ARGUMENT FROM) as a basis for the distinction between intentional (apparent, conceived, objective) existence and real existence. A mental act is false if the object has intentional existence only, true if it has both kinds of existence. He held the view that statements about future contingent events are neither true nor false. This leaves scope for free will but seems to set limits to God's foreknowledge.

Peter (the) Lombard (*c.* 1095–*c.* 1160) author of the (*Four Books of*) *Sentences* *c.* 1158. It is in the main a compilation of theological opinions of the Church Fathers and of more recent writers. It was the text most commonly used in the medieval universities, where most scholastics used it as a basis for their lectures. About 250 commentaries from the twelfth to the sixteenth century have survived. Some, including those of Aquinas and Duns Scotus, go beyond the confines of the text, and contain much else of independent philosophical interest.

Peter of Spain (*c.* 1215–77) scholastic theologian and philosopher, who held positions in Paris, Siena and his native Lisbon, before being elected pope (John XXI) in 1276. He is best known for his *Summulae logicales*, which combine traditional logic (Aristotle, Boethius) with an early presentation of the 'modern' logic. It was simply and clearly written, and was until the seventeenth century the logic text most widely used.

petitio principii Lat. appeal to the initial assumption. BEGGING THE QUESTION.

Phaenarete /fe'næretɪ/ a midwife, Socrates's mother.

phalakros Gr. bald head; bald man. *See* SORITES.

Phalén /fa'len (Sw.)/, Adolf (Krister) (1884–1931) professor at Uppsala 1916–31, and a leading member of the Uppsala School. For Phalén, the main task of philosophy was conceptual analysis, especially of basic concepts such as reality, time, knowledge, consciousness, etc. In many cases, such an analysis will reveal inconsistencies in our common-sense concepts, which were shaped for purposes other than purely theoretical or scientific ones. He argued in his critique of epistemological subjectivism (1910) that the classical problem of knowledge arises from inconsistent common-sense assumptions and therefore can have no solution. He showed, in a major work on the problem of knowledge in Hegel's philosophy (*Das Erkenntnisproblem in Hegels Philosophie* 1912), how the inconsistencies in Hegel spring from these inconsistent presuppositions. Other works discuss concepts of mind and consciousness, and deal extensively with Brentano, Meinong, Husserl and other contemporaries. In an essay on Hume's discussion of causality, Phalén argued that its ambiguities, like the ones generally besetting empiricism, arise from the failure to distinguish clearly between three kinds of inquiry: analysis of a concept, assessment of its validity, and explanation of its origin.

phallogocentrism *n.* a conflation of 'phallocentrism' and 'logocentrism' originating in some writings by Derrida. The word has been used by some writers for the centrality of the male influence on the shaping of both social relations and forms of discourse.

phallus (Gr. *phallos* penis) *n.* The word is sometimes used in a special sense due to the influence of Jacques Lacan. In his theory, the word denotes that which the young child believes to be lacking in its mother and desired by her. The child desires to be desired by its mother. Therefore, the child identifies itself with the phallus(!). In his *La signification du phallus* 1966 it is defined as the symbol of a lack, an absence, generally.

Pharisaism /'færɪseɪɪzm/ *n.* a Jewish religious movement which emerged in the second century BC; it aspired towards a piety stricter and more sincere than that of mainstream religion. The gospels attributed to the Pharisees moral blindness and religious hypocrisy. On the whole, however, their bad reputation seems undeserved.

phasis /'feɪsɪs/ *n.* Gr. saying, assertion.

phatic /'fætɪk/ (Gr. *phanai* to speak) *adj.* pertaining to what is said. The social anthropologist Bronislaw Malinowski introduced in 1923 the concept of phatic communion: speech that has the function of establishing social contact, a sense of belonging to a group, rather than merely conveying information or other messages. Similarly, one of the six basic functions of language distinguished by Roman Jakobson is the phatic function of maintaining communicative contact. J. L. Austin used the word in a different sense in his theory of SPEECH ACTS.

phenomenal *adj.* **1** pertaining to a phenomenon. **2** marvellous, remarkable.

phenomenalism *n.* an empiricist theory of human knowledge, according to which all that we know about the external world are data conveyed to us by sense-experience. We tend to assume that other things, for instance material objects, exist beyond these immediate data, but on the phenomenalist view, as proposed e.g. by Carnap and Ayer in the first half of the twentieth century, our beliefs and statements about such things can make sense only if they are reducible to beliefs or statements about sense-data.

Almost a century earlier, John Stuart Mill had suggested an analysis of the concept of a material object as the concept of a permanent possibility of sensory experiences. This implies that beliefs and statements about material objects can be reduced to beliefs and statements in terms of sense-data, so that Mill's view can also properly be described as phenomenalist.

About a century earlier again, Berkeley's denial of the existence of matter can be seen as implying a phenomenalist theory.

In present-day versions of phenomenalism, the claim is that all statements about things or states of affairs are ultimately reducible to statements about actual or possible sense-experiences. Some writers, however, have proposed phenomenalism not as a general theory of knowledge, but only as a theory of scientific knowledge.

phenomenal world (in Kantian philosophy) the world of experience, in contrast to the noumenal world.

phenomenology *n.* **1** In the twentieth century, *phenomenology* is used almost exclusively for the philosophical method and movement that had its origin in the work of Edmund Husserl (1859–1938). It is the attempt to describe our experience directly, as it is, separately from its origins and development, independently of the causal explanations that historians, sociologists or psychologists might give. Subsequently, Heidegger, Sartre and Merleau-Ponty pursued and continued to refine the phenomenological method, while by no means accepting Husserl's conclusions. **2** Earlier, the term had also been used in a similar sense by other philosophers like Brentano, Mach and Pfänder for a description or analysis of phenomena: the implied contrast is with inquiries that seek to go beyond that which is directly given in our experience. **3** Hegel's *Phänomenologie des Geistes* 1807 (*Phenomenology of Spirit*) is an account of how spirit gradually makes its appearance. The process begins by way of initial oppositions between itself and something else, and between different forms of consciousness and finally ends once all separation is overcome, with self-knowledge, i.e. absolute knowledge. **4** The word seems first to have been used by Lambert in his *Neues Organon* 1764 (The new Organon) for the inquiry into, or a theory of, sensory experience and, in general, how things appear to us, how they seem to be. This was one of the four main parts of his work. (The other three dealt with the laws of thought, with truth as opposed to error, and with the theory of meaning.) RSO

phenomenon (*sing.*); **phenomena** (*pl.*) (Gr. *phainomenon* appearance) *n.* (in philosophy) a *phenomenon* is a thing (a quality, a relation, a state of affairs, an event, etc.) as it appears to us, as it is perceived.

Phenomena, appearances, data, etc. are implicitly contrasted with the way things really are. This contrast gives rise to one of the fundamental problems of philosophy: whether or how far we can have knowledge of the way things really are.

In Kant's philosophy, awareness of a phenomenon is based on sense-experience, which involves sensory intuition. In contrast, we can have no direct awareness of a NOUMENON, since we have no intellectual intuition analogous to the sensory.

philautia /fɪˈlaʊtɪə/ *n.* Gr. self-love, egoism.

Philo /ˈfaɪləʊ/ **of Alexandria** (*c.* 25? BC–*c.* AD 45?) Jewish philosopher, who attempted to reconcile traditional Jewish belief with contemporary Greek philosophy, often by the use of allegorical interpretation of the Bible. His philosophical writings are strongly influenced by Plato and the Stoics. He is particularly noted for his doctrine of the *Logos*, the divine instrument of creation, which mediates between God and the world. In this and other respects, he greatly influenced early Christian writers. HT

Philolaus /fɪləˈlæʊs/ **of Croton** (*c.* 470–*c.* 390 BC) *See* PYTHAGORAS.

philology *n.* **1** 'The art and method of correcting ancient manuscripts' is an early definition. Other definitions are wider, extending beyond classical antiquity, and include not only textual criticism but also other kinds of inquiry, e.g. linguistics and hermeneutics.

Philology began with the Renaissance humanists. They gradually established increasingly reliable classical texts from poor manuscript copies. They revised doubtful attributions. They developed the art of distinguishing authentic historical documents from forged ones. Thus, Lorenzo Valla demonstrated that the so-called Donation of Constantine (used to justify papal claims to supremacy) was a fraud, and Isaac Casaubon showed that the manuscripts of the hermetic tradition dated from the first century, and were not early Egyptian. It has been said that the radical critique of traditional religion since the seventeenth century owes more to philology than to the rise of modern science.

2 Historical and comparative linguistics.

philosophe /fɪlozɔf (Fr.)/ (Fr. philosopher) *n.* The term is used especially for the philosophical writers of the French Enlightenment (Voltaire, Montesquieu, Helvétius, Diderot, Condorcet, Turgot, Holbach, etc.). Their writings were non-academic, intended for the educated public generally.

Philosopher, The Aristotle was often given this honorific epithet in the Middle Ages, in recognition of his remarkable theoretical achievements.

Philosopher's Stone a very special substance which, according to alchemist theory, has the power to turn baser substances into gold.

philosophia perennis /fɪləˈsɒfɪə pəˈrɛnɪs/ Lat. the perennial philosophy. The common philosophical heritage of mankind: a body of fundamental philosophical truths which can command universal assent. This notion occurs especially in neo-scholastic thought. Sometimes the claim is made that a particular system, e.g. that of Aquinas, pre-eminently contains the *philosophia perennis*. The expression can be traced to Augustinus Steuchius's book *De philosophia perenni* 1540, which attempted to reconcile ancient philosophy and Christian belief.

philosophical anthropology philosophical inquiry into, or theory of, human nature.

Philosophical Radicals a number of social critics and reformers in the first half of the nineteenth century, all influenced by Bentham's utilitarianism. Among them were James Mill, the economist David Ricardo, the lawyer Edwin Chadwick, and the classical historian George Grote.

philosophy (Gr. *philosophia* love of wisdom) *n.* This term is used in a variety of senses.

Only the most central ones are noted here.
1 Philosophy as an intellectual activity can be variously defined, depending on whether the emphasis is placed on its *method*, its *subject-matter* or its *purpose*.

The *method* of philosophy is rational inquiry.

As for the *subject-matter*, it was common in earlier times to bestow the name of philosophy on inquiry into many different subjects, provided that it was guided by canons of rationality. For instance, physics and indeed the natural sciences generally were called natural philosophy. The title of Newton's great work of 1687 illustrates this: 'The mathematical principles of natural *philosophy*'. Like physics, many other present-day disciplines began as branches of philosophy, and this process of separation is continuing. Nevertheless, it is often held that philosophy has as a distinctive subject-matter the most fundamental or general concepts and principles involved in thought, action and reality. It is also a common view that philosophical inquiry is a second-order inquiry which has for its subject-matter the concepts, theories and presuppositions present in various disciplines and in everyday life.

If philosophy is taken to be a pure disinterested search for knowledge, a quest undertaken for its own sake, there is nothing to add about its *purpose*. It has, however, been a common view that the activity of philosophizing should lead towards wisdom, virtue or happiness.
2 A theory arrived at as a result of philosophical inquiry.
3 A comprehensive view of reality and man's place in it.

Note: 'philosophy' is also used as the name of a particular subject of study in schools and universities. The content may vary markedly over time, between countries and between educational institutions. Whenever the recent or imminent death of philosophy is proclaimed, or the nature of philosophy is debated, it helps to have an indication whether this concerns the institutionalized discipline or a certain kind of inquiry or theory.

philosophy of . . . 'Philosophy of . . .' is multiply ambiguous. It can denote either a field of inquiry, or a theory. For instance, 'philosophy of mind' denotes a field of inquiry; 'Spinoza's philosophy of mind' denotes a theory.

Another type of ambiguity is exemplified by 'philosophy of history': it may denote an account of the general course of events over time, or the nature and methods of historiography.

Yet another type of ambiguity is exemplified by 'philosophy of religion', which can denote either a religious world-view or an inquiry into or theory of religious belief. Similarly, 'philosophy of law' can denote either a set of legal principles (probably on the basis of a rational theory of justice) or an inquiry into or theory of the nature of laws and legal systems.

phoneme /'fəʊniːm/ *n.* (in linguistics) a distinctive unit of sound in a natural language. Two occurrences of a sound may be regarded as tokens of the same phoneme (even if in fact they do not sound exactly alike) because of their contrastive relations to other sounds in the language, in the same way that two occurrences of a letter, from different fonts or by different hands, are seen as tokens of the same letter.

phoronomy /fɒ'rɒnəmɪ/ (Gr. *phora* rapid movement + *nomos* law) *n.* This eighteenth-century word, used by Kant, denotes what is now called kinematics, the theory of acceleration and velocity.

phrastic /'fræstɪk/ *See* NEUSTIC.

phrenology /frɪ'nɒlədʒɪ/ (Gr. *phrēn* mind) *n.* inquiry into, or theory of, correlations between a person's cranial features and psychological characteristics. It was proposed by F. J. Gall (1758–1828) and became popular in the early nineteenth century. Although scientific in spirit, the decisive weakness of the theory was its lack of empirical support. More progress was made when it became possible to investigate the brain, rather than the skull, more directly.

phronēsis /frəʊ'niːsɪs/ Gr. wisdom, good sense, good judgement, prudence *n.* one of the four CARDINAL VIRTUES.

phylogenesis /faɪləʊ'dʒɛnɪsɪs/ *n.* the development of a biological species.

physicalism *n.* **1** the view advocated by some logical positivists, especially Neurath (who also coined the term in 1931 and gave it currency), to the effect that the unified language of science must be a language which refers to material, physical entities, and in which all basic predicates are physical. It was part of this outlook that all meaningful language, including statements about mental and cultural phenomena, must be so reducible. In contrast, phenomenalism (Mach, Schlick, Ayer) takes the basic predicates and propositions to be about sense-data. The two views differ in their choice of basic propositions, but physicalism, in this sense, does not have to assume that the basic language is the language of physics. **2** The view that everything is constituted of the entities taken to be basic by the physical sciences, and that there are no regularities and laws that are independent of the ones that govern the basic physical entities. This is the modern version of materialism. The term physicalism has come to be used mainly in the philosophy of mind for the view that everything mental is really physical.

Physicalism used to be reductive. The view was that all statements about non-physical entities or properties could be translated into statements in the physical sciences (or, less restrictively, into statements assigning physical predicates to physical objects) or else should be rejected. Since the 1970s non-reductive variants of physicalism have been advanced: all that exists is physical, but it is not claimed that translatability into physicalistic language is always possible. In the philosophy of mind, this is often formulated by saying that mental properties are determined by or SUPERVENIENT on physical ones, but not reducible to them.

In the philosophy of mind, type-physicalism can be distinguished from token-physicalism. Type-physicalism is the view that kinds of mental states can be identified with kinds of physical states. Token-physicalism is the view that each and every token mental state is identical with some physical state, but allows that it may not be possible to identify mental types with physical types. Anomalous monism is a variety of token-physicalism that insists that no type–type identities between the physical and the mental are possible. *See* MONISM.

physico-theology *n.* This term (which literally means 'nature-theology') is well defined by the title of William Derham's *Physico-theology: a demonstration of the being and attributes of God from his works of creation* 1713.

The term *physico-theology* was in common philosophical use in the seventeenth and eighteenth centuries. It was above all the feature of apparent purposiveness of nature that formed the basis for the argument for God's existence, and this is why the more specific expressions *argument from design* and *teleological argument* eventually became the standard ones.

physiognomy *n.* inquiry into, or theory of, correlations between bodily features and psychological characteristics. The last theory of that kind to attract much attention from philosophers was the one proposed by Lavater 1775–8: a person's character can be read off in considerable detail from the details of the facial features. It gained considerable popularity. A witty critic was Lichtenberg (*Über Physiognomik*, 1788); but by the late 1790s Kant noted, in his *Anthropologie*, that this wave of intellectual fashion was subsiding.

physis /'faɪsɪs/ Gr. nature *n.* The standard contrasts are with *nomos*: law, custom, convention; and with *thesis*: something laid down, legislated, determined by an act of will.

Pico della Mirandola, Gianfrancesco /'piːko della mi'randola, dʒanfran'tʃɛsko (It.)/ (1469–1533) nephew of Giovanni Pico della Mirandola. *See* SCEPTICISM.

Pico della Mirandola, Giovanni /dʒo'vanni/ (1463–94) Renaissance thinker, associated with Marsilio Ficino and the academy of Florence. In his eclectic system, intended to overcome sectarian discord, he incorporated ideas from the university philosophy (scholastic-Aristotelian) and from hermetic and neo-Platonic writings. He also drew on the Kabbala, not only christianizing ideas from it, as earlier scholars had also done, but also by adopting cabbalistic methods of interpretation. But he did not accept occult mysteries uncritically, and wrote an attack on predictive astrology. In the 1870s the reading public was reminded of him through Walter Pater's questionable interpretation of him as an aesthetizing neo-pagan. The *Oration on the Dignity of Man* 1486 is the work by which he is now best known.

pietism /'paɪətɪzm/ *n.* a religious movement, mainly among Lutherans, which became influential in Germany especially in the first half of the eighteenth century. It is characterized by a strongly emotional individual religiosity in which prayer and contemplation feature prominently. Pietists could be accused of mawkish sentimentality, but to their credit remain the many orphanages and schools for the poor that they founded.

pious fraud deceit in the cause of religion.

plastic natures active forces which penetrate material nature, shape material objects, and make motion and organic life possible. The concept was used by Henry More, and again by Cudworth in *The True Intellectual System of the Universe* 1678 in their arguments against (atomistic) materialism. Since matter is inert and passive, there would be no activity with resultant movement and change, if nothing but matter were real.

platitude *n.* a truism. Many statements that used to be described as conceptually true, true *a priori*, etc., are among those called platitudes by some recent analytical philosophers. Their non-derogatory use of this word as a quasi-technical term may have begun with David Lewis in the mid-1960s.

Plato (427–347 BC) The first great systematic philosopher of the Western tradition, Plato belonged to an aristocratic family in Athens. After hearing lectures from the Heraclitean philosopher Cratylus, he became a devoted follower of Socrates. His family connections with leading members of the oligarchic party led him to consider a career in politics; but the excesses of the oligarchic government installed in 404 BC, and of the succeeding democratic government, caused him to withdraw from politics. He briefly retired to the city of Megara after Socrates was put to death in Athens in 399, and soon began to write Socratic dialogues at least in part to defend the memory of his master. About 387 he made a voyage to southern Italy and Sicily, where he made the acquaintance of Archytas, an influential Pythagorean philosopher-statesman, and of the ruling family of Syracuse. On his return to Athens, Plato founded the Academy, the first institution of general higher education in the West, which became home to leading mathematicians, scientists and philosophers. Twenty years later Plato was summoned back to Syracuse to help in the education of the young ruler Dionysius II, whom he hoped to convert to the philosophical life. The plan miscarried when Plato's supporter Dion was exiled, but Plato returned in around 360 to try to effect Dion's return to power – a plan which also failed. However, Plato had tried his best to implement some of his political ideas in the real world.

Plato wrote dramatic dialogues which often use Socrates as the chief character. All of them seem to have been preserved. Although the dating of the dialogues is subject to scholarly controversy, the following division into three groups appears to be plausible. The early dialogues seem to reflect Socrates's method and teachings (see SOCRATES), and often seek to define some virtue without reaching a satisfactory definition: the *Apology*, *Crito*, *Laches*, *Ion*, *Hippias Minor*, *Charmides*, *Protagoras*, *Lysis*, *Euthyphro*, *Gorgias*, *Euthydemus* and *Hippias Major*. The middle dialogues typically expound systematic theories often based on the Theory of Forms: the *Meno*, *Phaedo*, *Symposium*, *Menexenus*, *Cratylus*, *Republic* and *Phaedrus*. Some of the later dialogues examine problems of and interrelations between the Forms, as well as examining questions of knowledge, science, happiness and political science: the *Parmenides*, *Theaetetus*, *Sophist*, *Statesman*, *Timaeus*, *Critias*, *Philebus* and *Laws*. In the dialogues the figure of Socrates seems to change from a representation of the historical Socrates in the early dialogues to a mouthpiece for Plato in the middle dialogues, to a sometimes minor character in the later dialogues, which in fact come nearer to being treatises. The dialogue form, however, remains important for expressing the give-and-take of actual philosophical conversations, which for Plato represent the ideal pattern of instruction. Except in the *Parmenides*, Plato generally avoids technical discussions and tends to mix topics together in his works in a way which invites the exploration of related ideas.

The philosophy of Plato's 'middle period' is based on the theory of Forms. Distinguishing between knowledge and mere opinion, Plato holds that the former is possible only if there are absolute and changeless objects of knowledge. These are 'Forms', or ideal realities such as Justice itself, Holiness itself, Beauty itself, Equality itself. Sensible objects are 'called after' the corresponding Form because they 'participate in' that Form; e.g. Socrates is called just because he participates in Justice. Sensible objects never purely possess one property rather than its opposite. For instance, Socrates is not only just but unjust in some respects. But the Forms themselves never admit their opposites, being purely what they are, while sensible objects depend on Forms for whatever order and regularity they have. It is not clear exactly what terms have corresponding Forms. Plato prefers to discuss Forms corresponding to virtues, moral values (such as goodness) or mathematical concepts (such as equality); but there may be Forms corresponding to all or most general terms (including 'man', 'bed', 'ugly'). In any case, Plato seems to conceive the Forms as ideal exemplars that provide standards of judgement. Thus, to know the Form of Justice allows us to judge what acts or people are just. We know that Socrates is just because we somehow perceive his relation to Justice.

Plato holds that our souls are immortal and are reborn, according to the *Phaedo*, into different bodies. We have the ability to judge things by standards more perfect than any we experience. For instance, we understand what it is for things to be (perfectly) equal even though we never encounter perfectly equal things in experience. This ability must precede our use of the senses; and since we acquire our senses at birth, we must acquire our ability to make judgements about sensations before we are born. Accordingly, we must have had direct contact with the Forms, such as Equality, when our souls were out of our bodies before our present life. We are not at present completely aware of the Forms and their properties, so we must have forgotten them at birth, only to recollect them later as we use our senses. All learning of general truths, then, is recollection.

If learning is a process of recollection, the proper form of education is not teaching, but questioning to bring out knowledge the student already possesses. The art of questioning which Plato had learnt from Socrates as a method of refuting false opinions, he names 'dialectic' and recasts as a positive method: the questioner leads the learner on to see the inadequacy of his former opinions, and then to arrive at a more satisfactory view. By a process of induction the learner is led from particular insights to general truths. Ultimately the learner may be led to behold the Forms themselves and hence to grasp the first principles of all knowledge.

There are four levels of knowledge, corresponding to four levels of reality. The highest kind of knowledge is 'rational intuition', directed towards the Forms themselves. Next in order is 'understanding', or knowledge by deduction, which is directed towards mathematical objects such as triangles and exemplified in geometry; understanding presupposes a knowledge of first principles, namely the Forms. 'Belief' is a still lower kind of knowledge of physical objects. And shadows and reflections are images of physical objects which are known only by 'conjecture'. It is the task of the philosopher to lead the student upward towards knowledge of the Forms through dialectic. The motivation for the student is supplied by Love, which, attaching originally to a beautiful body, may yet be directed towards bodies in general, and then to laws and principles, until it draws the student towards the Forms themselves as the perfect exemplars of beauty and goodness.

In the *Republic* Plato criticizes both the Sophists and conservative moralists for their views on ethics: they are concerned only to show that justice brings one non-moral goods such as reputation and wealth, whereas they should demonstrate why justice is valuable for its own sake. Plato emphasizes the problem by raising the challenge of whether a just person could be happy even if he were unjustly tortured and put to death. He answers with the help of an elaborate analogy between an ideal city-state and the individual soul. An ideal state would have three classes: the guardians (rulers), the auxiliaries (soldiers), and workers. In the ideal state virtue would be found in the proper functioning of the parts, and justice in everyone's fulfilling his own duties and not meddling in those of others. Similarly the soul is composed of three parts: the reason, the spirited part, and the desiring part. When these function properly the individual is virtuous, and when each part does its assigned function, the individual is just. Moral failure occurs when the reason is subordinated to another part; and one cannot fail without damaging one's psychological health. Since the soul is more important than the body, a just person is always better off than an unjust person, no matter how successful the unjust person is in acquiring non-moral goods. But a person can be just either by habit or by philosophical knowledge. One who is just merely by habit may fall to the temptation to be unjust if there is an apparent opportunity to profit from injustice. Only the philosopher – who has beheld the Form of Justice – will be beyond temptation.

Plato's argument for justice provides not only a theory of ethics but also a model for the ideal state. In the ideal state philosophers will rule. They will be chosen by a process of testing and evaluation as they pass through various stages of education until they are 50 years of age. Having been thoroughly trained in mathematics and then in philosophy, they will be led to behold the Forms, after which they will be qualified to return to political life as guides for the state. They will exercise strict control over education, art, war, and even marriage, so as to keep out corrupting influences and to promote social harmony according to philosophical principles. The rulers will live in a commune in which women share leadership roles with men. Marriages will be arranged by a rigged lottery, and children will be raised in common nurseries. Since the rulers own all things in common they will have no desire to acquire private possessions but will put all their energies into ruling.

In the realm of art the rulers will censor productions to ensure they do not provide bad models of behaviour – such as the excessive emotional reactions of tragic heroes. Art is merely the imitation of an imitation and should therefore occupy a subordinate role in society, furthering the aims of the rulers. Despite Plato's disparaging view of art in the ideal state, he offers the basis of the first major theory of criticism when in the *Phaedrus* he notes that a composition should be like a living creature, exhibiting organic unity.

Plato's Theory of Forms seems to have come under fire in the Academy, and a series of problems and objections is recorded in the *Parmenides*. Most famous among the criticisms is the Third Man Argument, which Aristotle in his writings finds to be a valid objection. According to this argument, (1) everything that has a property has it because of a single cause, the Form; (2) the Form has the property in the highest degree; and (3) the Form is not identical with the things which have the property. According to principle (2) the many particular large things and the Form of Largeness all are large, and by principle (1) there must be a cause of largeness which, by principle (3), is not identical with any of the things that are large. But this must be a second Form of Largeness, Largeness_1, and so on. Although Plato seems to understand the steps of the argument, he makes no reply to it, only hinting that there may be some solution. The argument is interesting precisely because it seems to draw on key principles of the Theory of Forms to produce an absurd consequence.

In his later work Plato does not seem to abandon the Forms – although scholars are not united on this point – but explores their interrelations and potential applications. In the *Sophist* he argues that the Forms are 'woven together' in various ways. Some go together, such as Being and Motion, while others, such as Motion and Rest, do not mix at all. Most importantly, he gives an analysis of not-being as the Different. Thus when I say that motion is not rest, I am not saying that motion does not exist, but that it is different from rest. Plato goes on to analyse the sentence into subject and verb and to sketch a theory of truth whereby truth is the agreement of a sentence with the fact it describes. Although Plato's discussion is heavily based on metaphysics, it marks a major advance towards a conception of logical relations, and hence it prepares the way for the first logical system, that of his student Aristotle.

Before Plato, philosophy was either scientific theory about nature (as in the pre-Socratics), practical discussion of how to succeed in political life (the Sophists), or ethical theory (Socrates). Plato developed a comprehensive philosophy built around a central metaphysical theory, the Theory of Forms, which had implications for science, politics and ethics. Furthermore, since the Forms were in a sense values, he was able to combine facts and values, science and ethics into a single conception of the world. Although his dialectical method favoured open inquiry over fixed doctrine, he first conceived of knowledge as an ordered series of statements derived from first principles – i.e. he grasped the notion of science as a deductive system. And although Plato resisted the urge to divide philosophy into specialities such as ethics, epistemology and psychology, the architectonic nature of his vision and the range of his discussions helped to define such studies as essential parts of philosophy. Thus despite Plato's emphasis on shared and open-ended inquiry, he was also a systematic thinker who set the pattern of philosophy as a comprehensive explanation of all experience. DG

Method of citation: by page number in the edition published by Henricus Stephanus (Henri Etienne), Paris 1587, followed by one of the letters a–e, by which each page was divided into five equal sections. Good modern editions include this method of reference.

platonic love love of a non-sensuous kind. In platonic love the physical or intellectual beauty of the beloved is loved because it is seen as a manifestation of a higher, ideal kind of beauty. Socrates develops this idea in Plato's dialogue *Symposium*, claiming to have received it from a wise woman called Diotima.

Platonism *n.* **1** (from the Renaissance onwards) Plato's works were little known in the European Middle Ages, but were better known among Arabic and Jewish philosophers of the period. In the fifteenth century Greek scholars from Byzantium brought manuscripts of Plato's works to Italy, where they quickly aroused great interest, especially in Florence, where they were edited, translated (into Latin) and commented upon by Marsilio Ficino (1433–99) and Giovanni Pico della Mirandola (1463–94), who were members of Cosimo di Medici's Florentine Platonic Academy. The Platonism developed by Ficino and Pico into a *Theologia Platonica* was a religious philosophy, fusing elements from Plato's newly revived texts, those of the neo-Platonists, Plotinus and Proclus, of Philo Judaeus (who had written that Plato was Moses speaking Greek), and elements from the Jewish Cabbala and the hermetic writings, all of which were regarded as the most ancient wisdom of mankind that went back to Moses and Hermes. This Renaissance Platonism was presented as a Christian theosophy that included the biblical revelation, though authorities saw dangerous heretical tendencies in some of its teachings.

Another form of Christian Platonism was presented in England by John Colet and Thomas More in the sixteenth century. More used features of Plato's *Republic* in developing his ideal society in his *Utopia*. Various late sixteenth-century thinkers put together Platonic and Pythagorean mathematical ideas with mystical and religious views. Kepler, Galileo and others insisted that the world could be read in mathematical terms, and that God was the great geometer. The emphasis on mathematics as the language of science, in contrast to Aristotle's science based upon sensory qualities, emerged in good part from Renaissance Platonism. In fact the modern early mathematical physicists were called 'Platonists' by their opponents.

(*Cambridge Platonism*) In mid-seventeenth-century England a school of Platonic and neo-Platonic philosophy and theology developed at Cambridge, led by Henry More and Ralph Cudworth, which espoused a non-dogmatic rational religious outlook and metaphysical interpretation of modern science. Its leaders challenged the materialism and atheism they saw in the Cartesian theory, in the views of Hobbes and then of Spinoza. Isaac Newton employed some of their philosophical ideas in his theory of the physical world. Cambridge Platonism continued to be influential into the nineteenth century, when it was studied and modified and used by English Romantic poets and by the New England Transcendentalists, such as Ralph Waldo Emerson. Religious Platonism continued to be set forth in the twentieth century. One of its principal advocates was Dean W. R. Inge of St Paul's.

Starting in the late eighteenth century Hellenic scholars sought to separate Plato from the neo-Platonists and Cabbalists, and to study Plato's texts and ideas apart from later interpretations. Anything that smacked of neo-Platonism or Cabbalism was relegated to religion or theosophy, whereas genuine Platonism was pure philosophy. One tendency is to see the pure Plato as the source of the basic problems of philosophy, and to use the study of his writings as a way of getting into present philosophical concerns. Another tendency has been to see Plato in his Hellenic context, and to try to understand him as a purely pagan writer of antiquity rather than either as an inspirer of religious ideas in Judaism or in Christianity, or as the first analytic philosopher. In either case, Alfred North Whitehead's remark that all subsequent philosophy consists just of footnotes to Plato is one way of stating his importance, especially from the Renaissance onwards.

2 (in contemporary metaphysics) the term is used in twentieth-century philosophy as an alternative to the over-used term 'realism', for theories that accept the existence of abstract objects (numbers, properties, etc.), in contrast to nominalist theories, which only accept the existence of concrete individuals. Platonism takes abstract objects to exist independently of our thought (against conceptualism) and talk (against nominalism). RPO

pleasure principle the tendency to seek pleasure and avoid pain. In Freud's theory, this principle rules the Id, but is at least partly repressed by the 'reality principle'. The origin of this expression can be traced to G. Th. Fechner (1801–87), who used the German equivalent *Lustprinzip* in the defined sense in an article published in 1848. The theory that *all* action is determined by the prospect of pleasure is called (psychological) hedonism.

Plekhanov /pljɪˈxaːnof (Rus.)/, Georg Valentinovich (1856–1918) Russian social democrat and a leading exponent of Marxism in Russia. He opposed Bernstein's revisionism and Lenin's bolshevism. In his analysis of culture and society, he rejected vulgar materialism, and asserted that it is possible for human beings not to be entirely determined by economic forces in their theories and practices.

plenitude, principle of 'Every genuine possibility is actualized at some time.' This principle can be traced to ancient Platonism, and to Aristotle, who analysed modal notions temporally: the impossible is that which never occurs. The classical study of the principle is Arthur Lovejoy, *The Great Chain of Being* 1936. In his formulation, the principle is, 'No genuine potentiality of being can remain unfulfilled.' One consequence drawn from it is that the world exhibits no gaps, i.e. sudden transitions of level.

pleonasm /ˈpliːənæzm/ (Gr. *pleonasmos* surplus) *n.* an expression containing superfluous words.

pleonexia /pliːəˈneksɪə/ Gr. greed; desire for more than one's proper share; striving for an unfair advantage.

plērōma /pləˈrəʊmə/ Gr. fullness, plenitude *n.* a concept utilized in Gnostic and related cosmologies, and again in neo-Platonism. It refers to the spiritual or divine realm entire, which lacks nothing. Diverse elements within this realm may exile themselves and become lower-level HYPOSTASES. This in turn leads to a striving for reunion with the Absolute. HT

Plotinus /plɒˈtaɪnəs/ (205–70) the founder of neo-Platonism and, as such, an important influence in late classical, medieval Christian, Islamic and Renaissance thought. He studied under Ammonius Saccas in Alexandria, and from about 245 taught in Rome. His writings were edited by his student Porphyry as the six books of *Enneads*, i.e. six groups of nine treatises each.

He held that all modes of being are an outflowing from 'the One', an ultimate immaterial reality which he claimed that Plato was referring to in his dialogues, the *Parmenides* and – as 'the Good' – the *Republic*. These modes of being, in descending order of unity and value, are: mind (*nous*), soul (*psychē*) and nature (*physis*). His 'mind', like Aristotle's unmoved mover, or God, is thought thinking itself, within which are the 'forms' contemplated as a unity in a timeless way. His 'soul' is a lower and less unified version of mind, in which the forms must be contemplated separately and successively, a process which gives rise to space and time. His 'nature' is an even lower and less unified version of mind, in which the forms are seen only in a dream-like way, and which projects its dreams as the material world.

The individual human being is a microcosm of this entire process. Our 'minds' are normally concerned with the material world, or at best with individual ideas contemplated successively, but we can in ecstatic moments contemplate reality as a whole.

Plotinus's contribution to philosophy has been variously assessed. He creates a system out of Plato's philosophy which some readers believe to be what Plato intended, and which others decry as betraying Plato, who refused to present a system. Plotinus has also been praised by some, and attacked by others, for confirming his system by references to what were evidently personal experiences of a mystical kind. More recently some readers have come to appreciate the rigour of much of his argument, and the originality of his views on psychology and aesthetics. RB

Plutarch /ˈpluːtaːk/ (*c.* 48–*c.* 122) Greek biographer and moralist, from Chaeronea in Boeotia. He is best known for his parallel *Lives*, which give comparative accounts of the character and exploits of eminent Greeks and Romans. He was a prolific writer, and among his best-known and most influential works are the *Moralia*, a collection of essays. Some give moral advice, others discuss Platonic themes or argue against Stoic and Epicurean doctrines. In his discussions of religion, he operates with a single creator-God, but he makes much use of the notion of *daimons* to explain various religious experiences, including oracles. Since the Renaissance Plutarch's historical and moral writings have been widely read and appreciated. His influence can be seen in Montaigne, Shakespeare, Bacon, Hume, etc. He was the favourite author of the young Rousseau. HT/ed.

pneuma /ˈnjuːmə/ *n.* Gr. breath, spirit.

pneumatic *adj.* spiritual. A literal interpretation looks at the letter of what is written, a pneumatic interpretation at the spirit.

pneumatics /njuː'mætɪks/ *n. sing.* Leibniz's term for PNEUMATOLOGY as a branch of metaphysics.

pneumatology /njuːmə'tɒlədʒɪ/ *n.* **1** the branch of metaphysics that deals with the nature of spiritual beings, such as God, angels and the soul. The use of the term in this sense dates from the eighteenth century. **2** the theological doctrine of the Holy Spirit.

poiēsis /pɔɪ'iːsɪs/ Gr. making, producing *n.* An activity which results in creating a product. Plato and Aristotle contrast *poiēsis* with *praxis, doing* something. Excellent making requires skill (*technē*); excellent doing requires virtue (*aretē*). According to Aristotle, the former is acquired by practice, the latter by knowledge.

Poincaré, Henri /pwɛ̃kaʀe (Fr.)/ (1854–1912) French mathematician, physicist and philosopher of science. His best-known philosophical doctrine is 'conventionalism'. Nineteenth-century mathematicians had discovered alternative geometries to that of Euclid. This discovery called into question the then prevailing Kantian view that (Euclid's) geometry can be known *a priori*, independently of experience, and yet represents substantive or 'synthetic' knowledge of the structure of space. Poincaré advocated a modified Kantian position. It is logically possible that a non-Euclidean geometry describes the structure of space better than Euclid's. However, because Euclid's geometry is by far the simplest, physicists will always retain it as the geometry most appropriate for them. They will retain it, not because they know *a priori* that it is true, but because it contains the simplest geometric conventions. This view was undermined by the general theory of relativity, which incorporates a non-Euclidean geometry. AM

polis (*sing.*), ***poleis*** (*pl.*) Gr. a city-state (in ancient Greece) *n.*

Polish notation a bracket-free notation in symbolic logic, devised in the early 1920s by Jan Łukasiewicz. Operations are symbolized by prefixes. In propositional logic we have:

negation	~p	Np
conjunction	p & q	Kpq
disjunction	p ∨ q	Apq
conditional	p ⊃ q	Cpq

For example, *(p & q)* ⊃ *r* becomes *CKpqr*, and *(p & q)* ⊃ [~*r* ∨ *(p* ∨ *q)*] becomes *CKpqANrApq*. A variant notation, convenient in certain contexts, symbolizes the operations by suffixes.

political realism *See* REALISM.

polyadic *See* MONADIC OPERATOR.

polymath /'pɔlɪmæθ/ *n.* a person with an extensive knowledge of many branches of learning.

polysemy /pə'lɪsəmɪ/ *n.* the existence of more than one meaning for a linguistic expression; for example 'plot', which can mean a piece of land, or the main events in a story. (If it has exactly two meanings, it is properly called ambiguous; if more than two, multiply ambiguous; but these terminological distinctions are not strictly observed.) **polysemous** *adj.*

polysyllogism *n.* a chain of categorical syllogisms, in which the conclusion of one is used as a premiss in the next.

polytheism /'pɒlɪθiːɪzm; pɒlɪ'θiːɪzm/ *n.* the doctrine that there are many gods that may be worshipped. *See also* HENOTHEISM.

Pomponazzi /pɔmpɔ'natsɪ (It.)/, Pietro (1462–1525) Italian philosopher who taught at Padua, Ferrara and Bologna, often regarded as the most eminent of the Renaissance philosophers. Using Aristotelian principles, he argued in his work on the immortality of the soul (published in 1516) that the doctrine, although acceptable as an article of faith, was rationally indefensible. It was also morally dubious, because with the hope of reward and fear of punishment goes a servile mentality that is contrary to the very nature of virtue. The celebrated controversy around this work reverberated for a long time. His most important work was published posthumously (earlier publication would have put his life in danger). Its title was *On the Causes of Natural Effects*. It contained cogent refutations of the beliefs, then rampant in Europe, in demons, witchcraft, magical cures and miracles. He did not reject astrology, since he ranked the influence of planets as physical.

pons asinorum /pɒnz æsɪˈnɔːrəm/ Lat. the asses' bridge. This term, of ancient origin, came to be variously understood (or misunderstood), as follows. **1** a hurdle for dunces. A place where an ass, supposed to be stupid, would baulk. The expression, thus understood, has been thought to refer to the fifth proposition with its proof in the first book of Euclid's *Elements*. But it has also been thought to refer to the 47th proposition of that book, i.e. Pythagoras's theorem. **2** a help for dunces: a bridge-like diagram used already by Alexander of Aphrodisias, to show how to construct a passage from premisses to a given conclusion in a syllogism.

Popper /ˈpɔpər (Gm.)/, Sir Karl Raimund (1902–94) Austrian philosopher, who after emigration in the late 1930s taught in Christchurch, New Zealand, and after the Second World War at the London School of Economics. He is best known for his work in the philosophy of science and for his *The Open Society and Its Enemies* 1945 (5th rev. edn 1966).

Central to Popper's work is the theory of knowledge, which in his view is best studied by looking at the growth of scientific knowledge. Popper, inspired by Einstein's revolutionary overthrow of the work of Isaac Newton – the most impressive work in science until then – saw science as growing through conjecture and refutation. Science can aspire to tell us truths about the world. But its status is always tentative: while we aim at truth, we can never be sure that we have reached it.

Popper shared with the logical positivists of the Vienna Circle a strong interest in formal logic and in natural science, which was seen as a powerful exemplar of rationality. But he disagreed with many of their substantive views.

Popper stressed that testability was the hallmark of science, and he was critical of Freud and of Adler for claiming that their psychological theories were confirmed in situations where in fact they had not been genuinely put to the test. He was also critical of Marxists who had deprived Marx's theory of its scientific character by modifying it so that it could no longer be refuted by any actual historical developments. A theory has no scientific status unless it is falsifiable, i.e. unless it can be put to a test which could possibly refute it.

Falsifiability is a criterion of the scientific character of a theory. This may seem to be a parallel to the logical positivists' verifiability criterion, but this is not the case. Verifiability was for them a criterion of meaning. Popper was not concerned with meaning, and stressed that metaphysical statements (meaningless, according to the logical positivists) – which are not testable – may none the less be meaningful and that some had played an important role in the development of science.

Popper offered a dramatic solution to the classical problem of induction. David Hume had shown that inductive procedures are invalid, and yet induction seems to be the basic method of science, in that individual instances are taken to confirm general hypotheses. On Popper's account, science does not depend on induction, since it is not confirmation but refutation that is at the core of scientific method. The so-called problem of induction simply falls by the wayside.

Popper's approach to knowledge is also biologically orientated, and he has played a significant role in the development of 'evolutionary epistemology'. He argued that expectations – in part biologically based – play an important role in our knowledge and in the process of perception. There is a parallel with Kant; but for Popper, these expectations – including expectations about causality – are psychological, rather than categories of the understanding. Further, they are fallible, rather than giving us knowledge that is necessarily true. Popper also argued that there are continuities between human and animal problem-solving and learning by trial and error, and he draws parallels between his epistemology and Darwinian approaches within evolutionary theory. Popper has, however, insisted that human knowledge can be regarded as an element of an objectively existing 'third world' that is neither physical nor mental, but is constituted by the products of the human mind.

Popper's account of science, which also belongs to this third realm, gives a prominent role to the creative imagination; in this respect, he brings science closer to the popular image of artistic creativity. In work published in the late 1950s, he generalized his earlier emphasis upon falsifiability, stressing the importance of openness to criticism. Rational appraisal could thus be undertaken in areas other than science.

These ideas, and more technical arguments in epistemology and the philosophy of science, are treated in *The Logic of Scientific Discovery*, *Conjectures and Refutations*, *Objective Knowledge*, and the three-volume *Postscript to The Logic of Scientific Discovery*.

Popper is also known for his work on political philosophy. His *The Poverty of Historicism* is a critique of various widely accepted approaches to the methodology of the social sciences. Popper was especially critical of those who saw the social sciences as concerned with the discovery of long-term unconditional trends. Popper emphasized the conditional character of scientific prediction – its dependence upon universal laws and 'initial conditions'. He also defended methodological INDIVIDUALISM. This work was, in part, a settling of accounts with ideas influential in his native Austria; in part, an application of his own ideas about the character of science and of explanation to the problems of the social sciences.

Popper's *The Open Society and Its Enemies* is perhaps his best-known work. It was written during the Second World War, and sets out a case for liberal democracy by way of a detailed criticism of Plato and of Marx. Popper drew attention to illiberal aspects of Plato's views, and also took issue with the idea that anyone could possess the knowledge needed by the philosopher-rulers of Plato's *Republic*. Popper's own more positive ideas about politics stressed the fallibility of our knowledge and that our actions – and policy measures – always have unintended consequences. He proposed that we should adopt a strategy of 'piecemeal social engineering', in which attempts to solve our collective problems are followed up by the critical scrutiny of their actual outcomes: a process in which all citizens may play a part. Popper also offered a detailed critique of Marx's work. In part this draws on the theory of knowledge; in part Popper offers a step-by-step criticism of some of Marx's key ideas, and in part he criticizes any attempt to argue that there is a moral message inherent within the direction taken by human history. By contrast, Popper argues that while there is no intrinsic meaning to history, we can attempt to give history an ethical significance through political action.

Popper has also made many other important contributions to philosophy. He has argued for indeterminism and for a realistic interpretation of science, including quantum mechanics. He has written on the interpretation of probability theory and on natural deduction. He has written at some length on the mind–body problem, where he defends a form of interactionism (see notably *The Self and Its Brain* 1978, 1985, co-authored with John Eccles). Other themes include reductionism in science, which he values as a method, but which he thinks is seldom entirely successful; the status of evolutionary theory; the theory of language; and the methodology of the social sciences. He has also discussed the interpretation of the pre-Socratic philosophers. While Popper did not set out to develop a philosophical system, there are important and systematic interconnections between the different aspects of his views.

Popper's work has found an enthusiastic following among non-specialists. He rejects the view that philosophy is a self-contained technical specialism; rather, he believes that philosophical ideas have an important influence over practical affairs, and that we all take for granted ideas which would benefit from criticism. By intention, his style is simple and much of his work is accessible to the educated lay reader.

The reception of his work among professional philosophers has been rather mixed. Popper is recognized as an important figure, and many ideas of which he was initially an isolated champion have now become almost universally accepted. However, he has commonly been treated just as a philosopher of science, rather than as someone whose work on science is part of a wider project in epistemology and metaphysics. Within the philosophy of science, his work has come under criticism from many directions, including several writers once close to him, such as Feyerabend and Lakatos; his claim to have solved the problem of induction is not widely accepted. JSH

Porphyrian tree a device designed by Porphyry to show how reality and our concepts are ordered. Take a concept, such as substance (this is the classical illustration). It can be placed at the top of a finite tree with dichotomous branching, where each lower level is obtained by adding a specific difference (Figure 4).

Porphyry /ˈpɔːfɪrɪ/ (*c.* 232–305) disciple and biographer of Plotinus and editor of his works. He wrote a wide variety of works, moral and philological, and commentaries on Plato, Aristotle and Ptolemy. His introduction to his commentary on Aristotle's *Categories* (translated into Latin by Boethius), known as the *Isagoge* (Gr. introduction), became the basis for the teaching of logic in the Middle Ages, with its 'Porphyrian tree'. He improved on the theory of PREDICABLES. His many writings include an attack on Christian doctrine, and a plea, in *De abstinentia*, for a very strict kind of vegetarianism.

Port-Royal /pɔːtˈrɔɪəl (Eng.); pɔʀ-ʀwajal (Fr.)/ a monastery about 30 km south-west of Paris. With its growth, it was re-established under the same name in Paris in 1625, but use of the old premises was resumed in 1648. They were demolished in 1710, in the course of Louis XIV's persecution of the Jansenists. Attached to it, in various capacities, were a large number of members of the Arnauld family, most notably the abbess Angélique (1591–1661) and her brother Antoine (1612–94). He was the leading defender of Jansenism and,

Figure 4 Porphyrian tree

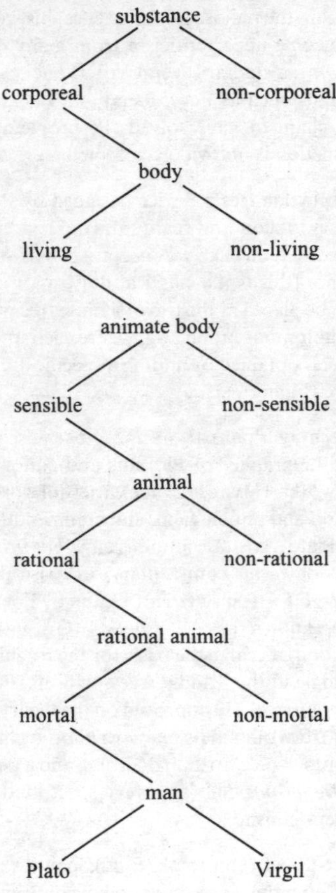

together with Pierre Nicole (1625–95), author of a textbook, *La logique ou l'art de penser* (Logic, or the art of thinking) 1662, 4th revised edn 1683, intended for use at Port-Royal and known as *The Port-Royal Logic*. It includes syllogistics, propositional logic (as transmitted from the Stoics by medieval authors), and Descartes's rules of method. It was the most widely used logic text well into the nineteenth century. Among the works emanating from this circle were a vast number of writings in defence of Jansenism, a universal grammar by Arnauld and Claude Lancelot (1615–95), Nicole's *Essais de morale* 1671–8 (Moral essays), and Pascal's *Lettres provinciales* 1657–8, a famous polemic against the morality of Jesuit confessors and moral theologians.

Posidonius /pɒsɪˈdəʊnɪəs/ (*c.* 135–*c.* 50 BC) the leading Stoic philosopher after Panaetius, against whom he reasserted the Stoic doctrine of universal conflagration and recurrence, and the claims of astrology and soothsaying. He modified Stoic orthodoxy by including Platonic and Aristotelian doctrines. He held high office at Rhodes, travelled widely, and was a polymath, leaving behind writings of encyclopedic scope on geography, history, physics, astronomy, psychology, etc., but none of them is extant.

positive /ˈpɔzɪtɪv/ (Lat. *ponere, positum* to put, to lay down) **1** *Positive* laws, moral rules or standards stand in contrast to *natural* ones. The positive ones result from a human or divine act of legislation or a decision, and may be seen as arbitrary, while the norms that are natural spring from the very nature of things. The positive law of a human society is the law which is created or enforced by human decisions or conventions.

This usage of *positive* was common in the seventeenth and eighteenth centuries, and is not entirely obsolete. It occurs in Cudworth, who writes of the distinction between things naturally good and evil on the one hand, and things positively good and evil on the other. He rejected the view that 'moral good and evil are *positive* things, good or bad because they are commanded or forbidden', and maintained that they are so 'in their own *nature*'.

In a closely related sense, a moral code or a legal code can be called positive in the sense that it is generally acknowledged as authoritative within a community or that there is general conformity to it.

Knowledge of what is positive in this sense is empirical. One has to find out what laws have been promulgated, or what 'the done thing' is within a community. In contrast, at least some of that which is natural can be known by the use of one's reason. This is why *positive* and *rational* can also be taken as contrasting terms. A positive law may lack rational justification.

Note: Posit*ive* law (etc.) ought to have been called posit*ed* law, as noted by SOTO. But for erring scribes, the medieval Latin *ius positivism*, which is anomalous, should have been *ius positum*.

2 Some writers distinguish *positive theology* or *positive religion*, ultimately supported by direct revelation or by earthly authority, from rational theology or religion. Again a contrast is implied between the *positive* and the *rational*.

3 Auguste Comte (1798–1857), the founder of philosophical positivism, described genuine knowledge as *positive* in the sense that it concerns itself with 'brute facts', that is, with whatever is given to us through experience. He contrasted the positive description and scientific explanation of facts with metaphysical and speculative pseudo-explanations.

4 Entirely distinct from all the above is the sense of *positive* which implies a contrast with *negative*. In these uses, *affirmative* can often be used as a synonym.

5 There are various further senses of *positive*. In mathematics, positive numbers are distinguished from negative numbers. In grammar, the positive form of an adjective, e.g. *wise*, is contrasted with the comparative and superlative forms, *wiser* and *wisest*.

positive freedom *See* NEGATIVE FREEDOM.

positive rights **1** rights recognized by positive law. The contrast is with *natural* rights, which do not depend on such recognition for their existence. **2** a person's right that another party do something. The contrast is with a *negative* right – a person's right that another party refrain from doing something.

positive utilitarianism *See* UTILITARIANISM.

positivism *n.* **1** *Legal positivism* is the theory that the law of the state is based on the will of the holder of sovereign power in the state. This will comes to expression primarily in acts of legislation and (tacit) authoritative acceptance of judicial decisions. The idea of a higher law is regarded as irrelevant from a legal point of view, although not from a moral point of view. 'The existence of a law is one thing; its merit or demerit another', according to John Austin (1790–1859) who, following Bentham, is the most important proponent of the theory in the anglophone world.

2 *Moral positivism*: theological moral positivism, also known as theological voluntarism, or as the divine command theory, is the theory that God's arbitrary commands make certain actions right and others wrong. Sociological moral positivism is defined as follows in Karl Popper's *The Open Society and its Enemies:* 'the theory that there is no moral standard but the one which exists; that what is, is reasonable and good; and therefore, that might is right.' By 'the moral standard which exists' is meant the one actually prevailing in a society. At first sight, theories of this kind have a strong point in their apparent realism, in that they refrain from making any assumptions of a higher law. They also at first sight have a weak point in their apparent conformism and submissiveness to the powers that be.

3 *Positivist philosophy*: beginning with Auguste Comte, *positive philosophy* and *positivism* are used to designate a world-view which is conceived of as being in tune with modern science, and which accordingly rejects superstition, religion, and metaphysics as pre-scientific forms of thought which will cede to positive science as mankind continues its progress.

According to positivist theories of knowledge, all knowledge is ultimately based on sense-experience. There cannot be different kinds of knowledge. All genuine inquiry is concerned with the description and explanation of empirical facts. There is therefore no difference in principle between the methods of the physical and the social sciences, for instance.

Empiricist philosophers like Francis Bacon and David Hume can be regarded as precursors of positivism. In the nineteenth century important representatives, apart from Comte, were Herbert Spencer, Ernst Haeckel, Richard Avenarius and Ernst Mach. Positivist ideas gained a foothold in the public mind, and were accepted by many radical philosophers and progressive intellectuals: in England, for instance, there were George Lewes, George Eliot, John Stuart Mill, etc. From the 1850s onward, Comtean positivism gained a marked influence in France, and came to expression in anti-clerical and anti-conservative politics. This was even more the case all over Latin America. The ideas behind the revolution in Brazil in 1889 were positivist, and the Brazilian flag carries the positivist motto 'Order and Progress'.

In sharp contrast, there is no comparable political dimension in the predominant variety of twentieth-century positivism, that is, the philosophical outlook advocated by members of the VIENNA CIRCLE, e.g. Schlick, Carnap, Neurath, and, under their influence, such British philosophers as A. J. Ayer. It became known as *logical positivism*, a label first given to the movement in articles by E. Kaila and Å. Petzäll, two Nordic sympathizers, around 1930. This tendency, also known as logical empiricism, differed from earlier versions in its approach to the exact sciences (logic, mathematics, geometry, etc.) but agreed with the earlier varieties in its empiricism and emphatic rejection of metaphysics.

Positivism has been strongly attacked by theologians, Marxist-Leninists, feminists, etc. for being atheistic, bourgeois, androcentric, etc. 'Positivism' is one of those philosophical terms which, like 'metaphysics', 'reductionism' and 'scholasticism', have come to be freely used for polemical purposes in senses that do not readily allow a clear definition.

Explicit avowals of allegiance to positivism and empiricism have become less common in the later decades of the twentieth century, but theories of a positivist or empiricist inspiration remain at the centre of philosophical interest.

positivism dispute an important debate about the nature of the social sciences that took place in Germany in the 1960s. A number of major contributions were collected in a volume published in 1969 (*Der Positivismusstreit in der deutschen Soziologie*, transl. as *The Positivism Dispute in German Sociology*). It was a controversy between critical rationalism (Albert, Popper) and critical theory (Adorno, Habermas) about objectivity and value-freedom, about the methods of social sciences, and about the social and political role played by social science.

possibilism *See* ACTUALISM.

possible worlds An early theoretical use of the concept occurs in Malebranche *Traité de la nature et de la grâce* (*Treatise on Nature and Grace*) 1674, I, §13; *Entretiens sur la métaphysique* 1688, 2,3 (Dialogues on metaphysics): our world is one among the many possible worlds that God could have created. This world, which he did create, differs from the others by the greater simplicity of its laws. The concept is also important in Leibniz's philosophy. In the *Theodicy* 1710 he argues that our actual world, having been created by God, a being with all perfections, is the best of all the worlds that he might have created, i.e. the best possible world.

When explaining the modal concepts of possibility, contingency and necessity, the following pattern of explanation, originating with Leibniz, has proved to be very attractive: a proposition p is necessary if p is true in all possible worlds; a proposition p is possible if p is true in some possible world. The advantage of this pattern of analysis is that the relations between modal concepts are, in a sense, reduced to the relations between the concepts of 'all' and 'some', which are accounted for in modern predicate logic.

Many contemporary philosophers and logicians find the idiom of possible worlds convenient but regard it as a figurative mode of expression only, whilst others, among whom David Lewis is foremost, argue that there *is* a plurality of worlds.

post hoc ergo propter hoc /ˈpəʊst hɔk ˈɜːgəʊ ˈprɔptə hɔk/ Lat. after this, therefore because of this. Inferences of this kind are unsound.

post-industrial society a term first used by Daniel Bell in a lecture in Boston in 1962, entitled 'The post-industrial society: a speculative view of the United States in 1985'. It gained currency through his book *The Coming of Post-Industrial Society* 1973. The ongoing transition from industrial society will lead to a society with the following characteristics: (1) supply of services (health, education, public administration) is predominant, and production of material goods in agriculture and manufacturing industry no longer absorbs the majority of the work force; (2) a new division of labour gives a central place to technicians and professionals; (3) a more immediate influence of theory on society; (4) long-term forecasting of technological change and its social impact; (5) scientific methods of decision-making, rather than intuitive ones based on moral or cultural traditions.

post-modern *adj.* 'Modern' can be used to designate various post-medieval historical periods. Also, for each historical period described as modern, there are many different features (styles, trends, doctrines) that can be considered essential to its modern character. Moreover, 'post' may suggest either a break or a continuation.

It follows that 'post-modern' and 'post-modernism' can mean many different things, and an author who wishes to be understood will have to explain the intended sense. This precaution is often neglected. Many writers begin with an admission that they have no clear definition of post-modernism and that it is not clear what is covered by the term, but then proceed to celebrate it at length – a curious procedure. There have been complaints of 'vacuous academic posturing' in this context.

Some clusters of meaning can, however, be discerned. When Jean Baudrillard (1929–), French sociologist, cultural critic and media intellectual, claims that contemporary culture is post-modern, the word denotes fragmentation and promiscuous trivialization of values, symbols, images: its most characteristic manifestation is the commercial advertisements shown in television broadcasts.

In architecture, where the word first gained currency, post-modernism denotes a rejection of the functionalism and brutalism of modern architecture (high-rise slums; impersonal box-like office blocks), together with a preference for aimless eclecticism. In the arts, 'post-modernism' denotes a break with, or a continuation of, modernism. It is said that whereas modernism assumes that there is hidden meaning or truth and is engaged in a search for it, post-modernism, able to recognize absurdity when it sees it, has recourse to pastiche, many-layered irony, flippancy, etc.

In philosophy, Lyotard's influential *The Postmodern Condition* 1979 uses the term to designate 'the deconstruction of the METANARRATIVES of modernity'.

postulate /ˈpɒstjulɪt/ *n.*; /ˈpɒstjʊleɪt/ *vb.* (Lat. *postulatum* requirement) In Euclid, five postulates are added to the definitions and the axioms. The distinction between axioms and postulates is not made explicit, but the axioms, also called common notions, are general truths regarded as self-evident, whilst the postulates are specific to geometry. Since then, the term has been used variously. The basic idea is that a postulate need not or cannot be proved.

In contemporary work on formal theories a similar distinction is made between the axioms of the logical part of the theory, and those of the non-logical part, which are called postulates. Some writers have used 'postulate' for those basic assumptions which assert the existence of something, and 'axiom' for those which do not. Others reserve the word 'postulate' for *practical* principles, i.e. assumptions about what it is possible to *do*, and use 'axiom' for *theoretical* principles.

Kant described the assumptions of God, freedom and immortality as postulates of practical reason. These practical postulates are requirements which, in Kant's theory, a person must be entitled to regard as possible to satisfy, since otherwise it would be impossible to fulfil one's moral duty. But the practical postulates cannot be accepted from a theoretical standpoint, only from a practical standpoint, when the person is regarded as an agent.

potentiality *n.* (in Aristotle) a power within a thing which strives to become actual, manifest itself. In *Metaphysics* Book Θ, the *locus classicus*, the key examples given by Aristotle are biological. A spider is a potential weaver of webs. This is true even if some, many, or indeed most spiders are not actual weavers – perhaps most perish before they reach the weaving stage.

S is potentially P implies *it is possible that S become P.* But the converse does not hold.

Ant. actuality.

pour soi /puʀ swa (Fr.)/ Fr. for itself, for oneself. *See* *AN SICH*.

power set The power set of a given set S is the set of all the subsets of S. For example, let S be the set {1,2,3}. Here is a list of all the subsets of S: {0}, {1}, {2}, {3}, {1,2}, {1,3}, {2,3}, {1,2,3}.

These subsets are the elements of the power set of S. S has three elements, and the power set of S has $2^3 = 8$ elements. It is easy to show that in general, if S has n elements, then the power set of S will have 2^n elements.

The concept of a power set also applies to infinite sets. It can be proved that the power set of a given infinite set S has a cardinality greater than that of S itself. That is, there is no one-to-one correspondence between the elements of S, and the elements of the power set of S. In turn, the power set of S has a power set greater than it, and so on. It follows that there is an infinite number of different orders of infinity.

practical (Gr. *praktikos* pertaining to action) *adj.* The *practical* is whatever relates to action, in contrast to the *theoretical* which relates to thought.

Note: To call an activity a *practice* suggests that it is customary or habitual; to use 'practice' without such a connotation, for activity more generally, usually reveals an influence from Marxist theory.

practical philosophy/theoretical philosophy This distinction reflects the contrast between action and contemplation, and is at least as old as Aristotle. In modern times, Christian Wolff assigned ethics, economics and politics to practical philosophy, and let theoretical philosophy comprise ontology, psychology, cosmology and theology – a structuring clearly discernible in Kant's *Critique of Pure Reason*.

practice *See* PRACTICAL.

pragmatic paradox a statement which, although self-consistent, is such that the act of making it shows it to be false: for instance, the statement made by saying 'I remember nothing at all' or 'No words ever pass my lips'. *See also* SELF-REFUTATION.

pragmatics (Gr. *pragma* deed, action) *n. sing.* a branch of the study of linguistic symbols. Pragmatics can be defined as the study of symbols in their relation to the speakers, listeners and social contexts. Pragmatics is contrasted with *syntax* (originally *syntactics*), the study of the interrelation of symbols; and *semantics*, the study of their relation to that which is symbolized. This terminology became established in the 1930s through the writings of Charles Morris.

pragmatism *n.* Pragmatism can be briefly described as the theory that a proposition is true if holding it to be so is practically successful or advantageous. Pragmatism began in the early 1870s, with C. S. Peirce's adoption of Alexander Bain's suggestion that beliefs are habits of acting rather than representations of reality. This suggestion led William James to think of a true belief as one which leads to successful action, to a theory of truth as 'what works'. The counter-intuitive consequences of this theory have led many people (notably Bertrand Russell) to claim that pragmatists confuse the pursuit of truth with the pursuit of pleasure. Pragmatists, however, do not see this as a confusion. On the naturalistic, Darwinian view put forward by John Dewey there is no such thing as the disinterested pursuit of truth: no interesting separation between practical deliberation and theoretical inquiry. All thinking is a matter of problem-solving, and we can simply abandon accounts of inquiry which rely on the notion of 'representation of reality'. James and Dewey thought that many of the traditional problems of philosophy were created by the uncritical use of dualisms (theory–practice, reality–appearance, mind–body, etc.) which should be repudiated, and that critics of pragmatism tended to take these out-of-date dualisms for granted. Analogies have often been found between the anti-foundationalist, anti-essentialist, contextualist tenor of James's and Dewey's philosophy and similar motifs in the later writings of Wittgenstein. In recent decades many theses associated with James's pragmatism and Dewey's naturalism have been defended in the writings of contemporary American philosophers including W. V. O. Quine, Donald Davidson, Hilary Putnam, Richard Rorty and others. RR

praxeology *n.* the name given by T. Kotarbinski to the general theory of efficient action in his *Praxiology* 1963, which analyses action-concepts (simple, complex, co-operative, etc.) and aims to establish a 'grammar of action', i.e. rules for successful action, on the basis of empirical inquiry.

The term was introduced by A. Espinas in the 1890s for a general theory of action, and used in a similar sense by the economist L. von Mises in *Nationalökonomie* 1940. Alternative spelling: *praxiology*.

praxis (Gr. *praxis* action, doing, activity) *n.* action, activity, contrasted by Aristotle with *poiēsis* and *theoria*.

Praxis is an important concept in Marx. In the *Economic and Philosophical Manuscripts* he sometimes contrasts it with mere labour: it is for him and later Marxist writers (e.g. Labriola, Gramsci, Lukács and Sartre) the free, conscious, creative, essentially human activity, alone capable of generating knowledge and a new and better social order. Habermas reserves the term for communicative interaction between people, which is governed by moral norms, and contrasts praxis with instrumental action, e.g. in the production of commodities, which is governed by technical rules.

precepts of justice The three traditional precepts of justice (*praecepta iuris*) are: *honeste vivere, neminem laedere, suum cuique tribuere*, that is: live in a morally upright manner, do harm to nobody, render to each what is his own (or: what is due to him).

These three precepts have a long history. They occur in Ulpian (d. 228), one of the leading authorities in Roman Law, and were included at the beginning of Emperor Justinian's *Institutions*, first published in 533. This was a textbook of jurisprudence prepared by a committee of Roman lawyers and scholars under the auspices of the Emperor. It has been in constant use since the Middle Ages.

precognition *n.* PARANORMAL knowledge of future events.

pre-critical *adj.* The word is mainly used to refer to Kant's early philosophy, before he developed the ideas presented in the *Critique of Pure Reason* 1781.

predestination *n.* According to the theological doctrine of predestination, which takes its main scriptural support from Romans 8 and 9 and Ephesians 1, God has already decided for each soul whether it will be saved or condemned. This doctrine can be found in Augustine and his many followers in the Middle Ages, in the Protestant reformers Luther, Zwingli and Calvin, in the Thirty-Nine Articles of the Church of England, Jansenius, Pascal, etc. It is rejected in Pelagianism and Arminianism, and in many theologies formulated in recent centuries.

predicables *n. pl.* These are the types of general term that can be used as predicates. In the *Topics* 1: 4,5,8, Aristotle distinguishes five (see Table 15). The theory of predicables that flourished in medieval scholasticism was based on Boethius's Latin translation of Porphyry's introduction to his commentary on Aristotle's *Categories*. There the division, somewhat revised, is as in Table 16.

predicament *n.* (in medieval logic) category. The word comes from the Latin *praedicamentum*, used by Boethius to translate the Greek *katēgoria*.

predicate *n.* that which is asserted or denied of the subject in a sentence; that which is asserted or denied of the thing(s) referred to in a sentence.

predicate logic originated with Frege, and has proved remarkably fruitful. First-order predicate logic adds to propositional logic the logic of: (1) sentences that ascribe a predicate to an individual (e.g., *Socrates is wise*, which can be symbolized Ws); (2) sentences that ascribe a relation to individuals (e.g., *Plato was a disciple of Socrates*, which can be symbolized Dps); (3) quantified sentences which say that a certain predicate or relation applies to some individual (e.g., *At least one person is wise*, which can be symbolized $(\exists x)Wx$); (4) quantified sentences which say that a certain predicate or relation applies to every individual (e.g., *Every philosopher is wise* can be symbolized $(\forall x)(Px \supset Wx)$); (5)

Table 15 The predicables (1)

Greek	*Latin*	*English*
horos	*definitio*	definition of the essence (e.g. man is a rational animal)
idion	*proprium*	a distinctive property (e.g. man is a laughing animal)
genos	*genus*	genus (e.g. man is an animal)
diaphora	*differentia*	a differentiating property (e.g. man is rational)
symbebēkos	*accidens*	an accidental property (e.g. man is white)

Table 16 The predicables (2)

Greek	*Latin*	*English*
genos	*genus*	genus
eidos	*species*	species
diaphora	*differentia*	a differentiating property
idion	*proprium*	a distinctive property
symbebēkos	*accidens*	an accidental property

multiply-quantified sentences in which the variables stand for individuals (e.g., *Everything is caused by something*, which can be symbolized $(\forall x)(\exists y)(Cxy)$).

All the sentences above are about individual entities. Second-order predicate logic adds to the above the logic of sentences about predicates and relations. *There is a predicate that applies both to Socrates and Plato*, can be symbolized $(\exists F)(Fs\ \&\ Fp)$; *There is a property that belongs to everything* can be symbolized $(\exists F)(\forall x)Fx$. *Syn.* functional calculus, predicate calculus, logic of quantification.

predicative *See* ATTRIBUTIVE.

prediction paradox A teacher announces to the class that there will be a surprise test some day during the following week. This, the argument goes, is totally impossible. For, the pupils argue, if the test has not been given before Friday, it is bound to be given on Friday, and will not then come as a surprise. Therefore, it cannot be given on Friday. The last possible day when the test can be given is therefore Thursday. But by the same reasoning, it cannot be given on Thursday either, and again, by parity of reasoning, it cannot be given on any day of the week. It follows that it is impossible to give this surprise test. And yet, it seems perfectly possible.

The paradox has been traced to Stockholm in the early 1940s. The authorities announced that some day during the following week there would be an unexpected air-raid alarm at which everyone should go to an assigned air-raid shelter, as part of a civil-defence exercise. It was then observed by a high-school mathematics teacher that this seemed totally impossible. The paradox came to notice internationally, probably through one of his pupils who, a few years later, was a student at Princeton.

preface paradox In the preface to his latest book, the author modestly warns that he has good reasons for thinking that some of the opinions in the book (call them O_1, O_2, O_3, . . . O_n), are mistaken. And yet, the author does not believe that O_1 is mistaken – if he did, he would have revised the text; nor that O_2 is mistaken – for the same reason; and so on. So the author believes not only that there is *some* mistake, but also that there is *none*!

The paradox of the preface was formulated by D. C. Makinson in an article with that title in *Analysis* 25 (1965), pp. 205–7.

preference According to preference-utilitarianism, satisfaction of preferences is intrinsically good, and should be maximized. But do *all* kinds of preferences deserve equally to be taken into account?

In *Taking Rights Seriously* 1977 (2nd rev. edn 1978), Ronald Dworkin distinguishes *personal* preferences from *external* preferences. A personal preference is a preference about what I do or get; an external preference is a preference about what other people do or get. Dworkin argues that the right of individuals to equal consideration and respect concerning the assignment of goods and opportunities means that their personal preferences are to be respected, but not their external ones. External preferences should be ignored, in order to avoid 'double counting': in a utilitarian calculation in which everyone is to count for one, my wish to be rich should be weighed in, and so should another person's wish to be rich. But my wish that the other person be poor should not be weighed in. In the debate, critics have voiced doubts about finding a clear line of demarcation between the two kinds of preference.

preference-utilitarianism moral theory according to which the good consists in the satisfaction of people's preferences, and the rightness of an action depends directly or indirectly on its being productive of such satisfaction. Like other kinds of consequentialism, the theory has satisficing (SATISFICE) and maximizing variants. The latter are the more common ones: the more people get what they want, the better. *Syn.* preference-consequentialism.

premise, premiss *n.* A premise or premiss is a statement which in an argument is not itself inferred but belongs to a set of statements *from* which a conclusion is inferred.

prenex normal form A formula in predicate logic is said to be in prenex normal form if all quantifiers are clustered at the beginning of the formula (hence the 'pre-') and every variable in the open sentence that constitutes the remaining part of the formula is bound (hence the '-nex' from Lat. *nexus* bond) by a quantifier.

It can be proved that for every formula in predicate logic there is an equivalent formula in prenex normal form. For many important proofs about predicate logic it is therefore enough to consider formulae in that form.

prescience /'presɪəns/ *n.* foreknowledge.

prescientific /priːsaɪən'tɪfɪk/ *adj.* pertaining to a stage prior or inferior to science.

prescription *n.* **1** a piece of advice, an instruction, a rule, relating to conduct. **2** in law, the creation or extinction of the possibility of bringing an action because of the lapse of a period of time.

prescriptivism *n.* Prescriptivism is a theory of the language of morals proposed by R. M. Hare. Its central thesis is that moral judgements are essentially action-guiding.

Hare's *The Language of Morals* 1952 distinguishes two kinds of meaning that the statements in our language can have: descriptive and evaluative. Statements with evaluative meaning can be used to guide action. In this respect, they are similar to imperatives. Moral statements have evaluative meaning. They differ, however, from other statements that have an action-guiding force by also being universalizable: when making a moral judgement about a particular matter, we imply that the same judgement also applies in relevantly similar circumstances, and there is scope for rational criticism in that a person who refuses to apply the same evaluation in relevantly similar circumstances is guilty of inconsistency.

Moral principles cannot, however, be

criticized as being inconsistent with matters of fact, since statements of fact cannot alone imply ought-statements. For the same reason the evaluative meaning of a statement is not implied solely by its descriptive meaning. It follows that our moral principles cannot have an ultimate justification in matters of fact. Ultimately, adopting a moral principle is a matter of personal commitment.

presence, metaphysics of *See* METAPHYSICS OF PRESENCE.

pre-Socratic philosophy The earliest Western philosophers were bold innovators who for the first time attempted to explain natural phenomena in exclusively natural terms. Breaking away from mythological explanation, these early Greek thinkers sought simple material principles which could account for the complexity of the world. Although the pre-Socratics formed a small group of thinkers from widely scattered Greek city-states, their ideas seem to have been widely disseminated among Greek intellectuals. The pre-Socratics typically dealt with natural philosophy, i.e. with issues that would today be dealt with largely by natural science. They often described the creation of a 'cosmos' or world-order from pre-existing matter and, in connection with some theory of matter and change, explained astronomical, meteorological, geological and zoological phenomena. They flourished in the sixth and fifth centuries BC, but the term 'pre-Socratic' is not strictly chronological, being used also for contemporaries of Socrates who were unaffected by the Socratic revolution in philosophy – a revolution that made human and ethical issues central to philosophical discussions.

One of the main problems in dealing with the pre-Socratics is the scarcity of evidence. No writing of a pre-Socratic philosopher has survived intact, and scholars can assemble only separate quotations ('fragments') of their actual words. In some cases, moreover, it is not clear whether the fragments are direct quotations or paraphrases, or what the original context was. In addition to studying the fragments, however, we can consult the works of ancient philosophers who had read the pre-Socratics' works. Here Aristotle is the best source, since he often deals at length and philosophically with his predecessors' thought. His colleague Theophrastus wrote a long treatise on the history of philosophical views on various topics, which unfortunately is lost. But most later collections of philosophers' views (doxographies) draw on Theophrastus's study, either directly or indirectly. In addition, from the Hellenistic period onwards there existed a tradition of philosophical biography, which supplies some information – not all of it reliable. In general, scholars place the most emphasis on the fragments of pre-Socratics; with secondary sources they use 'source criticism' to sort out the contributions – and distortions – of different interpreters in a tradition. Thus it is a difficult task to reconstruct pre-Socratic views, but with the aid of modern historical techniques we can understand the pre-Socratics better than our ancient secondary sources did.

The history of pre-Socratic thought shows a dialectical development. The philosophers of Miletus – Thales, Anaximander and Anaximenes – all seem to have explained natural phenomena as the result of a differentiation of an original material substance or *archē*: water, the boundless, or air, respectively. For the Pythagoreans, by contrast, everything was in some sense number. Heraclitus implicitly criticizes the appeal to a single *archē* by showing that if a single substance changes into all other substances, the original substance is no more real than its successors; what is real is not the original substance, but the law of transformation.

Parmenides and the Eleatic School, on the other hand, reject process on the grounds that any state that presupposes not-being is impossible, and change presupposes coming to be from not-being.

After Parmenides, natural philosophers rule out the kind of transformation of substances envisaged by the Milesians and Heraclitus: the basic substances must not come into being or perish – but there must be a plurality of them to account for change. Changes will then consist of temporary rearrangements of everlasting substances. Thus Empedocles posits four everlasting elements, Anaxagoras an indefinite number of elemental stuffs, and the atomists an infinite number of everlasting discrete material particles. Throughout the history of pre-Socratic thought certain derivative theories, especially of meteorological phenomena (i.e. of the phenomena in the sky generally), remained fairly constant; but theories of matter and the cosmos showed wide variations in response to perceived theoretical problems.

In the pre-Socratics, philosophy is largely scientific inquiry, and for their approach to science they have been both praised and blamed – praised for their interest in empirical research as against religious speculation, and blamed for speculating rather than conducting empirical research. It is true that the pre-Socratics were not rigorous observers or experimenters, but we should remember that theory is an important part of science, and the pre-Socratics did produce increasingly complex theories which aimed at explaining empirical phenomena. Their theories were designed to meet theoretical objections rather than to facilitate empirical inquiries, but even so they did anticipate many modern theories, including basic number theory, basic music theory, the theory of elements and chemical combination, the theory of evolution, cultural anthropology, the explanation of the phases of the moon and solar and lunar eclipses, and the atomic theory of matter.

Perhaps their most important contribution, however, is not to be found in any concrete advance, but in an attitude they embody: their single-minded and uninhibited pursuit of truth through reason established an ideal for all future philosophy. *See also* ANAXAGORAS, ANAXIMANDER; ANAXIMENES, DEMOCRITUS, EMPEDOCLES, HERACLITUS, LEUCIPPUS, MELISSUS, PARMENIDES, PYTHAGORAS, THALES, XENOPHANES, ZENO. DG

presupposition *n. p presupposes q* can be distinguished from *p entails q* as follows: if q is a necessary condition for the truth, simply, of p, we say that *p entails q*. If q is a necessary condition for the truth-or-falsity of p, we say that *p presupposes q*. This is how P. F. Strawson explained the distinction in his *Introduction to Logical Theory* 1952. To illustrate the point: consider 'Jack beats his wife' and 'Jack does not beat his wife'. The question of which of the two statements is true does not arise if Jack has no wife. Each statement presupposes that Jack has a wife. This is contrary to Russell's analysis, according to which each statement entails that Jack has a wife and, since Jack does not, each statement entails a falsehood, and hence each is false.

pretend *vb.* (in older usage) to *affirm*, to *claim* – without any connotation of insincerity or deceit.

prevarication /prɪværɪˈkeɪʃən/ (Lat. *praevaricari* to straddle) *n.* betraying a client by colluding with the opposing party; in a wider sense: evasion of issues by deception or equivocation.

Price /praɪs/, Henry Habberley (1899–1985) professor of philosophy at Oxford 1935–59. *Perception* 1932 and later works give an empiricist account of our knowledge of the external world by means of a theory of sense-data. He also took a positive interest in parapsychology. Among his other works are *Hume's Theory of the External World* 1940 and *Essays in the Philosophy of Religion* 1972.

Price, Richard (1723–91) Price was a Presbyterian minister. He published works on probability and life insurance which were soon put to practical use. He was a political radical whose writings in support of the American (1776) and French (1789) revolutions were widely read. As a moral philosopher, his *Review of the Principal Questions and Difficulties in Morals* 1758 was the most important defence of ethical rationalism in response to the objections raised by his friend David Hume. Price took the concept of obligation to be basic to morality, objective, and *a priori*, i.e. not based on sense-experience but grasped by rational insight.

Prichard /ˈprɪtʃəd/, Harold Arthur (1871–1947) English philosopher, professor at Oxford 1928–37. He cast doubt on the possibility of 'moral theory', arguing that our insight into our moral duties can only rest on direct intuition. An influential formulation of this view was 'Does Moral Philosophy Rest on a Mistake?' 1912, reprinted in *Moral Obligation* 1949. In the theory of knowledge, he rejected Kantianism in favour of a more realist view.

Priestley /ˈpriːstlɪ/, Joseph (1733–1804) an advocate of Enlightenment ideas, in opposition to the established religious and political order. Priestley was at first a Presbyterian minister, but eventually became a Unitarian. In 1782 he published a *History of the Corruptions of Christianity*. He was very successful and highly esteemed as a teacher in dissenting academies. His writings on educational reform opposed the idea of a uniform educational system, and advocated a modernized curriculum, in which theology and classics would be reduced and other subjects, especially history, promoted in order to meet the needs of society. Priestley is now best known for his scientific interests: he studied the nature of electricity and was one of the discoverers of oxygen.

Philosophically, Priestley was particularly influenced by Hartley's associationism. He regarded it as superior to the theories of Reid and other Scottish contemporaries in which explanations are made in terms of a large number of instinctive beliefs which, in Priestley's view, can and should be explained in terms of mental associations. Priestley developed this associationism into a defence of both materialism and determinism. He has been described as the founder of the modern doctrine of the perfectibility of man. His belief in human progress came to expression through his political writings, which advocated individual liberty, complete religious toleration (extending it, unlike Locke, even to atheists and Roman Catholics), democracy (*Essay on the First Principles of Government and the Nature of . . . Liberty* 1769) and later, opposed by Burke, the ideals of the French Revolution.

prima facie /praɪmə ˈfeɪʃɪ/ Lat. at first appearance, at first view; prior to closer investigation.

primary and secondary qualities This is a division between qualities which are objectively present in the world, entirely independently of any perceiving mind, and those which are subjective and mind-dependent, although caused by the object perceived. In ancient times, a distinction of this kind was made by Democritus, and in the modern era, with the birth of modern science, it can be found in Galileo, Descartes, Boyle and Newton. There are, however, two conceptions of secondary qualities. They can be understood as directly experienced *sensory qualities*, or as *powers* to produce certain experiences.

In Locke's *Essay Concerning Human Understanding* 1690, solidity, shape, extension, motion, rest and number are said to be primary qualities, which inhere in the external object; the secondary qualities are the powers in objects to affect our senses, to produce experiences of sensory qualities (colour, sound, etc.). In other authors secondary qualities are identified with the directly experienced sensory qualities.

The background to the primary/secondary distinction is a conception of the physical world as being tasteless, odourless and colourless, describable in terms of particles and forces, and as being conceived as it really is by disregarding our subjective reactions to it. There is some plausibility in the view that the real world is the world of primary qualities, which would be there even if we were not. But it can be argued that this view merely gives a privileged status to the sense of touch. Berkeley and later phenomenalists instead took the view that *all* sensible qualities are equally mind-dependent.

The distinction has many facets – starting with Hume, philosophers have compared values to secondary qualities – and it remains on the philosophical agenda. In the 1990s, the discussion is often in terms of *response-dependent* concepts. *See also* QUALITIES.

prime matter (in Aristotelian philosophy) the mere potentiality for receiving forms.

JM

prime mover (in Aristotelian philosophy) God, seen as the efficient and final cause of the universe. JM

prisoner's dilemma Two prisoners, A and B, are interrogated by police. They cannot communicate with each other. The police need a confession from at least one of the prisoners. In the following variant of the original story, the following three conditions apply: (1) if neither prisoner confesses, both will be acquitted; (2) if both prisoners confess, both will be sentenced to two years in prison; (3) if one prisoner confesses and the other does not, the one who confesses will be acquitted and get a substantial reward, and the one who does not confess will be sentenced to ten years in prison.

In this situation, A would reason as follows: 'Suppose B confesses. Then, if I confess, I will get two years, and if I do not confess, I will get ten years. So, in this case, I am better off if I confess. But suppose B does not confess. Then, if I confess, I will be acquitted and get a reward, and if I do not confess, I will be acquitted but get no reward. So, in this case, I am also better off if I confess.'

So, on the strength of this reasoning, A is better off if A confesses, no matter what B does. (Confession is said to be a *dominant* strategy for A.) Since the situation is entirely symmetrical, B will conduct the same reasoning, and conclude that he too ought to confess. It seems then entirely rational for each of them to confess. This will put them in prison for two years. And yet, if neither had confessed, they would both have been acquitted. The upshot is that the 'rational' decision does not lead to the best outcome.

The assertion that the outcome is not the best is standardly explained in terms of *pareto-superiority*: it means that there is another possible outcome that makes at least one party – in this case both – better off without making any party worse off.

The details of the story can vary. What is essential is that A and B each rank the four outcomes in this order of preference: acquittal with reward > acquittal without

Figure 5 Prisoner's dilemma

	A does not confess	A confesses
B does not confess	second best for both	best for A worst for B
B confesses	best for B worst for A	third best for both

reward > two years in prison > ten years in prison.

Generalizing, the same problem arises whenever the outcomes of the decisions are ranked in the same way and the parties cannot influence each other. This can be illustrated by a diagram, as in Figure 5. Many other situations produce a similar ordering of preferences, for instance when two hostile countries, who do not communicate between themselves, deliberate about nuclear disarmament.

The problem arising from this type of situation was first noted *c.* 1950 by the social psychologist Merrill Flood and the economist Melvin Dresher. A. W. Tucker provided the standard illustration. It has been at the centre of a wide-ranging debate in decision theory and in moral and political philosophy. It is not in essence a problem about egoism and altruism: the problem arises as soon as the parties' preference ordering is the one given in Figure 5, and this is possible also between altruistic agents. The problem is one of cooperation and non-cooperation: rational deliberation in this type of situation leads to a decision not to cooperate, even though this will produce a worse outcome for both parties than a decision by each to cooperate. It is a situation in which individual rationality is also collective irrationality.

The problem-situation changes if the two parties A and B think that they will be in a similar quandary *vis-à-vis* each other on further occasions. Then an additional consideration enters into the reasoning of each: 'If I, A, let B down this time, then I may be worse off next time than if I do not.' In such circumstances it may be rational for each party to cooperate.

Syn. exchange dilemma.

privacy In political philosophy and jurisprudence, writers in the United States use 'privacy' in a special sense, for the rights of an individual, and particularly those that are supposed to be recognized in the Constitution of the United States (especially in its First, Fourth and Fifth Amendments) and which can therefore be upheld by the US Supreme Court to protect individuals from legislative or judicial interference. Privacy thus understood can be defined as sovereignty over personal decisions, a right to individual autonomy. *See also* PUBLIC AND PRIVATE.

private language argument an argument that appears to be proposed in Wittgenstein's *Philosophical Investigations* 1953. To use a language is a rule-governed activity. The question is in what sense, if any, a completely isolated individual can be said to follow (or violate) a rule.

Wittgenstein distinguished between habits and rules. An isolated individual can of course have certain *habits*, but continuation or discontinuation of these is not a matter of being right or wrong. It is possible to distinguish between what is correct and incorrect only if a *rule* can be invoked; but following or breaking a rule makes sense only if there is social interaction and communication, and in this sense there can be no such thing as solitary rule-following. Since the use of language consists in following (at least for the most part) the rules of the language, it follows that there cannot be a private language.

From this follows that using a language is inconsistent with solipsism, and generally with the view that we can use language to talk about things that are in principle inaccessible to others. This has wide-ranging implications for traditional theories of knowledge, which tend to assume that knowledge is erected on the basis of experiences that are strictly private.

Since the 1950s there has been a continuing debate, re-activated in the 1980s through Kripke's discussion in his *Wittgenstein and Rule-Following*, about what Wittgenstein meant, and whether what he meant is tenable.

proairesis /prəʊˈaɪrəsɪs/ (Gr. choice, preference) *n.* There is an important discussion in Aristotle's *Nicomachean Ethics* 3, 3 1111^a–1113^a, where this is defined as desire, guided by deliberation, for something that is in our power. Also written *prohairesis*.

pro-attitude *n.* a favourable attitude. The word gained currency through P. Nowell-Smith, *Ethics* 1954, but it was already in use in the 1930s.

probabilism *n.* **1** (in moral theology) the view that, given conflicting opinions on a particular moral question, it is permissible to follow any probable opinion (usually one supported by a theologian whose views are considered to carry some authority), even if an opposing opinion is more probable. Probabilism in this sense was accepted by a number of influential Roman Catholic moral theologians, chiefly Jesuits, especially in the sixteenth and seventeenth centuries. This doctrine, and the moral laxity to which it led, was strongly attacked by Pascal in his *Lettres provinciales*. **2** (in epistemology) The term is now used for various theories of knowledge and scientific method in which the concept of probability has a central position. **3** (in moral philosophy) Consequentialist theories, according to which it is the probable and not the actual consequences of an action that are relevant when determining its rightness, are sometimes called probabilism, with *actualism* as a contrasting term.

probability, theories of Probability, unlike truth, comes in degrees. It is either true or false that it will rain tomorrow, whereas it may be more or less probable that it will rain. Games of chance led to an interest in the mathematics of probability – to an interest in such questions as, 'If the probability of throwing a six with a die is 1 in 6, what is the probability of throwing two sixes in a row?' This in turn led to the development of probability calculus.

Typical axioms of the calculus are (where 'P(p)' is read as 'the probability of p'): (1) $0 \leq P(p) \leq 1$; (2) if p entails q, then $P(p) \leq P(q)$ (probability is at least preserved across entailment); (3) $P(p \vee q) = P(p) + P(q) - P(p \,\&\, q)$ (the probability of a disjunction is the sum of the probability of each disjunct minus the probability of their conjunction). There are a number of different interpretations of this formal calculus.

We can think of probability as a measure of degree of belief. This is often called the subjective interpretation of probability. On this interpretation, the probability of rain tomorrow for me is simply the degree of belief I give to its raining tomorrow. Here, degree of belief is not thought of as something measured by strength of feeling, but in terms of betting behaviour. For me to give a 0.7 degree of belief to there being rain tomorrow is, roughly, for me to regard 70 cents as the fair price for a bet that returns $1 if it rains tomorrow, and nothing if it does not.

If we interpret degree of belief in terms of betting behaviour it can be proved that people whose degrees of belief violate the axioms of the probability calculus can have a DUTCH BOOK made against them. For instance, if they give $p \vee q$ a greater degree of belief than the sum of the degrees of belief they give to p and to q, minus the degree of belief they give to p & q, there will be a set of bets such that if they pay what they regard as the fair price for each bet, they must lose money. Thus, if one takes the possibility of having a Dutch book made against one to be a sufficient condition for having an irrational set of degrees of belief, degrees of belief must obey the calculus *provided* they are rational.

We can also think of probability as a measure of the degree of support a body of evidence gives to a hypothesis, often written P(h/e). If I say that there is a 0.7 probability of rain tomorrow, what I mean on this view is that relative to my evidence, or perhaps relative to all the available evidence, there is a 0.7 probability of rain tomorrow. The axioms of the calculus are then thought of as having an explicit or implicit relativity built into them. For instance, instead of 'If p entails q, then $P(p) \leq P(q)$', we have 'If p entails q, then $P(p/e) \leq P(q/e)$'. We can connect this interpretation to the one in terms of degree of belief as follows: the support e gives to h is the degree of belief that someone ought to give to h if e is all they know. It is then possible to draw on this connection and the Dutch book argument mentioned above to show that the notion of degree of support obeys the calculus.

Frequency interpretations of probability are also interpretations that see a relational notion as central: they offer accounts of the probability of something's being F, given it is G. The simplest version, the finite frequency theory, holds that the probability of F given G, P(F given G) = the number of Fs that are G divided by the number of Gs, that is, the relative frequency of Fs among the Gs. It is a simple exercise in arithmetic to show that this interpretation satisfies the axioms of the calculus.

The finite frequency theory cannot handle cases where there are no Gs, and also contradicts our sense that it is possible for a finite frequency to fail to correspond to the real probability. For instance, a fair coin C could land heads on both of the two tosses that it is ever subjected to and yet still be fair. But then P(C lands heads given C is tossed) = 0.5 (because it is a fair coin), and yet the relative frequency of heads is one. Thus, the finite frequency interpretation has been largely superseded by the long run relative frequency interpretation: P(F given G) = the limit that the relative frequency of Fs among Gs would approach were there indefinitely many Gs. This interpretation does, however, raise a number of difficult issues to do with specifying the nature of the long run that it appeals to – the most famous of which is encapsulated in Keynes's remark that in the long run we are all dead.

Finally, there is the interpretation of probability as an objective (i.e. non-epistemic), single-case (i.e. non-relational) property of events called 'chance'. This property is thought of as a theoretical property. It is the property that explains relative frequencies, that relative frequencies give good evidence for; and knowledge of this property settles the right degree of belief to have, without itself being either some kind of relative frequency or some degree of belief. The nature of chance and whether we are entitled to believe in it is a matter of current controversy. FJ

problematic /prɒblə'mætɪk/ **1** *adj.* (in traditional logic) a problematic judgement is one which represents a state of affairs as merely possible. In Kant's table of judgements in *Critique of Pure Reason* B100, it is one of the three modalities together with the apodeictic and the assertoric. **2** *adj.* (generally) doubtful; uncertain. **3** *n.* In the English translation of 1969 of Althusser's *For Marx* this word was introduced as a noun, to signify a system of interrelated concepts, a theoretical or ideological framework. It is, broadly, a synonym to 'paradigm' (in Kuhn's sense) or 'episteme' (in Foucault's sense). The word is also used as a noun in its original German sense (*Problematik*) to denote a set of interrelated problems.

Proclus (AD 410–85) neo-Platonist philosopher, head of the Athenian School from 437. Much of his work takes the form of commentaries on Plato, among which those on the *Timaeus* and the *Parmenides* are of particular historical significance. His *Elements of Theology* and *Platonic Theology* are comprehensive statements of late neo-Platonist metaphysics, giving a detailed and subtle account of how the One, the absolute reality, relates to other levels of reality, down to matter, the bottom level. The neo-Platonism he represented was a metaphysics that also had a religious (non-Christian) aspect. This is why some decades after his death the Emperor Justinian closed the School of Athena, which had flourished for about nine centuries. His systematic idealist metaphysics had a considerable influence in medieval, Renaissance and later philosophy, from Eriugena to Schelling.

HT/ed.

proem /'prəʊɛm/ *n.* preface, introduction. *See also* RHETORIC.

pro et contra Lat. for and against.

prohairetic logic the logic of preference and choice; the inquiry into, or theory of, the formal properties of preference-relations. *See also* PROAIRESIS.

projectibility *n.* Projectible properties are the ones that can be used in inductive reasoning: they are the properties in respect of which we rightly anticipate that unexamined objects will resemble examined ones. With reference to GOODMAN'S PARADOX, green is a projectible property, grue is not.

Other kinds of examples can be given. Suppose we want to confirm that all panthers have whiskers. It is difficult to get a good sample of panthers: they are elusive. So we consider instead the property of being-a-panther-or-a-rabbit. Now it is easy to get a good sample that can be safely examined, and we do find that all the examined samples have whiskers. This gives strong support for the hypothesis that all panthers-or-rabbits have whiskers, and so we have good grounds for thinking that all panthers have whiskers – although we have not examined any panther!

Something has obviously gone wrong. The composite property (panther-or-rabbit) is, like grue, not projectible, according to Nelson Goodman, who introduced the concept. The problem is to find adequate criteria for projectibility. Goodman suggested entrenchment, i.e. the concept should already be part of our conceptual stock. Green, rabbit, panther, are entrenched. Critics have doubted whether this conceptual conservatism is the appropriate answer.

projectivism *n.* No situation is objectively ghastly: the fact of the matter is that in certain situations we feel aghast. This exemplifies the basic idea of projectivism. It is a theory that certain properties which we ascribe to their bearers do not really belong there, but are projections of subjective states. An important source of inspiration for this approach was Hume, who wrote of 'the mind's propensity to spread itself upon external objects' (*Treatise of Human Nature*, 1,3,14, paragraph 24).

In metaethics, projectivist accounts of the moral properties we ascribe to actions, persons or states of affairs have been proposed since the late nineteenth century, with an even earlier anticipation in Hume. A refined version is presented by Simon Blackburn in his *Spreading the Word* 1984.

prolegomenon /prəʊlɪ'gɒmɪnən/ (*sing.*); **prolegomena** /-ə/ (*pl.*) (Gr. *prolegomenon* something said in advance) *n.* a prefatory essay; an introductory discourse(s). Among well-known works whose titles include this word are Grotius's Prolegomena, i.e. introduction, to his *De jure belli ac pacis* 1625 (On the law of war and peace), and Kant's *Prolegomena zu einer jeden künftigen Metaphysik die als Wissenschaft wird auftreten können* 1783 (Prolegomena to every future metaphysics that will be able to present itself as a science).

prolepsis /prəʊ'lɛpsɪs/ (*sing.*); **prolepses** /-iːz/ (*pl.*) (Gr. *prolēpsis* anticipation) *n.* **1** (in Stoic epistemology) general ideas which we have a disposition to form, antecedent to experience. **2** (in ancient rhetoric) anticipating and replying to an objection. **3** (in literary theory) anticipations of various kinds, e.g. 'flashforward' in a novel.

pronoia Gr. forethought, providence *n.* (in Stoic philosophy) divine providence, destiny.

proof /'pruːf/ *n.* the conclusive establishing of the truth of a proposition. In a *direct proof*, the truth of a proposition p is established by validly deriving p from true premisses. In an *indirect proof*, the truth of p is established by disproving not-p.

Notice that 'proof' (like 'prove', 'provable', etc) is a success-word. To prove one's case is to succeed in establishing one's case, and is different from merely arguing one's case, i.e. seeking to establish one's case. Similarly, to refute (or disprove) a claim is to succeed in showing its falsity, and is more than merely arguing against it.

Note: In 'the proof of the pudding is in the eating', the word 'proof' means *test.*

proof theory A main branch of modern logic founded by David Hilbert (1862–1943) as a tool for carrying out his programme in the foundations of mathematics. Hilbert wanted to justify classical mathematics by establishing its consistency. More precisely, he identified a finitary part of mathematics, dealing only with finite objects and finite processes, and aimed to show by the finitary means available in such a mathematics that the use of transfinite principles can never lead to results that contradict the finitary part of mathematics. He hoped that this should be possible by formalizing mathematics and then studying the proofs of the resulting formal system. This hope seemed to be dashed when Gödel showed in what is called his second incompleteness theorem that the consistency of a system can never be proved by using only principles that occur in the system, because the finitary means Hilbert had in mind all occurred in the system whose consistency he wanted to prove.

However, a few years after Gödel's result, Gerhard Gentzen was able to prove the consistency of elementary mathematics by using principles that went beyond those available in that system but which nevertheless had a finitary character. Most proof theory had been concerned with extending Gentzen's result to stronger mathematical systems, which has required the invention of even stronger finitary principles, but it has not been possible to establish the consistency of full mathematical analysis in this way.

Gentzen's consistency result depended on certain general insights about the nature of proofs, which to many logicians have seemed more interesting than their applications in carrying out a modified Hilbert programme. This has led to the emergence of the conception of a *general proof theory*, in which various properties of proofs are studied in their own right, or because of their general philosophical interest. Especially Gentzen's way of analysing proofs, which resulted in two new kinds of logical systems, viz. systems of NATURAL DEDUCTION and calculi of SEQUENTS, have attracted great attention. Of particular interest is the result that proofs within these systems can be written in a certain normal form, which can roughly be characterized by saying that the normal proofs do not make detours of certain kinds. This result, which has several important corollaries, has been extended to various logics during the last decades. Some of the results have a special bearing on intuitionistic logic and accord well with semantical ideas according to which the meaning of a sentence is explained in terms of what counts as a proof of the sentence. DPR

propaedeutic /prəʊpɪ'djuːtɪk/ (Gr. *pro-* before + *paideutikos* pertaining to education) *n.*, *adj.* (concerning) preparatory instruction.

proper part A part P of a whole W is a proper part if and only if some part of W is distinct from P.

proper subset A subset S of a set W is a proper subset if and only if some member of W is not a member of S.

property *n.* **1** in a wide sense, a quality, attribute or characteristic that belongs to something. In language, properties are expressed by predicates. In a narrower sense, properties are distinguished from relations: they are attributes designated by a non-relational predicate. Aristotle reserved the term for those attributes which are non-essential but belong to all members of a species (*Topics* $101^{b}19$–24; $102^{a}18$–23). **2** right of ownership over something; something over which there is a right of ownership. **3** In seventeenth-century writings (e.g. Hobbes and Locke), the word is often used in a wide sense which includes everything that can be said to be a person's own or belong to a person. In this wide sense, a person's property includes not only material possessions, but also life, liberty, actions, labour, body, mind, reputation, etc. This is often misunderstood. To call these things a person's property implies that those things are especially close to the individual who has them, and it implies that an action impairing them constitutes a wrong, an injury. But it does not imply that all these things can or should be seen as marketable commodities.

propitiate /prə'pɪʃɪeɪt/ *vb.* to placate, to appease, to conciliate (especially divine powers).

proposition (the Lat. *proponere* and cognates originally carried the sense of 'putting forward') *n.* **1** Different sentences are said to express the same proposition: for instance, the French 'il pleut' and the German 'es regnet' express the same proposition as the English 'it is raining'. Propositions are commonly said to be the bearers of truth and falsity. Sentences used to express commands, questions, etc. do not express propositions. When we say that a person knows that p, believes that p, doubts that p, affirms that p, denies that p, etc., the letter p stands for a proposition. **2** In older logic and rhetoric, the term *proposition* was used to designate the thesis put forward for the purpose of argument or proof. Thus, the theorems in Euclid's *Elementa* are called propositions. Each is stated initially, and then the proof is given. The last line of the proof, i.e. the conclusion, is a re-statement of the proposition, and the reader is reminded of that fact by the abbreviation Q.E.D (Lat. *quod erat demonstrandum* which was to be proved).

propositional attitude To hope, fear, wish, regret, that p is to have an attitude to the proposition p, and has therefore been called a propositional attitude, first by Bertrand Russell in *An Inquiry into Meaning and Truth* 1940. (In 1918, he had been reluctant to use the expression, since 'attitude' is a psychological term.) He applied the expression also to believing, thinking, knowing, etc. that p. Common to all *propositional attitude contexts* is that they are intensional, that is, expressions with the same denotation cannot freely be exchanged *salva veritate* (i.e. without change of truth-value). For instance: *Oedipus hopes that Iocasta will become his wife* is true; Iocasta is his mother (i.e. 'Iocasta' and 'Oedipus's mother' have the same denotation); but *Oedipus hopes that his mother will become his wife* is false.

propositional calculus a fundamental branch of modern logic, concerned with argument-forms whose validity depends on the connectives by which compound propositions are formed from simple ones. The propositional connectives usually considered are the ones taken to correspond to 'and', 'or', 'if – then' and 'not', in so far as these words can be understood TRUTH-FUNCTIONally. Truth-tables and truth-table tests of validity of argument-forms are standardly associated with systems of propositional logic. *Syn.* sentential calculus, sentential logic.

propositional function *See* OPEN SENTENCE.

propositional logic *See* PROPOSITIONAL CALCULUS.

prosentential theory of truth the view that, in ordinary English, 'it is true', 'that is true' relate to sentences in the same way that pronouns relate to nouns (or to quantifiers). A leading representative of this view is Dorothy Grover (1936–) in *A Prosentential Theory of Truth* 1992.

Protagoras of Abdera /prəʊˈtæɡərəs əv ˈæbdərə/ (*c.* 485–*c.* 415 BC) the greatest of the Sophists, a teacher of rhetoric and politics. Extant information is very limited: only a few fragments remain. He proclaimed the thesis that 'Man is the measure of all things'. It seems that this implies some form of relativism. He held that an insightful person never punishes for the sake of retribution, but only in order to deter from further crime. His views are discussed in Plato's dialogues *Protagoras* and *Theaetetus*.

Protagoras's paradox An ancient anecdote relates that Euathlos, who was poor, received tuition in law and rhetoric from Protagoras, on the understanding that he would pay tuition fees if and only if he won his first court case. Having finished his course of study, he carefully avoided taking any cases. Protagoras sued for payment of tuition fees, and argued before the court: 'If I win this case, Euathlos will have to pay. If I do not win, he will still have to pay (since he has then won his first court case). So, in either case, he has to pay.' Euathlos, contesting the claim, argued: 'If I win, I do not have to pay. If I do not win, I still do not have to pay (since I will then not have won my first court case). So, in either case, I do not have to pay.'

protasis /ˈprɒtəsɪs/ *n.* the antecedent in a conditional statement. The correlated term for the consequent is APODOSIS. Aristotle uses *protasis* to mean premiss.

Protestantism *n.* in the modern era, the third major division of Christianity, the others being the Roman Catholic and Eastern Orthodox churches.

As a religious movement, Protestantism is usually taken to have its beginning in Martin Luther's publication of 95 theses in 1517. They gave expression to a certain theological standpoint, but also criticized religious practices devoted more to profit than to piety. This was the beginning of a chain of events that led, in many countries in Europe, to the establishment of churches and congregations independently of Rome.

The most influential versions of early Protestant theology were those of Luther and Calvin. Monastic institutions, clerical celibacy, the cult of saints, etc., and a number of traditional doctrines concerning the authority of Scripture and of the Holy See, were rejected. Two theological conceptions, prominent in St Paul and St Augustine, were given special emphasis: the corruption of human nature, and the justification through faith bestowed on a person as a free and unmerited gift from God.

Protestant views were advanced by some pre-Reformation thinkers, most importantly John Wyclif and Johan Hus.

protocol sentence, protocol statement (Gm. *Protokollsatz*; a *Protokoll* is a minute, a record of proceedings) The term *Protokollsatz* was used in articles by Neurath and by Carnap in the journal *Erkenntnis* 1932 and was adopted by members of the Vienna Circle for the basic statements in which they took all knowledge to have its ultimate foundation: theory-free reports of immediate sense-experience, or statements directly recording the perception of a physical object by a particular observer at a particular time. A near synonym is *observation-statement*. *See also* NEURATH.

prōton pseudos /ˈprəʊtɒn ˈsjuːdɒs/ Gr. the first thing false; the initial error; the first false step.

Proudhon /prudɔ̃ (Fr.)/, Pierre-Joseph (1809–65) an early advocate of non-centralist anti-authoritarian socialism. In his first important work, *What is Property?* 1840, he condemned private property: 'property is theft'. He did not advocate state ownership, like Marx (who attacked his *Philosophy of Poverty* 1846 in *The Poverty of Philosophy* 1847), but argued for temporary use-rights and small-scale cooperative forms of control. Proudhon advocated world federalism, reduction of the role of state government in favour of local self-managing associations. The local associations would be the basic political unit, and the state ought to be replaced by a decentralized federation with limited powers. This was a major point of difference between him and Marx. Proudhon's ideas formed a basis for syndicalism and anarchism, and had a considerable political influence which declined, however, after 1917. Nevertheless, he anticipated certain ideas of self-management widely discussed in the 1960s and 1970s, e.g. that all employees in large industries should participate in management. His general view of philosophy was similar to Comte's: mankind has progressed from a religious stage, through a speculative stage, and is now reaching the higher stage of reason and science.

Quite curious, though of limited influence, were his strongly anti-feminist views. In *La Pornocratie* ('Pornocracy') he argued that legal equality between the sexes would lead to the gradual disappearance of marriage, since the emancipation of women would make them financially independent of men, and they would not wish to be married once they no longer needed a husband for financial support. The result would be general prostitution.

prove *See* PROOF.

prudence Gr. *sophia*; Lat. *prudentia n.* one of the four CARDINAL VIRTUES.

pseudo- /ˈsjuːdəʊ/ (Gr. *pseudēs* false, unreal) a word element signifying that the other part of the compound is spurious or deceptive. For example, the word *pseudo-problem* was used by logical positivists in their dismissal of traditional problems of philosophy, such as those of idealism v. realism, or the existence of other minds.

pseudo-Dionysius the author of writings incorrectly attributed to Dionysius Areopagita.

psi /psaɪ; saɪ/ the letter ψ in the Greek alphabet. It has various uses as a symbol. Parapsychological phenomena are sometimes called psi-phenomena.

psyche /ˈsaɪkɪ/ *n.* (Gr. *psychē* that in virtue of which a being is animate; the soul) mind.

psychic 1 *adj.* mental; pertaining to the mind. 2 *n.* a person claimed (or claiming) to have paranormal mental powers.

psychical research *See* PARAPSYCHOLOGY.

psychoanalysis *n.* Sigmund Freud (1856–1939) coined the term in 1896 and used it to designate his *theory* of the mind, as well as a certain *method of investigation*, and again a certain *therapeutic method*. The primary aim was to deal with neuroses and psychoses. Freud held that these are caused by memories of painful experiences which are 'repressed', confined to the unconscious level of the individual's mind. By bringing them to awareness, relief or cure can be achieved. The method by which they are brought out consists in conversation sessions between analyst and patient in which the patient's resistance is gradually overcome.

The painful memories that have been repressed are, according to Freud, always the same (*see* OEDIPUS COMPLEX), or at least of the same kind, i.e. childhood sex-related traumas. Freud held that the mind has a tripartite structure. The Id (Lat. it) consists of instincts and drives and is governed by the pleasure principle. It sets the young child on a collision course with reality, and the Ego, governed by the reality principle, comes into being, controlling the Id. The Superego exercises a censoring function. Its origin is in the internalization of parental prohibitions; it is often unconscious but comes to expression in feelings of guilt and shame.

During the twentieth century the psychoanalytic movement, which accepts and applies theories and methods that stem from Freud, has had its strongest growth in the United States. It has developed in various directions, often under considerable strain because of a persistent tendency, from Freud to Lacan, to deal with divergent views in terms of orthodoxy and heresy and to engage in schisms and excommunications. In the early days, psychoanalysis provoked much hostile criticism, which has not abated. Many critics still regard it more as an illness than as a cure. At the theoretical level, the main objection is that its hypotheses, if at all testable, do not pass tests at all well. At the practical level, the main objection is that the success rate of its therapeutic methods is poor. The main response to these criticisms is that they are based on a misunderstanding of what the theory and practice of psychoanalysis aim to achieve.

The psychoanalytic strategy of 'unmasking' and going beyond appearances has been a powerful source of inspiration for many twentieth-century schools of thought. Freud has been described as one of the 'masters of suspicion', along with Nietzsche and Marx.

psychokinesis /saikəʊkɪˈniːsɪs/ (Gr. *psychē* + *kinēsis* movement) *See* TELEKINESIS.

psychological egoism the theory that all motivation is self-interested. *See also* EGOISM.

psychological hedonism the theory that all action aims at attaining pleasure for the agent. In a formulation of John Stuart Mill: all actions are determined by pleasure and pain in prospect, pains and pleasures to which we look forward as the consequences of our acts. (Mill held that this, as a universal truth, can in no way be maintained.) The classical objections are those of Butler.

psychologism *n.* in general, the reduction of the concepts and assumptions of a certain field (religion, epistemology, politics, etc.) to psychological concepts, descriptions and explanations. The term is used more frequently by opponents than by adherents.

Especially, the reduction of logic to psychology. Psychologism in this sense is an attempt to explain the laws of *logic* as general statements about the functioning of mind, as proposed, for instance, by John Stuart Mill in his influential *System of Logic* 1843. This and other psychologistic theories of logic, like those of Erdmann and Sigwart, were criticized by Frege (*Foundations of Arithmetic* 1884) and Husserl (*Logical Investigations I* 1900). The main objection is that the propositions of logic appear with an implicit claim to necessary truth, but propositions describing or explaining the workings of a mind are at best only contingently true.

The term has also been used to characterize a certain way of interpreting Kant's critical philosophy. Psychologistic interpretations of Kant maintain that his theory of knowledge in *Critique of Pure Reason*, with its doctrines concerning the *a priori* forms of sensory intuition (i.e. space and time) and categories of the understanding (twelve in all), is an exercise in introspective armchair psychology, which may need correction in the light of empirical findings. A conception of epistemology as ultimately a branch of empirical inquiry is also present in some late twentieth-century theories of knowledge, e.g. Quine's 'naturalized epistemology'.

psychology *n.* inquiry into, or theory of, mental phenomena.

In the eighteenth century, Christian Wolff introduced the term *psychologia* and made a distinction, widely accepted, between two kinds: empirical and rational. From the mid-nineteenth century on, empirical psychology began to be established as an academic discipline in its own right. Rational psychology was a branch of metaphysics; its main questions concerned the relation between mind and body, the substantiality of the soul, and the immateriality and incorruptibility (and thus immortality) of the soul. In the *Critique of Pure Reason*, Kant argued in a subsection of the Transcendental Dialectic, entitled 'The Paralogisms of Pure Reason', that the attempt to construct a rational psychology goes beyond the limits of possible knowledge.

In current usage, the word 'psychology' straddles uneasily the discourse/object distinction: does 'Hume's psychology' refer to Hume's mind or Hume's theory of the mind?

psychophysical parallelism the theory that mind and body are distinct, that they cannot interact, but that for every mental occurrence there is a corresponding physical occurrence, and vice versa. Among its representatives are Spinoza and Leibniz. Leibniz illustrated the theory by a simile. Mind and body are like two clock-faces. Neither influences the other, but they tell the same time because they are driven by one clockwork not accessible to us. This theory is different from EPIPHENOMENALISM.

public and private 1 (in law and jurisprudence) *public law* concerns the activities of governmental authorities; it is traditionally distinguished from *private law*, which concerns the rights and correlative obligations of persons in their dealings with each other.

2 (in modern feminist writings) the public/private dichotomy (distinction, division, dualism) is between the non-domestic, especially the political realm, and the domestic one. Some feminist writers are said to 'challenge the public/private dichotomy'. This may be an inaccurate way of saying that they object to the exclusion of women from public life (politics, the professions, etc.), or it may be an accurate way of saying that in their view nothing is private, but everything belongs to the public sphere.

public choice the study of the nature and limits of rationality in collective non-market decision-making. The problems arising under headings such as PRISONER'S DILEMMA and VOTING PARADOX are among those investigated.

Pufendorf /ˈpuːfəndɔːf (Eng.); ˈpuːfəndɔrf (Gm.)/, Samuel (1632–94) German writer on politics and history; professor in Heidelberg and Lund, later court historiographer in Stockholm and Berlin; together with Grotius, the founder of the Modern Natural Law tradition, in which individual rights have a prominent place. His major work was *De jure naturae et gentium* Lund 1672, 2nd rev. edn Frankfurt 1684 (On the law of nature and nations).

This work contains a theory of moral entities, distinct from physical and mental entities, which come into being by 'imposition', i.e. acts of volition. His view that the concept of obligation makes no sense without a commanding law-giver was opposed to Grotius's teachings, and was in turn attacked by Leibniz, his most important critic.

Pufendorf's social contract theory, which combines elements from Grotius and Hobbes, operates with an assumption of a state of nature, without any civil authority, in which everyone is free (i.e. under nobody else's authority) and equal (in respect of authority) to all others. Life in this state is, however, dangerous and unpleasant. There is therefore a rational ground for accepting a principle of sociability, the central principle in his theory. Accordingly individuals, who have innate rights (some of which can be transferred, chiefly by promising, while others are inalienable), enter into a series of agreements to form a society, lay down a constitution, and appoint a ruler or ruling body. Apart from the obligation to obey civil authority, in return for guarantees of common security and safety, Pufendorf also discusses a series of other problems that arise in a theory of justice: war and peace, punishment, marriage, transactions based on contract, private property, etc.

He summed up the main content of the major work in a shorter work, *De officio hominis et civis* 1673 (On the duty of man and citizen), omitting, however, the more theoretical discussions concerning moral entities, moral powers, etc. The shorter work deals mainly with the duties of justice, but it was widely used as a textbook on ethics in general, although little is said of other kinds of duties and virtues. It was a publishing success: by the 1770s, there were about 150 editions and translations, and a vast number of imitations. Locke and Rousseau were among the many who recommended it as particularly suitable for the study of moral philosophy.

puncept *n.* a conceptual pun. Puncepts are cultivated especially by Derrida and other practitioners of DECONSTRUCTION. Examples: (1) 'herstory'; (2) '*DIFFÉRANCE*'; (3) 'intersexion' (which can suggest intersection, interaction between the sexes, androgyny, etc.); (4) '*des tours de Babel*' (used by Derrida to play on the polysemy of '*des*' (some, about, from), of '*tours*' (towers, turns, tropes, journeys), and when the phrase is spoken there is also *détour*, *détours*, etc., etc.).

While the puns of the Victorian drawing-room – sometimes insipid or plainly silly – were meant for light-hearted amusement, it must not be thought that puncepts are such. Deconstructionists intend them to serve a purpose, by subverting tidy rationality and keeping one's thoughts in a state of fluctuating suspense.

The word is a neologism, created by the American literary theorist Gregory Ulmer (1944–).

pure theory of law a theory of the nature of positive law, proposed by Hans KELSEN in the early 1930s. Its main tenets are: (1) every law is, or can be reduced to, a rule connecting a kind of action with a sanction; (2) the connection between the two is normative, expressed by an 'ought'; this oughtness is a category of its own, not reducible to psychological or sociological concepts; (3) the legal validity of a rule depends on the validity of its origin. The validity of the origin must depend on a higher legal norm again, and this regress can be terminated only by postulating a basic norm (e.g. a written constitution) whose validity is underived; (4) a legally valid rule need not be morally valid.

The theory is called 'pure' on the ground that it has no improper admixture from ethics, psychology or the social sciences.

Putnam /ˈpʌtnəm/, Hilary (1926–) A leading American philosopher, professor of modern mathematics and mathematical logic at Harvard from 1976, Hilary Putnam was educated at the University of Pennsylvania and the University of California at Los Angeles, where he was a student of Reichenbach. Putnam began his career working in the fields of logic, philosophy of science, and mathematics; a mark of his accomplishment in the last of these is that in 1956/7 he co-authored a solution to Hilbert's Tenth Problem concerning Diophantine equations. From the mid-1960s onwards, however, Putnam became increasingly involved in general philosophy of language and philosophy of mind.

During this time he wrote a number of articles that have had very considerable influence within analytical philosophy. In one group he proposed that beliefs and desires be regarded as computational states of systems organized to function in various ways. The computer analogy in Putnam's 'functionalist' theory of mind (presented in 'Psychological predicates' 1967 and other essays collected in *Mind, Language and Reality* 1975) promised to bypass traditional problems of dualism and materialism. It did this by suggesting that the nature of the medium in which mental states are realized is no more relevant to their character as beliefs, say, than is the embodiment of a computer program relevant to its nature as an adding procedure.

Another influential idea developed in publications of this period is 'semantic externalism'. In several essays, including 'Is semantics possible?' 1970 and 'The meaning of "meaning" ' 1975, Putnam argued, contrary to what was then orthodox in philosophical semantics, that at least for certain classes of expressions, in particular natural-kind terms, the reference of an expression is not a function of ideas or descriptions associated with it in the minds of the speakers (hence INTERNALISM). The traditional 'sense' attaching to a term such as 'lemon', e.g. small, oval, yellow, sour-tasting object growing on trees, etc., may be matched by things that are not lemons, and may fail to pick out actual lemons, since for whatever reason some lemons may not possess those features. Instead, Putnam argued, we should recognize that our linguistic practices include intentions to refer to things having a common constitution, whether or not most speakers are able to specify it. Thus the referent of 'lemon' (in one use of that term) is fruit of *Citrus limon*, further specifiable botanically and genetically. Similarly the referent of 'water' in standard usage is the substance identified by chemists as H_2O (give or take small quantities of other compounds), notwithstanding that few speakers know it to be such; commonly and continuously we defer to experts – this resulting from a tacit 'division of linguistic labour'.

Although many of his ideas have been widely adopted, Putnam has distanced himself from much of the work he inspired. This is in part because he believes it misinterprets his original claims, but also he now repudiates, and effectively criticizes, some of his earlier ideas. An instance is the rejection in *Representation and Reality* 1988 of the FUNCTIONALISM which he had originated. His practice of challenging philosophical theses with which he is commonly associated has led to the view that Putnam suffers from philosophical inconstancy. This has seemed to many to be dramatically the case so far as issues of realism and anti-realism in metaphysics are concerned. Once thought of as a scientific realist, since the late 1970s Putnam has been a prominent critic of what he describes as 'metaphysical realism', preferring instead a view which rejects the intelligibility of a participant-transcendent conception of the relation between thought and reality.

The essays collected in *Realism with a Human Face* 1990 and *Words and Life* 1994 develop this perspectival realism, showing that it is more continuous than at odds with his earlier work, and linking it with interpretations of Aristotle and the American pragmatists – in particular Dewey and James. Increasingly Putnam also addresses issues in moral and social philosophy and in aesthetics. This is consonant with his general humanist metaphysics and with his sense of the public role of philosophy. In the later work, Judaic theism is a further element, made explicit in his Gifford Lectures, *Renewing Philosophy* 1992. JH

Pyrrho /ˈpɪrəʊ/ **of Elis** (*c.* 360–*c.* 272 BC) the founder of the sceptical tradition. In order to achieve *ataraxia*, peace of mind, he recommended *epochē*, the suspension of judgement, since good reasons can be found not only for any opinion, but also against it.

No writings are extant. It was Aenesidemus, two centuries later, who revived his fame and claimed him as a founder of genuine sceptical philosophy. His views are known chiefly through Sextus Empiricus.

Pyrrhonism *n.* a near-synonym of *scepticism*, sometimes used only for its more radical form. The Pyrrhonist achieves peace of mind by finding that the arguments for and against an opinion balance evenly.

Pythagoras /paɪˈθæɡərəs/ (of Samos) (*c.* 570–495 BC), **and the Pythagoreans** Pythagoras was an early Greek philosopher who left the island of Samos off the coast of Asia Minor for Croton in southern Italy about 530 BC. Since he wrote nothing, it is hard to determine what his actual philosophical beliefs were. It is clear that he believed in metempsychosis (the rebirth of the soul in other bodies) and that he established societies in southern Italy which had political influence and followed a strict way of life. The way of life included the practice of moral virtues such as self-control, training of the memory, and ritual taboos such as a prohibition on eating beans. Pythagoras was thought to have miraculous powers and to have a divine nature, one mark of which was supposed to be his golden thigh. He was not a mathematician in the strict sense and it is doubtful that he was the first Greek either to discover the so-called Pythagorean theorem (it was used practically by the Babylonians at a much earlier date) or to offer any rigorous proof of it. However, he did venerate the power of number in ordering the world as represented in the mystical tetractys (the numbers 1–4 whose sum equals the number 10, which was taken to be 'perfect'). He may have been aware that the musical intervals of the octave, fourth and fifth were governed by ratios of whole numbers (these intervals can be heard between strings whose lengths are in the ratios 1:2, 3:4, and 2:3 respectively). This may have led him to believe that the heavenly bodies produce music in accord with the ratios of their speeds of revolution, the doctrine of the harmony of the spheres.

After Pythagoras's death, Pythagorean societies underwent some turmoil and finally died out completely in the 300s BC. However, already in that century Pythagoras came to be regarded by some as the source of all true philosophy, and in the succeeding centuries numerous works were forged both in his name and in the name of other Pythagoreans, primarily to support the belief that many of the doctrines of Plato and Aristotle had in fact been derived from the Pythagoreans.

Pythagoras's most famous successors were both from southern Italy: Philolaus of Croton (*c.* 470–390 BC) and Archytas of Tarentum (*fl.* 400–350 BC). A few genuine fragments of their work survive, but there are also many fragments from spurious works. Philolaus was the first Pythagorean to write a book. This book was the primary source for Aristotle's account of Pythagoreanism and influenced Plato's *Philebus*. The book began with an account of the origin of the cosmos and dealt with topics in astronomy, medicine and psychology. Philolaus argued that the cosmos and everything in it were composed of limiters (structural and ordering elements, e.g. shapes) and unlimiteds (that which is structured and ordered, e.g. material elements such as earth or water). These limiters and unlimiteds are bound together according to a harmony that can be expressed mathematically; true knowledge of reality stems from an understanding of these numerical relationships. He was the first to suggest that the Earth was a planet. It orbited along with the sun, moon, five planets, fixed stars, and counter-Earth (thus making the perfect number ten) around a central fire.

Little is known about Archytas's general philosophical principles, but it is clear that he thought that mathematical studies such as astronomy, geometry, arithmetic and music were crucial to understanding reality. Unlike Philolaus and Pythagoras himself, Archytas was a true mathematician; there are detailed reports about his proposed solution to problems such as the doubling of a cube. He was especially interested in the mathematics of music theory and developed a theory of acoustics.

Pythagoras's fame grew with the passage of time, as did the veneration of him as the source of all true philosophy by writers in the Platonic tradition, who are therefore often called neo-Pythagoreans. Nicomachus of Gerasa wrote several books on mathematics and music, including his *Introduction to Arithmetic*. The neo-Platonist Iamblichus of Chalcis (AD 250–330) wrote an account of the Pythagorean way of life, based on earlier sources, which was the first of a ten-volume sequence on Pythagorean doctrine. The glorification of Pythagoras by such authors influenced the later Western intellectual tradition, and eventually the term Pythagorean was applied to any thinker who sees the natural world as ordered according to pleasing mathematical relationships (e.g. Kepler). CH

Q

Q.E.D. abbreviation for QUOD ERAT DEMONSTRANDUM.

q.v. abbreviation for QUOD VIDE.

qua /kwaː; 'kweɪ/ *adv.* as; in the character of; in the capacity of.

quad, tree in the

There was a young man who said, 'God,
I find it exceedingly odd
that this tree I see
Should continue to be
When there's no one about in the Quad.'

Reply,
'Dear Sir:
Your astonishment's odd:
I am always about in the Quad.
And that's why the tree
Will continue to be
Since observed by
  Yours faithfully,
    GOD.'

These limericks, written by Ronald Knox (1888–1957), prominent Oxford author and Roman Catholic thinker, clarify a central point in Berkeley's philosophy.

quadrivium /kwɒd'rɪvɪəm/ (Lat. place where four roads meet) Arithmetic, music, geometry and astronomy, as subjects of instruction, were together called the *quadrivium.* In the school curriculum that had become established in the early Middle Ages, they were the four higher disciplines undertaken after the TRIVIUM which consisted of grammar, rhetoric and dialectic. Together these were the seven LIBERAL ARTS.

quaestio-form /'kwaɪstɪəʊ fɔːm/ the form in which many philosophical and theological works from the thirteenth to the fifteenth century were presented. The matter to be discussed is divided into a series of connected but discrete 'questions', each of which can be answered yes or no. Each question is then treated following the same basic pattern (although there are many variations, especially in late medieval works): the author begins with arguments (from reason and/or authority) for the opposite answer to that which he will defend; there follows a short statement, usually from an authority, in favour of his preferred answer, prefaced by the words *sed contra* ('but against these'). Next, the author gives his own detailed arguments for his solution. Finally he rebuts, one by one, the arguments with which he began in favour of the opposite solution. JM

quale /'kwɑːlɪ; 'kweɪlɪ/ (*sing.*); **qualia** / 'kwɑːlɪə, 'kweɪlɪə/ (*pl.*) (Lat. *qualis* of such a kind) *n.* a quality, as it is immediately felt or perceived; the introspectible, phenomenal character of a mental state or event. Examples of qualia are the hurtfulness of pain, greenness, loudness.

The term was introduced by pragmatist philosophers to denote something that is neither private nor public, but neutral; but a quale has sometimes been differently characterized, as something which in contrast to objects and events is private in the sense that it can be experienced by one person only. *Percept* and *sense-datum* are near-synonyms to quale.

qualitas occulta /'kwɒlɪtəs ɒk'ʌltə/ (*sing.*);

qualitates occultae (*pl.*) Lat. OCCULT QUALITY.

qualities *n. pl.* in modern philosophy, the distinction between the primary and secondary qualities is in the first instance associated with Locke. In his account, *primary qualities* are physical qualities which belong to material objects independently of any perceiver. Examples of primary qualities are impenetrability, extension, shape, motion, rest, texture, number. *Secondary qualities* are powers in material objects which bring forth a sensation in a perceiver. Examples of secondary qualities are colours, heat and cold.

Locke's distinction was derived from the contemporary physical sciences (Galileo, Boyle), but distinctions along similar lines can be found in Aristotle, and were reintroduced in Western philosophy via Averroës.

The term *tertiary quality* is used less frequently, and has been used in a number of different ways. *See also* PRIMARY AND SECONDARY QUALITIES; TERTIARY QUALITIES.

quality of propositions In traditional logic, the quality of propositions consists in their being affirmative or negative. Among categorical propositions, *All S is P* and *Some S is P* are affirmative, *No S is P* and *Some S is not P* are negative.

quantification *n.* the application of a quantifier to a sentence. In formal logic, this amounts to the binding of a free variable in an open sentence.

quantifier *n.* In ordinary language, quantifiers are words like *all*, *every*, *each*, *any*, *most*, *many*, *some*, *no*, etc. In formal logic, quantifiers are operators that turn an open sentence into a sentence to which a truth-value can be assigned. Given, for instance, the open sentence *x is corruptible*, the application of a quantifier like 'for most x' will produce a genuine sentence: *for most x, x is corruptible*, i.e. *most things are corruptible*.

Similarly, 'for some x' or 'there is at least one x such that' will turn the open sentence *x is corruptible* into *for some x, x is corruptible* or *there is at least one x such that x is corruptible*, i.e. *something is corruptible*. In the standard symbolism of predicate logic, this is represented by use of the existential quantifier: (∃x)(corruptible x). Again, *everything is corruptible* is represented in predicate logic by use of the universal quantifier: (∀x) (corruptible x). An alternative notation is (x)(corruptible x).

For various reasons, including the strong interest in the foundations of mathematics, modern logicians have given more attention to the universal and the existential quantifiers than to the other kinds. *See also* EXISTENTIAL QUANTIFIER; UNIVERSAL QUANTIFIER.

quantifier shift fallacy The fallacious inference e.g. from *everything has a cause* to *there is one cause for everything* can be symbolized:

$$\frac{(\forall x)(\exists y)(\text{ y causes x})}{(\exists y)(\forall x)(\text{ y causes x})}$$

The quantifiers have changed place, hence the name. Another example of the same fallacy is this: *Every boy loves some girl* (i.e. some girl or other), therefore *Some girl* (a universally popular one) *is loved by every boy*.

This fallacy can be regarded as a special case of fallacies due to the rearrangement of operators, so we could talk more generally of operator shift fallacies. A case in point is fallacious inferences of the form: Possibly not p, therefore Not possibly p.

Some important classical arguments, among them the one at the beginning of Aristotle's *Nicomachean Ethics* ($1094^{a}1$–26) and Aquinas's FIVE WAYS, are often held to be fallacious in this way, but this remains a matter for philosophical debate.

quantity of propositions In traditional logic, the quantity of propositions consists in their being universal or particular. Among categorical propositions, *All S is P* and *No S is P* are universal, *Some S is P* and *Some S is not P* are particular.

quantum logic a logical system that differs from the ordinary or 'classical' logic. One way of stating the difference is that quantum logic lacks the law of distribution: A & (B ∨ C) implies (A & B) ∨ (A & C), and consequently it also lacks various other laws that would imply distribution. The logic is recommended on the grounds that it makes better sense of quantum theory than classical logic does. This claim is controversial.

A quantum logic was proposed by Birkhoff and von Neumann in the 1930s, another one by Reichenbach, and one more recently by Hilary Putnam.

quasi-ordering a binary relation which is REFLEXIVE and TRANSITIVE.

quaternio terminorum /kwəˈtɜːnɪəʊ tɜːmɪˈnɔːrəm/ Lat. a quadruplet of terms. A kind of fallacious syllogistic inference; for example: *Some nurses are angels. All angels have wings. Therefore, some nurses have wings.*

If 'angel' is given the same sense in the two premisses, they become implausible, but do imply the conclusion. If 'angel' is given different senses in the two premisses (metaphorical in the first, literal in the second), they become plausible, but do not imply the conclusion, because the reasoning now involves four terms, i.e. *nurse*, $angel_1$, $angel_2$, *wing*.

Usually, either the premisses are plausible but do not imply the conclusion, or the premisses are not plausible but do imply the conclusion. It is one or the other, but not both. The fallacy consists in supposing that it can be both.

This is also known as the fallacy of four terms, or the four-term fallacy. It is a fallacy of equivocation.

queerness /ˈkwɪənɪs/, **argument from** In the debate concerning the objectivity of morals, John Mackie argued in his *Ethics: Inventing Right and Wrong* 1977 that objective values would have to be entities or qualities or relations of a very strange kind, utterly different from anything else in the universe. Also, our awareness of them would have to be utterly different from the ordinary ways in which we know other kinds of things. For the fact that such an objective value-feature was present would by itself have a motivating force on us to do or omit something, unlike ordinary objective facts which are in themselves neutral or inert. The very queerness of these allegedly objective value-facts makes their existence unbelievable. Mackie infers that our common belief in the objectivity of moral values is mistaken.

quid /kwɪd/ Lat. what; something.

quiddity /ˈkwɪdɪtɪ/ (Lat. *quidditas* whatness) *n.* what a thing is, its essence; in contrast to its HAECCEITY.

quietism /ˈkwaɪətizm/ *n.* a religious attitude of passive receptivity to divine illumination. The term was first used in the latter half of the seventeenth century to describe the attitude of certain Roman Catholic mystics and of certain pietists.

Quine /kwaɪn/, Willard Van Orman (1908–) American philosopher. During sojourns in Europe in the early 1930s Quine's philosophical development was influenced by his contacts with Polish logicians and with members of the Vienna Circle. He was professor of philosophy at Harvard University from 1948. The main aim of his philosophical work has been to develop a theory that would be congenial to a naturalistic and empiricist world-view. Earlier attempts had their problems; an important step in Quine's attempt to overcome them came with the article 'Two Dogmas of Empiricism' 1951, where he rejected the analytic/synthetic dichotomy, and the reduction of all meaningful statements to statements about immediate experiences. A comprehensive statement came with *Word and Object* 1960, a remarkably influential work. In it he developed a broadly materialist and extensionalist outlook: first-order predicate logic and set theory provide a framework sufficient for the articulation of our knowledge of the world. Among other works may be mentioned *The Ways of Paradox* 1966, *The Roots of Reference* 1974, *Quiddities* 1987, and *Pursuit of Truth* 1990. ed.

A philosophical self-portrait: Our intake of information about the world consists only of the triggering of our nerve endings by light rays and molecules from our environment, plus perhaps some kinaesthetic clues to the ups and downs in our path. This neural intake on each occasion is related to that on other occasions by *perceptual similarity* in varying degrees. Psychologists can test this subjective relation, in humans and others, by the conditioning and extinction of responses.

We and other animals expect perceptually similar intakes to be followed by intakes that are likewise perceptually similar to one another. Expecting this is induction, and is the basis of all learning. Thanks to natural selection, which has moulded our innate standards of perceptual similarity in favour of survival, these expectations commonly come true.

Various animals have vocal signals that they associate with distinctive ranges of neural intakes grouped by perceptual similarity. People have them in abundance, and I call them *observation sentences*. Examples are 'It's cold', 'It's snowing'; also such terms as 'Dog', 'Mama', 'Milk', 'Red', which at first are to be seen as sentences on a par with the others.

We learn to combine observation sentences into *observation categoricals*, which are generalized expressions of conditional expectation: thus 'When it's snowing, it's cold'. Here is the germ of natural science, and indeed of the experimental method. The categorical is the law or hypothesis to be tested, the snowy scene is the experimental condition of the test, and cold is the predicted observation.

Words that we first learn as observation sentences or as parts thereof, and carry over into observation categoricals, eventually get recombined along with new ones to form the theoretical sentences of natural science. Thanks to this sharing of vocabulary, various familiar and unfamiliar observation categoricals come to be logically implied by various blocks of theory. Herein lies the empirical test of theory by experiment. If an observation that fulfils the first clause of the implied observation categorical fails to fulfil the other, then the block of theory that implied the categorical is refuted. One or another of its sentences must be revoked. Usually one of them is suspect at the start, motivating the test.

Mathematics, in so far as applied, is of a piece with natural science; for the applied mathematical sentences are in the block of sentences that jointly imply the categorical. Mathematics thus imbibes empirical content in so far as applied. The proverbial necessity of mathematical truth resides merely in our exempting the mathematical sentences when choosing which one of a refuted block of sentences to revoke. We exempt them because changing them would reverberate excessively through science.

With omission of much detail, then, the chain from theory to its subject-matter in the world is this: sets of theoretical sentences logically imply observation categoricals, which are built of observation sentences, which are conditioned to ranges of neural intake. It is sentences first and last, irrespective of what objects may be denoted by terms and variables inside the sentences. Logical implication relates sentences purely by logical structure, after all, without regard to what objects their terms denote; and observation sentences are associated simply as wholes with neural intake, again without regard to what objects they may eventually be thought of as referring to. Hence our evidence for our theory of the world is independent of what things our theory says there are. Our knowledge of the world hinges only on our neural intake, on our association of observation sentences with it, and on the logical structure of our overall theory. Objects figure only as neutral nodes in that logical structure.

Conceptualization is human, and of a piece with language. Our reification even of sticks and stones is part of it. To ask what they really are, apart from our conceptualization, is to ask for truth without language. It is up to science itself in the broadest sense to tell us what there is, in its own best terms and subject to correction in the light of scientific progress. Elementary particles, sticks, stones, numbers, classes – such are the denotata of the terms of science and the values of its variables. There is no deeper sense of 'reality' than the sense in which it is the business of science itself, by its self-corrective hypothetico-deductive method of conceptualization and experiment, to seek the essence of reality.

WQ

quintessence /kwɪn'tesəns/ (Lat. *quinta essentia* fifth essence) *n.* a fifth essence or element, in addition to the traditional four: fire, earth, water, air. According to Aristotle, it is in the nature of these four to move up or down. Everything sublunary is made up of them. The natural movement of the heavenly bodies, however, is circular and hence more perfect, so they must be made up of a different, fifth kind of stuff. In the Middle Ages, this fifth essence was taken to be a heavenly substance needed to explain, *inter alia*, the transmission of light. The concept was also used in alchemist theorizing.

The current non-philosophical meaning of the word in everyday language is entirely different: a thing's innermost nature or most essential character. *See also* EMPEDOCLES.

Quintilianus /kwɪntɪlɪ'ɑːnəs/, Marcus Fabius (c. 35–100) author of the authoritative ancient work on rhetoric, the *Institutio oratoria*.

quod erat demonstrandum /'kwɒd 'ɛræt dɛmən'strændʊm/ Lat. which was to be proved; a phrase, usually abbreviated Q. E. D., traditionally tagged at the end of a proof (e.g. in Euclid) as a reminder that the last line of the proof, the conclusion, is identical with the proposition initially stated.

quodlibet Lat. anything; whatever you please.

quod vide Lat. which see; often abbreviated q.v.

quotation marks These can be used to indicate: (1) that a word or expression is named. Thus we write *dogs have four legs* and *'dogs' has four letters*, and we write *'snow is white' is true if and only if snow is white*; (2) that the words are quoted, and not the author's own, e.g. 'Don't come back,' said Jill to Jack; (3) that the author wishes to distance himself from the use of the words. For instance, 'shudder quotes' suggest that the words quoted should inspire some kind of dismay.

R

racecourse paradox *See* ZENO OF ELEA.

racism *n.* **1** the doctrine that ascribes to another race inferior or dangerous qualities. The doctrine is frequently linked with the view that in dealings with the other race, its inferiority or its dangerousness justifies exemption from the usual moral restraints. **2** the practice of discriminating on grounds of race to the disadvantage of the members of the other race.

Racists often regard the other race as biologically, intellectually or morally inferior – but not always. Hostile sentiments against Jews, Chinese, etc. have sometimes arisen from fear of their supposed racial superiority in certain respects.

radical (Lat. *radix* root) *adj.* **1** fundamental, thoroughgoing. When Bentham writes that one's 'radical mental constitution is connate', 'radical' means the same as 'fundamental'. (He does *not* assert that radicalism is innate!) **2** favouring major change, especially social and political. Theories, movements, parties are so described. In France, radicalism has been a general term for liberalism, republicanism and secularism. A prominent philosophical representative was Alain, e.g. in his *Eléments d'une doctrine radicale* 1925 (Elements of a radical doctrine).

radical interpretation *See* RADICAL TRANSLATION.

radical philosophy a philosophical tendency, primarily in Britain, arising in the late 1960s, in opposition to the predominance of analytical philosophy in the universities. The object of discontent was the 'sterile and complacent' nature of academic philosophy and its role as a part of 'dominant bourgeois culture'. The preferred alternatives have on the whole been on the political left. In the 1980s, an interest in feminist philosophy became more pronounced. An important forum has been the journal *Radical Philosophy* (1972–).

It was a different group of philosophers who were called PHILOSOPHICAL RADICALS in the early nineteenth century.

radical translation 'translation of the language of a hitherto untouched people' (Quine, *Word and Object* 1960, p. 28), i.e. where the language is completely unknown, where no cues or clues are known in advance, and where there are no bilingual interpreters.

A radical translator or interpreter (i.e. one who has to start completely from scratch) will know only certain 'external' facts, and has the problem of what meaning or content to attribute to the words of the person who speaks the entirely foreign language.

Such a translator will collect linguistic data in order to compile a bilingual dictionary (and, presumably, also a grammar). One datum may be the observation that when a rabbit jumps past, the informant points in that direction and utters the sound 'gavagai'. This is some evidence for the hypothesis that 'gavagai' means the same as 'rabbit', but the evidence can also be a basis for many other possible hypotheses about the meaning of the sound. Generalizing, it can be argued that many entirely different dictionaries and grammars may have a perfect fit to the observed data (whose number is always finite), so that we are never in a position to claim that one translation is *the* correct one. This is the thesis, advocated by Quine, of the indeterminacy of translation.

Ramsey /'ræmzɪ/, F(rank) P(lumpton) (1903–30) Cambridge philosopher. He proposed important improvements to Russell's and Whitehead's *Principia Mathematica* which were incorporated in the second edition. His theories in the philosophy of science and in probability theory continue to attract interest and have remained influential. In a ground-breaking paper of 1921 he proposed a 'deflationary' theory of truth: 'p' and 'p is true' are equivalent, and argued that the theory could be used to rule out pragmatist theories ('p is true' means, roughly, that belief in p works well) and coherence theories. Ramsey's central essays have been collected by D. H. Mellor in *Philosophical Papers* 1990.

Ramsey-sentence a sentence that results from (a) replacing a term in a sentence with a variable and (b) prefixing the sentence with an existential quantifier that binds the variable. The technique was devised by Frank Ramsey (*The Foundations of Mathematics* 1931, pp. 212–36) for the purpose of eliminating theoretical terms in science, but of course can also be used in other contexts.

According to functionalism in the philosophy of mind, mental concepts can be eliminated by means of Ramsey-sentences. To take an example (simplified) for illustrative purposes, the sentence 'pain is caused by pin-pricks and causes loud cries' can be replaced by 'there is an x such that x is caused by pin-pricks and x causes loud cries'.

The technique has also been applied in analyses of legal concepts. The basic idea is that a right can be analysed as something which has certain legal effects, and comes into being due to certain operative facts (such as payment of a sum of money, or long possession). It has been suggested that in this way the question of what rights are in themselves becomes redundant.

Ramus /'rɑːməs/, Peter (1515–72) French philosopher, the first dean of the non-university body of professors that later became known as Collège de France. He turned to Protestantism in the early 1560s. In that decade he spent time away from Paris, but, having returned, he was a victim of the St Bartholomew's Day massacre. Ramus became the leading figure of a movement vehemently opposing, in a vast number of books and editions, the traditional Aristotelian doctrines, university curricula, and methods of organizing and conveying information. The polemical onslaught was impartially directed both at the subtle and at the over-subtle theories of scholastic logic. Ramism had a remarkably pervasive influence, evident in new methods of instruction and new kinds of textbook, but, philosophically, later scholars have found in Ramism more heat than light.

Rand, Ayn /rænd, aɪn/ (1905–82) American writer of Russian origin. Her so-called philosophy of objectivism condemns altruism and extols selfishness and individual achievement.

range *n.* The range of a function is the set of values that it takes for the different values of its arguments. The set of arguments is called the domain of the function.

Examples: if the variable x in the function x^2 represents real numbers (i.e. the domain of the function is the set of real numbers), then the range of the function is the set of non-negative real numbers.

ratiocination /rætɪɒsɪ'neɪʃən/ *n.* process of reasoning.

rational *adj.* pertaining to the faculty of reason. In philosophy, the use of this word frequently implies a contrast with experience. Depending on the context, the implied contrast may be with religious revelation, ordinary sensory experience, emotion, etc. In practical contexts, rationality is the adaptation of means to ends. Rationality in the choice of means for an end is not to be confused with selfishness. It is possible to be rational in the pursuit of altruistic ends.

rationalism *n.* in general, a theory or practice which claims to be based on rational principles. **1** In philosophy the word is mainly used to designate a certain kind of theory of knowledge, according to which knowledge properly so called springs from the operations of the faculty of reason, rather than being based on experience. Descartes, Spinoza and Leibniz count as the major rationalist philosophers. Rationalism is commonly contrasted with EMPIRICISM. **2** more generally, in the nineteenth century and since: views which emphasize the authority of human reason and conscience. Rationalism in this sense can be described as a cast of mind: all kinds of phenomena are attributed to natural rather than miraculous causes, religious beliefs are seen as expressions of human aspirations, and in morality the ultimate appeal is to conscience and not to any external divine or human authority. It is in this sense that certain organizations with secularist aims styled themselves rationalist. *See also* CRITICAL RATIONALISM; ECONOMIC RATIONALISM; ETHICAL RATIONALISM.

rationalization *n.* **1** rational explanation. **2** spurious rational explanation (of human conduct). This modern usage, in which the term denotes an explanation of actions designed to make them seem more rational than they are, has its origins in psychoanalytic theory and can be traced to an article, 'Rationalization in everyday life' in the *Journal of Abnormal Psychology 3* (1908) by Ernest Jones, a disciple of Freud. It is in this sense of the word that 'the reason given for an action may be no more than a rationalization'. **3** organization of efficient means for given ends: (a) rational organization of economic activity, aimed at eliminating waste in processes of production, transport, communication, etc.; (b) the development of more efficient political, social and economic structures. Max Weber saw capitalism and bureaucracy as rationalizing stages in the history of human society.

rational number a number which can be represented as a common fraction, i.e. as a ratio of two integers. Examples are 1/2; 3/5; 7/4. Real numbers which cannot be so represented are called IRRATIONAL NUMBERS.

rational psychology philosophical inquiry into, or theory of, the soul and the mind; one of the main branches of traditional metaphysics. It is contrasted with empirical psychology, which is based on observation, formation of hypotheses, experiment, etc.

rational religion religious belief founded on reason alone. It is also called NATURAL RELIGION.

rational theology philosophical inquiry into, or theory of, the objects of religious belief, independently of any revelation. Also called natural theology. *See also* NATURAL RELIGION.

raven paradox *See* CONFIRMATION.

Rawls /rɔːlz/, John (1921–) American moral and political philosopher. Rawls held teaching positions at Princeton, Cornell, and Massachusetts Institute of Technology, and has since 1962 been professor at Harvard University. His book, *A Theory of Justice*, is widely regarded as the most significant work in political theory published in this century. All of Rawls's writings, beginning with his earliest papers in the 1950s on punishment, the foundations of ethics, and fairness, share a fundamental concern with questions of social or distributive justice. In *A Theory of Justice* 1971 Rawls attempted to develop the main conclusions of his earlier work into a single, comprehensive defence of a particular conception of social justice: 'justice as fairness'. In so doing, he hoped to present a substantial alternative to utilitarianism, which he regarded as the dominant moral philosophy. He also sought to revive the social contract tradition in political theory, offering his own theory as a contractarian defence of liberal principles of justice.

A just society, according to Rawls, is one whose basic structure conforms to the two principles of 'justice as fairness': *First principle*. Each person is to have an equal right to the most extensive total system of equal basic liberties compatible with a similar system of liberty for all. *Second principle*. Social and economic inequalities are to be arranged so that they are both: (1) to the greatest benefit of the least advantaged, consistent with the just savings principle, and (2) attached to offices and positions open to all under conditions of fair equality of opportunity.

The principles come, in Rawls's terminology, in 'lexical' order: the first principle, upholding individual liberty, has priority over the second, known as the 'difference principle'. Therefore, basic liberties such as freedom of speech and freedom of worship may not be infringed to improve the condition of the least advantaged members of society; however, granted this proviso, institutions should be designed to raise the welfare of the worst off. The reference to the just savings principle signals that the welfare of future generations is also an important consideration: what a society saves, and what burdens it thereby imposes, are matters of justice.

The general conception of justice embodied by the two principles, as governed by the priority rule, may be expressed in a sentence: 'All social primary goods – liberty and opportunity, income and wealth, and the bases of self-respect – are to be distributed equally, unless an unequal distribution of any or all of these goods is to the advantage of the least favoured.'

The justification Rawls offers for this conclusion is the most controversial aspect of his theory. He argues that 'justice as fairness' is to be preferred to all other conceptions of justice because it is the one which we would choose from a hypothetical starting point called the 'original position'. Here, because we would not have any knowledge of our own interests, preferences or attachments, we would be forced to choose impartially. From behind this 'veil of ignorance', as rational persons, we would reject utilitarian, intuitionist, perfectionist and egoist alternatives, leaving 'justice as fairness' as the only reasonable option. Moreover, adopting the 'maximin' criterion for making choices under conditions of uncertainty, we would always rank alternatives by their worst possible outcomes, opting for the alternative whose worst outcome is superior to the worst outcome of any other. This conservative strategy makes 'justice as fairness' the most attractive principle because it guarantees basic liberties and maximizes the condition of the least advantaged.

Rawls's theory has been widely criticized. Some, like John Harsanyi, argue that Rawls's contractarian method properly applied should generate utilitarian conclusions of the sort Rawls rejects. Others have found the conclusions attractive but the method unpersuasive. A more fundamental critique comes from Robert Nozick who, in *Anarchy, State and Utopia* 1974, maintains that Rawls's theory rests on premisses which are unacceptable because they fail to recognize the separateness of persons, and the rights of individuals to self-ownership and to ownership of acquired property. From a quite different perspective, communitarian writers like Michael Sandel in *Liberalism and the Limits of Justice* 1982 have complained of the individualist bias of Rawls's theory which leads him to overvalue justice and neglect the value of community.

Rawls has subsequently responded to the communitarian challenge by reinterpreting his theory as a political conception of justice suitable for contemporary liberal democracies, rather than a universal theory. He now maintains that his conception of justice is the one which is most likely to attract support from diverse groups and so build an 'overlapping consensus' in pluralist societies. It is therefore best able to preserve stability and social unity over time. A substantial restatement of his theory is offered in his book *Political Liberalism* 1993, which recasts his political philosophy as a response to the modern condition of diversity and value pluralism. CK

real definition In the traditional theories of definition, a real definition of a thing states its essential properties, in contrast to a nominal definition, which explains the meaning of a word.

realism *n.* The meaning of 'realism' varies with the context in which it is used. Two important senses, which sometimes combine, are (1) an attitude of 'hard-headedness', not being given to speculation and illusion, but keeping a firm grasp of what is actually the case, in short, a *realistic* attitude; and (2) a theory that entities of a certain category exist mind-independently, i.e. independently of what we believe or feel about them – in short, a *realist* theory.

These usages, and a few others, are noted below.

1 a theory to the effect that entities of a certain category or kind exist independently of what we think. A consequence of realism in this sense is that the entities are there to be discovered, and that ignorance and error is possible. For example (a–e): (a) *ontological realism*: a theory of what there is. Realists accept the idea that we live in a world that exists independently of us and our thoughts, and hence that some facts may be beyond our grasp, in the sense that we are unable to confirm that they obtain. *Syn.* metaphysical realism. *See also* INTERNALISM. (b) *conceptual realism*: the view that universals exist independently and objectively, and do not owe their existence to the particular individuals of which they are attributes, nor to being conceived by a mind. Originating in Plato's theory of forms, the theory was formulated in the Middle Ages and standardly contrasted with nominalism and conceptualism. A well-known modern proponent of this view is Frege. *See also* UNIVERSALS, THE MEDIEVAL PROBLEM OF. (c) *scientific realism*: the view that most of the theoretical entities, such as electrons and quarks, which are postulated in a true scientific theory to explain observable phenomena are real, independently existing things. This is in opposition to operationalism and instrumentalism. Some writers use 'scientific realism' in a more general sense, for various kinds of realism that are in harmony with a scientific world-view. (d) *modal realism*: the view that there are modal facts, i.e. facts properly described by sentences of the form 'necessarily p' or 'possibly p', which are real and independent of our thought and language. 'Modal realism' is often used especially for David Lewis's theory, or for a particular thesis included in his theory, viz. that possible worlds are as real as the actual world. (e) *moral realism*: (i) the view that there are moral facts independent of our beliefs or attitudes. Synonyms or near-synonyms are *moral objectivism* and *moral cognitivism*. *Ant.* moral irrealism, moral anti-objectivism, moral non-cognitivism. (ii) the view that there are moral facts independent of the will of divine or of human law-givers. *Ant.* voluntarism. Sometimes *moral realism* is used in an entirely different sense, for a realistic view of human character and conduct.

2 *semantic realism*. Every declarative statement has a definite truth-value, true or false, even if there is no way for us to know which it is. That is, the principle of bivalence is accepted. The opposite view, often called simply anti-realism, which has a prominent advocate in Michael Dummett, rejects the principle of bivalence: it makes no sense to talk of truths that can in no way be verified; a statement cannot be said to be true or false unless there is, in principle, some means available to us by which its assertion or denial can be warranted.

3 *epistemological realism*: the view that a mind-independent world exists in combination with the view that in perception we mentally grasp qualities and objects that are part of that world. The contrast is with idealism, according to which ultimate reality is mind, and the external physical world a mind-dependent construct. Early in the twentieth century, there emerged a number of explicitly realist reactions against idealism, for instance from Moore and Alexander in England, but also elsewhere: in Scandinavia from the Uppsala School, and in the United States from the New Realists and Critical Realists.

4 *legal realism*. The aim of the realist schools that flourished in the first half of the twentieth century was to purge legal thought of political and religious ideology and instead to develop a legal theory that could serve as a sound basis for legislative and judicial decisions. In the pursuit of this aim, the Scandinavian realists undertook a logical and conceptual analysis and critique of basic legal concepts, whilst the American realists gave more emphasis to social and psychological inquiry.

5 *political realism*: at least three senses can be distinguished: (a) the empirical, value-free, approach to the study of politics; (b) the view that politics is or ought to be the art of the possible. Realists of this kind tend to accept the constraints imposed by existing conditions and to act within that framework, in contrast to those who choose to resist; (c) the view that moral considerations ought to be irrelevant to political decisions; that only power and self-interest count; that might is right.

6 In literature and the arts, realism is a style that aims to keep imagination within bounds and to avoid embellishments, in order to keep faith with the way things really are, presenting commonplace events in the lives of ordinary people. In prose fiction, Honoré Balzac (*Illusions perdues* 1837–43 (Lost illusions)), Gustave Flaubert (*Madame Bovary* 1857), George Eliot (*Middlemarch* 1871–2), Theodor Fontane (*Effi Briest* 1895) are early prominent representatives of this tendency, and, in painting, Courbet and Manet. 'Socialist realism' is an aesthetic and literary style, endorsed by Stalin in the early 1930s as the only one suitable for communist society, and coercively imposed in the Soviet Union and its satellites.

realist *n.* **1** a person who accepts a realist theory. **2** a person who adopts a realistic attitude: aware of the facts, not given to illusions, not easily deceived by appearances or wishful thinking.

realization *n.* (in contemporary philosophy of science and philosophy of mind) **1** Assuming the appropriate time and place, the theory 'somebody around here has stolen from the rich and given the loot to the poor' is made true by Robin Hood and his activities. This can also be expressed by saying that Robin Hood is a realization of the theory.

This usage emerged around 1970. The motivation for it lies in a certain view about the role of theoretical entities in science. If they are viewed as posits hypothesized to stand in certain relations in scientific theories framed in terms of them, it is useful to have a term for the entities (if any) that stand in the hypothesized relations. They are said to be a realization of the theory.
2 The term has since been widely used especially in the philosophy of mind. For instance, according to FUNCTIONALISM, having a mind is a matter of having states that stand in a complex of relations, typically causal ones. Physicalists claim that the states that stand in these relations are states of the brain, and these states are then said to be a realization of the relevant functional organization.

realm of ends *See* KINGDOM OF ENDS.

real number a rational or irrational number.

reason of state statecraft, *Realpolitik*, political expediency. Appeals to 'reason of state' in political decision-making imply that ordinary moral constraints do not apply. Machiavelli's *The Prince* presents this view; in European history, Richelieu and Bismarck are taken as typical representatives. The concept is present in ancient historians, e.g. Thucydides, but the expression (first as *ragione dello stato* (It.) and *raison d'état* (Fr.)) dates from the sixteenth century.

receive *vb.* (in older usage) to *accept*. A received opinion is a generally accepted opinion.

recollection, argument from an argument for the pre-existence of the soul. *See* ANAMNESIS.

reduce (Lat. *reducere* to bring back) **1** (in twentieth-century philosophy) to reduce Xs to Ys is to show that Xs are *nothing but* Ys. The aim is to give an account of Xs in terms of Ys, which are given a privileged status. It is often the physical world that is given ontological priority, but in itself reductionism is not necessarily materialist. It is possible to distinguish reductions of different, albeit related kinds: (a) identification of objects with objects, events with events, properties with properties. For example: genes are nothing but DNA molecules. A flash of lightning is nothing but an electric discharge. Heat is mean kinetic energy of molecule movements. Another example is the identification of mental occurrences with those observed by means of microscopes, oscilloscopes, etc.; (b) the *reduction of a theory* is the explanation of it by another theory, usually considered to be more fundamental. In this sense, the Mendelian laws of genetics can be reduced to molecular biology. The common-sense 'theory' we have of thermometers and temperatures can be reduced to the kinetic theory of matter. According to the reductionist view called methodological individualism the laws established in the social sciences can be reduced to psychological laws concerning the behaviour of individuals. Theory-reduction often presupposes, but does not require, that the concept or entities of the reduced theory are themselves reduced; (c) examples of *semantic reduction* can be obtained by replacing statements about social facts with statements about individuals, as when statements about the 1.9 children of an average family are replaced by statements about the number of children of actual families. Another example is the empiricist thesis that all meaningful statements are equivalent to some logical construct upon terms that refer to immediate experience; (d) the claim that yellow is nothing but light of a certain wavelength can be used as an example of *causal reduction*.

The word *reductionism* came into frequent use in the mid-twentieth century. Some writers use it loosely to express disapproval of any theory that appears to be scientific.

Philosophers who favour a certain ontological monism (usually materialist) find reductionist theses inviting, but it is becoming generally acknowledged that there are considerable problems in giving them coherent and plausible formulations. To mention just one problem: the higher-level concept of 'a nation going to war' cannot be explained in terms of any *one* complicated set of physical facts, since going to war can be done in many different ways. And it will not do to say that going to war consists in doing this *or* that *or* that . . . (i.e. a disjunction of complexes of physical facts), because we cannot know what to include in the lower-level disjunction unless we already grasp the higher-level concept independently. In order to overcome these difficulties, many philosophers in the late twentieth century try to formulate theories (e.g. about the mind) that are monistic without being reductionist. The higher-level entities are said to be supervenient (SUPERVENIENCE) (or consequential) upon the basic ones, but not reducible to them.

2 (in Aristotelian logic) the validity of syllogisms of the second and third figures is proved by *reduction* to syllogisms of the first figure, which are assumed to be valid from the outset. Direct reduction (*anagoge*) relies on principles of *conversion*; indirect reduction (*apagoge*) also uses the principle of *antilogism*.

3 (in Husserlian phenomenology) reduction is a procedure that enables us to see things directly as they are, without any presuppositions or preconceptions. There are two kinds: (a) eidetic reduction, done by prescinding from the actuality of something given and thus gaining a 'mere possibility'. That is, any question or assumption about the real existence of the given is disregarded, so as to intuit the essence by itself; (b) transcendental reduction, which moves from matters of fact to transcendental subjectivity and world-constitution, i.e. to ultimate presuppositions of thought and reality.

reductio ad absurdum /rɪˈdʌktɪəʊ æd əbˈsɜːdəm/ refutation of an assumption by deriving a contradiction (or otherwise necessarily false conclusion) from it. In formal logic, the rule of *reductio ad absurdum*, called the rule of ~ -introduction (negation-introduction), is that if a contradiction of the form (q & ~q) is derivable from a set of premisses that includes p, then ~p is derivable from the set of premisses that remains after the removal of p.

reduction *See* REDUCE.

redundancy *n.* using more words in a discourse than necessary; a defect, according to classical rhetoric. But not everything superfluous calls for removal, because (1) certain errors in transmission or interpretation of a message are detectable only if the message contains redundant parts, (2) in standard logical systems, if A implies C, then A with the addition of any formula B also implies C. So, whatever else may be said against redundancy, adding a redundant premiss to a valid inference does not make the inference invalid.

reference *n.* **1** the relation between a referring expression and that to which it refers. Referring expressions are names, like 'Julius Caesar', or definite descriptions, like 'the conqueror of Gaul'. **2** that to which a referring expression refers.

It is possible for different names or descriptive phrases to have the same reference. 'The evening star' and 'the morning star' both *refer* to the planet Venus, and yet the two phrases do not *mean* the same: we say that their sense (or their meaning) is different. Frege clarified the distinction in these terms in his famous article '*Über Sinn und Bedeutung*' 1892 (On sense and reference).

A near-synonym of *reference*, in certain contexts, is DENOTATION. 'Evening star' *denotes* the planet Venus. In contrast, the CONNOTATION of 'evening star' is the characteristics which the expression signifies (roughly: heavenly body making an appearance in the evening).

Reference generates problems: one is how names (and words generally) can be made to connect with things; another is how names (Pegasus, for instance) can connect with things that do not exist. There are various theories of reference. Description theories, inspired by Frege, take a name to be an abbreviation of a DEFINITE DESCRIPTION. Cluster theories (Wittgenstein, Searle) take a name to refer to one or other among a number of definite descriptions. The CAUSAL THEORY OF REFERENCE is a third type.

Some writers insist on a terminological distinction: words denote, people refer. One would then say that the word 'horse' denotes that animal, but people refer to that animal when they use the word 'horse'.

referential *See* ATTRIBUTIVE.

referential opacity, referential transparency *See* TRANSPARENCY.

reflection presents to us the operations of our own mind, according to Locke, *Essay Concerning Human Understanding* 2,1,4, who contrasts it with sensation, by which we have sensory impressions from external things. Sensation and reflection are the two sources for all our ideas, according to Locke.

reflective equilibrium How are we to tell whether a moral theory is correct? Scientific tests are inapplicable. Appeals to immediate insight are dubious. For reasons like these, Rawls (*A Theory of Justice*, pp. 48–51) puts forward as a suitable criterion of adequacy for a moral theory what he calls a reflective equilibrium. We start with moral principles that we believe in; but in certain cases they will lead to judgements that clash with our considered moral judgement. We then modify, according to what seems most reasonable, our judgements or our principles. This gradual process of modification continues until the difficulties have been removed. The criterion of adequacy is, in other words, internal coherence. An existing equilibrium may, however, be upset by new circumstances and require renewed reflection.

reflexive *adj.* A relation R is said to be *reflexive* if and only if for any individual x, Rxx. For example, being equal to itself is a reflexive relation.

A relation R is said to be *irreflexive* if and only if for any individual x, not-Rxx. An example is that 'ancestor of' is irreflexive; that is, nobody can be his own ancestor.

A relation R which is neither reflexive nor irreflexive is said to be *non-reflexive*. An example is the relation of loving. Self-love is possible, and so is other-love: if A is in love, it is still an open question whether the object of A's love is A or someone else.

One can distinguish weak (or quasi-) from strong (or strict) reflexivity. R is weakly reflexive or quasi-reflexive if and only if Rxx holds for every x that stands in the relation R at all. For example: x has *the same length as* itself, but only if x has any length at all. Weak reflexivity means that Rxx holds for every x in a given domain. In contrast, strong reflexivity means that Rxx holds for every x in every domain. **reflexivity** *n.*

Reformation the religious movement in the sixteenth century which had for its object the reform of certain practices and doctrines of the Roman Catholic Church, and which led to the establishment of the Protestant churches.

The historically most important reformers were Martin Luther (1483–1546) and John Calvin (1509–64). Note that the term *Reformed* is used only for certain Calvinist churches.

refute *vb.* To refute a proposition is to disprove it: to show that it is false. What is true is never refuted, as Socrates pointed out in Plato's dialogue *Gorgias* (473^b11). What is true may be denied, but a mere denial does not refute a statement, for the same reason that a mere assertion does not amount to a proof. An easy way to see the difference is this: in order to deny an accusation, all one needs to do is to say so. But in order to refute it, more is needed.

regulative *See* CONSTITUTIVE.

Reichenbach /ˈraɪçənbax (Gm.)/, Hans (1891–1953) German philosopher who taught at Stuttgart from 1920, and was a professor in Berlin 1926–33. Forced into exile, he held academic positions in Istanbul 1933–8, and in Los Angeles 1938–53. He shared the empiricist outlook represented by the Vienna Circle, and edited the journal *Erkenntnis* together with Carnap and von Neurath.

Inspired by the new physics, Reichenbach developed a strong interest in the concepts of space and time, and the related problems of the foundations of geometry and physics. Kant's view that synthetic truths *a priori* constitute such foundations had, according to him, been conclusively refuted by modern geometry and relativity theory. He proposed a logic for quantum theory with three values (true, indeterminate, false), and made significant contributions to the logic of probability and induction. Much of this work is technical, but he was always concerned to explain his outlook in non-technical terms, as in *The Rise of Scientific Philosophy* 1951.

Reid /riːd/, Thomas (1710–96) Scottish philosopher; taught at King's College, Aberdeen 1751–64; professor of moral philosophy in succession to Adam Smith at the University of Glasgow 1764–80.

The philosophical tradition known as 'Scottish Common Sense Philosophy', while closely linked with earlier moral sense theories (cf. Francis Hutcheson), has its direct origins in the comprehensive criticism that Reid levelled against more or less the whole of modern philosophy in his three main works, *An Inquiry into the Human Mind on the Principles of Common Sense* 1764, *Essays on the Intellectual Powers of Man* 1785, and *Essays on the Active Powers of Man* 1788. From René Descartes via Nicolas Malebranche, John Locke and George Berkeley to Reid's own time, philosophical views of how the human mind acquires knowledge of the world that enables people to conduct the business of life had become, as Reid saw it, more and more at variance with common understanding. In personal life, in society and in science, humanity displays a capacity for knowledge and for being guided by this knowledge. It was the task of philosophy to explain how this was possible, and philosophy, in Reid's view, had failed to do so.

Philosophers had been misled by the triumph of natural sciences into drawing an analogy between matter and mind, and thus to using the methods of these sciences to explain both the cognitive and the active faculties of the mind. The very language that was being used in talking of mental phenomena was 'physicalistic', as we might say. The mental world was thus said to be composed of elements (ideas), and the composition was explained in spatial and mechanistic terms. Although few philosophers were materialists in the strict sense, most tended to understand the connection between ideas, passions, the will and behaviour in causal or quasi-causal terms. When driven to its final, absurd conclusions, which Reid found in the work of David Hume, modern philosophy had created a phantom-world of so-called 'ideas' that sprang from objects of observation; the self was a conglomeration of perceived ideas; and the will as the source of action was nothing but the balance of impulses at any given moment.

This was Reid's understanding of modern philosophy, which he considered not only false but dangerous. It was false on several counts. Reid saw no empirical evidence to support the analogy between mind and body. On the contrary, it is common experience that mental representation of the external world is inherently different from spatial phenomena, so that the process from sensation to idea must be understood in terms other than those of causation. This is further underlined by the obvious fact that the mind is itself highly active in the perception of both external and internal sensations. All perception is judgemental. It is equally at variance with experience to suggest that the mind perceives only simple, discrete ideas from which it composes complex ones. The mind generally perceives complex objects immediately and only reaches their simpler components through analysis.

The danger that Reid saw in modern philosophy was its sceptical tendency in knowledge and, consequently, in morals. The suggestion that the immediate objects of the mind are ideas led to a hopeless search for guarantees that the supposed ideas adequately represent their objects, but all proposed guarantors – such as God – must themselves be apprehended through ideas. And if the self is dissolved into a sequence of events, then there may be no inherent connection between 'acts of will' and behaviour, and hence no way of ascribing moral responsibility.

The characteristic Common Sense approach to these problems is to point out that sceptics like Hume are of necessity inconsistent in their scepticism. In the very living of life and the discussion of philosophy with other people, sceptics are affirming what their theories deny or question, namely the existence of a stable external world, of other minds, of the continuity of their own minds, and of their own and other people's ability to ascribe and accept responsibility for actions. We can understand all of this by proper empirical observation and philosophical analysis of the activity of the mind. Reid's realism was far from 'naive'. He did not suppose that the real world is spontaneously disclosed to the sober common mind. All minds, including the common, are *active* in their approach to the world, and only philosophical analysis of mental activity can explain how the world is apprehended. Reid's major positive contribution to philosophy is a detailed account of the various innate powers of the mind, especially instincts; the ability instantly and without reasoning to form judgements or shape beliefs about objects of perception; and the ability to form a number of 'first principles of common sense'. The principles of common sense are not themselves subject to any form of proof; they form the necessary presuppositions for all other cognitive activity.

On this basis Reid put forward a theory of free will and rational agency which encompassed two 'Rational Principles of Action', viz. rational self-love and a regard for duty. Moral philosophy investigates the system of duty which Reid, in accordance with the common natural-law tradition, divided into three areas: duties to God, to oneself, and to others. Set within a teleological framework and an ideal of the moral progress of humanity, Reid's moral theory led to a utopian leaning in politics. The latter has only become known recently from Reid's manuscripts, as has his work in mathematics and in most branches of the sciences (*Practical Ethics* 1990; *Reid on the Animate Creation* 1995).

Reid's work became immensely influential in France and in America in the first half of the nineteenth century, though it was often overshadowed by that of his disciple, Dugald Stewart. KHA

reification /riːɪfɪ'keɪʃən; reɪɪfɪ'keɪʃən/ (Lat. *res* thing + *facere* to make) *n.* the turning of something into a thing or object; the error which consists in treating as a 'thing' something which is not one. Hypostatization, treating an abstract entity as if it were concrete, is a case in point.

The use of this word normally reveals an influence from Hegelian-Marxist theory. It owes its currency to Georg Lukács's *History and Class-Consciousness*. (Marx did not use the word, but the concept of 'commodity fetishism' is in *Das Kapital*, vol. I.) In one sense of the word, reification occurs when something (an object or a human being) is treated, in theory or in practice, as an object or a marketable commodity. In a related sense of the word, reification occurs when something that depends on human decision and action, for instance an institution or a social practice, is treated as if it cannot be so affected, but somehow has an independent existence of its own, like an external object.

Lukács used this concept in his rejection of sociology. In his view, sociology is conceived as the inquiry into an objectively existing social reality – that is, sociology reifies it.

The word has come to be used rather loosely in certain types of social and political discourse, as a general expression of disapproval.

reincarnation /riːɪnkaː'neɪʃən/ *n.* rebirth of the soul in a new body.

Reinhold /'rɑinhɔlt (Gm.)/, Karl Leonhard (1758–1823) Of Austrian origin, Reinhold left for Germany at the age of 25 and converted to Protestantism. He was a professor in Jena from 1787 and then in Kiel from 1794. He established his reputation as a philosopher by his clear accounts of Kant's critical philosophy, by which it first became more widely known to the educated public. His own philosophy was developed from a Kantian basis, as in his *Versuch einer neuen Theorie des menschlichen Vorstellungsvermögens* 1789 (Essay on a new theory of the faculty of representation of the human mind).

reism /'reɪɪzm/ (Lat. *res* thing(s)) *n.* an ontological and semantic theory, based on the assumption that the world consists of individual concrete objects. Abstract properties and states-of-affairs are not part of the furniture of the world. This view was held by Brentano (but rejected by Meinong). A leading advocate of the theory, the Polish philosopher Tadeusz Kotarbinski (1886–1981), preferred the term *concretism*. He differed from Brentano by giving the theory an anti-metaphysical and materialist slant.

relation *n.* In contemporary logic, relations are treated as predicates of pairs, triplets, quadruplets, and generally n-tuplets of individuals. In the same way that one-place predicates are sometimes identified with classes of individuals, so two-place predicates (relations between two individuals) can be identified with classes of ordered pairs, and n-place predicates (relations between n individuals) with classes of ordered n-tuplets.

For some important properties of two-place predicates, see also REFLEXIVE; SYMMETRIC(AL) and TRANSITIVE.

relations, external/internal Whether a husband wears a hat or does not wear a hat makes no difference to his being a husband – so the relation between being a husband and wearing a hat is *external*. But whether a husband gets a divorce or does not get a divorce makes a difference to his being a husband – so the relation between being a husband and having a wife is *internal*. The distinction is close to that between essential and accidental properties. Wearing a hat is accidental to being a husband, being married is essential.

Philosophers in the Hegelian tradition, especially Bradley and Bosanquet, argued that all relations are internal. That view implies that the full truth about one individual object or person will be an account of all those things without which that individual would not be what it is, i.e. an account of absolutely everything. The truth is the whole, as Hegel said. This view was attacked by Moore and Russell and other anti-idealists early in the twentieth century.

relations of ideas a concept in Hume's theory of knowledge, contrasted with matters of fact. Relations of ideas are non-contingent and our knowledge of them is *a priori*. Matters of fact are contingent, and are known *a posteriori*.

relative *adj.* To say of something simply that it is relative is uninformative, since everything stands in some relation or other to something else. If there is any exception to this, there is at most one: the ABSOLUTE, which stands in no relation to anything else.

That which depends on something else for its existence can be said to be relative, or conditioned, in contrast to that which exists independently of all else, the absolute or unconditioned.

relativism *n.* a word that seems to have come into use towards the end of the nineteenth century. An early occurrence can be found in the English philosopher John Grote in 1865. Husserl used the word in his *Logical Investigations* 1900, arguing against psychologism that it implies (truth-) relativism. *See* CULTURAL RELATIVISM; ETHICAL RELATIVISM; KNOWLEDGE-RELATIVISM; TRUTH-RELATIVISM.

relativity, linguistic *See* WHORF.

relevance logic According to standard or classical systems of logic, every statement of the form *if p and not-p, then q* is true, and the corresponding inference *p, not-p, therefore q* is valid. For example, the following inference would be accepted as valid: '2 + 2 = 5, 2 + 2 ≠ 5; therefore the moon is made of green cheese'. This is so because all that is required for validity of an inference in classical logic is that it be impossible for the premisses to be true and the conclusion false. (Similarly, with terminology adapted, for validity of implications.) This requirement makes all inferences with inconsistent premisses valid.

From a common-sense point of view, the systems of logic that accept this seem excessively tolerant, and, virtually since the inception of standard systems, attempts have been made to design systems without such paradoxical principles. Many early attempts failed as they were too restrictive or generated paradoxes of their own. Other systems were more successful; one important class of these has become known as relevance logics. The first major work along these lines was A. R. Anderson and N. Belnap, *Entailment* 1975. S. Read, *The Logic of Relevance* 1988 provides an introduction to this area.

Relevance logicians hold that more should be required for validity, the extra ingredient being explained in various ways. One is that the premisses be genuinely inconsistent with the negation of the conclusion. Another is that the premisses and the conclusion have something in common or, in other words, that the premisses should be relevant to the conclusion. Hence the name relevance logic.

This may seem a reasonable demand. The ongoing debate has, however, shown it to be more difficult than expected for relevance logics to dislodge classical logic from its entrenched position.

Some recent writers make a distinction between relev*ance* logic and relev*ant* logic. Relevance logics, the ones on which Anderson and Belnap concentrated, formulate certain stringent conditions for relevance. *Relevant* logics encompass a much wider sweep of systems conforming to the weak requirement of variable sharing for implicational formulae. Whether such a terminological distinction will become generally adopted remains doubtful, however, especially since there is an ambiguity in 'relevant logic'. RSY

relevant *n.* 1 bearing upon the matter in hand or the point at issue. A statement, a consideration, etc. that is said to be relevant, must be understood to be relevant to something: *relevance* is always relational. *Ant.* irrelevant.

A sentence connective like implication: *p implies q*, and the corresponding conditional: *if p then q*, exhibits relevance if p is relevant to q, for instance, if p and q have some component or content in common. A system of logic is said to be relevant if all valid implications of the system exhibit relevance. This leads to a new sense of 'relevant':

2 belonging to or pertaining to a system of RELEVANCE LOGIC. In this sense, *relevant implication*, for instance, is implication which is valid according to a system of relevance logic.

For example: conjunctions of the form (p & ~p) do not relevantly imply an arbitrarily chosen statement q, because q may have nothing to do with p, share no content with p. This is in contrast to standard, classical or intuitionist logic, according to which a conjunction with contradictory conjuncts implies any statement whatever. *Ant.* standard, classical, non-relevant. RSY

reliabilism *n.* (in recent epistemology) a kind of analysis of what it is to *have a justified belief that p*, or of what it is *to know that p*. One kind of reliabilism is that justified belief is belief based on *reasons* of a kind that tend to ground true beliefs. Another kind of reliabilism is that justified belief is belief resulting from *processes* of a kind that tend to result in true beliefs.

Renaissance /rɪˈneɪsəns; rɪˈneɪsɑ̃s/ a period of intellectual history, commencing in Italy in the fourteenth century, elsewhere somewhat later. It was then that much of the cultural heritage from classical Greek times was rediscovered, partly by the discovery of manuscripts that had lain unknown or neglected for centuries, partly by translations into Latin or vernacular languages. There emerged a new tendency to imitate the diction of classical Latin writers, in order to restore the purity of language which was thought to have been subsequently neglected, and there was a growing interest not only in alchemy, astrology and other inquiries of an occult nature, but also in scientific inquiry. Renaissance philosophers such as Lorenzo Valla (1407–57), Marsilio Ficino (1433–99), Pietro Pomponazzi (1462–1525), Giovanni Pico della Mirandola (1463–94) and Erasmus of Rotterdam (*c.* 1466–1536) were critical of university (i.e. scholastic) learning, which was, broadly speaking, Aristotelian and Christian, and had more sympathy with less orthodox neo-Platonic, Stoic and even Epicurean ideas. The Renaissance saw a stimulation of intellectual life and the first growth of modern science. But the attacks on arid logic-chopping (and on the non-classical Latin of the logicians) contributed to a decline in the quality of logical theory for many centuries. The revitalized Latin style and concern for pure (especially Ciceronian) Latinity set high standards, and the difficulty of satisfying them may have contributed to the gradual disappearance of Latin as a common language of the learned.

repentance two kinds of repentance, hatred of one's past crime or sin, are distinguished, especially in traditional Christian theology: *attrition* springs from fear of God's just retribution; *contrition* springs from love towards God.

reprobate **1** *vb.* to condemn. **2** *n.* a person condemned. In predestinarian theology, human beings are either *elect* and will be saved, or *reprobate* and will be eternally punished.

reproduction *n.* The process (or the outcome of the process) by which members of a biological species bring into being other members of that species.

In Marxist-influenced social theory the term is used in a wider sense to designate the process (or the outcome of the process) by which a society continues to exist. Education, for instance, can be described as part of a reproductive process, being a device for providing a supply of compliant workers for industry.

repugnancy *n.* (in older usage, e.g. in Locke) (logical) incompatibility. The word is occasionally used as a technical term. In Anderson and Belnap, *Entailment* 1975, *manifest repugnancy* denotes conjunctions of atomic propositions and their negations, i.e. of the form (p_1 & $\sim p_1$ & p_2 & $\sim p_2$ & . . . p_n & $\sim p_n$).

res /reɪs/ Lat. thing *n.* in medieval philosophy, one of the TRANSCENDENTALS.

It is not easy to define a notion as general as this. Avicenna's proposal (*Philosophia prima* 1,5,25) should not be despised: 'a thing is that about which something true can be said'. Another plausible statement, about 1,000 years later, by Ruth Barcan Marcus (*Modalities* 1993, p. 224) is that things are what can properly enter into an identity relation.

Rescher /ˈreʃə/, Nicholas (1928–) Rescher came from his native Germany to the United States in 1938, and has been professor in Pittsburgh since 1961. The number of his publications is remarkable, and includes around 50 books, dealing with historical and theoretical aspects of most areas of philosophy and logic, from problems of social justice to medieval Arabic logic.

Rescher's theory of knowledge is a kind of pragmatism. It rules out the idea that we can test our theories against an objective reality to which there is direct access. It differs from the original 'utilitarian' pragmatism, which takes a theory to be true (or justified) if its acceptance is useful. Instead, Rescher's pragmatism is methodological: a theory is taken to be true (or justified) if it is based on the application of methods which have proved themselves by their usefulness – for instance, by successful predictions. A further important constraint is coherence. We should accept those theoretical perspectives that are capable of long-term survival, and, within a theoretical perspective, we should accept as true those propositions which together provide a coherent picture of the world.

res cogitans /ˈreɪs ˈkəʊdʒɪtænz/ (Lat. *res* thing; *cogitans* thinking) something that thinks; in Descartes, thinking substance, mind.

res extensa /ˈreɪs ɪksˈtɛnsə/ (Lat. *res* thing; *extensa* extended) something that has extension in space. In Descartes, material substance, matter.

res nullius /reɪs 'nʊlɪəs/ (Lat. *res* thing; *nullius* nobody's) nobody's property; an unowned thing.

restricted quantification *Every man is mortal* can be represented in two different ways: (1) for every man, that man is mortal: (∀x:Man x) (Mortal x); (2) for every thing, if that thing is a man then it is mortal: (∀x) (If Man x, then Mortal x). In the first case, the quantifier applies to the restricted domain of men only. In the second case, the quantifier can apply to wider domains, including the *unrestricted* domain of absolutely everything.

restrictive utilitarianism *See* UTILITARIANISM, RESTRICTIVE.

retroduction *See* ABDUCTION.

revealed religion traditionally contrasted with NATURAL RELIGION by having its basis in REVELATION.

revelation *n.* disclosure; unveiling. In religion and the philosophy of religion, the direct communication addressed to human beings from a divine being concerning the existence, attributes or will of that being, or giving other information of high significance. The act of communicating, and its content, is known primarily by experience (a vision, a voice, etc.) and secondarily by oral or written tradition.

revisionism *n.* Marxist theory that deviates from orthodox communist party dogma. In the late nineteenth century, Eduard Bernstein's (1850–1932) efforts were so described, chiefly by his opponents. He argued that Marx's theory had at least in part been refuted by actual developments. For instance, the evidence was not forthcoming for the thesis that the crisis and collapse of capitalism was inevitable and imminent. He concluded that working-class politics should no longer aim at a violent revolution, but at socialist and welfare-state reforms. Bebel, Kautsky, Liebknecht, Luxemburg, Zetkin, Lenin and others denounced this as petty-bourgeois opportunism.

Soon after the war, Stalin condemned Titoism for being revisionist, and made it a capital offence. Generally, the term has been used by orthodox communists to condemn the attempts to develop a Marxist theory that would make concessions to reformist and democratic ideals.

'Revisionism' has also been used in other contexts where a revision is proposed (for good reasons, or bad), and especially in historiography. For instance, historians who in the 1960s challenged the current view of the role played by the United States in the Cold War were called revisionists. The attempts, common to certain leftist 'anti-zionists' and rightist anti-semites, to deny Nazi crimes, or exculpate the criminals, or blame the victims, are also so described.

revolution *n.* In older usage, this word preserved its literal meaning of a turnaround, a revolving, a change, of political or social conditions, but not necessarily a sudden, abrupt or violent one. The current sense of major, or indeed violent, upheaval developed after 1789.

rhetoric *n.* the study of how to use language well, especially when addressing an audience. In ancient times it was divided into three kinds: (1) judicial, with *justice* in view; (2) political/deliberative, arguing in terms of expediency or *utility*; (3) epideictic, practised in panegyrics, eulogies, etc., attributing praise (and blame), where the key concept was *nobility*.

The standard teaching recognized five different parts of a speech (see Table 17).

There was another five-fold division (not correlated to the one in Table 17) of the tasks to be practised by the learner (see Table 18).

Table 17 The parts of a speech

English	*Greek*	*Latin*
proemium	*prooimion*	*exordium*
narration; statement of fact	*diēgēsis*	*narratio*
confirmation; proof	*pistis*	*confirmatio*
refutation	*lysis*	*refutatio*
peroration	*epilogus*	*peroratio*

Table 18 Five tasks to be mastered by an orator

English	*Greek*	*Latin*
invention; discovery	*heuresis*	*inventio*
disposition; organization	*taxis*	*dispositio*
style	*lexis*	*elocutio*
memory	*mnēmē*	*memoria*
delivery	*hypokrisis*	*actio*

The most important ancient writings on rhetoric are those of Artistotle, Theophrastus, Hermagoras (2nd century BC), the anonymous author *ad Herennium*, Cicero, and Quintilian (*c.* 35–100).

Rhetoric was defined as the art of using language *well* (*ars bene loquendi*), in contrast to grammar, which was defined as the art of using language *correctly* (*ars recte loquendi*). Both were among the seven liberal arts in the medieval curriculum.

rhizome /ˈraɪzəʊm/ (Gr. *rhizōma* root, root-system) *n.* **1** a root: Empedocles used this word for the four ultimate elements. **2** a sprawling network of roots. Deleuze and Guattari introduced this biological metaphor in contrasting opposition to another one – the tree of Porphyry. The latter is tidy, with a trunk, branches, and a fixed hierarchical order. In contrast, a rhizome is a untidy network with modes, knots, etc. The contrast symbolizes different styles of thought and writing. The two authors stress especially that rhizomes differ from structures. Structures are definable, rhizomes are multidimensional and grow in an irregular manner, so that standard criteria of theoretical adequacy do not apply.

Richard's /riʃaʀ (Fr.)/ **paradox** The paradox, proposed by the French mathematician Jules Richard (1862–1956) in 1905, can be formulated as follows: let E be the set of all non-terminating decimal numbers that can be designated in a finite number of words. For instance, the non-terminating decimal number 0.3333333 . . . can be designated in a finite number of words, i.e. 'one third'; and 'the ratio between the diagonal and the side of a square' is another example. Since these designations are all made up of a finite number of words, they can be arranged lexicographically, and therefore they form a denumerable set. The numbers designated, the members of the set E, can accordingly be listed in a sequence that will have this form:

$$
\begin{array}{llll}
1 & 0.\ x_{11}\ x_{12}\ x_{13}\ x_{14} \ldots\ldots\ x_{1n} & \ldots \\
2 & 0.\ x_{21}\ x_{22}\ x_{23}\ x_{24} \ldots\ldots\ x_{2n} & \ldots \\
3 & 0.\ x_{31}\ x_{32}\ x_{33}\ x_{34} \ldots\ldots\ x_{3n} & \ldots \\
\vdots & & \\
k & 0.\ x_{k1}\ x_{k2}\ x_{k3}\ x_{k4} \ldots\ldots\ x_{kn} & \ldots \\
\vdots & &
\end{array}
$$

Now, change the 'diagonal' number

$$0.\ x_{11}\ x_{22}\ x_{33}\ x_{44} \ldots\ldots\ x_{kk} \ldots$$

by replacing all 8s and 9s with 1s, and replacing all other digits x_{ii} with $x_{ii} + 1$.

Finally, consider the number obtained as a result of this change. It has just been designated in a finite number of words. So it is *somewhere* in the list. But we have defined it so that it differs from every number in the list. So it is *nowhere* in the list.

Rickert /'rikɛrt/, Heinrich (1856–1936) German neo-Kantian philosopher, professor in Freiburg and later in Heidelberg. Whereas Kant had distinguished two realms for reason, the theoretical and the practical, Rickert, like other neo-Kantians, distinguished several. Each of them is linked to a fundamental distinctive value-concept. Rational inquiry or logic has truth; aesthetics has beauty; mysticism has impersonal holiness; ethics has moral rightness; eroticism has felicity; religion has personal sanctification. Each basic value-concept yields a criterion of adequacy or truth appropriate to its realm. As indicated by the title of his best-known work, *Die Grenzen der naturwissenschaftlichen Begriffsbildung* 1st edn 1896, 5th edn 1929 (The limits of concept-formation in the natural sciences), he held that the concepts and assumptions of the natural sciences do not have general application, agreeing with Windelband and Dilthey that there is a radical difference between the natural and cultural sciences. The former aim at general propositions, and do not presuppose particular assumptions about values. The latter, among them pre-eminently historiography, do not have generality as their aim. Historical studies deal with the particular, so selection of facts is inevitable, and such selection cannot but rest on value-assumptions. These should not, however, be individual and arbitrary, but should be those that can be recognized as common cultural values, and, ideally, as the common values of a universal culture.

Ricoeur /ʀikœʀ (Fr.)/, Paul (1913–) French philosopher. During his philosophical education in France in the 1930s he concentrated on the history of philosophy, especially the ancient Greeks. Kant and Hegel were major influences in France at this time. Just before the Second World War, he met and was influenced by Gabriel Marcel. During five years as a prisoner in a German prisoner-of-war camp for French officers, he read the works of Karl Jaspers and Edmund Husserl. After his repatriation in 1945, he wrote books on Jaspers and Gabriel Marcel. He also translated Husserl's *Ideen* (*Ideas*) into French and published it along with his explanatory notes and commentary. In 1950, Ricoeur published his first major work, *Le Volontaire et l'involontaire* (The voluntary and involuntary; transl. as *Freedom and Nature*) which was heavily influenced by Husserl's 'eidetic' method. This is a method that calls for a careful conceptual analysis, in this case of the will or willing, which sets aside all empirical knowledge or hypotheses and concentrates on the conceptual structure of willing. The choice of the will as the object of investigation was a sign of the influence of Gabriel Marcel, and the book was intended to serve as a refutation of Sartre's *L'Etre et le néant* 1943 (Being and nothingness). His principal thesis is that every aspect of willing is reciprocal with a corresponding aspect of the involuntary. This is contrary to Sartre's notion of an absolute freedom which is in no way conditioned by the world or any other kind of necessity. The 'eidetic' analysis of the will reveals three 'moments': decision, voluntary movement, and consent. Each of these can be understood only in relation to the correlated moment of the involuntary: motives, the body as resistance, and the necessities imposed by one's character, one's unconscious, and life itself as represented by birth and death.

The Husserlian 'eidetic' analysis practised by Ricoeur requires him to 'bracket', i.e. disregard, both transcendence and evil. He treats the latter problem in *Finitude et culpabilité* 1960 (Finitude and guilt) of which the first part, *L'Homme faillible* (Fallible man) deals with the theoretical question 'How is evil possible?' while the second part, *La Symbolique du mal* (The symbolism of evil) addresses the question of how evil is expressed and described. Ricoeur, influenced by Kant, gives a transcendental answer to the first question: there is a disproportion in man which always leaves a gap between his possibilities and his actuality. This disproportion creates a 'fragility' which makes evil possible. Our condition is to always seek more possessions, more power, and more appreciation and esteem. These desires are never satisfied. He answers the second question by saying that evil is always expressed symbolically or metaphorically: stain, burden, being lost. The myths of the origin of the world – of which the Adamic myth in the Old Testament is a prime example – are the first-order explanations of how evil came to be in the world. This study of the symbolism of evil redirected Ricoeur's interests from a philosophical anthropology towards the hermeneutics which characterizes his philosophy from 1960 to 1990.

In the early 1960s, Ricoeur's interest in symbols and interpretation was extended to include Freudian symbolism and psychoanalytic interpretation. His book *De l'Interprétation: Essai sur Freud* 1965 (transl. as *Freud and Philosophy*) contains a long reading of Freud and a philosophical and hermeneutical analysis of his work. Ricoeur's thesis is that Freud's 'mixed language' of force and meaning is appropriate for his subject-matter, 'the semantics of desire', i.e. how desires, including unconscious desires, are expressed in language. Against certain Anglo-American critics of Freud, Ricoeur argues that psychoanalysis is not an observational but a hermeneutic science.

In the late 1960s, Ricoeur's interests expanded from symbols and psychoanalytic interpretation to hermeneutics in general and the problem of metaphor in particular. His *La Métaphore vive* 1975 (The live metaphor; transl. as *The Rule of Metaphor*) is a virtual encyclopedia of theories of metaphor from Aristotle to the latest French and American theories. His central thesis is that the power of metaphor lies in their capacity to redescribe the world. He says that poetry and fiction have this power on the level of the text.

Ricoeur's interest in the creation of meaning and the interpretation of texts is expanded yet again in his three-volume work *Temps et récit* 1983–5 (*Time and Narrative*). He begins with a thorough analysis of St Augustine's aporias (seemingly insoluble difficulties) with the concept of time and Aristotle's theory of the construction of narratives. His thesis is that 'time becomes human time to the extent that it is organized after the manner of a narrative; narrative, in turn, is meaningful to the extent that it portrays the features of temporal experience'. This thesis is tested in the second part of the first volume against theories of historical narrative. In the second volume, Ricoeur reviews some of the main contemporary theories of fictional narratives, with special attention to their treatment of temporality. In the final volume, he reviews the writings on time of philosophers such as Kant, Hegel, Heidegger and Husserl. His conclusion is that none of the philosophical attempts to describe and explain temporality is successful in overcoming the aporias discovered by St Augustine. Narratives are essentially temporal, and temporality can only be described and recaptured in the narratives of history and fiction.

In *Soi-même comme un autre* 1990 (Oneself as an other) Ricoeur returns to and expands his earlier philosophical anthropology. He is concerned with the problem of personal identity and the relation between the self and the other. His detailed studies include a semantics of action, a pragmatics of action, narrative identity, and a theoretical essay on the foundation of ethics. He develops a dialectic between a teleological ethics which has its grounding in the universal desire to 'live the good life with and for others in just institutions', and a morality of norms inspired by Kant's formalism.

In sum, Paul Ricoeur's work, spanning over sixty years, is difficult to categorize. All his writings are informed by the history of philosophy, give careful credit to the authors he has read and by whom he has been influenced, and exemplify a generosity of spirit to philosophical mentors and opponents alike. In his style is evident a search for dialogue between views that are generally taken to be polar opposites. In his view, philosophy is always a reflection on experience which is already there: philosophy starts nothing and is not foundational. Its task is to adjudicate among conflicting interpretations, each of which claims to be absolute. CR

right *n.* **1** a power (an ability, a faculty), belonging to a person, to bring about a change in the moral or legal situation (for instance, by creating an obligation for oneself or someone else, by waiving a claim, by authorizing another person to bring about a change, etc.). To have a right is, so to speak, to be in control, morally or legally. **2** permissibility. In this sense, to have a right to do x means that it is not wrong to do x. **3** permissibility in combination with prohibition of interference. In this sense, to have a right to do x means that it is not wrong to do x, and that it is wrong for others to interfere.

Closely related to these concepts of a right to *do* something there are also concepts of a right to *possess* something, a right to *receive* something, and a right that another agent do or forbear doing something. *See also* POSITIVE RIGHTS.

The adjective 'right' has a different denotation. It can *be* right that B be helped by A even if B *has* no right to be helped by A. Conversely, some ethical theories, though not all, allow for a right to do wrong: A can *have* a right to, say, evict a poor tenant, even if this would not *be* right.

rights of privacy *See* PRIVACY.

rigid designator An expression is a rigid designator if it designates the same entity in every possible world in which the entity exists.

According to a theory, proposed in opposition to the received Russellian view, by Saul Kripke ('Naming and Necessity', in D. Davidson and G. Harman (eds), *Semantics of Natural Language* 1972; *Naming and Necessity* 1980) and Hilary Putnam, proper names like 'Socrates', 'Napoleon', etc. and names of natural kinds like 'gold', 'cow', etc. are rigid designators.

In the actual world, Margaret Thatcher was in 1985 the Prime Minister of Great Britain. But it could have been otherwise, and then someone else would have been Prime Minister. So, it is not necessarily the case that she is the Prime Minister at that time, and hence 'Prime Minister' is not a rigid designator. In contrast, Kripke argues, no one else could have been Margaret Thatcher, so 'Margaret Thatcher' is a rigid designator.

rigorism *n.* strictness, inflexibility. The term is sometimes used to describe Kant's view of moral duty.

romanticism *n.* a cluster concept chiefly used to characterize tendencies in literature, music and the visual arts that reached their full flourish in the early decades of the nineteenth century. However, certain sets of philosophical ideas can also be described as romantic.

In areas of artistic endeavour, romanticism meant an emphasis on sincerity, originality, individuality, imagination, spontaneity, emotionalism, and self-expression. The neoclassical ideals of harmony and restraint were rejected, and so were the Enlightenment ideals of rationality and universality. The romantic genius is above all a free, unfettered spirit. It has been said that the spirit of classicism is serene, romanticism troubled: Goethe contrasted sickly romanticism with healthy classicism. A. W. Schlegel, who gave currency to the word in lectures given in Vienna 1809–11, contrasted classical poetry, which is in possession of its object, with romantic poetry, which is a poetry of longing.

Other ingredients also enter the clusters of what is considered distinctively romantic. Non-rational aspects of human thought and action were celebrated: rational analysis or empirical inquiry were subordinated to a reliance on feeling and non-rational intuition (we can know nature only by communing with it, not by intellectually analysing it) and, consonant with this attitude, nature-philosophy replaces science. In politics, universalism (as expressed in Schiller's *Ode to Joy*) came under strong pressure from nationalism.

In political thought, one strand of romanticism was reactionary. The ideal of society as an association of individuals who are by nature free and equal was rejected, in favour of the ideal of an organic community with traditional roots, where everyone knows his place: instead of forward-looking progressivism, backward-looking medievalism; instead of codification of the law, continued adherence to ill-defined legal custom, on the grounds that it represents the accumulated wisdom of the common people.

Another strand was radical, vehemently opposing the repression of individuals and individuality brought about by political and bureaucratic forces, and by established convention in society. It was writers of this generation that were the first to advocate free love. At the extreme, there was excessive individualism, a one-sided preoccupation with private, as opposed to common, values, and a celebration of artistic genius, supposedly entitled to exemption from the constraints of common decency.

Articulations of romantic ideas can be found in Hamann, Herder, Jacobi, Friedrich Schlegel, and philosophizing poets such as Hölderlin, Novalis, Shelley and Coleridge. Among major philosophers Schelling was the most typical representative, but other German idealists and their followers in other countries adopted these notions, and the tendencies described are by no means defunct.

Rorty, Richard (1931–) PhD (Yale) 1956, taught philosophy at Wellesley College for three years, at Princeton University for 21 years, since 1982 University Professor of Humanities at the University of Virginia.

A philosophical self-portrait: In the 1960s I wrote some articles on the nature of philosophy and edited a collection called *The Linguistic Turn: Recent Essays in Metaphilosophy* 1967. In my introduction to this collection I tried, and failed, to explain what was so important about linguistic method in philosophy. In an afterword to *The Linguistic Turn* written in 1990, I argued that the idea of 'linguistic method in philosophy' had been a chimera, but that ceasing to speak of consciousness or experience, and speaking instead of language, had constituted genuine philosophical progress.

In the 1960s and 1970s I defended a quasi-materialist solution to the mind–body problem. I tried, in a number of articles on the philosophy of mind, to develop and extend the 'psychological nominalism' which I had gleaned from Wilfrid Sellars. This was followed in the later 1970s by an attempt to combine Sellars with Quine, in order to formulate a generalized criticism of the notion that knowledge was a matter of mental or linguistic representation of reality. This anti-representationalism was the principal thesis of *Philosophy and the Mirror of Nature* 1979, a book which went on to argue that the end of representationalism meant the end of epistemologically-centred philosophy (though not of philosophy itself). Essays elaborating on some of the points made in that book were collected in *Consequences of Pragmatism* 1982.

In my 1989 book *Contingency, Irony and Solidarity*, as well as in two volumes of papers written during the 1980s – *Objectivity, Relativism and Truth* and *Essays on Heidegger and Others* (both published in 1991), I tried to bring together the anti-representationalist doctrines common to James, Dewey, Davidson and Wittgenstein with some similar doctrines shared by Nietzsche, Heidegger and Derrida. The main argument is that once one puts aside foundationalism, representationalism, and the sterile quarrels between 'realists' and 'anti-realists', one comes to see philosophy as continuous with science on one side and with literature on the other. I have also argued that the traditional tasks of moral philosophy should be taken over by literature and by political experimentation.

Although frequently accused of raving irrationalism and unconscionable frivolity by the political right, and of insufficient radicalism, as well as premature anti-communism, by the political left, I think of myself as sharing John Dewey's political attitudes and hopes, as well as his pragmatism. In my most recent work, I have been trying to distinguish what is living from what is dead in Dewey's thought. RR

Rosmini /rozmiːni (It.)/ **(-Serbati)**, Antonio (1797–1855) Italian priest, educator and philosopher. In his numerous philosophical writings, he aimed at a synthesis and reconciliation between Catholic doctrine and modern philosophical, social and political tendencies.

Ross, Alf (1899–1979) Professor of law at Copenhagen 1938–69, he wrote extensively in the areas of legal and political philosophy. In the 1920s he was mainly influenced by Kelsen, and in the 1930s by Hägerström, sharing their anti-conservative and democratic sympathies and their view that the difference between analysis and advocacy should be strictly observed. His definitive theory of normative concepts, developed later, retained the non-cognitivist view of first-order statements about legal and moral rights and duties first developed by Hägerström, i.e. that they have no truth-value, but are similar to imperatives or optatives. Second-order statements, on the other hand, i.e. statements that a certain rule is 'valid' and applicable within a particular jurisdiction, *are* true or false: they are predictions about what courts and officials will do. At this point, Ross shows an affinity with American Realism in his *Directives and Norms* 1968, and differs markedly from other Scandinavian realists.

Ross's paradox The paradox rests on two very plausible assumptions: (1) p implies p or q (this is a theorem in standard propositional logic); and (2) if you ought to see to it that p, and if p implies q, then you ought to see to it that q (this is a plausible principle of deontic logic).

We have then: *This letter is posted* implies *This letter is posted or it is destroyed.* Suppose now that you ought to see to it that this letter is posted. In that case, you ought to see to it that this letter is posted or this letter is destroyed. But that can be accomplished by destroying the letter. It seems, then, that destroying the letter both is and is not ruled out by the initial ought-statement (you ought to see to it that this letter is posted).

The paradox was first formulated by Alf Ross in 'Imperatives and Logic', *Theoria 7* (1941).

Ross, William David (1877–1971) was of Scottish descent, but his academic life was spent in Oxford. He had two main fields of interest in philosophy: one was Aristotle. He was editor-in-chief of the Oxford translation of Aristotle's works, and himself translated the *Metaphysics* and the *Nicomachean Ethics*. His other main field of interest was moral philosophy. In *The Right and the Good* 1930 and *Foundations of Ethics* 1939 he criticized utilitarianism, including G. E. Moore's 'ideal' version, on the grounds that it recognizes only one kind of moral duty, i.e. to promote a maximum of good, and fails to recognize the other kinds, for instance the duty to make good whatever injuries one has caused, the duty of gratitude, the duty to keep one's promises, etc. We have direct and certain insight that these are moral duties. Ross calls them *prima facie* duties, because they are immediately recognized as such. Ross is then faced with the problem of how to act in a particular instance, when duties pull in different directions. His answer is that one's actual duty, the duty proper, is that *prima facie* duty that has most weight. It is not possible to formulate a theory about how to weigh them, any more than how best to strike a particular ball in a game of cricket, and there is always the possibility of error: as in cricket, agents will rely on their best judgement, informed by experience. Ross's theory can be described as intuitionist in the sense that we can directly discern what *prima facie* duties there are, and pluralist in that there is no *one* basic moral principle.

Rougier /ʀuʒje (Fr.)/, Louis (1889–1982) Rougier wrote extensively on epistemology and problems in the philosophy of science in an anti-metaphysical empiricist vein. In France he was the leading representative of logical positivism (*La Métaphysique et le langage* 1960 (Metaphysics and language)). His philosophical influence was limited because of his dubious political stance during the war and the prevailing anti-empiricist intellectual climate in post-war France.

Rousseau /ˈruːsəʊ (Eng.); ruso (Fr.)/, Jean-Jacques (1712–78) philosopher of history and writer on politics, music and education, at once a central figure in the eighteenth-century Enlightenment and its most formidable contemporary critic. Fiercely proud of his citizenship of the Republic of Geneva, he decried as despotic other notions of political authority, from monarchical to parliamentary rule, on the grounds of their merely representing the people and thereby depriving them of the liberty of governing themselves. This notion of popular sovereignty was embraced in theory, though not in practice, by republicans of all denominations in the course of the French Revolution, when Rousseau came to be regarded as its prophet and his remains were transferred to the Panthéon in Paris.

In his lifetime, Rousseau was as famous as Voltaire and Diderot for his eloquence and range of interests. He was, *inter alia*, a composer and the author of a substantial dictionary of music, and he also wrote at length on botany. His *The New Héloïse* 1761 was the most widely read novel of his age and his *Emile* 1762 the most significant work on education after Plato's *Republic*, while his posthumously published *Confes-*

sions were the most important autobiography since St Augustine's, and his *Reveries du promeneur solitaire* 1782 (The reveries of the solitary walker) the most notable source of late eighteenth-century romanticism. For several years associated with the *philosophes* of Paris and himself a major contributor to Diderot's *Encyclopédie*, he broke with this vanguard of the Enlightenment from the mid-1750s on account of his profound faith in God and his delight in the divine spectacle of Nature, as distinct from what he took to be the atheism and scepticism of his contemporaries. The opening line of *Emile* articulates the guiding thread of his whole philosophy of history: 'Everything is good when it springs from the hands of our Creator; everything degenerates when shaped by the hands of man.'

Rousseau's first *Discourse on the Arts and Sciences* 1750 put that doctrine in terms of the corruption of morals due to the trappings of culture, 'spread like garlands of flowers round the iron chains' by which the human race has been weighed down. Ancient Sparta had been militarily and politically vigorous on account of its lack of artistic and scientific sophistication, he claimed, but Athens, the most civilized state of antiquity, had decayed into despotism through its excess of luxury, which in turn had corrupted the Roman Republic, even while generating the progressive grandeur of the Roman Empire.

In his more substantial second *Discourse on Inequality* 1755 Rousseau pursued such themes in social and economic terms instead, attempting to explain the origins of the family, private property and agriculture by way of a conjectural history of the human race. In criticizing modern natural law theories which had portrayed the foundations of the civil state as overcoming the deficiencies of the state of nature, he contended that the establishment of property and government had deformed our nature, estranging individuals from themselves and from each other, by making them sociable, exciting their *AMOUR-PROPRE* rather than their *AMOUR DE SOI*. No major thinker of the Enlightenment believed more passionately than Rousseau that our nature must originally have been benign. No one was more convinced that the metamorphosis of our species, in changing us from simple animals similar to apes, into rich men and paupers who behaved like vampires and sheep, had brought us out of a naturally free state into a condition of domestic slavery.

In his *Letter to d'Alembert* on the theatre of 1758 and his *Essay on the Origin of Languages* and *Government of Poland*, dating from the early 1760s and early 1770s respectively, he argued that the inhabitants of the modern world and particularly of large cities had rendered themselves passive spectators of political and religious dramas staged by cunning rulers whose aim was to maintain the ascendancy of their secular and spiritual authority, while keeping their subjects apart. In the *Social Contract* 1762 he attempted to breathe fresh life into the collective and fraternal attractions of ancient republics and the constitution of Geneva, through the doctrine of the GENERAL WILL, which he identified with the public interest of citizens acting as a legislative sovereign assembly. He insisted that both moral and civil liberty, which he thought attainable just in conditions of relative economic equality, could only be promoted within states whose members were obedient to laws they prescribed to themselves.

If, for different reasons, Kant and other republicans would later be drawn to such principles, Rousseau himself was averse to any political programme which might seek to realize them in practice, claiming that even the liberty of the whole of humanity was no warrant for violence or revolution.

Instead of devising a plan of instruction which might promote fraternity, he devoted his *Emile* to a scheme of domestic education which would allow the impulses of children to develop naturally, with as little interference from their tutors as possible.

When in 1762, to escape persecution from the authorities, Rousseau was obliged to leave France, where he had lived for most of the preceding thirty years, he found that it was his religious rather than his political ideas which occasioned official censure. In a celebrated section of Book 4 of *Emile*, 'The Profession of Faith of the Savoyard Vicar', he had made an eloquent case against atheism and materialism, which he had imagined would win the approval of all true Christian believers, only to find both the Catholic establishment of France and the Calvinist ministry of Geneva outraged by his appeal to a natural religion, shorn of all sectarian churches and scriptures.

In his later years, after returning to France in 1767, he found himself more drawn to communion with Nature than with other men, and the most lyrical pages of all his writings, in his *Reveries*, express the joys of solitude, the raptures of drifting imagination and the wonders of a natural wilderness uncultivated by mankind.

Rousseau's great influence, particularly over political radicals and romantics, is due in part to the eloquence of his style, as was recognized by Kant, who thought it difficult to read him critically because of his seductive prose. In attempting to open his heart to his readers, he sought to excite their own generous impulses and to inspire their good faith; to his critics he seemed insufferably vain and the author of his own martyrdom. In rejecting the doctrine of original sin, he ascribed the evils of the world not to human nature but to human history, so that in the eyes of his followers he appeared to offer hope of an earthly redemption, by way of comprehensive social change or individual self-reliance. RW

Royce /rɔɪs/, Josiah (1855–1916) American philosopher, who held teaching positions at Johns Hopkins University and, from 1882, at Harvard University. In the final version of his monistic absolute idealism, the Absolute was conceived as a communicative network of individual minds. Through his many writings on religion, literature, history and above all metaphysics, he exercised a considerable influence in his time.

Ruggiero, Guido de *See* DE RUGGIERO.

rule-consequentialism *See* RULE-UTILITARIANISM.

rule-following, problem of What rules of logic, law, morality, etiquette, grammar, of the road, of games, etc. have in common is that they apply to an indefinite number of possible situations. We think that it is possible to learn them, to be aware of them, and to apply them. But there are problems with these natural assumptions.

One problem is how we can learn a rule. It seems that the basis available is a finite number of instances in which a rule is said to be applied. But from a finite number of instances, it is possible to extrapolate to any of an indefinite number of different general rules. Supposing, however, that having learnt a rule we know it: how exactly can that knowledge be characterized? This is also relevant for the distinction between merely conforming to a rule, which can be done unwittingly, and following a rule, which is done intentionally.

These problems were first brought to the fore through Wittgenstein's *Philosophical Investigations* 1953. They have inspired the formulation of a new kind of scepticism: traditional scepticism concerns *truth*; rule-scepticism concerns *meaning*. According to one interpretation, argued by Kripke in a book on the subject published in 1982, Wittgenstein held that there is no fact of the matter corresponding to any statement ascribing a meaning to a word: statements of the form 'in English, the word "W" means M' are neither true nor false. For this view, 'rule-irrealism' seems indeed more apt than 'rule-scepticism'. This reading of Wittgenstein provoked renewed interest and stimulated a lively debate from the early 1980s, involving Crispin Wright, Philip Pettit, Paul Boghossian *et al.*

rule of inference In axiomatized systems of logic, the rules of inference indicate permissible ways of deriving theorems from theorems. In natural deduction systems, the rules of inference indicate permissible ways of deriving a conclusion from preceding assumptions. As examples can be mentioned: modus ponens, which permits the introduction of a formula B, given the formulae A and A ⊃ B; and the rule of uniform substitution, which permits replacing every occurrence of a propositional letter 'p' in a formula with another, say, 'q'.

rule-utilitarianism *n.* Instead of looking at the value of the consequences of *a particular act*, rule-utilitarianism determines the rightness of an act by a different method. First, the best rule of conduct is found. This is done by finding the value of the consequences of *following a particular rule*. The rule the following of which has the best overall consequences is the best rule. Secondly, the right action is the one which conforms with the best rule. Among early proponents were John Austin (*The Province of Jurisprudence* 1832) and John Stuart Mill (*Utilitarianism* 1861).

One problem with rule-utilitarianism is this: it invites us to consider the value of the consequences of the *general* following of a particular rule. Suppose the consequences of the general following of rule R are optimal. We can say that R is the best rule, and that everyone ought to follow that rule. But how ought one to act if people generally are not likely to follow that rule? To illustrate: suppose that for every country the best traffic rule is to keep to the right. According to rule-utilitarianism, I ought to keep to the right. Suppose I am in Britain and know that people generally will keep to the left . . . Ought I *really* to keep to the right?

Another problem is that the best rules would not be simple. The best rule for promise-keeping would be of the form: 'Always keep your promises, except . . .' (where the list of exceptions would be very long). This led the American philosopher David Lyons to argue, in *Forms and Limits of Utilitarianism* 1965, that a plausible formulation of rule-utilitarianism would make it recommend the same actions as would act-utilitarianism, so the two kinds are 'extensionally equivalent' and there is no practical difference between the two. Currently, rule-utilitarian formulations seem on the whole to be out of favour, but there are attempts to rehabilitate them.

Russell, Bertrand Arthur William, 3rd Earl Russell (1872–1970) with G. E. Moore, the founder of analytic philosophy in England. He was a student and later a fellow of Trinity College, Cambridge, 1890–1901; a lecturer at Cambridge 1910–16, when he was dismissed for his pacifism; and became again a fellow of Trinity College in 1944. He had a long and chequered career as an academic, a political activist, an educationist, a social reformer, a free-thinker and a pacifist. He stood unsuccessfully for Parliament, campaigned for nuclear disarmament, was sent to prison, founded a progressive school, became embroiled in several lawsuits, was married four times, and progressed from being an *enfant terrible* and scourge of the establishment to being accepted as a grand old man of philosophy and letters, a Nobel Prize winner (1950) and a member of the Order of Merit. During all this time he wrote voluminously, producing a flood of serious philosophical work and popular journalism, all written with grace and charm.

His greatest early work and probably his most lasting contribution to philosophy was in mathematical logic, where his co-operation with A. N. Whitehead resulted in the monumental and formidable *Principia Mathematica* 1910–13, an attempt to reduce mathematics to logic. Underlying this, as well as most of his other philosophical writings, was the assumption, voiced as early as 1900, that 'all sound philosophy should begin with an analysis of propositions'. This analysis is seen in two papers much read and discussed: a 1905 paper, 'On Denoting', which offers an explanation by way of a rephrasing of how we can sensibly say something about what does not exist when we use what he called a DEFINITE DESCRIPTION in a sentence such as 'the present King of France is bald'; and a 1910 paper which distinguishes between the knowledge we might have of something or somebody, such as Paris or President Clinton, which is based on direct acquaintance, and the knowledge which is based only on some description, such as 'the capital of France' or 'the president of the United States'. Russell's own view was that the only things we can in fact know by acquaintance are basic items such as sense-data, mental images, thoughts and feelings.

A more technical example of this analysis is provided by his 'Theory of Types' introduced in 1903 to solve certain paradoxes which he had encountered in reading the mathematicians Frege and Cantor. The puzzle was that the apparently genuine question whether the class of all classes which are not members of themselves is itself a member of itself, is illegitimate because it leads to contradictions. For, if this class *is* a member of itself – as, e.g., a catalogue of catalogues is a catalogue – then it should not be in this class (which is reserved for those which are not members of themselves) and, therefore, *is not* a member of itself; but if it *is not* a member of itself – as, e.g., a group of men is not a man – then it should be in this class and, therefore, *is* a member of itself. Russell's solution was to suggest a hierarchy of types of things, placing limits on what can be sensibly said. Thus we can sensibly say, e.g., 'Russell is a famous philosopher', but not 'A group of men is a famous philosopher'; and we can sensibly say 'A group of men split into opposing parties', but not 'Russell split into opposing parties'.

Because his examination of the language in which we express our ideas often resulted in a rephrasing of this language to bring out what he considered its correct logic, and because he thought that we can make discoveries about the general structure of the world from this correct logical form which would mirror it – a view which partly arose from the assumption that the meaning of a word is the object which it stands for and which led him to a frequent use of Ockham's razor for the elimination of apparently unnecessary entities – he thought that the proper task of analysis was to abandon everyday expressions and to build an ideal logically correct language. It was this view which gave him such a high opinion of his famous pupil Wittgenstein's early work, *Tractatus Logico-Philosophicus*, which favoured an ideal language, and such a low opinion of his later work, *Philosophical Investigations*, which stuck to everyday language. Because he was also an empiricist, Russell argued that the values of the variables in this structure-revealing logical language would be filled in from our experience. In mathematics these values would be supplied, for example, by what we already know such numbers as 'one', 'two', 'three' to mean, while in science and everyday life they would consist of those things which can be known by acquaintance, such things as sense-data and mental images. Everything else in either mathematics or scientific and everyday knowledge would be built up by what he called 'logical construction' from these basic data, as was shown for the former in *Principia Mathematica* and for the latter in such works as *Our Knowledge of the External World* 1914, *The Philosophy of Logical Atomism* 1918 and *Human Knowledge: Its Scope and Limits* 1948. What can be known by acquaintance is certain, whereas what can be known only by description is inferred and problematic, so the mottos which may enable us to reach the certainty which Russell, like Descartes, always sought should be 'Whenever possible, substitute constructions out of known entities for inferences to unknown entities' and 'Every proposition which we can understand must be composed wholly out of constituents with which we are acquainted.'

Early in life Russell published what has become one of the most popular introductions to philosophy for students, *The Problems of Philosophy* 1912, and towards the end he produced a useful guide to his life's philosophical progress, *My Philosophical Development* 1959. AW

Russell's paradox It seems reasonable to suppose that every set is either a member of itself or not a member of itself. Consider the set consisting of all and only those sets which are not members of themselves. Call this set W. That is, any set which is not a member of itself is in W, and any set which *is* a member of itself is not in W. Now let us ask, is W a member of itself or not? Suppose it is: then as we have just seen, it is not in W; i.e. it *is not* a member of itself. Suppose now that it is not a member of itself; then it is in W, i.e. it *is* a member of itself. Hence W is a member of itself if and only if it is not a member of itself; and this is self-contradictory.

This result is known as *Russell's paradox* or *Russell's antinomy*. It was first formulated by Bertrand Russell in his work *The Principles of Mathematics* in 1903. Its importance was that it showed that a contradiction could be derived from natural assumptions of set theory, and that therefore they would have to be modified. In particular, it showed that the *axiom of comprehension* (which states that for every property expressible in the notation of set theory, there is a set consisting of all and only those things which possess that property) would require modification; for non-self-membership is definable in the notation of set theory, but the assumption that there is a set consisting of all and only those sets which possess it leads to a contradiction. A number of alternative bases for set theory, from which Russell's paradox cannot be derived, have since been formulated.

GH/PR

Ryle /raɪl/, Gilbert (1900–76) Professor of philosophy at Oxford, successor to G. E. Moore as editor of the philosophical journal *Mind*, Ryle was one of the most influential figures in British philosophy in the 1950s and 1960s. An early interest in the nature of philosophy and its appropriate technique and methods, based not only on the British tradition of Hume and, later, Moore and Russell, but also on the continental tradition of Brentano, Meinong and Husserl, led him to a view of philosophical argument as conceptual analysis and to a search for criteria to distinguish the sensible from the nonsensical. This view was sometimes likened to a sort of logical geography which tried both to expose the mistaken conceptual maps of other philosophers and to chart the correct locations of our ordinary concepts. Sometimes it was likened to a placing in their correct categories of those concepts which had been the victim of other philosophers' 'category-mistakes'. His most famous exemplification of this came in *The Concept of Mind* 1949, whose principal argument was directed against the Cartesian view of the mind as a kind of non-physical entity related in some mysterious way to the physical body – a view stigmatized as the myth of 'the ghost in the machine'. In its place he favoured a philosophical behaviourism: statements that use mental terms are like promissory notes which can be redeemed in the hard cash of physical terms in statements about behaviour and behavioural dispositions. The book also contained a version of an earlier influential paper which distinguished *knowing how* to do something from *knowing that* such and such is the case; as well as argument against sense-data as objects in perception, and images as objects in memory and imagination. Further similar critical work was carried out in *Dilemmas* 1954. In his last years, Ryle published a series of papers on the nature of thought which were collected posthumously in *On Thinking* 1979. AW

S

Sabellianism A heresy named after Sabellius (*fl. c.* AD 200–220), which stressed God's unity, in opposition to the trinitarian doctrine that God is three persons (in one), which eventually became the orthodox one. According to this heresy, which also tends towards DOCETISM, the Father, the Son and the Holy Ghost are not distinct persons. They are only different modes of God, in the same way as the sun is bright, hot and round. Similar views were favoured by Michael Servetus (1509–53), who fell foul both of the Spanish Inquisition and of Calvin, and by the Swedish mystic Emanuel Swedenborg (1688–1772), etc.

sacrificium intellectus /sækrə'fɪsiəm ɪntə'lektəs/ Lat. sacrifice of the intellect; silencing the voice of reason, in favour in blind faith. This is part of the duty owed by Jesuits who have taken a vow of obedience, according to Ignatius Loyola: 'What seems white to my eyes is black if the Church so decides', and it is more generally recommended as a part of religious submission. It was in that spirit that some theologians accepted the dogma of papal infallibility *ex cathedra*, declared at the Vatican Council 1870, and the expression was frequently used in the contemporary polemic. Reason may be renounced submissively, in fulfilment of a religious duty of humility, but followers of many cults and ideologies renounce reason with alacrity, not from duty but from inclination.

Sade /sad (Fr.)/, Marquis de (Donatien-Alphonse-François, Comte de Sade) (1740–1814). De Sade engaged in various sexual perversions, including those which involve the inflicting of pain. Being mentally unbalanced, he was held in confinement for lengthy periods. His novels and short stories contain graphic descriptions of a remarkable variety of sexual practices. He also wrote *La Philosophie dans le boudoir* 1793 (Philosophy in the bedroom).

The apparent amoralism in his writings, which celebrate the unrestrained self-indulgent search for self-gratification, is the natural result of pursuing Enlightenment ideals, in the view of Horkheimer and Adorno in their *Dialektik der Aufklärung* 1947 (*Dialectic of Enlightenment*). It is an astonishing claim, and not uncontroversial.

Saint-Simon /sæsimɔ̃ (Fr.)/, Claude-Henri de Rouvroy, Comte de (1760–1825) French social theorist and reformer. Appealing to recent scientific findings (Cabanis, Bichat), he divided people into three main types: doers, thinkers and feelers. Workers, managers and administrators belong to the first class; scientists to the second; artists, poets, religious and ethical teachers to the third. They were also the ones who would propagate the simple message of universal brotherly love which would replace traditional religion. The disregard of these innate differences in favour of a misguided egalitarianism had been a great mistake; they were in fact the foundation for a solid social edifice, within which all members can spend their energies on developing their innate potential, and not on mutual conflict. General prosperity would then soon follow.

As for the organization of society, Saint-Simon believed that an enlightened people would generally develop the habit of deferring to those in whom they could recognize greater ability (as is the practice among scientists). The love of dominion over others would evaporate, and the energy spent in such a way would be redirected for better use. Most of the functions of the state could be fulfilled by managers, administrators and organizers. Thus, centralized state power would wither away and be reduced to a bare minimum, mainly to prevent crime, which would be very rare since its causes – poverty, for instance – would have been largely eliminated. The broad masses would no longer be subjects and underlings, but co-workers. These ideas were presented in writings from the 1820s, and further developed by his disciples S. A. Bazard (1791–1832) and B. P. Enfantin (1796–1864).

salus populi suprema lex (esto) /ˈsæləs ˈpɔpjʊliː sʊˈpriːmə leks ˈestəʊ/ Lat. let the welfare of the people be the highest law.

salva veritate /ˈsælvə vɛrɪˈtaːteɪ/ Lat. with truth being preserved. The replacement in a sentence of one expression with another *salva veritate* means that the truth-value remains the same after the change.

Sanches, Francisco (1551–1623) (or **Sanchez**) professor at Toulouse from 1585, first in philosophy but later elevated to a chair in medicine. His best-known work is the witty and incisive *Quod nihil scitur* 1581 (That nothing is known). It attacks the ruling scholastic Aristotelianism, with its excessive confidence in syllogisms. Sanches's scepticism is not nihilistic but moderate. He rejects claims to certainty: we understand nothing completely, and we are not in a position to maintain that our propositions are infallible. But theories can be provisionally accepted as they seem plausible. Sanches was in this work one of the first to formulate a modern conception of scientific method.

Sanches, whose ancestors had fled from Portugal, is not to be confused with the learned Spanish Jesuit, Thomas Sanchez (d. 1610), best known for his *De matrimonio* 1592 (On marriage), a treatise in moral theology which discusses cases of conscience in explicit detail.

sanction *n.* a consequence that is attached to an action by a law. On the whole, since Justinian's *INSTITUTIONS* (2,1,10), the term is reserved for consequences unwelcome to the person at the receiving end, i.e. penalties. A fine for drunkenness is a sanction, but a hangover is not – except metaphorically. Bentham, however, used the term in a wider sense, and distinguished in his *Introduction to the Principles of Morals and Legislation* 1789 four kinds of sanction (i.e. rewards or penalties): physical, moral (i.e. popular reactions), political, and religious.

Santayana /sæntɪˈænə/, George (1863–1952) Spanish by blood and nationality, regarded as an American philosopher (also poet, novelist and social critic) since he wrote all his many works in English, Santayana was a notable figure in the great Harvard department of philosophy at the turn of the century (as a younger colleague of William James), and developed his thought (sometimes by negative reaction) in an essentially American context. Santayana lived in America from the age of nine till he was almost 50, when he caused amazement by resigning his Harvard post and settling eventually in Rome. There he composed the great final statement of his philosophy in *Scepticism and Animal Faith* 1923 and the four volumes of *Realms of Being* 1927–40.

Philosophy, he contended, had been too preoccupied with problems of scepticism; rather, it should start from beliefs which it is mere dishonesty to pretend to doubt, and which we should frankly call knowledge since we believe them true and reliably generated. On this basis we find that there are four basic 'realms' (categories) of being: matter (the flux of physical reality), spirit (the consciousness produced in animal brains as they map the environment and organize behaviour – not physical itself but totally dependent upon brain activity), essence (the eternal system of possible types and things which may or may not be actualized from time to time in matter or in spirit) and truth (the total known or unknown character of the world).

Influential in American philosophical naturalism and critical realism, and in rejection of idealism, he is often also associated with America's most distinctive philosophy, pragmatism. But while he agreed that most of our 'truth' in practice consists of useful symbols rather than of a transcription of what exists independently, he insisted that there is also a more literal truth of which science and philosophy may give glimpses.

Santayana's philosophy receives less attention from academic philosophers now than is its due, perhaps because his lush style suggests mere 'poetry'. In fact, he developed an extraordinarily well-worked-out total philosophical system covering ethics, epistemology, metaphysics, theory of mind, etc. On scepticism and knowledge he anticipates more recent developments, while his derivation of ideals of rationality and spirituality from a purely naturalistic ontology has scarcely been caught up with. His somewhat paradoxical stance towards his Catholic background prompted Bertrand Russell's quip that Santayana believes that there is no God and that Mary is his mother. TSP

sapere aude! /'sæpəreɪ 'aʊdeɪ/ Lat. dare to use your reason! These words from Horace were adopted by a Society of the Friends of Truth formed in Berlin in 1736. Its constitution demanded that nothing should be accepted as true without adequate reason. In his famous essay 'What is Enlightenment?' of 1784, Kant suggested that these words could serve as the motto for the Enlightenment. *See also* ETHICS OF BELIEF.

sapientia Lat. wisdom, prudence *n.* One of the four CARDINAL VIRTUES.

Sapir–Whorf /seɪpiə'wɔːf/ **hypothesis** *See* WHORF.

Sartre /sartrə (Fr.)/, Jean-Paul (1905–80) Jean-Paul Sartre, French philosopher, playwright and social critic, was the leading advocate of existentialism. At the heart of his philosophy was a powerful notion of freedom and an uncompromising sense of personal responsibility. In the oppressive conditions of the Nazi occupation and during the embattled years following the Second World War, Sartre insisted that people are responsible for what they make of themselves no matter what the conditions, even in war. Thirty years later, Sartre stated in an interview a few years before his death that he never ceased to believe that 'in the end one is always responsible for what is made of one', a slight revision of his earlier, brasher slogan, 'man makes himself'. To be sure, as a student of Hegel and Marx – and fully conscious of his own physical frailty and the tragedies of the war – Sartre had to be well aware of the many constraints and obstacles to human freedom, but, as a Cartesian, he never deviated from Descartes's classical portrait of human consciousness as free and distinct from the physical universe it inhabited. One is never free of one's 'situation', Sartre tells us, but one is always free to 'negate' that situation and to try to change it. To be human, to be conscious, is to be free to imagine, free to choose, and responsible for one's life.

In his early work, Sartre followed Husserl's phenomenology and established the groundwork for much of what was to follow: his celebration of our remarkable freedom to imagine the world as being other than it is and his denial that the self is 'in' consciousness, much less identical to it. Our perceptions of the world, he argues, are always permeated by imagination, so that we are always aware of options and alternatives. The self, he suggests in *La Transcendance de l'ego* 1936 (*The Transcendence of the Ego*), is out there 'in the world, like the self of another'. The self is an ongoing project in the world, not simply self-consciousness as such ('I think, therefore I am'). This preliminary defence of freedom and the separation of self and consciousness provide the framework for Sartre's greatest philosophical treatise, *L'Etre et le néant* 1943 (*Being and Nothingness*).

The structure of *Being and Nothingness* is clearly Cartesian, despite the strong influence of Heidegger at the time. On the one hand, there is consciousness ('being-for-itself' or *pour soi*) and on the other, the existence of mere things ('being-in-itself' or *en soi*). Sartre describes consciousness as 'nothing' – 'not a thing' and with Husserl's notion of 'intentionality' – the idea that consciousness is always directed at an object; he avoids all talk of objects as being 'in' consciousness and denies that consciousness is or could be part of the causal order. Consciousness is not a 'thing' and is outside the causal order of the world. Consciousness is 'a wind blowing from nowhere towards the world'. It is through the nothingness of consciousness that negation comes into the world – our ability to imagine the world as being other than it is and the inescapable necessity of imagining ourselves as being other than we seem to be. Thus consciousness 'always is what it is not, and is not what it is' – a playful paradox which refers to the fact that we are always in the process of 'transcending' ourselves.

Sartre defines his ontology in terms of the opposition of 'being-in-itself' and 'being-for-itself' and the tension between the fact that we always find ourselves in a particular situation defined by a body of facts that we may not have chosen – our 'FACTICITY' – and our ability to transcend that facticity, imagine and choose, which constitutes our transcendence. We may find ourselves confronting certain facts – poor health, a war, advancing age, being Jewish in an anti-semitic society – but it is always up to us what to make of these facts and how to respond to them. We may occupy a distinctive social role as a policeman or a waiter, but we are always something more; we always transcend such positions. When we try to pretend that we are identical to our roles or the captive of our situations, we are in 'bad faith'. It is bad faith to see ourselves as something fixed and settled, defined by 'human nature', but it is also bad faith to ignore the always restrictive facts and circumstances within which all choices must be made. We are always trying to define ourselves, but we are always an 'open question', a self not yet made. Thus, Sartre tells us, we have a frustrated desire to be God, to be both in-itself and for-itself, defined and free.

Sartre also defines a third ontological category which he calls 'being-for-others'. It is not derivative in that our knowledge of others is not inferred, e.g. by some argument by analogy, from the behaviour of others. Our experience of other people is first of all the experience of *being looked at*, not spectatorship or curiosity. Someone 'catches us in the act', and we define ourselves in their terms. In his *Saint Genet* 1953, Sartre describes the conversion of the ten-year-old Genet into a thief when he is so caught by 'the look' of another. So, too, we 'catch' one another in the judgements we make: these judgements become an inescapable ingredient in our sense of ourselves. Our dependence on them can lead to conflicts so basic that in his play *Huis clos* 1943 (*No Exit*) Sartre has one of his characters utter the famous line, 'Hell is other people'.

After the war Sartre turned increasingly to politics and in his *Critique de la raison dialectique* 1960 (Critique of dialectical reason) he defended Marxism in accordance with existentialist principles. This required a rejection of materialist determinism and an account of political solidarity that had been lacking in *Being and Nothingness*. Not surprisingly, Sartre found the possibility of such solidarity in revolutionary engagement. In accordance with revolutionary principles, Sartre turned down the Nobel Prize in 1964. RSO

satisfaction *n.* a relation between an OPEN SENTENCE and arbitrary objects in a domain. An object satisfies an open sentence if and only if the open sentence is true of the object. For example, Socrates satisfies '_____ is a philosopher', because it is true that Socrates is a philosopher. Similarly, the ordered pair ⟨Romeo, Juliet⟩ satisfies '_____ loves _____', because it is true that the first member of the pair loves the second. As it happens, other ordered pairs, including ⟨Juliet, Romeo⟩, do so too.

The concept is used in logical semantics. That an interpretation satisfies a certain formula (or set of formulae) is another way of saying that the interpretation is a model of the formula (or set of formulae) or, in other words, that the formula (or set of formulae) is true under the interpretation.

Tarski was the first to use the word in this technical sense. Satisfaction is an important auxiliary notion in his definition of truth in formalized languages. To achieve generality, he took the objects related to an open sentence to be members of an infinite sequence.

satisfice *vb.* to obtain an outcome that is good enough. Satisficing action can be contrasted with maximizing action, which seeks the biggest, or with optimizing action, which seeks the best.

In recent decades doubts have arisen about the view that in all rational decision-making the agent seeks the best result. Instead, it is argued, it is often rational to seek to satisfice, i.e. to get a result that is good enough although not necessarily the best.

The term was introduced by Herbert A. Simon in his *Models of Man* 1957.

Saussure /sosyːʀ (Fr.)/, Ferdinand de (1857–1913) Swiss linguist. His structuralist theory of language was published posthumously from lecture notes. The leading idea of the theory is that linguistic signs derive their meaning not from the objects, entities, occurrences, etc. which they may signify by linguistic convention, but from their relationships to other signs in the language, from their position within the system. The theory can be generalized to apply to symbolism generally, and even beyond, and has been important for STRUCTURALISM.

At the extreme, a structuralist theory of language would omit the relation to entities outside the system, and stress coherence rather than correspondence.

Savigny /ˈzavɪnji (Gm.)/, Friedrich Carl von (1779–1861) the founder of the historical school in the philosophy of law; professor at the University of Berlin 1810–42. In his *Vom Beruf unserer Zeit für Gesetzgebung und Rechtswissenschaft* 1814 (Of the vocation of our age for legislation and jurisprudence) he opposed the efforts to codify positive law. The artificial imposition of a comprehensive legal code would necessarily be out of step with the popular will. If the law is to be in tune with the people's sense of justice, it should grow organically by gradual change, in the same way as language, customs, political traditions. Savigny was of course not opposed to changes in the law, but regarded the project of an overall codification as a folly, comparable to the codification of a living language. Savigny was aware that as the law inevitably becomes more technical, it becomes impracticable for the people at large to participate directly in the process of legal development. This does not, however, prevent access to the common sense of justice, which can be interpreted via three main sources: popular custom, laws of long standing that were generally accepted, and jurisprudential opinion, which would normally be a reliable interpretation of the people's will. Savigny is usually taken to represent the romantic view of the importance of the national spirit, in contrast to the eighteenth-century emphasis on universal reason. But in his writings on positive law, which in Germany was the received Roman civil law, little attention was given to the popular sense of legal justice: the emphasis was on the interpretation of past sources of law and of a legal system which, although received in Germany, was of foreign origin.

Scandinavian Realism a school of legal philosophy that flourished chiefly in Sweden and Denmark from the 1920s. Beginning with A. Hägerström, its aim was to remove ideological and metaphysical assumptions from legal theory and practice, by way of critical analysis of fundamental legal concepts. Other prominent representatives were V. Lundstedt, A. Ross (*Directives and Norms* 1958) and K. Olivecrona (*Law as Fact*, 2nd edn, 1971).

scepticism /ˈskɛptɪsɪzm/ (Gr. *skeptikos* investigating, inquiring) *n.* the view that nothing can be known with certainty; that at best, there can only be some private probable opinion.

According to ancient tradition, Pyrrho of Elis was the first sceptical philosopher. It was, however, in the Academy that scepticism flourished for the first time, and through the ages scepticism has often been called academic philosophy. This happened under Arcesilaus in the third century BC. He took strong exception to the Stoic doctrine that impressions that seem to a person to be irresistible and beyond doubt must be true. Probability alone can be our guide to life. This outlook was amplified by Carneades a century later. A third phase of the ancient sceptical tradition developed with Aenesidemus (first century BC), who thought that the academics had compromised their scepticism by actually proposing certain *dogmata* (tenets). It seems that he wanted to return to the Pyrrhonian version, giving emphasis to scepticism as a way of life in which serene peace of mind, *ataraxia*, is achieved by suspension of judgement, *epochē*. It was at this stage that the term *dogmatism* came to be regularly used as the opposite to scepticism. There now emerged a dichotomy between two kinds of scepticism: one suspends judgement, and in particular does not even affirm or deny that certainty is possible; the other does not go so far, but recognizes the fallibility of all judgements and rules out the possibility of certain knowledge. Hume, like many before him, called the more radical kind Pyrrhonian, in contradistinction to the mitigated, academic kind which he favoured (*Enquiry Concerning Human Understanding* 1748, Section 12).

There are hardly any writings extant from any of these thinkers, nor from Agrippa (third century), who is said to have reduced Aenesidemus's ten 'tropes', i.e. modes of conducting sceptical arguments, to five. Our principal source of information is Sextus Empiricus (third century), whose *Pyrrhonienses Hypotyposes (Outlines of Pyrrhonism*) and *Adversus Mathematicos* (*Against the Dogmatists*) have been preserved. HT/ed.

As a philosophical attitude, scepticism was almost unknown in the Middle Ages. It reappeared in the Renaissance partly as a result of the rediscovery of the ancient texts of the Greek sceptic Sextus Empiricus, and partly because these sceptical questions were relevant to the religious battles of the time over the justification of religious knowledge.

The first complete translation of Sextus, in the 1560s, was presented as the decisive answer to Calvinism – if nothing could be known, Calvinism could not be known to be true. Catholics pressed sceptical questions against Protestants and vice versa. But even earlier, in 1520, the arguments of Sextus had been used by Gianfrancesco Pico della Mirandola (1469–1533), the nephew of Giovanni, against astrology, divination, chiromancy and other superstitions, then rampant at all levels of society, but also against the more respectable theories of the time, all in order to secure a place for religious faith. At the same time, Erasmus of Rotterdam (1466–1536) was using sceptical arguments against Luther's severe dogmatism. Michel de Montaigne used Sextus's arguments in his lengthy essay, 'Apology for Raimond Sebond' 1576. Montaigne in his rambling style challenged any knowledge-claims in philosophy, science and theology by raising sceptical doubts about sense-knowledge and reasoning. He pressed the sceptical demand for a guaranteed criterion of true knowledge before any truths could be established. Since we cannot find any criterion, all we can do is suspend judgement, and accept whatever truths God gives us. Montaigne coupled his presentation of complete scepticism with an appeal, whether sincere or not, to faith, and said that he would remain a Catholic since to justify changing religion would require knowledge that he did not possess.

The problems raised by Montaigne and presented in the revived texts of Sextus, and to a lesser extent in Cicero's *Academica*, created a sceptical crisis. They became the fundamental concern of modern philosophy. Descartes tried to set forth a philosophy based on a truth so certain as to allow for no sceptical doubts, and on a criterion that whatever is clearly and distinctly conceived is true. Subsequent sceptics in the seventeenth century – Gassendi, Foucher, Huet, Glanvill, Bayle – undermined each newly proposed answer, and showed that every philosophical system was 'big with contradiction and absurdity'. The sceptical arguments of Bayle and their amplification and extension by Hume have constituted the challenge that each subsequent philosophical system has sought to overcome. RPO

Scheler /ˈʃeɪlə (Eng.); ˈʃelər (Gm.)/, Max (1874–1928) Scheler taught at Jena and Berlin, and after the war at Cologne. He was influenced by Husserl's phenomenology. In a major work on ethical formalism and substantive value-ethics (*Der Formalismus in der Ethik und die materiale Wertethik* 1913–16 (Formalism in ethics and substantive ethics of values)) he argued against Kant's theory because of its formalistic and moralistic character. Values are to be understood in analogy with secondary qualities, like colours. Scheler took the analogy further than is commonly done: in the same way that people lose the ability to discriminate colours at dusk, so it is possible that in a cultural dusk, people become blind to values. The experience of value is neither sensory nor intellectual, but emotional. It is a mistake to believe that all knowledge is based on the senses and the intellect.

Scheler follows Brentano in ascribing intentionality to emotions: they relate to something that has value, in a manner parallel to the way in which a perception relates to something that has a sensory quality. Feelings that lack this intentionality are not value-experiences proper. 'Reactive' emotional states, e.g. lust for revenge, do not have a value immanent in the feeling. Scheler distinguishes different kinds of emotion: those of a sensory kind (e.g. pain); vital emotions, linked to the body, e.g. a sense of vitality or of tiredness; mental emotions, e.g. sadness, joy, sorrow; spiritual emotions, e.g. blessedness or despair.

For each of these four levels there are correlated contrasts of basic value-concepts (see Table 19).

Table 19 Types of emotions (Scheler)

sensory	pleasant	unpleasant
vital	noble	base
mental	right	wrong
	beautiful	ugly
	true	false
spiritual	sacred	profane

Scheler further claimed that there is an *a priori* ranking order of these levels, and uses this to explain *moral* value. The level of bodily senses is lower, the personal feelings located in 'the human heart' are higher. Moral good consists in preferring the higher to the lower.

Scheler linked to this framework psychological analyses of different personality types and their sense of values, an account in which the basic notions of love and hate play an important part.

Schelling /'ʃɛlɪŋ/, Friedrich Wilhelm Joseph (1775–1854) When a student in Tübingen from 1790, Hegel and Hölderlin were among his friends. In 1798 he became professor of philosophy at Jena, shortly before Fichte left, and was in close contact with the Schlegel brothers, Novalis, and other representatives of romantic literature. He held chairs at Würzburg, Erlangen and Munich (1820–41) and then accepted an invitation to fill a chair in Berlin, where in the 1830s the authorities had become concerned over the radical critiques of traditional Christianity from Hegelian writers like Bruno Bauer and D. F. Strauss, and wanted Schelling's influence to counterbalance theirs.

In emphatic opposition to the mechanism and materialism presupposed in scientific theorizing, Schelling asserted that the physical world and its processes are suffused with mind. Nature is mind in the process of becoming conscious. Mind (or the self), on the other hand, is something which in its cognitive, rational activity, creates nature. This is the main thesis of his *System der transcendentalen Idealismus* 1800 (System of transcendental idealism). In this view, nothing in nature is completely lifeless. There is no radical difference between the organic and the inorganic. Nature is unconscious mind; mind is conscious nature. Attempts to explain life in purely mechanistic, lifeless terms are doomed: the life-force is an ultimate element. The theory did not stop at the programmatic level: Schelling's nature-philosophy deals in detail with magnetism (said to be the general form of particularity), the contrast between the light (male in its essence) and the heavy and inert (essentially female) etc. Romantic authors found inspiration in speculations of this kind, and so did certain scientists such as Lorenz Oken (1774–1851), originator of the hypothesis that all organic life arose from primeval slime.

Predominant in Schelling's philosophy is the aesthetic perspective. History is seen as a drama, apparently confused, but moving towards a *dénouement* in which the Absolute reveals itself. The highest values are not practical or moral, but artistic. The universe is a work of art; God is an artist. The central value in religion is the beauty of the religious (especially medieval-catholic) tradition; what is wrong with anti-religious critics is their philistine lack of aesthetic appreciation.

These ideas were incorporated in Schelling's philosophy of identity, in which the contrast between subject and object (which he identifies with the contrasts ideal/real, spirit/nature, mind/matter, etc.) is overcome in ultimate reality, i.e. the Absolute. Schelling claimed affinity with Spinoza, and with the neo-Platonic tradition as represented e.g. by Giordano Bruno. The absolute manifests itself in 'potencies': on the nature side, the main ones are matter, movement and organism; these are present in all natural phenomena. On the side of mind, they are intuition, intellect, reason.

Later, Schelling modified the theory to remove its pantheistic implications and bring it closer to orthodox religion. He gave greater emphasis to the separation of the natural world from the Absolute. In this he was influenced by Franz von Baader and by the mystical writings of Jacob Böhme. The differentiation of everything finite and individual from the primordial unity of the Absolute must be thought of as a spontaneous act of freedom, ultimately incomprehensible for a variety of reasons – for one thing, that act does not occur at any time, since time, and the world, is a result of that act.

schema /ˈskiːmə/ (*sing.*); **schemata** /ˈskiːmətə/ (*pl.*) Kant uses the word in a technical sense when he argues, in the *Critique of Pure Reason* (B176–B187), that in order to apply non-empirical concepts to empirical facts a mediating representation is necessary. Such a third element he calls a *schema*.

In the ordinary case there is, according to Kant, a certain homogeneity between concept and object; hence, to apply the concept of circularity to a plate is fairly unproblematic.

There is no similar homogeneity in the application of concepts such as the categories and the forms of intuition. To apply, e.g., the category of causality to a sequence of events, so that we regard one event as a cause, another as the effect, is more problematic, because the concept of causality involves necessity, but necessity is not an element in our experience, which only tells us that first there is something and then something else.

Our use of schemata, in this case transcendental schemata, explains how we can apply the categories to empirical facts. The transcendental schemata are non-empirical ('intellectual') in one respect, empirical ('sensible') in another.

Kant reviews the categories (the pure concepts of the understanding) and indicates their correlated schemata. For example, the schema for *causality* is *temporal succession according to a rule*; the schema for *necessity* is *existence of an object at all times*, etc. **schematism** *n.*

Schiller, F(erdinand) C(anning) S(cott) (1864–1937) British philosopher who taught at Oxford but later moved to Los Angeles. He called his philosophy humanism: it rejects the idea of an independently existing objective world, and was seen by him as a generalization of pragmatism.

Schiller /ˈʃɪlər (Gm.)/, (Johann Christoph) Friedrich (1759–1805) German playwright, poet, historian and philosopher. His plays have given him literary immortality. In a major essay, *Über Anmuth und Würde* 1793 (*On Grace and Dignity*), he criticized Kant's moral theory because of its one-sided emphasis on the dignity of man, a conception linked to the sense of duty. But, Schiller argued, a person who is torn between duty and inclination is in a state of disharmony, although we will feel respect for persons who follow the path of duty. At a higher level of character development, this inner tension disappears and morality becomes second nature; we find a harmonious character; it is graceful and has an immediate appeal for us. In his *Über die ästhetische Erziehung des Menschen, in einer Reihe von Briefen* 1794–5 (Letters on the aesthetic education of man) he discussed the obstacles hindering the full unfolding of true human nature. There is discord within the individual where man's sensuous nature and his rational and moral nature pull in different directions. Human nature is also thwarted and stunted in its free growth due to external circumstances. The division of functions and of labour leads to overspecialization and one-dimensionality. It creates a closed mind; it destroys generous impulses. A free, republican, political society can come into being only if its citizens achieve a higher culture. This is possible, Schiller argues, even in adverse circumstances. Through art, an individual can reach harmony and a many-sided development of his potential. In aesthetic life, sensuous nature can be uncoercively elevated and brought into harmony with man's higher, rational and moral nature; art enables the individual to lead a richer life. Indeed, the aesthetic faculty of the soul is as fundamental as sense and intellect, the two faculties recognized by Kant. In these and other essays, Schiller also developed a typology of artistic temperaments. His continued reflection on the relation between mind and reality led him away from Kant towards a more subjectivist theory of knowledge.

schism /'sɪzm; 'skɪzm/ (Gr. *schisma* a split, a division; cf. Gr. *schizein* to split) *n.* a division into mutually opposed parties arising from doctrinal differences within a church, sect, political party, club, school of psychoanalysis, etc.

The split between the Eastern and the Western Church in 1054, when the Patriarch in Constantinople, Michael Cerularius, and Pope Leo IX excommunicated each other, is known as the 'great schism'. Attempts to bridge it are still in progress. The split in the Roman Catholic Church (1378–1417), when rival popes resided in Rome and Avignon, is also so called.

Schleiermacher /'ʃlaɪərmaxər (Gm.)/, Friedrich (Ernst Daniel) (1768–1834) German theologian and preacher; he was a student at Halle, and later taught there. From 1810 he was professor of theology at the University of Berlin. In his first important publication, *Über die Religion* ... 1st edn 1799, rev. 3rd edn 1821 (*On religion: Speeches to its Cultured Despisers*), a series of addresses to non-believers, he argued that religion in the true sense is 'feeling and intuition of the universe', 'a sense for the infinite in the finite'. This description suggests that romantic philosophy need not be antithetical to Christianity, even if the paths towards the infinite are differently conceived. In this can be traced an influence of his friend Friedrich von Schlegel, a leading figure in the romantic movement.

Schleiermacher was later to define religion as a feeling, a feeling of absolute dependence, a feeling which, latent or manifest, is present in everyone. Religious doctrines are attempts, more or less adequate, to bring this sense to expression. This was the new way in which Schleiermacher tried to overcome the major crisis facing religion and theology as a consequence of the eighteenth-century critique. The reliability and authority of revelation, scripture, miracles and tradition could not be taken for granted; basing religion on reason alone had turned out to be highly problematic;

and limiting religion exclusively to its moral message, as Kant had tried to do, was inadequate. Schleiermacher's undogmatic theology, attuned to modern culture, set the tone for much Protestant theology. It was only a century later, with Karl Barth and Emil Brunner, that the opposition could launch a counter-offensive.

In the development of hermeneutics, the art of interpretation, Schleiermacher has come to be regarded as an innovator. Traditionally, hermeneutics had dealt chiefly with religious and legal documents. Schleiermacher went further: the aim was to formulate a general method for interpreting a text, a method for eliminating misunderstanding. He saw one important aspect of texts to be that they are their authors' 'externalized thoughts'. Hence, to interpret a text correctly it is necessary to go beyond it and, so to speak, to put oneself in the shoes of the person behind the text. The HERMENEUTIC CIRCLE is, in this instance, that the text can be understood only as a part of the author's overall life; and the life can be understood only by understanding its particular episodes, including the writing of the text. This psychological view of hermeneutics was later adopted by Dilthey, but rejected by Gadamer.

Schlick /ʃlik (Gm.)/, Moritz (1882–1936) born in Berlin, studied physics there under Max Planck, and was also a student in Heidelberg and Lausanne. He held chairs in Rostock, Kiel and, from 1922, in Vienna. In Vienna he was the initiator and leading participant of the Vienna Circle, and many of the central tenets of its logical positivism were also his, notably the VERIFIABILITY PRINCIPLE. His philosophical interests included epistemology, philosophy of science, and ethics. Early influences came from Mach and Poincaré, later ones from Wittgenstein's *Tractatus* and Carnap. In a number of articles, brought together as *Gesammelte Aufsätze* 1938 (Collected essays), he adopted a strong empiricist position, but held that empirical knowledge is about the form of experiences, not about their incommunicable content. He argued that most of the classical problems of philosophy are pseudo-problems, since all genuine problems are either of a mathematical-logical nature, or susceptible to empirical scientific inquiry. This implied that philosophy had reached a turning-point, or rather an end, with the insight that it has no domain of its own. He differed, however, from other logical positivists by regarding ethics as an empirical discipline, and in *Fragen der Ethik* 1930 (Problems of ethics) he analysed the concept of moral goodness in terms of what is approved by society, something which can be established by means of empirical inquiry; the same applies to the concept of the morally required, which he analysed in terms of what is on the whole desired by society.

Schmidt, Caspar *See* STIRNER.

Schmitt /ʃmit/, Carl (1888–1985) German legal and political theorist. His early thinking was influenced by the reactionary-Catholic ideas that had gained ground after 1815. During the Weimar and Nazi periods in Germany, he gained prominence as an acute political analyst.

With a keen sense for the weak points in liberal and democratic theory, Schmitt rejected as unrealistic both the ideals of parliamentary democracy and the ideal of a peaceful international world-order. Instead, the relation friend/foe emerged as the basic category in his political theory: antagonism is the basic category of politics. He rejected as illusory the idea that conflict can be reduced by compromise or consensus or rendered non-violent in the forms of economic competition or public debate.

Schmitt's analytical and critical powers

were not, however, equally applied to a critique of reactionary, fascist and nationalist ideology and practice; he was an apologist for these. One signal instance is his essay 'Der Führer schützt das Recht' 1934 (The Fuehrer protects the legal order), published in the wake of Hitler's assassination campaign against the Röhm faction. On the whole, he viewed Nazi brutality, war of conquest, and mass murder with equanimity. But it would be a mistake to describe his theorizing as a value-free exercise in political realism. There are many implicit or explicit value-judgements in his writings, although they shifted over time as he modified his stance to fit in with the values of what he took to be the winning side.

Schmitt's allegiance to the powers that be, and the political bias of most of his theoretical work, have not discouraged a number of post-war political theorists, both right and left, from being favourably disposed towards his ideas.

scholasticism /skəˈlæstɪsɪzm/ *n.* university philosophy; academic philosophy: philosophy of the kind cultivated in the schools (i.e. the medieval Christian universities). One important feature that distinguished scholastic from monastic learning was the practice of disputations and the prevalence of learned disputes. Sometimes, 'scholastic' would be used as a synonym of 'dialectic'.

Among the leading scholastic philosophers were John Duns Scotus, Thomas Aquinas and William of Ockham. From the Renaissance onwards, scholasticism became a byword for excessive cavilling, needless subtlety, turgidity, obscurity, etc. The association between scholasticism and Roman Catholic theology and philosophy was a further reason for condemnation by writers such as Locke, Pufendorf, Hegel, etc.

As the climate of opinion on these matters has changed in the course of the twentieth century, there has been a revival of scholarly interest in medieval thought. The more extreme attitudes for and against have virtually disappeared, and the quality of research – notably into medieval logic – has vastly improved. JM

Scholz /ʃɔlts (Gm.)/, Heinrich (1884–1956) German philosopher, professor at Münster from 1928. He pioneered in Germany an analytical approach to the philosophy of religion. In the spirit of Leibniz, Bolzano and Frege, he developed a formalized account of metaphysics in *Metaphysik als strenge Wissenschaft* 1941 (Metaphysics as an exact science). In mid-career, mathematical logic became his central area of interest. In his view, set out in the posthumous *Mathesis universalis* 1961, the laws of logic are truths about reality known directly by rational intuition.

school (Gr. *scholē* leisure) *n.* **1** In the Middle Ages, the Latin *schola* initially denoted a body of teachers and scholars, devoted to higher learning.
2 what is called a school of philosophy consists of two or more philosophers between whom there is contact and similarity of outlook.

Philosophers who are said to belong to a school in this sense usually deny it, and emphasize their differences, perhaps for fear of being thought unoriginal. This brings to mind 'The Law of Social Appearances' formulated by the English satirist Michael Frayn: 'The homogeneity of a group seen from outside is in inverse proportion to the heterogeneity seen from within,' or 'Likeness is in the eye of the unlike; the like see nothing but their unlikeness.'

Schopenhauer /ˈʃəʊpənhaʊə/ (Eng.); ˈʃoːpənhaʊər (Gm.)/, Arthur (1788–1860) German philosopher, most famous for his pessimist philosophy of the Will which he articulated in opposition to the optimistic philosophical system of Hegel. His influence on many great writers was remarkable; among them were Leo Tolstoy, Thomas Hardy, Thomas Mann, Richard Wagner, Sigmund Freud, Friedrich Nietzsche and Ludwig Wittgenstein.

Schopenhauer's philosophical system is an ingenious synthesis of Platonism, Kantianism and Eastern philosophy (especially that of the Buddhist tradition). The primary statement of this system occurs in *Die Welt als Wille und Vorstellung* 1818, 2nd rev. edn 1844 (*The World as Will and Representation*) which builds on his earlier dissertation, *Über die vierfache Wurzel des Satzes vom zureichende Grunde* 1813 (*On the Fourfold Root of the Principle of Sufficient Reason*). Schopenhauer never disavowed any claim that he made in these works, nor, for that matter, in his other early work on vision and colours (1815). Thus, all Schopenhauer's subsequent works further defended and developed the system set forth in *The World as Will and Representation*. His later works include: 'On the Will in Nature' 1836, republished with 'On the Foundation of Morality' in *Die beiden Grundprobleme der Ethik* 1841 (*The Two Fundamental Problems of Ethics*); a second edition of *The World as Will and Representation* which included a second volume of supplementary essays (1844); a revised and enlarged edition of *On the Fourfold Root* . . . 1847; and another collection of essays, *Parerga and Paralipomena* 1851.

He builds his system on the Kantian distinction between the noumenal world (the 'thing-in-itself') and the phenomenal world (the world of our everyday experience). The phenomenal world is 'the world as representation', the world as constituted by our conscious, perceiving minds. The world of representation is governed, according to Schopenhauer, by the principle of sufficient reason. In his account, this is the principle that every object in the phenomenal world is determined by its relations to all other objects. Like Kant, Schopenhauer rejects the application of such a principle to the relation between the phenomenal and noumenal worlds.

The noumenal world is the reality that underlies the world as representation. Unlike Kant, who claimed that the thing-in-itself was inaccessible to human knowledge, Schopenhauer claimed that we have immediate access to one noumenon, i.e. one's own will, which is the object of inner experience. As a phenomenon, it is identical with the body and its actions. Our inner experience also gives us insight into the nature of the inner life of reality. This inner life is will, and we are encouraged to view natural processes like a tree's growth, as well as our own behaviour, as manifesting will. Since we cannot live, either intellectually or emotionally, with the thought that the thing-in-itself is unknowable, and since will is the only thing other than phenomena of which we have knowledge, the will must therefore be the thing-in-itself. Schopenhauer accepts Kant's claim that the thing-in-itself is unity; the will, the reality that underlies all phenomena, is so also, because plurality applies only to space and time and we have no grounds for ascribing it to the noumenon.

Schopenhauer incorporates Platonism into his system in his account of natural kinds. Despite the fact that all phenomenal objects are manifestations of the same will, we observe that phenomenal objects are of various kinds, with various kinds standing in a definite relationship to one another. Schopenhauer explains this by invoking Plato's Ideas (or Forms). The Platonic Ideas are the eternal archetypes for the particular, transient objects that we observe in the phenomenal world. After a fashion, the Platonic Ideas bridge the world as will and the world as representation.

Because each particular manifests a particular idea, we are able, at times, to observe something universal within them. Aesthetic experience is the context in which we recognize the universal within the particular object. When we behold an object in this way, we see it as beautiful. At the same time, the sense of self changes, in that in the experience of art, the sense of individuality, with its associated suffering, is to some extent overcome. We come closer to a universal will-less consciousness. This is above all the case with music. It is the purest form of art, and has a special status, since it expresses ultimate reality immediately, without intervening universals or platonic forms.

According to Schopenhauer, this transformation of one's individual selfhood is the primary respite that human beings have from the tribulation of willing. Although will is what we essentially are, it is also the ultimate cause of our suffering. Will produces conflict among individuals, deludes us into believing that obtaining what we want is important, continually stimulates new desires, and generally inspires acts of evil. The will causes us to suffer and to inflict suffering. Aesthetic experience, particularly of music, provides an occasional reprieve, but aesthetic experience is short-lived.

Schopenhauer's thoroughgoing pessimism was neatly condensed in his turning *Welt* (world) into an acronym: *Weh* (woe), *Elend* (misery), *Leid* (suffering), *Tod* (death). The only secure salvation from a life of continual suffering is renunciation of the will. More or less following the Four Noble Truths of Buddhism, Schopenhauer argues that: (1) life consists of suffering; (2) suffering is caused by desire; (3) suffering can cease only through elimination of desire; and (4) the saintly life is the way to eliminate desire. Schopenhauer's formula for the saintly life was extremely ascetic, involving absolute chastity, mortification of the body, and poverty. His critics observed that there was nothing of this in his own life. Schopenhauer, however, accepted the testimony of the world's mystics that such a life is supremely blissful.

Although his system centres around individual misery and salvation, Schopenhauer does also have an ethical theory. To state the principle of morality is easy, he asserts. It is: 'harm nobody, but help others as much as you can'. But to find a basis for morality is difficult: what reason could one have for not following one's egoistic, anti-moral impulses? The answer, he argues, is to be found in metaphysics: at the level of reality, there can be no distinction between individual selves, so in reality I harm myself as much as I harm others; and if I refuse to help another I am forgoing something I myself need.

The quality of Schopenhauer's prose is unequalled among German philosophers, and is indeed outstanding. He was also a master of eloquent invective. The targets of his wrath were legion: among them were loud noise-making, the French language, religion, and the leading academic philosophers of his time – Fichte, Schelling and, above all, Hegel. Sometimes he overstepped the bounds: his anti-semitic and misogynist outbursts are not to his credit.

Schopenhauer was strikingly innovative in a number of respects. He was a philosophical pioneer in espousing voluntarism, the view that will is the fundamental metaphysical principle underlying all reality. Convinced that knowledge is subordinate to will, Schopenhauer introduced a conception of the unconscious that influenced Freudian psychoanalytic theory. He was the first major European philosopher seriously to pursue a study of Eastern philosophical systems; and his insistence that moral maxims and universal principles are ineffective remedies for the tribulations of the will is a precursor of more radical critiques of morality. KHI

Schütz /ʃʊts (Eng.); ʃyts (Gm.)/, Alfred (1899–1959) Austrian social theorist, in exile from 1939 in the USA, where he held a chair at the New School of Social Research in New York from 1952. He was an early opponent of positivism and behaviourism in the human and social sciences, and inspired phenomenological sociology by insisting that the basis for sociological analysis must be the way that people subjectively view their social environment, that is, their immediate common-sense view, as suggested by the title of his *Der sinnhafte Aufbau der sozialen Welt* 1932 (transl. as *The Phenomenology of the Social World*). However, he later abandoned its methodological individualism. His concept of 'the social construction of reality' (this is the title of a work, influenced by his ideas, by P. Berger and T. Luckmann 1966) need not be taken as a denial of an independent reality.

Schweitzer /ˈʃvaɪtsər (Gm.)/, Albert (1875–1965) German theologian, musician, musicologist, physician, humanitarian and philosopher. In his liberal-Protestant theological writings he reviewed the quest, initiated in the eighteenth century, for the historical Jesus, arguing that our historical knowledge of this enigmatic person is very limited. His *Kulturphilosophie* 1923 deals with the decline of Western civilization and with the problem of how human civilization can survive at all: a precondition is the recognition of the ethical principle of reverence for life. This principle can be given a metaphysical justification in that the life that ought to be respected is not merely that of another individual being, but is also, in a deeper sense, one of which each individual is a joint participant.

science *n.* Even in writings as recent as those of Locke and Hume there are many passages where the words 'science', 'scientific', etc., derived from *scientia* (the Latin equivalent of the Greek *epistēmē*), are reserved for knowledge of what is necessarily the case. Such knowledge is acquired by rational intuition or by demonstration. This usage goes back to Plato and Aristotle.

Well into the eighteenth century, what we call natural science was usually called natural philosophy.

scientia media /ˈʃɪentɪə ˈmɛdɪə/ Lat. intermediate (or middle) knowledge. *See also* MOLINA.

scientific realism *See* REALISM.

scientism *n.* the belief that the methods of the natural sciences are applicable in all inquiry, especially in the human and social sciences. **scientistic** *adj.*

scope, ambiguity of The statement *it is not the case that p implies q* is ambiguous. If we let '~' stand for 'it is not the case that', the statement can be symbolized either ~(*p implies q*) or (~*p implies q*). The scope of the negation-operator makes the difference. Also, the statement *If someone shows courage we will win* is ambiguous. It can mean either 'There is someone such that if he shows courage we will win' or 'If anyone shows courage we will win'. The first can be true even if some show of courage does not lead to a win; the second is true only if every show of courage leads to a win. In standard symbolism, the difference is that between $(\exists x)(Fx \supset p)$ and $(\exists x)(Fx) \supset p$. In the first, p is within the scope of the quantifier, in the second, p is outside.

Erroneous inferences due to such ambiguities can be described as fallacies of scope.

Scotism *n.* the philosophical and theological tradition inspired by the thought of John Duns Scotus. It was cultivated especially among the Franciscans, and officially accepted as authoritative in 1633. This was one factor that contributed to its importance in the universities in Roman Catholic countries, especially in the sixteenth to eighteenth centuries.

Scottish Enlightenment a cultural and intellectual movement in eighteenth-century Scotland. A prominent characteristic was the belief in improvement and progress in various areas: education, the arts, the human and natural sciences, agriculture and commerce. In religion, it was in opposition to the dour orthodox Calvinism dominant in the Church of Scotland early in the century. The major philosophical writers were Francis Hutcheson, David Hume, Adam Smith, Adam Ferguson, Thomas Reid and Dugald Stewart.

Scotus /ˈskəʊtəs/ *See* DUNS SCOTUS; ERIUGENA.

sea-battle *See* FUTURE CONTINGENTS.

Searle /sɜːl/, John (1932–)

A philosophical self-portrait: I cannot remember a time when I was not interested in philosophical questions, but I began university work in the subject at Wisconsin. The teacher there who most influenced me was Julius Weinberg. I left Wisconsin for Oxford on a Rhodes Scholarship at the age of 19 at the end of my junior year, and subsequently received all of my university degrees from Oxford. After I got my B.A. I had my first teaching job as a lecturer at Christ Church. I was in Oxford both as a student and as a don from 1952–9. This was a golden age in Oxford philosophy and I was very much influenced by the philosophical activity of the time, especially by two of my teachers, J. L. Austin and P. F. Strawson.

My earliest work was in the philosophy of language, and a good deal of it was an attempt to develop a general theory of speech acts. I made extensive use of insights already developed by other Oxford philosophers, especially Austin. In 1959 I completed my D. Phil. degree and took a position at the University of California, Berkeley, where I have been teaching ever since, except for numerous visiting positions in the US, Europe, and South America. My first published article was 'Proper names' *Mind 67* (1958) which I wrote as a discussion paper for my tutor, Peter Strawson, in 1955. Among my other early articles, perhaps the most controversial were, 'How to derive "Ought" from "Is"' *Philosophical Review 73* (1964), 'What is a Speech Act?' (*Philosophy in America* 1965) and 'Meaning and Speech Acts' *Philosophical Review 71* (1962). In 'How to derive "Ought" from "Is"' I tacked the then prevailing linguistic version of the fact/value dichotomy from the point of view of the theory of speech acts. This article caused a great deal of controversy, but nothing has led me to doubt its fundamental claim, namely that the traditional metaphysical distinction between fact and value cannot be captured by the linguistic distinction between 'evaluative' and 'descriptive' because all such speech act notions are already normative.

My work on speech acts eventually culminated in my first book, *Speech Acts: An Essay in the Philosophy of Language* 1969. The theme of this book is that speaking a language is engaging in a rule-governed form of behaviour, and that the basic unit of linguistic communication is the speech act. As a consequence of this approach, most of the problems in the philosophy of language, such as those concerning reference and meaning, are really aspects of the theory of speech acts. All human linguistic communication is the performance of speech acts. The primary aim of this book is to develop an analysis of illocutionary acts, such as promises, statements, commands, pledges, apologies, and to show how this approach could be applied to a number of philosophical problems.

Speech Acts is largely concerned with literal and serious uses of language, but this leaves a number of questions unanswered concerning metaphor, fiction, indirect speech acts, etc. I attempted to deal with these problems in a number of subsequent articles, and these were eventually collected in my second philosophical volume, *Expression and Meaning* 1979. The general thesis of *Expression and Meaning* is that the apparatus of intentionality that was used in the original theory of speech acts could deal with such other questions as those concerning metaphor, fiction, indirection, etc. In my view the most important article in this volume is the 'Taxonomy of Illocutionary Acts' in which I claim that there are not an infinite or indefinite number of things one can do with language. Rather, in the speech act line of business, there are exactly five possible basic types of illocutionary acts: assertives, directives, commissives, expressives and declarations.

The theory of language I developed had made extensive use of mentalistic notions, such as belief, desire, and intention, and the use of these philosophically troubling notions eventually led me to undertake a full-scale analysis of these and other mental concepts in my book, *Intentionality: An Essay in the Philosophy of Mind* 1983. This book is an attempt to advance a general theory of intentionality. I attempt to account for a great many forms of intentionality: beliefs, desires, intentional actions, perceptions, memories, etc., using a rather simple apparatus, including such notions as conditions of satisfaction, direction of fit, propositional content, psychological mode, intentional causation, the holistic network of intentionality, and so on.

In both *Expression and Meaning* and *Intentionality*, I advance a thesis that all representational phenomena, such as those one finds in intentional states and speech acts, require a set of nonrepresentational 'background' capacities for their functioning. The interpretation of a speech act or of an intentional state is only fixed relative to a set of biologically and culturally conditioned background capacities. All meaning and intentionality only function against a set of capacities that are not themselves part of meaning and intentionality.

In the late 1970s I became very interested in the then-developing new discipline of cognitive science. It seemed to me that cognitive science promised an exciting break with the sterile behaviourism that had plagued academic psychology. But, unfortunately, in the early days at least it suffered from a misunderstanding of the relationship between computers and brains. I refuted the idea that the brain is a digital computer and that the mind is a computer program in an article which became the topic of much controversy and debate, 'Minds, brains and programs' (*Behavioral and Brain Sciences* 1980). In this article, I advanced the now well-known Chinese Room Argument. The argument is this: If implementing a computer program were sufficient for understanding, then implementing a computer program for answering questions in Chinese should be sufficient for understanding Chinese. But this is plainly not the case, as is shown by the fact that if we imagine a person who knows no Chinese, such as myself, locked in a room, carrying out rules for giving Chinese symbol responses in answer to Chinese symbol questions, there is no way, just from the computer program, that I could gain an understanding of Chinese. From the outside I might appear to have a perfect knowledge of Chinese, but from inside, where understanding takes place, I understand nothing of Chinese. The force of this argument has been debated extensively in the literature, and there must be at least a couple of hundred published discussions of it, but nothing in this literature has led me to suppose that the Chinese Room Argument is anything less than a decisive refutation of the more ambitious claims of artificial intelligence.

My debates with artificial intelligence, as well as my other work in the philosophy of mind, led to my BBC Reith Lectures of 1984, published as *Minds, Brains and Science*. Here, I not only continued the debate about the Chinese Room, but also dealt with several more traditional problems in the philosophy of mind, such as the mind–body problem, and the problem of free will.

In 1992 I published *The Rediscovery of the Mind*, a further development of my views in the philosophy of mind. In this book, and in a series of articles that preceded it, I advance the thesis that an understanding of consciousness is essential to an understanding of mental phenomena and that much of the inadequacy of contemporary cognitive science and philosophy of mind derives from a failure to come to terms with the fact of consciousness as a subjective, qualitative biological phenomenon. About the mind–body problem, I advocated the thesis that the problem has a simple solution: mental states are caused by neurophysiological processes in the brain and are themselves higher-level features of the brain. I call this view, 'biological naturalism'. This book also extends the criticism of the computational theory of the mind: Except in the rare cases where a conscious agent is computing a function, say by doing arithmetic problems, 'computation' does not name an intrinsic process going on in nature but an observer relative phenomenon. A system only computes relative to the assignment of a computational interpretation to it by an outside observer. This shows that the thesis that the brain is a digital computer is incoherent: If it claims that the brain is intrinsically a digital computer the answer is that it is trivially false, because nothing is intrinsically a digital computer. If it claims that a computational interpretation can be assigned to the brain, it is empty because a computational interpretation can be assigned to any process whatever.

My more recent *The Construction of Social Reality* 1995 uses materials from my earlier work to try to answer fundamental questions in the foundations of the social sciences. What is the ontology of social reality? And in particular, how can it be the case that there is an objective reality of money, property, marriage, government, etc., which in some sense exists only by human agreement or human convention? This book provides a detailed analysis of the ontology of social and institutional reality. It also contains a defence of external realism, the idea that there is a real world that exists independently of our representations, and a defence of the correspondence theory of truth, the idea that statements are typically true, if and only if they correspond to facts in the world independently of the statement.

In addition to purely professional philosophical work, I have been active in issues of general cultural concern. I have published several articles on higher education, a book on student unrest, *The Campus War* 1971, and engaged in debates with literary theorists. JSE

secondary qualities *See* PRIMARY AND SECONDARY QUALITIES; QUALITIES.

secular *adj.* **1** non-religious, worldly. **2** used of a non-member of a religious order: secular clergy are clergy not bound by monastic vows.

secularization *n.* **1** the abandoning of religious assumptions or practices. 2 deconsecration (for instance, of a building).

secundum quid /sɪ'kʊndəm 'kwɪd/ Lat. in a certain respect; according to something, relative to something. The contrasting term is *simpliciter* (simply; without qualification; absolutely).

This expression is used, *inter alia*, in the traditional labelling of fallacies. Fallacies *secundum quid* are those that neglect a necessary qualification. One type infers from something stated without qualification to something which holds only under certain conditions (*a dicto simpliciter ad dictum secundum quid*). The other type infers in the opposite direction, from something that holds under a certain condition to something that holds without qualification (*a dicto secundum quid ad dictum simpliciter*).

self-contradiction *n.* a self-contradictory proposition is one which logically implies both some proposition p and its negation, not-p, and hence the conjunction (p and not-p).

It is commonly taken for granted that all propositions of the form (p and not-p), and therefore all self-contradictions, cannot be true but must be false. Many philosophical refutations consist of showing that a proposed view leads to self-contradiction.

self-realization *n.* This consists in bringing to actuality whatever is potentially present in the self. Certain theories, especially in romantic philosophy, take self-realization to be the highest good, and the stifling of a person's potential to be a great evil.

This doctrine, if proposed without qualification, seems problematic. We would not normally think that the stifling of certain tendencies in a potential axe-murderer is a great evil. One qualification often introduced is that the self, whose realization is the highest good, is a person's *true* self.

self-refutation *n.* An utterance is said to be self-refuting if it is possible, as soon as it has been made, for the hearer to infer that it cannot be true. For instance, a person's utterance: 'I never say a word' cannot be both made and true. This is an example of a *pragmatic* self-refutation: the act of asserting shows that what is asserted is false. There are also *logically* self-refuting propositions. For example, a statement which gives rise to the LIAR PARADOX logically implies its own falsity and hence implies a contradiction.

A self-defeating statement is not the same as a self-refuting statement. A self-defeating statement is a prediction which, by being made, brings about a situation in which it is false. For instance, in a market the publication of a prediction that a certain commodity will be scarce can be self-defeating, since it may bring about an increase in supply. Conversely, the publication of a prediction that a certain bank cannot meet its commitments can be self-fulfilling.

Sellars /'sɛləz/, Roy Wood (1880–1973) American philosopher, who taught at the University of Michigan. He argued for CRITICAL REALISM in epistemology, and for a modern, humanist re-interpretation of religion.

Sellars, Wilfrid (1912–89) American philosopher, son of Roy Wood Sellars, for many years professor at the University of Pittsburgh, and the author of a very influential paper, 'Empiricism and the Philosophy of Mind' 1956. In this paper Sellars put forward the doctrine of 'psychological nominalism', viz. that 'all awareness ... is a linguistic affair'. He argued that the empiricist tradition, especially in Hume's notion of 'sense-impression' and in the later notion of 'sense-data', had systematically confused that which causes a belief with the content of that belief. In *Science, Perception and*

Reality 1963 and *Science and Metaphysics* 1967, Sellars set out a very complex quasi-Kantian account of knowledge and truth. This combined a coherentist and holist view of inquiry with an account (adapted from Wittgenstein's *Tractatus*) of true sentences as picturing reality. These books also put forward an original exploration of the relations between theoretical, practical and moral reasoning. Sellars was one of the few important analytic philosophers who had an extensive and detailed knowledge of the history of philosophy, and his *Essays in Philosophy and its History* 1974 contain original interpretations of Plato, Descartes and Kant. RR

semantic (Gr. *sēma* sign) *adj.* pertaining to the meaning of signs and symbols, especially linguistic ones (i.e. words and sentences).

semantic ascent the shift from talking *in* certain terms to talking *about* them. Examples are the shifts: from 'There are wombats in Tasmania' to ' "Wombat" ' is true of some creatures in Tasmania'; from 'Malmö is a city' to ' "Malmö" is the name of a city'; from discussing the whiteness of snow to discussing the truth of 'Snow is white'. The shift from the material to the formal mode is a case of semantic ascent. The term was introduced by W. V. O. Quine in the last section of *Word and Object* 1960.

semantic realism *See* REALISM.

semantics *n. sing.* **1** a discipline concerned with inquiry into the meaning of symbols, and especially linguistic meaning. Semantics in this sense is often contrasted with syntax (or, less commonly, syntactics), which deals with structures, and pragmatics, which deals with the use of symbols in their relation to speakers, listeners and social context.
2 The object of the inquiry just mentioned.
3 A semantics for a system of formal logic is specified by a set of clauses which state what is to count as an *interpretation* of the formulae of the system, what is to count as *truth* in an interpretation, and hence what it is for a formula to be *valid*, for one formula to *entail* another, for a set of formulae to be *inconsistent*.

The system itself is characterized independently through its syntax, specified by a set of clauses which state what is to count as symbols, as a well-formed formula, as axioms, and as rules of inference.

For example, the semantics for standard propositional logic contains a clause that the sentence-letters can be assigned one of the truth-values T or F, and a number of clauses specifying how the truth-value of a compound sentence depends on the truth-values of its components. The semantics for predicate logic has additional clauses that to an individual variable is assigned one object from the domain, that to a monadic predicate-letter is assigned a set of individuals from the domain, etc.

semantic tableau /ˈtæbləʊ/ a method of proof in elementary logic to show that a set of formulae is inconsistent. It is probably the simplest of all proof procedures for elementary logic, and it is very easily shown to be complete (COMPLETENESS). The method was devised by E. W. Beth (1908–64) and has gradually been gaining acceptance since the 1960s.

semiology *See* SEMIOTICS.

semiotics (Gr. *sēmeion* sign) *n. sing.* **1** Semiotics is the name given by Charles Morris to the general inquiry into, or theory of, linguistic meaning. He distinguished three branches, which he called syntactics, semantics and pragmatics.
2 Semiotics (or *semiology*) is also the name used for an even more general inquiry into, or theory of, signs. The area studied in-

cludes various forms of action and communication, indeed anything that is capable of interpretation. Accordingly, there are rival conceptions of what such a study would be about. It might include verbal and non-verbal communication alike: not only speech and writing, but also gestures, clothing, architectural designs, works of art, film, etc. The term is sometimes used for a particular theoretical approach, especially that represented by French structuralists.

Peirce used the word 'semiotics'; Saussure, 'semiology'. Other terms have been proposed but have not become firmly established, e.g. 'significs'. There are striking differences between the American and the French conceptions of what to expect from semiotics.

Semiotics (*la sémiotique*) is quite different from 'the semiotic' (*le sémiotique*), which in Lacan's terminology stands for an inchoate, pre-verbal phase of signifying mental activity, which precedes the symbolic phase in which there is awareness of the contrast between a signifying subject and a signified object. The semiotic is superseded but not eliminated, and is capable of disrupting the symbolic.

semi-Pelagianism *n.* a theological doctrine and movement that flourished in the fourth and fifth centuries. The term is used to denote a position intermediate between the Pauline–Augustinian doctrine of the corruption of human nature after the Fall, and the very liberal Pelagianism. It accepts the doctrine of original sin and the necessity of divine grace for salvation, contrary to Pelagianism, but in order to salvage God's justice, it rejects the doctrine of man's total inability to do something for his salvation, a doctrine which seems to imply predestination and fatalism. From the sixth century it was condemned as heretical. Much later, Arminians were accused of semi-Pelagianism by Calvinists, Jesuits by Jansenists, etc.

sempiternal /sɛmpɪˈtɜːnəl/ *adj.* everlasting.

Seneca /ˈsɛnɪkə/, Lucius Annaeus (*c.* 5 BC–AD 65) dramatist, satirist and philosopher, educated in Rome, of Iberian ancestry. The main concern of his writings was ethical, as represented by his moral letters (*Letters to Lucilius*) and his moral essays; (Stoic) logic and physics were assigned a secondary role even in his *Physical Problems*. In his ethical writings he draws freely not only on the teachings of the Stoics, but also on those of the Epicurean and other schools. Seneca gives persuasive analyses of the problems of life and how to confront them wisely. His writings with their vivid depictions of vice and virtue have exercised a remarkable influence on Western thought since the Renaissance.

sense and reference Two referring expressions can refer to the same entity, and still have different senses. The standard example in Frege's celebrated article '*Über Sinn und Bedeutung*' 1892 (On sense and reference) are the two expressions 'the evening star' and 'the morning star'. They refer to the same object, i.e. the planet Venus, but differ in sense. This is why the proposition 'the evening star is the morning star' provides useful information, whilst neither 'the evening star is the evening star' nor 'the morning star is the morning star' does.

The distinction has much in common with the one between connotation and denotation, and with the one between intension and extension.

Frege held that the distinction applies not only to definite descriptions but also to predicates, and to proper names, e.g. 'Alexander the Great', 'Joe Blow', 'Cicero', etc. This is why the sentence 'Cicero is Tully' provides useful information to someone whose knowledge of the Roman statesman and writer is incomplete. Also, if in the sentence 'Cicero died in 43 BC' the name 'Cicero' is replaced by another expression with the same reference, e.g. 'the prosecutor of Catiline', the resulting sentence will have the same truth-value as the original one.

Frege also applied the distinction to sentences. Sentences also can differ in sense but have the same reference. Indeed, he held that all true sentences have the same reference, i.e. to 'the true', and all false ones to 'the false'. This part of his theory has gained few adherents, but for terms, the sense–reference distinction has come to be generally accepted.

sense-datum (*sing.*); **sense-data** (*pl.*) (Lat. *datum* given) *n.* an immediate object of sensory perception.

We can have sensory experiences of things which do not exist. The recipient of a heavy blow may see stars; there are no stars visible, but there is something that the victim sees: a sense-datum. Many philosophers have argued that sense-data are the immediate object of all sensory perception.

The term denotes at least some of the things earlier writers had referred to as *ideas of sense* (Locke), *ideas* and *sensible qualities* (Berkeley), *impressions* (Hume). The term gained currency around 1910 through the writings of G. E. Moore and Bertrand Russell, but had been used well before then by other writers, e.g. A. C. Fraser, Josiah Royce, and William James in *Principles of Psychology* 1890.

sensibility *n.* **1** delicacy of taste and feeling; sensitivity. **2** faculty of sensory perception. In Kant, things are given to us by means of sensibility: it is a receptive faculty, contrasted with the intellect, the faculty of thought.

sensible *adj.* **1** pertaining to the world of sense-experience. In Kant's philosophy, the sensible world is the world of which it is possible to have empirical knowledge, i.e. knowledge based on sensory intuition, in contrast to the intelligible world which, since we have no direct rational intuition, is unknowable.
2 showing good sense or judgement.

sensible knave Hume notes in his *Enquiry Concerning the Principles of Morals* (at the end of Section 9, Part 2) that the general observance of the rules of justice is of general benefit, but that it may seem as if a sensible knave (i.e. a shrewd scoundrel) can benefit even more by making exceptions in his own favour. This leads to the question, asked already in Book I of Plato's *Republic*, why a man who may seem to be a loser by his integrity should nevertheless act honestly.

sensum (*sing.*); **sensa** (*pl.*) *n.* something sensed. *See* SENSE-DATUM.

Sentences *See* PETER (THE) LOMBARD.

sentential calculus propositional calculus.

sentential logic propositional logic.

sentiment *n.* **1** opinion. When Hume talks of 'unfeigned sentiments', he means opinions declared without disguise. **2** feeling, emotion.

The two senses are distinct. Opinions are true or false, emotions are not.

Note: Sentimental and its cognates usually connote certain kinds of feeling: the tender ones. Depending on the context, sentimentality can connote refinement, emotionalism, mawkishness, etc.

separateness of persons It is an objection against many versions of utilitarianism that it does not allow for the 'separateness of persons', that it fails to recognize people as distinct individuals.

The argument is this: according to utilitarianism, right action is such action as tends to promote the good, for instance, maximal satisfaction of desires. But, it is objected, the theory is indifferent to the question of *whose* desires are satisfied. It allows for one person's loss to be offset by another person's greater gain, and it is only the net sum total that ultimately matters. A recognition of the 'separateness of persons' is needed to put constraints on such trade-offs.

The expression was introduced, and this line of argument revived, by John Rawls in *A Theory of Justice*.

sequents, calculus of a formalization of first-order logic, developed by Gentzen and closely linked to systems of natural deduction. In this calculus, sequents are expressions written in the form $A_1, A_2, \ldots A_n \rightarrow B_1, B_2, \ldots B_m$. Here, the set of As is called the *antecedent* and the set of Bs the *succedent* of the sequent. The intended interpretation of the sequent is that of an entailment from the *conjunction* of the As to the *disjunction* of the Bs. That is, the sequent is valid if and only if the truth of all the As implies the truth of at least one B.

Examples of rules in the sequent calculus are

$$\frac{\Gamma \rightarrow \Delta}{\Gamma, A \rightarrow \Delta}$$

i.e. the validity of the first sequent implies the validity of the second; and

$$\frac{\Gamma \rightarrow A \quad \Gamma, A \rightarrow \Delta}{\Gamma \rightarrow \Delta}$$

i.e. the validity of the first two sequents implies the validity of the last.

The use of sequents has allowed for developments of remarkable power and elegance in PROOF THEORY.

serial *adj.* a relation R is serial if and only if it is: irreflexive, i.e. $Rxy \supset \sim(x = y)$; transitive, i.e. $Rxy \& Ryz \supset Rxz$; connected, i.e. $Rxy \vee Ryx \vee x = y$.

seriality *n.* **1** the character of a serial relation. **2** the character of a series.

series *n.* **1** (in mathematics) Given a sequence of numbers, $a_0, a_1, a_2, a_3, \ldots$, a series is the sequence of the partial sums of the initial segments. The first member of the series is a_0, the second is $(a_0 + a_1)$, the third is $(a_0 + a_1 + a_2)$, and so on. If the members of the series converge to a limit, the limit is called the sum of the series; if they do not, the series is said to be divergent. **2** (in social theory) In French nineteenth-century positivist sociology, *série* was used to denote a social group or category. Later, Sartre used 'series' and 'group' as contrasting terms. A series is a plurality of isolated individuals; a collection of individuals in a temporary and contingent gathering who do not interact, e.g. a (French) bus queue (*Critique of Dialectical Reason* Book 1, chapter 4, sec. 1). A broadcast audience is another kind of series, an 'indirect gathering'. Yet another kind are the individual buyers and sellers in a market. Sartre contrasts series with groups, in which individuals stand in relations of reciprocity, cooperation, mutual recognition, and are capable of solidarity and coordinated collective action.

sexism *n.* disposition to regard one sex – one's own – as intellectually, morally or biologically superior to the other, and to approve of inequalities that favour members of the supposedly superior sex.

In standard usage, a person who considers the *other* sex to be superior is rarely called sexist. For the most part, it is men who are said to be sexist. The use of the word in this sense, introduced in analogy with *racism*, seems to have gained currency through Kate Millett's *Sexual Politics* 1969.

Sextus Empiricus (*c.* 150–*c.* 225) ancient

sceptic. His name indicates that he was a physician who based his practice on clinical observation rather than received medical doctrine. Two of his works, written in Greek, have come down to us: *Pyrrhonienses Hypotyposes* (*Outlines of Pyrrhonism*), and *Adversus Mathematicos* (*Against the Dogmatists*). They present the arguments and views of the sceptical philosophers and are our main source of knowledge of these. He described scepticism both as a way of life by which ATARAXIA could be attained, and as a philosophy which questions the knowledge-claims made in the areas of logic, science, ethics and religion. A few of the difficulties brought up by the sceptics were contrived or spurious, but most have remained on the philosophical agenda since Sextus's writings were published in Latin in the sixteenth century.

Shaftesbury /ˈʃɑːftsbərɪ/, Anthony Ashley Cooper, 3rd Earl of (1671–1713) author of philosophical discourses on beauty, virtue and religion, much esteemed for their polished elegance. He was the grandson of Locke's patron, the first Earl of Shaftesbury, and Locke had a hand in his early education. He presented eloquent arguments against egoistic theories of motivation which were associated with the names of Epicurus and Hobbes, but also presupposed by the prevailing theological morality in its doctrine of rewards and punishments in a future state. Against this, Shaftesbury argued that we have by nature a sense of beauty and an inclination towards good. To allow these natural dispositions to unfold leads to personal happiness. Morality is independent of religion. He was well known for his view that satire and ridicule can serve as a test of truth: a belief not abandoned in the face of jesting irreverence is more likely to be true. Shaftesbury's ideas, including the parallel between a sense of beauty and a sense of moral good, influenced Hutcheson, who developed a theory of a moral sense. Mandeville and Berkeley (in *Alciphron* 1732) were important early critics. Shaftesbury's main writings, including *Inquiry Concerning Virtue and Merit*, were published under the collective title *Characteristics of Men, Manners, Opinions, Times* 1711.

Sheffer's stroke (properly: Sheffer's stroke function) a binary truth-function, normally symbolized by a vertical stroke and usually read as *not both p and q*. Its truth-table is set out in Table 20.

Table 20 Truth-table for Sheffer's stroke

p	q	p | q
T	T	F
T	F	T
F	T	T
F	F	T

All truth-functions can be expressed with this binary truth-function alone: ~p, the negation of p, is equivalent to p | p, and p ∨ q, the disjunction of p and q, is equivalent to (p | p) | (q | q).

There is another binary truth-function p ↓ q which is also alone sufficient. It is usually read *neither p nor q*, and its values are F, F, F, T.

Shelley /ˈʃɛlɪ/, Percy Bysshe /ˈpɜrsɪ bɪʃ/ (1792–1822) Shelley was not only a romantic poet; he also wrote *The Necessity of Atheism* 1811 and *A Refutation of Deism* 1814, defending in these and other writings the radical ideas of the Enlightenment in favour of individual liberty and social justice. He did not, however, accept materialism, but opted for an idealism in tune with romantic philosophy, according to which, at a deeper level, all minds are parts of an infinite universal mind.

Sidgwick /'sɪdʒwɪk/, Henry (1838–1900) a fellow of Trinity College, and from 1883 professor of moral philosophy at Cambridge. Driven by the problem of how to find a foundation for a morality independently of religion, he presented, in his *Methods of Ethics* 1874 (7th rev. edn 1907), incisive analyses of basic principles that can be adopted in our moral thinking: egoism, intuitionism and utilitarianism. The upshot of his careful discussion is that we are committed to accepting conflicting basic principles. For instance, moral universalism, implied by utilitarianism, may require unreasonable self-sacrifice, contrary to egoism, here understood as a natural concern for one's own welfare. We can only hope that they will not ultimately clash in practice, but there can be no guarantee. Sidgwick's treatment of utilitarianism is the starting point for the present-day discussions of this moral theory.

Sidgwick was interested in scientific inquiry into paranormal phenomena, and was a founding member of the Society for Psychical Research.

Siger /'ziːgər (Gm.)/ **of Brabant** (*c.* 1240–*c.* 1285) among the more radical thinkers who took an interest in the Aristotelian tradition transmitted via Islamic and Jewish authors, especially through Averroes. Controversy arose, especially concerning two doctrines ascribed to Aristotle but not easily compatible with Christianity: that the world has no beginning in time; and that there is one unitary human intellect and hence no individual immortality of the soul. Siger was accused of maintaining a doctrine of 'double truth' – one religious, one philosophical. One of his critics was Aquinas, in *On the Unity of the Intellect against the Averroists* 1270.

simpliciter /sɪm'plɪsɪtə/ Lat. simply, unqualifiedly, by itself.

Simplicius /sɪm'plɪʃəs/ (early 6th century) neo-Platonic philosopher, attached to the Academy in Athens until its closure in 529. In his commentaries on Aristotle and Epictetus, at once scholarly and edifying, he tried to show the consonance of their writings with (neo)Platonic doctrine. His writings had a marked influence on medieval and Renaissance thought.

simplification *n.* an inference from a conjunction to a conjunct:

$$\frac{p \,\&\, q}{p} \qquad \frac{p \,\&\, q}{q}$$

In natural deduction systems, the rule permitting this inference is usually called &-elimination.

sine qua non /'saɪnɪ kweɪ nɒn; 'sɪnɪ kwaː nɒn/ Lat. without which not. A condition *sine qua non* is a necessary condition.

Singer, Peter (1946–)

A philosophical self-portrait: The ultimate practical question is: 'How are we to live?' To give a general answer to such a broad question is, however, a daunting task, and most of my writing has focused on more specific practical questions.

I am probably best known for *Animal Liberation* 1st edn 1975, 2nd edn 1990, a book that gave its title to a worldwide movement. The essential philosophical view it maintains is simple but revolutionary. Species is, in itself, as irrelevant to moral status as race or sex. Hence all beings with interests are entitled to equal consideration: that is, we should not give their interests any less consideration than we give to the similar interests of members of our own species. Taken seriously, this conclusion requires radical changes in almost every interaction we have with animals, including our diet, our economy, and our relations with the natural environment.

To say that this idea is revolutionary

is not to say that it was especially novel. Similar ideas can be found, for instance, in Henry Salt's *Animals' Rights*, first published in 1892. My contribution was to restate this view clearly and rigorously, and to illustrate that alternative views are based on self-interest, either naked or disguised by religious or other myths.

My broader credo can be found in *Practical Ethics* 1st edn 1979, 2nd edn 1993. Here the treatment of animals receives its proper place, as one among several major ethical issues. I approach each issue by seeking the solution that has the best consequences for all affected. By 'best consequences', I understand that which satisfies the most preferences, weighted in accordance with the strength of the preferences. Thus my ethical position is a form of preference-utilitarianism.

In *Practical Ethics* I apply this ethic to such issues as equality (both between humans, and between humans and non-human animals), abortion, euthanasia and infanticide, the obligations of the wealthy to those who are living in poverty, the refugee question, our interactions with non-human beings and ecological systems, and obedience to the law. A non-speciesist and consequentialist approach to these issues leads to striking conclusions. It offers a clear-cut account of why abortion is ethically justifiable, and an equally clear condemnation of our failure to share our wealth with people who are in desperate need.

Some of my conclusions have been found shocking, and not only in respect of animals. In Germany, my advocacy of active euthanasia for severely disabled newborn infants has generated heated controversy. I first discussed this in *Practical Ethics*; later, as co-author, with Helga Kuhse, in *Should the Baby Live?* 1985; and most recently in *Rethinking Life and Death* 1995. Perhaps it is only to be expected, though, that there should be heated opposition to an ethic that challenges the hitherto generally accepted ethical superiority of human beings, and the traditional view of the sanctity of human life. PS

singular proposition a subject-predicate proposition in which the subject term is a singular term.

singular term a name of an individual or, more generally, an expression used to denote a single individual.

Proper names, like 'Socrates', are singular terms. Other expressions whose function it is to refer to exactly one individual are also so called: for instance, demonstratives like 'this philosopher' and definite descriptions like 'the teacher of Plato'.

Sinn /zin/ *n.* Gm. meaning; sense (of a linguistic expression).

sistology *n.* the inquiry into, or theory of, items in general. It includes the study of things that exist (ontology) as well as things that do not exist but (in Meinong's terminology) subsist. The concept and the word are due to Richard Sylvan.

situation ethics an ethical-religious outlook which rejects the anxious legalistic observance of rules, and stresses the importance of the particular features of a situation. Our decisions should be guided not by rule-worship but by a concern about the consequences of the particular act, and especially how it will affect others. The formulation of this liberal religious ethic was more homiletic than theoretic. Its leading representative, Joseph Fletcher, gave an outline in *Situation Ethics* 1966.

skepticism American spelling of SCEPTICISM.

Skinner, B(urrhus) F(rederick) (1904–90) American behavioural psychologist, who taught at the universities of Minnesota,

Indiana and Harvard 1948–74. He was a pioneer in the area of programmed learning. In *Walden 2* 1948 he proposed that techniques of psychological reinforcement, which are, after all, practised in all educative endeavour, could be used systematically to create a better society. This view, that ideally human beings – for the sake of common welfare – should be subject to behaviour modification programmes controlled by expert psychologists, provoked a lively controversy. *Beyond Freedom and Dignity* 1971 rejects the traditional view that human beings can be autonomous and that they can be held responsible for their actions. 'A scientific analysis shifts both the responsibility and the achievement to the environment.' Among his other books are *Science and Human Behavior* 1953 and *About Behaviorism* 1974.

Skolem–Löwenheim theorem *See* LÖWENHEIM–SKOLEM THEOREM.

slave-morality *n.* an important concept in Nietzsche's *Genealogy of Morals*. He contrasts the servile and unhealthy mind-set of the downtrodden and contemptible with the free and healthy mentality of the naturally well-born, the natural aristocrats of the human race. Those who belong to the lower sort reject, through their leaders, the 'priests', the contrast between good and bad (in a non-moral sense) and replace it with the contrast between good and evil (in a moral sense). The masters, the healthy ones, are regarded as evil oppressors; the slaves, the misbegotten ones, are regarded as victims of injustice. Historically, the better sort were induced by the 'priests' to develop a sense of guilt and sin, and this is how slave-morality could gain hegemony with the success of certain religions, pre-eminently Judaism and Christianity.

Smart, J(ohn) J(amieson) C(arswell) (1920–)

A philosophical self-portrait: After studies at the universities of Glasgow and Oxford, I became professor of philosophy at the University of Adelaide, and subsequently at the Australian National University. My first published article was on time, and over the years I have written a good deal on space, time and space-time, and also on the temporal asymmetry of the world. These writings point to the contrast between what can be called the 'Strawsonian-Aristotelian' view of objects as three-dimensional and persisting in time and the four-dimensional space-time view of the world which is of course implied by the special and general theories of relativity realistically understood. I like to see the world Spinozistically *sub specie aeternitatis*, construed by eliminating tenses and other indexicals from metaphysical discourse, and also by eliminating anthropocentric notions such as those of the secondary qualities, or at least putting them in their place in a physicalist world-view.

At Oxford I was much influenced by Gilbert Ryle, and was naturally attracted by Ryle's behaviouristic and dispositional approach to the philosophy of mind. This removed mystery but, perhaps unlike Ryle, it seemed to me that one should look to cybernetics and neurophysiological psychology to explain behaviour. Ryle had trouble over giving a convincing account of perceptual sensations and mental images which do not seem to be mere dispositions but actual processes. There was much discussion of this between myself and two philosophically profound colleagues at the University of Adelaide, U. T. Place and C. B. Martin. I attempted to refute from a Rylean point of view the identity theory of sensations and brain processes that Place was developing, but I soon found that Place's thesis could not be refuted and since the thesis was congenial have ever since enthusiastically argued for a physicalist theory of mind. Later D. M. Armstrong and David Lewis proved valuable allies. I also defended realism in the philosophy of science, arguing that if an instrumentalism or phenomenalism were correct there would have to be cosmic coincidences. However, I have also defended a regularity view of laws of nature, but tried to distinguish two sorts of cosmic coincidences – the simple (good) ones and the complicated (bad) ones.

In ethics I have argued strongly for act-utilitarianism as married to (roughly speaking) a non-cognitivist metaethics, a metaethical view for which I have also argued. In philosophy of logic Quine has exercised a strong influence, with an account of possibility only in terms of consistency (in the sense of first-order predicate logic) with contextually agreed background assumptions. This metaphysical distrust of modality and counterfactuals led to a rejection of causality and causal theories of time. I have also been interested in Davidson's truth-theories, and have tried to defend metaphysical realism against philosophers such as Putnam and Dummett. In philosophical method my view is that plausibility in the light of total science is a proper touchstone of metaphysical truth.

Publications include: *Philosophy and Scientific Realism* 1963; 'An Outline of a System of Utilitarian Ethics' in J. J. C. Smart and Bernard Williams, *Utilitarianism: For and Against* 1973; *Ethics, Persuasion and Truth* 1984; *Essays Metaphysical and Moral* 1987; *Our Place in the Universe* 1989. JSM

Smith, Adam (1723–90) educated at Glasgow University under Francis Hutcheson and at Balliol College, Oxford; professor at Glasgow 1751–64. Subsequently, he spent about ten years studying and writing *The Wealth of Nations* 1776.

Smith is commonly seen as the founder of political economy. This is only partly true. First, there was a great deal of political economy before him, though nothing as methodical, wide-ranging and philosophically sophisticated as *The Wealth of Nations*. Secondly, Smith was in fact a philosopher who tried to construct a general system of the moral and social sciences in which political economy was but one part. The philosophical foundations were laid in the *Theory of Moral Sentiments* 1759, but a major part concerning the theory of law and government was never finished to Smith's satisfaction and he burnt the manuscript before he died. Consequently the connection between the two major published works can only be partially reconstructed on the basis of two sets of students' notes from his 'Lectures on Jurisprudence' at Glasgow (1762–3? and 1764).

The basis for Smith's moral philosophy is a social theory of moral personality. He rejects the idea of Hutcheson and others that moral agency hinges on a special moral sense, offering instead explanations based on empirically ascertainable features of the mind. He follows his great friend, David Hume, in rejecting the suggestion of Samuel Clarke and others that moral judgement and motivation are forms of rational inference; and he ignores religious ideas of conscience as either an infusion by, or a response to, the deity. For Smith, formation of the moral self begins with others. In explaining this, he invokes dialogic and dramatic notions of great sophistication.

Both inclination and need lead people to interact; interaction depends on observation and appreciation of others and their situation, and this is facilitated by the universal tendency sympathetically to put oneself in the position of the other and 'compare' reactions. Awareness of being the object of other people's observation and assessment generally leads the individual to pre-empt this process by self-observation and self-assessment; people internalize the spectator. The internal spectator will therefore often prompt such adjustment of behaviour as would otherwise be demanded by external spectators in order to satisfy the inclination to, or the need for, agreement or conformity. This process of mutual adjustment through sympathetic search for a common standpoint of course often fails, and leads to the quest for an ideal judgement transcending the various limitations of knowledge, bias, etc. of those actually involved. Once we begin a dialogue with such an imagined ideal of an impartial spectator, we have a moral conscience.

The features of personality and lines of action which people approve and disapprove of in others and in themselves will vary from one culture and period to another. A major task for philosophy is accordingly to look at humanity historically and comparatively. But this will make it apparent that there is one sphere of human reaction in which there is a great deal in common between all of humankind, namely *moral* approval and disapproval (as opposed to, say, aesthetic or religious reactions to others). The moral philosopher is thus able to identify a number of basic virtues and vices, the tone and composition of which will vary significantly, but which are nevertheless universally recognizable and comparable.

Within the sphere of morals, one element has a special status. When the spectator, whether the actual or the imagined impartial one, sympathetically enters into the situation of an agent, the result is approval or disapproval of the agent's judgement and action. When the agent is trying to promote the good or the welfare of someone, whether self or other, the spectatorial approval or disapproval will tend to vary from one person to the next; for while we tend to agree on what is good in broad outline, we have great difficulty agreeing on what is good for particular persons in specific situations. By contrast, people tend to agree on what is harmful not only in general but also in specific cases. The negative virtue of avoiding injury is *justice*, and justice is the foundation of law and is the subject of jurisprudence. The attributes and actions that are protected when people are just, i.e. abstain from injury, are their rights. The concept of rights is thus dependent on the concept of personality, and the latter inevitably varies from one stage of society to the next. Smith rejects the idea of a state of nature; human life is social life and there will therefore always be recognition of rights to physical, moral and some kind of social personality.

In Smith's view, humanity can be divided into four broad stages of social development, according to the extent of the concept of the person and, consequently, the scope of rights recognized. Among hunters and gatherers nothing much is recognized beyond what immediately sustains the physical and moral person, i.e. food, shelter, personal freedom and social recognition ('reputation', as Smith calls it). Dramatic extensions of the person are produced by 'shepherds' (nomads) with the recognition of property in food and tools much beyond what is required for each individual and his or her immediate dependants; and, again, with recognition of property in land in the agricultural stage. The most abstract extension of the concept of personality happens in commercial society with the full development of contractual entitlements (including money for labour) and ownership of purely symbolic property (paper money, credits) as parts of what a person is. Each of these developments requires strengthening of government to protect the new rights, and when this is effective, people's pursuit of their needs will form the system of exchange that is the subject of political economy.

Criticism of moral and legal practices, in Smith's view, must be internal to a given stage of society; yet such criticism has some universal features, namely the formal requirement of impartiality (amounting to universality) and, secondly, the primacy of avoiding injury. Smith's historical and critical concerns are thus intimately connected.

Smith also contributed to rhetoric, the theory of language, aesthetics, history and philosophy of science, and other fields.

KHA

Smuts /smuts (Af.)/, Jan (1870–1950) South African statesman and philosopher. *See* HOLISM.

social contract theory the theory that individuals, by nature free and equal, agree to renounce part of their natural liberty by entering into civil society and constituting a political authority to which they subject themselves for the sake of the advantages provided by civil society. The right to rule and the obligation to obey derive from the agreement; such an agreement is called a social contract.

As a piece of conjectural prehistory, the theory is rather implausible, but as a theory of the scope and limits of state authority and the individual's obligation it has proved very attractive. In ancient times Protagoras, Hippias, Lycophron and other Sophists favoured a theory of this kind. In the modern era, it was proposed in various forms by many political thinkers including Hobbes, Pufendorf, Locke and Rousseau. Present-day philosophers, among them John Rawls and David Gauthier, have revived the tradition: a just society is one that would satisfy the clauses of a contract that rational human agents under certain specified conditions would be prepared to agree to.

Social Darwinism Darwin's theory has been used to support the belief that nature does well by the process of natural selection, a competition in which the fittest survive. This process is not disturbed by extraneous interference since, as far as the theory is concerned, there is nothing extraneous. The view known as Social Darwinism holds a similar view of human society: it too does well by competitive processes in which the fittest survive, and which are not disturbed by extraneous interference aimed to help the less fit.

Views of this kind emerged towards the end of the nineteenth century. They were advocated by a number of writers in the social sciences, and by many politicians and captains of industry. In practice, this outlook that the weak should be left to their fate may, with suitable qualifications, have some limited validity for competition in sports and in commerce. But if the weaker party is an oppressed race, a conquered nation, an impoverished social class, or an individual afflicted by illness or handicap, the view is both theoretically and morally very dubious.

socialism *n.* a theory and a movement advocating public ownership of the more important means of production.

socialist realism the aesthetic theory of Marxism-Leninism, officially imposed in the Soviet Union in 1934, and later in the post-war Soviet bloc.

It demands that the artist represent reality in its revolutionary development and educate the working class in the spirit of socialism. It was brutally reaffirmed in 1948.

social virtues virtues exercised in actions that affect other persons. Justice and benevolence are social virtues. Many moral theories take all virtues to be social: moral concerns are concerns that involve other people. The view that there are non-social virtues can be found in Aristotle and Hume.

Hume counts prudence and serenity among them.

Socinianism /səʊ'sɪnɪənɪzm/ *n.* a doctrine and religious movement named after its originator, the Italian Protestant theologian Fausto Sozzini (1539–1604) (Lat. Faustus Socinus). It deviates from orthodox forms of Catholicism and Protestantism. The traditional doctrine of atonement, to the effect that Christ by his suffering deflected God's wrath, is rejected. Also rejected is the doctrine of the divinity of Christ. Christ is seen as a sinless human being, appointed by God to be a teacher and a model of perfection. The study of his life and teachings and of Scripture will lead the believer to repentance and salvation. Exposed to persecution in many countries, Socinianism found refuge in Poland, where it had its centre in Rakow, and in Lithuania, until it was proscribed in 1658. Its influence led to the development of UNITARIANISM.

sociobiology *n.* the study of the biological basis of social behaviour. Much of the study concerns non-human organisms, e.g. ants and bees, but some sociobiologists also attempt to (1) explain human social phenomena by processes of natural selection; (2) reduce cultural and social theory to biological theory; (3) establish a kind of ethical naturalism. It attracted attention through the writings of E. O. Wilson: *Sociobiology* 1975; *On Human Nature* 1978; (with C. J. Lumsden) *Genes, Mind and Culture* 1981. These writings provoked a lively debate about the alleged or actual moral and political implications of the theory. See, e.g., Peter Singer, *The Expanding Circle* 1981; Roger Trigg, *The Shaping of Man* 1982.

sociology *n.* the scientific study of human groups and societies.

Note: The word was created by Auguste Comte; he 'regretted its hybrid character', and John Stuart Mill called the new word a 'convenient barbarism' in his *Logic* 1843, because of the uncouth combination of Latin (socio-) and Greek (-logy) word-elements.

sociology of knowledge inquiry into, or theory of, human knowledge, regarded as a social phenomenon.

Many theories under this heading have a relativist tendency, asserting, e.g., that claims to objective validity are illusory, that all knowledge-claims are ultimately nothing but reflections of the social position of a social class or expressions of its class interests; or that knowledge is nothing but what is so defined by powerful interest-groups in a society; but it is of course possible to investigate belief-systems in a society even without these particular presuppositions.

Socrates /'sɒkrətiːz/ (469–399 BC) Socrates of Athens 'called philosophy down from heaven', turning it away from theories about nature towards inquiry into ethics. He shared with his contemporaries the Sophists a concern for practical issues and particularly for education; but he questioned the extravagant claims of some Sophists that they could teach virtue. He himself paid special attention to questions of moral education and moral character, and he seems to have held that the pursuit of moral improvement was the most important human task.

Although Socrates wrote nothing, his followers made him the subject of a unique literary genre, the Socratic dialogue. Consequently he is both the best known and the least known of ancient philosophers: we are able to see how he operated and to glimpse his personality, but always through someone else's eyes. We see clearly that for Socrates, philosophy was not merely a set of doctrines but a way of life. Living in accordance with philosophical principles,

Socrates had no time to earn a living for himself and, unlike the Sophists who had broken with Greek tradition in this respect, he refused to accept payment for his teaching – indeed he denied that he was a teacher. Being puzzled by a statement of the priestess at Delphi that no one was wiser than he, Socrates felt compelled to discover the meaning of the statement. By questioning men who had the reputation of wisdom, he came to see that he was wiser than they, because unlike them he did not claim to know what he did not know. He thus came to regard his examinations of individuals as a mission from God. He was also inspired by a divine voice which warned him against wrong actions. Socrates finally gave his life for his principles when, put on trial on a charge of impiety and corrupting the youth of Athens, he refused to renounce his way of life.

The main sources for Socrates's views are (1) Plato's dialogues, particularly his earlier dialogues depicting him in fictional conversations, which, however, seem to reflect his method and views; (2) Xenophon's Socratic works; (3) Aristophanes's comedy *The Clouds*, which portrays him as a charlatan working in the tradition of the Sophists and the pre-Socratic philosophers; and (4) Aristotle's remarks about him. A number of other Socratics besides Plato and Xenophon wrote Socratic dialogues which are lost. Of our sources, Plato seems to provide the best picture, both for its vivid portrait of Socrates's character and for its philosophical depth. Differences between Socrates's doctrines and methods (and particularly his social attitudes) and those that Plato expresses in his mature works, seem to indicate that Plato is not merely producing an alter ego in the character of Socrates.

What is most characteristic of Socrates is not a set of doctrines but a *method* of inquiry. He typically seeks from his partner in discussion a general definition of some virtue. When the partner proposes a definition which meets his requirements, he asks questions not always obviously connected with the definition. Socrates then typically produces a contradiction from the partner's responses, which he takes as grounds for rejecting the definition. This process of examination, known as *elenchus* (refutation), tests the consistency of the partner's opinions and, Socrates maintains, his character. Socrates claims not to know the answers to the questions he asks, but to be seeking the truth along with his partner. In his conversations Socrates notoriously uses irony, including a complex irony in which what he says is both not true in a superficial sense and true in a deeper sense.

Against this foreground of questioning there is a background of doctrines and assumptions that drive the Socratic method. Socrates allows us to glimpse his own views as puzzling statements often called the *Socratic paradoxes*. His most important view is that virtue is knowledge, a claim Socrates often hints at by invoking the 'craft analogy', comparing virtues to crafts such as horse-training and navigation, i.e. practices which reliably produce beneficial results by a rational process. But unlike a craft, virtue is not teachable. Socrates also holds that no one does wrong willingly, that no one can harm a good man, that it is worse to do wrong than to suffer it, that virtue is necessary and sufficient for happiness, and that all the virtues are somehow one. Although Socrates does not usually argue for his views, he seems to expect that differing views will be shown to be untenable by the elenchus, i.e. his process of cross-examination. In any case, he does have a positive ethical theory based at least in part on a moral psychology. Socrates seems to challenge the interpreter to find the unstated connections between his paradoxical doctrines.

On one possible interpretation Socrates does indeed lack philosophical knowledge, but he has a partial knowledge based on the elenchus. This knowledge is sufficient for virtue, for by revealing what we do not know it shows us that there is no reason to value anything but goods of the soul – i.e. good states of the soul rather than goods of the body such as beauty, or external goods such as wealth. We naturally seek what is best, and thus when we realize what is truly best we have no desire to attain external goods by evil means. Nor can anyone harm us, for the only true harm is damage to our souls, which are in our own power. Thus elenctic knowledge leads us to make correct value-judgements and hence to act rightly. Nevertheless, such knowledge is no stronger than the latest refutation of a false view, so that the philosopher must literally learn along with his partner in discussion. Consequently, virtue by itself is not teachable in the traditional sense of teaching; and the several virtues we normally think of as distinct capacities, such as courage, self-control and piety, are really manifestations of a single knowledge of good and evil.

In turning away from the natural inquiries of pre-Socratic philosophers and in challenging the claims of the Sophists to teach virtue, Socrates turned philosophy towards ethics. He demanded rigorous argumentation and tireless examination of basic principles, and for the first time presented philosophy as a dialogue to be carried on in a social context, rather than as solitary investigation and reflection. Above all, he insisted on addressing immediate social problems, which for him revolved around the need for effective moral education. He inspired the great schools of the following generations – the Academy of Plato, with its offshoot, the Lyceum of Aristotle, where ethical questions suggested metaphysical answers; the Cynics (claiming descent from the Socratic Antisthenes), who saw in Socrates a rebel against conventions; the Stoics (claiming descent from the Cynics), who saw in Socrates the exemplary wise man; and the sceptics, who saw in Socrates a questioner with no answers. For all of them Socrates embodied an ideal in which philosophy was not simply a theoretical doctrine but a way of life – indeed the good life itself. DG

Socratic fallacy This term was introduced by P. T. Geach for the view – rejected by Geach as erroneous – that one knows whether something is F only if one can give a definition of what it is to be F.

Socratic irony self-depreciation through pretended ignorance in a discussion, feigned in order to advance the search for truth.

Socratic method consists in asking questions that will prompt reflection, which in turn will produce knowledge – or awareness of one's own ignorance.

Socratic paradoxes *See* SOCRATES.

solipsism /'sɒlɪpsɪzm/ (Lat. *solus* alone + *ipse* oneself) *n.* **1** (in ontology) the view that nothing exists except one's own self and the contents of its consciousness. **2** (in epistemology) the view that nothing can be known except one's own self and the contents of its consciousness.

In an older sense, solipsism means egoism, the view that nothing is to be valued except one's own interests and pleasures. This usage occurs e.g. in Kant's *Critique of Practical Reason* 3, §3.

Solon /'səʊlɒn/ (*c.* 640–558 BC) the wise lawgiver of ancient Athens.

somatic (Gr. *sōma* body) *adj.* bodily; pertaining to the human body.

sophia /səʊ'faɪə/ Gr. intellectual excellence, wisdom *n.*

Sophie the young woman destined to become the devoted wife of Emile in Rousseau's work *Emile*. Rousseau's blatant 'sexism' caused consternation even in his time – Mary Wollstonecraft was an important critic – and it has again attracted much unfavourable attention in late twentieth-century feminist philosophy.

sophism *n.* **1** an argument which seems valid but is not. Aristotle studied such fallacies in his *De sophisticis elenchis* (Sophistical refutations). They have always attracted the attention of philosophers and logicians but were particularly the subject of intense study in the second half of the twelfth century, when the term was used non-derogatorily for various paradoxes which were the basis for exercises in disputations. **2** a piece of SOPHISTRY. JM/ed.

sophist (Gr. *sophistēs* a wise, knowledgeable person; an expert) *n.* in ancient Greece, a teacher of the more advanced disciplines of study, e.g. grammar, rhetoric, law.

It was through the sophists (and Socrates) that philosophy turned from the study of nature to the study of man. They brought to the fore the contrast between nature (*physis*) and convention (*nomos*). The idea that many things that we take for granted as being natural and therefore beyond our control, including our morality, customs and laws, are in fact conventional, has obvious radical implications.

The activities of these experts could have a certain unsettling effect within the narrow confines of the ancient Greek city-states. The sophists, being travelling teachers especially of rhetoric (the art of persuasion), were outsiders engaging in a new form of enterprise based on private initiative, and their teachings could make a difference to political life. The adverse reactions against them could resemble those of a traditional society into which modern advertising techniques are suddenly introduced.

Plato attacked many of their theories and activities, and this is the origin of the pejorative connotation associated with *sophist* and its cognates. Although he shows respect for some of them, like Protagoras and Gorgias, he disapproved of the sophists generally for two major reasons. One was that they charged fees for their services; the other was that they taught sophistry: how to get the better of an argument by fair means or foul, independently of the real merits of the case. In a similar spirit, Aristotle wrote (*De sophisticis elenchis* 1,1, 165ᵃ22) that a sophist is a person who derives pecuniary gain from appearing to be wise without actually being wise.

It was argued by Grote in the nineteenth century and by others since, e.g. Popper in *The Open Society and Its Enemies* 1945, that the poor overall reputation of the sophists was politically inspired, due to Plato's aristocratic abhorrence of the moral universalism and democratic sympathies of many sophists. The conflict between the sophists and their enemies was construed as a precursor to the conflict between democratic egalitarianism and various kinds of political elitism: aristocratic, conservative, even fascist. This interpretation and evaluation have been subject to lively controversy.

sophistication *n.* **1** refinement; intricacy; worldly wisdom. **2** adulteration; employment of sophistry, etc. This older derogatory sense is now obsolete.

sophistry *n.* reasoning which is plausible, fallacious and dishonest.

Sophroniscus /sɒfrə'nɪskəs/ sculptor, father of Socrates.

sōphrosynē /sɒ'frɒsɪneɪ/ Gr. self-control, being sensible; *n.* also translated as *moderation* and *temperance n.* One of the four CARDINAL VIRTUES. *See also* TEMPERANCE.

Sorge /ˈzɔrgə (Gm.)/ Gm. care; concern; sorrow *n.* a key concept in Heidegger's thought. It relates to three basic elements of an individual's *Dasein*: (1) the contingency of the individual's existence (i.e. the possibility of death) which comes to awareness through *Angst* (anxiety, dread); (2) *Geworfenheit* (thrown-ness), i.e. the sheer contingency of one's existence; (3) decline, decay.

sorites /sɒˈraɪtiːs/ (Gr. *sōritēs* a heaper, from *soros* a heap) *n.* a sequence of syllogisms or, more generally, a sequence of arguments, in which the (unstated) conclusion of one is a premiss in the next.

sorites paradox One grain of sand does not make a heap, nor do two. Adding one more does not help either; and so on. It seems that at no point can a number of grains become a heap. And yet, if the number is large enough, there *is* a heap. Similarly, a young person does not become old one day later: that day he is still not old. Nor does he become old the following day either. It seems that nobody ever grows old; and yet, many people *do*.

Conversely, a person who is not bald does not become bald by removing one hair; a heap of sand remains a heap even if one grain is removed, etc.

Usually both variants of the paradox are called 'sorites'. Occasionally the term is reserved for the first variant only, and the second is then called *phalakros* (= the bald man).

soteriology /sɒtɪərɪˈɒlədʒɪ/ (Gr. *sōtēr* saviour) *n.* (theological) doctrine of salvation.

Soto /soto (Sp.)/, Domingo de (1494–1560) Spanish Dominican, best known as the author of a major and widely used treatise *De justitia et jure* 1556 (On justice and law). He taught at Salamanca. His general standpoint was Thomist, although he accepted some of Duns Scotus's theories. He was an important early counter-reformer, arguing against the Protestant doctrine of grace.

spatial *adj.* pertaining to space.

species (*sing.* and *pl.*) (Lat. *species* appearance, form, kind, from *specere* to look, to behold) *n.* **1** A species is a class of individuals of a certain sort, e.g. man, horse, donkey, which have an essential property in common. Different species may belong to the same *genus*. Within one genus, different species are contraries in the sense that an object that belongs to the genus belongs to exactly one species. **2** The concepts of genera and species have long been used in the biological sciences. Linnaeus (1707–78) took a species to consist of *similar* individuals. The modern definitions since Buffon (1707–88) differ, in that they include interbreeding and reproductive isolation. **3** In the medieval, especially the Thomist, theory of knowledge, a *species* is something intermediate, between the external object and the mind. The motivation for this concept is two-fold: (a) the external object is material, but the grasp of the mind is not; and (b) objects are particular, whilst the mind contemplates universals. By means of the species, the act of cognition and the object of cognition can come together. The theory of species was rejected by William of Ockham, who taught that knowledge is of individuals and that we have direct knowledge of them. **4** In medieval thought, 'species' was also used in contrast to substance. Thus, bread and wine are the two species of the eucharist: they remain constant although, according to the dogma of transubstantiation, the substance changes. JM/ed.

speciesism /ˈspiːʃiːzɪzm/ *n.* the theory and practice that assigns a privileged position to mankind, such that we are entitled to treat members of other species in a way in which it would be wrong to treat members of our own.

The word, used chiefly by opponents of speciesism, was created in analogy with *racism* by Richard Ryder in his 'Experiments on Animals', in S. and R. Godlovitch and J. Harris (eds), *Animals, Men, and Morals* 1972, and gained wider currency through Peter Singer's review of that book, 'Animal Liberation', *New York Review of Books 20* (5 April 1973), and in Singer's *Animal Liberation* (1st edn 1975; 2nd edn 1990).

specious /ˈspiːʃəs/ *adj.* **1** plausible, but misleading. **2** apparent, but not real.

Older usage is different: Locke, Hume and others regularly use *specious* to mean plausible or apparent, without any implication of error or illusion. When these writers describe an argument as specious, they usually imply that it is a plausible one.

specious present a short time-span, within which all moments seem to be directly experienced; a duration that seems like a now.

spectator, impartial *See* IDEAL OBSERVER.

speculative *adj.* **1** theoretical (in contrast to practical). **2** non-empirical (in contrast to empirical). **3** conjectural, uncertain.

speech acts Jurisprudentialists have long realized what the philosopher Gilbert Ryle later emphasized: that often in doing one thing, e.g. excluding someone from a club, we are thereby doing another, e.g. insulting him, and bringing about another, e.g. hurting his feelings. The current application of this insight to speech acts was due to the work of J. L. Austin (1911–60) on the uses of language. In his William James lectures 1955, posthumously published as *How to Do Things with Words*, he distinguished between three things we might be doing, what he called performing three kinds of speech acts, in making an utterance. First, in making certain noises (a phonetic act), which are also words put into a certain grammatical construction (a phatic act) and with a certain meaning (a rhetic act), we *say* something and also *do* something: namely, perform an act of saying something (a *locutionary* act which includes these three subacts), e.g. 'That job does not pay well.' Secondly, *in* saying this, that is, performing a locutionary act, we generally also, because of certain conventions, *do* something else (perform an *illocutionary* act), e.g. we advise or warn a student against taking that job, which is not itself merely an act of saying something. Our locution may be said to have the 'force' of such an illocution, e.g. as advice or a warning. Thirdly, *by* saying so and so, that is, performing a locutionary act and, hence, also doing such and such, that is, performing an illocutionary act, we may, designedly or not, achieve certain non-conventional effects (perform a *perlocutionary* act), e.g. persuade the student not to take that job. Austin concluded his lectures with lists of what he considered different species of illocutionary acts, such as verdictives (e.g. grade, acquit), exercitives (e.g. warn, advise), commissives (e.g. promise, bet), behabitives (e.g. apologize, welcome) and expositives (e.g. affirm, define).

To all appearances speech-act theory has its origin in Anglo-American linguistic philosophy, but since the 1980s there has been a growing awareness of interesting anticipations in the work of philosophers influenced by Brentano or Husserl, such as Anton Marty (1847–1914) and Adolf Reinach (1883–1917). AW

Spencer /ˈspɛnsə/, Herbert (1820–1903) English philosopher, originator of a general evolutionist philosophy, an anti-conservative in religion and politics.

From his youth, Spencer's interests were in the direction of science and engineering (he invented a tachometer) rather than the humanities, and his education did not include classical languages. In contrast to other contemporary intellectuals, he did not lose his faith – he never had any. Combining a powerful intellect with a lucid style, he was a successful journalist in the quality press: he wrote for many magazines, among them the *Westminster Review*, a leading liberal and radical periodical, at the time edited by George Eliot (Mary Ann Evans), and was for a number of years in the mid-century assistant editor-in-chief of the *Economist*.

In the early 1850s he announced a 20-year plan to publish a series of works under the general title *System of Synthetic Philosophy*. Most of the volumes were actually published, although it took longer than planned.

In *First Principles*, Spencer argues that ultimate reality is unknowable. We cannot know the ultimate nature of that which is manifested to us (§35). Only its manifestations, which we experience as relations of Matter, Motion and Force, can be known. These are but symbols of the unknown reality. He criticizes a number of religious and metaphysical theories, among them theism, which presuppose that something of ultimate reality can be known.

The sciences try to establish general laws on the basis of observation of particular data. The method of science is first and foremost induction. The task of philosophy is to reach a synthesis, to establish a general theory for which the laws discovered by the sciences form a basis. This philosophical theory can formulate the most general laws and principles of the universe. Spencer's attempt to develop a comprehensive philosophical system rested on the assumption that the sciences had already progressed sufficiently to make such a synthesis possible.

In his theory, the general characterization of change is provided by the Law of Evolution. He formulates this law in terms of complexity and integration. Evolution consists in change from a state of simplicity, homogeneity, uniformity, to a state of greater complexity, heterogeneity, variety, in which the different parts combine and interact within an integrated whole. Examples can be found in the physical, biological, psychological and social sciences. Every evolutionary process is a change from homogeneity to integrated heterogeneity. This applies, for instance, to the evolution from a seed to a plant. As the seed develops, different parts of the plant come into being, and so does a 'division of labour' between them. Similarly, social evolution consists in a change from a homogeneous primitive society to a complex advanced society, in which different parts of the social whole fulfil different functions.

Changes in an opposite direction do, however, occur: there are many instances of decay, disintegration, death, etc. In such cases, the parts of a complex are not properly integrated, and drift apart.

In many contexts, Spencer seems to have adopted the view that change, for instance biological evolution, psychological development or social progress, must by natural necessity pass through various evolutionary stages, so that external intervention is futile or harmful. This is one of the reasons why he strongly opposed government intervention to regulate trade, social welfare measures, etc. The title of his book *The Man versus the State* 1884 is revealing. Spencer's political theory strongly asserts the rights of individuals against governments; but it is also a source of inspiration for Social Darwinism.

Spengler /ˈʃpɛŋlər (Gm.)/, Oswald (1880–1936) The work that made his fame, *Der Untergang des Abendlandes: Umriss einer Morphologie der Weltgeschichte* (1918–22) (The decline of the West: Outline of a morphology of world history), is a gloomy prophecy of doom of Western civilization as we know it, and became a runaway best-seller. He described various aspects and achievements of the great civilizations through history (on his count, there were eight), distilling for each of them a particular style or essence. But no civilization is immortal: each has a limited life-span of roughly one millennium. As for the European or Western civilization, the symptoms of decline preceding an imminent collapse are unmistakable: the prevailing power of money; the dominance of the mass media, especially the gutter press; the eclecticism and lack of original genius in all fields of cultural and intellectual endeavour – all these are clearly discernible signs of decay.

Sweeping generalizations by which whole civilizations are diagnosed and compared proved again to be a recipe for popular success through Arnold Toynbee's *A Study of History*.

Spinoza /spɪˈnəʊzə/, Benedict de (1632–77) born in Amsterdam to parents of 'marrano' origin (Jews forced to profess Christianity in Spain or Portugal) who had fled to Amsterdam, where they were permitted freedom of worship. His public expression of doubts concerning central tenets of Judaism led to his excommunication in 1656. He supported himself by grinding lenses and giving lessons in philosophy. He continued his own studies in philosophy and was attracted by Cartesianism, which was then rapidly gaining adherents in the Dutch universities despite the resistance of the Aristotelians. What attracted him was the rigorous reasoning and the systematization of the world-view that was being developed by scientists like Galileo.

Spinoza's first publication expounded Descartes's philosophy in geometric style, beginning with axioms and definitions, and demonstrating everything else from that basis (*Descartes' Principles of Philosophy* 1663). At this stage Spinoza had clearly worked out the main ideas of his own philosophy: he disagreed significantly with Descartes. He made some key disagreements explicit in the preface: he did not think either the human mind or the human body was a substance, i.e. a thing capable of existing and acting independently of other things; he did not think people have free will; he did not think there is anything which surpasses human understanding. If we wish to discover truth in the sciences and solve the difficult problems of metaphysics, we must proceed in a way different from Descartes's. Spinoza undertook this work of exposition because he felt that his own philosophy was so different from any accepted view that he could not safely publish it without first persuading his country's leaders that he had mastered the thought of his most important predecessor.

In 1665, with the first draft of the *Ethics* nearly complete, Spinoza set it aside to work on his *Tractatus Theologico-Politicus* (*Theological-Political Treatise*), a defence of the freedom of thought and expression, published in 1670. Here his own philosophical views come to expression more clearly than in the earlier work, although there is some doubt whether he is completely open about his own views. The early chapters of the work deal with traditional theological topics: prophecy, divine law, miracles, and the principles of scriptural interpretation. Spinoza is highly critical of Old Testament theology, rejecting as anthropomorphic even such fundamental prophetic teachings as the doctrine that God is a lawgiver, which he finds incompatible with God's omnipotence. He is largely silent about the New Testament, though the few things he does say about it have contributed to the suspicions about his candour. His own conception of God identifies God with the fundamental scientific laws of nature, which explain all phenomena occurring in nature. This excludes any possibility of miracles (where a miracle is understood as a divine interference with the natural order of things).

An important contribution of this work is its theory of scriptural interpretation. To understand the Bible, Spinoza argues, we must approach it as we would any other text, without presupposing as a principle of interpretation that what it says must be true; we must know the grammar, vocabulary and stylistic peculiarities of the language in which it was written; we must organize its teachings on various topics, and note passages which seem inconsistent or obscure; we must know the circumstances under which each book was written, how it was transmitted to us, and how it became part of the canon. If we examine the Bible according to these principles, he contends, we will conclude that it is the work of many human authors, who had very different and imperfect ideas about God, and were often writing many centuries after the events they described (relying on documents now lost); that it has been transmitted to us in a very corrupted form; and that often we simply have no idea of what it means. So we should take it as a guide only with respect to its most fundamental moral teachings, disregarding its theology and any principles of conduct which it does not teach repeatedly. We should learn from the Bible to practise justice and love our neighbours as ourselves. Nothing else matters. No one else in the seventeenth century wrote so boldly. This aspect of Spinoza's teaching exercised a strong influence on the eighteenth-century Enlightenment.

In its political portions, the *Theological-Political Treatise* shows strongly the influence of Hobbes, though Spinoza often reaches un-Hobbesian conclusions. He starts by imagining a state of nature, a condition in which people live without any civil authority. He contends that people's competitiveness and liability to irrational emotions would make this a condition of radical insecurity, poverty, misery and ignorance, so in their own interest people would have to form a government to restrain their behaviour, accepting a limitation on their natural freedom for the sake of the benefits they can expect from life in an organized society. Since Spinoza rejects the notion of a prescriptive natural law, which would impose constraints on what people could justly do, theoretically the rights of this government would be absolute. But because Spinoza holds that natural right is coextensive with power, and because the power of government depends ultimately on the voluntary cooperation of the people, in practice the rights of government would be limited. A tyrannical government which oppresses its subjects necessarily destroys its own power, and thereby its right. Spinoza concludes by arguing that to preserve itself and its power, government must allow extensive liberty. Perhaps the most striking difference from Hobbes is that Spinoza defends democracy as the most natural and stable form of government.

Spinoza intended the *Theological-Political Treatise* partly as support for the tolerant, republican policies of the DeWitt government, which faced strong opposition from the Calvinist clergy and monarchists supporting the Prince of Orange. But part of his intent was probably to defend his break with Judaism, and part, no doubt, was to prepare readers for the more systematic and rigorous presentation of his ideas which he intended to make in the *Ethics*. His biblical criticism tends to undermine confidence in revelation, making room for an argument which appeals only to human reason. He also hoped to explain in a somewhat more popular way his austere, impersonal conception of God. But the uproar which greeted the *Treatise* made it impossible to publish the *Ethics* in his lifetime.

The *Ethics* appeared (along with his correspondence and fragments of three unfinished works) in a collection of *Posthumous Works* published in 1677; it is divided into five parts.

Part I seeks to prove that God exists and acts necessarily, that he is the cause of all things, that all things are 'in' God, without whom they can neither be nor be conceived, and that God has predetermined all things, not by the freedom of his will, but by the absolute necessity of his nature. Since proofs of the existence of God play a central role in Spinoza's system, it is surprising that he was accused of atheism. But Spinoza's denial of personality to God, his insistence that God has no intellect, no will, no purposes and no emotions, has made his God seem rather remote, a God only a philosopher could love. This is not the God of Abraham, Isaac and Jacob. A central doctrine of Part I is that there is exactly one substance, God, in which everything else exists as a mode. There is much debate about what this means; one plausible interpretation is by way of the *Theological-Political Treatise*, as equivalent to saying that there is one system of fundamental scientific laws from which everything which happens in nature can in some way be deduced.

Part II argues that, of the infinite attributes God possesses, we know two, thought and extension, and that a mode of thought and a mode of extension are the same thing, expressed in a different way. Since the human mind and the human body are modes of thought and extension respectively, this implies that they are the same thing, considered now under the attribute of thought, now under the attribute of extension. It also implies that any physical object, as a mode of extension, must be identical with some mode of thought, must 'have a mind' in more or less the same sense that the human body has a mind. Does this imply that stones think, or feel pain? Probably not. What it does seem to imply is that they have life, in a broad sense of that term: they have a tendency to persist in being the entity they are. This theory would seem to explain why the mind would die with the body, and hence to defend one of the heresies which led to Spinoza's excommunication. It surprises many readers of the *Ethics*, then, to find that in Part V Spinoza claims that there is a part of the mind which is not destroyed with the body, but survives its death. Spinoza scholars have puzzled about this, without reaching any satisfactory explanation.

Part III argues that all human actions and emotions can be understood as instances of general laws of nature, which are as necessary as the theorems of geometry. The fundamental law is the tendency of each thing to persist in its being and increase its power of action. The fact that all other patterns of human behaviour follow from this principle is supposed to encourage us not to curse or condemn or mock human weaknesses such as hatred, anger or jealousy, but to try to moderate them, using the understanding of human psychology that the system supplies.

Part IV develops a code of conduct on the basis of the striving each thing has to preserve its being. Because Spinoza rejects the notion of a prescriptive natural law, he holds that it is permissible for us to do whatever we judge will contribute to our advantage. But what contributes most to our advantage is maximizing our understanding of God (i.e. Nature). Not only is this most satisfying intrinsically, it also enables us to minimize the conflicts with others that are made inevitable by the human liability to the passions, conflicts which are the greatest obstacle to our achieving a satisfactory life. Conversely, nothing is more useful to us than other members of our species, when they are guided by reason. We should seek to win others to the life of reason by love and nobility.

Part V sketches a therapy by which we can hope to control our own tendencies to irrationality, and concludes with a description of the intellectual love of God, which constitutes man's greatest good. Though Spinoza evidently had some personal difficulty suffering fools gladly, for the most part he appears to have succeeded in living according to his own ethical theory; hence he became, for later generations, the prototype of that supposed impossibility, the virtuous atheist. EC

spirit *n.* 1 a constituent element of an individual. In ancient times spirit was identified or closely connected with breathing. The words for spirit and breath were the same in Greek (*pneuma*) and in Hebrew (*ruach*). 2 an independently existing non-material being.

In older usage, the word *ghost* was a synonym in both senses.

In ancient speculation, spirit was thought of as something airy or vaporous. On continued reflection, philosophers came to understand that the genuinely spiritual must be immaterial. But, to ask Kant's question in *Dreams of a Spirit-Seer* 1766, can an immaterial thing exist *at* an instant, *during* a period of time, or *in* some place? Those who believe that it is possible for a ghost to pay visits to its favourite haunt and for spirits of the dead, now living in another realm, to be contacted, are committed to an affirmative answer. A negative answer is implied in classical and modern materialism, and many other philosophical theories.

spiritism *n.* beliefs and practices that include the assumption that each person has a spirit that can remain in existence after death, and that communication with it is possible. A person with the special ability to establish contact is called a medium (or, in New-Age jargon, a 'channeller').

The belief is ancient but, like *spiritualism*, the word came into use in the mid-nineteenth century.

spiritualism *n.* 1 ontological idealism; immaterialism. The term is sometimes used especially for French eclectic nineteenth-century idealism (Maine de Biran, Cousin, Ravaisson, etc.), or for Italian nineteenth- and twentieth-century idealism which emerged in opposition to ILLUMINISM and, later, to POSITIVISM. 2 SPIRITISM.

spontaneous *adj.* In everyday usage, a synonym of *unreflective*, but classical philosophers (e.g. Leibniz, Kant) use it in a different sense closer to the etymology of the word: a spontaneous action is one which originates with the agent; freedom, in contrast to determination by external forces, is the spontaneity of an intelligent being.

square of opposition a simple design showing the logical relations between concepts or between basic propositional forms. The best known is the one for categorical propositions in traditional syllogistic logic (Figure 6).

The relations are: (1) implication (here also called subalternation), symbolized by an arrow; (2) contrariety (the two statements cannot both be true, but can both be false); (3) subcontrariety (the two statements cannot both be false, but can both be true); (4) contradiction (of the two statements, one is true and the other is false).

Similar squares can be drawn in order conveniently to represent relations between propositions of other kinds, for instance, as in Figure 7.

Figure 6 Square of opposition (1)

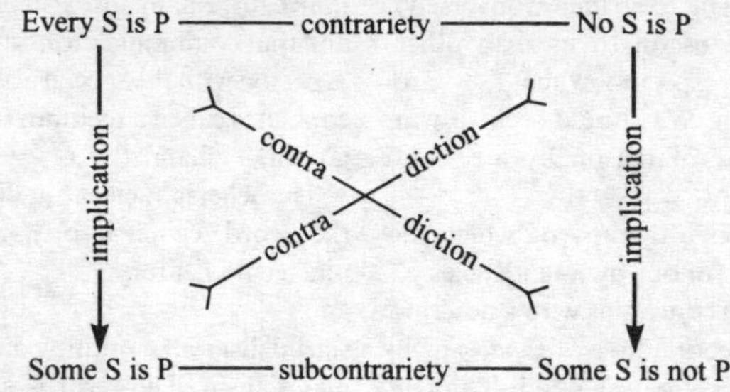

Figure 7 Square of opposition (2)

$(\forall x)(Fx \supset Gx)$ — $(\forall x)(Fx \supset \sim Gx)$

contra — diction

contra — diction

$(\exists x)(Fx \,\&\, Gx)$ — $(\exists x)(Fx \,\&\, \sim Gx)$

Figure 8 Square of opposition (3)

necessarily p — **necessarily not-p**

implication — contra — diction — contra — diction — implication

possibly p — **possibly not-p**

This square differs from the one preceding by having fewer relations.

The square for modal notions can be drawn as in Figure 8.

By extending this square to a hexagon, some additional relations can be made perspicuous, as in Figure 9.

stadium paradox *See* ZENO OF ELEA.

Stagirite /ˈstædʒɪraɪt/, **the** a by-name for Aristotle, derived from Stageira, his place of birth.

state of nature the condition in which, according to many theories, human beings would find themselves in the absence of civil authority.

Since ancient times political thinkers have found this concept useful in their analysis of what is lawful and just by nature, independently of human conventions and decisions. Such an analysis would in turn be relevant also for civil society, since at least some of the rights or duties existing naturally would retain their validity independently of subsequent conventions and decisions.

Different from the question of what is lawful and just by nature is the question of how individuals living in a state of nature would actually conduct themselves. Would they conform to the precepts of natural justice? From what we know of human nature we can easily work out, according to most classical political philosophers, e.g. Hobbes and Locke, that in the absence of civil authority there would be conflicts but no reasonable way to resolve them. In the state of nature, therefore, we cannot expect to coexist peacefully with others. But

Figure 9 An expanded square of opposition

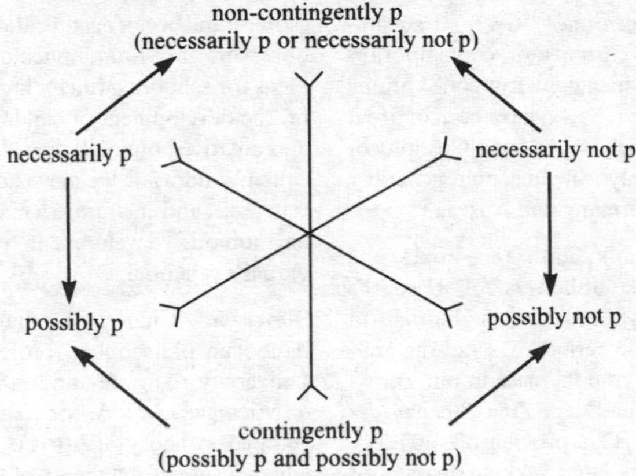

peaceful coexistence is a precondition for obtaining most necessities and conveniences of life. Consequently, we will find it desirable to leave the state of nature: we will prefer to live in a society under civil authority. Kant went even further, arguing that if we were in a state of nature, leaving it would be our duty, a demand of reason.

One of the objections against the view that conflict is inevitable in the state of nature, is that this view depends on a false view of human nature. The tendencies that lead human beings into conflict are not inherent in human nature, but arise only in human beings corrupted by civilization (Rousseau) or by economic exploitation (Marxism). Indeed, the argument goes, if these corrupting influences are eliminated, peaceful coexistence and the cooperation necessary for securing the necessities and conveniences of life will result, and remove or strongly reduce the need for civil authority.

status quo /ˈsteɪtəs ˈkwəʊ/ short for the Latin *status quo ante* the same state, the same condition, as before. A defender of the *status quo* wants to leave things as they are; an opponent of the *status quo* wants change.

Stebbing, (Lizzie) Susan (1885–1943) After studies in Cambridge, where the logician W. E. Johnson and G. E. Moore influenced her most, she taught philosophy at Bedford College in London from 1915 and became professor there in 1933. Her writings, inspired by the ideals of clarity and rationality, include *A Modern Introduction to Logic* 2nd edn 1933. *Philosophy and the Physicists* 1937 criticizes the philosophical mystifications of some eminent scientists.

Stegmüller /ˈʃtekmylər (Gm.)/, Wolfgang (1923–91) Austrian-German philosopher, professor at Munich from 1958. He held a leading position in Germany as a representative of analytical philosophy. In the philosophy of science his work was initially inspired by Carnap and Hempel, but in the early 1970s he adopted a new outlook, influenced in part by Thomas Kuhn: scientific theories should not be regarded as sets of statements, but rather as structures of a distinctive kind (*The Structuralist View of Theories* 1979). The many editions of his *Hauptströmungen der Gegenwartsphilosophie* (Main currents of contemporary philosophy), which grew from one volume in 1952 to four 1987–9, have been of great significance for the revival of philosophy of science and analytical philosophy generally in post-war Germany and Austria.

Stein /ʃtaɪn (Gm.)/, Edith (1891–1942) one of the earliest followers of Husserl's phenomenology, and his first *Assistent* in Freiburg. In the period 1914–22 she analysed empathy and its place in our knowledge of the mind, e.g. *Zum Problem der Einfühlung* 1917 (The problem of empathy), and offered in a later work an analysis of the distinction between causality and motivation, and of the differentiation of psychology from the humanities. Of Jewish origin, she converted to Roman Catholicism in 1922 and became a Carmelite nun in 1933. In a later major work on ontology, *Endliches und Ewiges Sein* 1935–6 (Finite and eternal being), she endeavoured to combine phenomenology and Thomism.

Steiner /'staɪnə (Eng.); 'ʃtaɪnər (Gm.)/, Rudolf (1861–1925) German thinker and theosophist, born in what was then Hungary and is currently Croatia. He held a prominent position in the theosophical movement at the beginning of the century, but broke away to develop an alternative system of thought, and of mental and bodily culture, which he called anthroposophy. Its organizational centre in Dornach (near Basel) in Switzerland is named Goetheanum, a clear indication of the strong influence of Goethe's nature-philosophy on Steiner, who rejected mainstream mechanistic and materialistic science, which he considered to be at best one-sided and in need of a more organic and spiritual supplementation. Genuine knowledge, he thought, must always include intuitive and aesthetic elements. Although Steiner's anthroposophical system is replete with esoteric and occult mystifications, impartial observers have found much of value in his ideas for schooling (including an emphasis on the development of children's aesthetic and creative potential), practised in the so-called Waldorf or Steiner schools. The aim is to assist and encourage a many-sided and harmonious development of the individual's potential.

Stevenson, Charles L(eslie) (1908–79) American philosopher, professor at Yale University 1939–46 and at the University of Michigan, Ann Arbor 1946–77. He developed a theory of EMOTIVE MEANING which he used for a theory of PERSUASIVE DEFINITION. His *Ethics and Language* 1944 gave a full and closely argued articulation of the emotivist (EMOTIVISM) theory of ethics, with its sharp distinction between cognitive uses of language (to state facts and give reasons) and non-cognitive uses (to express attitudes and exercise an influence). The salient point is that the language of ethics is primarily of the latter kind: an ethical statement typically expresses emotions and attitudes, and it is used to influence the addressee. This does not, however, rule out that both kinds of meaning, emotive and factual, may be jointly present in a statement.

Stewart, Dugald /'stjʊət, 'duːgəld/ (1753–1828) educated at the University of Edinburgh, where he first taught mathematics and later became professor of moral philosophy in succession to Adam Ferguson, 1785–1810.

While disliking the term 'common sense' in philosophy, Stewart rightly saw himself as an heir to Reid in his basic philosophical outlook; but he was an eclectic philosopher who was also much influenced by others, especially Adam Smith. To a greater degree than Reid, Stewart promoted the view that a science of 'the fundamental laws of human belief' could be developed inductively – in the same way as the natural sciences. Stewart drew historicist conclusions from the idea of the moral perfectibility of humanity, in contrast to Reid's utopian leanings, and one can see his philosophy of mind as part of an overall defence against political radicalism in the context of British reactions to the French Revolution.

Stewart was enormously influential in his own time, thanks to his popular lectures and his numerous works – and the prominence of many of his students: the founders of the *Edinburgh Review*, literary men as different as Sir Walter Scott and James Mill, foreign luminaries such as Benjamin Constant, and many more. Stewart was also immensely popular in France and America for a couple of generations. The combined effect of his and Reid's philosophy led to the idea of a 'Common Sense school', often simply known as 'the Scottish school'.

KHA

Stilpo of Megara (*c.* 380–*c.* 300 BC) said to have taught that every true proposition asserts identity between subject and predicate. If that were not the case, the subject would be infinitely divisible as further predicates are progressively asserted of it, and could then not be a substance. Hence the universe must consist of solipsistic monads (or be a single, self-conscious plenum). He also gave this an ethical interpretation: an individual should aim at self-sufficiency and emotional unperturbedness. GT

stipulative definition a declaration of an intention to assign a particular meaning to a new expression, or to assign a new meaning to an existing expression. This is done for the sake of convenience, for instance in order to have a shorter word to replace a more complex phrase. A stipulative definition can be convenient or inconvenient but cannot be correct or incorrect.

Stirner /'ʃtɪrnər (Gm.)/, Max (= Caspar Schmidt) (1806–56) journalist and teacher in Berlin, advocate of an extremely radical individualism in his *Der Einzige und sein Eigenthum* 1845 (The individual and his own). Only the individual self exists, and its basic form of activity is appropriative; everything is done and ought to be done only for one's own sake, even at the expense of other egos, which must look after themselves. Underpinning the theory is a broad historical sweep of a Hegelian kind but with an anti-Hegelian content. His later *Geschichte der Reaktion* 1852 (History of reaction) sharply attacks the established social and political order, but is mainly a compilation of extracts from other writers (Burke, Comte, etc.). There is a lengthy polemic against him in Marx and Engels's *The German Ideology*.

Stoa *See* STOICISM.

stochastic /stɒ'kæstɪk/ (Gr. *stokhazesthai* to aim at) *adj.* random; pertaining to a probability distribution.

Stoicism /'stəʊɪsɪzm/ *n.* one of the most popular philosophical systems in the Hellenistic and Roman periods. It was founded by Zeno of Citium about 300 BC, and named after the Porch or Arcade (Stoa) in which he taught at Athens. As a school it lasted at least until the third century AD, but as a system it influenced Christian thinkers until much later, and was revived in the Renaissance. More recently there has been much interest particularly in Stoic logic. After Zeno, the most important ancient Stoics were Cleanthes (331–232 BC), Chrysippus (*c.* 280–206 BC), Panaetius (185–*c.* 110 BC), Posidonius (*c.* 135–51 BC). The major late Stoics were Roman: Seneca (*c.* 5 BC–AD 65), Epictetus (*c.* 55–*c.* 135) and Marcus Aurelius (121–180).

Zeno and the other earlier Stoics divided philosophy into logic (including epistemology), physics (including theology) and ethics. Their logic was based on the possibility of *katalēpsis*, i.e. direct grasp or perception of the external world. They acknowledged both that the bodily senses can be deceived and that false judgements can be made about perceptions, but believed that these difficulties could be obviated by calm reflection. In this way mental conception could be made to correspond exactly to the external world. In their effort to explain how language can be (but often is not) an accurate representation of reality, they extended Aristotelian logic by formulating principles of propositional logic, and they also anticipated a number of modern epistemological problems. They also began to establish what eventually became the traditional grammatical categories of European languages.

Their physics is a materialist, though not atomistic or atheistic, system. They believed that matter is the only reality, and that the different substances in the universe are produced by different degrees of tension in matter. (It has been suggested that they anticipated the modern physical notion of a 'field of force'.) The whole universe is formed and guided by a *logos*, or reason, which is itself composed of matter in its finest degree of tension. This logos can be understood as God, as nature, as fate and as providence. The individual human mind is a 'seed' of the logos, and the purpose of an individual life is a progressive grasp of, and adaptation to, the overall purposes of the universe. The Stoics believed that the regularity of the natural world provided evidence for these purposes, and in this way they formulated an argument from design for the existence of gods, or God. Their way of arguing is presented in Cicero's *De natura deorum* (On the nature of the gods). The earlier Stoics also spoke of a cosmic cycle, in which God, acting as fire, brings the world into existence and then destroys it, but this notion was evidently dropped by later members of the school.

Stoic ethics defines virtue as living and acting in accordance with logos. It is intrinsically connected with logic and physics, in that only a clear grasp of reality allows a person to be virtuous. Evil is defined negatively as not living and acting in accordance with logos, i.e. as a kind of ignorance. Some Stoics claimed that, apart from virtue, all other aspects of life were ethically indifferent (*adiaphoron*). Most, however, suggested that some aspects (e.g. health) were 'to be chosen', whereas others (e.g. illness and pain) were 'to be avoided', in that the former are more conducive to virtue than the latter. All believed that one should not regret any unavoidable suffering or deprivation, as these were clearly part of the overall purpose of things. They thus advocated *apatheia* (passionlessness) as the most desirable state of mind. It is this which has led to the popular understanding of Stoicism as a kind of stiff-upper-lip attitude to the world.

Panaetius in particular adapted Stoicism to the outlook of members of the Roman ruling class. He modified the idea that only one who is fully in harmony with the logos can truly be called virtuous, by suggesting that many others can be 'making progress' towards that ideal. The ideal of conformity with logos implied an ethical cosmopolitanism: all human beings are by nature fellow-citizens of one world, divided only by artificial convention. Some Roman Stoics tended to assimilate this message with the goals of Roman imperialism. Stoicism encouraged an attitude of steadfastness and inner resistance in a period of autocratic oppression in imperial Rome, and provided above all a rhetoric of individual responsibility and self-reliance which, e.g. through the tragedies, letters and treatises of Seneca and the meditations of Marcus Aurelius, has greatly influenced much modern literature. RB

Strato of Lampsacus /ˈstrɑːtəʊ əv ˈlæmpsəkəs/ (*c.* 340–269 BC) head of the Lyceum, the peripatetic school in Athens, after Theophrastus. He made important revisions to Aristotle's theories, and rejected the view that natural phenomena are to be explained teleologically, i.e. in terms of some supposed purpose. Especially, he thought that there is no need to postulate a divine creator or designer beyond nature in order to explain the entire world-order. His preferred alternative explanation was in terms of an inherent dynamism. This outlook, which is certainly compatible with (and perhaps even implies) atheism, seems to have had a limited influence in ancient times, but it did attract the positive interest of Bayle, Hume and other Enlightenment thinkers.

Strauss /ʃtraʊs (Gm.)/, David Friedrich (1808–74) German theologian and philosopher. His *Das Leben Jesu kritisch bearbeitet* 1835–6 (The life of Jesus critically examined) argued that our historical knowledge of Jesus is highly uncertain. The gospels and the tradition stemming from them should be seen as an expression of the spirit of a religious community at a certain time. This need not, however, prevent it from also having personal and ethical relevance for other times and circumstances. By this work, in which religious supranaturalism is altogether rejected and Christianity is regarded at the same level as poetry or myth, he achieved notoriety among the orthodox, and fame among the radicals and liberals. His early thought, influenced by a Hegelian approach to history, gradually turned in a positivist and materialist direction.

Strauss, Leo (1899–1973) political thinker and intellectual historian of German-Jewish origin, in exile in the USA from 1938, professor of political science at the University of Chicago 1949–68. He was an eloquent critic of mediocrity and the various manifestations of mass culture, deploring the waning of interest in cultural and intellectual achievements. In Strauss's view (*Natural Right and History* 1952), political thought in the modern era, from Machiavelli, Hobbes, Locke and onwards, had gradually reduced the moral dimensions of political life, first to a minimal ethics clearly exemplified in Hobbes, and eventually to a complete elimination as in more recent theories of politics. These modern theories, some positivist, some historicist, inspired by Hegel, have in common a refusal to pass judgement. Against this, Strauss favoured a morally enriched political theory, as in classical natural law theory of the kind represented by Aquinas. As an intellectual historian, he urged that texts be read naively, taken on their merits, with respect for (though not necessarily assent to) their own truth-claims, but he also held (*Persecution and the Art of Writing* 1952) that much of the real message of classical political texts is esoteric, hidden between the lines – a view that remains highly controversial. Many American political theorists of a conservative bent have been influenced by his ideas to such an extent that they can be regarded as forming a school.

Strawson /ˈstrɔːsən/, P(eter) F(rederick) (1919–) English philosopher, fellow of University College, Oxford from 1948, fellow of Magdalen College and successor to Ryle as professor of philosophy 1968–87, one of the leading representatives of Oxford analytical and linguistic philosophy in the post-war era. In an article ('Truth' 1950) he argued that we use 'true' to express our endorsement of a statement, in opposition to the correspondence theory. Another article, 'On Referring' 1950, developed an important criticism of Russell's theory of descriptions. According to Russell, statements about the (non-existent) present King of France – e.g. 'the present King of France is bald' – are false, because they can be analysed as conjunctions in which one conjunct – i.e. 'someone is at present King of France' – is false. Against this, Strawson urged that Russellian logic does not do justice to ordinary language: ordinary-language statements about the present King of France presuppose his existence, but that one must not identify PRESUPPOSITION (as Russell does) with implication.

In *Individuals* 1959 and *The Bounds of Sense* 1966 (the latter proposing a theory of Kantian inspiration), Strawson distinguishes revisionary metaphysics from his own project of a descriptive metaphysics, which is an analysis of the basic categories and linguistic structures we employ in our thinking about the world and our descriptions of it. In order to talk and think about the world in the way we do, we have to assume that the world contains basic particulars: material objects form one basic category, persons another. They are basic because they are identifiable and re-identifiable; this is how they differ from particulars of other categories: events, states of affairs. Another basic category is that of abstract entities, universals.

Strawson's views have an anti-reductionist slant. He argues, e.g., that our conception of personhood is an irreducible subcategory of basic particulars, and he opposes both the attempts to analyse particulars as mere conglomerates of properties, and the theories that ascribe reality to particulars only.

strict implication *See* IMPLICATION, STRICT.

structuralism *n.* a kind of inquiry or theory predominantly concerned with the description of structures. Less attention is given to the genetic or historical dimensions of the subject-matter. The approach is often linked to an assumption that structures – relationships between particulars – rather than the particulars themselves, are basic to reality, to human knowledge, or both.

The term is mainly used for a particular school or movement in which the names of Saussure, Piaget, Lévi-Strauss and Barthes are prominent, and in which the structures discussed are for the most part mental, linguistic, social or literary. In general terms, there are three characteristics by which structures differ from mere aggregates: (1) the nature of an element depends, at least in part, on its place in the structure, i.e. its interrelations with other elements (holism); (2) the structure is not static, but allows for change from within. For instance, new sentences can be created within a language-structure (dynamism); (3) the characteristics of the structure can be understood without reference to factors external to it. We can understand the function of a word, say 'dog', within a language-structure independently of whether any dogs exist (autarchy).

In France, the influence of structuralism reached its zenith in the 1960s. It was preoccupied with unmasking: things are not what they seem; psychological, social, political phenomena should not be taken at face value, but should be understood as determined by structures often hidden from view. In the French debate this meant a rejection of the conceptions of individual autonomy that are present in existentialist, Marxist-humanist, religious and liberal thought. Instead, individuals were seen as mere place-holders in social networks or structures, and the idea that they are human subjects, i.e. agents whose decisions can influence the course of social events, was regarded as an illusion. The structuralists, for the most part politically to the left, frequently used their theoretical approach for a critique of 'bourgeois' culture and society.

Suárez /ˈswaːrɛz (Eng.); ˈswarɛθ (Sp.)/, Francisco (1548–1617) Born in Spain, Suárez spent most of his life, apart from five years in Rome, on the Iberian peninsula, where he taught at Coimbra from 1597 to 1616. He died in Lisbon. He became a Jesuit at the age of 16, and is still regarded as the principal Jesuit theologian.

He was prodigiously erudite and had a thorough knowledge of the medieval theologians and of the Church fathers. He is also a characteristically modern author, in that he handles questions one at a time, systematically and exhaustively; this is by contrast with the academic writing of the Middle Ages, which was dominated by commentaries and was thus, in the main, neither systematic nor exhaustive. Another modern characteristic is Suárez's integration of the analytical and the historical; again, the systematic consideration of the history of a question was absent during the Middle Ages. His *Disputationes Metaphysicae* 1597 was the first systematic treatment of metaphysics which did not follow the sequence of topics in Aristotle; because of its organization and its systematic nature, it was to set the scene for a whole genre of metaphysical writing reaching well towards the end of the eighteenth century. Leibniz and Wolff were among those strongly influenced.

On the question of how to harmonize divine foreknowledge and human freedom, Suárez proposed a theory of 'middle knowledge' similar to Molina's.

In the philosophy of law, his major work was *De legibus ac Deo legislatore* 1612 (a work to which a decade later Grotius was to acknowledge his indebtedness). Suárez partly adopted, partly modified Aquinas's views, and at times even opposed them. He retained the important division of four kinds of law: eternal, divine, natural, and human. He argued that Aquinas's analysis of law (a precept of reason directed to the common good) was incomplete in being too intellectualist and omitting the concept of obligation, which in turn presupposes a concept of a (legislative) act of will. GW

subalternation *n.* In syllogistic logic, there are two laws of subalternation. *Every S is P* implies *Some S is P*, and *No S is P* implies *Some S is not P*. In each of these two implications, the first statement can be called *superaltern* and the second *subaltern*.

subconscious *n.*, *adj.* Some writers use this term as a synonym for *unconscious*, others in a more special sense, referring to mental contents of which one is only dimly aware.

subcontraries *n. pl.* Two categorical propositions that cannot be false together but can be true together are subcontraries. This logical relation holds between affirmative and negative particular propositions: *Some S is P* and *Some S is not P*.

More generally, two propositions which cannot be false together but can be true together can be called subcontraries. **subcontrariety** *n.*

subject *n.* The origin of this word and its cognates is the Latin word *subjectum* (something put underneath), which was introduced as the equivalent of the Greek *hypokeimenon* and conveys the idea of an under-carriage, a substratum; the original meaning of the word is accordingly quite close to that of substance. This word and its cognates are used in many different senses, of which only a few are noted here.
1 In a sentence, the subject-term denotes the bearer of a property, and the predicate denotes the property. The subject is that

about which something is said. **2** In other contexts, subject and object are the correlated notions: (a) In ancient and medieval philosophy, the meanings of 'subject' and 'substance' were the same or closely related: it is something actually existing out there, for instance, a tree. In contrast, that which is thrown up before the mind, the tree as a mental content, was called the object. This usage is still to be found in Descartes; (b) In modern philosophy, the meaning of this pair has become more or less reversed. If we think of the self or the mind as something that 'underlies' its various perceptions, thoughts, feelings, etc., that is, something which thinks, feels, perceives, is aware of, etc., it is natural to use subject to mean self or mind, and to use object for that which stands over against the mind. This sense of subject (an individual mind or an individual with a mind) became established in the eighteenth century.

subjective *adj.* **1** a subjective experience is introspective, i.e. it is a subject's direct experience of itself, in contrast to experience of things and states external to the subject. **2** more generally, subjective is that which belongs to any subject conceived as a self, a mind. **3** in another sense, similar to the above, but more restricted, subjective is that which belongs to one, or a number of subjects, but not necessarily to all. **4** what is subjective is a mere matter of personal taste or preference; lacking in truth or validity; arbitrary.

It is often taken for granted that it is legitimate to criticize a belief or opinion for being 'subjective'; but that depends on what is meant. In the *first two* senses above, the criticism only amounts to saying that someone holds the opinion, which is not much of an objection. In the *third* sense, it amounts to saying that not everyone agrees, which is not a serious objection either. In the *fourth* sense, there is actually an objection, but to be effective it will of course have to be backed by reasons.

subjective idealism **1** a theory of knowledge: that a subject can know nothing except its own ideas. **2** an ontology: that nothing exists except minds and their ideas.

Berkeley argued for both.

subjective right *See* RIGHT.

subjectivism *n.* **1** (in epistemology) the view that the mind can know nothing but itself: whatever is known is the form, or content, or product of consciousness.
2 (in ontology) the view that ultimate reality is a subject (i.e. a conscious mind).
3 (in ethics) the view that evaluations depend for their truth-value on the existence of certain opinions or attitudes. For instance, one kind of ethical subjectivist theory is that which holds that a state of affairs is desirable if and only if it is desired by a subject (myself, or a majority, or a sovereign body in a society, etc.). Subjectivism in this sense is a kind of ETHICAL NATURALISM.

'Subjectivism' is sometimes used in an entirely different sense, as a synonym for NON-COGNITIVISM.

subjunctive conditionals a class of conditional statements. For example, 'If Jack had had any sense, he would have proposed to Jill'. These conditionals are called subjunctive because in Latin they would employ subjunctive verb-forms. (In English, there are few subjunctive forms, and auxiliary verbs are used instead.)

Conditionals of this kind often express causal connections, and interpretations of them are central to the contemporary analysis of laws of nature. Many subjunctive conditionals are counterfactual. In the example above, it is understood that Jack's having any sense is contrary to fact. But there are subjunctive conditionals which are not counterfactuals, i.e. those of the form 'If it were to be the case that p, then it would be the case that q'.

sublapsarianism /sʌblæp'sɛərɪənɪzm/ *n.* INFRALAPSARIANISM.

sublation *n.* a word specially devised to translate Hegel's *Aufhebung*: the overcoming of the contrast between a thesis and its antithesis in their synthesis. The German word suggests cancellation, elevation, supersession.

sublimation /sʌblɪm'eɪʃən/ *n.* **1** (in chemistry) the direct transformation of a substance from solid to vaporous form. **2** (in psychoanalysis) the transformation of a repressed sexual drive into a more elevated (intellectual, artistic, ethical, religious) quest.

sublime /sə'blaɪm/ *n.*, *adj.* awesome grandeur (of a personal character, of a work of art, of nature), contrasted in eighteenth-century aesthetics (Burke, Kant) with the beautiful. The classical treatment is *On the Sublime*, a work from the first century. Longinus is commonly given as the name of its author.

subliminal /sə'blɪmɪnəl/ *adj.* below the threshold of conscious perception.

subsist *vb.* This word is used as a translation of Meinong's *bestehen* to signify a mode of being which, according to his theory of objects, belongs to non-existent or abstract things and states of affairs which can nevertheless be objects of thought. Golden mountains, unicorns, numbers and propositions are examples of entities that subsist although they do not exist.

sub specie aeternitatis /sʌb 'spiːʃɪi aɪtɜːnɪ'taːtɪs/ Lat. under the aspect of eternity. The expression is Spinoza's. He uses it in his *Ethics* to characterize the highest form of knowledge, which he calls intuitive knowledge, in which things are seen from the standpoint of timelessness or eternity.

substance (Lat. *substantia*. This was the equivalent, first proposed by Seneca, of the Greek word *hypostasis*) *n.* The first of Aristotle's categories. Primary substances are individuals, this man or that horse; secondary substances are species – the classes of individuals of a certain sort (e.g. man, horse, donkey) – and genera, the classes of species, e.g. animal. The primary ones *can exist on their own*, in contrast to qualities, relations, etc., which need substances to carry them.

Another distinctive feature of substances is that they *can have contrary properties*. It is the same horse that is young or old; an animal can be a cat or a dog. A further feature is that they are *logical subjects*: they can have properties, relations, etc. ascribed to them, but are not themselves attributes of anything.

In the modern era, the philosophical concept of substance is first and foremost a concept of that which needs nothing else for its existence: substance is that which has independent existence. In this primary sense, Descartes holds that there can then be only one substance, i.e. God. But in a secondary sense, he holds that there are two (created) substances: mind and matter. They can be called substances because, apart from the fact that they are created by God, they have independent existence. For Spinoza, there can be only one substance. It may be called God or Nature – each of these words signifies something that we conceive of as having independent existence. Mind and matter are the two aspects, called attributes by Spinoza, under which we are able to have knowledge of what there is. Leibniz assumes a multitude of created individual substances, monads, each of them independent of all the others. JM

substitution, rule of a rule of inference in

formal systems: (1) a rule which allows for uniform replacement of a sentence-letter by any formula, and of a name-letter by any term. (There is a similar, more complex, rule for predicate-letters.) Replacements of this kind in a valid formula preserve validity; in an entailment they preserve entailment; in an inconsistent set they preserve inconsistency; (2) a rule of substitution of equivalent expressions: let the formula A contain a subformula X, and let B be the same as A, except that B contains Y where A contains X. Then, if X and Y are equivalent, so are A and B.

The similar rule for names is that one name can replace another name if they have the same extension. For predicates, the rule is that one predicate can replace another predicate, if they have the same extension.

substitutional quantification *See* OBJECTUAL QUANTIFICATION.

subvenience /səb'viːnjəns/ *See* SUPERVENIENCE.

succedent *n.* the expression on the right-hand side of a sequent in Gentzen's sequent calculus.

sui generis /'suːɪ 'dʒɛnərɪs/ Lat. of its own (distinctive) kind.

sui juris /'suːɪ 'dʒʊərɪs/ Lat. of (or in) one's own right; being legally in charge of oneself: being able to act with legal effect and being legally responsible for one's actions. *Ant. alieni juris*, i.e. being under the legal authority of someone else (e.g. a parent, a husband).

Summa contra Gentiles /'sʊmə 'kɒntrə dʒɛn'tɪːleɪz/, ***Summa Theologiae*** /'sʊmə θɪə'ləʊdʒɪeɪ/ *See* AQUINAS.

summum bonum /'sʊmʊm 'bəʊnʊm/ Lat. the highest good.

super *prep.* Lat. above, over.

superaltern *n.* a categorical proposition which implies another categorical proposition. *See* SUBALTERNATION.

superego *n.* in psychoanalytic theory (the term was introduced by Freud in 1923), the internalized, censoring and repressive part of the mind. It develops from the need to suppress the desire of every little boy to seduce his mother. This need arises as a consequence of the acceptance of the father's authority. But the superego is generated not only by the Oedipus complex, but also generally by the social and educational influences on the child. It manifests itself in conscience, shame and guilt, and controls desires and impulses of the Ego (constituted by adaptation to the external world) and helps the Ego to repress parts of the Id (the instinctive drives which, left to themselves, lead to conflict with the external physical and social world).

supererogation (Lat. *super* + *rogare* to ask) acting beyond the call of duty. The performance of a supererogatory act is good but not required; its non-performance is not morally bad. According to certain moral theories, supererogation is impossible. Most utilitarians (consequentialists) hold that it is our duty to act in the best way. Any other action is contrary to duty, and hence morally bad. Kant also conceives of duty in such a manner as to rule out the possibility of supererogation. **supererogatory** *adj.*

superlative (Lat. *super* + *latus* carried, brought) *adj.*, *n.* to the highest degree; something of the highest degree. In grammar, superlatives of adjectives and adverbs are usually expressed by the suffix '*-(e)st*', or by '*most*'; e.g. *wisest* is the superlative of *wise*, *most wisely* is the superlative of *wisely*.

Note: 'Superlative entities' has been used (in the early 1990s) for entities whose existence need not be postulated, that is, for ontologically redundant or superfluous entities (like Ryle's 'ghost in the machine') which can be cut away by Ockham's razor. The viability of the use of the word in this new sense is questionable.

superman *n.* from German *Übermensch*, a new and better type of human being, heralded in Nietzsche's *Thus Spake Zarathustra*. Some translators of Nietzsche prefer *overman*.

supernatural *adj.*, *n.* Supernatural beings exist above or beyond nature, where 'nature' is to be understood in a wide sense, to take in all of space and time and everything existing within that framework, i.e. the whole of the physical universe. It is especially in the context of religious belief that the concept of the supernatural has been used.

If scientists (or non-scientists) discover a new type of wave, a new force, a strange phenomenon in a remote galaxy, the very fact that it was there to be discovered makes it a natural phenomenon which may in due course be described in science textbooks. Supernatural beings run no risk of having their existence disclosed by scientific or everyday observation.

superstition *n.* false religion; belief in ghosts, demons, secret powers, etc., often combined with practices intended to manipulate or influence them.

supervaluation *n.* A supervaluation is a way of assigning truth-values to sentences of a formal language which admits of the possibility that sentences be neither true nor false. It thus allows for violations of the principle of bivalence, but accepts as logical truths the same sentences which are so accepted in standard semantics (for instance, the law of excluded middle).

By way of example, consider the problem of future contingents. In order to determine the truth-value of the claim 'There will be a sea-battle tomorrow', the supervaluationist considers the various ways in which the future could unfold. One possibility is that the future will make the claim true – there could be a sea-battle tomorrow; another possibility is that the future will render the claim false. In the absence of a unique truth-value assignment (True, or False), the claim is assigned a value that is neither True nor False in a supervaluation. On the other hand, no matter how the future unfolds, it will always be true that either there is or there is not a sea-battle tomorrow; as a consequence, the claim 'There will be a sea-battle tomorrow or there will not be' will be assigned the value True in a supervaluation, as it would in the standard classical valuation.

Supervaluations, first described by Bas van Fraassen in 'Singular terms, truth-value gaps, and free logic', *Journal of Philosophy 63* (1966), seem well suited to formally represent Aristotle's position on future contingents. Other areas where they may apply are vagueness, and presupposition-failure (e.g. a sentence like 'The present King of France is bald', which incorrectly presupposes that there is a present King of France). DH

supervenience /suːpəˈviːnjəns/ (Lat. *super* + *venire* to come) *n.* a relation of dependency between properties at different levels that is neither logical nor causal.

In general, if the *subvenient* properties, those at the lower level, are the same, then the correlated properties at the higher level, the *supervenient* ones, cannot differ. Yet the supervenient properties cannot be defined in terms of, or otherwise reduced to, the subvenient ones.

The concept of supervenience was first articulated by G. E. Moore in 'The Conception of Intrinsic Value', *Philosophical Studies* 1922. He held that intrinsic value supervenes on natural properties in that (1) it is not identical with any natural properties, and (2) two things that have the same natural properties cannot differ in intrinsic value.

Moore did not use the word 'supervenience', but it was used in this sense in Oxford in the 1940s (for instance, by Ryle in an article in *Philosophy* 1946), and its use became established with R. M. Hare's *The Language of Morals* 1952. In his view, supervenience-relations hold generally between descriptive and evaluative predicates, although evaluative predicates cannot be defined in terms of descriptive ones only.

Donald Davidson later used the concept of supervenience to account for the relation between mental and physical events: 'there cannot be two events alike in all physical respects but differing in some mental respects' ('Mental Events', *Essays on Actions and Events* 1980).

Subsequently, various distinctions have been recognized. Jaegwon Kim, in 'Concepts of Supervenience', *Philosophy and Phenomenological Research* 45 (1984–5), began by distinguishing two kinds of supervenience, weak and strong. S is *weakly* supervenient on B ('B' for basis) means that if two things have the same B-properties, they must have the same S-properties. For instance, if the moral goodness of St Francis is supervenient on having certain dispositions, then any other person who has the same dispositions is also morally good. But in a possible world that is 'morally dead' (i.e. in which no moral concepts apply) there could be those dispositions but no moral goodness. This is ruled out if S is *strongly* supervenient on B. In that case, if an individual in one possible world has those dispositions and an individual in another possible world has them too, then they also have the same supervenient property of moral goodness. Further distinctions among concepts of supervenience have been made along these lines.

Philosophers in the latter half of the twentieth century who incline towards materialism find supervenience-concepts useful. Analyses in terms of supervenience make it possible to admit a range of concepts without having to admit the real existence of non-material entities or non-natural realms of being. Thus, facts/values, body/mind, individuals/collectives and othercontrasting categories are seen as subvenient/supervenient pairs of conceptual ranges.

supposition *n.* **1** (in contemporary usage) a proposition assumed but not asserted in the context of a piece of reasoning. **2** (in medieval logic) the *suppositio* of a term (literally, that which is 'posited under') is that to which the term applies, its extension or denotation, in contrast to the *significatio* (intension or connotation). But *suppositio* was also used to account for the use/mention distinction: the *material* supposition is the word itself, the *formal* one is the meaning of the word.

supra *adj.* Lat. above, over.

supralapsarianism /suːprəlæp'sɛərɪənɪzm/ (Lat. *supra* + *lapsus* a slide, a fall) *n.* the view that God had already decided before the Fall whom to save and whom to condemn. *See also* INFRALAPSARIANISM.

supranaturalism *n.* a doctrine which assumes the existence of supernatural entities.

surprise examination, also **surprise hanging**, **surprise party** *See* PREDICTION PARADOX.

surrealism /sə'rɪəlɪzm/ (Fr. *sur* above) *n.* an aesthetic movement in the creative arts. It radically challenged established conventions as well as the standards or norms of sense and coherence in grammar, logic, pictorial representations, etc., often in dreamlike flights of imagination. Artistic effect was sought by apparently bizarre, incoherent or hallucinatory techniques.

This trend had its inception with a manifesto published in 1924 by the French writer André Breton. Among its early prominent representatives, many of whom came from Dada, were the French writer Louis Aragon; a number of painters such as the Spaniard Salvador Dali, the Belgian René Magritte and the German Max Ernst; and film directors, e.g. Luis Buñuel. Its influence on the creative arts in the twentieth century has been considerable. Occasionally, surrealism has also been interpreted as having an ethical message of personal liberation and responsibility.

The word was coined by Guillaume Apollinaire, who gave the subtitle 'drame surréaliste' to his *Les Mamelles de Tirésias* 1917.

suum /ˈsuːʊm/ Lat. one's own. Cf. *meum* mine; *tuum* yours; etc. *pron.*

suum cuique tribuere /ˈsuːʊm ˈkwiːkwe trɪbˈwɛːrɪ/ Lat. award to each what is his; i.e. his own or his due. One of the three classical PRECEPTS OF JUSTICE.

s.v. Lat. *sub voce*: under the (head-)word.

Swedenborg /ˈswiːdənbɔːg (Eng.); ˈsvedənbɔrj (Sw.)/, Emanuel (1688–1772) Swedish mining engineer, inventor, scientist, and philosopher of science of great ability, and a prolific writer in these areas. After a religious crisis in the mid-1740s, he wrote a vast number of religious works, among which the best known are *De Coelo ... et de Inferno* 1758 (On heaven and hell); *Arcana coelestia* (8 vols) 1749–56 (The heavenly secrets); and *Vera Christiana Religio* 1771 (The true Christian religion). He believed that by a special dispensation his mind had been opened up to the other world so that he could gain and communicate knowledge of it and of the spirits dwelling therein. He found supporting evidence for his religious ideas by means of minute allegorical interpretations which give a spiritual counterpart to what Scripture presents in a grosser form. The principal assumptions behind this mode of interpretation are (1) that, understood literally, much of Scripture is false and (2) Scripture cannot be false. His doctrine is an unorthodox variety of Christianity, and its followers are organized in the Church of the New Jerusalem. Eminent writers like William Blake, August Strindberg and W. B. Yeats have been influenced by his visionary ideas, as was the family of Henry and William James. In philosophy his name remains known mainly because the *Arcana* provoked Kant to write *Dreams of a Spirit-Seer* 1766.

syllepsis /sɪˈlɛpsɪs/ (Gr. *syn-* with + *lēpsis* a taking) *n.* **1** (in rhetoric) a figure of speech in which a word is associated with two (or more) other words, but in different senses, as in 'She opened the door and her heart to the poor boy', or 'He took his briefcase and a taxi'. *Syn.* zeugma. **2** (in grammar) the use of a word that is associated but not in grammatical agreement with two (or more) other words, as in 'Neither he nor we are pleased'. **3** (in recent semiotics) an account rendered according to some principle other than temporal sequence (e.g. a description of the setting of one's childhood summer holidays).

syllogism /ˈsɪlədʒɪzm/ *n.* **1** an argument in which a conclusion follows from several premisses. This definition by Aristotle (*Prior Analytics* 24^b 18–20) implies: (a) that syllogisms are *valid* arguments; (b) that they have *two or more* premisses; (c) that *none* of the premisses is *redundant*.

While his definition places no restriction on the form that a syllogism's premisses or conclusion may take, he himself gave detailed attention to syllogisms containing CATEGORICAL propositions only. These are known as categorical syllogisms. All categorical syllogisms are reducible to one or other of the following forms of *perfect* syllogism. (The letters S, M and P are place-holders for *terms*, i.e. noun-like expressions, referring to some kind of thing.):

(1) Every S is a M   Every M is a P
Every S is a P

(2) Every S is a M   No M is a P
No S is a P

(3) Some S is a M   Every M is a P
Some S is a P

(4) Some S is a M   No M is a P
Some S is not a P

All categorical syllogisms fall into one of three *figures* as in Table 21.

Table 21 The three figures

I	II	III
S-M M-P	S-M P-M	M-S M-P
S-P	S-P	S-P

In the first figure the middle term, i.e. the one common to the two premisses, is the predicate of one premiss, and the subject of another premiss. In the second figure, the middle term is the predicate in both premisses. In the third figure, the middle term is the subject in both premisses.

Within each figure there are different *moods*, in that there are four different kinds of categorical proposition into which the terms S, M and P may enter. Thus, the four syllogisms above are all in the same figure, but in different moods.

Aristotle showed that all the syllogisms in the second and third figures can be reduced to one or other of the four syllogisms in the first figure. He also showed that in the first figure there are two syllogisms that can be reduced to one or other of the remaining two. If the latter are assumed to be valid argument-forms, the reductions prove that all the other syllogisms are so too.

Aristotle's way of distinguishing the figures does not take into account the order of the two premisses. If it is taken into account, four figures are obtained. The fourth is called the Galenian figure, since it was traditionally – but according to Łukasiewicz incorrectly – attributed to Galen (see Table 22).

Table 22 The four figures

I	II	III	IV
M-P S-M	P-M S-M	M-P M-S	P-M M-S
S-P	S-P	S-P	S-P

In Aristotle's terminology, every syllogism is a valid inference. Later, the word 'syllogism' was used in wider senses:

2 an argument, valid or invalid, containing only categorical propositions, and having *two or more* premisses.

3 an argument, valid or invalid, containing only categorical propositions, and having *exactly two* premisses.

4 There are also arguments called syllogisms in which the premisses are not categorical propositions. This is the case especially for two kinds of valid arguments (note that p, q and r are place-holders for statements, not for terms):

A *disjunctive syllogism* is an argument of this form:

p or q   not p
q

A *hypothetical syllogism* is an argument of this form:

If p then q   If q then r
If p then r

5 A *modal syllogism* is a syllogism in which

a premiss or a conclusion is a modal proposition.

6 A *practical syllogism* is often taken to be one in which the conclusion is a proposition about what ought to be done. But it has been argued, especially by G. E. M. Anscombe, that a practical syllogism is one in which the conclusion is an action or decision, and that this is the authentic Aristotelian conception. PTH

symbol *n.* **1** an object or a shape, taken to represent something else. **2** an authoritative statement of religious faith; a creed.

symbolic *n.* one of the three psychological orders (the imaginary, the symbolic, the real) in Lacan's psychoanalytic theory.

symbolic logic formal logic which makes use of special symbols and not only of expressions in English or some other natural language.

symmetric(al) *adj.* A relation R between two elements x and y is *symmetric* if and only if Rxy implies Ryx. For instance, the relation *being married to* is symmetric, because if A is married to B then B is married to A.

A relation R between two elements x and y is *asymmetric* if and only if Rxy implies not-Ryx. For instance, the relation *older than* is asymmetric, because if A is older than B, then it is not the case that B is older than A.

A relation R between two elements is *non-symmetric* if and only if Rxy does not imply Ryx and does not imply not-Ryx, in other words it is neither symmetric nor asymmetric. For instance, *loves* is non-symmetric, because if A loves B we cannot infer that B loves A, nor that B does not love A.

A relation R between two elements x and y is *anti-symmetrical* if and only if Rxy and Ryx jointly imply that x and y are identical. An example is the relation *not greater than* between two numbers. The two statements 'A is not greater than B' and 'B is not greater than A' jointly imply that A = B.

sympathy (Gr. *syn-* with + *pathos* feeling) *n.* **1** benevolent concern. **2** the disposition to have the same sentiments that we see in others.

In *Treatise of Human Nature*, 2,1,11, Hume explains that on seeing, for instance, a sense of joy in another person, we have an idea of the joy of that person. Merely to have such an idea would not be sympathy; but there are certain near-universal mechanisms of the mind that in cases like these bestow vivacity on the idea and so convert it into an impression. (In Hume's theory, ideas and impressions do not differ in content, but only in force and vivacity.) That is, we share the joy, at least to some degree. This is sympathy: the propensity to feel and think in tune with the feelings and opinions that we observe in others. This propensity is part of human nature.

In *The Theory of Moral Sentiments*, 1,1,1, Adam Smith has a similar concept: 'we often derive sorrow from the sorrow of others'. But his explanation, in terms of an imaginary change of situation, seems different from Hume's.

syncategorematic /sɪnkætɪgɔrɪ'mætɪk/ *adj.* Expressions described thus are those parts of a sentence which do not refer, such as *every*, *some*, *except*, *if*, *only*, etc. JM

synchronic /sɪn'krɒnɪk/ (Gr. *syn-* with + *chronos* time) *adj.* pertaining to what obtains at a time, without reference to the passage of time. The term gained currency through Ferdinand de SAUSSURE who used them to distinguish two kinds of linguistic memory: one concerned with the evolution of language, the other with its structure. *Ant.* DIACHRONIC.

syncretism /'sɪŋkrətɪzm/ *n.* the tendency,

especially in religion, to combine elements from different belief-systems.

synderesis /sɪndɪ'riːsɪs/ *n.* (in medieval philosophy) the immediate grasp of the principles of right and wrong. The concept gained its place as a central topic in medieval thought through Peter Lombard's *Sentences*. Distinctions between *synderesis* and *conscientia* (conscience) were made in various ways. Usually *synderesis* was understood as the insight into the general and fundamental principles of right action, and *conscientia*, in contrast, was the faculty of applying moral principles in deliberation: it was possible for conscience to err.

The Greek word *syneidēsis* occurs in St Jerome's (*c.* 340–420) commentary on Ezekiel, to designate a conscience of which a spark remains even in a sinner like Cain. The word in Jerome was later mistranscribed as *synteresis* (= preservation; observance of a law or principle) or *synderesis*. By the thirteenth century the error had become established.

synecdoche /sɪ'nɛkdəkɪ/ (Gr. *synekdochē* taking up, accepting, a thing and all it entails) *n.* a rhetorical figure (a kind of metonymy) in which a part is used to signify the whole, a species to signify a genus, a singular to signify a plural, or vice versa; e.g. 'the crown' meaning the government; 'the law' meaning the police.

synonym /'sɪnənɪm/ *n.* Two linguistic expressions that belong to the same language and have the same meaning are synonyms. Usually it is words and parts of sentences that are said to be synonyms, rather than whole sentences. Two expressions with the same meaning which belong to different natural languages – like *Junggeselle* and *bachelor* – are not usually called synonyms. **synonymous** *adj.*, **synonymy** *n.*

syntactics *n. sing.* the study of the syntax of a language. Charles Morris used this term, along with semantics and pragmatics. The word is now rarely used and instead *syntax* is preferred.

syntax (Gr. *syntaxis* arranging in order) *n.* **1** The syntax of a natural language consists of the rules that govern the formation and structure of sentences in the language, but *syntax* is also used for the study of those rules. **2** The syntax of a system of formal logic consists of the *formation rules*, which specify what is to count as a well-formed formula in the system. However, rules of a different kind are also said to belong to the syntax of a formal language: in an axiomatic system, the *transformation rules* or rules of inference which specify how new theorems can be derived; in a natural deduction system, the rules of inference that specify what counts as a correct sequent; in a system based on semantic tableaux, the rules that specify what sets of formulae count as inconsistent. These rules can in principle be formulated without any regard to what meaning, if any, is assigned to the formulae.

Again, *syntax* can also refer to the study of the properties of a system specified by these rules, and in this sense syntax is a branch of metalogic.

In a related sense, the syntax of a sentence is its grammatical structure.

synthesis /'sɪnθɪsɪs/ (Gr. *synthesis* putting, placing together) *n.* a combination of separate parts into a unified whole.

synthetic /sɪn'θɛtɪk/ *adj.* *See* ANALYTIC.

system (Gr. *systēma* a whole composed of parts) *n.* **1** an organized, structured whole. **2** theory. The use of the word in this sense was common in the past, and can be found e.g. in Locke, Hume and Adam Smith.

systematic *adj.* **1** organized, structured; in contrast to jumbled, disorganized, haphazard. **2** theoretical. In this sense, the contrast is often with *historical*. A systematic treatment of subject-matter provides a theory; a historical treatment will place the subject-matter in its historical setting.

systematic ambiguity a term sometimes used to designate a particular kind of ambiguity: in Russell's theory of types, the same formula can represent other formulae which are like it except that the individual variables contained in it belong to a different type.

Others have used *systematic ambiguity* for the feature, described by Aristotle, of words like *healthy*: a person can be healthy, but not in the same sense that food can be healthy. Aristotle saw a connection between the different senses in that both are called healthy because there is some relation to one and the same thing, i.e. health.

T

tabula rasa /ˈtæbjʊlə ˈrɑːsə/ Lat. a blank tablet; a clean slate. The state of the human mind at birth, according to ancient Stoics and modern empiricists, e.g. Locke.

Tarski /ˈtɑːskɪ (Eng.); ˈtarskɪ (Po.)/, Alfred (né Tajtelbaum) (1902–83) Polish logician, who taught in Warsaw 1925–39 and the University of California at Berkeley 1942–68. His achievements in logic, universally admired, are for the most part of a rather technical nature, but especially his discussion of truth in 'The concept of truth in formalized languages' 1933 and 'The semantic conception of truth' 1944 have attracted wider philosophical attention.

Tarski argued that one constraint on any adequate theory of truth is that the theory should yield theorems of this kind: ' "Snow is white" in English is true if and only if snow is white'; ' "La neige est blanche" in French is true if and only if snow is white'; etc. Sentences of this form are called T-sentences. They are not themselves the theory of truth, but they should be implied by an adequate theory of truth. The theory that Tarski actually proposed cannot be outlined here. Its philosophical interest relates in the first instance to the study of formalized languages. Others, chiefly Donald Davidson, have adapted Tarski's approach to apply to natural languages.

tautology /tɔːˈtɒlədʒɪ/ (Gr. *to auto legein* to say the same) *n.* **1** (in grammar) a pleonasm, redundancy of expression, needless repetition, as in 'to descend down', 'people's democracy', 'binary dichotomization'. **2** (in logic) a formula which takes the value *true* for all assignments of truth-values to its atomic expressions. A simple example is the tautological formula (p ∨ ~p). Also, a statement in ordinary language which exemplifies a tautological formula can be called a tautology. Thus, 'It is raining or it is not raining' is said to be a tautology, since it exemplifies (p ∨ ~p). All tautologies are necessary truths, but the view that all necessary truths are tautologies is open to serious doubt. **3** The theorems of propositional logic (p & p) ≡ p and (p ∨ p) ≡ p are sometimes called laws of tautology.

taxonomy *n.* **1** systematic classification; systematic division into classes. **2** inquiry into, or theory of, the principles and methods of classification.

Taylor, A(lfred) E(dward) (1869–1945) British philosopher, whose main interests were in religion, metaphysics and ethics; his standpoint was broadly idealist. Author of a number of works, including *Plato* 1926, an exposition of Plato's dialogues, and *Does God Exist?* 1943.

Taylor, Charles (1931–) Canadian philosopher, who has held chairs at Oxford and at McGill University (Montreal); author of *Hegel* 1975. In *The Sources of the Self* 1989 and *The Ethics of Authenticity* 1992 he argues against the failure of modern moral and political thought to recognize how individuals are embedded in cultural and social contexts, and develops a COMMUNITARIAN view. Pointing to the significance of the subtler languages of poetry and religion, he opposes the flattening of perspective in philosophical materialism and 'post-modern' deconstructionism.

Taylorism *n.* the theory and practice of organizing industrial production for maximal efficiency, by standardization of products, specialization of labouring tasks, etc. An important method of improving efficiency is time-and-motion studies. Named after the US engineer Frederick Winslow Taylor (1856–1915), commonly regarded as the originator of scientific management.

technē /ˈtɛknɪ/ Gr. skill, art, craft, knowing how *n.* Possession of such a skill enables one to *produce* something, and it is possible to have such know-how on the basis of experience, even if one is ignorant of the general principles. Aristotle contrasts it with *epistēmē*, knowing *that* something is the case, and *why* it is.

technocracy /tɛkˈnɒkrəsɪ/ *n.* a political system dominated by governmental and private-enterprise bureaucracies, whose policies are directed towards technological efficiency. It has been claimed by James Burnham, Kenneth Galbraith, Daniel Bell et al., that modern societies increasingly fit this description, and that the importance of traditional political structures and bodies (democracy; parliaments) is declining. The term came into use in the 1920s.

Teilhard de Chardin /tɛjaʀ də ʃaʀdɛ̃ (Fr.)/, Pierre (1881–1955) French paleontologist, Jesuit and philosopher. Influenced by Bergsonian philosophy, his aim was to harmonize a theory of cosmic (not only biological) evolution with Christian thought. He proposed that in the same way that the living organisms on Earth can be conceived together as one entity, the biosphere, so the phenomena of self-conscious mental activity can be said to form together a noosphere, a thinking layer, as it were. In the continuing evolutionary process, the diversity and conflicts within each sphere will be replaced by increasing integration, and at the end – the Omega point – conscious individual minds will be submerged, in the same way as the cells in the body, into an integrated conscious whole, all fused together in a cosmic-divine consciousness.

His religious superiors found his ideas, best known through *Le Phénomène humain* 1955 (The phenomenon of man), unorthodox, and so did scientists, albeit for different reasons: P. B. Medawar, for instance, expressed his misgivings in a famous review in *Mind* 1961 (reprinted in his *The Art of the Soluble* 1967 and *Pluto's Republic* 1982).

tele- a word element derived from Greek, *tēle-*, which connotes distance, being far away, as in *telegraph*; or *tele-*, which connotes goal, purpose, end, as in *teleology*.

telekinesis /tɛlɪkɪˈniːsɪs/ (Gr. *tēle-* + *kinēsis* movement) *n.* setting in motion a material body (other than one's own) by a mental act without any physical intermediary; one kind of phenomenon investigated by parapsychology. Alleged instances of telekinesis (causing a pot-plant to fly away from a window-sill, for instance) turn out to be fraudulent or, at best, unverified. **telekinetic** *adj. Syn.* psychokinesis.

teleological (Gr. *telos* purpose) *adj.* pertaining to purposiveness; purposive. The word was coined by Christian Wolff.

teleological argument(s) for God's existence These are also known as argument(s) from design. They start with observations, especially of the regularities in the operations of nature and of the adaptation of means to ends; infer that this order must be a product of design; and take this to establish the existence of a supernatural intelligent being, usually identified with God.

Arguments of this kind were used by ancient Stoics such as Chrysippus, and occur e.g. in Cicero's *De natura deorum* (On the nature of the gods). Thomas Aquinas's Fifth Way (*Summa Theologiae* 1a, q2, art.

3) gives a version of the argument. Since the end of the Middle Ages, the writers who undertook to establish God's existence by rational argument have made frequent, eloquent and persuasive use of it. In the eighteenth century, however, the now classical objections to the argument were raised by David Hume in his *Dialogues Concerning Natural Religion* 1779, and by Immanuel Kant in his *Critique of Pure Reason* 1781 (especially chapter 3, section 6 of the Transcendental Dialectic, which has the heading 'Impossibility of a physico-theological proof').

The objections were disregarded by later advocates of the argument, e.g. William Paley in his *Natural Theology* 1802 and the authors of the *Bridgewater Treatises* in the 1830s, and even today many writers fail to take them seriously. On the other hand, the objections to the argument were reinforced with the publication of Darwin's *Origin of Species* 1859, as the theory of natural selection provided a scientific explanation of how apparent purposiveness in nature could exist without a designer. *See also* PHYSICO-THEOLOGY.

teleological ethics This expression can be used in two clearly different senses, as follows. **1** a theory which takes purposes or ends as the basis for principles of evaluation and of conduct. Aristotelian ethics is teleological in this sense. What is good or bad in relation to character and conduct is established on the basis of purposes or functions assumed to be inherent in human nature. These are held to be discoverable by observation and reflection on human nature, in analogy with the way that we find purposes or functions in biological contexts, where we assume that the proper development for a seed is to grow into a mature plant, and where we assume that a good eye is one that sees well. **2** a theory that the rightness of an action depends only on the value of consequences. This sense of 'teleological' was introduced in the 1930s, with 'deontological' as the contrasting term for the view that the value of the consequences does not always alone determine what is right. In this terminology, 'utilitarian' theories (e.g. Bentham's and Mill's) form one sub-class of teleological theories. Subsequently, 'consequentialism' was introduced in this more general sense, and seems preferable.

teleological explanation Human action can be explained in terms of purposes: the diver's return to the surface, for instance, is explained by his desire to breathe, and the student's assiduous pursuit of learning is for the sake of achieving enlightenment – or pursuing a career. Generally, when something (which need not be a human action) is explained in terms of a purpose, i.e. that for the sake of which it comes about, or exists, or has a certain feature, or operates, the explanation is teleological.

There are two kinds of teleological explanation. One is in terms of the purposes of an agent: a demon, a spirit, a God. Such non-human agents, usually invisible, are supposed to act for a purpose in the same way that human beings do. The other is in terms of purposes that are *immanent* or inherent, either in the thing whose properties or activities are to be explained, or in the system to which that thing belongs.

Teleological explanation is also called explanation in terms of *final causes*, and is often contrasted with explanation in terms of *efficient causes*.

Teleological explanation had an important basis in Aristotle's *Physics*, Book 2, but was sharply criticized when modern science and philosophy began in the seventeenth century. Spinoza, for instance, condemned such explanations (*Ethics*, Book 1, Appendix) for being anthropomorphic and for providing an *ASYLUM IGNORANTIAE*.

teleology *n.* **1** a theory which describes or explains in terms of purposes. **2** purposiveness (of a natural organism or system).

telepathy *n.* immediate awareness of the thoughts, feelings, etc. of another mind, not arising from ordinary observation or inference.

Claims to extrasensory communication are extremely dubious, and remarkable coincidences occur in its absence.

Telesio / tɪˈleɪzɪəʊ (Eng.); tɛˈlɛsjɔ (It.)/, Bernardino (1509–88) Italian anti-Aristotelian philosopher, who advocated a naturalistic approach to scientific inquiry, and an ethics founded on the basic urge for self-preservation.

teletransportation *n.* 'travelling' by electronic means.

In one story, proposed as a thought-experiment, a scanner records the exact state of every cell in my body, destroys the cells, but transmits the information by radio to a receiver (located at the antipodes, or on Mars) which uses the information together with new matter to create a perfect replica. The outcome of the process is exactly as it would have been if I had been moved physically by the speed of the radio waves.

This is a thought-experiment devised by Derek Parfit in chapter 10 of *Reasons and Persons* 1984 in the course of his exploration of the concept of personal identity over time. Does teletransportation convey *me* to the point of arrival as more familiar modes of transport do? And who am (or are) I, if the scanner works as described above, except that it does not destroy anything?

telos / ˈtelɔs/ Gr. end-point, aim, goal, purpose of activity *n.* complete, final state of affairs; 'that for the sake of which something is done' (Aristotle, *Physics*, Book 2,3 194b33).

temperament (Lat. *temperamentum* proper mixture) *n.* **1** a proportionate mixture or balancing of ingredients. **2** (in traditional Hippocratic-Galenic medicine) a certain combination of the four cardinal humours (bodily fluids) which was supposed to determine a person's physical and mental character; in so far as one of the fluids was preponderant, the temperament would be sanguine, phlegmatic, melancholic or choleric. **3** characteristic frame of mind or disposition of a person. **4** excitability; moodiness. **5** in music, the manner of tuning an instrument with a fixed pitch (organs, pianos, etc.): *pure temperament* provides for some pure intervals but will not sound equally well in all keys; *equal temperament* offers versatility at the expense of purity, by dividing the scale into 12 equal semitones.

temperance (Gr. *sōphrosynē*; Lat. *temperantia*) *n.* one of the four CARDINAL VIRTUES: the control of one's appetites and desires. It is also called self-control or moderation. Aristotle (*Nicomachean Ethics*) limits the application of the term to the control of bodily appetites.

temporal (Lat. *tempus* time) *adj.* **1** pertaining to the present life in this world, in contrast to eternal life (after death). **2** secular, in contrast to ecclesiastical. **3** pertaining to time.

tense logic the logic of the concepts of past, present and future, and other temporal concepts. Among its characteristic constants are 'it was the case that', 'it is now the case that', 'it will be the case that'. *Syn.* temporal logic.

tension *n.* not a technical term in philosophy, but sometimes used as a polite euphemism when a theory is criticized for being self-contradictory or inconsistent.

teratology /tɛrəˈtɒlədʒɪ/ (Gr. *teras* monster) *n.* **1** the study of monstrosities and abnormalities. **2** a collection of tales about fantastic creatures.

term (Lat. *terminus* boundary, end-point) *n.* **1** Originally the subject and the predicate of a categorical proposition were called terms – because they were at the end-points of the sentence. **2** In contemporary logic, 'term' or 'singular term' is used as a synonym of 'name' or 'referring expression'. In a sentence, terms name or refer to something, in contrast to predicates which signify a property or relation of that which is named or referred to by the term(s). The sentence 'Socrates is wise' contains the term 'Socrates' and the predicate 'wise'. The sentence 'Plato's teacher is wise' contains the same predicate, and the term 'Plato's teacher'. The sentence 'Socrates was the teacher of Plato' can be analysed as containing two terms, and a two-place predicate.

terminus ad quem /ˈtɜːmɪnəs æd kwɛm/ Lat. the end-point up to which. A boundary in time, marking the latest possible occurrence of a certain event.

terminus a quo /ˈtɜːmɪnəs ɑː kwəʊ/ Lat. the end-point from which. A boundary in time marking the earliest possible occurrence of a certain event.

ternary *adj.* three-place; triadic. *See also* MONADIC PREDICATE.

tertiary qualities **1** the power of an object to cause a change in another object. The concept, though not the expression, was introduced by Locke in his *Essay Concerning Human Understanding* 2,8,10–25, in contradistinction to primary and secondary qualities. The tertiary qualities are powers, dispositional properties, such as the power of *aqua regia* to dissolve gold, of the sun to melt wax or produce a suntan, etc. **2** Since the late nineteenth century, economic, aesthetic and other qualities have sometimes been called tertiary qualities, since their relation to the primary or secondary qualities of an object is regarded as one of dependence or supervenience.

tertium comparationis /ˈtɜːʃəm; ˈtɜːtɪəm kɒmpərəˈʃəʊnɪs/ Lat. the third element of a comparison; that in respect of which two things are compared.

tertium non datur /ˈtɜːʃəm; ˈtɜːtɪəm nɔn ˈdaːtə/ Lat. there is no third (thing). This is a way of saying, in Latin, that two alternatives exhaust what is possible. Especially in logic, the theorem $(p \vee \sim p)$ is known as the law of the excluded middle.

tertium quid /ˈtɜːʃəm; ˈtɜːtɪəm kwɪd/ Lat. some third (thing).

Tertullian /tɜːˈtʌlɪən/ (*c.* 160–*c.* 220) the first major Church father to write in Latin. Born in Carthage, he was trained in rhetoric and in the law. He went to Rome, where he became a convert to Christianity (*c.* 196). After his return to Carthage, he reacted against what he saw as the worldliness of the Church, became a leader of the ascetic Montanist movement, and advocated in one of his numerous writings, *inter alia*, a strict sexual morality, urging that young girls wear a veil in public, opposing remarriage, etc. His apologetic writings contain striking and memorable formulations: 'What has Athens to do with Jerusalem?', and (about the incarnation) 'it is certain because it is impossible'. In his philosophical writings, e.g. *Treatise against Hermogenes*, he argued against the theory that matter is eternal, in support of the doctrine of creation. His treatise *De Anima* (On the soul) agrees with standard Christian doctrine in its rejection of the Platonist and Gnostic doctrines of the pre-existence and reincarnation of the soul. He was not hostile to all pagan philosophy, and found much of value in Seneca's version of Stoicism, but he nevertheless resisted the 'Hellenization' of Christianity.

tetrachotomy /tɛtrə'kɒtəmɪ/ *n.* division into four parts.

textualism *n.* **1** the tendency to put the text alone in focus, neglecting its social or historical setting. This is an obstacle to an adequate understanding of most writings on society and politics, but also of most philosophical writings. **2** the view that it is impossible to get beyond the text. The term has been used polemically by Richard Rorty against those who deny that we can get beyond texts to reality – a counterpart to the nineteenth-century view that we cannot get beyond ideas to reality. His criticism is directed against 'post-structuralist' theorists such as Paul de Man, Derrida and Foucault.

Thales /'θeɪliːz/ (*fl.* 585 BC) Renowned as the first philosopher, Thales of Miletus is said to have made water the *archē* or material source of all things. He was included in all the varying lists of the Seven Sages of Greece, described as a mathematician, engineer, astronomer and statesman. Even the early Greeks had little reliable information about him, but they report his views that the Earth floats on water like a raft, and that the magnet has a soul. These are views which provide potential explanations of natural events. He was thus the first thinker to try to give naturalistic explanations to natural phenomena. The philosophical tradition begun by him was continued by his fellow Milesians, Anaximander and Anaximenes. DG

theism /'θiːɪzm/ (Gr. *theos* god) *n.* the belief that there is one God, a personal being with every perfection (perfect power, perfect knowledge, perfect goodness, perfect justice, etc.); creator of the world, manifested in the world, interacting with the world, but nevertheless existing entirely separately from the world; a being that is the one and only proper object of worship and obedience. Theism is common to Judaism, Christianity and Islam.

Theism can be contrasted with a variety of views: (1) the view that there is *one* God is rejected by *polytheism*, which claims that there are many gods; in contrast, traditional Western religions are also said to be *monotheistic*; (2) the view that God is a *personal* being is rejected as anthropomorphic in some philosophical systems, which rather conceive of God as an absolute, non-personal being; (3) the view that God is *distinct from the world* is rejected by *pantheism*, which identifies God and the world; (4) the view that God *interacts* with the world is rejected by *deism*, which ascribes to God a decisive role in originating the world, but none in keeping the world going; (5) the denial of the existence of any divine being is called *atheism*; (6) the suspension of judgement on the question whether theism is true is called *agnosticism*.

Many of the *teleological*, *cosmological*, *ontological*, *moral*, etc. arguments for the existence of God are intended to establish theism.

Note: It was not until the nineteenth century that 'theism' and 'deism' acquired their current senses, as defined above. When 'theism' first came into philosophical use through Cudworth, it was defined as meaning what is now called deism. Kant's definitions (*Critique of Pure Reason* A631, B659) were different again. He distinguished deism, i.e. transcendental theology, which claims knowledge of an original being only through pure reason, from theism, i.e. natural theology, which claims knowledge of such a being also by means of concepts borrowed from nature.

thematize *vb.* to turn something into a topic of inquiry or discussion. The word is a recent import from the German *thematisieren*.

theocracy /θɪ'ɒkrəsɪ/ (Gr. *theos* god +

-*kratia* power, might, strength) *n.* **1** a form of government in which God is recognized as the supreme civil ruler, whose laws are interpreted by priests or other divinely guided officials. **2** a form of government by ecclesiastical authorities who claim divine commission. A form of government is only called theocratic if the divine commission is claimed for an ecclesiastical authority. The monarchic theory of the divine right of kings is not called theocratic, nor is the democratic theory of the people's sacred or indeed divine right to rule itself. **3** a state or commonwealth under any such form of government.

theodicy /θɪ'ɒdɪsɪ/ (Gr. *theos* god + *dikē* right, justice) *n.* explanation of how God's perfect goodness, justice, wisdom, power and other perfections are compatible with the existence of evil in this world: that is, a theory which purports to solve the problem of evil.

The French equivalent of the word was created by Leibniz and used in the title of his *Essais de théodicée sur la bonté de Dieu, la liberté de l'homme et l'origine du mal* 1710 (Theodicy: Essays on God's goodness, man's freedom, and the origin of evil).

Kant wrote an essay arguing that all philosophical theodicies are doomed to failure (1793), but even two centuries later there is a lively philosophical debate on this issue.

In French, the term is sometimes used inaccurately to signify natural or rational theology generally.

theogony /θɪ'ɒgənɪ/ (Gr. *theogonia* birth of gods) *n.* **1** origin of the gods. **2** genealogy of the gods, i.e. an account of their ancestry, as in Hesiod's *Theogony* (*c.* 800 BC).

theological utilitarianism *See* UTILITARIANISM, THEOLOGICAL.

theology /θɪ'ɒlədʒɪ/ *n.* **1** inquiry into, or systematic account and explanation of, the teachings and practices that constitute a religious tradition or doctrine, based on the general acceptance of their validity. In this sense, there is Christian, Jewish, etc. theology. **2** natural theology, also called rational theology, does not proceed from religious assumptions but seeks to establish a doctrine of God on the basis of reason and experience alone without appeal to revelation.

theomachy /θɪ'ɒməkɪ/ (Gr. *theomachia*) *n.* battle with or among the gods.

theophany /θɪ'ɒfənɪ/ (Gr. *theophaneia*) *n.* manifestation of God or a god to man, by actual appearance.

Theophrastus /θɪə'fræstəs/ (*c.* 372–*c.* 287 BC) a great polymath, disciple and colleague of Aristotle, and his successor as head of the peripatetic school. His writings, of which most are lost, contain incisive objections to Aristotle's metaphysics. Two treatises on botany are extant, together with a number of shorter scientific writings, and so are a number of character sketches that inspired many later writers, notably La Bruyère.

Theophrastus Redivivus Lat. Theophrastus brought back to life. This is the title (the name alludes to Aristotle's disciple) of a work which gives a comprehensive survey of arguments in favour of atheism and of past thinkers who proposed them. The earliest known appearance of this work by an unknown, probably French, author was in 1659. For almost a century it circulated widely but clandestinely in manuscript copies. The first critical edition was published in Florence in 1981.

theorem *n.* a formula or a proposition that can be proved within a system of logic, mathematics, geometry, etc.

In axiomatized systems of logic, axioms are distinguished from theorems, and both are called theses; but it also happens that 'theorem' is used to include axioms as well.

theoretical entity an entity not itself observable, but postulated in a scientific theory in order to explain observed entities and processes. The same applies to the term 'theoretical property'.

theoretical philosophy *See* PRACTICAL PHILOSOPHY.

theory (Gr. *theōria* viewing; speculation; contemplation) *n.* a set of propositions which provides principles of analysis or explanation of a subject-matter. Even a single proposition can be called a theory.

In philosophy, the contrasts theory/practice, theoretical reason/practical reason, etc. are often conceived of as a contrast between passivity and activity: the theoretical knower is a passive contemplator, a recipient of food for thought; the practical agent is an active doer.

Since the 1980s, 'theory' is used in some academic contexts (chiefly in literary and cultural studies) not as a general concept, but for a particular kind of theory, inspired by thinkers like Lacan, Foucault and Derrida, usually with a tendency towards relativism in respect of knowledge and interpretation.

theory-laden *adj.* The thesis that observation is theory-laden states that it is impossible to observe without making any theoretical assumptions. The observations will reflect these assumptions. The most extreme form of the thesis leads to the doctrine of the INCOMMENSURABILITY of theories: observation cannot help to decide between theories because different theories generate different observations and there are no 'neutral' observations to which an appeal might be made. Its most extreme form also leads to the view that observers with different theories 'inhabit different worlds'. The view that the world we inhabit depends upon our theory is a kind of idealism, since it assumes that what we take to be the world depends for its existence upon us and our theories. AM

theory of knowledge *See* EPISTEMOLOGY.

theory of numbers *See* NUMBER THEORY.

theory of truth *See* TRUTH.

theosophy /θɪ'ɔsəfɪ/ *n.* The earliest use of the word was for the teachings of Ammonius of Alexandria (160–242), the founder of neo-Platonism, and his followers. A central tenet was that of the essential unity underlying rival religions and philosophies. Allegory and myth played an important part in the esoteric teachings of this school: and the insight gained through these would allow man to become morally and spiritually elevated to higher forms of being.

Later, the term designated more generally a higher wisdom concerning the divine and spiritual matters achieved at least in part through mystical experience. The writings of Jacob Böhme or Emanuel Swedenborg are theosophical in this sense.

More recently, the word often denotes the eclectic mixture of ideas, derived from Hinduism, Buddhism and Gnosticism, in the writings of Helena Blavatsky (1831–91) and promoted by the Theosophical Society, founded by her in 1875.

theriomorphism /θɪərɪəʊ'mɔːfɪzm/ (Gr. *thērion* wild beast) *n.* ascription of animal characteristics to non-animal beings. The representation of gods in animal form, as in ancient Egypt, is theriomorphic.

Theses on Feuerbach a set of 11 short comments on Ludwig Feuerbach's materialist philosophy, which is criticized for its neglect of practice. The eleventh thesis is often quoted: 'Philosophers have given different interpretations of the world; the point is to change it.' They were written by Marx in the mid-1840s and first published by Engels in 1888.

Theseus /'θiːsɪəs/, **the ship of** The ship by which Theseus, the semi-mythical hero of ancient Athens, accomplished his rescue mission was put on public display in Athens and, as the need arose, new planks, boards, sails, ropes, etc. replaced the old, until one day none of the original parts of the ship remained. Is this *repaired* ship still the *same* ship?

The story occurs in Plutarch's *Lives* (Life of Theseus 22–23). In Hobbes's *De Corpore* (Book 2, chapter 11, section 7) a further question is raised: suppose that all the old planks, boards, etc. were preserved and eventually combined into a ship, like the original one. Is this *restored* ship still the same ship?

If the answer to both questions is yes, two ships would be numerically the same, which is absurd. But on what reasonable grounds can the answer to either question be no? The story helps to analyse problems of identity: what is it to be *one and the same* thing?

thesis /θiːsɪs/ (*sing.*), **theses** /θiːsiːs/ (*pl.*) (Gr. *thesis* position; positing) *n.* a proposition. Especially: **1** an axiom or a theorem of a formal system. **2** a proposition presented for purposes of proof, or for consideration. **3** In medieval times it became standard university practice that a candidate for a degree would defend one thesis or several theses in public disputations. From this developed a new sense of the word: a dissertation (sometimes of considerable length) presented in order to qualify for a degree.

thesis eleven *See* THESES ON FEUERBACH.

thetic /'θɛtɪk/ *adj.* In Fichte's philosophy, a thetic ('positing') judgement affirms something as being self-identical (and not as being identical with or different from something else). The act by which the self posits itself is a thetic judgement: it affirms self-identity but also existence.

thin/full, thin/thick a 'thick' concept or description includes particular features and circumstances; a 'thin' one is couched in general and abstract terms.

Bernard Williams distinguishes 'thick' moral concepts (e.g. *courage*) from 'thin' ones (e.g. *right*) in his *Ethics and the Limits of Philosophy* 1985, but the usage seems to have begun with John Rawls who, in *A Theory of Justice*, section 60, contrasts two kinds of theory of the good: a thin theory, restricted to bare essentials, and a full theory. But when a later writer contrasts 'thin facts' with thicker ones, and uses phrases like 'thick principles' and 'thin rational agents', it seems the point has been stretched too far.

thing-in-itself (*sing.*) **things-in-themselves** (*pl.*) *n.* these terms and their opposites *thing-for-us*, (*pl.*) *things-for-us*, are used by Kant to distinguish an object as it is conceived to exist independently of any relation to a knowing subject, from that same object as something knowable by us.

third man argument an objection to Plato's theory of forms, first developed by 'Parmenides' in Plato's dialogue *Parmenides*, but given its most familiar shape by Aristotle.

According to the theory, a form is something that all things with a certain characteristic have in common. Thus, beauty is something that all beautiful things have in common. The form of man-ness is something that all men have in common. But the forms are also thought of as ideal paradigms: the form of beauty is most beautiful, and has therefore something in common with other beautiful things. Similarly, the form of man has something in common with other men. That common element is yet another form, a 'third man'.

In a similar way we get a fourth, fifth, and indeed an infinite series.

Thomas Aquinas *See* AQUINAS.

Thomasius /to'mazius (Gm.)/, Christian (1655–1728) German eclectic philosopher and academic lawyer, who taught first at Leipzig and from 1690 in Halle. He attacked the traditional university philosophy for being pedantic, dogmatic and Aristotelian, and favoured a moral philosophy that could be of practical use. In line with this was his promotion of the vernacular: he was the first to lecture in German instead of Latin, and in the 1690s he published four textbooks in German: on introductory and applied logic, and on introductory and applied ethics. Inspired by Grotius and Pufendorf, he set out to develop a natural law theory on a rational basis without appealing to (although in a manner consonant with) revelation, in two major works, first in 1688, and then in *Fundamenta iuris naturae et gentium* 1705 (Foundations of the law of nature and nations). In the latter, he argued against the traditional view that our reason is able to rule our will. He also proposed that the precepts of the law of nature are not like the commands of a superior, but like the counsel of a wise father interested in our well-being. They fall into three classes: (i) the *honestum*, i.e. the self-regarding duties and virtues; (ii) the *decorum*, i.e. what is proper and becoming in dealings with others; and (iii) the *justum*, i.e. the perfect duties to others. Each has a basic principle: (i) you can safely do to yourself what you would want others to do to you; (ii) do for others what you would want them to do to you; (iii) do not do to others what you would not want them to do to you (or, in an alternative formulation: respect others' rights). His pietism was marked by a special fervour in the period 1694–1705, and there is even a theosophical strand in his *Versuch vom Wesen des Geistes* 1699 (Essay on the nature of spirit). His opposition to judicial torture and the prosecution of witchcraft, and his advocacy of wide-ranging religious toleration, are among the reasons for his reputation as the first major figure of the German Enlightenment.

Thomism *n.* the philosophy that takes the thought of St Thomas Aquinas as its authoritative source. Modernized versions are often called neo-Thomism.

Thoreau /'θɔːrəʊ, θɔː'rəʊ/, Henry David (1817–62) along with Emerson, the best-known of the 'New England transcendentalists'. An intellectual of uncommonly broad culture, Thoreau was above all the advocate of values like creative spontaneity, which can flourish best in isolated communion with nature, and the message of *Walden or Life in the Woods* 1854 is one of individualist anarchism. His influential essay 'Civil Disobedience' 1849 is an emphatic assertion of the authority of one's conscience against that of the state.

Thrasymachus /θræ'sɪməkəs/ a character in Plato's dialogue *The Republic*, Book 1, who represents an immoralism dismissive of moral constraints on the pursuit of self-interest: if those who are strong can benefit from exploiting the weak, it would be foolish of them not to do so.

tilde /'tɪldə/ *n.* the symbol ~. It is a symbol for propositional negation: $\sim p$ can be read *it is not the case that p*. The angle $\neg$ is also so used.

Tillich /'tɪlɪk (Eng.); 'tiliç (Gm.)/, Paul (1886–1965) German Protestant theologian, from 1933 in exile in the United States, where he taught at Union Theological Seminary in New York, at Harvard and at Chicago. His philosophical theology sees religion as 'ultimate concern'. The central concepts of Christianity are interpreted as symbols giving the terms for answers to questions of ultimate significance to a person. In a culture, the things that really matter for an individual come to expression in different cultural forms – art, law, community, etc., none of which is directly religious, but each of which may contain elements of fundamental concern. A popular bestseller inspired by Tillich is J. A. T. Robinson, *Honest to God* 1963. Among Tillich's numerous writings are *Systematic Theology* 1951–63, in three volumes, of which the first is the most philosophical, and *Morality and Beyond* 1963.

timarchy *See* TIMOCRACY.

timocracy (Gr. *timē* price, value, honour + *-kratia* ruling power) *n.* **1** (in Aristotle) a society in which a property qualification determines the citizens' share in government and other civic rights and obligations (*Politics*, Book 4). **2** (in Plato) a society ruled by those who have most honour and where the rulers are motivated by a love of honour (*Republic*, 545b). *Syn.* timarchy.

timology *n.* **1** theory of value, axiology. **2** a kind of, or a branch of, a general theory of value.

The term, not in current use, was coined in 1902 by Kreibig, a disciple of Brentano, and was used by Meinong in *Über emotionale Präsentation* 1916 (On emotive presentation) to distinguish the theory of economic and ethical value from the theory of value in three other areas: logic, aesthetics, and hedonics. John Laird used the term for his objectivist axiology in *The Idea of Value* 1929.

Timon /ˈtaɪmən/ **of Phlius** (*c.* 320–230 BC) a follower of Pyrrho; satirized philosophers such as Plato, Aristotle and Arcesilaus, in the cause of Pyrrhonian scepticism. He was a witty satirist, but only fragments remain of his prolific output.

Tindal /ˈtɪndəl/, Matthew (1657?–1733) described himself as a 'Christian deist'. He advocated his deism in a vast number of pamphlets and books, of which the most important is *Christianity as Old as Creation* 1730. As the title implies, nothing revealed through Moses, the prophets, Jesus, etc. adds anything that affects the substance of what a Christian should believe. As the subtitle of that work explained, the gospel is only a *re-publication* of truths which could be grasped before it appeared, since all valid religious doctrines can be based on reason alone, independently of any revelation. He also attacked parts of the Bible, and many traditional doctrines and practices of the churches, on moral grounds, for being contrary to reason.

to hēgemonikon Gr. that which rules; that which directs. A technical term in Stoicism: the ruling faculty of the soul, conceived to be a rational principle. In ethical theories inspired by Stoicism, the term is used to denote moral conscience.

token/type *n.* the contrast between *token* and *type* is most easily explained by means of an example. On the next line:

dog, dog, dog

there is *one* word, i.e. one particular *type*, but in another sense there are *three* words, i.e. three *tokens*, all of the same type. The tokens are specimens, instances, of a type.

This pair of terms was introduced by C. S. Peirce.

token-reflexive *adj.*, *n.* words like *I*, *here*, *yonder*, *now*, *last week*, whose reference is determined by the circumstances of their being uttered. *See also* INDEXICAL.

Toland /ˈtəʊlənd/, John (1670–1722) Irish deist, best known as the author of *Christianity not Mysterious* 1696, in which he argued that all true belief is in harmony with and within the bounds of reason, but that mysteries are not. In his writings on religion he moved towards pantheism (and created the term), and expressed doubts about the biblical canon and the literal truth of the Bible. An influence from Spinoza is likely. In one of the *Letters to Serena*, Toland argued that motion is essential to matter, a view that undercuts the arguments for the existence of a being that initially pushes inert matter into motion.

tolerance, principle of If logic and mathematics are ultimately based on convention, it cannot be said that a certain system is correct and another incorrect. One's preference for one system over another must be based on other considerations, and as with conventions in other areas (games, manners, etiquette) there is scope for tolerance. This was the view of Carnap, who gave the principle its name.

toleration, paradox of If the intolerant are tolerated, they may prevail and make an end to toleration. But if they are not tolerated, one has already made an end to toleration.

Tönnies /ˈtœnis (Gm.)/, Friedrich (1855–1936) German philosopher and sociologist, who taught at the University of Kiel from 1881 to 1933. He was a leading Hobbes scholar, and saw Hobbes's social theory as an outline of a new kind of impersonal and competitive society of isolated individuals, in contrast to traditional society imbued with community values. This contrast played a central role in Tönnies's own social theory. *See also* GEMEINSCHAFT.

Topics One of the works of Aristotle, part of the *Organon*. It may have been devised as a handbook for debating contests, but also contains logical material, e.g. rules for proper definitions.

topology (Gr. *topos* place) *n.* **1** *point set topology*: a branch of mathematics which studies limits, continuity and other mathematical properties of point sets. **2** *algebraic topology*: a branch of geometry which studies properties that remain invariant under continuous stretching, bending, twisting, etc.

topos *n.* a stock topic; an established theme within an intellectual or literary tradition.

totalitarianism *n.* the total control of all aspects of life that are actually or potentially of political significance. The term was first used in the 1920s by Italian fascists for their own political goals, and later applied to Nazism and to Soviet communism. The word began to be used pejoratively in the 1940s.

tout court /tu kuːʀ/ Fr. briefly.

Toynbee /ˈtɔɪnbiː/, Arnold (Joseph) (1889–1975) English historian, author of *A Study of History*, a large-scale and impressive account of the origin, rise, decline and fall of the 21 civilizations which, in his view, can be identified in human history. Toynbee also tried to establish general explanatory laws derived from this basis. It has been objected that this inductive method is unpromising, and that there is no clear criterion for what is to count as one civilization. Professional historians have been only moderately impressed, pointing to inaccuracies or errors in this grandly designed work. Controversy has also been provoked by Toynbee's low opinion of certain existing traditions and cultures.

The work, in ten volumes (1934–54), was supplemented with two additional volumes containing reconsiderations and replies to critics. There is a two-volume abridgement (1946; 1957), and another in one volume (1972).

tractarian *adj.* **1** pertaining to the principles or tenets held by a number of High Churchmen in the Church of England

(from *Tracts for the Times*, a series of pamphlets written by J. H. Newman and others, published at Oxford 1833–41).
2 pertaining to Wittgenstein's *Tractatus Logico-Philosophicus*.

Tractatus Logico-Philosophicus Lat. a logical-philosophical treatise. *See* WITTGENSTEIN.

Tractatus Theologico-Philosophicus Lat. a theological-philosophical treatise. *See* SPINOZA.

transcend *vb.* to go beyond, to be beyond.

transcendent /træn'sɛndənt/ *adj.* **1** The general meaning of the word is 'going beyond' or 'being beyond'. It is used in many contexts. For instance, in medieval philosophy God is said to transcend himself when he creates the world.
2 The word is used particularly and frequently in the sense of being beyond the limits of any possible experience; beyond the limits of the world of experience.

There can be no *knowledge* of anything transcendent, according to Kant. A large number of representatives of nineteenth-century positivism agreed, albeit for reasons different from his. A famous expression of their view is Du Bois-Reymond's slogan, *Ignorabimus* (Lat. we shall remain ignorant, *viz.* of the ultimate nature of reality): science can only describe phenomena but cannot genuinely explain them. Spencer's theory of The Unknowable is another example. This agnosticism is rejected by philosophers who maintain that we possess ways of knowing other than the sensory way, and that what lies beyond the world of experience need not be unknowable.

The question whether *there is* anything transcendent, beyond the world of experience, is answered in the negative by materialists since the eighteenth century. A negative answer has also been given by some of the twentieth-century philosophers who gave philosophy a linguistic turn. The argument is: certain conditions have to be met in order that the expressions we use in our language make sense. These conditions are not satisfied by assertions that something transcendent, e.g. God, exists. Therefore, such assertions do not make sense. Since they do not make sense, they cannot be true. The conditions said by empiricists to be necessary are to the effect that only expressions whose meaning can be reduced to sensory experience make sense. A clear instance of this approach is the logical positivism of Carnap, Schlick, Ayer, etc. The upshot is that no assertion that implies the existence of something transcendent can be true.

One line of argument for the opposite view is that the material world, nature, the world of experience, the world open to scientific inquiry, cannot be ultimately self-sufficient or self-explanatory, but must, in its totality, be assumed to stand in some relation of dependency which, accordingly, must be transcendent. *Ant.* IMMANENT.

transcendental /trænsən'dɛntəl/ *adj., n.* **1** In medieval philosophy, the transcendentals are those entities which transcend the boundary between any two categories (in the Aristotelian sense) and thus are coextensive with being (*ens*). They were usually held to be one (*unum*), good (*bonum*), true (*verum*), self-identity; some thinkers added beautiful (*pulchrum*), something (*aliquid*) and thing (*res*). **2** Kant sharply distinguished between the transcendental and the transcendent, and since then the two words are usually differentiated in philosophical writing. In Kant's *Critique of Pure Reason* the transcendental is that which pertains to the necessary, *a priori*, conditions of knowledge. Transcendental philosophy is for Kant an inquiry into the necessary presuppositions of knowledge, and the result of the inquiry is a theory of the scope and objective validity of human knowledge.

Transcendental Aesthetic This and *Transcendental Logic*, *Transcendental Analytic* and *Transcendental Dialectic* are the most important divisions in Kant's *Critique of Pure Reason*. The main division is the one between *Transcendental Aesthetic*, which deals with the *a priori* conditions (Space and Time) of sensory intuition, and *Transcendental Logic*, which deals with the *a priori* conditions of our intellectual and reasoning faculties.

Transcendental Logic is, in turn, divided into two main parts. The *Transcendental Analytic* deals with the concepts and principles of the faculty of understanding (the intellect) without which no object can be thought, and without which there can be no empirical knowledge. It is in this division that Kant introduces *inter alia* his concept of categories (i.e. the pure concepts of the understanding). The *Transcendental Dialectic* deals with the illusions of reason, which originate in its natural tendency to rise above its proper station. This division contains Kant's discussion of the Paralogism, the Antinomy, and the Ideal of Pure Reason, designed to refute the traditional claims to rational philosophical knowledge of, respectively, the soul, the world and God.

Transcendental Analytic *See* TRANSCENDENTAL AESTHETIC.

transcendental argument For Kant, the term *transcendental* signifies such knowledge as concerns the *a priori* conditions of knowledge. By extension from this Kantian sense, the expression *transcendental argument* came to be adopted in a more general sense. Its recent vogue originated with one single passage in P. F. Strawson's *Individuals* 1959, where he argued that our activity of identifying and re-identifying particulars presupposes that *material object* is a basic category in our conception of the world, so that doubts about the existence of material objects cannot be sustained. Strawson characterized this argument as a transcendental one, and this gave currency to the expression, which was for quite some time freely used by many philosophers to denote arguments which derive necessary conditions for a theory or a practice, and especially for the use of certain concepts or categories. A transcendental argument is, then, an argument showing that a certain fundamental condition *must obtain* – or *must be supposed to obtain* – for some type of experience, discourse or practice (which is itself taken for granted) to make sense or have any validity. These usages differ from Kant's in that it is not assumed that the fundamental condition is a synthetic *a priori* truth.

transcendental deduction In older jurisprudential terminology, a deduction establishes the legal, in contradistinction to the factual, grounds for action in a court of law. Kant uses the term in a broader sense: the deduction of the pure concepts of the understanding (the categories) consists in justifying the use of these concepts. The way to justify the use of most concepts is by appeal to experience, but here the situation is different, since the concepts in question are applied *a priori*, independently of experience. This is why the deduction is said to be transcendental.

Transcendental Dialectic *See* TRANSCENDENTAL AESTHETIC.

transcendental idealism a central doctrine in Kant's Critical philosophy. In the *Critique of Pure Reason*, he defines it as follows: 'By transcendental idealism I mean the doctrine that appearances are to be regarded as being, one and all, representations only, not things in themselves, and that time and space are therefore only sensible forms of our intuition, not determinations given as existing by themselves, nor conditions of objects viewed as things in themselves.'

transcendental illusion a term used by Kant for the illusions of traditional metaphysics; they are illusions, natural and inevitable (in the same way as the large appearance of the moon at its rising), arising from the inherent tendency of human reason to trespass beyond its boundaries. The aim of the Transcendental Dialectic is to expose their illusory character.

transcendentalism *n.* a name given to the rather heterogeneous outlooks of a number of thinkers and writers in New England (USA) whose work was influenced by the rise of romanticism in philosophy and poetry (Goethe, Novalis, Cousin; Wordsworth, Coleridge, Carlyle). Many of them were Unitarians or secular humanists, and many of them were advocates of radical social reforms. Its leading names were Ralph Waldo Emerson (1803–82) and Henry Thoreau (1817–62). They rejected modern materialism and saw the phenomena of nature as carrying a message of a higher, spiritual truth.

Transcendental Logic *See* TRANSCENDENTAL AESTHETIC.

transcendental number a real number that is not ALGEBRAIC. Most real numbers are transcendental; only a few of them have names; best known are the numbers π and e (Euler's constant).

transcendental object (in Kant's philosophy) the thing-in-itself; that which we must assume to be the underlying unknown ground of what we know through sense-experience.

transcendental philosophy the Critical philosophy of Kant; the philosophy of Fichte and the early Schelling; the philosophy of certain neo-Kantians.

transfinite numbers the numbers assigned to sets with infinitely many elements. As Cantor discovered, infinite sets are not all equally large; on the contrary, the number of different transfinite numbers is itself transfinite.

transitive *adj.* **1** An example of a *transitive* relation is the relation 'greater than': if A is greater than B and B is greater than C, then A is greater than C. In general, a relation R is said to be *transitive* if and only if for any individuals x,y,z in the relevant domain, *Rxy and Ryz* implies *Rxz*.

In contrast, a relation R is said to be *intransitive* if and only if for any individuals x,y,z in the relevant domain, *Rxy and Ryz* implies *not-Rxz*. An example is the relation 'father of': if A is the father of B and B is the father of C, then A is not the father of C.

A relation R which is neither transitive nor intransitive is said to be *non-transitive*, i.e. *Rxy* and *Ryz* does not imply *Rxz* and does not imply ~*Rxz*. An example is love: if A loves B and B loves C, we can infer neither that A loves C, nor that A does not love C.

2 In grammar, transitive verbs are contrasted with intransitive verbs. Transitive verbs need an object, as in *S loves O*. Intransitive verbs cannot take an object, as in *S arrives*, *S smiles*; they combine in a sentence with only one noun. Transitive verbs allow for an equivalent passive construction *O is loved by S*, but intransitive verbs do not.

translation *See* INTERPRETATION.

translation, radical *See* RADICAL TRANSLATION.

transparency/opacity If 'X is Y' is a true statement of identity, in the sense that 'X' and 'Y' denote precisely the same object, it might seem that replacing 'X' by 'Y' in any statement would be bound to leave the truth-value of that statement unchanged. There appear, however, to be many exceptions to this. For example, the Taj Mahal is the tomb of Mumtaz Mahal, but replacing 'the Taj Mahal' with 'the tomb of Mumtaz Mahal' in 'John believes that the Taj Mahal is in Agra' may well transform a true statement into a false one, for John may believe that the Taj Mahal is in Agra but that Mumtaz Mahal lies buried elsewhere. A statement whose truth-value can be changed by replacing some referring expression in it by some other expression which stands for the same thing is said to provide a *referentially opaque* context for that expression. If its truth-value cannot be changed in this way, it is said to provide a *transparent* context for that expression, which is then said to occur *purely referentially* in it.

The use of the term 'opaque' derives from W. V. O. Quine's essay 'Reference and Modality', included in his *From a Logical Point of View* 1953. The question of which contexts are referentially opaque, and why, has been much discussed since then, and was also vigorously debated, using a different terminology, by medieval logicians. GH

transposition *n.* (in propositional logic) Also called *contraposition*, this term means that the two component sentences of a conditional are negated *and* change places. Thus, by transposition, (p ⊃ q) becomes (~q ⊃ ~p). In standard systems, the first implies the second. The second also implies the first, since the standard systems allow for elimination of double negation. Accordingly, the two inference-patterns are valid:

If p then q	If not-p then not-q
If not-p then not-q	If p then q

transubstantiation *n.* the doctrine, advocated as early as the ninth century by the Benedictine Paschasius Radbertus, which interprets Jesus' words 'this is my body' (Mark 14,22–25; Matthew 26,26–29; Luke 22,15–20) to mean that in the Eucharist the properties of the bread and wine remain but the substance is replaced by that of Christ. This is in striking contrast to the standard Aristotelian account of change, according to which the substance remains but acquires different properties. The doctrine of transubstantiation became established in Roman Catholicism from the Fourth Lateran Council (1215). Its classical formulation was offered by Aquinas. It was reaffirmed by the Council of Trent (1545–63) in a resolution of 1551, and again in a papal encyclical of 1965. During the Reformation it was much debated and was eventually rejected by Anglicans, who in the seventeenth and eighteenth centuries often stressed it as a decisive point of difference from Roman Catholicism.

transworld depravity The notion of transworld depravity is a technical one, introduced by Alvin Plantinga in the course of his attempted proof that the existence of evil is consistent with the existence of an omnipotent, omniscient and omnibenevolent God. His argument is a version of the so-called Free-Will Defence, and is set out in Plantinga's *The Nature of Necessity* 1974 and *God, Freedom and Evil* 1974.

An agent suffers from transworld depravity if, and only if, any possible world in which that agent is created by God is a world in which the agent freely performs at least one morally wrong action.

In the course of his attempted proof, Plantinga argues (1) that some possible worlds containing free agents are worlds which, even granted his omnipotence, God cannot create; and (2) that all those possible worlds in which free agents always, but freely, choose to do right might be in this category because all possible free agents might be transworld-depraved. Pertinent criticism of Plantinga's argument is offered by J. L. Mackie in his *The Miracle of Theism* 1982. *See also* FREE-WILL DEFENCE; POSSIBLE WORLDS; THEODICY. JB

tree in the quad *See* QUAD, TREE IN THE.

Trendelenburg /trɛn'dɛːlənbʊrk (Gm.)/ Adolf (1802–72) German philosopher, professor in Berlin from 1833, best known for his rehabilitation of Aristotelian philosophy and his opposition to Hegel.

Trendelenburg gap In his major work, *Logische Untersuchungen* 1840 (Logical investigations), Trendelenburg argued that Kant had considered two alternatives: either that space applies to phenomena only, or that space applies to things-in-themselves only, and had left a gap by omitting a third possibility, viz. that space is both subjective and objective. His objection was rejected by Kuno Fischer, a leading historian of modern philosophy. The ensuing debate about the interpretation and validity of Kant's TRANSCENDENTAL AESTHETIC was intense, sometimes even acrimonious, and engaged many of the leading philosophers in Germany in the closing decades of the nineteenth century.

trichotomy /traɪ'kɒtəmɪ/ *n.* division into three parts.

trinitarianism *n.* the Christian doctrine that God is a personal being, consisting of a trinity made up of *three* persons: the Father, the Son and the Holy Spirit.

Christians have often had problems coming to grips with this doctrine. It is often described as a 'mystery' which human beings cannot hope fully to understand but must accept on faith. Those who subscribe to *unitarianism* reject it, and it is not accepted in SOCIANISM and ARIANISM. Adherents to the doctrine have tried different ways of understanding the nature of personhood and of the relation between the three persons, which led to the development of philosophical theories that are of interest in their own right. Many of these attempts have been rejected as heresies both by the Roman Catholic and by major Protestant churches.

tripod /'traɪpɒd/ *n.* a three-legged stool; especially the one from which the Pythia, priestess of the temple at Delphi in ancient Greece, delivered her oracular sayings.

tripos /'traɪpɒs/ *n.* final honours examination at the University of Cambridge.

tritheism *n.* the doctrine that there are three gods, a heretical form of trinitarianism.

trivium /'trɪvɪəm/ (Lat. *trivium* a crossroads (where three roads meet); commonplace) *n.* Grammar, rhetoric and dialectic, together called the *trivium*, were the first three disciplines in the school curriculum that had become established by the ninth century. The remaining four were called the QUADRIVIUM, and together they made up the seven liberal arts.

trolley problem a much-discussed problem in applied ethics: the driver of a runaway tram can only steer from one narrow track on to another; five men are working on one track and one man on the other; anyone on the track the tram enters is bound to be killed. In this instance, it seems right to opt for the lesser evil, and sacrifice one innocent life rather than five. In contrast, suppose that, instead of a tram about to run over five innocent victims, there is a fanatical mob intent on killing five innocent hostages – would it be right to save them by framing and condemning one innocent person?

The example was presented by Philippa Foot in an article entitled 'The problem of abortion and the doctrine of double effect'

1967, reprinted in her book *Virtues and Vices*.

trope (Gr. *tropos* turn; turn of speech) *n.* **1** (in rhetoric and grammar) a kind of figurative, non-literal, use of words which achieves its effect by deviating from the standard meaning of the words used. Hyperbole, irony, litotes, metaphor, metonymy, simile and synecdoche are tropes. **2** The main arguments for scepticism advanced by Aenesidemus, Agrippa and other ancient sceptics were called tropes. **3** (in contemporary ontology) abstract particulars. An example would be the redness of a particular red surface, or the wisdom of a particular person like Socrates. These entities inhabit a particular position in space and time, but although they monopolize such a position they are not concrete: they are abstract in that they almost always come in clusters and can be grasped only by means of abstraction. According to the ontological theory proposed by D. C. Williams, who also gave the term this new meaning, in 'On the Elements of Being', *Review of Metaphysics* 7 (1953), the ultimate constituents of reality are tropes, a theory anticipated early in the century by G. F. Stout. This ontology has since been developed in Keith Campbell, *Abstract Particulars* 1990.

trophic (Gr. *trophē* nourishment) *adj.* pertaining to nutrition.

tropic *See* NEUSTIC.

truism *n.* an obviously true statement.

truth *n.* 'What is truth?' asked Pilate, but a dictionary is not where the answer should be expected. The truth in which philosophers are chiefly interested is an attribute of beliefs, opinions, theories, doctrines, statements, etc. The proper contrast is with *falsity*. In other senses of the word, the proper contrast is with what is fake, spurious, insincere, faithless, etc. *See also* LOGICAL TRUTH.

truth, theories of The oldest theory is the Correspondence Theory. Aristotle's early formulation in *Metaphysics* 1077^b26 was: 'to say of what is that it is, or of what is not that it is not, is true'. Contemporary versions phrase it as '"p" is true if and only if p'. The intervening period usually preferred to hold that something is true if it corresponds with something else. Controversy about the theory has usually been three-fold: what is it that is true – is it a belief, proposition, statement, sentence, or what?; what is it that this corresponds with – is it a state of affairs, situation, reality, fact, or what?; and what exactly is the relation called 'correspondence' between what is true and what makes it true?

The Coherence Theory was an alternative proposed originally by the great rationalist system-building metaphysicians, such as Leibniz, Spinoza, Hegel and Bradley, but also advocated in a somewhat different form by such logical positivists as Neurath and Hempel, who took mathematics as their model. According to the Coherence Theory the truth of a proposition consists in its being part of a comprehensive system in which it (according to certain idealist theories) entails every other proposition, or (according to certain positivist theories) it is consistent with every other proposition. For the rationalists the system constitutes the whole of reality; for some logical positivists it is the system accepted by contemporary scientists.

The nineteenth century produced the Pragmatist Theory of the American philosophers C. S. Pierce and William James, according to which an idea (that is, an opinion, belief or statement) is true if it works, if accepting it brings success.

The twentieth century saw the introduction of, first, the Logical Superfluity

Theory, due to Frege and Ramsey, which holds that to say *that so and so is true* is to say no more than *that so and so* – the word 'true' being superfluous; secondly, Tarski's Semantic Theory, suggested mainly for artificial languages, which stresses the equivalence ' "p" if and only if p', where the first p is a name of a sentence and the second p is the sentence itself; and, thirdly, what might be called 'non-descriptivist' theories, which argue that to say that something is true is not to say anything about this something, but to assess, praise, accept or concede it. AW

truth-apt *adj.* capable of being true or false. A sentence which, on one view, lacks truth-value (e.g. The present King of France is bald) is still truth-apt: it has one, if France has a King.

truth-function *n.* a function whose arguments are truth-values and whose values are truth-values.

The connectives of standard propositional logic are truth-functional operators. For instance, the truth-value of a conjunction of two propositions p, q, depends entirely on the truth-value of p and q respectively, according to the truth-table in Table 23.

Table 23 Truth-table for a truth-functional connective (conjunction)

p	q	p & q
T	T	T
T	F	F
F	T	F
F	F	F

As can be seen, if p and q are both assigned the value T, then the value of their conjunction is T. If p is assigned the value T and q is assigned the value F, then the value of their conjunction is F. And so on.

In ordinary language, the propositional connective 'and' is usually truth-functional. But some propositional connectives are not. For instance, in the statement: 'Jill fell ill because Jack came back', 'because' is not truth-functional.

Here, the truth-value of the proposition is not entirely determined by the truth-value of its two component statements: given that Jill did fall ill and that Jack did return, it is still an open question whether the first was *because* of the second. The truth-table for this compound proposition, symbolized 'I because B', is given in Table 24.

Table 24 Truth-table for a non-truth-functional connective

I	B	I because B
T	T	?
T	F	F
F	T	F
F	F	F

truth-relativism *n.* This is the view that a belief or opinion cannot be said to be true simply, but only true relative to a species, a conceptual scheme, a social practice, a social group, or a person. To illustrate with the last-mentioned kind: whenever a person, X, says or thinks: 'p is true', this can only mean 'p is true for X'. This view has the absurd consequence that if A believes that *p is true* and B believes that *p is not true*, there is no contradiction between what A and B believe!

truth-table *n.* a display in tabular form of the truth-value of a compound statement or formula, given the truth-value of its components.

truth-value *n.* *truth* and *falsity* are the two standard truth-values. In an extended sense, the values introduced in many-valued logical systems can also be called truth-values. Such systems reject the principle of bivalence, that every proposition is either true or false.

T-sentence Examples of T-sentences are: 'The sentence "Snow is white" is true in English if and only if snow is white'; and 'The sentence "La neige est blanche" is true in French if and only if snow is white.' Their general form is: 'The sentence S is true in L if and only if P', where S denotes a sentence, L is a language, and P is a translation of the sentence S into the language in which the T-sentence is formulated (which, in the two examples above, is English).

Alfred Tarski claimed that an adequate definition of truth for a language could be given if one could give a T-sentence for each sentence of the language. Usually this cannot be done because the number of possible sentences of a language is infinite. However, for certain formal languages Tarski was able to formulate a finite definition and to prove that it logically implied every T-sentence for the language. AM

Tugendhat /ˈtuːgənthat (Gm.)/, Ernst (1930–) professor of philosophy in Heidelberg 1966–75, then in Starnberg, and in Berlin since 1980. His earlier writings are strongly influenced by Husserl and Heidegger. A stay at the University of Michigan in the mid-1960s, and a close study of the later Wittgenstein, led his thinking in a new, linguistic direction: the focus of philosophy should no longer be reality, as in ancient times, nor consciousness, as in the modern era; instead, language should be the centre of philosophical attention. Tugendhat turned from the mentalistic analysis of acts and intentions to a semantic analysis of propositions. He has, however, brought this closer to the great themes of traditional philosophy than most anglophone philosophers, as can be seen in his *Traditional and Analytical Philosophy* 1982. At the same time, he has shown distrust of the metaphysics of consciousness and self-consciousness which flourished in the German idealist tradition (Fichte, Schelling, Hegel, etc.). Thus, *Selbstbewusstsein und Selbstbestimmung* 1979 (Self-consciousness and self-determination) uses techniques of analytical philosophy to resolve or dissolve many of their problems. This philosophical development is also a move away from ontology and epistemology towards a greater emphasis on problems of ethics. In Tugendhat's view, self-consciousness arises from the development of ethical concepts: the moral ought and one's sense of self are constituted concurrently. But morality is socially determined, and a more absolute foundation for ethics is not available: he rejects both traditional transcendent foundations of ethics, and modern transcendental ones, such as Habermas's. BC

tuism *n.* altruism. (Now used only in the compound NON-TUISH.)

tu quoque /ˈtuː ˈkwəʊkwɪ/ Lat. you too. A short way of saying that the person objecting is equally vulnerable to the objection proffered. *See also ARGUMENTUM AD HOMINEM.*

Turing, Alan Mathison (1912–54) made significant contributions to mathematics, cryptanalysis, logic, philosophy, and biology. He is best known for his pioneering work in the areas of computer science and cognitive science. Appointed to a Fellowship at King's College, Cambridge, in 1935, he was recruited for the war effort in 1939 when he worked as a cryptanalyst, breaking German codes. After the war he continued his research at the National Physical Laboratory, where he designed one of the first electronic computers, and at the University of Manchester.

The 'Turing machine', which he described in 1936, was the notional computing machine on which subsequent stored-program digital computers are modelled. A Turing machine consists of a potentially infinite paper tape that bears a single stream of discrete (e.g. binary) symbols and is scanned by a read-write head that moves left or right, one symbol at a time, erasing and writing symbols on the tape under the control of a program. Turing proved that a single machine, known as a universal machine, can be programmed to simulate any other Turing machine, and argued that every effective mathematical method can be carried out by this universal machine (*see* CHURCH'S THESIS; CHURCH'S THEOREM). He widened the concept of computability with his notion of O-machines or 'oracle' machines (1939), which perform computations on discrete symbols but cannot be simulated by a universal Turing machine. His pioneering work in computer intelligence included chess algorithms, the idea that 'intellectual activity consists . . . of search', and (anticipating modern CONNECTIONISM) 'paper' simulations of 'unorganized machines' – networks of neuron-like elements connected together largely at random which learn through a process of 'training'. Turing proposed that the brain is a digital computing machine, suggesting that the cortex at birth is an unorganized machine which through 'training' becomes organized 'into a universal machine or something like it'. He argued that the question 'Can machines think?' be replaced by 'Can a machine play the imitation game satisfactorily?' This game is now known as the 'Turing test': a human player attempts to distinguish between a computer and another human on the basis of their verbal responses, not necessarily truthful, to questions. The suggestion is that a computer that plays the game satisfactorily emulates the human intellect. JCD

turnstile *n.* The single turnstile in '$\vdash$ A' means that A is a theorem; 'B $\vdash$ A' means that A is a syntactic consequence of, derivable from, B. The double turnstile in '$\models$A' means that A is logically valid; 'B $\models$ A' means that A is a semantic consequence of B.

These symbols are used with reference to a formal system, and this can be made explicit: for instance, '$\vdash_{S4}$ A' means that A is a theorem in a formal system called S4.

The single turnstile was introduced by Frege as an assertion sign, to distinguish an assertion from a mere propositional content. Its present use began with Kleene and Rosser in the mid-1930s. The double turnstile was introduced by Kleene in the mid-1950s.

turp /tɜːp/ *n.* a unit of disvalue, in analogy with 'util' or 'hedon', a unit of value in utilitarian calculations.

Twardowski /tvar'dɔvski/ (Pȯ.), Kazimierz (1866–1938) After studies under Brentano in Vienna, Twardowski held a chair in Lwów from 1905 to 1930. Already in the 1890s, his analysis of mental acts and their contents led him to a rejection of psychologism. His analyses explored the conceptual geography of our mental concepts; he rejected materialist theories, and defended an anti-relativist theory of knowledge. In spirit and in content his views have much in common with the British analytical tradition from Moore to Ryle, and he is commonly regarded as the founder of Polish analytic philosophy. Twardowski's insistence on clarity and his distaste for nebulous speculation set the tone for much of twentieth-century Polish philosophy.

Twin Earth We use the word 'water' to pick out a kind of stuff which we associate with certain distinctive features: being an odourless, colourless liquid, falling from the sky, and filling the oceans, for instance.

A natural suggestion is that the word 'water' is short for something like this definite description: 'the odourless, colourless liquid that falls from the sky as rain and fills the ocean'.

Hilary Putnam raised a major problem for this view with his parable of Twin Earth. Twin Earth is very like Earth; in particular, it has an odourless, colourless liquid that falls from the sky and fills the ocean. The big difference is that the odourless, colourless stuff that does all this is not H_2O, as it is in our world, but XYZ, a different liquid compound altogether, despite its superficial similarities to H_2O.

Briefly, Putnam's point is that if 'water' were an abbreviated definite description, Twin Earth would contain water, and clearly it does not. Putnam suggests that we should think of 'water' – and natural-kind terms in general – not as short for long definite descriptions, but as names for the kind in common to certain exemplars that played a special role in introducing the natural-kind term. Twin Earth has no water because it does not have the stuff in common to the exemplars *we* used to introduce the term 'water'. FJ

tychism /'taɪkɪzm/ (Gr. *tychē* chance; coincidence) *n.* the doctrine that there is genuine chance or spontaneity in the world. C. S. Peirce created the term for his view that there are random events in the world. The laws of nature are probable and imprecise. He did also believe, however, that the laws move towards greater fixity, so that nature as a whole is gradually becoming more regular and uniform.

type *See* TOKEN/TYPE.

types, theory of a logical theory, originally proposed by Bertrand Russell in the early years of the twentieth century. Its main thrust is to rule out as ill-formed and therefore meaningless certain kinds of statement.

The basic assumption of the theory is that the elements of a set, and the set itself, are at different levels. At the lowest level, the elements are individuals. At the next level we have sets of individuals; at the next level again, sets of sets of individuals, and so on. All items on one level are said to be of the same type.

The general idea is that every level (except the ground level) is inhabited by sets which *have* elements from the next lower level, and which *are* elements of sets at the next higher level.

It follows from this restriction that there can be no set of all sets, and there can be no set which has itself as a member. Statements which imply the contrary are ill-formed. Accordingly, Russell's paradox, which presupposes that a set can have itself as a member, cannot arise. There are, however, problematic features in this theory of types and, in later developments, other ways have been tried to avoid the paradox.

Note: A language in which transgressions of the kind mentioned are ruled out, is sometimes said to 'contain' a theory of types.

tyranny (Gr. *tyrannos* tyrant) the oppressive rule of one person (a *tyrant*). In Plato's *Republic*, Book 8, it is described as arising naturally from tendencies inherent in democracy. In Aristotle's *Politics*, Book 5, it is the degenerate form of monarchy, condemned in his *Nicomachean Ethics* Book 8, 1160^b. The original meaning of the word was probably 'king'. In ancient Greece, the usurpers called tyrants were not all oppressors.

U

Übermensch /ˈyːbɛrmɛnʃ/ *See* SUPERMAN.

ubiety /juːˈbaɪətɪ/ (Lat. *ubi* where) *n.* location (literally: whereness).

ubiquity /juːˈbɪkwɪtɪ/ (Lat. *ubique* everywhere) *n.* the property of being everywhere at the same time. Commonly regarded as a divine attribute.

Ueberweg /ˈyːbərveːk (Gm.)/, Friedrich (1826–71) professor in Königsberg from 1862, editor-in-chief of the first major encyclopedic reference work for the history of philosophy. His name has remained on the many subsequent revised editions, which also contain very extensive bibliographical information.

Unamuno /unaˈmuno (Sp.)/, Miguel de (1864–1937) Spanish poet, philosopher and man of letters. Professor of Greek at Salamanca from 1891. *The Tragic Sense of Life* 1913 and *The Agony of Christianity* 1931 have affinities with existentialist thought.

uncertainty principle a result in quantum theory, established by Werner Heisenberg: at a given time it may be possible to measure the *position* of an electron with a very high degree of accuracy; and it is possible to measure its *momentum* (and hence velocity) with a very high degree of accuracy; but, beyond a certain limit, it is not possible to measure both together with a very high degree of accuracy.

It is often thought that this result implies a rejection of determinism, i.e. the principle that every event is fully determined by antecedent causes. Whether this *is* implied is a disputed matter. There is a useful discussion in Ernest Nagel, *The Structure of Science* 1961, chapter 10.

unconditioned *adj.* depending on nothing else for its existence. *Syn.* absolute.

unconscious *adj.* Mental phenomena that a person has without being aware of them on the occasion of their occurrence are said to be unconscious. The concept became common in nineteenth-century thought and plays a prominent part in the theories of Schopenhauer and von Hartmann. In the twentieth century, the concept of the unconscious is at the core of psychoanalytic theory and practice. It is conceived as the location of that which has been repressed by the superego, as distinct from what has not reached the level of full consciousness, the subconscious.

If there is a close conceptual link between consciousness and mind, the view that something can be both unconscious and mental is problematic.

underdetermination *n.* Different theories using different theoretical concepts, but both well supported empirically, are said to be underdetermined by the empirical evidence, and the same applies to theories that are mutually incompatible but fit all the available evidence.

understanding *n.* **1** a faculty of the mind, also called intellect. **2** a mental activity, involving interpretation. **3** a method of gaining knowledge, appropriate in the human sciences, and contrasted with the method characteristic of the natural sciences: experimental testing of hypotheses. This contrast was particularly insisted on in the writings of Dilthey and Windelband. *See also* HERMENEUTICS.

undistributed middle, fallacy of *See* DISTRIBUTION OF TERMS.

unexpected examination, etc. *See* PREDICTION PARADOX for the paradoxes of the unexpected examination, execution, hanging, etc.

unio mystica /ˈjuːnɪəʊ ˈmɪstɪkə/ Lat. mystical union, i.e. with the divine, achieved in religious contemplation.

Unitarianism *n.* a religious movement and belief-system in the Christian tradition, which arose after the Protestant Reformation. It rejects the dogma of the trinity: common to its various strands is the insistence on the oneness of God and the denial of the divinity of Christ and the Holy Spirit. The positive attitude to rationality and tolerance in matters of doctrine is also characteristic. Doubts about the authenticity of orthodox trinitarianism had been raised by Michael Servetus, Fausto Sozzini (Socinus), Hugo Grotius, John Milton, Samuel Clarke, Richard Price, Joseph Priestley, etc., but it was only in the eighteenth century that congregations and churches clearly identifiable as Unitarian came into being in the English-speaking countries.

unity of science This was an ideal of the logical positivists, advocated particularly by Otto Neurath. They thought or hoped that all the different sciences might be unified into a vast hierarchy, in which the characteristic laws of any science would be explicable from the laws of the science preceding it in the hierarchy. Thus, sub-atomic physics would explain atomic physics, atomic physics would explain molecular physics, molecular physics would explain chemistry and biochemistry, and so forth until the hierarchy even included sciences such as biology or economics or anthropology. It is also associated with the doctrine that all sciences share the same methods – the 'unity of method' thesis. AM

universal *n.* a universal is something shared by different particular objects. For instance, a wheel, a dinner plate and a ring are all circular. What they have in common, circularity, is a universal. The objects that are circular are said to be *instances* of the universal, or to *instantiate* or *exemplify* or *partake* of it. *See also* UNIVERSALS, THE MEDIEVAL PROBLEM OF.

universal, concrete In idealist philosophy, such as Bradley's, a universal is something that unites different individuals. An abstract universal, roughly a concept like *horse*, does not have individual existence, but it applies to horses which do, and in this sense provides unity in diversity. A concrete universal is itself something that has individual existence, e.g. a society: again there is unity in diversity.

universal generalization In predicate logic, let A be a formula containing a free variable x. The universal generalization of A is (∀x) A. For instance, the universal generalization of (Fx ⊃ Gx) is (∀x) (Fx ⊃ Gx). This corresponds to an inference from a premiss true of any arbitrarily chosen individual, to a conclusion about every individual.

universal instantiation In predicate logic, A is the universal instantiation of (∀x) A. This corresponds to an inference from a premiss true of every individual, to a conclusion about a particular individual.

universalism *n.* **1** (in ethics) the view that all human beings are morally equal in the sense that membership of a certain tribe, class, caste, nation, race, etc. as such neither justi-

fies special consideration nor excuses lack of consideration. *Ant.* particularism.
2 (in theology) the view that in the fullness of time everyone will be saved and that there will be a 'restoration of all things' – *see* APOCATASTASIS. This view, advocated by Origen (*c.* 185–254), Schleiermacher (1768–1834) and fairly widely accepted in twentieth-century religion, is contrary to traditional Christian theology which insists on the eternity of hell. *Ant.* particularism.

universalizability *n.* In Kant's moral philosophy, the principle of morality, also called the Categorical Imperative, can be described as a universalizability principle. It can be formulated: 'Let the principle on which you act always be such that you are at the same time able to will that it be a universal rule of conduct.'

Kant used this as a negative criterion: an act that fails to satisfy this principle is not morally right. In particular, it is not right to make exceptions and 'cut corners' in one's own favour.

R. M. Hare analyses moral statements as a kind of prescriptive statements (i.e. statements which provide answers to the question of what one ought to do). The moral statements differ from the non-moral prescriptive statements in that they are universalizable. To say that a person *morally* ought to do something implies that anyone in relevantly similar circumstances ought to do it.

universal proposition **1** a categorical proposition of the form *Every S is P*, or of the form *No S is P*. **2** in predicate logic, an open sentence bound by a universal quantifier.

universal quantifier an operator in predicate logic, usually written (x) or (∀x). It can be read 'For all x . . .'.

For instance, (∀x) (Philosopher x ⊃ Wise x) would be read 'For all x, if x is a philosopher then x is wise' or 'Every philosopher is wise'.

universals, the medieval problem of By the 'problem of universals' historians of philosophy mean the question of whether universals are things or merely words. For instance, all men belong to the species Man, and 'man' is a universal term (as opposed to 'Socrates' or 'this man', which are words referring to an individual). Is this species in some sense a thing, unitary and yet common to all men (the view of realists), or are words the only universals (as nominalists hold)? Plato not only considered that universals are real: he argued that they alone truly exist. Although he rejected this notion of Platonic universals or 'Ideas', Aristotle analysed individuals as consisting of a form, which makes them the sort of thing they are (a man or a dog or a stone), and matter. These forms are universal, and intellectual knowledge is based on the mind's power to abstract them from individuals.

Both Plato's and Aristotle's positions are, therefore, realist. It was not until the twelfth century that the nominalist views began to be proposed. Probably they originated from a certain approach to the exegesis of Porphyry's *Isagoge* and Aristotle's *Categories*. Instead of reading these works as if they were about things, some interpreters, among them probably Roscelin (*c.* 1045–*c.* 1120) began to treat them as discussions of words. Porphyry's chapters on genera and species would therefore be interpreted, like the rest of his treatise, as discussions of words. Roscelin's one-time pupil, Abelard, rejected this approach *except* for the case of universals (species and genera). In his work it became a philosophical, rather than merely an interpretative, principle. He did not for a moment doubt that the Aristotelian and Porphyrean hierarchy of species and genera correctly describes the structure of the world. But he insisted that no thing is a universal. Every thing is an individual, but there are words (such as 'man' and 'stone') which are invented in order to be predicable of many things of the same sort. Abelard also made clear that when he claimed that words are universals, he did not mean words in the physical sense (vibrations in the air), but words seen as bearers of meaning. He tried to introduce a new technical term to refer to words in this sense – *sermo* (*pl. sermones*) ('speech') – but his contemporaries seem to have preferred the more common *nomen* (*pl. nomina*) ('name'), and it is probably from this that the description 'nominalists' (*nominales*) is derived.

The nominalism of Abelard and his followers was never more than the position of one philosophical faction in the twelfth century. In the thirteenth century, as Aristotle's writings on the soul and metaphysics became known, nominalism all but disappeared. With Aristotle as a guide, such thinkers as Thomas Aquinas, Duns Scotus and their contemporaries elaborated various sophisticated forms of realism. They recognized universals as really existent; if they had not, the whole theory of intellectual cognition, founded on Aristotle's, would have collapsed. But they did not think that, for instance, the species Man, by which I am a man, is an entity distinct in reality from me – rather, it can be distinguished from me only by reason or (as Scotus argued) 'formally'.

In the early fourteenth century, however, nominalism was revived by William of Ockham. In consistency, he rejected the Aristotelian idea that intellectual knowledge was gained from our minds being informed by universals ('intelligible species') derived from the objects perceived. Reversing the order in Thomist and Scotist accounts of cognition, Ockham argued that our knowledge of the external world *begins* from a grasp of individuals. Ockham's nominalism was shared by another influential fourteenth-century thinker, John Buridan, and was developed in a variety of different directions by later medieval philosophers. JM

univocal /jʊˈnɪvəkəl/ *adj.* (of words) having one meaning only, unambiguous.

unlimited *adj.* lacking a quantitative limit, being indefinitely large or indefinitely small. This is the present-day usage. In classical philosophy, however, *unlimited* had the more general sense of *indefinite, indeterminate*.

unrestricted quantification *See* RESTRICTED QUANTIFICATION.

Uppsala School a philosophical school influential in Sweden in the first half of the twentieth century. It saw the central task of philosophy as one of analysis and radical critique of the concepts and assumptions of common sense and science, and approached this task in a decidedly anti-metaphysical spirit. In moral, social and legal philosophy, it stressed the fact/value and fact/norm dualisms. Its main representatives were Axel Hägerström and Adolf Phalén. They influenced philosophers such as Konrad Marc-Wogau and Anders Wedberg, author of a history of philosophy in which an analytical approach is adopted; theologians (e.g. Anders Nygren); philosophers of law (e.g. Karl Olivecrona); and economists (e.g. Gunnar Myrdal).

use/mention Compare: 'What is the meaning of being?' with 'What is the meaning of "being"?' These are two entirely different questions. In the first, the word 'being' is *used*, in the second it is *mentioned*.

Similarly, we *use* the word 'dog' to refer to the canine species or members of it, as in the sentence: 'The dog is a bug-ridden barking brute,' but we *mention* the word 'dog' to refer to the word itself: 'In standard English, "dog" is used to refer to a bug-ridden barking brute.'

Typically, a word that is *mentioned* is placed between quotation marks; sometimes it is instead italicized or underlined.

The second example above stems from a humorous 'dissertation' by the German satirist Kurt Tucholsky. His claim that it is in Leibniz has not been verified.

Note: Quine may have been the first to use this pair of terms to mark the distinction, in 1940.

utilitarian **1** *n.* a person whose theory or practice is in accordance with utilitarianism. **2** *adj.* pertaining to utilitarianism. Note that 'utilitarian' is not a synonym for 'right', 'useful', 'beneficial' or 'welfare-promoting'.

utilitarianism /jʊtɪlɪˈtɛərɪənɪzm/ *n.* a moral theory according to which an action is right if and only if it conforms to the principle of utility. Bentham formulated the principle of utility as part of such a theory in *Introduction to the Principles of Morals and Legislation* 1789. An action conforms to the principle of utility if and only if its performance will be more productive of pleasure or happiness, or more preventive of pain or unhappiness, than any alternative. Instead of 'pleasure' and 'happiness', the word 'welfare' is also apt: the value of the consequences of an action is determined solely by the welfare of individuals.

A characteristic feature of Bentham's theory is the idea that the rightness of an action *entirely* depends on the value of its consequences. This is why the theory is also described as consequentialist. Bentham's theory differs from certain other varieties of utilitarianism (or consequentialism) by its distinctive assumption that the standard of value is pleasure and the absence of pain; by being an act-utilitarian (ACT-UTILITARIANISM) theory; and by its maximizing assumption that an action is not right unless it tends towards the optimal outcome.

The view that utilitarianism is unable to accommodate any values except the crass, gross or materialistic ones is mistaken.

Since the 1960s, many writers have used *consequentialism* instead of *utilitarianism* for the view that the rightness of an action *entirely* depends on the value of its consequences. Many writers now restrict the word utilitarianism to denote certain *kinds* of consequentialism, especially Bentham's and Mill's. Currently there is terminological diversity, and the varieties of utilitarianism mentioned elsewhere are also described as varieties of consequentialism.

utilitarianism, act- *See* ACT-UTILITARIANISM.

utilitarianism, attitude- *See* UTILITARIANISM, INDIRECT.

utilitarianism, hedonistic a utilitarian theory which assumes that the rightness of an action depends entirely on the amount of *pleasure* it tends to produce and the amount of pain it tends to prevent. Bentham's utilitarianism is hedonistic. Although he describes the good not only as pleasure, but also as happiness, benefit, advantage, etc., he treats these concepts as more or less synonymous, and seems to think of them as reducible to pleasure. John Stuart Mill's utilitarianism, also described as hedonistic, differs importantly from Bentham's in taking some pleasures to be higher than other ones, so that when considering the values of the consequences of an action, not only the quantity but also the quality of pleasure has to be considered. This complicates the summing up, or may even make it impossible.

utilitarianism, ideal a utilitarian theory which denies that the sole object of moral concern is the maximizing of pleasure or happiness. In G. E. Moore's version of ideal utilitarianism in *Principia Ethica* 1903, it is aesthetic experiences and relations of friendship that have intrinsic value, and therefore ought to be sought and promoted, while consciousness of pain, hatred or contempt of what is good or beautiful, and the love, admiration, or enjoyment of what is evil or ugly are the three things that have intrinsic disvalue and therefore should be shunned and prevented.

It was Hastings Rashdall (1858–1924) in *The Theory of Good and Evil* 1907 who first used 'ideal utilitarianism' for non-hedonistic utilitarianism of this kind.

utilitarianism, indirect a kind of utilitarianism which recognizes that an agent is more likely to act rightly by developing the right attitudes, habits, principles, and acting on them, than by trying to calculate the value of the consequences before deciding to act. This indirect utilitarianism is so called because it bears on actions only indirectly. *See also* UTILITARIANISM, RESTRICTIVE.

utilitarianism, negative/positive Positive utilitarianism recommends the promotion or maximizing of intrinsic value, negative utilitarianism recommends the reduction or minimizing of intrinsic disvalue. At first sight, the negative kind may seem reasonable and more modest in what it recommends. But one way of minimizing human misery is by putting all human beings out of their misery. This course of action is usually considered unacceptable. This has led to a search for reformulations of negative utilitarianism, or to its rejection.

utilitarianism, restricted *See* RULE-UTILITARIANISM.

utilitarianism, restrictive Restrictive utilitarianism is the view that the right action is the one that maximizes objectively probable value. So, when *evaluating* an agent's decision, this is the criterion of rightness that should be applied. But it does not follow that when *deliberating*, the agent should engage in a calculation in order to work out how to maximize objectively probable value; that may indeed be counterproductive. The right decision may be more safely reached by not consciously aiming at it. Instead, an agent in whom certain attitudes and character traits have been developed (for instance, an immediate bent towards honesty and fairness), and who acts in character, may be more likely to take the right decision than an agent who perpetually engages in casuistic deliberation. *Syn.* indirect utilitarianism.

utilitarianism, rule- *See* RULE-UTILITARIANISM.

utilitarianism, theological Theological and non-theological varieties of utilitaranism agree on the account of the *rightness* of an action: the rightness depends entirely on the value of its consequences. But there is a difference in respect of the notion of *moral duty*.

Although our knowledge of God is very limited, we know that he is perfectly benevolent, so there can be no doubt that he desires the maximum happiness for his creatures. We can safely assume that he desires us always to act so as to promote this end. For us, his desire is a command, and the actions commanded by God are our duties. In this way, theological utilitarians (Paley, Austin) can explain why doing the right thing is a duty. In their view that there can be no duty without a command, they agree with Bentham and with many earlier writers on theology and jurisprudence. Bentham's own utilitarianism is non-theological and has therefore no place for a notion of *moral duty*, but only for the notions of *right*, *wrong*, *ought*, *ought not*, and others of that kind.

Utopia /juːˈtəʊpɪə/ (Gr. *outopia* no place and *eutopia* good place) The word was created by Thomas More as part of the title of his book *De optimae rei publicae statu deque nova insula utopia* 1516 (On the best government and on the new island *Utopia*), which describes in detail a society with ideal political structures and an ideal way of life. The word has since been used to denote ideal social and political conditions, and writings that describe such conditions. Other early modern works in the genre were Campanella's *City of the Sun*, and Bacon's *New Atlantis*.

V

vague /veɪɡ/ *adj.* At what line on the spectrum does red turn to pink, or orange? How many hairs can remain on the head of a bald person? No definite answer seems possible: hence expressions like *red* and *bald* are said to be *vague*.

Vagueness is of great philosophical interest because it seems to be inconsistent with the view that every proposition is true or false. Suppose that few hairs are left on Jack's scalp. Is it true that he is bald? Is it false?

An expression can be unspecific without being vague. For instance, 'dog' can denote canines of various breeds. This need not cause any difficulty in determining whether a particular animal is a dog. Also, an expression can be ambiguous without being vague. For instance, 'doctor' can designate a person with a PhD degree, or a medical practitioner. After disambiguation there need be no difficulty in determining whether a particular person is a doctor.

The use of vague expressions need not be a fault. Aristotle rightly observed that 'it is the mark of an educated person to look for precision . . . just so far as the nature of the subject-matter admits' (*Nicomachean Ethics* 1,3 1094^{b}23). *See also* SORITES.

Vaihinger /ˈfaiɪŋər (Gm.)/, Hans (1852–1933) professor in Halle 1882–1906, founder of the Kant Society in Germany and of the journal *Kant-Studien* (1894–). Inspired by Kant's view that the Ideas of Reason have a regulative but not a constitutive employment, so that, for instance, we conduct psychological inquiry *as if* there is an immaterial self at the core (although there can be no knowledge of such a thing), he developed in his *Die Philosophie des Als-Ob* 1911 (The philosophy of As-If) a general fictionalism: values, ideals, scientific theories and concepts are fictions, many of them self-inconsistent or at any rate without any objective basis. We can recognize this and at the same time recognize that such fictions serve us well.

validity /ˈvælɪdɪtɪ/ *n.* **1** A *valid argument* or inference is one in which the conclusion follows from the premisses. A necessary condition for validity is that it is impossible for the premisses to be true and the conclusion false. This means that valid arguments or inferences preserve truth. In modern logic, such truth-preservation is usually also accepted as a sufficient condition for validity. But RELEVANCE LOGICS add further conditions.

Validity (of arguments and inferences) is not the same as truth. Let P stand for the premiss(es) of the argument, and C for the conclusion. The argument has the form: 'P, therefore C'. The argument is said to be valid or invalid, but cannot be said to be true or false. It is its constituent propositions, including its premiss(es) and conclusion, that are true or false.

2 A *valid formula* in a logical system is a formula that is true under every interpretation. That is, every appropriate and uniform replacement of its variables yields a true sentence. Thus, $p \supset (q \supset p)$ is a valid formula, since the result of replacing p with some sentence and q with some sentence is inevitably a true sentence. $(\forall x)Fx \supset (\exists x)Fx$

is a valid formula, since the result of replacing F with some predicate and x with any individual is inevitably a true sentence.

In contexts other than logic and analysis of arguments, usage is more flexible, so that principles and theories can be said to be valid or invalid, but can also be said to be true or false.

Valla /'vælə (Eng.); 'valla (It.)/, Lorenzo (1407–57) Renaissance humanist. His philosophical dialogues attempt to combine Christian and Epicurean principles. A dialogue on free will, later discussed by Leibniz, deals with the question of how human freedom of choice is compatible with God's foreknowledge. Valla was one of the leading writers to attack scholastic logic, accusing it of being needlessly preoccupied with trifles and written in a Latin both artificial and barbarous.

valorize *vb.* to set or maintain a floor price, i.e. a minimum price of a commodity. This original use of the term, in the context of commodity trading, dates from the nineteenth century; it could carry the suggestion of price-fixing.

In late twentieth-century French, *valoriser* has come to be used in the general sense of assigning a high value, a positive value, to something. Its meaning is then the same as 'appreciate', 'evaluate favourably'. But it is also used neutrally in the same sense as 'evaluate'. Some writers now use 'valorize' in these senses.

valuation *n.* **1** assigning an economic value to a commodity, real property, a service, etc. **2** a value-judgement, saying of some object or state of affairs that it is good, bad or indifferent.
3 (in logic) a valuation of a formula consists in (a) assigning 'values' (i.e. a truth-value or something denoted) to the atomic variables in the formula and (b) working out the value of the formula itself, by applying the rules laid down in the semantics for the system.

In standard propositional logic, the atomic variables are the propositional letters p,q,r. . . . A row in a truth-table assigns a 'value': True or False, to each of them. The truth-value of the whole formula is obtained by the rules laid down in the semantics for the system, for instance the rule that ~A has the value False if and only if A has the value True; A & B has the value True if and only if A has the value True and B has the value True, etc.

In first-order predicate logic, there are also individual variables x,y,z. . . . The 'values' of these are individuals from a given domain (on the objectual view) or names (on the substitutional view). Again, the rules laid down in the semantics for the system make it possible to work out the truth-value of the whole formula.

The assignment of values to the variables, and the working out of the value of the formula, is also called an interpretation of the formula. If for every interpretation the formula is true, the formula is said to be valid.

The semantics of a formal system is sometimes called the valuation of the system.

value-freedom *n.* The thesis that science is *value-free*, or *value-neutral*, means that scientific research *alone* cannot establish whether an object, an action, a state of affairs, etc. is good, bad or indifferent. Scientists can verify, for instance, that strychnine is a poison. But can they establish that it is *bad* to ingest strychnine? That would require a further assumption: that your health or life is to be valued. But that assumption is not based on scientific inquiry. So, the argument goes, scientific inquiry can yield descriptions, explanations, and predictions, but not value-judgements.

When applied to the human and social

sciences, the thesis that science is value-free has been particularly controversial. Max Weber advocated this thesis early in the twentieth century. He was critical of the frequent attempts to present particular political, moral and religious ideologies as if they were backed by the authority of science. 'There is a sharp difference between empirical knowledge and value-judgements.' 'It can never be a task for an empirical science to determine binding norms and ideals.' 'Politics does not belong in the lecture-hall.' He argued in '*Die "Objektivität" sozialwissenschaftlicher und sozialpolitischer Erkenntnis*' 1904 (The 'objectivity' of knowledge in social science and social policy) and in '*Wissenschaft als Beruf*' 1918 (Science as a profession) that value-judgements cannot have that kind of backing, on the ground that science is capable of objectivity while value-judgements are essentially subjective. But the value-freedom thesis can be seen simply as a plea for a division of labour: between the function of a scientist and that of a responsible citizen, together with a recognition that a scientist can and should remain a responsible citizen also. Opponents have rejected this, arguing that such a separation of tasks is not feasible, since values inevitably enter into all inquiry.

Defenders of the thesis have also held that it is beneficial, by discouraging the intellectually dishonest promotion of ideology in the guise of science. Opponents of the thesis (e.g. Noam Chomsky) have also held that it is harmful, by encouraging the morally dishonest refusal to take responsibility for the direction and the results of scientific inquiry.

value-judgement *n.* a statement saying of something that it is, in some respect, good or bad.

The earliest use of this general term (or, to be precise, of its German equivalent – *Werturteil*) can be traced to the nineteenth century. 'Value' primarily signified economic value. The extended sense of 'value' was an innovation. It came about as the development of theories of economic value inspired Lotze, Meinong, von Ehrenfels, and many others, to create a general theory of value. In *System der Werttheorie* 1897 (System of value theory) Ehrenfels asserted that 'by now, "ethical values" no longer sounds strange'. As recently as 1941, Norman Kemp Smith called 'value-judgement' a modern term in his *The Philosophy of David Hume*.

Note that 'value' can occur as a mistranslation of its French counterpart '*valeur*', when this word is used in the sense of '(semantic) meaning': 'la valeur d'un mot' means, roughly, 'the meaning of a word'.

value-neutrality *See* VALUE-FREEDOM.

variable *n.* in formal logic, an expression representing an unspecified member of a set. For instance, in propositional logic, the letters p,q,r, etc. are conventionally used as propositional variables, representing some proposition or other. In predicate logic, x,y,z are conventionally used as individual variables, representing some individual or other.

In contrast, constants are expressions with a specified meaning. For instance, in propositional logic, connectives like ~ (negation) and & (conjunction) are constants.

In predicate logic, a variable is said to be *bound* if it falls within the scope of its quantifier, and *free* if it is not bound. In the expression Rxy (x stands in the relation R to y), there is no quantifier, so both x and y are free variables. In the expression (∀x)(Rxy) (everything stands in the relation R to y), x is bound and y is free. In the expression (∀x)(∀y)(Rxy) (everything stands in the relation R to everything), both x and y are bound.

vat, brain in a The way the world presents itself to us depends on how it impinges on our sense-organs. Virtual reality machines exploit this fact. They use computers to generate stimulations at our peripheries which are like those produced in normal cases by seeing trees, standing in the sun, and so on. As a result we seem to see trees, feel the sun on our skin and so on, while in reality being inside a laboratory. This was anticipated in the brain-in-a-vat thought experiment, much discussed by philosophers. We imagine an envatted brain which receives at its peripheries exactly the stimulation a normal embodied brain receives, and which generates at its peripheries exactly the outputs a normally embodied brain generates (the outputs which normally lead to limb movement and so on). The brain in a vat would have subjective experiences 'of' an external world, and of moving around in it exactly like ours.

The example is used to make vivid the challenge of scepticism about the external world. If my experiences would be exactly the same were I a brain in a vat, how then can I know that I am not a brain in a vat? Some philosophers, however, deny that my experiences, and those of an envatted replica of my brain, could be the same. The argument is that the nature of experience is inextricably tied into the causal connections between one's experience and one's surroundings, and hence that, because my experiences and the envatted brain's have quite different causal connections to surroundings, our experiences would not be the same.

An ancestor to the brain-in-a-vat story is Descartes's suggestion in the first *Meditation* that the entire world is a fiction generated by an evil genius. FJ

Vattimo /ˈvatimo (It.)/, Gianni (1936–) professor of philosophy at the University of Turin since 1982, a leading representative of 'post-modern' thought in Italy. Significant for his own thought is that of Nietzsche and Heidegger. His style of writing is less enigmatic than that of his French counterparts. He uses a concept of 'weak thought' and 'weak ontology', e.g. in *La fine della modernitá* 1985 (The end of modernity). It opposes the search for stable foundations for knowledge and the strict assertion of a metaphysical theory, typical of modernist thought, and does not impose itself, but reflects the experienced world in a manner appropriate to the 'post-modern' world. One important feature of this world is the central role of mass communication, which has affected people's sense of reality. Further, multiplicity and variety characterize this world: there is no central core of reality or authority. In the mass media, we can 'switch channels' at will; in language, we regard dialects and the standard language as equally legitimate; in history, we abandon the myth of one stream of historical progress; etc. The disorientation generated by this is liberating; it helps in our quest for emancipation.

veil of appearance an important conception in many philosophies: the real world, reality, is not the world as it appears to us; the veil of appearance hides reality from view. It was Schopenhauer who imported this metaphor (the veil of Maya) from Indian thought. The world of individuality and multiplicity is ultimately illusory. If the veil can be penetrated at all and true insight attained, it is by means of metaphysical reflection or mystical experience.

Venn diagrams a kind of logic diagram, named after their inventor, the Cambridge logician John Venn (1834–1923). Their principal use is in testing the validity of inferences involving categorical propositions, but with slight modifications they can also be used in other branches of logic.

Each term is represented by a circle. Non-existence is indicated by shading. For example, *Every S is M* is represented in Figure 10.

Figure 10 A Venn diagram (1)

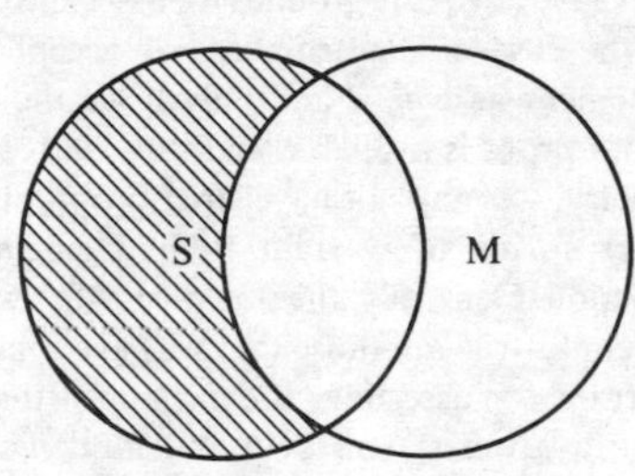

And the two premisses, *Every S is M* and *No M is P* can be combined so as to display that they imply *No S is P*, as in Figure 11.

Figure 11 A Venn diagram (2)

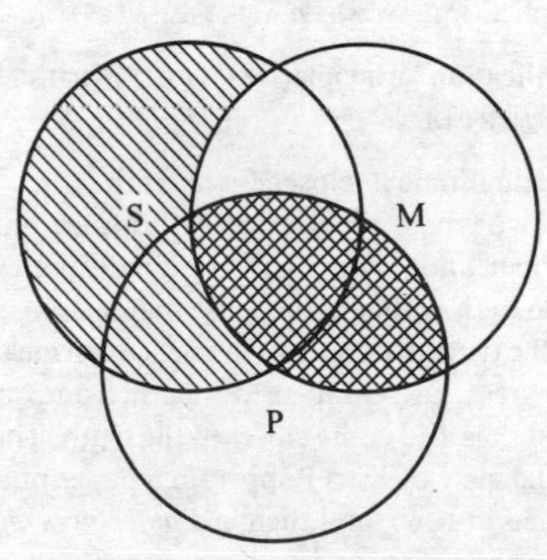

Every circle or, generally, every closed curve, intersects with every other circle or closed curve in a Venn diagram. This is in contrast to other kinds of logic diagrams, for instance those named after the Swiss mathematician Leonhard Euler (1707–83), which represent the five basic relations between extensions of terms as in Figure 12.

Figure 12 Euler diagrams

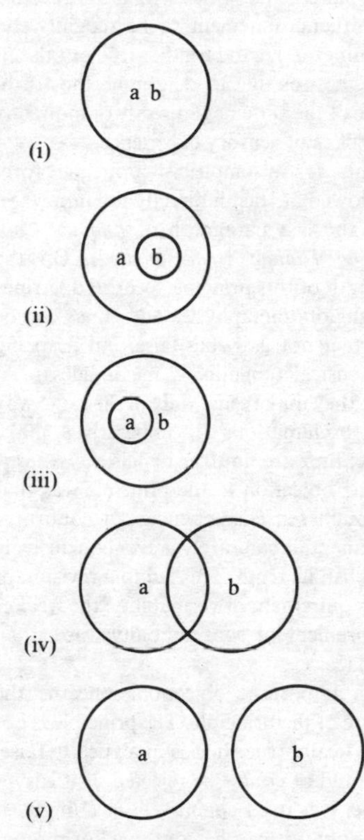

veridical /vɪˈrɪdɪkəl/ *adj.* not illusory. The word is used for sense-perceptions in which things are perceived as they are.

verifiability principle also called the verification principle, a distinctive and central tenet of logical positivism. It assumes that all (cognitively) meaningful statements can be divided into two broad classes. One contains the statements that are analytically true or analytically false, i.e. true, or false entirely in virtue of their meaning. The other contains synthetic statements. The verifiability principle formulates a criterion of meaningfulness of such statements, which is that in order for a synthetic statement to be (cognitively) meaningful, i.e. to be either true or false, it must be possible to determine the truth-value of the statement directly or indirectly by means of sensory experience.

This is an empiricist principle foreshadowed at least indirectly in Hume (see, e.g., the last paragraph of *Enquiry Concerning Human Understanding*). On the strength of this principle, central doctrines of religion, metaphysics and ethics can be rejected, not as being false, but as being nonsensical (cognitively meaningless). At best, they make sense only in the same way that exclamations or imperatives make sense; they are not true or false.

One objection to the principle was that although sense-experience can confirm a statement, it can rarely if ever conclusively establish its truth. This led to a revision of the requirement of verifiability: the weaker requirement of confirmability was put in its place.

An important objection concerns the nature of the principle. The principle is not analytically true. If it is analytically false, it should of course be rejected. If it is synthetic, it is itself cognitively meaningful if and only if it can be confirmed or disconfirmed by sense-experience. But this is not possible. So, if we accept the principle as true, we are committed to rejecting it as nonsensical. One response to this objection is that the principle is not to be accepted as true, but merely as a useful proposal, a stipulation. But this response has its own problems. Difficulties of this kind arise also with other formulations of empiricism. *See also* VERIFICATIONISM.

verifiable *adj.* capable of verification.

verification *n.* ascertaining that a proposition (a theory, an opinion, etc.) is true.

verificationism *n.* As a theory of meaning and truth, verificationism, usually associated with the name of Michael Dummett, is the view that to accept a statement as true is to have adequate grounds for asserting it. In the case of mathematics, we accept a statement as true if and only if we think that a proof is available. In other kinds of inquiry, we may not have strict proof, but other forms of warrant fulfil a similar function. Generally, the statements that we accept as true are those that we have some warrant for asserting. It can happen that both a given statement p and its denial, not-p, lack warranted assertibility. Goldbach's conjecture is an obvious example. If truth is understood in terms of warranted assertibility, there will be statements that we neither accept as true nor reject as false, since in either case the backing is absent. Therefore, on this verificationist view, the law of BIVALENCE does not have general application. *See also* ANTI-REALISM.

verification principle *See* VERIFIABILITY PRINCIPLE.

verisimilitude *n.* closeness to truth.

Two rival theories may both be imperfect, and yet one can be rationally preferable to the other in the sense that it is closer to the truth. So changes in science can mean progress, in so far as we learn from our mistakes and come closer to the truth. This is the view of Karl Popper; in a paper published in 1960, and then in *Conjectures and Refutations* 1963 and other writings, he proposed a precise analysis of verisimilitude, that is, how to spell out the conditions under which one proposition is closer to the truth than another. It is to be noted that Popper's analysis is not in terms of degrees of truth, and it makes a sharp distinction between verisimilitude and probability. His theory provoked a lively debate, in which Imre Lakatos, Pavel Tichý, Graham Oddie and others raised important objections to it.

vérité de fait; vérité de raison /veʀite də fɛ; veʀite də ʀɛzɔ̃ (Fr.)/ Fr. truth of fact/truth of reason. This pair of terms was used by Leibniz to distinguish contingent truths about matters of fact from the necessary truths of mathematics and logic.

Verstehen /fɛrˈʃteːən (Gm.)/ Gm. understanding *n.* Dilthey defined *Verstehen* as the procedure by which we infer something internal from external signs. It is an indirect way of knowing, contrasted to the direct approach of empirical science. *Verstehen* is not, however, to be identified with empathy, but with the understanding of meanings, values and purposes. Max Weber, influenced by Dilthey and Rickert, argued that, especially in the social sciences, causal explanation alone would omit crucial aspects: in order to grasp the sense of what is going on, understanding is needed.

verum sequitur ad quodlibet /ˈvɪərəm ˈsekwɪtə æd ˈkwɒdlɪbɛt/ Lat. the true follows from anything. This is the principle that a logically true proposition can be validly derived from any premiss. Like EX FALSO QUODLIBET, the principle is part of standard logical systems, but rejected in relevance logic.

vicious circle /ˈvɪʃəs ˈsɜːkl/ (Lat. *circulus vitiosus*) **1** reasoning which uses a premiss to prove (usually through a number of intermediate steps) a conclusion, but which also uses the conclusion to prove the premiss. **2** a definition in which the definiendum (the expression that is to be defined) is used in the definiens (the defining expression). Especially in mathematics and logic, impredicative definitions, in which the definiens refers to a domain of which the definiendum is an element, are viciously circular. It was Henri Poincaré who first used the expression '*cercle vicieux*' in his rejection of definitions of this particular kind.

Vicious Circle Principle 'Whatever involves all of a collection must not be one of the collection.' Influenced by Henri Poincaré, Bertrand Russell offered this in *Principia Mathematica* as one of his formulations of the principle. It was designed to obstruct the generation of paradoxes like Russell's Paradox, The Liar, etc., by ruling out concepts whose definitions involve a vicious circle.

vicissitude /vɪˈsɪsɪtjuːd/ (Lat. *vicissim* in turn) *n.* a turning, a change (of fortune). The word is not related to 'vice', 'vicious' or 'vitiate', and does not mean misfortune. The vicissitudes of life are for better, for worse, or neither.

Vico /ˈviːko (It.)/, Giambattista (1668–1744) professor at the University of Naples from 1699. Vico began as a Cartesian, but became dissatisfied with the devaluation of social and historical knowledge implicit in the Cartesian emphasis on 'clear and distinct ideas', which favours the exact sciences. He argued that those parts of the exact sciences that yield certain knowledge are only those that *we* construct. This principle, that we can know only what we have made, known as the *verum-factum* theory, leaves scope for historical knowledge. Vico can indeed be regarded as the founder of the philosophy of history as a branch of philosophical inquiry, through his *La scienza nuova* 1725 (The new science), rev. edns 1730 and 1744. The full title is *Principi di una scienza nuova d'intorno all commune nature delle nazioni* (The principles of a new science of the common nature of nations). It presents what he took to be general laws for the development of languages, laws, religions, and the rise and decline of nations, all of which is ultimately determined by divine providence for purposes that we cannot fully discern.

Vienna Circle The Vienna Circle was a group of analytical philosophers of a scientific and mathematical turn of mind, who met in Moritz Schlick's private Saturday morning seminars in Vienna from 1923, and whose outlook is generally described as logical positivism. Educated in the scientific and anti-metaphysical tradition of Mach and Poincaré, their thinking was early on influenced by Schlick's *Allgemeine Erkenntnislehre* 1918 (General theory of knowledge) and Wittgenstein's *Tractatus Logico-Philosophicus* 1921, both of which regarded the task of philosophy as the logical clarification of the basic concepts expressed in ordinary and in scientific language. Among the members of the group were Viktor Kraft and Rudolf Carnap, both interested in an analysis of the language of science, an interest best illustrated in Carnap's *Der logische Aufbau der Welt* 1928 (The logical construction of the world); Otto Neurath in economics and sociology; Herbert Feigl in psychology; and Friedrich Waismann in mathematics. The group's approach to philosophy was advertised in a pamphlet, *Wissenschaftliche Weltauffassung – der Wiener Kreis* 1929 (A scientific world-view – the Vienna Circle), in a series of congresses, and in a journal, *Erkenntnis* 1930–39. Its introduction to England was mainly due to A. J. Ayer's widely read *Language, Truth and Logic* 1936, 2nd rev. edn 1946.

The Circle's concerns were not confined to topics of academic philosophy. One of the four main objectives listed in the manifesto was educational and social reform. The reformist, welfarist and democratic political attitudes of those associated with the Circle aroused suspicion, hostility or hatred from communists, right-wing reactionaries and national socialists. Almost without exception the leading logical positivists in Austria and Germany went into exile to escape the Nazi regime, and in the 1940s the Circle had faded away as a group, though some of its ideas have continued to live in later analytic philosophy.

Their aim was a unity of science expressed in a common language to be reached by a logical analysis and, hence, a clarification of the statements made in the various sciences. In this clarification they adopted a VERIFIABILITY PRINCIPLE of meaning which accepted two kinds of statements as meaningful: the analytic ones (plus their negations), and those whose truth or falsity can be tested by perceptual experience. Other statements were rejected as unscientific and, indeed, as cognitively meaningless. These included not only some speculations in science, such as those about phlogiston and the aether, but also the whole of traditional metaphysics. However, they accepted logical and mathematical statements as meaningful, though not verifiable by perceptual experience, and this is why their positivism was distinguished from earlier forms by the epithet 'logical'.

AW

virtual *adj.* potential (in contrast to actual). In general, that which is potential but not actual is called virtual, especially if its actualization is imminent or very likely. *See also* EMINENT.

virtue *n.* **1** In a general sense, a virtue is a quality or a power. The dormitive virtue of morphine is the quality or power it has to send people to sleep.

2 In a more specific sense, a virtue is an excellence, a good quality in a person. In *Nicomachean Ethics*, 2,6 1107[a] 1ff, Aristotle defines virtue as a settled disposition of the mind which determines choice, and essentially consists in observing the mean relative to us, a mean rationally determined, that is, as a man of practical wisdom would determine it. (Practical wisdom is good sense in the conduct of one's life in general.)

Aristotle enumerates in Books 3–5 of the Nicomachean ethics a number of INTELLECTUAL VIRTUES and a number of moral virtues. *See* Table 25.

A more recent enumeration and discussion of good personal qualities is given by Hume in his *Enquiry Concerning the Principles of Morals* 1751. *See also* ARETĒ and CARDINAL VIRTUES.

virtue epistemology **1** a variety of reliabilism in the theory of knowledge. Virtue epistemology takes knowledge to be justified true belief, and regards a belief as justified if it results from a reliable process. The reliable process consists, according to virtue epistemology, in the exercise of the appropriate cognitive faculties (the senses, memory, ability to infer, etc.), given that the condition for exercising these faculties is appropriate. These cognitive faculties are called virtues because of their reliability. Thus, a person's belief that there is a pot of gold in the corner is justified if the person can see, touch, assay, etc. the substance, since the cognitive faculties are properly applied. The belief is not justified if it is based on wishful thinking, or arising from a state of inebriation.

This variety of reliabilism has been developed since the mid-1980s, especially by Ernest Sosa and Alvin Plantinga.

2 the investigation of the personal qualities that make for success in the acquisition of knowledge. In this sense, 'virtue epistemology' designates a branch of psychology and sociology.

virtue-ethics *n.* ethical theory in which the concept of virtue is fundamental, in contrast to rule- or duty-based moral theories. The relative merits of the two kinds of moral outlook have emerged as a main topic of debate in moral philosophy since the 1970s. Until then, moral philosophy had for a long time been mainly concerned with right conduct rather than good character. Traditional religious morality and Kant's moral theory are often contrasted with virtue-ethics, of which Aristotle is seen as the main philosophical representative. The contrast is sometimes marked by reserving 'morality' (and cognates) for the 'Kantian' or duty-based approach, and 'ethics' (and cognates) for the 'Aristotelian' or virtue-based one.

vitalism *n.* the view that the understanding of life requires an explanatory principle entirely different from those otherwise employed in the natural sciences: in addition to the substances and forces recognized in

Table 25 The moral virtues in the *Nicomachean Ethics*

bravery, valour (*andreia*)

self-control (temperance) in respect of bodily pleasure (*sōphrosynē*)

generosity (liberality) (*eleutheriotēs*)

magnificence (*megaloprepeia*)

self-respect or pride (proper sense of one's own worth and honour) (*megalopsychia*)

(modesty: *see* AIDŌS)

the nameless virtue of having some ambition, though not in excess

gentleness or good temper (including the ability to control one's anger) (*praotēs*)

friendliness (*philia*)

truthfulness (the medium between boastfulness and self-depreciation)

wittiness (*eutrapelia*)

justice (*dikaiosynē*)

the physical sciences there is a special life-force. This view was held by German romantic nature-philosophers, and later by Hans Driesch (1867–1941), who used the term *entelechy*. Henri Bergson (1859–1941) called it *élan vital* (vital impulse). Vitalism is not now accepted in the biological sciences.

Völkerpsychologie /ˈfœlkərpsyçologiː (Gm.)/ Gm. ethnopsychology *n.* inquiry into or theory of the intellectual and cultural manifestations characteristic of a society. This term is also the title of a major work by Wilhelm Wundt (1832–1920). In his view, the mental life of an individual cannot be fully understood unless it is seen in relation to the language, art, myth, custom, traditions, political and social institutions, etc. of the people to which the individual belongs. These are investigated at length in the ten volumes of this work, published 1900–1920. Before Wundt, the term had been used since the mid-nineteenth century. Vico, Lazarus, Steinthal and Glogau can be regarded as precursors to Wundt in this kind of inquiry.

volonté générale; volonté de tous /vɔlɔ̃te ʒeneʀal; vɔlɔ̃te də tʊs (Fr.)/ Fr. general will; will of all. Two concepts contrasted in Rousseau's *Contrat social* 1762 (Social contract). The general will, distilled from the particular wills of the citizens, is always right. The will of all, in contrast, can be wrong and when it is it ought to be disregarded. The general will is always directed towards that which is truly in the citizens' interest. The will of all, in contrast, is directed towards that which the citizens may favour even if it is not really in their interest.

Voltaire /vɔltɛːʀ (Fr.)/, François Marie Arouet de (1694–1778) French playwright, historian, polemicist and *philosophe*. His brilliant wit and his passion for justice made him perhaps the most influential of all the writers of the French Enlightenment. During a sojourn in England 1726–9, he found social and political conditions that compared favourably with French absolute monarchy, increasing pauperism, enforced religious uniformity, and strict censorship. In *Letters Concerning the English Nation* (also entitled *Philosophical Letters*), published in translation 1733 and in his original French the year after, he gave an engaging presentation of the empiricist philosophy (Locke), political constitutionalism, and deism, which all flourished in England. His *Eléments de la philosophie de Newton* 1738 contributed to the rejection in France of Cartesian physics in favour of Newton's. His classical short novel *Candide* 1759, still widely read, deals with the problem of evil, and contains many satirical allusions to the optimistic thesis of Leibniz's *Theodicy* that no world could be better than ours. In April that year, Hume wrote to Adam Smith: 'Voltaire has lately publish'd a small work called *Candide*, ou l'optimisme. It is full of sprightliness & impiety, & is indeed a satyre upon providence, under pretext of criticizing the Leibnitian system.' Unlike some of the more radical *philosophes*, Voltaire did not reject all religious belief, but he was an eloquent advocate of toleration, and uncompromising in his campaign against the crass superstitions, the brutal persecutions, and the miscarriages of justice that were committed, inspired or condoned by the Roman Catholic Church: he coined against it the famous slogan *Ecrasez l'infâme*.

voluntarism (Lat. *voluntas* will) *n.* This term is used for various theories in which the will is a central concept. For instance: **1** theological moral voluntarism: that God's arbitrary will determines what is morally good or bad. This view is also known as the Divine Command Theory; another name for it is theological moral positivism. **2** (in legal and moral philosophy) the view that obligations (legal or moral) can arise for a person only by means of a voluntary undertaking, typically by means of a promise voluntarily given by the person. In moral philosophy, this view can be found e.g. in R. P. Wolff (*In Defense of Anarchism* 1970) and R. Nozick (*Anarchy, State, and Utopia* 1974), but it is foreshadowed in Modern Natural Law theory from the mid-seventeenth century on. **3** The theory that the law of the state is the will of the sovereign legislator and derives whatever binding force it has from this fact. This view is also known as the *will-theory*; another name for it is legal positivism.

von Wright *See* WRIGHT.

voting paradoxes **1** logical problems inherent in collective decision-making. Two examples can serve as illustrations:

I. Three parties (individuals or groups) have a choice of more than two candidates, options, etc. For a simple illustration, assume that there are three, and call them A, B and C.

It is assumed that each party has a definite preference for each pair of options, so that, for instance for the pair A,B each party either prefers A to B or B to A. (This is the assumption of connectedness, i.e. that all the options stand pairwise in some preference-relation.) It is also assumed that if a party prefers A to B, and prefers B to C, then that party prefers A to C. (This is the assumption of transitivity.)

Suppose now that the three parties – call them I, II and III – have their preferences as in Table 26.

It is readily seen from this table that, collectively, there is among the three parties a majority favouring A over B, a majority favouring B over C, but a majority favouring C over A. So, although each of the individuals' preferences is transitive, their collective preferences are not.

Table 26 A voting pattern (1)

Parties	*I*	*II*	*III*
number of votes	20	20	20
most preferred option	A	B	C
second preferred option	B	C	A
least preferred option	C	A	B

This shows that the principle of majority rule, i.e. that the majority's preferred option ought to prevail, cannot be applied, since no option is preferred over the other two by a majority.

This important voting paradox was discovered by Condorcet in 1785 and named after him.

II. Another problem is that even if one candidate gets the greatest number of votes, the most preferred candidate may get the smallest number of votes, as in Table 27.

Table 27 A voting pattern (2)

Parties	*I*	*II*	*III*	*IV*
number of votes	16	19	23	2
most preferred option	A	B	C	A
second preferred option	B	A	A	C
least preferred option	C	C	B	B

Here, 18 voters put A first, 19 put B first and 23 put C first. So A gets the fewest votes, C the most votes. And yet (as can also be seen from the table) 41 prefer A to B, 35 prefer B to C, and 37 prefer A to C, so that of the 60 voters, 37 would rather have A than C.

These and similar results constitute a serious difficulty for conceptions like Rousseau's *volonté générale* and *volonté de tous*, and for the idea, often mouthed by politicians and journalists, that the electorate has given the winning political party a mandate to enact certain policies.

2 The term 'voting paradox' is also used for a different kind of problem: my vote is extremely unlikely to make any difference to the outcome. So it is rational for me not to take the trouble to vote but to spend my time more agreeably or more usefully. The same reasoning is equally valid for every potential voter. But if most or all potential voters do not vote, the outcome may be one that most or all potential voters do not desire.

vulgar *adj.* common; commonly accepted; popular. The word is now used pejoratively, but was often used without derogatory overtones by writers in the seventeenth and eighteenth centuries.

For instance, Cudworth's 'the vulgar physiology of the soul' is the common view of mental phenomena, i.e. what some writers now call 'folk psychology'. Hume's 'vulgar systems of morality' are the moral theories generally accepted at the time. Similarly, 'the vulgar' were the common people, and the expression was not necessarily disparaging.

Waismann /ˈvaɪsman (Gm.)/, Friedrich (1896–1959) a member of the Vienna Circle and an assistant to Moritz Schlick. He went into exile, lectured for a short period in Cambridge, and after 1939 in Oxford. He was close to Wittgenstein and came to be regarded as a representative of 'linguistic philosophy', gradually abandoning some of the tenets of logical positivism, including the strict distinction between analytic and synthetic statements (*The Principles of Linguistic Philosophy* 1965, 1994). Against the phenomenalist versions of logical positivism he developed a novel argument, by introducing the concept of 'open texture': statements about material objects can never be identical with a set of statements about sense-data, for the object may surprise us by showing an unexpected new feature, not previously experienced.

Watson /ˈwɒtsən/, John B(roadus) (1878–1958) professor of psychology at Johns Hopkins University until 1920. Early in his scientific career he investigated experimentally animal behaviour and learning, arriving at the view that the mind cannot be a proper object of scientific inquiry: scientific psychology has to be a study of observable behaviour. He called this view behaviourism. The method would ensure that psychological inquiry would do what we expect scientific inquiry to achieve: it will be objective, and it will enable us to predict and control behaviour. He also, to a greater extent than later behaviourists, held the view that all behaviour is analysable as complexes of stimuli and responses.

weakness of will *See* AKRASIA.

weak order(ing) a binary relation which is TRANSITIVE and strongly CONNECTED.

Weber /ˈveɪbə (Eng.); ˈveːbər (Gm.)/, Max (1864–1920) a leading figure in the intellectual and political life of Wilhelmine Germany. He held chairs at Freiburg, Heidelberg and Munich, but a nervous ailment interrupted his academic career; he was nevertheless an influential contributor to a wide range of academic and political debates. His work has had a lasting influence on modern political thought and on the development of sociology.

The greater part of his academic writing was concerned with the development and the significance of the rationalization of all spheres of life which Weber regarded as a distinctive feature of life of the modern West. The development of modern rational capitalism in particular depended on the accumulation of wealth for investment, which in turn required an impulse to accumulate far beyond what might be required for personal consumption. In *Die protestantische Ethik und der Geist des Kapitalismus* 1904–5 (*The Protestant ethic and the spirit of capitalism*) he traced the early development of this impulse to the practice of a worldly asceticism, promoted by some of the Protestant churches, which treated methodical work as a calling and limited the enjoyment of its product. This was followed by studies of the major world religions in which Weber explored the failure of non-Western civilizations to develop an equivalent capitalist spirit.

Another aspect of this perceived uniqueness of the modern West concerned the development of a distinctively rational mode of legitimation of political power. In contrast to forms of rule resting on an appeal to tradition or loyalty to a charismatic leader, Weber claimed that the West had developed a form of rule based on the rationality of impersonal rules and procedures: administrators were to be appointed on the basis of competence rather than patronage, and the validity of law was to be judged by the procedural correctness of the manner in which it had been instituted rather than its substantive content. As a result, Western governments achieved a historically unprecedented degree of administrative efficiency.

Rationalization in its broadest sense had, in Weber's view, induced a sense of 'disenchantment of the world' (*Entzauberung der Welt*), with the rejection of traditional customs and belief-systems in favour of a modern scientific world-view. In its sociopolitical aspect, rationalization led to a world that valued instrumental rationality as an end in itself, irrespective of the substantive ends it might be expected to serve. Government bureaucracy itself was an example: while it might have been developed to further the ends of government, it tended to acquire a power and a momentum that resisted political control and stifled social innovation. Weber held the view that political principles were ultimately a matter for decision and commitment, with no possible foundation in reason or in history. He argued, consistently with this, for the VALUE-FREEDOM of academic inquiry.

Weber did, however, see life in terms of a struggle between powerful individuals, groups, and – especially in the modern period – nations. If Germany was to succeed in this struggle it required political leaders capable both of overcoming the conservatism of bureaucracy and of mobilizing support around the pursuit of national objectives. Weber therefore advocated a liberal political system, not because of any belief in the rights of the individual, but rather as a means of representing competing values and securing a working accommodation between them. He also favoured mass democracy as a means of developing charismatic political leaders, capable of defining national objectives and of generating the popular support needed to curb the excessive power of the bureaucracy and impose their will on it in pursuit of those objectives. BHI

Weil /vej (Fr.); vaıl (Gm.)/, Simone (1909–43) From a well-to-do Jewish Parisian background, Weil was guided by ALAIN in her studies of philosophy. In the 1930s she became a convert, first to left-wing syndicalism – she took leave from her teaching position in a *lycée* to become a factory worker – and, after a mystical experience in 1938, to Christianity. She actively sided with the government against the rebels in the Spanish Civil War and later with the Free French against the Germans and their collaborators.

Her writings have two major themes: one sociopolitical, one religious. In her critique of modern society and its ideologies, she rejected the quasi-mystical cult of productive labour that loomed large in communist ideology and objected to the ideal of 'the revolution', as having in fact merely replaced traditional faith to become a substitute 'opium for the masses'. On the other hand, she also condemned the dehumanizing and soul-destroying effects of capitalist modes of production and consumption. There was also, in her view, a serious threat to significant human values from the increasing power of the state and of other bureaucratic structures. This growth had begun centuries ago in France, and had become truly excessive with the development of technology.

Because of its essential basis in competition and conflict, modern civilization was ill-suited to satisfy basic human needs: order, freedom, obedience, responsibility, equality, hierarchy, honour, punishment, freedom of thought, security, property, truth. Note that Weil described these items as needs, and not as rights – a concept which, in her view, serves to legitimize and entrench conflict. A remedy for the individual's rootlessness, alienation and psychological fragmentation can be found in the integrative and restoring power of genuine and meaningful labour. These views were put forward not as mere pronouncements, but supported by argument.

In her religious writings, which stressed the importance of stillness, humility, and obedience to divine love, Weil was influenced by neo-Platonic, Christian and Jewish mystical traditions.

Some of the published posthumous selections from her writings are *La Pésanteur et la grâce* 1947 (*Gravity and Grace*); *L'Enracinement* 1949 (*The Need for Roots*); and *Oppression et liberté* 1955 (*Oppression and Liberty*).

well-formed formula an expression which satisfies the formation rules of a formal system. These rules are recursive: they specify simple well-formed formulae, and the manner in which the more complex ones can be constructed from less complex ones. It is therefore always possible to determine effectively whether a formula is well-formed. The well-formed formulae are those which can be given an interpretation within the system. Of the well-formed formulae some, but not all, are axioms or theorems. According to the usual formation rules, 'p', '~p', 'p & q', 'p ⊃ (q ⊃ p)' and '(∀x)Fx' are well-formed, whereas '&p' 'p~' and 'Fx(∀x)' are ill-formed.

Weltanschauung /ˈvɛltanʃaʊʊŋ (Gm.)/ Gm. world-view; world-outlook *n.* a comprehensive philosophical view of the world and man's place in it.

Weltschmerz /ˈvɛltʃmɛrts/ Gm. 'world-pain', cosmic suffering *n.* a sorrowful mood, a generalized despondency, arising from a sense of disappointment with the world.

Wesen /ˈveɪzən (Eng.); ˈveːzən (Gm.)/ Gm. essence, nature; a being *n.*

Wesensschau /veɪzənˈʃaʊ (Eng.); ˈveːzən-sʃaʊ (Gm.) Gm. intuition of an essence *n.* the direct mental grasp of a concept or an essence; an important concept in Husserl's phenomenology.

Westermarck /ˈwestəmɑːk (Eng.); ˈvɛs-tɛrmark (Sw.)/, Edward (1862–1939) social anthropologist and moral philosopher, born in Finland, of Swedish descent. His fieldwork was in Morocco in the 1890s, and he later occupied academic positions in sociology and philosophy in London, Helsinki and Åbo. Most interesting from a philosophical point of view are the early chapters of *The Origin and Development of the Moral Ideas* 1906 and *Ethical Relativity* 1932. He attacked objectivist theories of ethics, arguing that the moral qualities we ascribe to actions and states of affairs must be understood as projections of subjective states, i.e. emotions. In some places it seems that he took ethical statements to be factual statements about our susceptibility to react to a situation with a certain emotion, and thus true or false, but there are also suggestions of an ERROR THEORY and some statements suggest the more radical NON-COGNITIVISM that Hägerström was to formulate unequivocally in 1911. Like many other anti-objectivists in ethics, Westermarck rejected ethical objectivisms, like the Christian and the Kantian ones, not only on theoretical but also on moral grounds: with an insight into the subjective nature of ethics, people would be less given to moralistic condemnation, and would become more open-minded and tolerant.

wff abbreviation of *well-formed formula.*

Whewell /ˈhjuːəl/, William (1794–1866) fellow and, from 1841, Master of Trinity College, Cambridge. Whewell was a polymath: he translated Goethe and Schiller; attacked the political radicalism of utilitarians and liberals; wrote on ethics, natural theology, gothic architecture and university reform. His main claim to fame, however, is as a physicist and a pioneer historian and philosopher of science. Influenced by Kant, Whewell claimed that geometry and the fundamental laws of (Newtonian) mechanics are necessary truths. The progress of science takes place through the incorporation of several known laws from different fields into a single, more comprehensive theory, as Galileo's and Kepler's laws had both been incorporated into Newton's theory. Whewell called this 'consilience of inductions' and claimed that no theory which achieved it had subsequently been found to be false. AM/ed.

Whichcote, Benjamin 1609–83) The guiding spirit of the Cambridge Platonists, theologically tolerant, Whichcote exercised a considerable influence through lectures and sermons. He wrote nothing for publication, and what has been published is based on his manuscripts and notes taken by his hearers. The main thrust of his ethical philosophy was rationalistic: the light of reason can discern the goodness or badness, rightness or wrongness, that belongs to an action or a state of affairs. The edge was against theological moral voluntarism, i.e. the view that the rules of morality are merely the commands of a most powerful being.

Whitehead /ˈwaɪthɛd/, Alfred North (1861–1947) English mathematician and philosopher, he became in 1884 a fellow of Trinity College, Cambridge, where he taught Bertrand Russell. Later, they jointly wrote *Principia Mathematica* 1910–13. In the period 1910–24 he taught in London, and devoted himself mainly to the philosophy of science, writing *Science and the Modern World* 1925. In 1924 he accepted a chair in philosophy at Harvard University, where he elaborated his metaphysics (*Process and Reality* 1929). It rejects the traditional metaphysical concept of substance in favour of process: what we call a thing is nothing but a recurrent confluence of events or processes.

wholism /ˈhəʊlɪzm/ *See* HOLISM.

Whorf /wɔːf/, Benjamin Lee (1897–1941) An eminent linguist and researcher of Aztec, Mayan and other languages, partly self-taught, Whorf later studied with the linguist Edward Sapir (1884–1939) and contributed importantly to the articulation of Sapir's 'principle of linguistic relativity', commonly known as the Sapir–Whorf hypothesis: the structure of one's language has a decisive influence on how one understands reality and behaves in respect to it. Different grammars produce different world-views: metaphysics depends on syntax. Whorf's support for this thesis was developed in a series of writings, collected in *Language, Thought, and Reality* (ed. John B. Carroll) 1956, by his comparing modern European languages and indigenous language, especially that of the Hopi Indians in North America. For instance, where we and our grammar structure our universe in the forms of space and time and regard time as linear, Hopi language and metaphysics does not include an equivalent to our concept of time, but has as its basis a dichotomy between the manifest (the present and past, revealed to the senses) and the unmanifest (the mental and the future).

The theory that one's grammar determines one's metaphysics had already been proposed in a less extreme form, without any implicit relativism, by Wilhelm von Humboldt (1767–1835) and other nineteenth-century linguists; it was often noted, for instance, how our subject/predicate structures run parallel to a metaphysics of substance and accident. 'If Aristotle had spoken Chinese or Dacotan, he would have had to adopt an entirely different logic or at any rate an entirely different theory of categories' (Fritz Mauthner, *Kritik der Sprache* 1902 (*Critique of Language*), vol. 3, p. 4). Whorf's research was intended to articulate the thesis more accurately and give it a secure empirical basis. The Sapir–Whorf hypothesis has, however, been the subject of much debate, and few would now accept it without qualification.

wide content *See* INTERNALISM.

William of Ockham *See* OCKHAM.

will-theory *See* VOLUNTARISM.

will to power **1** an important concept in Nietzsche's philosophy. **2** the title of a book which Nietzsche planned but subsequently decided not to write. **3** the title of a posthumous book containing a collection of unpublished manuscript notes by Nietzsche. The editors (his sister Elisabeth Förster-Nietzsche and his admirer H. Köselitz, who used the pseudonym Peter Gast) made the dubious claim that it represented the content of the book that Nietzsche had once planned to write. In fact, many of the notes probably express ideas which occurred to Nietzsche but which on further reflection he rejected or considered unfit for publication.

Windelband /ˈvɪndəlbant (Gm.)/, Wilhelm (1848–1915) German neo-Kantian philosopher, prominent also as a historian of philosophy. Having taught in various universities, he became professor in Heidelberg in 1903. In his view, Kant had developed his critical philosophy with the sciences only in mind. This was unduly narrow. The critical philosophy should be developed as a general theory of the organizing value-principles that underlie, respectively, theory, practice, and aesthetic experience. Windelband also stressed, in his *Geschichte und Naturwissenschaft* 1894 (History and natural science), published in *Präludien*, a collection of his essays, the specific character of cultural and historical inquiry, which is IDIOGRAPHIC and entirely different in aim from scientific theory which is NOMOTHETIC. This important distinction is between forms of inquiry, and not necessarily between different objects of inquiry.

wisdom *n.* one of the four CARDINAL VIRTUES.

Wisdom /ˈwɪzdəm/, (Arthur) John (Terence Dibben) (1904–93) English philosopher, who taught at Cambridge from 1934 and became professor of philosophy there in 1952; an important representative of analytical and linguistic philosophy. *Other Minds* 1952 gives a subtle analysis and refutation of sceptical doubts about knowledge-claims generally and about other minds in particular. Much of his work, strongly influenced by Wittgenstein, is meta-philosophical: a reflection on why philosophers tend to say very strange things, and on the nature of analysis and insight in philosophy. Other collections of articles of his are *Philosophy and Psycho-Analysis* 1953 and *Paradox and Discovery* 1965.

without *prep.* (in older usage) outside, external to. For instance, Locke raises the question how bodies without us can in any way affect our senses, and Berkeley contrasts that which exists only in the mind from what exists without it.

Wittgenstein /ˈvɪtgənʃtaɪn (Gm.)/, Ludwig (1889–1951) studied engineering in Berlin and Manchester, became interested in the philosophical foundations of mathematics, went to Cambridge in 1911 to work with Bertrand Russell, served in the Austrian army in the First World War, and developed the theory of language and logic which he published in 1922 in his first book, the *Tractatus Logico-Philosophicus* (transl. C. K. Ogden 1922; transl. D. F. Pears & B. F. McGuinness, 1st edn 1961, 2nd edn 1974). He then abandoned philosophy and did not return to it until the late 1920s, when he discussed his theory with some of the philosophers of the Vienna Circle. He returned to Cambridge in 1929, and after Moore's retirement was professor of philosophy there 1939–47. In this later period he elaborated a second, very different philosophy which made its first appearance in his posthumous book, *Philosophical Investigations* (transl. G. E. M. Anscombe, 1st edn 1953; 3rd edn 1969). This work has since been followed by many volumes extracted from notes which he had not prepared for publication.

His first book is plainly enigmatic, and the true significance of his later writings is even more difficult to fathom, though they have been appreciated by people without any philosophical training. All his work bears the stamp of genius, but that is not enough to explain the paradox that a philosopher who writes esoterically can convey something to readers unfamiliar with the problems with which he is dealing. Part of the explanation is that he is evidently taking apart a philosophical tradition which goes back to antiquity. That is a way of treating the past which can now be found in many other disciplines, and so, even when the set of doctrines that he is dismantling has not been identified, he can still be read with sympathy and an intuitive understanding.

His aim in the *Tractatus* was to develop a theory which would show how language succeeds in doing what it can do, and which would also demonstrate the limits of its competence. Since language expresses thought, this task can be regarded as an investigation of the limits of thought, a linguistic variant of Kant's first Critique. On the constructive side it produced two theses: the propositions of factual language are pictures, and the propositions of logic are tautologies. Its negative effect was to put moral, religious and aesthetic discourse, and even philosophical theorizing, beyond the limits of language.

When he wrote about 'the limits of language' he meant 'the limits of factual language', and so his negative conclusion could be read in two opposite ways. It could be taken as an exaltation of factual and scientific discourse with an implied devaluation of all other uses of language, including philosophical discourse: that is how the philosophers of the Vienna Circle took it. But there is also another, less iconoclastic interpretation: the other types of discourse are merely banished from the realm of factuality and the implication is not that they have no role in our lives but only that they must not be seen as failed attempts at factuality. The first interpretation is positivistic and the second is anti-scientistic.

If philosophy is not factual, it is questionable whether what the *Tractatus* offers is really a *theory* of language. Wittgenstein was always aware of the marginal position of philosophy. It had no subject-matter of its own and it lay far out on the edge of other modes of thought which did have their own subject-matters. It was a critique of thought conducted through a critique of language, and its most striking conclusion was that the great philosophical systems of the past were not really theories at all, but only varying ways of representing the world, like styles of painting. Why then was it not itself just another way of representing the world, with no authority to determine the status of its rivals?

The challenge which the *Tractatus* issued

to itself remained unanswered until the early 1930s, when Wittgenstein developed a new philosophical method and a new view of its results. Whatever the precise status of the 'theory' of the *Tractatus*, it certainly offered a single, uniform account of the essence of language. In his later work this result is rejected and so too is the method by which it was reached. He now saw language as a motley of many different practices irreducible to a single basic pattern. The character of each practice or 'language-game' is not something hidden and waiting to be revealed by logical analysis, but something lying open to view on the surface. It is simply determined by what we do with our words and by the circumstances to which we adapt our uses of them.

He had come to see his task as the description of all this material *without any attempt to theorize about it*; that gave his results an ordinary factual basis. But now the question was what made them philosophical rather than a contribution to social anthropology. His answer was an application of the leading idea of Freudian psychology to the history of thought. A philosophical theory, according to him, is an intellectual misconstrual of what we ourselves do with words. We yield to the temptation to assimilate one language-game to another and we make a theoretical mistake which has no effect on our practice but which is very deep and stubborn. We actually see our own practice in the wrong way. Consequently, it is never enough merely to be told where we went astray. We have to indulge the erroneous tendency to the full and it will then neutralize itself by its own evident absurdity.

The new method produced important results in several different fields. Its effect on the philosophy of language is most easily appreciated; the simple structures identified by the classical theories were replaced by detailed descriptions of the endless variety of our linguistic practices. The new method also aspired to transform the philosophy of mathematics and the philosophy of mind, with far-reaching consequences in epistemology and ontology. These developments are more difficult to characterize briefly.

In the philosophy of mathematics he was opposed to the idea that we discover objective truths. Any system that we seem to find is ultimately our own construction; the appearance of independent objectivity is only an effect of the procedures which come naturally to us and are then reinforced by rigorous training.

The philosophy of mind, which had been recessive in his early work, soon took the centre of the stage. There were several reasons for this development. He had always been fascinated by solipsism and his therapeutic treatment of it, which is sketchy in the *Tractatus*, is elaborated at great length in his later work. But his investigation of meaning also led him back to the philosophy of mind because any down-to-earth description of our uses of words must take account of our intentions. Now our success in carrying out our intentions stands in need of criteria, and he argued that no criteria would be available in the solipsist's private world of sensations disconnected from the physical world.

This was far more than a critique of solipsism, because traditional philosophies of perception assume that we can start from an original position in which we are able to describe our sensations in a language that is not supported by any connections with our physical environment or with other speakers of the same language in it. If Wittgenstein is right, this whole way of developing epistemology and ontology should be rejected.

His rearrangement of the accepted priorities is his great philosophical achievement. Man is the measure of all things but his standards are dependent on the world to which they are applied. DPE

Wolff /wʊlf (Eng.); vɔlf (Gm.)/, Christian (1679–1754) German rationalist Enlightenment philosopher, professor at Halle from 1706. His doctoral dissertation, presented at Leipzig in 1703 with the title 'Universal practical philosophy, set out mathematically', attracted Leibniz's interest and the two corresponded until Leibniz's death in 1716. Opposition to his rationalism from pietist colleagues led to expulsion by royal decree in 1723. He then taught at Marburg from 1723 until 1740, when the new king, Frederick II, reinstated him at Halle. Wolff acquired a remarkable reputation: he was a member of most of the major learned academies and had a large number of followers. He was a prolific writer: in one large set of volumes (1713–25), covering virtually all branches of philosophy, he 'taught philosophy to speak German'. They were based on his lectures at Halle, a new university where, in the modern manner, lectures were given in German. A larger set (1728–55), less popular in its style, presented his system in Latin. These writings were published in many editions and translations and made him the most influential academic philosopher of the eighteenth century. He established *Gründlichkeit* (thoroughness and accuracy) as an important philosophical virtue, and his influence in this respect gave German philosophy a flavour different from the French blend of elegance and superficiality. Wolff's philosophical theories were hardly original, but his systematization of the various branches of philosophy was widely adopted and determined the structure of many later theories, including Kant's.

Wollaston /ˈwʊləstən/, William (1660–1724) English philosopher, author of *The Religion of Nature Delineated* 1722, which defends a religion and an ethics based on reason alone. His natural religion relies on arguments from design to prove the existence of a divine being. He gave a special slant to his ethical rationalism – the view that our reason gives us direct insight into the rightness or wrongness of kinds of actions – by assimilating wrongdoing to the telling of a falsehood. This was criticized by Hutcheson in section 3 of *Illustrations on the Moral Sense* 1728 and by Hume in *Treatise of Human Nature* 1740, 3,1,1.

Wollstonecraft /ˈwʊlstənkrɑːft/, Mary (1759–97) English social philosopher, novelist, translator and journalist. Her travel diaries reveal her as an acute observer of social and political conditions. She was the first to reply to Burke's condemnation of the French Revolution with her *A Vindication of the Rights of Men* 1790. She also wrote *Thoughts on the Education of Daughters* 1787, and the work that has given her lasting fame, *A Vindication of the Rights of Woman* 1792. Its main argument, presented with passion and cogency, is for sexual equality. She put special emphasis on education, protesting against a system that kept women in a state of ignorance.

world in contemporary analytical philosophy the word is often used for a possible world, a possible situation. For instance, a comparison 'across worlds' is a comparison between different possible states of affairs.

Wright /vɒn ˈraɪt (Eng.); fɔn ˈvrɪgt (Sw.)/ Georg Henrik von (1916–) Finnish philosopher, professor of philosophy at Helsinki 1946–61, at Cambridge (where he succeeded Wittgenstein) 1948–51, member of the Academy of Finland from 1961. One of the key persons in charge of the posthumous editing of Wittgenstein's writings, von Wright is known also as an important philosopher in his own right. He wrote on the logic of induction, and pioneered the modern developments in DEONTIC LOGIC and in preference logic (*The Logic of Preference* 1963). *The Varieties of Goodness* 1963 offers a comprehensive conceptual analysis. *Explanation and Understanding* 1971 defends the view that the methods of natural science differ significantly from those of the humanities. In his analysis of the concept of causality, he has argued that our everyday and scientific concepts of causal connections between events depend on a more basic concept of what it is for a human agent to act (*Causality and Determinism* 1974). In later writings, some of which are collected in *The Tree of Knowledge and Other Essays* 1993, von Wright has laid more stress than is common among analytical philosophers on humanistic values, and on the limitations of science and technology. Through his writings on literature, culture and society he has gained a position as a prominent public intellectual, especially in Finland and Sweden.

Wyclif /'wɪklɪf/, John (*c.* 1328–84) A scholastic theologian, philosopher and prolific writer, Wyclif had studied at Oxford where he soon became a popular teacher and, in 1360, Master of Balliol College. He inspired the first heretical movement in England, the Lollards, and it was his supporters who first prepared an English version of the Bible (episcopally repressed in 1408).

Wyclif's theological views had contentious political implications. He argued that dominion, be it secular or ecclesiastical, could be properly exercised only if the lord, temporal or spiritual, who exercised it was in a state of grace. This also applied to the holding of church property and to the administration of sacraments. It could therefore be permissible for the secular power to take control of church property. Wyclif also attracted hostility from the orthodox establishment because of his implicit rejection of the doctrine of transubstantiation. He was led to this view through his philosophical realism, inspired by his reading of Plato and Augustine: universals exist prior to, and independently of, particulars. In Bohemia, Johan Hus adopted many of Wyclif's theological and political ideas. YP/ed.

XYZ

Xenocrates /zɛ'nɒkrətiːz/ (396–314 BC) succeeded Speusippus in 339 as head of Plato's Academy. He is said to have given a Pythagorean interpretation of the theory of Forms, and to have originated the classical division of philosophical inquiry into logic (or dialectic), physics and ethics.

Xenophanes /zɛ'nɒfəniːz/ (*c.* 570–*c.* 475 BC) ancient Greek philosopher of Colophon in Ionia who criticized traditional views of the gods and developed a rational theology to replace them.

An exile from his homeland, he travelled in Sicily reciting his poetry, in which he discussed theology, natural philosophy and human knowledge. Human knowledge cannot arrive at certain truth, but amounts only to opinion. Nevertheless, mortals can arrive at a better understanding through seeking truth. Unlike other philosophers of his age, he recognized that theories, including his own, were conjectural and liable to doubt, even if they embody the best reasoning possible on the subject.

In his philosophy of nature, Xenophanes makes the boundary between earth and sky limitless, with earth reaching downward without end. A new sun comes into being every day and moves on endlessly. Everything comes to be from earth and water, which at one time covered the Earth – as one can see from fossils of marine creatures which have been found on land – while at another time earth predominates over water in a cosmic cycle.

Xenophanes broke new ground with his radical challenge to traditional anthropomorphic religion and with his new concept of a transcendent God. Thus, he complains that the epic poets make the gods guilty of immorality, and humans in general make the gods in their own image:

But mortals think the gods are born,
and have dress and voice and form like unto them.
But if cattle and horses and lions with hands
could draw and accomplish works like men,
horses like to horses and cattle like to cattle
would draw the forms of gods and fashion bodies
just as they themselves had, every one. (fr. 15)
Africans say the gods are snub-nosed and black,
Thracians say they are blue-eyed and red-haired. (fr. 16)

But in reality there is one God, unlike humans in body and mind, who, remaining motionless, causes change by thought alone. And all of him sees, thinks, and hears. DG

Xenophon /'zɛnəfɔn/ (*c.* 430–354 BC) gives in his *Memorabilia* and in his *Apology* a picture of Socrates rather different from Plato's. He also wrote works on domestic economy, politics, history, etc. Notable is his *Cyropedia*, presenting the education of Cyrus, the Persian Emperor, as an example worth following.

yoga /'jəʊgə/ (Sans. harnessing, yoking) *n.* **1** a Hindu system of ascetic and mystical discipline which aims at developing full mastery over oneself, overcoming individual imperfections and limitations and ultimately achieving a union with the absolute. **2** a system of Hindu philosophy that underpins and explains yogic practices.

yon /jɒn/, **yonder** /'jɒndə/ over there. At the time of writing, the news media report that a leader of intellectual fashion has declared that *post-* has had its day, and is now elaborating on *trans*politics, *trans*aesthetics, *trans*economics, etc.

Many prefixes point away in some direction. Since the early 1980s, *post-* has been extremely popular ('post-feminism', 'post-industrialism', 'post-capitalism', etc.). Those keen to use this one should not forget the hyphen: if it is omitted, the innocent bystander who sees the words 'post modernism' might ask where to send it.

Post-, *trans-* and *meta-* direct us to the *after*, the *beyond* and the *above*, respectively. But these are not the only directions available. The pseud in breathless search for modish prefixes should remember that *over* has been out of fashion in recent decades, with *super-* and *hyper-* relegated to suburban shopping centres, and may be ready for a comeback, together with *sub-* and *hypo-* and other companions in the happy family of prefixes.

Zarathustra /zærə'θuːstrə/ the founder of a religion called *Zoroastrianism*, after its founder, whose name was rendered in Greek as Zoroaster. The religion is also called Mazdaism, after Ahura Mazda, the supreme deity, and in India, Parsism, since its followers there were Persians, driven into exile by Muslim persecution. The chief doctrine of the *Zend-Avesta*, the sacred writing of this faith, is dualistic: there is an opposition between good and evil, light and darkness, spirit and matter, and a constant struggle between them; man is free to decide between these and is exhorted to make the right choice: justice, purity, loving care for the good creation (plants, animals, fellow human beings). After resurrection, the righteous go to heaven and the wicked to the dark abyss.

It is usually said that Zarathustra lived in the early sixth century BC, but recent authoritative opinions place him before 1000 BC: according to some, probably around 1200 BC; according to others, a few hundred years earlier again.

Zeitgeist /'tsaitgaist (Gm.)/ (Gm. *Zeit* time +*Geist* spirit) *n.* the spirit of a time; the prevailing mentality of a particular period of time, especially as expressed in art, literature, philosophy, etc.

Note: Matthew Arnold's use of 'Time-Spirit' in *Literature and Dogma* 1873 has not taken on.

Zen a variant of Buddhism according to which various methods, partly practical, partly meditative, under the guidance of a master, will enable the disciple to achieve a 'sudden awakening' to a higher kind of insight. This tradition of Buddhism is primarily Japanese; it is to some extent antinomian and anti-intellectual, at least in some popularized versions, and this may in part explain its attraction in the West. It is sometimes, among Japanese philosophers, likened to the teachings of Heidegger.

Zeno of Citium /'ziːnəʊ əv 'sɪtɪəm/ (*c.* 332–*c.* 265 BC) the founder of Stoicism. He lectured in the painted porch (*stoa poikilē*) by the central market-place in Athens, and this is why the tradition that began with him was called Stoic. He taught that peace of mind would not be achieved by sceptical *epochē* (suspension of judgement), nor by accepting the Epicurean view that the world is without a purpose and is governed by chance. Instead, what is needed is to rise to insight into the objectively existing reason that structures all reality. With such understanding it is possible to attain APATHY, liberation from enslavement to one's passions.

Zeno of Elea /'ziːnəʊ əv 'iːlɪə/ (*fl. c.* 450 BC) ancient Greek philosopher, who supported the theory of his master Parmenides by arguing against motion and against plurality. He did this, probably in one single book. Only a few fragments remain, and our main secondary source is Aristotle's *Physics*, Book 6, chapter 9.

Against plurality, Zeno maintained that the assumption that there are many things leads to contradictory conclusions, for instance to the conclusions that things are both limited and unlimited in number. For on the one hand there are just as many things as there are, but on the other hand, between any two things there will always be a third. Furthermore, if there are many things, they must be both so small as not to have size, and so large as to be unlimited.

Zeno also argued against motion in four famous arguments: (1) according to the 'Racecourse' (or 'Dichotomy'), one cannot ever reach the finishing line, because one must first arrive at a point halfway along the course, then a point halfway along the second half of the course, and then a point halfway along the remainder, and so on, with the result that one will never arrive at the finishing line; (2) Achilles, the fleetest of men, races against the tortoise, the slowest of quadrupeds. He gives the tortoise a head start, but can never overtake the tortoise, because he must always arrive at a point just left behind by the tortoise; (3) the 'Arrow' asserts that every body is at rest when it occupies the position in which it is, but at every instant a flying arrow occupies the position in which it is; hence it is always at rest; (4) the 'Moving Rows' (or 'Stadium') uses problems about the relative motion of three rows of bodies, two of which are moving in contrary directions, to produce the absurd consequence that the same rows are moving with different speeds.

Parmenides's theory that Zeno set out to defend has the obvious implication that our senses cannot be trusted, and other arguments of Zeno were also designed to establish that point. One of them, 'the millet seed', is that if a bushel of seeds makes a noise when dropped, then the drop of a single seed must also make a noise. But it does not, and this shows that our sense of hearing is not to be trusted. This paradox can, however, be given a different interpretation. *See* MILLET SEED PARADOX.

Plato and other ancient sources generally understood Zeno to be defending Parmenides's theory that reality is one and changeless, against charges that such a theory had impossible consequences. To Parmenides's critics Zeno replies that the assumptions of plurality and motion have absurd consequences. Zeno's arguments against infinite divisibility seem to have influenced the atomists in the construction of their theory. His use of destructive arguments inspired some Sophists to practise arguing both sides of a case, and led Aristotle to call Zeno the father of dialectic. Aristotle used Zeno's arguments to sharpen his own theories of space, time and change.

DG/ed.

Zeno's paradoxes *See* ZENO OF ELEA.

zetetic /zəˈtɛtɪk/ (Gr. *zētein* to search, to inquire) *adj.*, *n.* seeking, inquiring. Sceptics take this to be what distinguishes them from the dogmatists. Occasionally the word is used as a synonym for 'sceptic'.

zeugma /ˈzjuːgmə/ (Gr. *zeugma* yoke) *n.* **1** (in grammar) a construction in which a word is associated with two others, although appropriate only to one, as in 'to wage war and peace'. **2** (in rhetoric) a figure of speech in which a word is associated with two others, in different senses, as when an eighteenth-century Protestant writer complained that Catholic maids tempt the lads 'to embrace them and their religion together'. Also used as a synonym of SYLLEPSIS.

A SHORT LIST OF TITLES IN PRINT

The list that follows is not a general guide to the philosophical literature. It serves a humbler purpose: to make it easier to find philosophical writings mentioned in the entries in this dictionary which are available in English and currently in print, and a few more. Books that are out of print can be tracked via library catalogues and second-hand booksellers. Some of the writings have been published in many different editions. There are, for instance, about twelve different editions in print in English of Machiavelli's *The Prince*, and more than twice as many of Thoreau's *Walden*. To include them all would make the list too long, so in some cases it became an unfortunate necessity to omit many good editions and mention only a few. Books available only in facsimile reprints form a special category, from which only some of the less expensive ones have been included here.

If an item, contrary to reasonable expectation, is not included in this list, the reason is most probably that it is out of print or is available only in very expensive editions or facsimile reprints. It can, of course, still be found through library catalogues or trade catalogues.

It is important to keep in mind that the list which follows gives the year of publication of a *recent* edition, likely to be available from booksellers. (In contrast, the dictionary entries as a rule give the year of *original* publication.) The year of publication advertised for recent editions can vary slightly between countries (mainly between the UK and the USA) and between hardback and paperback editions. Also, the year printed in the book may differ slightly from the year of release as reported in the trade catalogues on which it was necessary to rely in the preparation of this list. It should be remembered that the most recent printing need not be the most recent edition, since reissues of older editions are often given a new date.

For the sake of simplicity, place of publication is omitted for Oxford University Press books published in Oxford, and the same applies to certain British and North American releases with imprints such as 'Cambridge', 'Everyman', 'Penguin', 'Routledge', 'Verso'.

The main sources used to compile this list are: lists of 'Books Received' in recent philosophy journals, publishers' catalogues, and trade catalogues.

The inventory that follows should be reasonably reliable and up to date but, as we are reminded by Aristotle, it is a mark of good breeding not to expect greater precision than the subject-matter permits: for one thing, new editions are published, and published books go out of print.

As explained, the list does not provide a general guide to the philosophical literature. Such a guide could by itself be a full-length book. Nevertheless, readers may find the following information of some use.

REFERENCE WORKS: GENERAL

The Encyclopedia of Philosophy, ed. E. Craig, 10 vols, was published by Routledge in mid-1998. It supersedes the earlier *Encyclopedia of Philosophy*, ed. P. Edwards, 8 vols, published by The Macmillan Co. in 1967 (with a supplementary volume 1996) which nevertheless remains useful.

REFERENCE WORKS: BY AREA

Works of this kind are being published by various publishers. Philosophia (Munich) has published *Handbook of Metaphysics and Ontology* (2 vols). From Garland there is *Encyclopedia of Ethics* (2 vols). Blackwell has issued a series of 'Companions' to *Aesthetics*, *American Thought*, *Bioethics*, *Cognitive Science*, *Contemporary Political Philosophy*, *Continental Philosophy*, *Epistemology*, *Ethics*, *Feminist Philosophy*, *Metaphysics*, *Philosophy of Language*, *Philosophy of Law and Legal Theory*, *Philosophy of Mind*, *Philosophy of Religion*, *Philosophy of Science*. Most of these 'Companions' have entries by headwords in alphabetical order, but some contain articles grouped by subject.

REFERENCE WORKS ABOUT INDIVIDUAL PHILOSOPHERS

The series of Blackwell Philosopher Dictionaries includes a *Hegel Dictionary*, *A Hobbes Dictionary*, *A Wittgenstein Dictionary*, and works with similar titles covering Descartes, Locke, Rousseau, etc. Each contains a comprehensive bibliography.

The Library of Living Philosophers (edited 1938–81 by Paul Schilpp, and from 1981 jointly with him and later singly by Louis E. Hahn, and published by Open Court, Chicago) includes works published or shortly forthcoming about these eminent twentieth-century thinkers: Ayer, Blanshard, Broad, Buber, Carnap, Cassirer, Chisholm, Danto, Davidson, Dewey, Dummett, Einstein, Gadamer, Marjorie Greene, Hartshorne, Hintikka, Jaspers, C. I. Lewis, Marcel, Moore, Seyyed Hossein Nasr, Popper, Quine, Radhakrishnan, Ricoeur, Richard Rorty, Russell, Santayana, Sartre, P. F. Strawson, von Wright, Paul Weiss, and Whitehead. The works are entitled *The Philosophy of* [*name*] and contain an autobiography, a number of articles discussing the philosopher's work, a 'Reply to Critics', and a bibliography.

A number of reputable publishers have in recent years published collections of articles that present and discuss the thought of one philosopher and provide relevant bibliographical information. Those published by Cambridge University Press are styled 'Companions' although, strictly speaking, they are not reference works. Published so far are Companions to Aquinas, Aristotle, Bacon, Berkeley, Descartes, Duns Scotus, Foucault, Frege, Freud, Galileo, Habermas, Hegel, Heidegger, Hobbes, Hume, Husserl, James, Kant, Kierkegaard, Leibniz, Locke, Malebranche, Marx, Mill, Nietzsche, Ockham, Peirce, Plato, Plotinus, Quine, Rousseau, Russell, Sartre, Schopenhauer, Spinoza and Wittgenstein.

MONOGRAPHS ABOUT INDIVIDUAL PHILOSOPHERS

Two useful series, in which the books are of more modest size but provide good introductions to the work of individual thinkers, are the series 'Modern Masters' (Fontana) and 'Past Masters' (Oxford University Press). The volumes in the series 'Arguments of the Philosophers' (Routledge) discuss the thought of the philosophers at greater length.

HISTORIES OF PHILOSOPHY

A comprehensive standard work is Frederick Copleston, *A History of Philosophy* (9 vols, 1947–75; also in 3 vols). There are many shorter works: Bertrand Russell's well-known *History of Western Philosophy* (1945, many later edns) is readable and engaging, but not reliable in every particular.

Many works cover a certain period of the history of philosophy. Eight such works, each with different authors, are part of a series published by Oxford University Press under the collective title 'A History of Western Philosophy'. Of these eight, one deserves special mention, since it covers a relatively neglected area: B. P. Copenhaver and C. S. Schmitt, *Renaissance Philosophy*, 1992. For the same reason, mention should be made of *The Cambridge Translations of Renaissance Philosophical Texts* (ed. J. Kraye), from Cambridge University Press, which has also published collective works *The Cambridge History of Medieval Philosophy,—of Later Medieval Philosophy,—of Later Renaissance Philosophy,—of Seventeenth-Century Philosophy* (2 vols), and more are forthcoming.

The volumes that together make up the *Routledge History of Philosophy* each contain 10–15 chapters by different contributors.

W. K. C. Guthrie, *A History of Greek Philosophy*, 6 vols, Cambridge University Press, 1962–81, has established itself as the standard major work in its field.

John Passmore's survey *A Hundred Years of Philosophy* (reissued by Penguin Books in 1994), which covers the period from Mill to Wittgenstein, is continued in his *Recent Philosophers*, Duckworth, 1985.

WORKS BY INDIVIDUAL PHILOSOPHERS

All the works of the *ancient* philosophers are published in bilingual editions (Greek/English; Latin/English) in the major series called the Loeb Classical Library (Harvard University Press/Heinemann). Most ancient philosophical works are also available in other – and in some cases better – translations, for instance the ones recently published in the Oxford World Classics series, but for reasons of space only a few are listed below. For the Presocratic philosophers, *Early Greek Philosophy* (transl. J. Barnes, Penguin), is a good source. Note that this list does not aim at giving all the principal works of a philosopher, but only those which can be supposed to be currently in print.

Abelard, Peter *Dialogue of a Philosopher with a Jew and a Christian*. Toronto: Pontifical Institute of Mediaeval Studies, 1979.

——*Ethical Writings* (transl. Spade). Indianapolis, IN: Hackett, 1995.

Adorno, Theodor *The Culture Industry*. Routledge, 1991.

——*Minima moralia*. London: Verso, 1997.

——*Negative Dialectics*. Routledge, 1990; New York: Continuum, 1982.

——*The Problems of Moral Philosophy*. Oxford: Polity Press, 2000.

——E. Frenkel-Brunswik, M. Jahoda, P.

Sanford *The Authoritarian Personality*. London: Norton, 1994; New York: Norton, 1993.

Adorno, Theodor: see also Horkheimer.

Alembert, Jean d' *Preliminary Discourse to the Encyclopedia*, (Transl. R. N. Schwab). Chicago, IL: University of Chicago Press, 1995.

Alexander of Aphrodisias *On Fate*. London: Duckworth, 1984.

Althusser, Louis *For Marx*. Verso, 1996.

——*Lenin and philosophy*. New York: Monthly Review, 1978.

——*Philosophy and the Spontaneous Philosophy of the Scientists and Other Essays*. Verso, 1990.

——*Writings on Pscyhoanalysis*. New York: Columbia University Press, 1999.

Althusser, Louis and E. Balibar *Reading Capital*. Verso, 1997.

Anderson, A. R. and N. Belnap *Entailment*, 2 vols. Princeton, NJ: Princeton University Press, 1975, 1992.

Anselm of Canterbury *Monologion and Proslogion,* (transl. T. Williams). Indianapolis, IN: Hackett, 1996.

Apel, Karl-Otto *Charles Peirce: From Pragmatism to Pragmaticism*. Buffalo, NY: Prometheus, 1995.

——*Ethics and the Theory of Rationality*, Atlantic Highlands, NJ: Humanities Press, 1996.

——*From a Transcendental-Semiotic Point of View*. Manchester: Manchester University Press, 1998.

——*Towards a Transcendental Semiotics*. Atlantic Highlands, NJ: Humanities Press, 1996.

——*Towards a Transformation of Philosophy*. Milwaukee, WI: Marquette University Press, 1998.

——*Understanding and Explanation*. Cambridge, MA: MIT Press, 1984.

AQUINAS:

——*Summa contra gentiles* (ed. A. C. Pegis et al.). Notre Dame, IN: University of Notre Dame Press, 1975.

——*Summa Theologiae* (ed. T. Gilby et al.). London: Blackfriars and Eyre & Spottiswoode, 1963–75.

There are also many editions with selections from them dealing with specific topics, and of other writings of his.

Arendt, Hanna *The Human Condition*. Chicago, IL: University of Chicago Press; Magnolia, MA: Peter Smith, 1990.

——*On Revolution*. New York: Viking Penguin, 1991.

——*On Violence*. New York: Harcourt Brace, 1970.

ARISTOTLE:

The standard translation is now *The Complete Works of Aristotle: The Revised Oxford Translation*, (ed. Jonathan Barnes) Princeton, NJ: Princeton University Press, 1984. Single works by Aristotle are also available in a number of other good translations. e.g. *Nicomachean Ethics* (transl. J. Thomson, rev. H. Tredennick), Penguin, or *Nicomachean Ethics* (transl. T. Irwin, 2nd rev. ed.), Indianapolis, IN: Hackett, 2000; *Physics* (transl. R. Waterfield, ed. D. Bostock), Oxford University Press; *Politics* (transl. T. Sinclair, rev. T. J. Saunders), Penguin – to mention only a few.

Armstrong, David M. *A Materialist Theory of the Mind*, rev. edn. Routledge, 1994.

——*A World of States of Affairs*. Cambridge University Press, 1997.

——*What is a Law of Nature?* Cambridge University Press, 1985.

Arnauld, Antoine and Pierre Nicole, *Logic or the Art of Thinking*. Cambridge University Press, 1996.

Arnold, Matthew *Culture and Anarchy*. (ed.

S. Collini). Cambridge University Press, 1993; (ed. S. Lipman), New Haven, NJ: Yale University Press, 1993.

——*Literature and Dogma*. New York: AMS, 1970 (reprint).

Aron, Raymond *The Opium of the Intellectuals*. Greenwood, 1977.

Augustine *Against the Academicians* and *The Teacher* (transl. P. King). Indianapolis, IN: Hackett, 1995.

——*City of God* (transl. H. Bettenson), Penguin, 1984.

——*Confessions*. There are at least seven different translations into English in print, among them *Confessions* (transl. H. Chadwick), Oxford University Press (World's Classics), 1998, and *Confessions* (transl. R. S. Pine-Coffin), Penguin, 1970.

——*On the Free Choice of the Will* (transl. T. Williams). Indianapolis, IN: Hackett, 1993.

Austin, J. L. *How to do Things with Words*. Oxford University Press, 1976.

——*Philosophical Papers*, 3rd rev. edn. Oxford University Press, 1979.

——*Sense and Sensibilia*. New York: Oxford University Press, 1979.

Austin, John *The Province of Jurisprudence* (ed. W. D. Rumble). Cambridge University Press, 1995.

——*The Province of Jurisprudence* (ed. H. L. A. Hart). Indianapolis, IN: Hackett, 1998.

Averroes *The Incoherence of the Incoherence* (Tahafut Al-Tahafut). London: Gibb Memorial Trust, 1978.

Ayer, A. J. *The Central Questions of Philosophy*. Penguin, 1991.

——*Foundations of Empirical Knowledge*. London: Macmillan, 1964.

——*Language, Truth and Logic*. Peter Smith, 1990; New York: Dover, 1946.

——*Metaphysics and Common Sense*. London: Jones & Bartlett, 1994.

——*Philosophy in the Twentieth Century*. London: Phoenix, 1992.

——*The Problem of Knowledge*. Penguin, 1990.

Bachelard, Gaston *Dialectic of Duration*. Manchester: Clinamen Press, 2000.

——*Formation of the Scientific Spirit*. Manchester: Clinamen Press, 2001.

——*On Poetic Imagination and Reverie*. Dallas, TX: Spring Publishers, 1988.

——*The Psychoanalysis of Fire*. London: Quartet, 1999.

Bachofen, J. J. *Myth, Religion and Mother-Right*. Princeton, NJ: Princeton University Press, 1992.

BACON, FRANCIS:

Bacon's philosophical writings are published singly or in different combinations in many different editions. The ones mentioned here are only a small sample. The complete nineteenth-century edition of his works by Spedding et al. will gradually be superseded by a new one from Oxford University Press.

Bacon, Francis *Essays*. Penguin, 1986; Everyman, 1994.

——*The New Atlantis*. Kila, MT: Kessinger, 1992.

——*The New Atlantis and the Great Instauration*. Wheeling, IL: Harlan Davidson, 1989.

——*The New Organon*. Cambridge University Press, 2000.

——*Novum Organum*. Chicago, IL: Open Court, 1994.

Barnes, Jonathan *Early Greek Philosophy*. Penguin, 1987.

Barrow, John and Frank Tipler *The Anthropic Cosmological Principle*. New York: Oxford University Press, 1988.

Barth, Karl *Church Dogmatics*, 6 vols. Edinburgh: T. & T. Clark, 1956–69.

——*The Epistle to the Romans*. Magnolia, MA: Peter Smith, 1991.

Barthes, Roland *The Fashion System*.

Berkeley, CA: University of California Press, 1990.
——*Mythologies*. London: Cape, 1972.
——*The Semiotic Challenge*. Berkeley, CA: University of California Press, 1994.
Barzun, James *A Stroll with William James*. Chicago, IL: University of Chicago Press, 1984.
Bataille, Georges *Absence of Myth*. London: Verso; New York: Norton, 1994.
——*The Accursed Share*, 3 vols. New York: Zone, 1988, 1991.
——*The Inner Experience*. Albany, NY: State University of New York Press, 1988.
——*Literature and Evil*. New York: M. Boyars, 1986.
——*On Nietzsche*. Paragon, 1993.
——*Theory of Religion*. New York: Zone, 1992.
Bayle, Pierre *The Historical and Critical Dictionary. Selections* (ed. R. Popkin). Indianapolis, IN: Hackett, 1991.
Beauvoir, Simone de *The Second Sex*. Everyman, 1997.
Beccaria, Cesare *On Crimes and Punishments* (transl. D. Young). Indianapolis, IN: Hackett, 1986.
Bell, Daniel *The Coming of Post-Industrial Society*. New York: Basic Books, 1976.

BENTHAM, JEREMY:

The publication, now by Oxford University Press, of the standard edition, *The Collected Works of Jeremy Bentham*, is in progress. Among inexpensive editions can be mentioned:

Bentham, Jeremy *A Fragment on Government* (ed. J. H. Burns and H. L. A. Hart). Cambridge University Press, 1988.
——*Handbook of Political Fallacies*. New York: Harper Bros., 1962.
——*An Introduction to the Principles of Morals and Legislation*. New York: Hafner, 1970.
——*An Introduction to the Principles of Morals and Legislation*. Oxford University Press, 1996.
Bergson, Henri *Creative Evolution*. Lanham, MD: University Press of America, 1984.
——*Creative Mind: Introduction to Metaphysics*. New York: Citadel, 1992.
——*Duration and Simultaneity*, Manchester: Clinamen Press, 1999.
——*An Introduction to Metaphysics* (transl. T. E. Hulme). Indianapolis, IN: Hackett, 1998.
——*Matter and Memory*. New York: Zone, 1991.
——*The Two Sources of Morality and Religion*. Notre Dame, IN: University of Notre Dame Press, 1977.

BERKELEY, GEORGE:

The standard edition is *The Works of George Berkeley* (eds A. A. Luce and T. E. Jessop), in nine volumes. His writings are published singly or in various combinations in a number of editions, of which only a few can be mentioned here:

Berkeley, George *De Motu* (Latin and English) and *The Analyst*. Dordrecht: Kluwer, 1992.
——*Philosophical Works* (ed. M. Ayers), London: Everyman, 1993. Contains also *De Motu* (in translation), etc.
——*Principles of Human Knowledge*. (ed. J. Dancy). Oxford University Press, 1998; (ed. K. Winkler), Indianapolis, IN: Hackett, 1982.
——*Principles of Human Knowledge* and *Three Dialogues Between Hylas and Philonous* (ed. R. Woolhouse). Penguin, 1988.
——*Principles of Human Knowledge* and *Three Dialogues*. New York: Oxford University Press, 1996.

——*Three Dialogues Between Hylas and Philonous* (ed. J. Dancy). Oxford University Press 1998; (ed. D. Hilbert and J. Perry) Claremont, CA: Arete, 1994; (ed. R. M. Adams) Indianapolis, IN: Hackett, 1988.

Berlin, Isaiah *Against the Current*. New York: Viking Penguin, 1982.

——*Concepts and Categories*. Oxford University Press, 1980; New York: Viking Penguin, 1981.

——*The Crooked Timber of Humanity* (ed. Henry Hardy). London: Fontana, 1994.

——*Four Essays On Liberty*. Oxford University Press, 1990; Fontana, 1995.

——*Karl Marx*. 4th edn. Oxford University Press, 1978.

——*The Magus of the North: J. G. Hamann and the Origins of Modern Irrationalism*. London: Murray, 1993.

——*Russian Thinkers*. Penguin, 1994.

——*Vico and Herder*, London: Hogarth, 1992.

Blackburn, Simon *Spreading the Word*. Oxford University Press, 1984.

Bloch, Ernst *Natural Law and Human Dignity*. Cambridge, MA: MIT Press, 1987.

——*The Principle of Hope*, 3 vols. Oxford: Blackwell, 1986; Cambridge, MA: MIT Press, 1986.

Blondel, Maurice *Action: Essay on a Critique of Life and a Science of Practice*. Notre Dame, IN: University of Notre Dame Press, 1984.

Bodin, Jean *On Sovereignty* (ed. J. H. Franklin). Cambridge University Press, 1992.

Boethius *The Consolation of Philosophy*. Penguin, 1969.

Boethius: see also under Cicero.

Boethius of Dacia *On the Supreme Good* (and other writings). Toronto: Pontifical Institute of Mediaeval Studies, 1987.

Bonaventure *Journey of the Mind to God*. Indianapolis, IN: Hackett, 1993.

Bosanquet, Bernard *History of Aesthetics*. Charlottesville, VA: Lincoln-Rembrandt, 1986.

——*The Philosophical Theory of the State*, 2nd edn. Charlottesville, VA: Lincoln-Rembrandt, 1986; Gregg, 1993.

Bossuet, Jacques *Politics Drawn From the Very Words of Holy Scripture* (ed. P. Riley). Cambridge University Press, 1991.

Boyle, Robert *Free Enquiry into the Vulgarly Received Notion of Nature*. Cambridge University Press, 1997.

——*The Sceptical Chemist*. Kila, MT: Kessinger, 1992.

——*Selected Philosophical Papers* (ed. M. A. Stewart). Indianapolis, IN: Hackett, 1991.

Braddon-Mitchell, D. and Jackson, F., *Philosophy of Mind and Cognition*. Oxford: Blackwell, 1996.

Bradley, F. H. *Ethical Studies*. Oxford: Clarendon Press, 1988.

——*Writings on Logic and Metaphysics*. Oxford University Press, 1994.

Brentano, Franz *Descriptive Psychology*. Routledge 1995.

——*Psychology From an Empirical Standpoint*. Routledge, 1995.

Bridgman, P. W. *The Logic of Modern Physics*. Salem, NH: Ayer (reprint).

Bruno, Giordano, *Cause, Principle and Unity, and Essays on Magic*. Cambridge University Press, 1998.

Buber, Martin *I and Thou*. Edinburgh: T. & T. Clark, 1984; New York: Scribner, 1978.

——*On Intersubjectivity and Cultural Creativity*. Chicago: University of Chicago Press, 1992.

BURKE, EDMUND:

The publication by Oxford University Press of the *Writings and Speeches* is in progress. Among inexpensive editions can be mentioned the following:

Burke, Edmund *Philosophical Enquiry into the Origin of our Ideas of the Sublime and the Beautiful*. There are many editions. The details for a few of them are: Notre Dame, IN: University of Notre Dame Press, 1968; Charlottesville, VA: Lincoln-Rembrandt, 1986; Oxford: Blackwell, 1987; Oxford University Press, 1998.

——*Reflections on the Revolution in France*. There are many editions, among them: Penguin, 1982; Indianapolis, IN: Hackett, 1987; Oxford Oxford University Press, 1993.

Butler, Joseph *Analogy of Religion*. Charlottesville, VA: Lincoln-Rembrandt, 1986.

——*Fifteen Sermons Preached in the Rolls Chapel* (ed. J. Bernard). Charlottesville, VA: Lincoln-Rembrandt, 1986.

——*Five Sermons and Dissertation on the Nature of Virtue*. Indianapolis, IN: Hackett, 1985.

Cabet, Etienne *History and Constitution of the Icarian Community*. New York: AMS (reprint, 1917).

Calvin, Jean *Institutes of the Christian Religion*. Edinburgh, T. & T. Clark, 1980; Grand Rapids, MI: Eerdmans, 1989.

Campanella, Tommaso *City of the Sun*. London: Journeyman Press, 1981; Berkeley, CA: University of California Press, 1982.

——*A Defense of Galileo*. Notre Dame, IN: University of Notre Dame Press, 1994.

Camus, Albert *The Myth of Sisyphus*. Penguin, 1990; New York: Random House, 1991.

——*The Plague*. Penguin, 1989; Routledge 1990; New York: Random House, 1991.

——*The Rebel*. Penguin, 1990; New York: Random House, 1991.

Carnap, Rudolf *Meaning and Necessity*. Chicago: University of Chicago Press, 1988.

——*Philosophy and Logical Syntax*. Bristol: Thoemmes, 1996 (reprint).

Carroll, Lewis *Complete Works*. Penguin, 1988; London: Nonesuch Press, 1989; New York: Random House, 1979; Westminster, MD: McKay, 1993.

——*Pillow Problems* and *A Tangled Tale*. New York: Dover.

——*Symbolic Logic* and *The Game of Logic*. New York: Dover.

Cassirer, Ernst *Language and Myth*. New York: Dover.

——The Metaphysics of Symbolic Forms. New Haven, CT: Yale University Press, 1961.

——*The Myth of the State*. New Haven, CT: Yale University Press, 1961.

——*The Philosophy of Symbolic Forms*, 4 vols. New Haven, CT: Yale University Press, 1958–1996.

——*Substance and Function*. New York: Dover, 1995.

Castoriadis, Cornelius *The Imaginary Institution of Society*. Cambridge: Polity; Cambridge, MA: MIT Press, 1987.

——*Philosophy, Politics, Autonomy*. New York: Oxford University Press, 1991.

Chalmers, Alan *What is this thing called science?* 3rd rev. ed. St. Lucia, Q'ld: Queensland University Press; Buckingham: Open University Press; Indianapolis, IN: Hackett, 1999.

Charron, Pierre *De la Sagesse* (transl. as:) *The Wisdom of Pierre Charron*. Westport, CT: Greenwood, 1979.

Chisholm, Roderick *Brentano and Intrinsic Value*. Cambridge University Press, 1986.

Chodorow, Nancy *Feminism and Psychoanalytic Theory*. New Haven, CT: Yale University Press, 1991.

Chomsky, Noam *Cartesian Linguistics*. Lanham, MD: University Press of America, 1983.

——*Knowledge of Language*. Westport, CT: Praeger, 1986.

——*Language and Mind*. New York: Harcourt, Brace, 1972.

——*Rules and Representations*. Oxford: Blackwell; New York: Columbia University Press, 1982.

——*Syntactic Structures*. The Hague: Mouton, 1978.

Church, Alonzo *Introduction to Mathematical Logic*. Princeton, NJ: Princeton University Press, 1956.

Churchland, Patricia A. *Neurophysiology*. Cambridge, MA: MIT Press, 1989.

Churchland, Paul M. *Matter and Consciousness*. Cambridge, MA: MIT Press, 1988.

Cicero *On Duties* (ed. M. Griffin and M. Atkins). Cambridge University Press, 1991.

——*On the Nature of the Gods* (transl. H. C. McGregor) Penguin, 1972; (transl. P. Walsh), Oxford University Press, 1998.

Cicero and Boethius *On Fate* and *Consolation of Philosophy*. Warminster, Wilts.: Aris & Philips, 1991.

Cixous, Hélène and C. Clément *The Newly-Born Woman*. Minneapolis, MN: University of Minnesota Press, 1986.

Cixous, Hélène: see also Sellers.

Clarke, Samuel, *A Demonstration of the Being and Attributes of God*. Cambridge University Press, 1998.

Cohen, Morris R. *An Introduction to Logic*. Indianapolis, IN: Hackett, 1993.

——*Law and Social Order*. New Brunswick, NJ: Transaction, 1982.

——*Reason and Nature*. New York: Dover, 1978.

Collingwood, R. G. *An Essay on Metaphysics*, rev. edn. Oxford University Press, 1998.

——*Essays in Political Philosophy*. Oxford University Press, 1995.

——*The Idea of History*. rev. edn. Oxford: Clarendon Press, 1994.

——*The Idea of Nature*. New York: Galaxy Books, 1965; Westport, CT: Greenwood, 1986.

——*The New Leviathan*. rev. edn. Oxford: Clarendon Press, 1993.

——*The Principles of Art*. Oxford University Press, 1974.

——*The Principles of History and other Writings in the Philosophy of History*. Oxford: Clarendon Press, 1999.

Collins, Anthony *A Discourse Concerning Ridicule and Irony in Writing*. New York: AMS (reprint, 1970).

Condillac, Etienne Bonnot de *Philosophical Writings*. Hillsdale, NJ: Lawrence Erlbaum, 1987.

Constant, Benjamin *Political Writings*. Cambridge University Press, 1988.

Copernicus, Nicolaus *On the Revolutions*. Baltimore, MD: Johns Hopkins University Press, 1992.

Croce, Benedetto *The Aesthetic as the Science of Expression and of the Linguistic in General*. Cambridge University Press, 1992.

——*Guide to Aesthetics*. Indianapolis, IN: Hackett, 1995.

——*My Philosophy and Other Essays*. New York: AMS (reprint, 1949).

Cudworth, Ralph *A Treatise Concerning Eternal and Immutable Morality*. Cambridge University Press, 1996.

Davidson D. & Harman, G. (eds) *Semantics of Natural Language*. Dordrecht: Reidel, 1972.

Davidson, Donald *Essays on Actions and Events*. Oxford University Press, 1980.

——*Inquiries into Truth and Interpretation*. Oxford University Press, 1984.

Dawkins, Richard *The Blind Watchmaker*. rev. edn. Penguin; New York: Norton, 1996.

——*Climbing Mount Improbable*. New York: Norton, 1996; Penguin, 1997.

——*The Selfish Gene*, 2nd edn. New York: Oxford University Press, 1990.

De Ruggiero, Guido *The History of Euro-*

pean Liberalism. Magnolia, MA: Peter Smith, 1981.

Deleuze, Gilles *Bergsonism*. Cambridge, MA: MIT Press, 1988.

——*Cinema 1; Cinema 2*. London: Athlone; Minneapolis, MN: University of Minnesota Press, 1986, 1989.

——*Difference and Repetition*. London: Athlone, 1994; New York. Columbia University Press, 1993.

——*Expressionism in Philosophy: Spinoza*. Cambridge, MA: MIT Press, 1990.

——*The Fold: Leibniz and the Baroque*. London: Athlone, 1993; Minneapolis, MN: University of Minnesota Press, 1992.

——*Foucault*. London: Athlone, 1988.

——*The Logic of Sense*. London: Athlone, 1990; New York: Columbia University Press, 1993.

——*Nietzsche and Philosophy*. London: Athlone, 1986; New York, Columbia University Press, 1985.

Deleuze, Gilles and F. Guattari *Anti-Oedipus*. London: Athlone, 1984; Minneapolis, MN: University of Minnesota Press, 1983.

——*Nomadology*, new edn. Edinburgh: AK Press, 1994.

——*A Thousand Plateaus*. London: Athlone; Minneapolis, MN: University of Minnesota Press, 1987.

——*What is Philosophy?* Oxford: Blackwell; New York, Columbia University Press, 1994.

Derham, William *Physico-theology: a demonstration of the being and attributes of God from his works of creation*. Salem, NH: Ayer (reprint), 1978.

Derrida, Jacques *Aporias*. Cambridge University Press, 1994.

——*Archive Fever: A Freudian Impression*, Chicago, IL: University of Chicago Press, 1996.

——*Cinders*. Lincoln, NE: University of Nebraska Press, 1992.

——*Dissemination*. London: Athlone, 1993; Chicago, IL: University of Chicago Press, 1983.

——*Glas*. Lincoln, NE: University of Nebraska Press, 1990.

——*Margins of Philosophy*. Hemel Hempstead: Harvester; Chicago, IL: University of Chicago Press, 1984.

——*Monolingualism of the Other OR the Prosthesis of Origin*, Stanford, CA: Stanford University Press, 1999.

——*Of Grammatology*. Corrected Edition. Baltimore, MD: Johns Hopkins University Press, 1997.

——*Positions*. London: Athlone, 1987; Chicago, IL: University of Chicago Press, 1982.

——*The Postcard*. Chicago, IL: University of Chicago Press, 1987.

——*Speech and Phenomena and Other Essays on Husserl's Theory of Signs*. Evanston, IL: Northwestern University Press, 1973.

——*Spurs: Nietzsche's Styles*. Chicago, IL: University of Chicago Press, 1981.

——*The Truth in Painting*. Chicago, IL: University of Chicago Press, 1987.

——*Writing and Difference*. Routledge, 1990; Chicago, IL: University of Chicago Press, 1980.

DESCARTES, RENÉ:

Among the many translations, recent ones include:

Descartes, René *Discourse on the method of conducting one's reason and seeking the truth in the sciences*. Bilingual edn. transl. and introd. G. Heffernan, Notre Dame, IN: University of Notre Dame Press, 1994.

——*Discourse on Method and Meditations on First Philosophy*. New Haven, CT: Yale University Press, 1996.

——*Discourse on Method and Related Writings*. London: Penguin, 1999.

——*Meditations on First Philosophy*. Cambridge University Press, 1996.

——*Passions of the Soul* (transl. S. Voss). Indianapolis, IN: Hackett, 1989.

——*Philosophical Writings*, 3 vols. Cambridge University Press, 1985–91.

——*Selected Philosophical Writings*, Cambridge University Press, 1988.

——*The World and Other Writings* (ed. S. Gaukroger). Cambridge University Press, 1998.

Dewey, John *The Child and the Curriculum*. Chicago, IL: University of Chicago Press, 1990.

——*A Common Faith*. New Haven, CT: Yale University Press, 1934.

——*Democracy and Education*. New York: Prentice-Hall, 1995.

——*The Essential Dewey* (eds. L. A. Hickman and T. M. Alexander). 2 vols. Bloomington, IN: Indiana University Press, 1998.

——*Experience and Nature*. Chicago, IL: Open Court, 1977.

——*How We Think*. New York: Dover, 1997.

——*Human Nature and Conduct*. abridg, edn. Carbondale, IL: Southern Illinois University Press, 1988.

——*The School and Society*. Carbondale, IL: Southern Illinois University Press, 1988.

Diderot, Denis *Thoughts on the Interpretation of Nature and other philosophical works*. Manchester: Clinamen Press, 1999.

Driesch, Hans *Psychical Research: The Science of the Super-Normal*. Salem, NH: Ayer (reprint), 1975.

——*The Science and Philosophy of the Organism*, 2 vols. Salem, NH: Ayer (reprint).

Duhem, Pierre *The Aim and Structure of Physical Theory*. Princeton, NJ: Princeton University Press, 1991.

Dummett, Michael *Frege and Other Philosophers*. Oxford University Press, 1996.

——*Frege: Philosophy of Language*, 2nd edn. London: Duckworth, 1982; Cambridge, MA: Harvard University Press, 1993.

——*Frege: Philosophy of Mathematics*. London: Duckworth, 1991.

——*The Interpretation of Frege's Philosophy*. London: Duckworth, 1982; Cambridge, MA: Harvard University Press, 1981.

——*The Logical Basis of Metaphysics*. London: Duckworth; Cambridge, MA: Harvard University Press, 1991.

——*The Seas of Language*. Oxford: Clarendon Press, 1996.

——*Truth and Other Enigmas*. London: Duckworth, 1982; Cambridge, MA: Harvard University Press, 1978.

Durkheim, Emile *The Division of Labor in Society*. Basingstoke: Macmillan, 1985; New York: Simon & Schuster, 1997.

——*The Elementary Forms of Religious Life*. New York: Free Press, 1995.

——*The Rules of Sociological Method*. Basingstoke: Macmillan; New York: Free Press, 1982.

——*Suicide*. Routledge, 1990; New York: Free Press, 1997.

Dworkin, Ronald *Law's Empire*. London: Fontana; Cambridge, MA: Belknap/Harvard University Press, 1986.

——*Life's Dominion*. London: HarperCollins, 1995; New York: Random House, 1994.

——*A Matter of Principle*. Oxford University Press, 1986; Cambridge, MA: Harvard University Press, 1985.

——*Taking Rights Seriously*, 2nd edn. London: Duckworth, 1978; Cambridge, MA: Harvard University Press, 1977.

Eccles, John: see Popper.

Emerson, Ralph Waldo *Antislavery Writings*. New Haven, CT: Yale University Press, 1995.

Engels, Friedrich *Anti-Dühring*. London: Lawrence & Wishart, 1955; Chicago, IL: C. H. Kerr, 1984.

——*The Dialectics of Nature*. London: Lawrence & Wishart, 1977.

——*Ludwig Feuerbach and the Outcome of Classical German Philosophy*. New York: International Publishers Co. 1988.

——*Socialism: utopian and scientific*. London: Central Books, 1979; New York: Pathfinder, 1989; Chicago, IL: C. H. Kerr.

Epictetus *Enchiridion* (also *Manual*, or *Handbook*). Indianapolis, IN: Hackett; San Francisco, CA: HarperCollins, 1994.

Epicurus *The Epicurus Reader* (eds B. Inwood and L. P. Gerson). Indianapolis, IN: Hackett, 1994.

Eriugena, John *Periphyseon*. Washington, DC: Dumbarton Oaks, 1987.

Feigl, H. and W. Sellars (eds) *Readings in Philosophical Analysis*. Atascadero, CA: Ridgeview, 1981.

Fénelon, François *Telemachus* (ed. P. Riley). Cambridge University Press, 1994.

Ferguson, Adam *Essay on the History of Civil Society*. New Brunswick, NJ: Transaction, 1980.

Feuerbach, Ludwig *The Essence of Christianity* (transl. George Eliot). New York: Harper, 1957; Buffalo, NY: Prometheus, 1989.

——*Principles of the Philosophy of the Future*. Indianapolis, IN: Hackett, 1986.

Feyerabend, Paul *Against Method*, 3rd rev. edn. Verso, 1993.

——*Farewell to Reason*. Verso, 1987.

——*Philosophical Papers*, 2 vols. Cambridge University Press, 1985.

——*Philosophical Papers*, vol. 3. Cambridge University Press, 1999.

——*Three Dialogues on Knowledge*. Oxford: Blackwell, 1991.

Fichte, Johann Gottlieb *Early Philosophical Writings*. Ithaca, NY: Cornell University Press, 1992.

——*Foundations of Natural Right*. Cambridge University Press, 2000.

——*Foundations of Transcendental Philosophy*. Ithaca, NY: Cornell University Press, 1993.

——*Introductions to the* Wissenschaftslehre *and Other Writings (1797–1800)*. Indianapolis, IN: Hackett, 1994.

——*Science of Knowledge with First and Second Introductions* (transl. Heath and Lachs). Cambridge University Press, 1982.

——*Vocation of Man* (transl. Preuss). Indianapolis, IN: Hackett, 1987.

Ficino, Marsilio *Book of Life*, rev. ed. Woodstock, CO: Spring, 1994.

Filmer, Robert *Patriarcha* (ed. J. P. Somerville). Cambridge University Press, 1991.

Fletcher, Joseph *Situation Ethics: The New Morality*, Louisville, KY: Westminster/John Knox, 1966.

Fodor, J. and E. LePore (eds) *Holism: A Shopper's Guide*. Oxford: Blackwell, 1992.

Fodor, Jerry *The Elm and the Expert*. Cambridge, MA: MIT Press, 1994.

——*The Language of Thought*. Cambridge, MA: Harvard University Press, 1979.

——*Modularity of Mind*. Cambridge, MA: MIT Press, 1983.

——*Psychosemantics*. Cambridge, MA: MIT Press, 1989.

——*A Theory of Content and Other Essays*. Cambridge, MA: MIT Press, 1992.

Foucault, Michel *The Archeology of Knowledge*. Routledge, 1990; New York: Pantheon, 1982.

——*The Birth of the Clinic*. Routledge, 1990; New York: Random House, 1994.

——*Discipline and Punish*. Penguin, 1991; New York: Random House, 1979.

——*The Foucault Reader* (ed. P. Rabinow). Penguin, 1991; New York: Pantheon, 1984.

——*The History of Sexuality*, 3 vols. Penguin, 1988, 1990; New York: Random House, 1981–90.

——*Madness and Civilisation*. Routledge, 1990; New York: Random House, 1988.

——*The Order of Things*. Routledge, 1990; New York: Random House, 1994.

——*Religion and Culture*. Manchester: Manchester University Press, 1999.

Fourier, Charles *Utopian Vision: Selected Texts*. Columbia, MO: University of Missouri Press, 1984.

Frankena, William *Ethics*. 2nd edn. Englewood Cliffs, NJ: Prentice-Hall, 1988.

Frege, Gottlob Frege's well-known *Foundations of Arithmetic* and *Philosophical Writings* seem to be out of print. There is, however, *The Frege Reader* (ed. M. Beaney), Blackwell, 1997.

Freud, Sigmund *Freud's Complete Psychological Works* (ed. J. Strachey), 24 vols. New York: Norton, 1976, is the standard edition. There are also other collections of letters and papers. Many of the individual works are in print in a variety of editions.

Gadamer, Hans-Georg *Reason in the Age of Science*. Cambridge, MA: MIT Press, 1982.

——*Truth and Method*, rev. edn. London: Sheed & Ward; New York: Continuum Publishing, 1993.

Galileo *Dialogue concerning the two chief world systems*. Berkeley, CA: University of California Press, 1967; New York: Dover.

Gauthier, David *Morals By Agreement*. Oxford University Press, 1987.

Geach, Peter *Logic Matters*. Berkeley, CA: University of California Press, 1972.

Gehlen, Arnold *Man: His Nature and Place in the World*. New York: Columbia University Press, 1988.

Gellner, Ernest *Words and Things*, rev. edn. Routledge, 1979.

Geulincx, Arnold *Metaphysics*. Christoffel Press, 1999.

Gilligan, Carol *In a Different Voice*. rev. edn. Cambridge, MA: Harvard University Press, 1993.

——*Mapping the Moral Domain*. Cambridge, MA: Harvard University Press, 1990.

Gilson, Etienne *The Spirit of Mediaeval Philosophy*. Notre Dame, IN: University of Notre Dame Press, 1991.

Godwin, William *An Enquiry Concerning the Principles of Political Justice*. Penguin, 1976.

Goodman, Nelson *Fact, Fiction and Forecast*, 4th edn. Cambridge, MA: Harvard University Press, 1983.

——*Languages of Art*, 2nd edn. Indianapolis, IN: Hackett, 1988.

——*The Structure of Appearance*. Dordrecht: Kluwer, 1977.

——*Ways of Worldmaking*. Indianapolis, IN: Hackett, 1988.

Gramsci, Antonio *Letters from Prison*, 2 vols. New York. Columbia University Press, 1994.

——*Pre-Prison Writings*. Cambridge University Press, 1994.

Green, Thomas Hill *Lectures on the Principles of Political Obligation*. Cambridge University Press, 1986.

——*Prolegomena to Ethics*. Charlottesville, VA: Lincoln-Rembrandt, 1986.

Greimas, Algirdas *Narrative, semiotics and cognitive discourses*. London: Pinter Publishers, 1990.

——*Structural Semantics*. Lincoln, NE: University of Nebraska Press, 1983.

Greimas, Algirdas and J. Courtés *Semiotics and Language: An analytical dictionary*. Bloomington, IN: Indiana University Press, 1983.

Grice, Paul *Studies in the Ways of Words*. Cambridge, MA: Harvard University Press, 1991.

Grover, Dorothy *A Prosentential Theory of Truth*. Princeton, NJ: Princeton University Press, 1992.

Habermas, Jürgen *Communication and the Evolution of Society*. Cambridge: Polity 1991; Boston, MA: Beacon Press, 1979.

——*The Inclusion of the Other*. Cambridge, MA: MIT Press, 1998.

——*Justification and Application*. Cambridge: Polity, 1995; Cambridge, MA: MIT Press, 1993.

——*Knowledge and Human Interests*. Cambridge: Polity 1986; Boston, MA: Beacon Press, 1971.

——*Legitimation Crisis*. Cambridge: Polity 1988; Boston, MA: Beacon Press, 1975.

——*Moral Consciousness and Communicative Action*. Cambridge: Polity; Cambridge, MA: MIT Press, 1992.

——*On the Pragmatics of Communication*. Cambridge, MA: MIT Press, 1998.

——*The Philosophical Discourse of Modernity*. Cambridge: Polity; Cambridge, MA: MIT Press, 1990.

——*Postmetaphysical Thinking*. Cambridge: Polity, 1994.

——*The Structural Transformation of the Public Sphere*. Cambridge: Polity, 1992; Cambridge, MA: MIT Press, 1991.

——*Theory of Communicative Action*, 2 vols. Cambridge: Polity, 1986, 1989; Boston, MA: Beacon Press, 1985, 1989.

Haeckel, Ernst *The Riddle of the Universe*. Buffalo, NY: Prometheus, 1991.

Hägerström, Axel *Inquiries into the Nature of Law and Morals*. Stockholm: Almqvist & Wiksell, 1953.

Hampshire, Stuart *Morality and Conflict*. Cambridge, MA: Harvard University Press, 1984.

——*Thought and Action*, 2nd edn. Notre Dame, IN: University of Notre Dame Press, 1981.

Hanslick, Eduard *On the Musically Beautiful*. Indianapolis, IN: Hackett, 1986.

Hare, R. M. *Freedom and Reason*. Oxford: Clarendon Press, 1965.

——*The Language of Morals*. Oxford: Clarendon Press, 1964.

——*Moral Thinking*. Oxford: Clarendon Press, 1981.

——*Objective Prescriptions and Other Essays*. Oxford: Clarendon Press, 1999.

——*Sorting Out Ethics*. Oxford University Press, 1997.

Harrington, James *The Commonwealth of Oceana* (ed. J. Pocock). Cambridge University Press, 1992.

Hart, H. L. A. *The Concept of Law*. Oxford: Clarendon Press, 1961, 2nd rev. edn 1997.

——*Law, Liberty and Morality*. Oxford University Press, 1968; Stanford, CA: Stanford University Press, 1963.

——*Punishment and Responsibility*. Oxford University Press, 1968.

Hartley, David *Observations on Man*, 2 vols. Charlottesville, VA: Lincoln-Rembrandt, 1986.

Hayek, F. A. *The Constitution of Liberty*. Routledge, 1990; Chicago, IL: University of Chicago Press, 1978.

——*The Counter-Revolution of Science*. Indianapolis, IN: Liberty Fund, 1980.

——*Individualism and Economic Order*. Chicago, IL: University of Chicago Press, 1980.

——*Law, Legislation and Liberty*, 2 vols. Routledge, 1993; Chicago, IL: University of Chicago Press, 1978.

——*The Road to Serfdom*. Routledge, 1991; Chicago, IL: University of Chicago Press, 1994.

Hegel, Georg Wilhelm Friedrich *Aesthetics* (transl. T. M. Knox), 2 vols. Oxford University Press, 1988.

——*Elements of the Philosophy of Religion* (ed. P. Hodgson). Berkeley, CA: University of California Press, 1987.

——*Elements of the Philosophy of Right*.

(transl. Nisbet) Cambridge University Press, 1991.

——*Encyclopedia of the Philosophical Sciences in Outline*. New York: Continuum Publishing, 1992.

——*Lectures on the History of Philosophy* (transl. E. S. Haldane and F. Simson; intr. F. Beiser), 3 vols. Lincoln, NE: University of Nebraska Press, 1995.

——*Logic* (= Encyclopaedia I) (transl. Geraets). Indianapolis, IN: Hackett, 1991.

——*Logic* (transl. W. Wallace) (= Encyclopaedia I). 3rd rev. edn. Oxford University Press, 1975.

——*Phenomenology of Spirit* (transl. A. V. Miller). Oxford University Press; New York: Galaxy Books, 1979.

——*Philosophy of Mind* (= Encyclopaedia III) (transl. W. Wallace and A. V. Miller). Oxford University Press, 1971.

——*Philosophy of Nature,* 3 vols (= Encyclopaedia II) (transl. M. J. Petry). Atlantic Highlands, NJ: Humanities Press, 1976.

——*Philosophy of Right* (transl. Knox). Oxford: Clarendon Press; New York: Oxford University Press, 1967.

——*Science of Logic* (transl. A. V. Miller). Atlantic Highlands, NJ: Humanities Press, 1989.

Heidegger, Martin *Basic Concepts*. Bloomington, IN: Indiana University Press, 1998.

——*Basic Writings*, 2nd rev. edn. Routledge, 1993; San Francisco, CA: HarperCollins, 1992.

——*Being and Time*. Oxford: Blackwell, 1978; San Francisco, CA: HarperCollins, 1962.

——*The Concept of Time*. Oxford: Blackwell, 1992.

——*Hegel's Phenomenology of Spirit*. Bloomington, IN: Indiana University Press, 1994.

——*History of the Concept of Time: Prolegomena*. Bloomington, IN: Indiana University Press, 1992.

——*Introduction to Metaphysics*. New Haven, CT: Yale University Press, 1974.

——*Kant and the Problem of Metaphysics* (transl. R. Taft), 5th enl. edn. Bloomington, IN: Indiana University Press, 1990.

——*Nietzsche*, 2 vols. Edinburgh: T. & T. Clark, 1990; San Francisco, CA: HarperCollins, 1991.

——*On the Way to Language*. New York: HarperCollins, 1982.

——*Pathmarks*. Cambridge University Press, 1998.

——*Poetry, Language, Thought*. New York: HarperCollins, 1975.

——*The Question Concerning Technology*. New York: HarperCollins, 1982.

——*What is Called Thinking?* New York: HarperCollins, 1976.

Hempel, Carl *Philosophy of Natural Science*. Englewood Cliffs, NJ: Prentice-Hall, 1966.

Herder, Johann Gottfried *Against Pure Reason* (Selections). Minneapolis, MN: Augsburg Fortress, 1992.

Herder, Johann Gottfried see also Rousseau.

Hilbert, David *The Foundations of Geometry*, 2nd edn. Chicago, IL: Open Court, 1980.

Hobbes, Thomas *De cive* [Latin, 1 vol. and English, 1 vol.]. Oxford: Oxford University Press, 1984.

——*Human Nature and De Corpore Politico* (ed. J. C. A. Gaskin). Oxford University Press, 1994.

——*Leviathan* (ed. C. B. MacPherson). Penguin, 1982.

——*Leviathan* (ed. E. Curley). Indianapolis, IN: Hackett, 1994.

——*Leviathan* (ed. R. Tuck). rev. edn. Cambridge University Press, 1996.

——*Leviathan* (ed. J. C. A. Gaskin). Oxford: Oxford University Press, 1996.

——*On the Citizen* (ed. R. Tuck and M. Silverthorne). Cambridge University Press, 1998.

——*Philosophical Rudiments concerning Government and Society*. [This is the English version of *De cive*.]

Holbach *System of Nature*. Manchester: Clinamen Press, 1999.

Horkheimer, Max *Critique of Instrumental Reason*. New York: Continuum Publishing, 1974.

Horkheimer, M. and T. Adorno *The Dialectic of Enlightenment*. London: Verso, 1979; New York: Continuum Publishing, 1975.

Humboldt, Wilhelm von *The Limits of State Action* (transl. Burrow). Indianapolis, IN: Liberty Fund, 1993.

——*On Language*. Cambridge University Press, 1999.

——*The Sphere and Duties of Government* (transl. Coulthard). Bristol: Thoemmes, 1996).

HUME, DAVID:

There is no modern standard edition of Hume's collected works. One is being prepared: *The Clarendon Edition of the Works of David Hume*; and one volume is already in print: *An Enquiry Concerning the Principles of Morals* (ed. T. Beauchamp), Oxford University Press, 1998. There are many editions of individual works, among them the following:

Hume, David *Dialogues Concerning Natural Religion* (ed. J. M. Bell). Penguin, 1990.

——*Dialogues Concerning Natural Religion* (ed. N. Kemp Smith). London: Nelson, 1947.

——*Dialogues Concerning Natural Religion* and *The Natural History of Religion* (ed. Gaskin). Oxford University Press, 1994.

——*Enquiry Concerning Human Understanding* and *Enquiry Concerning the Principles of Morals*. The edition most frequently cited has been: *Enquiries Concerning Human Understanding and Concerning the Principles of Morals* (ed. L. A. Selby-Bigge, rev. edn. P. H. Nidditch) Oxford University Press, 1975. The second half of that volume is likely to be superseded by *An Enquiry Concerning the Principles of Morals* (ed. T. Beauchamp). Oxford University Press, 1999.

——*Essays, Moral, Political, and Literary* (ed. E. Miller). rev. edn. Indianapolis, IN: Liberty Fund, 1987.

——*The Natural History of Religion*. Stanford, CA: Stanford University Press, 1957.

——*Political Essays* (ed. Haakonssen). Cambridge University Press, 1994.

——*Treatise of Human Nature*. The edition most frequently cited has been that of L. A. Selby-Bigge, rev. by P. H. Nidditch, Oxford University Press, 1978. It is likely to be superseded by that of D. F. and M. Norton, Oxford University Press, 2000.

Husserl, Edmund *Ideas Pertaining to a Pure Phenomenology and to a Phenomenological Philosophy*. Vol. 1, The Hague: Nijhoff, 1983, vol. 2, Dordrecht: Kluwer, 1990.

Hutcheson, Francis *On Human Nature* (ed. T. Mautner). Cambridge University Press, 1993.

——*On the Nature and Conduct of the Passions*. Manchester: Clinamen Press, 2000.

——*An Inquiry into the Original of our Ideas of Beauty and Virtue*. Charlottesville, VA: Lincoln-Rembrandt, 1986 (reprint of 4th edn).

Hyppolite, Jean *Introduction to Hegel's Philosophy of History*. Gainesville, FL: University of Florida Press, 1996.

——*Logic and Existence*. Albany, NY: State University of New York Press, 1997.

Ingarden, Roman *The Ontology of the Work of Art*. Athens, OH: Ohio University Press, 1989.

Irigaray, Luce *Je, tu, nous: Toward a Culture of Difference*. Routledge, 1993.

——*Sexes and Genealogies*. New York, Columbia University Press, 1992.

——*Speculum*. Ithaca, NY: Cornell University Press, 1985.

——*This Sex Which is Not One*. Ithaca, NY: Cornell University Press, 1985.

Irigaray, Luce: see also Whitford.

Jacobi, Friedrich Heinrich *The Main Philosophical Writings and the Novel Allwill*. Toronto: McGill-Queen's University Press, 1995.

JAMES, WILLIAM:

The standard edition, *The Works of William James*, is published by Harvard University Press. What follows is only a small selection of current editions:

James, William *Essays in Radical Empiricism*. Lincoln, NE: University of Nebraska Press, 1996.

——*A Pluralistic Universe*. Lincoln, NE: University of Nebraska Press, 1997.

——*Pragmatism*. Indianapolis, IN: Hackett, 1988.

——*Principles of Psychology*. New York: Dover; Cambridge, MA: Harvard University Press, 1983.

——*Some Problems of Philosophy*. Lincoln, NE: University of Nebraska Press, 1996.

——*The Varieties of Religious Experience*. Penguin, 1983.

——*The Will to Believe and Other Essays in Popular Philosophy*. Magnolia, MA: Peter Smith, 1990.

Jaspers, Karl *The Origin and Goal of History*. Westport, CT: Greenwood, 1977.

——*Way to Wisdom*. New Haven, CT: Yale University Press, 1954.

Justinian *Institutes*. London: Duckworth; Ithaca, NY: Cornell University Press; 1987.

KANT, IMMANUEL:

The Cambridge University Press has commenced publication of *The Works of Immanuel Kant*, which can be expected to become the standard edition in English.

Kant, Immanuel *The Conflict of the Faculties* (transl. M. Gregor) Lincoln, NE: University of Nebraska Press, 1993.

——*Critique of Judgment* (transl. W. S. Pluhar). Indianapolis, IN: Hackett, 1987.

——*Critique of Practical Reason* (transl. L. W. Beck) 3rd edn. New York: Macmillan, 1993.

——*Critique of Practical Reason* (transl. M. Gregor). Cambridge University Press, 1997.

——*Critique of Practical Reason* (transl. H. W. Cassirer). Milwaukee, WI: Marquette University Press, 1998.

——*Critique of Pure Reason* (transl. N. Kemp Smith), 2nd edn. London: Macmillan, 1933; New York: St Martin, 1969.

——*Critique of Pure Reason* (transl. W. S. Pluhar). Indianapolis, IN: Hackett, 1996.

——*Critique of Pure Reason* (ed. and transl. P. Guyer and A. W. Wood). Cambridge University Press, 1998.

——*Dreams of a Spirit-Seer* is contained in the volume *Theoretical Philosophy 1755–1770*. Cambridge University Press, 1992. There is one older translation (from 1900), recently reprinted by Thoemmes Press, Bristol.

——*Grundlegung zur Metaphysik der Sitten*. Good translations currently available are: *Foundations of the Metaphysics of Morals* (transl. L.W. Beck) 2nd ed. London: Macmillan, 1990; *Groundwork of the Metaphysics of Morals* (transl. M. Gregor), Cambridge University Press,

1997; *Groundwork of the Metaphysics of Morals* (transl. H. Paton). New York: HarperCollins, 1964, also published under the title *The Moral Law*. Routledge, 1992.

——*Metaphysics of Morals* (transl. M. Gregor). Cambridge University Press, 1996.

——*Observations on the Feeling of the Beautiful and the Sublime*. Berkeley, CA: University of California Press, 1991.

——*The One Possible Basis for a Demonstration of the Existence of God* (transl. G. Treash). Lincoln, NE: University of Nebraska Press, 1994.

——*Philosophical Writings* (ed. Behler). New York: Continuum Publishing, 1992.

——*Political Writings* (ed. H. Reiss, transl. H. B. Nisbet). Cambridge University Press, 1991.

——*Practical Philosophy* (ed. M. Gregor). Cambridge: Cambridge University Press, 1997. (This volume contains the major works and shorter articles in the area of moral philosophy.)

——*Prolegomena to any Future Metaphysics* (transl. P. Carus). Indianapolis, IN: Hackett, 1977; Chicago, IL: Open Court, 1985; (ed. G. Hatfield), Cambridge: Cambridge University Press, 1997.

——*Religion and Rational Theology* (transl. George di Giovanni and Allen Wood, ed. Allen Wood). Cambridge University Press, 1996.

——*Religion within the Boundaries of Mere Reason, and other writings*. Cambridge University Press, 1998.

——*Religion Within the Limits of Reason Alone* (transl. T. M. Greene and H. H. Hudson). New York: Harper & Row, 1960.

Kelsen, Hans *Introduction to the Problems of Legal Theory* (transl. by B. L. and S. Paulson, of the first edn of *Die reine Rechtslehre* (The pure theory of law).). Oxford University Press, 1997.

——*An Introduction to the Problems of Legal Theory* (translation of the 1st edn of *The Pure Theory of Law*). Oxford University Press, 1997.

——*The Pure Theory of Law*. Magnolia, MA: Peter Smith, 1990.

Kierkegaard, Søren *The Concept of Anxiety*. Princeton, NJ: Princeton University Press, 1980.

——*The Concept of Irony*. Princeton, NJ: Princeton University Press, 1991.

——*Concluding Unscientific Postscript*, 2 vols. Princeton, NJ: Princeton University Press, 1992.

——*Either-Or* (Abridged edn). Penguin, 1992.

Kohlberg, Lawrence *Child Psychology and Childhood Education*. Penguin, 1989.

——*Moral Stages*. Farmington, CT: Karger, 1983.

Kojève, Alexandre *Introduction to the Reading of Hegel*. New York: Basic Books, 1969.

Kripke, Saul *Naming and Necessity*. Oxford: Blackwell, 1986; Cambridge, MA: Harvard University Press, 1982.

——*Wittgenstein on Rules and Private Language*. Oxford: Blackwell; Cambridge, MA: Harvard University Press, 1984.

Kristeva, Julia *Black Sun*. New York, Columbia University Press, 1992.

——*Desire in Language*. Oxford: Blackwell; New York, Columbia University Press, 1982.

——*Language the Unknown*. New York, Columbia University Press, 1991.

——*Powers of Horror*. New York, Columbia University Press, 1984.

——*Proust and the Sense of Time*. London: Faber; New York, Columbia University Press, 1993.

——*The Revolution in Poetic Language*. New York, Columbia University Press, 1984.

——*Strangers to Ourselves*. Harvester Wheatsheaf: New York, Columbia University Press, 1991.

——*Tales of Love*. New York, Columbia University Press, 1989.

Kropotkin, Peter *Mutual Aid: A Factor of Evolution*. Concord, MA: Paul & Co., 1988.

Kruschwitz, R. and R. Roberts (eds). *The Virtues: contemporary essays on moral character*. Belmont, CA: Wadsworth, 1987.

Kuhn, Thomas *The Structure of Scientific Revolutions*, 3rd edn. Chicago, IL: University of Chicago Press, 1996.

Lacan, Jacques *Ecrits*. Routledge, 1980; New York: Norton, 1982.

——*Speech and Language in Psychoanalysis*. Baltimore, MD: Johns Hopkins University Press, 1981.

La Mettrie *Machine Man and Other Writings*. Cambridge University Press, 1996.

——*Man a Machine and Man a Plant*. Indianapolis, IN: Hackett, 1994.

Lange, Friedrich Albert *The History of Materialism*. Salem, NH: Ayer, 1980 (reprint).

La Rochefoucauld, François de *Maxims* (ed. and transl. L. W. Tancock). Penguin, 1982.

Le Doeuff, Michèle *Hipparchia's Choice*. Oxford: Blackwell, 1991.

——*The Philosophical Imaginary*. Stanford, CA: Stanford University Press, 1990.

Leibniz, Gottfried Wilhelm *Discourse on Metaphysics*. This work has been published either singly or together with other philosophical writings in a number of different editions: Chicago, IL: Open Court, 1973; New York: St Martin, 1989; Manchester: Manchester University Press, 1990; Indianapolis, IN: Hackett, 1991; Everyman, 1991; etc.

——*Monadology* (ed. N. Rescher). Pittsburgh, PA: University of Pittsburgh Press, 1991; Routledge, 1992.

——*New Essays on Human Understanding*. Cambridge University Press, 1996.

——*Philosophical Essays* (transl. and ed. R. Ariew and D. Garber). Indianapolis, IN: Hackett, 1989.

——*Philosophical Texts* (transl. and ed. R. Woolhouse and R. Francks). Oxford University Press, 1998.

——*Political Writings* (ed. P. Riley). Cambridge University Press, 1988.

——*Theodicy*. Chicago, IL: Open Court, 1988.

Leopold, Aldo *Sand County Almanac*. New York: Oxford University Press, 1989; Oxford University Press, 1992; New York: Ballantine, 1986.

Leslie, John *The End of the World*. Routledge, 1998.

——*Modern Cosmology and Philosophy*, Buffalo, NY: Prometheus, 1988.

——*Universes*. Routledge, 1990.

Lessing, Gotthold Ephraim *Laocoon*. Baltimore, MD: Johns Hopkins University Press, 1984.

——*Nathan the Wise*. New York: Continuum Publishing, 1992.

——*Theological Writings* (incl. *The Education of the Human Race*). Stanford, CA: Stanford University Press, 1957.

Lévi-Strauss, Claude *The Elementary Structures of Kinship*. Boston, MA: Beacon Press, 1969.

——*The Savage Mind*. Chicago, IL: University of Chicago Press, 1968.

——*Tristes Tropiques*. Penguin, 1992.

Levinas, Emmanuel *Alterity and Transcendence*. London: Athlone, 1999.

——*Basic Philosophical Writings*. Bloomington, IN: Indiana University Press, 1996.

——*Collected Philosophical Papers*. The Hague: Nijhoff, 1987.

——*Entre nous. Essays on Thinking-of-the-*

Other. New York: Columbia University Press, 1998.
——*Outside the Subject*. London: Athlone, 1993.
——*Proper Names*. London: Athlone, 1997.
——*Totality and Infinity*. Pittsburgh, PA: Duquesne University Press, 1969.
Lewis, C. I. *Mind and the World Order*. New York: Dover, 1990.
Lewis, David *Counterfactuals*. Oxford: Blackwell 1981.
——*On the Plurality of Worlds*. Oxford: Blackwell, 1986.
——*Papers in Metaphysics and Epistemology*. Cambridge University Press, 1999.
——*Philosophical Papers*, 2 vols. New York: Oxford University Press, 1983, 1987.
Lichtenberg, Georg Christoph *Aphorisms*. Penguin, 1990.
Lloyd, Genevieve *The Man of Reason*. 2nd edn. Routledge; Minneapolis, MN: University of Minnesota Press, 1993.

LOCKE, JOHN:
The Clarendon Edition of the Works of John Locke contains all his correspondence, but as yet few of his published works. There are many other editions of his collected and single works. Those edited by Laslett and Nidditch (listed below) deserve special mention because of the high standard of editing.

Locke, John *An Essay Concerning Human Understanding* (ed. P. Nidditch). Oxford University Press, 1975. [Parts of Nidditch's editorial material, including his useful glossary, are omitted from the current paperback edn, 1979].
——*A Letter Concerning Toleration*. Indianapolis, IN: Hackett, 1993.
——*The Reasonableness of Christianity* (ed. J. Higgins-Biddle). Oxford University Press, 1999.
——*Some Thoughts Concerning Education* (ed. Yolton), Oxford University Press, 2000.
——*Two Treatises of Government* (ed. P. Laslett). Cambridge University Press, 1988.
Longinus *On Great Writing* (= *On the Sublime*). Indianapolis, IN: Hackett, 1991.
Lovejoy, Arthur *The Great Chain of Being*. Cambridge, MA: Harvard University Press, 1972.
Lovelock, James *The Ages of Gaia*, 2nd edn. Oxford University Press. 1995; New York: Norton, 1988.
——*Gaia*. Oxford University Press, 1995.
Lucretius *De rerum natura* is variously transl. as *On the Nature of Things*, *On the Nature of the Universe*, *The Way Things Are,* etc.
Lukács, George *History and Class-Consciousness*. Cambridge, MA: MIT Press, 1971; London: Merlin Press, 1975.
Lyotard, Jean-François *The Differend*. Manchester: Manchester University Press; Minneapolis, MN: University of Minnesota Press, 1984.
——*The Inhuman*. Cambridge: Polity, 1993; Stanford, CA: Stanford University Press, 1992.
——*The Libidinal Economy*. London: Athlone; Bloomington, IN: Indiana University Press, 1993.
——*The Post-Modern Condition*. Manchester: Manchester University Press; Minneapolis, MN: University of Minnesota Press, 1984.
Mach, Ernst *Contributions to the Analysis of Sensations*. Chicago, IL: Open Court, 1987.
Machiavelli, Niccolò *The Discourses*. Penguin, 1984; Oxford University Press, 1997; Chicago, IL: University of Chicago Press, 1996.
——*The Prince*. There are at least a dozen different editions in English currently in print: Penguin, Oxford, Cambridge, Hackett, Chicago, Yale, etc.

——*Selected Political Writings* (ed. D. Wootton). Indianapolis, IN: Hackett, 1994.

McGuinness, Brian *Wittgenstein, A Life: Young Ludwig (1889–1921)*. London: Duckworth, 1988.

MacIntyre, Alasdair *After Virtue*, 2nd edn. Notre Dame, IN: University of Notre Dame Press, 1984.

——*Against the Self-images of the Age*. London: Duckworth, 1995.

——*Dependent Rational Animals*, London: Duckworth, 1999.

——*A Short History of Ethics*. (1967) rev. ed. Routledge, 1998; Notre Dame, IN: University of Notre Dame Press, 1997.

——*Three Rival Versions of Moral Enquiry*. London: Duckworth, 1991; Notre Dame, IN: University of Notre Dame Press, 1992.

——*Whose Justice? Which Rationality?* London: Duckworth, 1988; Notre Dame, IN: University of Notre Dame Press, 1989.

Mackie, John *The Cement of the Universe*. Oxford: Clarendon Press, 1999.

——*Ethics: Inventing right and wrong*. Penguin, 1990.

——*The Miracle of Theism.* Oxford University Press, 1982.

MacPherson, C. B. *The Life and Times of Liberal Democracy*. Oxford University Press, 1977.

——*The Political Theory of Possessive Individualism*. Oxford University Press, 1964.

——*The Real World of Democracy*. Oxford University Press, 1972; Concord, Ontario: House of Anansi, 1992.

McTaggart, J. M. E. *The Nature of Existence*. Cambridge University Press, 1988.

——*Some Dogmas of Religion* (1930). Bristol: Thoemmes, 1997.

Maimonides, Moses, *Guide for the Perplexed* Penguin, 1988; Indianapolis, IN: Hackett, 1995.

Maistre, Joseph de *Considerations on France* (ed. R. Lebrun). Cambridge University Press, 1995.

Malebranche, Nicholas *Dialogues on Metaphysics and on Religion*. Cambridge University Press, 1997.

——*Philosophical Selections*. Indianapolis, IN: Hackett, 1992.

——*The Search after Truth*. Cambridge University Press, 1997.

——*Treatise on Ethics* (transl. C. Walton). Dordrecht: Kluwer, 1992.

——*Treatise on Nature and Grace* (translation of the 1st edition, by P. Riley). Oxford University Press, 1992.

Malthus, Thomas *Essay on the Principle of Population* (ed. D. Winch). Cambridge University Press, 1992.

Mandeville, Bernard *The Fable of the Bees*, 2 vols. Indianapolis, IN: Liberty Fund, 1988. [Reprint of the F. B. Kaye edition, Oxford, 1924].

——*The Fable of the Bees* (ed. P. Harth). Penguin, 1989; (ed. E. J. Hundert) Indianapolis, IN: Hackett, 1997.

Marcus, Ruth Barcan *Modalities*. New York: Oxford University Press, 1995.

Marcuse, Herbert *Eros and Civilization*. Routledge, 1998.

——*One-Dimensional Man*. Routledge, 1991.

——*Reason and Revolution*, 2nd ed. Routledge, 2000; Amherst, NY: Humanity Press, 1999.

Maritain, Jacques *Man and the State*, rev. edn. Washington, DC: Catholic University of America Press, 1998.

Marsilius (Marsiglio) of Padua *Defensor minor* [a shorter statement of *Defensor pacis*] and *De translatione imperii*. Cambridge University Press, 1993.

——*Defensor Pacis*. University of Toronto Press, 1980.

Marx, Karl *Capital,* 3 vols. Penguin, 1992–3.

——*A Contribution to the Critique of Polit-*

ical Economy. London: Lawrence & Wishart, 1983; New York: International Publishers, 1989.

——*Economic and Philosophical Manuscripts.* New York: International Publishers, 1964.

——*Grundrisse: Foundations of the Critique of Political Economy*. Penguin, 1993.

——*Selected Writings* (ed. D. McLellan). Oxford University Press, 1977.

Marx, K. and F. Engels *The Communist Manifesto*. There are about 15 different separate editions of this short work, e.g. *The Communist Manifesto* (ed. D. McLellan), Oxford University Press, 1998, but it is also included in many collections.

Mendelssohn, Moses *Jerusalem*. Hanover, NH: University Press of New England, 1983.

——*Philosophical writings*. Cambridge University Press, 1997.

——*Phädon*. Salem, NH: Ayer (reprint).

Merleau-Ponty, Maurice *The Phenomenology of Perception*. Routledge, 1995.

——*The Structure of Behavior*. Pittsburgh, PA: Duquesne University Press, 1983.

MILL, JOHN STUART:

The standard edition is *The Collected Works of John Stuart Mill*, published by the University of Toronto Press. There is a vast number of editions of single works, of which only a few can be mentioned here:

Mill, John Stuart *Autobiography*. Penguin, 1990.

Mill's *On Liberty, Utilitarianism*, and other writings on ethics and politics are available in a number of different editions, in various combinations. Among them are:

Mill, John Stuart *On Liberty* (ed. Gertrude Himmelfarb). Penguin, 1974.

——*On Liberty* (ed. E. Alexander), Broadview Press, 1999.

——*On Liberty, Considerations on Representative Government*. Everyman, 1992.

——*On Liberty, The Subjection of Women, Chapters on Socialism* (ed. Stefan Collini). Cambridge University Press, 1989.

——*On Liberty, Utilitarianism, Considerations on Representative Government, The Subjection of Women* (ed. John Gray). Oxford University Press (World's Classics), 1998.

——*Principles of Political Economy*. Oxford University Press, 1994.

——*Principles of Political Economy*. Penguin, 1986.

——*The Subjection of Women*. Indianapolis, IN: Hackett, 1988.

——*System of Logic*. 8th edn. Charlottesville, VA: Lincoln-Rembrandt, 1986 (reprint).

——*Three Essays On Religion*. Amherst, NY: Prometheus, 1998.

——*Utilitarianism*. (ed. R. Crisp). Oxford University Press, 1998.

——*Utilitarianism, On Liberty, Considerations on Representative Government*. Everyman, 1993.

——*Utilitarianism, in: J. S. Mill and Jeremy Bentham, Utilitarianism and Other Essays* (ed. A. Ryan). Penguin, 1987.

Millett, Kate *Sexual Politics*. Penguin; Virago, 1996.

Monk, Ray *Wittgenstein: The Duty of Genius*. London: Cape; New York: Free Press, 1990; Penguin, 1991.

Montaigne, Michel de *An Apology for Raymond Sebond* (ed. M. A. Screech). Penguin, 1987.

——*The Complete Essays* (ed. D. Frame). Stanford, CA: Stanford University Press, 1988.

——*The Complete Essays* (ed. M. A. Screech). Penguin, 1993.

——*The Complete Works* (ed. D. Frame). Stanford, CA: Stanford University Press, 1987.

Montesquieu *The Persian Letters*. Penguin, 1973.
——*The Spirit of the Laws*. Cambridge University Press, 1989.
Moore, G. E. *Principia Ethica*, 2nd rev. edn. Cambridge University Press, 1993.
More, Henry *Enthusiasmus triumphatus, or a brief discourse of the nature, causes, kinds, and cure of enthusiasm*. New York: AMS Press (reprint), 1966.
——*Manual of Metaphysics*, Part I. Hildesheim: Olms, 1995.
More, Thomas *Utopia*. There are at least 15 editions currently in print, including Cambridge, Marquette and Yale university presses; Dover, 1997; Everyman 1994; Hackett, 1999; St Martin's, 1995; Transaction, 1996.
Mortley, R. (ed.) *French Philosophers in Conversation*. Routledge, 1991.
Naess, Arne *Ecology, Community, and Lifestyle*. Cambridge University Press, 1990.
Nagel, Ernest *The Structure of Science*. Indianapolis, IN: Hackett, 1979.
Nagel, Thomas *Equality and Partiality*. New York: Oxford University Press, 1991.
——*The Last Word*. New York: Oxford University Press, 1997.
——*Mortal Questions*. Cambridge University Press, 1991.
——*The Possibility of Altruism*. Princeton, NJ: Princeton University Press, 1991.
——*The View from Nowhere*. New York: Oxford University Press, 1989.
Newton, Isaac *The Principia: Mathematical Principles of Natural Philosophy*. Berkeley and Los Angeles, CA: University of California Press, 1999.
——*Optics*. New York: Dover, 1952.

NIETZSCHE, FRIEDRICH:
Of the many translations into English, those made since the mid-century are on the whole to be preferred. An edition of the complete works in English translation is being published by Stanford University Press.

Nietzsche, Friedrich *Beyond Good and Evil* (transl. R. J. Hollingdale). Penguin, 1990; (transl. W. Kaufmann). New York, Random House, 1989.
——*The Birth of Tragedy* (transl. S. Whiteside). Penguin, 1994.
——*The Birth of Tragedy and Other Writings* (ed. and transl. R. Guess and R. Speirs). Cambridge University Press, 1999.
——*Daybreak* (ed. and transl. M. Clark and B. Leiter). Cambridge University Press, 1997.
——*Daybreak* (transl. R. J. Hollingdale). Cambridge University Press, 1997.
——*Ecce homo* (transl. R. J. Hollingdale). Penguin, 1993.
——*The Gay Science* (transl. W. Kaufmann). New York: Random House, 1974.
——*Genealogy of Morals* (transl. W. Kaufmann). New York: Random House, 1989.
——*Human, All Too Human* (transl. M. Faber) Penguin, 1994; (transl. R. J. Hollingdale) Cambridge University Press, 1996; (transl. M. Faber, with S. Lehmann) Lincoln, NE: University of Nebraska Press 1996; (transl. G. Handwerk) Stanford, CA: Stanford University Press, 1997.
——*On the Genealogy of Morality* (transl. M. Clark and A. Swensen). Indianapolis, IN: Hackett, 1998.
——*On the Genealogy of Morals* (transl. D. Smith) Oxford University Press, 1997.
——*On the Genealogy of Morality and Other Writings* (ed. K. Ansell-Pearson and C. Diethe). Cambridge University Press, 1994.
——*Thus Spake Zarathustra* (transl. R. J. Hollingdale) Penguin, 1969; (transl. W.

Kaufmann) New York: Random House, 1995.
——*Twilight of the Idols* (transl. R. Polt). Indianapolis, IN: Hackett, 1997.
——*Twilight of the Idols* (transl. D. Lange), Oxford University Press, 1998.
——*Twilight of the Idols* and *The Anti-Christ* (transl. R. J. Hollingdale). Penguin, 1990.
——*Unfashionable Observations* (transl. R. T. Gray). Stanford, CA: Stanford University Press; Cambridge University Press, 1998.
——*Untimely Meditations* (transl. R. J. Hollingdale). Cambridge University Press, 1997.
Nozick, Robert *Anarchy, State, and Utopia*. New York: Basic Books, 1977; Oxford: Blackwell, 1978.
——*The Examined Life*. New York: Simon & Schuster, 1990.
——*The Nature of Rationality*. Princeton, NJ: Princeton University Press, 1993.
——*Philosophical Explanations*. Cambridge, MA: Belknap/Harvard University Press, 1981; Oxford University Press, 1984.
Nussbaum, Martha *The Fragility of Goodness*. Cambridge University Press, 1986.
——*Love's Knowledge*. Oxford University Press; New York: Oxford University Press, 1992.
——*The Therapy of Desire*. Princeton, NJ: Princeton University Press, 1994.
Oakeshott, Michael *Experience and Its Modes*. Cambridge University Press, 1986.
——*On Human Conduct*. Oxford University Press, 1991.
——*Rationalism in Politics*. Indianapolis, IN: Liberty Fund, 1991.
Ockham, William of *Philosophical Writings* 2nd ed. Indianapolis, IN: Hackett, 1990.
——*A Letter to the Friars Minor and Other Writings* (transl. J. Kilcullen). Cambirdge University Press, 1995.
——*Predestination* (and other writings) (eds N. Kretzmann and M. M. Adams), 2nd edn. Indianapolis, IN: Hackett, 1983.
——*A Short Discourse on Tyrannical Government* (ed. A. S. McGrade). Cambridge University Press, 1992.
Okin, Susan Muller *Women in Western Political Thought*, rev. edn. Princeton, NJ: Princeton University Press, 1992.
Olivecrona, Karl *Law as Fact*, 2nd rev. edn. London: Stevens, 1971.
Owen, Robert *A New View of Society*, Penguin, 1991.
Paine, Thomas *The Age of Reason*. New York: Random House, 1993.
——*Common Sense*. Penguin, 1982.
——*Common Sense and The Rights of Man*. New York: NAL-Dutton, 1984.
——*Political Writings* (ed. B. Kuklick). Cambridge University Press, 1989.
——*The Rights of Man*. There are many editions, e.g. with the imprints Citadel, 1977; Everyman, 1993; Hackett, 1992; Penguin, 1984.
Paley, William *Natural Theology, or evidences of the existence and attributes of the Deity, collected from the appearance of nature*. Lincoln-Rembrandt, 1986.
Pareto, Vilfredo *The Mind and Society* (1935). New York: AMS (reprint).
Parfit, Derek *Reasons and Persons*. Oxford University Press, 1984, rev. edn. 1987.
Pascal, Blaise *Pensées* (transl. A. J. Krailsheimer). Penguin, 1970.
——*Pensées and Other Writings* (transl. Honor Levi). New York: Oxford University Press, 1995.
——*Provincial Letters* (transl. A. J. Krailsheimer). Penguin, 1967.
Passmore, John *A Hundred Years of Philosophy*. Penguin, 1994.
——*Man's Responsibility for Nature*. London: Duckworth, 1974.
——*The Perfectibility of Man*. London:

Duckworth, 1972; New York: Macmillan, 1978.
——*Recent Philosophers*. London: Duckworth, 1988; Chicago, IL: Open Court, 1991.
——*Science and Its Critics*. London: Duckworth, 1978.
——*Serious Art*. London: Duckworth; Chicago, IL: Open Court, 1991.
Pears, D. F. *The False Prison*, vol. 1, 1987; vol. 2, 1988. Oxford University Press.
Pico della Mirandola, Giovanni *On the Dignity of Man and other writings*. Indianapolis, IN: Hackett, 1998.
Plantinga, Alvin *God, Freedom and Evil*. Grand Rapids, MI: Eerdmans, 1978.
——*The Nature of Necessity*. Oxford: Clarendon Press, 1979.

PLATO:
The standard edition of the complete dialogues was for a long time *The Dialogues of Plato* (transl. Jowett), Oxford University Press. More recent are *The Collected Dialogues of Plato* edited by E. Hamilton and H. Cairns, New York: Pantheon (The Bollingen Series), and Plato: *The Complete Works* (eds. J. M. Cooper and D. S. Hutchinson). All the dialogues are also available in various translations, separately or in volumes containing a select few. For instance, there are about ten different versions of *The Republic* in print (including recent translations by D. Lee (Penguin) and R. Waterfield (Oxford University Press); at least four different versions of *Gorgias*; at least five of *Phaedo*; at least six of *Theaetetus*, etc. Limitations of space preclude a full enumeration.

Popper, Karl *Conjectures and Refutations*, Routledge, 1990.
——*The Logic of Scientific Discovery*. Routledge, 1992.
——*Objective Knowledge*. Oxford University Press, 1972.
——*The Open Society and Its Enemies*, 2 vols. Routledge, 1990, 1968; Princeton, NJ: Princeton University Press, 1966, 1991.
——*The Open Universe* (part of *Postscript* to *The Logic of Scientific Discovery*). Routledge, 1991.
——*The Poverty of Historicism*, 2nd edn. Routledge, 1991.
——*Unended Quest*. Routledge, 1992.
Popper, Karl and John Eccles *The Self and Its Brain*. Routledge, 1990.
Price, Richard *Review of the Principal Questions and Difficulties in Morals*. Charlottesville, VA: Lincoln-Rembrandt, 1986.
Priest, Graham *In Contradiction*. Dordrecht: Kluwer, 1987.
Priest, G., R. Sylvan and J. Norman (eds.). *Paraconsistent Logic*. Munich: Philosophia, 1989.
Priestley, Joseph *Political Writings*. Cambridge University Press, 1993.
Proclus *Elements of Theology*. Edmonds, WA: Holmes, 1993.
——*Platonic Theology*. Yonkers, NY: Selene, 1985, 1986.
Proudhon, Pierre-Joseph *What is Property?* Cambridge University Press, 1994.
Pufendorf, Samuel *On the Duty of Man and Citizen* (ed. J. Tully, transl. M. Silverthorne). Cambridge University Press, 1991.
Putnam, Hilary *Mathematics, Matter, and Method* (= Philosophical Papers, vol. 1). Cambridge University Press, 1979.
——*Mind, Language and Reality* (= Philosophical Papers, vol. 2). Cambridge University Press, 1979.
——*Realism with a Human Face*. Cambridge, MA: Harvard University Press, 1992.
——*Reason, Truth and History* (= Philosophical Papers, vol. 3). Cambridge University Press, 1991.

——*Renewing Philosophy*. Cambridge, MA: Harvard University Press, 1993.
——*Representation and Reality*. Cambridge, MA: MIT Press, 1991.
——*Words and Life*. Cambridge, MA: Harvard University Press, 1994.
Quine, Willard van Orman *From a Logical Point of View*, 2nd rev. edn. Cambridge, MA: Harvard University Press, 1980.
——*From Stimulus to Science*. Cambridge, MA: Harvard University Press, 1995.
——*Ontological Relativity and Other Essays*. New York: Columbia University Press, 1977.
——*Pursuit of Truth,* rev. edn. Cambridge, MA: Harvard University Press, 1992.
——*Quiddities*. Cambridge, MA: Harvard University Press, 1987; Penguin, 1990.
——*The Roots of Reference*. Chicago, IL: Open Court, 1990.
——*The Ways of Paradox*, rev. edn. Cambridge, MA: Harvard University Press, 1976.
——*Word and Object*. Cambridge, MA: MIT Press, 1960.
Ramsey, Frank *Philosophical Papers*. Cambridge University Press, 1990.
Rawls, John *Political Liberalism*. New York: Columbia University Press, 1993.
——*Collected Papers*. Cambridge, MA: Harvard University Press, 1999.
Read, Stephen *Relevant Logic*. Oxford: Blackwell, 1989.
Reichenbach, Hans *The Direction of Time*, Berkeley, CA: University of California Press, 1991.
Reid, Thomas *Essays on the Active Powers of Man*. Charlottesville, VA: Lincoln-Rembrandt, 1986.
——*Essays on the Intellectual Powers of Man*. Charlottesville, VA: Lincoln-Rembrandt, 1986.
——*An Inquiry into the Human Mind on the Principles of Common Sense*. (ed. D. Brookes). Edinburgh: Edinburgh University Press; University Park, PA: Pennsylvania University Press, 1997.
——*An Inquiry into the Human Mind on the Principles of Common Sense*, Indianapolis, IN: Hackett, 1983.
——*Practical Ethics* (ed. K. Haakonssen). Princeton, NJ: Princeton University Press, 1990.
——*Thomas Reid on the Animate Creation* (ed. P. Wood). Edinburgh: Edinburgh University Press, 1996; University Park, PA: Pennsylvania State University Press, 1995.
Reinhold, Karl Leonhard *The Fundamental Concepts and Principles of Ethics*, in: Roehr, S., *A Primer on German Enlightenment*. Columbia, MO: University of Missouri Press, 1995.
Rickert, Heinrich *The Limits of Concept Formation in Natural Science* (abridged edn). Cambridge University Press, 1986.
Ricoeur, Paul *Critique and Conviction*. Oxford: Polity, 1997.
——*Fallible Man*. Bronx, NY: Fordham University Press, 1986.
——*Freedom and Nature: the Voluntary and the Involuntary*. Evanston, IL: Northwestern University Press, 1966.
——*Freud and Philosophy*. New Haven, CT: Yale University Press, 1977.
——*From Text to Action*. Evanston, IL: Northwestern University Press; London: Athlone, 1991.
——*The Just* (transl. D. Pellauer). Chicago, IL: The University of Chicago Press, 2000.
——*Oneself as an Other*. Chicago, IL: University of Chicago Press, 1992.
——*The Rule of Metaphor*. Routledge, 1994; University of Toronto Press, 1987.
——*Time and Narrative*, 3 vols. Chicago, IL: University of Chicago Press, 1990.
Robinson, John *Honest to God*. London: SCM Press; Louisville, KY: Westminster/John Knox, 1963.

Rorty, Richard *Consequences of Pragmatism*. Hemel Hempstead: Harvester Press, 1982.
——*Contingency, Irony and Solidarity*. Cambridge University Press, 1989.
——*Essays on Heidegger and Others* (= Philosophical Papers, vol. 2). Cambridge University Press, 1991.
——*The Linguistic Turn: Recent Essays in Metaphilosophy* (1st edn 1967). 2nd rev. edn. Chicago, IL: University of Chicago Press, 1992.
——*Objectivity, Relativism and Truth* (= Philosophical Papers, vol. 1). Cambridge University Press, 1991.
——*Philosophy and the Mirror of Nature*. Princeton, NJ: Princeton University Press, 1979; Oxford: Blackwell, 1998.
——*Truth and Progress* (= Philosophical Papers, vol. 3). Cambridge University Press, 1998.
Rosmini, Antonio: Translations by D. Cleary and T. Watson of many of his works have in recent years been published by Rosmini House, Durham.
Ross, W. D. *The Right and the Good*. Indianapolis, IN: Hackett, 1988.

ROUSSEAU, JEAN-JACQUES:
Of the two translations of *Emile*, Bloom's is more recent. A number of different editions contain Rousseau's shorter works in various combinations.

Rousseau, Jean-Jacques *A Discourse on Inequality* (transl. M. Cranston). Penguin, 1984.
——*Discourse on the Origin of Inequality* (transl. D. Cress). Indianapolis, IN: Hackett, 1992.
——*Discourse on the Origin of Inequality*. Oxford University Press, 1994.
——*Emile* (transl. A. Bloom). New York: Basic Books, 1979; Penguin, 1991.
——*Emile* (transl. B. Foxley). Everyman, 1992.
——*Government of Poland*. Indianapolis, IN: Hackett, 1985.
——*La nouvelle Héloïse, or Julie, or The New Eloise*. University Park, PA: Pennsylvania State University Press, 1987.
——*On the Origin of Language*. Chicago, IL: University of Chicago Press, 1986.
——*On the Social Contract* (transl. Masters), New York: St Martin's, 1978.
——*Reveries of the Solitary Walker* (transl. C. Butterworth). Indianapolis, IN: Hackett, 1992.
——*The Reveries of the Solitary Walker* (transl. P. France). Penguin, 1979.
——*The Social Contract* (transl. M. Cranston). Penguin, 1984.
——*The Social Contract* (transl. D. Cress), rev. edn. Indianapolis, IN: Hackett, 1988.
Rousseau, J.-J. and J. G. Herder *Essay on the Origin of Languages and First and Second Discourses*. New York: HarperCollins, 1988.

Ruskin, John *Modern Painters*, London: Deutsch, 1989.

RUSSELL, BERTRAND:
He wrote 70 books and a vast number of articles, occasional writings and letters, all of which have been or will be published in the McMaster University edition of *The Collected Papers of Bertrand Russell*.

Russell, Bertrand *The Analysis of Matter*. Routledge, 1992.
——*The Analysis of Mind*. Routledge, 1992.
——*A History of Western Philosophy*. Routledge, 1991; New York: Simon & Schuster, 1984.
——*Human Knowledge: Its Scope and Limits*. Routledge, 1992.
——*An Inquiry into Meaning and Truth*. Routledge, 1992.

——*Introduction to Mathematical Philosophy* (1919). Routledge, 1993.
——*Logic and Knowledge: Essays 1901–1950*. Routledge, 1988.
——*My Philosophical Development*. Routledge; New York: Dover, 1993.
——*Our Knowledge of the External World*. Routledge, 1993.
——*Philosophical Essays*. Routledge, 1994.
——*The Philosophy of Logical Atomism*. Chicago, IL: Open Court, 1986.
——*Principles of Mathematics* (1903). Routledge, 1992.
——*Principles of Social Reconstruction*, London: Routledge, 1997.
——*The Problems of Philosophy*. Oxford University Press, 1967; Indianapolis, IN: Hackett, 1990.
——*Religion and Science*. New York: Oxford University Press, 1997.
——*Sceptical Essays*. Routledge, 1992.
——*Why I am Not a Christian*. Routledge, 1992; New York: Simon & Schuster, 1967.
Russell, B. & A. N. Whitehead: see Whitehead.
Ryle, Gilbert *The Concept of Mind* (1949). Penguin, 1990; Chicago, IL: University of Chicago Press, 1984.
Sade (Marquis de) *Justine, Philosophy in the Bedroom, and Other Writings*. London: Arrow Books; New York: Grove Atlantic, 1990.
Salt, Henry *Animals' Rights*, rev. edn. Arundel, West Sussex: Centaur Press, 1980.
Sanches, Francisco *Quod nihil scitur*. Cambridge University Press, 1988.
Sandel, Michael *Liberalism and the Limits of Justice*. Cambridge University Press, 1988.
Santayana, George *Reason in Science*. New York: Dover, 1983.
——*The Sense of Beauty*. Cambridge. MA: MIT Press, 1988.
Sartre, Jean-Paul *Being and Nothingness*. Routledge, 1990; New York: Pocket Books, 1996.
——*Critique of Dialectical Reason*, 2 vols. Verso, 1982, 1991.
——*Existentialism and Humanism*. London: Eyre Methuen, 1974.
——*No Exit*. Routledge, 1990; New York: Random House, 1989.
——*The Psychology of the Imagination*. New York: Citadel Press, 1986.
——*Saint Genet*. London: Heinemann, 1988; New York: Pantheon, 1983.
——*Sketch for a Theory of the Emotions*. Routledge, 1994.
Savigny, Friedrich Carl von *On the Vocation of Our Age for Legislation and Jurisprudence*. Salem, NH: Ayer (reprint).
Scheler, Max *Formalism in Ethics and Non-Formal Ethics of Values*. Evanston, IL: Northwestern University Press, 1973.
——*On Feeling, Knowing, and Valuing*. Chicago, IL: University of Chicago Press, 1992.
——*Ressentiment*. Milwaukee, WI: Marquette University Press, 1994.
——*Selected Philosophical Essays*. Evanston, IL: Northwestern University Press, 1973.
Schelling, F. W. J. *On the History of Modern Philosophy* (transl. A. Bowie). Cambridge University Press, 1994.
——*System of Transcendental Idealism*. Charlottesville, VA: University Press of Virginia, 1988.
Schiller, Friedrich *Essays*. New York: Continuum Publishing, 1993.
——*On the Aesthetic Education of Man*. Oxford University Press, 1982.
Schleiermacher, Friedrich *Hermeneutics and Criticism*. Cambridge University Press, 1998.
——*On Religion*. Cambridge University Press, 1996.
——*On Religion. Speeches to Its Cultured Despisers*. Cambridge University Press;

Louisville, KY: Westminster/John Knox, 1994.

Schlick, Moritz *General Theory of Knowledge*. Chicago, IL: Open Court, 1985.

Schopenhauer, Arthur *Essays and Aphorisms* (transl. R. J. Hollingdale). Penguin, 1973.

——*On the Basis of Morality* (transl. E. J. F. Payne). Indianapolis, IN: Hackett, 1996.

——*On the Fourfold Root of the Principle of Sufficient Reason*. Chicago, IL: Open Court, 1977.

——*On Vision and Colours* (transl. E. J. F. Payne). Providence, RI: Berg, 1994.

——*Prize Essay on the Freedom of the Will* (transl. E. J. Payne). Cambridge University Press, 1999.

——*Schopenhauer's Early Fourfold Root* (transl. and ed. F. C. White). Aldershot: Ashgate, 1997.

——*The World as Will and Representation* (transl. E. J. F. Payne). New York: Dover, 1967.

Schütz, Alfred *The Structures of the Life-World*. Evanston, IL: Northwestern University Press, 1989.

Schwarz, Stephen (ed.) *Naming, Necessity, and Natural Kinds*. Ithaca: NY: Cornell University Press, 1977.

Schweitzer, Albert *Philosophy of Civilization*. Buffalo, NY: Prometheus, 1987.

——*The Teaching of Reverence for Life*. New York: Holt, Rinehart & Winston, 1965; New York: Irvington, 1992.

Searle, John *The Construction of Social Reality*. Penguin; New York: Free Press, 1995.

——*Expression and Meaning: Studies in the theory of speech acts*. Cambridge University Press, 1986.

——*Intentionality: An Essay in the Philosophy of Mind*. Cambridge University Press, 1983.

——*Minds, Brains and Science*. Cambridge, MA: Harvard University Press, 1985; Penguin, 1992.

——*The Rediscovery of the Mind*. Cambridge, MA: MIT Press, 1994.

——*Speech Acts: An Essay in the Philosophy of Language*. Cambridge University Press, 1970.

Sellars, Wilfrid *Science and Metaphysics*. Atascadero, CA: Ridgeview, 1993.

——*Science, Perception and Reality*. Atascadero, CA: Ridgeview, 1991.

Sellers, Susan (ed.) *The Hélène Cixous Reader*. Routledge, 1994.

Sextus Empiricus *Against the Ethicists* (transl. R. Bett). Oxford University Press, 1997.

——*Against the Grammarians* (transl. D. Blank). Oxford University Press, 1998.

——*Outlines of Pyrrhonism* (transl. B. Mates). Oxford University Press, 1996.

——*Outlines of Scepticism* (transl. J. Annas and J. Barnes). Cambridge University Press, 2000.

Shaftesbury (Anthony Ashley Cooper, Third Earl of Shaftesbury) *Characteristicks of Men, Manners, Opinions, Times* (ed. P. Ayres). Cambridge University Press, 1999.

——*Characteristicks of Men, Manners, Opinions, Times* (ed. L. Klein). Oxford University Press, 1999.

The complete works, in English together with translations into German, are being published by Frommann-Holzboog, Stuttgart.

Shelley, Percy Bysshe *The Necessity of Atheism* (and other writings). Everyman, 1995.

Sidgwick, Henry *The Methods of Ethics*. Indianapolis, IN: Hackett, 1981.

——*Practical Ethics*. Oxford University Press, 1998.

Simon, Herbert *Reason in Human Affairs*. Stanford, CA: Stanford University Press, 1983.

Singer, Peter *Animal Liberation*, 2nd edn. Random House, 1990; London: Pimlico, 1995.

——*How Are We to Live?* Oxford University Press, 1997.

——*Practical Ethics*, 2nd edn. Cambridge University Press, 1993.

Skinner, B. F. *About Behaviorism*. London: Pimlico, 1999; New York: Random House, 1976.

Slote, Michael *From Morality to Virtue*. New York: Oxford University Press, 1995.

Smart, J. J. C. *Ethics, Persuasion and Truth*. Routledge, 1984.

Smart, J. J. C. and J. Haldane *Atheism and Theism*. Oxford: Blackwell, 1996.

Smart, J. J. C. and B. Williams *Utilitarianism: For and Against*. Cambridge University Press, 1973.

SMITH, ADAM:

The definitive edition of Smith's work is 'The Glasgow Edition' published in seven volumes by Oxford University Press. Paperback reprints of some of these volumes have been published by Liberty Fund.

Spencer, Herbert *The Man versus the State* (and other political writings). Indianapolis, IN: Liberty Fund, 1982.

——*Political Writings* (including *The Man versus the State*). Cambridge University Press, 1993.

——*The Principles of Ethics*, 2 vols. Indianapolis, IN: Liberty Fund, 1978.

Spengler, Oswald *The Decline of the West*. New York: Knopf, 1945.

SPINOZA, BARUCH:

The more recent translations of the *Ethics* by Curley (Princeton University Press (hb) and Penguin (pb)), by Shirley (Hackett), or by Parkinson (Oxford University Press) are preferable to the older ones. As for other writings by Spinoza, preference should at present be given to those translated by Curley (Princeton) or by Shirley (Hackett).

Spinoza, B. *Ethics* (transl. Curley). Penguin, 1996.

——*Ethics* (transl. Shirley). rev. edn. Indianapolis, IN: Hackett, 1998.

——*A Spinoza Reader: The Ethics and Other Works* (ed. E. Curley). Princeton, NJ: Princeton University Press, 1994.

——*Theological-Political Treatise* (transl. Shirley). Indianopolis, IN: Hackett, 1998.

——*Tractatus Theologico-Politicus* (transl. Shirley). New York: Brill, 1991.

Stalin, Joseph *Dialectical and Historical Materialism*. London: Communist Party of Britain Marxist-Leninist, 1986.

Stein, Edith *On the Problem of Empathy*. Washington, DC: ICS Publications, 1989.

Stich, Stephen *Deconstructing the Mind*. Oxford University Press, 1998.

——*The Fragmentation of Reason*. Cambridge, MA: MIT Press, 1993.

——*From Folk Psychology to Cognitive Science: the case against belief*. Cambridge, MA: MIT Press, 1985.

Stirner, Max *The Ego and Its Own* (ed. D. Leopold). Cambridge University Press, 1995.

Strauss, David Friedrich *The Life of Jesus* (transl. George Eliot). Mifflintown, PA: Sigler, 1994.

Strauss, Leo *Persecution and the Art of Writing*. Chicago: IL: University of Chicago Press, 1988.

Strawson, P. F. *Entity and Identity*. Oxford University Press, 1997.

——*Individuals*. Routledge, 1971.

Taylor, Charles *The Ethics of Authenticity*. Cambridge, MA: Harvard University Press, 1992.

——*Hegel*. Cambridge University Press, 1977.

——*The Sources of the Self*. Cambridge University Press, 1992.

Thoreau, Henry *Walden or Life in the Woods*. New York: Norton, 1992; London: Everyman, 1992 (There is a vast number of other good editions.)

Tillich, Paul *Morality and Beyond*. Louisville, KY: Westminster Press, 1995.

——*Systematic Theology*, 3 vols. Chicago, IL: University of Chicago Press, 1973–76.

Tocqueville, Alexis de *Democracy in America*. Among the many editions are: New York: Random House, 1990; Lanham, MD: Rowman & Littlefield, 1992; Everyman, 1994.

Toland, John *Christianity Not Mysterious*. Dublin: Lilliput Press, 1997.

Tönnies, Friedrich *Community and Society*. New Brunswick, NJ: Transaction, 1988.

Tugendhat, Ernst *Self-Consciousness and Self-Determination*. Cambridge, MA: MIT Press, 1989.

Vattimo, Gianni *The Adventure of Difference*. Cambridge: Polity; Baltimore, MD: Johns Hopkins University Press, 1993.

——*Belief*. Oxford: Polity Press, 1999.

——*Beyond Interpretation: the meaning of hermeneutics for philosophy*. Cambridge: Polity, 1997.

——*The End of Modernity*. Cambridge: Polity, 1991; Baltimore, MD: Johns Hopkins University Press, 1989.

——*The Transparent Society*. Cambridge: Polity; Baltimore, MD: Johns Hopkins University Press, 1991.

Vico, Giambattista *The New Science*. Ithaca, NY: Cornell University Press, 1984.

——*New Science* (transl. D. Marsh). Penguin, 1999.

——*On the Study Methods of Our Time*. Ithaca, NY: Cornell University Press, 1990.

Voltaire *Candide* (transl. R. Pearson), Oxford University Press, 1998; (transl. D. Wootton) Indianapolis, IN: Hackett, 2000. Other translations have the imprints Blackwell, 1988; Penguin, 1990; Everyman, 1992.

——*Letters on England*. Penguin, 1980.

——*Letters Concerning the English Nation*. Oxford University Press, 1994.

——*Philosophical Dictionary*. Penguin, 1984.

Watson, John *Behaviorism*. New Brunswick, NJ: Transaction, 1997.

Weber, Max *The Protestant Ethic and the Spirit of Capitalism*. Routledge, 1987; Los Angeles, CA: Roxbury, 1998; Englewood Cliffs, NJ: Prentice-Hall, 1977; Regnery, 1997.

Weil, Simone *Gravity and Grace*. Routledge, 1992; University of Nebraska Press, 1997.

——*The Need for Roots*. Routledge, 1995.

——*Oppression and Liberty*. Amherst, MA: University of Massachusetts Press, 1988.

Whewell, William *Theory of Scientific Method*. Indianapolis, IN: Hackett, 1989.

Whitehead, Alfred North *Process and Reality*. New York: Free Press, 1985.

——*Science and the Modern World*. New York: Free Press, 1985.

Whitehead, A. N. and B. Russell *Principia Mathematica*. Cambridge University Press, 1962.

Whitford, Margaret *Luce Irigaray: Philosophy in the feminine*. Routledge, 1991.

Whitford, Margaret (ed.) *The Irigaray Reader*. Oxford: Blackwell, 1991.

Williams, Bernard *Ethics and the Limits of Philosophy*. London: Fontana; Cambridge, MA: Harvard University Press, 1985.

Wilson, E. O. *On Human Nature*, Cambridge, MA: Harvard University Press, 1988; Penguin, 1995.

Wimsatt, K. and M. Beardsley *The Verbal Icon*. Lexington, KY: University Press of Kentucky, 1967.

Wittgenstein, Ludwig *On Certainty* (ed. G. E. M. Anscombe). Oxford: Blackwell, 1988; New York: HarperCollins, 1972.

——*Philosophical Grammar* (ed. R. Rhees). Oxford: Blackwell, 1986.

——*Philosophical Investigations* (ed. G. E. M. Anscombe), 3rd rev. edn. Oxford: Blackwell, 1997; Englewood Cliffs, NJ: Prentice-Hall, 1973.

——*Remarks on the Foundations of Mathematics* (ed. G. E. M. Anscombe, R. Rhees and G. H. von Wright) rev. edn. Cambridge, MA: MIT Press, 1983.

——*Remarks on the Philosophy of Psychology*, 2 vols (ed. G. E. M. Anscombe, G. H. von Wright and H. Nyman). Oxford: Blackwell, 1983.

——*Tractatus Logico-Philosophicus* (transl. C. K. Ogden, 1922). Routledge, 1981.

——*Tractatus Logico-Philosophicus* (transl. D. F. Pears and B. F. McGuinness, 1961). Routledge, 1975; Atlantic Highlands, NJ: Humanities Press, 1961.

——*Zettel*. Oxford: Blackwell, 1981; Berkeley, CA: University of California Press, 1967.

Wittgenstein: see also Pears, McGuinness, Monk.

Wolff, Robert Paul *In Defense of Anarchism*. rev. edn. Berkeley, CA: University of California Press, 1998.

Wollstonecraft, Mary *Thoughts on the Education of Daughters*. Bristol: Thoemmes, 1996.

——*A Vindication of the Rights of Men and A Vindication of the Rights of Woman*. Cambridge University Press, 1995.

——*A Vindication of the Rights of Men*. New York: Cassell, 1994.

——*A Vindication of the Rights of Woman* (rev. edn). Penguin, 1992; also Oxford University Press 1998; Dover, 1996; Everyman, 1995.

Wright, Elizabeth (ed.) *Feminism and Psychoanalysis*. Oxford: Blackwell, 1992.

Xenophon *The Education of Cyrus*. Everyman, 1994.

——*The Shorter Socratic Writings*. Ithaca, NY: Cornell University Press, 1996.

READ MORE IN PENGUIN

In every corner of the world, on every subject under the sun, Penguin represents quality and variety – the very best in publishing today.

For complete information about books available from Penguin – including Puffins, Penguin Classics and Arkana – and how to order them, write to us at the appropriate address below. Please note that for copyright reasons the selection of books varies from country to country.

In the United Kingdom: Please write to *Dept. EP, Penguin Books Ltd, Bath Road, Harmondsworth, West Drayton, Middlesex UB7 ODA*

In the United States: Please write to *Consumer Sales, Penguin Putnam Inc., P.O. Box 12289 Dept. B, Newark, New Jersey 07101-5289.* VISA and MasterCard holders call 1-800-788-6262 to order Penguin titles

In Canada: Please write to *Penguin Books Canada Ltd, 10 Alcorn Avenue, Suite 300, Toronto, Ontario M4V 3B2*

In Australia: Please write to *Penguin Books Australia Ltd, P.O. Box 257, Ringwood, Victoria 3134*

In New Zealand: Please write to *Penguin Books (NZ) Ltd, Private Bag 102902, North Shore Mail Centre, Auckland 10*

In India: Please write to *Penguin Books India Pvt Ltd, 11 Community Centre, Panchsheel Park, New Delhi 110017*

In the Netherlands: Please write to *Penguin Books Netherlands bv, Postbus 3507, NL-1001 AH Amsterdam*

In Germany: Please write to *Penguin Books Deutschland GmbH, Metzlerstrasse 26, 60594 Frankfurt am Main*

In Spain: Please write to *Penguin Books S. A., Bravo Murillo 19, 1° B, 28015 Madrid*

In Italy: Please write to *Penguin Italia s.r.l., Via Benedetto Croce 2, 20094 Corsico, Milano*

In France: Please write to *Penguin France, Le Carré Wilson, 62 rue Benjamin Baillaud, 31500 Toulouse*

In Japan: Please write to *Penguin Books Japan Ltd, Kaneko Building, 2-3-25 Koraku, Bunkyo-Ku, Tokyo 112*

In South Africa: Please write to *Penguin Books South Africa (Pty) Ltd, Private Bag X14, Parkview, 2122 Johannesburg*

READ MORE IN PENGUIN

LANGUAGE/LINGUISTICS

Language Play David Crystal

We all use language to communicate information, but it is language play which is truly central to our lives. Full of puns, groan-worthy gags and witty repartee, this book restores the fun to the study of language. It also demonstrates why all these things are essential elements of what makes us human.

Swearing Geoffrey Hughes

'A deliciously filthy trawl among taboo words across the ages and the globe' *Observer*. 'Erudite and entertaining' Penelope Lively, *Daily Telegraph*

The Language Instinct Stephen Pinker

'Dazzling . . . Pinker's big idea is that language is an instinct, as innate to us as flying is to geese . . . Words can hardly do justice to the superlative range and liveliness of Pinker's investigations' *Independent*. 'He does for language what David Attenborough does for animals, explaining difficult scientific concepts so easily that they are indeed absorbed as a transparent stream of words' John Gribbin

Mother Tongue Bill Bryson

'A delightful, amusing and provoking survey, a joyful celebration of our wonderful language, which is packed with curiosities and enlightenment on every page' *Sunday Express*. 'A gold mine of language-anecdote. A surprise on every page . . . enthralling' *Observer*

Longman Guide to English Usage
Sidney Greenbaum and Janet Whitcut

Containing 5000 entries compiled by leading authorities on modern English, this invaluable reference work clarifies every kind of usage problem, giving expert advice on points of grammar, meaning, style, spelling, pronunciation and punctuation.

READ MORE IN PENGUIN

PSYCHOLOGY

How the Mind Works Steven Pinker

This brilliant and controversial book explains what the mind is, how it evolved, and how it allows us to see, think, feel, interact, enjoy the arts and ponder the mysteries of life. 'To have read [the book] is to have consulted a first draft of the structural plan of the human psyche . . . a glittering *tour de force*' *Spectator*

The Uses of Enchantment Bruno Bettelheim

'Bruno Bettelheim's tour of fairy stories, with all their psychoanalytic connotations brought out into the open, is a feast of understanding' *New Statesman & Society*. 'Everything that Bettelheim writes about children, particularly about children's involvement in fiction, seems profound and illuminating' *Sunday Times*

Evolution in Mind Henry Plotkin
An Introduction to Evolutionary Psychology

Evolutionary theory holds a vital key to understanding ourselves. In proposing a more revolutionary approach to psychology, Professor Plotkin vividly demonstrates how an evolutionary perspective brings us closer to understanding what it is to be human.

The Man Who Loved a Polar Bear Robert U. Akeret

'Six fascinating case histories related with wit and humanity by the veteran psychotherapist Robert Akeret . . . a remarkable tour to the wilder shores of the human mind' *Daily Mail*

Private Myths: Dreams and Dreaming Anthony Stevens

'Its case for dreaming as something more universally significant than a tour across our personal playgrounds of guilt and misery is eloquently persuasive . . . [a] hugely absorbing study – its surface criss-crossed with innumerable avenues into science, anthropology and religion' *Spectator*

READ MORE IN PENGUIN

PSYCHOLOGY

Closing the Asylum Peter Barham

'A dispassionate, objective analysis of the changes in the way we care for the mentally ill. It offers no simple solutions but makes clear that "care in the community" is not so easy to implement as some seem to believe' *The Times Educational Supplement*

Child Behaviour Dorothy Einon

Covering the psychology of childcare, this book traces every key theme of child behaviour from birth to adolescence. Dorothy Einon discusses what, at any age, it is reasonable to expect of a child, how to keep things in perspective, and the most interesting and rewarding aspect of parenthood – bringing up a happy, well-adjusted child.

Bereavement Colin Murray Parkes

This classic text enables us to understand grief and grieving. How is bereavement affected by age, gender, personal psychology and culture? What are the signs of pathological grieving which can lead to mental illness? And how can carers provide genuine help without interfering with the painful but necessary 'work' of mourning?

Edward de Bono's Textbook of Wisdom

Edward de Bono shows how traditional thinking methods designed by the 'Gang of Three' (Socrates, Plato and Aristotle) are too rigid to cope with a complex and changing world. He recognizes that our brains deserve that we do better with them, and uses his gift for simplicity to get readers' thoughts to flow along fresh lines.

The Care of the Self Michel Foucault
The History of Sexuality Volume 3

Foucault examines the transformation of sexual discourse from the Hellenistic to the Roman world in an enquiry which 'bristles with provocative insights into the tangled liaison of sex and self' *The Times Higher Education Supplement*

READ MORE IN PENGUIN 

POLITICS AND SOCIAL SCIENCES

The Unconscious Civilization John Ralston Saul

In this powerfully argued critique, John Ralston Saul shows how corporatism has become the dominant ideology of our time, cutting across all sectors as well as the political spectrum. The result is an increasingly conformist society in which citizens are reduced to passive bystanders.

A Class Act Andrew Adonis and Stephen Pollard

'Will Britain escape from ancient and modern injustice? A necessary first step is to read and take seriously this ... description of the condition of our country. Andrew Adonis and Stephen Pollard here destroy the myth that Britain is a classless society' *The Times Higher Education Supplement*

Accountable to None Simon Jenkins

'An important book, because it brings together, with an insider's authority and anecdotage, both a narrative of domestic Thatcherism and a polemic against its pretensions . . . an indispensable guide to the corruptions of power and language which have sustained the illusion that Thatcherism was an attack on "government"' *Guardian*

Structural Anthropology Volumes 1–2 Claude Lévi-Strauss

'That the complex ensemble of Lévi-Strauss's achievement . . . is one of the most original and intellectually exciting of the present age seems undeniable. No one seriously interested in language or literature, in sociology or psychology, can afford to ignore it' George Steiner

Invitation to Sociology Peter L. Berger

Without belittling its scientific procedures Professor Berger stresses the humanistic affinity of sociology with history and philosophy. It is a discipline which encourages a fuller awareness of the human world . . . with the purpose of bettering it.

READ MORE IN PENGUIN

POLITICS AND SOCIAL SCIENCES

Anatomy of a Miracle Patti Waldmeir

The peaceful birth of black majority rule in South Africa has been seen by many as a miracle – or at least political magic. 'This book is a brilliant, vivid account of this extraordinary transformation' *Financial Times*

A Sin Against the Future Vivien Stern

Do prisons contribute to a better, safer world? Or are they a threat to democracy, as increasingly punitive measures are brought in to deal with rising crime? This timely account examines different styles of incarceration around the world and presents a powerful case for radical change.

The United States of Anger Gavin Esler

'First-rate . . . an even-handed and astute account of the United States today, sure in its judgements and sensitive in its approach' *Scotland on Sunday*. 'In sharply written, often amusing portraits of this disconnected America far from the capital, Esler probes this state of anger' *The Times*

Killing Rage: Ending Racism bell hooks

Addressing race and racism in American society from a black and a feminist standpoint, bell hooks covers a broad spectrum of issues. In the title essay she writes about the 'killing rage' – the intense anger caused by everyday instances of racism – finding in that rage a positive inner strength to create productive change.

'Just like a Girl' Sue Sharpe

Sue Sharpe's unprecedented research and analysis of the attitudes and hopes of teenage girls from four London schools has become a classic of its kind. This new edition focuses on girls in the nineties and represents their views on education, work, marriage, gender roles, feminism and women's rights.

READ MORE IN PENGUIN

PHILOSOPHY

Brainchildren Daniel C. Dennett

Philosophy of mind has been profoundly affected by this century's scientific advances, and thinking about thinking – how and why the mind works, its very existence – can seem baffling. Here eminent philosopher and cognitive scientist Daniel C. Dennett has provided an eloquent guide through some of the mental and moral mazes.

Language, Truth and Logic A. J. Ayer

The classic text which founded logical positivism and modern British philosophy, *Language, Truth and Logic* swept away the cobwebs and revitalized British philosophy.

The Penguin Dictionary of Philosophy Edited by Thomas Mautner

This dictionary encompasses all aspects of Western philosophy from 600 BC to the present day. With contributions from over a hundred leading philosophers, this dictionary will prove the ideal reference for any student or teacher of philosophy as well as for all those with a general interest in the subject.

Labyrinths of Reason William Poundstone

'The world and what is in it, even what people say to you, will not seem the same after plunging into *Labyrinths of Reason* . . . holds up the deepest philosophical questions for scrutiny in a way that irresistibly sweeps readers on' *New Scientist*

Metaphysics as a Guide to Morals Iris Murdoch

'This is philosophy dragged from the cloister, dusted down and made freshly relevant to suffering and egoism, death and religious ecstasy . . . and how we feel compassion for others' *Guardian*

Philosophy Football Mark Perryman

The amazing tale of a make-believe team, *Philosophy Football* is the story of what might have happened to the world's greatest thinkers if their brains had been in their boots instead of their heads . . .

READ MORE IN PENGUIN

REFERENCE

The Penguin Dictionary of Troublesome Words Bill Bryson

Why should you avoid discussing the *weather conditions*? Can a married woman be celibate? Why is it eccentric to talk about the aroma of a cowshed? A straightforward guide to the pitfalls and hotly disputed issues in standard written English.

Swearing Geoffrey Hughes

'A deliciously filthy trawl among taboo words across the ages and the globe' Valentine Cunningham, *Observer*, Books of the Year. 'Erudite and entertaining' Penelope Lively, *Daily Telegraph*, Books of the Year.

Medicines: A Guide for Everybody Peter Parish

Now in its seventh edition and completely revised and updated, this bestselling guide is written in ordinary language for the ordinary reader yet will prove indispensable to anyone involved in health care: nurses, pharmacists, opticians, social workers and doctors.

Media Law Geoffrey Robertson QC and Andrew Nichol

Crisp and authoritative surveys explain the up-to-date position on defamation, obscenity, official secrecy, copyright and confidentiality, contempt of court, the protection of privacy and much more.

The Penguin Careers Guide
Anna Alston and Anne Daniel; Consultant Editor: Ruth Miller

As the concept of a 'job for life' wanes, this guide encourages you to think broadly about occupational areas as well as describing day-to-day work and detailing the latest developments and qualifications such as NVQs. Special features include possibilities for working part-time and job-sharing, returning to work after a break and an assessment of the current position of women.

READ MORE IN PENGUIN 

REFERENCE

The Penguin Dictionary of the Third Reich
James Taylor and Warren Shaw

This dictionary provides a full background to the rise of Nazism and the role of Germany in the Second World War. Among the areas covered are the major figures from Nazi politics, arts and industry, the German Resistance, the politics of race and the Nuremberg trials.

The Penguin Biographical Dictionary of Women

This stimulating, informative and entirely new Penguin dictionary of women from all over the world, through the ages, contains over 1,600 clear and concise biographies on major figures from politicians, saints and scientists to poets, film stars and writers.

Roget's Thesaurus of English Words and Phrases
Edited by Betty Kirkpatrick

This new edition of Roget's classic work, now brought up to date for the nineties, will increase anyone's command of the English language. Fully cross-referenced, it includes synonyms of every kind (formal or colloquial, idiomatic and figurative) for almost 900 headings. It is a must for writers and utterly fascinating for any English speaker.

The Penguin Dictionary of International Relations
Graham Evans and Jeffrey Newnham

International relations have undergone a revolution since the end of the Cold War. This new world disorder is fully reflected in this new Penguin dictionary, which is extensively cross-referenced with a select bibliography to aid further study.

The Penguin Guide to Synonyms and Related Words
S. I. Hayakawa

'More helpful than a thesaurus, more humane than a dictionary, the *Guide to Synonyms and Related Words* maps linguistic boundaries with precision, sensitivity to nuance and, on occasion, dry wit' *The Times Literary Supplement*